RESEARCH HANDBOOK ON INTERNATIONAL BANKING AND GOVERNANCE

RESEARCH HANDBOOK ON INTERNATIONAL
BANKING AND GOVERNANCE

Research Handbook on International Banking and Governance

Edited by

James R. Barth

Auburn University and Milken Institute, USA

Chen Lin

Chinese University of Hong Kong

Clas Wihlborg

Chapman University, USA

Edward Elgar
Cheltenham, UK • Northampton, MA, USA

Published by
Edward Elgar Publishing Limited
The Lypiatts
15 Lansdown Road
Cheltenham
Glos GL50 2JA
UK

Edward Elgar Publishing, Inc.
William Pratt House
9 Dewey Court
Northampton
Massachusetts 01060
USA

A catalogue record for this book
is available from the British Library

Library of Congress Control Number: 2011932867

ISBN 978 1 84980 293 2 (cased)

Typeset by Servis Filmsetting Ltd, Stockport, Cheshire
Printed and bound by MPG Books Group, UK

Contents

Contributors

Emrah Arbak is a researcher at the Financial Institutions, Prudential Policy and Tax Unit at the Centre for European Policy Studies (CEPS), Belgium, chiefly specializing in financial services, corporate governance and public finance issues.

Francesca Arnaboldi is Assistant Professor at the University of Milan, Italy.

Rym Ayadi is Senior Research Fellow and Head of Research of the Financial Institutions, Prudential Policy and Tax Unit at the Centre for European Policy Studies (CEPS), Belgium.

James R. Barth is the Lowder Eminent Scholar in Finance at Auburn University, USA, a Senior Finance Fellow at the Milken Institute, USA, Fellow of the Wharton Financial Institutions Center, USA, and Co-Editor of the *Journal of Financial Economic Policy*.

Tom Berglund is Professor of Applied Microeconomics and the Theory of the Firm, Department of Economics, Hanken School of Economics, Helsinki, Finland and Helsinki Center of Economic Research.

Arnoud W.A. Boot is Professor of Corporate Finance and Financial Markets at the University of Amsterdam and Director of the Amsterdam Center for Law and Economics, the Netherlands. He is a member of the Dutch Social Economic Council and the Bank Council of the Dutch Central Bank.

Don Brash holds a number of directorships, including that of the ANZ National Bank, the largest bank in New Zealand. He is also Adjunct Professor of Banking at the Auckland University of Technology. He was Governor of the Reserve Bank of New Zealand from 1988 to 2002.

Barbara Casu is Reader in Banking and Finance and member of the Centre for Banking Research at Cass Business School, City University London, UK.

Yuan Chang is Assistant Professor in the Department of Business Education at National Changhua University of Education, Taiwan.

Heungsik Choe is President, Hana Institute of Finance, Korea.

J. Kimball Dietrich is Associate Professor of Finance and Business Economics at the Marshall School of Business at the University of Southern California, USA.

Walter Dolde is Associate Professor of Finance at the University of Connecticut – Stamford, USA.

Rients Galema is a PhD student in the Institute of Economics, Econometrics and Finance at the University of Groningen, the Netherlands.

Shubhashis Gangopadhyay is Research Director of the India Development Foundation, Dean of the School of Humanities and Social Sciences of Shiv Nadar University, Uttar Pradesh, India and Malmsten Visiting Professor at the University of Gothenburg, Sweden.

Claudia Girardone is Reader in Finance at the Essex Business School, University of Essex, UK. Her research focus is on modelling bank efficiency and productivity and competition issues in the banking sector.

Paul A. Gompers, Professor of Business Administration at the Harvard Business School, USA, specializes in research on financial issues related to start-up, high growth, and newly public companies.

Yufeng Gong is a PhD candidate in law and finance of Shanghai University of Finance and Economics, China.

Charles A.E. Goodhart, CBE, FBA is a member of the Financial Markets Group at the London School of Economics, UK.

Willem Pieter De Groen is a research assistant at the Financial Institutions, Prudential Policy and Tax Unit at the Centre for European Policy Studies (CEPS), Belgium.

Benton E. Gup is Chair of Banking at the University of Alabama, USA.

Jens Hagendorff is Senior Lecturer in Banking and Finance at the University of Edinburgh, UK.

Iftekhar Hasan is the E. Gerald Corrigan Professor of Finance at Fordham University, USA.

Richard J. Herring is the Jacob Safra Professor of International Banking at the Wharton School, University of Pennsylvania, USA, where he is also founding Director of the Wharton Financial Institutions Center.

Andreas G.F. Hoepner is a Lecturer in Banking and Finance at the School of Management of the University of St Andrews, UK.

Joel Houston is the William D. Hussey Professor of Business Administration at the University of Florida, USA.

Jennifer Itzkowitz is an Assistant Professor of Finance at Seton Hall University, USA.

John D. Knopf is an Associate Professor and Ackerman Scholar at the University of Connecticut, USA.

Satoshi Koibuchi is Associate Professor of Finance, Faculty of Commerce, Chuo University, Tokyo, Japan.

Rosa M. Lastra is Professor in International Financial and Monetary Law at the Centre for Commercial Law Studies (CCLS), School of Law, Queen Mary, University of London, UK.

Byungyoon Lee is a Fellow at the Korea Institute of Finance.

Robert Lensink is Professor of Finance and Financial Markets at the University of Groningen and Professor of Finance and Development at Wageningen University, the Netherlands.

Li Li is in the School of International Trade and Economics at the University of International Business and Economics, Beijing, China.

Chen Lin is a Full Professor in the Department of Finance at Chinese University of Hong Kong.

Yue Ma is Professor and Head of the Economics Department, Lingnan University, Hong Kong.

Peter MacKay is Associate Professor in the Department of Finance at Hong Kong University of Science and Technology.

Matej Marinč is Assistant Professor in the Faculty of Economics at the University of Ljubljana, Slovenia and Amsterdam Centre for Law and Economics, University of Amsterdam, the Netherlands.

David G. Mayes is the BNZ Professor of Finance and Director of the NZ Governance Centre at the University of Auckland, New Zealand.

Roy Mersland has extensive international management, consulting, and research experience in more than 20 countries in Latin America, Asia, Africa, and Europe.

Rakesh Mohan is Professor in the Practice of International Economics and Finance at the School of Management and Senior Fellow in the Jackson Institute for Global Affairs at Yale University, USA.

Philip Molyneux is Professor in Banking and Finance and Head of Bangor Business School at Bangor University, UK.

Andy Mullineux is Professor of Global Finance and Director of the Global Finance Research Group and the Finance Group of the Department of Accounting and Finance in the Birmingham Business School at the University of Birmingham, UK.

Andy Naranjo is the Emerson-Merrill Lynch Associate Professor of Finance and the Associate Director of the Center for International Business Education and Research at the University of Florida, USA.

Ajay A. Palvia is a Financial Economist in the Policy Analysis Division of the Office of the Comptroller of the Currency (OCC), USA.

Apanard P. Prabha is an economist in the Financial Research group at the Milken Institute, USA. She is also an Adjunct Assistant Professor of Economics at the University of Illinois at Springfield, USA.

Hilton L. Root, an academic and policy specialist in governance, complexity, international political economy, and development, is a member of the faculty at the School of Public Policy, George Mason University, USA.

Wanvimol Sawangngoenyuang is a researcher at the Economic Research Department of the Bank of Thailand.

S.K. Shanthi is Chair Professor at the Union Bank Centre for Banking Excellence, Great Lakes Institute of Management, Chennai, India.

Chung-Hua Shen is Professor in the Department of Finance of National Taiwan University.

Frank M. Song is a Professor of Economics and Finance in the School of Economics and Finance, University of Hong Kong.

Liang Song is Assistant Professor of Accounting at the School of Business and Economics, Michigan Technological University, USA.

Kenneth R. Spong is an Assistant Vice-President and Economist in the Banking Research Department at the Federal Reserve Bank of Kansas City, USA.

Tientip Subhanij is Chief Researcher of the Economic Research Department of the Bank of Thailand and concurrently Head of the Capital Market Research Institute of the Stock Exchange of Thailand.

Richard J. Sullivan is a Senior Economist in the Payments System function of the Economic Research Department at the Federal Reserve Bank of Kansas City, USA.

Francesco Vallascas is Lecturer in Banking and Finance at the University of Leeds, UK, and is on leave from the University of Cagliari, Sardinia, where he is a lecturer in financial intermediation.

Peter J. Wallison holds the Arthur F. Burns Chair in Financial Policy Studies and is co-director of the American Enterprise Unit (AEI) program on Financial Policy Studies.

Ingo Walter is Dean of the Faculty and the Seymour Milstein Professor of Finance, Corporate Governance and Ethics at the Stern School of Business, New York University, USA.

Lawrence J. White is Arthur E. Imperatore Professor of Economics at New York University's Stern School of Business, USA, and Deputy Chair of the Economics Department at Stern.

Clas Wihlborg holds the Fletcher Jones Chair of International Business at the Argyros School of Business and Economics, Chapman University, USA.

Thomas D. Willett is the Horton Professor of Economics at Claremont Graduate University, USA and Claremont McKenna College, and Director of the Claremont Institute of Economic Policy Studies and of its China-Asia Pacific Political Economy Program.

John O.S. Wilson is Professor of Banking and Finance and Director of Research in the Management School at the University of St Andrews, UK. He is Associate Editor of the *British Accounting Review* and *European Journal of Finance*.

Yuhai Xuan is an Assistant Professor of Business Administration in the Finance Unit of the Harvard Business School, USA.

Zhongfei Zhou is the Deputy President and Professor of Law of Shanghai University of Finance and Economics.

Foreword 1

The financial crisis that started in the summer of 2007 has underlined the importance of banks in the economy. This *Handbook* is edited by three leaders in the field. It is a timely and important contribution. Understanding how banks operate, their weaknesses and strengths, is important for practitioners and regulators, as well as scholars and students of banking. The book contains contributions by distinguished authors from all over the world.

The coverage of the chapters is excellent. Part I is concerned with ownership, efficiency and stability. These are crucial topics that form the core of our understanding of banking. There is a wide range of ownership structures around the world ranging from public to private ownership, as well as mutual and other structures. These differ in terms of their operating efficiency and their stability. The first six chapters provide a broad perspective on these different aspects. Part II contains five chapters that investigate one of the most discussed aspects of the crisis, the relationship between compensation practices and bank performance and risk. They consider what happened in the crisis and how compensation should be structured going forward.

One of the most discussed issues over the years in the field of banking is the roles of market discipline and regulation. Part III considers the former, while Part IV focuses on the latter. There are a number of ways in which the market disciplines banks. The two most important, which are covered in depth here, are the provision of information and the possibility of bank resolution. In most recent crises, large banks have been saved by governments to prevent contagion. This is the 'too big to fail' problem that stops banks from being resolved. These topics are considered in the five chapters in Part III. The five chapters in Part IV consider the complement of market discipline, which is government regulation and supervision. The particular forms that these should take after the experience of the crisis are considered in depth and for emerging countries as well as developed countries.

The remaining three parts consider a broad variety of topics. The four chapters in Part V focus on financial innovations, strategy and social responsibility. Part VI has chapters on community banks, mutual funds, venture capital and microfinance institutions. Finally, Part VII considers governance and related issues in New Zealand, Europe, Japan, Korea, China, Thailand and India.

Franklin Allen

Nippon Life Professor of Finance; Professor of Economics

Finance Department

Wharton School

University of Pennsylvania

Philadelphia, PA, USA

Foreword 2

The 2007–2009 crisis in world financial markets, triggered by defaults on subprime mortgages in the US, and the 2010–2011 crisis in the euro zone, raise questions about macroeconomic policy, financial stability, the design of financial regulation and supervision, and the corporate governance of banks and other financial institutions. Interventions by the official authorities, including massive recapitalization of some of the world's largest banks, underscore that the stability of individual banks has been at risk. Moreover, there has been considerable concern about systemic risk; that is, problems at individual banks have threatened the stability of the banking and financial system as a whole, especially after the collapse of Lehman Brothers in September 2008.

The recent financial crisis clearly shows the importance of having a well-conceived and coherent system and an institutional structure that help to prevent such crises from occurring in the first place and to resolve a crisis once it has occurred. Such a system did not exist when the crisis started in August 2007.

However, in the decade before the crisis started in 2007, several proposals on how to create such an institutional structure had been under discussion among academics, bankers and regulators. Unfortunately, the existence of relatively benign economic conditions in which banks were highly profitable, and the prevalence of a relatively close relationship between regulators and bankers ('regulatory capture'), prevented the implementation of these proposals.

The recent financial crisis has created a new momentum for designing and implementing a new regulatory and supervisory structure which will make the occurrence of crises less likely and the resolution easier once a crisis has occurred. New proposals are currently being discussed internationally under the auspices of, primarily, the Basel Committee on Banking Supervision, the Financial Stability Board and the European Commission. These proposals focus on: (1) a substantial increase of bank capital requirements, including the use of contingent capital instruments as a way of strengthening market discipline; (2) the design of credible resolution or 'prompt corrective action' schemes which would require bank supervisors to take prespecified actions when bank capital starts to decline and to close or to restructure financially a bank when capital falls below the lowest threshold or trigger point; (3) the creation of more adequate deposit insurance systems characterized by risk-related insurance pricing and immediate payout of insured deposits in the case of a bank failure; (4) a more adequate measurement and monitoring of systemic risk in the banking and financial system; and (5) the design of executive compensation schemes for top management of banks focusing more on longer-term performance.

These reform proposals have the explicit goal of limiting guarantees and moral hazard in the banking and financial system, thereby enhancing the incentive compatibility of financial regulation and supervision. The existence of explicit deposit insurance systems, as well as implicit guarantees associated with the perception that (large) banks will almost always be bailed out by the government, is creating perverse incentives towards increased risk-taking and a reduction of bank capital ratios. In order to address this moral hazard problem it is essential to reduce the need for government-provided bailouts.

In this volume, the *Research Handbook on International Banking and Governance*, the recent financial crisis is analyzed with governance as the unifying theme. The central question is how corporate governance arrangements of banks and other financial institutions affect risk-taking, performance and behavior of financial institutions more generally.

In most countries governments impose various regulations on banks to ensure a safe and sound banking system. As the editors note in their 'introduction and overview' chapter, corporate governance on the one hand and regulatory and supervisory governance on the other hand should be viewed as complements, with the same goal of producing prudential banking practices. The appropriate mix between the two types of governance is a debatable issue and, therefore, one that merits further enquiry.

The present volume aims at providing a contribution to this debate by exploring the role of governance studied under seven main themes: (1) ownership, efficiency and stability; (2) compensation, performance and risk; (3) market discipline: prerequisites and effectiveness; (4) governance, regulation and supervision; (5) governance, strategy and social responsibility; (6) governance in non-bank financial institutions; and (7) regional and country studies.

Through its broad scope of issues related to the corporate governance of banks and other financial institutions, analyzed from the background of the recent financial crisis, this new volume provides a timely and thorough perspective on how to reform the financial system in order to make future banking crises far less likely. Moreover, given the fact that the volume contains contributions from internationally recognized scholars, coming from the US, Europe, Asia and elsewhere, it provides excellent reading material for academics, students, bankers, regulators and supervisors, and others who have a genuine interest in the question of how to ensure banking and financial stability in the future.

Harald Benink
Professor of Banking and Finance
Tilburg University
Tilburg, the Netherlands
Chairman, European Shadow Financial Regulatory Committee

Foreword 3

After the massive failures in governance during the first decade of the twenty-first century – starting with Enron, Worldcom and Parmalat and building to an impressive crescendo with the global financial crisis of 2007–2009 – this edited volume by Professors Barth, Lin and Wihlborg on banking and governance could not possibly be published at a more timely moment.

Banks matter. They mobilize resources, allocate capital, monitor the use of that capital, provide risk management tools, and facilitate payments. When banks do their jobs well, societies benefit as credit flows to those with the best entrepreneurial ideas. As a result, people enjoy faster and more inclusive economic growth. But, when banks do their jobs poorly, societies suffer as credit – and hence economic opportunity – flows to the rich and powerful rather than to the innovative and energetic. And, with poorly functioning banks, credit too frequently pours into activities that generate quick bonuses or other perquisites for bank executives at the expense of long-run economic prosperity and stability.

Since banks matter, the governance of banks matters, as the recent crisis demonstrated all too well. Many economists and policymakers assumed that privately owned financial institutions would look after their own interests and in the process help society. But this view is based on the belief that those making decisions for the financial institutions are maximizing shareholder value. That is, this free-market approach assumes financial institutions are well governed. However, rather than maximizing the value of the institution to shareholders, executives maximized the value of the financial institution to executives, which often deviated wildly from the goals of shareholders. Executives used their influence over the board of directors to obtain enormous bonuses regardless of long-run performance. Indeed, some received lavish compensation despite the wretched performance of the financial institutions under their charge. Shareholders were simply unable to force financial institution executives to behave in the best interests of shareholders. The crisis cannot be understood without recognizing the breakdown in governance.

What accounts for the breakdown in the governance of the financial system? Diffuse shareholders and creditors have a hard time influencing what happens inside firms, and banks are particularly difficult for outsiders to influence because of their opacity. Although information problems are present in all sectors, they are particularly acute in finance. For example, consider sales as an indicator of quality. If Apple sells lots of iPods over a few years, this is a reasonable signal of the product's quality. But if a bank makes lots of loans over a few years, this does not necessarily provide accurate information about the quality of those loans. It is exceptionally difficult to discern the value of financial instruments and hence the quality of the financial firms holding those securities. Thus, the opacity of financial firms hinders effective governance. Since investors cannot easily figure out the condition and activities of financial firms, insiders – executives and large shareholders – can more easily exploit other investors and use the firm to achieve their own ends.

This challenge – addressing governance problems in finance that have been enormously costly to shareholders and taxpayers – is the focus of this volume. Private markets do not effectively govern financial intermediaries. This deficiency in private governance arises both because of market failures and because of bad policies and regulations that dissuade private investors from energetically monitoring the activities of financial institutions. Thus, the volume examines the role of financial policies and regulations in fostering better governance of financial institutions. The present volume excels at laying out the issues that affect both private and official governance of financial intermediaries, covering the existing literature and offering new perspectives.

Alas, who governs the financial regulators – the Guardians of Finance? Just as there are consequential challenges associated with designing policies, regulations and laws that induce the executives of financial institutions to behave in the best interests of shareholders rather than in the narrow, private interests of the executives, there are serious challenges associated with designing institutions to compel the Guardians of Finance, such as the Federal Reserve, the Securities and Exchange Commission and the Federal Deposit Insurance Corporation, to behave in the best interests of the public rather than in the narrow, private interests of individual regulators. Just as sound governance of banks is crucial for getting well-functioning banks, sound governance of the regulators is crucial for getting sound financial sector policies.

As we, along with Jim Barth, show in *Guardians of Finance: Making Regulators Work For Us* (MIT Press, 2012), the most recent and earlier crises were marked by regulators failing to act in the public interest. As with governing banks, the problem is that the insiders have much greater information than outsiders, where the outsider in the case of regulation is the public. Regulators have access to confidential information, and it is hard for the public or legislators to know what regulators knew and when they learned it. And regulation is extraordinarily complex, so it is difficult for a public with limited information to assess the quality of bank regulation. Just as the amount of loans is a poor metric of the quality of banking services, so the number of regulations, regulatory bodies and regulators is a poor signal of the quality of financial regulation.

In sum, governance mechanisms in finance need a careful rethinking. This volume represents a valuable contribution to this process. As we continue, we would stress that good governance is so important in finance that the governance of the financial regulatory agencies themselves should be an integral part of this rethinking.

Gerard Caprio
William Brough Professor of Economics and
Chair, Center for Development Economics, William College
Williamstown, MA, USA

Ross Levine
James and Merryl Tisch Professor of Economics and
Director, William R. Rhodes Center for International
Economics and Finance, Brown University
Providence, RI, USA and the NBER

Introduction and overview
James R. Barth, Chen Lin and Clas Wihlborg

This book is aimed at researchers and students of financial institutions in academia as well as in private financial institutions and public regulatory and supervisory authorities. Its objective is to bring the reader to the frontier of research on governance of financial institutions by interpreting and reviewing current research, as well as to push the frontier by presenting original research on new aspects of financial institution governance. To inspire future research the book also includes chapters on governance policy issues that require more attention by researchers.

The recent financial crisis has stimulated a debate on governance of financial institutions as well as research on effects of governance arrangements on the risk-taking, performance and behavior of financial institutions more generally. Furthermore, researchers are asking how regulation, legislation, politics and other factors influence governance of financial institutions and, thereby, their behavior in different dimensions. The contents of this book reflect this variety of research on financial institutions with governance as the unifying theme.

For many countries around the world the recent financial crisis was the worst they had experienced since the Great Depression of the 1930s. Financial institutions clearly were the center of attention as a large number of them either failed or were bailed out by governments during 2007 to 2010. The lengthy list of distressed institutions includes Citigroup, Bank of America, American International Group, Fannie Mae and Freddie Mac in the United States; PNB Paribas, Crédit Agricole and Société Générale in France; Commerzbank and Bayerische Landesbank in Germany; Allied Irish Bank and Bank of Ireland in Ireland; Royal Bank of Scotland, Lloyds Bank and Northern Rock in the United Kingdom; and UBS in Switzerland. More institutions may be added to the list as the process of dealing with still other troubled institutions continues to move ahead. Not surprisingly, these disturbing developments have led to numerous official and unofficial studies assessing what went wrong with financial institutions in so many countries, as well as to rethinking what is the most appropriate way to regulate such institutions to contain risk-taking behavior and to prevent taxpayer bailouts.

Some studies examining the causes of the US crisis have focused on macroeconomic factors such as low interest rates due to huge global capital inflows and an excessively easy monetary policy from 2002 to 2006. It is argued that this low interest rate environment led to a tremendous surge of credit into the housing sector, via mortgages and various other securities backed by mortgages, as investors in the United States and abroad sought higher returns. As a result of the unprecedented availability of funds for housing coupled with extremely lax lending standards for home buyers, home prices soared to unsustainable levels and then collapsed beginning in 2006. This triggered a mortgage market meltdown and a severe economic recession.

Given the dominant size of the US economy, these adverse developments in the financial and real sectors exacerbated financial problems occurring in many other parts of the globe as US imports declined and investors abroad suffered losses on all the securities they had purchased backed by US home mortgages. To make matters worse, the financial regulatory authorities in the United States and elsewhere failed to detect, or ignored, numerous emerging signs warning of impending troubles. The authorities thus failed to take decisive and timely action to limit the severity of the financial crises so many countries experienced. Once they did start taking action in the midst of the widening and deepening global crisis there was substantial uncertainty as to exactly what was being done and over what time period. This uncertainty only contributed to the inability of financial markets to function normally.

Several chapters in this volume present views of the causes of the crisis. It is inevitable that more studies will be conducted focusing on the role that various factors played in such a devastating financial crisis and the appropriate financial reforms needed to reduce, if not entirely prevent, both the likelihood and the severity of future crises in countries everywhere. Some countries have already responded to the crisis by enacting financial reforms. The United States, for example, enacted the Dodd–Frank Wall Street Reform and Consumer Protection Act in July 2010. Such reforms have already been subjected to careful scrutiny as new regulations are implemented and enforced over time.

Although macroeconomic factors have dominated the explanations for previous financial crises around the world, the recent crisis has focused attention on a number of microeconomic factors, including corporate governance of financial institutions; financial innovation in securitization and derivatives; and behavior and incentives of policymakers, regulators and supervisors. These factors are clearly interdependent, as emphasized in many chapters in this volume.

Corporate governance is an important field of research in finance and economics but so far only a few, relatively recent studies have focused on the corporate governance of banks and other financial institutions. While there have been many studies on the role of corporate governance in explaining the financial performance (e.g., stock return performance) of non-financial firms over time, those focusing solely on banks have been somewhat rare until relatively recently. The depth of the most recent global financial crisis, however, has generated substantially more interest in examining whether differences in the risk-taking behavior of individual banks can be explained by differences in the corporate governance practices at these institutions. The main concern in this regard is that, as with any corporation, conflicts of interest may arise between the top managers of a bank and its shareholders. If not kept in check, the managers may behave in ways that benefit themselves or those close to them at the expense of shareholders. In addition, if allowed, shareholders or a subset of controlling shareholders may influence a bank to engage in excessively risky activities at the expense of other stakeholders, like depositors (or the deposit insurer) and debt holders.

The conflict of interest between shareholders and other stakeholders may be particularly important in banking and financial services more generally because the public and politicians attach social value to particular financial services, such as real estate financing, payment services, consumer credit services and household exposure to risk on financial positions, including deposits.

Obviously, it is important that effort be devoted to mitigating the costs to shareholders and to other stakeholders in a bank from various potential conflicts of interest. It is the role of the board of directors in particular to mitigate costs to shareholders through the promotion and enforcement of good corporate governance practices. If not corrected, poor corporate governance at banks will adversely affect their performance and hence stock market valuation, and thereby adversely affect the availability and cost of credit to their customers. It will also raise the cost of capital to such banks. Poor corporate governance, moreover, may lead to excessive risk-taking behavior by banks, and thereby increase the risk of not only individual bank failures but also the risk of collapse of a country's entire banking system. More generally, and even worse, given the overriding importance of banks for mobilizing and allocating societies' scarce savings to the most productive projects, poor corporate governance of banks can impede overall economic growth and development in countries by producing less efficient and less stable financial intermediation.

To the extent that banks and other financial institutions provide services that are considered socially valuable or harmful, the activities of a well-governed bank from the shareholders' point of view will stand in conflict with or be insufficient relative to perceptions of the public interest. For this reason the financial sector in most countries is subject to a combination of support and regulatory constraints complicating the task of governance as well as the evaluation of what is good governance. Good governance from the shareholders' point of view need not coincide with public and political perceptions of good governance.

The fact that banks, especially in emerging market economies, are so important in helping finance a country's growth and development and that they receive various benefits from the government (e.g., deposit insurance and lender-of-last resort support) has led most individuals to conclude that simply relying on good corporate governance practices is insufficient. Instead, most individuals have concluded that it is also necessary to impose various regulations on banks to better ensure a safe and sound banking system. As a result, there are a variety of regulations and supervisory practices that govern the behavior of banks, ranging from entry to activity restrictions, capital requirements, ownership restrictions, and merger and acquisition restrictions. Corporate governance and regulatory and supervisory governance therefore should be viewed as complements with the same goal of producing prudential banking practices. The appropriate mix between the two types of governance, unfortunately, is a debatable issue and therefore one that merits still further enquiry.

The purpose of this book is to explore the role of governance, both internal and external, in explaining risk-taking and other aspects of the behavior of financial institutions, as well as to explore market and policy factors that explain the objectives and quality of governance. In light of the recent and severe global crisis it is important to identify the underlying causes of the crises in different countries. Only through analyses of the kind presented in this volume can one hope to implement the financial reforms necessary and sufficient to reduce the likelihood and severity of future crises.

This volume is divided into seven parts with governance as the unifying theme:

- Part I   Ownership, Efficiency and Stability.
- Part II   Compensation, Performance and Risk.
- Part III Market Discipline: Prerequisites and Effectiveness.
- Part IV   Governance, Regulation and Supervision.

- Part V   Governance, Strategy and Social Responsibility.
- Part VI   Governance in Non-Bank Financial Institutions.
- Part VII   Regional and Country Studies.

The first two parts take governance characteristics as given, and focus on analyses of the impact of these characteristics on the performance and risk of the financial system in Part I, and on performance of individual financial institutions in Part II. The delimitation between these two parts is not as sharp as it may at first seem. There is substantial overlap between the themes just as there is overlap between macro-prudential and micro-prudential regulation of financial activity.

Parts III and IV consider governance characteristics as endogenous and determined in interaction with market processes, regulation and supervision. Part III focuses on the role of market discipline in shaping risk-taking incentives of managers of financial institutions and the role of the regulatory and legislative frameworks in strengthening or weakening these incentives. Part IV focuses on the role of and effectiveness of regulation and supervision from a macro-prudential as well as a micro-prudential perspective. There is naturally an overlap between chapters in the two parts. Market discipline and direct regulation of financial activities can be viewed as substitutes for influencing governance of risk-taking. However, legislation and regulation can also be aimed at strengthening market discipline as opposed to being solely aimed at restricting risk-taking activities. The role of externalities and market failures for risk-taking is a crucial factor influencing conflicts of interest between shareholders' and social objectives in both parts. A focus on market discipline in Part III is motivated by market failures created by policy and regulatory intervention in financial markets, while regulation and supervision in Part IV are motivated by other sources of market failures.

In Part V strategic objectives of financial institutions, including social responsibility, are viewed as important aspects of corporate governance. This part includes empirically oriented chapters on merger and acquisition policy, and social responsibility as a potential departure from shareholder wealth maximization.

Most of the analysis in Parts I–V applies not only to banking in the traditional sense but also to all financial institutions participating in markets for direct and indirect credit. Nevertheless, we include in Part VI a group of chapters analyzing governance and behavior of financial institutions with governance structures that differ from traditional corporations. The types of institutions covered are community banks, venture capital firms, open-end and closed-end funds, which are compared from a governance point of view, and microfinance institutions in developing countries.

Lastly, Part VII includes chapters focusing on governance issues in particular regions and countries. While some of the chapters analyze general governance characteristics in a region, others focus on a particular issue that can be considered specific to governance in a region or country. A broad group of countries is covered without an attempt at global completeness. Nevertheless, each country or region included has important lessons for governance or it represents a particular approach to governance. The regions and countries included are New Zealand, the European Union, Japan, South Korea, China, Thailand and India.

We turn now to a brief summary of each chapter within the seven parts.

PART I: OWNERSHIP, EFFICIENCY AND STABILITY

The first chapter in this part, 'Bank governance: concepts and measurements', by Frank Song and Li Li, reviews the corporate governance mechanisms of the banking sector and discusses the empirical evidence on the relation between bank governance and perform-ance and the relation between bank governance and risk-taking. Moreover, the authors propose a corporate governance index, which captures four different aspects (i.e., board structure, ownership structure, executive compensation and information disclosure transparency) of bank governance. The index is composed based on a sample of 225 banks from 48 countries over the period 2004–2006.

Using the ownership data of more than 11 000 banks around the world, Iftekhar Hasan and Liang Song examine the causes and consequences of bank ownership struc-ture in Chapter 2, 'Bank ownership and performance: a global perspective'. They find strong evidence that banks tend to have a more concentrated ownership in countries with weaker investor protection and banking regulation. Moreover, they find that larger control rights by the controlling shareholder help to improve bank performance, espe-cially in the financial crisis period. These findings shed light on the policy implications for financial crises.

In Chapter 3, 'Is there a conflict between competition and financial stability?', Barbara Casu, Claudia Girardone and Philip Molyneux provide a thorough discussion on the risk-taking implications of banking competition, an important external govern-ance mechanism in the banking sector. The chapter reviews the theoretical debates on competition and the risk-taking incentives of banks. It then summarizes the empirical findings in the literature and discusses difficulties and practical issues in measuring bank competition and risk-taking. Various types of bank competition measures (e.g., concen-tration ratio, Herfindahl index, H-statistics, Lerner index, and persistence of profit) and bank risk-taking measures (e.g., loan loss provisions, Z-score, probability of default) are discussed in detail in the chapter.

The empirical evidence on bank competition and risk-taking is mixed, as reviewed in the previous chapter. But, more specifically, what is the impact of banking sector compe-tition on bank operating efficiency? Chen Lin, Yue Ma and Frank Song analyze this issue in Chapter 4, 'What drives bank operating efficiency? The role of bank competition and credit information sharing'. The chapter examines the impact of bank competition and information sharing via credit registries or private bureaus on bank operating efficiency. Using data for 1200 banks across 69 countries, the authors find strong evidence that both bank concentration and regulatory entry barriers reduce bank operating efficiency. Moreover, they find that credit information sharing enhances bank operating efficiency and attenuates the negative effect of bank concentration and entry barriers on bank effi-ciency. They also find that supervisory independence and bank information disclosure are positively associated with bank efficiency, whereas state ownership of the banking sector is negatively associated with bank operating efficiency.

Using micro-oriented loan level data, Joel Houston, Jennifer Itzkowitz and Andy Naranjo examine the implications of information costs, cross-country differences in legal and regulatory costs, and banking sector competition on pricing of syndicated loans in Chapter 5, 'Corporate borrower nationality and global presence: cross-country evidence on the pricing of syndicated bank loans'. Using a unique sample of 13 000 loans issued to more than 4000 firms across ten countries, they find that the borrower's nationality, global presence, size and loan type are important determinants of loan pricing. The results suggest the existence of a considerable international segmentation in the syndicated loan market and the importance of information costs and legal and regulatory costs in shaping loan contracts.

The last chapter in this part, Chapter 6 by Benton Gup, offers some policy suggestions for reform. The chapter, 'Lessons learned from recent financial crises', argues that the four key factors that contributed to the recent financial crisis in the United States are population growth, new laws and government-sponsored entities (i.e., Fannie Mae and Freddie Mac), increased liquidity and securitization. As regards policy recommendations, the chapter suggests that lenders should avoid excessive financial leverage, concentrated loan portfolios and high-risk borrowers, and be aware of interest rate risks.

PART II: COMPENSATION, PERFORMANCE AND RISK

Poor managerial incentives are widely referred to as one of the fundamental causes of the recent financial crisis. Chapters in this part examine the link between managerial incentives and bank risk-taking and offer important evidence with respect to the ongoing regulatory reforms on compensation structure in the financial sector. In the first chapter (Chapter 7) of this part, 'Bank ownership and risk taking: improving corporate governance in banking after the crisis', Kenneth Spong and Richard Sullivan examine the impact of managerial ownership on bank risk-taking. Using a sample of state-chartered banks in the Kansas City Federal Reserve District, they find that bank stock ownership by hired managers is positively associated with bank risk-taking, whereas managers' personal wealth concentration in bank investment is negatively associated with bank risk-taking. They also find that a larger share of cash bonus in managerial compensation tends to reduce bank risk-taking.

In Chapter 8, 'Executive compensation and risk-taking in European banking', Rym Ayadi, Emrah Arbak and Willem Pieter De Groen find similar results in a sample of 53 large banks in the European Union across the sample period 1999–2009. Specifically, they find that a long-term incentive plan is associated with more bank risk-taking and default likelihood. However, they do not find any significant impact of option plans and annual bonuses on bank risk-taking.

Jens Hagendorff and Francesco Vallascas provide a thorough review of the empirical literature on executive compensation and bank risk-taking in Chapter 9, 'CEO pay and risk-taking in banking: the roles of bonus plans and deferred compensation in curbing bank risk-taking'. They point out that most existing work focuses on equity-linked chief executive officer (CEO) compensation (mainly share and option grants), while non-equity-type CEO compensation schemes (e.g., pensions and other forms of deferred compensation) are largely overlooked. The chapter calls for more research on the relation between debt-linked components of CEO compensation and bank risk-taking.

In a related chapter (Chapter 10), 'Bank failures and CEO compensation', Walter Dolde and John Knopf examine the link between CEO compensation and the likelihood of bank failure using a large sample of 766 publicly traded banks and thrifts in the United States. They find somewhat surprising results that higher stock and options awards to

CEOs reduced the likelihood of failure of institutions during the financial crisis of 2008–2010. On the other hand, they find that bonus compensation is positively associated with the probability of bank failure. They further suggest that regulators should take managerial compensation into account when setting Federal Deposit Insurance Corporation (FDIC) insurance premiums.

In Chapter 11, 'Restricting risk-taking by financial intermediaries through executive compensation', Tom Berglund argues that restricting risk-taking managerial incentives in normal circumstances results in a negative long-run effect for productivity in financial intermediation and, as a consequence, reduces economic growth. He proposes to include a clause in the CEO compensation contract that all performance-based compensation will automatically be cancelled should a situation of financial distress occur.

PART III: MARKET DISCIPLINE: PREREQUISITES AND EFFECTIVENESS

In the first chapter of this part, Chapter 12, 'The lost cause: the failure of the Financial Crisis Inquiry Commission', Peter Wallison argues that the recent financial crisis was not caused by failures in bank regulation or risk management among the large financial institutions. Instead, he argues that the root cause of the financial crisis was the US government's housing policies, a factor that has been overlooked in the majority report by the Financial Crisis Inquiry Commission.

In Chapter 13, 'Market discipline for financial institutions and markets for information', Apanard Prabha, Clas Wihlborg and Thomas Willett review the literature on the impact of market discipline on risk-taking in financial institutions and on timely information disclosure. They also analyze the causes of the market discipline failure in the recent financial crisis. In their view, the most important market failure of informativeness was that large financial institutions had the incentive to remain strategically opaque so that outside investors could not assess their solvency. They also discuss how different types of financial instruments (e.g., stock price indexes, credit default swaps and subordinated debt) provide more or less timely information. Finally, they lay out four 'informativeness principles' for regulators and policymakers to follow with the objective of strengthening the incentives of market participants to acquire, analyze, disclose and signal information.

In Chapter 14, 'Moral hazard, bank resolution and the protection of depositors', David Mayes examines the potential impact of deposit insurance schemes on the banking sector in the most recent financial crisis. He argues that deposit insurance needs to be explicit and limited in coverage so that it can provide a credible disincentive to bank risk-taking. The deposit insurance schemes should contain a special resolution regime that facilitates a quick and smooth resolution of banks before losses mount too high. He also suggests that regulators should implement a contingent capital policy to address the issues related to going-concern resolutions for the 'too big to fail' financial institutions.

In Chapter 15, 'The governance of "too big to fail" banks', Andy Mullineux points out that the corporate governance of 'too big to fail' banks is particularly problematic because of the implicit insurance provided by the government at the taxpayers' expense. The chapter then discusses the ongoing regulatory structural reform (e.g., Volcker Rule,

Dodd–Frank Act) in the banking sector. The chapter also calls for a regulatory mechanism that contains a special resolution regime for 'too big to fail' banks and a pre-funded deposit insurance scheme with risk-related premia.

In Chapter 16, 'Incentives to improve the corporate governance of risk in financial institutions', Richard Herring discusses in great detail the benefits and costs of two very important aspects of corporate governance of banks: executive compensation and contingent convertible bonds. He argues that reform should focus on the compensation components that are widely agreed to encourage risk-takers to disregard the long-term consequences of their risk-taking behavior. He also argues that a properly structured contingent convertible bond scheme will have a much more direct impact on risk-taking incentives because of the potential credible threat of massive dilution of shareholders' and managers' pay-offs.

PART IV: GOVERNANCE, REGULATION AND SUPERVISION

The first chapter (Chapter 17) in this part, 'The boundary problems in financial regulation', by Charles Goodhart and Rosa Lastra, emphasizes a generic problem of financial regulation caused by the porous boundaries between regulated and non-regulated firms and between different jurisdictions. Most financial services can be performed in several types of financial institutions without being constrained by the jurisdiction of the institution providing financial services. For this reason regulation of particular financial institutions within specific jurisdictions tends to lose effectiveness over time. If regulation increases the costs of performing certain functions, these functions tend to move to where they can be performed more cheaply.

Systemically important financial institutions (SIFIs) tend to be subject to less market discipline than smaller competitors, as noted in the previous section. There is now a debate about regulation specifically aimed at SIFIs. Ingo Walter proposes in Chapter 18, 'Financial architecture, prudential regulation and organizational structure', a regulatory dialectic for examining the issue of derisking the financial system by reducing the size and/or scope of SIFIs. Various policy proposals, including the so-called Volcker Rule imbedded in the US Dodd–Frank Financial Stability and Consumer Protection Act of 2010, are examined against benchmarks. The concluding section of the chapter proposes the appropriate role of activity restrictions and carve-outs in regulatory initiatives designed to address the 2007–2009 financial crisis – or the next one.

One narrative of the financial crisis is that poor corporate governance at financial institutions was a major cause of the crisis. In Chapter 19, 'Corporate governance and prudential regulation of banks: is there any connection?', Lawrence White argues that this narrative is largely misguided. Public policy should look to improved prudential regulation, rather than improved corporate governance, for restraining the excessively risky activities of systemically important financial institutions.

Hilton Root concludes in Chapter 20, 'The policy conundrum of financial market complexity', that neither the unpredictability nor the rapidity of the financial collapse of 2008 can be explained by the usual culprits: the housing bubble, executive pay, regulators, rating agencies, risk models and global imbalances. The collapse is compared to an avalanche that bears no relationship to the grain of sand that triggered it. To guide regulation policymakers should recognize that success will depend on a more refined knowledge of why some initial events may have prompted an avalanche, while others did not.

Chapter 21, 'The future of financial regulation: reflections from an emerging market perspective' by Rakesh Mohan, former Deputy Governor of the Reserve Bank of India, provides an emerging market perspective on the financial crisis and its causes. The objective is to analyze the emerging contours of regulation of financial institutions. A lesson drawn is that the intellectual basis of light-touch regulation does not hold. Accordingly, supervisors must supervise. Furthermore, in emerging markets in particular, the traditional virtues of prudent fiscal policy and stable monetary policy, along with the maintenance of sustainable external accounts, should not be lost sight of in the presence of highly flexible financial markets.[1]

PART V: GOVERNANCE, STRATEGY AND SOCIAL RESPONSIBILITY

The nature of governance of financial institutions has changed dramatically with the increased role of securities markets relative to traditional credit markets in the financing of corporations, small and medium-sized enterprises and financial institutions. Financial innovation in derivatives, for example, has augmented marketability further at the expense of relationship banking.

Arnoud Boot and Matej Marinč focus on a potential dark side of marketability in Chapter 22, 'Financial innovations, marketability and stability in banking'. Based on key insights from the relationship banking literature, including the potential complementarities and conflicts of interest between intermediated relationship banking activities and financial market (e.g., underwriting, securitization) activities, they argue that marketability has possibly led to an excessive proliferation of transaction-oriented banking (trading and financial market activities). They ask whether the proliferation of financial innovations might impact bank-based versus financial market-driven economies differently, and discuss structural changes in financial institutions that could reduce fragility.

In Chapter 23, 'Bank acquisitions and strategy since the GLB Act', J. Kimball Dietrich asks whether the increasingly market-oriented financial environment has induced increased diversification of financial firms, as reflected in acquisitions within the financial sector after 1999 when the Gramm–Leach–Bliley Act liberalized restrictions on 'conglomerization' of financial firms. He describes and calculates the relative use of the expanded powers of bank management boards by analyzing banks' and bank holding companies' mergers and acquisitions from 1999 to 2007. These data in combination with stock market performance data are used to assess the performance and risk of alternative bank strategies concerning diversification.

Interest in social, environmental, ethical and trust (SEET) issues in banking has grown rapidly during the last decade. Andreas Hoepner and John Wilson provide an overview of SEET issues in banking in Chapter 24, 'Social, environmental, ethical and trust (SEET) issues in banking: an overview'. International initiatives are introduced. The United Nations Principles for Responsible Investment first highlighted the importance of SEET issues to the financial services industry. A structured review of the small but important literature on SEET issues in banking is presented for the benefit of academics, policymakers and practitioners alike.

Corporate social responsibility (CSR) is an extended version of corporate govern-ance because companies with well-formed corporate governance systems take care of most CSR issues. Although banks are important to the economic system, there is little empirical evidence concerning the relationship between taking care of CSR and bank performance. Chung-Hua Shen and Yuan Chang fill this gap in Chapter 25, 'Corporate social responsibility, financial performance and selection bias: evidence from Taiwan's TWSE-listed banks'.

The tested hypothesis is that taking more care of CSR results in stronger monitor-ing of the managers' decisions and thus weakens the managers' incentives to extract resources from the firms. By employing several matching methods the authors construct a sample of CSR banks and matching non-CSR banks. The empirical results exhibit little evidence that on average CSR banks, representing the stakeholder model of governance, are outperformed by or outperform non-CSR banks representing the shareholder model of governance.

PART VI: GOVERNANCE IN NON-BANK FINANCIAL INSTITUTIONS

In the first chapter (Chapter 26) in this part, 'Management turnover, regulatory oversight and performance: evidence from community banks', Ajay Palvia from the Office of the Comptroller of the Currency exploits a unique panel of US community banks to examine the role of regulatory oversight in disciplining bank management. The results indicate that weak regulatory evaluations are associated with increased executive turnover after controlling for performance, financial condition and other controls. Further, executive turnover linked to weak regulatory evaluations is found to be positively related to future performance. Overall, the findings are consistent with the explanation that regulatory oversight can lead to improved bank governance.

The ability to reclaim resources from managers is perhaps the most direct way to moderate principal–agent relations. In Chapter 27, 'Redeemability as governance: a study of closed-end and open-end funds under common management', Peter MacKay uses performance data for closed-end and open-end funds to test the hypothesis that the difference in share redeemability across funds within a family induces managers to favor their open-end funds over their closed-end funds (favoritism). This might entail chan-neling superior trades and resources toward their open-end funds.

Paul Gompers and Yuhai Xuan examine the characteristics of acquisitions of private firms by public companies in Chapter 28, 'The role of venture capitalists in the acquisi-tion of private companies'. They explore the impact that venture capital backing has on the acquirer's characteristics, form of payment and announcement returns, as well as long-run stock price and operating performance. The analysis suggests that the acquirers of private venture capital-backed companies do not suffer any adverse selection problem and continue to have superior performance in the long run.

The last chapter in this part, by Rients Galema, Robert Lensink and Roy Mersland, reviews the literature on microfinance institutions (MFIs). Chapter 29, 'Governance and microfinance institutions', also provides new empirical evidence on governance and risk, an issue that has been almost completely neglected in the literature. Most previous papers concentrate on the relation between corporate governance and financial and social performance. In this empirical study the authors ask whether larger boards make less extreme decisions by testing whether the larger boards are associated with less return variability.

Another feature of previous empirical microfinance governance studies is that they have been guided by agency theories developed for corporations and Western non-governmental organizations (NGOs). While corporations maximize profits, MFIs have dual objectives. Furthermore, there are many different types of MFIs ranging from the most commercial banks to the least commercial NGO. They all have different trade-offs between financial and social objectives. This chapter calls for new theory on how optimal incentives throughout the institution can stimulate the MFI to reach its dual objectives, and shows how different funding structures create different governance problems.[2]

PART VII: REGIONAL AND COUNTRY STUDIES

This last part begins with a study of New Zealand. This country stands out as one putting strong reliance on market discipline to constrain risk-taking in comparison with most other industrialized countries. Don Brash, former Governor of the Reserve Bank of New Zealand, provides a review of the regulatory debate and the features of the regulatory structure in New Zealand in Chapter 30, 'Bank governance: the case of New Zealand'. Market discipline in the mainly foreign-owned banking system is achieved by means of an emphasis on disclosure rules, no deposit insurance and establishment of procedures for closing insolvent banks. There were no failures during the recent financial crisis. Nevertheless, there seems to be a trend towards adoption of regulatory features in common with other industrialized countries, partly as a result of the global reach of the Basel guidelines.

In Chapter 31, 'Corporate governance in European banking', Francesca Arnaboldi and Barbara Casu survey the corporate governance features of banking institutions in the EU-15 countries. Working on the notion that corporate governance is influenced by cultural values, the authors present an analysis clustering these European Union (EU) countries on the basis of their legal system, language family and proximity as indicators of cultural differences. The results highlight that cultural and legal differences are still strongly embedded in national cultural identities and that these seem to drive the majority of the differences in corporate governance arrangements. The pluralistic structure of EU banking systems, the varied nature of corporate governance arrangements and different business models represent a strength of the EU banking sector, but are also a factor that may hinder further integration and the emergence of a truly European banking model.

The Japanese model for bank restructuring featured prominently in the debate about financial sector reform in the United States and Europe during the recent crisis, as a model to avoid. Satoshi Koibuchi explores in Chapter 32, 'Debt forgiveness during Japan's lost decade', why the traditional bank-led corporate restructuring was one of the main contributors to the prolonged non-performing loan problem in Japan. The bank-led corporate restructuring was expected to function as a scheme to resolve the debt overhang problem but announcements of debt forgiveness tended to impact negatively the equity prices of the main banks. The Industrial Revitalization Corporation of Japan (IRCJ) successfully introduced a new rule for sharing the burdens of debt forgiveness in proportion to lenders' loan shares. The IRCJ significantly mitigated the excess burden of debt forgiveness on the main banks.

In Chapter 33, 'Corporate governance of banks in Korea', Heungsik Choe and Byungyoon Lee review the history of the board system adopted by Korean banks and bank holding companies, highlight problems in its application, and present solutions. The Best Practices for Outside Directors of Banks and Related Institutions were announced in January 2010, including several clauses aimed at enhancing the independence and expertise of directors. In a second step the Financial Services Commission (FSC) is trying to enact the Act on Corporate Governance of Financial Institutions to improve the governance system as a whole, including the board system, audit committee, executive directors, major shareholders and compliance officers of all the financial institutions. The authors review the FSC's proposals to improve the corporate governance of Korean banks and discuss how to improve them further.

Regulatory governance has been defined as the capacity to meet delegated objectives, and to provide protection from industry capture and political interference and respect for the regulatory agency to implement the broad goals and policies of the legislature. With this starting point Yufeng Gong and Zhongfei Zhou employ independence, accountability and transparency as criteria for analyzing the regulatory governance of the China Banking Regulatory Commission (CBRC) from a legal perspective. In Chapter 34, 'Banking regulatory governance in China: a legal perspective', the authors discuss advantages and disadvantages in Chinese banking legislation with respect to regulatory governance. They outline a legal framework for guaranteeing sound regulatory governance of the CBRC.

Turning to Chapter 35, 'Corporate governance and bank performance in Thailand', Tientip Subhanij and Wanvimol Sawangngoenyuang provide an overview of policies implemented by the Bank of Thailand to enhance corporate governance in banks, and an empirical analysis of the impact of corporate governance variables on bank performance. The analysis reveals that since 2000, as the number of independent directors relative to board size has increased, banks' performance has improved and the cost-to-income ratio has fallen. Other factors than corporate governance may also have contributed to the positive developments.

In the last chapter (Chapter 36) in this volume, 'Governance issues in Indian microfinance', Shubhashis Gangopadhyay and S.K. Shanthi ask what role governance plays in resolving fundamental questions regarding the operation of microfinance institutions (MFIs) in India in particular.[3] Is there enough justification for subsidizing the microfinance industry with public funds? Do increased interest rates exacerbate agency problems as detected by lower loan repayment rates and less profitability? Is there evidence of a trade-off between the depth of outreach to the poor and the pursuit of profitability or self-sustainability? Is there evidence of 'mission drift' in the functioning of MFIs? Reports of exorbitant profit-making by MFIs, households burdened with multiple loans, coercive recovery by MFI agents and, to top it all, suicides by defaulters created a furor in Indian government and policy circles. Draconian state ordinance followed by a national level set of recommendations may push a hitherto unregulated fast-growing sector into becoming a highly shackled industry of the pre-reform days.

The authors are deeply indebted to Dr Apanard P. Prabha for all her help in making sure this book was completed on time.

NOTES

1. Country studies referring to emerging market economies can be found in Chapters 34 (China), 35 (Thailand) and 36 (India).
2. Chapter 36 in Part VII provides further analysis of MFIs in India.
3. Governance issues in the microfinance industry are discussed in Chapter 29 as well.

PART I

OWNERSHIP, EFFICIENCY AND STABILITY

1 Bank governance: concepts and measurements
Frank M. Song and Li Li

1.1 BANK GOVERNANCE: SELECTED LITERATURE REVIEW

Corporate governance has long been a hot topic for research (see Shleifer and Vishny, 1997; Denis and McConnell, 2003, for survey). Despite the general focus on this topic, relatively limited attention has been paid to the corporate governance of banks (e.g., Macey and O'Hara, 2003; Levine, 2004; Adams and Mehran, 2005; Caprio et al., 2007; Dahya et al., 2008). This is strange, considering the fact that corporate governance of banks is not only important but also unique (Levine, 2004).

It is important to understand corporate governance of banks for several reasons. First of all, banks are themselves corporations. Sound corporate governance is essential for banks to perform efficiently. Moreover, since banks exert a strong impact on economic development (Levine, 1997, 2005), corporate governance of banks is crucial for growth and development. Banks play a central role in mobilizing social savings and channeling them to the most productive projects. Bank lending is a major source of external finance for other firms, especially in developing and emerging economies. Sound corporate governance of banks is essential for bank managers to allocate social capital efficiently and to enhance the performance of the economies. Banks also play a critical role in the corporate governance of other firms (Franks and Mayer, 2001; Santos and Rumble, 2006), as creditors of firms and, in many countries, as equity holders. Thus, it is also essential that banks themselves face sound corporate governance so that they can exert effective governance over the firms they fund.

The vulnerability of the banking system further emphasizes the importance of sound corporate governance. Since the banking system is extremely vulnerable to shocks, shortcomings in corporate governance of banks, if widespread, can destabilize the financial system and pose systematic risks to the real economy (OECD, 2006). It has been claimed that, to an important extent, the financial crisis of 2007–2010 can be attributed to the failures and weaknesses of corporate governance arrangements (Kirkpatrick, 2009). For example, the executive compensation arrangements have incentivized extreme risk-taking while not punishing failures, and have emphasized short-term interests while not aligning with the long-term nature of risk.

Corporate governance of banks is also unique. Banks have two special features that distinguish corporate governance of banks from that of other firms: opaqueness and regulation. First, banks generally are more opaque than non-financial firms. Although information asymmetries exist in all sectors, evidence suggests that information asymmetries between insiders and outsiders are much more serious in banks (Furfine, 2001; Morgan, 2002). The greater opacity in banks intensifies the agency problem. The opaqueness makes it difficult for diffuse depositors and shareholders to monitor bank managers, makes it more difficult to design executive compensation plans that align the interests of managers and shareholders, and makes it easier for insiders to exploit outside investors.

Second, banks are heavily regulated. Because of the importance of banks for the whole economy, and the high information asymmetries between insiders and outsiders, governments around the world impose an array of regulations on banks. Official regulations can be considered as an additional governance mechanism; they may also impact the role of traditional corporate governance mechanisms for banks (Levine, 2004).

For one thing, certain regulation policies limit the impact of traditional governance mechanisms. For example, governments in many countries restrict the concentration of bank ownership; they also restrict the ability of outsiders to purchase a substantial percentage of bank shares without regulatory approval; and in some countries, there may be constraints on who can own banks (e.g., limits on ownership by non-financial or non-bank firms) (Barth et al., 2006). Regulations also restrict competition in product markets by imposing regulatory restrictions on banks' entry, especially on foreign banks' entry (Levine, 2004).

Additionally, supervision, which ensures that banks comply with regulatory requirements, may play a general monitoring role which substitutes or complements other governance mechanisms. For example, direct supervision by governments substitutes internal governance of banks, while promoting private monitoring can complement bank internal governance (Li and Song, 2010). Deposit insurance schemes reduce the incentive of depositors as debt holders to monitor banks, and increase the incentive of bank managers to increase risk-taking (Billett et al., 1998).

Due to the importance of corporate governance of banks, and the uniqueness of corporate governance resulting from high opaqueness and official regulations, it is valuable to examine whether the standard corporate governance mechanisms that apply to non-financial firms are also valid for banks. It is also valuable to examine the effects of regulations as an additional governance mechanism. Moreover, since shareholders and regulators do not always share the same objectives, we can gain insight into the optimal design of regulation and corporate governance for regulators and banks by understanding the interaction of regulation and corporate governance.

In the following section, we introduce existing papers on corporate governance of banks. We first focus on papers considering standard corporate governance mechanisms of banks, then introduce papers investigating the impact of bank regulations and papers studying the interaction of regulation and corporate governance of banks.

1.1.1   Traditional Corporate Governance Mechanisms in Banking

Corporate governance and market value of banks

Most empirical studies on corporate governance exclude financial firms from their samples due to the special characteristics of financial firms. Ever since the Asian financial crisis, more attention has focused on corporate governance of financial sectors, especially banks. Empirical studies on corporate governance of banks mainly focus on bank holding companies (BHCs) in the US. Adams and Mehran (2003) compare the corporate governance of BHCs and manufacturing firms and find that governance structures of BHCs are different from those of manufacturing firms. For example, BHC board size (18.2 members versus 12.1 members) and the percentage of outside directors (68.7 percent versus 60.6 percent) are significantly larger on average than for manufacturing firms; and BHC boards on average have more committees (4.9 compared with 4.4) and meet slightly more frequently (7.9 times versus 7.6 times). Adams and Mehran (2003) also find that manufacturing firms rely more on stock options in chief executive officer (CEO) compensation, and insiders hold more shares in manufacturing firms than BHCs.

Contrary to the empirical evidence in non-financial firms that smaller boards are more effective and then induce an increase in performance, several studies show that it may not be true for banking firms (Adams and Mehran, 2002; Belkhir, 2009; Adams and Mehran, 2005). Adams and Mehran (2002) focus on the effect of board size on performance in a sample of 35 large BHCs during 1986–1999, and find that the natural logarithm of board size is positively and significantly related to Tobin's Q. Belkhir (2009) extends the sample to include BHCs and S&LHCs (saving and loan holding companies) and confirms the findings of Adams and Mehran (2002). He finds a positive relation between board size and measures of performance (Tobin's Q and return on assets) and suggests that this relation is only a spurious correlation due to the positive effect of mergers and acquisitions (M&A) on both board size and performance. Adams and Mehran (2005) further investigate the issue; they show that the positive relationship is not driven by M&A. However, they suggest that features of the BHCs' organizational form may make a larger board more desirable for these firms, and document that board size is significantly related to characteristics of BHC firms' structures. Even after controlling for the potential sources of endogeneity – M&A and BHC firms' structure – they do not find a negative relationship between board size and Tobin's Q.

Brook et al. (2000) study the determinants of a bank becoming a target for acquisition by another bank. They find that outside directors' equity ownership enhances enforcing managers to act in the interest of shareholders by accepting a takeover bid. Brewer et al. (2000) find that bid premiums offered for target banks increase with the proportion of independent outside directors. However, Pi and Timme (1993) and Adams and Mehran (2002) find that the proportion of outside directors is not related to performance measures.

Corporate governance and bank risk-taking

Risk-taking is a central issue for the banking industry. Many studies investigate the effects of corporate governance on bank risk-taking. According to traditional agency theory, bank shareholders have a preference for 'excessive risk' (Galai and Masulis, 1976; Jensen and Meckling, 1976; John et al., 1991) due to the limited liability and the 'moral hazard' problem, while managers are more risk-averse than shareholders because managers want to pursue private benefits of control and preserve non-diversifiable human capital in the banks they manage (Demsetz and Lehn, 1985; Kane, 1985). By monitoring managers effectively or aligning the incentives of managers with shareholders, corporate governance mechanisms induce managers to take value-enhancing risk.

However, better corporate governance could reduce managerial discretion, which results in lower risk-taking of banks. Burkart et al. (1997) point out that as the monitoring efforts exerted by large shareholders increase, managerial initiative to pursue new investment opportunities decreases. Moreover, in contrast to traditional agency theory which suggests that managers are risk-avoiders, the behavioral agency school argues that managers are prone to biases such as hubris, overoptimism and overconfidence (e.g., Wiseman and Gomez-Mejia, 1998). A recent paper by Ben-David et al. (2007) demonstrates that the financial executives are overconfident. Better corporate governance mechanisms can correct the over-risky investments by managers, suggesting that better corporate governance is related to lower bank risk-taking. Therefore, it is an empirical issue as to how corporate governance mechanisms influence bank risk-taking.

Pathan (2009) uses a sample of 212 large US BHCs over 1997–2004 (1534 observations) to examine the effects of board structure on bank risk-taking. Pathan (2009) finds that strong bank boards of small size positively affect bank risk-taking, and the CEO's power to control board decision negatively affects bank risk-taking. These results support the traditional agency theory and suggest that better corporate governance mechanisms promote bank risk-taking. However, Pathan's (2009) results also indicate that more independent boards lead to lower bank risk, which means that better monitoring of managers may reduce risk-taking of banks.

Several empirical studies explore the effects of incentive compensation on bank risk-taking, and show that stock option-based executive compensation leads to more risk-taking in banking (Chen et al., 2006; Mehran and Rosenberg, 2009). Specifically, Chen et al. (2006) examine the relation between option-based executive compensation and market measures of risk for commercial banks during the period of 1992–2000. They show that the structure of executive compensation induces risk-taking, and the stock of option-based wealth also induces risk-taking. Mehran and Rosenberg (2009) use a sample of 549 bank-years for publicly traded banks in the US from 1992 to 2002 to assess the effects of CEO stock options on three key corporate policies for banks: investment choice, amount of borrowing and level of capital. Mehran and Rosenberg (2009) find that grants of stock option lead CEOs to undertake riskier investments. Higher levels of option grants are associated with higher levels of equity volatility and asset volatility. However, as Houston and James (1995) indicate, incentive executive compensation will not necessarily result in high bank risk. Incentive compensation increases the charter value of banks (Houston and James, 1995), which induces managers to behave prudently and avoid bankruptcy.

International evidence
Most of the research mentioned above focuses on BHCs in the US. Some studies have attempted to explore the issue of corporate governance in banks outside the US. For example, Anderson and Campbell (2003) investigate corporate governance of Japanese banks. The results indicate that no relation exists between bank performance and non-routine executive turnover in the pre-crisis period (1985–1990); however, there is an observed significant relationship between turnover and performance in the post-crisis period (1991–1996). Konishi and Yasuda (2004) examine the determinants of risk-taking of commercial banks in Japan and find a non-linear relationship between the stable shareholders' ownership and bank risk. They find that the risk decreases initially with the ownership by stable shareholders, and then increases as the asset substitution effect dominates the effect of managerial entrenchment on bank risk. Das and Ghosh (2004) find a significant relation between bank performance and CEO turnover. They show that CEOs of poorly performing banks are likely to face higher turnover than CEOs of well-performing ones. Crespí et al. (2004) examine the governance mechanism in the Spanish bank sector and find that CEO turnover is more likely when firms are poorly managed and their economic returns are low, and this relationship is stronger for the sample of independent commercial banks than savings banks. Choe and Lee (2003)

examine the stock market response to banking reform and find unusual high abnormal returns related to events associated with outside directors. Pathan et al. (2008) also find that announcements of bank corporate governance reforms are generally associated with significant change in bank sector returns in Thailand.

Recently some cross-country studies have investigated corporate governance of banks around the world. Andrés and Vallelado (2008) employ information on the boards of directors of 69 commercial banks from six Organisation for Economic Co-operation and Development (OECD) countries for the period 1996–2006 to investigate the role of board of directors in banking. They analyze the monitoring and advising roles of boards and find an inverted U-shaped relation between bank board size and bank value, also an inverted U-shaped relation between the proportion of outside directors and valuation.

Several cross-country studies have examined the effects of ownership structure on bank performance (e.g., Caprio et al., 2007; Laeven and Levine, 2009; Magalhaes et al., 2008). Specifically, Caprio et al. (2007) construct a database covering 244 banks across 44 countries and trace the ownership of banks to identify the ultimate owners of bank capital and the degree of voting rights and cash flow rights concentration. They find that ownership structure and shareholder protection laws that influence non-financial firms impact bank valuation as well: larger cash flow rights by the controlling owner and stronger shareholder protection laws increase bank valuation. Laeven and Levine (2009) set up a sample of 279 banks across 48 countries to examine the effects of ownership structure on bank risk-taking. They find that banks with controlling shareholders are characterized by higher risk-taking than banks with dispersed ownership, which is consistent with the traditional agency theory. Laeven and Levine (2009) also find that the same regulation policy can have different effects on bank risk-taking, depending on banks' ownership structure. Magalhaes et al. (2008) construct a dataset on 423 banks around 39 countries for the period from 2000 to 2006 to investigate the relationship between ownership structure and bank risk-taking. Their analyses show that ownership concentration is more important than risk-taking to explain performance. They provide a cubic relationship between ownership concentration and bank performance. Such evidence is supportive of theoretical hypotheses of effective monitoring at low levels of ownership concentration, expropriation or loss of managerial discretion at moderate ownership concentration, and high costs of expropriation at high levels of ownership concentration.

Baumann and Nier (2004) make use of a dataset on about 600 banks across 31 countries for the period 1993–2000 to investigate information disclosure and bank risk. They construct a composite disclosure index from annual accounts of banks that provides information about disclosure at the bank level, and report that banks disclosing more information to investors show lower stock volatility than those disclosing less information. Tadesse (2003) provides cross-country evidence that more comprehensive, accurate and timely bank disclosure mitigates the likelihood of a systematic banking crisis. Barth et al. (2007) employ information on about 2000 banks from 72 countries to examine the relation between market discipline and bank performance. They find that better information disclosure, accounting standards, and external auditing and monitoring are related with higher bank profits and lower costs.

All the cross-country studies mentioned above focus on individual corporate governance mechanisms. Li and Song (2010) consider more comprehensive corporate governance mechanisms, including board structure, ownership structure, executive compensation and transparency, and construct a corporate governance score to assess the impacts of corporate governance mechanisms on bank performance. They construct a sample of 225 banks from 48 countries for the period of 2004–2006 to examine the effects of internal governance mechanisms on bank valuation and bank risk. They form four indices on board of directors, executive compensation, ownership concentration and transparency, respectively, and find that traditional governance mechanisms working in manufacturing firms also enhance bank value and bank profits. Li and Song (2010) also examine the effects of four internal governance mechanisms on risk-taking of banks. Contrary to the traditional agency theory, they find that better corporate governance reduces bank risk. Specifically, they find a negative relation between incentive compensation and bank insolvency risk, and a negative relation between concentrated ownership and the probability of bank insolvency. The positive effect of ownership concentration on bank risk is consistent with Burkart et al. (1997), who suggest that the monitoring efforts exerted by the large shareholders reduce the managerial incentive to take risk. They do not find a significant relation between transparency and bank risk.

1.1.2   Corporate Governance, Regulation and Interactions

Banks are heavily and pervasively regulated due to the importance of the banking industry to the financial and economic system. Regulations act as an extra governance mechanism and distinguish corporate governance of banking from that of other industries. However, most of the studies we introduced above have not considered the role of regulations, partly due to the absence of data for measuring cross-country regulations.

Ever since Barth et al. (2006) compiled a comprehensive cross-country database on bank regulations and supervisions (we will introduce the database and the measures of bank regulation and supervision in section 1.2), many empirical studies have investigated the role of regulations on bank performance using the database (Barth et al., 2004, 2006; Beck et al., 2006; Caprio et al., 2007; Li and Song, 2010; Lin et al., forthcoming), and several papers have considered the interaction mechanism between traditional governance and regulations (Caprio et al., 2007; Laeven and Levine, 2009; Li and Song, 2010).

Regulation and supervision aim to benefit the functioning of the banking system, ensure the stability of the financial system and promote economic growth. Barth et al. (2004) assess whether the effects of regulation and supervision are consistent with these objectives; specifically, they examine the relationship between various regulatory and supervisory activities and bank development, performance and stability. They find that, on the one hand, government policies which rely excessively on direct government supervision and regulation of bank activities at best do not impact bank performance, and sometimes even impede bank development. For example, in contrast to when banks can diversify into other financial activities, restricting bank activities is negatively related to bank development and stability; and barriers to foreign-bank entry are positively associated with bank fragility. On the other hand, they find that government policies which rely on guidelines that force accurate information disclosure and empower private-sector monitoring of banks work best to promote bank development, performance and stability. For example, they find that the private monitoring index is positively related with bank development and bank performance.

Beck et al. (2006) explore the issue of regulation on bank performance further, and consider the impacts of regulation and supervision policies on bank lending corruption. They compare two types of supervision policies: one is the traditional bank supervision approach, which involves empowering official supervisory agencies to monitor, discipline and influence banks directly; and the other is the supervision approach that focuses on empowering private monitoring of banks by forcing banks to disclose accurate information to the private sector. They employ the private monitoring index and supervisory power index from the bank regulation database of Barth et al. (2004, 2006) to measure these two types of supervision policies. The empirical results show that direct discipline and monitoring by bank supervisory agencies does not improve the integrity of bank lending. However, the supervisory strategy that focuses on empowering private monitoring of banks reduces the degree of bank corruption. Beck et al.'s (2006) results are consistent with those of Barth et al. (2004).

Official bank regulations may arise in part to restrain bank insiders from expropriating or misallocating bank resources, as argued in Caprio and Levine (2002). Thus, effective regulation may increase investor confidence regarding expropriation, and increase market valuations. However, since bank regulations aim to reduce systematic risk and ensure banking development, the interests of regulators are not always aligned with those of bank shareholders. Therefore, bank regulations may conflict with the interests of shareholders and reduce market valuations. Several studies consider the role of regulations and the possible interaction effects between regulation and governance when studying the corporate governance mechanism of banks (Caprio et al., 2007; Laeven and Levine, 2009; Li and Song, 2010).

Caprio et al. (2007) consider the impacts of regulation policies when assessing the effects of ownership structure on bank valuations. They examine the effects of ownership concentration, shareholder protection laws and bank regulations on bank valuation, together with the interaction between ownership structure and law. They find that larger cash flow rights by the controlling owner and stronger shareholder protection laws increase bank valuation, and they also find a substitution between law and ownership concentration. However, they do not find any significant effect of regulation on market valuation of banks.

Laeven and Levine (2009) consider the issue of bank risk-taking and examine the effects of ownership structure on bank risk-taking. They focus on conflicts between bank managers and owners over risk, and find that bank risk-taking is positively related with the comparative power of shareholders within the corporate governance structure of each bank, which is consistent with the traditional agency theory. Laeven and Levine (2009) also examine the interaction effects between ownership structure and regulation on bank risk-taking. They find that the relationship between bank risk and capital regulations, deposit insurance policies and bank activity restrictions depends on each bank's ownership structure, such that the actual sign of the marginal effect of regulation on risk varies with ownership concentration. The results suggest that the same regulation policy can have different effects on bank risk-taking, depending on the bank's ownership structure.

Li and Song (2010) consider the possible effects of regulation policies on internal governance arrangements of individual banks, and then examine the effects of internal governance mechanisms and regulations on bank performance. Consistent with

Barth et al. (2004) and Beck et al. (2006), Li and Song (2010) explore the impacts of two types of supervision policies and find that direct official supervision substitutes internal governance arrangements of individual banks, while promoting monitoring by the private sector enhances internal governance mechanisms of banks. They then consider the relationship between various internal governance mechanisms and bank valuations and risk-taking, and find that better arrangements of internal governance mechanisms including the board of directors, ownership structure, executive compensation and information disclosure increase the market valuation of banks as well as reducing bank risk-taking. They also find that the supervision approach which focuses on promoting monitoring of banks by the private sector not only increases market valuation of banks but also boosts the positive effects of internal governance on bank valuation.

1.2   MEASURES OF GOVERNANCE FOR BANKS

Adam Smith (1776) describes that when ownership and control of corporations are not fully coincident, there is potential for conflicts of interests between owners and controllers – the agency problem. Berle and Means (1932) argue that managers of a firm pursue interests of their own rather than those of shareholders. Corporate governance is a set of economic and institutional mechanisms to induce the self-interested controllers of a corporation to make decisions that maximize value for its owners (Denis and McConnell, 2003). Generally, there are two types of mechanisms to resolve the conflicts between owners and controllers. One type consists of internal mechanisms, including the board of directors, the ownership structure, executive compensation and financial disclosure. The second comprises external mechanisms, including the takeover market, the legal infrastructure and product market competition.

As for other firms, the classical principal–agent problem is clearly present in the case of banks, mainly through the conflicting interests between managers and owners. Therefore, like other firms, banks set up internal governance frameworks to deal with the principal–agent problem. At the same time, due to the negative externalities of bank failures, governments in all countries regulate banks heavily, with the aim to reduce systemic risks, increase financial stability and protect the interests of diverse depositors. Regulations act as an additional external governance force for banks, and they are critically important since certain external governance mechanisms, such as the takeover market and product market competition, are nearly absent in banking (Prowse, 1997; Levine, 2004). In the following subsections, we will introduce the measures of internal governance and external governance of banks respectively.

1.2.1   Internal Governance

Internal governance mechanisms
The board of directors, at the apex of the internal control system, is the bridge between management and shareholders. Shareholders can exert influence on the behavior of managers through the board of directors, to ensure that the company is run in their interests. Conventional wisdom suggests that a more independent board

of directors indicates better corporate governance. The Sarbanes–Oxley Act of 2002 requires that boards have audit committees that consist only of independent outside directors. The Codes of Best Practice issued in many countries have called for greater outside representation and the separation of the roles of CEO and chairman in the board of directors (Denis and McConnell, 2003). The Basel Committee on Banking Supervision (BCBS) has advocated a board of directors with an adequate number of independent directors (BCBS, 2006). The empirical results on US non-financial firms generally show that higher board independence is not related with superior firm performance, but is related with better decision-making on such issues as acquisitions and CEO turnover (Hermalin and Weisbach, 2003). However, cross-country studies mainly demonstrate a positive relationship between board independence and firm value (e.g., Klapper and Love, 2004; Dahya et al., 2008). Relatively few studies have examined the effects of board independence in the banking industry (e.g., Brewer et al., 2000; Adams and Mehran, 2005; Andrés and Vallelado, 2008), and the results are mixed.

Ownership structure is crucial to the value maximization of a firm. Equity held by concentrated shareholders and insiders can be a corporate governance mechanism to avoid the conflicts of interests between managers and shareholders. Shleifer and Vishny (1997) suggest that legal protection and concentrated ownership are essential for a good corporate governance system. However, ownership concentration may have either positive or negative effects on corporate governance. Concentrated ownership may solve the free-rider problem of monitoring managers. The greater control that the largest shareholders have leads them to take actions to increase the market value of the firm, benefiting all shareholders. On the other hand, concentrated ownership also gives the largest shareholders substantial discretionary power to pursue private benefits at the expense of other shareholders, potentially reducing the firm's value. Similarly, equity ownership by insiders can align interests of insiders with those of other shareholders, leading to higher firm value. However, higher ownership by insiders can result in higher managerial control, potentially entrenching managers. The US evidence regarding the ownership structure and firm performance is mixed, whereas concentrated ownership most often has positive effects on firm value in non-US firms (Denis and McConnell, 2003). Caprio et al. (2007) demonstrate that concentrated ownership is an important governance mechanism for banking. They find that larger cash flow rights of controlling shareholders boost bank valuation in 44 countries. Laeven and Levine (2009) find that the ultimate cash flow rights held by the controlling owner are related with greater bank risk-taking, and explain that higher ownership concentration aligns managers' risk-taking incentives with those of shareholders.

To align the interests of managers and shareholders, appropriately structured executive compensation, which is linked to both stock valuation and accounting-based performance measures, is necessary. Pay–performance sensitivity reflects the degree to which executive compensation aligns top executives' interests with those of shareholders. The bulk of pay–performance sensitivity comes through equity-based compensation such as stocks and options (Murphy, 1999; Core et al., 2003). Many empirical studies have demonstrated a positive relationship between equity-based compensation and firm value (e.g., Jensen and Murphy, 1990; Mehran, 1995). However, some researchers argue that options are a means of rent extraction if the executives have control of the board and use large option grants to extract wealth from shareholders (e.g., Core et al., 1999). Banks are reported as less likely to use managerial stock options in executive compensation than non-financial firms (Houston and James, 1992); however, banks in the US have increasingly employed stock option-based compensation following deregulation (Crawford et al., 1995; Chen et al., 2006). Chen et al. (2006) suggest that stock option-based compensation induces bank risk-taking.

Financial transparency and adequate information disclosure are crucial for corporate governance of firms (La Porta et al., 1998; Bushman and Smith, 2003). Sufficient, credible and timely information regarding the firm's operations, financial status, and the external environment facilitates shareholders to discipline and monitor managers, enables the board of directors to enhance shareholder value by advising on managerial decisions, and provides a basis for determining executive compensation plans designed to align executives' and shareholders' interests. One key to the provision of accurate information is the use of accurate accounting standards. La Porta et al. (1998) suggest that the accounting standard is an important element of corporate governance. Leutz and Verrecchia (2000) find that German firms that voluntarily adopt either the International Accounting Standards (IAS) or the US Generally Accepted Accounting Practices (GAAP) for their reporting show lower information asymmetry and higher stock liquidity compared with a control group of firms employing the German reporting regime. Baek et al. (2004) find that Korean firms that have higher disclosure quality suffer less in a financial crisis. Transparency is even more important for the banking industry since information asymmetries between insiders and outsiders are much more serious in banks than in non-financial firms (Furfine, 2001; Morgan, 2002). Studies find that improving bank disclosure and transparency benefits banks as well as the financial system (e.g., Jordan et al., 1999; Tadesse, 2003). Specifically, Jordan et al. (1999) show that improving bank disclosure during a banking crisis is not destabilizing, but instead provides conditions for market discipline to work more effectively. Tadesse (2003) provides cross-country evidence that more comprehensive, accurate and timely bank disclosure mitigates the likelihood of a systematic banking crisis.

Internal governance measurements

This subsection describes our method of building up a cross-country database of bank internal governance. The database provides the information on board structure, ownership structure, executive compensation and transparency standards from 2004 to 2006 for more than 200 publicly listed commercial banks and bank holding companies (BHCs) in 48 countries.

The process of setting up the database is as follows. First, data permitting, we collected the internal governance information of the ten largest publicly listed commercial banks and BHCs (as defined by the total assets at the end of 2006) in those countries covered by Barth et al.'s (2006) database on bank regulation and supervision. For every bank in the sample, we collected the information on board structure, ownership structure, executive compensation and transparency standards from 2004 to 2006. We intensively used banks' annual reports, proxy statements, regulated files and websites. Also, many national institutions (e.g., central banks and regulatory authorities) maintain websites that we used to search for the corporate governance data. Since many countries have fewer than ten publicly listed banks regarding which we could get information on

Table 1.1   Summary of variables used in corporate governance indices

Index	Variables
Board structure index	*Percent of INEDs on the board of directors* *Percent of INEDs on the audit committee* *No CEO/Chairman duality* *INED as board chairman*
Ownership structure index	*Percent of ownership held by the largest shareholder* *Percent of ownership held by the five largest shareholders* *Logarithm of value held by the largest shareholder* *Logarithm of value held by the five largest shareholders*
Executive compensation index	*Option scheme to top executives* *Option scheme to non-executive directors* *Share-based bonus* *Variable compensation*
Transparency index	*Big 4 as auditors* *Cross-listing in US* *Disclosure of executive compensation and shareholdings*

Note: This table lists the four corporate governance indices and the variables used to construct the indices. Variables are condensed to the respective index using principal component analysis.

corporate governance, the final sample consisted of 476 bank-year observations of 225 banks across 48 countries.

Second, we formulated internal governance indices based on the information collected. Referring to Song and Lei (2008), Bai et al. (2004) and Gompers et al. (2003), we constructed four indices (the board structure index, ownership structure index, executive compensation index and transparency index) from 15 corporate governance variables based on the internal governance mechanisms reviewed before. We used the principal component analysis to form our indices. Using the largest positive eigenvector, we generated an index score with mean of 0, and standard deviation of 1 for each of the four internal governance mechanisms. Credit Lyonnais Securities Asia (CLSA) (2001) and Gompers et al. (2003) construct a corporate governance index by adding one point to each variable when the variable improves corporate governance, and they get the index by summing up the points. Compared to CLSA (2001) and Gompers et al. (2003), the advantage of principal component indices is that equal weights for the individual variables are not specified. A disadvantage is that it is less transparent how a change in a variable changes the index. Table 1.1 provides a summary of the indices and variables. The following discusses the construction of the four internal governance indices.

The board structure index is constructed from four variables. *Percent of Independent Non-executive Directors (INEDs) on the board of directors* is the ratio of INEDs to board size as percentage. *Percent of INEDs on the audit committee* is the ratio of INEDs on the audit committee to committee size as percentage. *No CEO/Chairman duality* is a dummy variable with the value of 1 if the CEO is not the board chairman, 0 otherwise. *INED as board chairman* is a dummy variable which takes a value of 1 if an INED acts as board chairman, 0 otherwise. We use the largest positive eigenvector to generate the board structure index, which varies between −2 and 2.04 with a mean of 0 and median of −0.07, higher value indicating higher board independence.

The ownership structure index is constructed from four variables. *Percent of ownership held by the largest shareholder* is the total issued shares held by the largest shareholder in percentage. *Percent of ownership held by the five largest shareholders* is the total issued shares held by the top five shareholders, as a percentage. *Logarithm of value held by the largest shareholder* is the logarithm of shareholding value held by the largest shareholder. *Logarithm of value held by the five largest shareholders* is the logarithm of shareholding value held by the top five shareholders.

Information on the percentages of ownership held by the largest and five largest shareholders comes from the BankScope database. We complement the variables manually from annual reports and websites for the missing data. Values held by the largest shareholders are products of the fractions of ownership and market values of the banks. The ownership structure index ranges from −2.61 to 3.27, with a mean of 0 and median of −0.02, and with higher value indicating higher ownership concentration.

The executive compensation index is constructed from four dummy variables. *Option schemes to top executives* is a dummy variable which takes a value of 1 if a bank employs share option schemes to top executives, 0 otherwise. *Option schemes to non-executive directors*: many banks also employ share option schemes to non-executive directors. The dummy variable takes a value of 1 if a bank has such schemes, 0 otherwise. *Share-based bonus* measures whether there are share-based bonuses for top executives. It equals 1 if a bank has such bonuses, 0 otherwise. *Variable compensation* takes a value of 1 if top executives are paid variable compensation, 0 if their compensation is fixed. The executive compensation index ranges from −1.77 to 1.31 with a mean of 0 and median of 0.67, higher value indicating higher pay-sensitivity of executive compensation.

The transparency index is constructed from three variables. *Big 4 as auditors* is a dummy variable, which takes a value of 1 if a bank employs one of the Big 4 accounting firms (PricewaterhouseCoopers, Deloitte Touche Tomatsu, Ernst & Young, KPMG) as their auditors, 0 otherwise. *Cross-listing in US* is a dummy variable which identifies banks whose shares are traded either as a direct listing on a US stock exchange or as an American Depository Receipt (ADR). *Disclosure of executive compensation and shareholdings* is the sum of three dummy variables, which indicate whether the bank discloses information on top executive compensation, top executive shareholdings and directors' shareholdings, respectively. The three dummy variables take a value of 1 if the bank provides corresponding information for individuals, 0.5 if the bank provides information in aggregate, and 0 if no such information is provided. Disclosure of executive compensation and shareholdings ranges from 0 to 3, with higher values indicating better disclosure. The transparency index varies between −2.60 and 1.32, with the mean of 0 and median of −0.02, and with higher value indicating better transparency standard of the bank.

We construct an overall internal governance score (IG) based on the board structure index, ownership structure index, executive compensation index and transparency index. The IG score is generated by summing up the rankings of the four internal governance indices, and then normalizing to 0–100. The IG score gives an ordinal comparison of banks, with a mean of 45.23 and a median of 44.41, and with higher value indicating better corporate governance quality.

Internal governance of banks around the world

Table 1.2 provides information on board structure, ownership structure, executive compensation and transparency of banks around the world in 2006.

Board structure The average board size of the publicly listed banks in 2006 in our sample is 12. The minimal board has only three members, whereas the maximal board has 27 directors. The boards of directors on average have two executive directors (EDs), ten non-executive directors (NEDs), and six INEDs. The audit committee has four members on average, three of which are INEDs. The average percentage of INEDs on the board of directors is 50.41 percent, and that on the audit committee is 69.66 percent. The roles of CEO and board chairman are separate in 82.16 percent of the banks, and 34.27 percent of banks have an INED acting as board chairman.

There exist large cross-country differences in board structure. In our sample, banks in the Netherlands have the highest board independence (92.5 percent), whereas banks in Croatia have the lowest board independence (0). Banks in Australia, Canada, Israel, the Netherlands and the US typically have board independence higher than 75 percent; however, Croatia, the Czech Republic, Greece, Japan, Lithuania, the Philippines and Turkey have board independence lower than 25 percent in their largest publicly listed banks. Although banks in 16 of 45 countries have an audit committee with independence higher than 80 percent, banks in 13 of 45 counties have an audit committee with independence lower than 20 percent. The separation of board chairman and CEO is a common practice for banks in our sample to enhance their internal monitoring mechanism; however, the chairman position in US banks is unanimously undertaken by the CEO.

Ownership structure Panel B in Table 1.2 provides information on the ownership structure of banks. The largest shareholders of banks in Ireland, the US, Japan, Portugal, Canada, Australia, the United Kingdom and Belgium (in our sample) on average hold less than 15 percent ownership. However, the largest shareholders hold more than 50 percent of bank ownership in Lithuania, Germany, Argentina, India, Austria, the Czech Republic, Brazil, Belize, Poland, Croatia, Turkey and Slovakia. The five largest shareholders hold less than 15 percent of bank ownership in only two countries (Ireland and Canada), and they hold more than 50 percent of bank ownership in 25 of 45 countries. Overall, the cross-country average of ownership held by the largest shareholder is 36.74 percent, and that held by the five largest shareholders is 53.78 percent.

The ownership structure data indicate that widely held banks are the exception rather than the rule, which is consistent with Caprio et al. (2007). Using 10 percent as the criterion for ultimate controlling shareholder, Caprio et al. (2007) show that in the average country, 75 percent of the largest listed banks have an ultimate controlling shareholder.

Concentrated ownership has been suggested as an effective corporate governance mechanism. Shleifer and Vishny (1986) demonstrate that the monitoring role in a company is actually performed by large shareholders. Elston and Goldberg (2003) show

Table 1.2   Corporate governance of banks in 2006

Country	Panel A: Board structure					
	% of INEDs on the board	% of INEDs on the audit committee	No CEO/ chairman duality	INED as board chairman	Board structure index	N
Argentina	31.39	83.33	0	0	−0.95	4
Australia	82.98	95.83	1	1	1.58	6
Austria	39.22	33.33	1	0.33	−0.49	3
Belgium	50.90	69.84	1	0.33	0.09	3
Belize	71.43	100.00	1	0	0.48	1
Brazil	36.66	70.83	1	0.25	−0.26	4
Canada	81.41	100.00	1	0.89	1.49	9
Croatia	0.00	33.33	1	0	−1.58	1
Czech Republic	25.00	33.33	1	0	−1.08	1
Denmark	61.27	18.52	1	0.89	0.31	9
Finland	42.38	52.78	1	0.33	−0.24	3
Germany	49.04	37.22	1	0.67	0.04	9
Greece	23.83	67.42	0.55	0	−0.99	10
Hong Kong	34.29	84.40	0.8	0	−0.50	10
Hungary	60.00	60.00	1	1	0.78	1
Iceland	57.78	66.67	1	0	−0.11	2
India	48.40	47.33	0.4	0.1	−0.68	10
Ireland	66.46	100.00	1	1	1.29	4
Israel	80.43	100.00	1	0.25	0.89	4
Italy	67.65	72.00	1	0.6	0.68	5
Japan	20.49	58.33	0.75	0	−1.05	8
Jordan	38.03	33.33	0.5	0.17	−0.91	6
Korea, Rep. of	64.63	71.00	0.4	0.2	−0.04	5
Lebanon	29.17	37.50	1	0	−0.96	2
Lithuania	23.81	24.44	1	0	−1.19	3
Luxembourg	40.22	66.67	1	0.5	0.00	2
Malaysia	55.67	91.67	1	0.29	0.35	7
Malta	67.46	90.00	1	1	1.22	2
Netherlands	92.50	100.00	1	1	1.81	5
Pakistan	59.44	88.89	0.67	0.33	0.28	3
Philippines	24.53	45.19	0.89	0.11	−0.93	9
Poland	41.67	65.00	1	0.5	0.01	2
Portugal	63.64	20.00	1	0	−0.44	1
Romania	53.90	66.67	0.5	0.5	0.03	2
Saudi Arabia	73.33	88.89	1	1	1.32	3
Singapore	61.83	88.89	0.67	0	0.03	3
Slovakia	47.32	18.75	1	0.5	−0.32	2
South Africa	54.74	62.74	1	0.43	0.18	7
Spain	44.96	78.33	0.86	0	−0.32	7
Sri Lanka	55.56	66.67	1	0	−0.15	1
Sweden	51.92	77.78	1	0	−0.12	3
Thailand	43.55	100.00	1	0.1	0.02	10
Turkey	16.93	38.89	1	0	−1.19	3

Table 1.2 (continued)

Country	Panel A: Board structure					
	% of INEDs on the board	% of INEDs on the audit committee	No CEO/ chairman duality	INED as board chairman	Board structure index	N
United Kingdom	55.48	94.17	0.9	0.7	0.70	10
USA	77.33	100.00	0	0	0.12	7
Country mean	50.41	66.67	0.86	0.33	−0.02	213

Country	Panel B: Ownership structure					
	% ownership of largest shareholder	% ownership of five largest shareholders	Value held by largest shareholder	Value held by five largest shareholders	Ownership structure index	N
Argentina	55.04	76.26	6.22	6.66	0.31	4
Australia	10.51	34.34	7.37	8.55	−0.09	6
Austria	60.20	82.33	8.55	8.92	1.37	3
Belgium	14.47	39.29	8.64	9.42	0.45	3
Belize	70.50	75.54	5.31	5.38	0.05	1
Brazil	66.18	76.85	9.13	9.29	1.56	4
Canada	8.16	13.39	5.65	6.55	−1.09	9
Croatia	76.30	97.10	7.96	8.20	1.46	1
Czech Republic	60.35	75.92	8.28	8.51	1.16	1
Denmark	18.51	28.00	5.09	5.67	−1.09	9
Finland	28.08	46.15	6.15	6.82	−0.33	3
Germany	53.57	61.70	7.22	7.63	0.53	9
Greece	39.26	48.79	6.68	7.04	−0.02	10
Hong Kong	45.12	56.67	7.15	7.51	0.33	10
Hungary	22.60	37.79	8.07	8.59	0.25	1
Iceland	30.15	43.17	7.57	7.99	0.18	2
India	55.18	69.37	7.08	7.32	0.54	10
Ireland	5.78	9.79	6.81	7.30	−0.78	4
Israel	35.03	61.64	6.06	6.70	−0.11	4
Italy	34.50	53.25	8.21	9.00	0.68	5
Japan	6.73	21.86	7.25	8.47	−0.31	8
Jordan	26.21	51.88	4.50	5.48	−0.89	6
Korea, Rep. of	33.85	46.14	8.14	8.73	0.52	5
Lebanon	37.67	60.88	4.47	4.95	−0.76	2
Lithuania	53.03	75.21	4.66	5.17	−0.33	3
Luxembourg	35.73	67.18	5.05	5.67	−0.45	2
Malaysia	27.19	50.32	6.60	7.28	−0.11	7
Malta	25.90	44.77	4.46	5.00	−1.07	2
Netherlands	43.44	63.08	7.91	8.53	0.74	5
Pakistan	45.89	60.29	5.59	5.91	−0.25	3
Philippines	37.40	67.69	5.02	5.79	−0.41	9
Poland	73.00	81.42	8.40	8.51	1.39	2
Portugal	7.00	22.19	6.89	8.05	−0.46	1
Romania	36.66	47.92	6.69	6.90	−0.08	2

Table 1.2   (continued)

Country	Panel B: Ownership structure					
	% ownership of largest shareholder	% ownership of five largest shareholders	Value held by largest shareholder	Value held by five largest shareholders	Ownership structure index	N
Saudi Arabia	33.92	49.84	8.15	8.56	0.53	3
Singapore	18.99	55.98	7.93	9.01	0.47	3
Slovakia	84.82	92.37	5.88	5.98	0.64	2
South Africa	39.62	59.97	6.88	7.47	0.24	7
Spain	26.27	42.81	8.20	8.91	0.44	7
Sri Lanka	28.99	59.18	3.45	4.17	−1.24	1
Sweden	16.27	32.80	8.24	8.98	0.23	3
Thailand	26.01	44.90	5.45	6.17	−0.64	10
Turkey	80.78	87.69	7.70	7.80	1.27	3
United Kingdom	12.78	28.16	6.55	7.54	−0.49	10
USA	5.88	18.14	8.53	9.69	0.14	7
Country mean	36.74	53.78	6.80	7.37	0.10	213

Country	Panel C: Executive compensation					
	Share option scheme to top executives	Share option scheme to non-executive directors	Share-based bonus	Variable compensation	Executive compensation index	N
Argentina	0	0	0.25	0.5	−1.15	4
Australia	1	0	1	1	0.69	6
Austria	0	0	0.33	1	−0.65	3
Belgium	1	0	1	1	0.69	3
Belize	1	0	1	1	0.69	1
Brazil	0.5	0	0.75	0.75	−0.13	4
Canada	1	0.44	1	1	0.98	9
Croatia	0	0	1	1	−0.11	1
Czech Republic	0	0	1	1	−0.11	1
Denmark	0.56	0	0.67	0.89	−0.03	9
Finland	0.67	0	0.67	1	0.15	3
Germany	0.67	0.11	0.67	1	0.22	9
Greece	0.55	0	0.55	0.82	−0.20	10
Hong Kong	0.6	0.1	0.6	0.9	0.02	10
Hungary	1	1	1	1	1.35	1
Iceland	1	0	1	1	0.69	2
India	0.2	0	0.2	0.5	−1.03	10
Ireland	1	0	1	1	0.69	4
Israel	0.75	0	0.75	0.75	0.07	4
Italy	0.6	0	0.6	1	0.04	5
Japan	0.63	0.63	0.63	1	0.49	8
Jordan	0	0	0	1	−0.93	6
Korea, Rep. of	0.6	0.6	0.8	0.8	0.43	5

Table 1.2 (continued)

Country	Panel C: Executive compensation					
	Share option scheme to top executives	Share option scheme to non-executive directors	Share-based bonus	Variable compen-sation	Executive compen-sation index	N
Lebanon	0	0	0	1	−0.93	2
Lithuania	0	0	0	1	−0.93	3
Luxembourg	1	0.5	1	1	1.02	2
Malaysia	0.71	0.29	0.71	0.71	0.17	7
Malta	0	0	0	1	−0.93	2
Netherlands	0.8	0.2	1	1	0.66	5
Pakistan	0	0	0	0.67	−1.21	3
Philippines	0.11	0	0.11	0.78	−0.94	9
Poland	0.5	0	0.5	1	−0.12	2
Portugal	1	0	1	1	0.69	1
Romania	0.5	0	1	1	0.29	2
Saudi Arabia	0	0	0.33	0.33	−1.22	3
Singapore	1	0	1	1	0.69	3
Slovakia	0	0	0	1	−0.93	2
South Africa	1	0	1	1	0.69	7
Spain	0.43	0.29	0.57	1	0.07	7
Sri Lanka	1	0	1	1	0.69	1
Sweden	0.33	0	0.67	1	−0.12	3
Thailand	0.3	0	0.4	0.9	−0.45	10
Turkey	0	0	0	0.33	−1.50	3
United Kingdom	0.9	0	1	1	0.61	10
USA	1	0.43	1	1	0.97	7
Country mean	0.53	0.10	0.64	0.90	0.00	213

Country	Panel D: Transparency				
	Big 4 as auditors	Cross listing in US	Disclosure of executive compensation and shareholdings	Transparency index	N
Argentina	1	1	1.13	0.74	4
Australia	1	0.67	3	0.89	6
Austria	1	0.33	0.5	−0.35	3
Belgium	1	0.67	2.67	0.78	3
Belize	0	0	0	−2.48	1
Brazil	1	0.75	1.13	0.40	4
Canada	1	0 78	3	1.03	9
Croatia	1	0	0	−0.96	1
Czech Republic	1	1	3	1.33	1
Denmark	1	0.11	1.17	−0.44	9
Finland	0.67	0	2.33	−0.72	3
Germany	0.89	0.33	1.89	−0.08	9

Table 1.2   (continued)

Country	Panel D: Transparency				
	Big 4 as auditors	Cross listing in US	Disclosure of executive compensation and shareholdings	Transparency index	N
Greece	0.82	0.27	0.55	−0.70	10
Hong Kong	1	0.5	2.85	0.62	10
Hungary	1	1	2	1.01	1
Iceland	1	0	3	0.00	2
India	0.1	0.2	2.4	−1.30	10
Ireland	1	0.75	3	1.00	4
Israel	1	0.25	2	0.01	4
Italy	1	0.4	2.8	0.47	5
Japan	1	0.75	1	0.36	8
Jordan	1	0	2.33	−0.22	6
Korea Rep. of	1	0.8	0.9	0.40	5
Lebanon	1	0.5	0	−0.29	2
Lithuania	1	0	0.83	−0.69	3
Luxembourg	1	0	0.5	−0.80	2
Malaysia	1	0.14	1.14	−0.40	7
Malta	1	0	1.25	−0.56	2
Netherlands	1	0.4	2.4	0.34	5
Pakistan	0.67	0	2.33	−0.72	3
Philippines	0.11	0	2.5	−1.51	9
Poland	1	0.5	2.75	0.58	2
Portugal	1	0	1.5	−0.48	1
Romania	1	0	0.5	−0.80	2
Saudi Arabia	1	0	0.67	−0.75	3
Singapore	1	0.67	1.33	0.36	3
Slovakia	1	0	0	−0.96	2
South Africa	1	0.29	3	0.38	7
Spain	1	0.43	1.93	0.23	7
Sri Lanka	1	0	1	−0.64	1
Sweden	1	0	3	0.00	3
Thailand	0.9	0	2.45	−0.33	10
Turkey	1	1	1.33	0.80	3
United Kingdom	1	0.5	2.9	0.63	10
USA	1	1	3	1.33	7
Country mean	0.91	0.36	1.75	−0.06	213

Note: This table reports the corporate governance measures of publicly listed banks around the world in 2006. Panel A presents country averages of board structure variables and the board structure index. Panel B presents country averages of ownership structure variables and the ownership structure index. Panel C presents country averages of executive compensation variables and the executive compensation index. Panel D presents transparency variables and the transparency index. N indicates the number of banks for each country in 2006 in our sample.

that concentrated ownership leads to lower executive compensation. Caprio et al. (2007) display that concentrated ownership boosts bank valuation.

Executive compensation In the average country, 53 percent of banks provide option schemes to top executives in our sample. Only 10 percent of the banks provide option schemes to the NEDs; 64 percent of the banks provide share-based bonuses to top executives; and 90 percent of the banks provide both fixed and variable compensation to top executives.

Incentive compensation is an effective corporate governance mechanism to align the interests of top managers with those of shareholders. Jensen and Murphy (1990) suggest that equity-based rather than cash compensation gives managers the incentive to maximize firm value. Mehran (1995) demonstrates that equity-based compensation does motivate managers to enhance firm value, and that firm valuation is positively related to the percentage of equity-based compensation. A limitation of the executive compensation index is that, due to the scarcity of detailed executive compensation data and the mismatch of compensation data across the countries, we can only construct the executive compensation index based on four dummy variables. Nevertheless, it still reflects the main differences in executive compensation of banks across the countries.

Transparency Ninety-one percent of the publicly listed banks in the average country appoint one of the Big 4 accounting firms as their auditors. The banks in Belize, India and the Philippines in our sample generally do not appoint Big 4 accounting firms. Thirty-six percent of the banks in the average country have their shares traded either as a direct listing on a US stock exchange or as an ADR. More than half of the banks do not disclose detailed information on executive compensation; however, most of the banks provide detailed information on shareholdings of top managers and directors.[1]

Employing Big 4 accounting firms as auditors may bring positive effects to a firm's reputation in corporate governance and account reporting. Firms cross-listing on US exchanges are expected to conform to stricter regulations and accounting standards (US GAAP), and to provide more information to shareholders, which could improve governance and increase firm value. Mitton (2002) suggests that firms with a listed ADR have higher disclosure quality. Klapper and Love (2004) find that firm valuations are positively related with their Standard & Poor's (S&P) transparency rankings in emerging markets. Baumann and Nier (2004) report that banks disclosing more information to investors show lower measures of stock volatility than those disclosing less information.

1.2.2 External Governance

External governance is referred to as the control exercised by stakeholders and markets to enforce internal governance (Halme, 2000). Competition related to financial products and takeover activities should be external mechanisms for improving the corporate governance of banks, and official regulations represent an additional external governance force.

However, competition cannot act on its own; its sustainability depends on the regulatory environment. The opaqueness of banks can weaken competitive forces, affecting product competition and takeover activities (Levine, 2004). Levine (2004) indicates that product market competition is less frequent in the banking industry due to the personal relationships that banks establish with their clients.

Moreover, as Adams and Mehran (2003) suggest, the existence of regulation and the high leverage of banking firms may impede the effects of other external governance mechanisms to resolve the governance problems of banks. For example, despite active consolidation, there have been very few hostile takeover bids in the banking industry. The main reasons include that bank regulations often impose substantial delays on any hostile takeover bid, and regulations may also reduce block holders' incentives to monitor the boards of financial institutions. As a result, the absence of an active market for corporate control in the banking industry prevents better-performing banks from taking over the poorly performing ones and removing their boards.

In the following subsection, we introduce the measures of bank regulation as an external governance mechanism.

Bank regulation and supervision

There are two types of regulatory frameworks: the traditional regulation approach and the market-oriented regulation approach. The traditional regulation approach, reflecting the idea of the 'supervisory power view',[2] emphasizes the role of direct regulation and supervision from supervisory agencies in promoting bank behavior and avoiding banking crises. Influential international institutions, such as the Bank for International Settlements (BIS), the International Monetary Fund (IMF) and the World Bank, all encourage the development of powerful bank supervisory agencies with the authority to scrutinize and discipline banks. Basel II recommends regulatory practices that empower official supervisory agencies to discipline banks in Pillar 2.

Alternatively, as suggested by the 'private empowerment view',[3] supervisory authorities can increase their reliance on market discipline to oversee banks rather than depend on direct disciplining and intervention, which is the market-oriented regulation approach. It has recently been stressed that discipline from market participants complements and supports the regulatory practices of banks (DeYoung et al., 2001). Basel II pays attention to the issue of market discipline and develops Pillar 3, which recommends regulatory practices that empower private monitoring of banks by forcing them to disclose accurate information to private sectors.

Several studies find that the traditional regulation approach which empowers direct official supervision has no positive effect on bank development, weakens internal governance of banks and sometimes even undermines financial stability; however, the market-oriented regulation approach which encourages market discipline and private monitoring works best to promote bank development, enhance internal governance and accelerate economic growth (Barth et al., 2004, 2006; Beck et al., 2006; Laeven and Levine, 2009; Li and Song, 2010).

Measurements of bank regulation and supervision

Barth et al. (2006) set up a comprehensive cross-country database on bank regulation and supervision in more than 150 countries. The data are based upon surveys sent to national bank regulatory and supervisory authorities, with the first version of the database assembled in the late 1990s, the second version assembled in 2003 and the latest version set up in 2007. The surveys include both quantitative and descriptive questions.

Barth et al. (2006) compile the responses to the surveys and formulate a set of bank regulation and supervision indices. The dataset covers various regulation practices, including measures reflecting the traditional regulation approach and the market-oriented regulation approach, such as official supervisory power, private monitoring measures, capital requirements, restrictions on bank activities, restrictions on domestic and foreign bank entry, deposit insurance mechanisms and ownership restrictions.

Traditional regulation approach   Capital requirements, restrictions on bank activities, restrictions on domestic and foreign bank entry, ownership restrictions, and official supervisory power measures reflect the idea of the traditional regulation approach, which focuses on direct regulation and supervision of banks by supervisory authorities.

The official supervisory power index measures whether supervisory authorities possess the power to take corrective actions when confronted with violations of regulations or other imprudent behavior of banks. The index is constructed from 14 dummy variables that indicate whether bank supervisory authorities can take specific actions against bank management, owners or auditors in both normal times and times of distress. It includes information on whether the supervisory authorities can obtain bank information from external auditors, take legal action against auditors for negligence, force a bank to change its internal organizational structure, force banks to establish provisions against actual or potential losses as determined by the supervisory agency, suspend dividends, stop bonuses, halt management fees, supersede the legal rights of shareholders, and remove and replace managers and directors. Official supervisory power ranges from 4 to 14, and higher values indicate wider authority for bank supervisors.

Traditional approaches to bank regulation emphasize the positive features of capital adequacy requirements. The capital regulatory index represents the degree of stringency of the regulatory capital requirements. The index incorporates two different but complementary measures of capital stringency: overall capital stringency, which measures the extent of regulatory requirements regarding the amount of capital banks must hold; and initial capital stringency, which measures whether the source of funds that count as regulatory capital can include assets other than cash or government securities, and whether the regulatory or supervisory authorities verify the sources of capital. This capital regulatory index has a median value of 6 and ranges from a low of 3 to a high of 10, with a higher value indicating greater stringency.

Overall activities restrictiveness and financial conglomerates restrictiveness measure the degree of restriction on banking activities. Overall activities restrictiveness is an index reflecting the regulatory restrictions on banks from engaging in fee-based activities (securities market activities, insurance activities and real estate activities) other than traditional interest spread-based activities. Financial conglomerates restrictiveness reflects the degree of regulatory restrictiveness on the mixing of banking and commerce. A high index value means high restrictions on bank activities and financial conglomerates.

The degree of competition in banking depends importantly on entry barriers, both domestic and foreign. The database incorporates three measures to capture qualitatively the extent to which competition within the banking industry is restricted. The three measures all relate to the ability of existing or new domestic and foreign banks to enter the banking business within a country. The three measures are: (1) limitations on foreign bank entry or ownership, which reflects whether there are any limitations placed on the ownership of domestic banks by foreign banks and whether there are any limitations placed on the ability of foreign banks to enter the domestic banking industry; (2) entry into banking requirements, which measures the specific legal requirements for obtaining a license to operate as a bank; and (3) fraction of entry applications denied, which equals the fraction of applications denied.

Market-oriented regulation approach   Private monitoring measures, external govern-ance measures and the deposit insurance mechanisms reflect the idea of the market-oriented regulation approach, which focuses on promoting market discipline and private monitoring of banks.

The private monitoring index reflects the scope of supervisory authorities to encourage the discipline and monitoring of private sectors. It is constructed from nine dummy vari-ables to measure the degree to which bank supervisory agencies force banks to disclose accurate information to the public and induce private sector monitoring of banks. The private monitoring index includes information on whether banks must be audited by certified auditors, whether they must be rated by international rating agencies, whether bank directors and officials are legally liable for the accuracy of information disclosed to the public, whether banks must publish consolidated accounts, whether the income statement includes accrued or unpaid interest or principal on non-performing loans, whether subordinated debt is allowable as a part of regulatory capital, whether off-balance sheet items are disclosed to supervisors and the public, whether banks must disclose risk management procedures, whether there is no explicit deposit insurance and whether no actual insurance was paid out the last time a bank failed. The private monitoring index ranges from 0 to 9, with higher values indicating more empowering of private oversight.

Bank regulation and supervision around the world
Barth et al. (2006) summarize and compare the bank regulation and supervision prac-tices around the world in detail, therefore here we skip the introduction of bank regula-tion and supervision practices around the world.

1.2.3   Internal Governance, External Governance and Bank Performance

The traditional regulation approach which empowers direct official supervision has been criticized as having no positive effect on bank development and sometimes even under-mining financial stability; however, the market-oriented regulation approach which encourages market discipline and private monitoring has been proved to promote bank development and economic growth (Barth et al., 2004, 2006; Beck et al., 2006; Laeven and Levine, 2009). Laeven and Levine (2009) study the impact of national regulation on bank performance while considering the influence of banks' corporate governance structure and show that, depending on banks' ownership structure, the same regulation policy can have different effects on bank risk-taking. Li and Song (2010) find that the tra-ditional regulation approach tends to crowd out internal governance of banks, while the market-oriented regulation approach can enhance the internal governance mechanism. What is more, they find that the market-oriented regulation approach not only improves bank valuation, but also enhances the positive effects of internal governance on bank valuation.

NOTES

1. The medians of the three dummy variables which indicate whether the bank discloses top executive compensation, top executive shareholdings and directors' shareholdings are 0.5, 1 and 1, respectively.
2. The 'supervisory power view' (Beck et al., 2006) suggests direct disciplining and monitoring of banks by supervisory agencies, since private agents frequently lack the incentive and capability to monitor powerful banks.
3. The 'private empowerment view' (Beck et al., 2006) argues that the responsibility of supervisory agencies should be to enhance the ability and incentive of private agents to overcome information costs so that private agents can exert effective governance over banks.

REFERENCES

Adams, R.B. and H. Mehran (2002), 'Board structure and banking firm performance', Unpublished working paper, SSRN.

Adams, R. and H. Mehran (2003), 'Is corporate governance different for bank holding companies?', *FRNBY Economic Policy Review*, **9**(1), 123–142.

Adams, R.B. and H. Mehran (2005), 'Corporate performance, board structure and its determinants in the banking industry', working paper, Federal Reserve Bank of New York.

Anderson, C.W. and T.L. Campbell (2003), 'Corporate governance of Japanese banks', *Journal of Corporate Finance*, **189**, 1–28.

Andrés, P. and E. Vallelado (2008), 'Corporate governance in banking: the role of the board of directors', *Journal of Banking and Finance*, **32**, 2570–2580.

Baek, J.S., J.K. Kang and K.S. Park (2004), 'Corporate governance and firm value: evidence from the Korean financial crisis', *Journal of Financial Economics*, **71**, 265–313.

Bai, C.E., Q. Liu, J. Lu, F.M. Song and J.X. Zhang (2004), 'Corporate governance and firm valuation in China', *Journal of Comparative Economics*, **32**(4), 599–616.

Barth, J.R., G. Caprio and R. Levine (2004), 'Bank supervision and regulation: what works best?', *Journal of Financial Intermediation*, **2**, 205–248.

Barth, J.R., G. Caprio and R. Levine (2006), *Rethinking Bank Supervision and Regulation: Until Angels Govern*, Cambridge: Cambridge University Press.

Barth, J.R., J. Hai, V. Hartarska and T. Phumiwasana (2007), 'A cross-country analysis of bank performance: the role of external governance', in B. Gup (ed.), *Corporate Governance in Banking: An International Perspective*, Cheltenham, UK and Northampton, MA, USA: Edward Elgar.

Basel Committee on Banking Supervision (BCBS) (2006), 'Enhancing corporate governance for banking organisations', February, www.bis.org/publ/bcbs122.htm.

Baumann, U. and E. Nier (2004), 'Disclosure, volatility, and transparency: an empirical investigation into the value of bank disclosure', *FRBNY Economic Policy Review*, **9**, 65–87.

Beck, T., A. Demirgüç-Kunt and R. Levine (2006), 'Bank supervision and corruption in lending', *Journal of Monetary Economics*, **53**, 2131–2163.

Belkhir, M. (2009), 'Board of directors' size and performance in the banking industry', *International Journal of Managerial Finance*, **5**, 201–221.

Ben-David, I., J.R. Graham and C.R. Harvey (2007), 'Managerial overconfidence and corporate policies', NBER Working Paper 13711.

Berle, A. and G. Means (1932), *The Modern Corporation and Private Property*, New York: Macmillan.

Billett, M.T., J.A. Garfinkel and E.S. O'Neal (1998), 'The cost of market versus regulatory discipline in banking', *Journal of Financial Economics*, **3**, 333–358.

Brewer, E., W. Jackson and J. Jagtiani (2000), 'Impact of independent directors and the regulatory environment on bank merger prices: evidence from takeover activity in the 1990s', working paper, Federal Reserve Bank of Chicago.

Brook, Y., R.J. Hendershott and D. Lee (2000), 'Corporate governance and recent consolidation in the banking industry', *Journal of Corporate Finance*, **6**, 141–164.

Burkart, M., K. Gromb and F. Panunzi (1997), 'Large shareholders, monitoring, and fiduciary duty', *Quarterly Journal of Economics*, **112**, 693–728.
Bushman, R.M. and A.J. Smith (2003), 'Transparency, financial accounting information, and corporate governance', *FRBNY Economic Policy Review*, **9**, 65–87.
Caprio, G., L. Laeven and R. Levine (2007), 'Governance and bank valuation', *Journal of Financial Intermediation*, **16**, 584–617.
Caprio, G. and R. Levine (2002), 'Corporate governance in finance: concepts and international observations', in R.E. Litan, M. Pomerleano and V. Sundararajan (eds), *Financial Sector Governance: The Roles of the Public and Private Sectors*, Washington, DC: Brookings Institution Press.
Chen, C.R., T.L. Steiner and A.M. Whyte (2006), 'Does stock option-based executive compensation induce risk-taking? An analysis of the banking industry', *Journal of Banking and Finance*, **30**, 915–945.
Choe, H. and B.S. Lee (2003), 'Korean bank governance reform after the Asian financial crisis', *Pacific-Basin Finance Journal*, **4**, 483–508.
CLSA (2001), 'Saints and sinners: who's got religion?', in Amar Gill (ed.), *CG Watch: Corporate Governance in Emerging Markets*, Hong Kong: CLSA.
Core, J.E., W. Guay and D.F. Larcker (2003), 'Executive equity compensation and incentives: a survey', *FRBNY Economic Policy Review*, **9**, 24–47.
Core, J., R. Holthausen and D. Larcker (1999), 'Corporate governance, chief executive officer compensation, and firm performance', *Journal of Financial Economics*, **51**, 371–406.
Crawford, A.J., J.R. Ezzell and J.A. Miles (1995), 'Bank CEO pay–performance relations and the effects of deregulation', *Journal of Business*, **68**, 231–256.
Crespí, R., M.A. García-Cestona and V. Salas (2004), 'Governance mechanisms in Spanish financial intermediaries', *Journal of Banking and Finance*, **28**(10), 2311–2330.
Dahya, J., O. Dimitrov and J.J. McConnell (2008), 'Dominant shareholders, corporate boards, and corporate value: a cross-country analysis', *Journal of Financial Economics*, **87**, 73–100.
Das, A. and S. Ghosh (2004), 'Corporate governance in banking system: an empirical investigation', *Economic and Political Weekly*, 20 March.
Demsetz, H. and K. Lehn (1985), 'The structure of corporate ownership: causes and consequences', *Journal of Political Economy*, **93**, 1155–1177.
Denis, D.K. and J.J. McConnell (2003), 'International corporate governance', *Journal of Financial and Quantitative Analysis*, **38**, 1–36.
DeYoung, R., M. Flannery, W. Lang and S. Sorescu (2001), 'The information content of bank exam ratings and subordinated debt prices', *Journal of Money, Credit and Banking*, **33**, 900–925.
Elston, J.A. and L.G. Goldberg (2003), 'Executive compensation and agency costs in Germany', *Journal of Banking and Finance*, **27**, 1391–1410.
Franks, J. and C. Mayer (2001), 'Ownership and control of German corporations', *Review of Financial Studies*, **14**, 943–977.
Furfine, C.H. (2001), 'Banks as monitors of other banks: evidence from the overnight federal funds market', *Journal of Business*, **1**, 33–57.
Galai, D. and R. Masulis (1976), 'The option pricing model and the risk factor of stock', *Journal of Financial Economics*, **3**, 53–81.
Gompers, P.A., J.L. Ishii and A. Metrick (2003), 'Corporate governance and equity prices', *Quarterly Journal of Economics*, **118**, 107–155.
Halme, Liisa (2000), 'Bank corporate governance and financial stability', in Liisa Halme, C. Hawkesby, J. Healey, I. Saapar and F. Soussa (eds), *Financial Stability and Central Banks: Selected Issues for Financial Safety Nets and Market Discipline*, London: Centre for Central Banking Studies, Bank of England.
Hermalin, B.E. and M.S. Weisbach (2003), 'Boards of directors as an endogenously determined institution: a survey of the economic literature', *FRBNY Economic Policy Review*, **9**, 7–26.
Houston, J.F. and C. James (1992), 'Managerial ownership, turnover and risk-taking in banking', working paper, University of Florida, Gainesville, FL.
Houston, J.F. and C. James (1995), 'CEO compensation and bank risk: is compensation in banking structured to promote risk taking?', *Journal of Monetary Economics*, **36**, 405–431.
Jensen, M.C. and W.H. Meckling (1976), 'Theory of the firm: managerial behavior, agency costs and ownership structure', *Journal of Financial Economics*, **3**, 305–460.
Jensen, M.C. and K.J. Murphy (1990), 'CEO incentives: it's not how much you pay, but how', *Journal of Applied Corporate Finance*, **3**, 36–49.
John, K., T.A. John and L.W. Senbet (1991), 'Risk-shifting incentives of depository institutions: a new perspective on federal deposit insurance reform', *Journal of Banking and Finance*, **15**, 895–915.
Jordan, J.S., J. Peek and E.S. Rosengren (1999), 'The impact of greater bank disclosure amidst a banking crisis', working paper, Federal Reserve of Boston.

Kane, E. (1985), *The Gathering Crisis in Federal Deposit Insurance*, Cambridge, MA: MIT Press.
Kirkpatrick, G. (2009), 'The corporate governance lessons from the financial crisis', *Financial Market Trends*, No. 96, 1–30, available at: http://www.oecd.org/dataoecd/32/1/42229620.pdf.
Klapper, L. and I. Love (2004), 'Corporate governance, investor protection, and performance in emerging markets', *Journal of Corporate Finance*, **10**, 703–728.
Konishi, M. and Y. Yasuda (2004), 'Factors affecting bank risk-taking: evidence from Japan', *Journal of Banking and Finance*, **28**, 215–234.
La Porta, R., F. Lopez-de-Silanes, A. Shleifer and R.W. Vishny (1998), 'Law and finance', *Journal of Political Economy*, **106**, 1112–1155.
Laeven, L. and R. Levine (2009), 'Corporate governance, regulation, and bank risk taking', *Journal of Financial Economics*, **93**, 259–275.
Leutz, C. and R.E. Verrecchia (2000), 'The economic consequences of increased disclosure', *Journal of Accounting Research*, **38**, 92–124.
Levine, R. (1997), 'Financial development and economic growth: views and agenda', *Journal of Economic Literature*, **35**, 688–726.
Levine, R.E. (2004), 'The corporate governance of banks: a concise discussion of concepts and evidence', World Bank Policy Research Working Paper No. 3404.
Levine, R. (2005), 'Finance and growth: theory and evidence', in P. Aghion and S. Durlauf (eds), *Handbook of Economic Growth*, Amsterdam: North-Holland Elsevier Publishers.
Li, L. and F.M. Song (2010), 'Bank regulation and board independence: a cross-country analysis', working paper, University of Hong Kong.
Lin, C., Y. Ma and F.M. Song (forthcoming), 'What drives bank efficiency: the role of bank competition and credit information sharing', *Review of Financial Studies*.
Macey, J.R. and M. O'Hara (2003), 'The corporate governance of banks', *FRBNY Economic Policy Review*, **9**, 91–107.
Magalhaes, R., M. Gutiérrez Urtiaga and J.A. Tribo (2008), 'Banks' ownership structure, risk and performance', working paper, SSRN.
Mehran, H. (1995), 'Executive compensation structure, ownership, and firm performance', *Journal of Financial Economics*, **38**, 163–184.
Mehran, H. and J. Rosenberg (2009), 'The effects of CEO stock options on bank investment choice, borrowing, and capital', Federal Reserve Bank of New York Staff Reports No. 305.
Mitton, T. (2002), 'A cross-firm analysis of the impact of corporate governance on the East Asian financial crisis', *Journal of Financial Economics*, **64**, 215–241.
Morgan, D. (2002), 'Rating banks: risk and uncertainty in an opaque industry', *American Economic Review*, **92**, 874–888.
Murphy, K. (1999), 'Executive compensation', in O. Ashenfelter and D. Card (eds), *Handbook of Labor Economics*, Amsterdam: North-Holland.
OECD (2006), 'Policy brief on corporate governance of banks in Asia', paper for the Asian roundtable on corporate governance, Thailand, June.
Pathan, S. (2009), 'Strong boards, CEO power and bank risk-taking', *Journal of Banking and Finance*, **33**, 1340–1350.
Pathan, S., M. Skully and J. Wickramanayake (2008), 'Reforms in Thai bank governance: the aftermath of the Asian financial crisis', *International Review of Financial Analysis*, **17**, 345–362.
Pi, L. and S. Timme (1993), 'Corporate control and bank efficiency', *Journal of Banking and Finance*, **17**, 515–530.
Prowse, S. (1997), 'Corporate control in commercial banks', *Journal of Financial Research*, **20**, 509–527.
Santos, J.A.C. and A.S. Rumble (2006), 'The American keiretsu and universal banks: investing, voting and sitting on nonfinancials' corporate boards', *Journal of Financial Economics*, **80**, 419–454.
Shleifer, A. and R.W. Vishny (1986), 'Large shareholders and corporate control', *Journal of Political Economy*, **94**, 461–488.
Shleifer, A. and R.W. Vishny (1997), 'A survey of corporate governance', *Journal of Finance*, **52**, 737–783.
Smith, A. (1776), *An Inquiry into the Nature and Causes of the Wealth of Nations*, New York: Modern Library.
Song, F.M. and A.C.H. Lei (2008), 'Corporate governance, family ownership, and firm valuations in emerging markets: evidence from Hong Kong panel data', working paper, SSRN.
Tadesse, S. (2003), 'Bank fragility and disclosure: international evidence', working paper, Moore School of Business, University of South Carolina.
Wiseman, R.M. and L.R. Gomez-Mejia (1998), 'A behavioral agency model of managerial risk taking', *Academy of Management Review*, **23**, 133–153.

2 Bank ownership and performance: a global perspective
Iftekhar Hasan and Liang Song

2.1 INTRODUCTION

A large literature (e.g., Levine and Zervos, 1998; Beck et al., 2000; Levine et al., 2000; Claessens and Laeven, 2003) has shown that a well-functioning banking system is associated with higher economic growth by mobilizing and allocating funds efficiently and providing an important role in governing firms. Thus, how to govern banks effectively to improve bank performance becomes an important question because it is related to a country's economic development. In addition to shareholder protection laws and bank regulations, ownership structure is a very important governance mechanism for banks (Shleifer and Vishny, 1997; Caprio et al., 2007). In particular, concentrated ownership can reduce the incentive of controlling shareholders to expropriate corporate resources from firms (Jensen and Meckling, 1976). In our study, we assemble data on ownership of banks around the world to assess its impact on banks' performance. More importantly, superior corporate governance measured by concentrated ownership may be more critical in the financial crisis period because the decline in the expected return on investment may motivate controlling shareholders to expropriate more (Johnson et al., 2000; Mitton, 2002). Thus, we also examine whether the relationship between bank ownership and performance is more pronounced in a period of financial crisis.

Specifically, we construct a new database covering 11 888 publicly traded and private banks across 44 countries and trace the ownership of banks in 2006 to identify the controlling shareholders' voting rights.[1] We find that banks generally have a controlling owner with significant control rights. In our average country, only about 25 percent of the banks do not have a controlling shareholder with more than 10 percent shares. About 6 percent of the banks are controlled by the state, about 27 percent of the banks are controlled by foreign shareholders and about 43 percent of the banks are controlled by private parties. We also investigate the identity of the foreign controlling shareholders and the private controlling shareholders. The evidence shows that the majority of foreign and private controlling shareholders are financial firms. In addition, the evidence indicates that banks are more widely held in countries with stronger legal protection of shareholders and bank regulations. Finally, we find that banks with a more concentrated ownership have a better operating performance and this relationship is more significant in the financial crisis period of 2008.

Our study contributes to the literature in several ways. First, La Porta et al. (1999) show that the firms generally have a concentrated ownership internationally and are usually controlled by families or the state. Caprio et al. (2007) find similar results in the banking industry. La Porta et al. (2002) and Barth et al. (2001, 2004) document that government ownership of banks is large and pervasive worldwide. While these studies examine bank ownership, they do not cover detailed bank ownership structure or restrict their sample to a limited number of banks. For example, the sample of Caprio et al. (2007) only covers 244 banks across 44 countries by collecting data on the ten largest publicly listed banks in each country. In this chapter, we construct a database covering 11 888 publicly traded and private banks across 44 countries with detailed ownership structure data for each bank. Thus, we contribute to the existing literature by providing a more comprehensive picture of bank ownership structure all over the world.

Second, Caprio et al. (2007) look at the effects of the shares of the controlling owner on bank performance. However, they only include publicly listed banks in their sample and use stock price-related measures to gauge bank performance. It is still an empirical question whether larger control rights by the controlling owner help improve private bank performance. In this chapter, we complement and extend the existing literature by examining the influence of the percentage of shares held by controlling shareholders on both private and publicly traded banks' operating performance.

Finally, Johnson et al. (2000) and Mitton (2002) find that corporate governance had a stronger impact on the whole economy and non-financial firm performance during the East Asian financial crisis of 1997–1998. We contribute to this stream of literature by showing that superior corporate governance measured by concentrated ownership is more critical to determine bank performance in the financial crisis period of 2008.

The remainder of the chapter proceeds as follows. Section 2.2 describes the data. Section 2.3 reports the pattern of bank ownership around the world. Section 2.4 investigates the effects of bank ownership on bank performance. Section 2.5 provides robustness tests for the results provided in section 2.4. Section 2.6 examines the relationship between bank ownership and performance in the financial crisis period. Section 2.7 summarizes the conclusions.

2.2 DATA AND VARIABLES

2.2.1 Sample

To conduct our analyses, we need data on bank ownership, bank performance, and other bank-specific and country characteristics. Our data about banks are from the Fitch-IBCA Bankscope dataset that provides bank-level annual financial information for 179 countries around the world. We collect data on bank holding companies and commercial banks in the year 2006 in those countries for which we can find data on shareholder rights in La Porta et al. (2002). Our sample period only covers one year because it is particularly difficult to construct the data of bank ownership (Caprio et al., 2007). The final sample consists of 11 888 publicly traded and private banks across 44 countries.

2.2.2 Variables

Our key variable is the control rights of the controlling shareholder. We define the variable *Controlling Share* as the percentage of shares owned by the controlling shareholder. Following La Porta et al. (1999, 2002), if a bank has a controlling owner who owns 10 percent or more, we classify the bank as having a concentrated ownership (the dummy variable *Widely Held* is equal to zero), otherwise it is widely held (the dummy variable *Widely Held* is equal to one).

We divide banks with a concentrated ownership into three categories and define three dummy variables correspondingly. First, the dummy variable *State Controlled* is equal to one if the controlling shareholder is the state, otherwise zero. Second, the dummy variable *Foreign Controlled* is equal to one if the controlling shareholder is from a foreign country, otherwise zero. Finally, the dummy variable *Private Controlled* is equal to one if the controlling shareholder is not a type mentioned before, otherwise zero.

We also define several variables related to the identity of the foreign and private controlling owner as below. First, the dummy variable *Foreign (Private) Family Controlled* is equal to one if the foreign (private) controlling shareholder is a family or individual, otherwise zero. Second, the dummy variable *Foreign (Private) Financial Controlled* is equal to one if the foreign (private) controlling shareholder is a financial institution such as a bank, insurance company and so on, and otherwise zero. Third, the dummy variable *Foreign (Private) Corporation Controlled* is equal to one if the foreign (private) controlling shareholder is a corporation, otherwise zero. Fourth, the dummy variable *Foreign (Private) Foundation Controlled* is equal to one if the foreign (private) controlling shareholder is a foundation, a research institute or a voting trust, otherwise zero. Finally, the dummy variable *Foreign (Private) Other Controlled* is equal to one if the controlling shareholder is not a type mentioned before, otherwise zero.

In the above definitions, we only define the variables to examine the identity of foreign controlling shareholders. To obtain a more precise picture about bank foreign ownership, we define several variables related to the identity of the biggest foreign owner as below, even if the biggest foreign owner is not the controlling shareholder. Specifically, we define the variable *Foreign Ownership* as the percentage of shares held by the biggest foreign shareholder. Then, we divide banks with at least one foreign shareholder into five categories and define five dummy variables correspondingly. First, the dummy variable *Foreign Family Owned* is equal to one if the biggest foreign shareholder is a family or individual, otherwise zero. Second, the dummy variable *Foreign Financial Owned* is equal to one if the biggest foreign shareholder is a financial institution such as a bank, insurance company and so on, and otherwise zero. Third, the dummy variable *Foreign Corporation Owned* is equal to one if the biggest foreign shareholder is a corporation, otherwise zero. Fourth, the dummy variable *Foreign Foundation Owned* is equal to one if the biggest foreign shareholder is a foundation, a research institute or a voting trust, otherwise zero. Finally, the dummy variable *Foreign Other Owned* is equal to one if the biggest foreign shareholder is not a type mentioned before, otherwise zero.

To measure bank performance, we use operating performance measures such as return on assets (*ROA*) and return on equity (*ROE*). To control for the banks' growth opportunity, we define the variable *Loan Growth* as the bank's one-year loan growth. The variable *Firm Size* is defined as the logarithm of the bank's total assets. The variable *Public* is equal to one if a bank is a publicly traded bank, otherwise zero.

We control for other governance mechanisms for banks such as legal protection of shareholders and official bank regulatory practices. Specifically, we control for the variable *Shareholder Rights*, which is the index to measure country-level shareholder protection from La Porta et al. (2002). According to La Porta et al. (2002):

The index is formed by adding 1 when: (1) the country allows shareholders to mail their proxy vote to the firm; (2) shareholders are not required to deposit their shares prior to the General Shareholders' Meeting; (3) cumulative voting or proportional representation of minorities in the board of directors is allowed; (4) an oppressed minorities mechanism is in place; (5) the minimum percentage of share capital that entitles a shareholder to call for an Extraordinary Shareholders' Meeting is less than or equal to 10 percent (the sample median); or (6) shareholders have preemptive rights that can only be waived by a shareholders' vote.

The higher value of this index means more protection of shareholders, which can improve banks' external governance and further their performance.

To control for the official bank regulatory environment, we use a series of variables from Barth et al. (2001, 2004, 2006) following Caprio et al. (2007). First, the variable *Supervisory Power* is an index to measure the power of the bank supervisory agency, which is formed by adding one for a positive response to each of the 14 questions. For example, the bank supervisory agency has more power if it does not need to get approved by the bank to meet with external auditors to discuss its report or force a bank to reorganize its internal structure. Greater bank regulatory power can reduce the management's incentive to expropriate resources from banks.

Second, the variable *Regulatory Restrictions* is an index to measure regulatory restrictions on the activities of banks such as securities market activities, insurance activities, real estate activities and the ownership of other non-financial firms. Greater regulatory bank activity restrictions can reduce the manager's potential mechanisms to expropriate bank resources.

Third, the variable *Capital Oversight* is an index to measure the level of regulatory oversight of bank capital. For example, a higher regulatory oversight may indicate the authorities' need to verify the sources of bank capital. Thus, greater regulatory oversight of bank capital may improve corporate governance.

Finally, the variable *Supervisory Independence* is an index to measure how independent the supervisory authority is. Beck et al. (2006) find that a more independent supervisory agency is associated with better governance of banks.

2.2.3   Summary Statistics

The Appendix describes the detailed definitions and sources of all variables. Table 2.1 provides the summary statistics of the main variables employed in this chapter. To avoid the influence of outliers, the variables such as *ROA, ROE, Loan Growth* and *Firm Size* are Winsorized at 1 percent. Caprio et al. (2007) construct a database covering 244 banks across 44 countries by collecting data on the ten largest publicly listed banks in each country. In this chapter, we construct a database covering 11 888 publicly traded and private banks across the same 44 countries. Thus, we include a lot of small banks in our sample. As shown, the mean value of the variable *Firm Size*, which is the logarithm of the bank's total assets, is 6.02. This value is much smaller than 16.404, which is reported by Caprio et al. (2007). The average value of the variable *Widely Held* is 0.79, which is bigger than 0.303, which is reported by Caprio et al. (2007). This result suggests that small banks are more likely to be widely held. In summary, our sample includes more small banks, and the distribution of bank ownership is significantly different compared

Table 2.1   Summary statistics

Variable	Observations	Mean	Std	Min.	Max.
ROA	11 888	0.01	0.02	−0.04	0.11
ROE	11 888	0.11	0.09	−0.21	0.41
Loan Growth	11 354	0.18	0.41	−0.29	3.12
Firm Size	11 888	6.02	2.41	0.19	18.27
Controlling Share	11 888	0.15	0.31	0.00	1.00
Widely Held	11 888	0.79	0.41	0.00	1.00
State Controlled	11 888	0.01	0.10	0.00	1.00
Foreign Controlled	11 888	0.06	0.24	0.00	1.00
Private Controlled	11 888	0.14	0.34	0.00	1.00
Foreign Ownership	11 888	0.17	0.37	0.00	1.00
Shareholder Rights	11 888	4.52	1.08	1.00	5.00
Supervisory Power	11 734	12.33	1.72	3.00	14.00
Regulatory Restrictions	11 745	11.20	2.01	5.00	14.00
Supervisory Independence	11 734	3.70	0.75	1.00	4.00
Capital Oversight	11 745	3.79	0.69	0.00	5.00

Note: This table presents the summary statistics of the main variables employed in this chapter. The detailed definitions and sources of these variables can be found in the Appendix.

to the findings reported in the existing literature. In the following section, we will examine the patterns of bank ownership in detail.

2.3   BANK OWNERSHIP AROUND THE WORLD

This section provides information about the extent to which bank ownership is concentrated and the identity of the controlling owner. Panel A of Table 2.2 provides the mean values of the bank control right variables by country. The results indicate that more than 90 percent of the banks in the United States are widely held. In other countries, more than 50 percent of banks have a controlling shareholder. The cross-country mean value of the variable *Widely Held* is 25 percent. This result suggests that in the average country, 75 percent of banks have a controlling shareholder with more than 10 percent shares, which is consistent with the finding based on the large bank sample by Caprio et al. (2007). However, Caprio et al. (2007) find that most large banks are controlled by the state and family. We find that in the average country, about 43 percent of banks are controlled by private parties, about 27 percent of banks are controlled by foreign owners, and about 6 percent of banks are controlled by the state. These results suggest that small banks have a different ownership structure compared to large banks.

Panels B and C of Table 2.2 provide information on the distribution of bank ownership by the shareholder protection index and bank regulation indexes. Specifically, for each of the five country-level indexes, we split the sample into countries with above-median and below-median value of each index. We report the corresponding bank ownership information in panel B and the test statistics about whether the ownership patterns differ significantly between high and low country level governance index countries in panel C.

Table 2.2 Distribution of bank control rights

Country	Controlling share	Widely held	State controlled	Foreign controlled	Private controlled	No. of banks
Panel A: Mean values of bank control rights by country						
Argentina	0.59	0.16	0.14	0.20	0.50	76
Australia	0.59	0.17	0.03	0.33	0.47	36
Austria	0.69	0.11	0.00	0.25	0.65	85
Brazil	0.59	0.22	0.07	0.27	0.44	134
Canada	0.46	0.44	0.00	0.36	0.20	45
Chile	0.43	0.38	0.00	0.18	0.44	39
Colombia	0.51	0.21	0.00	0.26	0.53	19
Denmark	0.32	0.49	0.00	0.06	0.45	78
Egypt	0.61	0.05	0.19	0.62	0.19	21
Finland	0.48	0.08	0.00	0.31	0.62	13
France	0.78	0.09	0.01	0.22	0.69	194
Germany	0.64	0.18	0.01	0.26	0.54	209
Greece	0.45	0.17	0.03	0.37	0.43	30
Hong Kong	0.65	0.12	0.00	0.59	0.29	49
India	0.49	0.17	0.39	0.09	0.36	70
Indonesia	0.59	0.09	0.15	0.45	0.32	53
Ireland	0.50	0.44	0.00	0.46	0.10	41
Israel	0.56	0.00	0.18	0.00	0.82	17
Italy	0.54	0.24	0.00	0.13	0.63	168
Japan	0.16	0.78	0.00	0.03	0.18	283
Jordan	0.28	0.18	0.00	0.45	0.36	11
Kenya	0.37	0.23	0.06	0.40	0.31	35
Korea, Rep. of	0.54	0.20	0.06	0.23	0.51	35
Malaysia	0.69	0.08	0.13	0.30	0.50	64
Mexico	0.57	0.30	0.02	0.28	0.40	43
Netherlands	0.71	0.17	0.00	0.39	0.44	71
Norway	0.62	0.25	0.10	0.15	0.50	20
Pakistan	0.39	0.14	0.10	0.29	0.50	42
Peru	0.68	0.22	0.00	0.72	0.06	18
Philippines	0.31	0.29	0.07	0.12	0.51	41
Portugal	0.59	0.28	0.00	0.34	0.38	29
Singapore	0.52	0.11	0.00	0.26	0.63	19
South Africa	0.65	0.11	0.11	0.21	0.58	38
Spain	0.60	0.13	0.00	0.35	0.51	82
Sri Lanka	0.36	0.30	0.15	0.10	0.45	20
Sweden	0.37	0.25	0.08	0.04	0.63	24
Switzerland	0.53	0.32	0.00	0.30	0.38	197
Taiwan	0.38	0.50	0.06	0.03	0.42	72
Thailand	0.37	0.19	0.16	0.34	0.31	32
Turkey	0.64	0.04	0.09	0.31	0.56	54
United Kingdom	0.43	0.47	0.01	0.25	0.29	167
USA	0.03	0.95	0.00	0.01	0.04	9065
Venezuela	0.36	0.50	0.00	0.11	0.39	36
Zimbabwe	0.62	0.08	0.31	0.23	0.38	13
Country mean	0.51	0.25	0.06	0.27	0.43	11 888

Table 2.2   (continued)

Country	Controlling share	Widely held	State controlled	Foreign controlled	Private controlled	No. of banks
Panel B: Mean values of bank control rights by country level investor protection and bank regulation indexes						
Low shareholder rights	0.56	0.23	0.03	0.25	0.50	1 752
High shareholder rights	0.08	0.89	0.01	0.03	0.08	10 136
Low supervisory power	0.57	0.23	0.04	0.22	0.51	1 320
High supervisory power	0.09	0.86	0.01	0.04	0.09	10 568
Low regulatory restrictions	0.57	0.24	0.02	0.27	0.47	1 580
High regulatory restrictions	0.08	0.87	0.01	0.03	0.09	10 308
Low supervisory independence	0.49	0.31	0.05	0.20	0.45	1 996
High supervisory independence	0.08	0.89	0.00	0.03	0.07	9 892
Low capital oversight	0.57	0.23	0.04	0.24	0.46	1 320
High capital oversight	0.09	0.86	0.01	0.03	0.09	10 568
Panel C: Test of mean values of bank control rights by country-level investor protection and bank regulation indexes						
Low versus high shareholder rights	72.30***	−77.26***	11.17***	36.73***	52.13***	11 888
Low versus high supervisory power	58.31***	−60.95***	11.81***	26.13***	45.10***	11 888
Low versus high regulatory restrictions	66.87***	−67.60***	5.81***	38.50***	44.07***	11 888
Low versus high supervisory independence	62.50***	−69.25***	18.63***	28.53***	48.73***	11 888
Low versus high capital oversight	66.29***	−68.23***	16.90***	34.32***	43.93***	11 888

Note: Panel A presents the mean values of bank control rights by country. Panel B presents the mean values of bank control rights by country-level investor protection and bank regulation indexes. Panel C presents the test statistics of the mean values by country-level investor protection and bank regulation indexes. The detailed definitions and sources of the variables can be found in the Appendix. The superscripts, ***, **, and * denote the 1%, 5%, and 10% levels of significance, respectively.

The results suggest that countries with above-median shareholder protection (89 percent of the banks are widely held) have more widely held banks than countries with below-median legal protection (23 percent of the banks are widely held). This difference is significant at the 1 percent level with t statistic −77.26. This result is consistent with

Caprio et al. (2007). We also find that countries with above-median value of the banking regulation indexes such as *Supervisory Power*, *Regulatory Restrictions*, *Capital Oversight* and *Supervisory Independence* have a significantly higher fraction of widely held banks than countries with below-median values of these indexes. These differences are all significant at the 1 percent level. These results suggest that greater bank regulation helps improve the banks' corporate governance. Thus, investors do not need the concentrated ownership to prevent managers from expropriating resources from firms.

We also find similar results in terms of the percentage of shares held by the banks' controlling shareholders. Specifically, banks' controlling shareholders in the countries with above-median value of the shareholder protection index and the banking regulation indexes such as *Supervisory Power*, *Regulatory Restrictions*, *Capital Oversight* and *Supervisory Independence* own a lower percentage of stock shares than countries with below-median values of these indexes. In addition, there is large cross-country variation in the average degree of control rights in our sample. For example, in Austria, the banks' controlling shareholders own 69 percent of shares on average. In the USA, the banks' controlling shareholders own 3 percent of shares on average.

Figure 2.1 illustrates how the percentage of shares held by the largest shareholder varies by the shareholder protection index and banking regulation indexes. Panel A, panel B, panel C, panel D, and panel E show the regression lines of the variable *Controlling Share* against the variables such as *Shareholder Protection*, *Supervisory Power*, *Regulatory Restrictions*, *Capital Oversight* and *Supervisory Independence*, respectively. As shown, banks' controlling shareholders in the countries with higher values of shareholder protection index and banking regulation indexes tend to have lower percentages of stock shares. The coefficient of the variables such as *Shareholder Protection*, *Supervisory Power*, *Regulatory Restrictions*, *Capital Oversight* and *Supervisory Independence* are all significant at 1 percent. This result is consistent with Caprio et al. (2007).

To make our results comparable to Caprio et al. (2007), we also investigate the identity of foreign and private controlling shareholders as reported in Tables 2.3 and 2.4. In Table 2.3, only banks with a foreign controlling shareholder are included. We find that the majority of foreign controlling shareholders are financial firms. In an average country, about 85 percent of foreign controlling shareholders are financial firms, about 8 percent of foreign controlling shareholders are corporations, about 4 percent of foreign controlling shareholders are foundations and almost 0 percent of foreign controlling shareholders are families.

In Table 2.4, only banks with a private controlling shareholder are included. We find that the majority of private controlling shareholders are financial firms. In an average country, about 50 percent of foreign controlling shareholders are financial firms, about 21 percent of foreign controlling shareholders are corporations, about 13 percent of foreign controlling shareholders are foundations and about 9 percent of foreign controlling shareholders are families.

Recently, bank foreign ownership has become more and more important. For example, Demirgüç-Kunt and Huizinga (2000) and Mian (2003) find that foreign ownership has a positive impact on bank performance. Thus, we provide information about the percentage of shares held by banks' largest foreign owners and their identity even if the largest foreign owner is not the biggest owner. Table 2.5 provides the mean values of shares held by the biggest foreign owner variables by country. We only include banks with at least

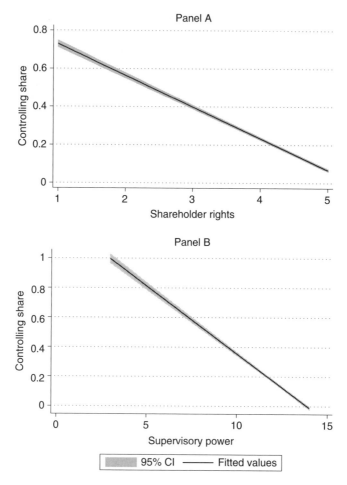

Note: Panel A, panel B, panel C, panel D, and panel E display the fitted regression lines of the variable *Controlling share* on the variables *Shareholder rights, Supervisory power, Regulatory restrictions, Supervisory independence* and *Capital oversight*, respectively.

Figure 2.1   Country-level governance indexes versus controlling share

one foreign owner. As shown, in the average country, the biggest foreign owner controls 42 percent of shares on average. This result suggests that about 71 percent of the banks' biggest foreign owners are financial firms, about 9 percent of the banks' biggest foreign owners are corporations, about 17 percent of the banks' biggest foreign owners are foundations and about 0 percent of the banks' biggest foreign owners are families.

We also summarize the association between the variables such as shareholder protection and bank regulation and the measures of bank performance. Panel A of Table 2.6 provides the median values of these variables by country. Panels B and C of Table 2.6 provide information on the distribution of bank performance variables by the shareholder protection index and bank regulation indexes. As discussed above, for each of the five country-level indexes, we split the sample into countries with above-median

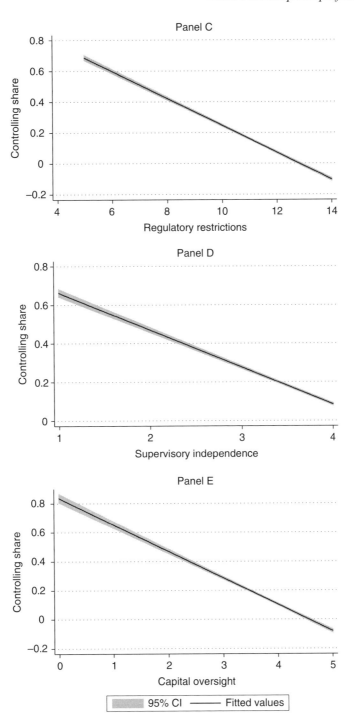

Figure 2.1 (continued)

Table 2.3   Distribution of the identity of bank foreign controlling shareholder

Country	Controlling share	Foreign family controlled	Foreign financial controlled	Foreign corporation controlled	Foreign foundation controlled	Foreign other controlled	No. of banks
Argentina	0.84	0.00	0.87	0.13	0.00	0.00	15
Australia	1.00	0.00	0.67	0.33	0.00	0.00	12
Austria	0.87	0.00	0.90	0.05	0.05	0.00	21
Brazil	0.80	0.00	0.78	0.19	0.03	0.00	36
Canada	0.87	0.00	0.94	0.00	0.06	0.00	16
Chile	0.93	0.00	1.00	0.00	0.00	0.00	7
Colombia	0.89	0.00	1.00	0.00	0.00	0.00	5
Denmark	0.90	0.00	1.00	0.00	0.00	0.00	5
Egypt	0.66	0.00	0.85	0.08	0.00	0.08	13
Finland	1.00	0.00	1.00	0.00	0.00	0.00	4
France	0.88	0.00	0.91	0.05	0.02	0.02	43
Germany	0.89	0.02	0.76	0.16	0.05	0.00	55
Greece	0.70	0.00	1.00	0.00	0.00	0.00	11
Hong Kong	0.73	0.00	1.00	0.00	0.00	0.00	29
India	0.28	0.00	0.50	0.33	0.17	0.00	6
Indonesia	0.70	0.00	0.75	0.08	0.13	0.04	24
Ireland	0.97	0.00	1.00	0.00	0.00	0.00	19
Israel	0.00	0.00	0.00	0.00	0.00	0.00	0
Italy	0.77	0.00	0.90	0.10	0.00	0.00	21
Japan	0.17	0.00	0.78	0.00	0.22	0.00	9
Jordan	0.45	0.00	0.80	0.00	0.20	0.00	5
Kenya	0.53	0.00	0.57	0.29	0.14	0.00	14
Korea, Rep. of	0.64	0.00	0.75	0.25	0.00	0.00	8
Malaysia	0.97	0.00	1.00	0.00	0.00	0.00	19
Mexico	0.71	0.00	1.00	0.00	0.00	0.00	12
Netherlands	0.90	0.00	0.89	0.11	0.00	0.00	28
Norway	1.00	0.00	1.00	0.00	0.00	0.00	3
Pakistan	0.56	0.00	0.42	0.33	0.17	0.08	12
Peru	0.87	0.00	0.85	0.15	0.00	0.00	13
Philippines	0.66	0.00	0.60	0.00	0.40	0.00	5
Portugal	0.66	0.00	0.90	0.10	0.00	0.00	10
Singapore	0.90	0.00	1.00	0.00	0.00	0.00	5
South Africa	0.82	0.00	1.00	0.00	0.00	0.00	8
Spain	0.73	0.00	0.79	0.10	0.10	0.00	29
Sri Lanka	0.15	0.00	1.00	0.00	0.00	0.00	2
Sweden	0.49	0.00	1.00	0.00	0.00	0.00	1
Switzerland	0.92	0.00	0.90	0.08	0.02	0.00	59
Taiwan	0.66	0.00	1.00	0.00	0.00	0.00	2
Thailand	0.51	0.00	0.82	0.00	0.18	0.00	11
Turkey	0.84	0.00	0.76	0.24	0.00	0.00	17
United Kingdom	0.82	0.00	0.90	0.05	0.02	0.02	41
USA	0.82	0.00	0.97	0.03	0.00	0.00	72
Venezuela	0.77	0.00	1.00	0.00	0.00	0.00	4
Zimbabwe	1.00	0.00	0.67	0.33	0.00	0.00	3
Country mean	0.73	0.00	0.85	0.08	0.04	0.01	734

Note: This table presents the identity of bank foreign controlling shareholders by country. Only banks with a foreign controlling shareholder are included. The detailed definitions and sources of the variables can be found in the Appendix. The superscripts, ***, **, and * denote the 1%, 5%, and 10% levels of significance, respectively.

Table 2.4   Distribution of the identity of bank private controlling shareholder

Country	Controlling share	Private family controlled	Private financial controlled	Private corporation controlled	Private foundation controlled	Private other controlled	No. of banks
Argentina	0.62	0.39	0.29	0.21	0.00	0.11	38
Australia	0.46	0.00	0.29	0.29	0.41	0.00	17
Austria	0.73	0.05	0.64	0.29	0.00	0.02	55
Brazil	0.71	0.10	0.31	0.44	0.07	0.08	59
Canada	0.67	0.11	0.56	0.11	0.22	0.00	9
Chile	0.60	0.00	0.59	0.29	0.12	0.00	17
Colombia	0.52	0.00	0.80	0.10	0.10	0.00	10
Denmark	0.54	0.03	0.49	0.06	0.31	0.11	35
Egypt	0.31	0.25	0.50	0.00	0.00	0.25	4
Finland	0.29	0.00	0.50	0.50	0.00	0.00	8
France	0.85	0.00	0.80	0.16	0.00	0.04	133
Germany	0.74	0.08	0.48	0.30	0.02	0.12	113
Greece	0.39	0.00	0.54	0.00	0.15	0.31	13
Hong Kong	0.75	0.14	0.64	0.21	0.00	0.00	14
India	0.59	0.28	0.48	0.08	0.00	0.16	25
Indonesia	0.52	0.06	0.29	0.35	0.12	0.18	17
Ireland	0.39	0.50	0.25	0.25	0.00	0.00	4
Israel	0.62	0.00	0.57	0.29	0.00	0.14	14
Italy	0.70	0.01	0.79	0.10	0.07	0.03	106
Japan	0.67	0.00	0.87	0.00	0.04	0.10	52
Jordan	0.19	0.25	0.25	0.00	0.50	0.00	4
Kenya	0.45	0.09	0.09	0.00	0.27	0.55	11
Korea, Rep. of	0.69	0.00	0.83	0.17	0.00	0.00	18
Malaysia	0.70	0.06	0.50	0.22	0.22	0.00	32
Mexico	0.89	0.00	0.71	0.18	0.06	0.06	17
Netherlands	0.81	0.00	0.55	0.13	0.26	0.06	31
Norway	0.87	0.20	0.70	0.10	0.00	0.00	10
Pakistan	0.35	0.14	0.33	0.05	0.19	0.29	21
Peru	1.00	0.00	0.00	1.00	0.00	0.00	1
Philippines	0.34	0.05	0.14	0.14	0.67	0.00	21
Portugal	0.95	0.18	0.55	0.27	0.00	0.00	11
Singapore	0.44	0.00	0.33	0.08	0.58	0.00	12
South Africa	0.68	0.00	0.45	0.18	0.09	0.27	22
Spain	0.66	0.10	0.81	0.05	0.05	0.00	42
Sri Lanka	0.39	0.11	0.67	0.22	0.00	0.00	9
Sweden	0.51	0.00	0.80	0.00	0.07	0.13	15
Switzerland	0.69	0.27	0.34	0.27	0.01	0.11	74
Taiwan	0.72	0.03	0.80	0.13	0.03	0.00	30
Thailand	0.40	0.00	0.20	0.20	0.40	0.20	10
Turkey	0.55	0.10	0.13	0.37	0.40	0.00	30
United Kingdom	0.77	0.06	0.65	0.21	0.02	0.06	48
USA	0.52	0.17	0.60	0.04	0.11	0.09	407
Venezuela	0.70	0.00	0.36	0.57	0.00	0.07	14
Zimbabwe	0.75	0.00	0.40	0.40	0.00	0.20	5
Country mean	0.61	0.09	0.50	0.21	0.13	0.08	1638

Note: This table presents the identity of bank private controlling shareholders by country. Only banks with a private controlling shareholder are included. The detailed definitions and sources of the variables can be found in the Appendix. The superscripts, ***, **, and * denote the 1%, 5%, and 10% levels of significance, respectively.

Table 2.5   Distribution of the identity of bank biggest foreign owner

Country	Foreign ownership	Foreign family owned	Foreign financial owned	Foreign corporation owned	Foreign foundation owned	Foreign other owned	No. of banks
Argentina	54.04	0.00	0.92	0.08	0.00	0.00	25
Australia	45.64	0.00	0.72	0.07	0.21	0.00	29
Austria	69.11	0.04	0.75	0.11	0.11	0.00	28
Brazil	57.50	0.00	0.69	0.16	0.16	0.00	51
Canada	53.15	0.00	0.85	0.00	0.15	0.00	27
Chile	47.83	0.00	0.88	0.00	0.12	0.00	17
Colombia	46.81	0.00	1.00	0.00	0.00	0.00	10
Denmark	9.96	0.00	0.41	0.00	0.59	0.00	51
Egypt	56.82	0.00	0.75	0.19	0.00	0.06	16
Finland	41.40	0.00	0.80	0.00	0.20	0.00	10
France	65.22	0.00	0.86	0.08	0.05	0.02	66
Germany	60.12	0.06	0.72	0.08	0.14	0.00	85
Greece	33.04	0.00	0.64	0.12	0.24	0.00	25
Hong Kong	63.38	0.00	0.93	0.00	0.08	0.00	40
India	6.67	0.00	0.49	0.17	0.30	0.04	53
Indonesia	54.36	0.00	0.67	0.12	0.18	0.03	33
Ireland	72.16	0.00	0.85	0.00	0.15	0.00	26
Israel	5.98	0.00	0.38	0.15	0.46	0.00	13
Italy	31.75	0.00	0.82	0.05	0.13	0.00	55
Japan	3.51	0.00	0.52	0.02	0.46	0.00	180
Jordan	27.99	0.10	0.50	0.30	0.10	0.00	10
Kenya	39.52	0.00	0.63	0.26	0.11	0.00	19
Korea, Rep. of	27.67	0.00	0.55	0.09	0.36	0.00	22
Malaysia	49.38	0.00	0.78	0.00	0.23	0.00	40
Mexico	61.16	0.00	0.86	0.00	0.14	0.00	14
Netherlands	67.10	0.00	0.85	0.15	0.00	0.00	40
Norway	53.08	0.00	0.67	0.00	0.33	0.00	6
Pakistan	28.48	0.00	0.44	0.20	0.08	0.28	25
Peru	86.94	0.00	0.85	0.15	0.00	0.00	13
Philippines	19.62	0.00	0.54	0.13	0.33	0.00	24
Portugal	48.22	0.00	0.69	0.13	0.19	0.00	16
Singapore	34.20	0.00	0.79	0.14	0.00	0.07	14
South Africa	43.42	0.00	0.82	0.00	0.18	0.00	17
Spain	48.53	0.00	0.71	0.13	0.16	0.00	45
Sri Lanka	7.86	0.00	0.56	0.22	0.22	0.00	9
Sweden	10.00	0.00	0.63	0.00	0.13	0.25	8
Switzerland	66.23	0.02	0.69	0.08	0.21	0.00	86
Taiwan	7.31	0.00	0.45	0.13	0.42	0.00	31
Thailand	26.05	0.00	0.63	0.00	0.37	0.00	27
Turkey	38.50	0.00	0.55	0.09	0.32	0.05	44
United Kingdom	57.28	0.00	0.90	0.03	0.05	0.02	61
USA	13.57	0.00	0.94	0.01	0.04	0.00	555
Venezuela	38.28	0.00	0.78	0.22	0.00	0.00	9
Zimbabwe	56.93	0.00	0.88	0.13	0.00	0.00	8
Country mean	41.72	0.00	0.71	0.09	0.17	0.02	1983

Note: This table presents the identity of bank biggest foreign owners by country. Only banks with foreign ownership are included. The detailed definitions and sources of the variables can be found in the Appendix. The superscripts, ***, **, and * denote the 1%, 5%, and 10% levels of significance, respectively.

Table 2.6 Distribution of investor protection index, bank regulation indexes and bank performance

Country	Shareholder rights	Supervisory power	Regulatory restrictions	Supervisory independence	Capital oversight	ROA	ROE	Loan growth
Panel A: Median values of bank performance by country								
Argentina	4	11	9	1	3	0.02	0.11	0.30
Australia	4	11	8	4	3	0.01	0.16	0.15
Austria	2	13	5	1	5	0.01	0.10	0.10
Brazil	3	14	10	1	5	0.02	0.18	0.23
Canada	5	6	7	4	4	0.01	0.11	0.09
Chile	5	10	11	1	3	0.01	0.11	0.17
Colombia	3					0.02	0.17	0.41
Denmark	2	8	8	1	2	0.02	0.16	0.27
Egypt	2	12	13	4	3	0.00	0.06	0.09
Finland	3	8	7	1	4	0.01	0.10	0.07
France	3	7	6	3	2	0.01	0.12	0.11
Germany	1	10	5	4	1	0.00	0.06	0.04
Greece	2	10	9	1	3	0.01	0.09	0.27
Hong Kong	5					0.01	0.13	0.08
India	5	8	10	3	3	0.01	0.16	0.30
Indonesia	2	12	14	2	5	0.01	0.13	0.13
Ireland	4	9	8	4	1	0.01	0.08	0.10
Israel	3	8	13	2	3	0.01	0.13	0.05
Italy	1	6	10	2	4	0.01	0.11	0.15
Japan	4	12	13	3	4	0.00	0.05	0.02
Jordan	1		11		5	0.02	0.14	0.21
Kenya	3	14	10	2	4	0.02	0.16	0.23
Korea, Rep. of	2	9	9	2	3	0.01	0.17	0.22

Table 2.6 (continued)

Country	Shareholder rights	Supervisory power	Regulatory restrictions	Supervisory independence	Capital oversight	ROA	ROE	Loan growth
Panel A: Median values of bank performance by country								
Malaysia	4	11	10	3	3	0.01	0.10	0.06
Mexico	1	9	12	1	4	0.02	0.12	0.27
Netherlands	2	8	6	4	3	0.01	0.13	0.09
Norway	4					0.01	0.15	0.19
Pakistan	5					0.02	0.21	0.26
Peru	3	12	8	3	3	0.02	0.23	0.15
Philippines	3	11	7	1	1	0.01	0.10	0.11
Portugal	3	13	9	4	3	0.01	0.12	0.14
Singapore	4	3	8	3	1	0.02	0.12	0.12
South Africa	5	4	8	2	4	0.02	0.24	0.26
Spain	4	9	7	3	4	0.01	0.09	0.23
Sri Lanka	3	11	7	2	0	0.01	0.15	0.27
Sweden	3	6	9	3	3	0.01	0.12	0.12
Switzerland	2	13	5	3	3	0.02	0.10	0.05
Taiwan	3	8	12	2	2	0.00	0.01	0.05
Thailand	2	10	9	2	4	0.01	0.08	0.08
Turkey	2	11	12	4	1	0.02	0.17	0.42
United Kingdom	5	11	5	4	3	0.01	0.12	0.15
USA	5	13	12	4	4	0.01	0.10	0.08
Venezuela	1	13	10	3	3	0.03	0.29	0.66
Zimbabwe	3					0.11	0.41	3.12
Country mean	3.09	9.84	9.03	2.55	3.05	0.01	0.14	0.24
Panel B: Median values of bank performance by country-level investor protection and bank regulation indexes								
Low shareholder rights	2					0.01	0.12	0.14
High shareholder rights	5					0.01	0.10	0.08
Low supervisory power		8				0.01	0.11	0.14

High supervisory power	13	0.01	0.10	0.09
Low regulatory restrictions	6	0.01	0.11	0.13
High regulatory restrictions	12	0.01	0.10	0.09
Low supervisory independence	2	0.01	0.11	0.13
High supervisory independence	4	0.01	0.10	0.09
Low capital oversight	3	0.01	0.12	0.14
High capital oversight	4	0.01	0.10	0.09

Panel C: Test of median values of bank performance by country-level investor protection and bank regulation indexes

Low versus high shareholder rights	−95.95***	4.61***	6.45***	109.03***
Low versus high supervisory power	−85.23***	−6.13***	2.23**	65.17***
Low versus high regulatory restrictions	−89.35***	−0.75	4.42***	64.25***
Low versus high supervisory independence	−107.79***	0.62	3.67***	71.35***
Low versus high capital oversight	−101.11***	0.28	5.44***	67.33***

Note: This table presents the median values of the investor protection index, bank regulation indexes, and bank performance by country. The detailed definitions and sources of the variables can be found in the Appendix. The superscripts, ***, **, and * denote the 1%, 5%, and 10% levels of significance, respectively.

and below-median value of each index. We report the corresponding bank perform-ance variables in panel B and the test statistics about whether the ownership patterns differ significantly between high and low country-level governance index countries in panel C.

The tests in Table 2.6 panel C indicate that there is no consistent pattern to bank per-formance measured by *ROA* across high and low levels of the country-level governance index and bank regulation indexes. However, we find some interesting results that banks in the countries with above-median value of the shareholder protection index and the banking regulation indexes such as *Supervisory Power, Regulatory Restrictions, Capital Oversight* and *Supervisory Independence* have lower performance measured by *ROE* than countries with below-median values of these indexes. The difference is significant at 1 percent. This result may be caused by higher ownership concentration in the countries with below-median value of the shareholder protection index and the banking regula-tion indexes as documented in Table 2.2. As shown, banks in the countries with above-median value of the shareholder protection index and the banking regulation indexes such as *Supervisory Power, Regulatory Restrictions, Capital Oversight* and *Supervisory Independence* have lower growth opportunity measured by *Loan Growth* than countries with below-median values of these indexes. The difference is significant at 1 percent. The reason may be that the countries with below-median value of the country-level govern-ance indexes are also emerging countries and banks in these countries have more growth opportunities.

2.4   BANK OWNERSHIP AND PERFORMANCE

To assess the impact of bank ownership structure on bank performance, we regress our dependent variables such as *ROA* and *ROE* against our key variable, the control rights of controlling shareholders (*Controlling Share*) and the control variables, the level of minority shareholders protection (*Shareholder Rights*), bank regulation policies such as *Supervisory Power, Regulatory Restrictions, Capital Oversight* and *Supervisory Independence*, and bank-specific characteristics such as *Loan Growth, State Controlled, Foreign Controlled* and *Private Controlled*. We add bank regulation indexes individually because they are highly correlated to each other. When we estimate our regressions, we use country random effects. The detailed model is as below:

ROA (ROE) = f (Controlling Share, Loan Growth, State Controlled, Foreign Controlled, Private Controlled, Public, Shareholder Rights, Supervisory Power, Regulatory Restrictions, Capital Oversight, Supervisory Independence).

As shown in Table 2.7, the coefficients of the variable *Controlling Share* are all signifi-cantly positive. This result indicates that higher levels of control rights by a controlling shareholder help improve bank operating performance, which is consistent with Caprio et al. (2007). This result suggests that concentrated ownership can reduce the incentive of controlling shareholders to expropriate corporate resources from firms. This result is not only statistically significant, but also economically significant. For example, using the coefficients reported in column 1 of Table 2.7, a one standard deviation increase

Table 2.7 Bank ownership and performance

	ROA				ROE			
	(1)	(2)	(3)	(4)	(5)	(6)	(7)	(8)
Controlling Share	0.0028***	0.0024***	0.0025***	0.0027***	0.0061*	0.0045***	0.0060***	0.0059***
	(6.73)	(5.25)	(5.01)	(5.89)	(1.86)	(5.26)	(5.89)	(4.93)
Loan Growth	−0.00001***	−0.00001***	−0.00001***	−0.00001***	−0.00005***	−0.00005***	−0.00005***	−0.00005***
	(−6.51)	(−6.75)	(−6.03)	(−6.99)	(−5.30)	(−5.51)	(−5.99)	(−5.01)
State Controlled	−0.0041	−0.0011	−0.0031	−0.0024	−0.0123	−0.0145	−0.0134	−0.0126
	(−0.59)	(−0.42)	(−0.67)	(−0.33)	(−0.99)	(−0.35)	(−0.77)	(−0.46)
Foreign Controlled	0.0021***	0.0012***	0.0013***	0.0020***	0.0045***	0.0041***	0.0035***	0.0036***
	(4.24)	(3.98)	(4.24)	(4.14)	(4.76)	(4.83)	(3.90)	(4.59)
Private Controlled	0.0011	0.0021	0.0014	0.0013	0.0073	0.0112	0.0100	0.0103
	(0.64)	(0.62)	(0.71)	(0.51)	(0.47)	(0.69)	(0.54)	(0.68)
Public Controlled	0.0009	0.0007	0.0010	0.0011	0.0069	0.0089	0.0074	0.0089
	(0.46)	(0.72)	(0.56)	(0.73)	(0.89)	(0.56)	(0.99)	(0.24)
Shareholder Rights	0.0012	0.0007	0.0009	0.0008	0.0016	0.0011	0.0016	0.0014
	(0.89)	(0.25)	(0.46)	(0.25)	(0.46)	(0.78)	(0.70)	(0.98)
Supervisory Power	0.0005***				0.0001			
	(5.86)				(0.17)			
Regulatory Restrictions		−0.0005				−0.0033		
		(−0.31)				(−0.78)		
Supervisory Independence			0.0015				0.0043	
			(0.87)				(0.88)	
Capital Oversight				0.0012				0.0034
				(0.41)				(0.98)
Observations	11215	11226	11215	11226	11215	11226	11215	11226
No. of countries	36	37	36	37	36	37	36	37

Note: The random effects are used. The detailed definitions and sources of the variables can be found in the Appendix. Numbers in parentheses represent t-values. The supe'scripts, ***, **, and * denote the 1%, 5%, and 10% levels of significance, respectively.

in *Controlling Share* causes an increase in *ROA* by 0.0028*0.31 or 0.000868, which is 8 percent of the mean value of *ROA* in our sample of banks.

We do not find a significant positive relationship between shareholder protection and bank operating performance, which is documented in Caprio et al. (2007). This may suggest that the shareholder protection only has a positive effect on large banks. We find that banks controlled by foreign shareholders have a better performance.

2.5   ROBUSTNESS TESTS

2.5.1   Simultaneous Causality Problems

Bank ownership structure may be endogenously determined by other factors, although La Porta et al. (2002) argue that ownership patterns do not change a lot over time. We address potential concerns about the endogeneity of our bank ownership structure measure following Caprio et al. (2007). Specifically, we use the average value of *Controlling Share* of other banks in the country as an instrument and the Baltagi (1981) error component two-stage least square random-effects estimator to estimate our regressions. As shown in Table 2.8, we obtain similar results and the same conclusion that a higher level of control rights by a controlling shareholder helps improve bank operating performance. This suggests that our main results are not biased by simultaneous causality problems.

2.5.2   Omitted Variable Problems

Controlling for other country-level characteristics
Because of our data limitation, we can only estimate our model cross-sectionally and cannot control for the country fixed effects. To make sure our results are not biased by the omitted variable problems, we control for a series of country characteristics. As shown in Table 2.9, we include the logarithm of real per capita gross domestic product (*Per Capita Income*), an index of contract enforcement (*Contract Enforcement*), an index of official corruption (*Corruption*), and an index of the law and order tradition of the country (*Law Tradition*). We obtain similar results and the same conclusion that a higher level of control rights by a controlling shareholder helps to improve bank operating performance. This suggests that our main results are not biased by country-level omitted variable problems.

Controlling for other firm-level characteristics
To make sure our results are not biased by the firm-level omitted variable problems, we control for a series of firm characteristics such as: (1) the variable *Capital Asset Ratio* (the capital asset ratio); (2) the variable *Loan Loss Provision Ratio* (the ratio of the bank's loan loss provisions to interest income); (3) the variable *Cost Income Ratio* (the ratio of total operating expenses to total operating income); (4) the variable *Liquidity Ratio* (the ratio of bank's liquid assets to liquid liabilities); and (5) the variable *Firm Size* (the logarithm of total assets of the bank). As shown in Table 2.10, our results are still robust. A higher percentage of shares held by a controlling shareholder helps to improve bank

Table 2.8 *Instrumental variable and bank performance*

	ROA				ROE			
	(1)	(2)	(3)	(4)	(5)	(6)	(7)	(8)
Controlling Share	0.0031***	0.0028***	0.0029***	0.0032***	0.0068***	0.0051*	0.0035***	0.0034***
	(5.24)	(5.01)	(5.89)	(5.24)	(5.25)	(1.89)	(5.26)	(4.24)
Loan Growth	−0.00002***	−0.00001***	−0.00001***	−0.00001***	−0.00003***	−0.00004***	−0.00005***	−0.00003***
	(−5.24)	(−4.92)	(−4.99)	(−6.14)	(−4.89)	(−5.04)	(−5.01)	(−4.83)
State Controlled	−0.0031	−0.0022	−0.0027	−0.0029	−0.0100	−0.0135	−0.0124	−0.0122
	(−0.89)	(−0.86)	(−0.24)	(−0.63)	(−0.35)	(−0.64)	(−0.37)	(−0.67)
Foreign Controlled	0.0013***	0.0015***	0.0009***	0.0026***	0.0050***	0.0047***	0.0041***	0.0035***
	(4.02)	(3.80)	(4.02)	(4.03)	(4.83)	(4.67)	(3.87)	(4.89)
Private Controlled	0.0009	0.0017	0.0018	0.0015	0.0068	0.0105	0.0104	0.0088
	(0.88)	(0.77)	(0.68)	(0.91)	(0.58)	(0.72)	(0.89)	(0.78)
Public	0.0008	0.0006	0.0011	0.0013	0.0058	0.0089	0.0067	0.0081
	(0.67)	(0.89)	(0.76)	(0.89)	(0.67)	(0.76)	(0.83)	(0.82)
Shareholder Rights	0.0021	0.0012	0.0016	0.0012	0.0012	0.0015	0.0012	0.0019
	(0.35)	(0.72)	(0.12)	(0.47)	(0.78)	(0.72)	(0.55)	(0.47)
Supervisory Power	0.0007				0.0003			
	(0.82)				(0.56)			
Regulatory Restrictions		−0.0002				−0.0031		
		(−0.80)				(−0.46)		
Supervisory Independence			0.0011***				0.0045	
			(5.81)				(0.99)	
Capital Oversight				0.0015				0.0045
				(0.79)				(0.34)
Observations	11215	11226	11215	11226	11215	11226	11215	11226
R-squared	0.25	0.26	0.27	0.22	0.29	0.31	0.30	0.24
No. of countries	36	37	36	37	36	37	36	37

Note: We use the average value of *Controlling Share* of other banks in the country as instrument and the Baltagi (1981) error component two-stage least square random-effects estimator to estimate our regressions. The detailed definitions and sources of the variables can be found in the Appendix. Numbers in parentheses represent t-values. The superscripts, ***, **, and * denote the 1%, 5%, and 10% levels of significance, respectively.

Table 2.9 Additional country-level controls

	ROA				ROE			
	(1)	(2)	(3)	(4)	(5)	(6)	(7)	(8)
Controlling Share	0.0031***	0.0027***	0.0029***	0.0023***	0.0068***	0.0078***	0.0055***	0.0035***
	(6.01)	(4.89)	(4.72)	(5.24)	(5.51)	(4.89)	(5.02)	(4.64)
Loan Growth	−0.00001***	−0.00001***	−0.00001***	−0.00001***	−0.00006***	−0.00003***	−0.00004***	−0.00002***
	(−6.03)	(−5.03)	(−4.89)	(−6.03)	(−5.25)	(−5.02)	(−5.24)	(−4.80)
State Controlled	−0.0024	−0.0018	−0.0028	−0.0015	−0.0103	−0.0126	−0.0124	−0.0105
	(−0.24)	(−0.89)	(−0.25)	(−0.45)	(−0.78)	(−0.45)	(−0.66)	(−0.57)
Foreign Controlled	0.0010***	0.0011***	0.0005***	0.0020***	0.0045***	0.0043***	0.0039***	0.0037***
	(3.90)	(3.99)	(4.00)	(3.89)	(4.79)	(4.89)	(3.99)	(4.94)
Private Controlled	0.0007	0.0014	0.0014	0.0013	0.0062	0.0101	0.0100	0.0081
	(0.91)	(0.79)	(0.74)	(0.84)	(0.78)	(0.73)	(0.80)	(0.74)
Public	0.0006	0.0009	0.0012	0.0013	0.0047	0.0067	0.0073	0.0084
	(0.56)	(0.98)	(0.87)	(0.67)	(0.59)	(0.89)	(0.90)	(0.90)
Shareholder Rights	0.0021	0.0014***	0.0016	0.0012	0.0011	0.0013***	0.0013	0.0010
	(0.72)	(4.46)	(0.80)	(0.82)	(0.71)	(4.89)	(0.45)	(0.90)
Per Capita Income	0.0048	0.0043	0.0051	0.0040	0.0026	0.0021	0.0029	0.0019
	(0.06)	(0.07)	(0.01)	(0.03)	(0.04)	(0.05)	(0.09)	(0.02)
Contract Enforcement	0.0025	0.0026	0.0020	0.0035	0.0104	0.0100	0.0109	0.0098
	(0.67)	(0.89)	(0.25)	(0.34)	(0.67)	(0.89)	(0.44)	(0.41)

Corruption	0.0030	0.0034	0.0037	0.0035	0.0109	0.0123	0.0121	0.0118
	(0.78)	(0.64)	(0.89)	(0.91)	(0.89)	(0.98)	(0.76)	(0.98)
Law Tradition	0.0024	0.0029	0.0031	0.0030	0.0100	0.0114	0.0109	0.0102
	(0.45)	(0.25)	(0.78)	(0.67)	(0.79)	(0.71)	(0.45)	(0.78)
Supervisory Power	0.0006				0.0004			
	(0.91)				(0.56)			
Regulatory Restrictions		0.0004***				−0.0036		
		(4.89)				(−0.63)		
Supervisory Independence			0.0010***				0.0021	
			(4.91)				(0.44)	
Capital Oversight				0.0005				0.0036
				(0.67)				(0.61)
Observations	11 215	11 226	11 215	11 226	11 215	11 226	11 215	11 226
No. of countries	36	37	36	37	36	37	36	37

Note: The random effects are used. The detailed definitions and sources of the variables can be found in the Appendix. Numbers in parentheses represent t-values. The superscripts, ***, **, and * denote the 1%, 5%, and 10% levels of significance, respectively.

Table 2.10 Additional bank-level controls

	ROA					ROE		
	(1)	(2)	(3)	(4)	(5)	(6)	(7)	(8)
Controlling Share	0.0035***	0.0041***	0.0037***	0.0047***	0.0051*	0.0051***	0.0067***	0.0078***
	(6.82)	(5.03)	(4.89)	(5.24)	(1.84)	(5.02)	(5.05)	(4.56)
Loan Growth	−0.00001	−0.00001***	−0.00001***	−0.00001***	−0.00003	−0.00006***	−0.00004***	−0.00007***
	(−0.93)	(−6.24)	(−4.82)	(−6.15)	(−0.78)	(−5.24)	(−5.41)	(−4.72)
State Controlled	−0.0034	−0.0021	−0.0027	−0.0034	−0.0101	−0.0124	−0.0121	−0.0113
	(−0.83)	(−0.65)	(−0.73)	(−0.67)	(−0.35)	(−0.45)	(−0.47)	(−0.24)
Foreign Controlled	0.0013***	0.0010***	0.0007***	0.0018***	0.0048***	0.0047***	0.0041***	0.0039***
	(4.02)	(3.89)	(4.14)	(3.92)	(4.20)	(4.67)	(3.89)	(4.90)
Private Controlled	0.0004	0.0013	0.0017	0.0012	0.0059	0.0098	0.0105	0.0077
	(0.56)	(0.47)	(0.89)	(0.78)	(0.89)	(0.68)	(0.75)	(0.65)
Public Controlled	0.0004	0.0010	0.0015	0.0014	0.0052	0.0076	0.0079	0.0089
	(0.36)	(0.78)	(0.92)	(0.56)	(0.78)	(0.45)	(0.56)	(0.98)
Shareholder Rights	0.0002	0.0004***	0.0006	0.0003	0.0025	0.0027***	0.0021	0.0013
	(0.35)	(4.41)	(0.51)	(0.38)	(0.78)	(5.98)	(0.24)	(0.45)
Capital Asset Ratio	−0.0017***	−0.0015***	−0.0018***	−0.0012***	−0.0051***	−0.0059***	−0.0071***	−0.0061***
	(−4.89)	(−4.78)	(−4.67)	(−4.89)	(−5.25)	(−5.89)	(−4.89)	(−5.35)
Loan Loss Provision Ratio	−0.0111***	−0.0118***	−0.0110***	−0.0111***	−0.0503***	−0.0514***	−0.0702***	−0.0681***
	(−4.78)	(−4.89)	(−4.31)	(−4.99)	(−5.01)	(−5.04)	(−4.67)	(−5.02)

	(1)	(2)	(3)	(4)	(5)	(6)	(7)	(8)
Cost Income Ratio	−0.0102	−0.0110	−0.0101	−0.0102	−0.0500	−0.0502	−0.0687	−0.0667
	(−0.89)	(−0.81)	(−0.34)	(−0.90)	(−0.61)	(−0.09)	(−0.31)	(−4.26)
Liquidity Ratio	0.0306	0.0310	0.0301	0.0304	0.1500	0.1503	0.1814	0.1824
	(0.25)	(0.67)	(0.54)	(0.76)	(0.87)	(0.11)	(0.67)	(0.31)
Firm Size	0.0002	0.0005	0.0003	0.0002	0.0015	0.0010	0.0012	0.0016
	(0.79)	(0.78)	(0.98)	(0.24)	(0.41)	(0.31)	(0.54)	(0.89)
Supervisory Power	0.0003***				0.0007			
	(4.82)				(0.56)			
Regulatory Restrictions		−0.0003				−0.0041		
		(−0.89)				(−0.81)		
Supervisory Independence			0.0021				0.0034	
			(0.52)				(0.56)	
Capital Oversight				0.0024				0.0031
				(0.89)				(0.36)
Observations	11 215	11 226	11 215	11 226	11 215	11 226	11 215	11 226
No. of countries	36	37	36	37	36	37	36	37

Note: The random effects are used. The detailed definitions and sources of the variables can be found in the Appendix. Numbers in parentheses represent t-values. The superscripts, ***, **, and * denote the 1%, 5%, and 10% levels of significance, respectively.

operating performance. This suggests that our main results are not biased by the firm-level omitted variable problems.

2.5.3   Other Robustness Tests

In this subsection, we examine whether our results are robust when we use different definitions of some of our variables and change the sample of countries and banks. Although the results are not reported, these are available upon request.

First, the US banks dominate our sample and may bias our estimation. To deal with this concern, we estimate our regressions in the sample excluding the US banks and obtain similar results and the same conclusions.

Second, Micco et al. (2007) find that bank state ownership, private ownership and foreign ownership only have significant influence on bank performance in developing countries and that these relationships do not show up in industrial countries. Thus, our results regarding the relationship between bank control rights and performance may also only exist in the developing country subsample or the industrial country subsample. To deal with this issue, we follow their approach and use the classification of the World Bank's World Development Indicators to divide our sample into the developing-country subsample and the industrial-country subsample. Our results are still robust in either of these two subsamples.

Third, we use 10 percent of a bank's ownership as the minimum level to classify that a bank is widely held in the above estimation. When we use 20 percent or 15 percent, we obtain similar results and the same conclusions.

Finally, we use *ROA* and *ROE* to measure bank operating performance. When we use other measures such as one-year change of *ROA* or *ROE*, our results are still robust.

2.6   BANK OWNERSHIP AND PERFORMANCE IN A PERIOD OF FINANCIAL CRISIS

Johnson et al. (2000) and Mitton (2002) find that superior corporate governance is more critical for non-financial firms in the Asian financial crisis period because the decline in the expected return on investment may motivate managers and controlling shareholders to expropriate more. In this section, we want to examine whether the relationship between bank ownership and performance is more pronounced in the recent 2008 financial crisis period. Specifically, we match our ownership data with the 2008 bank performance data. Because our ownership data are from 2006, we assume that bank ownership does not vary a lot over time.

As shown in Table 2.11, the coefficients of the variable *Controlling Share* are all significantly positive. This result indicates that higher levels of control rights by a controlling shareholder help to improve bank operating performance, even in a period of financial crisis. This result is not only statistically significant, but also economically significant. For example, using the coefficients reported in column 1 of Table 2.11, a one-standard deviation increase in *Controlling Share* causes an increase in *ROA* by 0.0034*0.31 or 0.001054, which is 10.54 percent of the mean value of *ROA* in our sample of banks. As noted above, in the normal period, a one-standard deviation increase in *Controlling*

Table 2.11   Bank ownership and performance in a period of financial crisis

	ROA				ROE			
	(1)	(2)	(3)	(4)	(5)	(6)	(7)	(8)
Controlling Share	0.0034***	0.0032***	0.0031***	0.0035***	0.0084*	0.0058***	0.0080***	0.0075***
	(4.83)	(4.98)	(4.04)	(4.35)	(1.88)	(5.04)	(5.01)	(4.78)
Loan Growth	−0.00001*	−0.00002*	−0.00001*	−0.00001*	−0.00003*	−0.00005*	−0.00004*	−0.00005*
	(−1.86)	(−1.87)	(−1.90)	(−1.91)	(−1.85)	(−1.87)	(−1.90)	(−1.88)
State Controlled	−0.0031	−0.0010	−0.0028	−0.0022	−0.0111	−0.0134	−0.0122	−0.0112
	(−0.89)	(−0.51)	(−0.87)	(−0.45)	(−0.87)	(−0.44)	(−0.67)	(−0.56)
Foreign Controlled	0.0019	0.0010	0.0011	0.0017	0.0040	0.0038	0.0032	0.0031
	(0.45)	(0.78)	(0.56)	(0.75)	(0.54)	(0.67)	(0.87)	(0.72)
Private Controlled	0.0010	0.0018	0.0012	0.0011	0.0070	0.0104	0.0098	0.0097
	(0.71)	(0.68)	(0.55)	(0.45)	(0.77)	(0.72)	(0.67)	(0.78)
Public	0.0003	0.0011	0.0010	0.0012	0.0057	0.0089	0.0067	0.0084
	(0.89)	(0.45)	(0.59)	(0.32)	(0.49)	(0.57)	(0.47)	(0.58)
Shareholder Rights	0.0010	0.0004	0.0005	0.0007	0.0013	0.0010	0.0013	0.0012
	(0.80)	(0.29)	(0.89)	(0.46)	(0.78)	(0.66)	(0.89)	(0.48)
Supervisory Power	0.0004				0.0001			
	(0.97)				(0.54)			
Regulatory Restrictions		−0.0004				−0.0030		
		(−0.78)				(−0.73)		
Supervisory Independence			0.0013***				0.0032	
			(4.82)				(0.56)	
Capital Oversight				0.0011				0.0031
				(0.39)				(0.71)
Observations	11114	11198	11114	11198	11114	11198	11114	11198
No. of countries	36	37	36	37	36	37	36	37

Note: The random effects are used. The detailed definitions and sources of the variables can be found in the Appendix. Numbers in parentheses represent t-values. The superscripts. ***, **, and * denote the 1%, 5%, and 10% levels of significance, respectively.

Share causes an increase in *ROA* by 0.0028*0.31 or 0.000868, which is 8 percent of the mean value of *ROA* in our sample of banks. Thus, the results suggest that the relationship between bank ownership and performance is more pronounced in the recent 2008 financial crisis period.

2.7   CONCLUSION

This chapter constructs a comprehensive dataset on the ownership of 11 888 publicly listed and private banks in 44 countries to identify banks' ownership structure and its impact on bank operating performance. This chapter finds that banks are more likely to have a concentrated ownership in the countries with weaker shareholder protection and bank regulations. This chapter also documents the patterns of bank controlling shareholders and foreign ownership. In addition, the evidence shows that larger control rights by the controlling owner help to improve bank operating performance and that this relationship is more pronounced in a period of financial crisis.

Our results imply that ownership structure is an important governance mechanism for banks, which is consistent with the existing literature (e.g., Shleifer and Vishny, 1997). Our chapter also has policy implications. The existing literature (e.g., Caprio et al., 2007) has shown that country-level shareholder protection and bank supervision have a positive impact on bank performance. However, it will take a very long time to conduct the legal reform and improve regulation in the banking industry. Our chapter shows that banks with a controlling shareholder have better performance. This may provide an alternative mechanism for policymakers to improve bank performance.

NOTE

1.   We do not focus on the cash flow ownership because the data are very difficult to obtain. In addition, Kalcheva and Lins (2007) argue that cash flow rights are highly correlated with control rights and the effect of control rights dominates.

REFERENCES

Baltagi, B.H. (1981), 'Simultaneous equations with error components', *Journal of Econometrics*, **17**, 189–200.
Barth, J.R., G. Caprio and R. Levine (2001), 'The regulation and supervision of banks around the world: a new database', in R.E. Litan and R. Herring (eds), *Brooking-Wharton Papers on Financial Services*, Washington, DC: Brookings Institution.
Barth, J.R., G. Caprio and R. Levine (2004), 'Bank regulation and supervision: what works best?', *Journal of Financial Intermediation*, **13**, 205–248.
Barth, J.R., G. Caprio and R. Levine (2006), *Rethinking Bank Regulation: Till Angels Govern*, New York: Cambridge University Press.
Beck, T., A. Demirgüç-Kunt and R. Levine (2006), 'Bank supervision and corruption in lending', *Journal of Monetary Economics*, **53**, 2131–2163.
Beck, T., R. Levine and N. Loayza (2000), 'Finance and the sources of growth', *Journal of Financial Economics*, **58**, 261–300.
Caprio, G., L. Laeven and R. Levine (2007), 'Governance and bank valuation', *Journal of Financial Intermediation*, **16**, 584–617.

Claessens, S. and L. Laeven (2003), 'Financial development, property rights, and growth', *Journal of Finance*, **58**, 2401–2436.

Demirgüç-Kunt, A. and H. Huizinga (2000), 'Determinants of commercial bank interest margins and profitability: some international evidence', *World Bank Economic Review*, **13**(2), 379–408.

Jensen, M. and W. Meckling (1976), 'Theory of the firm, managerial behavior, agency costs and ownership structure', *Journal of Financial Economics*, **3**, 305–360.

Johnson, S., P. Boone, A. Breach and E. Friedman (2000), 'Corporate governance in the Asian financial crisis, 1997–98', *Journal of Financial Economics*, **58**, 141–186.

Kalcheva, I. and K.V. Lins (2007), 'International evidence on cash holdings and expected managerial agency problems', *Review of Financial Studies*, **20**(4), 1088–1112.

La Porta, R., F. Lopez-de-Silanes and A. Shleifer (1999), 'Corporate ownership around the world', *Journal of Finance*, **54**, 471–517.

La Porta, R., F. Lopez-de-Silanes and A. Shleifer (2002), 'Government ownership of banks', *Journal of Finance*, **57**(1), 256–301.

Levine, R. (1999), 'Law, finance, and economic growth', *Journal of Financial Intermediation*, **8**, 8–35.

Levine, R., N. Loayza and T. Beck (2000), 'Financial intermediation and growth: causality and causes', *Journal of Monetary Economics*, **46**, 31–77.

Levine, R. and S. Zervos (1998), 'Stock markets, banks, and economic growth', *American Economic Review*, **88**, 537–558.

Mian, A. (2003), 'Foreign, private domestic, and government banks: new evidence from emerging markets', mimeo, University of Chicago.

Micco, A., U. Panizza and M. Yanẽz (2007), 'Bank ownership and performance: does politics matter?', *Journal of Banking and Finance*, **31**, 219–241.

Mitton, T. (2002), 'A cross-firm analysis of the impact of corporate governance on the East Asian financial crisis', *Journal of Financial Economics*, **64**, 215–241.

Shleifer, A. and R. Vishny (1997), 'A survey of corporate governance', *Journal of Finance*, **52**, 737–783.

APPENDIX

Table A2.1 Variable definitions and sources

Variable	Description
Shareholder Rights	According to La Porta et al. (2002): 'the index is formed by adding 1 when: (1) the country allows shareholders to mail their proxy vote to the firm; (2) shareholders are not required to deposit their shares prior to the General Shareholders' Meeting; (3) cumulative voting or proportional representation of minorities in the board of directors is allowed; (4) an oppressed minorities mechanism is in place; (5) the minimum percentage of share capital that entitles a shareholder to call for an Extraordinary Shareholders' Meeting is less than or equal to 10 percent (the sample median); or (6) shareholders have preemptive rights that can only be waived by a shareholders' vote. The index ranges from 0 to 6.' Source: La Porta et al. (2002).
Supervisory Power	According to Barth et al. (2004, 2006): 'this Index of official supervisory power is formed by adding one for an affirmative response to each for the following 14 questions. 1. Does the supervisory agency have the right to meet with external auditors to discuss their report without the approval of the bank? 2. Are auditors required by law to communicate directly to the supervisory agency any presumed involvement of bank directors or senior managers in elicit activities, fraud, or insider abuse? 3. Can supervisors take legal action against external auditors for negligence? 4. Can the supervisory authority force a bank to change its internal organizational structure? 5. Are off-balance sheet items disclosed to supervisors? 6. Can the supervisory agency order the bank's directors or management to constitute provisions to cover actual or potential losses? 7. Can the supervisory agency suspend the directors' decision to distribute: (a) Dividends? (b) Bonuses? (c) Management fees? 8. Can the supervisory agency legally declare – such that this declaration supersedes the rights of bank shareholders – that a bank is insolvent? 9. Does the Banking Law give authority to the supervisory agency to intervene – that is, suspend some or all ownership rights – [in] a problem bank? 10. Regarding bank restructuring and reorganization, can the supervisory agency or any other government agency do the following: (a) Supersede shareholder rights? (b) Remove and replace management? (c) Remove and replace directors?' Source: Barth et al. (2004, 2006).
Regulatory Restrictions	An index to measure regulatory restrictions on the activities of banks such as securities market activities, insurance activities, real estate activities and the ownership of non-financial firms. Source: Barth et al. (2004).
Capital Oversight	According to Barth et al. (2004): 'this index includes information on the following questions. 1. Is the minimum capital–asset ratio requirement risk weighted in line with the Basel guidelines? 2. Does the minimum ratio vary as a function of market risk? 3. Are market values of loan losses not realized in accounting books deducted from capital? 4. Are unrealized losses in securities portfolios deducted? 5. Are unrealized foreign exchange losses deducted? 6. What fraction of revaluation gains is allowed as part of capital? 7. Are the sources of funds to be used as capital verified by the regulatory/supervisory authorities? 8. Can the initial disbursement or subsequent injections of capital be done with assets other than cash or government securities? 9. Can initial disbursement of capital be done with borrowed funds?' Source: Barth et al. (2004).
Supervisory Independence	An index to measure how independent the supervisory authority is. Source: Barth et al. (2004).
Per Capita Income	The logarithm of real per capita gross domestic product. Source: World Development Indicators.
Contract Enforcement	An index of contract enforcement. Source: Levine (1999).

Corruption	An index of official corruption. Source: Levine (1999).
Law Tradition	An index of the law and order tradition of the country. Source: Levine (1999).
Controlling Share	The percentage of shares owned by its controlling shareholder. Source: Our own calculation.
Widely Held	It is equal to zero if a bank has a controlling owner with more than 10 percent ownership, otherwise one. Source: Our own calculation.
State Controlled	It is equal to one if the controlling shareholder is the state, otherwise zero. Source: Our own calculation.
Foreign Controlled	It is equal to one if the controlling shareholder is from a foreign country, otherwise zero. Source: Our own calculation.
Private Controlled	It is equal to one if the controlling shareholder is private parties, otherwise zero. Source: Our own calculation.
Public	It is equal to one if a bank is a publicly traded bank, otherwise zero. Source: Bankscope.
Foreign (Private) Family Controlled	It is equal to one if the foreign (private) controlling shareholder is a family or individual, otherwise zero. Source: Our own calculation.
Foreign (Private) Financial Controlled	It is equal to one if the foreign (private) controlling shareholder is a financial institution such as a bank, insurance company etc., and otherwise zero. Source: Our own calculation.
Foreign (Private) Corporation Controlled	It is equal to one if the foreign (private) controlling shareholder is a corporation, otherwise zero. Source: Our own calculation.
Foreign (Private) Foundation Controlled	It is equal to one if the foreign (private) controlling shareholder is a foundation, a research institute or a voting trust, otherwise zero. Source: Our own calculation.
Foreign (Private) Other Controlled	It is equal to one if the foreign (private) controlling shareholder is not a type mentioned before, otherwise zero. Source: Our own calculation.
Foreign Ownership	The percentage of shares held by the biggest foreign shareholder. Source: Our own calculation.
Foreign Widely Owned	It is equal to one if the percentage of shares held by the biggest foreign shareholder is more than zero and less than ten. Source: Our own calculation.
Foreign Family Owned	It is equal to one if the biggest foreign shareholder is a family or individual, otherwise zero. Source: Our own calculation.
Foreign State Owned	It is equal to one if the biggest foreign shareholder is the state, otherwise zero. Source: Our own calculation.
Foreign Corporation Owned	It is equal to one if the biggest foreign shareholder is a corporation, otherwise zero. Source: Our own calculation.
Foreign Foundation Owned	It is equal to one if the biggest foreign shareholder is a foundation, a research institute or a voting trust, otherwise zero. Source: Our own calculation.
Foreign Other Owned	It is equal to one if the biggest foreign shareholder is not a type mentioned before, otherwise zero. Source: Our own calculation.
ROA	Return on assets. Source: Bankscope.
ROE	Return on equity. Source: Bankscope.
Loan Growth	The bank's one-year loan growth. Source: Bankscope.
Firm Size	The logarithm of the bank's total assets. Source: Bankscope.
Capital Asset Ratio	The capital asset ratio. Source: Bankscope.
Loan Loss Provision Ratio	The ratio of the bank's loan loss provisions to interest income. Source: Bankscope.

3 Is there a conflict between competition and financial stability?

Barbara Casu, Claudia Girardone and Philip Molyneux

3.1 INTRODUCTION

Crises in the global financial system have impacted severely on many banking sectors with institutions experiencing major losses and necessitating raising additional capital privately or through their respective national governments (via various rescue and bailout schemes).[1] The failure of depositors, investors and regulators to discipline banks adequately has led various commentators to reconsider the links between bank stability and changes in the competitive environment.[2]

While there is an established literature on the measurement of competition and its implications for bank performance, the literature on competition and financial stability is less developed.[3] Two views are outlined in the literature. The first, known as the competition-fragility (charter or franchise value) view, argues that banks earn monopoly rents in uncompetitive markets resulting in higher profits, capital ratios and charter values. This makes them better placed to withstand demand- or supply-side shocks and discourages excessive risk-taking (Allen and Gale, 2000, 2004; Carletti, 2008). The second, referred to as the competition-stability view, argues that competition leads to less fragility. The argument goes that in concentrated banking systems with low levels of competition, the market power of incumbent banks results in higher interest rates for borrowers, making it more difficult for them to repay loans. These higher interest rates increase the incentives for borrowers to take on greater risk in search of higher returns. This, in turn, increases the possibility of the non-repayment of loans and the default risk of bank portfolios, making the financial system less stable (Boyd and De Nicolo, 2005). Also, large banks are often deemed to be too big, too interconnected or too complex to fail, and thus they obtain implicit (or explicit) subsidies via government safety nets. This may further increase moral hazard and encourage large banks to take on excessive risks, leading to instability (Herring and Carmassi, 2010; Beck et al., 2010; Demirgüç-Kunt and Huizinga, 2010).[4]

This chapter aims to provide an overview of the competition-stability/fragility literature. First we outline the theoretical arguments that focus on competition and the risk-taking incentives of banks. Then we discuss the empirical evidence and note some of the difficulties associated with measuring competition and risk in banking markets. The final section concludes and suggests areas for future research.

3.2 THEORETICAL LITERATURE

Up to the 1980s there appeared to be a general consensus that competition worsened banking sector stability (Carletti, 2010), the main argument being that competition led to excessive risk-taking on the assets (loans) side of banks' balance sheets, which caused a higher likelihood of individual bank's failure. More recently, studies have shown that competition may be beneficial to banks' portfolio risk. The traditional theoretical set-up assumes that the allocation of bank assets is determined by solving a portfolio problem emphasizing the liability side of the balance sheet. Upon confronting greater competition on the deposit side, banks tend to increase their offered rate to attract depositors. When paying higher deposit rates, neglecting the effects of competition in the loans market, banks' earnings decline. In order to cover lost profits, banks will tend to accept more risky investments. In contrast, when competition is restrained, banks exercise market power by paying lower deposit rates and therefore can increase their profits. As a result, banks in relatively uncompetitive markets are less willing to invest in low-probability, high-return projects. As a consequence, bank failure is less likely.

Matutes and Vives (2000) developed a theoretical model to assess the connection between competition in the deposit market and bank risk-taking incentives. The study focused on one side of the balance sheet, and any effects of competition for loans and investment projects were disregarded. After developing the model and building different scenarios, the authors concluded that when competition is intense and portfolio risk is observable, banks will not want to take on risk on the assets side if the deposit rate is constrained by a ceiling rate, because bank assets and liabilities are complementary. If portfolio risk is unobservable, or moral hazard exists (as is likely), this means depositors do not realize how deposit rates and asset allocations determine expected returns and/or the probability of bank failure. In such an environment banks will take on maximal asset risk. In a world with flat-premium deposit insurance, banks will become aggressive competitors and take maximal assets risk when competition for deposits is intense because depositors have no incentive to penalize bank risk-taking behaviour. With the introduction of risk-based deposit insurance, the authors argue, banks will take on minimal asset risk because risk-based insurance schemes make banks fully liable.

Another strand of the theoretical literature assumes that banks solve an optimal contracting problem. Here the modelling framework captures competition on both sides of the bank balance sheet. In less competitive deposits markets, banks can earn greater rents (as noted above). However, banks can also charge higher rates in the lending market. The less competitive the market, the higher the interest rates borrowers pay. Facing higher rates, borrowers tend to invest in more risky projects and therefore their probability of default increases. This risk mechanism is further exacerbated by moral hazard on the borrowers' side. As a result, banks become more risky in a less competitive market.

Koskela and Stenbacka (2000) develop a model that focuses on mean-shifting investment technologies to investigate the relationship between credit market competition and bank risk-taking. They argue that the introduction of competition in bank credit markets will lower interest rates charged to borrowers and thus result in higher investments without increasing the equilibrium probability of borrower default. It is also important to note that in their model investments are assumed to be financed by debt, and this assumption generates strong limited liability effects. Where investment projects are financed by both debt and equity, limited liability effects are mitigated and competition reduces risks even further. The result also holds in the presence of credit rationing.

Unlike Matutes and Vives (2000) and Koskela and Stenbacka (2000), who focus on one side of bank balance sheets, Boyd and De Nicolo (2005) develop a model that allows for the existence of competition on both the deposits and the loans side. These authors assume that project risk is determined by the interest rate charged to borrowers. The portfolio problem is transformed into a contracting problem with the existence of moral hazard. Banks with market power will pay lower rates on deposits and charge higher rates on loans. In this context, portfolio theory suggests that banks have less incentive to take on risk because they can earn monopoly profits: namely, lower competition leads to greater stability. However, the contracting problem provides competition with a new role. Higher loan rates force borrowers to seek more risky projects, which create greater portfolio risks for (monopoly) banks, as such less competition increases risk. The same mechanism runs in the opposite direction, as competitive banks will offer lower loan rates and therefore reduce moral hazard problems. Banks, as a result, face lower risks because their borrowers are less likely to pursue risky investments.

More recently Martinez-Miera and Repullo (2009) suggest a non-linear relationship between bank competition and stability. They argue that the competition-stability view advocated by Boyd and De Nicolo (2005) does not necessarily hold when loan defaults are imperfectly correlated. Heightened competition may reduce borrowers' probability of default (risk-shifting effect), but it may also reduce the interest payments from performing loans, which serves as a buffer to cover loan losses (margin effect). They find evidence of a U-shaped relationship between competition (measured by the number of banks) and bank stability. In highly concentrated markets the risk-shifting effect dominates and more competition reduces bank risk, while in very competitive markets the margin effect dominates and the increased competition erodes banks' franchise value and hence increases risks.

In the 2007–2008 banking crisis it has become apparent that large banks are often deemed to be too big, too interconnected or too complex to fail. In these cases they obtain implicit (or explicit) subsidies via government safety nets that may further increase moral hazard and encourage large banks to take on excessive risks, leading to financial instability (O'Hara and Shaw, 1990; Stern and Feldman, 2004; Brown and Dinç, 2011; Herring and Carmassi, 2010; Beck et al., 2010; Demirgüç-Kunt and Huizinga, 2010).

3.3 BANK COMPETITION AND RISK: EMPIRICAL EVIDENCE

One of the earliest studies on competition and risk-taking is by Rhoades and Rutz (1982) on US banking. They investigated the so-called 'quiet life' hypothesis: banks operating in concentrated markets prefer risk avoidance in order to enjoy a 'quiet life'. To put this more formally, in a less competitive environment banks have to make less effort to maximize operating efficiency. Rhoades and Rutz (1982) examine whether banks with more market power take on less risk than those operating in competitive banking environments. Using a large sample of 6500 unit banks operating between 1969 and 1978, they employ the volatility of return on assets (ROA) to measure overall risk (and various other indicators including the ratio of equity to assets, total loans to total assets and net loan losses to total loans). The three-bank deposit concentration ratio is used to measure bank market power. The results reveal that concentration is negatively and statistically correlated with three out of the four risk indicators. This suggests that banks with greater market power tend to reduce their risk-taking. Keeley (1990) employs the market value of bank capital-to-asset ratios and interest rates on large Certificates of Deposit (CDs) to proxy for bank risk. Keeley (1990) examines 150 large bank holding companies (which accounted for 40 per cent of all bank assets in the US over 1970 to 1986). The author observes a general decline in the market value of bank capital-to-asset ratios over the study period, which coincided with the time when restrictions on branching, multi-bank holding companies and interstate expansion were removed in the US. In order to measure market power, Keeley (1990) uses Tobin's Q (the ratio of market to book value of assets). Banks with greater market power are assumed to have higher market-to-book ratios. To conduct the empirical tests, Keeley (1990) estimates two sets of regressions. The first relates market power to the removal of branching restrictions and the second relates it to bank risk and (again) to the relaxation on interstate branching laws. The main finding is that banks with less market power (lower market-to-book assets) tend to take on greater risks (lower capital-to-asset ratios, and paying higher rates on large CDs). In sum, bank competition encourages risk-taking.

In a similar vein, Dick (2006) uses the ratio of loan charge-offs to total loans and loan-loss provisions to total loans to measure risk and branching relaxation as a proxy for market competition. It is argued that banks are expected to take on more risk when allowed to expand their operations across states because geographic diversification may provide a hedge against increased risk. Dick (2006) focuses her attentions on the full removal of US geographic branching restrictions in 1994. The results indicate that branch deregulation led to an increase in loan charge-offs. Competition, therefore, appears to increase credit risk.

In contrast to the results reported above, which suggest a positive link between bank competition and risk, a variety of other studies have come to the opposite conclusion. Jayaratne and Strahan (1998), for instance, find that the relaxation of branching restrictions in the US significantly reduced risk. Using aggregate state-level data from 1975 to 1992 they show that non-performing loans, net loan charge-offs and loan-loss provisions are all negatively and significantly correlated to intrastate branching indicators. Jayaratne and Strahan (1998) estimate the fall in loan-loss provisions after branching barriers are lifted to be around 48 per cent on average. The authors argue that competition helped bank managers to screen and monitor their borrowers better, leading to more cautious lending. Competition, therefore, appears to reduce the probability of bank failure.

De Nicolo (2000) examines the relationships between bank size, charter value and risk using a sample of 826 banks from 21 advanced economies over the period 1988 to 1998. He uses the Z-index as an indicator of risk[5] which is regressed against bank size measured by bank assets. The analysis reveals that banks of larger size tend to have lower charter values and a higher probability of insolvency. As larger banks are more likely to have market power, the findings imply that competitive banks are less risky. (Although it is widely recognized that size may not be a good indicator of bank market power.)

Extending their previous work, De Nicolo et al. (2004) study the effects of consolidation on risk-taking using a sample of banks from 100 countries between 1993 and 2000. First the study relates bank size to risk (measured using the Z-index). There is some evidence that large banks exhibit higher levels of risk-taking, a finding consistent with

De Nicolo (2000). Secondly, the study uses country-level data to investigate whether market concentration increases the probability of systemic risk. Drawing from the evidence of risk-taking at the firm level, De Nicolo et al. (2004) suggest that consolidation increases the probability of failure. The study also finds that systemic risk could decline if the level of market and policy transparency increases (reducing moral hazard). Greater transparency enhances monitoring and this incentivizes banks to manage their risk more effectively.

Boyd et al. (2006) employ two bank samples to investigate competition and risk issues empirically. The first sample consists of 2500 US banks operating in rural areas in 2003, and the second sample consists of a panel data set of about 2600 banks in 134 non-industrialized countries for 1993–2004. In the first part of the analysis, the authors regress the Z-index against a country-level deposits concentration measure (Herfindahl index),[6] in addition to various bank- and county-specific effects. The results show that deposit concentration is negatively and statistically correlated with the Z-index, suggesting that more concentrated banking systems are associated with higher risk. The approach is then extended to the international sample of banks. Here the researchers use three concentration ratios, based on deposits, loans and assets. After controlling for bank and country differences, the regression results are similar to those obtained from the US sample. Specifically, deposits, loans and assets concentration are all negatively and highly correlated with the Z-index. The authors also find that bank size is negatively related to the Z-index, indicating that larger banks face greater risks. All in all the results are in line with the findings of De Nicolo (2000) and De Nicolo et al. (2004).

Yeyati and Micco (2007) study the link between competition and risk for banks in eight Latin American countries. The authors use the Panzar and Rosse (1987) H-statistic as a proxy for competition[7] and the Z-index as a measure for bank risk. Higher values of the H-statistic are associated with a more competitive banking environment. Yeyati and Micco (2007) find a negative link between H-statistics and the inverse of the Z-index. The results indicate that competition leads to less risky activities.

As is probably becoming apparent, empirical evidence in support of the competition-fragility and competition-stability views is rather mixed. This is also confirmed by the most recent empirical literature. Jiménez et al. (2010) find that risks decrease with an increase in bank market power, whereas Turk-Ariss (2010) finds that competition leads to instability. Uhde and Heimeshoff (2009), using aggregated data for EU-25 countries, show that national banking market concentration has a negative impact on the stability of European banking systems. Berger et al. (2009) examine market power and risk issues using a sample of over 8000 banks across 23 developed countries over 1999 and 2005 and, using a standard Lerner index measure of competition,[8] find that banks with a greater degree of market power also have less overall risk exposure. The results provide limited support to both the competition-fragility and competition-stability views in that market power increases credit risk, but banks with greater market power face lower risks. Zhao et al. (2009, 2010) assess the extent to which deregulatory measures aimed at promoting competition lead to increased risk-taking in Indian banking. The results suggest that competition encourages increased risk-taking.

Overall, as in the theoretical literature, there is no consensus as to the relationship between competition and risk in banking. One of the reasons for this may be due to the fact that studies use different competition measures and risk indicators, as well as varying bank samples and methodologies. The following section highlights some of the methodological issues associated with measuring competition in banking. First we look at market structure and see how this is linked to competition and then we focus on the non-structural or new empirical industrial organization (NEIO) competition measures. Finally, we look at the consistency of competition indicators and link them to bank risk.

3.4 MARKET STRUCTURE AND COMPETITION IN BANKING

Structural indicators of competition are typified by measures of industry concentration such as n-firm concentration ratios and the Herfindahl index. These measures aim to reflect the implications of the number and size distribution of firms in the industry for the nature of competition, using a relatively simple numerical indicator. Both the number of firms and their size distribution (in other words, the degree of inequality in firm sizes) are important. Traditional industrial organization theory suggests that increased industry concentration lowers the cost of collusion (smaller numbers of firms make it easier to fix prices) resulting in anti-competitive behaviour and excess profits. This theory has found an empirical counterpart in the structure–conduct–performance (SCP) paradigm. Over time, variations of the SCP hypothesis have emerged, most noticeably studies that test whether the traditional SCP paradigm (collusion) or the competing 'efficiency hypothesis' hold (see Smirlock, 1985; Evanoff and Fortier, 1988).

The efficiency hypothesis states that if there is a positive relationship between concentration and bank profits/prices this may not necessarily be the result of anti-competitive behaviour, but can be explained by the superior operating efficiency of large banks. Overall, the earlier US literature tends to find evidence that the traditional paradigm holds, although later studies that test the aforementioned competing hypotheses tend to reject the traditional paradigm in favour of the efficiency hypothesis (see Gilbert, 1984; Berger, 1995; Berger et al., 2004). Overall, however, the question as to whether a positive relationship between industry concentration and performance (however measured, whether by profits or prices) reflects collusion or efficiency has never been resolved empirically (Goddard et al., 2007; Dick and Hannan, 2010).

An extensive theoretical literature on oligopoly behaviour has long recognized that major firms in concentrated markets can compete aggressively with one another, and this usually involves firms having to guess the price and quantity reactions to strategic moves made by each other (so-called conjectural variations). In these games, the competitive environment is determined by the strategic reactions (or conduct) of firms and not by the structure of the market. Drawing on such insights theorists have posited that in contestable markets the competitive behaviour of firms is determined by (actual and potential) entry and exit conditions (proxied by the extent to which prior investments represent sunk costs). The argument goes that markets with low entry and exit conditions are faced with a higher threat of entry by new firms, and incumbent firms behave competitively to deter entry (Baumol, 1982; Baumol et al., 1982). As such, the structural features of the market are irrelevant in determining competitive behaviour and it is entry and exit conditions that matter. A contestable market may have only two firms, but if entry and exit are costless, then the incumbent firms are likely to operate competitively so as to deter potential entrants. Like in the case of competing oligopolists, the competitive features of a contestable market cannot be measured using structural indicators. Consequently, researchers have proposed alternative non-structural measures of competition.

3.5   NON-STRUCTURAL MEASURES OF COMPETITION IN BANKING

Criticisms of the SCP paradigm have led to a shift away from the presumption that structure is the most important determinant of the level of competition. Instead, some economists have argued that the strategies (conduct) of individual firms are equally, if not more, important. Theories that focus primarily on strategy and conduct are subsumed under the general heading of the new industrial organization (NIO). According to this approach, firms are not seen as passive entities, similar in every respect except size. Instead they are active decision-makers, capable of implementing a wide range of diverse strategies. Game theory, which deals with decision-making in situations of interdependence and uncertainty, is an important tool in the armoury of the NIO theorists. Theories have been developed to explore situations in which firms choose from a plethora of strategies, with the choices repeated over either finite or infinite time horizons (Schmalensee, 1982).

The NIO approach has found an empirical counterpart in the new empirical industrial organization (NEIO). Here, in order to measure the conduct of firms, a variety of non-structural measures of competition typically based on the measure of monopoly (or market) power have been developed. In particular, these include measures of competition between oligopolists, such as Iwata (1974), and those that test for competitive behaviour in contestable markets, such as Bresnahan (1982), Lau (1982) and Panzar and Rosse (1987). These indicators have been developed from (static) theory of the firm models under equilibrium conditions and mainly use some form of price mark-up over a competitive benchmark, such as price over marginal cost for the Lerner index and price over marginal revenue for the Bresnahan measure, as indicators of competitive behaviour. The main exception is the Panzar and Rosse (1987) indicator which measures the relationship between changes in factor input prices and revenues earned by firms.

The Iwata (1974) model provides a framework for estimating conjectural variation values for banks that supply homogenous products, and as far as we are aware has only been applied once to banking – by Shaffer and DiSalvo (1994), who found evidence of imperfectly competitive behaviour in a highly concentrated duopoly market. Wider use has been made of the measures suggested by Bresnahan (1982) and Lau (1982) using the empirical approach suggested in Bresnahan (1989). This approach requires a structural model of banking competition where a parameter representing the market power of banks is included. This parameter simply measures the extent to which the average firm's marginal revenue varies from the demand schedule and therefore represents the degree of market power of banks in the sample. This approach was first applied to the banking industry by Shaffer (1989), on the US loan market and the Canadian banking industry, respectively. Examples of this approach to measuring competition in banking systems include studies on Finnish banking by Suominen (1994); on various European countries by Neven and Röller (1999) and Bikker and Haaf (2002); on Italian banking by Coccorese (1998) and Angelini and Cetorelli (2000); on Dutch consumer credit markets by Toolsema (2002); on Portuguese banking by Canhoto (2004); and on Japanese banking by Uchida and Tsutsui (2005). Most of this literature finds little evidence of market power in banking systems, apart from Neven and Röller (1999) who find significant monopoly collusive behaviour.

In addition to the aforementioned measures there is also an extensive literature that uses the Panzar and Rosse (1987) approach to investigate competitive conditions in European banking and elsewhere. Molyneux et al. (1994), Bikker and Groeneveld (2000), De Bandt and Davis (2000), Weill (2004), Koutsomanoli-Filippaki and Staikouras (2004), Casu and Girardone (2006) and Goddard and Wilson (2006) all find that monopolistic competition is prevalent across various European banking systems. Other cross-country studies, including Claessens and Laeven (2004), Goddard and Wilson (2009), Bikker et al. (2009) and Schaeck et al. (2009), suggest the same. Despite changes to the methodological approach to estimating the Rosse–Panzar statistic (Goddard and Wilson, 2009; Bikker et al., 2009), in virtually all studies evidence of monopolistic competition is prevalent. The main finding from the Rosse–Panzar literature is that monopolistic competition is widespread in banking, albeit that there is mixed evidence as to whether competition is generally increasing.

Other studies use the Lerner index – the difference between price and marginal cost divided by price – to measure market power in banking. Carbó et al. (2003) use the Lerner index to examine competition in regional banking markets in Spain and find evidence of increases in market power over the late 1990s, a finding confirmed by Maudos and De Guevara's (2004) study of interest margins in European banking. De Guevara and Maudos (2007) use the Lerner index to find evidence of increases in market power in Spanish banking from the mid-1990s to 2002. Other recent single-country studies include that of Koetter et al. (2008) on US bank holding companies between 1986 and 2005: the study finds that competition has declined over the study period. Koetter and Poghosyan (2009) study different technology features of German banks over 1994 to 2004 and find that greater bank market power increases bank profitability but also fosters risk (higher corporate defaults). More recently Fungacova et al. (2010) examine market power in Russian banking between 2001 and 2007 and find modest levels of competition improvement over the period. Furthermore, their estimates of the Lerner index are similar to those found for more developed banking systems.

Various researchers have also turned their attention to large cross-country studies of market power. Such studies have often been linked to efficiency issues. Maudos and De Guevara (2007), for instance, use a funding adjusted Lerner index measure to look at EU-15 banking systems over 1993 and 2002 where they find a positive link between market power and bank cost efficiency (rejecting the 'quiet life' hypothesis). Hainz et al. (2008) use the Lerner index to examine the link between competition and collateral across 70 countries and find that competition reduces the need for collateral.

Another recently introduced competition measure is that of Boone (2008). The measure is based on the efficiency hypothesis proposed by Demsetz (1973) which stresses that industry performance is an endogenous function of the growth of efficient firms. Put simply, the indicator gauges the strength of the relation between efficiency (measured in terms of average cost) and performance (measured in terms of profitability). In general, this indicator is based on the efficient structure hypothesis that associates performance with differences in efficiency. Under this hypothesis, more efficient banks (i.e., banks with lower marginal costs) achieve superior performance in terms of higher profits at the expense of their less efficient counterparts and this attracts greater market shares. This effect is monotonically increasing in the degree of competition when firms interact more aggressively and when entry barriers decline. The Boone indicator theoretically underpins the findings of Stiroh (2000) and Stiroh and Strahan (2003), who state that increased competition allows banking markets to transfer considerable portions of assets from low- to high-profit banks.

As shown theoretically in Boone (2008), the reallocation effect is a general feature of intensifying competition, so that the indicator can be seen as a robust measure of competition. While different forces can cause increases in competition – for instance, increases in the number of suppliers of banking services via lower entry cost, more aggressive interaction between banks, or banks' relative inefficiencies – as long as the reallocation conditions holds, the indicator remains valid. As the industry becomes more competitive, given a certain level of efficiency of each individual bank, the profits of the more efficient banks increase relative to those of less efficient banks. Schaeck and Čihák (2010) note that the Boone indicator has a number of appealing qualities compared with other competition measures. Unlike the Panzar and Rosse (1987) H-statistic the Boone indicator does not impose restrictive assumptions about the banking market being in long-run equilibrium. What is important for the Boone indicator is how aggressively the more efficient banks exploit their cost advantage to reallocate profits away from the least efficient banks in the market. Various recent studies such as Van Leuvensteijn et al. (2007), Maslovych (2009) and Schaeck and Čihák (2010) have applied the Boone indicator to banking markets, although there remains some scepticism as to the efficacy of this new measure (Schiersch and Schmidt-Ehmcke, 2010).

Another strand of empirical research that seeks to evaluate the competitive stance of markets is the persistence of profit (POP) literature which focuses on the dynamics of profitability, recognizing the possibility that markets are out of equilibrium at the moment they are observed. The persistence of profit hypothesis developed by Mueller (1977, 1986) is that entry and exit are sufficiently free to eliminate any abnormal profit quickly, and that all firms' profit rates tend to converge towards the same long-run average value. The alternative is that some incumbent firms possess the capability to prevent imitation, or retard or block entry (inhibiting competition). If so, abnormal profit tends to persist from year to year, and differences in firm-level long-run average profit rates may be sustained indefinitely. There is a substantial manufacturing POP literature (Goddard and Wilson, 1999). However, only a handful of studies investigate POP in banking. Goddard et al. (2004a, 2004b) find that despite intensifying competition there is significant persistence of abnormal bank profits in European banking over 1992 to 1998. Carbó and Fernandez (2007) also find weak evidence of persistence in bank spreads in Europe. In a study of 65 banking systems, Goddard et al. (forthcoming) find that persistence of bank profit appears to be weaker for banks in developing countries than for those in developed countries, suggesting that competition is lower in the latter. The study also finds that persistence of profit is stronger when entry barriers are high (Goddard et al., 2011).

3.6   COMPARING COMPETITION MEASURES

A major limitation of the extant literature is that there has been little work comparing the consistency of the aforementioned competition measures. There are two exceptions. First, Bikker and Bos (2004) examine both structural and non-structural measures of competition in European, Japanese and US banking between 1990 and 2003. They conclude that structural developments as well as data availability issues are likely to 'reduce the reliability of the Bresnahan approach' to measuring competition in banking markets. Although not explicitly stated, the tenor of their argument appears to provide support for the consistency of the Panzar and Rosse H-measure. The second study, by Carbó et al. (2009), focuses on comparing five competition indicators (net interest margin, return on assets – ROA, Lerner index, Panzar and Rosse H-statistic and the Herfindahl index) for 14 European Union (EU) countries between 1995 and 2001. The main finding is that these different measures of competition regularly give conflicting predictions of competitive behaviour across countries, within countries and over time.

3.7   BANKING STABILITY (RISK) MEASURES

Another issue relates to the measure of bank risk or stability. As discussed already, the empirical literature chooses a range of bank risk measures including loan-loss provisions and loan-loss reserves ratios derived from bank accounting information. Higher levels of reserves or provisions are suggestive of greater banking risk. Typically provisions data (being a flow) are more volatile than reserves measures. We would argue that banks with higher levels of reserves (or provisions) have an expectation of higher future risk and are therefore suggesting higher probability of default. Of course, a limitation associated with using measures calculated from accounting data is that even assuming that they accurately reflect portfolio quality, managers are likely to have some timing discretion over these measures, and there is evidence that such discretion is exercised in a manner that minimizes regulatory costs. In addition, measurement of risk is also problematic, especially for those institutions that do not have frequently traded securities. As the majority of banks in most jurisdictions do not have publicly traded securities, studies empirically investigating large samples of banks typically have had to resort to the use of accounting measures of banking risk. Recently researchers have sought to use 'new' market-based bank risk indicators such as Moody's KMV expected default frequency (EDF) and five-year cumulative probability of default (PD_{5Y}) indicators (Fiordelisi et al., 2010 [2011]). Both EDF and PD_{5Y} refer to the probability of default (PD) within the short and medium terms (one and five years, respectively) so these account for all risks. Both variables are free from managerial discretion and are estimated through an economic cycle (i.e., PD estimates are long-run probabilities of default which take into consideration upturns and downturns in the economy). However, as far as we are aware, these preferred banking risk indicators have not yet been linked to the competitive environment.

3.8   CONCLUSION

The ongoing impact of the 2007–2008 banking crisis continues to raise policy questions relating, among other things, to the relationship between banking sector competition and stability. Those commentators studying the causes of the crisis want to know whether excessive competition led to excessive risk-taking that fuelled a credit boom and the eventual collapse of credit markets. Policymakers also are interested in what impact government support has had on the competitive stance of the sector, and how this translated (if at all) into risk-taking propensity. Our review of the literature on competition and the risk-taking incentives of banks suggests no consensus view. It is unclear whether the competition-stability or the competition-fragility view holds. Furthermore, interpretation of much of the previous empirical literature is controversial given the apparent lack of consistency in competition and risk measures used, as well as the different methodologies and samples chosen. Future areas of research should perhaps focus on arriving at measures that provide more accurate indicators of bank risk – such as a broader use of market-based indicators – and more effort should be made to derive consistent competition indicators.

Post-crisis, anecdotal evidence points to less competition and a risk-averse banking sector, suggesting that the competition-fragility view is now prevalent in developed banking systems at least. It will be a major future challenge for researchers to derive competition and risk indicators that provide any consensus view. Another challenging area that may be worth investigating is the possible cyclicality of such relationships in major banking systems.

NOTES

1. Brunnermeier (2009) provides an excellent overview of the crisis.
2. A number of studies propose new forms of regulation to restore and maintain the stability of the financial system. See Stern School volumes by Acharya and Richardson (2009) and Acharya et al. (2010), and the Centre for Economic Policy Studies (CEPS) Report produced by Carmassi et al. (2010). Stephanou (2010) discusses a number of ways in which the market can be used by supervisors to assess bank risk and discipline the activities of bank managers.
3. Northcott (2004), Berger et al. (2004), Degryse and Ongena (2008) and Dick and Hannan (2010) provide reviews of the theoretical and empirical competition literature. Beck et al. (2010), Carletti (2010) and Vives (2010) provide excellent overviews of the theoretical and empirical relationship between competition and financial stability.
4. Also see O'Hara and Shaw (1990), Stern and Feldman (2004) and Brown and Dinç (2011).
5. The Z-index has been used widely in previous empirical literature concerned with the measurement and determinants of the safety and soundness of financial institutions (Iannotta et al., 2007; Garcia-Marco and Robles-Fernández, 2008; Hesse and Čihák, 2007; Beck et al., forthcoming). The Z-index is calculated as:

$$Z = \frac{ROA + E/A}{\sigma(ROA)},$$

where ROA is the bank's return on assets, E/A represents the equity to total assets ratio and $\sigma(ROA)$ is the standard deviation of return on assets.
6. The Herfindahl–Hirschman (HH) index is calculated as:

$$HH = \sum_{i=1}^{N} s_i^2$$

where s_i is the market share of bank i, and N is the total number of banks in the industry. For an industry that consists of a single monopoly producer, HH = 1. A monopolist has a market share of $s_1 = 1$. Therefore $s_1^2 = 1$, ensuring HH = 1. For an industry with N banks, the maximum possible value of the Herfindahl–Hirschman index is HH = 1, and the minimum possible value is HH = $1/N$.

7. The H-statistic is calculated from a reduced form revenue equation in which factor price inputs and bank outputs are related. Since this approach observes bank's reaction to changes in input prices, the H-statistic equals the sum of the coefficients of input price factors in respect of bank revenue. When H is equal to 1, it indicates perfect competition; and $0 < H < 1$ indicates monopolistic competition. H can be interpreted as a continuous measure of the level of competition, in particular between 0 and 1, in the sense that higher values of H indicate stronger competition than lower values.

8. The Lerner index (Lerner, 1934) measures the mark-up of price over marginal costs and is therefore an indicator of the degree of market power. It is calculated as: $Lerner_{it} = (P_{it} - MC_{it})/P_{it}$, where P_{it} is the price of total assets (usually proxied by the ratio of total revenues to total assets for bank i at time t), MC_{it} is the marginal cost of bank i at time t. Marginal cost is usually derived from the differentiation of a trans-log cost function. A value of the Lerner index equal to zero indicates perfect competition, while a value of one indicates monopoly.

REFERENCES

Acharya, V., T.F. Cooley, M. Richardson and I. Walter (2010), *Real Time Solutions for US Financial Reform*, New York: Stern School of Business.

Acharya, V. and M. Richardson (eds) (2009), *Restoring Financial Stability: How to Repair a Failed System?* New York: John Wiley & Sons.

Allen, F. and D. Gale (2000), *Comparing Financial Systems*, Cambridge, MA: MIT Press.

Allen, F. and D. Gale (2004), 'Competition and financial stability', *Journal of Money, Credit, and Banking*, **36**, 433–480.

Angelini, P. and N. Cetorelli (2000), 'Bank competition and regulatory reform: the case of the Italian banking industry', Federal Reserve Bank of Chicago, Working Paper Series, Research Development, WP. 99–32.

Baumol, W.J. (1982), 'Contestable markets: an uprising in the theory of industry structure', *American Economic Review*, **72**, 1–15.

Baumol, W.J., J.C. Panzar and R.D. Willig (1982), *Contestable Markets and the Theory of Industry Structure*, San Diego, CA: Harcourt Brace Jovanovich.

Beck, T., D. Coyle, M. Dewatripoint, X. Freixas and P. Seabright (2010), 'Bailing out the banks: reconciling stability and competition', London: Centre for Economic Policy Research.

Beck, T., H. Hesse, T. Kick and N. von Westernhagen (forthcoming), 'Bank ownership and stability: evidence from Germany', Bundesbank Working Paper Series.

Berger, A.N. (1995), 'The profit–structure relationship in banking: tests of market power and efficient structure hypotheses', *Journal of Money, Credit and Banking*, **27**, 404–431.

Berger, A.N., A. Demirgüç-Kunt, R. Levine and J.C. Haubrich (2004), 'Bank concentration and competition', *Journal of Money, Credit and Banking*, **36**, 433–451.

Berger, A.N., L.F. Klapper and R. Turk-Ariss (2009), 'Bank competition and financial stability', *Journal of Financial Services Research*, **35**, 99–118.

Bikker, J.A and J.W.B. Bos (2004), 'Trends in competition and profitability in the banking industry: a basic framework', Paper presented for the 25th SUERF Colloquium, Madrid, 14–16 October.

Bikker, J.A. and J.M. Groeneveld (2000), 'Competition and concentration in the EU banking industry', *Kredit und Kapital*, **33**, 62–98.

Bikker, J.A. and K. Haaf (2002), 'Competition, concentration and their relationship: an empirical analysis of the banking industry', *Journal of Banking and Finance*, **26**, 2191–2214.

Bikker, J.A., S. Shaffer and L. Spierdijk (2009), 'Assessing competition with the Panzar–Rosse model: the role of scale, costs, and equilibrium', DNB Working Papers 225, Netherlands Central Bank, Research Department.

Boone, J. (2008), 'A new way to measure competition', *Economic Journal*, **118**, 1245–1261.

Boyd, J. and G. De Nicolo (2005), 'The theory of bank risk taking revisited', *Journal of Finance*, **60**, 1329–1343.

Boyd, J.H., G. De Nicolo and A.M. Jalal (2006), 'Bank risk-taking and competition revisited: new theory and new evidence', IMF Working Paper WP/06/297.

Bresnahan, T.F. (1982), 'The oligopoly solution concept is identified', *Economic Letters*, **10**, 87–92.

Bresnahan, T.F. (1989), 'Empirical studies in industries with market power', in R. Schmalensee and R. Willig (eds), *Handbook of Industrial Organisation*, vol. II, New York: North-Holland, pp. 1010–1057.

Brown, C.O. and I.S. Dinç (2011), 'Too many to fail? Evidence of regulatory forbearance when the banking sector is weak', *Review of Financial Studies*, **24** (4), 1378–1405.

Brunnermeier, M.K. (2009), 'Deciphering the liquidity and credit crunch 2007–08', *Journal of Economic Perspectives*, **23**, 77–100.

Canhoto, A. (2004), 'Portuguese banking: a structural model of competition in the deposits market', *Review of Financial Economics*, **13**, 41–63.

Carbó, S. and F. Fernandez (2007), 'The determinants of bank margins in European banking', *Journal of Banking and Finance*, **31**, 2043–2063.

Carbó, S., D. Humphrey, J. Maudos and P. Molyneux (2009), 'Cross-country comparisons of competition and pricing power in European banking', *Journal of International Money and Finance*, **28**, 115–134.

Carbó, S., D. Humphrey and F. Rodríguez (2003) 'Deregulation, bank competition and regional growth', *Regional Studies*, **37**, 227–237.

Carletti, E. (2008), 'Competition and regulation in banking', in A.W.A. Boot and A. Thakor (eds), *Handbook of Financial Intermediation and Banking*, Amsterdam: Elsevier.

Carletti, E. (2010), 'Competition, concentration and stability in the banking sector', Istituto Luigi Einaudi per gli Studi Bancari Finanziari e Assicurativi (IstEin), Working Paper 2010, Number 8 Research Project: European Banking Competition, available at www.istein.eu/.

Carmassi, J., E. Lucchetti and S. Micossi (2010), 'Overcoming too-big-to-fail: a regulatory framework to limit moral hazard and free riding in the financial sector', Brussels: Centre for European Policy Studies.

Casu, B. and C. Girardone (2006), 'Bank competition, concentration and efficiency in the single European market', *Manchester School*, **74**, 441–468.

Claessens, S. and L. Laeven (2004), 'What drives bank competition? Some international evidence', *Journal of Money, Credit, and Banking*, **36**, 563–583.

Coccorese, P. (1998), 'Competition among dominant firms in concentrated markets: evidence from the Italian banking industry', Centro Studi in Economia e Finanza, Working Paper 89, Napoli: CSEF.

De Bandt, O. and P. Davis (2000), 'Competition, contestability and market structure in European banking sectors on the eve of EMU', *Journal of Banking and Finance*, **24**, 1045–1066.

De Guevara, J. and J. Maudos (2007), 'Explanatory factors of market power in the banking system', *Manchester School*, **75**, 275–296.

Degryse, H. and S. Ongena (2008), 'Competition and regulation in the banking sector: a review of the empirical evidence on the sources of bank rents', in A.W.A. Boot and A. Thakor (eds), *Handbook of Financial Intermediation and Banking*, Amsterdam: Elsevier.

De Nicolo, G. (2000), 'Size, charter value and risk in banking: an international perspective', International Finance Discussion No. 689, Board of Governors of the Federal Reserve System.

De Nicolo, G., P. Bartholomew, J. Zaman and M. Zephirin (2004), 'Bank consolidation, internationalization and conglomeration: trends and implications for financial risk', *Financial Markets, Institutions and Instruments*, **13**, 173–217.

Demirgüç-Kunt, A. and H. Huizinga (2010), 'Are banks too-big-to-fail or too big to save? International evidence from equity prices and CDS spreads', World Bank Policy Research Paper Number 5360.

Demsetz, H. (1973), 'Industry structure, market rivalry and public policy', *Journal of Law and Economics*, **16**, 1–9.

Dick, A.A. (2006), 'Nationwide branching and its impact on market structure, quality and bank performance', *Journal of Business*, **79**, 567–592.

Dick, A.A. and T.H. Hannan (2010), 'Competition and antitrust in banking', in A.N. Berger, P. Molyneux and J.O.S. Wilson (eds), *Oxford Handbook of Banking*, Oxford: Oxford University Press.

Evanoff, D.D and D.L. Fortier (1988), 'Re-evaluation of the structure–conduct–performance paradigm in banking', *Journal of Financial Services Research*, **1**, 277–294.

Fiordelisi, F., D. Marques-Ibanez and P. Molyneux (2010), 'Efficiency and risk in European banking', European Central Bank Working Paper Series 1211, Frankfurt, European Central Bank; also (2011), *Journal of Banking and Finance*, **35**, 1315–1326.

Fungacova, Z., L. Solanko and L. Weill (2010), 'Market power in the Russian banking industry', Bank of Finland (BOFIT) Discussion Paper, No. 3/2010. Helsinki: Bank of Finland.

Garcia-Marco, T. and M.D. Robles-Fernández (2008), 'Risk-taking behaviour and ownership in the banking industry: the Spanish evidence', *Journal of Economics and Business*, **60**, 332–354.

Gilbert, R.A. (1984), 'Bank market structure and competition: a survey', *Journal of Money, Credit and Banking*, **16**, 617–645.

Goddard, J., P. Molyneux and J.O.S. Wilson (2004a), 'Dynamics of growth and profitability in banking', *Journal of Money, Credit and Banking*, **36**, 1069–1090.

Goddard, J., P. Molyneux and J.O.S. Wilson (2004b), 'The profitability of European banks: a cross-sectional and dynamic panel analysis', *Manchester School*, **72**, 363–381.

Goddard, J., P. Molyneux, J.O.S. Wilson and M. Tavakoli (2007), 'European banking: an overview', *Journal of Banking and Finance*, **31**, 1911–1935.

Goddard, J., P. Molyneux, H. Liu and J.O.S. Wilson (2011), 'The persistence of bank profit', *Journal of Banking and Finance*, **35**, 2881–2890.

Goddard, J., P. Molyneux, H. Liu and J.O.S. Wilson (forthcoming), 'Do bank profits converge?', *European Financial Management*.

Goddard, J. and J.O.S. Wilson (1999), 'Persistence of profit: a new empirical interpretation', *International Journal of Industrial Organization*, **17**, 663–687.

Goddard, J.A and J.O.S Wilson (2006), 'Measuring competition in banking: a disequilibrium approach', Working Paper, University of Wales, Bangor.

Goddard, J.A. and J.O.S Wilson (2009), 'Competition in banking: a dis-equilibrium approach', *Journal of Banking and Finance*, **33**, 2282–2292.

Hainz, C., L. Weill and C.J. Godlewski (2008), 'Bank competition and collateral: theory and evidence', Bank of Finland Research Discussion Paper, No. 27/2008, December, Helsinki: Bank of Finland.

Herring, R.J. and J. Carmassi (2010), 'The corporate structure of international financial conglomerates: complexity and its implications for safety and soundness', in A.N. Berger, P. Molyneux and J.O.S. Wilson (eds), *Oxford Handbook of Banking*, Oxford: Oxford University Press.

Hesse, H. and M. Čihák (2007), 'Cooperative banks and financial stability', IMF Working Paper WP/07/02.

Iannotta, G., G. Nocera and A. Sironi (2007), 'Ownership structure, risk and performance in the European banking industry', *Journal of Banking and Finance*, **31**, 2127–2149.

Iwata, G. (1974), 'Measurement of conjectural variations in oligopoly', *Econometrica*, **42**, 947–966.

Jayaratne, J. and P.E. Strahan (1998), 'Entry restrictions, industry evolution, and dynamic efficiency: evidence from commercial banking', *Journal of Law and Economics*, **41**, 239–273.

Jiménez, G., J. Lopez and J. Saurina (2010), 'How does competition impact on bank risk taking?', Banco De Espana Working Paper 1005.

Keeley, M.C. (1990), 'Deposit insurance, risk and market power in banking', *American Economic Review*, **80**, 1183–1200.

Koetter, M., J. Kolari and L. Spierdijk (2008), 'Efficient competition? Testing the "quiet life" of US banks with adjusted Lerner indices', *Proceedings of the 44th Bank Structure and Competition Conference*, Federal Reserve Bank of Chicago.

Koetter, M. and T. Poghosyan (2009), 'The identification of technology regimes in banking: implications for the market power–fragility nexus', *Journal of Banking and Finance*, **33**, 1413–1422.

Koskela, E. and R. Stenbacka (2000), 'Is there a trade-off between bank competition and financial fragility?', *Journal of Banking and Finance*, **24**, 1853–1873.

Koutsomanoli-Filippaki, N. and C. Staikouras (2004), 'Competition in the new European banking landscape', paper presented at the Money, Macro and Finance 36th Annual Conference, Cass Business School, London, 6–8 September.

Lau, L. (1982), 'On identifying the degree of competitiveness from industry price and output data', *Economics Letters*, **10**, 93–99.

Lerner, A.P. (1934), 'The concept of monopoly and the measurement of monopoly power', *Review of Economic Studies*, **1**, 157–175.

Martinez-Miera, D. and R. Repullo (2009), 'Does competition reduce the risk of bank failure?', Centre for Economic Policy Research Working Paper DP6669, London: CEPR.

Maslovych, M. (2009), 'The Boone indicator as a measure of competition in the banking sector: the case of Ukraine', MA Thesis, Kiev School of Economics, Ukraine.

Matutes, C. and X. Vives (2000), 'Imperfect competition, risk taking and competition in banking', *European Economic Review*, **44**, 1–34.

Maudos, J. and J.F. De Guevara (2004), 'Factors explaining the interest margin in the banking sectors of the European Union', *Journal of Banking and Finance*, **28**, 2259–2281.

Maudos, J. and J.F. De Guevara (2007), 'The cost of market power in the European banking sectors: social welfare cost vs. cost inefficiency', *Journal of Banking and Finance*, **31**, 2103–2125.

Molyneux, P., D.M. Lloyd-Williams and J. Thornton (1994), 'Competitive conditions in European banking', *Journal of Banking and Finance*, **18**, 445–459.

Mueller, D.C. (1977), 'The persistence of profits above the norm', *Economica*, **44**, 369–380.

Mueller, D.C. (1986), *Profits in the Long Run*, Cambridge: Cambridge University Press.

Neven, D. and L.H. Röller (1999), 'An aggregate structural model of competition in the European banking industry', *International Journal of Industrial Organization*, **17**, 1059–1074.

Northcott, C.A. (2004), 'Competition in banking: a review of the literature', Bank of Canada, Working Paper, No. 2004-24.

O'Hara, M. and W. Shaw (1990), 'Deposit insurance and wealth effects: the value of being "too big to fail"', *Journal of Finance*, **45**, 1587–1600.

Panzar, J.C and J.N. Rosse (1987), 'Testing for "monopoly" equilibrium', *Journal of Industrial Economics*, **35**, 443–456.

Rhoades, S.A. and R.D. Rutz (1982), 'Market power and firm risk: a test of the "quiet life" hypothesis', *Journal of Monetary Economics*, **9**, 73–85.

Schaeck, K. and M. Čihák (2010), 'Competition, efficiency, and soundness in banking: an industrial organization perspective', European Banking Center Discussion Paper No. 2010-20S, 6 July, Tilburg University.

Schaeck, K., M. Čihák and M. Wolfe (2009), 'Are more competitive banking systems more stable?', *Journal of Money, Credit, and Banking*, **41**, 711–734.

Schiersch, A. and J. Schmidt-Ehmcke (2010), 'Empiricism meets theory: is the Boone-indicator applicable?', DIW Berlin Discussion Paper No. 1030, July, available at SSRN, http://ssrn.com/abstract=1641034.

Schmalensee, R.C. (1982), 'Antitrust and the new industrial economics', *American Economic Review, Papers and Proceedings*, **72**, 24–28.

Shaffer, S. (1989), 'Regulatory distortion of competition', Federal Reserve Bank of Philadelphia Working Paper 89-28.

Shaffer, S. and J. DiSalvo (1994), 'Conduct in a banking duopoly', *Journal of Banking and Finance*, **18**, 1063–1082.

Smirlock, M. (1985), 'Evidence of the (non) relationship between concentration and profitability in banking', *Journal of Money, Credit and Banking*, **17**, 69–83.

Stephanou, C. (2010), 'Re-thinking market discipline in banking: lessons from the financial crisis', World Bank Policy Research Working Paper, 5227.

Stern, G.H. and R.J. Feldman (2004), *Too Big to Fail: The Hazards of Bank Bailouts*, Washington, DC: Brookings Institution Press.

Stiroh, K.J. (2000), 'Compositional dynamics and the performance of the US banking industry', Federal Reserve Bank of New York Staff Report, No. 98.

Stiroh, K.J. and P.E. Strahan (2003), 'Competitive dynamics of deregulation: evidence from US banking', *Journal of Money, Credit and Banking*, **35**, 801–828.

Suominen, M. (1994), 'Measuring competition in banking: a two-product model', *Scandinavian Journal of Economics*, **96**, 95–110.

Toolsema, L. (2002), 'Competition in the Dutch consumer credit market', *Journal of Banking and Finance*, **26**, 2215–2229.

Turk-Ariss, R. (2010), 'On the implications of market power in banking: evidence from developing countries', *Journal of Banking and Finance*, **34**, 765–775.

Uchida, H. and Y. Tsutsui (2005), 'Has competition in the Japanese banking sector improved?', *Journal of Banking and Finance*, **29**, 419–439.

Uhde, A. and U. Heimeshoff (2009), 'Consolidation in banking and financial stability in Europe: empirical evidence', *Journal of Banking and Finance*, **33**, 1299–1311.

Van Leuvensteijn, M., J.A. Bikker, A. Van Rixtel and C. Kok-Sørensen (2007), 'A new approach to measuring competition in the loan markets of the Euro area', European Central Bank Working Paper, No. 768, June, Frankfurt: ECB.

Vives, X. (2010), 'Competition and stability in banking', IESE Business School Working Paper No. 852, April, Barcelona: IESE.

Weill, L. (2004), 'On the relationship between competition and efficiency in the EU banking sectors', *Kredit und Kapital*, **37**, 329–352.

Yeyati, E.L. and A. Micco (2007), 'Concentration and foreign penetration in Latin American banking sectors: impact on competition and risk', *Journal of Banking and Finance*, **31**, 1633–1647.

Zhao, T., B. Casu and A. Ferrari (2009), 'Competition and risk taking incentives in the lending market: an application to Indian banking', Centre for Banking Research Working Paper, WP-CBR-02-2009, London: Cass Business School.

Zhao, T., B. Casu and A. Ferrari (2010), 'The impact of regulatory reforms on cost structure, ownership and competition in Indian banking', *Journal of Banking and Finance*, **34**, 246–254.

4 What drives bank operating efficiency? The role of bank competition and credit information sharing

Chen Lin, Yue Ma and Frank M. Song

4.1 INTRODUCTION

Banking efficiency is essential for a well-functioning economy. Researches suggest that banks exert a first-order impact on economic growth and development (e.g., Levine, 1997). When banks operate efficiently by directing society's savings toward those enterprises with highest expected social returns and monitoring them carefully after lending, society's scarce resources are allocated more efficiently. This will in turn promote economic growth. By contrast, banks that simply operate with waste and inefficiency will slow economic growth and reduce society's economic welfare.

In this chapter, we study the effect of bank competition and credit information sharing on bank operation efficiency. Our study is motivated by the two recent global trends in the credit market. First, the unprecedented wave of consolidation of banks and financial institutions around the world in the decade 1998–2008 is intensifying the public policy and academic debates on the influences of concentration and competition in the banking sector (Berger et al., 2004).[1] Second, information sharing registries are becoming increasingly important elements of the institutional framework necessary to support a well-functioning and modern banking system (Miller, 2003). Many countries around the world have started to establish information sharing agencies in the past decade.[2] However, despite the great importance of the issue to both academics and policy makers, there is a lack of studies on the impacts of bank competition and information sharing and their interaction on bank operation efficiency.

In this study, we use bank-level accounting data of nearly 1200 banks across 69 countries from the BankScope database to construct an index of bank operation efficiency. We employ recently available survey data on bank concentration, supervision and regulation across 152 countries developed by Barth et al. (2006) to measure bank competition. Finally, we utilize a dataset of Djankov et al. (2007) and World Bank 'Doing Business' for 178 countries to measure credit information sharing mechanisms.[3] Among many important findings, we obtain the following three main results. First, banking competition as measured by lower banking industry asset (deposit) concentration and/or entry barriers enhances bank operation efficiency. This result supports the overall positive role of competition in improving bank performance. Second, information sharing mechanisms measured by the existence of credit registries and depth of credit information also increase bank operation efficiency, supporting the positive role of information sharing in banking operation. Third, information sharing further enhances the positive effect of bank competition and attenuates its negative effect on bank efficiency.

These findings have important implications for both academics and policy makers. Economists have long argued that competition generally facilitates efficiency by creating incentives for managers to perform and providing information to design appropriate incentive schemes (e.g., Hart, 1983; Scharfstein, 1988; Nickell, 1996; Allen and Gale, 2000; Vives, 2000).[4] By contrast, monopoly power induces inefficiency and waste. Similar arguments are made in banking. For example, Berger and Hannan (1998) argue that the monopoly power generated from market concentration may allow bank managers to relax their efforts. The concentration associated with monopoly power may also make it difficult to monitor manager effort because of a lack of benchmarks. Hence, they argue that banks are generally more efficient in a competitive banking environment.

However, an opposite view is that since banks are subject to serious asymmetric information problems, some monopoly power associated with banking provides incentives for bankers to collect and accumulate the borrower-specific information. By contrast, a more competitive banking market makes the information disperse, as each bank becomes informed about a smaller pool of borrowers. This reduces banks' screening ability and creates inefficiency as more low-quality borrowers obtain financing (Marquez, 2002). In addition, some monopoly power in banking allows the banks to build long-term repeated lending relationships with borrowers and possibly share in the future surplus generated by the borrower, which facilitates collecting information and monitoring of borrowers. In contrast, in a fully competitive market, banks may foresee a shorter duration of customer relationship and are not willing to incur necessary costs associated with overcoming informational problems as they cannot expect to share in the future surplus of the borrower. Therefore, credit market competition may be inimical to the formation of mutually beneficial relationships between firms and specific creditors (Petersen and Rajan, 1994, 1995). These arguments lead to the conclusion that banks may be less efficient in a competitive market as the information problem is less satisfactorily addressed.

Surprisingly, there are only a few empirical studies on the effect of bank competition on bank efficiency, and the existing evidence is mixed.[5] For example, Berger and Hannan (1998) find that in the US, banks with market power are related to lower bank efficiency. They attribute their findings to the high levels of market concentration allowing banks to charge prices in excess of competitive levels, and leading bank managers to slack or to pursue objectives other than profits.[6] By contrast, Maudos and de Guevara (2007) show the existence of a positive relationship between market power and cost X-efficiency for EU-15 countries over 1993–2002, and thereby reject the hypothesis that bank competition always enhances bank efficiency. However, they show that the welfare gains associated with a reduction in market power are greater than the loss of bank cost efficiency. Based on the analysis of a dataset consisting of 1400 banks across 72 countries, and indicators such as regulatory restrictions on bank competition and bank entry restrictions to measure the degree of bank competition, Demirgüç-Kunt et al. (2004) find that tighter regulations on bank entry, restrictions on bank activities, and regulations that inhibit the freedom of bankers to conduct their business all boost net interest margins (i.e., lower the intermediation efficiency according to their interpretation). However, they also find that the weak positive relationship between bank margins and concentration breaks down when controlling for a country's institutional development.

Given the ambiguity in both theory and evidence, it is important to re-examine the effect of bank competition on bank operation efficiency. In our empirical analysis, we examine whether bank competition generally promotes bank efficiency through its incentive effects or whether, due to an information problem, the effect of bank competition on bank efficiency could be negative. Our study suggests that the positive effect of bank competition on bank efficiency tends to dominate its negative effect, and supports the hypothesis that bank competition generally helps to enhance bank operation efficiency.

Our finding on the positive role of information sharing in bank operation efficiency is related to the small but growing credit information sharing literature. There are only a few theoretical studies on the role of credit information sharing in credit market performance. Pagano and Jappelli (1993) show that information sharing mechanisms reduce adverse selection by improving the pool of borrowers, and therefore improve bank efficiency in the allocation of credit. Padilla and Pagano (1997) show that information sharing institutions, through their incentive effects on curtailing imprudent behavior of borrowers, are also valuable in addressing moral hazard problems. In addition, they show that information sharing helps to reduce information rent that banks can otherwise extract from their clients, and reduce or even eliminate the information advantage of larger size banks, and therefore should enhance credit market competition. Some empirical studies confirm that credit registries help to reduce the selection costs of lenders by allowing them to predict individual loan defaults more accurately (e.g., Kallberg and Udell, 2003). There are also studies documenting evidence that information sharing affects bank lending, loan default, firms' access to credit, corruption in bank lending and bank risk-taking (e.g., Jappelli and Pagano, 2002; Brown et al., 2007; Barth et al., 2009; Houston et al., 2010). Recent cross-country evidence shows that private credit rises after improvements in creditor rights and in information sharing (Djankov et al., 2007).

However, the above-mentioned studies have not addressed the effect of information sharing mechanisms on bank operation efficiency directly. Our chapter provides the first empirical evidence on this important issue. In addition, we argue that information sharing mechanisms facilitate the positive effect of competition on bank efficiency as well as reduce the possible negative effect of competition on bank efficiency due to the information asymmetry problem. The later effect arises because the negative effect of bank competition on bank efficiency is likely due to disperse information and/or disincentives to build relationship banking in a competitive environment; and information sharing among banks could help to alleviate these concerns by reducing the information asymmetry problem. Therefore, information sharing enhances bank efficiency both directly through its effect on reducing the asymmetric information problem as well as indirectly through its effect on bank competition.

In addition to contributions to bank competition and information sharing literatures, we also contribute to the bank efficiency literature. There is an extensive literature on the efficiency of financial institutions (e.g., see an excellent survey by Berger and Humphrey (1997) on more than 130 empirical studies on efficiency). The bank efficiency literature mainly performs two tasks. The first task is to evaluate performance of banks and separate better-performing banks from worse ones. This is done by applying the non-parametric data envelope analysis (DEA) or parametric frontier analysis to banks or to branches within a bank. The second task is to use the efficiency measures to inform government policies, to improve managerial performance by identifying 'best practices' and 'worst practices', and to address other research issues. In performing the second task, the government policy-efficiency literature finds that deregulation of financial institutions can either improve or worsen efficiency, depending upon industry conditions prior to deregulation. However, the literature mostly focuses on the effect of deregulations on bank efficiency and ignores the impact of market institutions such as information sharing mechanisms and various aspects of bank supervision and regulations. We also perform instrumental variable (IV) analysis to address the possible endogeneity issue concerning the bank efficiency and market institutions. Finally, the two-stage bootstrapping non-parametric frontier method is used as a robustness test (following Simar and Wilson, 2007). The method allows random errors in the model and is able to correct for the estimation bias that the traditional DEA cannot deal with.[7]

Beyond our three major findings, we obtain some other results. We find that higher bank accounting quality and the independence of supervisory authorities are associated with greater bank efficiency. A banking system dominated by government ownership is associated with lower banking firm efficiency. Large and highly leveraged banks tend to have higher efficiency. Finally, a country with large size and higher gross domestic product (GDP) per capita seems to have more efficient banks while inflation is negatively associated with efficiency.

We perform a number of robustness tests on our results. Specifically, we expand our control variables by including major macroeconomic and institutional measures. We also provide some further corroborating evidence to support the hypothesis that bank competition and information sharing have causal impacts on the levels of bank operation efficiency by splitting samples according to country characteristics and studying their interaction effects. We find that information sharing and market competition work more effectively in enhancing bank efficiency in countries with a poor rule of law and lower income, suggesting that information sharing and bank competition to some extent substitute for the role of rule of law and country's stage of development in enhancing bank efficiency.

The rest of the chapter is organized as follows. Section 4.2 summarizes the theory concerning the effects of bank competition and information sharing on bank performance and the credit market. It also develops the key hypotheses on the effect of competition and information sharing on bank efficiency. Section 4.3 presents the data and defines the variables for the subsequent analysis. Section 4.4 presents the non-parametric data envelope analysis (DEA) methodology and discusses the empirical findings. It also provides robustness analysis of our major findings and some extensions. Section 4.5 concludes the chapter with discussions on some policy implications.

4.2   THEORY AND HYPOTHESIS

In this section, we summarize some of the main theoretical arguments on the effect of bank competition and credit information sharing on bank operation efficiency, and present our main hypotheses. Economic theory provides conflicting predictions on the effects of bank competition on bank efficiency. On the one hand, competition may enhance efficiency for the following three reasons. First, it is argued that the monopoly power generated from market concentration may allow managers to relax their efforts and enjoy a 'quiet life'.[8] Specifically, the difference between the actual price and competitive price would result in a monopoly rent, which provides a 'cushion', or a comfort zone to the managers. In the absence of other disciplining mechanisms, managers may allow unit costs to rise to consume part of this 'cushion' and still allow owners to earn economic profits without the full effort of cost minimization (Berger and Hannan, 1998). Therefore, a reduction in competitive pressure may result in lessened effort by managers to maximize operating efficiency. Second, the price 'cushion' and the lack of a performance benchmark in a concentrated market may simply blunt the economic signals that would normally force the changes in the management to keep costs low, allowing managers to persist in the positions for which they do not have comparative advantages (Berger and Hannan, 1998). In other words, the owners in a more competitive market are able to make a better assessment of managerial performance through benchmarking and consequently to change management if necessary. In this regard, market competitiveness can be viewed as a managerial incentive scheme to improve firm efficiency (Hart, 1983; Scharfstein, 1988; Vives, 2000). Third, monopoly power may allow the managers to grab a share of the monopoly rents through discretionary expenses or pursuit of objectives (e.g., empire building) other than firm profit maximization (Hermalin, 1992).

On the other hand, it is well known in the banking literature that banks are exposed to problems of information asymmetry (adverse selection and moral hazard), which can prevent the efficient allocation of credit (Leland and Pyle, 1977; Stiglitz and Weiss, 1981, 1988).[9] The information asymmetries between lender and borrower, as argued below, may result in a negative relationship between competition and efficiency. First, Marquez (2002) shows that borrower-specific information becomes more dispersed in a more competitive banking market, resulting in less effective borrower screening which could consequently reduce bank efficiency. Second, one way to reduce information asymmetries is to monitor the behaviors of borrowers over time, including repayment of loans and other transactions, through a long-term repeated lending relationship – relationship banking (Stiglitz and Weiss, 1981, 1988; Petersen and Rajan, 1994). Nevertheless, an increase in banking competition may reduce the expected length of customer relationship and consequently lead to inefficiency in bank lending. In addition, as argued by Petersen and Rajan (1994, 1995), banks with some monopoly power might have stronger incentives to incur the necessary costs associated with overcoming informational barriers and thereby allocate credit more efficiently. This is due to the fact that the lender has a lower expectation to share in the future surplus of the firm in a competitive banking sector, which forces the lender to break even on a period-by-period basis and therefore reduces the lender's incentives to overcome information barriers. Third, in a concentrated market, the potential economies of scale and economies of scope could result in a more efficient banking sector (e.g., see Amel et al., 2004).

Overall, the theory provides conflicting predictions on the effects of bank competition on bank efficiency. Based on the above arguments, we have our first pair of competing hypotheses as follows:

Hypothesis 1A   Higher concentration (less bank competition) in the banking sector is associated with lower bank efficiency.

Hypothesis 1B   Higher concentration (less bank competition) in the banking sector is associated with higher bank efficiency.

In their survey paper of banking concentration and competition, Berger et al. (2004) point out that bank competition is multifaceted insofar as it encompasses not only bank concentration but also regulatory restrictions, such as regulatory restrictions on competition, entry restrictions and other legal impediments that limit actual and potential bank competition. Therefore, we follow recent researchers (e.g., Barth et al., 2009) to use bank entry regulations as another measure of bank competition. In addition to the arguments presented above concerning the effect of bank competition on bank efficiency, further complications arise on the effect of bank entry barriers on bank efficiency. There are two competing theories on bank regulations (including bank entry regulations). The public interest theory of regulations argues that a benevolent government which pursues social welfare can promote bank efficiency and stability through effective screening of bank entry (Barth et al., 2006). In contrast, the private interest theory of regulations suggests that the industry incumbents will tend to demand entry barriers that create rents for themselves, since they typically face lower information and organization costs in a more concentrated market. In this theory, the regulation of entry could keep out the competitors and raise incumbents' rents (Djankov et al., 2002). Regulators, on the other hand, will be tempted to respond, both as a way to reward supporters, to help them maintain political control, and as a way to extract rents for their own benefits (Barth et al., 2006). As pointed out by Shleifer and Vishny (1993: 601): 'an important reason why many of these permits and regulations exist is probably to give officials the power to deny them and to collect bribes in return for providing the permits'. In this regard, the entry barrier will exert a negative impact on bank efficiency since the regulation has been used to maximize the bureaucrat's political and economic benefits rather than the bank's efficiency. Based on the above discussion, we therefore have our second pair of competing hypotheses as follows:

Hypothesis 2A   Higher entry barriers (less bank competition) in the banking sector are associated with lower bank efficiency.

Hypothesis 2B   Higher entry barriers (less bank competition) in the banking sector are associated with higher bank efficiency.

As can be seen from the discussion in the introduction, information asymmetries (adverse selection and moral hazard) play a critical role in determining bank efficiency. Information sharing registries (private bureau and/or public registry) are the institutional mechanisms developed by the banks and other lenders to mitigate the information asymmetry problem. Specifically, information sharing among lenders helps to reduce both the adverse selection and the moral hazard problems, for the following reasons. First, information sharing improves banks' knowledge of applicants' characteristics and permits more accurate predictions of repayment probability. This allows lenders to target and price their loans better, hence easing adverse selection problems. Pagano and Jappelli (1993) show that information sharing helps reduce adverse selection by improving the pool of borrowers. In their model, each bank has private information about local credit applicants but has no information about non-local credit applicants. Therefore, a bank faces adverse selection from the second group of potential borrowers. By sharing information, banks can also assess the quality of non-local credit seekers and lend to them as efficiently as they do with local borrowers. The information also allows banks to promote financial instruments and to set and manage credit limits better. In short, credit information sharing plays a key role in improving the efficiency of financial institutions by reducing loan processing costs as well as the time required to process loan applications (Miller, 2003).[10]

Second, credit registries also work as a borrower discipline device: every borrower knows that if he defaults, his reputation with all other potential lenders is ruined, cutting him off from credit or making it more expensive to get future credit. These mechanisms tighten borrowers' incentives to repay, hence reducing moral hazard. Therefore, we have the following hypothesis:

Hypothesis 3A   Information sharing mechanisms help enhance bank efficiency.

Finally, within the banking industry, credit information sharing mechanisms also enhance banking competition by reducing information rent that banks extract from their clients and leveling the informational playing field within the credit market. As we discussed earlier on, in the absence of information sharing, it would confer to the banks some market power over their customers if banks have private information about borrowers. The exchange of information among banks could reduce or even eliminate such an informational advantage of banks (Padilla and Pagano, 1997). Therefore we expect that information sharing mechanisms mitigate the negative impact of concentration and regulatory barriers on bank efficiency. These arguments lead to the following hypothesis:

Hypothesis 3B   Bank information sharing reduces the negative effect of bank concentration and entry barriers on bank efficiency.

In addition to the above three main hypotheses, we also examine other determinants of bank efficiency. Specifically, we include the banking sector ownership, supervisory power, independence of bank supervisor and bank accounting disclosure as additional banking sector controls in the analysis. We also include other bank-level and macro controls. The variables are discussed in detail in the next section.

4.3   DATA AND VARIABLES

4.3.1   The Sample

The dataset used in this study is compiled from three main sources: (1) the BankScope database provided by Bureau van Dijk and Fitch Ratings; (2) the Barth et al. (BCL henceforth) (2006) dataset on bank supervision and regulation in 152 countries; and (3) the Djankov et al. (DMS henceforth) (2007) and World Bank 'Doing Business' dataset on credit information sharing in 178 countries. Bank-level accounting information from 69 countries on about 1200 banks is from the BankScope database. The BankScope database has comprehensive coverage in most countries, accounting for over 90 percent of all banking assets in each country. Each bank report contains detailed balance sheet and income statement totaling up to 200 data items and 36 pre-calculated financial ratios. In this study, we mainly use the most recent data reported in the year 2006.[11] The banking competition and ownership data come from BCL (2006), and were compiled from a World Bank survey on bank regulation and supervision in 152 countries in 2003. The information-sharing variables come from DMS (2007) and the World Bank 'Doing Business' Dataset (World Bank, 2005), which contain data on information sharing credit institutions in 178 countries. Because of the incomplete overlap among the three datasets and missing firm-level and banking sector variables, the final sample used in our study includes 1181 banks in 69 countries all over the world. The list of the countries can be found in Table 4.3.

In addition to the three datasets mentioned above, we rely on two other data sources, the World Development Indicators (World Bank, 2004) and the World Governance Indicator compiled by Kaufmann et al. (2006), to control for macroeconomic and institutional factors that might affect the overall level of bank efficiency in a country. Tables 4.1 and 4.2 identify the data sources and provide brief descriptions and summary statistics of the key variables.

4.3.2 Bank Efficiency

We use the standard 'financial intermediation approach' to evaluate the relative efficiency of banks. The financial intermediation approach was originally developed by Sealey and Lindley (1977) and posits that total loans and securities are outputs, whereas deposits along with labor and physical capital are inputs.[12] The approach was thereafter widely adopted and used. Following the recent applications (e.g. Casu et al., 2004; Drake et al., 2006), we posit an intermediation model that has three inputs and three outputs. The inputs (X_i) are: $X1$ (total deposits + total money market funds + total other funding); $X2$ (personnel expenses: labor input); and $X3$ (total fixed assets: physical input). With respect to the three outputs (Y_i), we have: $Y1$ (total customer loans + total other lending); $Y2$ (total other earning assets: other interest-generating or fee-yielding assets such as bonds and investment securities); and $Y3$ (other, non-interest, income). The efficiency scores are evaluated using the data envelope analysis (DEA) method described in detail in section 4.4 below and are summarized across countries in Table 4.3. Standard deviation and confidence intervals are also reported.

As can be seen from the table, the efficiency scores vary across countries. The scores range from 0.35 (Albania) to 0.94 (Switzerland) with a mean of 0.765. At first glance, we can see that banks are relatively more efficient in more developed countries such as the US, the UK, Germany, France and Switzerland; while banks are relatively inefficient in less developed countries such as Albania, Ghana, Lithuania, Nigeria and the Philippines. Therefore, we will control for the GDP per capita in our regression analysis to isolate the impact of banking competition and information sharing on bank efficiency.

4.3.3 Competition

A key independent variable in our study is a measure of banking competition. Following Barth et al. (2009), we use several measures of bank competition. The first measure is the share of the five largest banks in total bank deposits (*Banking Concentration (Deposit)*) from BCL (2006) to measure banking concentration. Higher concentration indicates a lower degree of competitiveness within the banking industry. As a robustness check, we use the share of total assets held by the five largest banks in the industry (*Banking*

Table 4.1 Variable definitions and data sources

Variable	Definition	Original sources
Outputs of Banks		
Total Loans	Loans + total other lending (mil USD)	BankScope
Other Earning Assets	Total other earning assets (mil USD)	BankScope
Other Operating Income	Other operating income (mil USD)	BankScope
Inputs of Banks		
Total Deposits	Total deposits + total money market funding + total other funding (mil USD)	BankScope
Labor Input	Personnel expenses (mil USD)	BankScope
Capital Input	Fixed assets (mil USD)	BankScope
Bank Efficiency	Technical efficiency of the bank	Authors' calculation
Bank Size	Natural logarithm of total assets	BankScope
Bank Equity	The book value of equity divided by total assets	BankScope
Bank Concentration (Deposit)	The fraction of total deposits held by the five largest banks in the industry. The data are compiled based on a survey of banking regulators in 150 countries in 2001.	Barth et al. (2006)
Bank Concentration (Asset)	The fraction of total assets held by the five largest banks in the industry. The data are compiled based on a survey of banking regulators in 150 countries in 2001.	Barth et al. (2006)
Entry Barrier	Entry into banking requirement, which is a variable developed based on eight questions regarding whether various types of legal submission are required to obtain a banking license. Which of the following are legally required to be submitted before issuance of the banking license? (1) Draft by-laws? (2) Intended organization chart? (3) Financial projections for the first three years? (4) Financial information on main potential shareholders? (5) Background/experience of future directors? (6) Background/experience of future managers? (7) Sources of funds to be disbursed in the capitalization of the new bank? (8) Market differentiation intended for the new bank? The index ranges from 0 (low entry requirement) to 8 (high entry requirement). Higher values indicate greater stringency.	Barth et al. (2006)
Application Denied	The percentage of applications to enter banking that have been denied in the past five years. The data are compiled based on a survey of banking regulators in 150 countries in 2001.	Barth et al. (2006)
State Owned Bank	The fraction of the banking system's assets in banks that are 50 percent or more owned by government. The data are compiled based on a survey of banking regulators in 150 countries in 2003.	Barth et al. (2006)

Table 4.1 (continued)

Variable	Definition	Original Sources
Information Sharing	The variable equals one if an information sharing agency (public registry or private bureau) operates in the country by the end of 2005, zero otherwise.	Djankov et al. (2007), World Bank Doing Business database
Depth of Credit Information	An index measures the information contents of the credit information. A value of one is added to the index when a country's information agencies have each of these characteristics: (1) both positive credit information (for example, loan amounts and pattern of on-time repayments) and negative information (for example, late payments, number and amount of defaults and bankruptcies) are distributed; (2) data on both firms and individual borrowers are distributed; (3) data from retailers, trade creditors, or utilities, as well as from financial institutions, are distributed; (4) more than 2 years of historical data are distributed; (5) data are collected on all loans of value above 1% of income per capita; and (6) laws provide for borrowers' right to inspect their own data. The index ranges from 0 to 6, with higher values indicating the availability of more credit information, from either a public registry or a private bureau, to facilitate lending decisions.	Djankov et al. (2007), World Bank Doing Business database
Bank Accounting Disclosure	Whether the income statement includes accrued or unpaid interest or principal on performing and non-performing loans and whether banks are required to produce consolidated financial statements. Higher value indicates a more informative bank account.	Barth et al. (2006)
Official Supervisory Power	Principal component indicator of 14 dummy variables: (1) Does the supervisory agency have the right to meet with external auditors to discuss their report without the approval of the bank? (2) Are auditors required by law to communicate directly to the supervisory agency any presumed involvement of bank directors or senior managers in elicit activities, fraud, or insider abuse? (3) Can supervisors take legal action against external auditors for negligence? (4) Can the supervisory authority force a bank to change its internal organizational structure? (5) Are off-balance-sheet items disclosed to supervisors? (6) Can the supervisory agency order the bank's directors or management to constitute provisions to cover actual or potential losses? (7) Can the supervisory agency suspend the directors' decision to distribute: (a) Dividends? (b) Bonuses? (c) Management fees? (8) Can the supervisory agency legally declare – such that this declaration supersedes the rights of bank shareholders – that a bank is insolvent? (9) Does the Banking Law give authority to the supervisory agency to intervene – that is, suspend some or	Barth et al. (2006)

all ownership rights – in a problem bank? (10) Regarding bank restructuring and reorganization, can the supervisory agency or any other government agency do the following: (a) Supersede shareholder rights? (b) Remove and replace management? (c) Remove and replace directors?

Variable	Description	Source
Supervisory Independence	The degree to which the supervisory authority is protected by the legal system from the banking industry. The variable equals one if the supervisors are not legally liable for their actions (i.e. if a supervisor takes actions against a bank, the supervisor cannot be sued), and zero otherwise.	Barth et al. (2006)
Inflation	3-year average percentage inflation, GDP deflator	World Development Indicators (WDI)
GDP per Capita	Logarithm of gross domestic product per capita in year 2006	World Development Indicators (WDI)
GDP	Natural logarithm of gross domestic product in year 2006	World Development Indicators (WDI)
Voice and Accountability	The indicator measures the extent to which a country's citizens are able to participate in selecting their government, as well as freedom of expression, freedom of association, and free media. The value of year 2005 is used in this study. Higher values mean greater political rights.	Kaufmann et al. (2006)
Government Effectiveness	The indicator measures the quality of public services, the quality of the civil service and the degree of its independence from political pressures, the quality of policy formulation and implementation, and the credibility of the government's commitment to such policies. The value of year 2005 is used in this study. Higher values mean higher quality of public and civil service.	Kaufmann et al. (2006)
Rule of Law	The indicator measures the extent to which agents have confidence in and abide by the rules of society, and in particular the quality of contract enforcement, the police, and the courts, as well as the likelihood of crime and violence. The value of year 2005 is used in this study. Higher values mean stronger law and order.	Kaufmann et al. (2006)
Political Stability	The indicator measures the perceptions of the likelihood that the government will be destabilized or overthrown by unconstitutional or violent means, including political violence and terrorism. The value of year 2005 is used in this study. Higher values mean more stable political environment.	Kaufmann et al. (2006)
Quality of Regulation	The indicator measures the ability of the government to formulate and implement sound policies and regulations that permit and promote market competition and private-sector development. The value of year 2005 is used in this study. Higher values mean higher quality of regulation.	Kaufmann et al. (2006)
Control of Corruption	The indicator measures the extent to which public power is exercised for private gain, including both petty and grand forms of corruption, as well as 'capture' of the state by elites and private interests. The value of year 2005 is used in this study. Higher values indicate better control of corruption.	Kaufmann et al. (2006)

Table 4.2   Summary statistics

Variable	Mean	Median	SD	No. of banks
Panel A: Bank-level data				
Outputs of banks				
Total Loans	6.0	6.2	3.0	1181
Other Earning Assets	5.4	5.3	2.9	1181
Other Operating Incomes	2.7	2.4	2.6	1181
Inputs of banks				
Total Deposit	6.5	6.6	2.9	1181
Labor Input	2.6	2.5	2.5	1181
Capital Input	2.4	2.4	2.6	1181
Bank characteristics				
Bank Size	6.7	6.7	2.9	1181
Bank Equity	11.9	10.0	7.3	1181

Panel B: Banking sector variables				No. of countries
Information Sharing	0.9	1.0	0.3	69
Depth of Credit Information	4.0	5.0	1.9	69
Banking competition variables				
Bank Concentration (Assets)	0.7	0.7	0.2	67
Bank Concentration (Deposits)	0.7	0.7	0.2	67
Entry Barrier	7.4	8.0	1.0	69
Application Denied	16.0	3.3	24.6	55
Control variables				
Official Supervisory Power	10.7	11.0	2.3	69
Bank Accounting Disclosure	3.7	4.0	0.5	69
Supervisory Independence	0.6	1.0	0.5	69
State Owned Bank	14.5	5.1	19.5	69

Panel C: Other control variables				
Inflation	4.5	3.0	4.4	69
GDP per Capita	9.1	9.1	1.3	69
GDP	25.5	25.6	1.8	69
Control of Corruption	0.5	0.3	1.1	69
Government Effectiveness	0.6	0.7	1.0	69
Political Stability	0.2	0.3	0.9	69
Quality of Regulation	0.6	0.8	0.9	69
Rule of Law	0.5	0.5	1.0	69

Note: See Table 4.1 for variable definitions. SD denotes standard deviation. Panel A is bank-level data. Panels B and C are the country-level data. Summary statistics in Panel A are based on the logarithm terms of the variables.

Table 4.3   Banking efficiency score across countries

Country name	Mean (unweighted)	Weighted mean (by total loans)	Standard deviation	95% CI lower bound	95% CI upper bound
Albania	0.357	0.356	0.017	0.323	0.380
Argentina	0.686	0.685	0.056	0.584	0.762
Australia	0.758	0.768	0.015	0.712	0.773
Austria	0.843	0.863	0.032	0.789	0.892
Azerbaijan	0.507	0.508	0.029	0.459	0.551
Belarus	0.691	0.691	0.030	0.647	0.761
Belgium	0.936	0.936	0.010	0.913	0.955
Bolivia	0.606	0.579	0.020	0.541	0.613
Botswana	0.733	0.673	0.091	0.546	0.866
Brazil	0.748	0.793	0.017	0.738	0.807
Bulgaria	0.589	0.628	0.071	0.497	0.711
Canada	0.913	0.923	0.015	0.887	0.932
Chile	0.737	0.741	0.044	0.698	0.844
Colombia	0.574	0.593	0.032	0.535	0.639
Costa Rica	0.613	0.617	0.036	0.546	0.711
Czech Republic	0.648	0.648	0.012	0.646	0.656
Denmark	0.790	0.820	0.030	0.765	0.855
Ecuador	0.544	0.531	0.030	0.484	0.588
El Salvador	0.597	0.643	0.033	0.562	0.715
Estonia	0.591	0.591	0.041	0.533	0.657
Finland	0.909	0.912	0.017	0.849	0.921
France	0.906	0.920	0.016	0.874	0.930
Germany	0.899	0.922	0.027	0.847	0.944
Ghana	0.532	0.533	0.020	0.498	0.565
Greece	0.725	0.728	0.032	0.669	0.779
Guyana	0.534	0.534	0.027	0.492	0.592
Honduras	0.575	0.559	0.031	0.502	0.623
Hong Kong	0.813	0.831	0.023	0.765	0.852
Hungary	0.806	0.806	0.036	0.755	0.853
Iceland	0.926	0.925	0.011	0.891	0.931
India	0.690	0.733	0.038	0.674	0.794
Italy	0.860	0.868	0.011	0.835	0.876
Japan	0.821	0.853	0.046	0.771	0.902
Kazakhstan	0.564	0.615	0.049	0.550	0.695
Kenya	0.578	0.592	0.035	0.511	0.653
Korea, Rep. of	0.863	0.863	0.037	0.807	0.901
Latvia	0.514	0.542	0.041	0.422	0.599
Lithuania	0.435	0.470	0.120	0.211	0.591
Luxembourg	0.912	0.919	0.013	0.896	0.922
Macau	0.789	0.789	0.020	0.762	0.832
Macedonia (FYROM)	0.745	0.745	0.021	0.711	0.788
Malaysia	0.701	0.708	0.012	0.676	0.721
Mauritius	0.788	0.825	0.048	0.709	0.909
Morocco	0.608	0.608	0.036	0.574	0.749

Table 4.3 (continued)

Country name	Mean (unweighted)	Weighted mean (by total loans)	Standard deviation	95% CI lower bound	95% CI upper bound
Netherlands	0.666	0.679	0.048	0.587	0.730
New Zealand	0.705	0.712	0.011	0.705	0.713
Nigeria	0.446	0.456	0.024	0.406	0.495
Norway	0.903	0.903	0.002	0.896	0.904
Pakistan	0.515	0.553	0.027	0.516	0.620
Panama	0.690	0.718	0.039	0.632	0.769
Peru	0.555	0.536	0.048	0.463	0.650
Philippines	0.472	0.471	0.048	0.386	0.554
Poland	0.549	0.555	0.040	0.470	0.612
Portugal	0.874	0.874	0.027	0.806	0.891
Romania	0.610	0.604	0.042	0.533	0.676
Russian Federation	0.787	0.799	0.044	0.727	0.873
Singapore	0.862	0.861	0.034	0.789	0.886
Slovenia	0.667	0.667	0.008	0.657	0.674
South Africa	0.727	0.805	0.054	0.697	0.835
Spain	0.931	0.936	0.011	0.905	0.940
Sweden	0.806	0.805	0.015	0.754	0.810
Switzerland	0.940	0.939	0.052	0.756	0.963
Thailand	0.736	0.763	0.033	0.688	0.810
Trinidad and Tobago	0.650	0.656	0.049	0.598	0.773
Turkey	0.710	0.746	0.056	0.641	0.806
Ukraine	0.649	0.651	0.015	0.621	0.674
United Kingdom	0.902	0.931	0.026	0.871	0.951
USA	0.858	0.924	0.021	0.877	0.949
Venezuela	0.406	0.412	0.051	0.336	0.527
All	0.765	0.792	0.034	0.727	0.843

Note: A three-input and three-output financial intermediation model is constructed to measure the bank efficiency scores (see sections 4.3 and 4.4.2 for details). Estimation of weighted mean is based on Simar and Zelenyuk's (2007) group-wise heterogeneous sub-sampling procedure, with 2000 bootstrap replications both for bias-correction and for 95% confidence-interval (CI) estimation. Subsample size for each country l is given as $m_l = n_l^{0.7}$, n_l is the number of banks in country l. Weights are observed total loans of banks. Standard deviation and confidence intervals are for the weighted mean.

Concentration (Asset)) as an alternative measure. As discussed by Barth et al. (2009), bank competition encompasses not only bank concentration but also regulatory restrictions that limit actual and potential bank competition. Thus, we follow Barth et al. (2009) and include two additional measures to address this issue. The first variable measures the stringency of entry requirements into the banking industry (*Entry Barrier*). It is a variable constructed on the basis of eight questions regarding whether various types of legal submissions are required to obtain a banking license. The index ranges from 0 (low entry requirement) to 8 (high entry requirement), with higher values indicating greater stringency. The detailed definition can be found in Table 4.1. The second variable is the fraction of entry applications denied (*Application Denied*), which is the percentage of applications to enter banking that have been denied in the past five years. All these data are from BCL (2006).

4.3.4 Information Sharing

Another key independent variable in our analysis is credit information sharing. Based on the data available from DMS (2007) and the World Bank 'Doing Business' dataset, we include two variables to measure information sharing among lenders. The first dummy variable (*Information Sharing*) indicates whether an information sharing agency (public registry or private bureau) exists or not in 2005. The second variable (*Depth of Credit Information*) captures the difference in information contents across countries. The data are from the World Bank 'Doing Business' dataset. Specifically, the depth of credit information index measures rules affecting the scope, accessibility and quality of credit information available through either public or private credit registries. The six characteristics measured by the index include (Houston et al., 2010): (1) both positive credit information and negative information are distributed; (2) data on both firms and individual borrowers are distributed; (3) data from retailers, trade creditors or utilities, as well as from financial institutions, are distributed; (4) more than two years of historical data are distributed; (5) data are collected on all loans of value above 1 percent of income per capita; and (6) laws provide for borrowers' rights to inspect their own data. The index ranges from 0 to 6, with higher values indicating the availability of more credit information, from either a public registry or a private bureau, to facilitate lending decisions.

4.3.5 Additional Bank Controls

We also control for *Official Supervisory Power*, *Supervisory Independence*, *Bank Accounting Disclosure* and *State Owned Bank*. All the variables are from BCL (2006), and were compiled based on a World Bank survey on bank regulation and supervision in 152 countries in 2003. *Official Supervisory Power* is constructed from 14 dummy variables that indicate whether bank supervisors can take specific actions against bank management, bank owners and bank auditors both in normal times and times of distress. The detailed definition can be found in Table 4.1. High value indicates wider and stronger authority for bank supervisors.

Supervisory Independence is a dummy variable which measures the degree to which the supervisory authority is protected by the legal system from the banking industry. Specifically, the variable equals one if the supervisors are not legally liable for their actions, and zero otherwise. *Bank Accounting Disclosure* measures whether the income statement includes accrued or unpaid interest or principal on performing and non-performing loans and whether banks are required to produce consolidated financial statements. A higher value indicates more informative bank financial statements. We expect *Supervisory Independence* and *Bank Accounting Disclosure* to be positively associated with bank efficiency.

Private and foreign ownership in the banking sector may enhance bank efficiency due to a greater motivation in shaping appropriate managerial incentives, introducing more competition and maintaining a good reputation. By contrast, Sapienza (2004), Khwaja and Mian (2005) and La Porta et al. (2002) argue that state-owned banks are controlled by politicians who use the banks to maximize their own political and personal objectives such as providing jobs for political supporters and bailing out poorly performing state-owned enterprises (SOEs). Existing studies also provide evidence on the distortions in state-owned banks' lending practices (see, for example, Sapienza, 2004; Dinc, 2005). We therefore include one variable to measure the ownership structure of the banking industry. *State Owned Bank* is the fraction of the banking system's assets in banks that are 50 percent or more owned by the government. We expect that state ownership of the banking sector is negatively associated with bank efficiency.

We also control for *Bank Size* and *Bank Equity*. *Bank Size* equals the logarithm of total bank assets in millions of US dollars. Size may be an important determinant of bank efficiency if there are increasing returns to scale in banking. *Bank Equity* is the ratio of the book value of equity to total assets. It is argued that well-capitalized banks face lower bankruptcy costs, and hence lower funding costs and higher bank efficiency (Demirgüç-Kunt et al., 2004). We therefore expect that both bank size and bank equity are positively associated with bank efficiency.

4.3.6   Country Controls

The empirical analysis also includes several country-level variables to control for differences in economic development and institutions across countries. First, we include GDP per capita to capture the economic development of the region or country. Second, we include the natural logarithm of GDP to capture the size of the economy. We also control for the inflation of the economy. Furthermore, we include a series of other political and institutional quality indexes composed by Kaufmann et al. (2006) as a check on the robustness of the results. The indexes measure six different dimensions of governance, which include political stability, government effectiveness, regulatory quality, rule of law, voice and accountability, and control of corruption. We expect that banks tend to be more efficient in more developed countries and in countries with high-quality institutions.

4.4   EMPIRICAL RESULTS

4.4.1   Data Envelopment Analysis (DEA)

In this chapter, we apply a widely used non-parametric method (data envelopment analysis) along with second-stage regressions to examine the relationship between bank efficiency, information sharing, and competition. In the first-stage estimation, the DEA methodology computes an operational efficiency score for each bank in the sample. The second stage of the DEA estimates the determinants equation of the efficiency score.

The operational efficiency score for a bank is estimated as the fraction of actual inputs that is required for the bank to be located on the efficient frontier to produce the same level of output. Suppose the sample size is n and there are m inputs and s outputs for each bank. Denote $x_k = (x_{1k}, x_{2k}, \ldots, x_{mk})$ as an $m \times 1$ vector of inputs for bank k, $X = (x_1, x_2, \ldots, x_n)$ as an $m \times n$ matrix of inputs, $y_k = (y_{1k}, y_{2k}, \ldots, y_{sk})$ as an $s \times 1$ vector of outputs for bank k, and $Y = (y_1, y_2, \ldots, y_n)$ as an $s \times n$ matrix of outputs, respectively. The variable returns to scale DEA model can be expressed with the following n linear programming problems for each bank k ($k = 1, 2, \ldots, n$):

$$\text{Max}(\varphi_k \geq 1 \mid x_k, y_k, X, Y) = \text{Max}(\varphi_k \geq 1 \mid \varphi_k y_k \leq Y\lambda_k, X\lambda_k \leq x_k, \lambda_k \geq 0, I_1'\lambda_k = 1) \quad (4.1)$$

where I_1 denotes an $n \times 1$ vector of ones, φ_k denotes a scalar parameter, and $\lambda_k = (\lambda_{1k}, \lambda_{2k}, \ldots, \lambda_{nk})'$ denotes an $n \times 1$ non-negative vector of parameters.

The DEA model in (4.1) has an intuitive interpretation. For each bank k, a virtual output $Y\lambda_k$ is constructed as a weighted output of all the banks by choosing some non-negative weights $\lambda_k \geq 0$, $I_1'\lambda_k = 1$. It then seeks to expand the virtual output $Y\lambda_k$ as much as possible, subject to the inputs constraint of bank k: $X\lambda_k \leq x_k$. The virtual output $Y\lambda_k$ is then compared with the actual output y_k of bank k. If the maximized virtual output $Y\lambda_k$ is above the actual output of bank k by a scalar factor of $\varphi_k > 1$, then bank k is inefficient. Otherwise, bank k is located at the efficient frontier since $\varphi_k = 1$.

The input-oriented efficiency score is defined as $e_k = 1/\varphi_k$ ($0 \leq e_k \leq 1$) for bank k. Under the DEA method, a bank with an efficiency score of unity (100 percent) is located on the efficient frontier in the sense that its outputs cannot be further expanded without increasing its inputs. A bank with an efficiency score below 100 percent is relatively inefficient, suggesting that the bank can attain its current output level with fewer inputs. As discussed in section 4.3.2 above, in the first-stage estimation, we have three inputs and three outputs to estimate efficiency scores for each bank in the sample based on model (4.1).

In the second stage, we estimate the following equation to identify the determinants of the banking efficiency score e_k:

$$e_k = X_k\beta + u_k \quad (4.2)$$

where e_k is the efficiency score for bank k; X_k is a vector of explanatory variables including a constant term, which represent information sharing and competition proxies, as well as other control variables such as bank regulation, bank characteristics, and macroeconomic environment discussed in section 4.3; and u_k is an error term with a standard error of σ_u. Since efficiency scores e_k are truncated below from zero and above from unity, u_k is an error term with double-truncation. As a result, Simar and Wilson (2007) argue that the truncated regression estimation permits valid inference. We apply the standard maximum likelihood estimation with heteroskedasticity robust standards errors clustered by countries to allow for possible cross-section correlations. When clustering the standard errors by country, observations are not restricted to be independent within countries; rather, observations are required to be independent across countries. The assumption of clustering seems more reasonable in our context (Beck et al., 2006). We therefore follow them with clustering the standard errors by country.[13]

4.4.2 Information Sharing, Competition and Bank Efficiency

Using the DEA method described in section 4.4.1, we regress the bank efficiency measure on information sharing, bank competition and other control variables; that is, we run the following truncated regression:

$$e_k = f(\text{information sharing, bank competition, other control variables}) + u_k \quad (4.3)$$

where e_k is the bank efficiency score for bank k; other control variables include banking sector regulatory variables, government ownership of the banks, bank size, bank equity, macro variables such as inflation, GDP and GDP per capita.

The estimation results are presented in Table 4.4. The magnitude of the truncated regression coefficients cannot be simply interpreted as the marginal effects of a one-unit increase in the independent variables on the dependent variable, although the sign and statistical significance of the coefficients are similar to the linear regression interpretations. In order to get some sense of the magnitude of the effects, the coefficient estimates are transformed to represent the marginal effects evaluated at the means of the independent variables from the interval regressions. The marginal effect of a dummy variable is calculated as the discrete change in the expected value of the dependent variable as the dummy variable changes from 0 to 1.

In Table 4.4, the most important finding is that banking competition and information sharing increase bank efficiency. As can be seen in the table, the existence of an information sharing credit agency significantly increases bank efficiency, as indicated by the positive and statistically significant coefficients (at the 1 percent level) of *Information Sharing* in all model specifications. Specifically, the existence of the information sharing credit agency increases the bank efficiency by 12 percent to 15 percent. In addition, the coefficients of *Depth of Credit Information* are positive and statistically significant at the 1 percent level in all model specifications, suggesting that more credit information shared would lead to higher bank efficiency. Specifically, one unit increase in the *Depth of Credit Information* index (ranges from 0 to 6) is associated with a 5–6 percent increase in bank efficiency. All these results strongly support our Hypothesis 3A that information sharing mechanisms enhance bank efficiency.

The coefficients of *Bank Concentration (Deposit)* and *Bank Concentration (Asset)* are negative and statistically significant at the 5 percent level or less in all model specifications, suggesting that increased concentration (i.e., less competitiveness) results in a more severe problem of bank inefficiency. Specifically, a 10 percent increase in bank concentration reduces the bank efficiency by 0.23 percent to 0.3 percent. The coefficients of *Entry Barrier* and *Application Denied* are negative and statistically significant at the 5 percent level in all model specifications. All these results strongly support our Hypotheses 1A and 2A that higher banking concentration, higher entry barriers and more stringent entry restrictions are associated with lower bank efficiency. Overall, these results indicate that the efficiency gain of bank competition dominates its negative effect through information loss, resulting in a net positive impact of bank competition on efficiency.

Regarding the bank control variables, the coefficients of *Supervisory Independence* are positive and statistically significant at the 1 percent level across all models, indicating the importance of an independent supervisor in enhancing bank efficiency. Consistent with our expectation, better bank information disclosure is associated with higher bank efficiency, as indicated by the positive and statistically significant coefficients of *Bank Accounting Disclosure* across model specifications. State ownership of the banking sector, as we expected, is negatively associated with bank efficiency. In addition, *Bank Size* is positively associated with bank efficiency, suggesting the existence of increasing returns to scale in the banking sector. *Bank Equity*, as we expected, is positively associated with

Table 4.4 Information sharing, competition and bank efficiency

	(1)	(2)	(3)	(4)	(5)	(6)
Information Sharing	0.1277 [0.002]***			0.1311 [0.002]***	0.1368 [0.002]***	0.1454 [0.001]***
Depth of Credit Information	0.0585 [0.008]***			0.0534 [0.014]**	0.0525 [0.011]**	0.054 [0.010]***
Bank Concentration (Asset)		−0.0285 [0.006]***		−0.0239 [0.040]**	−0.0237 [0.043]**	
Bank Concentration (Deposit)			−0.0305 [0.012]**			−0.028 [0.023]**
Entry Barrier		−0.0206 [0.018]**	−0.0176 [0.036]**	−0.0204 [0.014]**	−0.0251 [0.011]**	−0.0209 [0.035]**
Application Denied		−0.0182 [0.026]**	−0.0181 [0.024]**		−0.0192 [0.037]**	−0.0187 [0.039]**
Control variables						
Official Supervisory Power	0.018 [0.091]*	0.016 [0.232]	0.0163 [0.208]	0.0182 [0.076]*	0.0167 [0.220]	0.0162 [0.235]
Supervisory Independence	0.0221 [0.009]***	0.0227 [0.006]***	0.0235 [0.008]***	0.0202 [0.012]**	0.0201 [0.017]**	0.02 [0.014]**
Bank Accounting Disclosure	0.0211 [0.026]**	0.019 [0.066]*	0.0217 [0.039]**	0.0219 [0.030]**	0.0193 [0.037]**	0.0219 [0.035]**
State Owned Bank	−0.0038 [0.038]**	−0.0039 [0.035]**	−0.0033 [0.080]*	−0.0043 [0.028]**	−0.0036 [0.044]**	−0.0031 [0.054]*
Bank Size	0.067 [0.052]*	0.0711 [0.037]**	0.0723 [0.035]**	0.082 [0.008]***	0.072 [0.045]**	0.07 [0.054]*
Bank Equity	0.0062 [0.026]**	0.0064 [0.027]**	0.0064 [0.023]**	0.0058 [0.058]*	0.0075 [0.036]**	0.0069 [0.045]**
Inflation	−0.0012 [0.043]**	−0.0019 [0.037]**	−0.0018 [0.045]**	−0.0012 [0.041]**	−0.0018 [0.032]**	−0.0011 [0.078]*
GDP per Capita	0.006 [0.026]**	0.0058 [0.029]**	0.0058 [0.030]**	0.0059 [0.031]**	0.0059 [0.030]**	0.0057 [0.032]**
GDP	0.0063 [0.031]**	0.0053 [0.138]	0.0068 [0.018]**	0.0065 [0.037]**	0.0063 [0.034]**	0.0075 [0.021]**
Constant	0.3112 [0.026]**	0.3293 [0.044]**	0.264 [0.076]*	0.313 [0.047]**	0.2927 [0.064]*	0.257 [0.069]*
Pseudo R^2	0.239	0.224	0.226	0.227	0.231	0.231
Log likelihood	1208.109	945.77	947.65	1190.15	953.66	954.52
Observations	1181	1005	1005	1173	1005	1005

Note: See Table 4.1 for variable definitions. The estimation is based on a truncated regression proposed by Simar and Wilson (2007). P-values are computed by the heteroskedasticity-robust standard errors clustered for countries and are presented in brackets. *, **, *** represent statistical significance at the 10%, 5% and 1% level respectively. The coefficient estimates are transformed to represent the marginal effects evaluated at the means of the independent variables from the interval regressions. The marginal effect of a dummy variable is calculated as the discrete change in the expected value of the dependent variable as the dummy variable changes from 0 to 1.

bank efficiency. With respect to the other macro controls, GDP per capita is positively associated with bank efficiency at the significance level 1 percent across models, indicating the importance of economic development in improving bank efficiency. Finally, inflation is negatively associated with bank efficiency and the GDP (proxy of the size of the economy) is positively associated with bank efficiency. The pseudo R square is about 24 percent, suggesting a reasonably good fitness of the models.

4.4.3 Information Sharing, Competition and Efficiency: Interaction Effects

As we discussed in section 4.2 on hypothesis development, information sharing mechanisms could also encourage a more competitive loan market because information sharing among banks could reduce the informational rents that banks extract from their clients within lending relationships. The exchange of information among banks could reduce or even eliminate the informational advantage of banks which possess more private information and consequently increase banking competition and bank efficiency. Therefore, we expect that the presence of good information sharing mechanisms attenuates the negative effect of bank concentration and bank entry barriers on bank efficiency. We consequently include several interaction terms between information sharing and competition measures to test for possible non-linear relationships between information sharing, bank competition and bank efficiency. More specifically, we add six interaction terms (i.e., three interaction terms between competition/entry barrier measures and information sharing dummy variable; another three interaction terms between competition/entry barrier and depth of credit information) to the regression models, respectively.[14] The empirical results are presented in Table 4.5.

As can be seen from the table, we find strong and consistent evidence that good information sharing mechanisms attenuate the negative effect of bank concentration and bank entry barriers on bank efficiency, as indicated by the positive and statistically significant interaction terms in all the model specifications. The evidence provides strong support to our Hypothesis 3B.

4.4.4 Robustness Tests: More Macro Controls

Next, we address the issue of potential omitted variables. Since the overall quality of the institutional environment might influence bank efficiency, we include a series of macro-institutional indexes in our model to test the robustness of the results. Specifically, we include the six components of World Governance Indexes (Kaufmann et al., 2006) to capture different aspects of the institutional environment (control of corruption, political stability, government effectiveness, quality of regulation, voice and accountability, and rule of law). The detailed definitions of the indexes can be found in Table 4.1. Because some indexes are highly correlated with each other, we include the indexes individually in the models. The results are presented in Table 4.6. Again, the marginal effects are reported.

As can be seen from the table, the empirical findings about banking competition and information sharing are very robust to the inclusion of other institutional variables. The concentration and entry barrier are significantly and negatively associated with bank efficiency. The coefficients of information sharing variables remain positive

Table 4.5   *The level and quality of information sharing – the interaction with competition variables*

	Level of information sharing			Quality of information content		
	(1)	(2)	(3)	(4)	(5)	(6)
Information Sharing	0.1129	0.1064	0.1715	0.1464	0.1291	0.1209
	[0.005]***	[0.003]***	[0.002]***	[0.002]***	[0.006]***	[0.004]***
Depth of Credit	0.0436	0.0419	0.0541	0.0466	0.0472	0.0387
Information	[0.018]**	[0.017]**	[0.012]**	[0.020]**	[0.011]**	[0.027]**
Bank Concentration	−0.0329	−0.0245	−0.0224	−0.0299	−0.0284	−0.0257
(Asset)	[0.027]**	[0.095]*	[0.089]*	[0.019]**	[0.098]*	[0.076]*
Entry Barrier	−0.0269	−0.0217	−0.0247	−0.0235	−0.0284	−0.0272
	[0.017]**	[0.017]**	[0.025]**	[0.026]**	[0.031]**	[0.022]**
Application Denied	−0.0178	−0.0154	−0.0217	−0.0231	−0.0196	−0.0239
	[0.032]**	[0.033]**	[0.040]**	[0.035]**	[0.037]**	[0.022]**
Information Sharing	0.0247					
× Bank Concen-	[0.025]**					
tration (Asset)						
Information Sharing		0.0180				
× Entry Barrier		[0.002]***				
Information Sharing			0.0083			
× Application Denied			[0.081]*			
Depth of Credit				0.0242		
Information ×				[0.014]**		
Bank Concen-						
tration (Asset)						
Depth of Credit					0.0250	
Information ×					[0.006]***	
Entry Barrier						
Depth of Credit						0.0074
Information ×						[0.037]**
Application Denied						
Control variables						
Official Supervisory	0.0124	0.0116	0.0172	0.0105	0.0155	0.0182
Power	[0.242]	[0.247]	[0.168]	[0.272]	[0.158]	[0.151]
Supervisory	0.0185	0.0192	0.0203	0.0185	0.0204	0.0219
Independence	[0.007]***	[0.003]***	[0.002]***	[0.004]***	[0.001]***	[0.001]***
Bank Accounting	0.0263	0.0265	0.0180	0.0253	0.0209	0.0152
Disclosure	[0.028]**	[0.013]**	[0.038]**	[0.042]**	[0.066]*	[0.018]**
State Owned Bank	−0.0038	−0.0049	−0.0036	−0.0044	−0.0044	−0.0031
	[0.027]**	[0.011]**	[0.032]**	[0.019]**	[0.016]**	[0.029]**
Bank Size	0.0729	0.0758	0.0705	0.0719	0.0737	0.0702
	[0.038]**	[0.025]**	[0.040]**	[0.039]**	[0.037]**	[0.043]**
Bank Equity	0.0080	0.0079	0.0081	0.0083	0.0082	0.0078
	[0.028]**	[0.032]**	[0.031]**	[0.022]**	[0.030]**	[0.038]**
Inflation	−0.0017	−0.0013	−0.0018	−0.0017	−0.0015	−0.0018
	[0.001]***	[0.015]**	[0.005]***	[0.002]***	[0.002]***	[0.002]***

Table 4.5   (continued)

	Level of information sharing			Quality of information content		
	(1)	(2)	(3)	(4)	(5)	(6)
GDP per Capita	0.0071	0.0067	0.0056	0.0078	0.0073	0.0070
	[0.018]**	[0.018]**	[0.030]**	[0.021]**	[0.013]**	[0.029]**
GDP	0.0046	0.0050	0.0067	0.0045	0.0039	0.0059
	[0.049]**	[0.040]**	[0.029]**	[0.048]**	[0.056]*	[0.039]**
Constant	0.3739	0.4737	0.3202	0.3426	0.3093	0.3135
	[0.049]**	[0.013]**	[0.093]*	[0.047]**	[0.021]**	[0.090]*
Pseudo R^2	0.233	0.235	0.231	0.233	0.233	0.233
Log likelihood	956.04	958.82	954.41	956.84	956.92	956.17
Observations	1005	1005	1005	1005	1005	1005

Note: See Table 4.1 for variable definitions. The estimation is based on a truncated regression proposed by Simar and Wilson (2007). The coefficient estimates are transformed to represent the marginal effects evaluated at the means of the independent variables from the interval regressions. P-values are computed by the heteroskedasticity-robust standard errors clustered for countries and are presented in brackets. *, **, *** represent statistical significance at the 10%, 5% and 1% level respectively.

and significant in all model specifications. Regarding the institutional controls, *Rule of Law* and *Quality of Regulation* are found to exert significant and positive impact on bank efficiency. *Control of Corruption* has a marginally significant and positive impact on bank efficiency. The coefficients of the other institutional variables are not statistically significant although the signs are positive. Regarding the other control variables, *Supervisory Independence* and *Bank Accounting Disclosure* continue to exert a positive effect on bank efficiency. State ownership of the banking sector is negatively associated with bank efficiency. *Bank Size* and *Bank Equity* are still positively associated with bank efficiency. Overall, the empirical results are very robust to the inclusion of more institutional variables.

4.4.5   Robustness Tests: Instrumental Variable Analysis

In our study, the potential for an endogeneity problem is less of a concern than in pure cross-country analysis because we are examining the impact of the competition environment of banking and the existence of information sharing institutions on performance of individual bank firms. It is not very likely that these firm-based measures of performance will affect the competition environment and institutions. Furthermore, among the countries with information sharing schemes, more than 85 percent of them set up the schemes five or more years prior to our sample period.

Nevertheless, we conduct some robustness tests using instrumental variable truncated regression analysis. Following Newey (1987), a consistent instrumental variable estimation for regressions with limited dependent variables is used. The empirical results are presented in Table 4.7.

We follow the recent literature in selecting instrumental variables (e.g. Beck et al., 2006; Barth et al., 2009). More specifically, we include legal origin (English, French,

Table 4.6   Robustness tests: more institutional controls

	(1)	(2)	(3)	(4)	(5)	(6)
Information Sharing	0.1161	0.1237	0.1212	0.1013	0.1232	0.1581
	[0.005]***	[0.003]***	[0.004]***	[0.007]***	[0.004]***	[0.000]***
Depth of Credit	0.0575	0.0581	0.0555	0.0672	0.0657	0.0753
Information	[0.014]**	[0.015]**	[0.014]**	[0.047]**	[0.014]**	[0.009]***
Bank Concentration	−0.0242	−0.0232	−0.0264	−0.0205	−0.0203	−0.0255
(Asset)	[0.038]**	[0.045]**	[0.026]**	[0.034]**	[0.035]**	[0.027]**
Entry Barrier	−0.0265	−0.0245	−0.0253	−0.0265	−0.0276	−0.0261
	[0.038]**	[0.031]**	[0.038]**	[0.031]**	[0.042]**	[0.036]**
Application Denied	−0.0181	−0.0173	−0.0179	−0.0216	−0.0186	−0.0185
	[0.036]**	[0.035]**	[0.034]**	[0.031]**	[0.032]**	[0.038]**
Control variables						
Official Supervisory	0.0158	0.0186	0.016	0.016	0.0158	0.0186
Power	[0.243]	[0.093]*	[0.232]	[0.1710]	[0.243]	[0.081]*
Supervisory	0.0203	0.024	0.0211	0.0182	0.0209	0.0224
Independence	[0.015]**	[0.013]**	[0.010]**	[0.017]**	[0.018]**	[0.020]**
Bank Accounting	0.0196	0.0176	0.018	0.0195	0.0183	0.0176
Disclosure	[0.018]**	[0.015]**	[0.020]**	[0.024]**	[0.025]**	[0.017]**
State Owned Bank	−0.0034	−0.0039	−0.004	−0.0038	−0.0036	−0.0039
	[0.044]**	[0.040]**	[0.036]**	[0.031]**	[0.042]**	[0.041]**
Bank Size	0.0711	0.0683	0.0718	0.0673	0.0711	0.0701
	[0.044]**	[0.058]*	[0.033]**	[0.055]*	[0.023]**	[0.029]**
Bank Equity	0.0078	0.0075	0.0069	0.0058	0.0072	0.0074
	[0.046]**	[0.047]**	[0.045]**	[0.043]**	[0.031]**	[0.041]**
Inflation	−0.0018	−0.0014	−0.0018	−0.0017	−0.0013	−0.0019
	[0.042]**	[0.104]	[0.039]**	[0.026]**	[0.051]*	[0.044]**
GDP per Capita	0.0051	0.0053	0.0055	0.0045	0.0055	0.0062
	[0.049]**	[0.044]**	[0.039]**	[0.036]**	[0.040]**	[0.028]**
GDP	0.0056	0.0063	0.0072	0.0057	0.0056	0.0056
	[0.043]**	[0.038]**	[0.041]**	[0.056]*	[0.038]**	[0.044]**
Control of	0.0541					
Corruption	[0.082]*					
Government		0.0442				
Effectiveness		[0.314]				
Political Stability			0.0312			
			[0.327]			
Quality of				0.0617		
Regulation				[0.030]**		
Rule of Law					0.0264	
					[0.027]**	
Voice and						0.0328
Accountability						[0.311]
Constant	0.3412	0.3322	0.3074	0.384	0.3222	0.2946
	[0.046]**	[0.050]*	[0.062]*	[0.036]**	[0.056]*	[0.075]*
Pseudo R²	0.232	0.231	0.231	0.236	0.231	0.231
Log likelihood	954.78	954.27	954.11	959.59	953.94	954.23
Observations	1005	1005	1005	1005	1005	1005

Table 4.6   (continued)

Note: Control of Corruption is an indicator which measures the extent to which public power is exercised for private gain, including both petty and grand forms of corruption, as well as 'capture' of the state by elites and private interests. Higher values indicate better control of corruption. *Government Effectiveness* is an indicator which measures the quality of public services, the quality of the civil service and the degree of its independence from political pressures, the quality of policy formulation and implementation, and the credibility of the government's commitment to such policies. Higher values mean higher quality of public and civil service. *Political Stability* is an indicator which measures the perceptions of the likelihood that the government will be destabilized or overthrown by unconstitutional or violent means, including political violence and terrorism. Higher values mean more stable political environment. *Quality of Regulation* is an indicator which measures the ability of the government to formulate and implement sound policies and regulations that permit and promote market competition and private-sector development. Higher values mean higher quality of regulation. *Rule of Law* is an indicator which measures the extent to which agents have confidence in and abide by the rules of society, and in particular the quality of contract enforcement, the police, and the courts, as well as the likelihood of crime and violence. Higher values mean stronger law and order. *Voice and Accountability* is an indicator which measures the extent to which a country's citizens are able to participate in selecting their government, as well as freedom of expression, freedom of association, and free media. Higher values mean greater political rights. The other variables are defined as previously. The estimation is based on truncated regression proposed by Simar and Wilson (2007). P-values are computed by the heteroskedasticity-robust standard errors clustered for countries and are presented in brackets. *, **, *** represent statistical significance at the 10%, 5% and 1% level respectively. The coefficient estimates are transformed to represent the marginal effects evaluated at the means of the independent variables from the interval regressions. The marginal effect of a dummy variable is calculated as the discrete change in the expected value of the dependent variable as the dummy variable changes from 0 to 1.

German and Nordic), latitude, ethnic fractionalization and religious composition as instrumental variables for the banking competition measures using data from DMS (2007). The detailed explanations about why these are potentially good instruments can be found in Beck et al. (2006) and Barth et al. (2009). All these instruments that we employ pass the test of the overidentifying restrictions and first-stage F-test.

As can be seen from the table, the empirical results are rather robust. The coefficients of *Information Sharing* and *Depth of Credit Information* remain positive and statistically significant. The results confirm our finding that information sharing mechanisms enhance bank efficiency. Similarly, the coefficients of *Banking Concentration* remain negative and statistically significant in all model specifications, indicating that banking competition improves bank efficiency. The coefficients of *Entry Barrier* and *Application Denied* are also negative and statistically significant across the model specifications. All these results bolster our finding that banking competition, in terms of lowering concentration, lowering entry barriers and imposing less stringent entry restrictions, is associated with higher bank efficiency.

In columns (4) to (9), we add six interaction terms (i.e., three interaction terms between competition/entry barrier measures and information sharing dummy variable; another three interaction terms between competition/entry barrier and depth of credit information) to the regression models, respectively. Consistent with our previous findings, we find strong and consistent evidence that good information sharing mechanisms attenuate the negative effect of bank concentration and bank entry barriers on bank efficiency, as indicated by the positive and statistically significant interaction terms in all the model specifications. The evidence therefore bolsters our Hypothesis 3B and previous findings.

Table 4.7 Robustness tests: instrumental variables estimation results

	Full sample estimation			The level and quality of information sharing – the interaction with competition variables					
				Level of information sharing			Quality of information content		
	(1)	(2)	(3)	(4)	(5)	(6)	(7)	(8)	(9)
Information Sharing	0.2640 [0.000]***		0.2743 [0.000]***	0.4016 [0.022]**	0.3099 [0.028]**	0.3997 [0.007]***	0.3418 [0.014]**	0.3807 [0.002]***	0.3665 [0.009]***
Depth of Credit Information	0.1180 [0.001]***		0.0957	0.1080	0.0919	0.0951	0.1258	0.1279	0.1220
Bank Concentration (Asset)		-0.0580 [0.003]***	-0.0496 [0.003]***	-0.0609 [0.027]**	-0.0479 [0.003]***	-0.0514 [0.002]***	-0.0572 [0.029]**	-0.0473 [0.001]***	-0.0521
Entry Barrier		-0.0427 [0.004]***	-0.0522 [0.006]***	-0.0723 [0.028]**	-0.0898 [0.024]**	-0.0991 [0.018]**	-0.0930 [0.079]*	-0.0818 [0.025]**	-0.0928 [0.063]*
Application Denied		-0.0376 [0.011]**	-0.0402 [0.017]**	-0.0633 [0.031]**	-0.0502 [0.054]*	-0.0601 [0.027]**	-0.0717 [0.044]**	-0.0792 [0.077]*	-0.0789 [0.007]***
Control variables									
Official Supervisory Power	0.0365 [0.251]	0.0023 [0.543]	0.0317 [0.207]	0.0313 [0.254]	0.0228 [0.157]	0.0318 [0.099]*	0.0312 [0.110]	0.0303 [0.084]*	0.0253 [0.133]
Supervisory Independence	0.0423 [0.005]***	0.0386 [0.010]***	0.0394 [0.003]***	0.0505 [0.002]***	0.0411 [0.001]***	0.0431 [0.001]***	0.0474 [0.005]***	0.0590 [0.001]***	0.0602 [0.000]***
Bank Accounting Disclosure	0.0165 [0.005]***	0.0174 [0.058]*	0.0182 [0.017]**	0.0177 [0.012]**	0.0145 [0.003]***	0.0174 [0.001]***	0.0182 [0.002]***	0.0243 [0.001]***	0.0136 [0.005]***

Table 4.7 (continued)

| | Full sample estimation | | | The level and quality of information sharing – the interaction with competition variables | | | | | |
| | | | | Level of information sharing | | | Quality of information content | | |
	(1)	(2)	(3)	(4)	(5)	(6)	(7)	(8)	(9)
Control variables									
State Owned Bank	−0.0078	−0.0081	−0.0076	−0.0046	−0.0067	−0.0078	−0.0073	−0.0077	−0.0043
	[0.026]**	[0.017]**	[0.017]**	[0.040]**	[0.013]**	[0.011]**	[0.018]**	[0.005]***	[0.032]**
Bank Size	0.0799	0.0896	0.0802	0.0821	0.0805	0.0798	0.0799	0.0779	0.0772
	[0.052]*	[0.037]**	[0.045]**	[0.018]**	[0.013]**	[0.002]***	[0.017]**	[0.018]**	[0.007]***
Bank Equity	0.0039	0.0039	0.0041	0.0038	0.0041	0.0040	0.0040	0.0042	0.0039
	[0.013]**	[0.017]**	[0.022]**	[0.003]***	[0.002]***	[0.002]***	[0.002]***	[0.001]***	[0.002]***
Inflation	−0.0025	−0.0026	−0.0015	−0.0033	−0.0020	−0.0037	−0.0029	−0.0028	−0.0025
	[0.021]**	[0.001]***	[0.039]**	[0.044]**	[0.034]**	[0.043]**	[0.041]**	[0.023]**	[0.047]**
GDP per Capita	0.0048	0.0077	0.0063	0.0058	0.0046	0.0055	0.0062	0.0079	0.0069
	[0.024]**	[0.040]**	[0.041]**	[0.046]**	[0.053]*	[0.049]**	[0.042]**	[0.015]**	[0.019]**
GDP	0.0132	0.0111	0.0082	0.0058	0.0052	0.0045	0.0063	0.0057	0.0047
	[0.001]***	[0.032]**	[0.021]**	[0.029]**	[0.030]**	[0.031]**	[0.042]**	[0.028]**	[0.047]**
Constant	0.6468	0.6595	0.5990	0.6472	0.6984	0.5397	0.6004	0.6761	0.8361
	[0.000]***	[0.026]**	[0.018]**	[0.034]**	[0.036]**	[0.080]*	[0.063]*	[0.039]**	[0.040]**

Interaction terms

	(1)	(2)	(3)	(4)	(5)	(6)	(7)	(8)	(9)
Information Sharing × Bank Concentration (Asset)				0.0669 [0.020]**					
Information Sharing × Entry Barrier					0.0100 [0.009]***				
Information Sharing × Application Denied						0.0102 [0.080]*			
Depth of Credit Information × Bank Concentration (Asset)							0.0186 [0.051]*		
Depth of Credit Information × Entry Barrier								0.0377 [0.005]***	
Depth of Credit Information × Application Denied									0.0132 [0.004]***
Pseudo R²	0.249	0.262	0.273	0.265	0.261	0.262	0.260	0.264	0.264
Log likelihood	1230.62	967.04	973.83	980.53	974.70	975.86	974.44	979.11	978.99
Observations	1181	1005	1005	1005	1005	1005	1005	1005	1005

Note: See Table 4.1 for variable definitions. Instrumental variables include ethnic fractionalization, latitude, religions, and legal origins. The estimation is based on a consistent IV estimation of limited dependent variable regressions (Newey, 1987; Wooldridge, 2002). P-values are computed by the heteroskedasticity-robust standard errors clustered for countries and are presented in brackets. *, **, *** represent statistical significance at the 10%, 5% and 1% level respectively. The coefficient estimates are transformed to represent the marginal effects evaluated at the means of the independent variables from the interval regressions. The marginal effect of a dummy is calculated as the discrete change in the expected value of the dependent variable as the dummy variable changes from 0 to 1.

Regarding the control variables, state ownership of the banking industry is negatively associated with bank efficiency. Bank information disclosure and supervisory independence enhance bank efficiency, as indicated by the positive and statistically significant coefficients across model specifications. Overall, the results are very consistent with our previous findings and predictions.

4.4.6   Robustness Tests: Estimation Based on Bootstrapping

The two-stage DEA method we have applied so far is a deterministic approach that does not allow random errors in the model (Berger and Humphrey, 1997). Recent development of the two-stage bootstrapping DEA (e.g., Simar and Wilson, 2007) introduces random disturbance into the model. In addition, Simar and Wilson (2007) show that their two-stage bootstrapping DEA is also a valid procedure to correct for potential estimation bias due to heteroskedascity and cross-sectional correlation documented in the previous literature. Therefore, we employ the two-stage bootstrapping DEA approach (Simar and Wilson, 2007) to test the robustness of our main results. This procedure can be implemented as follows.

1.   Stage I Estimation
   - Step 1. Estimate efficiency scores $\hat{e}_k$ based on (4.1) for all banks in the sample, $k = 1, 2, \ldots, n$.
   - Step 2. Estimate the parameter vector $\hat{\beta}$ and the standard error $\hat{\sigma}_u$ by the truncated regression model (4.2).
   - Step 3. Repeat the following four substeps B_1 times to obtain the bootstrapped $\{\hat{e}_{kb}^*\}$ ($k = 1, 2, \ldots, n$, and $b = 1, 2, \ldots, B_1$):
      Step 3.1. Randomly draw u_{kb}^* ($k = 1, 2, \ldots, n$) from N(0, $\hat{\sigma}_u^2$) distribution with left-truncation $(-\Sigma_j\beta_j X_{k,j})$ and right-truncation $(1 - \Sigma_j\beta_j X_{k,j})$.
      Step 3.2. Compute $e_{kb}^* = \Sigma_j\beta_j X_{k,j} + u_{kb}^*$ for $k = 1, 2, \ldots, n$.
      Step 3.3. Let $y_{kb}^* = y_k e_{kb}^*/\hat{e}_k$ for $k = 1, 2, \ldots, n$.
      Step 3.4. Replace Y by $Y_b^* = (y_{1b}^*, y_{2b}^*, \cdots, y_{nb}^*)$ in (4.1) and re-estimate $\hat{\varphi}_{kb}^* = $ Max$(\varphi_k \geq 1 \mid x_k, y_k, X, Y_b^*)$, and let $\hat{e}_{kb}^* = 1/\hat{\varphi}_{kb}^*$ for $k = 1, 2, \ldots, n$.
   - Step 4. Compute bias-corrected estimator $\hat{\hat{e}}_k = \hat{e}_k - BIAS(\hat{e}_k)$, where $BIAS(\hat{e}_k) = 1/B_1\Sigma_b\hat{e}_{kb}^* - \hat{e}_k$ (Simar and Wilson, 2000).
2.   Stage II Estimation
   - Step 5. Re-estimate the parameter vector $\hat{\hat{\beta}}$ and the standard error $\hat{\hat{\sigma}}_u$ by the truncated regression of $\hat{\hat{e}}_k$ on $X_{k,j}$ via model (4.2).
   - Step 6. Repeat the following three substeps B_2 times to obtain the bootstrapped $\{\hat{\beta}_b^*, \hat{\sigma}_b^*\}$, $b = 1, 2, \ldots, B_2$:
      Step 6.1. Randomly draw u_{kb}^{**} ($k = 1, 2, \ldots, n$) from $N(0, \hat{\hat{\sigma}}_u^2)$ distribution with left-truncation $(-\Sigma_j\hat{\hat{\beta}}_j X_{k,j})$ and right-truncation $(1 - \Sigma_j\hat{\hat{\beta}}_j X_{k,j})$.
      Step 6.2. Compute $e_{kb}^{**} = \Sigma_j\hat{\hat{\beta}}_j X_{k,j} + u_{kb}^{**}$ for $k = 1, 2, \ldots, n$.
      Step 6.3. Estimate the bootstrapped parameter vector $\hat{\hat{\beta}}_b^{**}$ and the standard error $\hat{\hat{\sigma}}_{ub}^{**}$ by the truncated regression of e_{kb}^{**} on $X_{k,j}$ via model (4.2).
   - Step 7. Use the bootstrapped parameter vector $\hat{\hat{\beta}}_b^{**}$ and the standard error $\hat{\hat{\sigma}}_{ub}^{**}$ to estimate the significance levels (p-values) of all the parameters. The empirical results are presented in Table 4.8.

Table 4.8 Robustness tests: estimation results based on bootstrapping DEA

	Basic equation	The level and quality of information sharing – the interaction with competition variables					
		Level of information sharing			Quality of information content		
	(1)	(2)	(3)	(4)	(5)	(6)	(7)
Information Sharing	0.1858 [0.002]***	0.2193 [0.006]***	0.2253 [0.002]***	0.2469 [0.007]***	0.2447 [0.004]***	0.2371 [0.005]***	0.2541 [0.005]***
Depth of Credit Information	0.0530 [0.000]***	0.0661 [0.003]***	0.0665 [0.002]***	0.0677 [0.003]***	0.0655 [0.001]***	0.0703 [0.003]***	0.0672 [0.005]***
Bank Concentration (Asset)	−0.0352 [0.008]***	−0.0460 [0.002]***	−0.0251 [0.009]***	−0.0265 [0.008]***	−0.0453 [0.003]***	−0.0392 [0.007]***	−0.0238 [0.008]***
Entry Barrier	−0.0218 [0.003]***	−0.0288 [0.042]**	−0.0260 [0.022]**	−0.0292 [0.049]**	−0.0292 [0.046]**	−0.0294 [0.044]**	−0.0301 [0.046]**
Application Denied	−0.0201 [0.033]**	−0.0319 [0.035]**	−0.0345 [0.037]**	−0.0279 [0.044]**	−0.0352 [0.031]**	−0.0383 [0.036]**	−0.0276 [0.032]**
Information Sharing × Bank Concentration (Asset)		0.0304 [0.024]**					
Information Sharing × Entry Barrier			0.0220 [0.016]**				
Information Sharing × Application Denied				0.0099 [0.078]*			
Depth of Credit Information × Bank Concentration (Asset)					0.0288 [0.032]**		
Depth of Credit Information × Entry Barrier						0.0338 [0.034]**	
Depth of Credit Information × Application Denied							0.0097 [0.046]**
Control variables							
Official Supervisory Power	0.0137 [0.235]	0.0163 [0.240]	0.0171 [0.220]	0.0173 [0.213]	0.0171 [0.193]	0.0175 [0.220]	0.0184 [0.213]
Supervisory Independence	0.0172 [0.007]***	0.0201 [0.018]**	0.0206 [0.016]**	0.0208 [0.024]**	0.0206 [0.010]***	0.0205 [0.014]**	0.0209 [0.012]**
Bank Accounting Disclosure	0.0175 [0.009]***	0.0226 [0.007]***	0.0225 [0.006]***	0.0233 [0.009]***	0.0228 [0.006]***	0.0229 [0.006]***	0.0231 [0.009]***
State Owned Bank	−0.0030 [0.037]**	−0.0038 [0.032]**	−0.0038 [0.021]**	−0.0039 [0.035]**	−0.0038 [0.023]**	−0.0039 [0.018]**	−0.0039 [0.042]**
Bank Size	0.0873 [0.045]**	0.1060 [0.016]**	0.1062 [0.017]**	0.1084 [0.005]***	0.1065 [0.031]**	0.1070 [0.032]**	0.1064 [0.007]***
Bank Equity	0.0089 [0.036]**	0.0108 [0.001]***	0.0105 [0.026]**	0.0102 [0.012]**	0.0104 [0.004]***	0.0105 [0.017]**	0.0106 [0.008]***
Inflation	−0.0023 [0.004]***	−0.0028 [0.002]***	−0.0024 [0.016]**	−0.0029 [0.002]***	−0.0026 [0.008]***	−0.0023 [0.002]***	−0.0027 [0.004]***

Table 4.8   (continued)

| | Basic equation | The level and quality of information sharing – the interaction with competition variables | | | | | |
| | | Level of information sharing | | | Quality of information content | | |
	(1)	(2)	(3)	(4)	(5)	(6)	(7)
GDP per Capita	0.0065	0.0086	0.0089	0.0090	0.0088	0.0077	0.0079
	[0.003]***	[0.032]**	[0.027]**	[0.026]**	[0.029]**	[0.032]**	[0.029]**
GDP	0.0067	0.0078	0.0084	0.0080	0.0074	0.0072	0.0076
	[0.004]***	[0.015]**	[0.013]**	[0.013]**	[0.009]***	[0.018]**	[0.013]**
Constant	0.2729	0.2557	0.3093	0.4317	0.2439	0.3253	0.2614
	[0.051]*	[0.022]**	[0.002]***	[0.013]**	[0.004]***	[0.012]**	[0.026]**
Pseudo R^2	0.234	0.249	0.251	0.249	0.243	0.225	0.233
Log likelihood	967.11	980.65	981.68	973.11	978.07	980.84	975.80
Observations	1005	1005	1005	1005	1005	1005	1005

Note: See Table 4.1 for variable definitions. The estimation is based on bootstrapping DEA developed by Simar and Wilson (2007). P-values are computed by the heteroskedasticity-robust standard errors clustered for countries and are presented in brackets. *, **, *** represent statistical significance at the 10%, 5% and 1% level respectively. The coefficient estimates are transformed to represent the marginal effects evaluated at the means of the independent variables from the interval regressions. The marginal effect of a dummy variable is calculated as the discrete change in the expected value of the dependent variable as the dummy variable changes from 0 to 1.

As can be seen from the table, the estimation yields very similar results. The coefficients of *Information Sharing* and *Depth of Credit Information* remain positive and statistically significant. The results confirm our finding that information sharing mechanisms enhance bank efficiency. The coefficients of *Banking Concentration*, *Entry Barrier* and *Application Denied* remain negative and statistically significant across the model specifications, suggesting that banking competition improves bank efficiency. All six interaction terms remain positive and statistically significant, suggesting that good information sharing mechanisms enhance the positive link between bank competition and efficiency. The findings on control variables are also highly consistent with our previous results.

4.4.7   Robustness Tests: Estimation Based on Three-Year Average Data

We test the robustness of the results using data over the 2004–2006 period. One advantage of using data averaged over the 2004–2006 period is that we smooth variables that vary over time (Demirgüç-Kunt et al., 2004). Both the inputs/outputs data in estimating bank efficiency scores and the independent variables are the three-year average data from 2004 to 2006. The banking regulation variables are time invariant because they are based on the survey in 2003. The empirical results are presented in Table 4.9.

As can be seen from Table 4.9, the results are highly robust to our previous findings. The empirical results strongly support our hypothesis that bank competition and information sharing enhance bank efficiency. Furthermore, information sharing reduces the negative impact of competition and enhances the positive link between competition and

Table 4.9 *Robustness tests: estimation results based on three-year (2004–2006) average data*

	Basic equation	The level and quality of information sharing – the interaction with competition variables					
		Level of information sharing			Quality of information content		
	(1)	(2)	(3)	(4)	(5)	(6)	(7)
Information Sharing	0.1250	0.1404	0.1415	0.1443	0.1383	0.1220	0.1144
	[0.001]***	[0.043]**	[0.018]**	[0.015]**	[0.010]**	[0.018]**	[0.019]**
Depth of Credit	0.0430	0.0391	0.0399	0.0454	0.0477	0.0594	0.0349
Information	[0.003]***	[0.005]***	[0.003]***	[0.003]***	[0.000]***	[0.015]**	[0.007]***
Bank Concentration	−0.0391	−0.0419	−0.0391	−0.0394	−0.0468	−0.0359	−0.0330
(Asset)	[0.014]**	[0.029]**	[0.024]**	[0.025]**	[0.007]***	[0.031]**	[0.050]*
Entry Barrier	−0.0121	−0.0130	−0.0159	−0.0118	−0.0119	−0.0183	−0.0123
	[0.012]**	[0.019]**	[0.014]**	[0.025]**	[0.023]**	[0.055]*	[0.024]**
Application Denied	−0.0322	−0.0353	−0.0324	−0.0471	−0.0338	−0.0321	−0.0493
	[0.007]***	[0.013]**	[0.014]**	[0.030]**	[0.014]**	[0.016]**	[0.015]**
Control variables							
Official Supervisory	0.0195	0.0178	0.0161	0.0198	0.0165	0.0189	0.0198
Power	[0.231]	[0.176]	[0.120]	[0.143]	[0.090]*	[0.152]	[0.144]
Supervisory	0.0128	0.0121	0.0117	0.0129	0.0119	0.0125	0.0132
Independence	[0.041]**	[0.001]***	[0.001]***	[0.004]***	[0.007]***	[0.006]***	[0.003]***
Bank Accounting	0.0172	0.0206	0.0228	0.0154	0.0205	0.0172	0.0144
Disclosure	[0.003]***	[0.011]**	[0.006]***	[0.025]**	[0.011]**	[0.018]**	[0.028]**
State Owned Bank	−0.0022	−0.0025	−0.0034	−0.0021	−0.0033	−0.0030	−0.0018
	[0.047]**	[0.045]**	[0.019]**	[0.052]*	[0.033]**	[0.036]**	[0.077]*
Bank Size	0.0494	0.0503	0.0525	0.0494	0.0501	0.0506	0.0491
	[0.045]**	[0.001]***	[0.008]***	[0.004]***	[0.006]***	[0.006]***	[0.000]***
Bank Equity	0.0042	0.0045	0.0047	0.0042	0.0044	0.0043	0.0040
	[0.036]**	[0.008]***	[0.007]***	[0.003]***	[0.008]***	[0.008]***	[0.001]***
Inflation	−0.0011	−0.0010	−0.0008	−0.0011	−0.0010	−0.0010	−0.0010
	[0.002]***	[0.009]***	[0.008]***	[0.002]***	[0.001]***	[0.003]***	[0.005]***
GDP per Capita	0.0098	0.0101	0.0093	0.0094	0.0107	0.0099	0.0103
	[0.003]***	[0.002]***	[0.003]***	[0.004]***	[0.002]***	[0.002]***	[0.002]***
GDP	0.0037	0.0030	0.0030	0.0041	0.0027	0.0029	0.0034
	[0.031]**	[0.039]**	[0.037]**	[0.024]**	[0.041]**	[0.040]**	[0.028]**
Constant	0.4751	0.4555	0.3293	0.3991	0.4817	0.5036	0.4016
	[0.050]**	[0.044]**	[0.009]***	[0.070]*	[0.034]**	[0.032]**	[0.077]*
Interaction terms							
Information Sharing × Bank Concentration (Asset)		0.0116 [0.038]**					
Information Sharing × Entry Barrier			0.0104 [0.007]***				
Information Sharing × Application Denied				0.0101 [0.059]*			
Depth of Credit Information × Bank Concentration (Asset)					0.0142 [0.010]***		

Table 4.9   (continued)

	Basic equation	The level and quality of information sharing – the interaction with competition variables					
		Level of information sharing			Quality of information content		
	(1)	(2)	(3)	(4)	(5)	(6)	(7)
Interaction terms							
Depth of Credit Information × *Entry Barrier*						0.0187 [0.033]**	
Depth of Credit Information × *Application Denied*							0.0056 [0.033]**
Pseudo R²	0.261	0.297	0.299	0.297	0.298	0.297	0.297
Log likelihood	984.43	985.22	987.97	984.71	986.34	985.26	985.35
Observations	1005	1005	1005	1005	1005	1005	1005

Note: See Table 4.1 for variable definitions. P-values are computed by the heteroskedasticity-robust standard errors clustered for countries and are presented in brackets. *, **, *** represent statistical significance at the 10%, 5% and 1% level respectively. The coefficient estimates are transformed to represent the marginal effects evaluated at the means of the independent variables from the interval regressions. The marginal effect of a dummy variable is calculated as the discrete change in the expected value of the dependent variable as the dummy variable changes from 0 to 1.

efficiency. The results confirm that our findings are not driven by market shock or out-liers in a specific year.

4.4.8   Further Exploration: Sample Splits

Based on our previous results, we find that better rule of law is associated with higher bank efficiency. We then split the sample into countries with better rule of law (the coun-tries with rule of law scores above the sample median) and poor rule of law (the countries with rule of law scores below the sample median) and explore the impacts of banking competition and information sharing on bank efficiency in each subsample. In addition, we split the sample into countries that are more developed (Organisation for Economic Co-operation and Development – OECD countries plus Hong Kong and South Korea) and those that are less developed (the other countries in the sample) and run regression analysis. The empirical results are presented in Table 4.10.

As can be seen in Table 4.10, both information sharing variables have much stronger impact on bank efficiency in countries with poor rule of law than in those countries with good rule of law. These results suggest that, to some extent, information sharing mecha-nisms serve as substitutes for good rule of law. In an environment with weak creditor rights protection and poor law enforcement, information sharing plays a more important role in enhancing bank efficiency through more effective and efficient screening and its disciplinary effect on borrowers in reducing moral hazard problems. Similarly, we find that information sharing variables have much stronger impact on bank efficiency in less developed countries than in more developed countries.

Table 4.10   Split sample estimations according to the rule of law and GDP per capita level

	Countries with good rule of law (1)	Countries with poor rule of law (2)	Countries with high GDP per capita (3)	Countries with low GDP per capita (4)
Information Sharing	0.0987	0.2732	0.1099	0.2495
	[0.003]***	[0.000]***	[0.008]***	[0.000]***
Depth of Credit	0.0301	0.0824	0.0378	0.0724
Information	[0.013]**	[0.000]***	[0.036]**	[0.000]***
Bank Concentration	−0.0270	−0.0489	−0.0114	−0.0246
(Asset)	[0.047]**	[0.032]**	[0.000]***	[0.043]**
Entry Barrier	−0.0107	−0.0150	−0.0227	−0.0263
	[0.046]**	[0.030]**	[0.049]**	[0.024]**
Application Denied	−0.0167	−0.0206	−0.0140	−0.0172
	[0.030]**	[0.006]***	[0.014]**	[0.032]**
Control variables				
Official Supervisory	0.0131	0.0179	0.0147	0.0161
Power	[0.188]	[0.353]	[0.031]**	[0.534]
Supervisory	0.0159	0.0164	0.0132	0.0151
Independence	[0.023]**	[0.000]***	[0.045]**	[0.016]**
Bank Accounting	0.0155	0.0184	0.0136	0.0177
Disclosure	[0.035]**	[0.000]***	[0.043]**	[0.002]***
State Owned Bank	−0.0020	−0.0038	−0.0030	−0.0048
	[0.021]**	[0.000]***	[0.002]***	[0.040]**
Bank Size	0.0812	0.0734	0.0716	0.0620
	[0.000]***	[0.000]***	[0.000]***	[0.000]***
Bank Equity	0.0053	0.0066	0.0070	0.0076
	[0.012]**	[0.000]***	[0.035]**	[0.000]***
Inflation	−0.0014	−0.0019	−0.0010	−0.0026
	[0.013]**	[0.000]***	[0.025]**	[0.042]**
GDP per Capita	0.0072	0.0089	0.0055	0.0041
	[0.007]***	[0.000]***	[0.005]***	[0.093]*
GDP	0.0054	0.0086	0.0046	0.0074
	[0.032]**	[0.121]	[0.003]***	[0.017]**
Constant	0.2590	0.2369	0.2654	0.2054
	[0.022]**	[0.034]**	[0.000]***	[0.045]**
Pseudo R^2	0.201	0.210	0.137	0.284
Log likelihood	459.03	548.27	327.23	688.82
Observations	499	506	374	631

Note: Columns (1) and (2) split the full sample of column (5) in Table 4.4 according to the variable of rule of law that is above the median level (with good rule of law, col. 1) or below the median (with poor rule of law, col. 2), respectively. Columns (3) and (4) split the full sample again into OECD countries plus Hong Kong and South Korea (high income countries, col. 3), and the remaining observations in the sample for column (4). The coefficients of the two variables related to information sharing, *Information Sharing* and *Depth of Credit Information*, are both significantly bigger at the 1% level in countries with poor rule of law (col. 2) and low income (col. 4) than those in countries with good rule of law (col. 1) and high income (col. 3), respectively. The estimation is based on truncated regression proposed by Simar and Wilson (2007). The coefficient estimates are transformed to represent the marginal effects evaluated at the means of the independent variables from the interval regressions. P-values are computed by the heteroskedasticity-robust standard errors clustered for countries and are presented in brackets. *, **, *** represent statistical significance at the 10%, 5% and 1% level respectively.

Bank concentration has less negative impacts on bank efficiency in countries with good rule of law and in more developed countries. This indicates the importance of legal environment and institutions in reducing the negative impact of bank concentration. The effects of *Entry Barrier* and *Application Denied*, however, are similar across the two types of countries.

4.5   CONCLUSION

Our chapter examines whether bank competition and credit information sharing help improve bank operation efficiency. We use three unique datasets: (1) the BankScope database provided by Bureau van Dijk and Fitch Ratings to measure bank operation efficiency; (2) the Barth et al. (2006) dataset on bank supervision and regulation in 152 countries to measure bank competition; (3) and the Djankov et al. (2007) and World Bank 'Doing Business' dataset in 178 countries to measure countries' information sharing mechanisms. The final matched sample includes nearly 1200 banks in 69 countries.

We find that both credit information sharing and banking competition enhance operating efficiency. Moreover, information sharing enhances the positive effect of bank competition and attenuates the negative effects of bank concentration and regulatory barriers on bank efficiency. We also find that larger banks and highly capitalized banks are generally associated with more bank efficiency. Finally, more developed countries with less inflation are usually associated with higher bank efficiency. Our findings are robust to controlling for different banking, macroeconomic, regulatory, and institutional factors and several endogeneity tests.

Although the institution and macroeconomic variables that have been identified in this chapter are out of control of the bank management, studying their effects on bank operation efficiency helps us to understand how these market institutions such as competition environment, credit information sharing, and laws and legal infrastructure affect banking firm efficiency. Our findings also suggest, to some extent, that the governments in various countries are able to raise bank efficiency by encouraging banking competition and promoting market institutions such as information sharing through public/private credit registries.

NOTES

1. According to Amel et al. (2004), over 10 000 financial firms were acquired in the major industrial countries from 1990 to 2001, including 246 deals in which the acquired firm had a market value greater than $1 billion.
2. According to Djankov et al. (2007), 54 countries in their survey of 129 countries set up some types of information sharing agencies in 1985–2005.
3. The World Bank Doing Business Survey collects data on the existence of public (i.e., government-owned) and private credit registries in a number of countries during the period 1978–2003. These registries collect information on credit histories and current indebtedness of various borrowers and share it with lenders. More details are in section 4.3 below.
4. It is generally believed that competition exerts downward pressure on costs, reduces slack, provides incentives for the efficient organization of production, and even drives innovation forward (e.g., see the arguments enunciated in Nickell, 1996).
5. There exists a large body of empirical studies on the relationship between bank concentration and prof-

itability (e.g., see a survey by Berger et al., 2004). Most studies find a positive statistical relationship between bank concentration and profitability. This positive relationship may be due to the market power of the concentrated banks. However, the evidence on the link between market power and efficiency effect is limited. Our study directly examines the effect of market power on bank efficiency.

6. These include objectives such as the expansion of staff or the reduction of risk below levels justified by maximization of shareholder value.
7. The traditional DEA approach implicitly assumes that all departures from the production frontier are due to technical inefficiency without regard to the potential impacts of measurement errors and other random noises. Such a restrictive assumption is relaxed in the stochastic frontier analysis (SFA) (Nguyen and Swanson, 2009). This was viewed as a comparative advantage of SFA relative to DEA.
8. The 'quiet life' argument is proposed by Hicks in his famous quote: 'the best of all monopoly profits is a quiet life' (Hicks, 1935).
9. Lenders are often unable to observe many characteristics of borrowers which are crucial in estimating the risk of default. This induces the adverse selection problems. After receiving the loan, the borrower may relax their effort to prevent default or take actions riskier than promised. This induces the moral hazard problems (Jappelli and Pagano, 2002).
10. According to some case studies reported by Miller (2003), the cost and time in allocating credit reduce significantly after the introduction of information sharing and credit scoring mechanisms. For instance, the loan processing time decreased from nine days to three days in a bank in Canada in 18 months since information sharing and credit scoring were implemented. The average processing time of a bank in the Netherlands decreased from 8–10 hours to 15 minutes for existing clients and 45 minutes for new clients. In a bank in the US, the average cost of processing a small business loan decreased from \$250 to \$100 after implementing the information sharing and credit scoring system.
11. To eliminate the influence of outliers the data were trimmed. The banks with the upper and lower 1 percent of the output–input ratios were excluded from our analysis. We also have extended our analysis to three-year (2004–2006) data and reported the three-year average results in Table 4.8. The findings with three-year average data are robust.
12. We have also used the 'profit approach' to measure bank operation efficiency, along the lines of Drake et al. (2006), and the results are robust.
13. The empirical results will be highly robust and even more significant without the country clustering effect.
14. We also split the sample into countries with an information sharing credit agency (or with high-quality information content) and without an information sharing credit agency (without high-quality information content) and explore the impact of banking concentration and entry barrier on bank efficiency in each subsample. The empirical results are very similar to the findings in the interaction-term regressions.

REFERENCES

Allen, Franklin and Douglas Gale (2000), *Comparing Financial Systems*, Cambridge, MA: MIT Press.

Amel, D., C. Barnes, F. Panetta and C. Salleo (2004), 'Consolidation and efficiency in the financial sector: a review of the international evidence', *Journal of Banking and Finance*, **28**, 2493–2513.

Barth, James R., Gerard Caprio and Ross Levine (2006), *Rethinking Bank Regulation: Till Angels Govern*, Cambridge: Cambridge University Press.

Barth, James, Chen Lin, Ping Lin and Frank Song (2009), 'Corruption in bank lending to firms: cross-country micro evidence on the beneficial role of competition and information sharing', *Journal of Financial Economics*, **91**, 361–388.

Beck, Thorsten, Asli Demirgüç-Kunt and Ross Levine (2006), 'Bank supervision and corruption in lending', *Journal of Monetary Economics*, **53**, 2131–2163.

Berger, Allen N., Asli Demirgüç-Kunt, Ross Levine and Joseph G. Haubrich (2004), 'Bank concentration and competition: an evolution in the making', *Journal of Money, Credit, and Banking*, **36**, 433–451.

Berger, Allen N. and Timothy H. Hannan (1998), 'The efficiency cost of market power in the banking industry: a test of the "quiet life" and related hypotheses', *Review of Economics and Statistics*, **80**, 454–465.

Berger, Allen N. and David B. Humphrey (1997), 'Efficiency of financial institutions: international survey and directions for future research', *European Journal of Operational Research*, **98**, 175–212.

Brown, Martin, Tullio Jappelli and Marco Pagano (2007), 'Information sharing and credit: firm-level evidence from transition countries', Centre for Studies in Economics and Finance, working paper no. 178, University of Salerno, Italy.

Casu, Barbara, Claudia Girardone and Philip Molyneux (2004), 'Productivity change in European banking: a comparison of parametric and non-parametric approaches', *Journal of Banking and Finance*, **28**, 2521–2540.

Demirgüç-Kunt, Asli, Luc Laeven and Ross Levine (2004), 'Regulations, market structure, institutions, and the cost of financial intermediation', *Journal of Money, Credit, and Banking*, **36**, 593–622.

Dinc, I.S. (2005), 'Politicians and banks: political influences on government-owned banks in emerging markets', *Journal of Financial Economics*, **77**, 453–479.

Djankov, Simeon, Rafael La Porta, Florencio Lopez-De-Silanes and Andrei Shleifer (2002), 'The regulation of entry', *Quarterly Journal of Economics*, **117**, 1–37.

Djankov, Simeon, Caralee McLiesh and Andrei Shleifer (2007), 'Private credit in 129 countries', *Journal of Financial Economics*, **84**, 299–329.

Drake, Leigh, Maximillian J.B. Hall and Richard Simper (2006), 'The impact of macroeconomic and regulatory factors on bank efficiency: a non-parametric analysis of Hong Kong's banking system', *Journal of Banking and Finance*, **30**, 1443–1466.

Hart, Oliver (1983), 'The market mechanism as an incentive scheme', *Bell Journal of Economics*, **14**, 367–382.

Hermalin, B.E. (1992), 'The effects of competition on executive behavior', *Rand Journal of Economics*, **23**, 350–365.

Hicks, J. (1935), 'Annual survey of economic theory: the theory of monopoly', *Econometrica*, **3**, 1–20.

Houston, Joel, Chen Lin, Ping Lin and Yue Ma (2010), 'Creditor rights, information sharing and bank risk taking', *Journal of Financial Economics*, **96**, 485–512.

Jappelli, Tullio and Marco Pagano (2002), 'Information sharing, lending and defaults: cross-country evidence', *Journal of Banking and Finance*, **26**, 2017–2045.

Kallberg, Jarl G. and Gregory F. Udell (2003), 'The value of private sector business credit information sharing: the US case', *Journal of Banking and Finance*, **27**, 449–469.

Kaufmann, Daniel, Aart Kraay and Massimo Mastruzzi (2006), '*Governance matters V: Worldwide governance indicators, 1996–2005*', World Bank.

Khwaja, A. and A. Mian (2005), 'Do lenders favor politically connected firms? Rent provision in an emerging financial market', *Quarterly Journal of Economics*, **120**, 1371–1411.

La Porta, Rafael, Florencio López de Silanes and Andrei Shleifer (2002), 'Government ownership of banks', *Journal of Finance*, **57**, 265–301.

Leland, D.N. and D.H. Pyle (1977), 'Information asymmetries, financial structure, and financial intermediation', *Journal of Finance*, **32**, 371–387.

Levine, Ross (1997), 'Financial development and economic growth: views and agenda', *Journal of Economic Literature*, **35**, 688–726.

Marquez, Robert (2002), 'Competition, adverse selection, and information dispersion in the banking industry', *Review of Financial Studies*, **15**, 901–926.

Maudos, Joaquin and Juan F. de Guevara (2007), 'The cost of market power in banking: social welfare loss vs. cost inefficiency', *Journal of Banking and Finance*, **31**, 2103–2125.

Miller, Margaret J. (2003), 'Credit reporting systems around the globe: the state of the art in public credit registries and private credit reporting firms', in Margaret J. Miller (ed.), *Credit Reporting Systems and the International Economy*, Cambridge, MA: MIT Press.

Newey, W.K. (1987), 'Efficient estimation of limited dependent variable models with endogenous explanatory variables', *Journal of Econometrics*, **36**, 231–250.

Nguyen, Giao and Peggy Swanson (2009), 'Firm characteristics, relative efficiency, and equity returns', *Journal of Financial and Quantitative Analysis*, **44**, 213–236.

Nickell, Stephen J. (1996), 'Competition and corporate performance', *Journal of Political Economy*, **104**(4), 724–746.

Padilla, A. Jorge and Marco Pagano (1997), 'Endogenous communication among lenders and entrepreneurial incentives', *Review of Financial Studies*, **10**, 205–236.

Pagano, Marco and Tullio Jappelli (1993), 'Information sharing in credit markets', *Journal of Finance*, **48**, 1694–1718.

Petersen, Mitchell and Raghuram Rajan (1994), 'The benefits of lending relationships: evidence from small business data', *Journal of Finance*, **47**, 3–37.

Petersen, Mitchell and Raghuram Rajan (1995), 'The effect of credit market competition on lending relationships', *Quarterly Journal of Economics*, **110**, 407–443.

Sapienza, P. (2004), 'The effects of government ownership on bank lending', *Journal of Financial Economics*, **72**, 357–384.

Scharfstein, D. (1988), 'Product-market competition and managerial slack', *Rand Journal of Economics*, **19**(1), 147–155.

Sealey, C.W. and J.T. Lindley (1977), 'Inputs, outputs and a theory of production and cost at depository financial institutions', *Journal of Finance*, **32**, 1251–1266.

Shleifer, Andrei and Robert W. Vishny (1993), 'Corruption', *Quarterly Journal of Economics*, **108**, 599–617.

Simar, L. and P. Wilson (2000), 'A general methodology for bootstrapping in nonparametric frontier models', *Journal of Applied Statistics*, **27**, 779–802.

Simar, L. and P. Wilson (2007), 'Estimation and inference in two-stage, semi-parametric models of production processes', *Journal of Econometrics*, **136**, 31–64.

Simar, L. and V. Zelenyuk (2007), 'Statistical inference for aggregates of Farrell-type efficiencies', *Journal of Applied Econometrics*, **22**, 1367–1394.

Stiglitz, J. and A. Weiss (1981), 'Credit rationing in markets with imperfections', *American Economic Review*, **71**, 393–410.

Stiglitz, J. and A. Weiss (1988), 'Banks as social accountants and screening devices for the allocation of credit', NBER working paper, no. 2710.

Vives, X. (2000), 'Corporate governance: does it matter?', in X. Vives (ed.), *Corporate Governance: Theoretical and Empirical Perspectives*, Cambridge: Cambridge University Press.

Wooldridge, J.M. (2002), *Econometric Analysis of Cross Section and Panel Data*, Cambridge, MA: MIT Press.

World Bank (2004), *World Development Indicators 2004*, Washington, DC: World Bank.

World Bank (2005), *Doing Business Data*, Washington, DC: World Bank.

5 Corporate borrower nationality and global presence: cross-country evidence on the pricing of syndicated bank loans

Joel Houston, Jennifer Itzkowitz and Andy Naranjo*

5.1 INTRODUCTION

The syndicated loan market is an important source of funding for firms around the world. Given the global nature of the syndicated loan market, a series of issues arise concerning the extent to which this market facilitates the flow of capital worldwide and the extent to which it is internationally integrated. With these issues in mind, we pose two questions in this chapter: what does the pricing of the syndicated loan market look like, and what are the factors that influence it? When thinking about these issues, it becomes immediately clear that globalization has often blurred the national identity of both lenders and borrowers. Many firms sell their goods and services throughout the world and/or own assets in countries outside of where they are headquartered. Likewise, many global lenders have operations and units throughout the world. One of the key contributions of our study is that we specifically control not just for the country in which the firms are headquartered or where the loan is syndicated, but we also take into account the extent to which the borrowers and lenders are linked in the different markets.

In contrast to what one might expect in an internationally integrated market, we find that loan pricing varies across countries and depends crucially on the borrower's nationality and global presence. Consistent with Carey and Nini's (2007) 'pricing puzzle', we also find that interest rate spreads on syndicated loans to corporate borrowers are significantly smaller in Europe than in the US. It is worth noting, however, that our study differs from Carey and Nini's in one important way. While their study focuses on the market in which the loans were syndicated, our analysis looks instead at another important issue: the borrower's and lender's nationality.[1] While there is arguably some correlation between the market of syndication and the nation in which the borrower and/or lender is headquartered, these distinctions prevent us from directly comparing our results to Carey and Nini's.

Moreover, our study also introduces a number of important firm-level controls that shed additional insights into the extent to which different types of firms are more or less globally integrated. Most notably, we find that the 'European discount' does not necessarily extend to the largest firms in our sample. Arguably these firms are in the best position to raise capital throughout the world, and are therefore able to capture any 'discounts' regardless of where they borrow. Moreover, we find that firms headquartered in North America that have significant assets or sales in Europe get the 'European discount' by using a European lead lender. This result suggests that foreign presence helps to reduce cross-border barriers. We also find that loan type matters. All else being equal, when North American firms borrow from European lenders via term loans, they pay lower spreads than when borrowing from North American lenders, consistent with the idea that term loans (transaction loans) are in a better position to take advantage of the foreign discount than lines of credit (relationship loans).

More broadly, our results can be viewed as part of a larger literature that provides conflicting evidence on whether financial markets are internationally integrated across countries and over time; see, for instance, Carey (2004), Bekaert et al. (2002a), Stulz (1999), Naranjo and Protopapadakis (1997), Bekaert and Harvey (1995), Chen and Knez (1995), Mittoo (1992) and Gultekin et al. (1989), among others.[2] Our study focuses on a period of time (1998–2004) in which banks have become more global in their operations as a result of technological innovations and reductions in regulatory barriers. Arguably, we might expect that the increased global reach of banks would facilitate increased integration within the syndicated loan market. At the same time, there are other forces that may be working to limit the integration of this market. These forces include information asymmetries, legal and regulatory barriers, and potentially different competitive environments.

Determining the factors that influence cross-border pricing of bank loans is particularly valuable to firms, banks and policymakers in their decision to raise capital, allocate resources and create regulations. For instance, investment and financing decisions depend on the degree of financial market integration.[3] With perfectly integrated international capital markets, firms can access external capital at the global cost of capital, even if the financial sector is less developed in their operating country.[4] The degree of financial market integration is also critical to the design and eventual success or failure of financial and monetary policies.

The remainder of the chapter is organized as follows. Section 5.2 provides a simple framework for understanding cross-country differences in the factors influencing the pricing of bank loans. Section 5.3 describes our data and provides summary statistics. In section 5.4, we investigate cross-country loan pricing. Section 5.5 provides some concluding remarks.

5.2 FACTORS INFLUENCING THE PRICING OF BANK LOANS

Banks take a variety of factors into account when pricing loans. Chief among these factors is the borrower's observed credit risk as well as the terms of the specific loan. Presumably, in a fully competitive and integrated loan market with no information costs, we would expect all lenders to charge the same rate on a given loan to a given borrower.

While the assumption of fully integrated markets with low information costs may apply to a subset of global firms that have ready access to capital worldwide, we might not expect this assumption to hold for the vast majority of borrowers for whom information costs are significant and are likely to vary considerably across lenders and across countries. As a result, it is reasonable to expect that information asymmetries, legal structures (including national laws, regulations and corporate governance practices), and competition may differentially affect lender choice and loan pricing across countries.[5]

Combining a mix of relationship lending and underwritten debt sold to outside banks, syndicated loans are an interesting hybrid of public and private debt. Relative to public debt and equity markets, bank loans often have a large private information component, and it is generally believed that lenders use a combination of 'soft' and 'hard' information when granting and pricing credit (e.g., Berger and Udell, 1995; Petersen and Rajan, 1994; Houston and James, 1996; Petersen and Rajan, 2002; Berger et al., 2003; Mian, 2006; Carey and Nini, 2007). If there are no costs or barriers to the movement and transmission of this information, these markets would likely be internationally integrated. However, both distance and borders may create information barriers, resulting in both a preference for domestic borrowing and segmented pricing. On the other hand, distance and borders are relative terms. For example, an American firm might be more able to borrow from a Japanese bank if the firm has a Japanese presence helping to alleviate information barriers across markets.

The institutional environment, which includes the competitive environment and the legal and regulatory environment, may also affect loan pricing.[6] Domestic banks share a common language and culture with domestic firms, and they are familiar with the regulatory conditions and accounting rules that govern a domestic firm. In addition, domestic banks may have a better understanding of local economic and political risks, and in the event of default may have a better understanding of the adjudication process. Recent work by Buch (2005) confirms the importance of borders. Looking at a sample of bank loans in five countries (France, Germany, Italy, the United Kingdom and the United States), she concludes that despite improvements in technology, banks tend to hold relatively few assets in foreign markets and that foreign holdings have not changed over time. Along these lines, Berger et al. (2003) hypothesize that local domestic lenders will continue to have a primary role in providing capital to small businesses and other informationally opaque borrowers. At the same time, they suggest that: 'services, such as syndicated loans to large borrowers, are more likely [than services such as cash management] to be provided by large, global institutions for which the home nations of these borrowers are of much less consequence to the demanders of the service'.

Although the concepts of distance and borders are inextricably linked, they are not perfectly related. Degryse and Ongena (2004) explain the usefulness of separating these concepts in assessing the geographical scope of financial markets. To the extent that 'distance' makes it harder to collect soft information, we would expect that banks that are closer to the borrowing firm in terms of physical distance would have an informational advantage. More specifically, being closer to the borrower makes it easier for the bank to meet with the managers and employees in person, observe operations and make more informed evaluations. Petersen and Rajan (2002) suggest that improvements in information technology may have led banks to rely more heavily on hard information such as financial statements and the firm's credit history. Consistent with this conjecture, the physical borrower–lender distance has increased for small and medium-sized firms in the United States. Contrary to Petersen and Rajan's finding, Degryse and Ongena (2005) find that distance between borrowers and lenders in Belgium has not changed over time and is still inversely related to loan interest rate. We do not attempt to reconcile these differences. Instead of focusing on the physical distance between borrower and lender, we evaluate the outcomes of these barriers caused by borders.

Despite the barriers created by borders, there may be some advantages to using a foreign lender. Firms may prefer global banks because of their global expertise. This expertise may come in at least two forms. First, to the extent that the borrower is a multinational firm, it may prefer a global bank that has expertise in many markets. Second, global banks may have deeper relationships with other banks. Larger loans require a broader (deeper or more liquid) loan base. Banks choose to syndicate loans to diversify their portfolio or because they may not have the capacity to lend the full amount (e.g., Simons, 1993). A working relationship with other banks may help global banks syndicate larger loans at considerably lower costs than local banks. In this regard, the factors that motivate a firm to use a foreign or global lender may be similar to the factors that lead a firm to become foreign listed (e.g., Pagano et al., 2002).

It follows that cross-country and cross-regional differences in the legal, regulatory and competitive environments for banks may affect a bank's ability to lend in different markets and may even produce systematic differences in loan pricing across markets. For example, anecdotal evidence suggests that the European syndicated loan market contains 'more banks competing for the business of big clients . . . The US market, by contrast, is dominated by a handful of powerful banks' (Wrighton, 2003). Stiff competition in the European market may drive prices down. Alternatively, lack of competition in the US may allow banks to keep prices at artificially high levels. Consistent with this conjecture, Carey and Nini (2007) find that loans syndicated in the UK are approximately 30 basis points cheaper than those syndicated in the US. Taken at face value, their results suggest that a lack of market integration combined with bank competition drives syndicated loan prices down in the European market.

Putting these various factors together, we develop a simple framework for understanding cross-country differences in loan prices. We begin by considering a firm (firm N) that is searching for a loan with a certain type of characteristics, L_N. The firm is deciding whether to borrow from a domestic lender, D, or a foreign lender, F. The price of the loan in both the domestic market (LP_{ND}) and in the foreign market (LP_{NF}) depends in part on the firm's characteristics (X_N), as well as the type of loan and terms of the loan (L_N). The price of the loan in the two markets also depends on the lender's information costs in the domestic and foreign markets (Φ_D and Φ_F, respectively) as well as the costs (or perhaps benefits) of the competitive, legal and regulatory environment faced by domestic and foreign lenders (θ_D and θ_F respectively). For simplicity, we refer to θ as the country effect.

The price of the loan in the domestic and foreign markets can be described as follows:

$$LP_{ND} = X_N + L_N + \Phi_D + \theta_D$$

$$LP_{NF} = X_N + L_N + \Phi_F + \theta_F$$

We assume that all else being equal, the borrower would choose the lender that offers the lowest price.

The above framework suggests different implications for different types of firms. First, firms with access to global capital markets are likely to be large firms or firms that have an international presence with foreign assets or sales. For these firms, we would expect that information costs in both markets are negligible, which suggests that $\Phi_D = \Phi_F = 0$. In this situation, the borrower's choice of lender would therefore depend on the relative country effects. In an environment where there is a level playing field where $\theta_D = \theta_F$, we would expect borrowers to be indifferent between the two markets, and we would expect loans to be priced similarly in the two markets. By contrast, if for these firms there is a significant difference in the country effects, we would expect most (if not all) borrowers to borrow in the market with the more favorable environment, and we would expect that lenders in that market would be able consistently to offer lower prices.

Second, firms with higher information costs and limited access to global capital markets are likely to be smaller firms and firms that do not have an international presence. For these firms, we would expect that information costs increase with distance, and we might expect that borders further increase information costs, all of which would suggest that $F_D < F_F$. In an environment where there is a level playing field ($q_D = q_F$), we would expect the information costs to dominate, which would suggest that these borrowers would overwhelmingly prefer domestic banks and that domestic lenders would be able to consistently offer lower prices. By contrast, trade-offs could possibly emerge if the competitive, legal and regulatory costs are lower in the foreign market. In those instances, we would expect to see that firms with relatively lower information costs may be more inclined to borrow in the foreign market. This potential trade-off may produce interesting cross-sectional differences within a given market. For example, we hypothesize that firms with a higher percentage of foreign assets and foreign sales may be more likely to borrow in the foreign market since, arguably, their foreign presence reduces distance, and thereby lowers the information costs associated with borrowing in the foreign market. On the other hand, firms with harder-to-value assets (such as firms with a higher proportion of intangible assets) may have much higher information costs when borrowing in foreign markets, which would increase the likelihood of using a domestic lender.

There are also three other key issues that will arise when we interpret our subsequent results. First, we might expect to see important differences depending on the type of loan. Our sample consists predominantly of loan packages, which often include term loans and/or lines of credit. Previous literature suggests that term loans are often viewed as more transaction driven, whereas lines of credit are considered more relationship driven (e.g., Berger and Udell, 1995). Therefore, we might expect the information costs to be lower for term loans, which all else being equal might translate into borrowers using foreign lenders for these transactions. We take this issue into account when examining the pricing of domestic and foreign loans.

5.3   DATA AND SUMMARY STATISTICS

5.3.1   Data

We gather loan information data from Reuters Loan Pricing Corporation's (LPC) DealScan database and financial firm-level data from Thomson's Worldscope database. From these databases, we obtain 13 103 loan packages issued to 4713 unique firms across ten countries over our sample period from January 1998 through October 2004.[7] We limit our sample to non-financial firms and to countries that have at least 100 deals that list the specific deal amount. The ten countries with sufficient preliminary data are:

Australia, Canada, France, Germany, Hong Kong, Japan, South Korea, Taiwan, the United Kingdom and the United States. However, in our subsequent syndicated loan pricing analysis, the Australasian firms fall out of our sample due to insufficient loan pricing data.[8] For the typical loan, DealScan includes the name and location of the borrower and the names of all of the lenders and their role in the loan contract at inception. Additionally, specific loan information includes amount of the loan (converted from the original currency to US dollars for comparison across countries), date of loan inception, projected maturity, loan type and purpose, and pricing.

The DealScan database is primarily composed of syndicated loans. Esty and Megginson (2003) explain that the structure of syndicates resemble pyramids with a few lead arrangers at the top and many participating banks (provider, participant, joint arranger, lender, underwriter, and so on) at the bottom.[9] During syndication, the arranging lenders meet with the borrower to assess credit quality, negotiate key terms and conditions, and prepare an information memorandum for participating banks. Once the key terms of the loan are negotiated, the arrangers become responsible for recruiting additional lenders, who are all party to one contract. This saves borrowers the cost of engaging multiple lenders and negotiating separate contracts. The lead bank of a syndicated loan typically holds a larger share of the loan (Kroszner and Strahan, 2001) and is believed to be better informed than the participant banks (Dennis and Mullineaux, 2000; Bharath et al., 2007; Sufi, 2007). DealScan divides lending banks into three categories for each loan: lead arrangers, agents and participants. While all leads are agents, not all agents are leads. Because of the critical role that lead arrangers play in information collection, monitoring and syndication, we focus on the banks that DealScan designates as lead arrangers, the more restrictive designation. For deals where a lead arranger is not defined, we recognize the agent banks as playing the primary role in syndication. Loans with more than one lender where no lender is designated as a lead or an agent are omitted from the sample.

Once the lead lenders of each deal are identified, we categorize the lead banks as foreign or domestic relative to the headquarters of the borrower's parent company. We use DealScan to identify the borrower's parent company and the location of its headquarters.[10] Foreign bank branches are not legally separate from the parent bank and thus maintain the full support of the parent bank's capital base and enjoy an equivalent credit rating. Foreign bank subsidiaries are frequently incorporated in one country, but a majority of ownership is held by the parent company which is located in a different country. For subsidiaries and branches, we determine bank location based on the nation of incorporation of the parent bank (as opposed to the location of the branch or subsidiary) as well.[11] The majority of leads that are designated as either foreign branches or foreign subsidiaries operate in Australia and Hong Kong.[12]

We then match the firms in the DealScan dataset with firms in the Worldscope database to obtain firm-level financial, sales, and other firm data. For firms to be considered a match, the nation in which their headquarters is located must be the same in both datasets. In addition, firms are considered to match if they have identical ticker symbols. Because ticker information is incomplete in the DealScan database, a second set of firms are matched by firm name.[13] This conservative matching procedure ensures that we only assign a match when the company is the same in both databases. Worldscope provides static company information, detailed annual reports, and exchange rates for publicly traded companies around the world. We convert all financial values to dollars and then clean the matched sample for errors and spurious matches by omitting cases in which the ratio of the loan amount to the total assets is greater than one and the ratio of foreign sales to total sales is greater than one. In Canada, Japan, Taiwan and the US, approximately 15 percent of the firms do not report intangible assets. We assume that if intangibles have been omitted, their value is $0.[14] The Worldscope database contains only firms that are publicly traded. As a result, the matched sample consists of firms that tend to be larger in size than those across the entire DealScan database.

In addition to basic balance sheet and income statement data, assets and sales information are delineated into distinct geographic segments. Firms discretionarily classify and report geographic segments, which results in the omission of some foreign sales or their combination into unusable segments. This tends to overemphasize the amount of domestic sales reported. Under-reporting of foreign sales and assets presence could bias the results from finding a relation between selecting a foreign lender and foreign presence, though we later show that this is not the case. Geographic segment data are aggregated using two different methods. First, the segments are pooled into one of two categories: domestic or foreign. Sales and assets are considered domestic if the segment description and the nation of the headquarters of the firm are the same. If the nation of the headquarters of the firm is not reported as one of the segment descriptions, then if the firm reports sales in the broader region in which the firm is headquartered, those sales are considered domestic. Second, we aggregate the geographic segment information for each firm into the following seven regions: North America; South America; Australasia; Western Europe; Africa and the Middle East; Eastern Europe and Central Asia; and other.

Many of the syndicated loan deals, or 'packages', are made up of multiple tranches, or loan 'facilities'. A typical package includes facilities of differing price, type and/or maturities (such as a one-year line of credit and a three-year term loan all originated on the same date). Sufi (2007) argues that investigating at the package level is appropriate to understand the choice of the lead lenders. First, all lenders, regardless of participation in an individual facility, are party to the same contract that is drafted at the time that the deal package is assembled. Second, treating multiple facilities as independent observations produces erroneously small standard errors. Consequently, we conduct our analysis of lead lender choice at the package level. However, our subsequent deal price analysis is necessarily investigated at the facility level.

5.3.2   Summary Statistics

Table 5.1 presents summary statistics of the data by country and by region. The sample is dominated by firms in the United States, followed by Japan, the United Kingdom, Taiwan and Canada. Companies located in Hong Kong and Korea average more than five deals each, while firms in the other countries average less than four deals. This table shows that both firm and lead bank characteristics differ by country and that some patterns are pervasive across countries. American and Japanese firms are the most likely to use domestic leads exclusively, suggesting that perhaps there is either a larger information barrier for firms in these countries or that these countries have deeper and more

Table 5.1   Summary statistics by country (1998–2004)

	Firms	Deals per firm	Firm characteristics					Lead bank characteristics		
			Firms with domestic leads only (%)	Firms with mixed leads (%)	Firms with foreign leads only (%)	Firms with foreign assets (%)	Firms with foreign sales (%)	Banks lending to nation	Banks w/HQ in nation	Banks w/ foreign loans (%)
Europe	315	2.74	28	39	33	53	83	283	159	79
France	57	3.79	34	43	24	12	91	153	57	77
Germany	49	3.12	28	39	33	54	91	104	64	82
United Kingdom	209	2.36	26	38	36	64	78	233	38	79
North America	3466	2.91	87	4	9	40	51	1062	723	19
Canada	123	2.23	54	11	35	55	72	99	32	85
United States	3343	2.83	88	4	8	39	51	1059	691	16
Australasia	932	2.95	75	6	19	31	44	569	284	38
Australia	88	2.88	41	23	36	48	55	122	23	56
Hong Kong	46	5.26	23	23	55	45	68	228	50	44
Japan	582	2.62	90	1	9	31	46	152	105	55
Korea	61	5.38	54	9	37	13	30	267	54	15
Taiwan	155	2.60	63	6	31	22	29	128	52	15

Notes: Firms are the number of distinct firms in the sample. Deals per firm are the average number of deals per firm in each country. In the 'Firm characteristics' panel, firms are included in the sample each year they take a syndicated loan and are only counted once per year. The 'Lead bank characteristics' panel details the bank characteristics for the banks determined to be leads of syndicated loans in the sample.

liquid markets that enable firms to raise sufficient funds domestically. It may also arise from other firm characteristics that vary between countries, which we address in our conditional analysis. Relative to firms in Japan and the United States, European companies are more likely to have foreign assets and sales and are less likely to rely exclusively on domestic lenders. The descriptive statistics also suggest that countries with higher foreign assets and sales are more likely to have a foreign lead present in the syndication process. Both foreign assets and foreign sales measure the foreign presence of a firm, which may serve to reduce information barriers that hinder using foreign banks. We test this hypothesis more extensively later.

Lead bank characteristics appear to roughly follow the same pattern as the firm characteristics. The US and Japan house the greatest number of banks. European and Canadian banks are involved in the highest percentage of international loans. Overall, Table 5.1 indicates that European firms and banks tend to be the most global.

Figure 5.1 lists countries in ascending order of the percentage of firms that use foreign lead lenders to arrange loan syndicates. Although the correlation is far from perfect, Figure 5.1 shows that as the percentage of firms using foreign leads increases, so does the percentage of firms that have foreign sales. This supports the hypothesis that a foreign presence may help firms to alleviate information problems created by borders and facilitate the use of international banks.

5.4   THE PRICING OF BANK LOANS: A GLOBAL PERSPECTIVE

Our earlier framework discussed in section 5.2 suggests that loan pricing is a function of borrower characteristics, loan characteristics, information costs and country effects. Borrowers obviously take these pricing differences into account when choosing between domestic and foreign lenders. In a local setting, recent work by Degryse and Ongena (2005) highlights the various ways in which distance, transaction and monitoring costs, and competition affect loan pricing. Focusing on a dataset of 15 000 bank loans from a large Belgian bank, they find that there is a negative correlation between distance and loan pricing, and a positive correlation between loan pricing and the firm's distance to competing banks. They conclude that borrower-borne transportation costs enable lenders to price-discriminate on the basis of distance.

In a more global context, a number of recent papers have tested for cross-country differences in loan pricing. Building on the growing literature related to law, finance and development (e.g., La Porta et al., 1997), Bae and Goyal (2003) find banks charge higher loan spreads in countries where property rights are weaker. Advancing this research, Qian and Strahan (2005) investigate the interaction of loan pricing and contractual terms in nearly 60 countries. Consistent with the law and finance framework, they find that differences in the legal and institutional environment influence the pricing of bank loans and the contractual terms of bank loans. Interestingly, after controlling for contractual terms, they argue that the legal and institutional environment only has a limited effect on loan pricing. They contend that 'Coasian bargaining' enables participants to impose contractual terms that mitigate the costs of a weak legal and institutional environment.

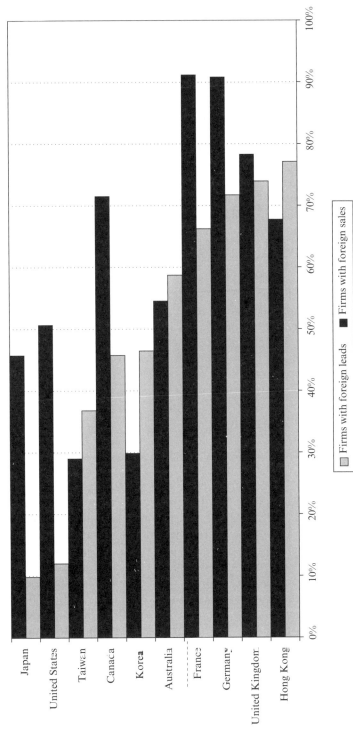

Figure 5.1 Percentage of firms that use foreign lead lenders to arrange loan syndicates

In a similar vein, Hao et al. (2005) examine the extent to which cross-country differences in bank regulation and supervision affect the pricing of both domestic and foreign loans. Looking at a sample of firms in 49 countries, they find that loan prices are influenced by both the level of banking concentration within the borrowing firm's country and the degree of 'banking–commerce integration'. This measure relates to whether or not banks in that country are able to own non-financial firms and/or whether non-financial firms are able to own banks. They find that domestic lenders charge lower rates in countries with a high degree of integration, but they find that this pricing advantage disappears in countries with a high degree of banking concentration (measured by the percentage of banking assets and deposits held by the top five banks in that country).

The previously discussed research recognizes that even if the market is perfectly integrated, firms may be required to pay differing amounts for loans as a result of country risks. Our chapter differs from this research by examining loan pricing in five relatively homogeneous nations. The countries we examine (Canada, France, Germany, the United Kingdom and the United States) are all democratic, first-world, developed nations. Further, the property rights index for each of the five countries falls within 10 percent of the highest possible property rights index assembled by Bae and Goyal (2003) (based on La Porta et al., 1998). All of the countries are in the top 20 percent of nations ranked by economic freedom according to the Heritage Foundation's 2000 Index of Economic Freedom (the property rights measure used by Qian and Strahan, 2005). Finally, of the 49 countries evaluated by Hao et al. (2005), Germany, the US and the UK rank lowest (in that order) for the degree of banking concentration. France ranks near the middle and Canada is among the countries with a high degree of banking concentration. To control for this variation, we include country dummies and run separate pricing regressions for Europe and North America. As a robustness test, we also estimate pricing models for each country.[15]

5.4.1 Syndicated Loan Pricing Analysis

The loan pricing analysis requires data adjustments and additional data. In particular, loan pricing is measured by the all-in spread of a drawn loan and differs by facility, not at the package level. Additionally, factors such as loan type and amount differ by facility, both of which affect pricing. We therefore conduct our loan pricing analysis at the individual facility level.[16] There are three costs associated with syndicating a loan. Arranging banks charge a one-time upfront fee for coordinating and managing the loan. Additionally, arranging banks charge an annual due diligence fee. The main cost comes in the form of the coupon payment, which is generally measured as an amount over LIBOR (London Interbank Offered Rate). The measure of loan price used, the all-in spread, consists of the coupon spread plus the annual fee. Unfortunately, pricing information is not available for the full matched sample of all countries. Requiring the all-in spread reduces the sample size and restricts the sample to loans made from banks in Europe and North America. Finally, for the smaller set of firms that have loan prices available, we collect bond rating information from Mergent's Fixed Investment Securities Database (FISD). Both Worldscope and FISD contain CUSIPs for many of the US firms. For US firms without CUSIPs and firms located internationally, we match the datasets using two criteria. Both the nation of incorporation and company name must be identical for firms to be considered a match.

Use of bond rating and bond rating migration closely follows Carey and Nini (2007). The most recent bond rating issued by either Moody's or S&P (Standard & Poor's) preceding the loan announcement and up to 30 days after the loan agreement is used as the bond rating prior to loan announcement. If both are provided, we use the lower of the two ratings. The rating following the loan announcement by up to one year is included in the specification as the change (migration) from the pre-loan rating. The final set of firms in the smaller 'pricing' dataset includes firms that are known to be unrated (by an indicator variable from the DealScan database) and rated firms for which we have bond rating information.

We begin our analysis by examining the conditional pricing of syndicated loans. Table 5.2 provides results from a series of ordinary least squares (OLS) regressions where the dependent variable is the all-in spread of drawn loans. In the first column, we control for the size of the facility, the borrower's credit rating, changes in the rating in the year following the loan origination date, the purpose of the loan, and year dummies. Further, we group the loans into three categories: type 1 includes term loans, type 2 includes lines of credit, and type 3 is all other types of loans.[17] We also include a dummy variable that indicates whether the deal includes a European lead bank. In the first two columns (1A–1B), we use presence of a European lead bank as our proxy for syndication in the European market. Consistent with Carey and Nini's (2007) 'European pricing puzzle', we find that after controlling for loan and borrower characteristics, deals with a European lead are significantly cheaper by 40.35 basis points. Carey and Nini (2007) surmise that the price differential is maintained because there remains a significant home bias where borrowers are reluctant (or perhaps unable) to borrow from foreign banks.

The second column of Table 5.2 (1B) excludes information regarding the specific bond ratings and instead breaks the firms into three credit categories: investment grade (AAA to BBB-), junk (BB+ to B-) and unrated. In this specification, we depart from the Carey and Nini (2007) framework and include the firm, lender and loan characteristics. As expected, we find that junk and unrated borrowers pay higher rates than investment-grade borrowers. We also find that larger firms and more profitable firms (as measured by ROA, return on assets) have lower spreads. Looking at the deal characteristics, we find a positive relation between spreads and syndicate size. Firms with foreign assets have lower spreads. In contrast, we find that firms that are foreign listed have higher spreads. Most notably, we find that even after controlling for these additional firm characteristics, the Carey–Nini 'puzzle' remains: deals with a European lead bank are still significantly cheaper by 32.16 basis points.

To explore further the source of this discount, we make a distinction between domestic European firms which borrow from a European lead bank, and foreign firms which borrow from a European lead bank. These results are presented in the next two columns of Table 5.2 (2A–2B). These results show that the benefits of borrowing from a European lead extend only to European borrowers. The last two columns of Table 5.2 (3A–3B) include a dummy variable that indicates whether the borrower is headquartered in a European country. Carey and Nini (2007) explain that because firms are most likely to syndicate loans in their home nation, this also represents a good proxy for the market of syndication. Including indicators both for the presence of a European lead and for the firm having its headquarters in Europe indicates that the benefits do not

Table 5.2 Influences on loan pricing (1998–2004)

	1A	1B	2A	2B	3A	3B
European Lead	−40.35 (0.000)***		3.86 (0.457)	0.03 (0.995)	−0.97 (0.838)	−6.41 (0.183)
Domestic European Lead		−32.16 (0.000)***				
European Company			−79.61 (0.000)***	−63.99 (0.000)***	−73.38 (0.000)***	−55.10 (0.000)***
Rated AAA to A+	−124.60 (0.000)***		−129.70 (0.000)***		−129.80 (0.000)***	
Rated A	−124.18 (0.000)***		−128.46 (0.000)***		−128.45 (0.000)***	
Rated A−	−120.96 (0.000)***		−126.04 (0.000)***		−126.34 (0.000)***	
Rated BBB+	−121.49 (0.000)***		−126.03 (0.000)***		−126.53 (0.000)***	
Rated BBB	−102.10 (0.000)***		−108.10 (0.000)***		−108.31 (0.000)***	
Rated BBB−	−77.31 (0.000)***		−80.89 (0.000)***		−80.91 (0.000)***	
Rated BB+	−50.76 (0.000)***		−57.47 (0.000)***		−57.32 (0.000)***	
Rated BB	−38.89 (0.000)***		−45.03 (0.000)***		−45.28 (0.000)***	
Rated BB−	−5.94 (0.432)		−10.60 (0.159)		−11.25 (0.135)	
Rated B+	−5.43 (0.389)		−8.19 (0.191)		−8.61 (0.169)	
Rating Improves 1 tick	18.22 (0.032)***		14.28 (0.090)***		13.93 (0.098)***	
Rating Improves 2 or 3	27.70 (0.022)***		20.65 (0.086)***		20.50 (0.088)***	
Rating Improves 4 ticks	−7.18 (0.712)		−8.64 (0.655)		8.96 (0.643)	
Rating Worsens 1 tick	18.17 (0.032)***		13.68 (0.104)		13.69 (0.104)	
Rating Worsens 2 or 3	38.31 (0.000)***		37.13 (0.000)***		36.70 (0.000)***	
Rating Worsens 4 ticks	103.15 (0.000)***		103.45 (0.000)***		102.45 (0.000)***	
Unrated	−33.50 (0.000)***	55.78 (0.000)***	−31.57 (0.000)***	59.06 (0.000)***	−30.54 (0.000)***	60.44 (0.000)
Junk		92.77 (0.000)***		93.23 (0.000)***		93.76 (0.000)***
Ln(Assets)		−11.83 (0.000)***		−12.46 (0.000)***		−11.89 (0.000)
Foreign Assets/Assets		−13.21 (0.050)***		−13.37 (0.046)***		−8.40 (0.211)***
Number of Leads		2.63 (0.104)		6.04 (0.000)***		5.83 (0.000)***

Foreign Listed		33.77 (0.000)***		34.30 (0.000)***		34.46 (0.000)***
Market-to-Book		−2.42 (0.038)***		−2.51 (0.000)***		−2.48 (0.000)***
Intangibles/Assets		−4.49 (0.437)		0.05 (0.993)		0.16 (0.977)***
Return on Assets		−65.61 (0.000)***		−65.88 (0.000)***		−65.87 (0.000)***
Debt Ratio		88.06 (0.000)***		85.63 (0.000)***		86.04 (0.000)
Ln(Facility Amount)	−27.70 (0.000)***	−20.99 (0.000)***	−26.42 (0.000)***	−20.08 (0.000)***	−26.06 (0.000)***	−20.41 (0.000)
Purpose 1	8.93 (0.028)***	8.57 (0.038)***	12.20 (0.003)***	10.44 (0.011)***	11.73 (0.004)***	10.06 (0.015)
Purpose 2	−2.45 (0.626)	−6.24 (0.213)	−1.52 (0.760)***	−5.70 (0.254)	−1.50 (0.764)	−5.62 (0.260)
Purpose 3	9.58 (0.003)***	8.97 (0.005)***	9.84 (0.002)***	9.21 (0.004)***	10.61 (0.001)***	9.97 (0.002)***
Purpose 4	−11.05 (0.000)***	−11.49 (0.000)***	−8.55 (0.004)***	−10.07 (0.001)***	−8.51 (0.004)***	−10.10 (0.001)**
Term Loan	−17.80 (0.034)***	−10.64 (0.196)	−19.74 (0.018)***	−11.63 (0.156)	−19.03 (0.022)***	−10.91 (0.183)
Line of Credit	−88.93 (0.000)***	−80.64 (0.000)***	−89.17 (0.000)***	−80.51 (0.000)***	−89.53 (0.000)***	−80.51 (0.000)***
Year = 98	−25.68 (0.000)***	−28.51 (0.000)***	−28.45 (0.000)***	−31.20 (0.000)***	−28.85 (0.000)***	−31.17 (0.000)***
Year = 99	−5.05 (0.212)	−4.82 (0.239)	−5.62 (0.162)	−5.38 (0.187)	−6.52 (0.104)	−5.97 (0.143)
Year = 01	8.93 (0.026)***	8.73 (0.029)***	9.40 (0.018)***	8.51 (0.032)***	8.94 (0.024)***	8.11 (0.042)***
Year = 02	28.98 (0.000)***	28.51 (0.000)***	28.94 (0.000)***	27.50 (0.000)***	28.29 (0.000)***	26.93 (0.000)***
Year = 03	35.86 (0.000)***	40.08 (0.000)***	35.34 (0.000)***	38.42 (0.000)***	34.71 (0.000)***	37.79 (0.000)
Year = 04	22.37 (0.000)***	27.56 (0.000)***	20.35 (0.000)***	24.40 (0.000)***	19.74 (0.000)***	24.06 (0.000)**
Intercept	433.71 (0.000)***	340.85 (0.000)***	428.45 (0.000)***	335.15 (0.000)***	427.54 (0.000)***	332.07 (0.000)***
Number of Obs.	10325	9699	10325	9699	10325	9699
R^2	0.39	0.42	0.39	0.43	0.39	0.43

Note: This table provides estimates from OLS regressions where the dependent variable is the all-in spread of a drawn loan. Analysis is done at the individual loan (facility) level. European Lead is an indicator that equals one if there at least one European lead present. Rating migrations represent the change in the firm's debt rating in the one year after the loan is issued. Both Assets and Facility Amounts represent the natural log of the total value. Foreign Assets are expressed as a ratio to total assets. Junk and Unrated are indicators equal to one if the firm's debt is rated below B+ or if the firm does not have a rating respectively. Market-to-Book is the firm's total assets minus total common equity plus market capitalization all divided by total assets. Return on Assets (ROA) is defined as net income divided by total assets. The number of leads is truncated to 5 for deals with more than 5 leads. Purpose indicators are included for each of the following categories: 1 = Takeovers and recapitalizations, 2 = Loans which finance ships, aircraft and special purpose vehicles, 3 = Project finance, 4 = Commercial paper backups, 5 = General corporate purpose (omitted category). P-values are reported below the coefficients in parentheses. *, **, *** indicate statistical significance at the 10%, 5% and 1% levels, respectively.

necessarily stem from borrowing from a European bank as much as from being from a European country.

5.4.2   A Closer Look at the Connection between Global Presence and Loan Pricing

As discussed in the previous subsection, European firms that use European lenders pay less for a loan relative to the price paid by an equivalent North American firm. In this subsection, we investigate if a European presence can help to overcome the barriers created by either information or legal structures to reduce the cost of loans. In other words, can North American firms take advantage of the European discount if they have a European presence?

Table 5.3 looks at loan pricing for the North American firms in our sample. Once again, we control for firm and loan characteristics, but we also take into account whether the borrower uses a European lender and the extent to which the firm has any European assets. The first two columns report regression results for the subsamples of firms without and with European assets, respectively. The coefficients on the firm and loan characteristic variables are generally as expected. Firms with lower bond ratings, lower levels of profitability, lower market-to-book ratios and higher debt ratios tend to pay more for loans. Loan prices tend to be smaller for larger loans and for lines of credit. We also observe a general increase in loan prices over time – this may be due to a combination of factors including interest rate trends at the macroeconomic level.

Most notably, we find that that the effects of having a European lender depend critically on whether the firm has any reported European assets. North American firms with no European assets pay a significant premium (just less than 16 basis points) when using a European lender. By contrast, North American firms that have European assets realize a significant discount (around 28 basis points) when using a European lender. This result suggests that North American firms can capture the 'European discount' as long as they have significant assets (or sales) in Europe. Thus, it appears that global assets may help reduce the information costs associated with borrowing in distant or foreign markets.

We might also expect that information costs may vary between small and large firms. To consider this issue, we also break the sample of North American firms into two other subcategories: large firms with assets above $15 billion and small firms with assets below $15 billion. The regression results for these subsamples are reported in columns 3 and 4 of Table 5.3. Once again, we find a significant difference in the loan pricing of European loans: small firms pay a small premium (significant at the 10 percent level) when using a European bank, whereas large firms receive the 'European discount' (of about 24 basis points).

Columns 5 and 6 present similar regression results that take both the size of the firm and its proportion of European assets jointly into account. We continue to observe that small firms with no European assets continue to pay a premium when using a European lender, but interestingly we find that even for small firms this premium becomes a discount when the firm has a significant portion of its assets (more than 25 percent) in Europe. We continue to observe an overall European discount for larger firms, and the discount appears to become larger as the firm holds a larger proportion of European assets. Columns 7 and 8 present similar results, but the key difference here is that instead of testing for the effects of having any European lead in the syndicate, we consider the effects of having only European leads in the syndicate. The results are robust to this alternative specification.

Overall, the results in Table 5.3 provide further support for the argument that European banks operate in a more competitive environment, but that information costs prevent some firms (small firms with limited European assets) from taking full advantage of the European discount.

Table 5.4 presents similar results from the perspective of European firms. Here we consider the impact of having a North American lender as part of the syndicate. Looking at the first two columns of Table 5.4, we see that when looking at the subsample of European firms without and with North American assets, there is no systematic effect of having a North American lender in the syndicate. However, when we break the sample into small and large firms, some important differences once again emerge. Small firms using a North American lead pay a premium, whereas large firms receive a discount. Most notably, the premium that small European firms pay for having a North American lender increases the higher its proportion of North American assets. This result suggests that European firms that hold fewer European assets begin to lose their European discount when they hold more foreign assets. One explanation for this result is that when analyzing information costs, lenders are more concerned with where your assets are than where the firm is headquartered. Moreover, the results in Table 5.4 provide some additional support to the argument that the lending market in Europe is more competitive and/or faces lower regulatory costs.

In our final set of tests, we further distinguish between term loans and lines of credit since the existing literature suggests that lines of credit are more relationship-based and have a higher information component. These results are reported in Table 5.5.

In this table, we see some interesting differences between term loans and lines of credit and between European and North American firms and banks. The first four columns of Table 5.5 focus on North American firms. We find that North American borrowers realize slightly more than a 40 basis point discount when they use a European lead for a term loan, but pay slightly more than a 25 basis point premium when they use a European lead on a line of credit. In both cases, we find that North American firms with more than 25 percent of their assets in Europe receive the largest benefits from having a European lender – although the discount remains larger for term loans. In the last four columns we see the effects for European firms of using a North American lender. We find that having a North American lender has no effect on the pricing of term loans to European firms, but that it slightly increases the price of a line of credit. This effect is more pronounced for the European firms that use a North American bank, even though they have no North American assets. Once again, these results confirm that while there may be some advantages to using a European lender, the European discount only seems to hold for borrowers with relatively low information costs.

5.5   CONCLUSIONS

We examine the pricing of loans for a large number of firms across countries and provide insights into the relative importance of information costs, cross-country differences

Table 5.3   *Effect of foreign leads and assets on pricing of loans to North American firms (1998–2004)*

	No European assets	With European assets	Small firms
European Lead Present	15.91 (0.016) **	−28.34 (0.004) ***	11.11 (0.079) *
No Eur. Assets * EL any			
1% – 25% Eur. Assets * EL any			
>25% Eur. Assets * EL any			
No Eur. Assets * EL only			
1% – 25% Eur. Assets * EL only			
>25% Eur. Assets * EL only			
Foreign Assets / Assets	4.44 (0.707)	−58.41 (0.000) ***	−6.74 (0.403)
Ln(Assets)	5.22 (0.032) **	7.75 (0.043) **	9.26 (0.000) ***
Number of Leads	−15.45 (0.000) ***	−8.76 (0.000) ***	−17.83 (0.000) ***
Junk	88.56 (0.000) ***	99.15 (0.000) ***	101.31 (0.000) ***
Unrated	51.27 (0.000) ***	71.75 (0.000) ***	63.53 (0.000) ***
Foreign Listed	41.08 (0.000) ***	20.54 (0.005) ***	41.33 (0.000) ***
Ln(Facility Amount)	−18.90 (0.000) ***	−22.08 (0.000) ***	−18.39 (0.000) ***
Market-to-Book	−1.79 (0.000) ***	−11.47 (0.000) ***	−2.54 (0.000) ***
Intangibles / Assets	2.21 (0.741)	−37.11 (0.015) **	2.66 (0.679)
ROA	−54.96 (0.000) ***	−101.16 (0.000) ***	−59.12 (0.000) ***
Debt Ratio	76.84 (0.000) ***	151.80 (0.000) ***	86.24 (0.000) ***
purpose 1	6.11 (0.222)	31.24 (0.001) ***	13.86 (0.003) ***
purpose 2	−6.42 (0.278)	−1.79 (0.880)	−7.01 (0.204)
purpose 3	−0.52 (0.890)	22.46 (0.002) ***	2.18 (0.532)
purpose 4	−11.65 (0.001) ***	−7.00 (0.285)	−9.73 (0.004) ***
Term Loan	−1.10 (0.915)	−35.90 (0.035) **	−20.78 (0.034) **
Line of Credit	−69.80 (0.000) ***	−113.30 (0.000) ***	−87.29 (0.000) ***
year = 98	−30.86 (0.000) ***	−43.68 (0.000) ***	−36.07 (0.000) ***
year = 99	−4.50 (0.355)	−17.03 (0.068) *	−6.40 (0.159)
year = 01	9.45 (0.051) *	11.56 (0.181)	11.11 (0.014) **
year = 02	24.14 (0.000) ***	36.02 (0.000) ***	24.40 (0.000) ***
year = 03	38.97 (0.000) ***	31.58 (0.001) ***	37.85 (0.000) ***
year = 04	26.06 (0.000) ***	19.61 (0.050) **	22.21 (0.000) ***
Intercept	349.36 (0.000) ***	349.93 (0.000) ***	360.03 (0.000) ***
Number of Obs.	6969	1967	7986
R^2	0.41	0.48	0.40

Note: The dependent variable in each OLS regression is the all-in spread on outstanding loan balances. Analysis is done at the individual loan (facility) level. Small firms have less than $15 billion in assets. Large firms have more than $15 billion in assets. European Lead (EL) *only* is an indicator that equals one if there are only European leads used. European Lead (EL) *any* is an indicator that equals one if there is at least one European lead present. EL only and EL any are interacted with European asset indicators. Assets and Facility Amount represent the natural log of the total value. Junk and Unrated are indicators equal to one if the firm's debt is rated below B+ or if the firm does not have a rating respectively. The omitted category is firms with investment grade ratings. Foreign Listed is an indicator for whether the firm's stock is listed on a foreign exchange. Market-to-Book is the firm's total assets minus total common equity plus market capitalization all divided by total assets. Return on Assets (ROA) is defined as net income divided by total assets. The number of leads is truncated to 5 for deals with more than 5 leads. Purpose is an indicator that the deal is from one of 5 categories. P-values are reported in parentheses. *, **, *** indicate statistical significance at the 10%, 5% and 1% levels, respectively.

Large firms	Small firms	Large firms	Small firms	Large firms
−24.31 (0.018) **				
	17.84 (0.017) **	−14.13 (0.251)		
	12.62 (0.331)	−46.08 (0.003) ***		
	−48.80 (0.019) **	−24.41 (0.590)		
			14.90 (0.131)	−18.60 (0.297)
			16.28 (0.307)	−111.95 (0.000) ***
			−66.38 (0.01) **	−38.64 (0.69)
−58.99 (0.004) ***				
−1.21 (0.763)	9.10 (0.000) ***	−0.64 (0.878)	9.84 (0.000) ***	−3.83 (0.321)
16.74 (0.002) ***	−17.90 (0.000) ***	18.84 (0.000) ***	−17.81 (0.000) ***	19.94 (0.000) ***
91.44 (0.000) ***	101.14 (0.000) ***	91.57 (0.000) ***	101.46 (0.000) ***	90.02 (0.000) ***
52.67 (0.000) ***	63.23 (0.000) ***	49.76 (0.000) ***	63.52 (0.000) ***	50.33 (0.000) ***
−20.42 (0.037) **	41.35 (0.000) ***	−24.82 (0.01) ***	41.14 (0.000) ***	−24.22 (0.011) **
−9.02 (0.003) ***	−18.46 (0.000) ***	−8.66 (0.005) ***	−18.51 (0.000) ***	−9.74 (0.002) ***
−0.30 (0.936)	−2.56 (0.000) ***	−2.91 (0.422)	−2.56 (0.000) ***	−3.01 (0.403)
−60.39 (0.002) ***	2.47 (0.701)	−60.54 (0.002) ***	2.19 (0.733)	−57.90 (0.003) ***
−61.04 (0.025) **	−59.08 (0.000) ***	−61.56 (0.024) **	−59.13 (0.000) ***	−63.08 (0.02) **
64.64 (0.007) ***	86.63 (0.000) ***	54.92 (0.020) **	86.68 (0.000) ***	56.88 (0.015) **
0.00 (1.000)	13.80 (0.003) ***	−2.38 (0.870)	13.63 (0.003) ***	−5.00 (0.73)
−5.22 (0.788)	−6.88 (0.212)	−5.10 (0.793)	−6.85 (0.215)	−15.33 (0.431)
47.70 (0.000) ***	1.94 (0.577)	47.11 (0.000) ***	1.73 (0.619)	47.89 (0.000) ***
−16.72 (0.039) **	−9.83 (0.004) ***	−18.76 (0.021) **	−10.02 (0.003) ***	−19.52 (0.015) **
47.44 (0.017) **	−20.43 (0.037) **	51.32 (0.010) **	−20.23 (0.038) **	49.04 (0.013) **
−75.03 (0.000) ***	−86.88 (0.000) ***	−73.38 (0.000) ***	−86.92 (0.000) ***	−74.83 (0.000) ***
−25.73 (0.071) *	−36.08 (0.000) ***	−26.63 (0.063) *	−35.99 (0.000) ***	−27.28 (0.056) *
−12.09 (0.369)	−6.38 (0.160)	−13.26 (0.328)	−6.47 (0.154)	−5.98 (0.66)
2.83 (0.812)	11.28 (0.012) **	2.34 (0.844)	11.31 (0.012) **	2.71 (0.819)
47.34 (0.000) ***	24.71 (0.000) ***	44.83 (0.000) ***	24.81 (0.000) ***	45.32 (0.000) ***
26.71 (0.022) **	37.88 (0.000) ***	24.47 (0.036) **	38.02 (0.000) ***	21.99 (0.058) *
32.16 (0.007) ***	22.36 (0.000) ***	29.89 (0.012) **	22.41 (0.000) ***	28.02 (0.017) **
2.74 (0.965)	360.27 (0.000)***	−19.02 (0.762)	359.11 (0.000) ***	−17.38 (0.78)
950	7986	950	7986	950
0.48	0.40	0.48	0.40	0.48

in legal and regulatory costs, and cross-country competition in bank lending. Our results suggest that there is considerable international segmentation in the syndicated loan market. We find that loan pricing varies across countries and depends crucially on the borrower's global presence, nationality, size and loan type. We find that loans to European firms are significantly cheaper than loans to North American firms by approximately 40 basis points in our sample. However, we further find that this discount varies considerably depending on the amount of sales and assets the firm has in Europe, the size of the borrower, and the type of loan. In this respect, our results indicate that the syndicated loan market is not internationally integrated, and that information costs and legal and regulatory costs have an important influence on where a firm borrows and the price that it pays.

Table 5.4   *Effect of foreign leads and assets on pricing of loans to European firms (1998–2004)*

	No N. Amer. assets	With N. Amer. assets	Small firms
North American Lead	2.99 (0.651)	16.91 (0.288)	22.47 (0.000) ***
No N. Amer. Assets * NAL any			
1% – 25% N. Amer. Assets * NAL any			
>25% N. Amer. Assets * NAL any			
No N. Amer. Assets * NAL only			
1% – 25% N. Amer. Assets * NAL only			
>25% N. Amer. Assets * NAL only			
Foreign Assets/Assets	2.20 (0.883)	2.10 (0.950)	42.70 (0.000) ***
Ln(Assets)	−4.02 (0.041) **	0.28 (0.964)	−1.32 (0.625)
Number of Leads	2.49 (0.257)	−15.03 (0.014) **	−8.97 (0.000) ***
Junk	52.96 (0.002) ***	57.10 (0.208)	50.08 (0.022) **
Unrated	56.26 (0.000) ***	29.82 (0.385)	52.49 (0.010) **
Foreign Listed	−3.23 (0.70)	−25.94 (0.142)	−27.76 (0.001) ***
Ln(Facility Amount)	−10.64 (0.000) ***	−14.31 (0.050) **	−11.51 (0.000) ***
Market-to-Book	0.61 (0.761)	2.59 (0.786)	−0.02 (0.991)
Intangibles/Assets	34.15 (0.021) **	−63.05 (0.141)	−14.18 (0.272)
ROA	−178.17 (0.000) ***	−244.21(0.019) **	−117.10 (0.000) ***
Debt Ratio	73.08 (0.000) ***	53.86 (0.342)	115.32 (0.000) ***
purpose 1	25.85 (0.004)***	43.01 (0.097) *	9.68 (0.264)
purpose 2	24.65 (0.037) **	18.91 (0.572)	28.23 (0.009) ***
purpose 3	94.03 (0.000) ***	131.56 (0.000) ***	102.58 (0.000) ***
purpose 4	13.97 (0.072) *	8.31 (0.676)	6.93 (0.350)
Term Loan	12.86 (0.400)	−23.31 (0.560)	−34.90 (0.044) **
Line of Credit	−14.46 (0.329)	−96.62 (0.014) **	−67.19 (0.000) ***
year = 98	−19.92 (0.106)	14.56 (0.630)	−19.47 (0.058) *
year = 99	−7.21 (0.489)	−5.00 (0.829)	3.43 (0.693)
year = 01	5.40 (0.540)	33.92 (0.222)	28.05 (0.001) ***
year = 02	26.19 (0.009) ***	26.60 (0.271)	21.54 (0.014) **
year = 03	48.67 (0.000) ***	84.91 (0.001) ***	33.64 (0.000) ***
year = 04	16.31 (0.125)	112.02 (0.000) ***	46.42 (0.000) ***
Intercept	76.89 (0.008) ***	209.33 (0.012) **	132.89 (0.000) ***
Number of Obs.	510	218	533
R²	0.49	0.54	0.56

Note: The dependent variable in each OLS regression is the all-in spread on outstanding loan balances. Analysis is done at the individual loan (facility) level. Small firms have less than $15 billion in assets. Large firms have more than $15 billion in assets. North American Lead (NAL) *only* is an indicator that equals one if there are only North American leads used. North American Lead (NAL) *any* is an indicator that equals one if there is at least one North American lead present. NAL only and NAL any are interacted with European asset indicators. Assets and Facility Amount represents the natural log of the total value. Junk and Unrated are indicators equal to one if the firm's debt is rated below B+ or if the firm does not have a rating respectively. The omitted category is firms with investment grade ratings. Foreign Listed is an indicator for whether the firm's stock is listed on a foreign exchange. Market-to-Book is the firm's total assets minus total common equity plus market capitalization all divided by total assets. Return on Assets (ROA) is defined as net income divided by total assets. The number of leads is truncated to 5 for deals with more than 5 leads. Purpose is an indicator that the deal is from one of 5 categories. P-values are reported in parentheses. *, **, *** indicate statistical significance at the 10%, 5% and 1% levels, respectively.

Large firms	Small firms	Large firms	Small firms	Large firms
−48.42 (0.009) ***				
	15.20 (0.030) **	−48.29 (0.015) **		
	30.39 (0.000) ***	−41.68 (0.096) *		
	54.83 (0.000) ***	−95.09 (0.021) **		
			−7.49 (0.536)	−100.79 (0.001) ***
			42.87 (0.001) ***	−5.91 (0.874)
			66.89 (0.000) ***	
9.28 (0.783)				
−9.59 (0.426)	−2.49 (0.370)	−11.06 (0.376)	−4.54 (0.119)	−10.82 (0.361)
7.18 (0.199)	−8.91 (0.000) ***	7.93 (0.157)	−4.09 (0.062) *	0.56 (0.92)
62.33 (0.061) *	40.89 (0.063) *	62.40 (0.068) *	38.71 (0.08) *	62.48 (0.054) *
56.46 (0.045) **	44.92 (0.029) **	62.31 (0.03) **	38.09 (0.065) *	66.46 (0.018) **
9.50 (0.624)	−18.63 (0.025) **	12.87 (0.507)	−20.22 (0.014) **	5.33 (0.78)
−16.27 (0.023) **	−9.87 (0.000) ***	−15.29 (0.034) **	−7.21 (0.012) **	−17.64 (0.013) **
−19.16 (0.318)	1.08 (0.541)	−19.94 (0.297)	0.67 (0.703)	−8.77 (0.653)
55.83 (0.343)	−21.17 (0.108)	53.40 (0.363)	−13.89 (0.286)	83.40 (0.149)
−341.51 (0.014) **	−136.08 (0.000) ***	−336.34 (0.017) **	−140.98 (0.000) ***	−294.60 (0.026) **
−25.62 (0.641)	108.17 (0.000) ***	−30.65 (0.550)	111.13 (0.000) ***	−51.84 (0.311)
35.79 (0.201)	11.87 (0.173)	38.60 (0.168)	13.00 (0.135)	33.31 (0.229)
10.33 (0.808)	30.36 (0.005) ***	17.86 (0.662)	26.99 (0.013) **	45.24 (0.271)
135.11 (0.000) ***	101.75 (0.000) ***	136.06 (0.000) ***	106.29 (0.000) ***	138.46 (0.000) ***
31.89 (0.125)	6.95 (0.348)	35.20 (0.091) *	7.68 (0.302)	20.11 (0.316)
55.02 (0.102)	−31.24 (0.071) *	56.04 (0.095) *	−39.31 (0.024) **	57.33 (0.085) *
−29.40 (0.334)	−61.94 (0.000) ***	−26.82 (0.377)	−68.48 (0.000) ***	−24.45 (0.415)
−4.57 (0.919)	−20.96 (0.042) **	−6.04 (0.892)	−16.80 (0.102)	−10.79 (0.807)
−19.85 (0.515)	2.73 (0.756)	−21.94 (0.465)	3.21 (0.713)	−45.25 (0.148)
−17.57 (0.540)	27.03 (0.001) ***	−12.82 (0.656)	26.52 (0.002) ***	−44.05 (0.125)
−25.96 (0.428)	21.95 (0.013) **	−25.40 (0.442)	27.75 (0.002) ***	−30.93 (0.341)
56.02 (0.039) **	36.93 (0.000) ***	57.96 (0.033) **	35.99 (0.000) ***	54.10 (0.044) **
38.65 (0.198)	48.87 (0.000) ***	38.28 (0.201)	46.77 (0.000) ***	37.67 (0.204)
246.11 (0.072) *	141.33 (0.000) ***	248.21 (0.081) *	147.48 (0.000) ***	252.87 (0.061) *
198	533	198	533	198
0.49	0.57	0.49	0.56	0.50

Table 5.5   Effect of foreign leads and assets on pricing of term loans and lines of credit (1998–2004)

	North American firms		
	Term loans	Term loans	Lines of credit
European Lead	−40.10 (0.000)***		25.67 (0.000)***
N. American Lead			
No European Assets * EL		−24.42 (0.062)*	
1% – 25% Eur Assets * EL		−64.60 (0.000)***	
>25% Eur Assets * EL		−78.17 (0.048)**	
No N. Amer. Assets * NAL			
1% – 25% N. Amer. Assets * NAL			
>25% N. Amer. Assets * NAL			
Ln(Assets)	−4.19 (0.091)*	−3.68 (0.142)	−16.87 (0.000)***
Number of Leads	2.88 (0.544)	3.25 (0.494)	7.48 (0.000)***
Junk	122.96 (0.000)***	122.97 (0.000)***	79.10 (0.000)***
Unrated	103.68 (0.000)***	104.20 (0.000)***	38.33 (0.000)***
Foreign Listed	55.20 (0.000)***	56.98 (0.000)***	27.51 (0.000)***
Ln(Facility Amount)	−10.14 (0.000)***	−10.53 (0.000)***	−23.06 (0.000)***
Market-to-Book	−3.28 (0.002)***	−3.40 (0.002)***	−1.73 (0.000)***
Intangibles / Assets	−59.73 (0.000)***	−60.63 (0.000)***	17.68 (0.003)***
ROA	−56.20 (0.000)***	−55.91 (0.000)***	−63.68 (0.000)***
Debt Ratio	79.30 (0.000)***	80.59 (0.000)***	90.97 (0.000)***
purpose 1	24.19 (0.013)**	24.77 (0.011)**	11.91 (0.011)**
purpose 2	−5.20 (0.633)	−4.61 (0.671)	2.52 (0.666)
purpose 3	26.08 (0.003)***	26.07 (0.003)***	−1.68 (0.594)
purpose 4	20.72 (0.021)**	20.78 (0.020)**	−15.70 (0.000)***
year = 98	−48.78 (0.000)***	−48.34 (0.000)***	−31.06 (0.000)***
year = 99	−24.70 (0.021)**	−24.14 (0.024)**	−1.84 (0.660)
year = 01	11.51 (0.299)	12.44 (0.262)	9.07 (0.024)**
year = 02	57.89 (0.000)***	58.77 (0.000)***	16.83 (0.000)***
year = 03	59.65 (0.000)***	60.19 (0.000)***	28.97 (0.000)***
year = 04	48.61 (0.000)***	48.71 (0.000)***	13.21 (0.004)***
Intercept	194.48 (0.000)***	190.83 (0.000)***	312.48 (0.000)***
Number of Obs.	2306	2306	6467
R^2	0.18	0.18	0.51

Note: The dependent variable in each OLS regression is the all-in spread on outstanding loan balances. Analysis is done at the individual loan (facility) level. European Lead (EL) only and North American Lead (NAL) only are indicators that equal one if there are only leads from the region used. European Lead any and North American Lead (NAL) any are indicators which equal one if there at least one lead from the region present. EL any, EL only, NAL any, and NAL only are interacted with European asset indicators. Assets and Facility Amount represent the natural log of the total value. Junk and Unrated are indicators equal to one if the firm's debt is rated below B+ or if the firm does not have a rating respectively. The omitted category is firms with investment grade ratings. Foreign Listed is an indicator for whether the firm's stock is listed on a foreign exchange. Market-to-Book is the firm's total assets minus total common equity plus market capitalization all divided by total assets. Return on Assets (ROA) is defined as net income divided by total assets. The number of leads is truncated to 5 for deals with more than 5 leads. Purpose is an indicator that the deal is from one of 5 categories. P-values are reported in parentheses. *, **, *** indicate statistical significance at the 10%, 5% and 1% levels, respectively.

North American firms	European firms			
Lines of credit	Term loans	Term loans	Lines of credit	Lines of credit
	0.06 (0.997)		11.94 (0.043)**	
29.57 (0.000)***				
38.17 (0.002)***				
−38.82 (0.050)**				
		−15.68 (0.368)		13.62 (0.044)**
		12.14 (0.638)		9.74 (0.223)
		17.64 (0.389)		10.15 (0.361)
−16.91 (0.000)***	11.46 (0.013)**	11.20 (0.015)**	−4.72 (0.019)**	−4.86 (0.017)**
7.62 (0.000)***	−6.03 (0.246)	−5.37 (0.311)	−2.06 (0.321)	−2.03 (0.331)
79.12 (0.000)***	73.75 (0.221)	63.93 (0.292)	33.90 (0.015)**	33.16 (0.019)**
38.42 (0.000)***	93.02 (0.105)	84.09 (0.145)	35.47 (0.004)***	35.23 (0.004)***
27.55 (0.000)***	3.18 (0.871)	3.80 (0.847)	−12.91 (0.081)*	−13.21 (0.076)*
−23.07 (0.000)***	−16.95 (0.006)***	−15.62 (0.012)**	−12.17 (0.000)***	−12.16 (0.000)***
−1.73 (0.000)***	−2.76 (0.674)	−1.26 (0.849)	−1.15 (0.561)	−1.29 (0.517)
17.72 (0.003)***	−32.36 (0.317)	−30.32 (0.349)	19.96 (0.158)	20.32 (0.154)
−63.57 (0.000)***	−36.19 (0.713)	−81.24 (0.433)	−169.85 (0.000)***	−168.05 (0.000)***
91.05 (0.000)***	95.23 (0.031)**	95.51 (0.030)**	58.59 (0.001)***	58.95 (0.001)***
11.80 (0.012)**	22.99 (0.329)	25.54 (0.280)	36.01 (0.000)***	36.01 (0.000)***
2.16 (0.711)	25.90 (0.315)	28.81 (0.265)	42.15 (0.001)***	42.03 (0.001)***
−1.94 (0.537)	154.57 (0.000)***	152.64 (0.000)***	75.84 (0.000)***	76.46 (0.000)***
−15.75 (0.000)***	50.58 (0.019)**	46.07 (0.034)**	7.02 (0.318)	7.19 (0.31)
−31.10 (0.000)***	−3.37 (0.916)	−12.19 (0.709)	−30.17 (0.007)***	−30.38 (0.007)***
−1.73 (0.680)	17.90 (0.435)	9.00 (0.707)	−12.36 (0.165)	−11.98 (0.181)
9.21 (0.022)**	32.62 (0.101)	30.03 (0.133)	4.47 (0.624)	4.30 (0.639)
17.20 (0.000)***	34.45 (0.113)	27.52 (0.217)	16.13 (0.081)*	16.43 (0.077)*
28.94 (0.000)***	64.55 (0.002)***	61.59 (0.004)***	44.46 (0.000)***	44.58 (0.000)***
13.26 (0.004)***	103.97 (0.000)***	101.40 (0.000)***	26.04 (0.008)***	25.80 (0.009)***
312.54 (0.000)***	−31.15 (0.676)	−25.47 (0.732)	121.16 (0.000)***	122.29 (0.000)***
6467	237	237	470	470
0.51	0.44	0.44	0.40	0.40

NOTES

*   We thank Dave Brown, Mark Carey, Mark Flannery, Chris James and Jay Ritter for their helpful comments and suggestions on an earlier version of this chapter.

1. This distinction stems in large part because their study uses loans from Dealogic's Loanware database (which includes the market of syndication), whereas our study utilizes Reuters Loan Pricing Corporation's (LPC) DealScan database, which includes the borrower's and lender's nationality, but does not include the market of syndication.

2. The generally accepted definition of market integration is that identical items should carry identical prices in all segments of an integrated market. In the context of financial markets, integration refers to the yield dispersion of an asset in a given market. Stulz (1981) defines capital markets as being integrated if assets with perfectly correlated returns have the same price, regardless of the location in which they trade. An equivalent definition is that assets that carry identical risks should be priced to have the same expected returns.

3. For example, McBrady and Shill (2007) find that even in the absence of operating incentives, borrowers opportunistically issue foreign currency-denominated bonds.

4. Foreign listings are also a mechanism for enhancing access to external capital markets – see, for instance, Pagano et al. (2002) and Lins et al. (2001) – and they can be viewed as firm-level liberalizations. Bekaert and Harvey (2000) and Bekaert et al. (2002b) provide detailed empirical evidence on the impact of countrywide liberalizations.

5. An extensive literature documents a home bias in the equities market, though these studies do not necessarily imply mispricing. Physical distance influences a variety of investing activities including choice of assets held (French and Poterba, 1991), actively managed US mutual funds (Coval and Moskowitz, 1999), portfolio choices of Americans (Huberman, 2001) and portfolio choices of Finns (Grinblatt and Keloharju, 2001).

6. Along these lines, a series of recent global bank regulation surveys by Barth et al. (2004, 2006, 2008) show that despite recent attempts to increase the global coordination of banking regulation, there remain significant regulatory gaps across countries. Given this environment, it is reasonable to presume that cross-country differences in banking regulations may encourage the flow of bank capital from markets that are heavily regulated to those markets that are less regulated. Supporting this conjecture, Houston et al. (2011) find evidence that banks are more likely to transfer capital to those markets that face less stringent financial regulations.

7. Although DealScan data are available prior to 1998, we begin our sample in 1998 because DealScan data prior to 1998 are incomplete for many deals that originate in Europe. Carey and Nini (2007) compare Loanware and DealScan and find that DealScan has incomplete data for approximately 80 percent of loans originated in Europe prior to 1998. From 1998–2002, the datasets have a 90 percent overlap if very small loans are omitted.

8. We refer to Canada and the US as North America; France, Germany and the UK as Europe; and Australia, Hong Kong, Japan, South Korea and Taiwan as both Asia and Australasia.

9. Including the few mentioned here, there are 88 distinct lender roles used in the dataset.

10. The practice of assigning the issuance of a subsidiary to its parent company is also employed by Henderson et al. (2006).

11. The results are robust to using the country of the branch or subsidiary.

12. In Australia, bank subsidiaries have foreign ownership of over 50 percent of the equity, but the majority of foreign bank subsidiaries in Australia have 100 percent foreign ownership (Sturm and Williams, 2004). The Hong Kong Monetary Authority lists many banks incorporated internationally that are licensed to operate in Hong Kong (http://www.info.gov.hk/hkma/eng/bank/index.htm). This list was compared to the lead banks in the sample. Banks licensed in Hong Kong but incorporated elsewhere are considered headquartered in the nation in which they are incorporated.

13. Firm names must be identical after abbreviation and punctuation are accounted for.

14. Omitting observations with missing intangibles does not materially change our results, but it reduces the sample size.

15. The country-level results are not tabulated, but they are similar to the regional-level reported results.

16. Other papers that investigate pricing at the individual facility level include Carey et al. (1998), Carey and Nini (2007), Qian and Strahan (2005), Hao et al. (2005), Bae and Goyal (2003) and Sufi (2007).

17. We confirm that the distribution of loan types in each country does not skew the results. Term loans carry the highest spreads in both Europe and North America and comprise just over 17 percent and 21 percent of the samples, respectively; 364-day facilities (type 2 loans) are the cheapest of the loan facilities and comprise 17 percent of the North American sample and 18 percent of the European sample.

REFERENCES

Bae, K. and V.K. Goyal (2003), 'Property rights protection and bank loan pricing', Hong Kong University, Working Paper.

Barth, James, Gerard Caprio and Ross Levine (2004), 'Bank regulation and supervision: what works best?', *Journal of Financial Intermediation*, **13**, 205–248.

Barth, James R., Gerard Caprio and Ross Levine (2006), *Rethinking Bank Regulation: Till Angels Govern*, Cambridge: Cambridge University Press.

Barth, James R., Gerard Caprio and Ross Levine (2008), 'Bank regulations are changing: for better or worse?', World Bank Policy Research Working Paper 4646.

Bekaert, Geert and Campbell Harvey (1995), 'Time-varying world market integration', *Journal of Finance*, **50**, 403–444.

Bekaert, Geert and Campbell Harvey (2000), 'Foreign speculators and emerging equity markets', *Journal of Finance*, **55**, 565–613.

Bekaert, Geert, Campbell Harvey and Robin Lumsdaine (2002a), 'Dating the integration of world equity markets', *Journal of Financial Economics*, **65**, 203–247.

Bekaert, Geert, Campbell Harvey and Christian Lundblad (2002b), 'Does liberalization spur growth?', Duke and Columbia Universities, Working Paper.

Berger, A.N., Q. Dai, S. Ongena and D.C. Smith (2003), 'To what extent will the banking industry be globalized? A study of bank nationality and reach in 20 European nations', *Journal of Banking and Finance*, **27**, 383–415.

Berger, A. and G. Udell (1995), 'Relationship lending and lines of credit in small firm finance', *Journal of Business*, **68**, 351–382.

Bharath, S., S. Dahiya, A. Saunders and A. Srinivasan (2007), 'So what do I get? The bank's view of lending relationships', *Journal of Financial Economics*, **85**, 368–419.

Buch, Claudia M. (2005), 'Distance and international banking', *Review of International Economics*, **13**, 787–804.

Carey, M. (2004), 'Global financial integration: a collection of new research', Board of Governors of the Federal Reserve System, Working Paper Number 821.

Carey, M. and G. Nini (2007), 'Is the corporate loan market globally integrated? A pricing puzzle', *Journal of Finance*, **62**, 2969–3007.

Carey, M., M. Post and S.A. Sharpe (1998), 'Does corporate lending by banks and finance companies differ? Evidence on specialization in private debt contracting', *Journal of Finance*, **53**, 845–878.

Chen, Zhiwu and Peter Knez (1995), 'Measurement of market integration and arbitrage', *Review of Financial Studies*, **8**, 287–325.

Coval, J.A. and T.J. Moskowitz (1999), 'Home bias at home: local equity preference in domestic portfolios', *Journal of Finance*, **54**, 2045–2073.

Degryse, H. and S. Ongena (2004), 'The impact of technology and regulation on the geographical scope of banking', *Oxford Review of Economic Policy*, **20**, 571–590.

Degryse, H. and S. Ongena (2005), 'Distance, lending relationships, and competition', *Journal of Finance*, **60**, 231–266.

Dennis, S.A. and D.J. Mullineaux (2000), 'Syndicated loans', *Journal of Financial Intermediation*, **9**, 404–426.

Esty, B.C. and W.L. Megginson (2003), 'Creditor rights enforcement and debt ownership structure: evidence from the global syndicated loan market', *Journal of Finance and Quantitative Analysis*, **38**, 37–59.

French, K. and J.M. Poterba (1991), 'International diversification and international equity markets', *American Economic Review*, **81**, 222–226.

Grinblatt, M. and M. Keloharju (2001), 'How distance, language and culture influence stockholdings and trade', *Journal of Finance*, **56**, 1053–1073.

Gultekin, Mustafa, N. Bulent Gultekin and Alessandro Penati (1989), 'Capital controls and international capital market segmentation: the evidence from the Japanese and American stock markets', *Journal of Finance*, **44**, 849–869.

Hao, L., D.K. Nandy and G.S. Roberts (2005), 'How bank regulation, supervision and lender identity impact loan pricing: a cross-country comparison', York University Working Paper.

Henderson, B.J., N. Jegadeesh and M.S. Weisbach (2006), 'World markets for raising new capital', *Journal of Financial Economics*, **82**, 63–101.

Houston, J. and C. James (1996), 'Bank information monopolies and the mix of private and public debt claims', *Journal of Finance*, **51**, 1863–1889.

Houston, J., C. Lin and Y. Ma (2011), 'Regulatory arbitrage and international bank flows', University of Florida Working Paper.

Huberman, G. (2001), 'Familiarity breeds investment', *Review of Financial Studies*, **14**, 659–680.

Kroszner, R.S. and P. Strahan (2001), 'Throwing good money after bad? Board connections and conflicts in bank lending', NBER Working Paper No. 8694.

La Porta, R., F. Lopez-de-Silanes, A. Shleifer and R.W. Vishny (1997), 'Legal determinants of external finance', *Journal of Finance*, **52**, 1131–1150.

La Porta, R., F. Lopez-de-Silanes, A. Shleifer and R.W. Vishny (1998), 'Law and finance', *Journal of Political Economy*, **106**, 1113–1155.

Lins, Karl, Deon Strickland and Marc Zenner (2001), 'Do non-US firms issue equity on US stock exchanges to relax capital constraints?', University of North Carolina, Working Paper.

McBrady, M.R. and M.J. Schill (2007), 'Foreign-currency-denominated borrowing in the absence of operating incentives', *Journal of Financial Economics*, **86**, 145–177.

Mian, Atif (2006), 'Distance constraints: the limits of foreign lending in poor economies', *Journal of Finance*, **61**, 1465–1505.

Mittoo, Usha (1992), 'Additional evidence on integration in the Canadian stock market', *Journal of Finance*, **47**, 2035–2054.

Naranjo, Andy and Aris Protopapadakis (1997), 'Financial market integration tests: an investigation using US equity markets', *Journal of International Financial Markets, Institutions and Money*, **7**, 93–135.

Pagano, M., A. Roell and J. Zechner (2002), 'The geography of equity listing: why do companies list abroad?', *Journal of Finance*, **57**, 2651–2694.

Petersen, M. and R. Rajan (1994), 'The benefits of lending relationships: evidence from small business data', *Journal of Finance*, **49**, 3–37.

Petersen, M. and R. Rajan (2002), 'Does distance still matter? The information revolution in small business lending', *Journal of Finance*, **57**, 2533–2570.

Qian, J. and P.E. Strahan (2005), 'How law and institutions shape financial contracts: the case of bank loans', Boston College Working Paper.

Simons, K. (1993), 'Why do banks syndicate loans?', *New England Economic Review of the Federal Reserve Bank of Boston*, 45–52.

Stulz, R. (1981), 'A model of international asset pricing', *Journal of Financial Economics*, **9**, 383–406.

Stulz, Rene (1999), 'Globalization, corporate finance, and the cost of capital', *Journal of Applied Corporate Finance*, **12**, 8–25.

Sturm, J. and B. Williams (2004), 'Foreign bank entry, deregulation and bank efficiency: lessons from the Australian experience', *Journal of Banking and Finance*, **28**, 1775–1799.

Sufi, A. (2007), 'Information asymmetry and financing arrangements: evidence from syndicated loans', *Journal of Finance*, **62**, 629–668.

Wrighton, Jo (2003), 'Who needs a bank, anyway? Do-it-yourself lenders clubs allow companies to arrange their own syndicated loans', *Wall Street Journal*, 17 December, p. C1.

6 Lessons learned from recent financial crises
Benton E. Gup

6.1 FORESIGHT FROM THE 1980S S&L CRISIS

William Seidman, former Chairman of both the Federal Deposit Insurance Corporation (FDIC) and the Resolution Trust Corporation (RTC), wrote a chapter in *History of the Eighties: Lessons for the Future* that was published by the FDIC in 1997.[1] More than 1600 banks failed during the 1980–1993 period that is associated with the savings and loan (S&L) crisis. He said that: 'The critical catalyst causing the institutional disruption around the world can be almost uniformly described by three words: real estate loans.' Most of the failures were attributed to construction and development (C&D) loans associated with commercial real estate.[2] Seidman went on to say that: 'the biggest danger for financial institutions is lending based on excessive optimism generated about certain kinds of lending that are the fashion of the day'.

Ten years after *History of the Eighties* was published, the United States experienced the worst financial and economic crisis since the Great Depression of the 1930s. Seidman's insights about 'real estate loans' and 'excessive optimism' were on target in explaining the economic and financial crisis that began in the United States in 2007. The US crisis also affected other countries.

This chapter asks what lessons we can learn from the crises in the US and other countries about real estate lending. To answer that question, the chapter is divided into three main sections. Section 6.2 examines four key factors that contributed to the recent crisis in the US. Section 6.3 focuses on real estate lending. Section 6.4 presents the conclusions.

6.2 FOUR KEY FACTORS CONTRIBUTING TO THE RECENT CRISIS IN THE US

Four key factors that contributed to the financial crisis in the US are: (1) population growth; (2) new laws and government-sponsored entities; (3) increased liquidity; and (4) securitization. The laws encouraged lenders to promote and fund home ownership for the increased population, with government backing for many of the mortgage loans. Many of the mortgage loans were then sold to other financial institutions in the US and abroad.

6.2.1 Population Growth

Between 1970 and 2007, the population of the United States increased from 205 million people to 301 million.[3] The population grew to 309.9 million in August 2010.[4] The additional 100+ million people have to live somewhere, and the states with the greatest increases in population were California, Florida and Georgia. These are among the states that experienced the largest booms and busts in real estate loans. Most of the population growth was in the South and Southwest states.

Another aspect of the population growth is the tendency toward urbanization. In other words, the population moved into large metropolitan areas such as Atlanta and Los Angeles. The increased population in restricted geographic areas boosted the demand for and prices of real estate in those areas.

Finally, the increased number of women in the workforce resulted in higher family incomes. This, in turn, allowed families to buy higher-priced homes. The average price of new homes sold in the United States increased from $42 100 in March 1975 to $329 400 in March 2007.[5] Following the financial crisis, the average price of new homes declined, and it was $242 900 in June 2010.

6.2.2   Laws and GSEs

Federal laws were enacted that encouraged banks to meet the credit needs of their growing communities. The laws include, but are not limited to, the following:

- The Community Reinvestment Act (1977) promoted home ownership.
- The Depository Institutions Deregulation and Monetary Control Act (1980) pre-empted state interest rate caps.
- The Alternative Mortgage Transaction Parity Act (1982) permitted variable interest rates and 'balloon' payments.
- The Taxpayer Relief Act (1997) eliminated capital gains on the sale of homes up to $500 000 for married couples. This law encouraged home owners to 'cash out' and refinance their homes.

Government-sponsored entities (GSEs) Fannie Mae and Freddie Mac bought more than 30.5 million home mortgages to support home ownership, and to increase their profits.

6.2.3   Increased Liquidity

The interest rates on conventional home mortgage loans peaked at 16.5 percent in 1981, and then gradually declined to 4.7 percent in December 2009.[6] Lower interest rates make home ownership more affordable. The demand for mortgage loans increases as the cost of borrowing falls.

The boom in mortgage lending was financed, in part, by 'shadow banks' – unregulated institutions including structured investment vehicles (SIVs), hedge funds, private equity funds and others. According to Federal Deposit Insurance Corporation (FDIC) Chairman Sheila Bair (2009), by early 2007, the level of financial intermediation undertaken in the shadow banking sector exceeded the level of activity in the traditional banking sectors.

Finally, sovereign wealth funds (e.g. from Abu Dhabi, Norway, Singapore) invested billions of dollars in Citigroup, Morgan Stanley, Merrill Lynch and other firms. The rapid expansion of credit is frequently followed by buoyant property prices.[7] Thus, the availability of funds at low prices helped to fuel the real estate boom.

6.2.4 Securitization

Securitization refers to the packaging and selling of loans. Securitization, which began in the 1970s, created liquidity for previously illiquid mortgage loans, credit card loans, and other types of loans. As a result of securitization, the basic business model of banking changed from originating and holding the loans that they made to originating and distributing the loans to other investors.

Moral hazard problem
The problem with securitization is that the originators of the loans get paid when the loans are sold. They have no equity or retained interest in the loans, which results in a moral hazard problem. The originators get paid regardless of whether the loans are repaid or defaulted. Thus, there is an incentive to sell high-risk loans.

High-risk loans
There are a wide variety of 'high-risk loans'. Consider the case of a $200 000, 2/28 adjustable rate mortgage (ARM) for 30 years. Suppose that the initial interest rate is 7.5 percent for the first two years, and then it becomes a variable interest rate based on prevailing market rates of interest. The 7.5 percent rate is sometimes called a 'teaser rate' to induce the borrower to take out the loan. For the first two years, the monthly payments are $1531. Suppose that interest rates increase to 10 percent in year three and 11.5 percent in year four. Monthly loan payments will increase to $1939 in year three and $2152 in the following year. The risk factor is that the borrower may not be able to pay an additional $621 monthly mortgage payment.

Option ARMs are another type of high-risk loans.[8] This type of loan may have a low 'teaser rate' for the first month, and then the option comes into play. The interest rate on some of these loans can be adjusted monthly. The borrower can make a payment that: (1) covers the principal and interest; or (2) covers the interest but not the principal; or (3) is a minimum payment based on the teaser rate that does not cover the interest or pay down the principal. In the latter case, the amount of the debt increases.

Increased financial leverage
Many of the securitized loans were held in SIVs, which did not have regulatory capital requirements like banks. Thus, securitization and SIVs increased the financial leverage of their parent bank holding companies.

6.3   REAL ESTATE LENDING

Real estate lending per se is not risky. However, it can be risky to banks and other lenders if: (1) excessive financial leverage is involved; (2) it represents a high concentration ratio of the loan portfolio; (3) the loans are made to high-risk borrowers; (4) real estate loans on a bank's books are subject to interest rate risk; (5) real estate bubbles have occurred in the past and will probably occur again in the future. This section examines five lessons learned from real estate lending in the United States and selected other countries.

Table 6.1   Real estate values

Panel A: 25-year $1 million commercial real estate loan @ 7% fixed rate

	Loan/Value 100%	Loan/Value 90%	Loan/Value 80%	Loan/Value 70%
25-year real estate loan	$1 000 000	$1 000 000	$1 000 000	$1 000 000
Initial asset value	$1 000 000	$1 111 111	$1 250 000	$1 428 571
Expected annual income	$85 810	$95 346	$107 263	$122 586

Panel B: Interest rates of interest increase 200 basis points to 9%

	Loan/Value 100%	Loan/Value 90%	Loan/Value 80%	Loan/Value 70%
25-year real estate loan	$1 000 000	$1 000 000	$1 000 000	$1 000 000
Present value of asset @ 9%	$842 877	$936 536	$1 053 602	$1 204 113
Asset value less loan amount	−$157 123	−$63 464	$53 602	$404 798
	Default likely	Default possible	Positive equity value	Positive equity value

6.3.1   Lesson 1: Financial Leverage – *Caveat Emptor*

This section examines the financial leverage associated with borrowers, loans, and banks. Financial leverage is a double-edged sword. It can be very beneficial, or it can be deadly.

Leveraged borrowers
Some corporate borrowers were highly leveraged. Bear Stearns, the former investment bank, had a leverage ratio of 33:1. In other words, it had $33 in investments and other assets for every $1 in capital. A $1 loss translates into a 100 percent loss of its capital. Bear Stearns faced failure from its losses in March 2008, and it was acquired by JPMorgan Chase. Hedge funds may have even higher leverage ratios (i.e., 50:1), which makes them very risky borrowers.

Many individual borrowers increased their financial leverage through repeated 'cashing out' and refinancing of their homes. The repeated refinancing of home mortgages resulted in an estimated $1.5 trillion in losses.[9]

Leveraged loans
Consider the case of a 25-year, $1 million commercial real estate loan with a 7 percent fixed rate of interest. As shown in Table 6.1, Panel A, if 100 percent of the value of the real estate is borrowed, the expected annual income from the real estate project is $85 810. If the borrower borrows 90 percent of the value of the property, then the initial value of the property is about $1.1 million ($1 000 000/.90 = $1 111 111). Similarly, if the borrower borrows 70 percent, the initial value of the property is about $1.4 million. The table also shows the expected annual incomes.

Suppose that market rates of interest increase 200 basis points to 9 percent. As shown in Panel B, the value of the property declines. In the case of the 100 percent loan–value ratio, the property is worth $157 123 less than the amount of the loan and default is likely. Similarly, when the loan–value ratio is 90 percent, default is likely. In both these cases, the property is worth less than the amount of the loan. Stated otherwise, the property is 'underwater'.

When the loan–value ratios are lower, the owner has a positive equity value, and will not default. The lesson to be learned here is that high loan–value ratios are risky, because the borrower is more likely to default if the property is underwater.

Leveraged lenders

Commercial banks are 'for-profit' corporations whose objectives include maximizing shareholders' wealth. The faster a bank can grow, the greater the potential profits. However, the success of its growth depends in part on how it is financed. An increasing number of banks are using non-core funding sources of funds. These include time deposits over $100 000, 'brokered deposits', and foreign office deposits. Banks also borrow funds from Federal Home Loan Banks. Non-core funding can increase a bank's financial leverage. It also increases its liquidity risk.[10]

Regulatory capital requirements limit the degree to which banks can be leveraged. In the first quarter of 2010, their risk-based core capital (leverage) ratio was 8.57 percent.[11] Core capital includes common equity capital plus non-cumulative perpetual preferred stock plus minority interest in consolidated subsidiaries, less goodwill and other ineligible intangible assets. It does not take many loan losses to wipe out the bank's capital. In simple terms, commercial banks have about $12 in loans and other assets for every $1 of capital.

Collectively, when a large number of highly leveraged borrowers default on their loans, it has a cascading effect on the banks. Thus, if highly leveraged borrowers default on loans to highly leveraged hedge funds, which in turn default on bank loans, there will be a large number of bank failures.

Bank failures in Iceland

Iceland is a small country with a population of about 300 700. According to the Central Intelligence Agency's *World Fact Book*:

> Much of Iceland's economic growth in recent years came as the result of a boom in domestic demand following the rapid expansion of the country's financial sector. Domestic banks expanded aggressively in foreign markets, and consumers and businesses borrowed heavily in foreign-currency loans, following the privatization of the sector in the early 2000s. Worsening global financial conditions throughout 2008 resulted in a sharp depreciation of the krona vis-a-vis [*sic*] other major currencies. The foreign exposure of Icelandic banks, whose loans and other assets totaled more than 10 times the country's GDP, became unsustainable. Iceland's three largest banks collapsed in late 2008.[12]

The main source of the boom was financial leverage: 'The country became a giant hedge fund. And once-restrained Icelandic households amassed debts exceeding 220% of disposable income – almost twice the proportion of American consumers.'[13]

6.3.2   Lesson 2: Diversification is Good, High Loan Concentrations is Bad for Banks

Federal bank regulators generally consider credit asset exposures greater than 25 percent of total risk-based capital to be a concentration.[14] Banks that specialize in particular lines of business, such as Colonial Bank, have higher concentrations.

Colonial Bank
Bobby Lowder created Colonial Bank in 1981 by acquiring a failed community bank – Southland Bancorp. His strategy was to build his deposit base by acquiring community banks, and by investing primarily in real estate loans.[15] The strategy was successful for many years. Colonial took advantage of the booming real estate markets in Florida, Georgia and Nevada. It operated 354 branches in Florida (57 percent of the branches), Alabama (26 percent), Georgia (5 percent), Nevada (6 percent), and Texas (6 percent).[16] The Colonial BancGroup, headquartered in Montgomery Alabama, had more than $26 billion in assets when it failed in 2009.

In 2008, 85 percent of Colonial's loan portfolio consisted of real estate loans: commercial real estate (34 percent), real estate construction (33 percent), and residential real estate (18 percent) loans.[17] In June 2009, commercial real estate loans were about 595 percent of Colonial's capital, and construction and development loans were 274 percent. When the real estate bubble burst, it did not take many loan losses to wipe out Colonial's capital.

'Diversification' means investing in assets whose returns are not perfectly positively correlated. Unfortunately for Colonial, the entire real estate market in the US was adversely affected by the financial and economic crisis. The states that suffered the most were those that had the greatest population growth. They included Florida, Georgia and Nevada, where Colonial's branches were located.

Colonial was the fifth-largest bank failure in US history. In August 2009, it was acquired by BB&T Corp., based in Winston Salem, NC.

6.3.3   Lesson 3: Loans Made to High-Risk Borrowers Are Risky

Subprime borrowers and mortgages
The financial crisis that began 2007 is commonly associated with subprime loans. The term 'subprime' refers to high-risk borrowers. Loans can be high risk because of borrower's low credit scores (i.e., FICO credit scores below 620), high debt-to-income ratios (i.e., greater than 50 percent), high debt-to-loan ratios, or other factors.[18]

Alt-A mortgages (i.e., Alternative A-rated mortgages) are riskier than 'prime'-rated mortgages, but less risky than subprime mortgages. Alt-A mortgages may lack full documentation, have higher loan-to-value ratios and debt-to-income ratios, or have other features that do not conform to GSEs' lending guidelines.

The delinquency on all residential real estate loans made by commercial banks soared from 1.6 percent in 2005 to 9.8 percent in the third quarter of 2009.[19] Similarly, the charge-off rates for commercial real estate loans increased from 1 percent to 8.7 percent.

The delinquency rate for prime adjustable rate mortgage (ARM) loans on one- to four-unit residential properties in March 2005 was 2 percent.[20] By March 2009, it had increased to 12 percent. In contrast, delinquent subprime adjustable rate mortgages during that same period almost tripled, soaring from about 10 percent to 27.6 percent.[21]

6.3.4   Lesson 4: Be Aware of Interest Rate Risk

Rising interest rates
Banks and other types of depository institutions generally finance their long-term assets with shorter-term liabilities. They profit from the difference between making long-term loans at high rates of interest and borrowing shorter-term funds at lower rates of interest. The difference between the two rates, called the net interest margin (NIM), is usually about 3 percent to 4 percent.

The S&L crisis of the 1980s was due to the fact that long-term mortgage loans were made at low fixed rates, and they were financed with short-term deposits. Then market rates of interest soared to record levels. During the 1976 to December 1981 period, 30-day Certificate of Deposit (CD) rates increased from 5.08 percent to 15.94 percent resulting in negative NIMs because of fixed-rate loans made at lower rates.[22]

Between 1980 and 1994, 1600 banks and savings institutions failed. As previously noted, mortgage rates of interest peaked at 16.5 percent in 1981, and then declined to less than 5 percent in November 2009. Banks and other lenders that make fixed-rate mortgage loans when market rates of interest are low, and then hold those loans instead of selling them, will be subject to interest rate risk (i.e., negative NIMs) when market rates of interest rise.

Interest rate risk can be mitigated by hedging with interest rate swaps or other instruments. There were 8099 FDIC-insured institutions in the United States in the third quarter, 2009.[23] However, only:

> 1110 insured US commercial banks reported derivatives activities at the end of the second quarter. Nonetheless, most derivatives activity in the US banking system continues to be dominated by a small group of large financial institutions. Five large commercial banks represent 97% of the total banking industry notional amounts and 88% of industry net current credit exposure.[24]

Lenders can also mitigate their interest rate risk by selling the long-term fixed rate loans to investors or government-backed entities, such as Fannie Mae and Freddie Mac, that are willing to hold them.

Accounting issues
FASB Statement No. 157, Fair Value Measurements, issued in September 2006, and FASB Statement No. 159, The Fair Value Option for Financial Assets and Financial Liabilities, issued in February 2007, became effective in 2008. Both FASB 157 and 159 will have an impact on their regulatory capital when market rates of interest change.[25] These accounting standards require banks to value their assets and liabilities in such a way that assets and liabilities reflect market prices.[26] Loans held for sale are marked to market. When market rates of interest increase, the market prices of long-term debt instruments such as bonds and fixed rate mortgages decline. If they decline sufficiently,

Table 6.2   The effects of funding maturities on the equity/asset capital ratio of 'Fair Value Hypothetical Bank'

Panel A: Bank's initial position ($ thousands)

Assets	Liabilities and equity	Equity/assets
$10 000 loan (20 years, 8% fixed rate, semiannually)	$9000 certificate of deposit (20 years, 5% fixed rate semiannually) $1000 equity	
Total assets $10 000	Total liabilities and equity $10 000	10% well capitalized

Panel B: The effects of funding maturities on the equity/asset capital ratio of 'Fair Value Hypothetical Bank', bank's position with alternative funding options ($ thousands)

Market rates of interest increase 100 basis points for both assets and liabilities	Alternative funding maturities	Equity/asset ratios when the bank is funded by CDs with different maturities
Assets (Market value) (20 years maturity)	Liabilities (Market value) (Maturity of CD)	Equity/assets
$9080 (20 years)	$7959.6 (20 years)	12.34% well capitalized
$9080 (20 years)	$8330.4 (10 years)	8.26% adequately capitalized
$9080 (20 years)	$8615.7 (5 years)	5.11% significantly undercapitalized
$9080 (20 years)	$8913.6 (1 year)	1.83% critically undercapitalized

they may wipe out a bank's regulatory capital. As shown in Table 6.2, Panel A, 'Fair Value Hypothetical Bank' is funding its long-term loan with a long-term deposit and it is well capitalized. However, this bank does not hedge its interest rate risk. Let us see what happens if market rates of interest increase 100 basis points, and the loan was funded with shorter-term sources of funds. As shown in Table 6.2, Panel B, the shorter the term of the funding sources, the more likely it is that the bank will be significantly undercapitalized – and that the bank will fail.

6.3.5   Lesson 5: Real Estate Bubbles Will Probably Occur Again

Real estate bubbles are not limited to the United States. There were real estate bubbles in Japan, Spain, Sweden and Thailand in the 1990s.[27]

Dubai

The most recent real estate bubble was in Dubai, located on the Persian Gulf coast. Dubai is one of seven emirates federated as the United Arab Emirates (UAE). It has a population of about 2.6 million. In 2000, if not before, Dubai began to engage in large-scale real estate projects with the intent of diversifying its economy and becoming a tourist destination and a global financial center. The large-scale real estate projects include one of the world's tallest skyscrapers (Emirates Towers), the most expensive hotel (Burj Al Arab), and large residential projects (Palm Islands, built into the Gulf) and other developments.

The basic idea was: 'build the real estate projects and the people will come and buy or occupy them'. However, the financial crisis that began in the US in 2007, falling oil prices and tighter credit had a chilling effect on Dubai's real estate projects. Some of the projects faltered, and the bubble burst.

The projects were run by Dubai's state-owned investment company, Dubai World. It wanted to restructure $26 billion in debt owed to global investors.[28] The global investors were surprised to learn that the Dubai government would not guarantee Dubai World's debts.[29] Investors with large exposures to Dubai World's debt include Abu Dhabi Commercial Bank,[30] Royal Bank of Scotland Group (UK), HSBC Holdings (UK), Barclays (UK), Lloyds Banking Group (UK), Standard Charter (UK) and ING Group (the Netherlands). Collectively, European banks had about $84 billion in exposure to UAE banks, including Dubai.[31]

6.4   CONCLUSIONS

Financial crises in the United States and elsewhere are commonly associated with real estate booms and busts. Memories tend to be short. Lenders and real estate developers either believe that they can 'cash out' before the problems occur again, or that such problems cannot happen to them. The odds are very high that there will be real estate booms and busts in the future. They may be localized in relatively small geographic areas, or they may have global aspects. Only time will tell.

Lenders and borrowers can avoid some of the problems associated with real estate lending by following the four lessons from previous crises that are presented here:

1. Both the borrower and the lender should avoid excessive financial leverage.
2. Proper diversification means avoiding high portfolio–loan concentrations, and investing in assets whose returns are not perfectly positively correlated.
3. Avoid highly leveraged loans, and high-risk borrowers. It follows that loans should only be made to borrowers that have a reasonable chance of repaying them in a timely fashion. This includes loans with adjustable rates of interest.
4. When market rates of interest are expected to increase, interest rate risk is a real threat to lenders that make long-term fixed-rate loans at low rates, and finance them with short-term sources of funds. Hedging can reduce some of that risk. Accounting rules for valuing traded assets add to interest rate risk for the large number of banks that do not hedge.

Lenders who want to maximize their growth rates and shareholder wealth, as well as high-risk borrowers, may not like these recommendations. They will result in fewer loans being made, lower rates of asset growth for the lenders, and lower profits. However, from a long-run macroeconomic point of view, the economy will be better off because of lower loan defaults and fewer bank failures.

NOTES

1. Seidman, William (1997), 'The world financial system: lessons learned and challenges ahead', in *History of the Eighties – Lessons for the Future*, Washington, DC: FDIC.
2. Burton, Steven K. (1999), 'Recent trends in construction lending practices', FDIC, *Bank Trends*, July, no. 99-01.
3. 'Statistical Abstract of the United States: 2009' (2009), US Department of Commerce, Table 2.
4. 'US and World Population Clock' (2009), US Census Bureau, http://www.census.gov/main/www/pop clock.html.
5. Census of Housing, US Census Bureau (2010), 'Median and average sales prices of new homes sold in United States', http://www.census.gov/const/uspricemon.pdf.
6. 'Statistical Abstract of the United States: 1992' (1992), US Department of Commerce, Table 806; 'Selected interest rates, Statistical Release H.15' (2009), Board of Governors of the Federal Reserve System, 7 December.
7. Borio, Claudio and Mathias Drehmann (2009), 'Assessing the risk of banking crises – revisited', *BIS Quarterly Review*, March, 29–46.
8. Heath, David (2009), 'Part two: WaMu: hometown bank turned predatory', *Seattle Times*, 28 October.
9. Khandani, Amir E., Andrew W. Lo and Robert C. Merton (2009), 'Systemic risk and the refinancing ratchet effect', 15 September, MIT Sloan Research Paper No. 4750-09; Harvard Business School Finance Working Paper No. 1472892, available at SSRN, http://ssrn.com/abstract=1472892.
10. Net non-core funding dependence ratio (NNCFD Ratio) and short-term net non-core funding dependence ratio (STNNCFD Ratio) are reported in the 'Uniform Bank Performance Report'; for additional analysis on this topic, see King, Thomas B., Daniel A. Nuxoll and Timothy J. Yeager (2005), 'Are the causes of bank distress changing? Can researchers keep up?', FDIC CFR Working Paper No. 2005-03, http://www.fdic.gov/bank/analytical/cfr/2005/wp2005/CFRWP_2005-03_nuxoll1.pdf.
11. 'FDIC Quarterly Banking Profile', 1st Quarter 2010, Table 1-A.
12. Central Intelligence Agency (2009), *The World Fact Book*, 'Iceland', https://www.cia.gov/library/publications/the-world-factbook/geos/ic.html.
13. Gumble, Peter (2008), 'Iceland: the country that became a hedge fund', CNNMoney.com., 1 December, http://money.cnn.com/2008/12/01/magazines/fortune/iceland_gumbel.fortune/.
14. Board of Governors of the Federal Reserve System (2010), Press Release, 'Federal financial regulatory agencies issue final guidance on correspondent concentration risks; Attachment: *Federal Register* notice for correspondent concentration risks guidance', 30 April.
15. O'Keef, Brian (2009), 'The man behind 2009's biggest bank bust', CNNMoney.com, 12 October.
16. Colonial BancGroup (2009), '2008 Annual Report'.
17. Ibid., p.51.
18. For additional information about FICO credit scores, see http://www.myfico.com/CreditEducation/. FICO is a product of the Fair Isaac Corporation.
19. 'Charge-off and delinquency rates on loans and leases at commercial banks' (2009), Federal Reserve Statistical Release, Third Quarter.
20. Delinquency rate refers to loans that are at least one payment past due, but it does not include loans in the process of foreclosure.
21. Federal Reserve Bank of Richmond (2009), 'US residential mortgage delinquency rates', http://www.richmondfed.org/banking/markets_trends_and_statistics/trends/pdf/delinquency_and_foreclosure_rates.pdf.
22. Board of Governors of the Federal Reserve System (2009), 'Federal Reserve Statistical Release H 15. Selected interest rates, historical data', http://www.federalreserve.gov/releases/h15/data.htm.
23. 'Quarterly Banking Profile, all institutions performance, third quarter 2009' (2009), FDIC, http://www2.fdic.gov/qbp/2009sep/qbpall.html.
24. 'OCC's Quarterly Report on Bank Trading and Derivatives Activities Second Quarter 2009' (2009), Comptroller of the Currency, http://www.occ.gov/deriv/deriv.htm.
25. 'Summary of Statement No. 159, The fair value option for financial assets and financial liabilities – including an amendment of FASB Statement No. 115' (2009), http://www.fasb.org/st/summary/stsum159.shtml.
26. For a detailed discussion of this issue, see Gup, Benton E. and Thomas Lutton (2009), 'Potential effects of fair value accounting on US bank regulatory capital', *Journal of Applied Finance*, **18**(1–2), 38–48.
27. Gup, Benton E. (1999), 'International banking crises: the real estate connection', in *International Banking Crises: Large-Scale Failures, Massive Government Intervention*, Westport, CT: Quorum Books.
28. Cummins, Chip, Dana Cimilluca and Sara Schaefer Muñoz (2009), 'Dubai's woes shake UAE region',

Wall Street Journal, 27 November, C1, C3; Lorade, Nikhil and Summer Said (2009), 'Dubai discusses debt revamp', *Wall Street Journal*, 1 December, C1, C3.
29.   Fennell, Edward (2009), 'Dubai's golden sands lose their lustre', *TimesOnLine*, 10 December, http://business.timesonline.co.uk/tol/business/law/article6950725.ece.
30.   Abu Dhabi is part of the UAE.
31.   'Dubai's debt reckoning' (2009), *Wall Street Journal*, 28–29 November, A14.

PART II

COMPENSATION, PERFORMANCE AND RISK

7 Bank ownership and risk taking: improving corporate governance in banking after the crisis

*Kenneth R. Spong and Richard J. Sullivan**

7.1 INTRODUCTION

The recent financial crisis, which started with the collapse in US subprime mortgage markets, has significantly disrupted the financial systems and economies in most major countries, making it the most severe crisis experienced in many years. Financial institutions and others greatly underestimated the risks they were taking and failed to prepare for the possibility of a financial breakdown. The depth of the crisis further forced public authorities to take a number of nearly unprecedented steps to support major financial institutions and markets.

While a variety of factors contributed to the crisis, many have suggested that a critical element was the lack of sound corporate governance at financial institutions. According to this view, deficiencies in corporate governance provided strong incentives to take on excessive risks. As an example, some claim that executive compensation at banks and securities firms was structured in a manner that rewarded short-term performance and high-risk strategies instead of long-term performance.

There are other reasons why governance and private discipline might have been considered inadequate and regarded as factors contributing to the crisis. Deposit insurance, financial regulation and the new policy actions taken during this crisis (expanded deposit insurance coverage, debt and money market fund guarantees, and broader liquidity assistance) have given depositors, creditors, stockholders and others substantial protection against the risks assumed by financial institutions. In response, these parties may not have played as much of a role in the discipline and governance of such institutions as they otherwise would have, and the institutions may have put less effort into managing their risk exposures. Even greater incentive issues may have existed for the largest financial institutions that were regarded as systemic threats to the financial system and thus treated as 'too big to fail' during this crisis.

These suggested shortcomings in corporate governance thus may have contributed to the crisis, although it may be hard to assess how much of a role they played. Another issue is what specific steps stockholders, directors, public authorities and others should take now to improve corporate governance in banking and thereby create a more resilient financial system. Given that the countries most affected by the crisis were already thought to have the best corporate governance, supervisory and legal frameworks, what assurance is there that any new steps will prove effective?

This chapter identifies some of the key aspects of the corporate governance framework for financial institutions and discusses what they tell us about possible reforms and improvements. Section 7.2 of the chapter reviews the theory and evidence relating to corporate governance and its role in the financial system. Section 7.3 examines the weaknesses in corporate governance that might have played a role in the crisis. Section 7.4 presents some research we have done that looks at the interplay among particular parts of bank governance systems. The concluding section, section 7.5, then looks at possible ways to strengthen corporate governance within the financial system.

7.2   CORPORATE GOVERNANCE AND ITS ROLE IN THE FINANCIAL SYSTEM

Corporate governance has been defined in a number of different ways.[1] One way of thinking about corporate governance is that it encompasses all the mechanisms, decision-making processes and contracts that help to ensure that the objectives of stockholders – and in some cases, other stakeholders – are met, while also directing how the various claims are settled within a corporation. Corporate governance thus encompasses the steps stockholders take to protect their interests; the role of the board of directors in setting the policies and direction of the firm; the incentives and constraints provided to managers and other employees for implementing such policies; and the influence that creditors, customers and others might exert over the firm's behavior.

A critical issue in the governance of any firm is how to get managers and other key players to maximize the value of the firm and act in the best interest of stockholders rather than pursuing their own personal interests. This issue is known as the principal–agent problem in finance, and it typically occurs when a manager is hired and paid a salary to run a company, while having little or no ownership stake in it (Jensen and Meckling, 1976). Without much stock, such managers will receive little direct benefit from actions they take to increase the firm's earnings and capital appreciation. This incentive problem may lead hired managers to act in ways less conducive to stockholder interests. For instance, a manager with only a fixed salary might simply put forth less effort than stockholders would desire. Many hired managers might also have a built-in aversion to taking acceptable business risks since they would not be fully rewarded for successful outcomes and, perhaps more importantly, their reputations and job security could be threatened by failures.

A number of market and corporate governance mechanisms can help to address some of these incentive issues. Managerial labor markets will encourage firms to offer competitive salaries and develop broader compensation packages for highly successful managers, thus helping to ensure that managers will be rewarded in some manner for their performance. Labor markets will also serve to punish managers that fail to serve stockholders, while giving other managers a chance to develop a reputation for performing well and thereby increase their marketability (Fama, 1980; Cannella et al., 1995).

From a corporate governance perspective, firms can do a number of things themselves to align better the interests of managers and stockholders. Managerial compensation can be expanded to include equity-based components, such as stock options and stock grants. Stock options, for instance, can provide a means of encouraging risk-averse managers to be more receptive to projects that entail some risk but have a reasonable probability of increasing the value of the firm. Stock grants can help give managers a similar incentive structure as other investors in the firm. To the extent that managers are encouraged or required to maintain notable amounts of stock in the firm, such holdings may further lead managers to consider what is best for the firm and its stockholders in terms of long-term performance.

After a certain point, though, significant stockholdings could also concentrate a manager's wealth in the shares of his or her firm. This lack of diversification could provide managers with a new incentive to be risk averse and avoid projects that have expected positive returns, but with some chance of loss. These diverse effects from stock options and grants give firms an opportunity to tailor and adjust compensation packages in whatever manner is thought most conducive to stockholder interests (DeYoung et al., 2010; Rogers, 2002; Coles et al., 2006). At the same time, it should also be recognized that corporate governance will be further complicated by the fact that the interests of individual stockholders are likely to vary substantially within a firm, according to the amount of stock ownership and policy influence each investor has and the investor's portfolio diversification and risk-return preferences.

Boards of directors also can play a key role in corporate governance by representing stockholders and establishing the overall policies and direction of the firm. Other board responsibilities generally include monitoring management, setting compensation policies for higher-level managers and overseeing other aspects of a firm's operations and risk management practices.[2] As a result, directors serve as another constraint on managers acting in their own interests rather than those of stockholders. How well directors perform this role will depend on such factors as the expertise and talents of the directors, the cost and complexity of monitoring, and the financial incentives directors may have to serve stockholders, including director fees and stock held in the firm.

A number of other parties, including creditors and customers, can influence or govern the operation of a firm. In particular, since creditors have a fixed claim against the firm, they will want to use contractual agreements and other provisions to protect themselves against a firm and its managers taking on new risks that might threaten the repayment of creditor claims.

In banking and certain other parts of the financial markets, corporate governance is further complicated by a number of factors that do not play as much of a role in other firms. These include the complexity and high leverage in many banks and the liquidity issues associated with deposits available on demand. The complexity and lack of transparency in bank operations and balance sheets make it harder for stockholders, directors and creditors to exert appropriate discipline over management, thus potentially giving managers some added leeway to pursue their own objectives. High leverage may further magnify the returns stockholders and managers could receive from successfully taking on more risk, consequently setting the stage for significant conflicts between stockholders and both creditors and depositors. The special nature of banking is also reflected in the fact that a substantial portion of a bank's deposit base can be withdrawn on demand, which gives depositors a unique disciplinary tool and creates liquidity issues for the bank.

While deposit insurance now provides a means of reducing these liquidity problems and protecting depositors and the financial system from panic, it introduces new governance problems and moral hazard issues. Because insured depositors no longer need to be concerned about a bank's condition or to even extract a price for higher risk exposures, bank managers and shareholders have an opportunity to take on more risk than would otherwise be possible. To prevent bankers from exploiting these risk-taking incentives, banking regulators must put themselves in the position of protecting insured depositors and monitoring risk taking at financial institutions. As a result, banking regulators become another component in the governance of banks.

Overall, governance in the financial marketplace thus consists of the interplay of all these different components – stockholders, directors, creditors and depositors, labor markets and compensation incentives, and regulators – and their efforts to guide managers toward selected objectives. There are a number of ways these components may reinforce each other or serve as substitute governance mechanisms. Moreover, given the wide variety of ownership, management and board structures across financial institutions, reliance on particular governance mechanisms may vary greatly from one institution to another.

7.3   THE CRISIS AND WEAKNESSES IN CORPORATE GOVERNANCE

Views on the role that corporate governance problems may have played in the financial crisis vary widely. According to Kirkpatrick (2009): 'the financial crisis can be to an important extent attributed to failures and weaknesses in corporate governance arrangements'.[3] In contrast, Acharya et al. (2009) state: 'Are the governance failures by themselves sufficient to cause a crisis of the magnitude we have seen? Most likely not.'[4] This recent corporate governance debate is being examined more closely through research based on a number of different governance factors, including comprehensive indicators of good corporate governance, executive compensation practices, the structure and effectiveness of boards of directors, and other incentives.

For a number of years, banking supervisors and international authorities have placed much emphasis on banks adopting sound corporate governance principles (Basel Committee on Bank Supervision, 1999; OECD, 1999).[5] In this regard, several studies have looked at more comprehensive measures of corporate governance and their relationship to the financial crisis. Beltratti and Stulz (2009), for instance, used subindices from the Riskmetrics Corporate Governance Quotient and several other corporate governance and shareholder protection indices. They did not find any consistent evidence to support a link between better corporate governance and better bank performance during the crisis and, in a few cases, banks with higher governance scores even performed worse. Adams (2009) compared financial and non-financial firms on a number of corporate governance characteristics and generally concluded that the governance of financial firms was comparable to that of non-financial firms. These studies thus suggest that financial institutions did not appear to have notable failings with regard to general governance standards suggested by corporate governance authorities and regulators.

A common public perception is that executive pay at financial institutions encouraged the excessive risk taking that led to the crisis. As a result, several policy steps have already been taken to address executive compensation, including the limitations imposed on institutions receiving funds under the Troubled Asset Relief Program, supervisory guidance issued by US regulators on sound compensation policies (*Federal Register*, 2010), and the Dodd–Frank Act provisions regarding non-binding shareholder votes and executive compensation committees and disclosures. The evidence linking compensation practices to the financial crisis, though, is mixed.

Fahlenbrach and Stulz (2010) find little to suggest that stock options and more sensitive pay led to worse performance during the crisis. At the large firms that suffered the most during the crisis, Fahlenbrach and Stulz (2010) and Nestor Advisors (2009) also assert that many of the executive officers had significant equity stakes and experienced substantial losses themselves from the crisis, thus indicating a corporate governance framework that should have had the desired link to long-term performance. Bebchuk et al. (2010), though, conclude that the top executives at Bear Stearns and Lehman Brothers did cash out much of their performance-based compensation over a number of years before their companies collapsed, and that such compensation may have provided incentives for excessive risk taking.

The crisis has also been attributed to weaknesses in the structure and effectiveness of boards of directors at financial institutions, and in looking back, one could easily claim that the directors at many institutions did not succeed in their oversight of management and risk management practices. Several recent studies, though, suggest that the usual ideas for improving the corporate governance role of boards, such as greater independence, had little effect or may have even been counterproductive during the crisis.

For instance, Nestor Advisors (2009) found that the major investment banks in the United States all had boards that met high standards of independence, and Adams (2009) and Erkens et al. (2009) concluded that the banks that had more independent boards suffered more during the crisis. Adams (2009) and Kirkpatrick (2009) even suggested that large financial firms may have gone too far and placed too many outside directors on the board without the expertise or capabilities to oversee complex financial operations. Ellul and Yerramilli (2010) provide some support for this view in a study of bank holding companies. They show that the companies which had lower risk exposures and fared better during the crisis had more active board risk committees and the independent directors on these committees had more previous banking experience. Consequently, the structure of a financial institution's board may not be as important from a corporate governance standpoint as the incentives and skills that the directors have.

One other concern in this crisis is that the governance of financial institutions may have been distorted by moral hazard problems associated with deposit insurance, 'too big to fail', and other forms of public support and protection. In this regard, managers, directors and investors – particularly at large institutions – may have been led to take on additional risk, knowing that the market would not fully discipline them for the increased risk and that public support would be available if needed. Before the crisis, Rime (2005) and Morgan and Stiroh (2005) found that banks considered to be 'too big to fail' received more favorable credit ratings than their condition would warrant and benefited from lower funding costs when compared to other banks.[6] As a result, the larger institutions that encountered significant problems during the crisis likely had the incentive and opportunity to take on more risk than other firms.

Given the considerable protection provided to highly leveraged and systemically important firms during this crisis, Nestor Advisors (2009) and Bolton et al. (2010) further argue that aligning the interests of executives with those of long-term stockholders will not be enough for sound corporate governance. Instead, they suggest that governance and financial incentives should be structured in a manner that will align executives more closely with a broader range of stakeholders, including creditors, depositors and other counterparties.

Although it seems obvious that shortcomings in corporate governance made a contribution to the crisis, the research above suggests that several of the standard and more basic ideas on corporate governance may not individually explain the crisis that well. A possible reason for this outcome is that corporate governance is a complex interaction of different parties and mechanisms, and it may not be easy to condense corporate governance into a few simple and testable relationships. Also, while sound corporate governance is important, moral hazard and financial incentive problems may subvert some of its positive influences and constraints on risk.

7.4 ANALYSIS OF CORPORATE GOVERNANCE AND RISK TAKING IN BANKS

We examine the corporate governance framework in banks and its effect on risk taking by looking at a sample of state-chartered banks in the Kansas City Federal Reserve District. Although these banks are typically small – each bank has total assets of under $1 billion – the banks have a considerable diversity in their ownership, management and board structures and, accordingly, their corporate governance frameworks. The management structure in the sample banks, for instance, ranges from banks with hired managers who have little or no stock ownership to banks with an owner-manager who controls virtually all of the bank's stock.[7]

Because our sample only contains community banks, various elements of the corporate governance framework we examine may not be directly applicable to larger banks that are more widely held and face the discipline of actively traded markets. However, the diversity of governance, management and ownership systems in our banks may provide a better look at how corporate governance works than would be the case for larger banks, which are much more similar to each other in their management and ownership structures. In addition, many of the financial incentives facing managers, owners and directors at community banks have their counterparts in the larger institutions and can provide a guide to some of the governance factors that may have contributed to the crisis.

We obtained much of our corporate governance information on the sample banks from state bank examination reports, and these data were first collected from 1994 examination reports and used previously in DeYoung et al. (2001) and Sullivan and Spong (2007). These reports have a confidential section for supervisors with a detailed description of the specific responsibilities of bank managers and other key policymakers, salaries and bonuses of officers, the amount of stock held by individual investors, the personal wealth and other characteristics of bank directors, and any family relationships among officers, directors and stockholders. Given the detailed and comprehensive nature of this information, a variety of corporate governance mechanisms can be examined together, thus providing a look at the interplay among such mechanisms. We also use the quarterly Reports of Condition and Income that banks file with their federal supervisor to derive performance data on each bank.

Table 7.1   Characteristics of sample banks

	Type of manager	
	Owner	Hired
Number of banks	110	160
Nonmetropolitan location*	81%	72%
Total assets (1994) (millions)**	$39	$57
Operating ROAA (1994)*	1.46%	1.62%
Average operating ROAA (1990–1994)	1.43%	1.52%

Notes:
Statistics are unweighted averages.
***,**,* indicate that a null hypothesis of no difference between the means of the owner-manager and hired-manager banks for the particular variable is rejected at a 1, 5 or 10 percent significance level.

7.4.1   Characteristics of Sample Banks and their Managers and Directors

The sample banks are separated into two groups, based on the ownership characteristics of the bank's top manager, who has responsibility for its daily operations.[8] There are 110 owner-manager banks in which the manager is a member of the ownership group with the largest stake in the bank. These banks are a useful reference group because the major owners and managers are the same and there should be no principal–agent conflicts. The remaining 160 observation are hired-manager banks, where the managers may have some ownership of the bank but are not part of the majority ownership group. The hired-manager banks are an important focus of analysis because these managers may be inclined to pursue their own interests rather than those of the owners and may have incentives for risk-averse behavior.

As seen in Table 7.1, the typical owner-manager bank is somewhat smaller, more likely to be in a rural location, and reported slightly lower returns than the average hired-manager bank. There is considerable diversity in the ownership and wealth characteristics of the top manager in these banks (Table 7.2). Among owner-manager banks, the manager personally owns on average 37 percent of the bank and the manager and family members together own 63 percent. At most hired-manager banks, the manager has little or no ownership stake: their ownership share averages only 3 percent and including the family only raises the average share to 4 percent.[9] A number of hired managers, though, have more significant holdings: 32 of the hired managers have ownership of 5 percent or greater, with a maximum of 39 percent.

With regard to measures of wealth, the average owner-manager is wealthier and has more wealth concentrated in the bank. The average net worth of owner-managers is $1.72 million, compared to $0.47 million for hired managers (Table 7.2). Owner-managers have a higher percentage of their wealth concentrated in their bank stockholdings, 86 percent on average, while for hired managers the average is 21 percent (Table 7.2).[10] Consequently, most owner-managers are far less diversified than the typical hired manager and are more closely linked to the fortunes of their banks.

Table 7.2 Ownership and wealth characteristics of daily managing officer

	Type of manager	
	Owner	Hired
Personal ownership stake in bank***	37%	3%
Personal plus family ownership stake in bank***	63%	4%
Personal net worth (millions)***	$1.72	$0.47
Value of bank investment as a percent of net worth***	86%	21%

Notes:
Statistics are unweighted averages across sample banks.
***,**,* indicate that a null hypothesis of no difference between the means of the owner-manager and hired-manager banks for the particular variable is rejected at a 1, 5 or 10 percent significance level.

In addition to ownership incentives, managers will also be influenced by their compensation and the manner in which it is structured.[11] Since few of the small banks in the sample have actively traded stock, management compensation generally takes the form of annual salaries and cash bonuses. The awarding of bonuses is often based on informal agreements and practices, and much of a bonus may be paid towards the end of the year, depending on how well the bank has performed that year. Thus, bonuses provide a general incentive for good performance – in terms of both generating earnings and controlling risk – and may not necessarily reflect a specific set of goals. Sixty-nine percent of sample banks paid cash bonuses to managers.[12] On average, 13 percent of total manager compensation took the form of bonuses, with a maximum of 74 percent.

Another influence on the operation and governance of the sample banks is their board of directors. There are a number of observable characteristics of bank boards that may affect how well the directors actively oversee their banks.[13] For the sample banks, these include director attendance rates, the level of director fees and their role in helping to attract capable and motivated board members, and the representation of independent or outside directors on the board. Independent directors, for example, may be able to offer specialized business expertise and dispassionate advice not otherwise available to the bank. On the other hand, insiders on the board are likely to have a strong financial motivation to see their bank do well and have more banking and financial expertise than most independent directors.

A particularly important board responsibility is monitoring managers, especially in the hired-manager sample banks. Since careful monitoring of hired managers requires time and effort, directors may need a strong financial incentive to bear these costs. Consequently, we assume that the board member most likely to play this role will be one who is part of the majority ownership group, and designate this person the principal monitor of the bank. Since it is not clear what this monitoring director's attitude toward risk taking will be, we look at what portion of this director's wealth is tied up in the bank and hypothesize that the less diversified the director is, the greater the incentive to limit managerial risk taking. For the hired-manager banks in our sample, the principal monitor's concentration of net worth in their bank investment averages 41 percent.

Table 7.3   Measures of risk in sample banks

	Type of manager	
	Owner	Hired
Equity-to-total asset ratio**	10.2%	9.4%
Non-current assets-to-total assets ratio*	0.906%	0.614%
Standard deviation of operating return on assets	0.787%	0.842%
Survival likelihood index	20.6	19.0

Notes:
Statistics are unweighted averages, based on 262 to 270 observations, depending on availability of data.
***,**,* indicate that a null hypothesis of no difference between the means of the owner-manager and hired-manager banks for the particular variable is rejected at a 1, 5 or 10 percent significance level.

7.4.2   Measures of Risk in the Sample Banks

We study four areas of bank risk. The first three relate to specific areas of risk: capital or leverage (an inverse measure of capital), credit quality and earnings variation. Capital, measured by the equity capital-to-total assets ratio, indicates the cushion provided by stockholders to absorb bank losses, and by itself, more capital implies less risk. With regard to credit quality, the ratio of non-current assets to total assets is an indicator of the level of risky loans in a bank.[14] Earnings variation, measured by the standard deviation of operating return on assets, indicates the ability of bank management to control risk exposures and produce steady earnings over time, with high earnings variation implying a more risky bank.[15]

The fourth measure of bank risk – a survival likelihood index – combines several indicators of risk and bank performance and thus provides a more complete picture of risk than such one-dimensional measures as capital, credit quality and earnings variation. In fact, the survival likelihood index incorporates three factors together: capitalization, the level of profitability, and fluctuations in income.[16] This index is defined as:

$$\frac{equity\ capital\text{-}to\text{-}total\ asset\ ratio\ +\ average\ value\ of\ operating\ return\ on\ assets}{standard\ deviation\ of\ operating\ return\ on\ assets}$$

The higher the value of the survival likelihood index, the lower the risk of the bank. Higher capital and higher returns would increase the index, while a higher standard deviation of operating return on assets would lower the index and imply more risk.

The survival likelihood index can also be viewed as a measure of the likelihood of failure, with a smaller value of the index associated with a greater chance of bank failure. This is of particular importance to stockholders and regulators since bank failure can wipe out a stockholder's investment, while exposing the bank insurance fund to loss.[17]

There is no clear picture of differences in bank risk between hired-manager and owner-manager banks on these four dimensions (Table 7.3). There is no statistical difference between these banks in terms of earnings fluctuations and survival likelihood. Credit risk and leverage are statistically different across these banks, with hired-manager banks more risky in terms of leverage, but owner-manager banks more risky in terms of credit risk. This suggests that overall risk is not very different for these two types of banks, but the incentives and preferences of owners and managers towards risk is leading to a different mix of risks.

7.4.3   Regression Analysis of Bank Risk

To gain a clearer understanding of the different corporate governance factors that affect risk taking and the interactions and trade-offs among such governance mechanisms, we employ multiple regression analysis. The model equation makes risk a function of several explanatory variables: the ownership share of the hired manager (when the bank has a hired manager); the ownership share of the owner-manager (when the bank has an owner-manager); the manager's ratio of bank investment to personal net worth; the share of cash bonuses in the manager's total compensation; the principal monitor's ratio of bank investment to personal net worth (for hired-manager banks only); selected measures of board of director oversight activity; and some control variables. These control variables include a bank's location (metropolitan or rural) and its asset size.

This multivariate approach especially helps to separate out the individual effects on bank risk taking of all the corporate governance mechanisms and financial incentives mentioned above as explanatory variables. In contrast, just looking at one of these variables alone might ignore important interactions or off-setting influences from other variables. An example of this is the different implications for risk taking from two aspects of bank stock ownership. Increased stock ownership, all else being equal, is likely to encourage greater risk taking, given one's increased claim on the returns from successful ventures. However, the more one's wealth is concentrated in the ownership of a bank, the less willing one will be to put this investment at a greater risk.

The regression results support the hypothesis that bank stock ownership by hired managers can help to overcome a tendency by them to take on less risk at their banks than would be desired by stockholders. The estimated relation between a hired manager's ownership and each of the four measures of bank risk is statistically significant, and indicates that as the hired manager's stock ownership rises, risk in their bank also rises (Table 7.4 and Figure 7.1).[18] In the case of owner-manager banks, stock ownership is significantly related only to credit risk, again suggesting a positive relationship. However, the estimated coefficient for owner managers (0.0087) is much smaller than that for hired managers (0.0314), indicating a much smaller economic effect for owner-managers. These results are consistent with limited principal–agent problems in owner-managed banks.

Our results are also consistent with the hypothesis that bank risk will decline as a manager's portfolio becomes more highly concentrated in his or her bank investment and the manager's fortunes thus become more closely linked to the bank's. Estimates show that manager wealth concentration is significantly and negatively related to leverage risk, credit problems as measured by non-current assets, earnings fluctuation and the risk of survival (Table 7.4 and Figure 7.2). The effect that wealth concentration has on bank risk, moreover, is economically important and of a similar magnitude to the impact of changes in managerial ownership (Sullivan and Spong, 2007). To the extent that stockholders and corporate governance authorities regard ownership structure as a key determinant of firm risk, they should also regard portfolio effects of comparable importance.

Table 7.4   Regression analysis of bank risk, wealth concentration, ownership structure, and board characteristics on bank risk

Type of risk	Leverage	Credit quality	Earnings variation	Bankruptcy
		Dependent variable		
	Equity capital/ total assets	Non-current assets/total assets	log (net earnings variation)	log (survival likelihood index)
Independent variable				
Personal plus family ownership stake of hired manager	−0.0950*** (0.0357)	0.0314** (0.0133)	1.6458** (0.7034)	−2.2408*** (0.7818)
Personal plus family ownership stake of owner manager	−0.0038 (0.0073)	0.0087** (0.0042)	0.0913 (0.1393)	−0.1124 (0.1549)
Manager's bank investment/net worth	0.0170** (0.0085)	−0.0022* (0.0012)	−0.1295** (0.0525)	0.1604*** (0.0586)
Manager's bank investment/net worth squared	−0.0035** (0.0018)			
Share of cash bonus in manager compensation	0.0212* (0.0124)	−0.0067* (0.0037)	0.2927 (0.2348)	−0.0721 (0.2405)
Principal monitor's bank investment/net worth	0.0180*** (0.0066)	−0.0013 (0.0013)	−0.0565 (0.0751)	0.1886** (0.0907)
Attendance rate at board of director meetings	0.0417 (0.0295)	0.0135 (0.0117)	0.7018 (0.7485)	−0.2270 (0.8096)
Share of insiders on board of directors	0.0002*** (0.0001)	−0.0001 (0.0000)	0.0004 (0.0016)	0.0016 (0.0017)
Average annual fees paid to board of directors	0.0000 (0.0000)	−0.0000 (0.0000)	0.0000 (0.0000)	−0.0000 (0.0000)
Non-metropolitan indicator variable	0.0068* (0.0037)	−0.0036 (0.0024)	−0.1567 (0.0952)	0.2507** (0.1066)
Total assets of bank	−0.0001* (0.0001)	−0.0000 (0.0000)		
Total assets of bank squared	0.0000*** (0.0000)	−0.0000 (0.0000)		
log (total assets of bank)			−0.1925*** (0.0506)	0.2078*** (0.0548)
Constant term	0.0270 (0.0279)	0.0011 (0.0114)	−3.6601*** (0.9279)	0.5339 (1.0356)
Observations	258	257	258	258
R-squared	0.183	0.083	0.115	0.118

Notes:
*** p < 0.01, ** p < 0.05, * p < 0.1.
Robust standard errors in parentheses.

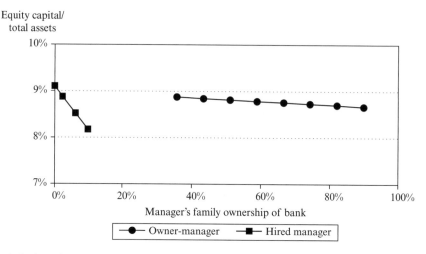

Notes: A rise in equity capital/total assets indicates a fall in leverage risk. Calculations based on regression (1) from Table 7.4. The range of a manager's family ownership of bank for each individual (owner-manager and hired manager) is the respective mean plus and minus one standard deviation, with a zero lower bound. Other than the manager's family ownership of bank, the independent variables are set to the means of hired-manager banks for hired managers and to the means of owner-manager banks for owner-managers.

Figure 7.1   Estimated effects of manager ownership on leverage risk

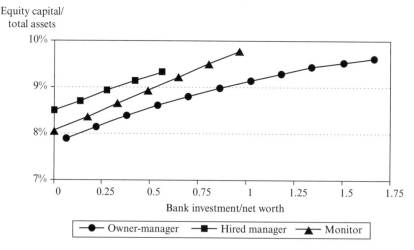

Notes: A rise in equity capital/total assets indicates a fall in leverage risk. Calculations based on regression (1) from Table 7.4. The range of bank investment/net worth for each individual (owner-manager, hired manager, and monitor) is the respective mean plus and minus one standard deviation, with a zero lower bound. Other than bank investment/net worth, the independent variables are set to the means of hired-manager banks for hired managers and monitors, and to the means of owner-manager banks for owner-managers.

Figure 7.2   Estimated effects of concentration of wealth on leverage risk

The share of cash bonuses in a manager's total compensation is statistically significant when bank risk is measured by leverage and by credit quality. In both cases, leverage risk and credit risk fall as the share of total manager compensation paid in cash bonuses rises. The direction and the statistical significance of these relationships may be tied to the high visibility of leverage and credit losses, which makes them good candidates for performance measures when determining incentive compensation at our sample banks.[19]

Results indicate that the more principal monitors have their wealth concentrated in their bank investment, the higher will be a bank's survival likelihood index and equity capital-to-total asset ratio. Thus, these monitors would appear to be influencing bank risk in a manner consistent with their own preferences. However, we find no relation between the principal monitor's wealth diversification and the credit risk or earnings variation of the bank, suggesting that major investors may have less influence over daily decisions in a bank compared to broader policy issues, such as the leverage of their bank.

In general, our measures of board activity are not statistically related to bank risk. The sole exception is that the share of insiders on the board of directors is positively related to the equity capital-to-total asset ratio. Having more insiders on sample bank boards is associated with less leverage risk. Thus, while outsiders may contribute to good governance, insiders with substantial financial exposure to bank risk appear to be willing and able to control at least one major type of bank risk.

Overall, these results suggest that governance and control of risk in a bank can come from a number of different sources. We find ownership to be an important factor influencing the behavior of managers, both in terms of giving hired managers an incentive to take risks more in keeping with stockholders' preferences, and in terms of linking managers more closely to the long-term performance and viability of their banks when these investments become a major part of their portfolios. Although the cash bonuses given to managers at the sample banks are not directly comparable to the type of compensation contracts at larger banks, we find some evidence that the prospect of receiving bonuses for good performance gives managers an incentive to avoid credit problems and to maintain and increase their bank's capital. While corporate governance has recently emphasized the importance of independent directors on bank boards, our results suggest that the most influential directors may be those with major stockholdings and a consequential incentive to invest the time and effort to be an effective director and develop the necessary financial expertise.

7.5   CONCLUDING COMMENTS

The recent crisis has raised a number of questions about the adequacy of corporate governance systems in financial institutions, and financial authorities have made a variety of suggestions for reforming and strengthening financial governance. Much of the research done in response to the crisis, though, suggests that corporate governance is a complex mechanism and that a comprehensive understanding of all the different elements of governance is necessary before effective policies can be developed.

Our analysis of corporate governance systems in smaller banks suggests that there are several different approaches that can be taken at financial institutions to ensure that stockholder interests are served and risk is managed within desired or acceptable parameters. In particular, we find several governance tools and financial incentives that influence the amount of risk taking in our sample banks. These include stock ownership by bank managers and their wealth diversification, the structure of managerial compensation, monitoring by directors and major stockholders, and the composition and characteristics of bank boards.

While it is difficult to say what risk levels may be appropriate from the standpoint of stockholders, depositors or regulators, we find that the key players in a bank will be most careful about managing risk if they have something significant at stake that could be lost as a result of poor decisions or changing financial conditions. These results reflect smaller institutions and a non-crisis period, but finding an effective means for controlling risk in ongoing operations is relevant to preparing any size or type of organization for more stressful conditions.

There are several corporate governance lessons that can be drawn from this crisis and from governance research. First, for corporate governance to be effective and create the right incentives, the public guarantees and assistance provided during this crisis – along with the moral hazard issues associated with deposit insurance and 'too big to fail' institutions – must be more limited in the future and addressed through tighter regulatory policies.

In addition, since it is hard to relate this crisis to one particular breakdown or shortcoming in corporate governance systems, coming up with simple rules for sound corporate governance may be difficult without also considering how an institution uses other governance tools. In the end, we find that governance works best when managers, directors and stockholders all have a significant personal stake in their decisions.

NOTES

*   The views expressed in this chapter are those of the authors and do not necessarily reflect those of the Federal Reserve Bank of Kansas City or the Federal Reserve System.
1. For several of these definitions, see Shleifer and Vishny (1997), Macey and O'Hara (2003) and Mülbert (2010).
2. For more on boards of directors and their fiduciary duties, see Macey and O'Hara (2003).
3. Kirkpatrick (2009: 2).
4. Acharya et al. (2009: 111).
5. There have also been other efforts to strengthen corporate governance on a broader level, including the Sarbanes–Oxley Act of 2002 and the new board and director requirements for companies listed on the New York Stock Exchange (NYSE) and NASDAQ.
6. Credit rating agencies explicitly adjust their ratings upward according to the probability that public authorities will step in and prevent financial institutions from defaulting on their obligations, with this probability being the greatest for institutions of systemic importance (see Moody's Investor Service, 2007).
7. For a more detailed description of these banks, see DeYoung et al. (2001). Our bank sample consisted of nearly 270 state-chartered banks after we removed a handful of banks because of missing data or significant changes in management or ownership during the time of the study.
8. We identify the manager as the person that examiners list as responsible on a daily basis for directing the operations of the bank. In most, but not all, cases this was the president or chief executive officer (CEO).
9. Often this ownership consisted of shares necessary for the hired manager to qualify as a member of the board of directors.
10. These wealth concentration numbers were calculated by comparing the value of a manager's investment in the bank to the net worth of this manager, as reported in the bank's examination report. The value of investment in the bank is the number of shares of common stock held, times the book value of bank capital per outstanding share. Since few of the banks had stock that was actively traded, book value was

used as a simple proxy for the value of stock in the sample banks. Control shares may be worth more, but book value gave a consistent measure across all stockholders and sample banks.

    This wealth concentration ratio will be subject to some measurement error, since the net worth figures in bank examinations are self-reported by directors or management and examiners do little to verify their accuracy. Also, several factors may influence what managers perceive to be their 'true' investment in the bank. For instance, managers or their holding companies commonly use debt financing to purchase major blocks of stock, thus raising the issue of whether their net investment would be the best measure to use. On the other hand, lenders often require personal guarantees on such debt, which would put much more at stake than the manager's net investment. We did not have consistent, current information on debt financing or personal guarantees, so we could not try to adjust for such factors. As a result, our wealth concentration ratios are approximations, and in some cases may even exceed one because of debt financing or misreporting of wealth. Overall, though, these numbers should provide a good, general guide to the wealth concentration of the major players in a bank's operations.

11. See Smith and Stulz (1985) and DeYoung et al. (2010) on designing manager compensation contracts to provide incentives to control risk.
12. Hired-manager banks more commonly paid bonuses, but the difference with owner-manager banks is not statistically significant.
13. One study found that banks with boards of directors that have poor attendance at board meetings and low bank ownership tend to be less efficient. See Spong et al. (1995).
14. Non-current assets include loans that are past due by 90 days or more, loans that are designated as no longer accruing interest, and real estate acquired by real estate foreclosure or as collateral for an unpaid loan.
15. Operating net income (return) is net income before taxes, securities gains/losses, and extraordinary items. Operating net income is a better reflection of a bank's business risk because business risk is determined by the variability of the demand for the bank's products and services, interest rate volatility, and the flexibility of the bank's asset and liability management. Operating net income focuses on the core business of the bank and eliminates fluctuations in income from variables that can be manipulated on a short-run basis. See Sinkey (1989: 408).
16. The index is based on the Z score in Boyd and Graham (1989). This represents the number of standard deviations below the mean that operating return on assets would have to fall in order to eliminate capital. This same ratio is sometimes called the distance-to-default.
17. Boyd and Graham (1989) consider the question of whether the survival likelihood index computed using accounting data or stock market data is a better measure of bankruptcy risk. They conclude that the accounting-based survival likelihood index conveys 'much of the same information that is in commercial paper ratings. The market [survival likelihood] indices do not. To the extent, therefore, that commercial paper ratings are useful measures of bankruptcy risk, these findings favor the use of a survival likelihood index computed with accounting data.'
18. In DeYoung et al. (2001), we also find that profit efficiency improved substantially at these banks as hired managers accumulated shares in their banks and became more closely aligned with stockholders. Profit efficiency reached its highest point when a hired manager had a 17 percent ownership share and then declined somewhat beyond that point, which might reflect a greater potential for stockholder conflicts and entrenchment or the limited number of hired-manager banks in that category.
19. Our other measures of bank risk (earning fluctuations and survival likelihood) can be meaningfully measured only over longer time periods.

REFERENCES

Acharya, V., T. Philippon, M. Richardson and N. Roubini (2009), 'The financial crisis of 2007–2009: causes and remedies', *Financial Markets, Institutions and Instruments*, **18**, 89–137.
Adams, R. (2009), 'Governance and the financial crisis', Finance Working Paper No. 248/2009 (April), European Corporate Governance Institute.
Basel Committee on Banking Supervision (1999), 'Enhancing corporate governance for banking organizations', Basel, Switzerland (revised in 2006 and 2010).
Bebchuk, L., A. Cohen and H. Spamann (2010), 'The wages of failure: executive compensation at Bear Stearns and Lehman 2000–2008', Discussion Paper No. 657 (revised 2/2010), Harvard Law School.
Beltratti, A. and R.M. Stulz (2009), 'Why did some banks perform better during the credit crisis? A cross-country study of the impact of governance and regulation', Finance Working Paper No. 254/2009 (July), European Corporate Governance Institute.

Bolton, P., H. Mehran and J. Shapiro (2010), 'Executive compensation and risk taking', paper presented at conference on Governance, Executive Compensation and Excessive Risk in the Financial Services Industry, Columbia University School of Business, 28 September.

Boyd, J.H. and S.L. Graham (1989), 'Bank holding company risk', in B. Gup (ed.), *Bank Mergers: Current Issues and Perspectives*, Boston, MA: Kluwer Academic Publishers.

Cannella, A., D. Fraser and D. Lee (1995), 'Firm failure and managerial labor markets: evidence from Texas banking', *Journal of Financial Economics*, **38**, 185–210.

Coles, J.L., N.D. Daniel and L. Naveen (2006), 'Managerial incentives and risk-taking', *Journal of Financial Economics*, **79**, 431–468.

DeYoung, R., E.Y. Peng and M. Yan (2010), 'Executive compensation and business policy choices at US commercial banks', Research Working Paper 10-02 (January), Federal Reserve Bank of Kansas City.

DeYoung, R., K. Spong and R.J. Sullivan (2001), 'Who's minding the store? Motivating and monitoring hired managers at small, closely held commercial banks', *Journal of Banking and Finance*, **25**, 1209–1243.

Ellul, A. and V. Yerramilli (2010), 'Stronger risk controls, lower risk: evidence from US bank holding companies', NBER Working Paper No. 16178 (July), National Bureau of Economic Research.

Erkens, D., M. Hung and P. Matos (2009), 'Corporate governance in the 2007–2008 financial crisis: evidence from financial institutions worldwide', Finance Working Paper No. 249/2009 (December), European Corporate Governance Institute.

Fahlenbrach, R. and R. Stulz (2010), 'Bank CEO incentives and the credit crisis', Fisher College of Business Working Paper Series, Ohio State University.

Fama, E. (1980), 'Agency problems and the theory of the firm', *Journal of Political Economy*, **88**, 288–307.

Federal Register (2010), 'Guidance on sound incentive compensation practices', Department of the Treasury (Office of the Comptroller of the Currency), Federal Reserve System, Federal Deposit Insurance Corporation, and Department of the Treasury (Office of Thrift Supervision). **75**(122), 25 June, 36395–36414.

Jensen, M. and W. Meckling (1976), 'Theory of the firm, managerial behavior, agency costs, and ownership structure', *Journal of Financial Economics*, **3**, 305–360.

Kirkpatrick, G. (2009), 'The corporate governance lessons from the financial crisis', *OECD Journal: Financial Market Trends*, **1**, 61–87.

Macey, J.R. and M. O'Hara (2003), 'The corporate governance of banks', Federal Reserve Bank of New York, *Economic Policy Review* (April), 91–107.

Moody's Investor Service (2007), 'Incorporation of joint-default analysis into Moody's Bank Ratings: a refined methodology'.

Morgan, D. and K. Stiroh (2005), 'Too big to fail after all these years', Staff Report No. 220 (September), Federal Reserve Bank of New York.

Mülbert, P.O. (2010), 'Corporate governance of banks after the financial crisis – theory, evidence, reforms', ECGI Working Paper Series in Law No. 151/2010, European Corporate Governance Institute.

Nestor Advisors Ltd (2009), 'Governance in crisis: a comparative case study of six US investment banks', NeAd Research Note 0109/April, London.

OECD (1999), 'OECD principles of corporate governance', Organisation for Economic Co-operation and Development, Paris (revised 2004).

Rime, B. (2005), 'Do "too big to fail" expectations boost large banks issuer ratings?', Systemic Stability Section, Swiss National Bank.

Rogers, D.A. (2002), 'Does executive portfolio structure affect risk management? CEO risk-taking incentives and corporate derivatives usage', *Journal of Banking and Finance*, **26**, 271–295.

Shleifer, A. and R. Vishny (1997), 'A survey of corporate governance', *Journal of Finance*, **52**, 737–784.

Sinkey, J.F. (1989), *Commercial Bank Financial Management*, New York: Macmillan.

Smith, C.W. and R.M. Stulz (1985), 'The determinants of firms' hedging policies', *Journal of Financial and Quantitative Analysis*, **20**, 391–404.

Spong, K., R.J. Sullivan and R. DeYoung (1995), 'What makes a bank efficient? A look at financial characteristics and management and ownership structure', *Financial Industry Perspectives* (December), Federal Reserve Bank of Kansas City.

Sullivan, R.J. and K.R. Spong (2007), 'Manager wealth concentration, ownership structure, and risk in commercial banks', *Journal of Financial Intermediation*, **16**, 229–248.

8 Executive compensation and risk-taking in European banking

Rym Ayadi, Emrah Arbak and Willem Pieter De Groen

8.1 INTRODUCTION

The financial crisis of 2007–2008 has revealed serious weaknesses in the corporate governance of major financial institutions and has led to severe public criticism of the role that executive compensation packages played in encouraging excessive risk-taking and myopic behaviour in the financial sector.

Although the remuneration schemes were not seen as the main cause of the financial crisis of 2007–2008, they were a major contributing factor. Indeed, the existing pay packages tend to provide bank executives with myopic incentives, such as bonuses that are either fully at the discretion of the management board or related to a narrow and short-term definition of company performance.[1] Such incentives lead to a race to inflate profits and, in most cases, excessive risk-taking.

In response to this concern, the European Commission announced in the Communication of 4 March 2009 for the Spring European Council on driving European recovery[2] that it would:

> (i) as a matter of urgency, address the impropriety of the remuneration framework in the financial sector with a view to curbing excessive risk-taking and short-termism, and (ii) as a second step, examine more broadly and report on current corporate governance practices in financial institutions, making recommendations including for legislative initiatives, where appropriate.

Immediately after the G20 London Summit, the Commission issued two recommendations in April 2009, one strengthening its 2004 Recommendation on remuneration of directors of listed companies and the second one addressing remuneration of risk-taking staff in the financial sector.[3] To remedy the potential short-termism of remuneration policies, the EC has recommended the member states to implement rules and principles to ensure that assessments consider multi-year performance and risks, including potential 'clawback' clauses to claim back any unjustified pay.[4] The July 2010 amendment to the Capital Requirements Directive ('CRD III') also imposes an obligation on credit institutions 'to have remuneration policies and practices that are consistent with and promote sound and effective risk management, accompanied by high level principles on sound remuneration' and to bring remuneration policy under the scope of supervisory review, allowing national supervisors to impose penalties In October 2010, the Committee of European Banking Supervisors (CEBS) published a draft guideline that was built on the High-level Principles for Remuneration Policies published in April 2009 in order to facilitate the EU-wide compliance of the remuneration principles, as required by the CDR III.[5] These responses were largely inspired by the principles in three broad areas: (1) active board involvement; (2) long-term risk- and performance-adjustment and deferral of bonuses; and (3) oversight by supervisory risk-assessment; issued by the Financial Stability Board (FSB) in April 2009 and endorsed at the G20 London Summit.

These principles gave way to the development of more detailed standards by September 2009 that were endorsed by the G20 in its Pittsburgh meeting. Serving as a model for most of the national and regional initiatives, the FSB's principles and standards cover various governance, performance- and risk-alignment, and oversight issues. The March 2010 FSB peer review highlighted international differences in various aspects, notably on the legal approach.[6] A key shortcoming has been the lack of progress in compliance with risk- and performance-adjustment principles and rules. The European Commission has also found that the implementation of its legal initiatives on remuneration has been at best partial and heterogeneous, with substantial differences between member states on the content and level of detail for the risk-adjustment, long-term alignment and disclosure requirements.[7]

To sum up, as a response to the financial crisis, there has been a clear policy drive to require banks and other financial institutions to incorporate more long-term-oriented and performance-contingent remuneration packages largely aimed to reduce excessive risk-taking.

Although several studies have investigated the remuneration–bank risk linkage within the US context, the focus has been on equity-based pay, such as option plans, and their impact on aligning interests of shareholders and management. The impacts of other types of compensation packages, such as annual bonuses or the so-called 'long-term performance incentives', on risk-taking have not been adequately investigated. In Europe, no empirical study has so far investigated the role of such policies on risk-taking of banking institutions.

The present chapter attempts to fill these gaps by using an empirical assessment of the relationship between a variety of bank risk measures and different aspects of compensation schemes, based on a novel database[8] on remuneration in the EU's most systematically important banks. Almost half of our dataset includes banks that are not listed on the stock market, which makes the capital market-based measures of risk that are widely used in the US studies inapplicable. Thus, an alternative measure of risk, which is based on widely available annual income statement and balance sheet information, is used as an indicator of failure likelihood.

Section 8.2 provides a summary of the literature on empirical studies that assess the impact of compensation on market-based risk measures. Two alternate hypotheses on the relationship between bank risk and compensation schemes are provided in section 8.3. The methodology and data used in the chapter are reviewed in section 8.4, which provides details on the model that links measures of risk to the various elements of compensation schemes while at the same time controlling for variables that are often thought to be influential in risk determination. In section 8.5 a series of tests are conducted to assess the relationship between bank risk and remuneration policies, paying attention to the possibility that the two parameters may be jointly determined. Section 8.6 concludes.

8.2 LITERATURE REVIEW[9]

Over the past decades, at least up until the US accounting scandals of 2000–2002, there has been a general call to tie management compensation packages to changes in a firm's equity value. First suggested by Berle and Means (1932 [1991]) and later formalized by Jensen and Meckling (1976), these calls have been based on the inefficiencies emanating from the separation of ownership and management of publicly owned corporations. According to theory, managers may have substantial discretion over the operations of a corporation, which may be used for their own benefit in a variety of ways, including empire building, entrenchment and so forth (Shleifer and Vishny, 1997). Performance-based pay schemes are put forward as a solution to align the interests of owners and managers. Accordingly, optimal compensation schemes reward (or punish) with the aim of providing incentives for managers to maximize the firm's shareholder value (Jensen and Murphy, 1990; Holmström and Tirole, 1993).

The use of stock options in financial institutions appears to have changed drastically over time. Houston and James (1995) show that the chief executive officers (CEOs) of US banks held fewer stock options and received a smaller proportion of their salaries in the form of stocks and options than CEOs in other industries in the 1980s and early 1990s. Contemporaneous studies have shown that the use of bonuses and stock options were greater in deregulated banking markets in the US during the 1990s (Crawford et al., 1995; Hubbard and Palia, 1995). Recent evidence, however, shows that performance-based pay has become more habitual in the financial services sector. Based on a survey of CEO compensation packages in US banks by the 2000s, Chen et al. (2006) confirm that the use of option-based schemes has exploded in recent years, with the value of stock options representing over one-third of total salaries of executives.

The main argument for opposing schemes that closely track stock market performance arises from their complete disregard of debt. The results of the classical agency theory noted above are applicable for full-equity firms with a dispersed ownership structure. However, most firms fulfil their funding needs at least partly by debt financing. The problem is that when debt financing is substantial, as is the case with banks, shareholders may have an incentive to shift an inappropriate amount of risk to the debt holders, as noted by Jensen and Meckling (1976). Much like the pay-offs from call options, the equity holders' returns are increasing with the riskiness of the underlying assets since the downside risks (beyond the value of the equity) are borne entirely by depositors (Saunders et al., 1990; John et al., 2000; Bebchuk and Spamann, 2010).

The moral hazard problem could be allayed if the depositors can monitor and impose sanctions on banks, for example by withdrawing their deposits. However, in theory, the deposit insurance schemes that are in place across the world weaken the depositors' incentives to monitor the banks adequately.[10] Thus, the stockholders can maintain an almost exclusive control over the management through the use of performance-related remuneration tools, potentially undermining the debt value of the bank and leading to excessive risk-taking.

Another argument against the prevalent use of stock-performance-based compensation schemes arises from the overly simplistic assumptions of the classical agency theory. Even for an all-equity firm, the idea of relying on stock performance to align incentives rests on the supposition that stock prices are an unbiased estimate of a firm's fundamentals and cannot be manipulated by managers. Recent corporate scandals and research have challenged the validity of these notions, bringing forth evidence that performance-based schemes may lead to short-termism and excessive risk-taking, especially in speculative markets (Bebchuk and Fried, 2004; Bolton et al., 2006a, 2006b, 2010).

Several studies have sought to establish a link between manager–shareholder incentive alignment and risk-taking. Saunders et al. (1990) show that managerial stock ownership has a positive impact on idiosyncratic risks borne by US banks. This result confirms the 'risk-taking' argument, implying that increasing managerial ownership augments risks as the incentives of managers and stockholders become similar. Mehran and Rosenberg (2007) also find evidence of increased risk-taking with a heavier use of stock options.[11] Using a cross-country study, Laeven and Levine (2009) document that risks are higher in banks that are owned by powerful shareholders, that is, those with large block-holders.

Other studies reach the opposite results. Chen et al. (1998) show that risk-taking is reduced with the size of option plans. The result could be explained by the argument put forth by Smith and Stulz (1985), who claim that as managerial ownership increases, managers become increasingly risk averse since their equity portfolios become less diversified. Using more recent data covering the compensation schemes in US banks right before and during the 2007–2008 crisis, Fahlenbrach and Stulz (2009) also find no evidence that greater sensitivity of executive pay to stock volatility has led to worse performance.

The closest study to ours is Chen et al. (2006), which assesses the relationship between the stock option plans and risk-taking in the US banking industry. According to the results of that study, while the option plans induce more risk-taking, the causality also runs in the opposite direction; that is, more risky banks are also more likely to offer option-based compensation. These findings confirm that even though risk and remuneration policies are jointly determined, schemes that align the interests of managers and shareholders may invite more risk-taking in banking, as long as the managers' portfolios remain well diversified.

8.3   HYPOTHESES ON RELATION BETWEEN EXECUTIVE COMPENSATION AND RISK-TAKING

In this section, we develop alternative hypotheses on the relationship between bank risk and compensation schemes. Implicit in the reforms that have been enacted in response to the 2007–2009 crisis is the view that the myopic incentives provided by the remuneration schemes have led to governance weaknesses and 'creative risk-taking'. Narayanan (1985) shows that short-termist incentives, such as annual profit-sharing plans, may augment risks when the managerial ability is private information. In such a case, the manager may select a project that yields short-term profits, expecting to improve the perceptions regarding their ability, without paying adequate attention to the firm's (and its shareholders') long-term interests. Armed with informational advantages about both their own values and the underlying values of their decisions, managers may also engage in hidden actions, which would affect the long-term valuation and short-term stock price, especially if they have substantial power over the board (Bebchuk and Fried, 2004; Bolton et al., 2006a). These arguments lead to the first hypothesis:

Hypothesis 1   Short-term incentives, such as annual bonuses and profit-sharing schemes, augment bank riskiness.

Turning to long-term performance incentives, to the extent that they serve to align the interests of stockholders and managers, option plans and performance plans could both augment risk-taking. These motives are particularly acute when depository insurance systems imply fixed premiums or for institutions that are 'too big to fail'. In either case, the managers can increase their expected returns from these packages by increasing bank risk to inefficient levels or increasing the value of their 'call options', shifting the risk to deposit insurance schemes or the tax payers.[12] This leads to the second hypothesis:

Hypothesis 2   Long-term performance-related pay packages that align the interests of shareholders and managers augment bank risks.

8.4   METHODOLOGY AND DATA

8.4.1   Risk Indicators

Two types of sources are used to assess risk in this chapter. First, we decompose the listed banks' stock performances to derive a number of measures, much as in Flannery and James (1984) and Chen and Chan (1989). The simplest market-based measure is the total stock volatility, or the standard deviation of the daily returns (total risk), calculated for each bank and for each year separately. Although useful in assessing the market's perception of risks, total risk is likely to incorporate risks that are well beyond bank-specific issues, such as the market conditions and economic environment. In order to measure the bank's exposures to these sources, which are additional elements of risk, the daily stock market returns are decomposed into exposure to banking sector volatility (systematic risk) and exposure to interest rate yields (interest risk). Lastly, the variation of the residual term, which is obtained once total variation is decomposed into the market and interest-rate exposure components, defines the final market-based measure, called the idiosyncratic risk as it provides an estimate of the volatility that is the bank's own doing.

The market-based measures described above are obtained by the estimation of a two-index model, which is defined as:

$$R_{jd} = \alpha + \beta_j^S STOXX_d + \beta_j^I I_d + u_{jd} \tag{8.1}$$

where R_{jd} is the total return on stock of bank j on day d, $STOXX_d$ is the return on the Dow Jones STOXX® Europe 600 Banking index, obtained from STOXX.com, and I_d is the daily one-year German bond yield, obtained from the German Bundesbank's statistics website. The four measures are then equivalent to the standard deviations of total returns, R_{jd}, and the error component, u_{jd}, described by the variables σ_j and σ_{uj}, respectively, as well as the coefficient estimates for systematic risk, β_j^S. For the interest-rate risk, the absolute value of the coefficient estimates for β_j^I are used since any exposure, whether it is positively or negatively correlated with the market rates, is considered risky.[13]

The daily stock pricing data for 1 January 1999 to 31 December 2009 were obtained from Yahoo Finance and Finanzen.net. The daily index data for Dow Jones STOXX® Europe 600 Banking index were downloaded from STOXX's website while the daily one-year German bond yields were obtained from the German Bundesbank's statistics website. For the total of 53 banks in our sample, 28 have stock listings for which pricing data are collected.

Since a significant proportion of the banks in our sample are not listed (25 out of 53 banks), an alternative risk measure is also necessary. Moreover, although the four measures provide a glimpse of the stock price volatility and responsiveness, they do not clearly capture default risks. Our second risk measure thus uses the widely available balance sheet information for the entire sample to develop the so-called 'Z-score', derived as in Boyd and Runkle (1993), which is a simple indicator of the risk of failure.

To derive the Z-score, suppose that failure occurs when the losses of bank j at year t cannot be entirely absorbed by equity, or when $\pi_{jt} + E_{jt} < 0$. Then, assuming that the bank's return on total assets (ROA), or π_{jt}/TA_{jt}, is normally distributed with mean μ_j, and standard deviation σ_j, the probability of failure is given as:

$$pr(\pi_{jt} < -E_{jt}) = pr(\pi_{jt}/TA_{jt} < -E_{jt}/TA_{jt}) = \int_{-\infty}^{Z_{jt}} \phi(r)\,dr \qquad (8.2)$$

where ϕ represents the standard normal distribution, r is the standardized return on assets and Z, or the Z-score, is the boundary that separates a healthy bank from an unhealthy one, described as the normalized equity ratio:

$$Z_{jt} = \frac{-(E_{jt}/TA_{jt}) - \mu_j}{\sigma_j}. \qquad (8.3)$$

Note that unlike most of the literature, a greater Z-score implies a greater probability of default and, therefore, a greater risk for the bank.[14]

To calculate the Z-scores and for other bank-specific variables Bureau Van Dijk's Bankscope database is used to obtain various balance sheet and income statement items for the years 1999–2009, including the total assets, equity and the return on assets.[15]

8.4.2   Remuneration Variables

All the indicators relating to the remuneration schemes are constructed by the Centre for European Policy Studies (CEPS) after an examination of the annual reports and governance reports of the sampled banks for the years 1999 to 2009. The database covers information on fixed salaries; long-term performance-related bonus packages, such as option plans and long-term performance incentives; and annual bonuses, which are dependent on short-term performance (i.e., annual profits).

The sample covers 53 banks, although the number of banks for which remuneration information data exist varies. The dataset also includes a significant number of multiple bank-year entries due to CEO replacements.[16]

Four different aspects of compensation schemes are covered by the CEPS database. The dummy variable *LTBONUS* identifies long-term bonus plans that reward the CEOs with cash or shares that are made conditional on multiple-year performance criteria. By definition, these bonus plans exclude option plans. Examples of such programmes include a variety of forward-looking incentive plans, such as the so-called 'long-term

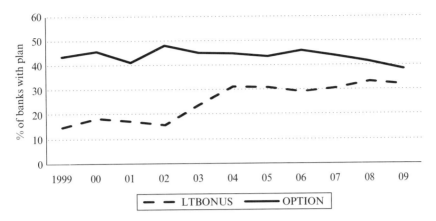

Figure 8.1   Evolution of the use of long-term performance and option plans

incentive plans', deferred bonus plans, performance share plans, or cash or share payments, all linked to some long-term (relative or absolute) company-wide performance.

The second dummy variable, *OPTION*, identifies the presence of a formal option plan for the CEOs. These plans are contracts that give chief executives and other management the right to buy a specific number of the company's shares at a fixed preset price within a certain period of time. The value of the stock option thus depends on the future prices of the stock. Stock option plans may provide similar incentives with certain long-term bonus plans, such as performance share plans with stock performance related criteria. However, the two variables are mutually exclusive since long-term benefits are made conditional on meeting targets and not granted at the onset of the program. When either of the two plans was not mentioned in the annual report of the bank for the specific year, the relevant dummy was set to zero.[17]

The evolution of the option plans and long-term bonus plans is depicted in Figure 8.1. As is clear from the figure, long-term bonus plans have become increasingly popular in recent years while the use of option plans has remained relatively constant within our sample. In particular, about 40 per cent of banks in our sample offer an option plan while slightly more than 30 per cent of all the banks (up from 15 per cent in earlier part of the decade) offer some form of long-term performance incentives.

In addition to these two dummy variables, our dataset also contains the amount of annual compensation provided to the chief executive officers as the base salary (*FIXED*) and annual bonus (*ANBONUS*). The share of annual bonus in total annual pay (*ANBONUS%*) was also calculated. The base salary is unconditional on company performance and is set by contractual agreement as part of the employment contract. Annual bonuses, on the other hand, are often granted at the discretion of the board of directors or the compensation committee. In most cases, they are performance dependent; however, the targets are annual and do not consider multiple-year criteria, as in profit sharing schemes or annual performance bonuses. Other components, such as value of long-term incentives, option plans, exit bonuses, 'golden parachutes', or other benefits in kind, such as company cars, housing allowance, medical insurance, pension payments, etc., are not included in this amount and are not a part of our database.[18]

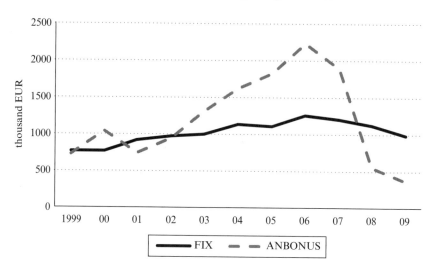

Figure 8.2   Evolution of the average fixed salary and annual bonus

The evolution of fixed salary and annual bonuses is depicted in Figure 8.2. The figure shows that the average fixed salary has increased only gradually, more or less in line with the overall price levels. Annual bonuses, however, increased rapidly after 2001, surpassing the total amount granted as fixed salary. This upward trend gave way to a rapid decline in 2006–2007 with the onset of the financial crisis. By the year-end 2009, annual bonuses amounted to less than half of fixed salary, or one-third of total annual cash pay, down from nearly double the fixed pay in 2006.

The measures of risk considered above are modelled as a function of various aspects of compensation schemes. We also control for firm-specific factors such as bank size, capital ratio, income diversification and type of bank.

The following model is used for the determination of risk:

$$Risk = f(\text{Compensation}, LN(TA), CAPITAL, NONINI, COOPERATIVE) \quad (8.4)$$

where:

Compensation	One of option plan dummy *(OPTION)*, long-term bonus dummy *(LTBONUS)*, or share of annual bonus in total annual pay *(ANBONUS%)*.
Risk	One of total risk (σ_j), idiosyncratic risk (σ_{uj}), systematic risk (β_j^s), interest-rate risk β_j^i, and indicator on default likelihood *(ZSCORE$_j$)*.
LN(TA)	The natural logarithm of total assets, used as a proxy for bank size.
CAPITAL%	The equity-to-assets ratio, used to measure financial soundness.
NONINT%	The share non-interest income in total income, used as a measure for broadened banking activity such as investment banking or off-balance-sheet activity.
COOPERATIVE	Dummy for cooperative banks, used to highlight potentially the role of traditional banking.

Table 8.1 Descriptive statistics

Variable	N	Mean	Median	Std. dev.	Min.	Max.
TOTAL RISK, σ_j	299	0.026	0.021	0.032	0.006	0.509
IDIOSYNCRATIC RISK, σ_{uj}	290	0.020	0.014	0.035	0.005	0.575
SYSTEMATIC RISK, β_j^s	290	0.909	0.949	0.367	0.003	2.254
INTEREST RISK, β_j^I	290	0.326	0.196	0.606	0.001	7.740
ZSCORE	619	−18.547	−15.745	15.273	0.798	−91.168
ANBONUS	208	1.230	0.800	1.472	0	8.149
ANBONUS%	208	0.399	0.477	0.267	0	0.876
LTBONUS	554	0.484	0	0.500	0	1
OPTION	546	0.438	0	0.497	0	1
CEO_YEARS	572	4.530	3.4	3.954	0	24
TA	619	335600	184887	422377	145	2586701
LN(TA)	619	11.714	12.128	1.836	4.977	14.766
CAPITAL%	552	0.054	0.047	0.038	−0.004	0.278
NONINT%	617	0.426	0.364	1.891	−34.786	23.490
COOPERATIVE	621	0.121	0	0.326	0	1

Notes: The first four risk measures are market-based, derived using a two-index model. *ZSCORE* indicates the likelihood of a bank failure, defined as the sum of capital ratio and average return on assets divided by the standard deviation of return on assets; *ANBONUS* is the total annual bonus (millions of euros); ANBONUS% is the percentage of annual bonus to total annual salary; *LTBONUS* is a dummy variable measuring long-term stock and cash remuneration; *OPTION* is a dummy variable indicating the presence of a formal option plan; *CEO_YEARS* is the total number of years a CEO is in position; *TA* is the total assets (in millions of euros); *LN(TA)* is the natural logarithm of total assets (in millions of euros); *CAPITAL%* is the equity-to-asset ratio; *NONINT%* is the percentage of income that is from non-interest sources; and *COOPERATIVE* is a dummy variable measuring type of bank effects.

A positive and significant sign on the compensation variables would signify that the relevant schemes are positively correlated with bank risks. Bank size, as measured by *LN(TA)*, may have a negative impact on riskiness if large banks are able to diversify their risks. Conversely, size may augment risks if larger banks take on activities that expose them to various components of risk. Larger banks may also be able to withstand elevated risks due to the market's belief that they will be saved, as hypothesized by the 'too-big-to-fail' argument. Capital ratios should be negatively correlated with risk, especially the failure likelihood, since they indicate additional absorption space in the event of an adverse shock. Banks with a greater share of non-interest income may also be able to diversify their risks (Demsetz and Strahan, 1997). More traditional banks, such as banks with lower non-interest income, cooperative or savings banks, may also have lower exposure to risk, as experience on banks following demutualization seems to suggest (Fraser and Zardkoohi, 1996).[19] Table 8.1 gives a detailed description of the variables used in the study.

8.5   RESULTS

8.5.1   OLS Regressions for Assessing Impact of Compensation on Risk-Taking

The effects of various compensation schemes on the two sets of risk measures are given in Table 8.2 and Table 8.3. In order to minimize the endogeneity problem arising from a two-way relationship between compensation schemes and risk, all of the exogenous variables are lagged.[20, 21] The dummy variables for years 2000 to 2008 have also been included to control for annual volatility in our risk measures. Moreover, for equations involving the option plans (*OPTION*), only listed banks are included in the regression to avoid biased estimates.

A quick glance through the two tables shows that the interaction between the remuneration variables and the risk may at times depend on the type of measure used. In each table, the regression models have been estimated using different compensation scheme parameters.[22] Table 8.2 gives the results for each of the market-based risk measures in separate groups of columns. In Table 8.3, two sets of regressions were run for each compensation parameter, with and without year dummies. The similarities between columns (1)–(3) and (4)–(6) show that the inclusion of year dummies changes little in our estimations.

Starting with the determinants of market-based risk, as summarized in Table 8.2, it is worthwhile to first note that among the depicted non-compensation variables, the total assets variable, *LN(TA)*, has a statistically significant and consistent impact on exposures to market volatility (systematic risk).[23] This means that larger banks develop activities that make their returns more closely aligned with other large banks in the sector.[24] In turn, well-capitalized banks appear to be subject to significantly less systematic risks although the results on other market-based risk measures are more mixed. Lastly, banks that engage more in less traditional activities with more non-interest income appear to be slightly more stable although the coefficient estimates are not significant enough to make a stronger statement.

Turning to the determinants of failure likelihoods, as measured by the *ZSCORE* indicator in Table 8.3, holding more capital reduces the default risk consistently across all regressions. Moreover, being large may increase default risks although the results are highly mixed. Banks that have more traditional lines of business, that is, those that rely less on non-interest income, appear to be sounder, although only slightly so. Lastly, cooperative banks are persistently and significantly less risky than their peers.[25]

Turning to the compensation variables, the dummy for long-term performance incentives (*LTBONUS*) appears to increase bank failure likelihood, as noted from columns (1) and (4) of Table 8.3. The second remuneration-related variable included in the study, the dummy option plans (*OPTION*), appears to have a contrasting impact. In particular, banks with option plans have greater market exposures (systematic risk), as noted in column (8) of Table 8.2. In contrast, banks with an option plan appear to face a lower default likelihood, as shown in columns (2) and (5) of Table 8.3. As for the third remuneration variable, the share of annual bonuses in total annual pay (*ANBONUS%*), the results summarized in the columns (3), (6), (9) and (12) of Table 8.2 unravel another intriguing result. Compensation packages that grant relatively larger annual bonuses (as opposed to fixed salaries) seem to reduce riskiness. The result is also surprising because

Table 8.2   Relation between market-based risk measures and compensation schemes

	(1)	(2)	(3)	(4)	(5)	(6)	(7)	(8)	(9)	(10)	(11)	(12)
	TOTAL RISK (σ_j)			IDIOSYNCRATIC RISK (σ_{uj})			SYSTEMATIC RISK (β_j^s)			INTEREST RISK (β_j^i)		
LTBONUS	−0.002 (0.006)	–	–	−0.002 (0.006)	–	–	0.046 (0.044)	–	–	0.045 (0.095)	–	–
OPTION	–	−0.009 (0.006)	–	–	−0.012 (0.007)	–	–	0.117** (0.050)	–	–	−0.170 (0.107)	–
ANBONUS%	–	–	−0.013*** (0.004)	–	–	−0.008** (0.003)	–	–	−0.254** (0.121)	–	–	−0.488*** (0.170)
LN(TA)	0.001 (0.002)	0.003 (0.003)	0.003*** (0.001)	−0.001 (0.003)	0.002 (0.003)	0.001 (0.001)	0.176*** (0.018)	0.153*** (0.020)	0.130*** (0.026)	−0.009 (0.039)	0.032 (0.043)	0.024 (0.037)
CAPITAL%	−0.000 (0.001)	0.000 (0.001)	−0.002*** (0.000)	0.000 (0.001)	0.000 (0.001)	−0.001*** (0.000)	−0.024** (0.010)	−0.030*** (0.010)	−0.060*** (0.012)	0.027 (0.022)	0.031 (0.022)	−0.022 (0.016)
NONINT%	−0.026 (0.020)	−0.026 (0.020)	−0.012** (0.005)	−0.033 (0.023)	−0.031 (0.022)	−0.016*** (0.005)	−0.103 (0.155)	−0.103 (0.154)	−0.188 (0.175)	−0.279 (0.338)	−0.204 (0.333)	−0.204 (0.246)
COOPERA-TIVE	−0.007 (0.011)	−0.007 (0.011)	−0.003 (0.003)	−0.005 (0.012)	−0.005 (0.012)	−0.000 (0.002)	0.017 (0.085)	0.019 (0.083)	−0.026 (0.083)	−0.225 (0.184)	−0.261 (0.179)	−0.240** (0.116)
Year dummies (2000–2008)	YES	YES	YES	YES	YES	YES	YES	YES	YES	YES	YES	YES
Observations	231	234	134	226	229	134	226	229	134	226	229	134
R-squared	0.096	0.098	0.628	0.066	0.071	0.704	0.491	0.496	0.352	0.249	0.263	0.611

Notes: Ordinary least squares (OLS) regression models with lagged (t − 1) exogenous variables. Constant terms and year dummies are suppressed for brevity. Numbers of observations in columns (3), (6), (9), and (12) are low due to limited amount of information on the amount granted as annual bonuses, *ANBONUS%*.
Standard errors in parentheses; ***, **, * represent significance at the 1%, 5%, 10% levels of p-values, respectively.

Table 8.3   Relation between bank failure (Z-score) and compensation schemes

	(1)	(2)	(3)	(4)	(5)	(6)
LTBONUS	3.143**	–	–	3.226**	–	–
	(1.510)			(1.527)		
OPTION	–	−3.895***	–	–	−3.902***	–
		(1.293)			(1.305)	
ANBONUS%	–	–	0.798	–	–	−2.611
			(2.761)			(3.638)
LN(TA)	−0.011	1.635***	−0.738	−0.035	1.901***	−0.487
	(0.530)	(0.504)	(0.742)	(0.544)	(0.531)	(0.786)
CAPITAL%	−1.722***	−1.892***	−2.101***	−1.749***	−1.997***	−2.282***
	(0.244)	(0.275)	(0.336)	(0.247)	(0.280)	(0.349)
NONINT%	0.005	−0.914	0.463	−0.013	−5.770	0.241
	(0.267)	(3.499)	(1.813)	(0.269)	(4.187)	(1.833)
COOPERATIVE	−8.331***	−5.505**	−5.773**	−8.323***	−5.262**	−6.227**
	(1.705)	(2.281)	(2.730)	(1.725)	(2.304)	(2.771)
Year dummies (2000–2008)	–	–	–	YES	YES	YES
Observations	413	244	153	413	244	153
R-squared	0.205	0.302	0.256	0.211	0.324	0.294

Notes: Ordinary least squares (OLS) regression models. Constant terms and year dummies are suppressed for brevity. Numbers of observations for columns for (4)–(5) and (9)–(10) are low due to limited amount of information on variable executive pay.
Standard errors in parentheses; ***, **, * represent significance at the 1%, 5% and 10% levels of p-values.

annual bonuses are often thought to contribute to more myopic risk-taking as they do not depend on long-term performance measures.

To explain these contrasted results, there are two arguments. First, long-term bonus plans could be more high-powered, unlike the option plans which tend to respond less to management decisions and increase market exposures, possibly arising from inherent incentives to 'beat the market' (Galai and Masulis, 1976).[26] At the same time, option plans may reduce default likelihood as they represent a significant proportion of the incomes of managers, rendering the managers' portfolios less diversified (Smith and Stulz, 1985).

These results may call for more qualitative analysis related to the design of the compensation packages including especially the characteristics of the scheme components, such as the share of cash versus equity pay, fixed versus variable pay, and the existence of bonus/malus, deferral or clawback schemes. Obviously these elements must be disclosed to allow peer review and monitoring over time.

8.5.2   Simultaneous Equation Estimates

In order to account for the role of bank riskiness in relation to the types of compensation schemes offered, we now turn to simultaneous equation regressions. When compensation schemes and the various sources of risk are jointly determined, the two endogenous variables are correlated with the error terms of equations where they appear as right-hand-side parameters. This also means that the error terms of the two equations are correlated. In consequence, the coefficient estimates for the relevant variables cannot be consistently estimated by the ordinary least squares (OLS) techniques. An alternative is to use the two-stage least squares (2SLS) method to first generate predicted values of each endogenous variable from the set of the remaining exogenous variables and then to use these instruments to estimate the original model.[27] For compensation equations that involve dichotomous variables, such as *OPTION* or *LTBONUS*, the estimations followed the continuous/probit model discussed in Maddala (1983, Ch. 7).

The model considered for compensation determination is as follows:

$$Compensation = f(Risk, LN(TA), CEO\_YEARS) \tag{8.5}$$

where *CEO_YEARS* gives the number of years that the chief executive has remained within the company. In addition to these variables, year dummies are also included to control for yearly impact of changing economic conditions on compensation schemes. The exogenous variables were not lagged in the simultaneous equation regressions since endogeneity is controlled for.

Risk is expected to have some impact on compensation schemes. In effect, it is expected that banks that have more failure likelihood would face troubles providing fixed salaries – that is, due to cash flow problems – and try to retain their executives by offering other alternatives, such as long-term or annual bonuses or option plans. Moreover, banks with heightened risk profile may have information advantages, partly explaining why they may survive with elevated levels of risk to begin with. In such cases, higher risk may be indicative of better opportunities to profit from option plans or other performance-based compensation plans, implying a positive relationship.

Tables 8.4 and 8.5 give the results of the simultaneous equations using the market-based measures of risk. It is easy to see the relationship between compensation and risks is different from the earlier results in Table 8.2. In particular, the various compensation variables have no significant impact on the four market-based measures. As far as the signs of coefficient estimates are considered, long-term performance bonus plans (*LTBONUS*) have a positive impact on all risk measures, which can be seen in columns (1) and (4) of Table 8.4 and Table 8.5. The option plans (*OPTION*) and annual bonuses (*ANBONUS%*), on the other hand, have generally a negative impact on all risk measures.

Going in the other direction, risk appears to have some role in determining compensation arrangements. In particular, banks with more systematic risk appear to be less likely to offer option plans, which can be seen from column (8) of Table 8.5. For other risk measures, the results are more mixed.

Larger banks appear to offer higher annual bonuses (*ANBONUS%*) as well as being more likely to offer both option plans (*OPTION*) and long term performance bonus plans (*LTBONUS*). This finding holds across almost all models, with the exception of the systematic risk equations.

CEOs with longer histories in their banks (i.e., those with greater *CEO_YEARS*) are less likely to receive option plans (*OPTION*) and, in several cases, annual bonuses (*ANBONUS%*). However, the results in Tables 8.4 and 8.5 are unable to highlight a

Table 8.4   Simultaneous equations for market variation and compensation schemes

Risk equations	(1)	(2)	(3)	(4)	(5)	(6)
	TOTAL RISK (σ_j)			IDIOSYNCRATIC RISK (σ_{uj})		
LTBONUS	0.058	–	–	0.066	–	–
	(0.211)			(0.309)		
OPTION	–	−0.004	–	–	−0.004	–
		(0.006)			(0.008)	
ANBONUS%	–	–	−0.193	–	–	−0.183
			(0.190)			(0.198)
LN(TA)	−0.041	0.005	0.003	−0.049	0.002	−0.001
	(0.151)	(0.006)	(0.009)	(0.223)	(0.008)	(0.009)
CAPITAL%	0.001	0.001	0.001	0.001	0.001	0.002
	(0.004)	(0.002)	(0.002)	(0.006)	(0.002)	(0.002)
NONINT%	−0.049	−0.021	0.032	−0.051	−0.025	0.029
	(0.110)	(0.015)	(0.056)	(0.131)	(0.018)	(0.059)
COOPERATIVE	0.032	−0.010	−0.033	0.035	−0.006	−0.030
	(0.144)	(0.009)	(0.027)	(0.189)	(0.010)	(0.029)
Year dummies (1999–2008)	YES	YES	YES	YES	YES	YES
Observations	282	286	179	262	266	173
R-squared	0.109	0.102	0.088	0.066	0.060	0.057

Compensation equations	(7) LTBONUS	(8) OPTION	(9) ANBONUS %	(10) LTBONUS	(11) OPTION	(12) ANBONUS %
TOTAL RISK (σ_j)	13.728	19.473	1.112	–	–	–
	(29.106)	(39.190)	(3.881)			
IDIOSYNCRATIC RISK (σ_{uj})	–	–	–	−3.257	8.122	−1.188
				(26.638)	(35.212)	(3.413)
LN(TA)	0.757***	0.797***	0.063**	0.739***	0.835***	0.044
	(0.104)	(0.103)	(0.030)	(0.135)	(0.134)	(0.037)
CEO_YEARS	−0.002	−0.021**	−0.003	−0.000	−0.020**	−0.002
	(0.008)	(0.010)	(0.002)	(0.008)	(0.009)	(0.002)
Year dummies (1999–2008)	YES	YES	YES	YES	YES	YES
Observations	282	286	179	275	279	175
R-squared	0.231(ps)	0.364(ps)	0.502	0.232(ps)	0.382(ps)	0.559

Notes:
Two-stage least square (2SLS) methods were used to estimate the simultaneous equation models. For the dichotomous equations in columns (1)–(4), the compensation equations were estimated using the continuous/probit model discussed in Maddala (1983, Ch. 7). Constant terms and year dummies are suppressed for brevity. Numbers of observations for columns (5)–(6) are low due to limited amount of information on variable executive pay.
Corrected standard errors in parentheses; ***, **, * represent significance at the 1%, 5% and 10% levels of p-values. For dichotomous value equations pseudo (ps) R-squares are reported.

Table 8.5   Simultaneous equations for market betas and compensation schemes

Risk equations	(1)	(2)	(3)	(4)	(5)	(6)
	SYSTEMATIC RISK (β_j^s)			INTEREST RISK (β_j^i)		
LTBONUS	0.312	–	–	1.422	–	–
	(1.478)			(6.265)		
OPTION	–	−0.012	–	–	−0.092	–
		(0.059)			(0.125)	
ANBONUS%	–	–	0.207	–	–	−2.459
			(0.996)			(2.924)
LN(TA)	−0.036	0.198***	0.101**	−1.033	0.076	−0.033
	(1.068)	(0.056)	(0.045)	(4.527)	(0.119)	(0.132)
CAPITAL%	−0.013	−0.018	−0.045***	0.054	0.046*	0.025
	(0.028)	(0.013)	(0.011)	(0.120)	(0.028)	(0.032)
NONINT%	−0.320	−0.187	−0.223	−0.739	−0.144	0.677
	(0.627)	(0.133)	(0.297)	(2.657)	(0.283)	(0.872)
COOPERATIVE	0.186	−0.008	0.034	0.619	−0.286*	−0.597
	(0.907)	(0.075)	(0.144)	(3.839)	(0.158)	(0.423)
Year dummies (1999–2008)	YES	YES	YES	YES	YES	YES
Observations	275	279	175	275	279	175
R-squared	0.465	0.469	0.232	0.279	0.283	0.058

Compensation equations	(7) LTBONUS	(8) OPTION	(9) ANBONUS %	(10) LTBONUS	(11) OPTION	(12) ANBONUS %
SYSTEMATIC RISK (β_j^s)	0.783	−6.397**	0.028	–	–	–
	(2.218)	(3.036)	(0.174)			
INTEREST RISK (β_j^i)	–	–	–	0.849	2.842	0.328
				(1.142)	(2.044)	(0.266)
LN(TA)	0.608	2.040***	0.052**	0.782***	0.916***	0.101**
	(0.415)	(0.593)	(0.026)	(0.109)	(0.143)	(0.045)
CEO_YEARS	−0.001	−0.020*	−0.002*	−0.002	−0.027**	−0.003
	(0.007)	(0.010)	(0.001)	(0.007)	(0.012)	(0.002)
Year dummies (1999–2008)	YES	YES	YES	YES	YES	YES
Observations	275	279	175	275	279	175
R-squared	0.233(ps)	0.405(ps)	0.558	0.234(ps)	0.394(ps)	0.078

Notes:
Two-stage least square (2SLS) methods were used to estimate the simultaneous equation models. For the dichotomous equations in columns (1)–(4), the compensation equations were estimated using the continuous/probit model discussed in Maddala (1983, Ch. 7). Constant terms and year dummies are suppressed for brevity. Numbers of observations for columns (5)–(6) are low due to limited amount of information on variable executive pay.
Standard errors in parentheses; ***, **, * represent significance at the 1%, 5% and 10% levels of p-values.
For dichotomous value equations pseudo (ps) R-squares are reported.

definitive relationship for the likelihood of obtaining (or accepting) long-term perform-ance bonus plans.

Table 8.6 provides the results for the simultaneous equation regressions for the bank failure indicator (*ZSCORE*).[28] As far as non-compensation variables are concerned, the findings are more or less in line with the market-based compensation models. Well-capitalized banks consistently have low default risks. Cooperative banks appear to be more stable than their commercial peers, although the results are weak for option plan regression (in columns (2) and (5)) since only listed banks were included in the sample. Larger banks (and/or their CEOs) have a preference for receiving non-fixed pay, which is clear from the persistently significant signs on *LN(TA)* in columns (3)–(5). CEOs with longer histories in their banks are less likely to receive long-term bonuses in exchange for option plans (and possibly for annual bonuses).

Perhaps the most striking finding of Table 8.6 relates to the long-term performance bonus plans, which appear to increase risk significantly. The consideration for endogene-ity appears not to have changed this relationship, as noted from the comparable estimate in column (1) of Table 8.3. In turn, no other compensation scheme properties, neither option plans nor annual bonus plans, have any significant impact on default likelihood.

Banks that have a greater likelihood of default are also less likely to offer long-term performance plans, notably option plans, possibly since the CEOs would be less likely to accept such plans. Moreover, troubled banks are more likely to offer bonus plans. This should also not be very surprising; banks that are in trouble often face cash flow problems, which make the payment of fixed benefits more difficult and, thus, less likely.

8.6   CONCLUSIONS

This study has used a novel database on executive pay in top European Union (EU) institutions to assess the role of CEO compensation in relation to bank riskiness. The database provides a variety of compensation scheme components, including long-term incentive bonus plans, option plans and the share of annual bonus pay in total annual pay. A number of market-based risk measures were also developed as indicators of total and idiosyncratic volatility as well as systematic and interest-rate exposures. Since the sample contains a significant number of unlisted banks, accounting information was used to develop a measure on bank failure likelihood.

Our analysis of CEOs' pay in top EU banks reveals the following striking result: although option plans and annual bonuses do not seem to increase risk, there is evidence that the so-called 'long-term performance bonus plans' augment the likelihood of default in banking. The result is robust to controlling for time (and the impact of the recent crisis) as well as potential sources of simultaneity between compensation and risk deter-mination. Other aspects of compensation packages, such as the presence of option plans or the level of annual bonuses in relation to fixed pay, do not seem to have a significant impact on risk-taking in banking.

Our results also uncover an inverse relationship between risk and compensation. In particular, systematic risk appears to decrease the likelihood of receiving an option plan. Moreover, banks that face difficulties appear to substitute annual bonuses for fixed sala-ries. Non-risk factors also contribute to the determination of compensation packages.

Table 8.6   *Simultaneous equations for failure likelihood (Z-score) and compensation schemes*

Risk equations	(1) ZSCORE	(2) ZSCORE	(3) ZSCORE
LTBONUS	3.445**	–	–
	(1.358)		
OPTION	–	0.968	–
		(1.290)	
ANBONUS%	–	–	−1.614
			(2.889)
LN(TA)	−2.246	0.010	−0.514
	(1.367)	(1.117)	(0.594)
CAPITAL%	−2.754***	−2.448***	−2.239***
	(0.389)	(0.348)	(0.276)
NON_INT%	0.109	−7.540**	−0.716
	(0.271)	(3.524)	(1.489)
COOPERATIVE	−7.232***	−2.599	−4.277**
	(2.045)	(2.181)	(2.131)
Year dummies (1999–2008)	–	–	–
Observations	514	309	205
R-squared	0.261	0.335	0.301

Compensation equations	(4) LTBONUS	(5) OPTION	(6) ANBONUS%
ZSCORE	−0.019*	−0.062***	0.004*
	(0.011)	(0.020)	(0.002)
LN(TA)	0.574***	0.876***	0.066***
	(0.068)	(0.093)	(0.015)
CEO_YEARS	0.016***	−0.016**	−0.001
	(0.006)	(0.007)	(0.001)
Year dummies (1999–2008)	YES	YES	YES
Observations	514	309	205
R-squared	0.194(ps)	0.365(ps)	0.517

Notes:
Two-stage least square (2SLS) methods were used to estimate the simultaneous equation models. For the dichotomous equations in columns (1)–(4), the compensation equations were estimated using the continuous/probit model discussed in Maddala (1983, Ch. 7). Constant terms and year dummies are suppressed for brevity. Numbers of observations for columns (5)–(6) are low due to limited amount of information on variable executive pay.
Standard errors in parentheses. ***, **, * represent significance at the 1%, 5% and 10% levels of p-values. For dichotomous value equations pseudo (ps) R squares are reported.

CEOs with a longer history in the bank are more likely to secure long-term bonuses and less likely to obtain options or annual bonuses.

To sum up, our results provide no backing to the hypothesis that short-term performance schemes, such as annual bonuses, augment risk-taking (as hypothesized in

Hypothesis 1). In addition, the results on long-term performance schemes are mixed: option plans do not necessarily lead to more (or less) risks; however, the so-called long-term performance bonus plans appear to increase default risks (partly confirming Hypothesis 2). Lastly, the compensation schemes have little (if any) impact on the volatility and market exposures of the stock prices of listed banks.

The contrasting results for the option and long-term bonus plans may be explained in several ways. It is possible – although unlikely – that the compensation amounts granted under option plans are much larger, implying a lower level of diversification for CEOs. It is also very likely that the way that these packages are negotiated has something to do with the findings. In effect, most of the so-called 'long-term performance incentive plans' are opaque schemes that are often granted at the discretion of the management board or the compensation committee. Lastly, long-term performance plans that are based on an accounting performance criterion may provide higher-powered incentives than stock-price-based plans since the latter are typically more volatile and exposed to non-bank-related risks.

To conclude, such results cast some doubt on the recent European policy actions on remuneration policy, and call for more research in this field to understand the full implications of the long- and short-term performance plans before reaching any conclusion on the risk-related incentives they provide.

NOTES

1. These concerns have also been echoed across the Atlantic by the US Treasury Secretary Geithner during his (6 June 2009) testimony to the Congress, who argued that: 'although many things caused this crisis, what happened to compensation and the incentives in creative risk taking did contribute in some institutions to the vulnerability that we saw in this financial crisis'.
2. Commission Communication of 4 March 2009 to the Spring European Council, 'Driving European Recovery', COM(2009) 114.
3. For more details, see the European Commission recommendations on remuneration policies in the financial services sector (2009/384/EC) and on remuneration of directors of listed companies (2009/385/EC), which were published in the *Official Journal of the European Union* on 30 March 2009.
4. Exactly how a past bonus payment may be categorized as 'unjustified' or how 'clawback' schemes may work in practice is not elaborated in the recommendation. The remuneration code implemented by the UK Financial Services Authority (FSA) in 2009 proposes that a substantial proportion of the bonus arrangements are realized as deferred payments linked to the future performance of the firm (Bell and Reenen, 2010).
5. The April 2009 CEBS High-level principles for Remuneration Policies is available at http://www.cebs.org/getdoc/34beb2e0-bdff-4b8e-979a-5115a482a7ba/High-level-principles-for-remuneration-policies.aspx. For the October 2010 CEBS Guidelines on Remuneration Policies and Practices, see http://www.cebs.org/documents/Publications/Consultation-papers/2010/CP42/CP42.aspx.
6. The FSB's 'Thematic review on compensation: peer review report', published on 30 March 2010, is available at http://www.financialstabilityboard.org/publications/r_100330a.pdf.
7. See report on the application by member states of the EU of the Commission 2009/384/EC, Recommendation on remuneration policies in the financial services sector, available at http://ec.europa.eu/internal_market/company/docs/directors-remun/com-2010-286-2_en.pdf.
8. CEPS internal database on executive compensation of European financial institutions.
9. See also Hagendorff and Vallascas (Chapter 9 in this volume) for a more detailed review of the literature on chief executive officer (CEO) pay and risk-taking in banking.
10. An alternative is to charge risk-sensitive insurance premiums to align banks' interests with those of the insurance scheme (Merton, 1977). However, the feasibility of the appropriately priced premiums could be challenged in the presence of asymmetric information (Chan et al., 1992).
11. Mehran and Rosenberg (2007) note that the results arise from risky project choices and not necessarily

through increased leverage, which would be the case if the managers were acting on behalf of stockholders to shift the risks to the debt holders, depositors and the deposit insurance schemes, as implied by the moral hazard literature reviewed above.

12. Alternatively, long-term performance-related packages may have little or no impact if they are very small in size when compared to the executives' fixed salaries and annual bonuses. Going in the other direction, managers may become risk-averse if the packages represent a significant proportion of the incomes of managers, rendering the managers' portfolios less diversified (Smith and Stulz, 1985). Moreover, certain types of long-term performance incentives may also be more aligned with depositors' interests, such as customer satisfaction, market access, and so on, potentially leading to more risk-aversion.

13. This is identical to the assumptions made by Chen et al. (2006). For the market risk, taking the absolute value of the coefficient estimate would have been immaterial since almost all coefficient estimates have a positive sign.

14. It is worth highlighting that the Z-score admits negative values in most cases – the only exceptions are when mean return on assets is negative. In most of the literature, a negated score that usually takes positive values has been used. However, this would mean that greater scores imply lower risk and would complicate with the market-based risk measures developed above. We have therefore used the lower bound for the standardized returns of a healthy bank in order to facilitate the interpretation and comparability of our risk measures.

15. The return on assets (ROA) is calculated as pre-tax profits divided by total assets. The mean and standard deviation of each bank's returns are estimated using the maximum amount of information that could be extracted from Bankscope, in most cases covering all the years 1995 to 2009.

16. Out of the total 621 bank-year observations, 148 observations (representing 74 CEO replacements) have double and six observations (two CEO replacements) have triple entries.

17. In this manner, our sample could in principle have Type II errors, that is, failing to identify the presence of an existing long-term bonus or option plan. However, these errors are highly unlikely since most banks have to report the presence of these plans for tax purposes.

18. Although some of the EU's banks, notably those in France, Germany and the UK, report detailed information on a wider range of remuneration packages, potential sources of inconsistencies arise when the entire sample is considered. For example, while most banks report the shares granted under their bonus plans, several details, such as exercise prices and various vesting limitations, are missing. For most banks, there are no details on deferred payments. There are some cases where long-term benefit plans include non-performance-related items, such as pension plans and savings units. There is, however, a substantial amount of consistency for profit-sharing plans and other items categorized under annual bonuses since these items are subject to taxation.

19. For more on the relative resilience of cooperative and savings banks, see Čihák and Hesse (2007), Ayadi et al. (2009) and Ayadi et al. (2010), among others.

20. However, endogeneity can still be a problem even with the lagged regressions if the causal relationships are long-lived and since the remuneration variables (especially the dummy variables *OPTION* and *LTBONUS*) are relatively persistent.

21. As noted above, there are many same year entries for banks that have hired a new executive in mid-year. To allow taking lags, the CEO with the greatest tenure was used to represent the entire year; all other CEO-related entries for that bank-year were dropped.

22. Models with more than a single compensation variable were also estimated. The results for these regressions do not change any of the results summarized here.

23. Apart from total assets in Table 8.2, the dummy year variables covering 2000 to 2007 (not shown in tables for brevity) also have significant and persistently negative signs for the total risk and interest rate risk components, implying that these risks have increased substantially in 2008 and 2009.

24. The finding that bank size augments systematic exposures was also obtained in Saunders et al. (1990) and Chen et al. (1998, 2006), among others.

25. Although a dummy for savings banks could not be used throughout the regression analysis for identification reasons, in all cases that a test could be done, the failure likelihoods for savings banks were found to be comparable with cooperative banks and substantially lower than commercial banks.

26. The risk-augmenting impact of option plans on systematic exposures is supported by other empirical findings for the US banking sector (Chen et al., 1998, 2006).

27. For more details on the two-stage instrumental variable estimator for systems of equations involving jointly determined variables, see Greene (1997, Ch. 16).

28. Year dummies were not included in the risk equations in Table 8.6. since they rendered the model unidentifiable. This is unlikely to be a major problem; as it is clear from a comparison of columns (1)–(3) with (4)–(6) in Table.8.3, the regression results do not change significantly with the inclusion of year dummies.

REFERENCES

Ayadi, R., D.T. Llewelyn, R.H. Schmidt, E. Arbak and W.P.D. Groen (2010), *Investigating Diversity in the Banking Sector in Europe: Key Developments, Performance and Role of Cooperative Banks*, Brussels: Centre for European Policy Studies (CEPS).

Ayadi, R., R.H. Schmidt, S. Carbo Valverde, E. Arbak and F. Rodriguez Fernandez (2009), *Investigating Diversity in the Banking Sector in Europe: The Performance and Role of Savings Banks*, Brussels: Centre for European Policy Studies (CEPS).

Bebchuk, L. and J. Fried (2004), *Pay without Performance: The Unfulfilled Promise of Executive Compensation*, Cambridge, MA and London: Harvard University Press.

Bebchuk, L.A. and H. Spamann (2010), 'Regulating bankers' pay', *Georgetown Law Journal*, **98**(2), 247–287.

Bell, B. and J.V. Reenen (2010), 'Bankers' bonuses: claw-back clauses are critical', http://www.voxeu.org/index.php?q=node/4986.

Berle, A.A. and G.C. Means (1932), *The Modern Corporation and Private Property*, New Brunswick, NJ: Transaction Publishers, reprinted 1991.

Bolton, P., H. Mehran and J. Shapiro (2010), 'Executive compensation and risk taking', Staff Reports, No. 456, Federal Reserve Bank of New York, June.

Bolton, P., J. Scheinkman and W. Xiong (2006a), 'Executive compensation and short-termist behaviour in speculative markets', *Review of Economic Studies*, **73**(3), 577–610.

Bolton, P., J. Scheinkman and W. Xiong (2006b), 'Pay for short-term performance: executive compensation in speculative markets', National Bureau of Economic Research, NBER Working Papers: 12107.

Boyd, J.H. and D.E. Runkle (1993), 'Size and performance of banking firms: testing the predictions of theory', *Journal of Monetary Economics*, **31**(1), 47–67.

Chan, Y.-S., S.I. Greenbaum and A.V. Thakor (1992), 'Is fairly priced deposit insurance possible?', *Journal of Finance*, **47**(1), 227–245.

Chen, C.R. and A. Chan (1989), 'Interest rate sensitivity, asymmetry, and the stock returns of financial institutions', *Financial Review*, **24**(3), 457–473.

Chen, C.R., T.L. Steiner and A.M. Whyte (1998), 'Risk-taking behavior and management ownership in depository institutions', *Journal of Financial Research*, **21**(1), 1–16.

Chen, C.R., T.L. Steiner and A.M. Whyte (2006), 'Does stock option-based executive compensation induce risk-taking? An analysis of the banking industry', *Journal of Banking and Finance*, **30**(3), 915–945.

Čihák, M. and H. Hesse (2007), 'Cooperative banks and financial stability', IMF Working Papers, No. WP/07/02, International Monetary Fund.

Crawford, A.J., J.R. Ezzell and J.A. Miles (1995), 'Bank CEO pay–performance relations and the effects of deregulation', *Journal of Business*, **68**(2), 231–256.

Demsetz, R.S. and P.E. Strahan (1997), 'Diversification, size, and risk at bank holding companies', *Journal of Money, Credit and Banking*, **29**(3), 300–313.

Fahlenbrach, R. and R.M. Stulz (2009), 'Bank CEO incentives and the credit crisis', National Bureau of Economic Research, NBER Working Papers: 15212.

Flannery, M.J. and C.M. James (1984), 'The effect of interest rate changes on the common stock returns of financial institutions', *Journal of Finance*, **39**(4), 1141–1153.

Fraser, D.R. and A. Zardkoohi (1996), 'Ownership structure, deregulation, and risk in the savings and loan industry', *Journal of Business Research*, **37**(1), 63–69.

Galai, D. and R.W. Masulis (1976), 'The option pricing model and the risk factor of stock', *Journal of Financial Economics*, **3**(1–2), 53–81.

Greene, W.H. (1997), *Econometric Analysis*, 3rd edition, Upper Saddle River, NJ: Prentice Hall.

Holmström, B. and J. Tirole (1993), 'Market liquidity and performance monitoring', *Journal of Political Economy*, **101**(4), 678–709.

Houston, J.F. and C. James (1995), 'CEO compensation and bank risk: is compensation in banking structured to promote risk taking?', *Journal of Monetary Economics*, **36**(2), 405–431.

Hubbard, R.G. and D. Palia (1995), 'Executive pay and performance: evidence from the US banking industry', *Journal of Financial Economics*, **39**(1), 105–130.

Jensen, M.C. and W.H. Meckling (1976), 'Theory of the firm: managerial behavior, agency costs and ownership structure', *Journal of Financial Economics*, **3**(4), 305–360.

Jensen, M.C. and K.J. Murphy (1990), 'Performance pay and top-management incentives', *Journal of Political Economy*, **98**(2), 225–264.

John, K., A. Saunders and L.W. Senbet (2000), 'A theory of bank regulation and management compensation', *Review of Financial Studies*, **13**(1), 95–125.

Laeven, L. and R. Levine (2009), 'Bank governance, regulation and risk taking', *Journal of Financial Economics*, **93**(2), 259–275.

Maddala, G.S. (1983), *Limited-Dependent and Qualitative Variables in Econometrics*, Cambridge, MA: Cambridge University Press.

Mehran, H. and J. Rosenberg (2007), 'The effect of employee stock options on bank investment choice, borrowing, and capital', Federal Reserve Bank of New York, Staff Reports: 305.

Merton, R.C. (1977), 'An analytic derivation of the cost of deposit insurance and loan guarantees: an application of modern option pricing theory', *Journal of Banking and Finance*, **1**(1), 3–11.

Narayanan, M.P. (1985), 'Managerial incentives for short-term results', *Journal of Finance*, **40**(5), 1469–1484.

Saunders, A., E. Strock and N.G. Travlos (1990), 'Ownership structure, deregulation, and bank risk taking', *Journal of Finance*, **45**(2), 643–654.

Shleifer, A. and R.W. Vishny (1997), 'A survey of corporate governance', *Journal of Finance*, **52**(2), 737–783.

Smith, C.W. and R.M. Stulz (1985), 'The determinants of firms' hedging policies', *Journal of Financial and Quantitative Analysis*, **20**(4), 391–405.

9 CEO pay and risk-taking in banking: the roles of bonus plans and deferred compensation in curbing bank risk-taking

Jens Hagendorff and Francesco Vallascas

9.1 INTRODUCTION

Executive compensation policy may serve as a mechanism to reduce conflicts between managers and shareholders over the deployment of corporate resources and the riskiness of the firm (Jensen and Meckling, 1976; Shleifer and Vishny, 1997). Public and academic interest in chief executive officer (CEO) compensation in the banking industry has increased exponentially in the aftermath of the financial crisis of 2007–2008. While this is partly motivated by public outrage over the levels of CEO remuneration in an industry that has become increasingly reliant on public funds, the view that the structure of executive pay has given rise to socially harmful risk-taking by banks is gaining ground. Thus, the use of incentive pay in banking is widely believed to have motivated excessive risk-taking and to have acted as a contributory factor to the recent financial crisis (e.g., Bebchuk and Spamann, 2009; IMF, 2010; Federal Reserve Bank, 2010).

Understanding the relationship between CEO pay and bank risk-taking matters. It matters because of the importance of banks to any monetary economy, and because taking risks is a key component of many of the activities performed by banks. Furthermore, optimally designed incentive compensation is essential to induce managerial effort by incentivizing bank CEOs to commit to risky but positive net present value (NPV) projects (Jensen and Meckling, 1976; Amihud and Lev, 1981; Smith and Stulz, 1985). Finally, understanding the pay–risk relationship also matters because CEO pay at banks has become subject to increasing levels of government intervention in the aftermath of the recent financial crisis.

As regards recent government interventions into pay in banking, Europe has taken a rather prescriptive approach to this, mainly by introducing caps or punitive taxes on CEO pay. For instance, in Germany CEO compensation at banks which receive state aid has been capped at 500000 euros. Dutch banks have agreed to limit cash bonuses to 100 percent of base salary. Both the UK and France have introduced a 50 percent tax on bonuses paid during 2009. Further, pending European Union (EU) legislation will dictate that bonus awards above a certain level must defer payment of a fixed fraction. In response to these EU guidelines, the UK's Financial Services Authority (FSA) has announced that at least 40 percent of bonus payments made to senior management at a wide range of financial services firms must be deferred for a period of at least three years from 2011. Further, non-equity based bonus payments to the CEOs of UK financial firms will be limited to 50 percent of total compensation, with the remainder payable in equity and equity-like instruments.

By comparison, the US approach to compensation has been more principle-based and less prescriptive. Excluded from the principle-based approach are banks which receive government support under the Troubled Asset Relief Program (TARP). At TARP recipients, executive compensation packages require approval from a paymaster until the funds have been completely repaid. However, generally the US approach to regulating CEO pay in banking is based on requiring banks to provide balanced risk-taking incentives to senior risk management staff. Nevertheless, the guidelines for senior executives at large banking organizations (LBOs) come close to dictating that bonuses be paid in equity-based instruments, that the payment be deferred and that vesting be performance-contingent. The US guidance on compensation practices as published by the Federal Reserve Bank (2010: 33) advises that:

> Incentive compensation arrangements for senior executives at LBOs are likely to be better balanced if they involve deferral of a substantial portion of the executives' incentive compensation over a multi-year period in a way that reduces the amount received in the event of poor performance, substantial use of multi-year performance periods, or both. Similarly, the compensation arrangements for senior executives at LBOs are likely to be better balanced if a significant portion of the incentive compensation of these executives is paid in the form of equity-linked instruments that vest over multiple years, with the number of instruments ultimately received dependent on the performance of the organization during the deferral period. (Federal Reserve Bank, 2010: 33)

While less prescriptive, the US approach to CEO pay in banking displays a similar preference for equity over non-equity types of compensation as European approaches. However, little is empirically actually known to date about the effects of non-equity types of pay on bank risk. Most importantly, recent empirical findings openly challenge the wisdom of paying bank CEOs with equity-like forms of compensation at the expense of non-equity-linked compensation. Non-equity-based forms of CEO compensation are widespread and include CEO bonus plans and CEO pension entitlements under a defined benefit scheme. Both CEO bonus payments (e.g., Noe et al., 1996; Balachandran et al., 2010) and CEO pension entitlements (e.g., Edmans and Liu, 2011; Wei and Yermack, 2010; Tung and Wang, 2010) have been linked to lower bank risk in recent academic work.

This chapter critically reviews existing empirical work on the relationship between CEO pay and bank risk-taking and argues that previous work has been too narrow in its focus on equity-linked CEO compensation (mainly share and option grants), while neglecting common forms of CEO compensation which are not equity-linked and which could make a valuable contribution to promoting socially optimal risk-taking by banks. Research which examines non-equity components of CEO compensation, particularly pensions and other forms of deferred compensation, is still in its infancy (see Balachandran et al., 2010; Wei and Yermack, forthcoming). However, many of the findings which are proffered by this stream of research are consistent with the view that, where equity-based pay encourages risk-taking, non-equity linked pay makes CEOs more risk-averse (see Edmans and Liu, 2011). This chapter argues that it is regrettable that not more is empirically known about the risk effects generated by non-equity (and essentially more debt-like) forms of compensation, and calls for debt-like components of CEO compensation to be examined in greater detail.

The remainder of this chapter is organized as follows. The next section provides an overview of the increasing importance of equity-linked compensation in the US banking industry over recent times and argues that empirical evidence supports the view that more equity-based compensation is linked to riskier banks. Section 9.3 makes the case for paying bank CEOs using bonus plans and deferred compensation and explains why non-equity forms of compensation offer a promising way of mitigating CEO appetite for risk and promoting socially responsible risk-taking in the banking industry. The final section offers some conclusions and policy implications.

9.2   EQUITY-LINKED COMPENSATION AND ITS EFFECT ON CEO RISK-TAKING

9.2.1   The State We Are In

Over recent decades, the use of equity-linked compensation has increased rapidly – both inside and outside the banking industry. Equity-linked CEO compensation takes the form of grants of the firm's shares as well as call options on the firm's equity. Option grants in particular make CEO wealth sensitive to risk-taking. Call options combine unlimited upside with limited downside potential and, therefore, provide convex CEO pay-offs linked to marginal increases in bank risk. DeYoung et al. (2010) show that the use of equity-linked compensation in US banking has increased so rapidly over the last decade that CEO pay-offs linked to increases in firm risk are now higher in the banking industry than in other industries. DeYoung et al. (2010) calculate that the average bank CEO saw their wealth increase by around $300 000 in 2004 as a result of a 0.01 percent increase in the standard deviation of stock return volatility. For US CEOs in non-financial firms, the dollar amount linked to marginal increases in risk was about a third less in 2004.

There are two explanations which are frequently cited for the marked increase in equity-linked compensation in US banking. Theoretical arguments over the optimal riskiness of a firm suggest that the use of risk-sensitive compensation is consistent with agency theory. Agency theory postulates that optimal executive compensation needs to align the interests of risk-averse managers with those of risk-neutral shareholders by motivating managers to commit to risk-increasing but positive NPV projects (Jensen and Meckling, 1976; Amihud and Lev, 1981; Smith and Stulz, 1985). CEO performance contracts need to motivate bank CEOs sufficiently to take advantage of this growing investment opportunity set (Smith and Watts, 1992; Mehran and Rosenberg, 2007). In most countries, the range of commercial activities that banking firms may engage in has increased to include various capital market activities as well as insurance underwriting. One way of motivating CEOs to participate in these new opportunities is to increase their share of equity-linked compensation in the banking industry. Put differently, increases in the risk sensitivity of executive compensation were designed to encourage bank managers to exploit various new financial activities, typically fee-based and more risky than traditional banking activities (see Stiroh, 2006), which deregulation had opened up. Mehran and Rosenberg (2007) and DeYoung et al. (2010) interpret the fact that large increases in equity-linked compensation can be found for US bank CEOs in the period immediately following the deregulation of banking activities as consistent with this view.

The second explanation for the increase in equity-linked compensation takes a more negative view of the role of bank CEO compensation packages and argues that CEO compensation has increasingly been designed to encourage CEOs to shift risk onto bond-holders and regulators. Since banks are leveraged institutions, shareholders benefit from higher-risk investment choices which increase the potential value of bank assets, while keeping the downside risk limited (John and John, 1993; Bebchuk and Spamann, 2009). Therefore, shareholders will use their control over incentive compensation in order to encourage higher risk-taking and, effectively, to shift risk onto bondholders (whose pay-offs will not increase with higher bank risk) and regulators (who guarantee the financial safety net which is likely to be called upon in the event of institutional failure).

The next section discusses the empirical literature on the risk effects of equity-linked compensation. A distinction is made between CEO option holdings (where the empirical evidence strongly suggests that these are linked to higher bank risk) and CEO sharehold-ings (whose risk effects are much less clear-cut).

9.2.2 Previous Literature on the Risk-Taking Effects of Equity-Linked Compensation

Previous work on the effects of CEO option holdings on bank risk-taking is relatively unambiguous with regard to the implications that option holdings have for the risk preferences of bank CEOs. Generally, the non-financial literature finds that increased sensitivity of CEO pay in remuneration packages causes CEOs to make riskier invest-ment choices (Rogers, 2002) and bind corporate resources to riskier activities (Nam et al., 2003; Coles et al., 2006; Rajgopal and Shevlin, 2002; Guay, 1999). In the US banking industry, the empirical evidence is also supportive of CEO option holdings being associ-ated with higher banking risk. Mehran and Rosenberg (2007) and DeYoung et al. (2010) show that when the sensitivity of option values to risk-taking is higher, banks engage in riskier types of activities. Chen et al. (2006) find a positive relationship between the value of stock options granted to CEOs and market measures of banking risk. Hagendorff and Vallascas (2011) show that bank CEOs whose wealth is more sensitive to risk-taking engage in bank mergers that increase the probability of default of the acquiring bank post-merger. One exception to the literature which is otherwise almost univocal in finding that equity-based CEO compensation has a risk-increasing effect is a recent study by Fahlenbrach and Stulz (2011). The authors are not able to find a link between equity-based risk incentives and the performance of bank stocks during the recent finan-cial crisis. Fahlenbrach and Stulz (2011) interpret their results as consistent with the view that there is no link between equity-based CEO compensation and pre-crisis CEO risk-taking.

Next to options, equity grants also provide a way of aligning managerial and share-holder interests. However, the implications of share ownership on bank riskiness are theoretically and empirically much more ambiguous than those of CEO option hold-ings. The main reason for this is that, unlike options, the CEO pay-offs linked to share holdings are not highly convex. On the one hand, this means that larger managerial shareholdings may well overcome CEO risk-aversion and incentivize CEOs to identify and commit to risky and positive NPV projects. However, on the other hand, larger

CEO shareholders will expose managers to company risk to a much larger degree than diversified shareholders and this could aggravate – rather than overcome – managerial risk-aversion (Smith and Stulz, 1985; Amihud and Lev, 1981).

DeYoung et al. (2010) find some evidence that high share ownership by the CEO reduces the riskiness of bank activities, while Mehran and Rosenberg (2007) do not detect any robust influence of CEO ownership on risk-taking. For the banking industry, Bliss and Rosen (2001) and Minnick et al. (2011) show that banks whose CEOs have a large shareholding in the bank that they run are less likely to engage in acquisitions. This is consistent with banks whose CEOs own a share of the bank's equity forgoing risky investment projects such as mergers and acquisitions (M&A).

In sum, the empirical evidence discussed above is inconsistent with the regulatory aim of employing more equity-based compensation to control managerial risk-appetite. The literature in this area only offers some limited evidence that CEO shareholdings may be associated with lower banking risk, while the consensus finding on option grants is that these are associated with measurable increases in bank risk.

9.3 NON-EQUITY-BASED COMPENSATION AND BANK RISK

Non-equity-based forms of compensation provide an interesting route to offer incentives to CEOs which, unlike equity-linked forms of compensation, are not characterized by the sort of convex pay-offs which reward increases in bank risk. Below, this section proffers a discussion of how CEO bonus plans and deferred compensation affect banking risk.

9.3.1 CEO Bonus Plans

CEO bonus plans are an interesting case. In sharp contrast to public opinion and also many of the regulatory proposals that emerge for the future regulation of pay in banking (some of these are discussed above), neither theoretical nor empirical work supports the view that CEO bonuses promote risk-taking in general (Smith and Stulz, 1985; Duru et al., 2005; Kim et al., 2008). The main reason for this is due to the pay-off structure of CEO bonus plans. A typical CEO cash bonus becomes payable once earnings-based targets are met over a one-year period. The key point is that above that threshold, the pay-off increases with performance up to a maximum pay-out (cap). Therefore, for bank performance above the threshold at which bonus payments become payable, CEO pay-offs from executive bonus plans are not convex with respect to performance. Duru et al. (2005) argue that earnings-based cash bonuses make managers seek stable cash flows to meet contractual debt obligations. The authors show that the costs of debt financing decrease at firms where CEOs receive higher cash bonus payments. Duru et al. argue that higher bonus payments reduce agency conflict with debt holders and, thus, lower the risk-shifting incentives in these firms.

Admittedly, one implication of the more or less binary pay-off structure of CEO bonus plans is that when firm performance is below the earnings-based threshold at which bonus payments become payable, the pay-off function for a CEO turns convex and will incentivize CEOs to take risk in order to secure a bonus payment (see Smith and Stulz,

1985). Kim et al. (2008) confirm these theoretical arguments by estimating the perform-ance thresholds underlying CEO bonus plans, and show that CEOs display increased risk-taking behavior where current levels of corporate performance place a CEO just underneath the performance threshold at which a bonus becomes payable.

Further, in the banking industry, the presence of regulation and safety nets means that there are two additional conditions under which CEO cash bonuses may indeed promote risk-shifting. First, cash bonuses aggravate risk-shifting incentives where the prospect of regulatory intervention is low (Noe et al., 1996). For instance, Webb (2008) argues that bank executives become more risk-averse where the intensity of regulatory monitoring is high. Consequently, where regulatory environments are less strict and regulatory inter-vention unlikely, executives will be more responsive to pay-based incentives to take on excess risk. Second, cash bonuses promote managerial risk-shifting at distressed banks (Noe et al., 1996; Benston and Evan, 2006). Since bonus payments to CEOs are solvency-contingent, they incentivize CEOs to engage in a 'gamble for resurrection' by engaging in risky projects whenever institutional default seems likely. In these cases, bonus payments insulate CEOs at distressed banks from the longer-term negative effects of high-risk, negative-NPV projects (Duru et al., 2005).

The narrow empirical literature available on the role of CEO bonus payments and bank risk reaches conflicting conclusions. Harjoto and Mullineaux (2003) report a positive association between bonus payments and the return volatility of bank equity. Balachandran et al. (2010) show evidence that the sum of bonus and other cash incen-tives reduces the probability of bank default. This is in contrast to Ayadi et al. (Chapter 8 in this volume) who show for a sample of European banks that the presence of long-term bonus plans is associated with higher risk (on the basis of Z-scores). Vallascas and Hagendorff (2010) examine the risk effects of CEO cash bonus plans for a sample of US and European banking firms. The results show that CEO cash bonuses reduce bank default risk. Consistent with the theoretical arguments proffered above, their results also show that the risk-reducing effect of CEO cash bonuses is particularly pronounced in stronger regulatory environments and for non-distressed financial institutions.

9.3.2   Deferred Compensation

One of the key features of CEO cash bonuses is that, because the pay-offs for CEOs are not convex functions of performance, they do not reward CEO risk-taking and, there-fore, have the potential to align managerial risk preferences more closely with those of debtholders. It follows from this that if there are benefits linked to aligning the interests of debtholders and management, these could equally be realized by paying CEOs directly with debt.

Debt as a form of executive remuneration is widespread. It tends to take the shape of deferred compensation, most notably in the form of defined benefit pensions (see Sundaram and Yermack, 2007; Wei and Yermack, 2010). These company promises of fixed sums at some future point in time are unfunded and unsecured CEO claims. In the US and many other countries, the deferred compensation claims of executives take no priority over the claims of other unsecured creditors in the event of bankruptcy. The value of deferred compensation claims by CEOs – also known as 'inside debt' (Jensen and Meckling, 1976) – can make up a substantial share of CEOs' overall remuneration.

Wei and Yermack (2010) report that out of the Standard & Poor's (S&P) 1500 firms, more than two-thirds of CEOs hold some form of inside debt, and that for those who hold inside debt, the holdings were worth an average of $5.7 million in 2006.

The key argument for why inside debt can play an important part as a remedy against CEO risk-shifting incentives is that rather than merely giving CEOs an interest in the survival of the firm (as solvency-contingent cash bonuses do), inside debt gives CEOs a financial interest in the liquidation value of the firm (Edmans and Liu, 2011). As explained above, where firms are close to failure, CEO cash bonuses may cause managers to engage in a 'gamble for resurrection' even if the most likely outcome of this gamble will be that firms will survive for one more period of bonus payments. Inside debt, by contrast, gives CEOs incentives not only to avoid institutional failure, but also to maintain high asset values such that company promises made to them as well as to other unsecured creditors can be honored.

A small number of empirical studies report evidence consistent with inside debt curbing CEO risk-taking behavior. Sundaram and Yermack (2007) find that large inside debt positions by a CEO reduce the probability of default on a firm's debt. More recently, Wei and Yermack (2010) examine the bond and share price reaction to the disclosure of inside debt holdings in 2007 as mandated by the Security and Exchange Commission (SEC). The authors find that large CEO pensions (as well as other forms of deferred payments to CEOs) are associated with gains for bondholders and losses for shareholders. Wei and Yermack (2010) argue that shareholder wealth losses in the time period after the disclosure of large inside debt holdings are consistent with the view that such holdings reduce firm risk and, therefore, the expected returns from holding equity.

Tung and Wang (2010) provide the hitherto only examination of the risk-taking effects of inside debt holdings in the banking industry. Their analysis is limited to the time period 2006–2008 and shows that bank CEOs with higher inside debt holdings engaged in less risk-taking before the financial crisis (as indicated by better stock market performance during the financial crisis).

There is a clear need for further research to look at the risk-taking effects of inside debt holdings over longer examination periods. The recently enhanced disclosure requirements by the SEC as regards deferred compensation claims by CEOs will provide a wealth of new opportunities for researchers to examine the effects of paying CEOs with debt. However, even before the enhanced disclosure requirements became active in 2007, the proxy statements filed with the SEC contain sufficient information to estimate the expected present value of a CEO's pension using actuarial computations (see Sundaram and Yermack, 2007). Some of the questions which future research should address relate to the conditions under which managerial holdings of inside debt have a risk-reducing effect, as discussed in the following two paragraphs.

One question which future research should address is whether the risk-reducing effects of inside debt reverse where banks are distressed and close to default. In other words, does debt-like compensation have a risk-inducing effect at risky banks, because the incentive effects of debt-like incentives are akin to those of equity at these institutions? Also, the personal circumstances and overall structure of CEO compensation will need to be taken into account to a larger degree by future research. Typically, pension entitlements make up the bulk of deferred compensation claims by CEOs. While the actuarial value of pension entitlements will be largest for CEOs close to retirement, the risk-reducing effects of similar levels of pension entitlements may well be largest for CEOs who are close to retirement. Further, a CEO with substantial amounts of equity-linked compensation will arguably be less likely to be concerned with pay-offs from a pension scheme and other types of deferred compensation. Consequently, for CEOs with large amounts of equity-linked pay, deferred compensation may not be effective in reducing banking risk. Ultimately, the question whether an optimal balance exists between equity and debt-based CEO compensation, and what this optimal balance is, should be addressed in future compensation research.

Relatedly, because defined benefit schemes give CEOs an interest in the asset value of the firm long after they retire, future research could also examine the effect of inside debt on CEO succession. It is conceivable that CEOs who are close to retirement with high inside debt holdings will be succeeded by a 'safe pair of hands' which are likely to pursue low-risk strategies. All of these are interesting questions which can be addressed using publicly available compensation data (at least of US bank CEOs).

If future work on inside debt holdings confirms the results reported above for the banking industry, this has important policy implications. Generally, the results based on pension data back the notion that deferred compensation should form an integral part of CEO compensation and that deferred compensation is most effective in curbing risk-shifting where the deferral period spans over many years (as in the case of defined benefit pensions).

9.4　CONCLUDING REMARKS

This chapter critically reviews the existing literature that links the structure of CEO compensation to bank risk-taking. While this literature has grown considerably in recent years, it remains solemnly focused on the role of equity-linked compensation. That is, previous work on banking almost exclusively examines the impact that paying CEOs with option and equity grants has on banking risk. This focus on equity-linked pay is regrettable, given that non-equity-linked forms of compensation bear the potential to rein in much of the socially suboptimal risk-taking in the banking industry which is now widely seen as a contributory factor to the recent financial crisis.

This chapter argues that while the extant work has made important contributions to aid a better understanding of the pay–risk relationship in banking, it should not be forgotten that non-equity-based forms of compensation warrant empirical investigation. This is because the pay-off structure of CEO bonus plans or deferred compensation is very different from that of equity-linked pay. The payment of CEO bonus plans is contingent on the bank remaining solvent, and the pay-out value of deferred compensation claims by a CEO is dependent on the liquidation value of the bank. In the case of CEO pension rights and other forms of deferred compensation, it could easily be argued that these CEO claims turn managers into bondholders who, because they join the ranks of the other unsecured creditors, have a financial interest to maintain high liquidation values of bank assets and, thus, low levels of risk. The work discussed in this chapter backs the notion that increasing the degree to which managerial interests are aligned with those of debtholders reduces the agency costs of debt and, therefore, lowers managerial incentives to shift risk.

As far as the role of CEO bonus plans is concerned, the work discussed in this chapter comes to conclusions which are inconsistent with many of the recent policy initiatives in the US as well as a number of European countries. The view underlying many of these initiatives is that high bonuses are undesirable and, in the case of many European economies, should be subject to high levels of taxation. A potentially risk-reducing role of CEO bonus plans has not entered the public debate on this matter. Similar arguments apply to the role of CEO pension entitlements. While deferred compensation is a key pillar of how payment practices at large banking firms are likely to be reformed, the role that pension entitlements can play in this context has not entered the public debate on this matter either.

Finally, the focus of existing work on the US means that cross-country differences in regulation and safety net subsidies to banking firms will not be adequately considered if empirical findings based on the US market are applied to other countries. For instance, it could be argued that in the presence of a generous and effective provision of a deposit insurance system such as the one provided by the Federal Deposit Insurance Corporation (FDIC) in the US, shareholders are less than adequately monitored by other bank creators and face more incentives to encourage bank risk-taking via CEO compensation contracts that are more sensitive to risk-taking.

Compensation at banking firms is an important topic. Previous research in this area has pointed out that equity-linked compensation in an industry that is highly leveraged and enjoys safety-net subsidies will aggravate risk-shifting incentives faced by CEOs. It will now be up to future work to understand how the structure of managerial compensation can be employed to cushion and manage CEO risk-taking incentives. Moving the focus away from equity and towards debt-like forms of CEO remuneration offers a promising route for this – for both researchers and policymakers.

REFERENCES

Amihud, Y. and B. Lev (1981), 'Risk reduction as a managerial motive for conglomerate mergers', *Bell Journal of Economics*, **12**, 605–617.

Balachandran, S., B. Kogut and H. Harnal (2010), 'The probability of default, excessive risk, and executive compensation: a study of financial services firms from 1995 to 2008', unpublished working paper, Columbia University.

Bebchuk, L.A. and H. Spamann (2009), 'Regulating bankers' pay', *Georgetown Law Journal*, **98**, 247–287.

Benston, G. and J. Evan (2006), 'Performance compensation contracts and CEOs' incentive to shift risk to debtholders: an empirical analysis', *Journal of Economics and Finance*, **30**, 70–92.

Bliss, R. and R. Rosen (2001), 'CEO compensation and bank mergers', *Journal of Financial Economics*, **61**, 107–138.

Chen, C.R., T.L. Steiner and A.M. Whyte (2006), 'Does stock option-based executive compensation induce risk-taking? An analysis of the banking industry', *Journal of Banking and Finance*, **30**, 915–945.

Coles, J.L., N.D. Daniel and L. Naveen (2006), 'Managerial incentives and risk-taking', *Journal of Financial Economics*, **79**, 431–468.

DeYoung, R., E.Y. Peng and M. Yan (2010), 'Executive compensation and policy choices at US commercial banks', Federal Reserve Bank of Kansas City Research Working Paper 10-02.

Duru, A., S.A. Mansi and D.M. Reeb (2005), 'Earnings-based bonus plans and the agency costs of debt', *Journal of Accounting and Public Policy*, **24**, 431–447.

Edmans, Alex and Q. Liu (2011), 'Inside debt', *Review of Finance*, **15**, 75–102.

Fahlenbrach, R. and R. Stulz (2011), 'Bank CEO incentives and the credit crisis', *Journal of Financial Economics*, **99**, 11–26.

Federal Reserve Bank (2010), 'Guidance on sound incentive compensation policies', Board of Governors of the Federal Reserve System, Washington, DC.

Guay, W.R. (1999), 'The sensitivity of CEO wealth to equity risk: an analysis of the magnitude and determinants', *Journal of Financial Economics*, **53**, 43–71.

Hagendorff, J. and F. Vallascas (2011), 'CEO pay incentives and risk-taking: evidence from bank acquisitions', *Journal of Corporate Finance*, **17**, 1078–1095.

Harjoto, M.A. and D.J. Mullineaux (2003), 'CEO compensation and the transformation of banking', *Journal of Financial Research*, **26**, 341–354.

IMF (2010), 'A fair and substantial contribution by the financial sector', Report for the G-20, International Monetary Fund, Washington, DC.

Jensen, M.C. and W.H. Meckling (1976), 'Theory of the firm: managerial behavior, agency costs and ownership structure', *Journal of Financial Economics*, **3**, 305–360.

John, T.A. and K. John (1993), 'Top-management compensation and capital structure', *Journal of Finance*, **48**, 949–974.

Kim, Y.S., J. Nam and J.H. Thornton Jr (2008), 'The effect of managerial bonus plans on corporate derivatives usage', *Journal of Multinational Financial Management*, **18**, 229–243.

Mehran, H. and J.V. Rosenberg (2007), 'The effect of employee stock options on bank investment choice, borrowing, and capital', Federal Reserve Bank of New York Staff Report No. 305.

Minnick, K., H. Unal and L. Yang (2011), 'Pay for performance? CEO compensation and acquirer returns in BHCs', *Review of Financial Studies*, **24**, 439–472.

Nam, J., R. Ottoo and J. Thornton Jr (2003), 'The effect of managerial incentives to bear risk on corporate investment and R&D investment', *Financial Review*, **38**, 77–101.

Noe, T.H., M.J. Rebello and L.D. Wall (1996), 'Managerial rents and regulatory intervention in troubled banks', *Journal of Banking and Finance*, **20**, 331–350.

Rajgopal, S. and T. Shevlin (2002), 'Empirical evidence on the relation between stock option compensation and risk-taking', *Journal of Accounting and Economics*, **33**, 145–171.

Rogers, D.A. (2002), 'Does executive portfolio structure affect risk management? CEO risk-taking incentives and corporate derivatives usage', *Journal of Banking and Finance*, **26**, 271–295.

Shleifer, A. and R. Vishny (1997), 'A survey of corporate governance', *Journal of Finance*, **52**, 737–783.

Smith, C.W. and R. M. Stulz (1985), 'The determinants of firms' hedging policies', *Journal of Financial and Quantitative Analysis*, **20**, 391–405.

Smith, C.W. and R.L. Watts (1992), 'The investment opportunity set and corporate financing, dividend, and compensation policies', *Journal of Financial Economics*, **32**, 263–292.

Stiroh, K. (2006), 'New evidence on the determinants of bank risk', *Journal of Financial Services Research*, **30**, 237–263.

Sundaram, R.K. and D.L. Yermack (2007), 'Pay me later: inside debt and its role in managerial compensation', *Journal of Finance*, **62**, 1551–1588.

Tung, F. and X. Wang (2010), 'Bank CEOs, inside debt compensation, and the global financial crisis', working paper.

Vallascas, F. and J. Hagendorff (2010), 'CEO remuneration and bank default risk: evidence from the US and Europe', unpublished working paper.

Webb, E. (2008), 'Regulator scrutiny and bank CEO incentives', *Journal of Financial Services Research*, **33**, 5–20.

Wei, C. and D. Yermack (2010), 'Deferred compensation, risk, and company value: investor reactions to CEO incentives', working paper, Federal Reserve Bank of New York.

Wei, C. and D. Yermack (forthcoming), 'Investor reactions to CEOs' inside debt incentives', *Review of Financial Studies*.

10 Bank failures and CEO compensation
Walter Dolde and John D. Knopf

10.1 INTRODUCTION

John et al. (2000) suggest that attention to capital ratios alone may not be an efficient way to regulate banks. They demonstrate theoretically that the structure of manager compensation plays an important role in bank risk-taking. These authors propose, therefore, that US Federal Deposit Insurance Corporation (FDIC) insurance premiums reflect each bank's compensation structure and the associated incentives to take risks which may result in failure.

In this chapter we examine the relationship between chief executive officer (CEO) compensation and the likelihood of failure for a large sample of publicly traded banks and thrifts in the USA. After controlling for capital ratios, we find that the structure of CEO compensation has a significant impact upon the probability of failure, consistent with John et al. (2000). Specifically, we split CEO compensation into salary, bonus and equity (stock awards and option awards). We find that salary and equity compensation are inversely related to failure, while bonus compensation is positively associated with the probability of failure. We attribute these findings to the incentive effects of different forms of compensation. If the firm fails, the manager may well be terminated, in which case the present value of future salary collapses. Similarly stock and option compensation may be indicative of the manager's equity in the firm, which also disintegrates in a failure. Bonuses are less likely to be serially correlated and are also more reflective of short-term performance, providing greater incentive for exposure to risk and insolvency.

10.2 RELATED LITERATURE

A growing literature relates bank risk-taking to components of corporate governance such as manager and director stock ownership, structure of manager compensation, and board structure. Additional research examines how bank regulation interacts with governance variables in affecting risk-taking.

10.2.1 Research on Risk and Compensation

We are unaware of any research directly linking managerial compensation with bank default rates. Cheng et al. (2010) examine the relationship between compensation and other proxies for risk-taking and compensation. For the period 1992 to 2008, they find that total compensation is significantly related to risk-taking in a way that the authors view as 'short-termism'. The result obtains after controlling for insider ownership, which provides incentives for a long-term decision horizon in the authors' view. Both compensation and risk-taking vary positively with the ownership share of institutional investors who 'tend to have short-termist preferences and the power to influence firm management policies'.

In early work, Crawford et al. (1995) find that bank CEO compensation became more sensitive to bank performance after the deregulation starting in 1982. Sensitivity increased for all three forms of compensation: stock ownership, stock options and cash compensation (salary and bonus). Prior to 1982 an increase in CEO compensation of $0.72 was associated with $1000 of wealth creation for shareholders. After deregulation, sensitivity rose sixfold to $4.72. The greatest increase occurred in option compensation, which was negligible before 1982 and $2.95 per $1000 afterwards. The results support a contracting hypothesis that the heightened sensitivity was intended to induce more risk-taking in the face of a richer set of positive net present value (NPV) opportunities.

In contrast to the characterization of Crawford et al. (1995), Houston and James (1995) find no evidence that compensation practices at the 134 largest commercial banks during 1980–1990 provided incentives for greater risk-taking. Compared to other industries, banking offers CEOs lower cash compensation, less frequent participation in stock option plans and lower levels of options held, and a smaller fraction of compensation in the form of grants of stocks and options. Within the cross-section of banks in the sample, equity-based incentives are positively associated with the value of a bank's charter, but not with risk-taking.

10.2.2 Research on Risk and Ownership Structure

Fahlenbrach and Stulz (2011) find better alignment of CEO and outside shareholder interests was negatively related to bank performance in the recent financial crisis. Greater insider ownership and greater sensitivity of CEO wealth to bank performance represent better alignment of interests. Furthermore, larger cash bonuses and larger option compensation were not negatively related to performance during the crisis. The authors note that options grants typically consist of options that are very much in the money relative to the likely future stock level at their long maturities. Hence time value and sensitivity to volatility is muted. The incentive effects of strongly in-the-money options differ little from the incentive effects of stock ownership. Fahlenbrach and Stulz conjecture an alternative reconciliation of poorer performance in better incentive-aligned banks. The financial crisis was unanticipated, including by bank CEOs. They had in place strategies designed to maximize shareholder value – and their personal wealth – in the market environment as they perceived it. There is no evidence that CEOs sold large numbers of shares or escaped large wealth losses.

Laeven and Levine (2009) examine the relationships among bank regulations, ownership structure and bank risk-taking. They find evidence that bank regulation may increase risk or decrease it, depending upon the ownership structure. For example, an index of regulatory capital stringency is related positively to a measure of bank stability (inverse of risk). But an interaction term with the power of insider control exhibits a negative coefficient, meaning that strong insider control offsets the direct stabilizing effect of regulation. Similarly, regulatory restrictions on bank activities foster stability with widely dispersed ownership. But an interaction term between restriction and insider power has a negative coefficient. In both the cases of capital stringency and activity restrictions, the effect of the regulation may be to increase risk for tightly controlled banks. The same phenomena are observed in relation to explicit deposit insurance.

10.2.3   Research on Risk and Compensation Structure

The empirical results of Mehran and Rosenberg (2008) for the years 1992–2002 contrast with the financial crisis results of Fahlenbrach and Stulz (2011) noted above. Mehran and Rosenberg find that stock option grants induce bank CEOs to undertake riskier investments, leading to higher equity and asset volatility. Perhaps counterintuitively, however, higher stock option grants are associated with lower leverage and increased capital levels. As an aside, the theoretical framework of John et al. (2000) cited at the beginning of this chapter calls for bonuses of bank managers to be an increasing function of bank capital. But John et al. offer a prescription that is not at present the standard course of treatment.

John and Qian (2003) report that pay–performance sensitivity of bank CEOs declines in bank leverage and in size. These empirical results are consistent with theoretical arguments that: (1) optimal sensitivity is lower with greater leverage to prevent risk-shifting; and (2) there is less information asymmetry in larger firms. The authors find that bank CEO compensation sensitivity is $4.70 per $1000 of change in shareholder value. A non-trivial part of this sensitivity derives from gains in the market value of stock and options holdings. This sensitivity estimate ($4.70) compares with $6 per $1000 for manufacturing firms (Murphy, 1999) which have lower leverage and are smaller than the John and Qian bank sample.

Of the reports reviewed above that find a positive relation between bank manager compensation and risk-taking, there is disagreement on the social welfare implications. Crawford et al. (1995) find the positive association beneficial, encouraging managers to undertake positive-NPV projects newly available after deregulation, along with the concomitant risks. But Cheng et al. (2010), Laevan and Levine (2009) and Mehran and Rosenberg (2008) infer the undertaking of excessive or unprofitable risk, consistent with moral hazard.

10.3   DATA

Other studies examining the relationship between compensation and risk-taking in the banking industry have used stock return variability or various balance sheet measures. Here we examine the relationship between compensation structure and the incidence of failure among financial institutions.

Our sample consists of all publicly traded banks and thrifts that in 2007 filed both financial reports and executive compensation information with the US Securities and Exchange Commission (SEC). The guidelines requiring detailed compensation reporting were promulgated in 2006. We take our data from SNL Securities, which collects and organizes data from SEC filings for all publicly traded banks and thrifts. After eliminating institutions with missing data, we arrive at a sample of 766 firms.

The FDIC provides a list of failed financial institutions that it takes over. We matched the FDIC failure data with the SEC compensation and financial reports. Many of the publicly traded banks were holding companies, mostly multi-bank, but some with a single bank subsidiary. We classified a multi-bank holding company as failed if any of its subsidiaries appeared on the FDIC list. We construct the variables below from these FDIC and SEC data; summary statistics appear in Panel A of Table 10.1.

- *Failure*: A dummy variable equal to 1, if the financial institution failed between January 2008 and August 2010, or equal to 0 otherwise. The mean for *Failure* in Table 10.1 is 0.055, meaning that 5.5 percent of our sample failed during the 32-month observation window.
- *Salary*: Reported base compensation of CEOs, including compensation earned but deferred at the recipient's election. The mean *Salary* for CEOs in our sample is $320 088 with a maximum of $1 500 000 and a minimum of $0.
- *Bonus*: Reported annual bonus, including compensation earned but deferred at the recipient's election. The mean *Bonus* of $76 619 is slightly less than a quarter of the mean *Salary*, but the maximum *Bonus* ($14 500 000) is almost ten times larger than the maximum *Salary* ($1 500 000). It is also interesting to note that the median *Bonus* is zero, thus fewer than half of the CEOs received a bonus in 2007.
- *Equity*: Reported fair value of both stock and option awards, including the full grant date fair value of all options, stock appreciation rights and similar equity-based compensation instruments that have option-like features. We combined equity and option compensation because a fair value measure was available only for their total, not for the components separately. In addition, most options grants are deep in the money relative to a reasonable future price, as pointed out by Fahlenbrach and Stulz (2011). To the extent that implicit value is a large part of the value of an options award, the incentive effect of the award is much the same as a stock award. *Equity* has the widest range of all of the compensation methods, with a minimum of zero and a maximum of $23 300 000. The median is zero and the mean is $319 740, about 87 percent of the mean *Salary*.
- *Compensation*: The sum of *Salary*, *Bonus*, *Equity* and any personal expenses paid by the firm, such as insurance premia or personal travel. *Compensation* has a mean of $946 444 and a range from $1 000 to $38 300 000.

For our regressions we construct variables which standardize our various forms of compensation as a percentage of *Compensation*. These variables are as follows:

- *Salary%*: Ratio of *Salary* to *Compensation*, with an average of 0.604 (60.4 percent).
- *Bonus%*: Ratio of *Bonus* to *Compensation*, with an average of 0.063 (6.3 percent).
- *Equity%*: Ratio of *Equity* to *Compensation*, with an average of 0.091 (9.1 percent).

We employ four control variables available via SNL from financial reports for 2007 filed with the SEC. These are all standard measures widely used in empirical finance research:

- *Log Total Assets*: Logarithm of reported total assets, a control for the size of the institution. There is broad empirical consensus that the incidence of financial

Table 10.1   Correlations among forms of compensation (Equity%, Salary% and Bonus%) and proxy for size (Log Total Assets)

Panel A: Mean, median, standard deviation, minimum and maximum for the variables used in our study

Variable	Obs.	Mean	Median	Std. Dev.	Min.	Max.
Failure	766	0.055	0	0.228	0	1
Salary ($)	766	320088	255057	206258	0	1500000
Bonus ($)	766	76619	0	607625	0	14500000
Equity ($)	766	366237	0	1852407	0	23300000
Compensation ($)	766	946444	413227	2561	1000	38300000
Salary%	766	0.604	0.632	0.218	0.000	1.100
Bonus%	766	0.063	0.000	0.106	0.000	0.698
Equity%	766	0.091	0	0.186	0	0.996
Total Assets (millions $)	766	1350	123	121000	38	2190000
Tier 1 Capital Ratio (%)	766	13.72	11.70	7.353	5.42	86.50
ROA (%)	766	0.609	0.76	1.092	-16.86	6.13
Price to Book	766	1.306	1.23	0.468	0.351	3.747

Panel B: Correlations among the following variables

	Equity%	Salary%	Bonus%	Log Total Assets
Equity%	1			
Salary%	-0.4897	1		
Bonus%	-0.0937	-0.2004	1	
Log Total Assets	0.6228	-0.5745	0.0112	1

Note: Failure is a dummy that equals 1 if the bank or thrift failed from January 2008 to August 2010 and 0 otherwise. The sample for this table consists of publicly traded US banks and thrifts that filed proxy statements with the SEC in 2007. *Equity($)*, *Salary($)* and *Bonus($)* are the dollar components of *Compensation($)* and *Equity%, Salary%* and *Bonus%* are the respective proportions. *Log Total Assets, Tier 1 Capital Ratio* and *ROA* are control variables measured at book value. *Price to Book* is the ratio of the market price of equity to the book value.

distress is negatively related to firm size. From Table 10.1, mean *Total Assets* is $1.35 billion, but the range is vast, $38 million to $2.19 trillion. (We show the mean of *Total Assets* for perspective in Table 10.1, but employ *Log Total Assets* in multivariate estimation.)

- *ROA*: Return on assets, equal to net income in ratio to average assets, a control for profitability. Empirically, more profitable firms are less likely to suffer financial distress. Mean and median *ROA* are 0.609 and 0.76, respectively
- *Tier 1 Capital Ratio*: The ratio of book value of equity and equivalents to assets, a control for leverage, a proxy for leverage decisions. Both finance theory and numerous empirical papers suggest that a higher capital ratio (lower leverage) is associated with reduced probability of financial distress. The mean *Tier 1 Capital Ratio* is 13.94 percent and the median is 11.70 percent, both well within the classification of a well-capitalized institution.
- *Price to Book*: The ratio of the share price to book value per share, a control for growth opportunities. Empirical results on the relation between *Tier 1 Capital Ratio* and financial distress are mixed. Firms with more growth opportunities may have comparative advantages at identifying and exploiting them as markets change. But high-growth firms also change more rapidly and are exposed to greater risk. *Price to Book* ranges from 0.35 to 3.75, with mean and median respectively at 1.31 and 1.23.

Panel B of Table 10.1 shows the correlations among the three components of compensation and *Log Total Assets*. *Log Total Assets* and *Equity%* are strongly positively associated with a correlation equal to 0.623. The correlation between size and *Salary%* is −0.575, indicating a strong negative relation. Small institutions rely almost exclusively on salary compensation, while larger banks shift the structure of compensation towards stock awards. Observed directly, the correlation between *Equity%* and *Salary%* is −0.490. There is some trade-off between *Bonus%* and *Salary%* within cash compensation, indicated by a correlation of −0.200.

10.4 RESULTS

We apply data on our cross-section of 766 depository institutions filing with the SEC for 2007 to examine the relationship between failure in the subsequent 32 months and the structure of CEO compensation, controlling for institution size, profitability, leverage and growth prospects. The dependent variable is binomial, taking the values of 1 if the institution failed during the observation window and 0 if it did not. Multivariate models testing hypotheses about binomial models require logit methods.

Table 10.2 presents the estimates for four logit regression models, including coefficients and probability values estimated using robust sandwich standard errors. All models include the same control variables from filed financial reports. They differ in that Models 1–3 include as an explanatory variable a single component of compensation, scaled by total compensation. Model 4 includes all three components.

Other things being equal, 1 percent higher compensation as stock or option awards reduces the probability of failure by 2.08 percent in Model 1 and by 2.64 percent in

Table 10.2   Logit regression results for bank and thrift failure

Variable	(1)	(2)	(3)	(4)
Equity%	−2.076			−2.636
	0.105			0.045
Salary%		−2.972		−3.025
		0.002		0.002
Bonus%			4.571	3.108
			0.003	0.034
Log Total Assets	0.0773	−0.2928	−0.064	−0.106
	0.549	0.017	0.489	0.432
Tier 1 Capital Ratio	−0.2392	−0.2451	−0.24	−0.2515
	0.003	0.001	0.001	0.001
ROA	−0.3376	−0.3587	−0.4324	−0.4335
	0.101	0.031	0.017	0.012
Price to Book	−0.008	−0.0102	−0.0092	−0.0111
	0.097	0.029	0.047	0.022
Intercept	0.1967	7.209	1.825	4.834
	0.931	0.003	0.311	0.053
Sample Size	766	766	766	766
R-square	0.1029	0.1258	0.1293	0.162
Chi-square	23.15	34.78	38.21	49.14

Notes:
In this table we report logit regression results. The dependent variable for all regressions is a dummy that equals 1 if the bank or thrift failed from January 2008 to August 2010 and 0 otherwise. The sample for this table consists of publicly traded US banks and thrifts that filed proxy statements with the SEC in 2007. The p-value is given below each coefficient value. P-values are estimated using robust sandwich standard errors.
Failure is a dummy that equals 1 if the bank or thrift failed from January 2008 to August 2010 and 0 otherwise. *Equity%*, *Salary%* and *Bonus%* are the proportions of CEO compensation that take those forms. *Log Total Assets*, *Tier I Capital Ratio* and *ROA* are control variables measured at book value. *Price to Book* is the ratio of the market price of equity to the book value.

Model 4. The coefficient in Model 1 just misses significance at the 10 percent level, while the p value for Model 4 is 0.045, that is, better than the 5 percent level. These results cannot be attributed to size, the negative association between size and financial distress, and the positive association between *Equity%* and *Failure*, because both models include a control variable for size (*Log Total Assets*). Stock and option compensation may be equivalent to a call option on the assets of the institution, but CEOs of banks and thrifts did not act that way during the financial crisis. Perhaps the incentive to take risk is not viewed unconditionally but rather as taking prudent risks according to circumstances.

The relationship between an extra 1 percent of compensation in the form of salary and failure is similar to but smaller than an extra 1 percent in salary. In Model 2 the coefficient of *Salary%* is −2.97 with a p value of 0.002. When all compensation components are present in Model 4, 1 percent more salary decreases the probability of failure by 3.03 percent (p = 0.002). Perhaps, too little attention is paid to executives' human capital in modeling CEO decision-making. Brookman and Thistle (2007) estimate that 58 percent of all CEO separations are involuntary. In the calmer times of two decades earlier, Warner et al. (1988) found that 28 percent of CEO separations were involuntary. Termination results in a large loss of human capital. At minimum there is an interruption in a large income stream. Beyond that, the stigma of termination reduces the probability of finding another job (Cannella et al., 1995). If a new position is offered, it may well be at a lower compensation level. There are strong financial reasons to avoid 'the career-ending mistake'. Note in addition that unvested stock and option grants are reversed in the case of termination.

Bonus% is significantly positively related to the incidence of failure. An extra percentage point of compensation in the form of bonus increases the probability of failure by 4.57 percent (Model 3, p = 0.003) or 3.11 percent (Model 4, p = 0.034). This result seems out of step with those for equity and salary compensation shares. Note that fewer than half of all institutions awarded a bonus in 2007 (median = 0 in Table 10.1). This low frequency makes a bonus akin to 'transitory income' in contrast to salary, which may be subject to inertia and regarded as 'permanent income' (Friedman, 1957). Permanent income has a larger behavioral influence than transitory income. A possibly related factor may be that, with the first signs of the ensuing financial crisis emerging in the last quarter of 2007 and the beginning of 2008, some CEOs may have negotiated for greater bonuses to offset potentially weak market performance of the broad stock market, which would drag down thrift share prices and the value of CEOs' own holdings in their firms. Thus higher bonuses in 2007 may not have provided an incentive for riskier behavior, but rather may have indicated an increased perception of difficult times ahead.

All of the control variables are significant in all models except *ROA* in Model 1 (p = 0.101) and *Log Total Assets* in Models 1, 3, and 4. Consistent with previous empirical research, *Tier 1 Capital Ratio* (low leverage) is associated with reduced incidence of *Failure*. Probability values are 0.003 or smaller in all models. Profitability (*ROA*) is negatively related to *Failure* in all models, at significance levels ranging from 0.014 to 0.101. Growth opportunities as proxied by *Price to Book* are significantly negative in all four models, at better than the 0.05 level except for Model 1 (p = 0.097).

Compared to the previous empirical research reviewed above, our results are most like those of Laeven and Levine (2009) in the case of an absence of a controlling insider ownership block. Cheng et al. (2010), Crawford et al. (1995), John and Qian (2003) and Mehran and Rosenberg (2008) generally find that most forms of CEO compensation are positively related to risk-taking, especially options awards. (Fahlenbrach and Stulz (2011) and Houston and James (1995) report that risk-taking is unrelated to compensation and its components.)

10.5 SUMMARY

We provide additional evidence on the impact of managerial compensation on risk-taking (failure), which should be of interest to investors and regulators. It is important to note that the nature of the measure of risk may make a difference in the empirical results for compensation and risk-taking. Incidence of failure captures only downside risk outcomes. Consistent with John et al. (2000), our evidence suggests that regulators who are particularly concerned about downside risk (failure) should consider managerial compensation when setting FDIC insurance premiums. The somewhat surprising empirical results of our study suggest that higher stock and options awards to CEOs reduced the likelihood of failure during the financial crisis of 2008–2010. The same is true for higher salary. Most of the rest of the empirical literature (Cheng et al., 2010; Crawford et al., 1995; John and Qian, 2003; Mehran and Rosenberg, 2008) finds a positive relation between these components of compensation and risk-taking. But none of those papers has the financial crisis in its sample periods and all examine two-sided risk measures, whereas failure represents only downside risk. We do find that larger bonuses are positively associated with the incidence of failure. This positive relation may not represent an incentive effect as much as negotiation for higher temporary pay in advance of a perceived riskier financial environment.

Our results are also important to investors. Greater stock return volatility and riskier decisions about investments and financing have both upside and downside potential. In a portfolio context, diversified investors desire exposure to the risks and returns of banking. CEOs who underinvest and, therefore, fail to seize positive-NPV opportunities may dissatisfy investors, even as they suit the goals of regulators. It is possible that bank CEOs are sensitive to both audiences, discriminating between strategies that raise risk generally and those with such a heavy downside that they might end in failure. Within the set of opportunities, strategies with less extreme downside risk (and some upside risk) may be favored, especially when general financial environment risk seems higher.

REFERENCES

Brookman, Jeff and Paul D. Thistle (2007), 'CEO tenure, the risk of termination and firm value', working paper, University of Nevada, Las Vegas.
Cannella, Albert A., Donald R. Fraser and D. Scott Lee (1995), 'Firm failure and managerial labor markets: evidence from Texas banking', *Journal of Financial Economics*, **38**, 185–210.
Cheng, Ing-Haw, Harrison Hong and Jose A. Scheinkman (2010), 'Yesterday's heroes: compensation and creative risk-taking', NBER Working Paper.
Crawford, Anthony J., John R. Ezzell and James A. Miles (1995), 'Bank CEO pay–performance relations and the effects of deregulation', *Journal of Business*, **68**, 231–256.
Fahlenbrach, Rüdiger and René Stulz (2011), 'Bank CEO incentives and the credit crisis', *Journal of Financial Economics*, **99**, 11–26.
Friedman, Milton (1957), *A Theory of the Consumption Function*, Princeton, NJ: Princeton University Press.
Houston, J.F. and C. James (1995), 'CEO compensation and bank risk: is compensation in banking structured to promote risk-taking?', *Journal of Monetary Economics*, **36**, 405–431.
John, Kose and Yiming Qian (2003), 'Incentive features in CEO compensation in the banking industry', *FRBNY Economic Policy Review*, April, 109–121.
John, Kose, Anthony Saunders and Lemma Senbet (2000), 'A theory of bank regulation and management compensation', *Review of Financial Studies*, **13**, 95–125.
Laeven, Luc and Ross Levine (2009), 'Bank governance, regulation and risk-taking', *Journal of Financial Economics*, **93**, 259–275.
Mehran and Rosenberg (2008), 'The effect of employee stock options on bank investment choice, borrowing and capital', Federal Reserve Bank of New York, Staff Report no. 305.
Murphy, K. (1999), 'Executive compensation', in Orley Ashenfelter and David Card (eds), *Handbook of Labor Economics*, Vol. 3, Amsterdam: North-Holland.
Warner, J.B., R.L. Watts and K.H. Wruck (1988), 'Stock prices and top management changes', *Journal of Financial Economics*, **30**, 461–492.

11 Restricting risk-taking by financial intermediaries through executive compensation

Tom Berglund

The financial crisis that started in 2007 and peaked in 2008–2009 clearly revealed that there are externalities in financial intermediation that markets as such are unable to handle. The question that governments and regulatory bodies around the world are trying to answer presently is how these externalities should be addressed. Finding appropriate solutions is not made easier by the fact that there is a strong popular sentiment against bankers in general, who are seen as the culprits for the fall in living standards as a consequence of the crisis in most countries around the world.

In the aftermath of the Great Depression in the 1930s demand for a strict banking regulation was triggered by deposit insurance that was introduced to stave off bank runs. In that crisis the existence of even sound banks was threatened by withdrawals from panic-stricken depositors. However, deposit insurance, that removed this threat, created a moral hazard problem: when banks are allowed to fund their activities with cheap deposits that are guaranteed by the government, excessive risk-taking by an individual bank will not be appropriately penalized by the market.

While this externality has been well known, and constitutes the basis for relatively strict banking supervision around the world, the new insight that the recent crisis has forcefully highlighted is that these externalities are not limited to deposit-taking banks. Big and highly interconnected financial institutions will be subject to externalities too, even if none of their funding comes in the form of deposits.

The reason why any big player in financial intermediation will be subject to negative externalities is that if this institution fails there will be costly repercussions for other players in financial intermediation.[1] Since these expected costs do not show up in the profit and loss statement of the individual bank, the value-maximizing risk-taking strategy for that institution will involve a higher level of risk than what is socially optimal.

It is well known in standard microeconomics that if the externalities can somehow be imposed on the firm as explicit costs, the socially optimal solution can be restored. In practice, though, measuring these externalities appropriately, and furthermore imposing the corresponding costs on the systemically important financial institutions (SIFIs) tend to be extremely difficult. In particular, the problem is made complicated by the fact that any proposed measurement scheme is likely to provide scope for sophisticated manipulation. Once banks know that certain indicators will increase their costs they will invent ways to conduct their business that minimize the impact on those specific indicators.

The alternative of allowing the supervisory authority to determine the systemic importance of big financial institutions without the use of any explicit formulas is also problematic. Regulators are likely to favour financial institutions that are run by persons that they themselves consider trustworthy, which will then allow these institutions to operate with lower costs than institutions that are run by persons unknown to the regulators. This will foster regulatory capture when big financial institutions will invest in improving their standing at the regulator, also by other means than by complying with the regulator's official recommendations.

An intensively discussed alternative, or complementary, route to address this issue is to regulate the incentives of chief executive officers (CEOs) of large financial institutions. The general idea in doing this is to prevent the top management that runs the day-to-day operations of the firm from being rewarded by owners in situations where owners will not carry the total expected costs for the firm's actions.

Fahlenbrach and Stulz (2009) studied 98 financial intermediaries over the recent financial crisis to see whether managers had incentive schemes that were better aligned with those of the firm's shareholders. Consistent with the above conjecture they found that the firms that were managed by CEOs with more equity-related compensation had a worse performance in the crisis than firms run by managers who had weaker shareholder incentives. Similiar results are obtained by Chesney et al. (2010) when explaining the level of write-downs in US financial firms in 2007–2008.

John et al. (2000) set up a simplified model for bank risk-taking in which they show that incorporating management incentives in the insurance premiums that banks should be charged to cover costs for exposure to systemic risk is indeed a better way to try to control bank risk-taking than exclusively through capital ratios.

From previous literature on management incentives it is well known that top management, in the absence of performance-related variable pay, tends to be too risk-averse from shareholders' point of view, the reason being that if the risk materializes there is no way for the management to convince the outside market that the loss was attributable to bad luck, bad management having no share in it. Since bad luck for this reason will hurt the CEO while good luck will have no impact on the CEO's compensation, the CEO will be inclined to avoid risks, even in cases where these risks are expected to be profitable for the firm (Holmström, 1982).

From a social point of view this reluctance to take risks is at least to some extent beneficial, as seen in the evidence reported in the Fahlenbrach and Stulz (2009) study. If shareholders are prevented from setting up incentives that will induce management to take socially costly risks, the resulting equilibrium may be closer to the socially optimal one than if shareholders are free to set the incentives so as to achieve alignment with their own personal interests.

What complicates the issue is the fact that incentives are relevant not only for risk-taking, but also for generating effort from key decision-makers. In a world where information and communication technology is subject to constant development, new business opportunities and new ways to conduct existing businesses more efficiently will frequently arise. Staying abreast with the development and grabbing the opportunities as they arise requires effort: initiatives have to be taken and the staff has to be motivated to take on new challenges. In the absence of monetary incentives, maintaining the status quo – that is, opting for defensive rather than expansionary measures – will easily become the most attractive strategy for the CEO.[2] This will create a welfare loss in two respects: existing services will be unnecessarily expensive, and the introduction of new services that would be beneficial for customers will be delayed.

Top management's efforts in today's financial intermediation are closely tied to issues related to the size of the business. The reason is economies of scale and scope created by new technology. Running a modern bank requires a substantial investment in appropriate software. Software intensive technology is usually connected with substantial fixed costs, that is, the costs for programming and testing the system; while the costs for adding customers to the system, once in operation, tend to be small in comparison. To exploit these economies of scale the financial intermediary has either to be big enough in itself or to buy the services from some other firm, a firm which in turn is able to operate on a scale that is big enough. While the first alternative contributes to making the intermediaries as such 'too big to fail', the latter alternative tends to make them 'interconnected' to a firm that may become too big to fail. Regulation of the CEO's incentives in one type of a firm may easily lead to behaviour that will reduce the problem in certain types of firms by recreating it in a new type of firm where the top management have the incentives to expand their business more aggressively.

In addition to risk-taking incentives in bank management compensation, another related compensation issue that has surfaced in the recent financial crisis is the size of the pay package for bank executives. In principle it is true that paying out large sums in compensation to management will reduce core equity and make the financial intermediary more exposed to risk. Thus it may make sense to restrict the size of the pay package when the intermediary's core equity is endangered. However, this does not constitute a good argument for setting some kind of a cap on bank top management compensation in general.

The reason why general caps on executive pay in financial intermediaries are likely to be counterproductive is that financial intermediaries are competing for talent in a market where there are lucrative alternatives.[3] Most potential candidates for a top job at a financial intermediary have already been able to accumulate substantial wealth of their own. They will thus have the opportunity to focus on managing this wealth instead of opting to work for a financial intermediary. To lure them to devote their time to running the large financial intermediary instead, the compensation must be high enough to trump the alternative of managing the private portfolio.[4]

A comparison with the level of executive compensation in industrial firms is misleading due to fundamental differences in the character of the business. Industrial firms are dealing in goods that tend to be unique in some sense. They have an established production process and established distribution channels. Any attempt by a talented potential CEO to set up a new competing business would be extremely risky. Given these differences in the character of the business we would expect CEOs of financial intermediaries to receive a higher income on average than their counterparts in equal-sized industrial firms.

A cap on executive pay in financial intermediation would, in other words, lead to a distortion in the allocation of managerial talent. Talent that would achieve more in terms of wealth creation in large financial intermediaries would end up in positions where their net contribution to total wealth would be smaller.[5]

From a risk reduction point of view a cap on executive pay makes no sense. By applying the Shapiro and Stiglitz (1984) efficiency wage model it is easily shown that the smaller the part of the economic rent of an employment relationship that an employee is awarded, the larger the likelihood that the employee misbehaves in a way that may terminate the employment relationship, if detected. Paying insufficient attention to potentially harmful risk-taking within the organization is one of the most likely types of managerial misbehaviour that could lead to termination of the employment relationship for the CEO of a financial institution. A high straight salary for the CEO, that will motivate the CEO to pay more attention to measures that discourage risk-taking, should thus correlate positively, rather than negatively, with more stringent risk controls in financial intermediaries. Consistent with this Fahlenbrach and Stulz (2009) found that banks that paid less to their CEOs suffered more from the financial crisis.

A much-discussed issue in management compensation for financial intermediaries is also the role of so-called 'golden parachutes', that is, severance pay for CEOs. It has been argued that they should be banned since they reward the management for bad behaviour, that is, strategies that make it difficult for the firm to continue on its own. While there may be some merit in this argument in some cases, there are other cases where a golden parachute is clearly beneficial since it reduces the incentives for CEOs who are no longer able to cope with the situation to hang on to their jobs, hoping for a stroke of good luck to pull them out of the difficulties.

This chapter discusses a number of aspects related to attempts to control risk-taking by financial intermediaries by regulating top management compensation. Although the fundamental idea of directly trying to impact upon the incentives of the decision-makers in financial institutions, so as to insulate them from pressures to act in their shareholders' interest at the expense of what is beneficial for society, carries some merit, there are a number of issues that make these kinds of proposals less attractive.

Restricting risk-taking incentives will normally also restrict incentives for valuable effort. Even if the role of top management effort is extremely difficult to measure it is generally accepted that top management effort is important to generate change in organizations. Since information processing is at the core of modern banking business, technological development will regularly require banks to adapt. This will require vigilance and effort from the top management. Preventing banks from rewarding the top management for well-invested effort will have negative long-run consequences for productivity in financial intermediation, and thus most likely for growth in standards of living for the society at large.

Putting general caps on executive compensation is not advisable either. The consequence of such caps is likely to be a migration of talent to related business areas, and in particular to private wealth management, with detrimental consequences to the banking sector.

Finally, it is interesting to note that if risk avoidance is what should drive management, compensation paying out a large part of the economic rent of the operations as a fixed sum to top management should give the strongest incentives for tight risk controls.

The main conclusion that the above arguments point to is that management incentives are something that regulators under normal circumstances should leave to shareholders; in practice, to the board of the company. However, when the likelihood is that the bank will run into serious financial trouble, that is, when the bank's equity nears depletion, and supervisory authorities have to step in to prevent 'gambling for resurrection', top management incentives should be addressed as well. CEO compensation contracts should be required to include a clause saying that all performance-based additional compensation will automatically be cancelled should that type of situation occur.[6] Strict rules limiting CEO compensation are, in other words, justified as a part of an early structured intervention scheme for banks.

NOTES

1. If this 'first-order' externality is expected to be much higher without government intervention we would expect a rational government to step in to reduce the externality, thus producing the same moral hazard problem as deposit insurance.
2. Competition between banks will not eliminate this problem if we assume that all banks are subject to the same restrictions concerning management incentives.
3. See for example Axelson and Bond (2009).
4. Even if the potential CEO would not have enough private wealth, it seems highly likely that in order for the person to be competent to run a large financial intermediary, that person would have to be well connected. Thus the person would most likely be able to set up a joint venture with other wealthy people in which the sums involved are big enough to guarantee a decent income for the potential candidate.
5. One may argue that the going for lesser talent would be beneficial for society since less-talented persons are easier to control from the regulator's point of view. However, the likelihood of unintended substantial mistakes that may endanger the business should be negatively correlated with managerial talent.
6. See European Shadow Financial Regulatory Committee (2009).

REFERENCES

Axelson, Ulf and Philip Bond (2009), 'Investment banking careers', EFA 2009 Bergen Meetings Paper, available at SSRN, http://ssrn.com/abstract=1343600.
Chesney, M., J. Stromberg and A.F. Wagner (2010), 'Risk-taking incentives, governance, and losses in the financial crisis', Swiss Finance Institute Research Paper No. 10-18, 2 November, available at SSRN: http://ssrn.com/abstract=1595343.
European Shadow Financial Regulatory Committee (2009), Statement No. 30, Warsaw, 21 September.
Fahlenbrach, R. and R. Stulz (2009), 'Bank CEO incentives and the credit crisis', Dice Center WP 2009-13 / Fisher College of Business WP 2009-03-013.
Holmström, B. (1982), 'Managerial incentive problems – a dynamic perspective', in *Essays in Economics and Management in Honor of Lars Wahlbeck*, Helsinki: Swedish School of Economics. (See also *Review of Economic Studies*, January 1999.)
John, K., A. Saunders and L.W. Senbet (2000), 'A theory of bank regulation and management compensation', *Review of Financial Studies*, **13**(Spring), 95–125.
Shapiro, Carl and Joseph E. Stiglitz (1984), 'Equilibrium unemployment as a worker discipline device', *American Economic Review*, **74**(3), 433–444.

PART III

MARKET DISCIPLINE: PREREQUISITES AND EFFECTIVENESS

12 The lost cause: the failure of the Financial Crisis Inquiry Commission

Peter J. Wallison

12.1 INTRODUCTION

In late January 2011, the US Financial Crisis Inquiry Commission issued its report on the 2008 financial crisis.[1] I was one of ten members on this Commission and wrote a dissenting statement that is available online through the American Enterprise Institute (AEI)[2] or through the Commission's website.[3] It is also available in hard copy, together with the full report and the other dissents, through the US Government Printing Office.[4] Three other Republicans on the Commission – Bill Thomas (who was also the Commission's vice-chair), Keith Hennessey and Douglas Holtz-Eakin – also dissented, and their dissent (the THH dissent) can also be found on the Commission's website.[5] In this chapter, I summarize my dissent and the logic on which it rested, offer a brief description of the deficiencies of the 500-page majority report, and explain why I could not join in the dissent of the three other Republicans.

Since the Commission's mandate was to explain what caused the financial crisis, my dissent focuses almost entirely on that question. George Santayana is often quoted for the aphorism that 'those who cannot remember the past are condemned to repeat it'. Attempting to identify the causes of the financial crisis, however, shows that Santayana's idea was a bit facile. Even if we know what happened in the past, there is still debate about what caused it to happen. The continuing appearance of revisionist histories about important events, such as the USA's Civil War or the Great Depression, testifies to the protean quality of the past. The difficult task for historians, economists and public policy specialists is to discern which, among a welter of possible causes, were the significant ones – the ones without which history would have been different.

Using this standard, I believe that the *sine qua non* of the financial crisis was the US government's housing policies; these fostered the creation of 27 million subprime and other risky loans – half of all mortgages in the United States – which were susceptible to default when the massive 1997–2007 housing bubble began to deflate. If the US government had not chosen this policy path – feeding the growth of a bubble of unprecedented size and an equally unprecedented number of weak and high-risk residential mortgages – I believe that the great financial crisis of 2008 would not have occurred. What follows is a brief summary of the argument in my dissenting statement.

The US government's housing policies were intended to increase homeownership by providing low-income borrowers with increased access to mortgage credit. Under legislation adopted by Congress in 1992, the Department of Housing and Urban Development (HUD) in both the Clinton and George W. Bush administrations carried on an intensive effort to reduce mortgage underwriting standards. HUD used: (1) the affordable-housing requirements imposed by Congress in 1992 on the government-sponsored enterprises

(GSEs) Fannie Mae and Freddie Mac; (2) its control over the policies of the Federal Housing Administration (FHA); and (3) a 'Best Practices Initiative' for subprime lenders and mortgage banks such as Countrywide, to encourage greater subprime and other high-risk lending.

Ultimately, all these entities, as well as insured banks covered by the Community Reinvestment Act (CRA), were compelled to compete for mortgage borrowers who were at or below the median income in the areas where they lived. This competition caused underwriting standards to decline, increased the numbers of high-risk loans far beyond what the market would have produced without government influence, and contributed importantly to the growth of the 1997–2007 housing bubble.

When the bubble began to deflate in mid-2007, the millions of low-quality loans produced by this competition began to default in unprecedented numbers. The effect of these defaults was exacerbated by the fact that few if any investors – including housing-market analysts – understood at the time that Fannie Mae and Freddie Mac had been acquiring large numbers of subprime and other high-risk loans to meet HUD's affordable-housing goals. Thus, when so many mortgages began to default in 2007, investors were shocked and fled the multitrillion-dollar market for private mortgage-backed securities (MBSs), dropping MBS values – and especially those MBSs backed by subprime and other risky loans – to fractions of their former prices. Mark-to-market accounting then required financial institutions to write down the value of their assets, reducing their capital and liquidity positions and causing great investor and creditor alarm.

In this environment, the government's rescue of Bear Stearns in March 2008 temporarily calmed investor fears but created significant moral hazard; investors and other market participants reasonably believed after the rescue of Bear that all large financial institutions would be rescued if they encountered financial difficulties. However, when Lehman Brothers – an investment bank even larger than Bear – was allowed to fail, market participants were shocked; suddenly, they were forced to consider the financial health of their counterparties, many of which appeared weakened by losses and the capital write-downs required by mark-to-market accounting. This caused a halt to lending and a hoarding of cash – a virtually unprecedented period of market paralysis and panic that characterized the financial crisis.[6]

12.2   FINDING THE CAUSE

Many commentators, as well as the Commission majority and the three Republican members of the Commission (Bill Thomas, Keith Hennessey and Douglas Holtz-Eakin, whom I shall call the THH dissenters), have expressed disagreement with my view of the causes of the financial crisis; they argue that the crisis was more complex and cannot be explained by any single cause. However, everyone agrees that the financial crisis had a single cause: the mortgage meltdown in late 2007 and the resulting delinquency and default of an unprecedented number of US mortgages. As the Commission majority said:

> While the vulnerabilities that created the potential for crisis were years in the making, it was the collapse of the housing bubble – fueled by low interest rates, easy and available credit, scant

regulation, and toxic mortgages – that was the spark that ignited a string of events, which led to a full-blown crisis in the fall of 2008.

Indeed, most of the Commission majority's report was taken up with anecdotes about how financial institution managers and regulators failed to recognize the growth of the housing bubble and prevent the build-up of non-traditional mortgages (NTMs) in the US financial system.

Since a mortgage meltdown was the acknowledged trigger of the financial crisis, a commission charged with determining what caused the financial crisis should want to find out why there was such a massive accumulation of NTMs – the 'toxic mortgages' described above – that defaulted when the bubble deflated. Why, for example, did the underwriting standards that had prevailed for many years in the US mortgage market suddenly begin to deteriorate in the early 1990s? If the financial crisis was in fact caused by the default of these mortgages, why these NTMs were created was clearly the key question for the Commission's inquiry. Unfortunately, neither the Commission majority nor the THH dissenters made any significant effort to address this central issue.

For example, the majority's report says only that the 'toxic mortgages' were 'fueled by low interest rates and easy and available credit'. Exactly how low interest rates and easy and available credit caused a decline in underwriting standards is never explained. Similarly, the THH dissenters say that: 'tightening credit spreads, overly optimistic assumptions about US housing prices, and flaws in primary and secondary mortgage markets led to poor origination practices'. How tightening credit spreads and the other factors led to 'poor origination practices' is never addressed. In effect, both the majority report and the THH dissenters treat the existence of 27 million weak loans as a 'given' – a starting point for which no explanation is required.

This is not a minor flaw in their arguments. It is a serious failure to address the one aspect of the financial crisis that distinguishes it from all previous financial disruptions and crises. Before the 2008 crisis, the United States had frequently experienced extended periods of low interest rates, large flows of funds from abroad and excessive optimism about the future of housing prices. We also had the same general regulatory and financial structure and a private financial system in which managements were expected to anticipate and act on risks to their firms. None of these conditions or factors, separately or together, had ever before resulted in a mortgage-based financial crisis. The one element in the 2008 financial crisis that was completely unprecedented was the presence of 27 million NTMs: never in the past were half of all mortgages in the United States in danger of delinquency and default when a housing bubble deflated. Treating this factor as a given is a classic case of ignoring the elephant in the room, and it prevented the Commission majority and the THH dissenters from gaining a clear understanding of the mechanism through which the 2008 crisis came about.

My dissent addresses this error. It attempts to explain why there were so many NTMs in the US financial system in 2008, how the massive number of these loans caused the extraordinary size and longevity of the 1997–2007 bubble, and how the collapse of the bubble and the private MBS market caused the weakness of financial institutions around the world.

12.3   THE DETERIORATION OF UNDERWRITING STANDARDS

It seems obvious that such a large number of NTMs could not have accumulated in the US financial system unless there had been a serious decline in mortgage underwriting standards. Why that decline occurred is a major piece of the crisis puzzle. For 50 years following World War II, US residential mortgages were solid assets, bought and held as investments by banks and other financial institutions in the United States and around the world. During this period, there were two major US housing bubbles – in 1979 and 1989 – but when they deflated they resulted only in local losses. If housing prices ever fell nationally – and this is a debated question – it was never more than by a small percentage. It again seems obvious that the reason for this stability was the existence of strong underwriting standards, requiring downpayments and good credit records for those who wanted to buy homes.

Why were previous (traditional) underwriting standards abandoned? As I discuss in my dissent, the deterioration of mortgage underwriting standards began in 1992, when Congress adopted the GSE (government-sponsored enterprise) Act and imposed what were called 'affordable housing (AH) goals' on Fannie Mae and Freddie Mac. Under these requirements, a certain percentage of mortgages purchased by Fannie and Freddie had to be loans to low- and moderate-income (LMI) borrowers – home buyers whose income was at or below the median income in the areas where they lived. This was the initial step in a US government social policy that eventually had the desired effect: it made substantial amounts of mortgage credit available to LMI borrowers for the first time, and it succeeded in increasing the homeownership rate in the United States from 64 percent (where it had been for 30 years) to more than 69 percent in 2004. However, this policy also created a ten-year housing bubble of unprecedented size, and the growth of the bubble – by suppressing delinquencies and defaults as housing prices climbed – fostered a large market for securitized NTMs held by financial institutions in the United States and around the world. When the bubble collapsed, these NTMs became the toxic assets that endangered the stability and solvency of many financial institutions and caused others to become insolvent or illiquid.

Initially, Congress set the AH goals at 30 percent: 30 percent of the loans the GSEs bought from originators had to be loans to LMI home buyers. In the succeeding 15 years, HUD tightened and extended these requirements so that by 2007, 55 percent of all loans had to qualify as affordable-housing loans to LMI borrowers. HUD also added various subgoals that required loans to borrowers at or below 80 percent and 60 percent of area median income, and these subgoals were enlarged even more substantially than the main LMI goal. Generally speaking, once the AH goals exceeded 50 percent, the GSEs had to find one goals-eligible mortgage for every prime mortgage they bought. Since not all NTMs were goals-eligible, the GSEs had to buy more NTMs than the goal requirement in order to be sure in any year that they exceeded the goal. As discussed in my dissent, this requirement forced Fannie and Freddie into adopting various schemes to manipulate their reported numbers by paying originators to defer delivering prime loans or temporarily 'renting' subprime loans from others in order to meet the goals for a particular year.

With HUD's increasingly aggressive affordable-housing requirements, and several entities competing for the same borrowers, it was simply not possible to find enough prime borrowers among the targeted LMI group to meet the government's demands without reducing mortgage underwriting standards. It is that simple. In my view, this is the only plausible explanation for why mortgage underwriting standards declined so significantly between 1992 and 2007.

To illustrate what happened to mortgage underwriting standards during this 15-year period, consider downpayment requirements. By 2000, Fannie Mae was offering to buy loans with zero downpayments. As described below, originators found that they could make loans to people with little or no downpayment resources and still sell those loans to Fannie or Freddie. Between 1997 and 2007, Fannie and Freddie bought over $1 trillion in mortgages with downpayments of 5 percent or less. In 1990, only one in 200 purchase money mortgages (that is, not refinances) had a downpayment requirement of less than 3 percent, but by 2007 almost 40 percent of all purchase money mortgages had downpayments of that size. The credit quality of borrowers also declined. Between 1997 and 2007, Fannie and Freddie bought $1.5 trillion in subprime loans and over $600 billion in loans with other deficiencies that would have made them unsalable in 1990.[7] Officials of Fannie and Freddie attended meetings of mortgage originators to ask for more subprime loans.[8]

12.4 HUD'S ROLE

Although there might be some question about whether HUD intended this result, and thus whether the decline in underwriting standards was a deliberate policy of the US government, HUD made no effort to hide its purposes. In statements over several years, the department made clear its intent to reduce mortgage underwriting standards. I have included three of these statements below, the first made in 2000 when HUD was increasing the affordable-housing goals for Fannie and Freddie:

> Lower-income and minority families have made major gains in access to the mortgage market in the 1990s. A variety of reasons have accounted for these gains, including improved housing affordability, enhanced enforcement of the Community Reinvestment Act, more flexible mortgage underwriting, and stepped-up enforcement of the Fair Housing Act. But most industry observers believe that one factor behind these gains has been the improved performance of Fannie Mae and Freddie Mac under HUD's affordable lending goals. HUD's recent increases in the goals for 2001–03 will encourage the GSEs to further step up their support for affordable lending.[9]

Similarly, in 2004, when HUD was again increasing the affordable-housing goals for Fannie and Freddie, the department stated:

> Millions of Americans with less than perfect credit or who cannot meet some of the tougher underwriting requirements of the prime market for reasons such as inadequate income documentation, limited downpayment or cash reserves, or the desire to take more cash out in a refinancing than conventional loans allow, rely on subprime lenders for access to mortgage financing. If the GSEs reach deeper into the subprime market, more borrowers will benefit from the advantages that greater stability and standardization create.[10]

Finally, the following statement appeared in a 2005 report commissioned by HUD:

> More liberal mortgage financing has contributed to the increase in demand for housing. During the 1990s, lenders have been encouraged by HUD and banking regulators to increase lending to low-income and minority households. The Community Reinvestment Act (CRA), Home Mortgage Disclosure Act (HMDA), government-sponsored enterprises (GSE) housing goals and fair lending laws have strongly encouraged mortgage brokers and lenders to market to low-income and minority borrowers. Sometimes these borrowers are higher risk, with blemished credit histories and high debt or simply little savings for a down payment. Lenders have responded with low down payment loan products and automated underwriting, which has allowed them to more carefully determine the risk of the loan.[11]

These statements are strong evidence that the decline in mortgage underwriting standards between 1992 and 2007 did not just happen; nor was it the result of low interest rates, flows of funds from abroad or any of the other events or conditions suggested by the Commission majority and the THH dissenters. HUD intended the direct effect of its policies, which placed Fannie and Freddie into competition with other government agencies and other financial institutions that were effectively under the government's control – all of which were seeking loans to the same LMI borrowers. Because there were only a limited number of prime borrowers among the low-income groups targeted by government social policies, all these competing entities had to lower their underwriting standards to find the borrowers they needed to meet their government-imposed quotas. That, in summary, is the discussion in my dissent on why there were so many subprime and other high-risk mortgages in the US financial system when the housing bubble deflated in 2007. In contrast, neither the majority report nor the THH dissenters had a plausible explanation for the decline in underwriting standards. In both cases, this decline was treated as something that happened as a result of low interest rates or greater capital availability, without any explanation of why these factors would have that effect. With that view, they could only – at best – tell half the story of the financial crisis.

12.5   THE MAJORITY REPORT

Because of its refusal to consider the reasons for the decline in underwriting standards, the Commission majority was forced to argue that the low quality of so many loans in the US financial system resulted from a failure to regulate loan originators, especially mortgage brokers. As is true throughout the majority report, the discussion in this area is critical of certain practices in the market but educes no data on how widespread these practices were or how significant they might have been in contributing to the financial crisis.

In any event, what the majority report failed to recognize or communicate is that brokers do not finance mortgages. Before they make a mortgage, they must have a buyer to provide the financing. The reason that brokers were so active during the housing boom is that they could always find a buyer for the mortgages they were originating – and most of the time that buyer was Fannie, Freddie, FHA, a subprime lender involved in a HUD program, or a bank that needed certain kinds of mortgages to comply with the CRA. If those government mandates had not existed – if the GSEs and others had not been required by law to buy affordable-housing loans – many fewer subprime and other risky mortgages would have been originated. Subprime lending would have remained what it was before 1992, a niche business. Instead, the Commission majority argued that the brokers were the source of the problem – as though regulating their activities was the solution to excessive subprime lending rather than ending the government mandates that made it possible for brokers, whether unscrupulous or honest, to find buyers for the subprime or other risky mortgages they originated.

The Commission majority ended this portion of its report by concluding that: 'there was untrammeled growth in risky mortgages. Unsustainable, toxic loans polluted the financial system and fueled the housing bubble'.[12] This statement is correct if one considers the 27 million subprime and other risky loans that existed in the US financial system before the financial crisis. However, the Commission majority failed to produce data that connect the abusive practices the report condemns, such as yield-spread premiums, to any given number of subprime or otherwise risky loans. Without these data, it is impossible for anyone to conclude that abusive lending practices or predatory lending had any significant effect on the financial crisis. This is true throughout the Commission majority's report. Because the majority refused to do a thorough analysis of why and how so many subprime and other risky loans were originated, they were left to claim that 'toxic loans polluted the financial system and fueled the housing bubble' without any supporting evidence.

There is some irony here. Although no statistics for the prevalence of predatory lending were ever produced, the Commission majority identified it as a cause of the housing bubble and, presumably, the financial crisis; yet, even though the Commission had data showing that Fannie and Freddie had made 12 million subprime and other risky loans – enough to drive them into insolvency – it concluded that the role of these two GSEs in the crisis was only 'marginal'. The political bias in this conclusion is clear.

12.6   THE COMMISSION MAJORITY'S TREATMENT OF FANNIE AND FREDDIE

In the preface to its report, the Commission majority stated:

> The GSEs participated in the expansion of subprime and other risky mortgages, but they followed rather than led Wall Street and other lenders in the rush for fool's gold. They purchased the highest rated non-GSE mortgage-backed securities and their participation in this market added helium to the housing balloon, but their purchases never represented a majority of the market.

This is a myth, but has become a widely believed fallacy. Even the administration's recent housing proposal states:

> Initially, Fannie Mae and Freddie Mac were largely on the sidelines while private markets generated increasingly risky mortgages . . . But as their combined market share declined – from nearly 70 percent of new originations in 2003 to 40 percent in 2006 – Fannie Mae and Freddie Mac pursued riskier business to raise their market share and increase profits.

These statements neatly encapsulate both the Commission majority's errors and the remarkable persistence of the false narrative about the financial crisis that both the Commission and the Obama administration have embraced. The facts demonstrate that Fannie and Freddie acquired the NTMs that eventually caused their insolvency and the financial crisis for only one reason – because of the AH goals – and not because they were seeking profits or attempting to recover market share.

The Commission majority's report focused almost entirely on the market for private mortgage-backed securities, which they called private label securities (PLS). This market included about 7.8 million securitized NTMs in 2008, less than one-third of the 27 million low-quality loans that were outstanding in 2008. The balance, about 19.2 million loans were held or guaranteed by Fannie and Freddie, FHA and other government holders, insured banks and savings and loans (S&Ls) covered by CRA, and Countrywide and other lenders that had pledged to reduce underwriting standards under a HUD program called the 'Best Practices Initiative'. The Commission majority also focused only on a short period in between 2004 and 2007, and virtually ignored everything that had happened in the mortgage market before that time. Both were serious errors. The 7.8 million NTMs that underlay the PLS were certainly contributors to the crisis, but their contribution was far less than the GSEs and other government-mandated buyers of these loans and, even more important, the whole PLS market would not have existed if the government-mandated buyers had not created an unprecedented housing bubble that grew for ten years between 1997 and 2007.

Most housing bubbles last only three or four years. This was true of the housing bubbles the USA experienced in 1979 and 1989. Both lasted about that long, and when they deflated caused only local housing losses, not the 30 percent national housing price decline the US has experienced. The reason that housing bubbles eventually deflate is that delinquencies start to show up, investors leave, the bubble flattens, and everyone else either gets out or licks their wounds. The 1997–2007 housing bubble lasted ten years because there was one investor in the market – the US government – that was following a social policy and was not worried about losses. Long after private investors would have left the market, HUD was still raising the affordable housing goals for the GSEs, and the GSEs were still meeting them by competing for NTMs with the FHA and the other institutions that were also subject to government mandates.

Housing prices continued to rise as a result of these government-backed investments, and when these prices rise they suppress delinquencies and defaults. This is because homeowners who cannot meet their mortgage obligations can usually refinance their mortgages (having acquired some equity in the home because of rising prices) or sell the home and pay off the mortgage. In addition, because of their inherent riskiness, most of the loans that were supported by rising prices carried high interest rates. Accordingly, investors were seeing pools of high-interest-rate loans that were not showing the delinquencies and defaults that would have been commensurate with the expected risks. This is what stimulated the growth of the PLS market beginning in the early 2000s. Nevertheless, this market did not pass $100 billion until 2002, about 4 percent of the entire housing market that year. At that point, the bubble was already five years old, longer than any bubble in the past century. But as the government continued to pump funds into affordable housing, the bubble continued to grow – and with it the attractiveness of PLS based on NTMs. By 2004, the PLS market had reached 15 percent of the entire housing market, and it continued to grow rapidly thereafter as investors in the US and abroad became avid buyers of assets that seemed to offer very high risk-adjusted returns.

Because the Commission majority did not consider any NTM purchases prior to 2003, they had no perspective on what Fannie and Freddie were doing before 2003, and could not see the contribution of government-mandated purchases to the growth of the bubble. In their report, the PLS market just appeared out of nowhere, for no particular reason, in 2003 or 2004. This led the Commission majority to accept and propagate the false idea that Fannie and Freddie followed Wall Street into subprime lending.

In fact, it was the other way around. Because of the affordable housing requirements, Fannie and Freddie had been buying subprime and other NTMs since the early 1990s. Indeed, the GSEs began to acquire high loan-to-value (LTV) mortgages (a kind of NTM) in 1994, shortly after the imposition of the AH goals, and by 2001 – before the private mortgage-backed securities (PMBS) market reached $100 billion in annual issuances – the GSEs had already acquired at least $700 billion in NTMs, including over $400 billion in subprime loans.[13] In 2002 alone, when the entire PLS market finally exceeded $100 billion for the first time (reaching $134 billion), the GSEs bought $206 billion in subprime loans and $66 billion in other NTMs.

In other words, it would be more accurate to say that Wall Street followed the GSEs into subprime lending. This was true in two ways: the GSEs were heavy buyers of subprime loans and other NTMs before there was any Wall Street securitization of NTMs; and the GSEs' purchases built the 1997–2007 housing bubble, which provided the necessary conditions (high yields and low delinquencies) which made the PLS market possible. The GSEs were also the largest buyers of the PLS backed by NTMs. As the majority report itself points out, their purchases reached 40 percent in 2004.[14]

In its effort to obscure the government's role in the financial crisis, the Commission majority does not even mention the statements by HUD quoted above – statements that show the department's unequivocal commitment to reducing underwriting standards – and it makes transparent efforts throughout its report to suggest that Fannie and Freddie were no more than marginal players in the accumulation of NTMs in the financial system.

There is a long and tedious effort in the majority's report to demonstrate that Fannie and Freddie got into trouble because they bought NTMs in order to make profits or to recover the market share they had lost to the PLS market in 2005 and 2006. This is what the majority described as: 'Fannie Mae's quest for bigger market share, profits, and bonuses, which led it to ramp up its exposure to risky loans and securities as the housing market was peaking'. Although various GSE officials are quoted to the effect that the AH goals were not the reason for these purchases, the documents say otherwise.

My dissent, based on these documents, shows unequivocally that market share was not a factor. Among other things: (1) the GSEs' market share did not increase in 2005 or 2006; (2) they did not lower their guarantee fees (G-fees), which would have made them more competitive and increased market share; (3) their regulator at that time (OFHEO, Office of Federal Housing Enterprise Oversight) did not want them to increase their risks and would not have allowed them to do it; and (4) their market share finally did increase in 2007, when the number of delinquent and defaulting mortgages had brought the PLS market to a halt, leaving Fannie and Freddie with a clear field to buy as many NTMs as they wanted. The fact that they then went ahead and purchased more NTMs – while everyone else had left the market because of the delinquencies of those very mortgages – shows again that their motive was the pressure to meet the AH goals, and not profit or market share.

Moreover, the idea that they bought mortgages for profit that only a few years later made them deeply insolvent is absurd on the face of it. Anyone who was observing the market at that time would have seen that delinquencies among NTMs were increasing rapidly. Other issuers – certainly as interested in profits as the GSEs – were abandoning the market entirely and trying desperately to hedge their NTM risks.

Finally, here is a statement from Fannie's 2006 10-K annual return, which makes clear that it was the affordable housing goals – and nothing else – that were the cause of their financial collapse:

> [W]e have made, and continue to make, significant adjustments to our mortgage loan sourcing and purchase strategies in an effort to meet HUD's increased housing goals and new subgoals. These strategies include entering into some purchase and securitization transactions with lower expected economic returns than our typical transactions. We have also relaxed some of our underwriting criteria to obtain goals-qualifying mortgage loans and increased our investments in higher-risk mortgage loan products that are more likely to serve the borrowers targeted by HUD's goals and subgoals, which could increase our credit losses.[15]

12.7   CONCLUSION

There is powerful evidence that the financial crisis was caused by government housing policies and not by a lack of regulation or the simultaneous failures of risk management among the world's largest financial institutions. Under these circumstances, as I state in my dissent, there is reason to doubt that the Dodd–Frank Act was necessary to prevent another financial crisis. It is more likely that a change in government housing policy would provide greater protection against another financial crisis than the Dodd–Frank Act, with none of the adverse effects that the Act is likely to have on economic growth in the United States.

NOTES

1. Financial Crisis Inquiry Commission (2011), *Final Report of the National Commission on the Causes of the Financial and Economic Crisis in the United States*, Washington, DC, January, http://c0182732.cdn1. cloudfiles.rackspacecloud.com/fcic_final_report_full.pdf, accessed 4 February 2011.
2. Wallison, Peter J. (2011), *Dissent from the Majority Report of the Financial Crisis Inquiry Commission*, Washington, DC: AEI, 26 January, www.aei.org/paper/100190.
3. Wallison, Peter J. (2011), *Financial Crisis Inquiry Commission Dissenting Statement*, Washington, DC, January, http://c0182732.cdn1.cloudfiles.rackspacecloud.com/fcic_final_report_wallison_dissent.pdf, accessed 4 February 2011.
4. See http://bookstore.gpo.gov.
5. Hennessey, Keith, Douglas Holtz-Eakin and Bill Thomas (2011), *Dissenting Statement of Commissioner Keith Hennessey, Commissioner Douglas Holtz-Eakin, and Vice Chairman Bill Thomas*, Washington, DC, January, http://c0182732.cdn1.cloudfiles.rackspacecloud.com/fcic_final_report_hennessey_holtz-eakin_ thomas_dissent.pdf, accessed 4 February, 2011.
6. Peter J. Wallison, *Dissent from the Majority Report of the Financial Crisis Inquiry Commission*.

7. Peter J. Wallison, *Dissent from the Majority Report of the Financial Crisis Inquiry Commission*, p. 65.
8. Ibid., p. 60.
9. US Department of Housing and Urban Development (2011), *HUD's Affordable Housing Goals for Fannie Mae and Freddie Mac*, Issue Brief No. V, Washington, DC, 5 January, www.huduser.org/Publications/PDF/gse.pdf, accessed 4 February 2011.
10. US Department of Housing and Urban Development (2004), *HUD's Housing Goals for the Federal National Mortgage Association (Fannie Mae) and the Federal Home Loan Mortgage Corporation (Freddie Mac) for the Years 2005–2008 and Amendments to HUD's Regulation of Fannie Mae and Freddie Mac*, Document 04-24101, Washington, DC, 2 November, http://www.govpulse.us/entries/2004/11/02/04-24101/hud-s-housing-goals-for-the-federal-national-mortgage-association-fannie-mae-and-the-federal-home-lo, accessed 8 February 2011.
11. US Department of Housing and Urban Development, Office of Policy Development and Research (2005), *Recent House Price Trends and Homeownership Affordability*, Washington, DC, May, 85, www.huduser.org/Publications/pdf/RecentHousePrice.pdf, accessed 4 February 2011.
12. Ibid., 101.
13. Wallison, *Dissent*, Table 7, p. 65.
14. FCIC, *Majority Report*, p. 123.
15. Fannie Mae 2006 10-K, p. 146.

13 Market discipline for financial institutions and markets for information

Apanard P. Prabha, Clas Wihlborg and Thomas D. Willett

13.1 INTRODUCTION

Under ideal conditions competitive markets should induce firms to adopt good governance procedures that lead to the maximization of shareholder value. Firms that do not approximate such behavior will face penalties in the form of lower profitability and higher costs of financing. Ultimately the wayward firms will be forced out of business or at least shrink or be taken over. Ideally market discipline would begin to come into play as soon as a firm begins to go astray, and markets would provide early warning signals and incentives in sufficient time for management to take corrective actions well before bankruptcy or financial market disruptions occur.

The recent global financial crisis has again shown that once concern arises in the markets they place enormous pressure on public as well as private sector entities. As we will document in sections 13.4 and 13.5, however, financial markets generally failed in the run-up to the crisis in terms of giving strong warning signals in a timely enough fashion for disaster to be avoided.

A major purpose of this chapter is to analyze why such early warning signals were not forthcoming and consider what, if anything, can be done to help induce financial markets to provide early warning signals that provide corrective discipline in advance of the generation of crisis conditions. We also consider theoretical arguments and empirical evidence on whether some types of financial instruments have tended to be better than others at providing early warning signals.

Forward-looking market signals are one aspect of market discipline provided by financial markets. Another aspect is incentives for risk-taking. Prices on financial instruments are based on forward-looking information and trading in financial markets is based on differences in perceptions and uncertainty about the future. Much of the theory of financial institutions views them as information intermediaries and risk managers.[1]

When economists observe a failure of market discipline in the sense of excessive risk-taking, a first impulse is usually to look for sources of government-induced moral hazard that has blunted the normal operation of market incentives. Undoubtedly this often plays an important role, but we argue that in the recent crisis it is far from the only factor at work.

Many economists have stressed that for market discipline to work there must be a group of monitors who have both access to sufficient reliable information and the incentives to gather and act on it. Moral hazard of course blunts these incentives, but even in its absence there are important conditions in many financial markets that also impede the generation of early market discipline. One difficulty is the merger mania that led to large financial conglomerates which in the view of many experts became not only 'too big to fail' (TBTF), but also too big and complex to manage.

Numerous recent books and articles on the crisis suggest that many high-level managers of large financial institutions had little idea of the risks that their institutions were taking on despite their access to internal information. In some cases this may have been due to some of the types of behavioral biases pointed to by studies in the rapidly growing field of behavioral economics and finance. For example, a manager may not want to look too hard at the processes which are generating high short-run profits. Creditors should not be subject to this wishful thinking inducing them not to do due diligence, but as outsiders it may be very difficult if not impossible for them to obtain the information necessary to make sound judgments about the overall risk levels of a large conglomerate financial firm.

In order to arrive at principles for government involvement in the regulation of financial markets and institutions, we review literature and evidence on market discipline before interpreting market discipline in terms of informativeness of financial market activity. This view is based on the assumption that 'available information' is endogenous relative to the regulatory framework and the structure of financial markets. The reason is that information is costly to acquire and absorb, as well as costly to disclose and signal from a financial institutions point of view. Thus, we reinterpret financial markets as markets providing incentives for acquiring and revealing information. With costly information there is no unambiguous concept of efficient markets, but we develop four 'informativeness principles' for regulators, supervisors and government action.

In section 13.2 we discuss and review the conceptual literature on market discipline with respect to risk-taking in financial institutions (FIs). The empirical literature is reviewed in section 13.3. Market discipline with respect to timeliness of information is discussed in section 13.4 where empirical evidence prior to the crisis and within the crisis is reviewed. We also discuss how different debt-based and equity-based financial instruments provide more or less timely information. In section 13.5 we discuss the behavior of credit default swap (CDS) spreads and equity prices around events associated with the insolvency of some financial institutions during the financial crisis of 2007–2009. An alternative view of financial markets as providing incentives to acquire and produce costly information is developed in section 13.6. This leads up to four 'informativeness principles' for public sector intervention presented in section 13.7. Concluding comments follow in section 13.8.

13.2 MARKET DISCIPLINE ON RISK-TAKING IN FINANCIAL INSTITUTIONS

There is a substantial literature on market discipline with respect to risk-taking in banking and FIs more generally. Two aspects are emphasized.[2] First, market discipline requires that the cost of funding reflects an FI's risk-taking in the sense of probability of default. Second, an FI's management must respond properly to the information provided by the costs of different sources of funding. In well-functioning markets the management of an FI would choose asset and liability positions that maximize shareholder value.

The first aspect of market discipline refers to pricing of default risk. It is well known that the limited liability of shareholders of corporations provides incentives for the latter to shift risk to creditors, and these incentives become stronger when equity capital is low. For this reason creditors of corporations in general have incentives to monitor default risk and 'loss given default' (LGD) and demand compensation for this risk. The credit risk premium can be viewed as the premium on a put option on the corporation's assets purchased by the shareholders with a strike price equal to value of the debt. If the credit risk premium on a corporation's debt is too low, shareholders have an incentive to take on too much relatively low-cost debt and increase default risk at the expense of debt holders.

The second aspect of market discipline refers to governance issues. For market discipline to be effective, the corporate governance structure must provide incentives for management to maximize shareholder value. These two aspects of market discipline are both part of what is often called direct market discipline in the banking literature. Indirect market discipline refers to the use of price signals with respect to risk being used by supervisors as indicators that may trigger intervention.[3]

Direct market discipline may fail in the financial industry for several reasons, providing arguments for regulation of risk-taking and supervision. Creditors may not be able to obtain information to assess an FI's riskiness. The opaqueness of banks in particular is often referred to as an argument for supervision of banks, based on the presumption that supervisors are better able to gather the information required to assess risk. The second common argument for market discipline failure is that an FI's creditors are explicitly or implicitly protected from losses in case of default. In particular, explicit insurance of banks' depositors reduces their incentives to monitor banks and to demand a risk premium on deposits. Implicit insurance exists if an FI's creditors expect to be bailed out in case of insolvency because the FI is considered 'too big to fail' or a government blanket guarantee is expected in case FIs face distress. Explicit and implicit insurance of creditors induces FIs to take on too much debt and to shift default risk to deposit insurance funds and/or taxpayers.

The recent financial crisis has also highlighted poor corporate governance as a source of market discipline failure. In particular, compensation schemes for executives as well as traders and risk managers have been blamed for excessive risk-taking. Several chapters in this volume address this issue.

The mentioned sources of market failure with respect to an FI's risk-taking may explain excessive risk-taking on the level of a particular FI. They provide the rationale for micro-prudential regulation.

An additional social concern with risk-taking is that the default of one FI has systemic consequences, meaning that one FI's failure or actions in response to distress increases the probability of other FIs' failure through contagion. Potential systemic consequences of an FI's failure provide the rationale for macro-prudential regulation and supervision. The systemic aspect of market discipline failure implies that potential system-wide losses of one FI's distress are not reflected in the risk premium for the individual FI. Contagion effects of one or more FI's distress are often viewed as externalities. Even if the credit risk of the individual FI is priced efficiently, externalities caused by an FI distress may exist.

The literature on different channels of contagion has expanded rapidly since the outbreak of the financial crisis in 2008. Prior to the crisis, contagion through runs on opaque banks and through interbank claims was considered the main source of systemic risk,[4] but other channels of contagion have been emphasized in recent literature.[5] This literature emphasizes that in the modern financial system where FIs rely on securities markets for funding, contagion arises as a result of price and liquidity effects of one bank's distress. The implementation of mark-to-market and fair value accounting has amplified the strength of contagion through the price and liquidity channels.

The policy concern with systemic financial crisis is amplified by the possibility that events in the financial sector cause substantial (real) effects on growth, employment and productivity. Although financial crises often originate outside the financial sector in, for example, a decline in economic activity or sharply falling asset prices, contagion through the financial system amplifies the real effects when FIs reduce the supply of credit and liquidity dries up.

13.3 EMPIRICAL EVIDENCE ON MARKET DISCIPLINE ON RISK-TAKING

There is a large literature asking whether there is market discipline in the sense that the cost of funding of banks and other financial institutions reflects their riskiness. Since a large part of banks' liabilities are insured by deposit insurance systems, the empirical literature focuses on yields of non-insured bank debt and equity returns. If yields do not respond to changes in the risk of an FI, market discipline is lacking either because market participants are unable to become informed about the risk of individual FIs or because there is implicit protection of debt.

Flannery (1998) reviews the early literature on private investors' ability to assess risk in banking. He concludes that bank share prices generally behave similarly to equity prices of non-financial firms and that bank liability investors also respond to changes in conditions of banks. The evidence refers to yields on certificates of deposit (CDs) as well as bank debentures. Even retail depositors seem to respond to insolvency problems of banks. Flannery and Sorescu (1996) come to similar conclusions with respect to subordinated debentures.

Flannery (1998) concludes that: 'there is little evidence that broadly contagious runs would be a problem for banks even in the absence of the federal safety net protection for depositors'. This conclusion refers only to the traditional source of contagion in banking and has no bearing on contagion through short-term borrowing in the securities markets.

A more recent literature focuses on subordinated debt as an instrument for imposing direct as well as indirect market discipline. Calomiris (1999), Evanoff and Wall (2000, 2001), Federal Reserve Board (1999), Jagtiani et al. (2002) and Levonian (2000) are examples of subordinated debt studies from a US perspective. Sironi (2003) uses evidence from subordinated debt issues by European banks. The general conclusion for the USA as well as for Europe is that investors in this kind of debt are sensitive to bank risk in the sense that they require a higher yield for banks that are perceived as relatively risky.

The mentioned empirical results must be interpreted with care. They do not imply that default risk of banks is efficiently priced, only that there is some effect on price. Furthermore, the measures of bank risk are based on different kinds of proxies obtained from publicly available accounting data such as capital ratios and asset types. Thus, one implicit, imperfect proxy for risk is regressed on other imperfect proxies for risk for opaque, relatively large banks. The results show that these proxies are correlated, however.

Evanoff et al. (2007) show that the sensitivity of subordinated yield spreads depends on the development of markets for the instruments. In a fully implemented mandatory subordinated debt program, liquidity of the markets would increase and, thereby, the sensitivity of yield spreads to risk.

There is evidence that the sensitivity of debt yields depends on the degree of implicit protection of banks' creditors. The results in Sironi (2003) indicate that subordinated debt yields of large 'too big to fail banks' are less sensitive to risk proxies than the yields of other banks. Perhaps surprisingly in light of bailout experiences in the recent financial crisis, Sironi finds that the perception of implicit 'too big to fail' guarantees weakened during the 1990s in Europe.

Other studies indicate that the value of the implicit subsidy provided to 'too big to fail' financial institutions is substantial. Hart and Zingales (2009) refer to a newspaper article[6] stating that the differential interest rate on interbank loans between large and small banks dropped from negative 8 points to negative 34 points after September 2008. Gandh and Lustig (2010) find that a long position in the stock portfolio of the largest US banks and a short position in the stock portfolio of the smallest banks underperforms an equally (beta) risky portfolio of non-financial firms by 8 percent. This difference reflects the extension of government implicit guarantees to large US banks.

Another type of evidence indicating that market discipline is relatively weak for 'too big to fail' banks comes from literature analyzing how risk-taking depends on explicit and implicit insurance of banks' creditors. This literature uses proxies for riskiness such as non-performing loans/capital, the volatility of equity returns, so-called z-scores and the incidence of banking crisis. These proxies are regressed on bank-specific variables, country-specific macro variables and country-specific institutional variables such as explicit deposit insurance coverage, proxies for implicit protection of creditors and governance variables for the country as well as the bank level.

Several empirical studies show that effects of explicit deposit insurance on banks' risk-taking depend on ownership, governance factors and other institutional characteristics of a country. Demirgüç-Kunt and Detragiache (2002), Barth et al. (2004) and Cull et al. (2005) find that high quality of domestic institutions and legal systems reduces the moral hazard effect of deposit insurance. Hovakimian et al. (2003) emphasize that effects of explicit deposit insurance depend on its design and credibility. Fernández and González (2005) find that the adverse effect on risk-taking can be reduced by enhancing the effectiveness of accounting and auditing systems. González (2005) suggests that the finding in some papers that deposit insurance reduces risk-taking can be explained by the positive impact of deposit insurance on banks' charter values in a strictly regulated environment.

Other studies including Angkinand and Wihlborg (2010), Gropp and Vesala (2004) and Nier and Baumann (2006) emphasize the role of implicit insurance as a contributing factor to failing market discipline on risk-taking of banks. Based on a sample of European banks, Gropp and Vesala (2004) find that explicit deposit insurance is associated with lower moral hazard and reduced risk-taking if banks have large uninsured liabilities and small assets relative to the total assets of a banking system. Angkinand and Wihlborg (2010) hypothesize and estimate a U-shaped relationship between explicit deposit insurance coverage and banks' risk-taking using country-level data. The U-shaped relationship implies that banks' incentives to shift risk to a deposit insurance fund is minimized by a deposit insurance system offering a partial deposit insurance coverage because market discipline is likely to be weak at low as well as high levels of deposit insurance coverage. The weak discipline at low levels is caused by a high likelihood that governments find themselves compelled to issue blanket guarantees to creditors of distressed banks, or to bail them out. The weak discipline at high levels is due to moral hazard generated by high deposit insurance coverage.

Nier and Baumann (2006) study the market discipline effect for individual banks. Risk-taking is measured by the share of non-performing loans in total assets, by provisions for non-performing loans and by the volatility of the bank's equity market return. Market discipline has several dimensions including the extent of explicit deposit protection on the country level, the amount of uninsured funding of a bank, and Fitch ratings of the expected extent of government support of a bank to capture implicit insurance. Their results indicate that lack of explicit deposit insurance and high amounts of uninsured deposits are likely to reduce risk-taking by increasing desired capital, while the likelihood of government support reduces market discipline both directly and through the effect on desired capital.

Risk-taking incentives of bank managers can be expected to depend on the objectives and, therefore, on the governance structures of banks. In the literature, it is usually assumed that managers in a 'high-quality' governance structure maximize shareholders' wealth while the incentives to serve the interests of other stakeholders are provided by market forces, law and regulation.

There is a limited number of studies on the impact of bank governance on risk-taking. Early studies were limited to US data. For instance, Saunders et al. (1990), using a sample of 38 bank holding companies in the US during 1978–1985, find a positive relation between managerial ownership and risk-taking. On the other hand, Chen et al. (1998) find a negative relation between managerial ownership and the level of risk, taking in a larger sample of 302 banks and savings institutions during the period 1988–1993. Their explanation is that managers become more risk-averse when their ownership stake increases. Risk-taking is measured by the volatility in daily stock returns and market interest rates.[7]

Related studies focus on the impact of ownership on risk-taking and performance. Several studies indicate that state ownership of banks leads to inefficiency and poor performance (e.g., La Porta et al., 1998) as a result of reduced exposure to market discipline in equity markets. Caprio and Martinez-Peria (2000), Barth et al. (2004), Berger et al. (2005) and Byström (2004) find evidence that state-owned banks are inclined towards higher risk-taking as captured by the ratio of non-performing loans to total loans and bank failure rates.

The large share of foreign ownership of the banking sectors in many emerging market economies in Eastern Europe and Latin America has stimulated research on the effects of foreign ownership on banking operations there. According to Lensink and Hermes (2004) the entry of foreign banks improves the performance of domestic banks although costs increase as well. However, the evidence with respect to effects of foreign ownership on banks' risk-taking is, not surprisingly, mixed since market discipline on foreign-owned banks would depend on host- as well as home-country factors.[8]

Caprio et al. (2007) and Barth et al. (2006) analyze whether the quality of bank governance across countries is influenced by rules with respect to shareholder rights and disclosure. They use the market to book values of banks as a proxy for quality of governance. The results show that greater transparency and stronger minority shareholder rights are associated with higher market values but also that concentration of ownership substitutes for shareholder protection. Fernández and González (2005) and Nier and Baumann (2006) find that greater disclosure and transparency strengthen market discipline and reduce risk-taking of banks.

The quality of governance can be expected to have an indirect impact on risk-taking by influencing management's response to capital regulation, deposit insurance coverage and restrictions on banks' activities. Laeven and Levine (2009) ask whether the marginal effects of these variables on risk-taking depend on concentration of ownership. They find that concentrated ownership is associated with relatively large marginal effects. Thus, the impact on market discipline of, for example, deposit insurance becomes less pronounced if ownership is disbursed.

Management turnover is often used as an indicator of the responsiveness of a governance system to market signals. In this vein, Čihák et al. (2009) analyze whether market discipline in the US banking industry is exerted through management turnover in response to market signals in equity and debt markets. Focusing on banks that are not large enough to enjoy substantial implicit protection through regulatory forbearance, the authors find that forced management turnover is associated with deteriorating bank soundness as reflected in reduced dividend payments and a decline in the share of non-insured deposits. A relatively high level of subordinated debt is also associated with turnover of management. These results indicate that bank governance is responsive to market signals in equity as well as deposit markets. The authors do not find evidence of improved performance and reduced risk after turnover, however.

In summary, there is strong evidence that a degree of market discipline on risk-taking is imposed by increased costs of funding for more risky FIs. Market discipline is weakened by explicit as well as implicit protection of FIs' creditors; in particular, implicit protection of 'too big to fail' banks. The evidence with respect to the impact of governance variables on risk-taking is more ambiguous. Theoretically, this ambiguity can be explained by interaction between governance characteristics and protection of FIs' creditors. Effective governance structures from shareholders' point of view can contribute to risk-shifting to deposit insurance funds and taxpayers when creditor protection is strong. Although the evidence indicates that market discipline works if there are creditors facing credible risk of losses, it is harder to draw strong conclusions about its effectiveness with respect to the incidence of bank failures and, in particular, the incidence of financial crises.

13.4   THE TIMELINESS OF MARKET DISCIPLINE

Failure of market discipline can be the result of FIs' cost of funding not reflecting available information about factors affecting the value of an FI's assets and its sources of funding. An important question for management as well as for supervisors is whether market prices related to an FI's cost of funding can provide early warnings about impending distress of individual FIs, as well as about the financial system as a whole in time for managers of FIs and governments to take action to stave off a crisis. According to research reviewed below and data presented in the next section, the recent crisis was clearly not widely foreseen even six months in advance by FI managers, nor by supervisors and central bankers. This observation is to some extent obvious since if a dramatic fall in asset values with all its consequences had been foreseen well in advance the crisis would most likely have been averted.

Market discipline obviously does not imply perfect foresight about the quality of an FI's portfolio. Absence of market discipline must be associated with a market failure as a reason for prices not reflecting information. A genuine lack of information is not a financial market failure while inefficiency in the pricing of available information is. The issue of market failure is more complicated than that, however, because 'available' information is itself a function of incentives to acquire and reveal information in financial markets. We emphasize this point in section 13.6 where we interpret financial markets as instruments for creating incentives for information production. Even when there is no market failure market discipline can be weak when the level of information is low.

The conclusion of the 'Turner Review' of the financial crisis published by the UK Financial Services Authority (FSA) (2009) is that market discipline, in the sense that market prices would provide early warning signals, 'cannot be expected to play a major role in constraining bank risk taking'. This conclusion in the Turner Review seems to contradict the results in several papers mentioned in the previous section, stating that yields on financial instruments issued by FIs could be used by supervisors as indicators of impending distress. The contradiction could be explained by the Turner Review's focus on early warnings of systemic crises, while the papers referred to in the previous section focused on market signals with respect to individual FIs' distress.

Evidence presented by Berger et al. (2000) leads to more ambiguous conclusions with respect to the ability of supervisors to assess developments and risk ahead of market participants. These authors conclude that market prices usually lead supervisors' access to information except after on-site bank examinations.

There are reasons to suspect that the pessimistic view of the timeliness of market signals relative to supervisors' access to information may be exaggerated even if one has a pessimistic view of the value of market signals as early warning indicators. This is because the record of regulation is also not strong. Supervisors and regulators certainly did not act with more foresight than markets in the initial stages of the recent crisis. The failure of supervisors in the Northern Rock case is well known and described by Hamalainen et al. (2008). Only a few weeks before the collapse of Northern Rock, the UK FSA gave the mortgage bank permission to lower its required capital by nearly 30 percent by adopting the 'Advanced Internal Measurement Approach' under Basel II. At the same time a simple leverage ratio indicated that the bank's capital had already declined substantially. There are similar examples in the US.

Another weakness of the Turner Review's conclusions is that they do not take into account that perceptions of strong protection of creditors of large FIs, in combination with absence of warning signals from supervisors on both sides of the Atlantic, may have contributed to both lax risk management practices and a relaxed attitude of investors to risk of FIs' distress. It is possible that a financial system with less implicit protection could provide more effective early warning signals. We return to this issue in section 13.6 where we argue that a fuller analysis of timeliness of information in market signals and regulatory implications must take into account that much information is costly for both market participants and supervisors.

Ratings agencies also failed to provide early warnings of the impending crisis in 2007. There is a literature on the timeliness of market signals relative to ratings changes for FIs. For example, Distinguin et al. (2006) analyze whether banks' stock returns reflect information about bank risk by asking whether the returns contribute to predictions of distress for individual banks in Europe. Distress is defined as a two-step decline in ratings within a year. They find weak predictive ability of stock returns with respect to ratings declines when controlling for a number of observable factors. But neither the market nor the ratings agencies have a strong record.

The literature discussed in the previous section on the responsiveness of subordinated yield spreads has a bearing on timeliness as well. The empirical articles include both time series and cross-section analysis. Results in the time dimension indicate that changes in factors influencing perceptions of risk trigger adjustment in yields. On these grounds Calomiris (1999), Flannery (1998), Evanoff and Wall (2001), Evanoff et al. (2007) and others have recommended that yield spreads should be used as an informative tool by supervisors. Thereby, the financial instruments would provide indirect market discipline.

Many countries' financial supervisors employ a variety of market and non-market signals to assess the health of banks including debt ratings, stock prices, estimated default frequencies (see below), market capitalization, asset volatility, subordinated debt yield spreads and analysts' opinions to complement information obtained from banks as noted by Furlong and Williams (2006).

There is a growing literature since the financial crisis on the timeliness of different market signals with respect to the increasing insolvency risk of FIs. Stock returns are generally viewed as an inferior predictor of distress relative to debt instruments for non-financial corporations, because limited liability of shareholders weakens the price effect of increasing insolvency risk and the incentives of shareholders to monitor this risk. Debt holders, on the other hand, have strong incentives to monitor insolvency risk since they must bear the losses once there is no equity capital. The price sensitivity of a debt instrument to insolvency risk would depend on the instrument's priority in insolvency. Subordinated debt yields are expected to be the first to indicate increasing insolvency risk since holders of this debt are the first to bear losses once equity capital is lost. However, we show below that this expected relationship did not hold up strongly in the recent crisis.

In the financial industry debt instruments may be less sensitive to insolvency risk than in other industries as a result of implicit creditor protection. In particular, creditors of large and complex banks, including holders of subordinated debt, already enjoyed a degree of 'too big to fail' protection before the crisis. The relative informativeness of equity prices and yields for FIs' debt instruments is therefore an open question.

Implicit protection affects the information value of credit default swap (CDS) spreads as well. CDS spreads have become a common tool for analysis of insolvency risk since the spread interpreted as a put option premium is a direct implicit measure of insolvency risk. The downside of the CDS spread as a measure of risk is that liquid markets for this instrument exist only for relatively few large FIs.

The implicit estimates of insolvency risk in CDS spreads are derived from standard option pricing models under the assumption of risk-neutrality with respect to pricing.

Other measures of insolvency risk like Moody KMV's Expected Default Frequency (EDF) based on equity price volatility, equity price and leverage do not depend on the risk-neutrality assumption. On these grounds Singh and Youssef (2010) view the ratio of the CDS spread to the EDF signal for an FI as the 'price of risk' for this FI. They analyze how this 'price of risk' for several FIs developed before and during the crisis.[9] They argue that during crisis periods measures of probability of default should be adjusted for increased 'price of risk'. For this reason CDS spreads may be biased proxies for insolvency risk during crisis periods. Both CDS spreads and EDF signals are sensitive to assumptions about loss given default (LGD).

Implicit estimates of probability of default in the debt market, besides CDS spreads, can be obtained from yields of subordinated debt (SND). These yields, like other debt instrument yields, have a disadvantage relative to CDS spreads in that they reflect interest rate risk as well as insolvency risk. This means that an assumption must be made about interest rate risk in order to derive an implicit measure of insolvency risk. Equity-based measures besides EDF are distance to default (DD) estimates and implicit estimates based on option prices for equity of FIs. Use of the latter is of course constrained by the existence of a liquid market for a particular stock. DD estimates require only equity prices, volatility and leverage information, which means that they can be obtained for all FIs with traded equity. The information value with respect to probability of default can be reduced by 'contamination' of a multitude of risk sources affecting equity prices with different implications for insolvency risk. Some sources of risk may have substantial effects on volatility but little impact on probability of default.

We turn now to empirical evidence about the relative timeliness and early warning properties of different market signals. Jagtiani and Lemieux (2001) examine the bond pricing behavior of bank holding companies in the period prior to failure of their bank subsidiaries during the sample period of 1980–1995, and conclude that debt holders can effectively monitor the banks in their sample. Lack of bond data at the time of the study limited the sample to five failed banks. For these banks the authors find that bond spreads rose as early as six quarters prior to failure, although spreads did not always change much.

Gropp et al. (2006) estimate DDs and implicit measures based on SND spreads for European banks well in advance of bank failures during the period of 1991–2001. They conclude that SND spreads have information value only close to a bank's distress, while DDs reveal insolvency risk six to 18 months in advance. Thus, the two measures may reflect different information. The authors also find evidence that the implicit safety net weakens the predictive power of SND spreads. Both measures improve predictions based on accounting information alone.

Stephanou (2010) looks at the performance of equity, debt, and five-year CDS for three US banks (Citigroup, Bear Stearns, Lehman Brothers) from 2006 to January 2009, and compares them with a market benchmark financial instrument capturing broader market-wide movements. The analysis indicates that the decline in prices of some bank instruments differentiated the three troubled financial institutions from the market benchmarks only a few months in advance of events defined as revelations of large losses in the financial system.[10] The first instruments to reveal bank-specific insolvency risk information were equity prices and CDS spreads, while SND and senior bond yields responded more slowly and weakly.

Hamalainen et al. (2008) use the UK mortgage bank Northern Rock's failure in September 2007 to compare the information in four measures of insolvency risk: DD, implied volatilities from equity option markets, CDS spreads and SND yields. They also analyze developments of equity prices, volume and volatility. The results conform with those in Gropp et al. (2006) in that equity-based indicators including DD and options on equity reveal impending distress before debt instrument-based indicators. The first indications of trouble appeared in February 2007, but Northern Rock could not be distinguished from eight other UK FIs until June 2007, three months before emergency lending was provided by the Bank of England. CDS spreads showed signs of impending distress in June 2007 followed by SND a month later when markets essentially shut down.

The evidence presented reveals that bank-specific indicators did not reveal information about impending distress until about three to six months ahead of failure or government intervention during the recent financial crisis. In all cases the timeliness of equity-based measures of insolvency risk was superior to debt-based measures including CDS spreads. Evidence from the 1990s and the early 2000s shows better timeliness of insolvency risk indicators with lead times up to 18 months. One explanation could be that investors during the recent systemic crisis could not identify which banks were subject to the most stress until very late. In fact, bank managers seem to have had little knowledge about their banks' exposure until large losses were realized. Citibank is a case in point. The chief executive officer (CEO) Vikram Pandit, who took over in December 2007, revised loss estimates repeatedly in spite of attempts to reveal relatively pessimistic information after having taken over the helm of the bank.

Any evaluation of timeliness depends on the time needed by managers or supervisors to take effective countermeasures when distress or crisis is impending. Hart and Zingales (2009, 2010) propose a trigger rule to issue equity capital based on CDS spreads. They show that if their rule had been applied to Bear Stearns, the investment bank would have had to raise equity in August 2007, eight months before it was rescued by J.P. Morgan. The authors argue that their trigger rule would have forced a number of US FIs to raise equity up to 12 months before distress occurred. This does not mean that the crisis would necessarily have been averted. The lack of differentiation of insolvency risk measures across FIs implies that the trigger most likely would have forced many FIs to raise equity at the same time in a market with little willingness to invest in FIs.

In the next section we present further evidence with respect to the early warning properties of CDS spreads and equity prices during the period 2007–2009. In relation to the studies reviewed above we expand the dataset to include European and Japanese banks. We also include data for a recently developed early warning measure geared towards providing a signal for the contribution of individual FIs to systemic risk. This measure, the marginal expected shortfall (MES), represents the expected loss an equity investor in an FI would suffer if the overall market declined substantially. Its function is to provide investors and supervisors with information about which FIs deserve particular scrutiny from a systemic perspective.

The MES is described in Brownlee and Engle (2010). It is an equity market-based signal and it depends on the volatility of an FI's equity price, the correlation with the market return and the co-movement of the tails of the distributions. Thus, it is designed to capture special characteristics of the tails of distributions associated with systemic shocks.

MES has been developed by a group of researchers at the Stern School of Business at New York University. There is a website where the MES of the 102 FIs is updated and analyzed on a weekly basis.[11] Relative to the previously mentioned indicators, the MES is expected to provide a signal ahead of the CDS spread since it is equity based, and it takes into account tail characteristics of distributions, the correlations with market returns and the relative size of an FI.

13.5   EVIDENCE OF MARKET PRICES AS EARLY WARNING SIGNALS OF THE FINANCIAL CRISIS OF 2007–2009

In this section we add to the evidence presented in the previous section about the timeliness of market signals during the recent crisis. The analysis is similar to Hamalainen et al. (2008) and Stephanou (2010), but we include data for a larger number of large financial institutions in the United States as well as in Europe and Japan, and we include data for the marginal expected shortfall for a few FIs in addition to data for CDS (credit default swap) spreads, SND (subordinated debt) yields and equity prices. We ask whether the market signals for individual distressed FIs relative to a composite signal for a peer group helped identify the downside risks ahead of events defined by the failure or bailout of the individual FIs.

Data for three financial instruments – stock price index, CDS spreads and SND yields – were collected for 19 FIs in the United States, 20 FIs in the EU and 7 in Japan. Table 13.1 shows that these FIs include commercial banks, investment banking firms, and insurance companies. In order to be included in our sample, an FI must have both stock prices and CDS data available.[12] A list for European and Japanese financial institutions is largely drawn from Ohno (2010).

Before looking at the data for market signals Figure 13.1 presents the timing of warning signs in the US housing market from 2003. As shown in Figure 13.1a, the annual growth rate of home prices increased at a declining rate after January 2006. The first month with declining home prices was January 2007. Figure 13.1b shows that both new and existing home sales started to fall after they had record high sales in late 2005. About the same time, subprime home mortgage originations started to decline, after increasing dramatically earlier in the decade. The prime home mortgage originations, on the other hand, did not fall until the third quarter of 2007 (Figures 13.1c and 13.1d).[13] The summer of 2007 is widely acknowledged as the starting point of the US subprime mortgage crisis. However, some housing indicators had shown market weakness as early as the beginning of 2006.[14]

Figures 13.2 and 13.3 present the development of equity prices, CDS spreads and SND yields from January 2006 through 2008 for Bear Stearns, Lehman Brothers, Bank of America and Citigroup in comparison with developments for a peer group. Bailout and failure events are marked in the figures. These events are listed in Table 13.2.

Figure 13.4 presents the MES for Bank of America and Citigroup relative to the average MES for 102 US FIs for the same period and events. AIG is compared to a peer group in Figure 13.5. In Figure 13.6 the EU and Japan are brought into the picture. Stock price indices for the EU, Japan and the US are compared around the events. The list of the US, EU and Japanese FIs included in the peer groups and the composite indices is shown in Table 13.1 above.

Table 13.1   Sample coverage

Name	Country	Sector
Bank of America	United States	Banks
Citigroup	United States	Banks
JPMorgan Chase and Company	United States	Banks
United States Bancorp	United States	Banks
Wells Fargo and Company	United States	Banks
American Express	United States	Financial Services
Bear Stearns	United States	Financial Services
Capital One Financial	United States	Financial Services
Goldman Sachs Group	United States	Financial Services
Lehman Brothers Holdings	United States	Financial Services
Merrill Lynch and Company	United States	Financial Services
Morgan Stanley	United States	Financial Services
Aetna	United States	Health Care Equipment & Service
American International Group	United States	Nonlife Insurance
Berkshire Hathaway	United States	Nonlife Insurance
Cigna	United States	Health Care Equipment & Service
Hartford Financial Services Group	United States	Nonlife Insurance
MetLife	United States	Life Insurance
Prudential Financial	United States	Life Insurance
Barclays	United Kingdom	Banks
Banco Santander	Spain	Banks
Banco Comercial Portugues	Portugal	Banks
Banque Nationale de Paris Paribas	France	Banks
Credit Suisse Group	Switzerland	Banks
Crédit Agricole	France	Banks
Commerzbank	Germany	Banks
Deutsche Bank	Germany	Banks
HSBC Holdings	United Kingdom	Banks
Lloyds Banking Group	United Kingdom	Banks
Royal Bank of Scotland Group	United Kingdom	Banks
Société Générale	France	Banks
Standard Chartered	United Kingdom	Banks
United Bank of Switzerland 'R'	Switzerland	Banks
Northern Rock	United Kingdom	Banks
AXA	France	Life Insurance
Aegon	Netherlands	Life Insurance
Aviva	United Kingdom	Life Insurance
ING Group	Netherlands	Life Insurance
Prudential	United Kingdom	Life Insurance
Mitsubishi UFJ Financial Group	Japan	Banks
Mizuho Financial Group	Japan	Banks
Sumitomo Mitsui Financial Group	Japan	Banks
Daiwa Securities Group	Japan	Financial Services
Nomura Holdings	Japan	Financial Services
Sompo Japan Insurance (Frankfurt)	Japan	Nonlife Insurance
Tokio Marine Holdings	Japan	Nonlife Insurance

The dotted lines in Figures 13.2–13.6 indicate the key institution-specific events listed in Table 13.2. Examination of the figures describing the developments of equity prices, CDS spreads, SND yields and MES data generates several observations, as follows.

Stock prices and CDS spreads performed in a similar way. Generally they provided forewarning of risks of these institutions relative to the peer group only a few months prior to the events. Subordinated debt spreads reacted at a slower rate, and remained relatively flat until the intervention occurred. According to evidence for Northern Rock presented in the previous section, the SND yield for Northern Rock seems to have reacted more clearly relative to its peer group but more slowly than the other signals (Hamalainen et al., 2008).

These observations are consistent with those reported in the previous section except that we cannot clearly distinguish between the timeliness of equity prices and CDS spreads. The reviewed literature found that equity-based prices generally reflected increased insolvency risk ahead of CDS spreads. A more refined analysis using statistical criteria for early warning signals may lead to a differentiation between the two instruments.

MES for Citigroup and Bank of America in Figure 13.4 seems to provide early warnings for insolvency risk of these two FIs well ahead of the other instruments. In particular, the MES of the two banks seem to diverge substantially from the average about four months ahead of the event BA/C-2 (28 October 2008 when Troubled Asset Relief Program or TARP funds were first allocated to Citigroup and Bank of America) while the divergence for equity prices and CDS spreads seems to occur only about two months in advance. MES depends on equity price volatility like the DD, EDF and equity option-based indicators discussed above. The relatively early warning of MES is consistent with the evidence presented in the previous section with respect to indicators depending on equity price volatility.

There is volatility in the different indicators of insolvency risk of individual FIs relative to the peer group. The indicators sometimes diverge for a brief period before they converge again. Thus, it is possible that specific trigger points for divergence of indicators relative to the peer group were reached well in advance of the final divergence before an event. This observation may explain why Hart and Zingales (2010) find that early warning signals provided information that could have been used by banks to strengthen their capital base around six months in advance. An in-depth analysis of the value of the indicators should consider both Type 1 and Type 2 errors.

The market signals largely failed to indicate the increased insolvency risk of Bear Stearns, the first of the FIs encountering distress in Figure 13.2. The markets were moderately successful in indicating the risks of Bank of America and Citigroup as well as AIG in Figures 13.3 and 13.5. It seems likely that Bear Stearns sensitized market participants to insolvency risk.

Markets seem to punish individual FIs harshly after their risks become apparent. The stock price falls abruptly and the spread of CDS and subordinated debt yields widens relative to peers.

Observation of developments in the US, the EU and Japan in Figure 13.6 shows that stock prices reacted the same way in all three regions, but CDS spreads diverged more although they moved in the same direction. The pattern for equity prices implies that the international linkages among FIs in the three regions were strong. The weaker reactions

(a) Change of home price (monthly data)

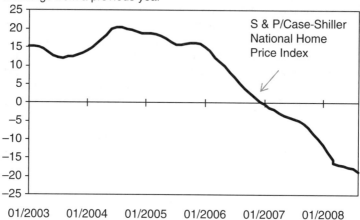

(c) Prime home mortgage originations

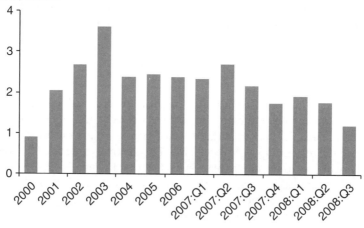

Note: The quarterly data for home mortgage originations are annualized.

Sources: Inside Mortgage Finance and Barth et al. (2010).

Figure 13.1 Warning signs in the US housing market

in CDS spreads in the EU and Japan to US events indicate that perceptions of insolvency risk diverged much more than those of the risk facing shareholders.

None of the market indicators aggregated over FIs revealed a serious systemic crisis approaching until early 2008. The stock market index, the average CDS spread, and the average MES revealed some negative information in July 2007 but they all recovered again before the trend-wise increase in risk began in 2008.

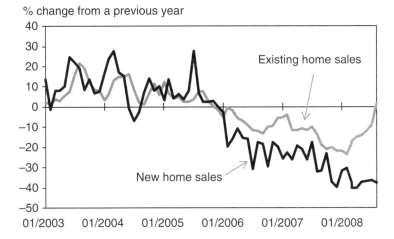

(b) Change of home sales (monthly data)

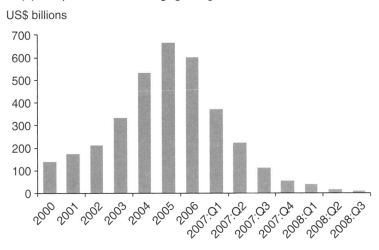

(d) Subprime home mortgage originations

Figure 13.1   (continued)

In summary, there is little doubt that while market signals provided some information they did not provide timely early warning about the impending distress of FIs during the pre-crisis year 2007 and the crisis years 2008 and 2009. The empirical evidence reviewed in previous sections indicates that early warnings from the market were more effective during the decades prior to the crisis. The fact that early warning signals failed prior to the recent crisis may help to explain why the crisis became so severe.

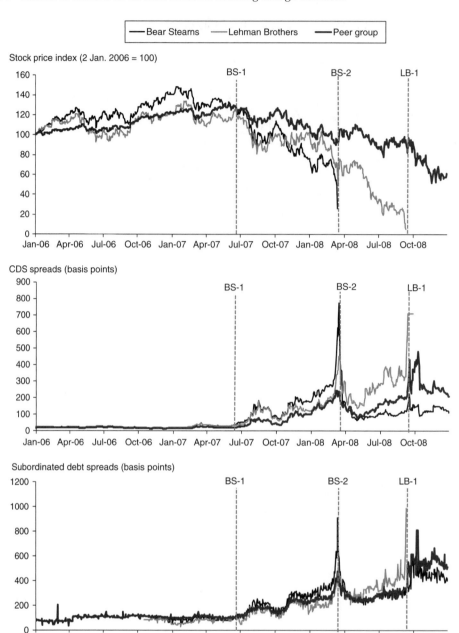

Notes: The vertical dot lines indicate key institution-specific events. See Table 13.2 for descriptions of these key events. Peer group includes American Express, Capital One, Goldman Sachs, JPMorgan, Merrill Lynch, Morgan Stanley, US Bank, and Wells Fargo.

Sources: Bloomberg, DataStream.

Figure 13.2   Selected closed investment banking firms

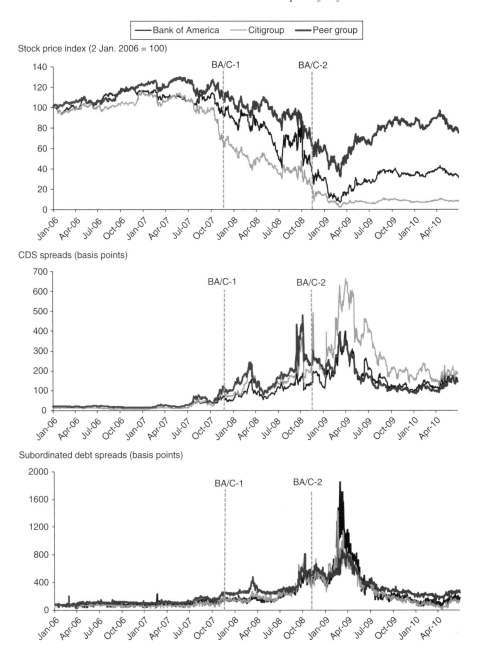

Notes: The vertical dot lines indicate key institution-specific events. See Table 13.2 for descriptions of these key events. Peer group includes American Express, Capital One, Goldman Sachs, JPMorgan, Merrill Lynch, Morgan Stanley, US Bank, and Wells Fargo.

Sources: Bloomberg, DataStream.

Figure 13.3 Selected US commercial banks that received government financial assistance

Table 13.2   Key events

Bear Stearns		
BS-1	7 June 2007	Bear Stearns informs investors that it is suspending redemptions from its High-Grade Structured Credit Strategies Enhanced Leverage Fund.
	31 July 2007	Bear Stearns liquidates two hedge funds that invested in various types of mortgage-backed securities.
BS-2	16 March 2008	JPMorgan Chase & Co. announces it is acquiring Bear Stearns for $2 per share.
Lehman Brothers		
LB-1	15 September 2008	Lehman Brothers files for Chapter 11 bankruptcy protection.
Northern Rock		
NR-1	14 September 2007	The Chancellor of the Exchequer authorizes the Bank of England to provide liquidity support for Northern Rock, the United Kingdom's fifth-largest mortgage lender.
NR-2	17 February 2008	Northern Rock is taken into state ownership by the Treasury of the United Kingdom.
Citigroup and Bank of America		
BA/C-1	5 November 2007	Citigroup CEO Chuck Prince resigns after an announcement that Citigroup may have to write down up to $11 billion in subprime bad debts.
	13 November 2007	Bank of America says it will have to write off $3 billion of subprime debt.
	5 June 2008	The Federal Reserve Board announces approval of the notice of Bank of America to acquire Countrywide Financial Corporation in an all-stock transaction worth approximately $4 billion.
BA/C-2	28 October 2008	TARP funds are initially allocated to Citigroup and Bank of America. Bank of America and Citigroup each receive $25 billion. Bank of America receives the second allocation of $20 billion on 9 January 2009, shortly after it acquires Merrill Lynch. Citigroup receives an additional $20 billion on 23 November 2008, after its stock price plummets 60% in one week.
	26 November 2008	The Federal Reserve Board announces approval of the notice of Bank of America Corporation to acquire Merrill Lynch & Co. for $50 billion.
American International Group (AIG)		
AIG-1	28 February 2008	AIG reports a fourth-quarter of 2007 net loss of $5.2 billion (the biggest loss to date), due largely to write down on mortgage-related investments. The company's financial products take a pretax charge of $11.12 billion from a net unrealized market valuation loss of its large credit default swap portfolio.
AIG-2	16 September 2008	The Federal Reserve Board authorizes the Federal Reserve Bank of New York to lend up to $85 billion to AIG, of which $40 billion is allocated from the TARP program on 25 November 2008.

Sources: Adapted from Federal Reserve Bank of St Louis and various other sources.

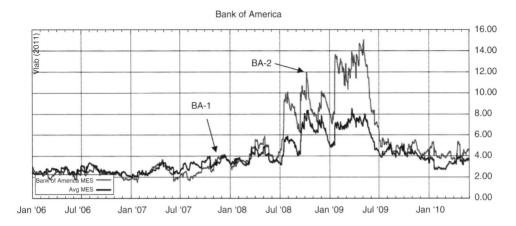

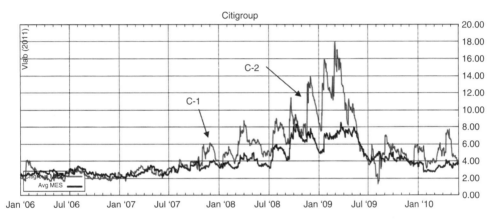

Source: Vlab, Stern School of Business, New York University.

Figure 13.4   Marginal expected shortfall (MES)

13.6   MARKET DISCIPLINE WITH RESPECT TO INFORMATIVENESS WITH COSTLY INFORMATION

An important property of effective market discipline is the informational efficiency of financial markets. As noted in section 13.4 in the discussion of timeliness of information, the question asked in most finance literature is whether 'available information' is fully reflected in prices. Available information is an ambiguous concept, however, and it should not be considered exogenous in an analysis of whether financial markets perform efficiently if information acquisition, analysis of information and information provision are costly. In this case a key function of financial markets is to provide incentives to acquire, analyze and disperse information, as noted in Wihlborg (1990). In this section we discuss how informational efficiency depends on informational incentives in financial markets. Financial regulation is likely to affect these incentives and, therefore,

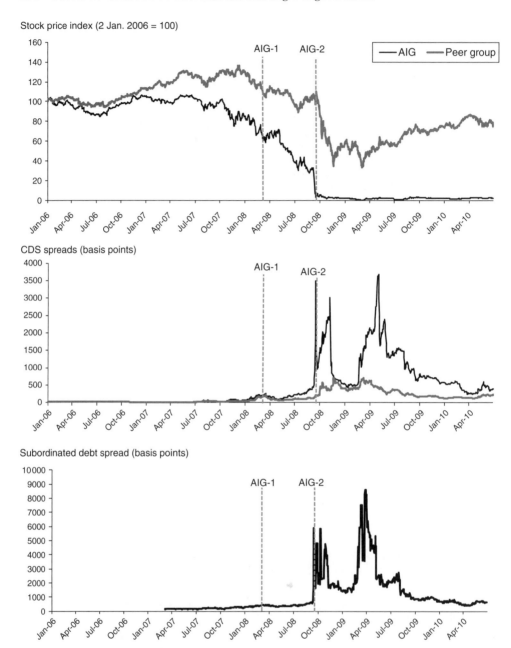

Notes: The vertical dot lines indicate key institution-specific events. See Table 13.2 for descriptions of these key events. Peer group includes Aetna, Berkshire Hathaway, Cigna, Hartford, MetLife, and Prudential.

Sources: Bloomberg, DataStream.

Figure 13.5   American International Group (AIG)

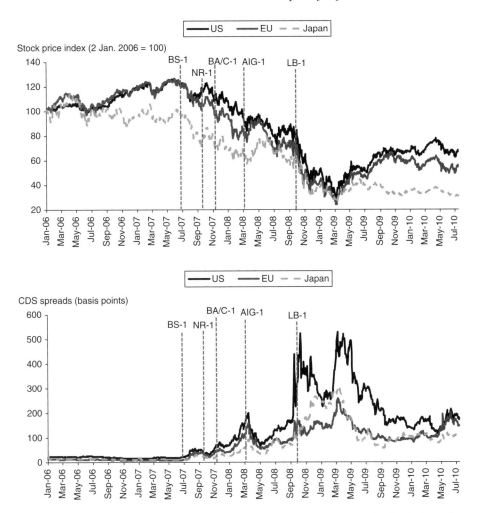

Notes: The vertical dot lines indicate key institution-specific events. See Table 13.2 for descriptions of these key events. The composite market signal is a simple average value of market indicators of financial institutions in the United States, European countries and Japan. A list of these financial institutions is shown in Table 13.1.

Sources: Bloomberg, DataStream.

Figure 13.6   Composite market signals

the information reflected in market prices. We discuss implications for financial market regulation of considering information to be costly and endogenous in section 13.7.

Grossman and Stiglitz (1980) demonstrate that informationally efficient markets cannot exist if information is costly. If all information is reflected in prices there is no incentive to acquire costly information, and if information is not acquired it cannot be reflected in prices unless information is freely available to insiders. They show that equilibrium prices with costly information will only partially reflect the costly information.

The degree to which the costly information is reflected depends on the cost of acquiring it. The information revelation to the uninformed remains imperfect and possibly incorrect as a result of confusion about different types of shocks that may cause price changes. There is some free-riding on the information acquired at a cost as a result of partial informativeness of prices. In financial markets the degree of free-riding would depend on the market micro structure.

There is little doubt that most information in the marketplace is costly, if not to acquire then to interpret and put to use. Michael Lewis (2010) demonstrates in his book *The Big Short: Inside the Doomsday Machine* that a few investors had sufficient information well in advance of the crisis about the risks associated with subprime mortgages. They were able to predict large-scale failures and an impending crash in the value of mortgage-backed securities years in advance. They also dared to invest based on their forecast. The investor stories also reveal that much research time was devoted to reading of prospectuses for mortgage-backed securities. Much relevant information seems to have been available but only a few investors had the time, patience and resources to go deeply into the information contained in these inaccessible documents. As a result, the investors going short hardly made a dent in the valuation of securities until large-scale failures of subprime mortgages became a reality. Other investors as well as supervisors seem to have remained under the illusion that real estate prices in the US could not decline. Market prices and yields on securities issued by FIs and supervisors' (non-) actions reflected this view.

Information about the overvaluation of mortgage-backed securities prior to the crisis was evidently available to the few investors able to invest resources in research and analysis, but prices did not reflect this information. Is this evidence of financial market inefficiency? And, if so, what is the appropriate regulatory response?

In the words of Llewellyn and Mayes (2003), efficiency with respect to yields on securities issued by FIs requires that there must exist monitors of FIs with sufficient incentives to become informed and to analyze this information. Even if financial markets are 'well-functioning' in terms of trading costs, opportunities and liquidity, the market for information used in pricing of securities may not function well. Monitoring is costly, and if these costs are very high a large number of potential investors will remain uninformed about sources of disturbances and risk-taking.

There is no unambiguous definition of what level and quality of information is required for financial markets to be called 'well-functioning' from an informational point of view. Demand as well as supply of information must be considered. Demand based on incentives to become informed is influenced, for example, by the existence of explicit and implicit protection of creditors of FIs. Supply based on incentives to make relevant information available to investors exists if an FI can reduce its cost of capital by revealing positive information affecting, for example, insolvency risk by means of disclosure and signaling. Such information revelation by high-quality FIs would also reveal that others are low-quality FIs.[15]

We noted above that the availability of information in the markets for mortgage-backed securities was limited to a few individuals in the run-up to the crisis. Similarly, it is clear from the data presented in the previous section that the available information about insolvency risk of major FIs was poor during the crisis. The available information would depend on a combination of demand and supply factors. It is important for policy to determine the weight of demand and supply factors in explaining the dearth of information about insolvency risk of FIs. We return to this issue and its regulatory implications below.

If there are incentives to become informed or to provide information, there is scope for 'information intermediaries' to develop to exploit economies of scale in the acquisition and analysis of information. Ratings agencies can be viewed as such intermediaries, charging the firm interested in supplying information by means of being rated. Their existence is evidence of demand as well as supply of information. Unfortunately, however, ratings agencies did not do a good job of providing correct and timely information to market participants.

Much economic analysis of regulation is based on the assumption that information is costless in well-functioning markets. An implication of this view is that there is a case for public policy action as soon as markets are not informationally efficient. However, if information is costly, the relevant question is how the best information can be made available for decision-makers at the lowest possible costs. Regulatory intervention can be justified if it can achieve a better resource allocation at a certain cost of information, or a certain resource allocation at a lower cost of information.

The benefit in terms of information of decentralized markets is that widely dispersed information and a variety of interpretations of information can be reflected in market prices that provide incentives for resource allocation. Trading in financial markets, in particular, is based on differences in information or in interpretations of existing information. The markets provide incentives for a variety of participants to become informed and put information to use in order to make profits. Financial decision-making by a centralized entity, on the other hand, may achieve some economies of scale in information gathering and analysis, but the range of available information will be limited.

In spite of the inevitable duplication of information costs occurring in decentralized markets, we assume in the following that informational efficiency depends on the demand side primarily on the number and variety of individuals engaged in acquisition and analysis of information. In other words, pluralism is an important source of informational efficiency in decentralized financial markets. On the supply side, informational efficiency would depend on the perceived costs and benefits for firms to disclose and signal relevant information honestly to the market. If there are strong incentives for all firms to remain opaque and actually to mislead, even when demand for information is strong, the case for government intervention is strong as well. Such government intervention could be regulatory constraints on risk-taking and examination of FIs' asset allocation by supervisors. Of course, one should also consider the political economy incentives that may lead to government failure.

13.7 'INFORMATIVENESS PRINCIPLES' FOR GOVERNMENT POLICY

The view of financial markets as instruments for creating incentives to acquire, analyze, disclose and signal information at a cost has implications for the regulation and supervision of financial markets and institutions, as well as for policy intervention in crisis situations. We offer the following four general 'informativeness principles' for regulation, supervision and government intervention in financial markets:

1. Regulation, supervision and intervention in financial markets should minimize disincentives for private market participants to acquire and analyze information, recognizing that a central agency cannot substitute for a multitude of agents to determine what information is relevant for evaluation of a securities and default risk.
2. Regulation, supervision and intervention should minimize disincentives for issuers of securities to provide and signal information about characteristics of the securities.
3. Regulation, supervision and intervention should aim at reducing information costs. Some kinds of information may be gathered by a government agency for purposes of supervision or to be made available to market participants. Such activities should not reduce incentives of private market participants to acquire other kinds of information.
4. Regulators and supervisors should help to identify market failures affecting particular types of information. In case there are such failures, disclosure rules may be implemented. It is necessary to recognize that forced disclosure carries with it incentives to obfuscate.

As stated, these principles are very general and they are not easily operationalized. We view efforts to do so as an important direction for further analysis. Here, we will conclude by trying to provide illustrations of the principles in operation with respect to FIs. Thereby, we also illustrate how current regulatory practices may have contributed to failures of market discipline with respect to availability of information as documented in previous sections.

The first 'informativeness principle' applies directly to explicit and implicit protection of depositors and other creditors of FIs. Such protection reduces the value of information about the insolvency risk of FIs.

Externalities associated with the insolvency of an FI can justify a degree of protection of depositors in particular, but if externalities can be addressed in other ways, implicit and explicit protection could be reduced. For example, specific insolvency law for FIs enabling them to be closed down with a minimum of systemic repercussions would reduce implicit protection by reducing the need for bailouts in crisis situations. We return to this issue below.

The empirical evidence presented in previous sections indicates quite clearly that protection of FIs' creditors reduces the information values of prices on debt-based financial instruments. Furthermore, the implicit protection of 'too big too fail' FIs implies that the informational efficiency of markets for these systemically important FIs is particularly low.

Implicit protection of FIs' creditors is relevant for the second 'informativeness principle' as well, since governments are most likely to bail out large financial institutions with complex interconnections with other FIs. The perceived bail out bias in favor of large, complex FIs implies that they obtain reduced costs of funding. Thus, the incentives to become large, complex and opaque seem to be strong. They have been strengthened further during the crisis.

In the early days of the crisis, liquidity in interbank markets and short-term markets for financing of FIs dried up. A major cause of this generalized seizing-up of the liquidity in the markets was widespread uncertainty about who had bad debt and how much. An informationally efficient market would have induced solvent FIs to signal and provide information about their quality. This would have allowed market participants to distinguish between solvent and distressed FIs. Thereby, the liquidity crunch would have become less severe for FIs with less default risk.

Why did financial markets fail in their informational role to provide incentives to reveal and signal relevant information about FIs? The role of implicit protection through expected bailouts has been mentioned. Although most bank managers would most likely try to avoid being bailed out, they would be hard pressed in times of crisis to say no to offers of aid available to competitors. Managers revealing positive information about probability of insolvency face the risk that they disqualify their FIs from aid. The Troubled Asset Relief Program (TARP), and other programs outside the US, included promises to make funds available to any FI in need. Such programs are likely to have discouraged the revelation of positive information about the financial health of FIs.

The design of lender of last resort (LOLR) facilities in central banks can also discourage information release of a positive nature if access to cheap LOLR funding is made conditional on the FI's financial health. Unlike TARP, the Federal Reserve cannot be strongly criticized on these grounds, however, since its lending facilities during the crisis were linked to specific types of assets rather than to the financial health of the FI.[16]

Another explanation for the lack of information of relevance for judging FIs' insolvency risk is that top management in large FIs simply did not know their exposures, as a result of the complexity of domestic and international interconnections as well as failures of internal risk management controls in a number of cases. Frequent updating of, for example, Citibank's loss estimates indicates lack of internal knowledge of this kind. One must ask: how can a bank operate with inability to grasp quickly its own exposures and potential losses? A reasonable explanation is that such knowledge does not have much value. If market participants do not penalize the bank for lack of information about risk and opaqueness, and the government is expected to bail out the bank if losses materialize, the efforts of bank management can be devoted towards other activities than information disclosure and signaling.

One aspect of proposals for 'living wills' is that they would force management to update exposure and interconnectedness information more or less continuously. However, one may question how well 'living wills' will achieve this objective if incentives to provide this information are weak. We return to this issue below in connection with the fourth 'informativeness principle'.

The third 'informativeness principle' refers to reducing costs of information. As mentioned, there are economies of scale in the collection of information. Thus, a central agency responsible for gathering and publishing certain kinds of information would economize on information costs. As noted, ratings agencies already perform this function, although the incentives of these agencies to disclose negative information have come under scrutiny.

A government agency responsible for information disclosure must be concerned that its information release does not reduce incentives of private market participants to gather additional relevant information. The centralized information gathering should therefore be restricted to uncontroversially relevant information that cannot be subject to widely different interpretations. It is possible that forecasting of some macroeconomic variables represents information of this nature.

The Basel rules for calculation of regulatory capital can be used to illustrate the dangers of centralization of rules for assessing risk. Basel II specifies in its standardized approach how risk weights should be allocated to different types of assets. The Internal Ratings Approach allows banks to use internal models for assessment of risk weights. Since the models must be approved by supervisors it is inevitable that internal models also become highly standardized. Furthermore, Basel II is complex and resource-consuming to implement.

One possible consequence of Basel II is that risk assessment becomes oriented towards satisfying the regulatory requirements. Since this activity is resource-consuming, the capacity to develop independent economically valid risk assessment declines. Incentives to develop credit evaluation models become geared towards satisfying the supervisor. As a result, diversity in risk assessment declines. Markets generally are more robust when a number of different views are present. If the risk assessment implied by Basel II is not economically valid, the bank is nevertheless hedged to some extent by having lived up to the supervisor's expectations. Thereby, the likelihood of being bailed out increases since large losses are no longer the fault of the bank alone.

Moral hazard created by explicit and implicit protection implies that intellectual power within the bank will be devoted to manipulating risk assessment for the purpose of reducing capital requirements rather than for the purpose of developing improved risk assessment. The incentive to reveal useful exposure information to market participants is not likely to be high under these circumstances. The most that will be revealed is what conforms to the information developed to satisfy the supervisor.

The fourth 'informativeness principle' refers to market failure with respect to information acquisition and release. As noted, regulation may be a source of market failure but there are no doubt other sources as well. For example, the conflict of interest facing ratings agencies, which are paid by borrowers, is often mentioned as an explanation for the poor performance with respect to ratings of mortgage-backed securities prior to the crisis.

The large number of layers of actors in a financial system characterized by trading in risk through securities markets relative to a bank-dominated financial system increases the number of potential agency conflicts that may have to be monitored from the point of view of information revelation or obfuscation.

Explicit and implicit guarantees have already been mentioned as sources of market failure with respect to both information acquisition and revelation. Information disclosure rules are often viewed as an antidote to information market failure, but if incentives to obtain, release and signal information are not present, disclosure may not be very effective. A particular type of information can be packaged along with other kinds of information in such a way that the information value becomes very low. A case in point is the prospectuses that must accompany issues of securities in the US in particular. These are often so long, complicated and overloaded with information that few readers are able to absorb the relevant information.

The strongest case for government involvement in the information process arises as a result of the potential systemic consequences of an FI's distress. The different channels of contagion in financial markets can be considered externalities. The individual FI has little incentive to provide information to the public about all its interconnections that could be channels of contagion. These interconnections are particularly important in case of distress of an FI. Without information about them an orderly closing of a large FI by a court or administrator without causing systemic effects is impossible. US bank insolvency procedures include the forming of a 'bridge bank' to keep critical operations going, and 'haircuts' for various non-insured creditors. These procedures have been implemented by the FDIC for many banks except the very large ones. Bailouts of large banks' creditors seem to be considered necessary because the information required to identify creditors which would take a haircut before a bridge bank could be reopened quickly is lacking. The administrator's or the court's access to the living will information mentioned above could help resolve this problem.

FIs may have incentives to obfuscate the information required by the supervisor in order to have it available in case an FI fails. Market discipline on the provision of this kind of information would seem to be ineffective since it would not be made publicly available. Investors with claims on FIs have a stake in the quality of the information, however. Therefore, market discipline could be utilized by supervisors to create incentives for FIs to provide relevant information if supervisors would publicize their assessment of the information they obtain.

13.8   CONCLUDING COMMENTS ON MARKET DISCIPLINE AND INFORMATIVENESS

It is not a controversial statement that market discipline on major financial institutions in the US and Europe failed in the run-up to the 2007–2009 financial crisis, and contributed to the depth of the crisis. A much harder question is why market discipline failed and what legal and regulatory reforms could improve market discipline in the future. Alternatively, policymakers may give up on market discipline and approach the financial sector by creating a much more interventionist regulatory structure.

We have reviewed literature on market discipline for financial institutions, distinguishing between market discipline on risk-taking and discipline in the sense of timely information being revealed in yields on securities such as equity and debt issued by the financial institutions. There is little doubt that market discipline failed to restrain excessive risk-taking and did not reveal relevant information about the insolvency risk of individual financial institutions as well as about systemic risk. Information was out there in the run-up to the crisis about factors influencing the values of mortgage-backed securities and the financial institutions holding them. Nevertheless, the stock markets tended to reward those financial institutions which turned out to be taking greater risks. This is essentially the logic underlying Charles Prince's infamous comment in a *Financial Times* interview on 10 July 2007 that as long as the music was still playing the banks needed to keep dancing.

In order to understand the sources of the failure of market discipline we take the view that a major role of financial markets is to provide incentives for investors to acquire costly information and for issuers of securities to disclose and signal relevant information. Both types of information production are costly and they affect the informativeness of securities prices with respect to risk-taking and factors influencing values.

The most important market failure of informativeness in our view is that major financial institutions seem to have had incentives to remain opaque and not to disclose information that would have helped investors assess the solvency of financial institutions. The puzzle is to determine why markets do not seem to provide sufficient incentives for high-quality institutions to reveal information that enables investors to identify their quality; why financial institutions issued opaque securities that required enormous investments of time and knowledge to evaluate; and why investors bought them.

Viewing financial markets as sources of incentives to produce information, we identified factors that may have created the failure of informativeness. Explicit and implicit protection of creditors is clearly such a factor. Furthermore, incentives for creating opaqueness are strengthened in times of systemic stress by the policy measures implemented to dampen the consequences of failures of financial institutions, as well as by the regulatory framework for capital adequacy. For example, the financial institutions disclosing low risk might not obtain the same kinds of subsidies that distressed financial institutions receive. The capital adequacy framework commits resources of financial institutions to satisfy formally the supervisory principles for risk evaluation, while at the same time taking risks that produce higher returns. Resources are drained from more effective economic risk evaluation and, as a result, the main objective of information revelation becomes to demonstrate abidance by the regulation.

In the last section we laid out four 'informativeness principles' for regulators, supervisors and government intervention in financial markets. These principles aim at creating incentives for information production and acquisition in order to improve market discipline. Disclosure rules without incentives to acquire, analyze, disclose and signal relevant information are likely to produce information that is nearly impossible to comprehend. Thus, financial markets will not be efficient in the sense that prices reflect the information that can be made available at a cost.

NOTES

1. A comprehensive theoretical view of financial institutions is presented in Bhattacharya and Thakor (1993).
2. See, for example, Benink and Wihlborg (2002).
3. The distinction between direct and indirect market discipline has been made by Flannery (1998). Literature on the two types of discipline is reviewed in the next section.
4. Diamond and Dybvig (1983) model contagious bank runs that occur after one bank's failure when depositors are unable to distinguish between solvent and insolvent banks.
5. See, for example, Brunnermeier et al. (2009) and Kashyap et al. (2008) for summaries of the new views of contagion.
6. Cho (2009) in the *Washington Post*, 28 August.
7. Anderson and Fraser (2000) argue that the different results can be explained by changes in the regulatory environment between the 1980s and the 1990s. These changes affected banks' charter values in the USA. In the Japanese banking sector Konishi and Yasuda (2004) observe that the relationship 'between the stable shareholders' ownership and bank risk is nonlinear'.
8. See, for example, Demirgüç-Kunt et al. (1998), Claessens et al. (2001), Barth et al. (2004) and Levine (2004).
9. Singh and Youssef also consider how different assumptions about time varying loss given default (LGD) affect the implicit price of risk.

10. The events were revelations of losses and capital injections in Citibank in November 2008 and February 2009, the Bear Sterns merger in March 2008 and the Lehman Brothers failure in September 2008.
11. http://vlab.stern,nyu.edu/analysis/RISK.
12. Sometimes CDS data are for a bank and stock prices for bank holding companies. One example: Nomura Securities and Nomura Holdings.
13. See Barth et al. (2010) for comprehensive analyses of the build-up and meltdown of the US mortgage market.
14. For discussion of the early identification of the looming crisis by some hedge funds see Lewis (2010).
15. After the first round of signaling quality, the relatively high quality among those who did not reveal information to begin with now have incentives to reveal information. The process continues until all FIs have revealed information.
16. In hindsight the Federal Reserve has been criticized for low-cost lending to relatively healthy FIs, although from an informational efficiency point of view the Federal Reserve's lending policies were sound.

REFERENCES

Anderson, Ronald C. and Donald R. Fraser (2000), 'Corporate control, bank risk taking, and the health of the banking industry', *Journal of Banking and Finance*, **24**, 1383–1398.
Angkinand, Apanard P. and Clas Wihlborg (2010), 'Deposit insurance coverage, ownership, and banks' risk-taking in emerging markets', *Journal of International Money and Finance*, **29**, 254–274.
Barth, James R., Gerard Caprio Jr. and Ross Levine (2004), 'The regulation and supervision: what works best?', *Journal of Financial Intermediation*, **13**, 205–248.
Barth, James R., Gerard Caprio Jr. and Ross Levine (2006), *Rethinking Bank Regulation: Till Angels Govern*, Cambridge: Cambridge University Press.
Barth, James, Tong Li, Wenling Lu, Triphon Phumiwasana and Glenn Yago (2010), *The Rise and Fall of the US Mortgage and Credit Market*, New York: Cambridge University Press.
Benink, Harald A. and Clas Wihlborg (2002), 'The new Basel Capital Accord: making it effective with stronger market discipline', *European Financial Management*, **8**, 103–115.
Berger, Allen N., George R.G. Clarke, Robert Cull, Leora F. Klapper and Gregory F. Udell (2005), 'Corporate governance and bank performance: a joint analysis of the static, selection, and dynamic effects of domestic, foreign, and state ownership', *Journal of Banking and Finance*, **29**, 2179–2221.
Berger, Allen N., Sally M. Davies and Mark J. Flannery (2000), 'Comparing market and supervisory assessments of bank performance: who knows what and when?', *Journal of Money, Credit and Banking*, **32**, 641–667.
Bhattacharya, Sudipto and Anjan V. Thakor (1993), 'Contemporary banking theory', *Journal of Financial Intermediation*, **3**, 2–50.
Brownlee, Christian T. and Robert Engle (2010), 'Volatility, correlation and systematic risk measurement', Department of Finance, Stern School of Business, New York University, available at http://vlab.stern,nyu.edu/analysis/RISK.
Brunnermeier, Markus, Andrew Crocket, Charles Goodhart, Martin Hellwig, Avinash D. Persaud and Hyun Shin (2009), 'The fundamental principles of financial regulation', Geneva Report on the World Economy 11.
Byström, Hans N.E. (2004), 'The market's view on the probability of banking sector failure: cross-country comparisons', *International Financial Markets, Institutions, and Money*, **14**, 419–438.
Calomiris, Charles (1999), 'Building an incentive compatible safety net', *Journal of Banking and Finance*, **23**(10), 1499–1519.
Caprio, Gerard, Luc Laeven and Ross Levine (2007), 'Ownership and bank valuation', *Journal of Financial Intermediation*, **16**, 584–617.
Caprio, Gerard and Maria Soledad Martinez-Peria (2000), 'Avoiding disaster: policies to reduce the risk of banking crises', Discussion Paper, Cairo: Egyptian Center for Economic Studies.
Chen, Carl R., Thomas L. Steiner and Anne Marie Whyte (1998), 'Risk-taking behavior and management ownership in depository institutions', *Journal of Financial Services Research*, **21**(1), 1–16.
Cho, David (2009), 'Behemoths born of the bailout reduce consumer choice, tempt corporate moral hazard', *Washington Post*, 28 August.
Čihák, M., A. Maechler, K. Schaeck and S. Stolz (2009), 'Who disciplines bank managers?', IMF Working Paper no. 272, International Monetary Fund.
Claessens, Stijn, Aslí Demirgüç-Kunt and Harry Huizinga (2001), 'How does foreign entry affect domestic banking markets?', *Journal of Banking and Finance*, **25**(5), 891–911.

Cull, Robert, Lemma W. Senbet and Marco Sorge (2005), 'Deposit insurance and financial development', *Journal of Money, Credit, and Banking*, **37**(1), 43–82.

Demirgüç-Kunt, Asli and Enrica Detragiache (2002), 'Does deposit insurance increase banking system stability? An empirical investigation', *Journal of Monetary Economics*, **49**, 1373–1406.

Demirgüç-Kunt, Asli, Ross Levine and Hong-Ghi Min (1998), 'Opening to foreign banks: stability, efficiency and growth', in A. Meltzer (ed.), *The Implications of Globalization of World Financial Markets*, Seoul: Bank of Korea.

Diamond, Douglas W. and Philip H. Dybvig (1983), 'Bank runs, deposit insurance, and liquidity', *Journal of Political Economy*, **91**(3), 401–419.

Distinguin, Isabelle, Philippe Rous and Amine Tarazi (2006), 'Market discipline and the use of stock market data to predict financial distress', *Journal of Financial Services Research*, **30**, 151–176.

Evanoff, Douglas D., Julapa Jagtiani and Taisuke Nakata (2007), 'The potential role of subordinated debt programs in enhancing market discipline in banking', Federal Reserve Bank of Kansas City Economic Research paper 07-07.

Evanoff, Douglas and Lawrence Wall (2000), 'Subordinated debt and bank capital reform', in Kaufman, George G. (ed), *Research in Financial Services: Private and Public Policy*, Vol. 12, Amsterdam: Elsevier, pp. 53–119.

Evanoff, Douglas and Lawrence Wall (2001), 'Sub-debt yield spreads as bank risk measures', *Journal of Financial Services Research*, **20**(2–3), 121–145.

Federal Reserve Board (1999), 'Using subordinated debt as an instrument of market discipline', Staff Study No 172, Washington, DC.

Fernández, Ana and Francisco González (2005), 'How accounting and auditing systems can counteract risk-shifting of safety-nets in banking: some international evidence', *Journal of Financial Stability*, **1**(4), 466–500.

Financial Services Authority (FSA) (2009), 'The Turner Review: a regulatory response to the global banking crisis'.

Flannery, Mark J. (1998), 'Using market information in prudential bank supervision: a review of the US empirical evidence', *Journal of Money, Credit and Banking*, **39**(3), 273–305.

Flannery, Mark J. and Sorin M. Sorescu (1996), 'Evidence of bank market discipline in subordinated debenture yields: 1983–1991', *Journal of Finance*, **52**(4), 1347–1377.

Furlong, F. and R. Williams (2006), 'Financial market signals and banking supervision: are current practices consistent with research findings?', *Federal Reserve Bank of San Francisco Economic Review*, 17–29.

Gandh, Priyank and Hannes Lustig (2010), 'Size anomalies in US bank stock returns: a fiscal explanation', NBER Working Paper No. 16553, National Bureau of Economic Research.

González, Francisco (2005), 'Bank regulation and risk-taking incentives: an international comparison of bank risk', *Journal of Banking and Finance*, **29**(5), 1153–1184.

Gropp, Reint and Jukka Vesala (2004), 'Deposit insurance, moral hazard and market monitoring', *Review of Finance*, **8**, 571–602.

Gropp, R., J. Vesala and G. Vulpes (2006), 'Equity and bond market signals as leading indicators of bank fragility', *Journal of Money, Credit and Banking*, **28**, 399–428.

Grossman, Sanford J. and Joseph E. Stiglitz (1980), 'On the impossibility of informationally efficient markets', *American Economic Review*, **70**(3), 393–408.

Hamalainen, Paul, Adrian Pop and Barry Howcroft (2008), 'Did the market signal impending problems at Northern Rock? An analysis of four financial instruments', Discussion Paper 2008–11, Department of Economics, Loughborough University.

Hart, Oliver and Luigi Zingales (2009), 'A new capital regulation for large financial institutions', University of Chicago Booth Working Paper No 09-36.

Hart, Oliver and Luigi Zingales (2010), 'How to improve the financial-reform law: a brief proposal to protect the system without stifling innovation', *City Journal*, 23 November.

Hovakimian, A., Edward Kane and Luc Laeven (2003), 'How country and safety-net characteristics affect bank risk shifting', *Journal of Financial Services Research*, **23**(3), 177–204.

Jagtiani, Julapa, George Kaufman and Catharine Lemieux (2002), 'The effect of credit risk on bank and bank holding company bond yields: evidence from the post-FDICIA period', *Journal of Financial Services Research*, **25**(4), 559–575.

Jagtiani, J. and C. Lemieux (2001), 'Market discipline prior to bank failure', *Journal of Economics and Business*, **53**, 313–324.

Kashyap, Anil K., Raghuram G. Rajan and Jeremy C. Stein (2008), 'Rethinking capital regulation', paper prepared for Federal Reserve Bank of Kansas City symposium on Maintaining Stability in a Changing Financial System, Jackson Hole, Wyoming, 21–23 August.

Konishi, Masaru and Yukihiro Yasuda (2004), 'Factors affecting bank risk-taking: evidence from Japan', *Journal of Banking and Finance*, **28**(1), 215–232.

La Porta, Rafael, Florencio Lopez-de-Silanes, Andrei Shleifer and Robert W. Vishny (1998), 'Law and Finance', *Journal of Political Economy*, **106**(6), 1113–1155.

Laeven, Luc and Ross Levine (2009), 'Bank governance, regulation and risk taking', *Journal of Financial Economics*, **93**, 259–275.

Lensink, Robert and Niels Hermes (2004), 'The short-term effects of foreign bank entry on domestic bank behavior: does economic development matter?', *Journal of Banking and Finance*, **28**(3), 553–568.

Levine, Ross (2004), 'Denying foreign bank entry: implications for bank interest margins', in Luis Antonio Ahumada and J. Rodrigo Fuentes (eds), *Banking Market Structure and Monetary Policy*, Santiago: Central Bank of Chile.

Levonian, M. (2000), 'Subordinated debt and quality of market discipline in banking', paper, Federal Reserve Bank of San Francisco.

Lewis, Michael (2010), *The Big Short: Inside the Doomsday Machine*, New York: W.W. Norton.

Llewellyn, David T. and David G. Mayes (2003), 'The role of market discipline in handling problem banks', Bank of Finland Discussion Paper No. 21, Helsinki.

Nier, Erlend and Ursel Baumann (2006), 'Market discipline, disclosure and moral hazard in banking', *Journal of Financial Intermediation*, **15**, 332–361.

Ohno, Sanae (2010), 'Liquidity crunch and interdependence among major financial institutions during global financial turmoil: evidence from credit default swap spread', presented at the Asia-Pacific Economic Association Conference.

Saunders, Anthony, Elizabeth Strock and Nickolaos G. Travlos (1990), 'Ownership structure, deregulation and bank risk taking', *Journal of Finance*, **45**(2), 643–654.

Singh, Manmohan and Karim Youssef (2010), 'Price of risk: recent evidence from large financials', IMF Working Paper No. 10/190, International Monetary Fund.

Sironi, A. (2003), 'Testing for market discipline in the European banking industry: evidence from subordinated debt issues', *Journal of Money, Credit, and Banking*, **35**, 443–472.

Stephanou, Constantinos (2010), 'Rethinking market discipline in banking: lessons from the financial crisis', Policy Research Working Paper, 5227, World Bank.

Wihlborg, Clas (1990), 'The incentive to acquire information and financial market efficiency', *Journal of Economic Behavior and Organization*, **13**(3), 347–365.

14 Moral hazard, bank resolution and the protection of depositors

David G. Mayes

14.1 INTRODUCTION

Depositor protection is normally organized through one of two schemes. It can take the form of insurance, provided by contributions by the banking system either before or after a bank failure according to rules laid down by the authorities, which normally include compulsory membership.[1] In other cases, particularly in Europe, it is provided in the form of a guarantee through a government agency, where the cost is either borne by the taxpayer or recovered from the surviving banks at a later date. In many countries, even under insurance, the scheme is also run by a government agency and, even where it is not, it is usually a government agency that determines when deposit insurance is triggered even if this goes through the courts. In the present crisis, however, governments have taken a much stronger role in protecting deposits and many have offered blanket guarantees. Even where such guarantees have not been offered the coverage of insurance schemes has been raised substantially (IADI, 2010).

Previously (IADI-BIS, 2008) deposit insurance was thought to have two main objectives.[2] The first was to protect those in society who could not really be expected to assess the risk of their banks and for whom the loss of their deposit would cause serious hardship. The second was to help ensure financial stability. With the rise in coverage it is the second reason that has become dominant and few ordinary depositors can expect to lose anything. However, this reflects a further widely held view that, in the event of crisis, depositors will not lose, irrespective of what the terms of the deposit insurance or guarantee scheme actually say. There is thus implicit systemic deposit insurance to add to the explicit schemes. While the explicit schemes may not have existed before the crisis, in Australia and New Zealand for example, the implicit schemes did (LaBrosse and Mayes, 2007) and the behaviour of the authorities in providing guarantees has borne this out in practice. Two schemes have thus been in place side by side in most countries: a limited explicit insurance directed at coping with the failure of the occasional small bank, and an implicit complete guarantee that will cut in if a major bank gets into difficulty or an important segment of the market is approaching failure.

What has happened in the present crisis is that the implicit schemes have become explicit, and hence the role of the limited schemes has disappeared. We are now at the phase in the crisis when authorities are looking ahead to the post-crisis 'normal' world and trying to sort out what the insurance or guarantee scheme should look like. New Zealand, for example, decided in October 2010, on the expiry of its temporary scheme, that guarantees would not be renewed after a transition arrangement for a few troubled institutions lasting until the end of 2011. Australia on the other hand decided to make its scheme permanent in October 2011, with some changes in its terms. Many of the previous explicit schemes have been shown to have major drawbacks (Mayes and Wood, 2008, covers the case of the UK). Some hurried measures to improve schemes and restore confidence have proved disastrously expensive (Ireland for example). In this chapter I discuss the factors that should affect the revision of deposit insurance schemes for the post-crisis world.

Deposit insurance has always led to worries about the moral hazard it might cause, as on the one hand banks may be prepared to take more risks if they think the depositor will be saved, and on the other hand funding will become more certain for banks as depositors will have less to fear from a bank failing and will hence have little incentive to monitor their activities. Now with the change in the coverage of deposits this problem is potentially enhanced and this chapter explores the consequences and suggests a way forward. That way forward is to return to the previous coverage as soon as the crisis is clearly past. However, despite all the discussion about moral hazard it is difficult to provide estimates of the contribution that the safety net and explicit parts of it make to increasing the risk propensity of banks. We have been able to observe the extensive risks that many banks took in the run up to the crisis, which threatened their solvency, but there is usually quite a long list of contributory causes, and moral hazard from the structure of deposit guarantees is only one of them. It is important to stress that it is not necessarily just that banks took increasing risks but also that the authorities relaxed their vigilance (see Demyanyk and van Hemert, 2008, and Garcia, 2010, for an analysis of both trends in the US).

Even so at present most countries have two classes of banks: those that can go through ordinary resolution processes and those which have to be maintained as a going concern because, to use the traditional phraseology, they are 'too big to fail' (TBTF). There has long been pressure to end TBTF (Stern and Feldman, 2004; Mayes et al., 2001) but until recently there has been little enthusiasm for seeing it through. Now there has been renewed interest, particularly in the UK (e.g. Tucker, 2010), where the Bank of England has sought 'going-concern resolution'. Now ideas for such resolution, labelled 'living wills' and 'funeral plans', are becoming accepted and feature in Financial Stability Board (FSB) recommendations (FSB, 2011a). New instruments for automatic recapitalization are being proposed (see Wall, 2009; AFME, 2010; Huertas, 2010) and, as in the case of CoCo bonds for the Lloyds Banking Group, have been implemented.[3] This chapter explores these ideas in some detail as part of the basis for advocating a return to the traditional model of deposit insurance, where it is a rarely used instrument that deals with the occasional small bank failure – clearly in a world where the moral hazard is not exploited.

There is a further aspect of guarantees revealed by the experience in Iceland: a bank or a group of banks may be 'too big to save' in the sense that the authorities do not have the resources to mount an orderly resolution (Mayes and Liuksila, 2004). Thus in the Icelandic case the borrowing power of the government was insufficient to recapitalize the banks that got into difficulty. Similarly the country could not afford to pay for all the deposits and transfer them to another provider while waiting to be repaid from the insolvency estate. The impact of this might not have mattered had it not been the case that the Icelandic banks were vigorously seeking deposits from overseas. Where these funds were raised through branches (in the European Union) the Icelandic authorities were still required to provide deposit insurance by European Union (EU) regulation (Iceland being a member of the EEA – European Economic Area – where EU law also applies).

Even though Iceland did not have the fiscal capacity to honour its obligations to foreign depositors, retail depositors have in the main been paid out in full by the authorities in the host countries, who have thereby succeeded to their claims against the insolvent banks. In order to try to ensure continuing confidence in the Icelandic banks after the failures and to enable repayment of foreign depositors, Iceland implemented depositor priority: depositors have first claim on the insolvency proceeds.[4]

The structure of the rest of the chapter is therefore as follows: section 14.2 considers the routes that are available for going-concern resolution, while section 14.3 considers what would need to change in the structure of the system to achieve it. Section 14.4 focuses on the key issue for depositors, how a resolution can be achieved with no material break in their access to their deposits. Section 14.5 expands the discussion to examine what problems cross-border banks pose for these developments and section 14.6 considers how countries can exit from the current special arrangements for deposit guarantees and near total insurance coverage. Section 14.7 sets out in light of this what a new framework for deposit insurance might look like.

14.2   ROUTES TO GOING-CONCERN RESOLUTION

The ideal outcome from the point of view of the authorities for resolving a troubled systemic bank is that the private sector recapitalizes it without the losses being absorbed by the taxpayer and that this process, while involving losses, does not lead to any loss of confidence in the financial system as a whole.[5] The current problem when a large bank runs out of capital, especially at a time of difficulty, generally is that the private sector cannot find – or is unwilling to find – the necessary funds, and governments are then faced with a choice over whether to step in and use taxpayers' money, or whether to let the bank fail and risk a serious threat to confidence and hence major contraction both in the financial system and the real economy.

The result in the present crisis has tended to be 'open bank assistance', that is, the government has provided capital for the bank and/or purchased distressed assets from the existing shareholders. Clearly this is only one example of going-concern resolution and, as in the Nordic crises, the existing shareholders may be written down to zero if the losses are sufficiently large that their capital has been exhausted. Going-concern resolution only requires that the parts of the business that are vital to financial stability continue operating uninterrupted, not that their ownership remains unchanged (Hüpkes, 2004b).

With a small bank it is relatively straightforward to achieve this ideal outcome, providing a bank is resolved early before losses mount, simply by applying the sorts of special resolution regime that exist in many countries. The regime, pioneered in the US, is perhaps most straightforwardly set out in the Banking Act 2009 in the UK. This was prepared, after extensive consultation and extensive review of other countries' schemes, to correct the serious difficulties the UK encountered in the present crisis. It is therefore something like current best practice. In such a regime there are three straightforward solutions for the treatment of small banks:

● The bank is placed in insolvency and the insured depositors are paid out through the deposit insurer, the insurer succeeding to the claims of the depositors.

- The deposits and other viable parts of the bank are transferred to another provider, with any unsaleable parts being left in the insolvency estate; the deposit insurer may have to contribute to any shortfall in financing and the authorities will select the acquirer on the basis of least cost to the insurer and the best chance of a viable future (all the normal conditions for registering a new bank would need to apply to the merged institution, including 'fit and proper persons' and so on).
- The parts of the bank that the authorities think can best be saved, in the sense of minimizing the loss to creditors, are placed in one or more bridge banks, run by the authorities, temporarily until they can be sold on to another provider.

The second of these is the normal choice, while a bridge bank is used if the authorities do not have enough time. The first is likely to apply only in the case of very small institutions. (Only a handful of the 400 or so banks that were resolved in the US in the period between the Lehman Brothers failure and November 2011 used either a direct pay-out or a bridge.[6]) Only if none of these three resolution techniques can be applied does the UK system offer the option of nationalization and a move from the ideal to taxpayer funding.

The problem of size comes when either the deposit insurance fund cannot afford to transfer the deposits or where the bank is so complicated that organizing the split into what must be continued in the interests of the stability of the system and what can be placed in the insolvency estate cannot be done in time. Some method has to be found to substitute private funds for public funds in these cases so that the bank can continue to function as a going concern.

Clearly simply raising the funds on the market is ruled out as that will already have been tried or contemplated, possibly even with a government guarantee. Indeed failure to raise such funds is normally the source of the failure of the bank. Similarly *ex post* capital-raising is not possible as the inability of the state to provide the bridging finance is the reason for the discussion. The choice therefore is between having some sort of private guarantee or insurance that can be drawn on, probably using foreign as well as domestic sources, or deriving the capital from the creditors.[7] The advantage of the creditor recapitalization is that the funds have already been paid and there is no need for an organization to have to pay out at a stage when markets are distressed. Furthermore there is always the danger that several banks have used the same insurer and if one or two large banks get into difficulty at the same time the insurer itself will fail (Rajan, 2009).

Creditor recapitalization can be effectively a debt-for-equity swap. It could be at two levels. A simple one would be to write down a set of junior creditors to the point that the bank returns to solvency. They would then be in the same position that they would in the event of insolvency, so they would not lose further by this action.[8] A second possibility is to write them down far enough that the bank becomes adequately recapitalized. In return for this further write-down the creditors would effectively become the equity holders of the recapitalized bank. The original shareholders would be written down to zero if the bank is insolvent.[9]

However such a scheme could also be applied even if shareholder capital had not reached zero but the bank had become undercapitalized. In this case junior debt could be turned into equity. There is some debate about whether this should be common equity or preference shares. The existing shareholders would have their holding diluted.

The key question is then what the trigger point should be and who would decide when the trigger should be pulled. The common assumption is that it should be the supervisory or regulatory authority which should decide (Brunnermeier et al., 2009). However, if it were a clearly objective measure then a bank could, for example, apply to the court for the trigger to be exercised rather in the same way that a commercial firm can make an application for bankruptcy under Chapter 11 in the US code. Since this is a capital injection it seems appropriate that the trigger should also be a capital ratio. Clearly this approach could be used more than once while there is sufficient debt available if the extent of the losses turns out to be underestimated.[10]

It would appear sensible to suggest that any such recapitalization should only be undertaken with debt which was sold with this option built in. It is already the case that subordinated debt holders can be written down in this manner in Denmark, and it was used in the case of Roskilde Bank in August 2008 when Danmarks Nationalbank intervened. Similarly the new CoCo bonds that have been issued by the Lloyds Banking Group have the contingency for conversion into equity written in.[11]

One of the key issues in making such a recapitalization work is that financial markets need to accept it. If it simply generates a series of close-out clauses and effectively excludes the bank from the payments system then clearly it will not work. The requirement at the heart of this discussion is that the resolution be performed in such a way that the bank remains a going concern. This worry that the resolution process may not permit the existing bank to continue has been raised in the context of the Norwegian legal framework (Mayes, 2009). The recapitalization needs to avoid generating any default. In other cases it may need to avoid generating a credit rating downgrade. If the authorities offer a guarantee for the recapitalized bank, this may be avoided.

The only country that has seriously contemplated using creditors to recapitalize the bank as part of the normal insolvency process is New Zealand (Harrison et al., 2007) and this is now being implemented.[12] Now the Basel Committee (2010) is considering the issue and has issued a discussion paper.

Hüpkes (2004b) pointed out that when a large bank gets into difficulty it is only certain parts or functions of the bank that need to be saved in order to promote continuing stability in the financial system as a whole. In addition to the normal deposit-taking activity described here, the bank may be of systemic importance elsewhere, perhaps as a market maker in some aspects of derivatives. However, tackling an institution in this way on a going-concern basis implies that it can readily be divided.

14.3   CHANGING THE STRUCTURE OF THE SYSTEM

In the present crisis, the initial response of the Bank of England (Tucker, 2009) to the problem of TBTF, or perhaps 'too complex or too interconnected to fail' (Knight, 2009), was that the organization should be required to restructure itself in such a way that this was no longer true. Stern and Feldman (2004) suggest a similar condition that no merger should be permitted in the banking industry unless the authorities can see how to resolve it in the case of a crisis. The Bank of England position was that the onus should be on the bank itself to explain how it can be restructured in some form of 'living will' (Tucker, 2010). The idea has been contested largely from the standpoint of practicality in the sense that one cannot be sure about whether the difficulties can be overcome until the particular nature of the crisis is clear. However, the idea that systems should become more robust with respect to the failure of a single institution has been widely considered (Brunnermeier et al., 2009).

One immediate concern for ease of resolution of a complex institution is the degree of separability of the various parts of the bank. With the holding company structure in the US, constituent banks are often separable. Insurance arms are often also free-standing but, where the bank runs an integrated operation, it may be very difficult to carve out parts even if they are not separately capitalized subsidiaries. The Hüpkes approach is therefore more like a set of rules for a traditional resolution, separating out those parts of the bank that must be kept operating from those that can go into the insolvency estate. If that approach can be applied and there are no close-out concerns, then the problem is much simpler (Hüpkes, 2009).

During 2011 the Financial Stability Board (FSB) has made considerable progress in setting out rules for the handling of what it labels SIFIs – systemically important financial institutions. Such institutions first of all need to have higher capitalization than other banks so that there is a bigger cushion that can be used in the event of problems and more time will be available to sort them out. Second, they must have in place recovery plans that enable them to return rapidly to satisfactory capitalization should such a problem strike. Last, they need to have resolution plans which set out how the authorities can resolve them in the event of failure, whether by breaking up, utilizing contingent capital or asset sales (FSB, 2011a).

14.4   NO MATERIAL BREAK IN ACCESS

A major lesson from the present crisis is that people are more inclined and much more able to run on a bank than was previously thought to be the case.[13] It is no longer true that there is a break between closure fairly early on Friday afternoon and opening on Monday morning during which period depositors cannot get at their accounts and so a resolution can be performed without inconveniencing them. Now Internet access and EFTPOS (electronic funds transfer at point of sale) makes it possible to access one's account at any time of day or night, and it is only a small proportion of customers who need to visit the bank personally in order to make a substantial withdrawal. However, closing a fairly substantial account would require a physical presence, even if the transaction is then electronic and not a pay-out in cash.

Traditional deposit protection focuses on removing the credit risk, but in the modern environment loss of liquidity could also have significant effects on people after only a few days (Kaufman, 2007). Hence people will run on the bank even if they only fear a problem of access. In the EU until recently they would have had every reason for such a run as the time allowed for a deposit pay-out was 90 days and even this could be renewed twice in the face of difficulty. Deposit insurers are now, therefore, trying to make sure that there is no material break in service should a bank fail. There is no accepted definition of what a material break is. In New Zealand operation is supposed to resume in the 'value day', and other countries aim to resolve the problem either overnight or over a weekend.

This has considerable implications for the nature of the resolution process for banks. Insured deposits need to be identifiable at the end of any day so that accounts can be divided into insured and uninsured portions (where necessary), any aggregation across accounts for a single holder performed, and so on. Similarly, the means of transferring deposits must be clearly established so that it can take place smoothly at the appointed time. This requires considerable prepositioning in the sense of the nature of bank computer systems. Small issues, such as whether if account numbers change payments into the previous number will still be picked up and rerouted without delay, all have to be addressed. Since these changes cannot be implemented just when the bank gets into difficulty, they have to be continuing characteristics of all banks' systems. The period of 2–3 months that the authorities hope they will have in preparing a resolution relate to establishing the problem, valuing the bank and finding suitable providers to take on the deposits and other parts of the bank. Hoping to complete due diligence in such a period is a tough task and almost certainly acquirers will be in for some surprises. If such smooth transitions cannot be made, the political attractiveness of open bank assistance or nationalization increases, with its associated moral hazard.

14.5 CROSS-BORDER CONCERNS

The systems of deposit insurance and the associated resolution and regulatory frameworks are national and are not well designed to handle financial institutions that run across borders, unless the component parts are effectively separate legal organizations that can operate on their own and can be resolved largely independently. Where foreign operations are small, the fact there are considerable difficulties in getting resolution regimes to work together can be coped with, albeit with various legal counterclaims after the event. However if the institutions are of significance in more than one country then the problems become serious. Each country needs to be able to manage the concerns for its domestic financial stability which stem from these organizations (Brunnermeier et al., 2009, set out the issues very clearly).

Deposit insurance is thus part of a wider concern. It is the problems with trying to organize a resolution that present the difficulty, rather than those of trying to coordinate the deposit insurance funds. While in the case of Fortis in October 2008 the Dutch and Belgian authorities did not agree on the best way forward, the fact that the Dutch authorities could step in and purchase the operations in their jurisdiction solved the crisis. They could manage this not simply because the Dutch operations were subsidiaries, but because they were distinct free-standing operations. ABN-AMRO, for example, which had been purchased by Fortis as part of a consortium purchase led by the Royal Bank of Scotland only the year before, had not been integrated into the rest of the group. Nationalization of course removed the need to use deposit insurance as the whole bank was acquired, but deposit insurance would not have been a problem in this regard as the insurance did not run across borders. It was ownership of the bank that ran across borders rather than bank operations.

The problem with the Icelandic banks was that it was the operations that ran across borders. The Icelandic banks, particularly Landsbanki through Icesave, were soliciting deposits from foreign countries, not to run matching lending activities in those countries but to finance their general operations. There was thus no self-sufficient operating entity that could readily be acquired even if this had been legally possible. In the case of Heritable Bank, a Landsbanki subsidiary, and Kaupthing, Singer & Friedlander's Edge business, both in the UK, however, the banking operations could be transferred to ING Direct because they were free-standing. As Internet banking operations they were somewhat easier to transfer and the deposit insurer (the Financial Services Compensation Scheme) could finance the transfer of insured deposits. The UK government decided that it would protect all deposits (i.e., those above the £50 000 coverage limit) to preserve financial stability, and hence there was no need to institute any complex splitting of accounts and to treat the various categories of depositors differently.

The EU is in a special position with deposit insurance because it wishes to encourage financial integration and hence allows branches of banks registered elsewhere in the EU or European Economic Area (EEA) to operate under the prudential supervision and deposit insurance of their home country, with the option of topping up to the level of the host country through the deposit insurer (Ayadi and Lastra, 2010). Other jurisdictions insist that all significant operations are locally incorporated and normally supervise branches as well as subsidiaries.[14] In the New Zealand case mentioned earlier, not only must all banks of systemic importance be locally incorporated and capitalized, but they must also be capable of operating on their own within the value day should the need arise (RBNZ, 2006).[15]

It is really the experience in Iceland that has shown the weakness of the EU system. The Icelandic banks were able to operate on a scale completely inconsistent with any possibility that their insurance fund could pay out in the event of a correlated shock: given the size and leverage of the three main banks, the chances were that a shock to any one of them would have brought the whole system into question. Furthermore the country was too small relative to the banks to be able to offer any other going-concern resolution to the three banks. What they were able to do was keep the domestic banking system in being by transferring domestic deposits and matching assets into new banks, and leaving foreign deposits and the remaining assets and liabilities in the insolvency estates. However in order to cover for the inability to deliver the insurance to foreign depositors that had been taken out, they instituted depositor preference. Thereby depositors ranked above other creditors in the resolution and the chances are that this will enable the depositors to be paid in full – eventually.[16] In the meantime the governments in the two countries most affected have paid out the retail depositors from their own funds and have succeeded to the claims of the insured depositors in the insolvency proceedings in Iceland.

In the circumstances this is a rather ingenious 'solution' and will confirm in retail depositors' minds that effectively all deposits are insured in a crisis. Iceland was also a little unusual in that large deposits formed about two-thirds of total deposits – in part perhaps because as a small country Iceland offered little other liquid domestic opportunity for such funds. The deposit guarantees and deposit preference therefore apply to these depositors as well. Indeed such an arrangement would be clearly necessary, otherwise the business sector might have come to a halt if all such deposits were caught up in the insolvency. The belief in who is likely to be rescued in these extreme circumstances is therefore likely to stretch widely.

The FSB (FSB, 2011b) has now listed 29 global-SIFIs (G-SIFIs) that are sufficiently important cross-border banks that special arrangements have to be put in place for their resolution and coordination of the actions of the various regulators and supervisory bodies involved (by the end of 2012). The aim is to ensure that no institution is then too big or too complex to handle.[17]

14.6   EXITING THE SPECIAL ARRANGEMENTS

Neither Australia nor New Zealand had deposit insurance in place at the start of the present crisis although there were active plans in Australia. As a result, when the crisis struck, much more extensive guarantees were required to instil the necessary confidence, with a guarantee in Australia and a $1 million dollar guarantee in New Zealand, both provided by the government, although this had to be paid for by the larger banks in New Zealand as was the case for deposits and wholesale funding over $1 million in Australia. The New Zealand scheme was temporary in character and needed to be changed if a longer-term scheme were required, whereas only some issues, such as coverage, need to be revisited in Australia before the crisis measures are unwound.

Exit clearly has to be timed carefully as it needs to occur when the crisis is past and no one thinks the banks are under threat, although it can be brought back in very rapidly. There is a clear problem for troubled banks. If deposit guarantees exist they can at least rely on those deposits and stand a better chance of raising other funding. Ending of the guarantees would simply result in the demise of the marginal banks just before the guarantee expired. The authorities therefore need to resolve any such marginal banks first. They either have to find sufficient capital that the ratings of the troubled banks rise and people believe them sound, or they will have to close in an orderly manner, which could involve a merger or acquisition of the relevant deposits by another provider.

In New Zealand this means that there are now very few institutions providing the riskier aspects of finance, such as secondary loans on property, as the finance company sector has largely disappeared through failure. Small institutions are singularly ill suited to this sector as many of the higher-risk items are quite large and problems in the property market tend to be correlated, hence ample capital cushions and diversification are required. In the US and some other jurisdictions, insurance premia for banks depend on the risk of the institution, so obtaining deposits becomes more expensive because of the higher premium that has to be paid. This may have relatively little impact on the cost of funds as such institutions have in any case to pay risk premia to depositors with such insurance (although it is sometimes argued that interest rates do not fully incorporate the risk or lenders would be frightened off).

There also has to be some degree of coordination in exit especially where banks or deposits can run across borders. As the crisis winds down, confidence only returns slowly, so people are likely to follow opportunities for greater safety, at least in the short run, even if there is a degree of interest cost to doing so. When there was little threat in Europe then countries could operate with differing levels of insurance and little arbitrage as a result. Now it is less clear, and in any case the agreement on minimum levels is EU-wide and any agreement to lower them would have to be EU-wide as well. Outside Europe there is no particular need for the smaller countries to wait for the large ones to act, and in Australasia, New Zealand has already ended its scheme (except for a transitional period for small non-bank institutions) before Australia concluded its review.

14.7   A NEW FRAMEWORK FOR DEPOSIT INSURANCE

Whereas most advanced countries could return to their previous arrangements once the crisis is over, the position is slightly different in Australia and New Zealand. Even with $25 000 coverage per bank a depositor could have $100 000 covered by placing the funds in four banks, which would cover the whole of the large majority of depositors completely. The big four banks in Australia already have what can be described as an implicit guarantee from the government. In those circumstances an insurance scheme would have a different meaning. The Australian guarantee would effectively apply to the New Zealand subsidiaries even though they might not be directly covered. Reputation risk would suggest that they could not let the subsidiaries fail while the parent tried to survive, and keeping the parent going through 'going-concern resolution' if the whole bank were in trouble would be likely to include the subsidiaries especially since their structure has a strong element of *ex ante* ring fencing.

In a sense therefore New Zealand is bound to be a free-rider on the Australian system on the one hand, or a sufferer from Australian problems on the other. Currently the New Zealand regulatory and resolution system is rather different from that in Australia. While the New Zealand system has been geared towards avoiding providing any public finance for the financial system in the event of failure, it is not so clear what would be done in Australia, with the likelihood being that some such finance would be provided. This provides a prima facie basis for difficulty as the resolution of subsidiaries in New Zealand would be based on creditor recapitalization while the Australian taxpayer would be keeping the parent in business.

If the large banks do not need deposit insurance because they will be 'bailed out' in a different manner, either through contingent capital or other forms of government intervention, then an insurance scheme would only apply to banks which are small enough that they could be allowed to enter insolvency or undergo transfers of deposits and other assets and liabilities through the resolution process. Both classes of bank need to pay for their protection in an equitable manner so that one class is not disadvantaged compared to the other. Where the contingent capital is provided through the market this is automatic in the case of large banks,[18] but if this comes through some form of government guarantee and requirement to hold more capital, the correct pricing is less obvious. The government guarantee ensures that creditors will not lose in the case of a failure – which is certainly a prima facie moral hazard. That will also entail that large banks with the same risk in their business as a smaller bank will nevertheless have a lower cost of finance. In sum this may be equitable, but the system is unlikely to have been designed with this in mind.

If only the small banks are in the insurance system then there is a danger of underfunding of deposit insurance unless premia are to be quite high, and the likelihood is that for any non-trivial failure the taxpayer will be called upon. In many funds banks do not really pay a premium but have to build the fund up to a level that is expected to provide enough cover. Contributions will be in proportion to the deposits insured and there will be a contributions holiday, or at least contributions will be lowered to the level where they simply meet the deposit insurer's ongoing costs, once the fund reaches the target level. In the US, despite the implicit guarantee for the largest banks, nevertheless all banks contribute to the scheme and this ensures its viability even through the difficulties of the present crisis.

If the large banks were excluded from a deposit insurance scheme in Australia the effect would be considerable. (Kiwibank would presumably be excluded in New Zealand as well, because the government as owner would be expected to recapitalize the bank in the event of difficulty as that is likely to be the least cost route.) Interestingly enough the guarantee implemented in the crisis in New Zealand was free for the small banks, but the large banks had to pay for it on a basis that roughly covered the expected risk.

In this new world the attempt to reduce moral hazard by 'constructive' ambiguity largely disappears. It is clear what will happen to banks of all sizes if they face an idiosyncratic failure. The smaller banks will go through the normal resolution regime, shareholders will be wiped out, insured depositors made whole with the insurance fund succeeding to their claims, and creditors will eventually be paid out according to the normal insolvency process. Systemic banks on the other hand will be allowed to continue their key operations, using either contingent capital or state support. If the threat to the system is general then the reaction becomes more difficult to judge.

Some countries issued blanket guarantees, some increased deposit insurance coverage markedly, while others simply bailed out the troubled banks. If there is no indication as to which of these routes will be followed next time then the ambiguity returns, but the unfortunate experience of Ireland in finding its guarantee is becoming cripplingly expensive suggests that countries may be more cautious next time (see Laeven and Valencia, 2008, for a general assessment).[19] It even applies to individual institutions as the chances are that the scale of a crisis may be misestimated. When the first small banks become insolvent the insurance fund can cope and ordinary procedures can be followed. At some point as the numbers mount, the authorities will become worried that there will be a systemic problem and more extensive guarantees will be issued. While shortly before the crisis it may be possible to rank banks in terms of when they might fail this would not apply to any longer-term guarantees that are arranged.

The Swiss authorities (Hüpkes, 2004a) are among the only ones to recognize that the structure of their banking system – with two very large banks, Credit Suisse and UBS – might mean that the deposit insurer was unable to cope with the failure. Thus while the system implemented in Switzerland in 2004 provided for the writing-down of claims in the manner described above and advocated in Mayes et al. (2001), an absolute limit of CHF4 billion was placed on the pay-out.[20] If this limit were reached then a haircut would be placed on all insured deposits to limit the pay-out to the maximum.

There is no reason why the Icelandic problems should recur in the EU if the countries were to set up a more Europe-wide system so as to eliminate the problem of large banks backed by small countries with limited ability to finance deposit insurance or deposit guarantee schemes. However, progress in this direction is slow. While more harmonization in the national systems is suggested (European Commission, 2010),[21] the idea that there should be EU-level insurance matched with EU-level supervision, still less EU-level regulation, has received very little support. The Federal Deposit Insurance Corporation (FDIC) was set up in 1935 after the finding in the US that the previous state deposit insurance schemes could not cope. Even if there were some sort of reinsurance scheme, so that smaller schemes could lay off the risk across the rest of the area, the system might be viable. However, it would not solve the issue that a country could not guarantee its own financial stability as branches of foreign banks within its territory would still be regulated, supervised and resolved by the home country whose interests might be very different.

The EU scheme (European Commission, 2010) is based on the idea that the member countries would cooperate but that there would be a funding cushion to handle large problems. There is no suggestion as yet that insurance coverage should return to pre-crisis levels, so the costs of important failures could be considerable. By offering a state back-up to deposit insurance funds in these circumstances the EU is building in an incentive to take greater risks – given the much more comprehensive capital and liquidity buffers that are being planned for the EU's implementation of 'Basel 3'.

The problem with a non-credible insurance scheme in a small country is that although it will work well in normal times with the occasional failure of a small bank, it is not going to be believable with much smaller banking problems than would be the case in a larger country. Thus the point at which state intervention and guarantees are required occurs much earlier. Ironically this may increase the moral hazard as it removes the prospective resolution from a technical set of rules to be followed by the appropriate agency, whose actions can be audited after the event for the compliance with the rule. It also increases the chance that the problem will be allowed to mount and action will be delayed when the authorities realize their systems will not be able to cope.

The only difference to this outcome would occur if recapitalization methods are required that automatically write down the existing shareholders and implement a debt-for-equity swap for sufficient of the bondholders that the bank becomes healthy again. The interesting feature of such recapitalizations for cross-border banks (indeed like any other bank) is that the bondholders will not necessarily be domestic and hence the recapitalization is likely to run across borders even without any attempt by governments to agree some burden sharing. A future system would therefore seem to need at least seven ingredients:

- It would need to be explicit and limited in coverage so that there is a believable disincentive to risk-taking.
- It would need to be funded up front and the size of the funds and any back-up arrangement through the state would need to be such that it could credibly cover the risks.
- It would relate to idiosyncratic failures in individual banks and not the looming failure of the whole banking system.
- It would cover a wide range of deposit takers.
- It would be accompanied by a special resolution regime that enabled speedy and smooth resolution of banks before losses mounted too far, using tools such as those set out in the UK Banking Act 2009.
- It would have a treatment of contingent capital such that going-concern resolutions were possible for larger banks without using government funds.
- It would need careful prepositioning so that depositors do not have any material break in access to their funds.

And it would be implemented as soon as the present crisis appeared to have passed and all existing troubled banks had been addressed.

NOTES

1. Risk-weighted contributions are rare and as a result there is an implicit subsidy from the less to the more risky banks, which might in itself encourage risk-taking and act as a moral hazard.
2. This is set out in the first of the Core Principles for best practice in deposit insurance developed jointly by the International Association of Deposit Insurers (IADI) and the Bank for International Settlements (BIS).
3. The conversion of these bonds is triggered when Tier 1 capital falls below 5 per cent.
4. The resolution of the three main Icelandic banks is of interest in that the authorities swept up domestic deposits, domestic loans and sufficient government recapitalization in new banks in order to keep the domestic financial system operating, while leaving the foreign loans and other creditors including foreign depositors to be dealt with through the insolvency.
5. Normally using the priority ranking for insolvency, so that the shareholders bear the first loss, then the junior unsecured creditors, then the senior creditors and so on.
6. There are other crucial aspects to such resolutions that do not lie at the heart of the present discussion but must be borne in mind. The most important of these is that deposits have to be transferred to a new provider as a working system. It may be that all the information can be transferred from the failing bank's computer system to that of the acquirer and that the depositors can obtain access to their accounts, but often it is not possible to dispense with either the failing bank's systems or many of its physical branches. This may mean that the residual bank has to run services for the transferred part of the bank until a final organization of such services can be achieved.
7. See Squam Lake Working Group (2009) and Wall (2009) for a recent exposition of the options.
8. This is by no means a new issue: Aghion et al. (1992) suggest it as the normal way to handle insolvency and Mayes et al. (2001) explore it as one of a number of ways to effect a bank resolution without involving public funds.
9. See Harrison et al. (2007) for a discussion of how this might be applied. Huertas (2010) points out that existing shareholders do not necessarily need to be written down – indeed this may be impossible without closing the bank in some jurisdictions. Their shares can be diluted to trivial proportions by the issue of new shares to the new owners providing the capital from the debt for equity swap.
10. Mayes et al. (2001) assume that this form of recapitalization would be a routine option, but others argue that it should only be used if financial stability is threatened (Squam Lake Working Group, 2009).
11. Tier 1 capital falls below 5 per cent.
12. This idea of Bank Creditor Recapitalization is now relabelled 'Open Bank Resolution' and the provisional detail of its implementation is set out in Hoskin and Woolford (2011).
13. Pictures of the queues outside Northern Rock in the UK are frequently shown in the media.
14. The EU also seeks to apply universality in resolution so that there is a single set of proceedings rather than the 'territoriality' applied in the US, which separates the proceedings in each jurisdiction.
15. New Zealand and Australia are heavily economically and financially integrated, in many respects more so than occurs in the EU.
16. EU regulation requires that domestic and foreign depositors are treated equally (unlike the domestic depositor preference in Australia).
17. The first failure of a G-SIFI, Dexia, occurred in October 2011, just before the last was published, but it was fortunately readily divisible into parts along national lines, although public funds were used by the Belgian government in purchasing the banking operations in Belgium.
18. Although we have seen persistent mispricing of risk in the run-up to the present crisis.
19. Guarantees proved relatively inexpensive in the Nordic crisis and were effective in re-establishing confidence in the banks, an example that was widely cited (Ingves and Hoelscher, 2005).
20. Since raised to CHF6 billion.
21. The European Commission proposal suggests that the idea of funds at a European level could be pursued in 2014. However, in the meantime the main purpose of the proposal is to suggest that each EU country should have to set up resolution funds that would be available in the event of a major failure. The implication is that such funds would involve government money and hence the full moral hazard would be built into the design of the system.

REFERENCES

Aghion, P., O. Hart and J. Moore (1992), 'The economics of bankruptcy reform', *Journal of Law, Economics and Organization*, **8**, 523–546.

Association for Financial Markets in Europe (AFME) (2010), *Prevention and Cure: Securing Financial Stability After the Crisis*, Annex 2 'Contingent Capital and Bail In', http://www.afme.eu/document.aspx?id=4360.

Ayadi, R. and R. Lastra (2010), 'Proposals for reforming deposit guarantee schemes in Europe', *Journal of Banking Regulation*, **11**(3), 210–222.

Basel Committee on Banking Supervision (2010), 'Proposal to ensure the loss absorbency of regulatory capital at the point of non-viability', Basel: BIS, August.

Brunnermeier, M., A. Crockett, C. Goodhart, A. Persaud and H.S. Shin (2009), *The Fundamental Principles of Financial Regulation*, 11th Geneva Papers on the World Economy, http://voxeu.org/index.Php?q=node/2796.

Demyanyk, Y. and O. van Hemert (2008), 'Understanding the subprime mortgage crisis', mimeo, Federal Reserve Bank of St Louis.

European Commission (2010), 'Bank Resolution Funds, Brussels', 26 May 2010, COM(2010) 254 final, http://ec.europa.eu/internal_market/bank/docs/crisis-management/funds/com2010_254_en.pdf.

Financial Stability Board (2011a), 'Key attributes: effective resolution regimes for financial institutions', October, available at http://www.financialstabilityboard.org/publications/r_111104cc.pdf.

Financial Stability Board (2011b), 'Policy measures to address systemically important financial institutions', 4 November, available at http://www.financialstabilityboard.org/publications/r_111104bb.pdf.

Garcia, G.G. (2010), 'Ignoring the red flags', paper presented at the symposium on Reforming the Governance of the Financial Sector, University of Auckland, September.

Harrison, I.G., A. Anderson and J. Twaddle (2007), 'Pre-positioning for effective resolution of bank failures', *Journal of Financial Stability*, **3**(4), 324–341.

Hoskin, K. and I. Woolford (2011), 'A primer on open bank resolution', *Reserve Bank of New Zealand Bulletin*, **74**(3), 5–10.

Huertas, T. (2010), 'The road to better resolution: from bail-out to bail-in', Bank of Slovenia conference, The Euro and the Financial Crisis, 6 September.

Hüpkes, E. (2004a), 'Learning lessons and implementing a new approach to bank insolvency resolution in Switzerland', in D. Mayes and A. Liuksila (eds), *Who Pays for Bank Insolvency?* Basingstoke: Palgrave-Macmillan.

Hüpkes, E. (2004b), 'Protect functions, not institutions', *Financial Regulator*, **9**, 43–49.

Hüpkes, E. (2009), 'Resolving crises in global financial institutions: the functional approach revisited', in J.R. LaBrosse, R. Olivares-Caminal and D. Singh (eds), *Financial Crisis Management and Bank Resolution*, London: Informa.

IADI (2010), 'Discussion paper on cross border deposit insurance issues raised by the global financial crisis', Basel: BIS.

IADI-BIS (2008), 'Core principles for effective deposit insurance systems', Basel: BIS, http://www.iadi.org/NewsRelease/JWGDI%20CBRG%20core%20principles_18_June.pdf.

Ingves, S. and D. Hoelscher (2005), 'The resolution of systemic banking crises', in D. Evanoff and G. Kaufman (eds), *Systemic Financial Crises: Resolving Large Bank Insolvencies*, Singapore: World Scientific.

Kaufman, G. (2007), 'Using efficient bank insolvency resolution to solve the deposit insurance problem', in A. Campbell, R. Labrosse, D. Mayes and D. Singh (eds), *Deposit Insurance*, Basingstoke: Palgrave-Macmillan.

Knight, M.D. (2009), 'Mitigating moral hazard in dealing with problem financial institutions: too big to fail? Too complex to fail? Too interconnected to fail?', in J.R. LaBrosse, R. Olivares-Caminal and D. Singh (eds), *Financial Crisis Management and Bank Resolution*, London: Informa.

LaBrosse, R. and D.G. Mayes (2007), 'Promoting financial stability through effective depositor protection: the case for explicit limited deposit insurance', in A. Campbell, R. LaBrosse, D. Mayes and D. Singh (eds), *Deposit Insurance*, Basingstoke: Palgrave-Macmillan.

Laeven, L. and F. Valencia (2008), 'The use of blanket guarantees in banking crises', IMF Working Paper 08/250.

Mayes, D.G. (2009), 'Banking crisis resolution policy: lessons from recent experience – which elements are needed for robust and efficient crisis resolution?', CESifo Working Paper 2823, October.

Mayes, D.G., L. Halme and A. Liuksila (2001), *Improving Banking Supervision*, Basingstoke: Palgrave.

Mayes, D. and A. Liuksila (2004), *Who Pays for Bank Insolvency?* Basingstoke: Palgrave-Macmillan

Mayes, D.G. and G.E. Wood (2008), 'Lessons from the Northern Rock episode', *Economic Internationale*, **114**, 5–27.

Rajan, R. (2009), 'Cycle-proof regulation', *The Economist*, 8 April, http://www.economist.com/business finance/displayStory.cfm?story_id=13446173>.

Reserve Bank of New Zealand (RBNZ) (2006), 'Outsourcing policy', Financial Stability Department Document BS11.
Squam Lake Working Group (2009), 'An expedited resolution mechanism for distressed financial firms: regulatory hybrid securities', Council on Foreign Relations Press, April, http://www.cfr.org/content/ publications/ attachments/Squam_Lake_Working_Paper3.pdf.
Stern, G. and R. Feldman (2004), *Too Big to Fail*, Washington, DC: Brookings Institution.
Tucker, P. (2009), 'The debate on financial system resilience: macroprudential instruments', Barclays Annual Lecture, London.
Tucker, P. (2010), *Resolution of Large and Complex Financial Institutions: The Big Issues*, available at http:// www.bankofengland.co.uk/publications/speeches/ 2010/speech431.pdf.
Wall, L.D. (2009), 'Prudential discipline for financial firms: micro, macro, and market regimes', paper presented at the Conference on Global Financial Crisis: Financial Sector Reform and Regulation, ADBI, Tokyo, 21–23 July.

15 The governance of 'too big to fail' banks
Andy Mullineux

15.1 INTRODUCTION

The 2007–2009 global financial crisis (GFC) revealed significant inadequacies in the corporate governance and the regulation and supervision of banks. Large, complex or interconnected banks, with the notable exception of Lehman Brothers in October 2008, were bailed out and/or merged with other banks because of the systemic risks they posed. They were judged too important to be allowed to fail, or 'too big to fail' (TBTF).

Many banks, including large ones (e.g., Merrill Lynch, an investment bank, and Washington Mutual, WaMu, a mortgage lender) were merged with others (Bank of America in these cases) to form even bigger banks, despite a regulatory rule that no bank in the US should have more than a 10 per cent market share. Concentration in banking in the US and elsewhere has thus increased. Bank bondholders (including providers of Tier 2 and some Tier 1 capital – see www.bis.org) have generally been protected (except in cases such as Lehman's and WaMu) and, post-Lehman, bank bond issuance has been guaranteed by governments in the EU and the US, and more widely.

Meanwhile, the Federal Deposit Insurance Corporation (FDIC) in the US has been able to allow numerous (non-TBTF) banks to fail under its bank resolution arrangements, with the protected deposits transferred to other banks promptly. In addition, the US deposit insurance (DI) cover was raised from US$100 000 to US$250 000 to reassure depositors. DI was effectively extended by the Fed (the Federal Reserve System, the US central banking system) to Money Market Mutual Funds (MMMFs) after a couple of large MMMFs 'broke the buck' when the value of their assets fell below that of their liabilities. Specialist investment banks merged with deposit-taking banks to gain access to the Fed's lender of last resort (LOLR) and other liquidity facilities, which were dramatically expanded using the Troubled Assets Relief Program (TARP) and other special asset purchase and loan schemes such as the Troubled Assets Loan Fund (TALF). This further increased the complexity of investment banks and marked an even greater departure from the 1933 Glass–Steagall Act, which had required a separation of investment banking from (deposit-taking) commercial banking.

The European Central Bank (ECB) concentrated primarily on providing liquidity at short- and medium-term maturities, but did buy Covered Bonds which underpinned German and Danish mortgage markets. The Bank of England (BoE) provided short-term liquidity, and engaged in quantitative easing, buying new issues of government bonds, but unlike the Fed did not engage extensively in credit easing, buying asset-backed securities, including mortgage-backed securities, from the US government-sponsored enterprises (GSEs) Fannie Mae and Freddie Mac.

15.2 STRUCTURAL REFORM TO MAKE BANKS SAFE

One possible solution to the TBTF problem might be to break up big and complex banks as part of a wide-ranging structural reform. One of the most fundamental and long-standing proposals is to prevent banks from using retail deposits to make loans; see Kay (2009) on 'narrow banking' and Kotlikoff (2010) on 'limited purpose banking'. Both see deposit-taking 'banks' operating a range of mutual funds, the safest of which effectively have 100 per cent liquid reserves, or 'narrow banking' as originally conceived by Henry Simons, Irving Fisher and Milton Friedman *inter alia* (Kotlikoff, 2010). This would dramatically reduce leveraging and lending, but a less dramatic, narrower banking solution could be sought.

Other structural solutions include the Volcker Rule (discussed below), an updated Glass–Steagall Act (discussed below) separating retail or commercial banking from investment banking, and simply breaking up big banks so that they do not have market shares in excess of, say, 10 per cent (by loan or other assets, or deposits). The aim would be to eliminate TBTF banks and increase competition, thus simplifying the regulation problem; but would such reform reduce banking cost efficiency?

Andrew Haldane has argued in speeches (www.bankofengland.co.uk) that the accumulated evidence on economies of scale and scope suggests that they are not sufficiently substantial to justify large and complex banks. A counter-argument is that 'universal banks', which combine commercial and investment banking, are more diversified and better able to weather business fluctuations.

The Glass–Steagall Act was passed in 1933 following a review of the causes of the financial crisis that generated the Great Depression. It was repealed in 1999 by the Gramm–Leach–Bliley Financial Services Modernization Act, and since then US banks have taken the opportunity to diversify their businesses. In the UK, diversification followed the 'Big Bang' financial reforms in 1986. As lessons were drawn from the GFC, the question of whether investment and commercial banking should again be separated, or whether some other structural reform was appropriate, was raised. One proposal was the Volcker Rule which was proposed by the G30 Report (2009) following the deliberations of a working group chaired by Paul Volcker, a former Chairman of the Fed. It recommended that deposit-insured banks, and possibly also specialist investment banks, should cease 'proprietary trading' on their own account in order to eliminate conflicts of interest with purchasers of securities they design and sell. It effectively aimed to separate 'banking' from hedge fund (HF) and private equity funds (PEF) activity.

'Prop trading' did not cause the crisis, but the interaction between banks (deposit-taking and investment), HFs and PEFs did create a 'shadow banking system' that borrowed short to lend long, and both HFs and PEFs participated in the increased leveraging and added to the demand for bank funding and collateralized debt obligations (CDOs) that lay at the heart of the crisis (Tett, 2009). The shadow banking system contracted dramatically following the failure of Lehman Brothers. Further, in April 2010, a US regulator, the Securities and Exchange Commission (SEC), alleged that Goldman Sachs' dealings with John Paulson's HF involved a conflict of interest with the purchases of the CDOs issued. This demonstrated that HFs were not mere 'innocent bystanders' after all, and that the 'prop desks' of investment banks were essentially internal HFs and

PEFs. As a result, conflicts of interest abounded (Augar, 2006, 2009). Further, HFs were significant holders of CDOs in the run-up to the GFC.

HF and PEF activity grew rapidly in the run-up to the GFC and then contracted sharply, especially in 2008, but assets under management in April 2010 were only 2 per cent below their October 2007 peak, having reached their post-crisis nadir in early 2009. It seemed prudent to regulate them more tightly; for the nature of crises may be similar, but the causes commonly differ (Reinhart and Rogoff, 2009). The EU agreed to tighten regulations on HFs and PFs in May 2010 and the US has also been considering tougher regulation involving more disclosure. The US has already tightened the regulation of MMMFs, crucial suppliers of funds to the shadow banking system. MMMFs had got into difficulties by investing increasingly in riskier assets in an attempt to raise returns and attract investors.

15.3 POST-GFC PROGRESS WITH REGULATORY AND STRUCTURAL REFORM IN THE UK AND THE US

The US passed the Dodd–Frank Wall Street Reform and Consumer Protection Act in July 2010. It contains a weakened version of the Volcker Rule and introduced a consumer protection agency, which is to be a semi-autonomous division of the Federal Reserve System, whose responsibility for the safety and soundness of the banking system is to be enhanced. Many of the regulatory details were to be decided by the various US regulatory agencies, which were not fundamentally rationalized. No fundamental restructuring of the banking industry beyond the Volcker Rule was required and so there was no return to the Glass–Steagall Act separation of investment and commercial banking. Large bonuses, particularly in investment banking, reappeared on Wall Street in 2009 as the banks quickly repaid government stakes in them in order to escape the attention of the government-appointed regulator of banking remuneration.

In contrast, the UK's Financial Services Authority (FSA), the regulator of investment and commercial banks and the wider financial sector, has issued a bank remuneration code designed to curb the incentivization of risk-taking through bonuses that are essentially guaranteed regardless of performance. In August 2010, it began to consult on the revisions to the code which are required by the EU's updated Capital Requirements Directive (CRD 3) and the UK's Financial Services Act 2010. In addition, HM Treasury (the UK finance ministry) began consulting in July 2010 on a restructuring of UK financial regulation (CM7874, 2010). It is proposed that the Bank of England, the central bank, takes over the prudential regulation of banks, alongside enhanced responsibility for the stability of the financial system, from the FSA. A new Consumer Protection and Markets Authority would be created to take over the regulation of markets and consumer protection from the FSA; and a separate body had already been established in 2010, the Consumer Financial Education Board (CFEB), to take over the FSA's role in raising consumer financial capability.

Thus, both the UK and the US aim to enhance the protection of retail consumers of financial services and products and to give a greater role to the central bank in regard to promoting financial stability. The lender of last resort has an incentive to protect the taxpayer against abuse of the liquidity insurance it provides, and so it is appropriate for the central bank (and any deposit insurance fund) to be involved in prudential regulation and supervision.

There remains a case, however, for separating retail consumer product and service regulation from 'microprudential' regulation, given that retail financial services are essentially a utility and TBTF banks control a large share of the market. This is particularly the case in the UK, but less so in the US so long as the '10 per cent rule' relating to bank deposit concentration is enforced there. In the run-up to the GFC the Fed and the FSA seemed to find it difficult to juggle their prudential supervision and consumer protection roles and both were criticized: the Fed for paying too little attention to its consumer protection role, and the FSA for paying too much attention to consumer protection at the expense of its prudential supervision role.

It seems possible that more substantial structural reform will emerge in the UK from the deliberations of the Independent Commission on Banking (ICB) set up by the new coalition government in June 2010 and due to report in September 2011. It is to be chaired by Sir John Vickers, former head of the Office of Fair Trading (OFT), the UK competition (antitrust) authority that currently also has responsibility for regulating consumer credit under the Consumer Credit Act 2006. Given the significantly more highly concentrated nature of UK banking (compared to the US), and the substantial increase in concentration that followed the mergers induced by the credit crunch in the UK, this is welcome, although it stops short of a full Competition Commission review of the banking industry.

If, as seems likely, shareholder-owned banks are to be allowed to continue to operate, then following the Commission's review and consequent restructuring, a separate retail banking (and insurance) utility regulator should be established; given that access to finance is just as much a 'citizen's right' in a developed economy as access to electricity and water supplies and other utilities. The retail banking (and insurance) regulator should also take over the regulation of consumer credit from the OFT.

15.4   THE CORPORATE GOVERNANCE OF SHAREHOLDER-OWNED, DEPOSIT-TAKING BANKS

Mutual ownership has a long tradition in banking, and it is a good model for delivering retail banking to households and small and medium-sized enterprises (SMEs) and assuring widespread access to finance (BSA, 2009). Local or state government and post office banks also play a significant role in many countries, such as Germany (Mullineux and Terberger, 2006). Shareholder-owned deposit-taking banks require special treatment because shareholders (increasingly including management) have interests that differ from those of depositors. The desire to maximize 'shareholder value' potentially leads to short-termism and risk-seeking behaviour. Bank depositors in contrast are risk-averse, for otherwise they would have instead bought bank shares (Mullineux, 2006).

The GFC made clear that, to prevent bank runs, DI needs to be comprehensive and access to deposits maintained. This implies that, as in the US, DI should be pre-funded (with risk-related premiums) as a means of 'taxing' risk-taking (Merton, 1977). If it is not pre-funded, there is no *ex ante* tax, only the threat of post-crisis levies. But how large should the DI funds be? The existing funds, even in the US, are clearly not big enough to protect depositors of TBTF banks, who have instead been revealed to enjoy insurance from taxpayers well above that provided to smaller banks through DI schemes.

How then can the TBTF banks be made to pay for the implicit taxpayer insurance they enjoy? Free implicit insurance gives TBTF banks the competitive advantage of cheaper funding as a result of higher credit ratings. It also creates a major moral hazard problem, leading banks into higher-risk strategies because they expect to be bailed out if bad outcomes result. This has been made abundantly clear by the bailouts during the GFC and made worse, along with the antitrust issues, by the resulting increase in concentration in banking. Hence, the TBTF problem has been worsened by the GFC and responses to it.

An improvement in the corporate governance of banks requires assigning special roles to independent directors (non-executive directors, NEDs), and possibly also auditors of banks, and greater institutional shareholder (Insts) 'engagement' (Walker, 2009). The bank board should also take responsibility for internal risk management.

The appropriate division of labour between NEDs and Insts is unclear and so is whether they can deliver remuneration restraint in banking. In the UK, the revised (in 2010) Corporate Governance Code and the new Stewardship Code (see Financial Reporting Council, FRC, http://www.frc.org.uk) attempt to resolve such issues in the case of banks and other companies. In addition, the Financial Services Authority (FSA) has laid down rules aimed at preventing remuneration packages from encouraging short-term risk-seeking. The best that can be hoped for is that 'clawbacks' of bonuses are introduced, more incentive-compatible remuneration packages are developed and introduced, and internal risk controls are improved.

The interests of retail depositors and other consumers of banking products and services also need to be protected. The high pre-crisis profitability of TBTF banks, and the quick return to bumper fees from underwriting and banking profits in investment banking after the crisis, along with widening interest rate spreads between lending and borrowing rates in retail and commercial banking, point to serious antitrust issues. A far-reaching competition authority review in the UK, and the rest of the EU and the US, is thus required. Recall, however, that the US has a rule preventing individual banks taking more than 10 per cent of US deposits, and note that the much more concentrated Australian and Canadian systems had a 'good crisis'. Were they better regulated, or just lucky? Both countries benefited from the global commodity boom in the last decade, it should be noted, but both have also undertaken substantial banking sector reforms in the last decade or so.

One possible solution to the corporate governance problem is to legislate to give banks a legal 'fiduciary duty' to depositors on a par with, or ahead of, that to shareholders (and other creditors), as proposed by Macey and O'Hara (2003). Another is to reduce or eliminate the limited liability of bank shareholders. Alternatively, all deposit-taking banks could become mutuals and be regulated accordingly, thereby resolving the conflict between shareholder and depositor interests and reducing the risk exposure of taxpayers. Such a solution to the fundamental corporate governance problem of shareholder-owned banks, however, seems even more unlikely than the fundamental restructuring of banking systems required to eliminate other conflicts of interest, and so we turn to the regulation of TBTF banks.

15.5   REGULATING TBTF BANKS

The approach of the US Federal Deposit Insurance Corporation (FDIC) to regulating non-TBTF banks, based on funded DI with risk-related premiums paid by banks and a prompt resolution regime for failing banks, works well. It allows numerous weak banks to be closed without inconveniencing depositors, thereby containing the moral hazard problem and eliminating bank runs. In contrast, not only depositors but also the bond-holders of TBTF banks (*pace* Lehman) were protected during the GFC; and so were the shareholders of bailed-out banks to a considerable extent.

Can a similar funded DI scheme, with risk-related premiums as in the US, be established for TBTF banks in Europe alongside a special resolution regime involving 'living wills', and is there a need for a European-level deposit insurance fund and/or a European-level bank resolution fund? The aim should be to devise a system where big banks can be allowed to fail and bondholders and shareholders are not underwritten by taxpayers. This would enhance the incentive of bondholders and shareholders to monitor bank management. It requires banks to have a pre-agreed plan (a 'living will') determining how they would be broken into parts, with perhaps some parts saved or sold and other parts closed, when a crisis occurs. For many banks, the 'living wills' would have to be agreed with regulators in more than one country, making international cooperation essential, particularly in Europe.

The advantage of a funded deposit insurance scheme with risk-related premiums is that funds are available to restructure failing TBTF banks, risk-taking is taxed, and the banks as a group need hold less in-house insurance (i.e., capital and liquid reserves). But, what would the fund be used for between crises, and can TBTF banks really be successfully restructured during crises? An alternative, or additional, option is to rely on enhanced capital and liquidity requirements for TBTF banks such as the July 2010 revised Basel III proposals (www.bis.org). But how much capital and liquidity is required to assure systemic stability without dramatically curbing lending (IIF, 2010)?

The eurozone crisis that erupted in April 2010 highlights another problem. European banks holding bonds issued by Greece, in particular, but also Spain (downgraded in late May) and Portugal clearly risk losses on their bond holdings. The consequences of this crisis are potentially much larger, however. Should any government including the USA be regarded as risk free? If not, the bonds that they issue should not have zero risk weightings under the proposed Basel III capital adequacy requirements. Instead, capital must be held against them. Further short-term papers issued by governments that are required to be held as part of liquidity ratios are not riskless either. Hence banks may need to hold more of the liquid reserves in cash, rather than Treasury bills. The increased capital and cash reserve holding will further reduce the banks' lending capacity, which has already been curbed dramatically by the collapse of securitization and the need to rely less on wholesale funding.

The Basel Committee is also working on the 'procyclicality issue' – the tendency of risk-related capital adequacy requirements and provisions against losses to rise in slumps and fall in booms – by proposing that capital and liquidity ratios vary over the 'cycle' and provisioning is forward-looking, or 'dynamic'. Spain was praised for its dynamic provisioning regime, but has now recognized that it was not tough enough on its savings banks, which had excessive exposure to property and construction markets. Further, prevailing accounting standards are creating an obstacle to widespread adoption of forward-looking provisioning due to concerns that the banks will simply use provisioning to smooth reported profits.

A pre-funded DI arrangement for TBTF banks seems unlikely to be agreed by all G20 countries, making it difficult for some to go it alone because it would put domestic banks at a competitive disadvantage. A 'second-best' solution is to require banks, like polluters, to pay for cleaning up the mess they create. US President Obama's proposed special levy on banks for 'as long as it takes' to recoup the costs of the crisis induced by the banks aims to make the 'polluters' pay and could potentially reduce moral hazard, because future miscreants would expect penalties *ex post*. Further, if capital ratios and special taxes are high enough on TBTF banks, then they may perhaps choose to downsize and to separate off, or sell, activities with higher capital requirements and thereby downscale and simplify their structures. The UK coalition government's budget in June 2010 introduced a levy on large banks to force them to contribute to the recovery from the crisis they helped cause.

A post-bailout windfall tax on banks, levied in early 2010 in the UK and France, seemed justified (and popular) because banks were operating with reduced competition, and benefiting from bumper fees from underwriting and broking increased government (and corporate) bond issuance to fund the bank bailouts and curb the 'Great Recession' in 2009. The focusing of the windfall taxes on investment banking was probably also correct, but populism dictated that employee bonuses, rather than bank profits, were taxed in the UK.

15.6   WHAT ELSE SHOULD BE DONE?

There is growing evidence of misreporting, as well as fraud. Misreporting of loan losses at Northern Rock was prosecuted by the Financial Services Authority (FSA) in July 2010, and the use of a Repo 105 accounting loophole by Lehman Brothers was identified in April 2010 by the Valukas (US Court Examiner) Report. Both pointed to continuing shortcomings in auditing. Such problems were supposed to have been resolved, post-Enron, by the 2002 Sarbanes–Oxley Act in the US and Financial Reporting Council (FRC) oversight of auditors in the UK. Auditing of banks was recognized in the 1989 UK Banking Act as being special because of the risk of sparking a bank run or failure if a bank's accounts are 'qualified'.

The financial innovations (CDOs and so on) at the heart of the crisis were clearly complex and often traded 'over the counter', that is, outside organized markets (exchanges). In 2009, the G20 agreed to require much more exchange trading of derivatives in order to reduce 'counterparty' risk exposures. The investment banks, which stood to lose a lot of fees, lobbied hard against the proposal and were supported by captains of US industry, who feared that the use of exchange-traded derivatives would tie up their liquidity because of 'margin requirements'. The 2010 US Dodd–Frank Act contained compromise requirements and the EU was working to match them in 2010.

Financial innovation itself should probably be regulated: at the retail level by the consumer protection regulator, and at the wholesale and market level by a capital markets regulator. As with pharmaceutical drugs, new financial innovations should be 'trialled' before widespread use, although the innovators will oppose this as they will fear loss of first-mover advantage since financial innovations are hard to patent because they tend to benefit from rapid widespread adoption, leading to the formation of new markets.

Short-termism remains an issue. Lord Turner (the FSA Chairman) has questioned the usefulness of much of the financial market trading (FSA, 2009), as did Tobin (1984). 'Tobin', trading or 'turnover' taxes have been considered on a number of occasions (e.g., in France), but will only work if applied uniformly in all major financial centres; and what would the funds be used for? A 'Robin Hood tax' to fund the World Bank, or aid to achieve the Millennium Goals, or just to boost government revenue? In June 2010, the German government announced that it would unilaterally introduce a financial 'turnover tax', having already introduced restrictions on the 'short-selling' of equities.

In April 2010, the International Monetary Fund (IMF) reported to the G20 on its deliberations on special financial taxes. It favoured a new tax related to the size of a bank's liabilities (net of insured deposits and more narrowly defined Tier 1 capital) to pay for future 'clean-ups', and an additional levy on profits above 'normal' and on 'high' pay, in preference to a trading or turnover (Tobin) tax. Revised proposals were submitted to the G20 in June 2010 (IMF, 2010). Widespread international agreement on tax levels and so on would be required. Canada and Japan immediately came out against the April proposals, and Australia and others were less than enthusiastic about them.

Canada prefers requiring banks to issue Conditional Convertible (CoCo) bonds (pioneered by Lloyds Banking Group in late 2009). CoCos are bonds that convert to ordinary shares at some trigger point. Further, the Basel Committee was concerned that attempts to agree on special bank taxes will be a distraction, leading to a delay in agreement on Basel III.

If banks were required to hold an agreed proportion of their liabilities as CoCos, then the bondholders would have an incentive to monitor banks' risk-taking. This relates to a long-standing proposal of the 'Shadow Basel Committee' (http://www.ceps.eu/content/european-shadow-financial-regulatory-committee-esfrc) that banks should be required to issue more bonds in order to subject themselves to monitoring by bondholders acting as informed debt holders. The CoCo proposal would increase the cost of bank funding, further reducing their capability to lend, or raise the cost of borrowing. The Institute of International Finance (IIF) issued its estimates of the substantial reduction in economic growth that would be caused by the sizeable (in its estimation) reductions in bank lending that would result (IIF, 2010). Stephen G. Ceccheti (Head of the Monetary and Economics Department at the Bank for International Settlements) alleged that the IIF estimates were much exaggerated (www.bis.org). Would one or both of the levies proposed by the IMF be used to build up a TBTF DI fund, as Sweden is doing with its bank levy, or will cash-strapped governments find other uses for the revenue raised? Further, should the tax levels be the same in well-established financial centres, such as London and New York, as in emerging capital markets?

More fundamentally, should interest and other payments on debt continue to be tax-deductible? If banks could not deduct the interest they pay for debt financing, then they would probably issue more equity. Bank lending might fall dramatically and SMEs would also borrow less, as they too would lose the tax deductibility of interest. There would be a shift to more venture capital-based financing and wider adoption of Islamic 'profit and loss sharing' principles. US households would also lose tax deductibility of interest on home loans, making overborrowing less likely in the future. A significantly smaller banking and financial system may however be just what is needed.

The TBTF banks, and indeed banking and financial systems, may in fact simply be 'too big to save'. The cost of stopping the GFC generating a second Great Depression has resulted in heavily indebted governments, so much so that a second round of bank rescues in Europe as a result of their exposure to risky government bonds, rather than the subprime mortgages this time, would be crippling, leading to years of significantly higher taxes and slower growth. There are seemingly limits to Keynesianism and the welfare state. The debt of the financial system in the eurozone was estimated to be 250 per cent of GDP on the eve of the crisis in 2007. That of the governments was estimated to be 67 per cent. Can governments and taxpayers afford the risk of having to bail out such a massive financial sector?

15.7   CONCLUSIONS

Hitherto, UK and US banks have 'got out of jail' virtually free. The US banks seem to have been spared far-reaching structural reform beyond a partial application of the Volcker Rule and a requirement that there should be substantially more issuance of exchange-traded, as opposed to bespoke, 'over the counter' derivatives, as part of the 2010 Dodd–Frank Act.

Augar (2006, 2008, 2009) has identified a string of conflicts of interest in investment and universal banks that have emerged in the wake of the UK's 'Big Bang' reforms of stockbroking in 1986 (Mullineux, 1987) and the banning of fixed commissions on Wall Street in the US in 1975. To make banks safe and protect consumers of banking products and services, the conflicts of interest should be eliminated, or managed through regulation and supervision. Their elimination would require substantial structural reform that separated broking, market making, underwriting and asset management, and more generally, the 'buy side' from the 'sell side' and the provision of 'advice' to purchasers of financial securities. Proprietary trading would have to be separated from trading on behalf of clients (the Volcker Rule) and retail deposits prevented from use in 'casino banking', which may additionally require a separation of investment from commercial banking. In other words, there would be a return to a pre-Big Bang model in London and a pre-1975 model in New York, but with the markets better regulated, and cartelistic arrangements such as fixed commissions eliminated.

To the extent, however, that economics of scale and scope and diversification effects can be demonstrated to be beneficial, then the universal banking model, combining investment and retail and commercial banking, can be justified, and instead the conflicts of interest would need to be as assiduously monitored for abuse. This would leave the system open to 'gaming' by banks seeking loopholes, 'regulatory capture' by banks of regulators, and disaster myopia (Guttentag and Herring, 1986) on the part of regulators and supervisors, as the time that elapses since the GFC increases.

In the UK, the government, strapped for cash as it is, may be tempted to minimize structural reform in order to maximize the 'franchise value' of banks, and thus the price of the bank shares it holds, prior to selling them. The ICB set up to explore structural reform options is to be 'independent', drawing on evidence from experts. The Which? consumer organization set up its own independent 'Future of Banking Commission' which reported in June 2010 (Which Report, 2010). It recommended: the establishment of special resolution regimes for banks ('living wills'); enhanced deposit insurance; and structural reform, going beyond the Volcker Rule, designed to eliminate the most important conflicts of interest in banking. It supported US and EU proposals to bring the majority of trading in derivatives (and other securities) onto organized exchanges, so that counterparty risks can be monitored and managed. It was generally supportive of developments in the bank prudential regulation, remuneration and corporate governance spheres and suggested some enhancements, especially in the consumer protection sphere. It thus urged the UK's coalition government-initiated 'independent' Banking Commission to pay particular attention to promoting effective competition in order to eliminate or manage conflicts of interest in banking and to protect consumers. A dedicated retail banking and insurance utility regulator may well be required to protect consumers of retail financial sector products and services.

REFERENCES

Augar, Philip (2006), *The Greed Merchants*, London: Penguin Books.

Augar, Philip (2008), *The Death of Gentlemanly Capitalism: The Rise and Fall of London's Investment Banks*, London: Penguin.

Augar, Philip (2009), *Chasing Alpha*, London: Vintage Books.

BSA (2009), 'Converting failed financial institutions into mutual organisations', September, Building Societies Association, London.

CM7874 (2010), 'A new approach to financial regulation: judgement, focus and stability', HM Treasury, London.

Dodd–Frank Wall Street Reform and Consumer Protection Act, Public Law No. 111-203, 12 Stat. 1376, 21 July 2010.

FSA (2009), 'The Turner Review: a regulatory response to the global financial services authority', London.

G30 (2009), 'Financial reform: a framework for financial stability', January, Group of Thirty, Washington, DC.

Guttentag, J.M. and R.J. Herring (1986), 'Disaster myopia in international banking', Essays in International Finance, No. 164 (September), Department of Economics, Princeton University.

IIF (2010), 'Comments by the Institute of International Finance on the Basel Committee for Banking Supervisions consultative documents', April, Institute of International Finance, Washington, DC.

IMF (2010), 'A fair and substantial contribution by the financial sector', International Monetary Fund, Washington, DC, http://www.imf.org/external/index.htm.

Kay, John (2009), 'Narrow banking: the reform of bank regulation', CSFI Report Number 88, September, Centre for the Study of Financial Innovation, London.

Kotlikoff, Laurence J. (2010), *Jimmy Stewart is Dead: Ending the World's Ongoing Financial Plague with Limited Purpose Banking*, Hoboken, NJ: John Wiley & Sons.

Macey, J.R. and M. O'Hara (2003), 'The corporate governance of banks', *Federal Reserve Bank of New York Economic Policy Review*, 9(1), 91–107.

Merton, Robert C. (1977), 'An analytic derivation of the cost of deposit insurance and loan guarantees: an application of option pricing theory', *Journal of Banking and Finance*, 1(June), 3–11.

Mullineux, A.W. (1987), *UK Banking after Deregulation*, Beckenham: Croom Helm.

Mullineux, Andy (2006), 'The corporate governance of banks', *Journal of Financial Regulation and Compliance*, 14(4), 375–382.

Mullineux, Andy and Eva Terberger (2006), 'The British banking system: a good role model for Germany', Anglo-German Foundation, London.

Reinhart, Carmen M. and Kenneth S. Rogoff (2009), *'This Time Is Different': Eight Centuries of Financial Folly*, Princeton, NJ: Princeton University Press.

Tett, Gillian (2009), *Fool's Gold*, London: Little Brown.

Tobin, James (1984), 'On the efficiency of the financial system', *Lloyds Bank Review*, **153**(July), 1–15.

Walker, Sir David (2009), 'A review of corporate governance in UK banks and other financial entities: final recommendations', H.M. Treasury, London.

Which? Report (2010), 'The Future of Banking Commission', London: Which?

16 Incentives to improve the corporate governance of risk in financial institutions

Richard J. Herring

16.1 INTRODUCTION

Although debates still rage over the causes of the financial crisis of 2007–2009, most analysts agree that faulty corporate governance of risk was a major contributing factor, if not the principal cause. Examples of failures in the governance of risk abound. An apparent lack of effective firm-wide oversight plagued many of the institutions that failed or required massive government intervention. Chief executive officers (CEOs) and boards appeared to have lacked an effective framework for imposing a consistent risk-appetite to constrain aggregate risk within acceptable limits.

This defect took many forms: an over-reliance on risk decisions taken at a low level in many product lines and trading desks without consideration of how such exposures might interact under various macroeconomic conditions; a failure to question the risks of particular strategies and, instead, a tendency to follow the herd in an attempt to grow revenues and market share with minimal attention to risk; a reluctance to question fundamental assumptions about basis risks and hedges; an astonishing disregard for the centuries-old challenge of funding long-term assets with short-term liabilities and for liquidity risk more generally; a tendency to override limits when they conflicted with revenue goals; an astonishing inability to track aggregate exposures over complex legal structures and product silos; and a failure to risk-adjust the price of internal transfers of funds and compensation more generally. As a result, the bonuses and compensation were real, but the profits were not.

Examples of these problems may be found in the bankruptcy of Lehman Brothers (Valukas, 2010), the losses sustained by UBS (UBS, 2008) and AIG (Special Inspector General for TARP, 2009), the collapse of Northern Rock (Kirkpatrick, 2009), the forced merger of Bear Stearns (Kirkpatrick, 2009; SEC, 2008), the collapse of Indy-Mac, WaMu (Office of the Inspector General, 2010; Kelly, 2008) and Wachovia (Corston, 2010), as well as the string of losses reported by Citibank (Special Inspector General for TARP, 2011), Merrill Lynch and Bank of America (SEC, 2010), which raised questions about whether corporate boards and senior management comprehended their exposures to subprime mortgage risks.[1]

These failures in the corporate governance of risk are all the more remarkable because supervisors have focused on this problem for more than a decade (BCBS, 1997, 1999a, 1999b, 2005, 2006, 2008, 2010a, 2010b; Joint Forum, 1998; Davies 2003). The 'Core Principles' of banking supervision (BCBS, 1997) even embed good corporate governance of risk as a key principle. Nonetheless, most of these efforts have focused on processes and procedures to ensure good corporate governance – largely a matter of getting the right information to the right decision-makers at the right time – as well as the structure of boards, usually emphasizing the role of non-executive directors on audit committees, risk committees and, more controversially in the United States, splitting the roles of CEO and chairman. Most of these recommendations for enhancing corporate governance seem sensible, although they have seldom drawn on lessons of what has actually gone wrong and, more generally, they lack any empirical support.

16.2   THE SCANT EMPIRICAL EVIDENCE

The press has often attributed good corporate governance to corporate culture, an elusive but important factor. *The Economist* (2010a) noted that two American institutions which appeared to come through the crisis better than their peers did so based on some very simple principles. JPMorgan Chase was said to hold to two basic principles: (1) do not hold too much of anything; and (2) only keep what you are sure will generate a decent risk-adjusted return. Goldman Sachs, which did require government assistance, but less than the other 'bulge bracket' investment banks, encouraged greater attention to risk by promoting senior traders to risk positions and, indeed, making such positions a stepping stone to the top echelons of management. This may not have cultivated prowess in public relations, but it did enable the firm to cut its losses and hedge its remaining risks while some of its competitors continued to build even larger exposures. Numerous other examples can be found, for example, contrasting the strong leadership at Credit Suisse with the disastrous performance of UBS, or the severe losses at Citigroup with the relative success of JPMorgan Chase. Strong leadership and a sound corporate culture undoubtedly matter, but it remains to be seen how these factors can be replicated, much less ensured by regulation or supervision. Moreover, the evidence remains largely anecdotal.

Recently Erkens et al. (2010) have attempted to fill the gap in our empirical knowledge of the impact of presumed good corporate governance principles on outcomes during the global financial crisis. Since the 1990s a series of official commissions, often formed in the wake of a shocking lapse in corporate governance, have transformed the rules for good corporate governance by placing much greater stress on transparency and accountability and on encouraging independent directors to take a constructive but independent view from that of management (Committee on Corporate Governance, 2000). *The Economist* (2010b) reports that the annual Booz & Company surveys of the world's biggest public companies show that firms now routinely separate the jobs of chairman and chief executive officer. In 2009, less than 12 percent of incoming CEOs were also made chairman of the board, compared with 48 percent in 2002. And CEOs are dismissed more frequently for poor performance, with the average tenure dropping from 8.1 years in 2000 to 6.3 years in 2009. Independent directors, too, have become more professional, at least in part because the Sarbanes–Oxley Act makes them personally liable for the statements they sign.

Yet we have no empirical evidence that these seemingly sensible changes have positively influenced the quality of decision-making. The financial crisis that engulfed the US and Western Europe presents an opportunity to see whether financial institutions that adopted good practices of corporate governance fared better than those that did not.

Erkens et al. (2010) conduct a comprehensive study of the performance during the crisis of 296 financial institutions from 30 countries with assets of more than $10 billion. They regress cumulative stock returns during the crisis on measures of corporate governance and control variables. They include three corporate governance factors: (1) board independence; (2) institutional ownership; and (3) the presence of large shareholders measured as of December 2006. They control for whether a firm is cross-listed on US stock exchanges, leverage, firm size, dummy variables indicating a firm's industry, home country, and the firm's stock return during 2006 in case performance during the crisis period reflects a reversal of pre-crisis performance.

Their analysis finds that firms with more independent directors and greater institutional share ownership experienced worse stock returns during the crisis period. They note that one potential explanation for the result is that boards and shareholders encouraged managers to increase shareholder returns through greater risk-taking before the crisis In further testing, however, they find that greater institutional ownership is consistent with greater pre-crisis risk-taking, but a higher proportion of independent directors is not. They test an alternative hypothesis about the negative role of the proportion of independent directors on stock performance based on the theory that independent directors, out of concern for their own reputations, pressured managers to raise additional equity capital to ensure capital adequacy and reduce bankruptcy risk.[2] This leads to a transfer of wealth from existing shareholders to debt holders (and potentially protects taxpayers). Erkens et al. (2010) found that the amount of capital raised during the crisis (scaled by total assets) did depend on corporate governance factors. Firms with a larger proportion of independent directors did, indeed, raise more equity capital. Moreover, they found that the relation between stock returns and the proportion of independent directors became insignificant once firms that raised equity capital were excluded from the sample.

The authors also explored the relation between firm performance during the crisis and country-level governance, measured as the quality of legal institutions and the extent of laws protecting shareholder rights. These factors proved insignificant, indicating that firm-level, not country-level, governance variables were more important in explaining outcomes during the crisis, which may be indirect confirmation of the popular view that strong leadership and corporate culture matter most.

Erkuns et al. then tried to determine whether additional corporate governance variables could explain stock returns. They tested the existence of a risk committee, the financial expertise of the board, and separation of the roles of CEO and chairman, as well as the percentage of shares owned by insiders. None of these additional variables proved significant or altered the explanatory power of the original two corporate governance measures: the percentage of ownership by institutional investors and the proportion of independent directors.

These results raise troubling questions about the presumptions underlying most recommendations for enhancing corporate governance. But more fundamentally, the results imply that good corporate governance of risk is much more than a box-checking exercise. A board may conform to all of the hallmarks of good corporate governance, yet may lack the incentives to adopt the risk management framework necessary to control and coordinate the activities of complex, cross-border financial institutions. In the next section, we turn to the question of incentives.

16.3   THE ROLE OF INCENTIVES IN GOOD CORPORATE GOVERNANCE OF RISK

16.3.1   Compensation

In general, the many suggestions for enhancing corporate governance of financial institutions seem sensible, but usually ignore the role of incentives. The one exception is the recent attention focused on compensation (European Commission, 2010; Turner, 2009; BCBS, 2011). Until the crisis, little attention was paid to the structure of remuneration either by the supervisory authorities or by firms (except, of course, for the importance of maintaining competitive incentives to attract and retain top talent). The crisis provided an abundance of examples that the structure of remuneration can create incentives for excessive risk-taking. As Turner notes:

> [P]ast remuneration policies, acting in combination with capital requirements and accounting rules, have created incentives for some executives and traders to take excessive risks and have resulted in large payments in reward for activities which seemed profit making at the time but subsequently proved harmful to the institution, and in some cases to the entire system.

Indeed, the consensus among regulators that badly designed compensation contributed to the crisis was echoed in the communiqué from the first meeting of the Group of 20 (2008), which pledged that: 'action needs to be taken, through voluntary effort or regulatory action, to avoid compensation schemes which reward excessive short-term returns or risk taking'. This was reinforced in the following Group of 20 (2009) Summit in Pittsburgh where the leaders announced: 'We committed to act together . . . to implement strong international compensation standards aimed at ending practices that lead to excessive risk-taking'.

The Financial Stability Forum (2009) published 'Principles for sound compensation practices' which placed heavy emphasis on the role of the board in the effective governance of compensation. Principle I required that: (1) the firm's board of directors must actively oversee the compensation system's design and operation; (2) the firm's board of directors must monitor and review the compensation system to ensure the system operates as intended; (3) staff engaged in financial and risk control must be independent, have appropriate authority, and be compensated in a manner that is independent of the business areas they oversee and commensurate with their key role in the firm. In the US, regulators have announced a joint proposed rulemaking to implement Section 956 of the Dodd–Frank Act, which prohibits incentive-based compensation arrangements that encourage inappropriate risk-taking, that are deemed to be excessive or that may lead to material losses.[3] The European Commission (2010) has made a similar proposal.

The Turner Review (Turner, 2009: 80) summarized what has become a broad consensus among regulators about appropriate remuneration principles:

> (1) Firms must ensure that their remuneration policies are consistent with effective risk management; (2) Remuneration committees . . . should reach independent judgments on the implications of remuneration for risk and risk management; (3) Remuneration should reflect an individual's record of compliance with risk management procedures, rules and appropriate culture, as well as financial measures of performance; (4) Financial measures used . . . should entail the adjustment of profit measures to reflect the relative riskiness of different activities; (5)

Table 16.1   Criteria for bad remuneration policies

Measurement of performance for the calculation of bonuses	Calculated on the basis of revenues, without any counterbalancing risk controls Does not take risk or capital cost into account Performance assessed entirely on the results for the current financial year Employee bonuses calculated solely on the basis of financial performance
Composition of the remuneration	Remuneration which has little or no fixed component Paid wholly in cash No deferral in the bonus element
Performance adjusted deferred compensation	Payout of the deferred element is not linked to the future performance of business undertaken in previous years Performance adjusted deferred compensation schemes can be waived/not enforced despite evidence of poor performance or wrongdoing
Governance	No independent oversight of remuneration policies or of remuneration awards to executives or senior staff No process, or no transparent process, for managing conflicts of interest Business areas can determine the compensation of staff in risk and compliance Staff have an ability to influence unduly the valuation of their own positions and hence the determination of performance measures. Ability also to front-load profit from transactions Incomplete separation of duties between front and back office: ability of the front office to influence back office procedures

Source: Annex to Sants (2008).

The predominant share (two thirds or more) of bonuses which exceed a significant level, should be paid in a deferred form . . . with a deferral period which is appropriate to the nature of the business and its risks; (6) Payment of deferred bonuses should be linked to financial performance during the deferral period.

Increasingly prescriptive rules, however, will set off a massive hunt for loopholes by legions of highly paid lawyers and investment bankers. Significant ownership of the firm by senior managers and the board does not guarantee effective governance of risk. Bear Stearns and Lehman Brothers boasted higher ownership by employees than any other financial institution. Moreover, even if we knew precisely how to compensate risk-takers, derivatives enable managers to undo virtually any constraint on compensation.[4]

Rather than specify highly prescriptive rules for compensation, regulators (and economists) would be on firmer ground to identify bad practices in remuneration. Consensus would be much easier to achieve and infractions might be easier to monitor. The Financial Services Authority (Sants, 2008) provided a very useful list of bad practices (see Table 16.1) that has the additional virtue of being much briefer than the 77 pages of proposed rulemaking on compensation proposed by regulators in the United States.

While attention to perverse incentives in compensation standards may curb unintended, excessive risk-taking and may even encourage employees to take a longer view of the risks to which they expose the institution, this approach will not ensure the implementation of appropriate, effective standards for the overall corporate governance of risk. This approach relies almost completely on supervisory discipline.[5] Some view this as a desirable and inevitable outcome. Turner (2009: 47), in his masterful review of the crisis, concludes that: 'Market discipline expressed via market prices cannot be expected to play a major role in constraining bank risk taking, and that the primary constraint needs to come from regulation and supervision'. This conclusion is backed up by an analysis of credit default swap (CDS) prices which indicated the relative riskiness of institutions but gave no indication in 2007 of the scale of problems ahead, and share prices that tended to reinforce management convictions that aggressive growth strategies were value-accretive. Moreover, he notes that market pressures from analysts and shareholders were more procyclical than capital regulation, and that although institutional investors expressed significant concerns about some risk-taking, they were ineffective in preventing it.

Two flaws undermine the force of Turner's conclusion. First, while markets may have shown little foresight, supervisors acted with even less. In one of the most egregious examples, the FSA permitted Northern Rock to adopt the Advanced Internal Measurement Approach to computing its capital requirements for mortgages, which lowered its required capital by about 30 percent that was to be paid out to shareholders. This decision was made just weeks before Northern Rock collapsed.

Second, moral hazard distorts market price signals by permitting creditors to assume they will be protected from loss if the worst happens, which enables shareholders to press for greater risk-taking without having to pay more for their credit. And, as Mervyn King, Governor of the Bank of England, has observed (Conway, 2009), the massive subsidies provided to banks by governments on both sides of the Atlantic have 'created possibly the biggest moral hazard in history'. He went on to express skepticism that tighter future regulations would be enough to prevent banks from generating financial crises so long as big banks enjoy an effective guarantee from the state.

The next two subsections examine reforms that could reduce moral hazard dramatically and restore market discipline as an effective force for enhanced corporate governance of risk.

16.3.2 Contingent Convertible Bonds (CoCos) as an Incentive for Improved Corporate Governance[6]

Research by Flannery (2005), Kashyap et al. (2008), D'Souza et al. (2009), Huertas (2009), Duffie (2010) and Hart and Zingales (2010) has highlighted the potential value of providing some form of contingent equity capital infusion for banks via either conversion of existing debt, insurance contracts or a rights offering as a buffer against loss. The Dodd–Frank Act mandates the Fed to study the scope for use of some minimum amount of contingent capital as part of regulatory capital requirements. The Basel Committee on Banking Supervision (BCBS, 2011) has set out standards that CoCos must meet to qualify as Tier 1 or Tier 2 capital. And the European Commission (2011) has proposed standards for debt bail-ins to avoid the use of taxpayer funds. Requiring a minimum amount of contingent capital certificates (CCCs) or CoCos – subordinated (sub) debt instruments that convert automatically into equity in adverse states of the world, and prior to reaching the regulatory insolvency intervention point – would have several advantages as a buffer against loss relative to traditional sub debt.

First, making subordinated debt convert into equity prior to bank insolvency eliminates the potential, politically charged issue of deciding whether to impose losses on debt holders after intervention – something most regulators were reluctant to do in the recent crisis. Since the subordinated debt has already converted to equity and will share in the losses suffered by equity holders, the issue is removed from consideration.

Second, because sub debt has converted to equity before insolvency, debt holders cannot withdraw their funds at their maturity dates, which itself might trigger an insolvency event, although they can sell their equity in the secondary market.

Third, because CoCos would credibly remain in the bank and suffer losses in insolvency states, *ex ante*, the prices of CoCos will accurately reflect their true risks. Given the widespread practice of bailing-out subordinated debt, sub debt can no longer serve this function.

Fourth, in the event conversion is triggered, CoCos will provide a better buffer against losses to depositors, counterparties and senior debtors than subordinated debt, since they will cease to accrue interest once they convert and therefore alleviate liquidity pressures on the bank to some extent.

Fifth, and most importantly, CoCos will incentivize boards and senior managers to strengthen the governance of risk to avoid dilution. Of course, if an institution waits too long, it may find that equity markets are closed to it or it can sell assets only at distressed prices. That is why a systemically important financial institution (SIFI) is likely to launch new issues or sell assets long before it approaches the CoCo conversion point. Of course, on occasion the firm may not be able to issue new equity or sell assets at any acceptable price, and the conversion is triggered. That would be unfortunate for the existing shareholders, but it automatically recapitalizes the SIFI at the expense of shareholders and holders of contingent capital, rather than the taxpayers.

D'Souza et al. (2009) emphasize that this potential dilution may be an important advantage of CoCos from two perspectives. First, it encourages banks voluntarily to raise additional equity capital to avoid conversion so that the effective equity buffer against loss will likely exceed the amount of CoCos issued. Second, the strong incentives for management to avoid conversion mean that CoCos are likely to trade more like fixed-income instruments than ordinary convertibles. Thus CoCos are likely to hold greater appeal to institutional investors, who tend to prefer low-risk debt instruments.[7] In Huertas's colorful phrase: 'To the common shareholder, contingent capital holds out the prospect of death by dilution and it can be anticipated that shareholders would task management to undertake the necessary measures to avoid dilution' (2009: 5). Thus appropriately designed CoCos can provide a strong incentive for enhanced corporate governance of risk.

To serve this important incentive function, CoCos must meet four key challenges:

1. Devising an appropriate trigger for conversion of CoCos into equity.
2. Determining the amount of CoCos relative to other balance sheet items.
3. Identifying the amount of CoCos that must be converted at the trigger point.
4. Setting the terms under which CoCos will be converted into equity.

Setting an appropriate trigger

An appropriate trigger must be accurate, timely and comprehensive in its valuation of the issuing firm (D'Souza et al., 2009). And the trigger should be defined so that it can be implemented in a predictable way, so that CoCo holders can price the risks inherent in the instrument at the time of its offering. This latter point has been emphasized by the ratings agencies that refuse to rate CoCos in which the conversion is contingent upon the decision of a regulator or bank management.

Some proposals for contingent capital (e.g., D'Souza et al., 2009; Hart and Zingales, 2010) assume that book values of the institution's equity relative to its assets, based on accounting reports and/or examinations by supervisors, would be used as a conversion trigger for CoCos. But book value is an accounting concept, subject to manipulation, and inevitably a lagging indicator of deterioration in a bank's balance sheet.[8] The problem of using book values as triggers is not just one of managerial dishonesty.[9] Regulators and supervisors have shown time and again that they are hesitant to opine negatively about SIFIs in public. Such forbearance leads to protracted delays in recognizing problems. Moreover, a central purpose of employing non-equity capital is to reinforce official supervision with market discipline.

What market-based measures could be employed as the trigger? The two obvious candidates are CDS spreads and stock price movements. CDS markets seem less desirable for the purpose of deriving triggers for two reasons. First, the markets are relatively shallow, and thus may be susceptible to manipulation. Second, the pricing of risk is not constant over time: an observed spread at one point in the business cycle, under one set of market conditions, can be indicative of a higher level of risk than that same spread observed at another time under a different set of business conditions.

Equity values, if used properly, would provide the best source of information on which to base triggers. Indeed, some of the best-known cases of the failures of large firms that surprised rating agencies and regulators were signaled long in advance by severe and persistent declines in the aggregate market value of their equity. KMV's rating of Enron's debt was the only one that correctly predicted a severe probability of default. The reason for its success was that the KMV model was based on the Black–Scholes approach to measuring default risk as a function of leverage (measured using market values) and asset risk (also derived from observed stock price volatility). Similarly, market value information about Lehman provided an early warning of its problems. Valukas (2010) shows that the combined value of the equity and the outstanding debt at Lehman was slipping over time during the spring and summer of 2008, so that it was actually less than the face value of Lehman's liabilities on several occasions in July and August of 2008. If Lehman had been required to issue CoCos, this substantial and protracted market decline in the equity value of Lehman would have produced conversion of debt into equity long before insolvency.

More importantly, the existence of a credible CoCo requirement would incentivize all large financial firms voluntarily to raise equity capital in large amounts before hitting the CoCo trigger. D'Souza et al. (2009) argue that even under the assumption of a 15 percent decline in share prices in reaction to an announcement of an equity offering, the dilution effects on stockholders would be much less from an equity offering than from a triggered conversion, provided that it is of sufficient size and on sufficiently favorable terms to the holders of the CoCos. In other words, managers who are maximizing the value of shareholders' claims in the firm will always have a strong incentive to prevent CoCos from triggering by strengthening the governance of risk and, if necessary, pre-emptively issuing equity into the market or selling assets, so long as the dilution effect of the CoCo conversion is sufficiently large.

The declining equity values are only reliable as rough measures of a SIFI's health if they are persistent and severe, and even then, they offer only a rough indication of the firm's financial health. Fortunately, that indication is good enough to serve as an effective trigger for CoCos if a 90-day moving average is employed to smooth fluctuations in share prices and reduce the noise in stock price signals. This would also make it more difficult for speculators to force a CoCo conversion.

Would a trigger based on the market value of capital relative to quasi-market value of the firm[10] be desirable based on the criteria of predictability, timeliness, comprehensiveness and accuracy? Clearly, it is a comprehensive measure of firm value (in fact, the market capitalization of a bank is 'the' comprehensive measure of value, which includes, in principle, the value of tangible and intangible assets as well as off-balance-sheet positions). Because market values of the shares of SIFIs are continuously observable in deeply traded equity markets – markets that continued to trade actively even during the depth of the financial crisis when many other markets ceased to function – a trigger based on equity valuation will be timely and predictable.

Will it also be accurate? Yes, so long as the demands placed on the measure are not excessive. Equity prices are not perfectly reliable, and they are particularly unreliable in detecting small valuation changes over short periods of time. They may also be subject to manipulation. For these reasons, some sacrifice of timeliness by relying on a moving average is useful. But for the purpose of constructing a credible, predictable, comprehensive and reasonably accurate measure of large swings in the market value of a SIFI, the market value of the firm is the only real possibility. So long as the user does not seek to achieve false precision, equity is reliable.

For example, suppose a trigger were defined as follows: the CoCo will convert from debt to equity if the ratio of the market cap of the bank to the quasi-market value of the bank falls to 4 percent. Assuming that the bank started with a prudent ratio of market cap to the quasi-market value of assets, a decline to this trigger would provide a reasonably accurate measure of a sustained decline in the value of the firm. Since the share prices are 90-day rolling averages, no SIFI could reasonably argue that the decline in the value of its equity was the product of market manipulation or irrational shareholder behavior.

The right amount and conversion price of CoCos

Because the efficacy of CoCos as an incentive device depends crucially on their dilutive effects on equity holders, it is important that CoCos be issued in sufficient quantity. For purposes of seeing how such a requirement might have worked during the crisis in which banks were required to hold a minimum of 2 percent common equity relative to risk-weighted assets (measured in book value terms), it seems plausible to propose that the minimum required amount of CoCos should have been set at 2 percent of the 'quasi market value' of the firm.[11] Note that a 4 percent trigger would set off a conversion of CoCos equal to 2 percent of the quasi-market value of the bank. This would imply a huge dilution of equity holders. All of the required CoCos should be converted when the ratio hits the trigger.

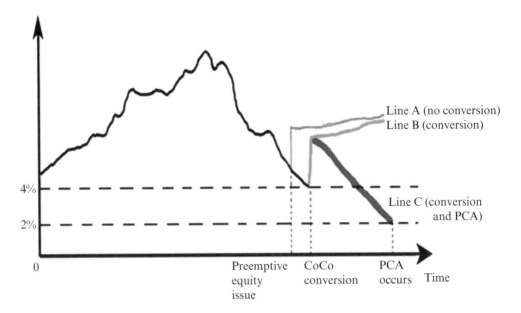

Figure 16.1   How a CoCo trigger will work

The conversion price should be a sufficient number of shares so that the market value of shares received is at least equal to the principal amount of the CoCos.[12] This would strengthen the incentives for improving the governance of risk and for management to voluntarily issue equity or sell assets to preempt conversion

An example of how CoCos would work
Figure 16.1 illustrates how the proposed CoCo trigger would work. As the market cap to quasi-market value of the firm falls, approaching the trigger, a firm like A (line A) might issue equity (or sell assets) to avoid hitting the trigger. If for some reason a firm like B is unable or unwilling to issue equity or sell assets, the conversion of CoCos is triggered (line B). This will result in massive dilution of existing shareholders, who will undoubtedly be angry, and the new shareholders who formerly held CoCos may be unhappy as well. Shareholder dissatisfaction on this scale is likely to lead to an ouster of the existing management and the installation of a new management team that will strengthen the governance of risk. And so CoCo conversion might enhance the virtually moribund market for corporate control of regulated financial institutions – an important element of market discipline that is largely ineffectual among regulated banks. It will certainly add further motivation to management to take corrective action before reaching the trigger.

This doubling of capital and reduction in liquidity pressures (and perhaps a new management team) may buy the firm enough time to restructure successfully. Finally, a firm C may be unable to use the additional capital and time to accomplish a restructuring or recapitalization, and so its value would continue to decline until prompt corrective action is triggered (line C).

Figure 16.2 shows the movement of the market cap to quasi-market value of assets from April 2006 to April 2010 for five SIFIs that did not require government support.

90-day rolling market cap to quasi-market value of assets
for large American financial institutions that did not receive major subsidies

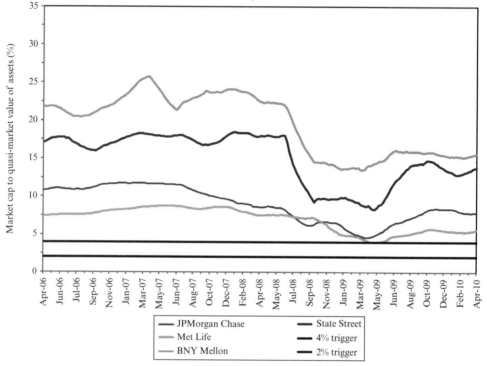

Figure 16.2   How a 2% CoCo requirement might have worked for US SIFIs that did not require intervention

Note that none of these institutions fell below the 4 percent ratio. If the CoCo requirement had been in place, only Goldman Sachs and Met Life might have triggered a conversion. The prospect of dilution would have almost certainly caused the managers of both firms to issue more equity or sell assets to avoid hitting the trigger.

Contrast Figure 16.2 with Figure 16.3, which shows the movement of the market cap to quasi-market value of assets ratio for ten banks that required substantial government support, were forced to merge or entered bankruptcy. Note that all of these firms breached the 4 percent ratio and in most cases did so many months before they were subject to intervention. It is particularly noteworthy that Bear Stearns, Lehman Brothers and AIG – all of which appeared to catch the supervisory authorities by surprise and were subject to different interventions, hastily improvised over sleepless weekends – had, in fact, fallen below the 4 percent trigger several months earlier. It is possible that a CoCo requirement might have induced these firms to higher standards of risk governance. At a minimum, it would have bought them additional time to prepare for an orderly resolution and would have been a clear warning to regulators to refine their rapid resolution plans.

In summary, a 4 percent trigger based on the ratio of the market cap to the quasi-market value of assets might have been an effective device for preventing the collapse

90-day rolling market cap to quasi market value of assets
US SIFIs that failed, were forced into mergers or received major SCAP infusions

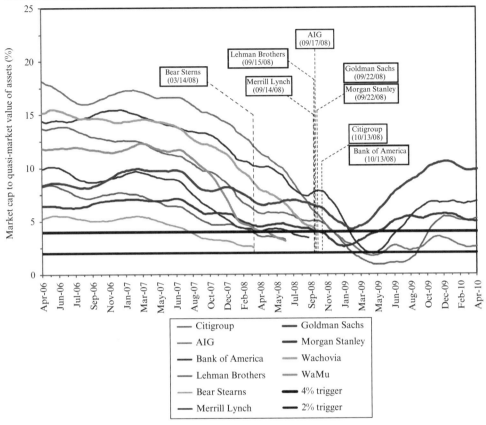

Figure 16.3   How a 2% CoCo requirement might have worked for US SIFIs that did require intervention

of all of these troubled SIFIs during the 2008–2009 crisis. Moreover, each of these institutions would have faced strong incentives pre-emptively to strengthen the corporate governance of risk and, if necessary, issue equity or sell assets to avoid triggering their CoCos months earlier. And the supervisors could not have claimed to be taken by surprise at the sudden collapse of these firms.

16.3.3   Rapid Resolution Plans as an Incentive for Improved Governance of Risk[13]

Even an effectively designed CoCo requirement will be less effective than it should be in the absence of a credible resolution policy for SIFIs. The 'Report and recommendations of the Cross-border Bank Resolution Group' (BCBS, 2010c) makes clear that even among the relatively few countries that have national frameworks for resolving financial institutions, none of them adequately addresses the problems that arise in the resolution of a purely domestic SIFI, much less a cross-border SIFI. The Group of Twenty (G20), meeting in Pittsburgh in 2009, instructed the Financial Stability Board to find a solution to this problem within a year. But a year later, at the Seoul meeting of the G20, the FSB reported that it needed much more time to find a workable solution.

Meanwhile the FSA in Britain (Huertas, 2010), the European Union (Commission Staff Working Document, 2009) and the Dodd–Frank Act in the US (House Committee on Financial Services, 2010) have proposed separate solutions to this problem, but none of them adequately addresses the problem of resolving a complex, international conglomerate. Unfortunately, the most worrisome SIFIs have precisely this profile. In the absence of a credible policy that would permit such an institution to be resolved without manageable spillovers to the rest of the financial system, governments will continue to execute enormously costly bailouts that will undermine some of the market discipline inherent in CoCos and diminish any prospect of market discipline from creditors. The result will be still more 'Zombie' institutions (Kane, 1989) that warehouse dead debt, weaken competitors, and cannot play a constructive role in economic recovery until, after sufficient subsidy,[14] they can absorb their losses and recapitalize.

Resolution planning

This regulatory tool is at least as important to systemic stability as the disaster recovery and business continuity plans that are now required of most large institutions. But the resolution plan must be carefully defined and, because SIFIs typically have complex international corporate structures, the plan must also be carefully reviewed by the college of supervisors (or crisis management group) formed to oversee the SIFI.[15] Although there will undoubtedly be considerable experimentation as members of the G20 fulfill their pledge to develop such plans, the FSB should make efforts to establish best practices as soon as possible; not only to minimize compliance costs for SIFIs, but also to ensure that the resolution plans yield comparable, useful results for each SIFI as a whole.

The resolution plan should begin with the assumption that the SIFI is insolvent under the regulatory definition of insolvency. This definition should be above the point of economic insolvency and standardized across countries because differing insolvency standards can lead to disorderly insolvencies or massive, improvised bailouts. The plan should be a joint undertaking of the institution, its board of directors and the principal supervisors. Although clearly the supervisors must have decisive control, it is equally important that the resolution plan be perceived as a fundamental part of good corporate governance.[16] The plan should contain several elements.

First, the SIFI must map its lines of business into the corporate entities that must undergo some sort of resolution process in the event of insolvency. Each of these separate entities and its location must be justified to the board of the SIFI and, ultimately, to the primary supervisors for each of the different lines of business and to the college of supervisors established for the SIFI. Fragmentation of lines of business across numerous legal entities will be difficult to justify to the board and the authorities because it would impede any attempt to salvage going-concern value from a line of business if it cannot be easily separated from the rest of the group and sold.[17] The resolution procedures must be described for each entity, including an estimate of how long they will take to complete.

The dialogue between the SIFI and its primary supervisor will inevitably be contentious because it will represent a dramatic change from past practice[18] and will cause the SIFI to focus on possibilities it would rather not contemplate.[19] As Lord Turner (Giles et al., 2009), Chairman of the Financial Services Authority in Britain, has noted: 'In the past, authorities around the world have tended to be tolerant of the proliferation of complex legal structures designed to maximize regulatory and tax arbitrage. Now we may have to demand clarity of legal structure.'[20]

Second, the SIFI must identify key interconnections across affiliates, such as cross-guarantees, stand-by lines of credit, contractual commitments or loans that link the fate of one affiliate to that of another. The plan should also identify operational interdependencies such as information technology, service agreements, staffing allocations, human resource and related support systems, trading and custody systems, as well as liquidity, and risk management procedures that would impede the separation of one unit from another.

Third, the SIFI should be required to develop and maintain a virtual data room that contains information that an administrator or resolution authority would require to make an expeditious resolution of the entity. This is likely to require investment in an improved management information system that provides details such as organizational structures, loan and counterparty exposures disaggregated by borrower or counterparty, and legal entity.[21] The SIFI must also identify key information, trading and custody systems, indicating where they are located, and the essential personnel to operate them. Plans must be made to make these systems available to all entities at home or abroad during the resolution process, whether they are operated by the SIFI or outsourced to a third party. As a practical matter, this may require that backup information technology (IT) operations be segregated in a separate subsidiary that could continue to function if the rest of the firm were to be resolved.

Fourth, the SIFI must identify any activities or units it regards as systemically important, and demonstrate how they could continue to operate during a resolution process. This will usually require that they be separately incorporated and made bankruptcy-remote so that they could easily be detached from the group if necessary in order to keep the systemically important function operating while other parts of the group are resolved.[22] Arrangements should also be in place to make a rapid transfer of customer accounts to another institution in the event of resolution.

Fifth, the SIFI must consider how its actions may affect exchanges, clearing-houses, custodians and other systemically important elements of the infrastructure. Ideally it should identify how it can disconnect from these highly automated systems without creating serious knock-on effects. This will require cooperation with these systemically important parts of the infrastructure. A particularly good example of a successful effort of this sort was the CHIPS (Clearing House Interbank Payment System) initiative enabling its bank participants and key central banks to withstand the simultaneous failure of its four largest participants.

Sixth, the SIFI must identify the procedures it would follow during resolution. This report should be quite detailed including, at a minimum, a list of bankruptcy attorneys and administrators who might be called upon, individuals who would be responsible for press releases and various notifications to counterparties and regulators, and a good-faith estimate of the time it would take to resolve each separately chartered entity.

Seventh, the resolution plan should be reviewed at least annually and updated if the institution executes a substantial merger or a restructuring introduces additional complexity.

The managers of the SIFI must demonstrate to their board of directors that the resolution plan is complete and feasible. Boards should recognize that oversight of resolution plans is as much their responsibility as oversight of business continuity plans. Indeed, when the SIFI approaches insolvency, the board's fiduciary duty becomes one of maximizing the bankruptcy estate that can be passed on to creditors.[23] If the board finds that the plan is excessively complex or time-consuming, it has a duty to require management to simplify the corporate structure of the firm, invest in more powerful IT systems or reduce the scope of its activities so that it can be resolved in a reasonable amount of time.[24] This will also give boards a strong incentive to enhance the corporate governance of risk.

This process may also have a useful side benefit. Considerable research in cognitive psychology shows that decision-makers are likely to be more risk-averse when they are forced to confront worst-case scenarios even if they consider them unlikely to happen.[25] This too should strengthen the emphasis on effective corporate governance of risk.

Next, the primary supervisor[26] must evaluate the resolution plan in cooperation with both any other domestic supervisors of business in which the firm may be active, and the international college of supervisors established for each SIFI. This group must certify that the plan is feasible, and the estimated time for the resolution is plausible and acceptable. In addition, it must ensure that all systemically important activities have been identified and properly insulated, so that they could be spun-off to another firm in the event of insolvency.[27] If the primary supervisor and the college of supervisors find the plan is not feasible or would take an unacceptable amount of time to execute, it should have the power to compel the SIFI to propose alternative options.

The SIFI might propose alternatives such as simplifying its corporate structure, improving its IT infrastructure, spinning off activities or placing a line of business in an affiliate with no financial connections to any other affiliates and financed completely by equity.[28]

The supervisory authorities, however, must have substantially greater resources than currently, and power to compel action if the SIFI does not propose an acceptable alternative. If they lack such power, no meaningful action is likely to be taken, and the entire exercise will become a senseless and costly ticking of boxes. It may even prove counterproductive to the extent that it encourages market participants to believe that a problem has been solved when in fact it has not. The temptation to cut corners will be severe because the process will be enormously costly for both SIFIs and the authorities. Yet these costs will surely be small relative to the very large support – direct loans, asset purchases, collateral swaps, guarantees, asset insurance and direct equity injections and indirect support – provided by American and European governments to their financial systems during the crisis.

Since many financial firms have become much too complex to take through any kind of resolution procedure in a reasonable amount of time, it seems naive to expect these firms to give up willingly the complexity that virtually assures them access to subsidies, a safety net and a competitive advantage over other smaller, less complex institutions, and so it is important that the process of resolution planning produces demonstrable improvements in the resolvability of these institutions. It may be necessary to appoint an independent commission to ensure that progress continues to be made.

Alternatively, Andrew Kuritzkes (2010) has suggested that a periodic tax of $1 million be levied on each subsidiary of a SIFI. The tax would be deferred for five years, with the first collection in 2015 to incentivize firms to simplify their legal structures. The tax would be collected at five-year intervals thereafter. Based on current legal structures, the costs to international financial conglomerates would be significant, ranging from $134 million to $2.6 billion for the top 30 financial conglomerates.[29] The tax could be justified by the negative externalities associated with cross-border activity, legal complexity and regulatory forum shopping. Others have suggested that capital requirements be calibrated to create similar incentives to simplify corporate structures, but capital requirements are already burdened with a number of objectives and have proven remarkably ineffectual in deterring risk-taking (IMF, 2009, Ch. 3, p. 7).

Imposing constraints on the size or structure of firms has traditionally been justified on grounds of competition policy, not as a way of enhancing financial stability. But what was once unthinkable is now being widely discussed. Governor of the Bank of England, Mervyn King (2009), former Governor of the Federal Reserve Board, Alan Greenspan (McKee and Lanman, 2009), and former US Secretary of State and Treasury, George Shultz (Wessel, 2009), have all said, in effect: 'Any bank that is too big to fail is simply too big'. Greenspan (2009) has also argued in addition that banks that are 'too big to fail' interfere with the creative destruction that is essential to a dynamic economy. Perhaps most surprisingly, Jamie Dimon (Sender, 2009), CEO of JPMorgan Chase, has endorsed a resolution mechanism that would wipe out shareholders and impose losses on creditors but protect the financial system when a SIFI fails: 'We think everything should be allowed to fail . . . but we need a resolution mechanism so that the system isn't destroyed. To dismantle a bank in a way that doesn't damage the system should be doable. It's better than being too big to fail.'[30]

During the process of evaluating resolution plans, the primary supervisor and the international college of supervisors[31] will gain an understanding of the regulations and tax provisions that provide SIFIs with incentives to adopt such complex corporate structures. It may be excessively optimistic to believe that these insights will help inform future regulatory, accounting and tax reforms, but it would be useful, nonetheless, to highlight some of the unintended consequences of regulatory actions in the hope that it might influence future reforms at the margin.

In addition, if a SIFI is involved in more than one line of business (as is invariably the case), the supervisors who oversee each of the important lines of business should be required to simulate a resolution each year under varying stress conditions. In this process, each supervisor must develop modes of cooperation with the others or make clear its intention to ring-fence the SIFI's operations within its domain. Unless supervisors within a single country can agree on how to resolve a SIFI, there is little hope of making progress in the much more complex international arena.

The primary supervisor must also conduct a similar exercise with the international college of supervisors and simulate a resolution annually under varying stress conditions. This will have the same virtues as the domestic exercise, and here too the supervisors will need to develop modes of cooperation or make clear their intent to ring-fence the portion they control. This will enable the other key supervisors to anticipate what might happen and make appropriate preparations. Although these commitments will not be legally binding, the supervisors' personal integrity will be on the line, so there will be a strong incentive to be candid.

Benefits of adopting rapid resolution plans

The potential benefits from developing resolution plans are substantial. First, the process should reduce moral hazard by making it clear to creditors and counterparties that a SIFI can be resolved in such a way that it may impose losses on them without catastrophic consequences for the rest of the financial system. An indication that this might have a powerful effect can be inferred from Moody's reaction (Croft and Jenkins, 2009) to the 'recovery and resolution plans' proposed in the UK. It warned the British authorities that such an approach 'would remove the necessity to support banks as banks would no longer be too interconnected or complex to fail. This could potentially result in rating downgrades where ratings currently incorporate a high degree of government support.' Of course, this benefit will be realized only to the extent that market participants believe a workable resolution plan exists and will be used. Equally importantly, they must believe that firms which are not required to have resolution plans are credibly excluded from bailouts.

Second, gaining approval of the resolution plan will cause SIFIs to enhance their governance of risk, simplify their corporate structures and make preparations so that less of the bankruptcy estate is consumed by a frantic, last-minute attempt to formulate and execute a resolution plan. These amounts can be quite substantial. The administrators of the Lehman bankruptcy (Cairns, 2009) have estimated that at least $75 billion was wasted because of the lack of any preparation for bankruptcy.

Third, developing the plan may cause SIFIs to reduce their risk exposures because of greater awareness by the board of directors, more thorough analysis by supervisors, and greater discipline by creditors and counterparties. This too is an important means of enhancing the governance of risk.

Fourth, a credible resolution plan will level the playing field between SIFIs and smaller, less complex institutions, so that profits and market share flow to institutions that provide the best services most efficiently rather than to institutions that benefit from the subsidy of an implicit guarantee.

Of course, resolution plans have both private and social costs in addition to the above benefits. Compliance costs will certainly increase significantly for SIFIs (and for supervisors, making it all the more important to provide them with adequate resources). But some of the upgrades in IT systems required should enable firms to manage their businesses more effectively, as well as facilitate a resolution.[32] Resolution plans may also reduce the efficiency with which the SIFI can deploy its capital and liquidity, but often these efficiencies have proven illusory in a crisis, when they are most needed. To the extent that capital and liquidity will be ring-fenced by regulators of other lines of the conglomerate's business (who believe their main duty is to protect the customers of the SIFI in their regulatory domain), they will be unwilling (or perhaps legally unable) to upstream capital or liquidity to a faltering parent.[33] Finally, a resolution plan may increase capital requirements and tax payments and lower profits to the extent that corporate simplification requires the elimination of entities used to engage in regulatory arbitrage and tax avoidance. But this is a private cost, not a social cost.

With regard to social costs, resolution plans could limit potential economies of scale and scope. But there is little evidence in the academic literature that economies of scale and scope outweigh the diseconomies of scale and scope that have become evident in the recent crisis.[34] In any event, technology-intensive activities, which offer genuine scale economies in some lines of business that involve heavy fixed costs, can be ring-fenced and operated as separate units from which firms of all sizes could benefit, much like the evolution of automated teller machines, which are now a shared network but began as proprietary systems. By reducing leverage, resolution plans may increase the costs of intermediation. But since excessive leverage is heavily implicated as a cause of the recent crisis, this may actually be a social benefit rather than a cost.

16.4   CONCLUDING COMMENT

The importance of effective corporate governance has long been recognized by regulators, but officials have been remarkably ineffectual in encouraging SIFIs to adopt practices that will ensure they have an effective framework for keeping aggregate risk within the firm's specified risk appetite. In part this stems from lack of attention to incentives for adopting effective governance of risk. Indeed, an indirect consequence of the tendency to bail out creditors of nearly every SIFI that suffers major losses is that it undermines incentives for creditors to encourage firms to enhance their governance of risk.

The attention to the structure of remuneration may help, although there is a danger that it may become much too prescriptive. It may be preferable to focus on compensation practices that are widely agreed to encourage risk-takers to disregard the longer-term consequences of their actions. These are simpler to monitor and sanction, although the competition for top talent will undoubtedly lead to a burst of innovations to circumvent the spirit of these regulations. But even an effective set of regulations on the structure of remuneration will not necessarily lead to the adoption of an effective framework for controlling risk. Two other innovations, however, may have a much stronger impact.

The adoption of a properly structured requirement for CoCos will have a much more direct impact on the incentives for adopting effective risk governance measures. The threat of massive dilution should focus boards and senior managements on improving their control of risk, and the holders of CoCos will be likely to monitor and price these efforts. Moreover, the introduction of a properly structured CoCo requirement is likely to resurrect the market for corporate control, which is virtually moribund in heavily regulated financial institutions and, under these circumstances, is likely to lead to a preference for managers who will impose effective risk controls.

Finally, the adoption of credible rapid resolution plans will strengthen the incentives provided by a CoCo requirement and will increase market discipline from other creditors as well, who have generally assumed that they will be bailed out in the event that a SIFI encounters excessive risks. Moreover, the process of establishing rapid resolution plans will enable supervisors and boards to gain a much deeper understanding of risk controls and vulnerabilities.

Samuel Johnson observed: '[W]hen a man knows he is to be hanged in a fortnight, it concentrates his mind wonderfully.' Similarly the existence of a credible way to resolve any SIFI will focus creditors, boards and managers of SIFIs on the importance of effective risk management and improve the corporate governance of risk.

NOTES

1. Of course, too much emphasis may be placed on faulty governance. No principles of corporate govern-ance can be expected to protect an institution fully against strategic errors or simply paying too much for an acquisition.
2. It should be noted that a decline in shareholder returns does not necessarily imply that the issuance of equity results in a destruction of the total value of the firm. Below I will suggest an alternative rationale for the pressure from independent directors to raise equity capital. As a firm approaches bankruptcy, the role of the directors shifts from representing the shareholders to protecting the assets of the firm for creditors who will become the new owners. In short, the independent directors have a fiduciary duty to protect the value of the bankruptcy estate. This will certainly not be rewarded by a rise in share prices, because shareholders at that stage place a high value on the option that they may be saved by a high-risk high-return investment and they will resist a transfer of wealth to creditors, but it will reduce the costs of financial distress that would otherwise diminish the value of the firm and possibly cause losses to taxpayers.
3. The 'Notice of proposed rulemaking on incentive based compensation arrangements' (2011) is 77 pages long.
4. For several examples see Dash (2011).
5. The reliance on supervisory discipline is not complete in all proposals because some advocate disclosure of compensation practices and, occasionally, a non-binding shareholder vote on compensation. But these disclosure measures will not result in effective market discipline unless an important class of stakeholders has an incentive to monitor the disclosures and take appropriate action if they seem inappropriate.
6. This subsection draws on Calomiris and Herring (2011) and on Claessens et al. (2010).
7. D'Souza et al. (2009) run simulations to show that the strong incentives for CoCo issuers to avoid conver-sion would make conversions extremely rare and thus they would have yields quite close to traditional subordinated debt.
8. For example, the Japanese banking system was insolvent for almost a decade while still satisfying its minimum book value capital requirements under the Basel standards.
9. And the complicity of accounting firms in window-dressing transactions, as shown in the Lehman Brothers case.
10. One of the main problems in determining the market value of a bank is estimating the value of the bank's assets, most of which are not actively traded. The quasi-market value attempts to estimate the market value of a bank's assets by making use of the balance sheet identity and adding the market value of the bank's shares to the face value of the bank's liabilities (under the assumption that it will not default). This measure is chosen because of its ease of computation on a continuous basis.
11. The crisis showed that the definition of the numerator, the risk-weighted denominator and the minimum acceptable ratio were completely inadequate. Nonetheless, for this retrospective examination of the crisis it is interesting to see whether the quasi-market value ratio would have been informative in separating SIFIs that would require intervention from SIFIs that did not. Basel III will require a much higher level of equity and the issuance of CoCos should be larger as well.
12. Two issues of contingent capital – one by Rabo Bank (a cooperative) and the other by Lloyds – have proven to be significantly more expensive than subordinated debt. But it is important to note that these issues present a very different incentive to the managers than what is contemplated in this proposal. In the case of Rabo Bank, there are no shareholders to be diluted, and in the case of Lloyds, the amount of contingent capital and the trigger do not provide sufficient motivation for managers to issue equity pre-emptively to avoid setting off the conversion trigger. Moreover, the issuance of these bonds during the crisis probably increased their cost.
13. This subsection draws on Herring (2009, 2010) and Claessens et al. (2010).
14. See Haldane (2009) for an analysis of the direct and indirect subsidies Western governments provided to SIFIs during the crisis, an amount equal to roughly 25 percent of world gross domestic product (GDP).
15. Within the last year, 'internationally-consistent firm-specific contingency and resolution plans' have been endorsed by the Group of Twenty (2009), experimented with by the FSA as recovery and resolution plans (known popularly as living wills), introduced by the US Treasury to Congress as rapid resolution plans and proposed in the Dodd Bill as funeral plans. The FSB Principles for Cross-Border Cooperation on Crisis Management of April 2009 commit national authorities from relevant home- and host-country jurisdictions to ensure that firms develop adequate resolution plans. The resolution plans will include both plans to be prepared in the first instance by each firm, to reduce its risk exposures and make its struc-ture more effective in a 'going-concern' scenario, and wind-down plans, to be prepared by the authorities, in a 'gone-concern' scenario (FSB, 2009). The FDIC (2010) has issued a notice of proposed rulemaking regarding 'Special reporting, analysis and contingent resolution plans at certain large insured deposi-

tory institutions'. Although the concept has been broadly endorsed, little has been written about what the details of such a plan should include. Exceptions are to be found in Avgouleas et al. (2010), Huertas (2010) and Herring (2009, 2010). This subsection draws heavily from Herring (2010).

16. Ron Feldman (2010) has argued that the planning must be driven by supervisors, not firms. Although supervisors must have the final word, much can be gained by maintaining a dialogue between the firm, its board and the authorities. His point that, to be effective, resolution plans must lead to changes in the operations of financial institutions and supervisors, before a crisis hits, is on the mark.

17. The collapse of Lehman Brothers presents a particularly good example of this problem. It had lines of business that were fragmented across numerous subsidiaries that were caught up in multiple insolvency procedures on three different continents with no prospect of reassembling the line of business even though this may have preserved substantial going-concern value.

18. Hüpkes (2009: 515) made the point clearly in an article titled 'Complicity in complexity: what to do about the "too-big-to-fail problem"', in which she argues that policymakers need to give more attention to how the complexity of an institution's legal structure affects the resolution process. She explains that the size of an institution is not the crux of the matter: 'Rather it is the complexity of large financial institutions that makes rapid and orderly wind-downs virtually impossible.'

19. The very rumor that a SIFI was making a resolution plan might set off a run in the absence of a general legal requirement that all SIFIs must do so. The legal obligation will enable the SIFI to do something it should be doing as a matter of good governance, without fear of undermining its reputation.

20. This notion has generated a considerable amount of controversy in Britain, with bankers generally taking the view that the supervisory authorities have no business monitoring their tax avoidance strategies. Alistair Darling, Chancellor of the Exchequer, has tartly responded (Giles et al., 2009): 'I do worry when an organization is structured for tax purposes rather than for the efficiency of its business and the strength of its business.'

21. This too is likely to be a contentious point as demonstrated by the years it has taken the Federal Deposit Insurance Corporation (FDIC) to gain authority to require insured banks to identify insured deposits to facilitate rapid pay-outs. Banks successfully resisted for a number of years, claiming that it would be an overwhelming technological challenge.

22. Hüpkes (2005) wrote about this in the context of global financial institutions, much like the SIFIs that are the focus of this chapter.

23. The absence of a credible plan would be presumptive evidence of a failure to carry out this fiduciary duty.

24. Precisely what is 'a reasonable amount of time' will likely change as the approach is implemented. The ultimate goal ought to be a plan that can be implemented over a weekend, but earlier iterations will clearly take much longer. Some have advocated the need for a twilight ('cotton wool') period between intervention and the decision to start liquidation to allow resolution to proceed more smoothly.

25. See Guttentag and Herring (1984) and the references cited therein.

26. In countries with a unified regulatory system, this is clear. In others, like the United States, it may not be unless the entity is a bank holding company or a financial services holding company. Clearly this is one of the first problems to be resolved if there is ambiguity about who has overall responsibility for an institution (e.g., AIG) or whether the primary supervisor is competent to carry out its duties (e.g., Lehman Brothers).

27. Hüpkes has emphasized this point repeatedly. See, for example, Hüpkes (2005).

28. One might question how these equity investments should be treated in computing consolidated minimum capital requirements. The equity investment should count fully because the purpose of imposing the equity requirement on these bits of the infrastructure, including the systemically important pieces, is to make them easy to detach from the failing institution. They should be relatively easy to sell because they are often systemically important parts of the infrastructure.

29. See Herring and Carmassi (2010).

30. The EU has a mechanism for taking account of competition policy in the case of a failing SIFI that receives state support. Former European Commissioner for Competition Neelie Kroes has required that Commerzbank, ING, the Royal Bank of Scotland and Lloyds downsize to compensate for the anti-competitive effects of the subsidies they have received. The EU Competition Commissioner can force banks to take a range of actions, including mandates to 'sell billions of euros of assets, close branches, cut balance sheets drastically, restrict payments to investors, executives and staff, and focus more narrowly on retail banking' (Reuters, 2009). The United States lacks any mechanism for considering such issues except in the merger approval process (which is often given short shrift in the case of a shotgun merger). And although the EU action is taken after the extension of a bailout, it seems preferable to the frequent US pattern of subsidizing the merger of a very large bank with another even larger bank with scant regard for competitive effects. See further Dewatripont et al. (2010).

31. If not actually integrated with the supervisory authority, the resolution authority should be represented at these discussions. It will have the greatest expertise regarding how to implement an ordinary resolution.

32. In a private comment, Robert Eisenbeis has pointed out that just as the preparations for Y2K enabled a number of banks to deal more effectively with the shock of 9/11, this improvement in IT systems may have unexpected benefits.
33. In this sense, the Basel Committee's long-time emphasis on consolidated regulation of minimum capital requirements may be deeply misleading. Similarly, the ratings agencies clearly misjudged the ability of AIG to upstream excess capital from its multiple insurance businesses to aid the holding company or a faltering affiliate.
34. See, for example, Berger and Mester (1997). Although there are numerous empirical studies that attempt to quantify economies of scale, all are subject to criticism because of the paucity of relevant data. This is, of course, particularly true for enormous banks. But it does seem clear that scale economies cannot be the main driving force behind the creation of trillion-dollar banks. A more robust and perhaps more relevant empirical regularity is that the compensation of senior executives tends to increase proportionately with scale (Frydman and Saks, 2007).

REFERENCES

Avgouleas, E., C. Goodhart and D. Schoenmaker (2010), 'Living wills as a catalyst for action', DSF Policy Papers No. 4, Duisenberg School of Finance, Amsterdam.
BCBS (1997), 'Core principles for effective banking supervision', April.
BCBS (1999a), 'Supervisory lessons to be drawn from the Asian crisis', Basel Committee on Banking Supervision Working Paper No. 2, June.
BCBS (1999b), 'Enhancing corporate governance for banking organisations', Consultative Document, September.
BCBS (2005), 'Enhancing corporate governance banking organisations', Consultative Document, July.
BCBS (2006), 'Enhancing corporate governance for banking organisations', Consultative Document, February.
BCBS (2008), 'Report of the Senior Supervisors Group', Consultative Document, Basel.
BCBS, (2010a), 'Principles for enhancing corporate governance', Consultative Document, March.
BCBS (2010b), 'Principles for enhancing corporate governance', Consultative Document, October.
BCBS (2010c), 'Report and recommendations of the Cross-border Bank Resolution Group', March.
BCBS (2011), 'Basel Committee issues final elements of the reforms to raise the quality of regulatory capital', Press Release, 13 January.
Berger, Allen and Loretta Mester (1997), 'Efficiency and productivity change in the US commercial banking industry: a comparison of the 1980s and 1990s', Federal Reserve Bank of Philadelphia Working Paper, No. 97-5.
Cairns, Ann (2009), 'Breaking the insolvency mould', *International Corporate Rescue*, 6(2), 115, available at http://www.chasecambria.com/site/journal/article.php?id=384.
Calomiris, Charles and Richard Herring (2011), 'Why and how to design an effective contingent capital requirement', working paper.
Claessens, Stijn, Richard Herring and Dirk Schoenmaker (2010), 'A safer world financial system: improving the resolution of systemic institutions', 12th Geneva Report on the World Economy, ICMB and CEPR.
Commission Staff Working Document (2009), 'An EU framework for cross-border crisis management in the banking sector', Document Accompanying the Communication from the Commission to the European Parliament, the Council, the European Economic and Social Committee, the European Court of Justice and the European Central Bank.
Committee on Corporate Governance (2000), 'The combined code, principles of good governance and code of best practice', Final Report from Cadbury and Greenbury Reports, May.
Conway, Edmund (2009), 'Mervyn King: bail-outs created "biggest moral hazard in history"', *Telegraph*, 20 October.
Corston, John (2010), Statement on 'Systemically important institutions and the issue of "too big to fail"', before the Financial Crisis Inquiry Commission, 1 September.
Croft, Jane and Patrick Jenkins (2009), 'Moody's warns over "living wills"', *Financial Times*, 23 September.
Dash, Eric (2011), 'Dealbook: hedging lets bankers skirt efforts to overhaul Pay', *New York Times*, 6 February.
Davies, Howard (2003), 'Corporate governance in financial institutions', speech delivered to International Monetary Conference, 3 June.
Dewatripont, Mathis, Gregory Nguyen, Petr Praet and Andre Sapir (2010), 'The role of state aid control in improving bank resolution in Europe', Bruegel Policy Contribution, Issues 2010/04, May.
D'Souza, Andre, Brian Foran, Gaye Erkan Hafez, Charles Himmelberg, Quan Mai, Jim Mannoia, Richard

Ramsden and Scott Romanoff (2009), 'Ending "Too Big To Fail"', Goldman Sachs Global Markets Institute, December.

Duffie, Darrell (2010), 'A contractual approach to restructuring financial institutions', in Kenneth Scott, George Shultz and John Taylor (eds), *Ending Government Bailouts as We Know Them*, Stanford, CA: Stanford University Press, Hoover Institution.

The Economist (2010a), 'A matter of principle, why some banks did much better than others', 11 February.

The Economist (2010b), 'Corporate constitutions, the world knows less about what makes for good corporate governance than it likes to think', 28 October.

Erkens, David, Mingyi Hung and Pedro Matos (2010), 'Corporate governance in the 2007–2008 financial crisis: evidence from financial institutions worldwide', Working Paper, Leventhal School of Accounting, Marshall School of Business, September.

European Commission (2010), 'Corporate governance in financial institutions and remuneration policies', 2 June.

European Commission (2011), 'Commission seeks views on possible EU framework to deal with future bank failures', Consultation Document, Brussels, 6 January.

Federal Deposit Insurance Corporation (FDIC) (2010), 'Special reporting, analysis and contingent resolution plans at certain large insured depository institutions', Notice of Proposed Rulemaking, May.

Feldman, Ron (2010), 'Forcing financial institutions change through credible recovery/resolution plans: an alternative to plan-now/implement later living wills', Economic Policy Paper 10-2, Federal Reserve Bank of Minneapolis, 6 May.

Financial Stability Board (FSB) (2009), 'Progress since the Pittsburgh Summit in implementing the G20 recommendations for strengthening financial stability', Report to G20 Finance Ministers and Governors, November.

Financial Stability Forum (2009), 'FSF principles for sound compensation practices', 2 April.

Flannery, Mark J. (2005), '"No pain, no gain": effecting market discipline via "reverse convertible debentures"', in Hal Scott (ed.), *Capital Adequacy beyond Basel: Banking, Securities, and Insurance*, Oxford: Oxford University Press.

Frydman, Carola and Raven Saks (2007), 'Executive compensation: a new view from a long-term perspective, 1936–2005', Federal Reserve Board Technical Report, no. 2007-35, available at http://www.federalreserve.gov/pubs/feds/2007/200735/200735abs.html.

Giles, Chris, George Parker and Patrick Jenkins (2009), 'Living wills to be forced on banks', *Financial Times*, 15 September.

Greenspan, Alan (2009), 'Speech to the Council on Foreign Relations', 15 October, available at http://www.cfr.org/publication/20417.

Group of Twenty (2008), 'Declaration: Summit on Financial Markets and the World Economy', 15 November.

Group of Twenty (2009), 'Leaders' statement: the Pittsburgh summit', 24–25 September.

Guttentag, Jack and Richard J. Herring (1984), 'Credit rationing and financial disorder', *Journal of Finance*, **39**, 1359–82.

Haldane, Andrew (2009), 'Banking on the state', presented at the 12th Annual Federal Reserve of Chicago International Banking Conference, 25 September, available at www.bankofengland.co.uk/publications/speeches/2009/ speech409.pdf.

Hart, Oliver and Luigi Zingales (2010), 'A new capital regulation for large financial institutions', FEEM Working Paper No. 124.2009, http://ssrn.com/ abstract=1533274.

Herring, Richard J. (2009), 'Wind-down plans as an alternative to bailouts', Pew Financial Reform Project, Briefing Paper No. 15.

Herring, Richard J. (2010), 'Wind-down plans as an alternative to bailouts: the cross-border challenges', in K. Scott, G. Shultz and J. Taylor (eds), *Ending Government Bailouts as We Know Them*, Stanford, CA: Hoover Institution Press, Stanford University.

Herring, Richard J. and Jacopo Carmassi (2010), 'The corporate structure of international financial conglomerates: complexity and its implications for safety and soundness', in A. Berger, P. Molyneux and J. Wilson (eds), *The Oxford Handbook of Banking*, Oxford: Oxford University Press.

House Committee on Financial Services (2010), 'Summary of the Dodd–Frank Wall Street Reform and Consumer Protection Act', June.

Huertas, Thomas (2009), 'Too big to fail, too complex to contemplate: what to do about systemically important firms', paper presented at the Financial Markets Group, London School of Economics, 15 September.

Huertas, Thomas (2010), 'Living wills: how can the concept be implemented?', in Richard J. Herring (ed.), *Cross Border Resolution of Large, Complex Financial Institutions*, Philadelphia, PA: Wharton Financial Institutions Center.

Hüpkes, Eva (2005), '"Too big to save": towards a functional approach to resolving crises in global financial institutions', in Douglas Evanoff and George Kaufman (eds), *Systemic Financial Crisis: Resolving Large Bank Insolvencies*, Singapore: World Scientific Publishing.

Hüpkes, Eva (2009), 'Complicity in complexity: what to do about the "too-big to-fail" problem', *Butterworth's Journal of International Banking and Financial Law*, October, 515–18.

International Monetary Fund (IMF) (2009), 'Detecting systemic risk', in *Responding to the Financial Crisis and Measuring Systemic Risks*, April Global Financial Stability Report, Washington, DC.

Joint Forum on Financial Conglomerates (1998), 'Supervision of financial conglomerates', February.

Kane, Edward (1989), *The S&L Insurance Mess: How Did It Happen?* Washington, DC: Urban Institute Press.

Kashyap, Anil, Raghuram Rajan and Jeremy Stein (2008), 'Rethinking capital regulation', paper presented at the Federal Reserve Bank of Kansas City Symposium, 'Maintaining Stability in a Changing World', 21–23 August, Jackson Hole, WY.

Kelly, Tom (2008), 'WaMu failed to heed lesson learned in 80's, the largest bank failure in US history', Inman News, 7 October.

King, M. (2009), Speech Delivered at the Lord Mayor's Banquet for Bankers and Merchants of the City of London at the Mansion House, 17 June.

Kirkpatrick, Grant (2009), 'The corporate governance lessons from the financial crisis', *OECD Financial Market Trends*, 1, 1–30.

Kuritzkes, Andrew (2010), 'A safer world financial system, improving the resolution of systemic institutions, Geneva report: discussion', overhead presentation at the Geneva Conference, 7 May.

McKee, Michael and Scott Lanman (2009), 'Greenspan says US should consider breaking up large banks', Bloomberg.com, 15 October.

Office of the Inspector General (2010), 'Evaluation of federal regulatory oversight of Washington Mutual Bank', Department of the Treasury, Federal Deposit Insurance Corporation, Report No. Eval-10-002, April.

Reuters (2009), 'EU competition chief readies ruling on bank bailouts', 16 October, available at http://www.nytimes.com/2009/10/17/business/global/17kroes.html?_r=1.

Sants, Hector (2008), 'Dear CEO letter on remuneration policies', FSA, 13 October.

SEC (2008), 'SEC's oversight of Bear Stearns and related entities: broker-dealer risk assessment program', Office of Inspector General, Report No. 446-B, 25 September.

SEC (2010), 'Investigation of the circumstances surrounding the SEC's proposed settlements with Bank of America, including a review of the court's rejection of the SEC's first proposed settlement and an analysis of the impact of Bank of America's status as a TARP recipient', Office of the Inspector General, Case No. OIG-522, 30 September.

Sender, Henry (2009), 'Dimon backs means to close down banks', *Financial Times*, 28 October.

Special Inspector General for TARP (2009), 'Factors affecting efforts to limit payments to AIG counterparties', 17 November.

Special Inspector General for TARP (2011), 'Extraordinary financial assistance provided to Citigroup, Inc', 13 January.

Turner, Adair (2009), 'The Turner Review, a regulatory response to the global banking crisis', FSA, March.

UBS (2008), 'Shareholder report on UBS's write-downs, Zurich, 18 April.

Valukas, Anton (2010), 'Report of Anton R. Valukas, Examiner for United States Bankruptcy Court, Southern District of New York', March.

Wessel, David (2009), 'Three theories on solving the "too big to fail" problem', *Wall Street Journal*, 29 October, available at http://professional.wsj.com/article/SB125668497563411667.html.

PART IV

GOVERNANCE, REGULATION AND SUPERVISION

17 The boundary problems in financial regulation
Charles A.E. Goodhart and Rosa M. Lastra*

17.1 INTRODUCTION

As with territorial waters and the exclusive economic zone in fishing disputes between countries, where you draw the line of regulation, protection and government assistance is contentious. Calls either to widen the net of regulation (and related protection) or to limit protection, for example to some set of 'narrow banks', have proliferated in response to the crisis.[1] The dichotomy between international (global) markets and institutions and national rules, exposing the limitations of the principle of national sovereignty, is a major challenge in the design of effective financial regulation.

From the point of view of governance, the first boundary problem can contribute to more complex organizational structures, increasing the opacity of the financial system. The second issue may affect the location of different financial activities and the structure of the financial sector in different countries, also adding a layer of complexity to the governance of financial institutions.

17.2 FIRST BOUNDARY PROBLEM: THE 'PERIMETER ISSUE', THE DISTINCTION BETWEEN REGULATED AND NON-REGULATED (OR LESS REGULATED) ENTITIES

The first boundary problem was examined at some length in the *National Institute Economic Review* (2008)[2] and in the Appendix to the so-called Geneva Report (2009),[3] focusing on cases where the non-regulated can provide a (partial) substitute for the services of the regulated.[4] The unregulated frequently depend on services, such as payment services, and on back-up lines of credit from the regulated. In the build-up to the crisis, there are plenty of examples of unregulated entities which were structured as 'associates', or offshoots, of the regulated ones.

If regulation is effective, it will constrain the regulated from achieving their preferred, unrestricted position, often by lowering their profitability and their return on capital. So the returns achievable within the regulated sector are likely to fall relative to those available on substitutes outside. There will be a switch of business from the regulated to the non-regulated sector.[5] In order to protect their own businesses, those in the regulated sector will seek to open up connected operations in the non-regulated sector, in order to catch the better opportunities there. The example of commercial banks setting up associated conduits, SIVs (structured investment vehicles) and hedge funds in the last credit bubble is a case in point.

But this condition is quite general. One of the more common proposals, at least in the past, for dealing with the various problems of financial regulation has been to try to limit deposit insurance and the safety net to a set of 'narrow banks', which would be constrained to hold only liquid and 'safe' assets. The idea is that this would provide safe deposits for the orphans and widows. Moreover, these narrow banks would run a clearing-house and keep the payments system in operation, whatever happened elsewhere. For all other financial institutions outside the narrow banking system, it would be a case of *caveat emptor*. They should be allowed to fail, without official support or taxpayer recapitalization.

In fact, in the UK something akin to a narrow banking system was put in place in the nineteenth century with the Post Office Savings Bank (POSB) and the Trustee Savings Bank (TSB). But the idea that the official safety net should have been restricted to the POSB and TSB was never seriously entertained. Nor could it have been. When a 'narrow bank' is constrained to holding liquid, safe assets, it is simultaneously prevented from earning higher returns, and thus from offering as high interest rates or other valuable services (such as overdrafts) to its depositors. Nor could the authorities in good conscience prevent the broader banks from setting up their own clearing-house. Thus the banking system outside the narrow banks would grow much faster under normal circumstances; it would provide most of the credit to the private sector, and participate in the key clearing and settlement processes in the economy.

This might be prevented by law, taking legal steps to prohibit broader banks from providing means of payment or establishing clearing and settlement systems of their own. There are at least four problems with such a move. First, it runs afoul of political economy considerations. As soon as a significant body of voters has an interest in the preservation of a class of financial intermediaries, they will demand, and receive, protection. Witness money market funds and 'breaking the buck' in the USA. Second, it is intrinsically illiberal. Third, it is often possible to get around such legal constraints, for example by having the broad bank pass all payment orders through an associated narrow bank. Fourth, the reasons for the authorities' concern with financial intermediaries, for better or worse, go well beyond insuring the maintenance of the basic payment system and the protection of small depositors. Neither Bear Stearns nor Fannie Mae had small depositors, or played an integral role in the basic payment system.

When a financial crisis does occur, it usually first attacks the unprotected sector, as occurred with SIVs and conduits in 2007. But the existence of the differential between the protected and unprotected sector then has the capacity to make the crisis worse. When panic and extreme risk-aversion take hold, the depositors in, and creditors to, the unprotected or weaker sector seek to withdraw their funds, and place these in the protected or stronger sector, thereby redoubling the pressures on the weak and unprotected sectors, which are then forced into fire sales of assets, and so on. The combination of a boundary between the protected and the unprotected, with greater constraints on the business of the regulated sector, almost guarantees a cycle of flows into the unregulated part of the system during cyclical expansions with sudden and dislocating reversals during crises.

The institutional criterion that typically governs financial regulation divides firms into banks, securities firms and insurance firms, among others, and then generally applies a separate set of rules for each type of institution (with banks bearing the heaviest regulatory cost), while leaving entities that perform similar services (e.g., the 'shadow banking system') outside the regulatory loop; and this approach has proven deficient during the crisis. The shadow banking system, which played a key role in the growth of the securitization market and is considered by many to be one of the causes of the crisis, is an example of this boundary problem.[6] While we mostly know what a bank is, the very expression 'shadow banking system' is imprecise and its contours are not clearly defined. According to Roubini, broker-dealers, hedge funds, private equity groups, structured investment vehicles and conduits, money market funds and non-bank mortgage lenders are all part of this shadow system.[7] Gary Gorton and Andrew Metrick believe that it was the (wholesale) run on the repo market during 2008, a run not so much on depository institutions as on the shadow banking system, that caused the crisis, and suggest that new regulation could improve the functioning of the shadow banking system by making it less vulnerable to panics and crises of confidence.[8]

Today's financial markets are characterized by the proliferation of financial conglomerates and complex financial groups and by the blurring of the frontiers between the types of business that financial firms undertake, thus rendering institutional classifications less meaningful. Supervision has traditionally been organized by institution, irrespective of the business function or range of functions that the institution undertakes. Inter-industry affiliation and inter-industry competition in the financial sector have suggested the need for enhanced consolidated supervision, and increased reliance on regulation by business function rather than by institution. Under a system of supervision by business function, supervisors focus on the type of business undertaken, regardless of which institutions are involved in that particular business. The Dutch supervisory model, introduced in the second half of 2002, provides an example of a functional model based on the objectives of supervision. The Dutch central bank (De Nederlandsche Bank, DNB) is the institution responsible for prudential supervision in the pursuit of financial stability. The Authority for Financial Markets (AFM) is the authority responsible for conduct of business supervision. Both supervisory authorities cover the full cross-sector width of financial markets (all institutions in banking, securities, insurance and pensions).[9]

Notwithstanding this functional–institutional boundary problem, whether we need to circumscribe government protection to a specified set of regulated institutions remains an issue of great importance. If regulation is to differ in intensity between the systemically important and the less so, then there is a need for (legal) clarity as to which falls into each camp. But the systemic importance of any financial intermediary may vary depending on circumstances. The definition of 'systemic importance' is fuzzy.

However, the recent crisis has shown that we must make a much greater effort to understand the emergence and existence of such systemic risks. We need greater transparency to be able to identify systemic risk in the first place. It is clear that some non-banks are systemically significant and that the potential provision of government assistance justifies the widening of the regulatory net. The problem is how to do it.

The issue of drawing boundaries for regulation-protection is not new. For instance, the Glass–Steagall Act of 1933 (named after its legislative sponsors, Carter Glass and Henry B. Steagall) established a clear boundary between commercial banks and investment banks in the USA, with government assistance typically confined to the former (even though there were some emergency provisions, such as section 13(3) of the Federal Reserve Act, which permitted the Fed to act as lender of last resort to non-depository financial institutions, a provision that became handy since it was activated in the rescues of Bear Stearns in March 2008 and of AIG in September 2008). Many provisions of Glass–Steagall were repealed by the passage of the Financial Modernization Act of 1999 (Gramm–Leach–Bliley Act).[10] Interestingly, this repeal, though hailed at the time as a major achievement, has been blamed by a few politicians and commentators for some of the problems that led the financial crisis.[11] Indeed, among the structural reforms suggested to deal with crises, some have proposed a return to Glass–Steagall, while narrow banking or mutual fund banking has been advocated by others.[12]

Given the link between regulation and government protection, financial institutions are somewhat reluctant to accept more intensive regulation as the price for protection. This explains why Goldman Sachs and Morgan Stanley did not apply to become bank holding companies until after the collapse of Lehman Brothers in September 2008. But regulation is costly and banks and other regulated financial institutions often try to game or circumvent the regulatory system, so as to reduce this cost. There often appears to be a trade-off between safety and profitability, with financial institutions willing to sacrifice safety in good times in order to enhance their profitability.[13]

How, in a regulatory system, can we combine the need to protect safety and soundness with the need to make a profit, and therefore to take risks? What is the difference between normal risk and excessive risk, and who defines it? These are perennial questions in financial regulation. While regulators – in a free market economy – should not be unduly concerned about profits (unless the lack of profits should threaten a desirable function) they should, however, worry about risks. As acknowledged, a regulator can always claim: 'If I am going to assist you on a rainy day, I need to oversee you on sunny days.'

Safe and sound banking and finance rests firstly upon good risk management and secondly on good risk control (by both the regulated and the regulators). In principle, only if management fails to control risks adequately should regulators intervene. However, it is difficult for regulators to know whether the institution has been or is being irresponsible unless they monitor on a regular basis. Any risk can grow to systemic proportions when its negative impact extends beyond an individual institution, affecting or threatening to affect by contagion many other institutions, often creating a disruption in the monetary system and an associated economic paralysis. Systemic risks seldom occur alone; they usually spread to other risks like wildfire and undermine confidence. Confidence and trust play an essential role in the financial system. Henry Thornton wrote in 1802:[14]

> Commercial credit may be defined to be that confidence which subsists among commercial men in respect to their mercantile affairs . . . In a society in which law and the sense of moral duty are weak, and property is consequently insecure, there will, of course be little confidence or credit, and there will also be little commerce.

Historical experience suggests that regulation, and more specifically governmental banking regulation, was often a by-product or reaction to crises or conflicts. In the United Kingdom, for instance, the shift from self-regulation to legal regulation in the field of financial services was prompted by a series of crises: the enactment of the 1979 Banking Act[15] followed the secondary banking crisis, and the 1987 Banking Act[16] was enacted following the Johnson Matthey Bankers failure. This is also the case in the United States, where both the creation of the Federal Reserve System (acting as lender of last resort) in 1913 and that of the Federal Deposit Insurance Corporation in 1933 were responses to financial crises. Similarly, in Spain the creation of the guarantee insurance funds (Fondos de Garantía de Depósitos) for banks and thrifts in 1977 was motivated by a banking crisis. At an international level, regulation has also been prompted by financial failure and crises. Regulation after crisis is a constant in the history of finance.[17]

In some instances there are regulated and unregulated entities performing similar types of business. This is the case for instance with investment companies (pools of funds), where the legislation in the USA (and other jurisdictions) separates the 'ins', that is, mutual funds falling in the US under the Investment Company Act of 1940, from the 'outs', such as hedge funds, which are not subject to the stricter requirements of the Act and other securities laws. In the EU, Alternative Investment Funds (AIFs) are defined as funds that are not harmonized under the Undertakings for Collective Investment in Transferable Securities (UCITS) Directive.[18]

Another twist in the boundary problem is the interaction that some unregulated (or lightly regulated) institutions have with regulated ones. For instance, rating agencies exert an extraordinary influence and power upon financial institutions and their regulators (not to mention politicians in countries where sovereign debt is downgraded, with the example of Greece in 2010 providing ample evidence on this point).

The boundary problem has particular implications with regard to capital requirements. Why should capital requirements be strictly imposed upon commercial banks (credit or depositary institutions) when the shadow banking system is engaged in similar types of risky activities? Moreover, emphasis on capital, important as it is as an indicator of soundness, should not be the sole tool in the regulators' armoury. As Robert Litan insightfully stated in the 1980s, regulators focus so much upon capital requirements because it is difficult to assess and control the quality of the asset portfolio and, of course, potential mismatches between the duration of liabilities and assets provide a cause for concern about liquidity management and controls.[19]

The boundary problem is also present with regard to lending limits, a traditional tool in banking regulation. We need to devise effective leverage limits that fulfil the same function that traditional lending limits have fulfilled in the past with regard to banks' overall exposures (including lending limits to insiders, subsidiaries and shareholders, and limits on large credit exposures).

Insofar as regulation is effective in forcing the regulated to shift from a preferred to a less desired position, it is likely to set up a boundary problem. This is, therefore, a common occurrence after, or response to, almost any regulatory imposition. A current (2010) example is the proposal to introduce additional regulatory controls on systemically important financial intermediaries (SIFIs). If SIFIs are to be penalized, there needs, on grounds of equity and fairness, to be some definition of and some criteria for what constitutes a SIFI – a complex exercise. But once such a definition is established and a clear boundary established, there will be an incentive for institutions to position themselves on one side or another of that boundary, whichever may seem more advantageous. Suppose that we started, say in a small country, with three banks, each with a third of deposits, and each regarded as too big to fail (TBTF), and the definition of a SIFI was a bank with over 20 per cent of total deposits. If each bank then split itself into two identical clones to avoid the tougher regulation, with similar portfolios and interbank linkages, would there have been much progress? Similarity can easily generate contagion. Indeed, regulation tends to encourage and to foster similarity in behaviour. Does it follow then that regulation thereby enhances the dangers of systemic collapse that its purpose should be to prevent? Does the desire to encourage all the regulated to adopt, and to harmonize with, the behaviour of the 'best' actually endanger the resilience of the system as a whole?

One extreme solution to the first boundary problem is to regulate either all financial entities alike or none at all.[20] Laissez-faire proponents of free banking have long advocated this system, suggesting a minimalist approach in which the only acceptable rules are those that promote competition (entry or licensing, bankruptcy rules to govern exit and others) or anti-fraud provisions. Such a laissez-faire system however is unrealistic, while the alternative – regulate all alike – is not feasible. This means that the boundary problem is likely to remain, and that any new rule will bring with it new boundary problems.

What should the regulators and supervisors then do? Again we quote from the Geneva Report:

> They should start by trying to list the key financial markets and systems in their own country. Having done so, they should review whether and which financial institutions are so important to the functioning of that market, or system, that their downfall, whether in the form of bankruptcy or major deleveraging, would seriously disrupt the operations of that market or system . . . In essence the financial supervisors have got to ask themselves, which financial institutions can be allowed to fail, and which cannot. Those that they claim cannot be allowed to fail, should be specifically regulated . . . Besides occasions of institutional downfall, regulators need to be concerned with such market failures as may lead to resource misallocations, e.g. in the guise of asset bubbles and busts.[21]

A criterion that divides institutions into those that can be allowed to fail and those that cannot (a criterion that draws on the 'too big to fail' doctrine and its variants, such as too interconnected to fail) needs to be well known and publicized *ex ante*, since only those institutions that cannot be allowed to fail (because of the need to protect essential functions such as the smooth functioning of the payment system) are to be protected and regulated. And since licensing is the first stage in the supervisory process, which acts as a filter in subsequent stages, the licensing requirements would be a relatively straightforward way to deal with this problem.[22] Of course, if enacted, any such rule dividing institutions into those that are allowed to fail and those that are not is likely to lead a legion of lawyers to look at it in microscopic detail so as to find loopholes.

> The more effective regulation is, the greater the incentive to find ways around it. With time and considerable money at stake, those within the regulatory boundary will find ways around any new regulation. The obvious danger is that the resultant dialectic between the regulator and the regulated will lead to increasing complexity, as the regulated find loop-holes which the regulators then move (slowly) to close. Basel I metamorphosed into Basel II [and now into Basel III]. So the process becomes ever more complex, almost certainly without becoming less porous.[23]

The above consideration suggests that any prescriptive rule-based approach needs to be complemented with more generic principles that respect the spirit of the law. Furthermore, national regulation alone will not suffice. Global problems require global solutions, which leads us into the next section.

17.3 SECOND BOUNDARY PROBLEM: THE CROSS-BORDER DIMENSION, THE BORDERS BETWEEN STATES OR JURISDICTIONS WITH DIFFERENT LEGAL SYSTEMS AND REGULATORY STRUCTURES

The second boundary of critical importance to the conduct of regulation is the border between states or jurisdictions, such as the European Union (EU), each with their own legal and regulatory structures, that is, the cross-border problem, which is rooted in the limitations of the principle of national sovereignty. Sovereignty as a supreme power is typically exerted over the territory of the state: the principle of territoriality.[24] So, the ongoing process of globalization and the frequency of cross-border movement of persons, capital, goods or services has major implications for the scope of unfettered sovereignty, which continues to shrink.[25]

Financial markets and institutions have grown international in recent years. However, supervision and crisis management generally remains nationally based, constrained by the domain of domestic jurisdictions. The cross-border expansion of banks (via mergers and acquisitions, joint ventures or the establishment of branches and subsidiaries) and the effective supervision of institutions operating in various jurisdictions present numerous challenges for financial regulators and supervisors. Though progress has been made with regard to the regulation and supervision of cross-border banks, notably via soft law rules (Basel Committee of Banking Supervision and others) and regional rules (European Commission rules), the cross-border resolution of banking crises remains a matter of intense policy and legal debate. Despite the many difficulties involved, efforts to develop international standards on cross-border bank resolution are currently under way.[26]

In a global financial system with (relatively) free movement of capital across borders, most financial transactions that are originated in one country can be executed in another. This means that any constraint, or tax, that is imposed on a financial transaction in a country can often be (easily) avoided by arranging for that same transaction to take place under the legal, tax and accounting jurisdiction of another country; sometimes, indeed often, under the aegis of a subsidiary or branch of exactly the same bank or intermediary as was involved in the initial country.

This tends to generate a race to the bottom, though not always, since the parties to a contract will prize legal certainty and contract reliability. (In this latter regard, Howell Jackson, drawing on the 'race to the bottom' versus 'race to the top' debate that has been a feature of corporate law scholarship in the United States – through the work of Roberta Romano and others – over the last 25 years, discusses the merits of regulatory competition in securities markets.[27]) Another aspect of this same syndrome is the call for 'a level playing field'. Any state which seeks to impose, unilaterally, tougher regulation than that in operation in some other country will face the accusation that the effect of the regulation will just be to benefit foreign competition with little, or no, restraining effect on the underlying transactions.

Moreover the cross-border concern may constrain the application of countercyclical regulation. Financial cycles, booms and busts differ in their intensity from country to country. Housing prices rose much more in Australia, Ireland, Spain, the UK and the USA than in Canada, Germany and Japan in the years 2002–2007. Bank credit expansion also differed considerably between countries. But if regulation becomes countercyclically tightened in the boom countries, will that not, in a global financial system, just lead to a transfer of such transactions offshore; and London has been at the centre of arranging such cross-border financial operations.

Financial globalization in general, and the cross-border activities of SIFIs in particular, mean that the 'level playing field' argument is advanced to oppose almost any unilateral regulatory initiative. The main response to this, of course, is to try to reach international agreement, and a whole structure of institutions and procedures has been established to try to take this forward, with varying degrees of success. Inevitably, and perhaps properly, this is a slow process.[28] Those who claimed that we were losing the potential momentum of the crisis for reforming financial regulation simply had no feel for the mechanics of the process. Moreover, any of the major financial countries, perhaps some three or four countries, can effectively veto any proposal that they do not like, so again the agreements will tend to represent the lowest common denominator, again perhaps desirably so.

Finally, there can be circumstances and instances when a regulator can take on the 'level playing field' argument and still be effective. An example can be enforcing a margin for housing LTV (loan-to-value) ratios by making lending for the required downpayment unsecured in a court of law. Another example is when the purpose of the additional constraint is to prevent excessive leverage and risk-taking by domestic banks, rather than trying to control credit expansion more widely (as financed by foreign banks).

There is no easy solution to the second boundary problem. The doctrine of multilayered governance, which discusses the allocation of regulatory powers at the national, regional (European) and international levels, provides a template to address some of these issues.[29] We need an interjurisdictional approach to financial regulation. Some rules and supervisory decisions must remain at the national level, while rules for a regional area, such as the European Union, ought to be regional. Yet, a global banking and financial system requires some binding international rules and an international system for the resolution of conflicts and crises. An analogy with football could be instructive in this regard. There are domestic leagues, ruled by national football associations; there is in Europe a Champions League of the best football clubs governed by the Union of European Football Associations (UEFA), and finally – though this is a competition among countries not clubs – there is the Fédération Internationale de Football Association (FIFA) and the World Cup. The challenge is to identify the criteria under which financial regulatory powers should be allocated and the different layers (including private mechanisms) that are needed. Effective enforcement remains the greatest challenge at the international level, since enforcement mechanisms have traditionally been nationally based. The conditioning of market access on the basis of compliance with some international rules could be an effective way of tackling some of these difficult cross-border issues.

Globalization and regionalization (in particular in the EU) have challenged the traditional law-making process, a development which is particularly relevant for the future of financial regulation:

> International financial soft-law is often a 'top-down' phenomenon with a two-layer implementation scheme. The rules are agreed by international financial standard setters and national authorities must implement them in their regulation of the financial industry. The financial

intermediaries are the 'final' addresses of those rules. Standards and uniform rules, however, can also be designed by the financial industry itself. Self-regulation, by definition, has a 'bottom-up' character.

International lawmaking relies upon a variety of sources. It is in the confluence of 'hard law' (legally enforceable rules), soft law of a 'public law' nature (which can complement, co-exist [with] or turn into hard law) and soft law of a 'private law' nature (comprising rules of practice, standards, usages and other forms of self-regulation as well as rules and principles agreed or proposed by scholars and experts) where the future of international financial and monetary law lies.[30]

17.4 CONCLUDING OBSERVATIONS

To conclude, border problems are pervasive, and complicate the application of regulatory measures both within and between countries. The prospective regulator will always need to be alert to the likely effect of shifts of business across such borders, and seek to mitigate them. But to some extent such cross-border business transfers are generic and the regulator or supervisor will just have to monitor and, up to a point, live with them. The perimeter issue remains a major challenge for regulators and supervisors, one that resurfaces again and again in the debate about derivatives, hedge funds, rating agencies and others. Progress towards an effective framework for cross-border crisis management and resolution is hampered by the two boundaries that we have discussed in this chapter. Regulation is most needed in good times, when rapid credit expansion and exuberant optimism cloud the sound exercise of judgment in risk management, yet regulation is typically designed in bad times, in response to a crisis. We need appropriate countercyclical regulation, bearing in mind the biblical story of Joseph in which provisions were gathered in good times to be used in bad times. Regulation and supervision should aim at protecting the interests of society (by identifying, preventing and containing systemic risk as well as by guaranteeing the operation of and access to critical banking and financial functions), rather than the interests of individuals or institutions. Notwithstanding the porous borders of financial regulation, we have to continue to make progress in redesigning finance so as to restore the faith in the financial market as an instrument for the wealth and development of nations.

NOTES

* This chapter was first published as 'Border problems', *Journal of International Economic Law*, **13**(3), Special Issue on 'The Quest for International Law in Financial Regulation and Monetary Affairs', (2010), 705–718, http://jiel.oxfordjournals.org/content/13/3/705.abstract. The authors are grateful to Thomas Cottier for valuable comments.

1. While in fisheries, it is a matter of defining jurisdiction – the basis of regulation – and the actual amount of regulation, including subsidies, is left to the particular jurisdiction, in finance the issues are more complex, for a number of reasons including the border problems analysed in this chapter.

2. See Goodhart, Charles (2008), 'The boundary problem in financial regulation', *National Institute Economic Review*, **206**(1), 48–55.

3. See Goodhart, Charles (2009), 'The boundary problem in financial regulation', Appendix A, in Markus K. Brunnermeier, Andrew Crockett, Charles Goodhart, Avinash Persaud and Hyun Song Shin (eds), *The Fundamental Principles of Financial Regulation*, 11th Geneva Report on the World Economy,

Geneva: International Center for Monetary and Banking Studies, ICMB and Centre for Economic Policy Research, CEPR.

4. The very definition of what constitutes financial regulation is contentious. While all companies are subject to some rules (general law concerning torts, contracts, property, and so on), some financial entities – notably commercial banks – are subject to more stringent 'financial rules' (concerning licensing, capital and liquidity requirements, lending limits, and so on) than others. It is in this context that the dichotomy between the regulated and non-regulated becomes significant. There is always concern that financial activities will migrate from banks to other kinds of companies (non-regulated or less regulated) to avoid the crackdown of more stringent financial rules, such as those of the US Dodd–Frank Act 2010 (Dodd–Frank Wall Street Reform and Consumer Protection Act, Pub. L. No. 111-203 (2010)) and of the new Basel Committee proposals. 'Defining the perimeter of regulation will continue to be a challenge, given the growing number of tax and regulatory incentives for firms to establish businesses in the shadows outside the regulated sector.' See Francesco Guerrera, Tom Braithwaite and Justin Baer (2010), 'Report on financial regulation', *Financial Times*, 1 July, quoting Charles Randell of law firm Slaughter & May.

5. Though in some cases, legal security will be preferred over higher profits.

6. See Lastra, Rosa M. and Geoffrey Wood (2010), 'The crisis of 2007–2009: nature, causes and reactions', *Journal of International Economic Law*, **13**(3), 531–550.

7. See Roubini, Nouriel (2008), 'The shadow banking system is unravelling: Roubini Column in the *Financial Times*. Such demise confirmed by Morgan and Goldman now being converted into banks', http://www.roubini.com/roubini-monitor/253696/the_shadow_banking_system_is_unravelling_roubini_column_in_the_financial_times_such_demise_confirmed_by_morgan_and_goldman_now_being_converted_into_banks, visited 4 August 2010.

8. See Gorton, Gary and Andrew Metrick (2009), 'Securitized banking and the run on the repo', NBER Working Paper No. w15223, August, http://papers.ssrn.com/sol3/papers.cfm?abstract_id=1454939, visited 4 August 2010.

9. See Lastra, Rosa M. (2006), *Legal Foundations of International Monetary Stability*, Oxford: Oxford University Press, Chapter 3.

10. Pub.L. 106-102, 113 Stat. 1338, enacted 12 November 1999.

11. In 1999 the revocation of Glass–Steagall drew few critics. One of the leading voices of dissent was Senator Byron L. Dorgan, Democrat of North Dakota. He warned that reversing Glass–Steagall and implementing the Republican-backed Gramm–Leach–Bliley Act was a mistake whose repercussions would be felt in the future. 'I think we will look back in ten years' time and say we should not have done this, but we did because we forgot the lessons of the past, and that that which is true in the 1930s is true in 2010', Mr Dorgan said in 1999. 'We have now decided in the name of modernization to forget the lessons of the past, of safety and of soundness.' Senator Richard Shelby of Alabama, now the ranking Republican on the Senate Banking Committee, voted against the Gramm–Leach–Bliley Act because of his concern that repealing Glass–Steagall would threaten the safety and soundness of the banking system. Mr Dorgan's views were echoed by then-Senator Barack Obama in 2008 as he campaigned for the presidency. See http://dealbook.blogs.nytimes.com/2009/11/12/10-years-later-looking-at-repeal-of-glass-steagall of 12 November 2009, accessed 10 May 2010.

12. The narrow banking proposals have been again endorsed by John Kay (2009), 'Narrow banking: the reform of banking regulation', Centre for the Study of Financial Innovation, 15 September, available at http://www.johnkay.com/wp-content/uploads/2009/12/JK-Narrow-Banking.pdf, accessed 4 August 2010, while Lawrence Kotlikoff (2010) has made a case for the mutualization of the financial industry in his book *Jimmy Stewart is Dead: Ending the World's Ongoing Financial Plague with Limited Purpose Banking*, Chichester: John Wiley & Sons.

13. See Goodhart, Charles (2010), 'How should we regulate the financial sector', in Richard Layard and Peter Boone (eds), *The Future of Finance: The LSE Report*, London: London School of Economics and Political Science.

14. Thornton, Henry (1802), *An Enquiry into the Nature and Effects of the Paper Credit of Great Britain*, London: J. Hatchard and F. and C. Rivington.

15. http://www.opsi.gov.uk/acts/acts1979/pdf/ukpga_19790037_en.pdf, accessed 30 August 2010.

16. http://www.opsi.gov.uk/acts/acts1987/pdf/ukpga_19870022_en.pdf, accessed 30 August 2010.

17. See Lastra, Rosa M. (1996), *Central Banking and Banking Regulation*, London: Financial Markets Group, London School of Economics and Political Science, Chapters 2 and 3.

18. See proposed Directive on Alternative Investment Funds, 21 April 2009, http://ec.europa.eu/internal_market/investment/docs/alternative_investments/fund_managers_proposal_en.pdf, accessed 4 August 2010.

19. See Litan, Robert E. (1986), 'Taking the dangers out of bank deregulation', *Brookings Review*, **4**(4), 3–12: 'Examinations are costly and time-consuming and the most important aspect of a bank's balance sheet,

the quality of its asset portfolio, is difficult to assess at any given time. Perhaps in recognition of those limitations, federal regulators are increasing capital requirements.'

20. See Goodhart, n. 3 above.
21. Ibid.
22. With regard to the four stages of the supervisory process: licensing, supervision stricto sensu, sanctioning and crisis management, as well as the difference between supervision and regulation, see Lastra, Chapter 2, n. 17 above.
23. See Goodhart, n. 3 above.
24. See Lastra, Rosa M. (2006), *Legal Foundations of International Monetary Stability*, Oxford: Oxford University Press, Chapter 1. Sovereignty is the supreme authority within a territory. The state is the political institution in which sovereignty is embodied. Sovereignty in the sense of contemporary public international law denotes the basic international legal status of a state that is not subject, within its territorial jurisdiction, to the governmental (executive, legislative or judicial) jurisdiction of a foreign state or to foreign law other than public international law. It forms part of the fundamental principles of general international law and it is considered to be one of the principal organizing concepts of international relations. Monetary sovereignty is a particular attribute of the general sovereignty of the state under international law. Some authors argue that the concept of monetary sovereignty predates by thousands of years the concept of political sovereignty that was developed in the Renaissance, since the authority to create money had been proclaimed by the rulers or priesthood of ancient civilizations (Sumer, India, Babylon, Persia, Egypt, Rome and others). However, the modern understanding of the attributes of sovereignty is rooted in the political thought that was developed in the Renaissance. Politics operated without this organizing principle in the Middle Ages.
25. See Stacey, Helen (2003) 'Relational Sovereignty', *Stanford Law Review*, **55**(2029), 2040–2051.
26. The Basel Cross Border Resolution Group issued a report and recommendations in March 2010, http://www.bis.org/publ/bcbs169.htm, accessed 4 August 2010. The International Monetary Fund issued a paper 'Resolution of cross border banks – a proposed framework for enhanced coordination' (to which one of us contributed) on 11 June 2010. See http://www.imf.org/external/np/pp/eng/2010/061110.pdf, accessed 22 July 2010. See generally Lastra, Rosa M. (ed.) (2011), *Cross Border Bank Insolvency*, Oxford: Oxford University Press.
27. Howell Jackson has advocated the advantages of legal certainty and reliability and the role of securities laws in creating strong capital markets. See, *inter alia*, Jackson, Howell E. (2001) 'Centralization, competition, and privatization in financial regulation', *Theoretical Inquiries in Law*, **2**(2), http://www.bepress.com/til/default/vol2/iss2/art4, accessed 3 July 2010.
28. The problem is a general one and in EU law outside of finance, for example in goods, it has been a matter of harmonizing only key points, but not entire areas. A level playing field in international finance calls for some international rules. Given the difficulties inherent in the regulation and harmonization of asset quality, the focus so far has been on capital, though in the aftermath of the crisis attention has also turned to other areas, such as liquidity and resolution.
29. For a more extensive discussion of this doctrine see the article by Rolf Weber (2010), 'Multilayered governance in international financial regulation and supervision', *Journal of International Economic Law*, **13**(3), 683–704.
30. See Lastra, Rosa M. (2006), *Legal Foundations of International Monetary Stability*, Oxford: Oxford University Press, pp. 500–501.

18 Financial architecture, prudential regulation and organizational structure

Ingo Walter

18.1 INTRODUCTION

As a general proposition, financial intermediaries cannot be allowed to impose politically unacceptable costs on society, either by failing individuals deemed worthy of protection in financial matters or by permitting firm-level failure to contaminate other financial institutions and, ultimately, the system as a whole. Protecting the system from misconduct and instability is in the public interest, and inevitably presents policymakers with difficult choices between financial efficiency and innovation on the one hand, and institutional and systemic safety and stability on the other, together with ensuring integrity and sound business conduct in financial dealings (see for example Acharya and Richardson, 2009; Acharya et al., 2011). And because the services provided by banks and other financial intermediaries as allocators of capital affect nearly everything else in the economy, regulatory failure quickly becomes traumatic, with important and often lasting consequences for the real sector.

The complexity of the financial services industry as a whole – and individual financial intermediaries themselves – has important and unique implications for the nature and effectiveness of financial regulation. Markets and institutions tend, perhaps more often than not, to run ahead of the regulators. And regulatory initiatives sometimes have consequences that were not and perhaps could not have been foreseen. Consequently, the linkage between systemic safety and soundness and the size and scope of financial institutions has been hotly debated after the financial crisis of 2007–2009. Is it possible to create a more robust financial system at minimum cost to society by correctly pricing systemic risk and charging financial firms for 'manufacturing' it? If political economy factors or governance limitations impede progress in this direction, should financial firms be restricted as to scale and/or scope in order to limit systemic risk? What could be gained? What could be lost?

Assessing the potential effects of size and scope in financial services firms – and the impact of restricting them – is as straightforward in concept as it is difficult to calibrate in practice. The positives include economies of scale, improvements in operating efficiency (including the impact of technology), cost economies of scope, revenue economies of scope, impact on market structure and pricing power, improved financial stability through diversification of revenue streams, improvements in the attraction and retention of human capital and, controversially, taxpayer support of systemic financial firms. The negatives include diseconomies of scale, higher operating costs due to increased size and complexity, diseconomies of scope on either the cost or revenue sides (or both), the impact of possible conflicts of interest on the franchise value of the firm, and a possible conglomerate discount in the share price. Bigger and broader is sometimes better, sometimes not. It all depends.

The evidence so far suggests rather limited prospects for firm-wide cost economies of scale and scope among major financial services firms in terms of overall cost structures, although they certainly exist in specific lines of activity. Operating economies seem to be the principal determinant of observed differences in cost levels among banks and non-bank financial institutions. Revenue economies of scope through cross-selling may well exist, but they are likely to apply very differently to specific client segments and product lines. Conflicts of interest can pose major risks for shareholders of multifunctional financial firms, which may materialize in civil or even criminal litigation and losses in franchise value. There is plenty of evidence that diversification across uncorrelated business streams promotes stability, although unexpected correlation spikes (as between insurance and investment banking) may arise from time to time and there is the specter of conglomerate discount that must be confronted.

This chapter proposes a regulatory dialectic for examining the issue of derisking the financial system by reducing the size and/or scope of 'systemically significant financial institutions', or SIFIs. This suggests four specific criteria against which policy options should be benchmarked. Various policy proposals, including the so-called Volcker Rule imbedded in the 2010 US Dodd–Frank Financial Stability and Consumer Protection Act of 2010, are examined against these benchmarks. The concluding section of the chapter proposes the appropriate role of activity restrictions and carve-outs in regulatory initiatives designed to address the 2007–2009 financial crisis – or the next one.

18.2   THE REGULATORY DIALECTIC

The regulatory dialectic in the financial services sector is both sophisticated and complex, and it often confronts heavily entrenched and politically well-connected players (and runs up against the personal financial interests of some of the brightest minds and biggest egos in business). The more complex the industry, the greater the challenge to sensible regulation, and this is probably most striking in the case of massive, complex, global financial services conglomerates that may be too hard to manage, too hard to oversee and govern, and almost certainly too hard to monitor and regulate. Consequently, the organizational structure and governance of financial firms invariably enters into the regulatory debate. There are perhaps two extremes.

First, if explicit and implicit subsidies of financial intermediaries such as 'too big to fail' support can be eliminated or properly 'taxed' so that the systemic externalities are successfully internalized, then the managements and boards of SIFIs will tend to rethink their strategies and structures and react accordingly, on balance becoming less systemic. There are two benefits: to society by reducing its exposure to systemic risk, and to shareholders by reducing or eliminating any conglomerate discount and allowing them to choose in which functions of financial intermediation to invest their capital as opposed to holding shares in financial conglomerates. This is the 'market discipline' approach to dealing with the link between organizational structure and systemic risk.

Second, if it is impossible for technical or political reasons to achieve full internalization of systemic risk into the microeconomics of the firms that create such risk – thereby precluding the market discipline solution – then imposing structural change by breaking up SIFIs represents a second-best alternative. Separation of commercial banking from principal investing and proprietary trading, managing private equity firms and hedge funds, and some businesses like commodities trading are a few examples. Some of the separated financial firms will nevertheless remain systemic, but they will be far narrower and more specialized, and therefore more amenable to competent functional oversight by specialized regulatory agencies.

If the market-discipline solution prevails and negative externalities associated with systemic risk are substantially internalized, then the issue of optimum organizational structure will resolve itself, and the associated incremental costs will be disseminated among the end-users of financial intermediation as well as shareholders in an efficient general equilibrium solution. If not, then structural reforms imposed by regulation necessarily become part of the toolkit for dealing with systemic risk emanating from the financial sector.

18.3   SYSTEMIC PERFORMANCE BENCHMARKS

In terms of their mandate from the public, regulators must strive to achieve maximum static and dynamic efficiency of the financial system as a whole. That is, they need to ensure both efficiency in financial flows and innovation in financial products and processes, and they need to promote the competitive viability of financial institutions that are subject to regulation. Simultaneously, they must safeguard the (micro-prudential) stability of key institutions and the (macro-prudential) stability of the financial system as a whole. In addition, they need to ensure what is considered 'acceptable' market conduct in order to retain confidence in financial integrity, including the politically sensitive implied social contract between financial institutions and unsophisticated clients (consumer protection).

More specifically, from the perspective of the public interest there are four key benchmarks against which financial systems should be calibrated:

1. Static efficiency. The metrics include the weighted mean spread between what ultimate savers (predominantly households) receive and what ultimate users of capital (households, non-financial businesses and governments) have to pay. That spread is heavily influenced by some composite of operating costs, regulatory costs, and intermediation losses.
2. Dynamic efficiency. Here the metrics are less transparent, and include product and process innovation and technology change in financial intermediation and the role of the financial system in promoting economic growth by continually allocating and denying capital to competing uses in the production function that drives the real economy.
3. Stability. The financial system itself should be sufficiently robust to withstand shocks that will inevitably emanate from the real sector from time to time, and the financial sector should be resistant to producing shocks of its own, which inevitably spill over into the real sector of the economy.
4. Competitiveness and robustness. In a macro sense, the financial sector is an industry like any other, and generates income, employment and international trade in services. Countries compete vigorously to maintain financial centers that add value in

this regard. New York and London are the dominant global wholesale hubs, arch-rivals and constantly under competitive pressure from insurgent financial centers, particularly as the contours of financial flows shift geographically. Key metrics include share of new debt and equity issues, secondary market trading volumes, exchange-traded and over-the-counter (OTC) derivatives volumes, assets under management, and mergers and acquisitions (M&A) deals advised.

These four benchmarks may well conflict with each other and involve trade-offs that are often hard to identify and measure. Nevertheless, options for financial reform – and particularly line-of-business or geographic constraints – that are in the public interest should be calibrated largely against these benchmarks. The results can usually be assessed only after some time has passed. And even then, they are invariably controversial, based on counterfactuals that will be put forward.

We also know that financial safety-net design is beset with difficulties such as moral hazard and adverse selection. This becomes especially problematic when products and activities shade into one another, when on- and off-balance sheet activities are involved, and when domestic, foreign and offshore business is conducted by financial firms for which the regulator is responsible. The problem of market conduct is no less difficult, when end-users of the system range across a broad spectrum of financial sophistication from mass-market retail clients to highly sophisticated, interprofessional trading counterparties. All the while, the system has to be sufficiently robust to avoid arbitrage across geographic or functional jurisdictions by firms that can afford the best legal minds and lobbyists that money can buy.

So far, the regulatory function in finance has been almost entirely a matter of national sovereignty. Yet banks and other financial firms can and do operate across national jurisdictions, and in offshore markets that can help them avoid significant parts of the regulatory net altogether. Regulatory burdens deemed excessive in one country can trigger migration of financial value-added that can significantly shift the gains from one financial center to another, encouraging regulatory laxity. Who is responsible? Should firms that operate across national borders be broken up into networks of national intermediaries so that those who carry the safely net get to do the regulating? What would be gained? What would be lost? In a highly competitive industry with multiple functional and geographic regulators, could this portend a global regulatory race to the bottom?

Only two years before the onset of the 2007–2009 global financial crisis, two major reports in the United States – one commissioned by then Treasury Secretary Henry Paulson (Committee on Capital Markets Regulation, 2006) and the other produced by McKinsey for officials of the City and State of New York (McKinsey, 2007) – argued for significant US deregulation to avoid losing large parts of wholesale financial intermediation to London and other financial centers based on evidence (much of it seriously flawed) that this migration was already well under way. The 'elegant whining' that permeated both reports was somewhat mistimed, coming as it did only months before the roof fell in on the US financial system, in part attributable to regulatory failures.

In going about their business in an environment where stiff competition runs across functional, institutional and geographic lines, regulators continuously face the possibility that 'inadequate' regulation will result in costly failures and, alternatively, that 'over-regulation' will create opportunity costs in the form of financial efficiencies or innovations not achieved, or in the relocation of firms and financial transactions to other regulatory regimes offering lower regulatory burdens. Since any improvements in financial stability can only be measured in terms of damage that did not occur and costs that were successfully avoided, the argumentation surrounding financial regulation is invariably based on 'what if' hypotheticals. In effect, regulators are constantly compelled to rethink the balance between financial efficiency and creativity on the one hand, and safety, stability and suitable market conduct in the financial system on the other.

In short, regulators face the daunting task of designing an 'optimum' regulatory and supervisory structure that provides the desired degree of stability at minimum cost to efficiency, innovation and competitiveness – and to do so in a highly politicized environment in a way that effectively aligns such policies among regulatory authorities functionally and internationally and avoids 'fault lines' across regulatory regimes. There are no easy answers. There are only 'better' and 'worse' solutions as perceived by the constituents to whom the regulators are ultimately accountable.

The financial history of the United States provides a good example of how difficult it is to strike the right balance in financial regulation. In commercial banking alone there were well over 15 000 failures during the twentieth century – 5000 during the Great Depression of the 1930s and an annual average of well over 100 some 50 years later during the 1980s (not including massive failures of thrift institutions and the $150 billion taxpayer bailout in the Savings & Loan debacle). And this was well before the 2007–2009 financial crisis. Outside the United States, mismanagement or outright fraud have left prominent names like Banco Ambrosiano, BCCI, Bank Bumiputra, Crédit Lyonnais, Barings, Herstatt, Schroder Münchmeyer Hengst, IKB, Fortis and Yamaichi Securities among the failed or seriously damaged over the years, plus essentially the entire Japanese banking system and those of Finland, Mexico, Norway and Sweden in the early 1990s. As well, the Asia crisis of the late 1990s led to major financial failures in Indonesia, Korea and Thailand, in some cases taking almost a decade to recover.

The financial crisis that began in 2007–2009 was basically a continuation of this long history of regulatory failure, complete with numerous failures of regulatory arbitrage (both functional and geographic), regulatory forbearance and the political capture of regulators by the institutions they were supposed to regulate – with enormous costs to the financial system and the economy as financial instability contaminated the real sector. On the other hand, it has been impossible to measure the benefits to the real economy that should be ascribed to the regulatory environment that ultimately led to serious problems.

Most of the regulators who were in command when their various ships hit the icebergs have acknowledged the policy shortcomings that contributed to the disasters, in sharp contrast to the senior managements and boards of the institutions directly involved. Perhaps the most respected and experienced observer of the US financial system, former Federal Reserve Chairman Paul Volcker, noted in a speech in April 2008 that:

> today's financial crisis is the culmination, as I count them, of at least five serious breakdowns of systemic significance in the past 25 years – on the average one every five years. Warning enough that something rather basic is amiss . . . Simply stated, the bright new financial system – for all its talented participants, for all its rich rewards – has failed the test of the market place . . . [A] demonstrably fragile financial system that has produced unimaginable wealth for some, while repeatedly risking a cascading breakdown of the system as a whole, needs repair and reform. (Volcker, 2008)

Volcker is clearly on target in terms of financial instability and its costs to society, but even he cannot document the counterfactual: how would the world have turned out – in terms of economic growth and other things people care about – if a bulletproof regulatory system had prevailed for the preceding half century, effectively impeding most of the efficiency and innovation that ultimately contributed to the instability? Would society have been better off? Volcker would surely concede this point, and probably suggest that we can do much better going forward.

Certainly the emergence of the financial system from the latest crisis has provided a window of opportunity to change the rules once again in the direction of the public interest. In the United States, the Congressional debates leading up to the Dodd–Frank Financial Stability and Consumer Protection Act of 2010 were pale imitations of the 1933 Pecora Hearings leading up to the bold reforms of the Banking Act of 1933, including the creation of deposit insurance and the Glass–Steagall provisions of the Act forcing a separation of functions and breaking up the universal banks. Some have argued that the chemistry of special-interest politics of US financial reform (including multifunctional financial firms that are even larger and more complex than they were before the crisis) assures a green light for financial institutions to go back to business as usual as quickly as possible even as they continue to benefit from taxpayer subsidies (Johnson, 2009). Defeatists have argued that it will take an even more devastating crisis, one that engulfs politics as well as finance and economics, to trigger a modern equivalent of the 1933 Pecora debates and create meaningful structural reforms in financial intermediation.

18.4 CALIBRATING STRUCTURAL OPTIONS AGAINST BENCHMARKS

There are three alternatives for regulating the scope of business of financial intermediaries going forward.

18.4.1 Modified Laissez-Faire

The first option is essentially maintaining the status quo and allowing banks or bank holding companies to engage in all forms of financial intermediation and principal investing worldwide, subject to certain firewalls and other safeguards. These safeguards will be duly modified to deal with systemic risk and incorporate the lessons of the financial crisis of 2007–2009. This option is the core of the Dodd–Frank Act in the US, and major regulators elsewhere have recommitted themselves to the universal banking or financial conglomerate model, that is, that bigger and broader are better. The core of the reforms involve much improved monitoring of the build-up of systemic risk in the financial architecture and a responsibility structure – in the United States the Systemic Risk Council chaired by the Secretary of the Treasury and comprising the Chairman of the Federal Reserve Board of Governors and the heads of the relevant regulatory agencies – which includes the power to intervene directly in markets and institutions deemed to create a serious systemic risk. Such pre-emptive action could include terminating or breaking up the affected firms. Complementing pre-emptive action is the orderly resolution of failed financial institutions, which likewise could lead to significant structural change as they are broken up or sold.

The remainder of the reforms focus on improved supervision and better pricing of systemic risk through higher capital ratios and surcharges for size and riskiness, which could trigger changes in the financial conglomerate business model. Pricing systemic risk using a combination of capital and liquidity requirements – and the cost of more intense regulatory supervision – has considerable promise. Effectively, these are 'taxes' intended to internalize the negative externalities created by firms that produce systemic risk. If boards and managements are doing their jobs, they will carefully re-examine the costs and benefits of remaining a massive financial conglomerate, for example, and find ways of escaping the newly imposed taxes – which will have to be agreed globally to prevent regulatory arbitrage. Skeptics point to weaknesses among financial institutions' boards (including extreme complexity that prevents boards from knowing what they need to know), the virtual absence of hostile takeovers in the financial services sector (i.e., the absence of a well-functioning market for corporate control in the financial sector), and the willingness of boards to live with the large discounts that seem to characterize financial conglomerates.

18.4.2   Geographic Fragmentation

Observers of the evolutionary approach to dealing with systemic risk remain concerned about global coordination and the avoidance of competitive distortions, as well as possible opportunity costs of impeding the globalization of finance and its contribution to world economic growth. National governments in countries such as the UK, Switzerland, Japan, France and the US ultimately support the safety net covering financial conglomerates and other systemic firms based in their jurisdictions. And in the case of large international firms based in small countries, the spillover from systemic risk to sovereign risk has become obvious. Governments therefore have an additional incentive to apply serious safety and soundness policies to their financial firms and then let the firms decide whether they should change their business models to avoid the costs. This incentive also suggests that most of the world's home-countries of systemic financial firms would have a great incentive for the kind of international regulatory harmonization and coordination needed to make it work.

Skeptics argue that most countries are so wedded to the universal banking and financial conglomerates model that they are unlikely to go along with the tougher regulatory architecture that may result in serious structural change. And practitioners argue that forcing structural change on systemic financial firms would be bad for global allocation of capital and risk, and new mechanisms would have to be found to preserve as much efficiency and innovation as possible in cross-border financial flows. Like protectionism in international trade, the costs of financial fragmentation could be significant, although these costs are often broadly dispersed and hard to measure. On the positive side, the threat of financial fragmentation and structural break-ups may have created a fear factor among politically powerful systemic firms, possibly undermining their resistance to other, less dramatic regulatory options.

18.4.3 Break-Ups, Ring-Fencing and Functional Carve-Outs

The argument is that key activities of investment banks, hedge funds, private equity firms and other parts of the 'shadow' financial system are incompatible with the special character of commercial banking, namely operating the payments system, taking deposits and making commercial loans, and serving as the transmission belt for monetary policy. These activities include underwriting and dealing in corporate debt and equities, asset-backed debt and certain other securities, derivatives of such securities including credit default swaps, principal investing and managing in-house hedge funds. These activities are also deemed incompatible with access to central bank discount facilities, debt guarantees and other sources of government support intended to safeguard the public utility attributes of commercial banking.

Under this option in the United States, for example, the investment banks that converted to bank holding companies in the 2007–2009 crisis to gain full access to the government safety net (Goldman Sachs and Morgan Stanley) would revert to broker-dealer status and would be functionally regulated as such alongside oversight by a systemic risk regulator. The investment banking divisions of commercial banks would be sold, floated or spun off to shareholders, and similarly regulated. Investment banking divisions of foreign financial conglomerates would have to be similarly divested or operate in the US as separately capitalized subsidiaries.

18.4.4 Balancing the Alternatives

Advocates of the last option suggest that the US Glass–Steagall constraints of 1933 may in fact have performed relatively well – when benchmarked against all three of the above criteria – for over half a century. The battle in the financial architecture between bank-based and capital-market-based finance, domestically and internationally, assured static and dynamic efficiency pressure on all financial intermediaries, and the system maintained basic stability in the face of major macro shocks and changing monetary standards. During this period, New York became the leading global center of finance, with London (benefiting from natural advantages such as time-zone overlaps and policy advantages such as light regulation and a thriving offshore market) as its only serious rival. All of the continental European financial centers, dominated as they were by universal banks, eventually dropped by the wayside as their own investment banking units (Deutsche Bank, UBS, Paribas, and so on) joined their chief global wholesale rivals in London and New York.

Meantime, under the 'separated' financial architecture investment banks gravitated to an integrated full-service model, complemented by boutiques, and thrived without access to central bank liquidity facilities or public bailouts in the case of failures like Barings in London or Peregrine Securities in Hong Kong. The same was true of buy-side specialists in the mutual fund business (e.g., Fidelity and Vanguard), pension funds (e.g., TIAA-CREF in the US and Hermes in the UK) and hedge funds (e.g., Soros and Tiger), although LTCM was a close call. Buy-side specialists helped prevent the perennial problem of multi-line firms trying to represent buyers and sellers simultaneously and the intractable conflicts of interest that result from them.

The survival and even prosperity of financial specialists in the presence of government-supported and subsidized bank holding companies suggests that a modern version of functional separation would not be ruinous when benchmarked against the three afore-mentioned criteria. The evidence remains mainly anecdotal, but it suggests that a powerful non-bank financial intermediation industry would quickly emerge following the break-up of financial conglomerates, one populated by relatively transparent financial firms that lend themselves to relatively straightforward oversight by functional regulators in tandem with a systemic risk regulator empowered to deal with banks as well as non-bank financial firms.

A less draconian approach to fundamental activity separation involves recognition that some types of financial activities should not be allowed within multifunctional financial firms deemed to be systemic and having powerful public utility characteristics. Among these activities are: (1) management of in-house hedge funds; (2) creating off-balance-sheet affiliates having no commercial purpose; (3) running large proprietary trading positions in cash securities and derivatives; and (4) acting as principal investors in non-financial activities such as real estate and private equity.

Financial conglomerates usually argue that such carve-outs will limit synergies that are essential to their business models, despite general lack of evidence that such synergies actually exist, as discussed earlier in this chapter. Indeed, it is likely that a host of non-bank financial firms will step up to conduct those activities that contribute static or dynamic gains without risking systemic consequences as long as they are appropriately regulated along functional lines with systemic risk oversight.

An alternative to functional carve-outs is to limit the size of financial conglomerates that incorporate commercial banking units, so that they are forced to become non-systemic. Metrics to achieve this could include market share caps, deposit or asset ceilings, and the like. This would not involve activity prohibitions, but size-constrained financial conglomerates would soon lose critical mass in specific areas of engagement, and presumably would try to focus on the most profitable ones and divest others. This could be a more market-aligned and elegant solution than specific activity carve-outs. Given limited evidence on the relationships between firm size and efficiency, stability and competitiveness, size constraints may have some merit.

The US Dodd–Frank Financial Reform and Consumer Protection Act of 2010 embodies a significant element of functional carve-outs in the form of the 'Volcker Rule', promulgated despite the fierce opposition of financial conglomerates. Essentially, financial institutions with access to government lender of last resort (Federal Reserve) facilities and performing a vital public utility role in the payments system and as a transmission belt for monetary policy should not be engaged in activities that generate systemic risk. Following vigorous debate, these prohibited activities include proprietary trading in financial instruments and their derivatives (except US government and municipal securities), and principal investing in hedge funds and private equity funds in excess of a cumulative total of 3 percent of core capital. Passage of the Volcker Rule quickly led to shut-downs and divestitures of proprietary trading desks, although the distinctions with respect to market-making and client-driven trading remained subject to debate. Nevertheless, the necessary risk-taking no longer allowed in bank-related financial firms quickly migrated to independent hedge funds and private equity firms without major disruptions in the market.

18.5   STABILITY BENEFITS AND CONGLOMERATE COSTS OF FUNCTIONAL DIVERSITY

There are two further issues. One is the notion that greater diversification of earnings attributable to multiple products, client-groups and geographies can create more stable, safer and ultimately more valuable financial institutions. The lower the correlations among the cash flows from the firm's various activities, the greater the benefits of diversification. The consequences should include higher credit quality and higher debt ratings (lower bankruptcy risk), therefore lower costs of financing than those faced by narrower, more focused firms, while greater earnings stability should bolster stock prices. In combination, these effects should reduce the cost of capital and enhance profitability, in addition to reducing bankruptcy risk and its potentially systemic effects. Consequently activity restrictions imposed on financial firms could actually increase systemic risk. Empirical research (e.g., Saunders and Walter, 1994) based on merger simulations suggests that this argument cannot be dismissed out of hand.

The second issue relates to a discount that seems to exist in the valuation of financial conglomerates, as it does in the case of non-financial conglomerates. That is, the shares of multi-product firms and business conglomerates tend to trade at prices lower than shares of more narrowly focused firms (all else being equal). There are two basic reasons why this 'conglomerate discount' seems to exist.

First, conglomerates tend to use capital inefficiently. This may be attributable to managerial discretion to engage in value-reducing projects, cross-subsidization of marginal or loss-making projects that drain resources from healthy businesses, misalignments in incentives between central and divisional managers, and the like. The bulk of value erosion in conglomerates is usually attributed to overinvestment in marginally profitable activities and cross-subsidization. This value loss may be smaller in cases where the multi-product firms are active in closely allied activities within the same industrial sector. If the internal capital market within conglomerates functions less efficiently than the external capital market, their shares ought to trade at a discount to the stand-alone value of their constituent businesses.

Empirical findings from research across broad ranges of non-financial businesses may well apply to diverse activities carried out by financial firms as well. If retail banking and wholesale banking and property and casualty (P&C) insurance are evolving into highly specialized, performance-driven businesses, for example, one may ask whether the kinds of conglomerate discounts found in industrial firms may not also apply to financial conglomerate structures – especially if centralized decision-making is becoming increasingly irrelevant to the requirements of the specific businesses.

A second possible source of a conglomerate discount is that investors in shares of conglomerates find it difficult to 'take a view' and add pure sectoral exposures to their portfolios. Investors may want to avoid such stocks in their efforts to construct efficient asset-allocation profiles. This is especially true of performance-driven managers of institutional equity portfolios who are under pressure to outperform cohorts or equity indexes. Why would a fund manager want to invest in yet another (closed-end) fund in the form of a conglomerate – one that may be active in retail banking, wholesale commercial banking, middle-market lending, private banking, corporate finance, trading, investment banking, asset management insurance and perhaps other businesses as well?

Both the capital-misallocation effect and the portfolio-selection effect may weaken investor demand for shares of universal banks and financial conglomerates, lower their equity prices, and produce a higher cost of capital than if the conglomerate discount were absent. This higher cost of capital would have a bearing on the competitive performance and profitability of the enterprise. It may wholly or partially offset some of the aforementioned benefits of conglomeration, such as greater stability and lower bankruptcy risk through diversification across business lines.

Recent large-scale empirical studies (Laeven and Levine, 2007; Schmid and Walter, 2009) have attempted to ascertain whether or not functional diversification is value-enhancing or value-destroying in the financial services sector. The studies are based on a large US dataset covering the period from the mid-1980s to the mid-2000s, when there was a substantial and persistent conglomerate discount among financial intermediaries, with the empirical results suggesting that it is diversification that causes the discount, and not that troubled firms diversify into other more promising areas. The studies also investigated the geographic dimension of diversification as well as the interaction between geographic scope and functional diversification, and concluded that the value destruction associated with functional diversification was not apparent in geographic diversification.

The conglomerate discount argument suggests that the application of functional restrictions on financial firms, whether imposed by the regulators or by boards reacting to significant increases in the pricing of systemic risk, carries with it a potential dividend in reducing the problem of conglomerate discount in the financial services sector.

18.6   CONCLUSIONS

Systemic risk issues after the financial crisis of 2007–2009 have focused heavily on so-called 'systemically important financial institutions' (SIFIs), a cohort of financial firms that is almost exclusively (but not necessarily) composed of large, complex and heavily interconnected financial conglomerates. This chapter has discussed the economic and strategic drivers of SIFIs – if such institutions generate significant systemic risk, it is important to understand how they get that way.

In conclusion, SIFIs increase shareholder value if they generate: (1) top-line gains which show up as market extension, increased market share, wider profit margins or successful cross-selling; (2) bottom-line gains related to lower costs due to economies of scale or improved operating efficiencies, usually reflected in improved cost-to-income ratios, as well as better tax efficiency; or (3) reductions in firm-specific exposure to risk associated with improved risk management or diversification of the firm across business streams, client segments or geographies whose revenue contributions are imperfectly correlated. In the process of achieving these gains both the size and complexity of SIFIs tend to create systemic risk which, if it is not internalized by means of correct pricing, represents a transfer of wealth from society at large to SIFI shareholders and employees. This is what happened during the financial crisis of 2007–2009 and is in the process of being addressed in the ongoing regulatory reforms.

The chapter then considered the requirements, from a public interest perspective on the financial architecture, by setting out key benchmarks – static and dynamic efficiency, stability and robustness, and competitiveness – and the trade-offs that exist between them. How SIFIs satisfy or detract from these benchmarks was examined. If SIFIs generate substantial systemic risk which needs to be addressed as a result of the 2007–2009 financial crisis, then it will be important to know what potential gains and losses are associated with subjecting these financial intermediaries to sharper regulations, higher capital and liquidity standards, or restrictions imposed on some of their activities. These impacts were calibrated against the performance benchmarks.

In this context, the chapter focused on some of the major regulatory initiatives following the 2007–2009 financial crisis, and in particular the US Dodd–Frank legislation of 2010, in terms of their possible impact on business models of SIFIs either in the form of mandatory activity carve-outs or as management responses to elimination of public subsidies through better pricing of systemic risk.

All things considered, the most defensible approach to improving the financial architecture by addressing systemic risk given the facts on the ground – and assuming it can be carried out in a disciplined, consistent, internationally coordinated and sustained manner with a firm eye to the public interest – is heavily reliant on market discipline. By being forced to pay a significant price for systemic risk, SIFIs such as universal banks and financial conglomerates will have to draw their own strategic conclusions in the context of the microeconomics and industrial organization of global wholesale financial intermediation. But this assumes that market discipline works effectively. Those who have become cynical about the political economy of regulation and 'regulatory capture' have continued to advocate specific activity carve-outs as a second-best alternative, and this has been reflected in the US Volcker Rule as well as continued debate about the future of SIFIs in the form of universal banks and financial conglomerates as a dominant form of organization in the financial architecture.

REFERENCES

Acharya, Viral, Thomas Cooley, Matthew Richardson and Ingo Walter (eds) (2011), *Regulating Wall Street*, New York: John Wiley & Sons.
Acharya, Viral and Matthew Richardson (eds) (2009), *Restoring Financial Stability*, New York: John Wiley & Sons.
Committee on Capital Markets Regulation (2006), 'Interim report of the Committee on Capital Markets Regulation' (the Paulson Report), Washington, DC: US Government Printing Office.
Laeven, Luc and Ross Levine (2007), 'Is there a diversification discount in financial conglomerates?', *Journal of Financial Economics*, **85**, 331–367.
McKinsey & Co. (2008), 'Sustaining New York's and US' global financial services leadership', report commissioned by Mayor Michael Bloomberg and Senator Charles Schumer, Mayor's Office of the City of New York, available at http://www.nyc.gov/html/om/pdf/ny-report-final.pdf.
Saunders, Anthony and Ingo Walter (1994), *Universal Banking in the United States*, New York: Oxford University Press.
Schmid, Markus M. and Ingo Walter (2009), 'Do financial conglomerates create or destroy economic value?', *Journal of Financial Intermediation*, April, 193–216.
Volcker, Paul A. (2008), Remarks at a meeting of the Economic Club of New York, 28 April, transcript at http://econclubny.org/files/Transcript_Volcker_April_2008.pdf.

19 Corporate governance and prudential regulation of banks: is there any connection?
Lawrence J. White

19.1 INTRODUCTION

In the aftermath of the financial crisis of 2007–2009, a number of 'narratives' about the causes of the crisis have developed. One specific narrative will be the topic of this chapter: that a major (if not the major) cause of the crisis was poor corporate governance of the largest banks and other large financial institutions of the United States. This narrative argues that the poor governance encouraged the senior managements of these institutions to undertake excessively risky strategies that may have benefitted these managements but that were not in the long-run interests of the shareholder-owners of these institutions. The strategies caused these institutions to 'blow up', and the financial crisis followed.

An immediate implication of this narrative is that better corporate governance – a better alignment of the interests of senior management with the interests of their shareholders – would have prevented (or at least ameliorated) the crisis, and that better governance is necessary for the prevention of future such crises. One manifestation of this belief is the inclusion of measures that are intended to improve corporate governance – especially for financial institutions – in the Dodd–Frank Wall Street Reform and Consumer Protection Act of 2010 (P.L. 111-203).

This chapter will argue that this corporate governance narrative is largely misguided and reflects an inadequate understanding of modern finance and financial theory.[1] This lacuna applies to the understanding of the role of debt and therefore leverage in a corporation's capital structure in potentially encouraging the owners of the corporation (who are protected by the 'limited liability' that is a part of the legal structure that pertains to corporations) to undertake more risky strategies than they would in the absence of the debt. If senior managements of corporations are properly representing and responding to the interests of their shareholders, then they ought – unless restrained by the debt holders or by prudential regulators – to be undertaking activities that might otherwise appear to be excessively risky.

Accordingly, even if corporate governance is improved in the future, this improvement is unlikely to play a major role in restraining risk-taking and thus avoiding future financial crises. Instead, future avoidance must rely on a different narrative: that excessive risk-taking (which *ex ante* may well have been in the interests of diversified shareholders) combined with excessive leverage (i.e., inadequate capital) by large, complex and interconnected financial institutions that were inadequately restrained by prudential regulation was the cause of the crisis. In turn, this calls for forestalling future financial crises the 'old-fashioned' way: through heightened, expanded and improved prudential regulation of these financial institutions, with a special emphasis on higher and better-measured capital requirements.[2]

This chapter will proceed as follows: because the concept of leverage is central to this chapter – for understanding the motives of corporate owners for excessive risk-taking and thus why poor corporate governance is not needed to explain the risky behavior and also why prudential regulation is appropriate for these large financial institutions – section 19.2 will review the concept and its implications, as well as illustrating the closely related concept of 'capital' for financial institutions. Section 19.3 will bring diversified owners, and then managers and corporate governance, into the discussion. Section 19.4 will provide a brief overview of prudential regulation and its central role in restraining excessive risk-taking by financial institutions. And section 19.5 offers a brief conclusion.

19.2   UNDERSTANDING LEVERAGE AND ITS IMPLICATIONS

19.2.1   A Balance Sheet Approach to Understanding Leverage

Although this chapter is primarily about financial institutions and their regulation, I will start somewhere else:[3] a stylized balance sheet for a roughly typical manufacturing corporation of the middle of the decade of the 2000s,[4] as portrayed in Figure 19.1a. That firm has assets of $100, consisting of plant, equipment, inventories, accounts receivable, cash on hand, and so on. Its direct obligations to creditors are $60, consisting of loans owed to banks, any bonds owed to bond investors, accounts payable, and so on. By simple subtraction, its net worth or owners' equity – the value of its assets minus the value of its direct obligations – is $40.

This firm has a leverage ratio – its ratio of assets to net worth – of 2.5 to 1. The sense of the leverage ratio can be seen in Figure 19.1b: if the firm's assets increase by $10 (to $110) – say, because it makes and retains operating profits of $10, or its assets simply appreciate by $10 – without an increase in its direct obligations, then its net worth also increases by $10 (to $50). Thus a 10 percent increase in the value of its assets results in a 25 percent increase in its net worth; this is a notion of 'leverage' that is comparable to the high school physics example of a plank and a fulcrum.[5]

Leverage also works in reverse, as in Figure 19.1c: a 10 percent decrease in the value of the firm's assets results in a 25 percent decrease in the value of its net worth.

Assets	Liabilities
$100 (plant, equip., inv., cash, etc.)	$60 (bank loans, bonds issued, accts. payable, etc.)
	$40 (net worth, owners' equity)

Net worth/assets: 40%
Leverage: 2.5/1

Figure 19.1a   The balance sheet of a typical manufacturing corporation

Assets	Liabilities
$110 $~~100~~ (plant, equip., *+10%* inv., cash, etc.)	$60 (bank loans, bonds issued, accts. payable, etc.)
	- *$50 $~~40~~* (net worth, owners' *+25%* equity)

Net worth/assets: 45%
Leverage: 2.2/1

Figure 19.1b   A modified balance sheet of a typical manufacturing corporation

Assets	Liabilities
$90 $~~100~~ (plant, equip., *–10%* inv., cash, etc.)	$60 (bank loans, bonds issued, accts. payable, etc.)
	- *$30 $~~40~~* (net worth, owners' *–25%* equity)

Net worth/assets: 33%
Leverage: 3/1

Figure 19.1c   Another modified balance sheet of a typical manufacturing corporation

These simple examples portray an important point: leverage and the (relative to assets) amount of net worth are inversely related to each other. Further, the relative amount of net worth is important for the lenders and creditors to the corporation because of the strictures of the legal system of 'limited liability' for the shareholder-owners: under limited liability, the shareholders cannot be required to support the company beyond their initial contributions.[6] Thus, in Figures 19.1a–19.1c, if the company's assets were to fall below $60 (which would wipe out its net worth) and thus be inadequate to cover the claims of the company's creditors, those creditors normally have no claim against the owners. The creditors will simply have to divide the (inadequate) assets among themselves to satisfy their claims, usually in a bankruptcy proceeding.

There is an important corollary, from the perspective of the owners of the borrowing corporation: limited liability means that they may not bear the full losses from the 'downside' of their corporation's risk-taking, if the losses are so large as to more than wipe out the corporation's net worth. In turn, this limited downside alters the owners' incentives for taking risks: the more that the owners do not bear the downside losses, the greater are their incentives for taking risks, since they get the full gains from the upside but are limited in the losses that they bear.[7] Since net worth is also owners' equity, the extent of net worth is also a measure of the disincentive for the owners to take large risks, since a larger net worth means that the owners have more to lose and are farther away from the limit on their losses that limited liability provides.

Accordingly, from the creditors' perspective, the level of a company's net worth represents the extent of the buffer that protects them against a decrease in the value of the company's assets that would expose them to a loss, as well as an indicator of the owners' disincentive for risk-taking. The thicker the buffer (other things being equal), the more assured the creditors should feel.

Creditors to non-financial corporations long ago figured out this crucial point about the importance of net worth: typically, when a bank makes a loan to a company, there are restrictions in the lending agreement that are intended to prevent the company from taking excessively risky actions, the downside of which would erode the company's net worth and thus place the lending bank at risk; and, as the company's net worth buffer becomes thinner, the bank's restrictions get tighter. Similarly, when a company sells bonds into the securities markets, the bond buyers (who are effectively lending their funds to the company) include covenants in the bond indenture that place the same kinds of restrictions on a company's actions.[8]

19.2.2 Leverage and Financial Institutions

The same basic ideas apply to a commercial bank or thrift institution: Figure 19.2a provides the stylized balance sheet of a well-capitalized bank or thrift. Its $100 of assets are primarily the loans that it makes and the bonds that it owns. Its direct obligations of $92 are primarily its deposits.[9] And, again, by simple subtraction, it has $8 of net worth or owners' equity. For financial institutions, this net worth is also called 'capital'. Note that 'capital' is not 'money', or 'cash' or 'liquidity'. It is net worth.[10] Although a bank can increase its 'capital' by getting a 'cash injection' from investors, the increase in capital occurs because the additional cash adds to the assets of the bank and therefore to its net worth. If the bank lends or invests the cash (and thus exchanges the cash for an equivalent amount of other assets), its capital is still augmented by the investors' infusion. By contrast, a loan of an equivalent amount of cash to the bank would not increase its capital (and would instead increase its leverage).

Note that this bank has a substantially thinner net worth (capital) buffer than does the manufacturing firm.[11] Equivalently, it is much more leveraged: 12.5 to 1. This is illustrated in Figure 19.2b: a 10 percent increase in the value of the bank's assets yields a 125 percent increase in the bank's capital.

Assets	Liabilities
$100 (loans, bonds, investments)	$92 (deposits)
	$8 (net worth, owners' equity, capital)

Capital/assets: 8%
Leverage: 12.5/1

Figure 19.2a   The balance sheet of a well-capitalized bank or thrift

Assets	Liabilities
$110 $~~100~~ (loans, bonds, +*10%* investments)	$92 (deposits)
	$18 $~~6~~ (net worth, owners' +*125%* equity, capital)

Capital/assets: 16%
Leverage: 6.1/1

Figure 19.2b   A modified balance sheet of a well-capitalized bank or thrift

Assets	Liabilities
$90 $~~100~~ (loans, bonds, –*10%* investments)	$92 (deposits)
	$–2 $~~6~~ (net worth, owners' –*125%* equity, capital)

Capital/assets: ?
Leverage: ?

Figure 19.2c   A balance sheet of an insolvent bank or thrift

Assets	Liabilities
$70 (loans, bonds, investments)	$92 (deposits)
	$–22 (net worth, owners' equity, capital)

Capital/assets: ?
Leverage: ?

Figure 19.2d   The balance sheet of a deeply insolvent bank or thrift

Again, leverage also works in reverse, as in Figure 19.2c: a 10 percent decrease in the value of the bank's assets more than wipes out its capital and renders it insolvent. A yet larger decrease in the value of its assets yields a yet deeper insolvency, as in Figure 19.2d.

The protections of limited liability apply to the shareholder-owners of banks and other depository institutions as well.[12] Accordingly, the greater leverage of financial institutions provides enhanced incentives for their owners to take risks at the potential expense

Assets	Liabilities
$100 (residential mortgages)	$96 (bonds, loans, c.p.)
	$4 (net worth, owners' equity, capital)

plus $200 of issued RMBS carrying the GSEs' guarantees

Capital/assets: 4% (1.3% if RMBS guarantees are included)

Leverage: 25/1 (75/1 if RMBS guarantees are included)

Figure 19.3   The balance sheet of Fannie Mae and Freddie Mac

of their depositor-creditors, since the owners gain all of the 'upside' from the successful outcomes of risk-taking but bear only part of the 'downside' (until their net worth is exhausted) from the unsuccessful outcomes. Unlike the lender-creditors to non-financial corporations, however, the depositor-creditors to depositories generally do not directly place restrictions on the risk-taking of the banks to which they have entrusted their deposits. Instead, government regulators are the entities that impose these restrictions. In an important sense, prudential regulation of depository institutions by government can be considered to be the public-sector counterpart to the restrictions and covenants that private-sector lender-creditors impose when lending to non-financial corporations.[13]

The balance sheets and leverage of two other categories of financial institution (circa 2007) are worth considering. Figure 19.3 portrays the (stylized) balance sheet of the two government-sponsored enterprises (GSEs): Fannie Mae and Freddie Mac. As can be seen, their on-balance-sheet ratio of capital to assets was only 4 percent; equivalently, their leverage was 25 to 1. This on-balance-sheet portrayal, however, neglects an important additional facet of the GSEs' operations: their issuance of the equivalent of an additional $200 of residential mortgage-backed securities (RMBSs). These securities carried the GSEs' guarantees to the RMBS investors that, in the event that the underlying mortgage borrowers defaulted on their obligations, the GSEs would keep the investors whole. If those contingent obligations are included (as they should be, since they represented contingent claims against which the GSEs' capital provided a buffer), their leverage was effectively 75 to 1.

Finally, Figure 19.4 portrays a (stylized) highly leveraged investment bank. Its $100 in assets are its investments in bonds, loans, shares of stock, real estate, and just about any other asset – real or financial. Its $97 in direct obligations are in the form of loans, bonds, commercial paper, and other obligations. By simple subtraction, it has only $3 in capital. The investment bank's leverage is 33.3 to 1. For both the GSEs and the investment bank, even modest (percentage) losses in the value of their assets would expose their creditors to losses.

Assets	Liabilities
$100 (loans, bonds, stocks, real estate, investments)	$97 (bonds, loans, com. paper)
	$3 (net worth, owners' equity, capital)

Capital/assets: 3%
Leverage: 33.3/1

Figure 19.4   The balance sheet of a highly leveraged investment bank

Table 19.1   The fifteen largest financial institutions in the US, 2007 (by asset size, 31 December 2007)

Rank	Financial institution	Category	Assets ($ billion)	Equity as a % of assets
1	Citigroup	Commercial bank	2182	5.2
2	Bank of America	Commercial bank	1716	8.6
3	JPMorgan Chase	Commercial bank	1562	7.9
4	Goldman Sachs	Investment bank	1120	3.8
5	American International Group	Insurance conglomerate	1061	9.0
6	Morgan Stanley	Investment bank	1045	3.0
7	Merrill Lynch	Investment bank	1020	3.1
8	Fannie Mae	GSE	883	5.0
9	Freddie Mac	GSE	794	3.4
10	Wachovia	Commercial bank	783	9.8
11	Lehman Brothers	Investment bank	691	3.3
12	Wells Fargo	Commercial bank	575	8.3
13	MetLife	Insurance	559	6.3
14	Prudential	Insurance	486	4.8
15	Bear Stearns	Investment bank	395	3.0

Note: The Federal Home Loan Bank System ($1272B in 2007) and TIAA-CREF ($420B in 2007) have been excluded from this list; if GE Capital were a standalone finance company, its asset size ($650B in 2007) would place it at no. 12.

Source: *Fortune 500*, 5 May 2008, and the Federal Housing Finance Agency (for Fannie Mae and Freddie Mac).

19.2.3   Some Real-World Illustrations

The balance sheet examples for the categories of financial firms just discussed may seem fanciful. They are not. Table 19.1 presents the relevant data for the 15 largest financial firms in the US as of year-end 2007.[14] As can be seen, their ratios of net worth (capital) to assets are roughly consistent with the examples.

19.2.4   A Summing Up

There are a number of clear lessons that emerge from this section:

1.   Leverage magnifies the (percentage) gains and losses for the owners of a leveraged enterprise.
2.   Leverage plus limited liability may distort the incentives of a corporation's owners toward taking on more risk than would be the case if the owners bore the full burden of the downside losses.
3.   The extent of the distortion depends on the amount of the owners' equity (i.e., net worth – or, in the case of a financial institution, its capital) relative to the potential risk-taking activity. If the owners' equity is relatively large and the risks are small, limited liability will have little or no effect on risk-taking; conversely, if the owners' equity is small and the risks are large, limited liability may well encourage risk-taking that would not otherwise occur if the owners bore the full downside consequences.

This last point is worth driving home with a simple numerical example. Suppose that the manufacturing company of Figure 19.1a has an opportunity for a 'bet' that may (net) yield +$5 or −$5 with equal probability. Since even the downside would be borne entirely by the owners (since their net worth of $40 would easily absorb the loss), then, if they are risk-neutral, they would be indifferent to this opportunity (since its expected value is $0); if they are risk-averse, they would forgo the opportunity.

Now suppose that the same +$5/−$5 (with equal probability) opportunity is presented to the bank of Figure 19.2a. Again, the owners will be the full bearers of the downside, and a similar decision calculus should hold.[15]

Finally, suppose that the same +$5/−$5 opportunity is presented to the investment bank of Figure 19.4. Now the owners gain the full +$5 upside gain, while (because of limited liability) they bear only −$3 of the −$5 loss. The expected value of this opportunity to the owners is now is +$1 (= +$5*0.5 − $3*0.5). Risk-neutral owners should welcome this opportunity; even mildly risk-averse owners should be interested. Equally important, the owners are indifferent to the size of the loss beyond −$3. Whether the possible loss is −$5 or −$50 or −$500 should be of no concern to the owners (so long as the probability of loss stays at 50 percent), although it would be of great concern to the institution's creditors. In essence, uneconomic opportunities (i.e., with expected values that are negative) would be of interest to the owners. Section 19.3 will expand on these lessons.

19.3   LEVERAGE, OWNERS, MANAGERS AND GOVERNANCE

The discussion in section 19.2 had no mention of corporate governance. The examples were all in terms of the incentives of the owners themselves. The important lesson is that leverage plus limited liability can alter the incentives of owners toward undertaking greater risk than if the owners bore all of the downside from risk-taking.

19.3.1   Owners, Risk-Taking and Diversification

One impediment to greater risk-taking might be risk aversion on the part of the owners. Suppose that, in the example at the end of section 19.2 of the +$5/−$5 (with equal probability) opportunity that was posed for the owners of the investment bank of Figure 19.4, all of the owners' net worth was solely invested in the equity of that institution. In that case, even though limited liability creates a positive expected value of the opportunity for the owners, they might nevertheless be reluctant to embrace it, since it would carry a 50 percent probability of wiping out their net worth.

Instead, however, suppose that the owners' net worth was spread across many such institutions: that the owners all had diversified portfolios that encompassed dozens of such institutions. Suppose further that each institution had a +$5/−$5 opportunity and that each of these opportunities was uncorrelated with the others – that is, that the outcome of each opportunity depended solely on its 50–50 equal probability and not on the outcomes of the others. In this case, unless the owners were extremely risk-averse, they should want their institutions to embrace the opportunities. On average the owners would gain, and the possibility that they would experience an overall loss would be quite small.[16] In essence, they would harvest the gains and walk away from the losses (and rediversify their portfolios), with the likelihood of an overall gain being quite high. Finally, recall that the owners would be unconcerned about the size of the loss and thus would be ready to embrace opportunities that were uneconomic.

This last point is worth restating: diversified owners have no special reasons for preserving the solvency of all of the companies in which they have ownership stakes. Instead, because of the downside protections of limited liability, their interests are for their companies to be operated with the maximum amount of leverage that those companies' creditors and/or regulators will allow and for the companies to embrace risky opportunities that offer positive expected outcomes for the owners, even if the opportunities are uneconomic when the creditors' losses are included and the downside outcomes would mean the insolvency or bankruptcy of some of the companies.

19.3.2   Managers and Governance

Let us now introduce a set of senior managers that are employed by the diversified owners. In so doing we have now created the potential issue of corporate governance: will the senior managers faithfully manage the corporation in the interests of the owners?[17]

There are at least three possible answers to this question that are relevant to this discussion of risk-taking:[18] (1) yes they will; (2) no they will not; they will take excessive risks; or (3) no they will not; they will refrain from taking risks that would be in the interests of diversified owners. We will address each possibility in turn.

(1) Yes they will
It is first worth considering the possibility (e.g., because of an appropriate incentive structure) that the managers do faithfully operate the company in the interests of its owners. In this case, as the earlier part of this section and the previous section have argued, diversified owners will want the managers to operate their companies at the maximum leverage that the companies' creditors and/or regulators will allow and to embrace risky oppor-

tunities that embody positive expected values for the owners even if (because of limited liability) the opportunities are not economic (i.e., because the expected downside outcomes, including the losses to creditors, exceed the expected upside gains to the owners).

Thus, even good governance will not rein in uneconomic risk-taking.

(2) No they will not; they will take excessive risks
It is surely possible that, because of poorly structured incentives and inadequate monitoring, the company's managers might embrace risky opportunities that rewarded the managers but that were uneconomic for the owners. This seems to be the case that is envisioned by those who believe in the 'poor corporate governance' narrative for the financial crisis and thus by the authors of the corporate governance sections of the Dodd–Frank Act.

In this case, better governance may reduce uneconomic risk-taking – but the lesson of case (1) is that better governance alone will not be sufficient to eliminate all uneconomic risk-taking. Further, there is evidence that the risk-taking by the large US financial institutions prior to the crisis of 2007–2009 was, *ex ante*, in the interests of the shareholder owners of these corporations.[19]

(3) No they will not; they will refrain from taking risks that would be in the interests of diversified owners
It is worth considering the third possibility, that managers might refrain from embracing risky opportunities that would otherwise be in the interests of the owners. Consider one of the standard reward structures for managers: they receive performance-based bonuses in the form of stock grants or stock options. If the managers are restricted from quickly selling the stock or options, then their portfolios are likely to become heavily unbalanced in the direction of their ownership position in their company; that is, they are unlikely (unless they are independently wealthy) to be well diversified. In that case, the managers become similar to the undiversified owners that were described in the early part of this section: if the managers are risk-averse, they may be reluctant to take the big risks that would have a positive expected value for the diversified owners, because the downside outcomes of those risks might greatly reduce the (undiversified) managers' net worths.

In this case, ironically, poor governance serves to rein in excessive risk-taking.

19.3.3 A Summing Up

It is clear that good corporate governance is far from a panacea for reining in excessive risk-taking by financial corporations. At best (case (2) above), it might help a little bit.

In short, something more than better corporate governance is needed to restrain excessive risk-taking by financial institutions. That something more is prudential regulation, to which I now turn.

19.4   PRUDENTIAL REGULATION

'Financial regulation' encompasses a wide range of activities and goals.[20] In this section I will focus on prudential regulation:[21] the regulatory effort to maintain the solvency of financial institutions. As was noted earlier, prudential regulation has been applied to a number of categories of financial institutions; however, I will confine my attention to the prudential regulation of depository institutions (which, for the purposes of brevity, I will describe as 'banks').[22]

19.4.1   The Arguments for Prudential Regulation

The arguments for the prudential regulation of banks start with the leverage and limited liability arguments of section 19.2. It is clear that creditors to a corporation need to be protected against the risk-taking incentives of the corporation's owners. For non-financial corporations, the creditors are expected to protect themselves. But for banks (and a number of other categories of financial institution) the creditors – for banks, these are primarily the depositors – are seen as unable to protect themselves adequately. Hence, there is a longstanding tradition (in the US, this tradition extends back at least to the 1860s[23]) of having government prudential regulation as the substitute protector for the depositors.

The arguments, specifically, for government prudential regulation of banks (instead of relying on depositors to protect themselves through covenants or other negotiated restrictions) are:

1. Banks are complex and difficult to understand – except (hopefully) by experts – even under the best of circumstances.[24]
2. Depositors – even commercial (i.e., business) depositors – tend to be relatively unsophisticated with respect to understanding the activities and finances of banks.
3. The primary liabilities that are issued by banks tend to be short-term demandable deposits, which the depositors expect to be liquid and available at short notice at par (i.e., they do not expect to bear losses); equivalently, there ought to be a safe place where relatively unsophisticated individuals (and businesses) can keep their money (and savings), as an alternative to cash that is stored in cookie jars or under mattresses.[25]
4. Typically, there are large numbers of depositors in a bank, and the levels or amounts of their deposits vary over time. Coordination among them, so as to agree on a set of covenants to impose on their bank – and to agree on who should do the necessary monitoring – would be far more difficult than is the case for bond covenants (where there is typically a trustee, as well as a few dominant block holders of the bonds that have been issued by any company) or bank loans to non-financial corporations (where there is typically a single bank or a consortium of a few banks).
5. Because of 1–4, banks are susceptible to runs:[26] if some depositors are unsure about the value of the bank's assets but are worried that the assets may be inadequate to satisfy all depositors' claims, those depositors may want to 'run' to the bank to withdraw their funds before other depositors get the same idea. Other depositors, seeing or hearing about the first group's actions, may similarly rush to withdraw their funds.
    This general depositor run on the bank can be exacerbated by the realization that even a solvent bank is relatively illiquid, in the sense that it has lent to its borrower customers almost all of the depositors' funds and keeps only a small amount of cash on hand to deal with 'normal' withdrawals. (Think of Jimmy Stewart's efforts, in the

movie *It's a Wonderful Life*, to stop his depositors' run by explaining to them that their money is not in the till but has been loaned to their neighbors.)

And, if depositors in the bank across the street see the run on the first bank and they fear that the same problems may apply to their bank as well, the depositors in this second bank may start a run on their bank. Thus a 'contagion' or 'cascade' of bank runs can develop.[27]

6. Since a bank that is subject to a run by its depositors cannot satisfy all of their demands for cash withdrawals, the bank must either close (declare bankruptcy or its equivalent) or suspend payment until it can liquidate its assets.[28] Either of these outcomes would be unsatisfactory to depositors, which can serve to heighten fears and exacerbate runs.

7. The closure of a bank because of insolvency will impose losses on relatively unsophisticated depositors. These losses may be considered to be unacceptable politically (as well as exacerbating the depositor nervousness that leads to runs).

8. The closure of a bank and the liquidation of its assets – which will mean calling in (i.e., requiring repayment) of its loans – may deprive local households and businesses of a significant source of credit. Even if there are alternative lending sources, the specialized knowledge that the bank has developed as to who is a creditworthy borrower (and who is not) may be lost, to the detriment of those creditworthy borrowers (who, at a minimum, will have to demonstrate anew their creditworthiness to another potential lender).[29]

The roles of a prudential regulator, a central bank and deposit insurance in maintaining a stable banking system can now be seen. Prudential regulation is intended to prevent the bank from becoming insolvent and thereby prevent depositors from being exposed to losses.[30] The central bank can lend (provide liquidity) to an otherwise illiquid but solvent bank, to help the bank deal with any temporary nervousness that might develop among its depositors.[31] And deposit insurance provides a back-up reassurance to depositors and thus serves as an additional backstop against bank runs, in the event that prudential regulation has failed to prevent the bank's insolvency.[32]

19.4.2   The Primary Tools of Prudential Regulation

Capital adequacy
Since the goal of prudential regulation is to maintain the solvency of banks – that is, to ensure that they have positive levels of capital – minimum capital levels (relative to the risks that are undertaken by the bank) are at the heart of any system of prudential regulation.[33] Equivalently (as is clear from section 19.2), this means limits on leverage.

For all financial institutions, capital levels are so thin that accurate measurements of the value of the institution's assets – and thus of its capital (because capital is determined by simple subtraction) – are crucial. An accounting system that relies primarily on market values for the determination of asset values (with some allowance for the vagaries of thin markets), rather than on historical costs or projected cash flows, is essential.

As a bank's capital buffer gets thinner, prudential regulators should progressively restrict its activities. At the limit of insolvency, the regulator must declare a receivership and take full control of the bank (see below). This system of progressive restrictions has come to be called 'prompt corrective action'.

Activities limitations
In principle, if prudential regulators could accurately ascertain the risks of all potential activities by a bank – including non-financial activities, such as owning and operating an automobile manufacturing facility, or a large department store – and could thereby assign the appropriate capital levels, then there would be no need for any restrictions on the activities of banks. More realistically, prudential regulators will be limited in their ability to ascertain the riskiness of most non-financial activities, and perhaps even of some financial activities, If prudential regulators cannot ascertain the riskiness of an activity, that activity ought not to be permitted for a bank.[34]

Managerial competency requirements
The failure of a bank – even a small, local bank – is clearly a more serious event than the failure of a corner delicatessen. Requiring that the senior managers of a bank demonstrate their competency at running a bank naturally follows.[35]

Close monitoring of the financial flows between a bank and its owners
Because it is too easy to loot a bank – to extract assets from the bank in a way that benefits its owners but that leaves the liability holders at risk (such as excessive dividends to the owners, or favorable loans to the owners, their families or their friends) – prudential regulators must closely monitor the financial flows between a bank and its owners (or their families, or their friends).

Adequate numbers of well-trained and well-paid regulators
Because prudential regulation involves sophisticated monitoring of sophisticated financial institutions, adequate numbers of well-trained and well-paid personnel to conduct this monitoring are essential.

A receivership regime for insolvent banks
Once a bank reaches insolvency, it must be placed in a receivership (usually operated by the regulator or the deposit insurer). The receivership extinguishes the rights of the owners and usually dismisses the senior management who 'drove the bank into the ditch'. The regulator can then decide whether the best course of action is to liquidate the bank or to find an acquirer.[36]

19.4.3   What Role for Improved Governance?

Is there room for improved governance as part of the prudential regulation of banks? The answer is 'yes'; but the full nuances of this 'yes' should be understood. First, improvements in governance can, at most, be just a modest part of prudential regulation.

Second, restraints in managerial risk-taking that would otherwise exceed the levels that are in the shareholders' interests are in the interests of the depositors (or the deposit insurer) as well as in the interests of shareholders.

But, third, the necessary restrictions on managerial risk-taking so as to enhance the prospects for solvency of the bank require much more extensive restrictions than those that would be in the interests of diversified shareholder-owners, and thus ought not to be considered to be part of a program of 'improved governance'.

19.5 CONCLUSION

Is there a relationship between corporate governance and the prudential regulation of banks? The answer must be, 'Yes; but just barely.' If the managers of banks are undertaking risky strategies that are beyond those that are in the interests of the banks' shareholder-owners, then improved corporate governance also serves the larger interests of society in preserving the solvency of banks.

But, as this chapter has argued, the diversified shareholder-owners will want their managers to undertake considerably more risk than is in society's interests. In that important sense, then, prudential regulation of banks must require bank managers to undertake less risk (and maintain higher levels of capital, and so on) than would otherwise be in their owners' interests. In that sense, good prudential regulation must (ironically) worsen the corporate governance of banks.

NOTES

1. Similar critiques can be found in Carpenter et al. (2011) and Fahlenbrach and Stulz (2011).
2. This line of argument can also be found in Acharya and Richardson (2009), Acharya et al. (2011) and White (2009b, 2010).
3. This section draws heavily on White (2009a).
4. The US Internal Revenue Service (IRS) publishes the aggregated balance sheets of corporations, drawn from their tax filings, in its annual publication *Statistics of Income*. For 2007, the latest year for which IRS data were available at the time of writing, the net worth to assets ratio for manufacturing corporations was about 35 percent. We use the 40 percent in Figure 19.1a primarily for simplicity of the arithmetic calculations.
5. In the United Kingdom and other countries that have a British orientation for their accounting and financial services, the term 'gearing' is used to convey the same concept. Since the physics of the transmission of force through a lever and through gears is similar, the use of the two terms to refer to the same balance sheet concept is not surprising.
6. By contrast, for a sole proprietorship or a partnership, the owner or owners are fully liable for the obligations of their company, up to the limits of personal bankruptcy.
7. Even in the absence of the limited liability protection for corporate shareholders, the limits that are created by personal bankruptcy generate the same kinds of incentives for risk-taking.
8. Although the financial markets long ago figured this out, the economics and finance literature was relatively late in understanding it. See, for example, Stiglitz and Weiss (1981).
9. This stylized balance sheet is best representative of a smaller bank or thrift. Larger banks are more likely to have other kinds of direct liabilities, such as bonds or repurchase agreements ('repos'), in addition to deposits.
10. This is a rough approximation. Especially with respect to prudential regulation, 'regulatory capital' includes other balance sheet entries that are not normally considered to be part of net worth.
11. It is worth noting, however, that there was a time in the middle of the nineteenth century – when bank capital ratios were in the same range as the net worth ratio of the manufacturing firm of Figure 19.1a; see, for example, Lown et al. (2000). Capital requirements declined over time to levels today that are in the range of Figure 19.2a. See also Keeley (1990).
12. Some thrifts and insurance companies are 'mutuals' and are (in principle) owned by their depositors or insureds. Similarly, credit unions are owned by their members who are also depositors and borrowers. The principle of limited liability extends to these categories of financial institutions as well, which

again places the burden on creditors when the institution's net worth is negative. For these institutions, however, the categories of 'creditor' (depositor or insured) may overlap with the category of 'owner'.

13.   It is worth noting that prudential regulation (prior to 2010) was also applied in the US to bank holding companies, insurance companies, money market mutual funds, defined-benefit pension funds and broker-dealers. The Dodd–Frank Act extends prudential regulation to large financial institutions that pose systemic risks more generally. An elaboration on the topic of prudential regulation will be provided in section 19.4.

14.   Year-end 2007 slightly precedes the March 2008 absorption of Bear Stearns by JPMorgan Chase, which was engineered and backed by the Federal Reserve and marked the first major manifestation of the shaki-ness of the largest, thinly capitalized financial institutions in the US.

15.   The depositors (unless they are covered by deposit insurance) and/or the deposit insurer, however, ought to be concerned by the substantial reduction in net worth that the downside outcome would yield, since there would then be only $3 of net worth, and another such opportunity could lead to the institution's insolvency.

16.   If an individual had a diversified portfolio of equal-sized investments in 50 such institutions and all 50 undertook these opportunities, then the likelihood of the individual's experiencing any overall loss at all would be only 3.2 percent, and the likelihood that the individual would experience a loss of 50 percent or greater to his/her net worth would be only 0.3 percent.

17.   Consideration of this issue extends back at least to Berle and Means (1932). Modern economics and finance consideration of it can be dated to Jensen and Meckling (1976) and Fama and Jensen (1983).

18.   I focus here on governance with respect to risk-taking. There are, of course, additional dimensions to the governance question, such as whether the senior managers may make simple choices (such as whether to merge with another company) that favor senior managers (who get more prestige, as well as more pay, from running a larger company) at the expense of owners (if the merged company is less profitable, and so on.

19.   Fahlenbrach and Stulz (2011), for example, find that the actions of the senior managers of the large US financial institutions prior to the crisis appear to have been in the *ex ante* interests of their shareholder-owners.

20.   In addition to prudential regulation, 'financial regulation' can encompass efforts to protect consumers from 'toxic' (harmful) financial products and services, protect them from fraud, require adequate infor-mation about financial products and services or about the finances of publicly traded companies, limit directly the prices and fees that can be charged by financial institutions, and so on.

21.   In the US the traditional phrase for this type of regulation has been 'safety-and-soundness' regulation. Outside of the US, however, 'prudential' regulation has been the common term, and it is now widely used in the US as well.

22.   Many of the arguments for and instruments of the prudential regulation of banks have their counterparts in the prudential regulation of other financial institutions.

23.   The National Currency Act of 1863 and the National Bank Act of 1864 created a national charter for banks and a national prudential regulator, the Comptroller of the Currency, to regulate them. Even before then, the states as charterers of banks saw banks as special and restricted their activities. Further, where states had created state-backed systems of deposit insurance (New York was the first to do so in 1829) they realized that they needed a system of regulation to try to contain the activities of banks that could put the deposit insurance system at risk.

24.   Morgan (2002) empirically demonstrates the validity of this argument.

25.   This last version is really an argument for deposit insurance; but then the deposit insurer would want a system of prudential regulation to protect itself.

26.   More formal discussions can be found in Diamond and Dybvig (1983), Postlewaite and Vives (1987) and Chen (1999).

27.   As became clear in September 2008, similar runs were possible by the short-term creditors to the thinly capitalized large investment banks in the US.

28.   And even for a solvent bank, the forced liquidation of its assets would likely yield losses and thus render it insolvent, generating losses for even the patient depositors.

29.   For example, Bernanke (1983) demonstrated that this was one of the major costs of the thousands of bank closures that accompanied the US economy's descent into the Great Depression of the 1930s.

30.   For a skeptical view as to the efficacy of prudential regulation, especially outside of the US context, see Barth et al. (2006).

31.   Of course, in lending to the bank, the central bank becomes a creditor to the bank; at a minimum the central bank will want adequate collateral for its loan and, more generally, it will want to assure itself of the solvency of the bank to which it is lending.

32.   For general arguments along these lines, see White (1991).

33.   Included in capital should be a 'slice' of subordinated debt and/or debt that converts to equity ('contin-gent capital') when capital levels decline.

34. However, that activity may well be appropriate for a non-financial holding company of a bank. See White (2009c) for a general argument along these lines.
35. US bank regulators require such competency on the part of the senior management for start-up (de novo) banks. And it remains an occasionally used tool for personnel removal at more seasoned banks.
36. The operation of a receivership is best envisioned as operating in conjunction with the deposit insurer: the deposit insurer pays off the insured depositors and then must deal with its consequent loss: the negative net worth 'hole' of the insolvent bank. The receiver tries to find the best route to maximizing the value of the remaining assets and thus minimizing the size of the deposit insurer's loss.

REFERENCES

Acharya, Viral V., Thomas F. Cooley, Matthew P. Richardson and Ingo Walter (eds) (2011), *Regulating Wall Street: The Dodd-Frank Act and the New Architecture of Global Finance*, Hoboken, NJ: Wiley.

Acharya, Viral V. and Matthew Richardson (eds) (2009), *Restoring Financial Stability: How to Repair a Failed System*, Hoboken, NJ: Wiley.

Barth, James R., Gerard Caprio Jr. and Ross Levine (2006), *Rethinking Bank Regulation: Till Angels Govern*, New York: Cambridge University Press.

Berle, Adolf A. and Gardiner C. Means (1932), *The Modern Corporation and Private Property*, New York: Macmillan.

Bernanke, Ben S. (1983), 'Nonmonetary effects of the financial crisis in the propagation of the Great Depression', *American Economic Review*, **73** (June), 257–276.

Carpenter, Jennifer, Thomas Cooley and Ingo Walter (2011), 'Reforming compensation and corporate governance', in Viral V. Acharya, Thomas F. Cooley, Matthew P. Richardson and Ingo Walter, (eds), *Regulating Wall Street: The Dodd–Frank Act and the New Architecture of Global Finance*, Hoboken, NJ: Wiley.

Chen, Yehning (1999), 'Banking panics: the role of the first-come, first-served rule and information externalities', *Journal of Political Economy*, **107**(October), 946–968.

Diamond, Douglas W. and Philip H. Dybvig (1983), 'Bank runs, deposit insurance, and liquidity', *Journal of Political Economy*, **91**(June), 401–419.

Fahlenbrach, Rudiger and Rene M. Stulz (2011), 'Bank CEO incentives and the credit crisis', *Journal of Financial Economics*, **99**(January), 11–26.

Fama, Eugene F. and Michael C. Jensen (1983), 'Separation of ownership and control', *Journal of Law and Economics*, **26**(October), 301–325.

Jensen, Michael C. and William H. Meckling (1976), 'Theory of the firm: managerial behavior, agency costs, and ownership structure', *Journal of Financial Economics*, **3**(October), 305–60.

Keeley, Michael (1990), 'Deposit insurance, risk, and market power in banking', *American Economic Review*, **80**(December), 1183–1200.

Lown, Cara S., Stavros Peristiani and Kenneth J. Robinson (2000), 'Capital regulation and depository institutions', in James R. Barth, R. Dan Brumbaugh Jr. and Glenn Yago (eds), *Restructuring Regulation and Financial Institutions*, Santa Monica, CA: Milken Institute Press.

Morgan, Donald P. (2002), 'Rating banks: risk and uncertainty in an opaque industry', *American Economic Review*, **92**(September), 874–888.

Postlewaite, Andrew and Xavier Vives (1987), 'Bank runs as an equilibrium phenomenon', *Journal of Political Economy*, **95**(June), 485–491.

Stiglitz, Joseph and Andrew Weiss (1981), 'Credit rationing in markets with imperfect information', *American Economic Review*, **71**(June), 393–410.

White, Lawrence J. (1991), *The S&L Debacle: Public Policy Lessons for Bank and Thrift Regulation*, New York: Oxford University Press.

White, Lawrence J. (2009a), 'The role of capital and leverage in the financial markets debacle of 2007–2008', *Mercatus on Policy*, **37**(February), 1–4.

White, Lawrence J. (2009b), 'Financial regulation: an agenda for reform', *Milken Institute Review*, **11**(First Quarter), 15–25.

White, Lawrence J. (2009c), 'Wal-Mart and banks: should the twain meet? A principles-based approach to the issues of the separation of banking and commerce', *Contemporary Economic Policy*, **27**(October), 440–449.

White, Lawrence J. (2010), 'Financial regulation and the current crisis: a guide for the antitrust community', in Bernard A. Nigro, Maureen K. Ohlhausen and Charles T. Compton (eds), *Competition as Public Policy*, Chicago, IL: American Bar Association.

20 The policy conundrum of financial market complexity
Hilton L. Root

Your own best footstep may unleash the very cascade that carries you away, and neither you nor anyone else can predict which grain will unleash the tiny or the cataclysmic alteration. (Kauffman, 1993)

20.1 ECONOMICS AND THE SAND PILE

A pile of sand. What could be a less likely metaphor for a global financial system that contains close to $200 trillion in assets worldwide? Yet an avalanche in that sand pile caused a colossal financial meltdown that destroyed at least 15 percent of national wealth in the United States alone.[1] Which grain of sand triggered the avalanche? We cannot know with certainty where it was or why it moved. Conventional risk models used by economists are poor at determining which set or category of transactions pushed the markets into a system-wide free fall, and they fail completely at expressing the market in collapse.

Because financial instruments such as mortgages, bonds and derivatives operate in several markets at the same time, they are subject not only to the internal dynamics inherent in those particular markets, but to interactive risks as well, emanating from the wider financial system. In fact, trading those financial instruments might have originated the interactive risks – they reflect correlations across activities and markets when losses in one area affect losses in another. The solutions are much harder to find than when discrete sectors or markets are affected.

The operative rule for policymakers who resort to social science is that one must know the cause of a problem in order to ensure against it. But that standard methodology was not effectual for the experts who sought the grain of sand in the aftermath of the 2008 financial collapse. The system's international internal dynamics are not observable by today's mathematical models, which had grown obsolete long before the collapse itself. Nonetheless, policymakers in charge of the clean-up have resorted to boilerplate platitudes in their response to the crisis, calling for increased regulation or insisting that the markets would sort themselves. This response oversimplifies the system-wide dynamics of the collapse.

20.2 THE OPEN ARCHITECTURE OF THE FINANCIAL SYSTEM

The 2007–2009 crash came after a decade of smaller financial collapses. Russia, East Asia, Brazil and the United States had experienced smaller collapses in an equally sudden fashion and without an explicit precipitating event. From that pattern of persistent and intermittent crises, one might have assumed that given time, one might witness the inevitability of an avalanche. Yet when it did come in 2008, it arrived just as unexpectedly and just as fast as the smaller ones before it. The world watched, transfixed and stunned. Until then, it had been presumed that the system's decentralized architecture and its responsiveness to price signals would enable it to absorb major shocks, and that the many supervisors and watchdogs engaged in oversight would take note of systemic risk long in advance of actual danger. The assumptions were false.

Yet none of the potential weaknesses, if measured in proportion to the size of the system itself, seemed large enough to threaten the entire system. So when the massive avalanche finally did occur, the professionals expected to find a cause that was just as large. Even the collapse of the housing market's subprime sector was not large enough by itself to cause the overall systemic collapse.

In each of the previous smaller meltdowns the precipitating event, discernable after the fact, was unrelated to the magnitude of the outcome – just as the size of the avalanche is unrelated to the grain of sand that triggered it. 'The same tiny grain of sand may unleash a tiny avalanche or the largest avalanche of the century', explains Stuart Kauffman. 'Big and little events can be triggered by the same kind of tiny cause. Poised systems need no massive mover to move massively' (Kauffman, 1993: 236). In 2008, the gurus of the financial system – thinking in terms of efficient market theory, equilibrium conditions, and random walks – did not foresee that large events could have small causes or that both small and large crashes could be triggered by small events.

20.3   THE DEMOCRATIZATION OF HIGH YIELD, A NEW COMPLEXITY AND THE GLOBAL FINANCIAL CRISIS

Where does the complexity come from that made the global financial crisis so intractable? Why did instability suddenly arrive, like a 'phase transition', similar to the way ice melts to liquid? Why were market participants unable to observe what they thought would be predictable milestones of system criticality? The financial system is itself a partial regime, comprising multiple systems of order that function simultaneously. A lesson drawn by evolutionary ecologists dealing with a parallel analytical problem – cross-scale effects – is that when what happens at one scale is affected by events at other scales, optimization models are likely to fail. Socio-ecological systems cannot be understood by studying only one scale because linkages across scales will determine how the system as a whole operates.[2]

Beginning in the 1970s the financial system was given responsibility for being an agent of social change when financial institutions were ordered to classify and issue loans according to the social identity of the recipient. Political leaders of modern democracies, not only in the United States, sought to allow their populations to access high yield financial services, once a privilege known only to elite consumers. Financial policy was politically designated to be a tool of social inclusiveness that would be less deleterious for the economy and less controversial politically than outright redistribution. Social stability could be strengthened if ordinary workers could be the beneficiaries of high-yield, high-volatility capitalism.

The decision to pursue democratic access to high yield as a vehicle of social inclusion was compatible with the social agendas of both US political parties: no one should be excluded from the benefits of high-achieving capitalism. Engaging wider sectors in capital accumulation was much more palatable than redistributing wealth, and it was something with which all politicians could agree. However, the democratization of high-yield financial capitalism ended the financial certainty upon which measures of risk were traditionally calculated.

The crisis that began in 2008 derives its complexity from the mixing of a sociopolitical risk with ordinary business risk. Overlooked was the fact that financial markets not only create wealth, they also liquidate wealth. Thus democratic capitalism exposed much wider segments of the population to the gains, as well as disturbances, of a financial system that remains delicately balanced on the edge of chaos. To avoid repeating the adverse consequences that contributed to the crisis, it is critical to understand that the democratizing of high-yield capital was a source of systemic risk and uncertainty. But it was a policy that was pursued in earnest beginning in the 1990s and therefore is not the grain of sand that precipitated the collapse.[3]

20.4   BEHAVORIAL ECONOMICS CAN OFFER CLUES TO THE MARKET'S INTERNAL DYNAMICS

Dissenting voices in economics have offered critical insights that modify the assumptions of the efficient market theory, the idealized view in which all the relevant information is already in today's prices, that each price change is independent of the last, and that yesterday's change will not influence today's price. The crisis of 2008 has taught us that the global financial system is a dynamic, open system that reacts most sensitively to its own internal dynamics.

Behavioral economics offers some useful insights into those dynamics; for instance, that bubbles and crashes are inherent to markets because the behaviors of the market participants generate their own sets of dynamics. What happens today does influence tomorrow's decisions. When one country invades another or refuses to abide by a treaty, potential partners will remember that refusal, which will shape their perceptions of its commitments for years, if not decades. Market participants are no different; they too have long memories. The stories they tell and the beliefs they hold about the behavior of others matter as much as do statistical probabilities. The behaviorist models demonstrate that market agents are less strategic and more emotional than traditional models anticipate (Shermer, 2007).[4]

The conventional models that presumed to transform risk into a deterministic, reversible process underestimated long-term interdependence. Historical evidence suggests that markets are not as self-contained as the models presume. It is unrealistic to assume the interchangeability of the future and the past. The reality is that prices cluster and January is traditionally bullish not because fundamentals of the global economy shift but because investors believe that other market participants routinely experience optimism at year opening. Participants have memories of past actions that condition how they read signals about the future; as a result price shifts do not exhibit statistical independence, nor are they normally distributed.

In a paper published in 1988, Vernon Smith et al. tested the assumption that if only experienced traders participated in the market, bubbles would be smaller and less frequent (Smith et al., 1988). They concluded that professionals are no better at steering the market toward normalcy than are uninformed novices. The study revealed that professional traders are not as economically rational as the efficient price theories presume. They are not quicker at learning, and they are no less likely than amateur traders to have irrational expectations. Such behavior causes price bubbles to be an empirical regularity of markets.

Questions about the internal dynamics of the market have never been at the top of the research agenda in finance. Why do traders speak of market 'optimism' and 'pessimism'? Do market participants trade on rumors and gossip, fears and expectations? Are markets self-propelling systems, or are they driven in large part by what investors believe about what other investors believe? Keynes compared traders to judges at a beauty pageant. Rather than selecting the faces they like best, they select the ones they believe are most likely to please the other judges.

The failure of one investor to cover a position is not supposed to spread throughout the system. And in conventional risk models, it takes only a minimal number of rational players to drive the market toward efficiency. But in real markets, when traders with vastly different expectations and goals fail to anticipate each other's actions, the outcomes are volatile. Volatility occurs because market participants lack common expectations. They come together with different time horizons; some may react with more immediacy than others. Information may not be immediately absorbed, which creates a dynamic that is different from the sum of its parts. Such internally generated time inconsistencies can have the same effect on prices as has the revelation of externally generated information that economists do pay attention to, such as the weakening of the labor market or a slowdown in capital expenditures. Conventional approaches, rooted as they are in an equilibrium framework, overemphasize exogenous shocks and disregard the system's self-generated internal dynamics.

20.5   RAPIDITY AND UNPREDICTABILITY

The financial crisis of 2008 has been explained as a story of ingenuous and shortsighted manipulation by the few against a poorly informed and gullible public. Alternatively, it is told as a tragedy of technocratic hubris and overreach by a crew of high-octane computational models from the hard sciences (Lohr, 2008). Arcane computations based on formidable mathematical models allowed a handful of professors to earn Wall Street salaries.

Only a few summers before the crash of 2008, economists and practitioners alike, the financial-sector experts, had touted system stability as an issue forever solved. That confidence in the fundamental soundness of the system was born from the success in dealing with the 1997 collapse of the Asian economies,[5] which regained their vigor in a few short years. Russia's markets collapsed in 1998, only to recover and usher in a decade of unprecedented growth. The experts had helped Brazil's markets revive after current account deficits led to a crash in 1998–1999. They had even averted a global recession despite the collapse of Long Term Capital Management (LTCM) in 1999, and the dot.coms in 2001, which had destroyed $5 trillion dollars in assets. But in 2008, Iceland's economy and banking system collapsed, and though the experts did not know it then, Iceland marked the beginning of system-wide failure. It was an avalanche, but not the grain of sand – not the cause of what followed.

The crash in the fall of 2008 is an anomaly to those who seek statistical regularity; unexpected and inexplicable to those closest to it. It was the culmination of a chain of events, no doubt, but not attributable to a single cause. In retrospect it is easy to identify accumulated excesses spanning a long period of time and to note that, yes, some industry models anticipated specific bubbles. (Many commentators within the real estate sector, for example, anticipated the burst in the US housing bubble.) But while we can identify the components of instability, hindsight will not help us identify that point when the system reached criticality. We do not yet fully understand the system's hard-to-discern internal dynamics, and thus we also cannot know which particular dynamic(s) contained sufficient risk to cause the system to experience an avalanche. The systemic risk only makes its appearance in the form of a collapse. The financial innovations of the 1970s and 1980s possessed their own internal dynamics that contributed to the system's criticality, but those sequences and linkages did not reveal themselves until after the crisis happened.

Alarmingly, financial systems replicate the behavior of other out-of-equilibrium, complex systems, such as the weather, 'where minor disturbances may lead to events, called avalanches, of all sizes' (Bak, 1999). A single random twitch can cause components in a complex system to disintegrate; and the links across such open systems can dramatically amplify the impact system-wide. Even a complete description of the vibrations within one component of the system will not provide an adequate understanding of how the impact is transferred across other components. Complex systems are known to self-organize into instability against all foresight and precaution.

Most conventional models of financial systems assume operational equilibrium. The market may actually seem stable until the very moment when it goes into a free fall – and then the models that described the market in its pre-crisis state lose their effectiveness at describing the state of crisis into which the market has succumbed. Most conventional models also have trouble coping with two of the most recurrent features of financial system volatility: the remarkable rapidity and unpredictability of meltdown. The conventional tools endorsed by the international financial community can rarely detect an imminent collapse. The East Asian economies collapsed only several weeks after an International Monetary Fund team gave the Thai and South Korean economies clean bills of health. Similarly, in the months before the collapse of the US financial system, the IMF issued a positive prognosis for global economic growth, expecting a quick recovery from a minor recession. Bear Stearns collapsed just days after its creditors on the overnight market refused to extend credit which the firm needed to cover positions it had taken during the trading day. Yet in each case, no one examined how close the system itself came to a total meltdown. Instead, they took comfort in their models, believing that a process of continuous financial innovation had proved robust against a series of system-shaking shocks. How can these same experts determine a course of action when they do not have the tools or the skills to understand what caused the whole system, stable for years, to collapse?

Another contributor to the 'fog' of crisis prevention and prediction is the general rule that the solutions to one crisis seem always to contain the seeds of the next. Models effective at depicting equilibrium conditions will rarely reveal when seemingly stable systems are about to become unpredictably dynamic. In the initial months after the 2008 financial collapse, for example, a number of US financial system experts proposed segregating the distressed assets (the non-performing loans), moving them off the balance sheets of the banks, and selling them at highly discounted values. If it were only a question of segregating the non-performing from the performing loans, the meltdown could have been reversed. But the proposal, which had seemed to work in East Asia in 1997, was abandoned because it quickly became apparent that the crisis was much larger than just the balance sheets of a few major financial institutions.

20.6   THE BLAME GAME: CAUSES AND CULPRITS

In the search for culprits, the most globally cited guilty party is the US financial system itself. From France to China, market liberalism has been attacked as the scourge behind the worldwide system collapse. Yet this same system was the global showcase for capitalism for more than two decades. Many of its primary characteristics, such as the secondary mortgage market, still attract active emulation throughout the world. In economic textbooks, the system is touted as a model of the laws of economics itself. Thus, the debates over the future of financial policy – and the apocalyptic claims predicting the end of US economic supremacy or the death of capitalism – are essentially debates about the future of economics. The battle for interpreting the past will determine how economics is taught and practiced in the future.

A few spectacularly corrupt financial institutions and rapacious individuals also received more than their share of the headlines. The full extent of criminal negligence is just coming to light; nevertheless, the crisis would have occurred with or without the insidious purveyors of Ponzi schemes and sellers of interest-only 'liar's loans'. Disclosing all the malfeasance in the world will not help diagnose the global system's sudden collapse.

The newly formed Obama administration in 2009 blamed the previous administration. Obama's Treasury Secretary, Timothy Geithner, blamed the previous Treasury Secretary, Henry Paulson, who in turn blamed the greed of the traders and the deafness of Congress. Other accounts highlight the failure of regulators, the failure of the rating agencies and the inappropriate remuneration in the financial services sector. Yesterday's heroes – Alan Greenspan, Robert Rubin and Larry Summers, once mentioned as the financial dream team of the 1990s – are today's villains.

Still others search for the one miscalculation that nudged the system to its tipping point. Some critics go back to the repeal in 1999 of Glass–Steagall Act, created after the Great Depression to separate deposit banking from commercial and investment banking. The repeal, they allege, created the mega-banks in the first place, those 'too big to fail' behemoths that received hundreds of billions in federal bailout funds. Others point to loosened credit policies after 2001, and still others to the decision to allow large financial institutions to increase their capital–lending ratios in 2004. There are those who point to the failure to bail out Lehman Brothers in 2008. Joseph Stiglitz proclaimed that a flawed economic philosophy, market liberalism and deregulation caused the collapse of democratic capitalism, and advocated democratic socialism in its stead (Stiglitz, 2009).

The list of potential culprits is as long as there are lists of financial sector experts. In our financial whodunit, we will look at the most frequently cited culprits and causes, from the most mundane – the inflated mortgage market and subprime lending, bank leveraging, the creation of 'too big to fail' banks, the conflicts within Freddie Mac and Fannie Mae – to the more exotic offenders, such as skyrocketing executive pay, rating agencies on hire from the firms they rated, risk models too esoteric for even market insiders to grasp, regulators who did not regulate, and the global imbalances perceived by the elite technocrats employed in finance ministries and international financial institutions. All of them became components of instability, but none of them alone explains the origins of the collapse.

20.6.1   The Inflated Mortgage Market and Subprime Lending

The mortgage market, long considered one of the most attractive features of the US financial system, tops almost everyone's list of culprits. How was it possible that this showcase system, praised and emulated for over 20 years, collapsed virtually overnight?

In short, the mortgage market evolved dramatically during the 1990s until it no longer resembled the system that would-be homeowners encountered in the 1980s. Back then, a mortgage applicant was required to pay at least 20 percent to 30 percent of the price of a home as a downpayment and this only after personal interviews and investigations into employment and credit history. The applicant had to have a particular credit and employment profile, one that excluded certain ethnic groups and professions. Even the lucky few who fell into the right categories had to wait months while their applications were evaluated.

Beginning in the mid-1990s, when loan writers had at their disposal the computational capabilities of supercomputers, a mortgage seeker had only to fill out an application. Formal interviews were eliminated, and individual risks were aggregated into categories according to a borrower's general risk profile. This lowered collateral requirements so that loans of hundreds of thousands of dollars could be obtained with less than 5 percent down. These mortgages could be arranged on the telephone or on the Internet within a matter of days.

This facilitated the creation of secondary markets in which the originating bank pooled and packaged its loans into securities. The streams of payments were divvied up and catalogued according to risk. The riskiest were backed by higher interest rates. The securitized loans were clustered together, repackaged and resold as a group to investors – and thus, the risk was transferred to the market. This process, called securitization, was consistent with the idea of financial deepening: by creating a larger risk pool, the securitization process made it possible to provide more loans to more people. The existence of this new class of mortgage-backed securities attracted in turn pools of investment capital much larger than what was traditionally available to homeowners. This brought down interest rates offered to individuals and reduced interest rate spreads.

A further deepening of the system occurred when credit default swaps were offered as insurance on the remote probability that the securitized instruments would default.[6] Credit default swaps were, in effect, derivatives created to allow investors to purchase insurance against default by issuers of those mortgage-backed securities. These could be customized according to a client's particular requirements.[7] From the perspective of the late 1980s, the new system looked safe, the capacity of the economy to put people in homes greatly expanded, the financial industry riding on the coat-tails of the mortgage industry became one of the most profitable in the United States. Investors worldwide wanted access to these securities and to the credit default swaps that insured them.

Politicians of both parties valued particularly the social dimension of these showcase arrangements, which allowed poorer and previously excluded individuals and families to become homeowners and fulfilled an ideological predilection of both the Clinton and Bush administrations to expand homeownership as a means of expanding the appeal of market capitalism. The expansion of homeownership became the centerpiece and most tangible example of the philosophy of democratic capitalism at work.

A more perfect sequence of risk-mitigating devices had never been seen. So what went wrong? For starters, the economy started to slow in 2007 and people who had bought under subprime conditions began having trouble making their mortgage payments. Initially, few observers believed that a collection of bad mortgages could bring the entire financial system to its knees. The problems were mostly in the periphery of the system, where, it was reasoned, they would remain. After all, how could several hundred billions of dollars in defaults topple a $5 trillion system? Even when the dollar amount of non-performing mortgages ballooned from about $200 billion to $400 billion, between 2006 and 2008, experts had little reason to fear that less than $1 trillion of losses in the mortgage market could bring a $200 trillion system to collapse (Puri, 2011). Just a few years earlier, the financial services industry had to mark down $5 trillion worth of technology stocks when a much bigger bubble had burst, but the economy quickly recovered.

Trying to find the origins of the crisis solely in the overheated housing market is problematic. This explanation disregards the hidden impact that the housing market slump was to have on other markets in which mortgage securities and credit default swaps were traded. On its own merits, the housing market bubble was not worrisome enough for analysts to fear the collapse of the whole system. But there are other independent factors to examine as possible culprits from the list of possible villains.

20.6.2 The Leverage Game

Many people blame the banks for taking the leverage game to new extremes. The banks, they say, tried to leverage securitization in ways that were not originally intended. Securitization itself is not a culprit among the components of instability, but excessive leveraging is.

Securitization is consistent with the democratization of high-yield financial capitalism. It deepened the financial system and dramatically increased homeownership. The idea behind securitizing mortgages is to transfer credit risk to the financial markets. After the crisis began, it was discovered that many of these securitized assets were actually never transferred. Banks had instead used them as collateral to bolster their own balance sheets in order to make more loans.

Why did the banks violate one of the cardinal benefits of financial innovation and not use securitization to transfer their risk to the credit markets? There is nothing new about the leverage game – banks make money by leveraging their deposits – but a change in the laws during 2004 allowed more money to be leveraged with less skin in the game. Regulatory loopholes permitted the loan originators to 'arbitrage the regulations' to inflate their balance sheets, essentially to inflate the value of their assets, and to look more solvent than they actually were.[8] Thus, the banks could lend more but put less of their own money on the line.[9]

How did excessive leverage and aggregate risk arise in a sector that is heavily regulated? And why did capital adequacy standards (reserve limits) fail to limit risk? Financial institutions were allowed to reduce the capital they held by moving assets to special investment vehicles they did not own, but to which they extended guarantees. A shadow banking system of hedge funds and bond dealers proliferated to allow banks to unload their riskier products while writing buy-back clauses so that the hedge funds could turn around and leverage the banks' triple-A ratings.[10] All this activity occurred under the watch of the regulators, leaving behind a trail of massive credit write-offs, regulatory infractions and poor long-term price performance.

But the capital markets offer many alternatives to banks, we are told, so why should we assume that what happens in one sector of the financial system would be enough to sink the entire system? We must keep searching to find an answer.

20.6.3   Large, Complex Financial Institutions

Another centerpiece of democratic capitalism was the creation of large, complex financial institutions. Post-crisis, the list included nearly insolvent organizations like Bank of America, Citi Group, Chase and Wells Fargo. The large, complex financial institutions emerged after Congress repealed the Glass–Steagall Act in 1999. Before the repeal, banks that accepted deposits in the United States were barred from investment banking or from underwriting bonds and equities. The commercial side of banking was separated from the investment side of the business to safeguard depositors' nest eggs from high-risk operations.

A massive lobbying campaign by the financial services industry helped end the separation of banking services. The logic was to put deposits to work more efficiently so that the public would receive higher returns by gaining access to investment opportunities previously available only to elite investment accounts. Allowing their depositors access to a wider range of investment alternatives would also enable the banks to manage better their own risk. The Securities and Exchange Commission allowed the newly created big banks to increase their debt-to-capital ratio from 12:1 to 30:0 in April 2004, escalating the race for high yields. Yields went up and depositors ended up with more money, but much of it in risky assets.

20.6.4   Government-Sponsored Enterprises

Those icons of democratic capitalism, Freddie Mac and Fannie Mae, these government-sponsored enterprises (GSEs), are designed as public–private partnerships with a social mission to buy and securitize mortgages.[11] Yet can an institution that enjoys a public mission and implicit government guarantee also have a profit-maximizing strategy? Before his appointment as one of President Obama's economic advisers, former Treasury Secretary Larry Summers wrote in the *Financial Times* that Freddie and Fannie were riddled with conflicts of interest that gave their chief executive officers (CEOs) a perverse incentive to gamble. He suggested replacing them with a new system of mortgage finance: either completely privatizing Fannie or making it completely public. As a hybrid, it combines many of the worst qualities of both socialism and capitalism by allowing a private interest to profit from an implicit federal government guarantee.

The flaw in the design concept rests with the fact that the public and private roles of these institutions are in conflict. The government implicitly guarantees private profits but socializes the risks, thus encouraging management to take on too much debt. The shareholders look the other way, assuming the government will bail them out with public money. Yet despite pointing out the flaws of government–private partnerships, the solutions to the financial crisis offer more, not less, of the same practice. Although considered to be a proven failure that has cost taxpayers nearly $150 billion in bailout funds, the share of new mortgages purchased by Freddie and Fannie since the crisis has increased to over 90 percent of all new mortgages.

20.6.5 Skyrocketing Executive Pay

Ironically, there is a dangerously undemocratic side to the quest for higher returns on behalf of the investing public. The fund managers became an interest group whose interests diverged sharply from the public's. Yet they acquired the resources and the status to assert that the rise of their industry, and its propagation, were essential to the well-being of the economy. The industry leaders gained the aura of being the economy's alpha males and females. Success in the financial sector gave bond salesmen the wherewithal to become global opinion leaders. James Wolfensohn became president of the World Bank; Michael Milken chaired an annual conference on the global economy attended by Nobel Prize winners, and people listened. Senators recalled being awed by the private fortune, said to be over $700 million, which Treasury Secretary Henry Paulson had acquired as a trader for Goldman Sachs. How could they know better? Perhaps that is why, in the aftermath of the financial collapse, Congress gave Paulson a blank check to manage and distribute the financial recovery funds with little oversight.

Yet post-crisis bonus and incentive schemes in the financial services area are now criticized as recipes for excessive risk-taking.[12] And there is considerable discussion of bringing executive compensation into closer alignment with the long-term performance of the products they offer to the public.[13] The problem is that the public, along with the bankers, is lured into the business sector with the highest returns. Bankers are not promoted on how much risk they avoid; their careers depend upon how much money they push out the door or bring in as transaction fees. Within the industry, operators hurt their career prospects if they go on record saying: 'I have reservations. I have hesitations. I'm not going to put my client's money in those assets.' As for the public, it was hard not to develop a taste for higher returns when one's neighbors were getting 5 percent or 6 percent and installing designer kitchens or buying new cars. But earning higher returns meant putting their investment funds in these innovative, high-risk products.

Critics who had strong reservations about the riskiness of the system found little appetite for their opinions. They were mocked by regulators and politicians who believed that because people were making money, even so much that at times it looked too good to be true, they should not second-guess the market or intervene. When Brooksley Born of the

Commodity Futures Trading Commission wanted to look into the risks of the derivative market, she was told her agency had no authority over derivatives and that her call for action was casting a 'shadow of regulatory uncertainty over an otherwise thriving market'. Meanwhile, the amount of private credit (debt) in the market increased about 100 percent between 2001 and 2008, and the government deficit ballooned.

There was another reason for the lax regulations. The regulators were government officials and, by definition, economic nationalists who wanted to keep the profits of industry at home. Financial capitals around the world competed to increase their share in the market, and one way to attract this very lucrative business was to have lower standards than a rival market. Raising standards too high could drive away business. Bankers in Frankfurt did not want to lose business to Dublin; Hong Kong did want to lose to Tokyo; Tokyo did not want to lose to Singapore. National regulators had an incentive to keep standards low because they wanted more business and they were unwilling to strengthen supervisory standards if it meant creating business for somebody else. National regulators have a dual job: they must protect investors, but they must also protect businesses and prevent them from moving overseas to more conducive environments. Considering the mixed objectives that national regulators are held responsible for, it is unrealistic to expect an optimal level of global regulation.

20.6.6   The Rating Agencies

In the early stages of the crisis, experts were sure that conflicts of interest among the rating agencies caused excessively rosy assessments that underestimated the inherent risks of financial innovation. What could have motivated their thinking when they assigned positive ratings to what in hindsight appear to have been highly dubious assets? The fact that the rating agencies – Moody's, Standard & Poor's and Fitch – were called National Recognized Statistical Rating Organizations gave the pubic heightened confidence in the objectivity of their assessments. Their dismal performance is generally attributed to their incentive structures. Rating agencies are paid by the issuers of securities who would bring in more business with positive ratings and turn over more business to the rating agencies. The costs of overly rosy assessments are born by the investors, while the agencies enjoy First Amendment protection, since their ratings are simply their opinions. However, these privately owned operations play a quasi-public role since their assessments are used by public agencies. Clearly, public policy would benefit by reforming the oligopolistic environment in which the rating agencies operate. But this simple observation overlooks a more subtle problem: the ratings of the collateralized debt obligations (CDOs) failed because the risk management models used by the rating agencies were flawed.

20.6.7   The Risk Models

The financial crisis of 2008 offers little basis for academics to take pride of place over their more practical-minded counterparts or to point fingers at practitioners and accuse them of shortsightedness or narrow self-interest. The conventional risk models used on Wall Street were built on the latest, celebrated economic logic – all based on the well-established efficient market hypothesis, which created an orthodoxy that emanated from halls of academe to the stock trading floors. It idealized a market in which all relevant information is already packed into a price. Yesterday's change will not influence today's movement or tomorrow's price; each change is independent from the last (Mandelbrot, 2004).

One such risk model was the Black–Scholes formula for valuing executive stock options. The idea was to use regressions to track past behavior and determine how stocks behave historically. The spreads from a variety of trades are regressed to their historical means; the larger spreads are assumed to decline, the smaller ones to increase. But after profits of $2.1 billion in a single year and capital subscriptions of $7 billion, something unpredictable happened at Long Term Capital Management. The effects of the Russian crisis caused spreads to diverge from their historic averages, leading the hedge fund to the verge of bankruptcy. According to the standard theories, the meltdown that brought down LTCM was a 1-in-5 billion freak accident, an anomaly. But the averages upon which the model was regressed were biased by an insufficiently short time period of 10–15 years, when most of the assets being tracked moved in one direction: up. Big price swings, it turned out, were more common than the model presumed.

The properties of a phenomenon in the physical world do not change by measuring it and publicizing the results. But in trading models, the measurement creates real-time feedback by dealers who short and distort, thereby altering the expectations and behaviors of other market participants. The models changed the statistical probabilities in the financial system, as participants responded by placing their bets in gigantic symphony – and moving from safety to crisis. For example, after the publication of the 'East Asian Miracle' study by the World Bank in 1993 and the mainstreaming of that phrase by the business media, a glut of investment capital poured into East Asia. But the timing was off and the safe investments had already been placed; when everyone pulled out, the region's economies collapsed in 1997.

Academic models of risk distribution are available to everyone in the world to use. Turn on your computer, and you would have the same information as someone in New York or London or Tokyo. With a click of the mouse, you can move assets just as fast as anyone else, but when everyone uses the same risk assessments, the money just as quickly moves in the same direction. When everyone puts their bets on the same place, the possibility increases that outliers – the fat tails far from the normal distribution – can wreak havoc with the system. The misperceptions shared by market participants clustered in certain urban financial centers are amplified.

Risk models work best when they assume that decision-makers are independent. When market participants across the globe have the same data on risk and returns, and employ the same optimization models, they end up with largely similar portfolios. Undervalued assets are quickly inflated and cause informational shifts, and these participants rush to the newly designated safe areas, creating new risks that condemn the market to cycles of instability (Persaud, 2000). The mix of computers with the human herd instinct produces ever larger bubbles that are now global in scale.

Because the traditional risk models treat the system as though it were closed and as though each outcome is only a matter of adding up the inputs, they fail to anticipate the large impacts of possible small causes: how the internal dynamics of one market can have multiplier effects across the entire system. And once the 2008 crisis began, the capability of these traditional risk models to function collapsed completely. They assumed a distribution of risk that was only realistic during the so-called normal period and could tell us little about the behavior of the risks once they shift in the direction of a crisis.

20.6.8   The Regulators

Why didn't the regulators, who were supposed to protect the public, try to deflate the housing bubble? Why did they not try to stop predatory lending? Many critics allege that the regulators were corrupted into complicity, but there is another perspective from which to understand their role. The regulators are just like the people who made the investments: enthusiastic, optimistic, forward-looking Americans. Regulators did not protect the public because they were part of it, as blind as everyone else. They believed the same illusions and myths, and when the fundamentals of the game seemed such that only a timid fool would stay away, they behaved like everyone else, acolytes enthusiastically sharing the exuberance and the hubris of the hour. When not conducting their own trades, they cheered for good fortunes of others.

Considerable social and ideological homogeneity made the industry myopic. The trading companies, as well as the regulators, were composed of people of virtually the same backgrounds, who attended the same schools and the same events, read the same columnists and cited the same books. It became doctrine that market behavior could be synchronized through private incentives in ways that would preserve and constantly 'grow' the system. The doctrine was sustained by two decades of almost continuous success at mitigating market fluctuations through innovations that seemed to enhance the resilience of the system. After all, the global system had survived six major threats in the previous decade: the Mexican peso collapse of 1994, the Asian crisis of 1997, the Russian meltdown of 1998, the Brazilian meltdown of 1998–1999, the collapse of Long Term Capital in 1991, and the dot.com crash of 2001. The regulators, like the traders in the trenches, fancied themselves to be battle-hardened members of the financial elite, insiders not by co-option, but because they believed in the same faulty models of risk. They did not imagine that each new mechanism designed to protect the system's underlying robustness also added to its complexity.

20.6.9   Perceived Global Imbalances

US financial authorities have insisted for years that global imbalances – such as a savings glut among America's principal East Asian trading partners – create market volatility by providing a storehouse of credit and thus inciting risky behavior by borrowers. But blaming the global crisis on the savers has not persuaded central bankers in Asia to change their ways. East Asian central banks started to hold dollar reserves to protect themselves from bank runs like those in 1997, when overseas investors decided to pull out of the region overnight to cover their losses at home. The affected countries – South Korea, Thailand, Indonesia and Japan – now advance the argument that foreign currency reserves are protection against the fickleness of global capital flows. While US financial officials adhere to the view that the excessive reserves will fuel another credit boom and lead to another cycle of instability, East Asia's central banks believe they protect themselves by building up currency reserves; and their relative success in weathering the storm of 2008 is likely to persuade their counterparts in other developing countries to do the same thing.[14]

Deeper scrutiny of this hypothesis by Barajas et al. shows that, historically, of 135 credit booms only 23 of them, or 17 percent, ended in a crisis. Banking crises were frequently preceded by episodes of lending booms (Barajas et al., 2007). Of the samples, those booms that inflated asset and real estate prices were most likely to end in crisis.

So it looks as if we have a found a culprit, at least for the inflated housing market. Who allowed those excesses to accumulate? Someone was not minding the store, and that someone was the Federal Reserve. The Federal Reserve (Fed) was the mastermind behind the lower interest rates that occurred regularly in 2007 and 2008. The Fed's monetary policy was one of the destabilizing forces, a contributor to the overall risk in the system. But do we have our suspect? The jury is clearly not convinced. Most plans for recovery anticipate an even larger role for the Fed to serve as a guarantor of system stability.

20.7   THE SAFETY AND SOUNDNESS OF THE SYSTEM: DO YOU TRUST THE FED TO MANAGE SYSTEMIC RISK?

The Federal Reserve is the most likely suspect of having created instability in at least one component of the financial market, but it cannot be labeled the grain of sand that triggered the collapse of the financial system. It was a contributor to systemic risk and uncertainty but not the trigger to the avalanche of the entire system.

The Fed's laissez-faire policy and low interest rates produced more mortgages, which were swept up and tiered and resold in successive waves of innovative, high-risk financial instruments that investors – at times the same ones who sold them in the first place – gambled against by purchasing credit derivatives. But as noted, there are a number of other culprits, or components of instability.

The Fed, however, is being heralded again as the most likely source of wisdom to protect the entire system. Apparently alone among federal agencies, it has the capacity and the wherewithal to act as the 'supercop' to protect the financial system from systemic risk.[15] If not the Fed, then who is better situated to police the entire system,[16] to say that this deal is no good but that deal is okay?

But on what criteria will Fed officials conduct inquiries when there is no consensus among the experts as to what constitutes systemic risk? Why should the Fed be granted overarching authority to regulate something it is incapable of defining? If the judgment of the supercop appears random, traders will innovate less; thus, giving the Fed such a big stick is tantamount to reducing the scope of financial innovation.

Certain critics of the Fed were outspoken long before the financial crisis unfolded. They argued that instead of more control, the Fed should be forced into daylight and its elitist culture ended. William Greider writes in *Secrets of the Temple*: 'were they not part of the secretive culture that sanctified the policy of too big to fail?' (Greider, 1989). Are they not purveyors to the cozy club of companies that enjoy proximity and privilege? Has there not been a revolving door between the private investment houses and the government agencies that are mandated to regulate them? Clearly the Fed failed to anticipate the systemic effects of two decades of credit expansion, a debt explosion and inflated valuations.

The Fed has essentially just one tool for dealing with risk: its control and supervision of the money supply. However, system risks are broader than any one segment of the system over which the Fed has jurisdiction. The risk arises from the trading of securities of all kinds across many markets. It arises when the complex web of intertwining securities causes the system to lock up because market participants cannot surmise the positions or risk exposures of their partners (Gorton, 2010). It arises when traders make trades in one segment of the market to cover positions they hold in another.

During the heyday of deregulation, market professionals believed that the threat of counterparty risk would lead to more effective risk management by firms. Before a congressional committee, Alan Greenspan, then Chairman of the Federal Reserve, argued in 1994 and again in 1998 that derivatives did not need to be regulated because the principle of counterparty risk would prompt market participants to regulate each other. After the meltdown the world looks different, and the same market professionals, Greenspan included, have argued that the crisis was a consequence of the actions of individual traders who solved their own problems by creating counterparty risk, which altered the nature of competition for others. Greenspan has since joined the consensus of his colleagues who believe the market is not and never will be a sufficiently adaptive environment to regulate itself. Having conceded in 2008 that, 'I found a flaw, I don't know how significant or permanent it is', in 2010 he asserts, 'I would not have done anything differently', and advocates no changes except for an end to Bush-era tax cuts.[17]

The topic of systemic risk and its elimination raises complex questions that traditional financial economics is not well prepared to answer. Can wholesale financial failure be eliminated? If not, how can we mitigate crisis? Will a bailout sow the seeds of the next crisis? Is it possible to regulate systemic risk? How should it be quantified? Is it even desirable to regulate systemic risk? One trader's risk may be another trader's opportunity. Can regulators learn to recognize system risk before the system is in crisis? Can anyone devise purely objective criteria for systemic risk, or is this a case of 'You'll know it when you see it'? And if that is true, would the appointment of a supercop, reputed for encouraging overconsumption and overborrowing, create so much uncertainty that it would deter not only dangerous financial growth but also innovation of the healthy kind? If the decisions of a central supervisor are so difficult to anticipate, would the increased uncertainty deter financial innovation of all types?

Only once we answer such questions will it be possible to obtain a consensus on the appropriate level of regulation. So far there are no feasible alternatives to expanding the Fed's oversight, but there is deep apprehension concerning the Fed's ability to perform in this new role without surrendering its status as a neutral player.

20.8   THE POLICY CONUNDRUM

Having examined the list of culprits, and dispensed with them one by one, it becomes evident that this is about all we can do: exclude possible grains of sand as causes of the avalanche. The financial system has gained almost impenetrable complexity over the past few decades, and we must study its increasingly turbulent dynamics to know more. Local economies are open systems, subject to system-wide effects. National economies are the components of a much larger system and subject to system-wide effects. Their own internal dynamics can in turn influence the wider system, with repercussions that may rebound upon it.

The next generation of regulators must target the system's most enduring characteristic and conundrum: its proclivity toward periodic, difficult-to-predict avalanches that result from its internal dynamics. Economists, mathematicians, social scientists, bankers, traders and politicians do not have the skills or tools to discern or anticipate how these systems fit together and how and why they will fail. We know this much already: that as a complex system, the financial system is sensitive to catastrophic failures from tiny causes (Hubler et al., 2007).[18]

Regulators must learn to ask what characterizes these avalanches. If they cannot discern the actual trigger, they can begin by examining possible causes: the kinds of initial events that might trigger an avalanche, the kinds of linkages and behaviors surrounding an event, potential thresholds that distinguish system meltdowns from nonevents (Tornell and Westermann, 2005).[19]

If Tornell and Westermann are correct, then it is crucial to re-examine the basis for both confidence in a financial system and the soundness of its financial institutions. Market risk is nested in political and social risk, while a nation's ability to exit a financial crisis is fundamentally a question of trust – of consent and credibility within the polity. It is the confidence in the underlying solidity of social institutions and the legitimacy of political institutions that constitutes the financial system's underlying strength, and the absence of such trust that causes polities which suffer deep social divides to have underdeveloped financial systems. Institutions that manage risk well, that can convert household risk into social risk rather than vice versa, become an essential defense against crisis contagion. Likewise, a government whose commitments to reform and payment of the national debt are credible exhibits firm social foundations. Significant amounts of debt can be sustained when financial policy has institutionalized public support behind it.

To return to the analogy of the grain of sand in the sand pile, we know that a grain of sand can affect the pile's internal dynamics. But we do not yet know if a particular grain of sand was consequential in its own right or because the pile was already in a state of criticality, at the edge of collapse, due to other, unobservable internal dynamics. Just as we do not therefore know which grain of sand may cause the avalanche, so we do not yet know which sand pile in a larger system is on the edge of a meltdown. We may in fact never be able to access this information. Thus, the best defense will be financial systems designed with multiple fail-safe faculties operating at different scales.

Although it is critical to keep the micro-evolutionary effects distinct from the macro ones for analytical purposes, because financial systems are open systems what happens at one level will have impacts on the wider global system, and what happens at the macro level will affect the micro level. Financial economics is now challenged to develop an approach to distinguish these two classes of phenomena while using the same body of theory to address both.

NOTES

1. The loss in US household wealth between December 2007 and December 2008 was 17 percent; because both stocks and homes are widely held, the losses were spread among the population. By the end of 2008, the Dow Jones Industrial Average was down 34 percent compared to a year earlier.
2. In a highly influential contribution to the study of environment and ecology Simon Levin argues that: 'the problem of pattern and scale is the central problem in ecology' (Levin, 1992: 1943). The regularities of the biosphere derive from interacting self-organizing processes rather than being parts of a unified or central-ized whole (Levin, 2009: 772). The structure and dynamics of one scale of a social-ecological system will depend on the dynamics of the system at scales above and below. For example social and political risks that are not effectively managed will prevent economic transitions to market-based resource distribu-tion. A state is similar to an ecological system being composed of a hierarchy of interconnected adaptive cycles that operate at multiple scales. Complexity exists because any one scale is linked to hierarchies that govern system-wide behavior. Economists are generally inclined to models that ignore the multi-scale structure of the economy. Ignoring cross-scale dynamics that are inevitable in economic systems causes failures to optimize adaptive evolution.
3. The antecedents of the policy can be found in the Community Reinvestment Act of 1979.
4. For a popular overview of behavioral economics see Shermer (2007) or Thaler and Sunstein (2008).
5. Between 1997 and 1998, Thailand, Indonesia and South Korea all suffered depletion of the current account, and depreciation and decline in real output.
6. Technically, credit default swaps are not insurance. They are not sold exclusively by insurance companies (AIG sold its through a non-insurance subsidiary, purposely to avoid regulation) and are unregulated. Nonetheless, insurance is a good analogy to explain the credit default swap transaction.
7. One of the problems encountered when these instruments started to malfunction was that they were non-standard; thus, it was impossible to benchmark the probabilities of similar but not identical issues.
8. Banks were also buying their own securities, as well as their own equities, so it looked as though they were making more money to increase the equity, or share value, of the firm, allowing shareholders to claim higher dividends.
9. Lehman Bros wrote mortgages, sold bonds, sold credit default swaps, and so on. Countrywide is a similar case. The demand for the mortgage-backed securities was so great that these vendors aggressively mar-keted the loans and bonds beyond their capacity to operate.
10. The shadow sector, which constitutes 70 percent of all financial assets, is essential to help rescue the system.
11. The residential mortgage market is approximately $10 trillion; 55 percent is securitized. The GSEs manage about $1.5 trillion and securitized $3.8 trillion; their leverage ratios are about 25:1
12. There have been calls for locking up bonuses in reserve accounts and permitting clawbacks.
13. Intermediation is efficient when gains created by specialists who augment market liquidity surpass the costs of their activity. Economists generally look the other way when considering the returns earned by financial intermediaries, believing that high returns reflect how efficiently capital is distributed to its most efficient use.
14. Educated opinion has advocated that Asians rebalance their economies through more effective social safety nets to reduce the need for saving; to provide support for the small and medium-sized enterprise sector to create new growth centers and encourage deeper and broader capital markets, especially bond markets; and above all to promote domestic consumption. No collective agreement seems likely on any of the above within the region.
15. An obvious innovation is for government to collect insurance premiums for the necessary bailout fund.
16. Senator Charles Grassley, Hearing Before the Committee on Finance: 'TARP oversight: a six month update', Statement of Ranking Member Charles Grassley. Can the Federal Reserve supervise systemi-cally risky companies without being embroiled in endless lobbying and litigation that compromises its independence? (http://finance.senate.gov/sitepages/hearing033109.htm, Senator Grassley calls Fed 'an appendage of the Treasury'.)
17. http://www.businessinsider.com/alen-greenspan-interview-2011-1.
18. Also see other works by A. Hubler and colleagues (Hubler et al. 2007; Foster et al., 2007).
19. Aarón Tornell reports that countries that embrace innovation grow fastest but are also more likely to experience a financial crisis. In crisis after crisis, the countries with open financial markets took the hardest hits. South Korea, for example, opened its stock markets to foreign hedge funds that eventually acquired half of the country's market capitalization. When the funds pulled out, values crashed. The countries that grow the fastest are the countries in which boom-and-bust cycles, and prosperity and crisis, are pairs, just like capitalism and collusion. Just as no one has found a way to deter short-term investment if they want to receive long-term flows, to eliminate fully the risk of high growth and financial fragility

we would have to close the financial markets. A high-growth economy without financial risks has yet to be discovered. Instead of trying to take the risk out of finance market economies, we need policies that anticipate the avalanches of financial market change. Gigantic perturbations may be a universal feature of system changes from which an increasingly optimized set of economic institutions is derived.

REFERENCES

Bak, Per (1999), *How Nature Works: The Science of Self-Organized Criticality*, New York: Springer.

Barajas, Adolfo, Giovanni Dell'Ariccia, and Andrei Levchenko (2007), *The Good, the Bad, and the Ugly*, Washington, DC: International Monetary Fund.

Foster, G., A. Hubler and K. Dahmen (2007), 'Resonant forcing of multidimensional chaotic map dynamics', *Physical Review E*, **75**(3, pt. 2), article 036212.

Gorton, Gary B. (2010), *Slapped by the Invisible Hand: The Panic of 2007*, New York: Oxford University Press.

Greider, William (1989), *Secrets of the Temple: How the Federal Reserve Runs the Country*, New York: Simon & Schuster.

Hubler, A., G. Foster and K. Phelps (2007), 'Managing chaos: thinking out of the box', *Complexity*, **12**, 10–13.

Kauffman, Stuart A. (1993), *The Origins of Order: Self-Organization and Selection in Evolution*, NewYork: Oxford University Press.

Levin, Simon (1992), 'The problem of pattern and scale', *Ecology*, **73**, 1943–1967.

Levin, Simon (2009), *The Princeton Guide to Ecology*, Princeton, NJ: Princeton University Press.

Lohr, Steve (2008), 'In modeling risk, the human factor was left out', 4 November.

Mandelbrot, Benoit B. (2004), *The (Mis)behavior of Markets: A Fractal View of Risk, Ruin, and Reward*, New York: Basic Books.

Persaud, Avinash (2000), *Sending the Herd off the Cliff Edge: The Disturbing Interaction between Herding and Market-Sensitive Risk Management Systems*, Washington, DC: Institute of International Finance.

Puri, Shilpa (2011), 'Distribution of global financial assets', *Markest in Motion* (Financial Technologies Knowledge Management Company Newsletter), **1**(44), 17 January.

Shermer, Michael (2007), *The Mind of the Market: Compassionate Apes, Competitive Humans, and Other Tales from Evolutionary Economics*, New York: Times Books.

Smith, V.L., G.L. Suchanek and A.W. Williams (1988), 'Bubbles, crashes and endogenous expectations in experimental spot asset markets', *Econometrica*, **56**, 1119–1151.

Stiglitz, Joseph E. (2009), 'Capitalist fools', *Vanity Fair*, **51**, 48.

Thaler, Richard H. and Cass R. Sunstein (2008), *Nudge: Improving Decisions About Health, Wealth, and Happiness*, New Haven, CT: Yale University Press.

Tornell, Aarón and Frank Westermann (2005), *Boom-Bust Cycles and Financial Liberalization*, Cambridge, MA: MIT.

21 The future of financial regulation: reflections from an emerging market perspective

*Rakesh Mohan**

21.1 INTRODUCTION

The world experienced the most severe financial and economic crisis in 2008–2009 since the Great Depression. Although the crisis originated in the subprime mortgage market in the United States, it then spread to Europe and later to the rest of the world. The speed of the contagion that spread across the world was perhaps unprecedented. What started off as a relatively limited crisis in the US housing mortgage sector turned successively into a widespread banking crisis in the United States and Europe, the breakdown of both domestic and international financial markets, and then later into a full-blown global economic crisis. Interestingly, however, although the emerging market economies (EMEs) in Asia and Latin America also suffered severe economic impacts from the crisis, their financial sectors exhibited relative stability. No important financial institutions in these economies were affected in any significant fashion. So this crisis should really be dubbed the North Atlantic financial crisis rather than a global financial crisis.

In any case, the fallout from this financial crisis could be an epoch-changing one for central banks and financial regulatory systems. The crisis occurred after an extended period dubbed the 'Great Moderation', a period characterized by high global growth, huge financial sector expansion and low product price inflation, but accompanied by steep growth in monetary aggregates and asset prices, along with volatility in exchange rates. The prevailing monetary policy orthodoxy was inflation targeting or variants thereof, and light-touch financial regulation. The price that the world has paid for the practice of such narrowly focused monetary policy, inadequate macroeconomic policy coordination, and neglect of financial regulation and supervision has been huge.

21.1.1 Dimensions of the Crisis

I focus first on the severity of the crisis. From an average annual growth rate of 4.1 percent between 2001 and 2008, world gross domestic product (GDP) growth fell to −0.7 percent in 2009. The unprecedented globally coordinated monetary and fiscal efforts launched after the Lehman episode have largely succeeded in averting the threat of an economic depression. Led by the rapid recovery of EMEs, world GDP growth is now estimated by the International Monetary Fund (IMF) (in its September 2011 World Economic Outlook) to have recovered to 5.1 percent in 2010. That the world was taken by surprise by the developments in 2008 and 2009 is shown by the fact that as late as July 2008 the IMF expected world GDP to grow by 3.9 percent in 2009. The reversal in expectations was so sudden that exactly a year later the forecast had been reversed to −1.4 percent for 2009. Similarly, the growth forecast for 2010 was as low as 1.9 percent in April 2009; the speed of the recovery taking place in 2010 was also unexpected. The world economy has been beset with extreme uncertainty during the recent crisis period.

Global credit write-downs were estimated by the IMF at US$2.8 trillion in the October 2009 Global Financial Stability Report (GFSR) (IMF, 2009b), but were revised to US$2.3 trillion in the October 2010 update (IMF, 2010b). Despite the ongoing recovery the overall costs of the crisis have still been massive. First, households have suffered a severe reduction in overall wealth due to the marked decline in property prices. Second, fiscal expansion of the G20 countries, relative to their 2007 levels, is of the order of about 6 percent of their GDP in both 2009 and 2010; US fiscal expansion is much higher at just under 10 percent of its GDP. Third, in containing the emerging North Atlantic financial crash in 2008–2009, the total support given to the financial sector in advanced economies was of the order of US$7 trillion, including capital injections into financial institutions by governments, purchase of assets by treasuries, central bank liquidity injections and other upfront government financing, though some of these expenditures will of course be recovered (IMF, 2009a, 2010a).

Fourth, despite this massive effort, unemployment levels still continue to be in the region of 10 percent or higher across the developed world and are expected to remain at such high levels for an extended period of time. As assessed by the IMF, output levels in advanced countries will never go back to the pre-crisis trends so there is a very large permanent output loss. Fifth, the average debt-to-GDP ratio for advanced economies is expected to increase to around 120 percent by 2015, implying very large long-term debt servicing costs and crowding-out of private activity (IMF, 2010a). Of course, this expected increase in debt cannot all be attributed to the financial crisis; some of it is certainly due to population ageing and the associated health and pension costs that are expected.

Sixth, we are also witnessing extended volatility in the exchange rates of major currencies and fragility in leading capital markets, leading to extended economic uncertainty and possible volatility in capital flows, with implications for financial stability.

So the cost of this crisis has been massive for the global economy, and its fiscal effects will be felt for some time to come. It is therefore very important that we identify the causes of the current crisis accurately so that we can think of and act on the longer-term implications for monetary policy and financial regulatory mechanisms. Consequent to the financial crisis of 2008–2009, along with the coordinated fiscal and monetary policy actions that were taken to avert a major crash, a comprehensive re-examination of the financial regulatory and supervisory framework is under way around the world. While some degree of normality has returned to global financial markets in 2009–2010, in view of the very heavy costs that the world has had to pay, it is essential that governments and regulatory authorities do not fall prey to the natural temptations of complacency that such return to normality could entail.

Against this backdrop, I first provide a brief interpretation of how the crisis arose in terms of shortcomings in the extant practice of monetary policy and financial regulation, and then attempt to analyze the emerging contours of regulation of financial institutions with an emphasis on the emerging challenges and dynamics.

21.2   WHAT WENT WRONG WITH THE FINANCIAL SYSTEM

21.2.1   Accommodative Monetary Policies

It is generally agreed that a variety of factors led to the crisis: developments in the sub-prime sector, excessive leverage in the financial system as a whole in recent years, lax financial regulation and supervision, and global macro imbalances. What I have been particularly interested in is the role of lax monetary policy in the advanced economies, and particularly that in the United States. In examining the waves of capital flows to emerging market economies that have occurred over the last 30 years, it is noteworthy that almost each wave has been preceded by loosening of monetary policy in the advanced economies, usually led by the US, followed by tightening leading to the reversal of capital flows. In the period after the dot.com crash, lax monetary policy led to excess liquidity and low interest rates worldwide. In previous episodes of such excess liquidity over the last 30 years it was emerging market economies that suffered from crises (CGFS, 2009).

But this time it rebounded on the North Atlantic economies. When there is an extended period of lax monetary policy and low interest rates, there is a natural search for yields leading to outward capital flows in search of higher yield. What happened during this recent period of monetary expansion is that with monetary policies being accommodative for an extended period in the US and other advanced economies, in addition to capital flows going outward in search of yields, the volume of liquidity generated was such that there was also a burst of financial innovation within these countries, so that higher yields could be obtained within. This search for higher yields within led to many of the irregularities observed. The consequence is that it is the advanced countries of the North Atlantic which have suffered from this financial crisis.

The other issue of note is that, partly because of large expansion in the global supply of goods from China and other EMEs – over the decade since around the turn of the century – the accommodative monetary policy and increased liquidity did not lead to higher inflation as measured by the Consumer Price Index (CPI), or even higher inflation expectations as conventionally measured. It did, of course, lead to huge increases in asset prices of different varieties, particularly housing and real estate, not just in the US and Europe but in other parts of the world as well.

Being particularly focused on CPI or on core inflation, central banks felt no pressure to tighten until very late because they were not observing increases in CPI, or in inflation expectations. Being against the prevailing orthodoxy, they avoided reacting to asset price growth, and even to supply-induced commodity price increases. To my mind, this is a major issue for central banks, financial regulators and academics to discuss. In the presence of low CPI inflation, central banks typically come under significant public and market pressure not to raise rates. In what circumstances should monetary policy take cognizance of variations in asset prices and in commodity prices, and how? And what should be the role of coordinated action through prudential regulation?[1]

21.2.2   Shortcomings in Financial Regulation and Supervision

There is actually much greater discussion going on internationally on the existing regulatory practices and the future of financial regulation and supervision than on monetary policy. The intensity of discussion is reflected in the plethora of reports that have been issued by authoritative sources, both official and non-official, in all the affected jurisdictions (CGD, 2010; CCMR, 2009; de Larosiere Report, 2009; Geneva Report, 2009; G20, 2009; G30, 2009; IIF, 2009; Turner Review, 2009; United Nations, 2009; United Kingdom, 2009; United States, 2009; Warwick Commission, 2009). What is common to all these dozen or so reports is the acknowledgement that regulation and supervision in the advanced economies was too lax in recent times, and that there needs to be considerable rethinking leading to much strengthened, and perhaps intrusive, regulation and supervision in the financial sector. Apart from the laxity in the supervision of banks there was a serious conceptual flaw in the approach to financial regulation. It was assumed that micro-prudential regulation and supervision of individual financial institutions would also ensure systemic stability of the financial system. This approach ignored the possibility of the fallacy of composition. The increase in complexity of interaction of financial markets with even sound financial institutions could have negative systemic effects through cumulative negative externalities. Thus there is clear recognition now of the need for contra-cyclical macro-prudential regulation, and of the need to reduce moral hazard posed by systemically important financial institutions (SIFIs).

At the root of such rethinking, though not always acknowledged as such, is really the questioning of the existing intellectual assumptions with respect to the functioning of markets, and the nature of financial risk. To quote the Turner Review (2009):

> At the core of these assumptions has been the theory of efficient and rational markets. Five propositions with implications for regulatory approach have followed:
>
> (i)   Market prices are good indicators of rationally evaluated economic value.
> (ii)   The development of securitized credit, since based on the creation of new and more liquid markets, has improved both allocative efficiency and financial stability.
> (iii) The risk characteristics of financial markets can be inferred from mathematical analysis, delivering robust quantitative measures of trading risk.
> (iv)   Market discipline can be used as an effective tool in constraining harmful risk taking.
> (v)   Financial innovation can be assumed to be beneficial since market competition would winnow out any innovations which did not deliver value added.
>
> Each of these assumptions is now subject to extensive challenge on both theoretical and empirical grounds, with potential implications for the appropriate design of regulation and for the role of regulatory authorities. (Turner Review, 2009: 30)

What were the specific developments in the financial system that arose from these broadly accepted intellectual assumptions that led to the ongoing global financial crisis?

Recurring financial crises: build-up of excessive leverage

Financial and banking crises have a long history, which is as old as the existence of the financial sector itself (Kindleberger and Aliber, 2005; Reinhart and Rogoff, 2009). All liquid markets can be susceptible to swings in sentiment, which can produce significant divergence from rational equilibrium prices. However, boom and bust in equity prices have surprisingly small consequences relative to boom and bust in credit instruments, unless investment in equity instruments is itself from heavily leveraged borrowed resources. What is common to almost all crises is the build-up of excessive leverage in the system and the inevitable bursting of the financial bubble that results from such leverage. What is ironic about the current crisis is that this excess leverage occurred over a period when greater consensus had developed through the Basel process on the need for and level of adequate capital required in banking institutions across all major jurisdictions. Furthermore, sophisticated financial risk management capabilities were also believed to have been developed within large financial institutions during this period of unusually high rapid growth in both the magnitude and the sophistication of the financial system. This had some perverse results.

First, because of the perceived increase in sophistication in the measurement of risk, high-quality risk capital in large banks could be as low as 2 percent of assets, even while complying with the Basel capital adequacy requirements. Second, large financial institutions could maintain lower high-quality capital because of the assumption that they had better risk management capacity than smaller, less sophisticated institutions. The thinking now is moving in the opposite direction: to reduce moral hazard, and to reduce systemic risk, it is being argued that SIFIs should be subject to higher capital requirements and they should be discouraged from becoming too big to fail.

With financial deregulation in key jurisdictions like the US and the UK, along with most other countries, financial institutions also grew in complexity. Financial conglomerates began to include all financial functions under one roof: banking, insurance, asset management, proprietary trading, investment banking, broking, and the like. The consequence has been inadequate appreciation and assessment of the emerging risks, both within institutions and system-wide. What were the factors that led to this emergence of excessive system-wide and institutional risk?

Growth in securitized credit and derivatives

Among the notable developments of the last decade has been the unprecedented explosive growth of securitized credit intermediation and associated derivatives (Yellen, 2009). The issuance, for example, of RMBSs (residential mortgage-backed securities) doubled from US$1.3 trillion to US$2.7 trillion between 2001 and 2003. The assumption underlying this development was that this constituted a mechanism that took risk off the balance sheets of banks, placing it with a diversified set of investors, and thereby serving to reduce banking system risks. As late as April 2006, the IMF's Global Financial Stability Report noted that this dispersion would help 'mitigate and absorb shocks to the financial system', with the result that 'improved resilience may be seen in fewer bank failures and more consistent credit provision'. The opposite actually transpired.

Although simple forms of securitization have existed for a long time, this assumption has already proved to be erroneous. Among the key functions of banks is maturity transformation: they intermediate shorter-term liabilities to fund longer-term assets in the non-financial sector. Banks are typically highly leveraged and hence trust and confidence is crucial to their functioning and stability. Traditionally, therefore, banks exercised sharp vigilance on the risk elements of their assets, which were typically illiquid, in order to ensure constant rollover of their shorter-term funding liabilities. What securitization does is to turn illiquid assets into liquid ones, which in theory then disperses risks from the banks' balance sheets and also reduces their requirements of banking capital. The incentive to monitor credit risk in the underlying assets also disappears. With assets themselves seen as liquid short-term instruments, they began to be funded by ultrashort-term liabilities, including even overnight repos whose volume increased manifold in recent years. The majority of holdings of securitized credit ended up, however, in the books of highly leveraged banks and bank-like institutions themselves, and hence risk got concentrated rather than being dispersed. Systemic risk increased because traded instruments are inherently more susceptible to price swings depending on changes in market sentiment, and much of this trading was in opaque over-the-counter (OTC) markets. Moreover, at low levels small changes in interest rates and yields result in greater volatility in prices. What emerged was a 'complex chain of multiple relationships between multiple institutions' (Turner Review, 2009) and hence the higher risk of contagion within the financial sector. Furthermore, liquidity risks in such markets were also not understood adequately. It was assumed that these liquid markets would always exist, and hence securitized assets were assumed to be inherently less risky than illiquid long-term credit assets.

Financial innovation arising from the search for yields compounded this problem as second-order derivatives proliferated. For example, CDO (collateralized debt obligation) issuance tripled between the first quarters of 2005 and 2007, reaching its peak of US$179 billion in the second quarter of 2007, before collapsing to US$5 billion by the fourth quarter of 2008. With the lack of transparency in OTC markets, their valuation became increasingly dependent on model valuation and credit ratings, rather than observable and transparent market valuation, and hence inherently more opaque. Thus, when problems arose in these markets and prices were not visible, valuation of the assets of banks and the shadow banking system became unobservable. Consequently, trust and confidence evaporated and markets froze.

Emergence of the shadow banking system

These problems were further compounded by the emergence of the largely unregulated shadow banking system that took assets off the banks' balance sheets, thereby reducing the latter's capital requirements. Ironically, the increased attention to capital adequacy in banks itself led to a poorly capitalized financial system overall. The complexity and magnitude of intra-financial sector transactions exploded over the decade preceding the crisis. For example, issuance of global credit derivatives increased from near zero in 2001 to over US$60 trillion in 2007; OTC interest rate derivatives grew from around zero in 1987 to about US$50 trillion in 1997 and US$400 trillion by 2007; global issuance of asset-backed securities (ABSs) went up from about US$500 billion in 1997 to over US$2 trillion; forex trading activity rose tenfold from about US$100 billion to US$1 trillion in 20 years between 1987 and 2007, doubling after 2002; and trading in oil futures increased from an equivalent of about 300 million barrels in 2005 to 1000 million barrels in 2007, more than ten times the volume of oil produced (Turner Review, 2009). Thus the financial sector was increasingly serving itself rather than any perceived needs of the real economy.

Given such an explosive increase in financial transactions unrelated to developments in the real economy, the financial sector exhibited high profits and growth, while doing relatively little for the non-financial sectors of the economy, which the financial sector exists to serve in principle. Compensation levels in the financial sector also exploded correspondingly, and talent got sucked in from other sectors as well. The debt of financial companies increased to levels exceeding the GDP of leading economies; in the UK, for example, financial sector debt increased from 40 percent of GDP in 1987 to 200 percent in 2007; and in the US from a similar 40 percent in 1987 to over 100 percent in 2007 (FSA, 2009). Thus, in the process of taking risks off balance sheets through securitization, these risks returned to the extended banking system itself and the original rationale for securitization was belied. Rather than reducing systemic risk, the system of complex securitization and associated derivatives only served to increase it. Moreover, it became increasingly difficult to trace where the risk ultimately lay.

Why is there high compensation in the financial sector?
There needs to be further questioning of the widespread discussion around compensation in the financial sector: is the compensation issue really a red herring? Is it not the excess profitability of financial institutions that has led to the very high compensation levels of their employees, along with the high returns to shareholders? If a firm has such high returns, they have to go somewhere: they are either distributed to shareholders or to the employees or to a combination of both, which is what has been happening. It is then difficult to restrict compensation levels as is being argued currently. Much of the discussion has veered off into the minutiae of compensation practices related to the various forms in which compensation is given. To my mind the real question relates to the high profitability observed in recent years in segments of the financial sector.

Therefore, the question really is: is there a lack of competition in the financial sector? And if so, why? Are there some regulatory provisions that restrain competition, or are there some entry barriers inherent in the structure of the financial industry? If there is no lack of competition, why do these profits not get competed down? And again, if the answer is indeed that there is a lack of competition, what can be done? What kind of competition policy measures would be relevant and applicable to the financial sector? Addressing these questions is probably more useful for dealing with the compensation issue than dealing directly with compensation patterns and levels would be.

The regulatory system was clearly behind the curve in taking account of these developments. Regulatory focus was on banks and not on the emerging shadow banking system, which the market was supposed to discipline. The procedures for calculating risk-based capital requirements underestimated the risks inherent in traded securitized instruments, thereby adding to the incentive for banks to securitize assets into traded instruments, which bore lower risk weights. The trading of these instruments has largely been in OTC markets that exhibit little transparency. As a result of this overall process, banks became effectively undercapitalized, and the leverage ratios of the unregulated shadow banking system and investment banks reached unsustainable levels. There was a clear failure of supervision. A good deal of the ongoing discussion on change in regulation is focused on this issue through mandating of increased capital requirements for higher-risk activities.

With the existence of low interest rates, mispriced low risk perceptions, and inherent incentives to originate lending and distribute securitized instruments, household indebtedness increased to unprecedented levels, particularly for housing. In both the US and the UK, the household debt-to-GDP ratio increased from an average of around 60 percent between the mid-1980s and 1990s to over 100 percent in the following decade (Turner Review, 2009). Demand for housing assets rose, and hence housing prices. Thus micro behavior led to increased systemic risk that was not adequately appreciated or understood, and hence not monitored by the authorities.

21.3   THE CHALLENGES AHEAD

The agenda that is being developed for the strengthening of financial sector regulation and supervision is ambitious. Contentious issues are arising both at domestic, national regulatory levels and at the international levels on regulatory cooperation. Whereas the principles that have been outlined for this regulatory overhaul are being increasingly well accepted, many challenges are emerging on their modes of implementation, and on their practicality.

21.3.1   Regulatory Structure and Macro-Prudential Regulation

A great deal of discussion is taking place in a number of jurisdictions on the changes needed in regulatory structure so that the probability of such a financial crisis arising again is minimized. The regulatory regimes have to be more effective over the cycle. There is general agreement on the need for putting in place a regime of macro-prudential regulation and financial stability oversight. The issue under discussion in different jurisdictions is: who will do it? Would it be a council of regulators, the central bank or the treasury? The core concern behind such discussion relates to the location of responsibility for maintaining financial stability. Should central banks be made responsible, and also accountable, for maintaining financial stability? Macro-prudential regulation is increasingly seen to be among the key means for maintaining financial stability. That requires the imposition of prudential regulations in the light of some macroeconomic or overall financial trends that need to be acted on. If the central bank is only a monetary authority and a separate agency, like the Financial Services Authority (FSA) of the UK, is responsible for financial regulation and supervision, how is coordination to be achieved so that such action can be implemented? The US has had a very fragmented regulatory structure, whereas the UK had placed all regulatory responsibilities for all segments of the financial sector in the unified FSA. In the rest of Europe monetary policy was centralized in the European Central Bank (ECB) but financial regulation has remained fragmented at national levels. The US Federal Reserve System has had significant regulatory responsibilities, but regulatory failures were significant in all North Atlantic financial systems, with the exception of Canada.

The ongoing efforts to undertake significant regulatory reform in the US, the UK and the eurozone illustrate the lack of consensus on what kind of regulatory structure constitutes best practice for promoting financial stability.

The UK is abandoning its experiment of completely separating financial regulation from the central bank, and the FSA is now being folded back into the Bank of England. The Governor of the Bank of England will now be responsible for monetary policy, financial regulation and financial stability, an arrangement similar to that prevailing in India. Consequent to the crisis it is felt that the central bank can better exercise its responsibility for financial stability if financial regulation also comes within its purview.

The US Treasury had initially proposed that all banking regulation be unified in a single agency, while placing greater responsibility on the US Federal Reserve for maintaining financial stability. Under the reform bill that has finally been passed, systemic risk will be formally assessed by a new Financial Services Oversight Council which will be composed of the main regulators and chaired by the Treasury Secretary. It will focus specially on SIFIs in order to prevent institutions from getting 'too big to fail'. Any emerging SIFIs, including non-banks, will be put under the regulation of the Federal Reserve (Fed). Regulatory jurisdiction has been simplified and clarified, with the Fed handling systemic institutions; the Office of the Comptroller of the Currency (OCC), national banks; and the Federal Deposit Insurance Corporation (FDIC), state banks. The only agency being eliminated is the Office of Thrift Supervision. It is yet to be seen how these new arrangements will function. What is clear, however, is that there is now much greater appreciation of the role of the central bank in maintaining financial stability and in regulating SIFIs of all varieties, not just banks.

Having worked in both the Indian central bank and the Treasury I really do not believe that effective macro-prudential oversight or financial stability oversight can be done without the central bank being at the helm of this activity. Any kind of group can be set up depending on the country's overall regulatory set-up, including the treasury and the heads of the other regulators. The central bank is the lender of last resort; it is also the only agency which has an overall view of the economy, along with exceptional stability in terms of staffing and continuity in thinking, relative to most treasuries. It also has its ear to the ground with respect to evolving developments in all financial markets if it does its job well as a monetary authority.

Our own experience is that the Reserve Bank of India, as both the monetary authority and the lead financial sector regulator, has been able to supplement its monetary policy very effectively with prudential actions on a consistent basis. It regularly monitors credit aggregates, including movements in sectoral credit. Consequently it could take macro-prudential action when it observed excess credit growth, both on an aggregate basis and in particular sectors like real estate and housing. So it increased the cash reserve ratio (CRR) to curb overall credit growth and imposed higher provisioning and risk weights for lending to the affected sectors. As part of its supervisory activities it also monitors the incremental credit deposit ratio carefully, and cautions banks when such a ratio is found to exceed acceptable norms. It is also able to do forward-looking countercyclical capital buffering through increases in loan loss provisioning when needed. Further, when it observed regulatory arbitrage being practiced by the lightly regulated non-bank finance companies (NBFCs) during 2005–2007 it took measures to tighten their regulation towards reducing their potential ability to do excess leverage. This experience is a valuable example for practicing the kind of proposals being put forward for implementing macro-prudential polices as supplements to monetary policy as normally practiced in a narrow fashion.

I do believe that given different countries with large variations in institutional legacies, traditions and systems, no one size can fit all. But at the same time, I think that the central bank does need to have a lead role as far as financial stability is concerned within any kind of arrangement that is deemed fit in a particular country. As a recent IMF paper notes:

> If one accepts the notion that, together, monetary policy and regulation provide a large set of cyclical tools, this raises the issue of how coordination is achieved between the monetary and the regulatory authorities, or whether the central bank should be in charge of both. The increasing trend toward separation of the two may well have to be reversed. Central banks are obvious candidates as macro prudential regulators. (Blanchard et al., 2010)

In any case there is a clear need for a comprehensive approach to regulatory risk in the financial sector, particularly as the perimeter of financial regulation is widened to encompass hitherto unregulated or lightly regulated entities such as hedge funds, credit rating agencies and other non-bank financial companies (CCMR, 2009).

21.3.2 Need for Higher Capital Adequacy

The various proposals that are under discussion with respect to enhanced capital requirements will lead to increased levels of regulatory capital over the economic cycle and extension of such capital requirements on bank-like institutions that are currently unregulated or lightly regulated. This will inevitably lead to lower profitability for equity investors.

In addition to the increases in basic capital adequacy that are being considered, other proposals under discussion include:

- Higher-quality Tier I capital to comprise only common shares and reserves.
- Higher-quality liquidity standards.
- Maintenance of countercyclical capital buffers.
- Countercyclical provisioning.
- Higher risk weights for trading and derivative activity.
- Higher capital and liquidity requirements for systemically important financial institutions (e.g., institutions with assets above some threshold level).
- Prescription of a maximum leverage ratio.

The bargaining power of banking institutions had become weak in the wake of the financial crisis: hence, there was little initial observable protest regarding such proposals. As the financial crisis has begun to be resolved, and some semblance of normalcy and profitability is returning to the financial sector, the financial industry is doing its utmost to resist the requirements for higher capital. Whatever the final result, the phase-in of these new requirements is certainly being delayed. It will be a challenge for regulators and governments to resist demands for further relaxation of the new capital requirements, both the enhanced minimum levels and the capital buffers proposed in good times.

Everyone seems to agree that there is a need to have increased levels of regulatory capital. But there is a need to analyze whether that implies lower profitability in the financial sector, though that in itself may not be such a bad idea for the maintenance of financial stability. There is still a need for greater understanding of its implications for the financial sector as a whole. Would more stringent capital requirements imply a slower pace of credit intermediation and overall lower economic growth? Or does it just mean that there will be less intra-financial-sector activity with negligible implications for the real economy? There is clearly a great need for working out the overall economic effects of the current recommendations related to the proposed regulatory overhaul. I understand that such impact studies are now being conducted by the Basel Committee on Banking Supervision (BCBS) and the Financial Stability Board (FSB) before the new capital standards are put in place. The influential private sector banking lobbying group, the Institute of International Finance, has meanwhile estimated that the combined loss in the US, the eurozone and Japan will amount to about 3 percent of GDP over five years on full implementation of the Basel proposals. It is important that these calculations should be scrutinized very carefully: what may cause slower expansion of the financial sector may not necessarily have similar effects in the real sectors of the economy.

21.3.3 Contra-Cyclical Capital Requirements

The proposal for provision of contra-cyclical capital will face significant implementation issues. Regulators will need to do significant technical work on the understanding of business cycles so that turning points can be recognized. What would be the triggers for changes in these capital buffers in either direction? Would these changes kick in in anticipation of business cycle turns or post facto? How formula- or rule-based would these changes be, so that regulated institutions know in advance themselves what they need to do? An additional issue in this sphere arises from the possibility of economic cycles occurring at different times in different jurisdictions. This would necessitate greater cross-border cooperation between home and host regulators in terms of applicable capital requirements for different segments of the same international financial conglomerate. An additional problem for EMEs would be the lack of adequate data for business cycle identification.

21.3.4 Macro-Prudential Regulation for Containing Systemic Risk

There is general agreement on macro-prudential regulations and the identification of systemic risks like the build-up of asset bubbles. However, considerable technical work will need to be done at both national and international levels on identifying what such risks are, what is systemic and what is not, and what kind of regulatory actions would be effective. In the recent experience, for example, there was ample awareness of the build-up of both global financial imbalances, and of the asset price bubble, but there was little agreement on what needed to be done. Even if adequate work is done on the identification of systemic risk, and on the regulatory measures necessary, what will be the enforcement methodology internationally? Within national regulatory systems, issues relating to inter-regulatory cooperation will also arise: who will be in charge of issuing early warning systems, and who will listen to them?

21.3.5 Extending the Perimeter of Regulation

There is general agreement on the extension of regulation on all systemically important institutions, markets and instruments. Here again there is an issue of implementation. How do we decide what is systemically important? Certainly, all financial institutions that have access to the central bank liquidity window or to whom the central bank can act as lender of last resort should be subject to capital regulation. Considerable debate has ranged around the regulation of hedge funds, which come in all sizes, shapes and forms. Some are large, but not leveraged; others can be both large and leveraged; and yet others can be small and leveraged, or otherwise. Whereas it may be that individual hedge funds or other equity pools are not systemically important, they may be so collectively. Furthermore, they could be collectively not important systemically in good times, but become so in times of extensive leveraging. The story is similar for markets and instruments. Thus the national and international regulatory system will have its work cut out in this regard. Excessive regulation could indeed snuff out entrepreneurship if not done carefully.

21.3.6   Securitization and Derivatives

As I have discussed, a great deal of debate has emerged around the issue of securitized credit and its offshoots. There is agreement on the need for attaching greater risk weights on securitized instruments and derivatives and on restricting the trading of standardized instruments on transparent trading platforms in order to reduce systemic risk. However, the broader issue of the utility of financial innovations remains to be addressed. Are many of these innovations largely unproductive and dysfunctional and do they need to be discouraged, or otherwise? That the explosion in the magnitude of such derivative instruments provided little benefit to the financial system or the economy as a whole is now clear. However, securitization is a time-honoured methodology that has done much to lubricate the financial system and to help in funding real economy needs at competitive costs. So how these instruments are regulated and how 'good' financial innovations will be winnowed from the 'bad' will be a challenge.

21.3.7   Systemically Important Financial Institutions

As the current global crisis has shown, whereas many of the large, complex financial institutions are global in nature, their regulation is national. Considerable discussion is now ongoing on how international regulatory cooperation can be enhanced. There appears to be a good degree of consensus that is emerging in the standard-setting bodies on the contours of enhanced regulation (BCBS, 2009a, 2009b; FSB, 2009; G20, 2009). But implementation of their recommendations will rest with national authorities and their respective legislatures. The US reform is clearly placing responsibility for regulation on the US Federal Reserve. The domestic debates taking place so far in national jurisdictions are much more fractious than in the international standard-setters; and the financial industry has much greater lobbying power within national borders and their respective legislatures and governments than in the largely technocratic standard-setters. Apart from the regulatory problems associated with ongoing institutions, even more difficult are the problems associated with cross-border resolution of failing institutions. The discussion on these issues has just begun.

There is increasing debate on institutions being 'too big to fail' (Scott et al., 2010). This is reflected in the renewed debate in the US on whether there should be some retreat to Glass–Steagall-type restrictions on the activities that are allowed among banking institutions. Should banking be boring? Whereas there would appear to be little support for bringing back the full separation of commercial and investment banks, broker-dealers and insurance companies, the emerging consensus that banks' activities in proprietary trading should be curbed (Volcker, 2010; Brady, 2010; Schultz, 2010) appears to have succeeded in the US financial reform. Banks have deposit insurance protection and also have access to lender of last resort facilities from the central bank. In times of liquidity stress they can receive liquidity from the central bank, whereas in times of insolvency it is deposit insurance that comes to their rescue. Thus, if banks' risk-taking activities result in stress, their losses are effectively socialized, and some curb on their excessive risk-taking activities is justified.

21.3.8   Volatility in Capital Flows

From the point of view of emerging market economies (EMEs), at the macro level, the volatility in capital flows has led to severe problems in both macro management and financial regulation (CGFS, 2009). These capital flows have been influenced significantly by the extant monetary policy regimes in developed countries and hence their volatility is not necessarily related to economic conditions in the receiving economies. Excess flows, sudden stops and reversals have significant effects on EME financial sectors, the working of their capital markets and asset prices, and hence their economies as a whole. Management of this volatility involves action in monetary policy, fiscal management, capital account management and also financial market regulation. This will remain a challenge since there is little international discussion on this issue. There is, however, increasing recognition that some degree of capital controls may be desirable in such circumstances (e.g., Commission on Growth and Development, 2010; Ostry et al., 2010).

In response to the crisis, monetary policy has been loosened substantially in major advanced economies since the second half of 2007. Policy rates have been cut to near zero levels, even lower than those in 2003–2004, and the financial systems have been flooded with large volumes of liquidity. Abundant liquidity is already being reflected in the return of capital flows to EMEs and this excess liquidity, if not withdrawn quickly, runs the risk of inducing the same excesses and imbalances that were witnessed during 2003–2007. Excess liquidity could also take the form of large capital flows to the EMEs and their likely recycling back to the advanced economies. As the global economy starts recovery, a calibrated exit from this unprecedented accommodative monetary policy will have to be ensured to avoid the recurrence of the financial crisis being experienced now.

21.4   KEY LESSONS FROM THE CRISIS

Let me now summarize. The emergence of the global financial crisis has led to a new wave of thinking on all issues related to both monetary policy and financial regulation.

The first lesson from the crisis is that the practice of both monetary policy and financial regulation had tended to become too formula-bound and hence too predictable. The prevailing monetary policy frameworks, essentially based on inflation targeting, have been found wanting. What should be the basis of new frameworks that also look at other issues related to the maintenance of financial stability? Furthermore, will the new frameworks necessitate less separation of monetary policy and financial regulation?

The second lesson is that the intellectual basis of light-touch regulation clearly does not hold. The financial world is highly susceptible to systemic risk, herd behavior and moral hazard, which require consistent regulatory intervention.

The third lesson is that within the new principles that are being debated, we should admit that in the face of unexpected developments that always arise in the financial sector, rules are not enough. There is an important role for the exercise of judgment by both monetary authorities and financial regulators.

The fourth lesson is that financial supervisors must supervise. Regulation by itself will not work. It must be enforced through active and intrusive supervision. Regulators must regulate and supervisors must supervise.

The final lesson is that the traditional virtues of prudent fiscal policy and stable monetary policy, along with the maintenance of sustainable external accounts, should not be lost sight of in the presence of highly flexible financial markets.

NOTES

* This chapter was delivered as the R.K. Talwar Memorial Lecture, Mumbai, 28 July 2010. The preparation of this chapter gained significantly from the many discussions held over the last few years with Y.V. Reddy, V. Leeladhar, Shyamala Gopinath and Usha Thorat, both before and during the crisis. I gratefully acknowledge the training I received from Anand Sinha, Prashant Saran, P.R. Ravi Mohan, T. Gopinath and Muneesh Kapur in the Reserve Bank. The chapter has also benefited from the G20 (2009) Working Group 1 report on 'Enhancing sound regulation and strengthening transparency'. The responsibility for views expressed is totally mine.

1. See Blanchard et al. (2010) for an excellent comprehensive discussion on possible new frameworks for monetary policy.

REFERENCES

Basel Committee on Banking Supervision (BCBS) (2009a), 'Strengthening the resilience of the banking sector', Consultative Document, Basel: Bank for International Settlements, available at http://www.bis.org/publ/bcbs164.pdf?noframes=1.

Basel Committee on Banking Supervision (BCBS) (2009b), 'International framework for liquidity risk measurement, standards and monitoring', Consultative Document, Basel: Bank for International Settlements, available at http://www.bis.org/publ/bcbs165.pdf?noframes=1.

Blanchard, Olivier, Giovanni Dell'Ariccia and Paolo Mauro (2010), 'Rethinking macroeconomic policy', Staff Position Note SPN/10/03, Washington, DC: International Monetary Fund.

Brady, Nicholas (2010), 'Fifty years in business: from Wall Street to the Treasury and beyond', in Kenneth Scott, G.P. Schultz and J.B. Taylor (eds), *Ending Government Bailouts As We Know Them*, Stanford, CA: Hoover Institution Press.

Commission on Growth and Development (CGD) (2010), 'Post crisis growth in developing countries: a special report of the Commission on Growth and Development on the implications of the 2008 financial crisis', Washington, DC: World Bank.

Committee on Capital Markets Regulation (CCMR) (2009), 'The global financial crisis: a plan for regulatory reform', New York: CCMR.

Committee on Global Financial System (CGFS) (2009), 'Capital flows and emerging market economies', Chairman – Rakesh Mohan, Basel: CGFS Paper No 33, Bank for International Settlements.

de Larosiere Report (2009), 'Report of the high-level group on financial supervision in the EU', Chairman – Jacques de Larosiere, Brussels, http://ec.europa.eu/commission_barroso/president/pdf/statement_20090225_en.pdf.

Financial Services Authority (FSA) (2009), 'A regulatory response to the global banking crisis', Discussion Paper 09/02, London: Financial Services Authority.

Financial Stability Board (FSB) (2009), 'Report of the Financial Stability Board to the G20 finance ministers and governors', Basel: Financial Stability Board, available at http://www.financialstabilityboard.org/publications/r_091107a.pdf.

G20 (2009), 'Report of the Working Group on Enhancing Sound Regulation and Strengthening Transparency', Co-Chairs – Tiff Macklem and Rakesh Mohan.

G30 (2009), 'Financial reform: a framework for financial stability', Chairman – Paul A. Volcker, Washington, DC, http://www.group30.org/pubs/reformreport.pdf.

Geneva Report (2009), 'The fundamental principles of financial regulation', Geneva Reports on the World

Economy 11 (by Markus Brunnermeier, Andrew Crocket, Charles Goodhart, Avinash D. Persaud and Hyun Shin), http://www.cepr.org/pubs/books/CEPR/booklist.asp?cvno=P197.

Institute of International Finance (IIF) (2009), 'Reform in the financial services industry: strengthening practices for a more stable system', Washington, DC.

International Monetary Fund (IMF) (2009a), 'The state of public finances cross country fiscal monitor: November 2009', Washington, DC.

International Monetary Fund (IMF) (2009b), 'Global financial stability report: market update', Washington, DC.

International Monetary Fund (IMF) (2010a), 'Global financial stability report: market update', January, Washington, DC.

International Monetary Fund (IMF) (2010b), 'World economic outlook update', July, Washington, DC.

Kindleberger, Charles P. and Robert Z. Aliber (2005), *Manias Panics and Crashes: A History of Financial Crises*, Basingstoke: Palgrave Macmillan.

Ostry, Jonathan D., Atish R. Ghosh, Karl Habermeier, Marcos Chamon, Mahvash S. Qureshi and Dennis B.S. Reinhardt (2010), 'Capital inflows: the role of controls', Staff Position Note SPN/10/04, International Monetary Fund.

Reinhart, Carmen M. and Kenneth S. Rogoff (2009), *This Time is Different*, Princeton, NJ: Princeton University Press.

Schultz, George P. (2010), 'Make failure tolerable', in Kenneth Scott, G.P. Schultz and J.A. Taylor (eds), *Ending Government Bailouts As We Know Them*, Stanford, CA: Hoover Institution Press.

Scott, Kenneth, George P. Schultz and John B. Taylor (2010), *Ending Government Bailouts As We Know Them*, Stanford, CA: Hoover Institution Press.

Turner Review (2009), 'The Turner Review: a regulatory response to the global banking crisis', by Lord Turner, Chairman, Financial Services Authority, UK, http://www.fsa.gov.uk/pubs/other/turner_review.pdf.

United Kingdom (2009), 'Reforming financial markets', London: HM Treasury, http://www.hm-treasury.gov.uk/d/reforming_financial_markets080709.pdf.

United Nations (2009), 'Report of the Commission of Experts of the President of the United Nations General Assembly on reforms of the international monetary and financial system', Chairman: Joseph Stiglitz, http://www.un.org/ga/econcrisissummit/docs/FinalReport_CoE.pdf.

United States (2009), *Financial Regulatory Reform: A New Foundation*, Washington, DC: US Department of the Treasury, http://www.financialstability.gov/docs/regs/FinalReport_web.pdf.

Volcker, Paul (2010), 'Financial reforms to end government bailouts as we know them', in Kenneth Scott, G.P. Schultz and J.A. Taylor (eds), *Ending Government Bailouts As We Know Them*, Stanford, CA: Hoover Institution Press.

Warwick Commission (2009), 'The Warwick Commission on International Financial Reform: in praise of unlevel playing fields', University of Warwick.

Yellen, Janet L. (2009), 'A Minsky meltdown: lessons for central bankers', available at http://www.frbsf.org/news/speeches/2009/0416.html.

PART V

GOVERNANCE, STRATEGY AND SOCIAL RESPONSIBILITY

22 Financial innovations, marketability and stability in banking
Arnoud W.A. Boot and Matej Marinč

22.1 INTRODUCTION

Having well-functioning financial institutions and markets is considered important for the economy at large. In this context it is important to look at the proliferation of financial innovations and ask what this has done to the functioning of the financial sector. When looking at the last few years with the financial crisis at the center of our attention, one is tempted to conclude that recent innovations like subprime mortgages and their repackaging in marketable securities have not contributed to the well functioning of the financial sector. But this conclusion might be premature.

The key question addressed in this chapter is therefore how financial innovations have affected the structure and stability of the financial services industry. A fundamental feature of recent financial innovations is that they are often aimed at augmenting marketability; see for example securitization and related products like credit default swaps (CDSs) and collateralized debt obligations (CDOs). Such marketability can augment diversification opportunities, yet as we will argue can also create instability. This is the focus of the chapter. We will argue that understanding the added value (and the downside) of financial innovations is important to understand the type of measures that might have to be taken. The point of view that we will advocate is that financial innovations have distinct value – and as such should be applauded – yet the institutional environment should be amended to control the negative effects that particularly the enhanced marketability might have induced.

Facilitating marketability is a core element of the most noteworthy innovations that have become infamous during the 2007–2009 financial crisis: for example, securitization resulting in securities like CDOs, asset-backed commercial paper (ABCP) and CDS. However, the mere fact that something becomes tradable can undermine commitment. For example, mortgages that become tradable might undermine the incentives of the originator to monitor the quality of borrowers. Or, more fundamentally, when markets exist for all kinds of real assets of a firm, the firm can more easily change direction in its strategy. This might be good, but could also lead to lack of commitment (and staying power), more impulsive decisions and possible herding. The last refers to the tendency to follow current fads. In banking, herding is particularly worrisome because it could create systemic risk, meaning that when all institutions make the same bets, risk exposures become more highly correlated and a simultaneous failure of institutions might become more likely.[1]

The enhanced marketability may also have led to a proliferation of transaction-oriented banking (trading and financial market activities) at the expense of more traditional relationship banking. Such an evolution is particularly relevant because financial systems are often characterized as being either bank-based (continental Europe) or financial market-driven (US, UK). In the former, bank financing and relationships are dominant, while direct funding from the financial market plays a more important role in the latter. Financial innovations may have affected these systems differently.

The distinction is not as sharp as the dichotomy might suggest; for example more than half of US businesses are bank-financed, and financial markets clearly play a role in continental Europe; hence no system is fully market- or bank-driven. Nevertheless, an interesting question is whether the more recent proliferation of financial innovations might impact those systems differently. One observation is that bank-based and financial market-driven systems might have become more alike. In particular, recent innovations – like securitization – have made banks' assets more marketable and increased the sensitivity of banks to financial market developments. Banks might have thus become a more integral part of financial markets. The more intertwined nature of banks and financial markets may have weakened the distinction between bank-based and financial market-driven systems. One could argue – as we will do – that bank-based systems have been impacted most because they had increased sensitivity to financial market developments, but were somewhat insulated from it before.

Considering the herding behavior and more impulsive decisions that financial markets may facilitate (and possibly the boom–bust nature of financial markets), we will argue that the increased linkages between banks and these markets have augmented instability in banking, and bank-based systems may have felt this most. From here we will point to institutional and regulatory changes that might be needed to improve the stability of the financial sector. One could say that the institutional structure (including regulation) has not kept up with the enhanced marketability and 'changeability' of the industry.

The organization of the chapter is as follows. We will first discuss in section 22.2 the key insights from the literature on financial intermediation, particularly the distinction between relationship banking and transaction banking. In section 22.3 we will argue that there is substantial complementarity between relationship banking activities and investment banking activities; the latter are typically seen as centered around financial markets. A point that we will be making here as well is that characterizing investment banking as purely transaction-oriented is too simplistic.

In sections 22.4 and 22.5 we discuss, respectively, the pros and cons of financial innovations. There is a core literature, discussed in section 22.4, that convincingly argues that financial innovations can play a positive role and contribute to economic growth. Financial innovations could however have a destabilizing impact; the financial crisis of 2007–2009 is arguably a manifestation of this. Section 22.5 therefore asks the question: what causes innovations to be potentially value-destructive? A fundamental feature that comes up here is the marketability that recent financial innovations typically aim for; marketability may have a dark side and create instability. Section 22.6 further expands on the downside of marketability. Marketability, leading to more transaction-oriented banking, may erode institutional franchise value which, as we will argue, is key to stability. This has implications for the desired structure of banking. Section 22.7 concludes.

22.2 RELATIONSHIP VERSUS TRANSACTION BANKING

Traditional commercial banks hold non-marketable or illiquid assets that are funded largely with deposits. There is typically little uncertainty about the value of these deposits which are often withdrawable on demand. The liquidity of bank liabilities stands in sharp contrast to that of their assets, reflecting the banks' *raison d'être*. By liquefying claims, banks facilitate the funding of projects that might otherwise be infeasible.[2]

The banks' assets are illiquid largely because of their information sensitivity. In originating and pricing loans, banks develop proprietary information. Subsequent monitoring of borrowers yields additional private information. The proprietary information inhibits the marketability of these loans. The access to information is the key to understanding the comparative advantage of banks (Diamond, 1984). In many of their activities, banks exploit their information and the related network of contacts.

One might be tempted to interpret modern banking as transaction-oriented. So does an investment bank – generally considered a prime example of modern banking – facilitate a firm's access to public capital markets? The investment bank's role could be interpreted as that of a broker; that is, matching buyers and sellers for the firms' securities. In this interpretation investment banks just facilitate transactions, which would confirm the transaction orientation of modern banking. The investment banks' added value would then be confined to their networks, that is, their ability to economize on search or matching costs. As a characterization of modern banking, however, this would describe their economic role too narrowly. Investment banks do more. Almost without exception investment banks underwrite those public issues, that is, absorb credit and/or placement risk. This brings an investment bank's role much closer to that of a commercial bank engaged in lending; the processing and absorption of risk is a typical intermediation function similar to that encountered in traditional bank lending.

In lending, a bank manages and absorbs risk (e.g., credit and liquidity risks) by issuing claims on its total assets with different characteristics from those encountered in its loan portfolio. In financial intermediation theory this is referred to as qualitative asset transformation.[3] Underwriting by an investment bank can be interpreted analogously; risk is (temporarily) absorbed and is channeled through to the claim holders of the investment bank. The role of investment banks is therefore more than purely brokerage. Underwriting requires information acquisition about the borrower which is supported by a relationship orientation. A relationship orientation will therefore still be present in investment banking, both in the direction of investors ('placement capacity') and toward borrowing firms.

Nevertheless, in a relative sense their involvement is more transaction-oriented. What will also be true is that in investment banking relationships depend much less on local presence. Public debt issues are relatively hands-off with few interactions between financiers and borrowers over time. The full menu of financing options for borrowers includes many other products with varying degrees of relationships. In the continuum between bank loans and public debt issues, we can find, for example, syndicated loans. These are offered by investment banks and commercial banks alike and involve several financiers per loan. Generally, only the lead banks have a relationship with the borrower, and the relationship intensity is somewhere in-between a bank loan and a public debt issue (see Dennis and Mullineaux, 2000; Sufi, 2007).[4]

As a caveat observe that within investment banks there is somewhat of a 'battle' between the client-driven activity that we have so far emphasized (involving underwriting, and so on), and proprietary trading that is purely transaction-oriented and has (virtually) no relationship component. In section 22.6 we will discuss this further.

We will now discuss the complementarities between more traditional relationship banking activities and investment banking, and point to the increased intertwined nature of banking and financial markets.

22.3   BANKS VERSUS CAPITAL MARKETS: COMPLEMENTARITIES

The standard view is that banks and markets compete, so that growth in one is at the expense of the other (e.g., Allen and Gale, 1995, 1997; Boot and Thakor, 1997). In this context Deidda and Fattouh (2008) show theoretically that both bank and stock market development have a positive effect on growth, but the growth impact of bank development is lower when there is a higher level of stock market development. What this shows is that dynamics of the interaction between banks and markets can have real effects. How banks and markets interact is therefore of great interest.

There is evidence that banks and financial markets do not just compete, but also are complementary. For example, the close monitoring role of banks might facilitate timely intervention. This feature of bank lending is valuable to the firm's bondholders as well. They might find it optimal to delegate efficiently the timely intervention task to the bank.[5]

Another manifestation of potential complementarities between bank lending and capital market activities is the increasing importance of securitization. Securitization is an example of unbundling of financial services and a more recent example of financial development. It is a process whereby assets are removed from a bank's balance sheet, so that a bank no longer permanently funds assets when they are securitized; instead, the investors buying asset-backed securities provide the funding. Asset-backed securities rather than deposits thus end up funding dedicated pools of bank-originated assets. Securitization decomposes the lending function such that banks no longer fully fund the assets, but continue to be involved in other primal lending activities, for example monitoring and servicing the borrowers. A potential benefit of securitization is better risk-sharing. The proliferation of securitization may however also be induced by regulatory arbitrage, for example as a vehicle to mitigate capital regulation; see section 22.4.

Central to the extensive academic work on securitization (see An et al., 2008) is the idea that it is not efficient for originators to offload completely the risks in the originated assets. The originating bank needs to maintain an economic interest in the assets to alleviate moral hazard concerns and induce sufficient effort on the originating bank's part in screening and monitoring. What this implies is that, even with securitization, banks should not become disengaged from the assets they originate. Banks still continue to provide the services involved in screening and monitoring borrowers, designing and pricing financial claims, and providing risk management and loan servicing support. As such, securitization preserves those functions that are at the core of the *raison d'être* for banks. This militates against the notion that securitization necessarily lessens the importance of banks.

As the subprime crisis of 2007–2009 has shown, this development was not without problems. The structure of real-world securitization transactions appears to have taken a rather fragile form. In particular, it is important to note that much of the securitization leading up to the crisis involved the financing of long-term assets with short-term funding, which induced substantial liquidity risk; for example as in ABCP conduits. While this liquidity risk was sometimes mitigated by liquidity guarantees (e.g., stand-by letters of credit and other refinancing commitments), the underwriting institutions often underestimated the risks involved and overstretched themselves.[6]

The eagerness of banks to securitize claims – and keep the 'repackaging machine' rolling – may have also adversely impacted the quality of loans that were originated (e.g., subprime lending). The originating institutions often also retained minimal residual risk. As a consequence, monitoring and screening incentives may have been further compromised (see Mian and Sufi, 2007).[7] Credit rating agencies played an important role in this process as well. Their willingness to provide favorable ratings clearly helped in growing this market.[8]

The 2007–2009 financial crisis brought securitization almost to a grinding halt. However, the risk diversification that securitization can accomplish appears to be of more than just ephemeral importance. Thus, we expect securitization to re-emerge, albeit possibly in a form that entails lower levels of liquidity risk, as well as lesser moral hazard in screening (loan underwriting standards) and monitoring. A caveat is that some of the activity in securitization may have been induced merely by capital arbitrage,[9] in which case its social value may be rather limited; the new Basel II capital requirements – and also the so-called Basel III amendments – might diminish such regulatory arbitrage.

Another effect of the interaction between banks and markets is that as markets evolve and entice bank borrowers away, banks have an incentive to create new products and services that combine services provided by markets with those provided by banks. This allows banks to 'follow their customers' to the market rather than losing them. There are numerous examples. For instance, when a borrower goes to the market to issue commercial paper, its bank can provide a back-up line of credit in order to guarantee refinancing. Securitization of various sorts is another example in that banks not only originate the loans that are pooled and securitized but they also buy various securitized tranches as investment securities. The impetus for such market-based activities grows stronger as interbank competition puts pressure on profit margins from traditional banking products, and the capital market provides access to greater liquidity and lower cost of capital for the bank's traditional borrowers. As a consequence, there is a natural propensity for banks to become increasingly integrated with markets, and a sort of unprecedented 'co-dependence' emerges that makes banking and capital market risks become increasingly intertwined. This could make banks more willing to engage in lending and hence improve access to financing, but also points at potentially a higher level of instability. One conclusion that we will draw is that this could improve access to finance under 'normal' circumstances, yet makes access more volatile and subject to the boom-and-bust nature of financial markets.

22.4 UNDERSTANDING THE PROS OF FINANCIAL INNOVATION

The notion that financial innovation is good for economic growth is based on the idea that such innovations will improve the allocation of capital. In the words of Fed Chairman Ben Bernanke: 'The increasing sophistication and depth of financial markets promote economic growth by allocating capital where it can be most productive' (Bernanke, 2007). This sounds politically correct, and by its very generality is difficult to refute. However, more specificity is needed. What precisely can be good about financial innovations? In a first-best world where information is available to all and everybody is capable of fully discerning all relevant attributes, financial innovations could help complete the market, that is, facilitate a complete set of Arrow–Debreu securities. This is the typical 'spanning' argument; financial innovations are good because they help complete the market.[10]

As a more or less immediate corollary, financial innovations might then help improve the allocation of capital. In more simple terms, a complete market allows individuals to hedge optimally (that is, smooth) their income over time. Given the higher level of predictability that results, they are more readily willing to invest their money for longer periods of time, facilitating more long-term investments.

Similarly, the tradability of debt and equity in financial markets allows investors to liquefy their holdings at any point in time (i.e., by selling their holdings to other investors) and helps in diversifying risks. In doing so firms might have easier access to long(er)-term financing. The wish to liquefy claims also helps explain the introduction of limited liability in equity-type contracts – an innovation by itself. It facilitates trading, and allows investors to liquefy claims on otherwise long-term investments (Michalopoulos et al., 2009). Liquidity therefore is valuable; yet, as we will see, it can simultaneously have some negative repercussions. More specifically, in a world with imperfections, agency and information problems lead to potential distortions that can create a 'dark side' of liquidity.[11]

22.4.1 Financial Innovations Also Valuable for Other Reasons

New securities are sometimes introduced to help overcome information asymmetries. While not really a new security, a debt claim may illustrate this. Such a claim might offer financing at lower cost than issuing equity because it is less information-sensitive (see Myers and Majluf, 1984). The idea is that an equity-type claim would suffer from a 'lemon' problem: outsiders would not be able to assess the value and hence refuse to provide funding since the firm could try to exploit a too optimistic view among potential investors about the firm. As put forward in Akerlof's (1970) famous paper, investors would be naive to buy a firm's equity at an average price, because only the below-average firms would happily be willing to sell the equity at that price. Investors thus face a problem of adverse selection and the market may break down.

Note that things might not be that bad if there is a very low cost in verifying the true state of nature which would help enforce the ensuing obligations. That is, if the lemon problem can be easily overcome by verifying the true state at relatively low cost, equity financing might be available. However, if the verification cost is high this may not work. The costly-state-verification literature has focused on *ex post* verification (Townsend, 1979); the firm may hide assets and refuse to repay outside financiers. A debt claim may help, since with debt (contrary to equity) verification is not always needed. That is, if debt is repaid (interest plus principal) there is no need to verify. If it is not repaid (or only in part) one needs to verify whether there is indeed a lack of resources. Having a debt contract in conjunction with a third party (for example, bankruptcy court) that can impose a stiff penalty on the firm if it falsely claims insufficiency of funds can solve the misrepresentation problem. Unless the debt is issued by a very risky firm the anticipated costs of verification are limited since in most cases the firm can and will repay (and no verification is needed). Note that in the case of external equity there is no fixed payment and verification is always needed. The upshot of this is that a debt security can be seen as a value-enhancing innovation to help facilitate access to funding (see the earlier contribution of Gale and Hellwig, 1984; and also Tirole, 2006).

The literature on financial innovation – also referred to as the security design literature – has come up with various other approaches to mitigate problems of information asymmetry. One that also rationalizes debt as a valuable security is Boot and Thakor (1993). They show that if information production costs are not excessive, introducing debt in the capital structure of firms could encourage information production in equity financial markets. This would then, via trading in the financial market, get prices closer to the underlying true value. The idea is that with debt in a firm's capital structure, equity becomes riskier, but importantly more information-sensitive. Hence, for (potential) equity holders the value of producing information about the firm goes up. More information is produced as a result, and prices are pushed towards their real values (see also Fulghieri and Lukin, 2001). All this would be good for resource allocation because mispricing is mitigated.[12]

Others have argued that a rights issue – again a financial innovation – could help solve the lemon problem (Heinkel and Schwartz, 1986; Balachandran et al., 2008). With a rights issue existing shareholders get the right to buy the newly issued shares. In essence, if only existing shareholders buy the new shares that a firm wants to issue, the pricing is not that important. Why? Observe that when shares are issued at a price that is too low, new shareholders get a windfall gain at the expense of existing shareholders. With a rights issue (in principle) the new shares go pro rata to the existing shareholders; gains and losses are now in the same hands, that is, internalized by the same group of investors. A rights issue may therefore allow the firm to raise new equity, while a 'normal' equity issue would have been infeasible because of a lemon problem. This is important because it highlights that existing shareholders might be prepared to continue to provide financing.[13]

The security design literature provides several other examples of financial innovations that could resolve particular agency and asymmetric information problems. For example, convertible bonds could give bondholders protection against risk-seeking behavior by shareholders. The idea is that in a situation where a lot of debt already exists, new debt financing might not be available because it might induce shareholders to favor excessive risk. That is, their leveraged claim gives shareholders an enormous upside potential if risks work out, while the downside is born by the debtholders. With convertible debt, debtholders will share in the upside if risks work out (i.e., conversion will then occur). As a consequence, incentives are more aligned because shareholders no longer exclusively get the upside and debtholders get part of the upside.

Other motivations for introducing financial innovations include regulatory arbitrage and minimizing transaction costs. Whether this is good or bad depends on the particular context. For example, innovations designed to bypass regulations (regulatory arbitrage) might be good if one considers those regulations undesirable.[14] But assuming that the regulation in question has merit – say, capital requirements imposed on banks – innovations that are only aimed at bypassing it should probably be viewed negatively.

Reducing transaction costs as a rationale for financial innovations can often be viewed more positively. If certain frictions – transaction costs – impede the optimal allocation of capital then innovations that reduce these seem optimal.[15] In this positive interpretation, innovations like credit default swaps (CDSs) and collateralized debt obligations (CDOs) would promote an optimal allocation of capital by reducing the cost of diversifying and reallocating risk. However, as Posen and Hinterschweiger (2009) note, during the period 2003–2008 the growth in over-the-counter (OTC) derivatives outpaced that of real investment by a factor of 12 (300 versus 25 percent). And after 2006 real investments stagnated while OTC derivatives arguably grew faster than ever. While this does not preclude that the proliferation of these financial instruments provided benefits also later in the boom, the negative effects on the robustness of the financial system – as observed in 2007–2009 – tend to refute this.

What emerges is that there are clear pros to financial innovation but negative effects cannot be excluded. In our view (see also the next section) this is related to the fast changes that innovations induce and the fact that existing institutions (including regulation) might not have adjusted to the new realities. In that type of environment innovations might become 'weapons of mass destruction' as Warren Buffet once remarked.[16]

We now elaborate further on the 'dark side' of financial innovation.

22.5   INNOVATIONS MIGHT BE PROBLEMATIC

Johnson and Kwak (2009) state that a financial innovation is only good if it 'enables an economically productive use of money that would not otherwise occur'. This statement makes it clear that financial innovations do not necessarily add value. This might particularly be the case when information asymmetries are present.

When information asymmetries are severe and particular contingencies are not contractible at all, having complete markets is infeasible. This happens when contingencies are not verifiable, and/or too costly to verify. Introducing a financial innovation might now have a much darker motivation. Financial innovations might be intended to fool market participants. An example might be the Dutch or UK market for life insurance products. On several occasions structural misselling has occurred with a common denominator: the presence of an excessive variety of product innovations that share one characteristic – complexity in conjunction with obscurity of costs relative to potential benefits.[17]

Financial innovations would then tend to worsen the allocation of capital. The more recent advances in securitization could be interpreted that way too. Initially securitization could have allowed for a wider access to investors, reduced funding costs and hence improved lending opportunities for banks. As stated earlier, this may well have been value-enhancing. There is a logic in fulfilling the demand for high investment grade securities by packaging mortgages, and selling the low-risk portion to (distant) investors. As long as the originators of the loans keep the more risky layer, they would still have a strong incentive to screen loan applicants and monitor them. What happened subsequently is less benign. It is clear that lending standards weakened (Keys et al., 2010).[18] In part this had little to do with securitization. The housing boom in the US seduced lenders into granting higher mortgages. As long as prices kept rising, loans could always be refinanced and/or sales of underlying houses would cover the outstanding mortgages. Where securitization did come into the picture is that the insatiable appetite for triple-A paper in the market pushed financial institutions into a high gear repacking mode, ultimately lowering standards even further. Also, in a desire to issue as much triple-A paper as possible, the more risky tranches of securitization structures were repackaged again, and more triple-A paper was squeezed out. All this packaging and repackaging led to very complicated securities. When the market finally started questioning the sustainability of the housing boom, the arcane securities were suddenly out of favor.[19]

Financial innovations often cause harm by reducing transparency, and this might be deliberate. The earlier example about life insurance, as stated, might be a good example. While securitization did create arcane products (the sequentially repacked claims), the objective of securitization might not have been to create this lack of transparency. The arcane nature of the end product might have been a side-effect of the sequential repackaging that was driven to 'squeeze out' as much triple-A paper as possible. In practice this may still have had the same effect: some market participants were fooled into trusting the quality of this highly rated paper (and the willingness of rating agencies to grant such high ratings did help; see also White, 2010).

The more fundamental observation, and the one already eluded to in the previous section, is that securitization is a financial innovation that intertwines banks with financial markets. Financial markets are however subject to booms and busts, and are heavily momentum driven. As long as momentum was there, the market's appetite could not be saturated, and much money could be made by putting the 'repackaging machines' into higher and higher gear. The important observation is that recent financial innovations are ways to augment marketability, and this is typically linked to financial markets, and those are subject to boom and busts.

22.5.1   Marketability and Excessive 'Changeability' are Key

Securitization has opened up the bank balance sheet. Many bank assets have potentially become marketable. This marketability is typically seen as something positive, but the links with the financial markets that this has created have made banks potentially more vulnerable vis-à-vis the volatility and momentum in financial markets. Moreover, marketability means that existing activities and risks can be changed almost instantaneously. Since financial markets go through cycles and are subjected to hypes and investor sentiments, the banks' decisions might become more momentum-driven; see also Shleifer and Vishny (2010). This adds further instability.[20]

One could frame the enhanced opportunities to change things almost instantaneously as a move to more 'footloose institutions'. What we mean by this is that corporations (or banks for that matter), due to the proliferation of financial markets and the increased marketability of their assets (creating a transaction orientation), become uprooted, meaning that they lose a degree of fixity and stability. This discussion is also related to the general corporate governance question on the rights of shareholders in the financial market. In related work by Boot et al. (2008), the emphasis is on the need to have some stable shareholders. The liquidity that stock markets provide may cause ownership to be changing all the time such that no stable and lasting link with shareholders comes about. Support and commitment to a particular strategy might then become weaker and more haphazard.[21] This could make firms more sensitive to short-term financial market pressures.[22]

22.6   DARK SIDE OF MARKETABILITY AND (LACK OF) INSTITUTIONAL FRANCHISE VALUE

Creating liquidity and opening up markets – that is, trading possibilities – is typically seen as something positive. But this is not always the case, as follows from the previous section. One application is the context first investigated by Amar Bhide (1993). His insight was that the liquidity of stock markets is typically considered a virtue, yet may have a dark side in that fully liquid stock markets encourage diffuse ownership, and this may undermine monitoring incentives (i.e., cause free-rider problems). Hence corporate control over managers might be lax, inducing inefficiencies. In other words, monitoring incentives typically require a large(r) and enduring stake in a company, yet this is at odds with liquidity. This suggests a trade-off between liquidity and a more enduring presence by committing not to sell.

In subsequent research, Bolton and von Thadden (1998) have shown that stock market liquidity may actually benefit from the simultaneous presence of a few block holders. That is, having some proportion of shares freely traded, but not all, may help create liquidity in the freely traded shares in part because the market knows that some investors have a more sizable and permanent (minority) stake that gives them an incentive to monitor. In this way some agency problems at the level of the firm might be mitigated. This is in line with the earlier discussed work of Boot et al. (2008) who focus on the pros and cons of (lack of) stability in the shareholder base particularly in the context of exchange-listed firms.

The costs of liquidity and/or marketability can be further emphasized in the context of financial sector stability. This can be linked to securitization (see earlier), but also to the stability of investment banks versus commercial (relationship-oriented) banks. Traditional relationship-oriented banks seem incentivized to build up institutional franchise value. Individuals are part of the organization as an entity, and not readily identifiable as individual stars. In other words, the value created is an integral part of the organizational entity and not portable as part of individuals.

Investment banks on the other hand, particularly their trading activities,[23] seem more based on the individual star concept with high marketability of individuals. As a consequence, less institutional franchise value is built up; individual franchise values dominate. If this is the only difference then a relationship banking institution has substantial implied franchise value, while the investment bank has little implied value, and hence

Keeley's (1990) analysis would suggest that an investment bank would take lots of risk, while the franchise value of a commercial bank would help curtail its risk-taking.[24]

Historically investment banks have solved the marketability problem (and the potential lack of institutional franchise value) by having partnerships. The partnership structure has two dimensions that could jointly resolve the marketability problem, and related opportunistic, risky behavior (and the star phenomenon):

- a partnership means that bankers have their personal wealth tied up in the business: they own the equity claim of the business;
- the partnership structure is such that the equity is not (optimally) marketable.

The latter implies that 'stars' cannot take their money out, or only at a reduced value. Implicitly, this means that non-portable franchise value is created, and this value is transferred over time to future partners. Interesting examples exist where institutions have made changes that have destroyed this structure. For example, with a go-public transformation (converting a partnership into a listed shareholder-owned company) the current partners effectively expropriate all franchise value that has been built up over time.[25] Even worse, once the partnership is gone, stars may no longer be 'under control'. Their financial interest is no longer tied to the firm. This elevates risk and reduces stability.

In commercial banking the enhanced marketability, and with it, transaction focus, may have opened the door for some type of 'star' phenomenon as well. Transactions as typically linked to marketability make it easier for individuals to stand up as being the sole 'inventor'. This may have induced opportunistic behavior, particularly as partnership structures in commercial banking have never been very common.

In any case, partnerships among major financial institutions are rare. Changes, whether in the form of financial innovations (products), processes (securitization) or institutional changes (the demise of a partnership in lieu of an exchange listing with marketable equity) all work in the same direction. They make things 'footloose' and in doing so could undermine stability.

22.7   PUTTING IT TOGETHER: WHAT TO CONCLUDE?

What has been shown is that financial innovations can be good from the perspective of completing markets, as well as from the perspective that focuses on overcoming asymmetric information and agency problems. Nevertheless, a much more negative picture can be drawn. The instability that they might cause is arguably even more worrisome. This red flag is related to the observation that financial innovations often aim at augmenting marketability, and intertwine banks and financial markets. This makes banks subject to the boom-and-bust nature of financial markets. Marketability definitely has a dark side; it potentially causes severe instability.[26]

We have emphasized potential complementarities between banks and financial markets. On the positive side one could say that financial innovations have possibly strengthened these complementarities. One could however easily draw a more negative conclusion. In the 2007–2009 financial crisis European banks have arguably been hit hardest. One interpretation is that the European financial sector started combining the worst of both worlds: it continued to be driven by banks, with their negative effects on renewal and entrepreneurship, yet these very same banks became intertwined with financial markets and as a consequence volatility increased and the benefits of stability disappeared.

We tend to subscribe to the conclusion that the marketability created in banking via financial innovations has created a very opportunistic environment prone to herding, fads and excessive risk-taking. More instability seems an inherent part of this new reality. Our discussion on the value of partnerships that actually may contain unwarranted opportunistic behavior, and its disappearance, points to the need to find some new 'fixed points' in the financial system; not everything can be fluid.

What comes out of this chapter is that we need to (learn to) deal with the instability that marketability brings. The institutional framework needs to adapt to this new reality, and that is what we mean by discovering new 'fixed points'.

NOTES

1. Risk taking might also become more cyclical. For example, Coval et al. (2009) find that the demand for senior tranches in securitized structures was high despite their high sensitivity to bad economic states. Investors were either lured by high ratings of such instruments or, alternatively, they were eager to upload systemic risk. And this was an industry wide phenomenon. Haensel and Krahnen (2007) show on a data set of European CDOs that banks that issued CDOs raised their systemic risk.
2. See Bhattacharya et al. (2004) for an overview of the modern literature on financial intermediation.
3. We do not focus on the costs and benefits of such mismatch on the banks' balance sheets. See Calomiris and Kahn (1991) and Diamond and Rajan (2001) for theories that rationalize jointly the asset and liability structures of banks.
4. It is important to note that the relationship aspect does not only involve funding, but also includes various other financial services, for example letters of credit, deposits, check clearing and cash management services. We will not focus on these services per se, but note that the information that banks obtain by offering multiple services to the same borrower might be valuable in lending (Degryse and Van Cayseele, 2000). For example, the use of checking and deposit accounts may help banks in assessing a firm's loan repayment capability. Thus, the scope of relationships may affect banks' comparative advantages.
5. To play this role well, banks may need to secure senior status. Seniority makes them willing to act tougher. To see this, observe first that the unsecured other debtholders need to be compensated for their subordinated status. This is directly related to the work on bargaining power and seniority; see the work of Gorton and Kahn (1993) and Berglöf and von Thadden (1994). The complementarity between bank lending and capital market funding is further highlighted in Diamond (1991), Hoshi et al. (1993) and Chemmanur and Fulghieri (1994). See Petersen and Rajan (1994) and Houston and James (1996) for empirical evidence, and Freixas and Rochet (2008) for a recent overview.
6. Most noteworthy are the bankruptcies among German *Länder* banks that were involved in providing liquidity guarantees. Risks were further elevated by enormous leverage in the securitization process.
7. Securitization is facilitated in part by credit enhancement, including partial guarantees by the arranger of a securitization transaction (and/or he holds on to the most risky layer of the transaction). In the recent credit crisis, this disciplining mechanism broke down; residual risks with the arranger appeared minimal, and were often framed as liquidity guarantees to off-balance street vehicles without appropriately realizing the inherent risks. That is, banks, while they might have believed that risk was offloaded, often had been underwriting the liquidity risk in securitization transactions by, for example, guaranteeing the refinancing of commercial paper in ABCP transactions via standby letters of credit. Such guarantees have generated profits for banks, but also created risks, as illustrated by the losses incurred by banks in the recent subprime crisis. The marketability of securitized claims has also been facilitated by accreditation by credit rating agencies (Boot et al., 2006). The role of rating agencies has been called into question with the 2007–2009 subprime lending crisis.
8. Allegations have been made about conflicts of interest for rating agencies arising from the fact that structured finance is (was) a source of ever-increasing income for them, which then corrupts their incentives for

accurately rating the issuers involved in structured finance (Cantor, 2004; Partnoy, 1999). In this context, Coffee and Sale (2008) point at the naivety to think that reputation-building incentives alone would keep credit rating agencies in check (see also Mathis et al., 2009).

9. Jones (2000) reviews the principal techniques for regulatory capital arbitrage invoked by Basel I standards. Calomiris and Mason (2004) provide evidence on regulatory arbitrage in the case of credit card securitization.

10. A complete market means that investors or consumers can 'contract' on any conceivable future state of the world, and in doing so create an optimal allocation. In the context of hedging, for example, such a complete market allows investors to neutralize whatever state-contingent risk they may face. What this means is that investors can tailor the state-dependent pay-offs to their precise preferences. Please note that one cannot automatically assume that introducing new securities in incomplete markets that give investors greater 'spanning' opportunities is by definition value-enhancing. Elul (1995) shows that adding a new security could have 'almost arbitrary effects on agents' utilities'.

11. We are not focusing here on innovations in trading platforms and trading practices in general (e.g., flash trading). Hendershott et al. (2010) argue that financial innovations in algorithmic trading (e.g., smart order routing, direct market access, crossing, co-location, global capacities) increase liquidity.

12. Hennessy (2009) shows that firms may issue securities that are less information-sensitive if the Akerlof (1970) lemon problem is severe. In that case, risk and information problems are overwhelming, and trying to carve out a relatively safe claim might be the only hope for obtaining external finance.

13. Note that this may not work in the presence of (too much) debt. With what is called 'debt overhang', new equity even from existing shareholders may not be forthcoming because it would give debtholders a windfall gain. This is the case particularly when the coupon on existing debt is fixed; these debtholders would then fully benefit from any infusion of equity. Existing equity holders would pay the price and possibly choose to resist a new equity issue. If debt could get renegotiated hand-in-hand with an equity infusion, this effect could be mitigated. It is also quite prevalent in banking where a government guarantee effectively makes debt available at low cost, while the guarantee is not priced. This induces risk-taking behavior and could make banks averse to raising new equity because it would benefit the government (i.e., lower the value of the guarantee).

14. Also tax evasion should be mentioned. Tax efficiency, to put it more neutrally, is central to many financial innovations. For example, the practice of financial engineering in order to design a security that has properties of equity but qualifies for interest deductibility for tax purposes; for example, trust-preferred securities that were mainly issued by bank holding companies for their favorable tax and regulatory treatment.

15. Tufano (2003) summarizes other motivations for introducing financial innovations along these lines.

16. So far we have not emphasized that many of these recent developments in innovation have been facilitated by developments in information technology (IT); particularly marketability has really been spurred by these IT developments. For a broader discussion of the impact of IT advances on banks and financial markets, see Frame and White (2009). The major revolution in IT technology induced innovation in both front offices and back offices. In front offices, IT technology enabled new channels of access to banking such as Internet banking. In addition, several new products have been created for borrowers such as factoring, leasing and asset-based lending (Berger and Udell, 2006). In back offices, the IT technology has possibly led to better assessment of risk also for more opaque small business lending. The example includes small businesses credit scoring techniques that were developed in the 1990s (see Berger et al., 2005, and Petersen and Rajan, 2002, for the impact of IT on the distance between bank and borrower). In addition, substantial changes occurred in payment technologies. Paper payments such as cash and checks were increasingly replaced by electronic payments such as debit and credit cards. Studies identify substantial cost reduction in processing of electronic payments from 1990 to 2000 (see Berger, 2003) and economies of scale (see Hancock et al., 1999). For markets, IT developments have led to fast and largely automated electronic trading. This has probably increased the frequency of trading and liquidity; however, much about its stability impact is as yet unknown.

17. Gabaix and Laibson (2006) analyze how producers (e.g., financial services firms) can exploit uninformed consumers by misrepresenting attributes. In Carlin (2009) complexity is added to discourage information production, intended to facilitate expropriation of investors. Henderson and Pearson (2009) show how innovations might be designed to fool market participants, and in doing so cause serious harm.

18. Parlour and Plantin (2008) analyze loan sales. In their view banks weight the benefits of loan sales in the form of additional flexibility to redeploy bank capital quickly with the drawbacks in the form of lower monitoring incentives. They show that loan sales would lead to excessive trading of highly rated securities but to insufficient liquidity in low-rated securities. Risk-weighted capital requirements may help in bringing liquidity to low-rated securities.

19. DeMarzo (2005) shows that pooling of securities is valuable due to diversification especially if the originator has limited information about the assets' quality. However, the informed financial institutions buy pooled assets and tranch them. By tranching the assets financial institutions make liquid and low-risk debt less sensitive to their private information.
20. Also replacing deposit funding by wholesale funding exposed banks to additional liquidity risk. Huang and Ratnovski (2011) show that the dark side of liquidity comes in the form of reduced incentives of wholesale funds providers to monitor their banks and this may trigger inefficient liquidation; see also Acharya et al. (2010). The main threat of a bank run may no longer come from demand deposits as in Diamond and Dybvig (1983), but rather from wholesale financiers or from bank borrowers that deplete their loan commitments (see Ivashina and Scharfstein, 2010; Gatev et al., 2009).
21. Another important area of research on the dark side of marketability is the work in economics that emphasizes that creating (interim) markets and trading opportunities might not necessarily be good. It could for example create time-inconsistency problems and complicate the feasibility of otherwise (*ex ante*) optimal commitments. In this context, the work of Jacklin (1987) is noteworthy. He showed that introducing trading opportunities at the intermediate point in time could destroy the liquidity insurance feature of demand deposit contracts in the Diamond and Dybvig (1983) framework.
22. The dark side of liquidity and possibility for quick changes in asset allocation is related to the work of Myers and Rajan (1998) who emphasize that the illiquidity of bank assets serves a useful purpose in that it reduces asset substitution moral hazard.
23. Many of the activities in an investment bank are relationship-based (see section 22.3); trading is typically not. In recent times, traders appear to have gained power within investment banks, for example more recent leaders of Goldman Sachs came from the trading side. In any case, we do not see the distinction between commercial banking and investment banking as an absolute dichotomy.
24. There is some value in the multitude of connections that are combined in the investment bank, but this is also pointing at externalities of failure (see Duffie, 2010).
25. Morrison and Wilhelm (2008) analyze the decisions of major US investment banks to go public. Investment banks were initially organized as partnerships. The opacity of partnerships and illiquidity of their shares allowed for successful mentoring and training in tacit uncontractible human skills, such as building relationships, negotiating mergers and acquisitions (M&A) deals and advising clients. They have argued that IT technology necessitated heavy investments and that that necessitated investment banks to go public. Potentially confirming this is that wholesale-oriented investment banks such as Morgan Stanley, for which tacit human capital was more important than IT technology, went public later than retail-oriented investment banks such as Merrill Lynch.
26. Other thoughts on instability and financial innovation are provided in Shiller (2008), Loayza and Ranciere (2005) and Brunnermeier et al. (2009). See also Frame and White (2002) on the difficulty of evaluating the added value of financial innovations.

REFERENCES

Acharya, V.V., D. Gale and T. Yorulmazer (2010), 'Rollover risk and market freezes', NBER Working Papers 15674, January.

Akerlof, G. (1970), 'The market for lemons: quality uncertainty and the market mechanism', *Quarterly Journal of Economics*, **84**(3), 488–500.

Allen, F. and D. Gale (1995), 'A welfare comparison of intermediaries and financial markets in Germany and the US', *European Economic Review*, **39**, 179–209.

Allen, F. and D. Gale (1997), 'Financial markets, intermediaries and intertemporal smoothing', *Journal of Political Economy*, **105**, 523–546.

An, X., Y. Deng and A.B. Saunders (2008), 'Subordination levels in structured financing', in A.W.A. Boot and A.V. Thakor (eds), *Handbook of Financial Intermediation*, Amsterdam: North-Holland.

Balachandran, B., R. Faff and M. Theobald (2008), 'Rights offerings, takeup, renounceability, and underwriting status', *Journal of Financial Economics*, **89**(2), 328–334.

Berger, A. (2003), 'The economic effects of technological progress: evidence from the banking industry', *Journal of Money, Credit and Banking*, **35**, 141–176.

Berger, A., W. Frame and N. Miller (2005), 'Credit scoring and the availability, price, and risk of small business credit', *Journal of Money, Banking, and Credit*, **37**, 191–222.

Berger, A.N. and G.F. Udell (2006), 'A more complete conceptual framework for SME finance', *Journal of Banking and Finance*, **30**, 2945–2966.

Berglöf, E. and E. von Thadden (1994), 'Short-term versus long-term interests: capital structure with multiple investors', *Quarterly Journal of Economics*, **109**(4), 1055–1084.

Bernanke, B. (2007), 'Regulation and financial innovation', Speech to the Federal Reserve Bank of Atlanta's 2007 Financial Markets Conference, Sea Island, Georgia, 15 May, http://www.federalreserve.gov/newsev ents/speech/bernanke20070515a.htm.

Bhattacharya S., A.W.A. Boot and A.V. Thakor (2004), *Credit, Intermediation and the Macro Economy: Models and Perspectives*, Oxford: Oxford University Press.

Bhide, A. (1993), 'The hidden cost of stock market liquidity', *Journal of Financial Economics*, **34**, 31–51.

Bolton, P. and E. von Thadden (1998), 'Blocks, liquidity and corporate control', *Journal of Finance*, **53**, 1–25.

Boot, A.W.A., R. Gopalan and A.V. Thakor (2008), 'Market liquidity, investor participation and managerial autonomy: why do firms go private?', *Journal of Finance*, **63**(4), 2013–2059.

Boot, A.W.A., T. Milbourn and A. Schmeits (2006), 'Credit ratings as coordination mechanisms', *Review of Financial Studies*, **19**(1), 81–118.

Boot, A.W.A. and A.V. Thakor (1993), 'Security design', *Journal of Finance*, **48**, 1349–1378.

Boot, A.W.A. and A.V. Thakor (1997), 'Banking scope and financial innovation', *Review of Financial Studies*, **10**, 1099–1131.

Brunnermeier, M., A. Crockett, C. Goodhart and H. Shin (2009), 'The fundamental principles of financial regulation', preliminary conference draft, Geneva Report on the World Economy, 11, International Center for Monetary and Banking Studies, Geneva, Switzerland.

Calomiris, C.W. and C. Kahn (1991), 'The role of demandable debt in structuring optimal banking arrangements', *American Economic Review*, **81**, 497–513.

Calomiris, C.W. and J.R. Mason (2004), 'Credit card securitization and regulatory arbitrage', *Journal of Financial Services Research*, **26**(1), 5–27.

Cantor, R. (2004), 'An introduction to recent research on credit ratings', *Journal of Banking and Finance*, **28**(11), 2565–2573.

Carlin, B.I. (2009), 'Strategic price complexity in retail financial markets', *Journal of Financial Economics*, **91**, 278–287.

Chemmanur, T.J. and P. Fulghieri (1994), 'Reputation, renegotiation, and the choice between bank loans and publicly traded debt', *Review of Financial Studies*, **7**(3), 475–506.

Coffee, J.C. and H.A. Sale (2008), 'Redesigning the SEC: does the Treasury have a better idea?', working paper, Columbia Center for Law and Economics Studies, No. 342.

Coval, J.D., J.W. Jurek and E. Stafford (2009), 'Economic catastrophe bonds', *American Economic Review*, **99**(3), 628–666.

Degryse, H. and P. Van Cayseele (2000), 'Relationship-lending within a bank-based system: evidence from European small-business data', *Journal of Financial Intermediation*, **9**, 90–109.

Deidda, L. and B. Fattouh (2008), 'Banks, financial markets and growth', *Journal of Financial Intermediation*, **17**(1), 6–36.

DeMarzo, P.M. (2005), 'The pooling and tranching of securities: a model of informed intermediation', *Review of Financial Studies*, **18**, 1–35.

Dennis, S. and D. Mullineaux (2000), 'Syndicated loans', *Journal of Financial Intermediation*, **9**, 404–426.

Diamond, D. (1984), 'Financial intermediation and delegated monitoring', *Review of Economic Studies*, **51**, 393–414.

Diamond, D. (1991), 'Monitoring and reputation: the choice between bank loans and directly placed debt', *Journal of Political Economy*, **99**, 689–721.

Diamond, D. and P. Dybvig (1983), 'Bank runs, deposit insurance and liquidity', *Journal of Political Economy*, **91**, 401–419.

Diamond, D. and R. Rajan (2001), 'Banks and liquidity', *American Economic Review*, **91**, 422–425.

Duffie, D. (2010), 'The failure mechanics of dealer banks', *Journal of Economic Perspectives*, **24**, 51–72.

Elul, R. (1995), 'Welfare effects of financial innovation in incomplete markets economies with several consumption goods', *Journal of Economic Theory*, **65**, 43–78.

Frame, W.S. and L.J. White (2002), 'Empirical studies of financial innovation: lots of talk, little action?', working paper, Federal Reserve Bank of Atlanta.

Frame, W.S. and L.J. White (2009), 'Technological change, financial innovation, and diffusion in banking', working paper, July.

Freixas, X. and J. Rochet (2008), *Microeconomics of Banking*, 2nd edition, Cambridge, MA: MIT Press.

Fulghieri, P. and D. Lukin (2001), 'Information production dilution cost and optimal security design', *Journal of Financial Economics*, **61**, 3–42.

Gabaix, X. and D. Laibson (2006), 'Shrouded attributes, consumer myopia, and information suppression in competitive markets', *Quarterly Journal of Economics*, **121**, 505–540.

Gale, D. and M. Hellwig (1984), 'Incentive-compatible debt contracts: the one-period problem', *Review of Economic Studies*, **52**(4), 647–663.

Gatev, E., T. Schuermann and P.E. Strahan (2009), 'Managing bank liquidity risk: how deposit–loan synergies vary with market conditions', *Review of Financial Studies*, **22**(3), 995–1020.

Gorton, G.B. and J.A. Kahn (1993), 'The design of bank loan contracts, collateral, and renegotiation', working paper, NBER, No. W4273.

Haensel, D. and J.P. Krahnen (2007), 'Does credit securitization reduce bank risk? Evidence from the European CDO market', 29 January, working paper, University of Frankfurt.

Hancock, D., D.B. Humphrey and J. Wilcox (1999), 'Cost reductions in electronic payments: the roles of consolidation, economies of scale, and technical change', *Journal of Banking and Finance*, **23**, 391–421.

Heinkel, R. and E.S. Schwartz (1986), 'Rights versus underwritten offerings: an asymmetric information approach', *Journal of Finance*, **41**(1), 1–18.

Hendershott, T., C. Jones and A. Menkveld (2010), 'Does algorithmic trading improve liquidity?', working paper, Tinbergen Institute/VU University of Amsterdam.

Henderson, B.J. and N.D. Pearson (2009), 'The dark side of financial innovation', working paper, EFA meetings in Bergen, Norway.

Hennessy, C. (2009), 'Security design, liquidity and the informational role of prices', working paper, LBS.

Hoshi, T., A. Kashyap and D. Scharfstein (1993), 'The choice between public and private debt: an analysis of post-deregulation corporate financing in Japan', working paper, NBER No. 4421.

Houston, J. and C. James (1996), 'Bank information monopolies and the mix of private and public debt claims', *Journal of Finance*, **51**(5), 1863–1889.

Huang, R. and L. Ratnovski (2011), 'The dark side of bank wholesale funding', *Journal of Financial Intermediation*, **20** (2), 248–263.

Ivashina, V. and D.S. Scharfstein (2010), 'Bank lending during the financial crisis of 2008', *Journal of Financial Economics*, **97**(3), 319–338.

Jacklin, C. (1987), 'Demand deposits, trading restrictions, and risk sharing', in E.D. Prescott and N. Wallace (eds), *Contractual Arrangements for Intertemporal Trade*, Minneapolis, MN: University of Minneapolis Press.

Johnson, S. and J. Kwak (2009), 'Finance: before the next meltdown', *DemocracyJournal.org*, Fall, 19–24.

Jones, D. (2000), 'Emerging problems with the Basel Capital Accord: regulatory capital arbitrage and related issues', *Journal of Banking and Finance*, **24**(1–2), 35–58.

Keeley, M. (1990), 'Deposit insurance, risk, and market power in banking', *American Economic Review*, **80**, 1183–1200.

Keys, B.J., T.K. Mukherjee, A. Seru and V. Vig (2010), 'Did securitization lead to lax screening? Evidence from subprime loans', *Quarterly Journal of Economics*, **125**(1), 307–362.

Loayza, N. and R. Ranciere (2005), 'Financial development, financial fragility, and growth', IMF Working Paper.

Mathis, J., J. McAndrews and J. Rochet (2009), 'Rating the raters: are reputation concerns powerful enough to discipline rating agencies?', *Journal of Monetary Economics*, **56**(5), 657–674.

Mian, A. and A. Sufi (2007), 'The consequences of mortgage credit expansion: evidence from the US mortgage default crisis', University of Chicago Working Paper.

Michalopoulos, S., L. Laeven and R. Levine (2009), 'Financial innovation and endogenous growth', NBER Working Paper 15356, September.

Morrison, A.D. and W.J. Wilhelm (2008), 'The demise of investment banking partnerships: theory and evidence', *Journal of Finance*, **63**(1), 311–350.

Myers, S. and N.S. Majluf (1984), 'Corporate financing and investment decisions when firms have information that investors do not have', *Journal of Financial Economics*, **13**(2), 187–221.

Myers, S.C. and R.G. Rajan (1998), 'The paradox of liquidity', *Quarterly Journal of Economics*, **113**(3), 733–771.

Parlour, C.A. and G. Plantin (2008), 'Loan sales and relationship banking', *Journal of Finance*, **63**(3), 1291–1314.

Partnoy, F. (1999), 'The Siskel and Ebert of financial markets: two thumbs down for the credit rating agencies', *Washington University Law Quarterly*, **77**, 619–712.

Petersen, M. and R.G. Rajan (1994), 'The benefits of lending relationships: evidence from small business data', *Journal of Finance*, **49**(1), 1367–1400.

Petersen, M. and R.G. Rajan (2002), 'Does distance still matter? The information revolution in small business lending', *Journal of Finance*, **57**, 2533–2570.

Posen, A. and M. Hinterschweiger (2009), 'How useful were recent financial innovations? There is reason to be skeptical', *Real Time Economic Issues Watch*, 7 May.

Shiller, R.J. (2008), 'Has financial innovation been discredited?', Project Syndicate.

Shleifer, A. and R.W. Vishny (2010), 'Unstable banking', *Journal of Financial Economics*, **97**, 306–318.

Sufi, A. (2007), 'Information asymmetry and financing arrangements: evidence from syndicated loans', *Journal of Finance*, **62**, 629–668.

Tirole, J. (2006), *The Theory of Corporate Finance*, Princeton, NJ: Princeton University Press.
Townsend, R. (1979), 'Optimal contracts and competitive markets with costly state verification', *Journal of Economic Theory*, **21**(2), 265–293.
Tufano, P. (2003), 'Financial innovation', in G. Constantinides, M. Harris and R. Stulz (eds), *The Handbook of the Economics of Finance*, New York: Elsevier, 307–335.
White, L.J. (2010), 'Markets: the credit rating agencies', *Journal of Economic Perspectives*, **24**(2), 211–226.

23 Bank acquisitions and strategy since the GLB Act
J. Kimball Dietrich

23.1 INTRODUCTION: BANK STRATEGY AND THE GRAMM–LEACH–BLILEY ACT

The Gramm–Leach–Bliley Act of 1999 (GLB Act) of the USA, also known as the Financial Modernization Act and in some policy discussions as the 'Deregulation Act', was largely an effort to allow commercial banks and bank holding companies (BHCs) to expand their operations beyond strict commercial banking activities, taking deposits and making loans. Acquisitions undertaken by banks and BHCs since 1999 can be viewed as allowing banks much greater flexibility in their strategies in the financial services industry (as discussed below). The goal of the Act was to balance the competitive position of US banks relative to international banks (so-called universal banks), allowed by foreign banking laws to engage in securities and insurance services, and US non-banks (and non-banking holding companies) like thrifts and finance companies, also allowed a wider range of non-bank activities than BHCs.

The primary provisions of the GLB Act were amendments to the Bank Holding Company Act of 1956 (BHC Act) as amended, and to Section 20 of the Federal Reserve Act (the Glass–Steagall Act) that limited banks and BHCs from underwriting corporate securities. The Bank Holding Company Act required BHCs to be regulated by the Federal Reserve Board (FRB) and that all acquisitions of BHCs satisfy the test that the acquired businesses were 'closely related to banking'. Insurance and securities services were legally deemed not closely related to banking. FRB approvals through time established a number of non-bank activities performed by companies that BHCs could acquire, such as leasing and financing companies, the FRB having found them to be closely related enough to commercial bank activities to be acceptable as acquisition targets (see Yeager et al., 2007).

A loophole emerged in the prohibition of securities-related services for banking corporations, since Section 20 of the Glass–Steagall Act prohibited commercial banks from earning a 'substantial' amount of revenue from underwriting activity, leaving the interpretation of 'substantial' to the FRB. In 1989, the FRB allowed commercial banks to underwrite corporate bonds and equity to a limited extent, and in 1996 the FRB increased its interpretation of what the definition of 'substantial' was, namely from 10 to 25 percent of revenue. Hence even before the repeal of Glass–Steagall in the GLB Act in 1999, many commercial banks became active in investment banking through what were called 'Section 20 subsidiaries'. This activity could be achieved through internal departments or through acquisitions.[1]

While US commercial banks and BHCs served a large number of diverse geographical markets for deposit and loan products, before 1999 the banking business for nearly all banks could reasonably be described as a business with narrowly defined strategic possibilities. The GLB Act enabled commercial banks and BHCs to expand not only into securities underwriting in an unlimited way through security firm subsidiaries, but also into insurance. The mechanism for this was the Act's creation of a new entity, financial holding companies (FHCs), distinguished from BHCs by being able to acquire and own businesses not meeting the 'closely related to banking' requirement of the BHC Act. This expansion of the strategic options available to commercial banks and BHC management and boards gave individual banking firms opportunities to pursue very different strategies through acquisitions of non-banking financial firms. Alternatives to growth through acquisitions available to BHCs included return of capital to investors or other distribution of cash. Stock repurchase strategies could correspond to a strategy of confining business activities to traditional banking or acquiring other banks and distributing cost savings from consolidation to shareholders.

The expansion of bank powers to offer an unlimited range of financial services is sometimes identified with forms of 'deregulation' of banking that led to increased risk. Some policymakers have called for the reinstatement of Glass–Steagall-type restrictions and repeal of the GLB Act. Many financial market observers assign partial responsibility for the financial crisis of 2007–2009 to the Act's deregulation.

This chapter analyzes the use of bank management and boards' use of the expanded authorities under the GLB Act in making acquisitions after 1999. These acquisitions can be described as defining banks' changing strategies over the period. I describe and calculate the relative use of these expanded powers by analyzing banks' and BHCs' mergers and acquisitions from 1999 to 2007 using the SDC Platinum database as described in the next section. These data are combined with CRSP on bank share performance and US Treasury disclosures on Troubled Asset Relief Program (TARP) loans during the crisis. These data will be used to assess the performance and risk of alternative bank strategies concerning diversification since the GLB Act.

23.2   DATA: SOURCES AND DESCRIPTION OF BANK ACQUISITION ACTIVITIES

There are large numbers of commercial banks and BHCs in the United States. The number of banks averaged above 13 000 from the 1930s and began to increase with loosened charter restrictions in the 1960s, reaching a peak of 14 434 in 1980.[2] The Monetary Control and Deregulation Act of 1980 marked the beginning of the deregulation of bank interest rate restrictions (Regulation Q) and opening of banking services competition to non-banks like thrifts. A characteristic of banking after 1980 has been consolidation of banks, for example across state boundaries as allowed by the Riegel–Neal Interstate Banking and Branching Efficiency Act of 1994. In 1999, at the time of the GLB Act's implementation, there were 8582 commercial banks and approximately 600 BHCs.

During the period 1999 to 2007, the total number of banks fell from 8582 to 7283, a decline that extended a trend in the US beginning in 1980. The main economic impulse for bank consolidation is cost economies possible with loosened limitations on bank acquisitions, reducing redundancy in facilities from services provided through branches that grew in the absence of interest-rate competition before 1980, and cross-state consolidation when allowed. The GLB Act, as discussed in the first section, however enabled

Table 23.1   Listed and unlisted banks and bank holding companies, transaction volume and total deal value 1999 to 2007

	1999 total listed	Listed 1999 with M&A activity	Unlisted 1999 with M&A activity	Total 1999 M&A activity	2007 total listed	Acquiror survived to 2007
Number of banks	453	216	236	452	261	161
Number of deals		1387	685	2072		1063
Deals with values		908	472	1380		
Total deal value*		$582905	$43905	$626810		$477825

Note: * Millions; not all deals include transaction values.

banks to acquire non-banks through forming FHCs. Since the Act was passed, the number of FHCs has increased from around 300 to nearly 500, while BHCs have also increased to around 1000 entities (Federal Reserve Board, 2006).

The merger, acquisition and stock repurchase activities of banks, BHCs and FHCs analyzed in this chapter are derived using the SDC Platinum dataset on mergers and acquisitions. The database, based on hundreds of sources, contains information on all deals over $1 million or 5 percent of a company and includes many small banks and BHCs. The SDC database contains 2072 mergers and acquisitions by banking firms from December 1999, when the GLB Act became effective, until December 2007. Data on about two-thirds of these transactions include transaction values (see Table 23.1; and see Figure 23.1 for a distribution of transaction values).

Most banks or BHCs in the United States are public companies, however many banks and BHCs are relatively small but are included in the SDC Platinum database. Many of these firms are so small that they do not meet the listing requirements for the major US exchanges, specifically the NASDAQ, American or New York stock exchanges or affiliates, hence are not included in the CRSP database of stock returns and other stock-related data. This presents a problem in matching merger, acquisition and stock repurchase transactions with data on listed companies. Table 23.1 provides summary statistics by trading classification in 1999 and total transactions between 1999 and 2007 in the combined SDC and CRSP data. In addition, the table provides the number of firms in the 1999 listed bank sample that survived until 2007, since some banks are acquired by other banks, fail or are delisted.

An interesting aspect of banks is that some smaller, unlisted banks grow and qualify for listing on the exchanges, while others are delisted due to bankruptcy, acquisition or a fall in share value below thresholds for listing. Banks listed in 2007 will therefore contain firms that have survived the entire period and new firms that have grown to qualify for listing due to merger activity and internal growth. Table 23.1 shows that of the 216 banks or BHCs listed in 1999, 161 'survived' until 2007 as a listed company. Less than half of the listed banks had mergers and acquisitions activity from 1999 to 2007, while the total

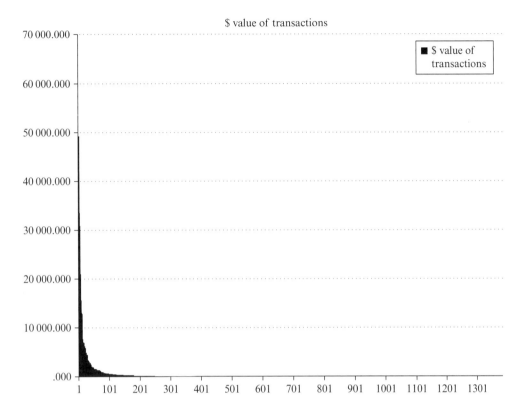

Figure 23.1   Histogram of transaction values

number of listed banks or BHCs fell by 2007 to 261. The other 100 bank companies that were listed, therefore, were either banks that were not engaged in acquisitions or smaller banks that grew to satisfy listing requirements over the period.

23.3   IMPACT OF GLB ON BANK STRATEGIES

To begin with an overview of bank strategic choices following GLB, Table 23.1 provides some basic facts. First, listed companies, generally larger banking firms, dominated acquisition activity, with more than twice as many deals and more than 13 times the dollar value of transactions as unlisted banking firms. Over the period from the GLB Act to 2007, over 2000 deals amounting to $627 billion occurred. In contrast, Table 23.2 shows that banking firms repurchased shares valued at $17 billion, mainly paid by larger, traded banking firms. Table 23.1 shows that over 450 bank firms were listed in 1999, and of those 216 acquired other firms.

Table 23.2 provides a list of stock buy-back transactions, also available from the SDC database. From the end of 1999 to 2007, banking firms returned $17 billion to shareholders. However, an analysis of listed firms' returned capital shows that these larger firms accounted for all but $1.25 billion of these buy-backs or returns of capital to investors,

Table 23.2   Stock repurchases by year and financial institution

	% equity purchased (annual maximum)	Value of buy-back (annual sum)	Total assets (annual sum)	Average of post % equity/TA
1999	7.10	2.836	714.700	5.2
TF Financial Corp	7.10	2.836	714.700	5.2
2000	9.60	106.418	13504.600	0.3
Central Bancorp Inc, MA	4.80	1.434	409.600	6.9
Co Vest Bancshares Inc, IL	2.30	1.025	553.500	7.9
Home Federal Bancorp, IN	5.00	3.876	832.200	8.8
Indian Village Bancorp Inc, OH	5.00	0.282	59.400	9.0
Integra Bank Corp	8.50	25.676	2468.200	11.2
Jacksonville Bancorp, TX	4.90	1.398	292.400	9.3
Mystic Financial Inc, MA	5.00	2.234	473.800	4.4
Redwood Empire Bancorp, CA	9.60	5.175	435.100	11.2
State Finl Svcs Corp, WI	6.60	6.154	1090.000	8.0
Trustmark Corp, Jackson, MS	4.90	58.600	6757.000	16.8
Wyman Park Bancorp, MD	5.00	0.564	133.400	4.2
2001	33.30	640.307	75968.900	−0.5
American National Bankshares	3.30	2.683	571.400	13.8
Banner Corp	5.00	7.800	1987.800	7.5
Berkshire Hills Bancorp Inc	5.00	18.513	3037.400	3.5
Capital Crossing BK, Boston, MA	33.30	15.480	737.300	4.2
Citizens Banking Corp, Flint, MI	6.30	55.689	7936.300	10.4
CoVest Bancshares Inc, IL	8.70	6.816	585.100	12.2
First Bancorp of Indiana Inc	6.60	2.216	185.300	16.9
First Federal Bancshares, IL	10.00	3.532	237.600	13.4
First South Bancorp Inc, NC	4.90	3.088	526.700	11.4
Heritage Financial Corp, WA	9.30	7.287	531.000	13.4
Home Financial Bancorp, Indiana	19.90	1.524	63.900	9.6
Independence Cmnty Bk Corp, NY	5.00	43.013	6871.000	11.9
InvestorsBancorp, Waukesha, WI	7.50	0.581	–	n/a
Jacksonville Bancorp, TX	4.90	1.414	301.500	9.1
Lincoln Bancorp, IN	15.60	10.397	498.600	11.3
Long Island Financial Corp, NY	10.00	1.939	275.100	6.3
M&T Bank Corp, Buffalo, NY		272.930	30924.500	n/a
MCB Financial Corp, California		3.000	206.200	n/a
Mystic Financial Inc, MA	5.20	5.621	1173.900	1.9
NBC Capital Corp	13.60	24.500	1009.500	15.4
North Valley Bancorp	5.00	3.525	550.600	12.2
Southern Missouri Bancorp Inc	5.00	0.897	240.500	7.1
TCF Financial Corp, MN	5.00	79.060	10666.400	14.1
Teche Holding Co, New Iberia, LA	5.00	1.661	452.900	7.0
TriCo Bancshares, Chico, CA	2.10	2.541	961.100	12.3
United Financial Corp, MT	6.10	1.453	330.500	6.8
United Security Bancorp, WA	10.00	6.863	533.000	11.6

Table 23.2   (continued)

	% equity purchased (annual maximum)	Value of buy-back (annual sum)	Total assets (annual sum)	Average of post % equity/TA
2001				
Vista Bancorp, Phillipsburg, NJ	3.90	4.600	695.300	16.3
Westamerica Bancorp	4.90	51.684	3878.500	25.9
2002	30.90	5182.788	730001.800	−0.3
Alliance Financial Corp, NY	8.60	6.300	562.900	11.9
Bank of America Corp	6.00	4706.200	679538.000	10.9
Banner Corp	5.00	10.381	2094.800	9.4
Berkshire Hills Bancorp Inc	5.00	5.017	1037.400	9.2
Bryn Mawr Bank Corp	5.00	5.855	469.000	23.7
Centennial Bancorp, Portland, OR	4.60	8.325	680.700	25.4
Central Bancorp Inc, MA	4.90	1.404	429.100	6.4
Central Valley Community	2.00	0.421	201.300	10.2
CFS Bancorp Inc	30.90	50.563	1732.900	6.5
First Bancorp, Troy, NC	12.90	8.336	928.800	6.1
First Mutual Bancshares Inc	19.60	15.799	687.100	9.4
HMN Financial, Rochester, MN	8.10	7.762	1414.500	3.3
Home Federal Bancorp, IN	5.00	3.434	845.300	7.7
Landmark Bancorp Inc	4.90	1.795	209.800	16.6
Local Financial Corp, OK	10.00	27.481	2584.600	9.6
Logansport Financial Corp	5.00	0.765	137.700	10.6
Mystic Financial Inc, MA	10.00	2.357	311.200	6.8
UnionBanCal Corp, CA	4.60	320.593	36136.700	18.4
2003	10.10	8467.033	702748.600	0.8
Associated Banc-Corp	5.00	71.600	12519.900	10.9
Bank of America Corp		8023.600	640105.000	n/a
Fidelity Bancorp, Pittsburgh, PA	5.00	4.665	1255.100	3.3
First Finl Bancorp	5.00	35.363	3986.300	16.9
First PacTrust Bancorp Inc	4.00	3.921	500.100	18.8
Heritage Financial Corp, WA	10.00	11.860	601.700	17.7
Laurel Capital Group Inc	5.10	1.973	307.300	11.9
Pathfinder Bancorp, Oswego, NY	6.10	2.338	278.500	12.9
Redwood Empire Bancorp, CA	10.10	11.713	525.900	19.8
UnionBanCal Corp, CA	4.40	300.000	42668.800	15.3
2004	9.50	393.948	35614.700	1.5
EFC Bancorp Inc, Elgin, IL	5.10	5.981	614.200	18.1
HCB Bancshares Inc, Camden, AR	4.70	1.058	276.400	7.8
Heritage Financial Corp, WA	9.50	13.332	594.600	21.4
IBERIABANK Corp	4.50	14.970	2009.300	15.8
M&T Bank Corp, Buffalo, NY	5.20	349.750	31139.100	20.5
North Central Bancshares, IA	9.10	5.436	461.600	11.8
Teche Holding Co, New Iberia, LA	5.00	3.421	519.500	12.5

Table 23.2   (continued)

	% equity purchased (annual maximum)	Value of buy-back (annual sum)	Total assets (annual sum)	Average of post % equity/TA
2005	5.30	2592.482	154 199.900	6.8
Colonial BancGroup Inc		30.000	15 834.500	n/a
Heritage Commerce Corp		10.000	1060.700	n/a
M&T Bank Corp, Buffalo, NY	4.30	520.750	52 886.900	21.9
Mellon Financial, Pittsburgh, PA	5.30	2023.750	83 580.000	20.6
Synergy Financial Group Inc	5.00	7.982	837.800	18.1
2006	2.00	1.180	378.800	15.3
Colonial Bankshares Inc	2.00	1.180	378.800	15.3
2007	5.40	97.487	8027.300	3.1
American Bancorp of NJ Inc	5.00	24.071	1068.600	42.8
Central Pacific Financial Corp	4.90	43.740	5563.600	15.3
First Clover Leaf Finl Corp	5.00	4.909	376.400	24.8
Legacy Bancorp Inc	5.00	7.963		n/a
Roma Financial Corp	20.00	15.849	887.200	57.8
Third Century Bancorp, IN	5.40	0.955	131.500	12.7
Grand total	33.30	17 484.479	1 721 159.300	

or 93 percent of the value of stock repurchases. The dollar volume of buy-backs is dominated by two very large listed firms; Bank of America and Mellon accounted for nearly all of this in three multibillion dollar transactions. In terms of the strategic significance of return cost savings to investors, the return of listed banking firms' invested capital was only 2.7 percent of acquisitions made by listed companies. This percentage is nearly identical to the amount of capital returned relative to acquisitions for smaller unlisted banking firms.

To assess the strategic impact of the greater strategic flexibility allowed to banking firms following the GLB Act, the most interesting question concerns the nature of the acquiring firms' targets. Our analysis of banking firms' acquisition of targets is in terms of Stardard Industrial Classification (SIC) codes of acquired firms. Table 23.3 provides a breakdown of banking firm acquisitions by individual four-digit SIC codes. SIC codes 6000 to 6999 identify all financial service firms. SIC codes below 6000 represent businesses from extractive industries (1000s), manufacturing of consumer or capital goods (roughly 2000 to 3000), transportation and utilities services (4000s), and wholesale and retail trade (5000s). The first panel of Table 23.3 indicates that banking firms acquired positions in 18 target firms in those non-financial categories. Examination of those transactions reveals that most of them were foreign minority interest acquisitions by major financial firms like Goldman Sachs.

Of the 117 acquisitions of non-financial firms with SIC codes above 6999 (7011 to 619B), well over half of them are concentrated under five SIC codes corresponding to software publishing (SIC 7372), Internet services (SIC 7375), business services not elsewhere classified (SIC 7389), accounting services (SIC 8721), and finally business

Table 23.3   Acquisitions by banks by SIC code by year

Acquisitions by commercial banks and financial holding companies by SIC codes 1041 to 5731 by year

Year	1041	2013	2092	2111	2731	2835	3544	3663	3711	3826	4512	4813	4832	4911	5651	5731
1999																
2000																
2001								1					1			
2002					1		1					1				1
2003	1															
2004										1						
2005									1							
2006		1	1			1					1			1		
2007				1										2	1	
Total	1	1	1	1	1	1	1	1	1	1	1	1	1	3	1	1

Acquisitions by commercial banks and financial holding companies by SIC codes 6000 to 6163 by year

Year	6000	6011	6021	6022	6029	6035	6036	6081	6091	6099	6141	6153	6159	6162	6163
1999															
2000	2	4	71	29	5	20	3			1	6	1	1	5	2
2001	4	2	106	37	7	27	7				3	4		1	
2002	3	1	89	17	2	23	4				2	1	2	4	
2003	3		78	19	3	29	5				3	1		8	
2004	2		135	36	5	33	2		1		4		1	12	4
2005	1		100	24	3	16	4				4			3	
2006			128	18	1	10	4		1		6			2	
2007	5		83	14	3	9		1			8		1	7	3
Total	20	7	790	194	29	167	29	1	2	1	36	7	5	42	9

Table 23.3 (continued)

Acquisitions by commercial banks and financial holding companies by SIC codes 6213 to 6799 by year

Year	6000	6211	6231	6282	6289	6311	6321	6331	6351	6361	6371	6411	6512	6531	6712	6719	6722	6726	6733	6798	6799
1999		1																			
2000	2	10		4		1		4				23		1	8		1	14			6
2001	4	4		9		11	1			1		9			9	5		8			18
2002	3	15		23	2	11		1		1		20			12			6			8
2003	3	9		26	1	11		1				40	1		6						
2004	2	4		14	3	7					3	10			3				1		4
2005	1	3	1	11	2	3	3	2	1			19	1		5		1	3	3	1	
2006		4		9	2	2						7			31		2		1		3
2007	5	5		19		2		1			1	7			40	1	1	2	2	2	4
Total	20	55	1	115	10	48	4	9	1	2	4	135	2	1	114	6	5	33	7	3	43

Acquisitions by commercial banks and financial holding companies by SIC codes 7011 to 619B by year

Year	7011	7261	7291	7353	7359	7371	7372	7373	7374	7375	7376	7377	7379	7389	8071	8721	8732	8741	8742	8748	619A	619B	Grand total
1999															1								2
2000					2		1	1		3		1		3			1			3	2		239
2001			1			1	3	1	1	2		3		2		6	1		1	1			296
2002							3		1	2	1	1		1						1	1	1	263
2003		1	1	3	1		1			1									2	1	1		264
2004							2		4	1			1			2				1			297
2005					3		1			5				1					1	6			226
2006	1						1		1				1	1		3		1		1	4		251
2007	1						2		1	2				4					2				234
Total	1	1	1	3	6	1	14	2	8	16	1	5	2	12	1	11	2	1	6	14	8	1	2072

consulting (SIC 8748). Altogether, bank firm acquisitions outside financial and real estate services numbered 135 out of 2702 deals, or less than 7 percent of the total merger activity by banks in the period 1999 to 2007. The remaining transactions were confined to financial services.

Banking firms engaging in mergers and acquisitions activity reported in the SDC database acquired 1151 deposit-taking firms from the GLB Act to 2007, namely 984 banks (SICs 6021 and 6022) and 167 thrifts (SIC 6035), or 55 percent of total transactions. Clearly these acquisitions represent further consolidation of deposit-taking firms and do not represent a major strategic shift in activity out of traditional banking. Examining the non-traded bank or smaller firm acquisitions over the period, a much higher percentage (90 percent of their acquisitions) are of other deposit-taking firms (banks and thrifts and bank holding companies). In terms of value, deposit-taking firms accounted for over 90 percent of non-traded banking firms' acquisitions.

Larger, listed firms follow a similar but slightly different pattern in concentrating acquisition activity in traditional banking activities. Most of their acquisitions, close to 70 percent, are in deposit-taking institutions, and an additional 8 percent in credit-related activities like credit cards or real estate lending that would likely have been approved by the FRB for a BHC before the GLB Act was passed. However, around 13 percent of the value of their acquisitions would not have been possible without the GLB Act, and an additional 1 percent in business services, including data processing, would likely have been reviewed by the FRB concerning its relation to banking. The conclusion is that most mergers and acquisitions activity for banking institutions for both smaller and larger banking firms has been in their traditional lines of business, but larger listed banks have diversified more into non-traditional activities than non-listed smaller banks.

As discussed above, a number of banks established securities businesses using the Section 20 exception based on a relatively low percentage of revenue from securities underwriting and other transactions. To investigate the role of banking firms established in the securities business before the GLB Act, we focus on the mergers and acquisitions activity of those firms. Fifteen Section 20 firms from Chaplinsky and Erwin (2009) are identified using their list of 34 Section 20 banking firms among the listed banking firms active in acquisitions according to the SDC data. Their list included many foreign banks that were not really restricted from securities activities but found it convenient to enter the business through their US affiliates. These US Section 20 firms are among the largest banks and financial firms in the US, including Bank of America, Citigroup, Chase Manhattan, JP Morgan, and so forth.[3]

These major firms with a presence in the securities business in 1999 continued to invest in that business segment. These large Section 20 firms were responsible for $404 billion in merger activity in securities firms. Unlike the average samples, only 54 percent of the Section 20 firm deals, accounting for 83 percent of the value of these transactions, were in deposit-taking or credit-related firms whose acquisitions were allowed before the GLB Act, while about one-sixth of their acquisitions (in terms of deals or value) were in securities firms. While the 15 Section 20 firms accounted for about 65 percent of the total value of mergers by all banking firms from 1999 to 2007, they accounted for 87 percent of the investment in securities firms made by listed banking firms over the period.

To summarize, banking firms in general have remained 'closely related to banking' defined as deposit-taking, lending and other credit-related activities. Larger banks, especially those which had established a presence in the securities business through Section 20 activities before 1999, have continued to dominate acquisitions in securities firms but have still invested most in traditional banking acquisitions. It is possible that their activities, measured in terms of percentage of revenues generated in underwriting and trading, would not have been possible under FRB interpretations of Section 20, but nonetheless, their actions since 1999 represent an expansion of an existing strategy already begun by the time 'deregulation' of banking activities occurred.

23.4   GLB AND BANK STRATEGIES AND RISK

The question of the effect of banks' securities and other businesses not 'closely related to banking' (like insurance activities) on market performance and risk has been assessed in a preliminary way in Akhigbe and Madura (2004). This chapter offers a preliminary analysis of the effects of entering the securities business on banking firms using two simple measures: comparative rates of return and standard deviations of firms that 'survived' as listed firms from 1999 to 2007 (thus ignoring firms that followed the strategy of selling to an acquiring firm) contrasting Section 20 firms with non-Section 20 firms. Secondly, I will assess the proportion of those two classes of firm that received Troubled Assets Relief Fund (TARP) injections of capital in 2007 and 2008.

The performance of the banking firms that existed over the period varies substantially but this variation does not seem to depend on bank acquisition strategies. Table 23.4 provides summary statistics on risks and returns for three classifications of banking firms. The firms consist of all firms that traded in both 1999 and at the end of 2007, since otherwise no comparable statistics could be computed for banks in general. No doubt there are some biases in this sample, given that many banking firms stopped trading over the period. However, the direction of bias is not clear. Some banks ceased trading because they were acquired, implying either that they were attractive to buyers because of their superior performance, or that they were targets offering opportunities because of inefficiencies and poor performance leading to low valuations. Firms trading at the end of the period but not in 1999 may have become listed because of a successful strategy increasing their value, while some firms not trading in 1999 may have failed or been delisted for poor performance. I present the data as background for discussion only.

While the population of all banking firms making acquisitions over the period 1999 to 2007 shown in Panel A of Table 23.4 performed slightly better than the subset of firms with Section 20 status in 1999 shown in Panel B, given the large variation in annual returns the differences do not seem significant. Their market risk, measured as the standard deviation of annualized monthly returns, is virtually identical. Finally, their market returns during the first six months of the financial crisis at the end of 2007 were virtually identical. Some smaller firms in Panel A did have a wider range of outcomes, but that observation supports little inference concerning strategy and market returns and risk.

Panel C of Table 23.4 shows the same return data for banking firms that survived from 1999 to 2007 but that made no acquisitions reflected in the SDC database. There are 71 of these firms with complete CRSP return data for the entire period. These firms

Table 23.4   Return and risk statistics for BHCs surviving 1999–2007

	Average	Minimum	Maximum
All BHC acquiror firms surviving			
Annualized returns to June 2007	0.0936	−0.0908	0.3227
Std. dev. of returns	0.0696	0.0419	0.1199
Return July–Dec 2007*	−0.0355	−0.2453	0.2770
Section 20 surviving			
Annualized returns to June 2007	0.0540	−0.0053	0.1032
Std. dev. of returns	0.0689	0.0613	0.0800
Return July–Dec 2007*	−0.0550	−0.1939	0.1040
Traded firms with no SDC acquisition deals surviving			
Annualized returns to June 2007	−0.0416	−0.3459	0.1163
Std. dev. of returns	0.0756	0.0340	0.2174
Return July–Dec 2007*	−0.0842	−0.8347	1.5052

Note: *Annualized 6-month return.

do demonstrate poorer average annualized returns over the entire time period, and a stronger negative impact of the 2007 financial crisis. It would be tempting to say that the strategy of no acquisitions, which could correspond to internal growth, paying out cash or struggling to survive, is on average less successful in market performance terms than firms active in acquisitions. This conclusion does warrant further examination since the reason for the differences in the traded firms in 1999 and 2007 can have multiple explanations, including failure, delisting and acquisition by another firm.

The focus of this research is on the impact of banking firm strategies entailing expansion into non-traditional banking activities, especially securities business. Table 23.5 provides a preliminary exploration of the relation between banking firm performance, risk and acquisition strategies outside of traditional banking. The table reports three regressions to provide examples of the general results of this investigation: two use linear regression of market returns and standard deviations to variables capturing the firms' non-bank acquisitions, and one reports a Probit estimation of the likelihood of a financial firms requiring TARP funds in the period after 2007.

The basic finding is that bank strategies with respect to non-bank mergers and acquisitions have little explanatory power either for average market returns or the two risk measures, standard deviations of returns and requiring TARP funds. TARP funds for banks represent both temporary needs for capital and government concerns about 'two big to fail' or 'sources of systemic risk'. I use TARP as both an explanatory variable in the market-data based regressions, and separately as a risk measure in relating bank strategies to government assessments of institutional risk.

Panel A reports a regression of market returns on Section 20 status and requiring TARP funds in 2007 or later together with the number of SIC codes 6200 acquisitions (securities firms) and SIC 6300 acquisitions (insurance firms). There is no statistical relation evidence in these estimations between acquisitions strategies, future TARP use, and established securities businesses and returns. The same is true between market risk

Table 23.5   Regression results

Panel A: Regression results: dependent variable annualized returns: returns of all firms trading in 1999 and 2007 with acquisitions

Explanatory variables	Coefficient	Std. error	t-statistic	Prob.
C	0.092932	0.007638	12.16684	0.0000
SEC20	0.014485	0.027136	0.533818	0.5944
TARP	−0.015425	0.011790	−1.308261	0.1931
NUM6200	−0.000199	0.002914	−0.068283	0.9457
NUM6300	0.002793	0.008281	0.337219	0.7365
R-squared	0.014847	Mean dependent var		0.087277
Adjusted R-squared	−0.015465	S.D. dependent var		0.064719
S.E. of regression	0.065218	Akaike info criterion		−2.585832
Sum squared resid	0.552938	Schwarz criterion		−2.478230
Log likelihood	179.5437	F-statistic		0.489800

Panel B: Regression results: dependent variable standard deviation of returns: deviations of returns of all firms trading in 1999 and 2007 with acquisitions

Variable	Coefficient	Std. error	t-statistic	Prob.
C	0.070594	0.001683	41.95701	0.0000
SEC20	−0.005328	0.005977	−0.891295	0.3744
TARP	−0.004236	0.002597	−1.630798	0.1054
NUM6200	0.000996	0.000642	1.552605	0.1229
NUM6300	0.000836	0.001824	0.458296	0.6475
R-squared	0.035944	Mean dependent var		0.069210
Adjusted R-squared	0.006281	S.D. dependent var		0.014412
S.E. of regression	0.014366	Akaike info criterion		−5.611544
Sum squared resid	0.026830	Schwarz criterion		−5.503941
Log likelihood	383.7792	F-statistic		1.211738
Durbin-Watson stat	2.290139	Prob(F-statistic)		0.308971

Panel C: Probit regression results: dependent variable TARP dummy TARP-No TARP 2007–2011 for all firms trading in 1999 and 2007 with acquisitions

Variable	Coefficient	Std. error	z-statistic	Prob.
C	0.703217	0.556300	1.264096	0.2062
RISK9907	−12.94795	7.986513	−1.621226	0.1050
NUM6200	0.074856	0.055956	1.337766	0.1810
Mean dependent var	0.444444	S.D. dependent var		0.498755
S.E. of regression	0.495152	Akaike info criterion		1.386715
Sum squared resid	32.36319	Schwarz criterion		1.451277
Log likelihood	−90.60327	Hannan-Quinn criter.		1.412951
Restr. log likelihood	−92.73981	Avg. log likelihood		−0.671135
LR statistic (2 df)	4.273079	McFadden R-squared		0.023038
Probability (LR stat)	0.118063			
Obs with Dep = 0	75	Total obs		135
Obs with Dep = 1	60			

measured as standard deviations and the same variables. The TARP variable is even negative (reduces risk) and nearly significant, though small.

A major policy question is whether the expansion and diversification of banking firms into services not 'closely related to banking' in the face of the financial crisis of 2007 to 2009 increased the firm's individual risk or systemic risk. Many banks were forced by stress to accept government capital infusions from the TARP program while several were forced to accept TARP funds at the beginning of the program implementation so as to remove the stigma of accepting government capital infusions.

I pursue this approach to analyzing the risks of banks' strategies to assess the significance of their diversification into non-banking activities to the likelihood that they were required to apply for TARP funding. Using data on TARP transactions, banks in my sample that required government funds during the crisis are compared to the classifications of their strategies in terms of mergers and acquisitions, as a source of both bank growth and diversification into non-banking. If banks accepting TARP funds are considered risky, strategies increasing the likelihood that a banking firm would accept those funds would explain some of the need for them. The Probit regression reported in Panel C uses banking firms' market risk measures and the number of securities firms acquisitions. Neither variable is significant at usual levels; the market risk measure actually reduces the likelihood of needing TARP funds.

Given that most banking firms have concentrated their acquisitions strategies in areas previously allowed under the pre-GLB regulation of banking holding companies, and in the face of the evidence discussed above, it is hard to maintain that the GLB Act unleashed bank managements and boards to make risky investments in financial segments that would increase their vulnerability to stress and crises. Most of the securities activities of banks seem to be connected to activities that existed prior to 1999, represented by the Section 20 banks.

23.5 CONCLUSIONS AND OPEN QUESTIONS

Banking firms were released from tight restrictions on their financial business through the GLB Act of 1999. However, most banks have not taken advantage of the opportunity to diversify their financial services strategy into previously prohibited activities like securities underwriting and insurance. In fact, the one-stop financial service firm remains an unfulfilled dream in the US. Instead, a number of larger firms have continued diversification strategies in place in 1999, and very few other firms have matched this approach.

A number of issues are of great interest and are not addressed in this analysis. One question is what is the best strategy or approach to maximize shareholder value given the underlying and apparently continuing economic logic of banking firms' consolidation. The question is whether internal growth, possible sale to an acquiring firm, or mergers and acquisitions that are either diversifying or not diversifying are better strategies. Another strategy is to maximize returns by returning as much cash to investors as possible; not only stock buy-backs but also through dividends. Exploring both of these questions requires a complete analysis of each bank's history and when it sold or was delisted, meaning an examination of different time periods for individual institutions. The comparison of banks with different lengths of measured performance requires assumptions about investors' alternative investment opportunities over the entire period of analysis. The impact of strategy on risk also requires a more thorough examination in terms of other measures of risk, like beta coefficients or bankruptcy, in the case of banks' usually forced sales.

A critical concern is the relation between banking firm strategy – internal growth, cash distributions, bank acquisitions, non-bank diversification allowed by GLB, and so forth – and compensation schemes for executives. Given the relatively homogeneous nature of the financial services business compared to non-banking businesses like manufacturing, non-bank services, mining, and so forth, the relationship between compensation and strategy choice, within the narrow bounds defined by the financial services industry, seems a rich area for analysis. Of course, this area has also been a major focus of post-crisis discussion.

The conclusion of this analysis is that the GLB Act's authorization of non-banking financial services to FHCs was not a major source of risk in the financial crisis of 2007–2009. Only a few banks used the expanded powers, and their performance is not in the aggregate different to that of banks in general. While individual failures are the focus of policy discussions, the major financial firm collapses like AIG, Merrill Lynch, Wachovia, and so forth do not provide evidence to contradict the conclusion that neither the GLB Act nor banking diversification in non-bank financial services caused the crisis.

NOTES

1. See Chaplinsky and Erwin (2009) for a description of these developments and their Table 1 (p. 385) for a list of commercial banks active in investment banking before 1999.
2. Source of bank numbers data is the Federal Deposit Insurance Corporation, Table CB01, 'Federal Deposit Insurance Corporation number of institutions, branches and total offices, FDIC-insured commercial banks, United States and other areas', www.fdic.gov, 13 February 2011.
3. The 1999 data reflect firms before they consolidated, so for example, Chase and JPMorgan Chase show up separately.

REFERENCES

Akhigbe, Aigbe and Jeff Madura (2004), 'Bank acquisitions securities firms: the early evidence', *Applied Financial Economics*, **14**, 485–496.
Chaplinsky, Susan and Gayle R. Erwin (2009), 'Great expectations: banks as equity underwriters', *Journal of Money and Banking*, **33**, 380–389.
Federal Reserve Board (2006), *Federal Reserve Bulletin*, Table 4, 'Nonfinancial characteristics of all reporting bank holding companies in the United States'.
Yeager, Timothy, Fred C. Yeager and Ellen Harshman (2007), 'The Financial Services Modernization Act: evolution or revolution', *Journal of Economics and Business*, **59**, 313–339.

24 Social, environmental, ethical and trust (SEET) issues in banking: an overview
*Andreas G.F. Hoepner and John O.S. Wilson**

24.1 INTRODUCTION

Banks play critical roles in every economy. They operate the payments system, are a source of credit for large parts of the economy, and (except in times of crisis) act as a safe haven for depositors' funds. The banking system aids in allocating resources from those in surplus (depositors) to those in deficit (borrowers) by transforming relatively small liquid deposits into larger illiquid loans. Via this intermediation process, banks help match deposit and loan supply and provide liquidity to an economy. If intermediation is undertaken in an efficient manner, then deposit and credit demands can be met at low cost, benefiting the parties concerned as well as the economy overall (via positive externalities including long-term economic growth and progress in human development). The recent financial crisis, however, has brought a focus on negative externalities in banking such as the contagious effects of bank failures and costs of government bailouts.

Tangential to these, but by no means less important, are social, environmental, ethical and trust issues (SEET). Over the last decade, corporate social responsibility has developed into an important strategy to enable firms to increase and smooth cash flows through consumer goodwill and loyalty, respectively (Carroll, 1999; Carroll and Shabana, 2010; Mintzberg, 1983). Consequently, a number of researchers have investigated the impact of corporate social responsibility or corporate environmental management on organizational performance (Becchetti et al., 2009; Griffin and Mahon, 1997; Margolis and Walsh, 2003; Orlitzky et al., 2003). While no conclusive result has been identified to date, it seems clear that SEET issues matter most in industries providing credence services. These industries (such as fund management, insurance or health care) provide services whose quality cannot easily be assessed until (often long) after consumption. This is because a judgement about quality requires the consumer to have highly specialized knowledge (Barnett, 2007; Hoepner et al., 2010; Siegel and Vitaliano, 2007).

While many bankers are familiar with trust issues surrounding the financial crisis, they might be less aware of scientific research, for instance, on environmental issues relevant to the financial services industry. Such issues already affect reinsurance firms via the increased pay-outs to clients in the aftermath of a series of recent environmental disasters. In the proceedings of the US National Academy of Sciences, Wackernagel et al. (2002) estimated that the world used up 21 per cent more resources than supplied by the planet on a renewable basis. This implies that the current generation is collectively borrowing resources from future generations without necessarily providing the proof of having sufficient collateral (i.e., technological progress) to pay the resources back (even without any interest).[1] Lord Nicholas Stern's (2006) extensive review of the Economics of Climate Change concludes as follows:

> The scientific evidence is now overwhelming: climate change is a serious global threat, and it demands an urgent global response . . . Using the results of formal economic models, the Review estimates that if we don't act, the overall costs and risks of climate change will be equivalent to losing at least 5% of global GDP each year, now and forever. If a wider range of risks and impacts is taken into account, the estimates of damage could rise to 20% of GDP or more. In contrast, the cost of action – reducing greenhouse gas emissions to avoid the worst impacts of climate change – can be limited to around 1% of GDP each year . . . Our actions now and over the coming decades could create [or avoid] risks of major disruption to economic and social activity, on a scale similar to those associated with the great wars and . . . it will be difficult or impossible to reverse these changes. (Stern, 2006: xv)

Stern's (2006) report resulted in enormous public interest and put increasing pressure on governments and businesses to consider climate change as a serious issue. For instance, *The Economist* commented on Stern's report suggesting the establishment of a worldwide insurance fund to insulate the global economy from the possible impact of climate change:

> [G]overnments should act not on the basis of the likeliest outcome from climate change but on the risk of something really catastrophic (such as the melting of Greenland's ice sheet, which would raise sea levels by six to seven metres). Just as people spend a small slice of their incomes on buying insurance on the off-chance that their house might burn down, and nations use a slice of taxpayers' money to pay for standing armies just in case a rival power might try to invade them, so the world should invest a small proportion of its resources in trying to avert the risk of boiling the planet. The costs are not huge. The dangers are. (*The Economist*, 2006: 1)

Besides the environment, issues such as poverty and human rights have received increasing attention over last decade (Barkemeyer et al., 2010). With the financial crisis of 2008 and 2009, turmoil in the global financial system impacted severely on the banking sector with many banks suffering large losses and necessitating the need to raise additional capital privately or through their respective national governments (via various rescue and bailout schemes).[2] The failure of investors, depositors and supervisors to discipline banks appropriately has led academics and policymakers to reconsider ethical issues. For instance, the perceived levels of greed and hubris in the financial system moved into central focus on the public agenda (Weitzner and Darroch, 2009).[3] Restoring stability and trust within the financial system will be a long process.

The rest of this chapter provides an overview of social, environmental, ethical and trust (SEET) issues in banking. It is structured as follows. Section 24.2 utilizes the Factiva database in order to illustrate the increasing relevance of SEET issues in banking over the last decade. In section 24.3 we examine three international initiatives which have been important in providing a focus for SEET issues. These initiatives are: the United Nations Environment Programme Finance Initiative (UNEP FI), the Equator Principles, and the United Nations-backed Principles for Responsible Investment (PRI). Section 24.4 provides a brief review and synthesis of the small but important literature on social, environmental and ethical (SEE) issues in banking, while section 24.5 uses the recent financial crisis as a backdrop to illustrate the importance of trust within the banking industry.[4] Section 24.6 provides a summary.

24.2 THE EMERGENCE OF SOCIAL, ENVIRONMENTAL, ETHICAL AND TRUST (SEET) ISSUES IN BANKING

In order to provide a general analysis of the increasing relevance of SEET issues in banking, we investigate the number of publications indexed in the Dow Jones Factiva database for certain themes over the last decade. This database offers access to current and archival news items from about 28 000 news sources from 157 countries. Factiva's coverage comprises all relevant types of news sources including newspapers, television channels, radio channels, newswires (e.g., Dow Jones, Reuters and the Associated Press) and magazines (e.g., *The Economist, Forbes*) (Factiva, 2010). Hence, the number of publications indexed in Factiva can be viewed as an indicator of the attention that a certain theme receives during a given period.

We searched for the key words 'bank' and at least one of the keywords 'social responsibility', 'climate change' and 'ethics' to approximate broadly the attention of English language news sources to social, environmental and ethical issues in banking.[5] Our search results displayed in Figure 24.1 yield an interesting insight. While the public interest in SEE issues in banking remained relatively stable between 2000 and 2004, it grew substantially afterwards. Overall, Factiva's news coverage of this theme grew by 784.7 per cent from 5916 news items in 2000 to 52 339 publications in 2009. Over the same period, Factiva's general coverage of any news item grew only by 113.3 per cent, and its coverage of bank-related stories increased by no more than 146.7 per cent (illustrated in Figures 24.2 and 24.3). This suggests that the attention to SEE issues in banking grew substantially and overproportionally in 2000–2009 (and especially 2005–2009).

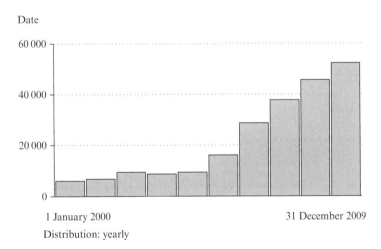

Date

1 January 2000   31 December 2009

Distribution: yearly

Note: This figure displays the annual number of publications indexed by Factiva for the search words 'bank' and 'social responsibility' or 'climate change' or 'ethics'. Factiva's global coverage of publications relating to this theme increased by 784.7% from 5916 in the year 2000 to 52 339 in the year 2009.

Source: Factiva (2010).

Figure 24.1 Factiva search hits for the keywords 'bank' and 'social responsibility' or 'climate change' or 'ethics'

Date

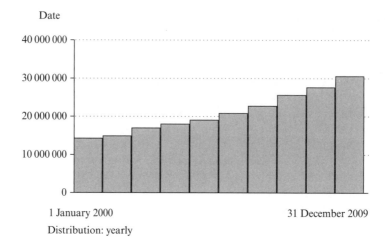

1 January 2000   31 December 2009

Distribution: yearly

Note: This figure displays the annual number of publications indexed by Factiva for the search word 'of'. We use the search word 'of' to approximate Factiva's general coverage of any theme. Factiva's global coverage of publications relating to any theme increased by 113.3% from 14 224 598 in the year 2000 to 30 338 449 in the year 2009.

Source: Factiva (2010).

Figure 24.2   Factiva search hits for the keyword 'of'

Date

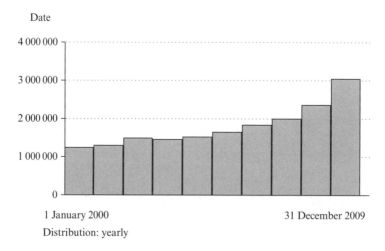

1 January 2000   31 December 2009

Distribution: yearly

Note: This figure displays the annual number of publications indexed by Factiva for the search word 'bank'. Factiva's global coverage of publications relating to this theme increased by 146.7% from 1 231 746 in the year 2000 to 3 038 237 in the year 2009.

Source: Factiva (2010).

Figure 24.3   Factiva search hits for the keyword 'bank'

Date

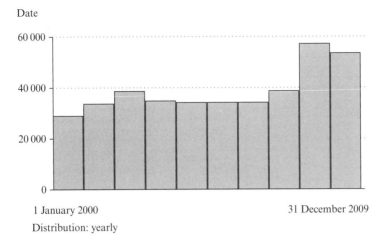

1 January 2000   31 December 2009

Distribution: yearly

Note: This figure displays the annual number of publications indexed by Factiva for the search words 'bank' and 'fear'. Factiva's global coverage of publications relating to this theme increased by 85.3% from 22 821 in the year 2000 to 53 403 in the year 2009. However, there was a 47.8% surge in coverage from 38 859 in 2007 to 57 033 in 2008.

Source: Factiva (2010).

Figure 24.4   Factiva search hits for the keywords 'bank' and 'fear'

The attention pattern to trust-related issues in banking behaved very differently in 2000–2009.[6] Overall, the attention to trust in banking grew underproportionally by only 85.3 per cent from 2000 to 2009. However, attention to trust in banking surged by 48.3 per cent in one single year from 2007 to 2008. These results are perhaps explained by the strong confidence of banks in the earlier years of the decade and the financial crisis of 2008. Interestingly, though, attention to trust fell a bit from 2008 to 2009. This indicates that financial markets might have a relatively short memory. Hence, concerns about trust might merely be temporary phenomena that appear but provoke a rather immediate reversal, since trust is a necessary condition for economic growth. In contrast to trust, the most important social, environmental and ethical issues like climate change appear to be systematic forces that transform the global environment in which financial markets operate.

To understand whether the increased attention towards SEE issues resulted overproportionally from any one of the social, environmental or ethical components, we compare the attention to each individual part. For this purpose, we conducted three searches on Factiva based on the keyword pairs: (1) 'bank' and 'social responsibility'; (2) 'bank' and 'climate change'; and (3) 'bank' and 'ethics'. Our search results are displayed in Figures 24.4–24.7. They show that attention to the social responsibility theme in banking has grown exponentially throughout the whole decade. This theme's growth is, with 877.9 per cent, roughly in line with SEE issues in general. Attention to the ethics theme in banking grew a little from 2000 to 2005, experienced a surge in attention in 2006, but has remained stable since. There seems to be no immediate explanation for this rather odd pattern, but this pattern and the overall moderate growth in attention to the ethics in banking theme

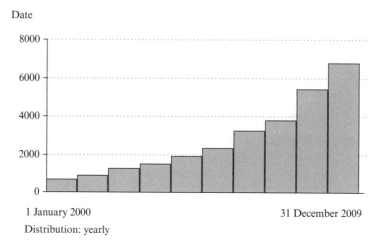

Note: This figure displays the annual number of publications indexed by Factiva for the search words 'bank' and 'social responsibility'. Factiva's global coverage of publications relating to this theme increased by 877.9% from 693 in the year 2000 to 6777 in the year 2009.

Source: Factiva (2010).

Figure 24.5   Factiva search hits for the keywords 'bank' and 'social responsibility'

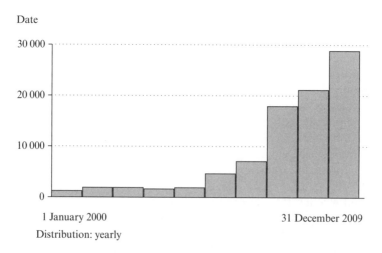

Note: This figure displays the annual number of publications indexed by Factiva for the search words 'Bank' and 'Climate Change'. Factiva's global coverage of publications relating to this theme increased by 2300.9% from 1191 in the year 2000 to 28 595 in the year 2009.

Source: Factiva (2010).

Figure 24.6   Factiva search hits for the keywords 'bank' and 'climate change'

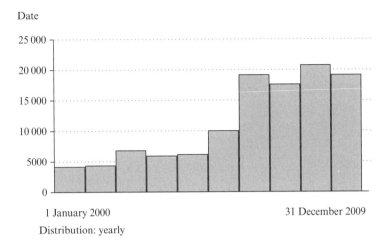

Date

Distribution: yearly

1 January 2000   31 December 2009

Note: This figure displays the annual number of publications indexed by Factiva for the search words 'bank' and 'ethics'. Factiva's global coverage of publications relating to this theme increased by 357.9% from 4164 in the year 2000 to 19069 in the year 2009.

Source: Factiva (2010).

Figure 24.7   Factiva search hits for the keywords 'bank' and 'ethics'

of 357.9 per cent indicate that ethical considerations have not yet fully found their way into banking. In contrast to ethics, the attention to climate change in relation to banking has similarities to a higher-order growth function and experienced an overall growth of 2300.9 per cent over the decade. Whereas very few news stories examined the climate change–banking relationship in the first part of the decade (2000–2004), considerable media attention existed from at least 2007. Comparing the absolute attention to the three themes highlights the relative loss of importance of the ethics theme in banking. While ethics received much more attention in banking than social responsibility or climate change at the beginning of the 2000s, it experienced considerably less attention in 2009.

24.3   INTERNATIONAL INITIATIVES AROUND SEET ISSUES IN BANKING

The recent attention to SEET issues in banking is related to three international initiatives.[7] These initiatives are: the United Nations Environment Programme Finance Initiative (UNEP FI); the Equator Principles; and the United Nations-backed Principles for Responsible Investment (PRI). The remainder of this section provides a brief overview of each of the aforementioned initiatives.

24.3.1   United Nations Environment Programme Finance Initiative (UNEP FI)

Originally referred to as the 'Banks Initiative', the United Nations Environment Programme Financial Institutions Initiative on the Environment (UNEP FII) was

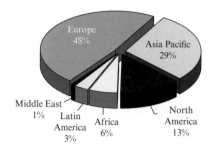

Source: UNEP FI (2010c).

Figure 24.8   UNEP FI signatories by region August 2010

launched in 1992. The intitiative aimed to develop a constructive dialogue between financial institutions about sustainable economic and environmental development. Initially, only a few commercial banks (Deutsche Bank, HSBC Holdings, Natwest, Royal Bank of Canada and Westpac) took part in the initiative, and they subsequently issued the UNEP Statement by Banks on the Environment and Sustainable Development. Signatories to their statement increased to 165 after five years (Kelly and Huhtala, 2001; Peters, 2003; UNEP FI, 2010b). The signatories of the UNEP Statement support sustainable development, environmental management and public awareness on environmental issues. Specifically, the declaration commences:

> We members of the financial services industry recognize that sustainable development depends upon a positive interaction between economic and social development, and environmental protection, to balance the interests of this and future generations. We further recognize that sustainable development is the collective responsibility of government, business, and individuals. We are committed to working cooperatively with these sectors within the framework of market mechanisms toward common environmental goals. (UNEP FI, 1997: 1)

In 2003 the UNEP FII merged with a similar initiative for insurance companies (the UNEP Insurance Industry Initiative) to form the United Nations Environment Programme Financial Initiative (UNEP FI). Its mission is: 'to identify, promote, and realise the adoption of best environmental and sustainability practice at all levels of financial institution operations' (UNEP FI, 2010a: 1). To fulfil its mission it aims to develop and promote linkages between sustainable and financial performance by carrying out a variety of activities. The activities of the UNEP FI include: research on the business case for the management of SEE issues (especially the internalization of environmental externalities); training and other capacity-building activities; and intensive networking activities. These activities are predominantly funded by fees from signatories (UNEP FI, 2010a, 2010c). At the time of writing (November 2010), around 200 financial institutions from over 40 countries are signatories of the UNEP FI. Of these signatories, 48 per cent emanate from Europe and 29 per cent from the Asia Pacific region (as shown in Figure 24.8). Only 13 per cent of the signatories are based in North American jurisdictions, illustrative of a rather low level of North American participation in this initiative.

24.3.2 The Equator Principles

In October 2002, nine international banks involved in project financing activities met with the World Bank Group's International Finance Corporation (IFC) to discuss ways in which the environmental and social risks associated with project finance could be assessed and managed. They concluded that a joint industry framework, which allowed for addressing these risks in any project financing context, would be beneficial for all parties involved. ABN Amro, Barclays, Citi and WestLB developed the Equator Principles, which were launched in June 2003 and initially adopted by ten banks. These banks comprised: ABN AMRO, Barclays, Citigroup, Crédit Lyonnais, Credit Suisse First Boston, HVB Group, Rabobank Group, Royal Bank of Scotland, WestLB and Westpac. In 2006, the Equator Principles were revised to extend their applicability and strengthen their requirements. By 2007, approximately 70 financial institutions had signed the Equator Principles. By the end of 2007, these institutions jointly provided more than 70 per cent of the project financing activities in emerging markets.

Signatories of the Equator Principles commit to providing project financing only to borrowers who comply with the Equator Principles' social and environmental policies. These policies require borrowers, for instance, to conduct an environmental and social assessment; develop social and environmental management systems; and establish, in partnership with local communities, procedures for consultation and grievance resolution. Signatories of the Equator Principles also commit to report annually on their own implementation of the Principles. In common with UNEP FI, the Equator Principles are funded mainly by their signatories. Another similarity between both initiatives is that the Equator Principles have more signatories from Europe than from North America. However, unlike the UNEP FI, more North American financial institutions signed the Equator Principles than counterparts located in the Asia Pacific region (Equator Principles, 2010; Watchman et al., 2006).

24.3.3 Principles for Responsible Investment (PRI)

In early 2005 the United Nations invited the world's largest institutional investors to develop the Principles for Responsible Investment. Twenty institutional investors from 12 countries responded to the invitation. Under the coordination of the UNEP FI and the UN Global Compact, they created a working group comprising 70 experts from the investment industry, academia, (inter)governmental organizations and civil society in April 2005. Nine months later, this working group had created the Principles for Responsible Investment (PRI), which were officially launched at the end of April 2006.

The PRI aim to reflect the core values of large institutional investors with long-term investment horizons. Hence, the PRI's board comprises only representatives from institutional investors and the UN. The principles can also be signed by investment managers and professional service firms (MacDonald et al., 2007; PRI, 2010a). Inspired by visions of fiduciary capitalism (Hawley and Williams, 2000), the principles provide a framework for institutional investors to consider the potential materiality of environmental, social and governance issues for their investment portfolios (Freshfields Bruckhaus Deringer, 2005; PRI, 2010a; UNEP FI, 2009). Specifically, signatories of the Principles for Responsible Investment commit to, among others, integrate environmental, social and

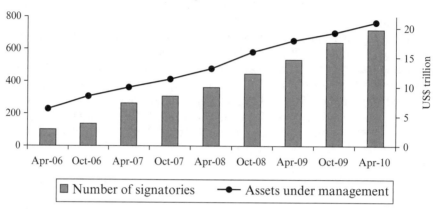

730 signatories, US$21 trillion AUM

Source: PRI (2010).

Figure 24.9   Growth of UN Principles for Responsible Investment (PRI)

corporate governance (ESG) criteria in their investment processes and active ownership policies; promote corporate disclosure on ESG issues; and report on their individual PRI implementation.

The PRI have been welcomed by the investment industry. In the first 28 months of their existence, the PRI have been signed by institutions with collective assets exceeding more than $15 trillion. This represents nearly 20 per cent of the worldwide assets under professional management (Maslakovic, 2008; PRI, 2008). In September 2010, the PRI had 805 signatories from 45 countries, which represent assets valued over $20 trillion as shown in Figure 24.9. In common with the UNEP FI, the majority of the PRI's signatories are based in Europe. The PRI also have more signatories from the Asia Pacific region than from North America. Initially, the PRI did not have a mandatory fee for signatories. However, a fee will be introduced in 2011 (PRI, 2010b, 2010c).

24.4   REVIEW OF EXISTING RESEARCH ON SEE ISSUES IN BANKING[8]

North American academics do not appear to have developed as much interest as their European counterparts in the professional initiatives surrounding SEE issues in banking. The vast majority of existing academic studies originate from Europe. Despite the geographical homogeneity in contributions to the literature, no cohesive literature on SEE issues in banking has developed. Consequently, in the review which follows, we had to collect studies from various corners of the academic sphere. The current incoherence of the literature is reflected in the lack of any previous literature review on the area, and in a low citation density between the studies published in the area. With this review, we aim to provide a synthesis of, and context to, existing work in order to bring some coherence to the literature.

We began our review process by searching the Web of Knowledge database and Google Scholar for academic literature using various combinations of search words describing SEE issues in banking. Subsequently, we checked all the references to, and citations of, the identified studies. Finally, we excluded all studies from our review which do not appear to be relevant, reliable and rigorously conducted. While we cannot reject the possibility that we have excluded a suitable study from our review, we are confident that our final sample of 24 studies represents a good approximation of the current population of relevant, reliable and rigorous academic studies on SEE issues in banking.

We categorize our 24 studies in the following four areas: (1) problems of, or with, SEE issues in banking; (2) opportunities of, or with, SEE issues in banking; (3) analysis of the SEE considerations and views of banks; and (4) effects of the consideration of SEE issues in banking. Table 24.1 provides a summary of the studies across each of these four categories. The remainder of this section provides a general review of this literature.

24.4.1   Problems of or with SEE Issues in Banking

Brown and Whysall (2010) explore the discrepancy between the notions that, on the one hand, the UK financial services industry is world class and that, on the other hand, its performance in peer reputation surveys is weak. The two authors posed their research question in winter of 2008–2009, but subsequently observed real world events to explain this discrepancy, when the fallout from the financial crisis severely damaged the reputation of the UK financial services industry. The financial crisis is also the main focus of Weitzner and Darroch's (2009) theoretical discussion. These authors argue that the financial crisis with its shadow banking system and opaque products was caused in part by human greed. They consider this especially problematic, since greed-motivated shadow systems and opaque financial services would be especially difficult to govern at the market and institutional level. Unfortunately, though, the authors leave their argument at the stage of a theoretical assertion, and do not support or test it with empirical data.

The lack of transparency of financial institutions is identified by Schrader (2006) with regard to SEE issues based on a 'mystery shopping' approach. Schrader finds that the majority of German financial advisors of large retail banks display no initiative in offering ethical investment products to (self-declared) ethically and environmentally concerned mystery shoppers. In fact, 19 per cent of the advisors even (falsely) deny the existence of ethical funds in their institution's portfolio. Due to such problems with the affinity of financial advisors and clients, Cowton (2002, 2010) welcomes new banking philosophies (such as those promoted by Triodos Bank), which aim to align more closely the values and characteristics of depositors and borrowers. Cowton also emphasizes the importance of integrity and responsibility in banking. Integrity is commonly a prerequisite of trust, and as such a minimum of integrity can be viewed as a necessary condition for a functioning banking system. Responsible behaviour of banks and bankers is simply necessary due to the enormous consequences which their actions can have for the global society, as illustrated by the recent financial crisis. For instance, the total cost of capital misallocations and other mistakes made in the global financial crisis, in part due to irresponsible behaviour, has been estimated to be around \$2.3 trillion (IMF, 2010).[9]

Table 24.1 Overview on existing research on SEE issues in banking

Study	Research question/task	Data	Method	Findings
Panel (i): Problems of/with SEE issues in banking				
Brown and Whysall (2010)	Exploration of the pre-credit crisis discrepancy in Britain's financial services being externally promoted as world class despite performing weakly on a peer reputation survey	Descriptive statistics	Theoretical discussion	The credit crisis is used to clarify the discrepancy with the peer reputation surveys being considered more accurate than the external promotion
Cowton (2002, 2010)	Exploration of ethical issues in banking with special focus on integrity, responsibility and affinity	Anecdotal evidence	Theoretical discussion	Author argues that integrity is a prerequisite of trust and as such a minimum of integrity is a necessary condition for a functioning banking system. Responsibility is relevant in current banking due to the enormous consequences which banking practices and problems can have on society and natural environment. Affinity relates to new banking practices offered for instance by Triodos and Islamic Banks to bring depositors and borrowers into a closer association to align their values and characteristics.
Schrader (2006)	Analysis of the transparency of ethical investment product offerings by large retail banks	21 mystery shopping consultations at 7 large retail banks in the area of Hannover, Germany	Mystery shopping	Study finds the majority of German financial advisors of large retail banks to display no initiative in offering an explicitly ethically and environmentally concerned mystery shopper existing ethical investment products in their financial institution's portfolio. 19% of the advisors even falsely denied

438

				the existence of ethical funds in their institution's portfolio
Weitzner and Darroch (2009)	Exploration of the relationship between greed and governance failures in financial markets and institutions	Anecdotal evidence	Theoretical discussion	Authors argue that '[t]he development of the shadow banking system and opaque products was motivated in part by greed. These developments made governance at both the institutional and market levels extremely difficult, if not impossible. In part the findings are limited by the current opacity of the markets and the dynamics of events.'

Panel (ii): Opportunities of/with SEE issues in banking

Argandoña (2009)	(1) Does the credit crisis have an ethical component? (2) Does ethics help to explain the crisis? (3) Could ethical actions have helped to avert the crisis?	Anecdotal evidence	Theoretical discussion	Study argues that 'the generalized [ethically based] practice of corporate social responsibility within financial institutions could have helped to reduce the magnitude of the crisis, perhaps not systematically but definitely in some organizations that have been most affected by the crisis.'
Coulson (2009)	Exploration of how banks might be able to contribute to environmental governance	Anecdotal evidence	Theoretical discussion	The author argues that banks should contribute to environmental governance by committing to the precautionary principle
Scholtens (2006)	Discussion of the transition mechanisms between finance and sustainability	Descriptive statistics	Theoretical discussion	Study argues that besides the potential pressures of public shareholders on corporations to support a sustainable development, these pressures could also come from private equity investors and banks (through their lending and project financing activities).

Table 24.1 (continued)

Study	Research question/task	Data	Method	Findings
Panel (iii): Analysis of the SEE considerations/views of banks				
Cowton and Thompson (2000)	Investigation of differences between banks which signed the UNEP FII Statement by Banks on the Environment & Sustainable Development and those which did not	57 survey responses from banks, of which 20 signed the UNEP FII Statement	Questionnaire	Study finds that signatories of UNEP FII Statement give more importance to environmental issues but this difference in importance is only significant for a few issues (e.g., usage of cleaner technologies, belief in sustainable development)
de la Cuesta-González et al. (2006)	Analysis of the CSR performance of Spanish banks	Four large Spanish banks (BBVA, SCH, Bankinter and B.Popular), whose joint market value represents over 30% of the IBEX 35	Index construction	Paper finds that the CSR performance of the four Spanish banks (especially BBVA and SCH) is relatively poor compared with banks from other countries.
Decker and Sale (2009)	Exploration of the understanding of and approach to CSR in financial institutions	6 individuals from financial institutions	Interviews	Authors suggest that financial institutions are motivated to engage in CSR to generate trust and manage reputational and regulatory risks
Hortacsu and Gunay (2008)	Exploration of the ethical views of bank managers	Convenience based sample of 32 Turkish bank managers	Questionnaire	Study finds managers to generally condemn illegal issues like bribery or corruption as unethical. Abuse of confidential information is also mainly considered unethical, while bankers are divided in their views on the ethicality of abuse of trust.

Study	Purpose	Data	Method	Findings
O'Sullivan and O'Dwyer (2009)	Exploration of the initiation and evolution of the Equator Principles especially focusing on issues of legitimacy	(1) Interviews with individuals from 9 NGOs within the BankTrack network (2) Informal discussions with individuals related to UNEP FI	In-depth interviews	Study argues that NGOs were a major force in the development of the Equator Principles but were subsequently disappointed about their implementation by many signatories.
Peneda Saraiva and Silva Serrasqueiro (2007)	Analysis of the supply of non-financial information on financial products offered in Portugal	32 Portuguese financial institutions	Questionnaire	Study finds only about a third of all financial institutions to provide social or environmental information on their financial products to their clients
Scholtens (2009)	Development of a framework to rate international banks' CSR performance	29 indicators of CSR in banking applied to 32 banks from 15 countries	Index construction	Study finds CSR performance of international banks to improve in general and in most indicators between 2000 and 2005
Statman (2004)	Comparison of society's and financial market's notion of fairness	Anecdotal evidence	Theoretical discussion	Paper argues that most financial market participants have free market understanding of fairness, which allows any business transaction 'regardless of excess, folly, or distance from the legal line', while only sufficiently socially responsible businesses meet society's notion of fairness.
Thompson and Cowton (2004)	Exploration of environmental considerations in bank lending decisions	57 survey responses from banks	Questionnaire	Study finds that environmental criteria are integrated in lending decisions predominantly as a means to manage risk. Ethical ideals, sustainable development concerns or bank image appear of secondary relevance in the decision to integrate environmental criteria in bank lending decisions in the mid-1990s.

Table 24.1 (continued)

Study	Research question/task	Data	Method	Findings
Panel (iii): Analysis of the SEE considerations/views of banks				
Weber et al. (2008)	Analysis of the integration of environmental risks into all phases of the credit risk management (rating, costing, pricing, monitoring and work-out)	50 European banks, of which 25 signed the UNEP FI statement	Questionnaire	Study finds that environmental risk is integrated by the vast majority of banks in rating stage. A majority of banks also include it in the monitoring and work-out stage. The consideration of environmental risks is significantly higher for signatories of the UNEP FI statement
Wright and Rwabizambuga (2006)	Exploration of why financial institutions signed the Equator Principles	Descriptive statistics	Theoretical discussion	Authors argue that financial institutions mainly signed the Equator Principles to signal 'devices for demonstrating positive credentials, with the aim of strengthening corporate reputation and organizational legitimacy'. They support their argument by indicating that signatories of Equator Principles are based (i) in countries with high political, civil and human rights, which tend to value CSR reputation more, and (ii) in countries with BankTrack NGOs pressuring banks to demonstrate organizational legitimacy.

Panel (iv): Effects of the consideration of SEE issues in banking

Callado-Muñoz and Utrero-Gonzalez (2011)	Analysis of 'the effects of CSR on the competitive outcome in the Spanish mortgage and deposit markets' based on a self-developed theoretical model, which predicts two testable hypotheses: 'Hypothesis 1: Savings banks will have a larger market share (in mortgages and deposits) relative to commercial banks provided that the valuation of CSR practices by consumers is significant'. 'Hypothesis 2: If consumers value CSR practices, interest rates will be less important in consumer decision making.'	Institutional level data on the CSR practices of savings banks and the deposit and mortgage granting activities of savings banks and commercial banks from 1999 to 2004 categorized by Spanish province	(1) Theoretical model (2) Numerous empirical analyses including an instrumental variable estimation and generalized method of moments estimation of their panel dataset as well as a simultaneous equation approach	Hypothesis 1 is mainly supported. The study finds that deposit consumers value CSR relating to cultural, environment and heritage activities, while mortgage consumers only value cultural CSR activities. Leisure, health, education and R&D related CSR activities do not appear to be significantly valued by consumers. Hypothesis 2 is also supported, as deposit or mortgage decisions do not appear to be significantly impacted by differences in real interest rates.
Hoepner et al. (2010)	Analysis of the effect of CSR on stock returns in the financial services industry	Sample of 43 financial institutions which were listed at least once among the 100 most sustainable companies announced at the World Economic Forum between 2005 and 2009	Carhart model based on financial services industry equities controlled for country effects	Paper finds the stock return of a portfolio of the most sustainable financial institutions to be insignificantly different from the industry benchmark.

443

Table 24.1   (continued)

Study	Research question/task	Data	Method	Findings
Panel (iv): Effects of the consideration of SEE issues in banking				
Llewellyn (2005)	Analysis of the reasons behind the higher ROEs of British banks compared with other European banks over the period 1992–2003	Descriptive statistics (no controls for accounting practices etc.)	Case study	Study argues that the stronger shareholder value focus of British banks explains the superior ROEs compared to the more stakeholder value focused European banks
Scholtens and Dam (2007)	Investigation of differences between banks adopting the Equator Principles and those not adopting them	87 banks involved in project financing, of which 31 adopted the Equator Principles	(1) t-tests for the comparison characteristics of adopters and non-adopters (2) Event study of the effect of signing the Equator Principles	(1) Adopters are found to be larger and experience a somewhat higher systematic risk than non-adopters. Adopters' accounting performance measures are worse, while their average daily stock return is significantly higher. Adopters display a significantly higher CSR performance in terms of stakeholder and environmental variables, while adopters' corporate governance ratings are higher but not at a statistically significant level. (2) Banks' share prices show no significant reaction to the adoption of the Equator Principles.

Shen and Chang (Chapter 25 in this volume)	Analysis of the relationship between CSR and financial performance of Taiwanese banks	Quarterly data for Taiwanese Stock Exchange listed banks 01/2002–06/2006	Comparison of CSR banks with matched non-CSR banks based on five different matching methods	Authors observe no significant difference between CSR and non-CSR banks
Simpson and Kohers (2002)	Analysis of the link between corporate social and financial performance in the banking industry	Community Reinvestment Act ratings and financial data for 385 US banks in 1993–94	Cross-sectional regression analysis	The study finds banks with a better Community Reinvestment Act rating to have a significantly higher ROA and significantly lower loan losses

Note: This table provides a structured overview on existing academic research on social, environmental and ethical (SEE) issues in banking. We attempt to provide structured information on each relevant and reliable study in the area, although we can, of course, not claim this table to be exhaustive. We categorize studies according to four topics: (1) Problems of/with SEE issues in banking; (2) Opportunities of/with SEE issues in banking; (3) Analysis of the SEE considerations/views of banks; (4) Effects of the consideration of SEE issues in banking. We associated one study with only one topic for space reasons but we acknowledge that some studies could have been allocated to several topics. Column one display the study information, whereby additional information on each study can be found in our reference list. The second column displays the research question(s) or research task(s) of a study, which relate to SEE issues in banking. Columns three and four present a brief description of the most advanced data source(s) and method(s) employed in the respective study. Column five gives a short overview on a study's findings.

Hortacsu and Gunay (2008) concur with Cowton regarding the importance of integrity and responsibility in banking. They nicely summarize the point as follows:

> The fiduciary dimension of the banking business creates a high potential for ethical violations and financial fraud leading to systemic crisis, regardless of national boundaries . . . The moral integrity of bank managers, as guardians of others' money, is crucial to the sustainability of the system. (Hortacsu and Gunay, 2008: 121)

24.4.2   Opportunities of or with SEE Issues in Banking

Argandoña (2009) discusses the very topical issue of ethics in the financial crisis. He asks whether the unethical behaviour of bankers can help to explain the financial crisis, and if more ethical behaviour could have at least mitigated the financial crisis to some degree. Based on a narrative theoretical exploration of these aforementioned questions, he arrives at the view that a stronger focus on an ethically based practice of corporate social responsibility (CSR) within financial institutions would have mitigated the financial crisis for three reasons. Firstly, CSR could have helped to prevent some unethical banking practices. Secondly, a wider practice of CSR within the financial services industry could have created a more long-term-focused and responsible business climate. Thirdly, CSR generally increases the level of trust in the business community. Since trust is one of the most valuable commodities for business, especially during crisis, CSR as a trust generator might have made a considerable difference.

Coulson (2009) and Scholtens (2006) discuss how banks can make positive contributions to a sustainable economic and environmental development through the consideration of SEE issues. Coulson (2009) argues that banks could mitigate many environmental problems if they would commit to the precautionary principle[10] in their lending activities. Scholtens (2006) suggests that banks, like public shareholders, could use their power to pressure corporations to apply more long-term sustainable business practices.

In common with large insurers and pension funds, many banks have large and diversified investment portfolios.[11] Consequently, the overall performance of the world's equity markets affects their investment return more than the performance of a small group of companies within these equity markets. Hence, whenever there are conflicts of interest between an individual company's short-term performance and the long-term performance of the world's equity markets (e.g., because individual companies are externalizing risks on the system), the interests of the overall equity market should be more relevant for most banks than individual interests. Consequently, banks have an incentive to lobby policymakers to develop and implement economic policies focusing on sustainable long-term growth instead of short-term profit maximization, since the latter can overheat economies and expose them to hidden long-term risks, as seen in the recent financial crisis (Hawley and Williams, 2000; Mattison et al., 2010).

24.4.3   Analysis of the SEE Considerations and Views of Banks

This subsection reviews the degree and the drivers of SEE considerations in the banking industry. Statman (2004) argues that bankers have a free market notion of fairness. He provides several examples to suggest that this notion allows any business transaction independently of its ethical implications or even its distance from the legal line. Society, however, has a more ethically inspired and even time-varying notion of fairness, which bankers need to understand to manage cash flow, reputation and legal risks. Hence, following Statman's view, banks would be expected to sign any SEE initiative for legitimizing reasons, but subsequently show a half-hearted commitment to implementation. This suggestion has been investigated with regard to the Equator Principles and the UNEP FI statement.

O'Sullivan and O'Dwyer's (2009) interviews with non-governmental organizations (NGOs) in the BankTrack network confirm this suggestion in the authors' view.[12] They argue that NGO activity was a major force in the development of the Equator Principles but that NGOs were disappointed with the subsequent implementation by many signatories. Wright and Rwabizambuga (2006) extend this argument. They illustrate a close relationship between the home countries of the campaigning NGOs and the signatories of the Equator Principles which does not appear to exist in the same form for the non-signatories. Consequentially, they conclude that organizational legitimacy is one driver for financial institutions to sign the Equator Principles. However, they also consider a second driver by comparing the home countries of signatories with the home countries of non-signatories. They find that signatories tend to be based in countries with higher political, civil and human rights. In those countries, consumers have more opportunities to express their views, which should make CSR reputation more beneficial. Decker and Sale's (2009) interviews lead them to complement this view that financial institutions use CSR to generate trust and manage reputational and regulatory risks.

With respect to bank lending decisions, Thompson and Cowton (2004) find that banks integrate SEE issues not so much to generate legitimacy or reputation, but simply to manage risks. Their survey finds that environmental criteria are integrated into lending decisions predominantly for risk management purposes. Ethical ideals, sustainable development concerns or bank image appear secondary to the surveyed bankers. In an earlier study of the same survey, the two authors find that signatories of the UNEP FII statement generally valued environmental issues higher than did non-signatories, but the difference was only significant for a few environmental issues (such as the use of cleaner energy) (Cowton and Thompson, 2000). Weber et al. (2008) offer more convincing results. They find signatories of the UNEP FI statement, the successor of the UNEP FII statement, to have a significantly higher incorporation of environmental risks in the credit risk management process. Similarly, Scholtens and Dam (2007) find signatories of the Equator Principles to have significantly better environmental and social performance ratings than non-signatories.

Scholtens (2009) also observes positive tendencies with respect to the overall CSR performance of international banks, which he finds to have improved on average and in the vast majority of individual indicators between 2000 and 2005. Weber et al. (2008) confirm this result, as they find the majority of European banks in their survey to have incorporated environmental risks in the rating, monitoring and work-out stage of their credit risk management process. De la Cuesta-González et al. (2006) and Peneda Saraiva and Silva Serrasqueiro (2007) find less positive results but these are limited to Iberian banks.

24.4.4   Effects of the Consideration of SEE Issues in Banking

The effects of SEE issues on banks have been largely unexplored to date. Llewellyn (2005) argues that the higher returns on equity (ROEs) of British banks compared to their European counterparts between 1992 and 2003 can be explained by the higher shareholder value focus of British banks. This argument (which is unfortunately not supported by any in-depth empirical analysis) implies that the consideration of SEE issues might have negative consequences for the financial performance of banks. Five studies have conducted robust and reliable empirical analysis of the relationship between the social and financial performance of banks to date (November 2010).

Simpson and Kohers (2002) analyse Community Reinvestment Act ratings of 385 US banks over the period 1993–1994. They find that a better rating leads to significantly higher returns on assets (ROAs) and significantly lower loan losses. More recently, Scholtens and Dam (2007) conduct an event study of banks signing the Equator Principles to explore whether the adoption of these principles has a significant effect on share price performance. The authors fail to find any significant relationship between social and financial performance. Similarly, Shen and Chang (Chapter 25 in this volume), using quarterly data covering the period 2002–2006, fail to find any convincing effect of CSR on financial performance of Taiwanese banks. Hoepner et al. (2010) analyse the financial performance effects of CSR across ten main industry sectors using industry-specific Carhart (1997) models with country controls.[13] While they can find significantly positive effects in other industries (e.g., healthcare), they do not observe any significant effect of CSR on the stock performance of financial institutions.

Rather than analysing the direct effect of CSR on financial performance, Callado-Muñoz and Utrero-Gonzalez (2011) investigate the effect of CSR on financial institutions' competitive outcomes in the deposit and mortgage markets. They develop a theoretical model from which they derive two testable hypotheses. First, they hypothesize that the more socially responsible Spanish savings banks will have larger market shares than less socially responsible commercial banking counterparts, if consumers significantly value CSR. Second, they assume that under the condition that consumers value CSR, interest rates will be less relevant to consumer decision-making. Based on a Spanish dataset from 1999 to 2004 and numerous advanced statistical analyses, they find their first hypothesis to be supported. Specifically, depositors appear to experience a significant value from CSR activities relating to cultural, environmental and heritage activities, while mortgage borrowers at least significantly value culturally related CSR. The second hypothesis also seems supported, since Spanish consumers' deposit and mortgage decisions do not appear to be significantly influenced by differences in real interest rates. Hence, it might be difficult for academics to identify significant effects on a bank's overall financial performance from the integration of SEE issues in banking activities (simply due to too much noise). However, banks considering SEE issues might experience significant effects on individual competitive outcomes.

24.5   TRUST IN BANKING AND THE FINANCIAL CRISIS

From late 2006, problems in the US residential mortgage market led to an increased number of foreclosures and defaults leading to the decline of the value of the securities backed by such assets (Gerardi et al., 2009).[14] The complex nature of the asset-backed (and other) securities and the lack of transparency of the banks' off-balance-sheet vehicles made it nearly impossible to value such assets (Bailey et al., 2008). Holders of investments backed by subprime mortgages did not know what they were worth, and banks became wary of lending to each other because they also did not know the extent of losses held in structured credit vehicles. Declines in property prices led to further declines in the value of securitized mortgage products and bank loan books (Foote et al., 2008). All in all, this culminated in a liquidity freeze in interbank markets and the subsequent credit crunch (Crouhy et al., 2008).

As the meltdown in financial markets continued, banking sector traumas were experienced around the globe. The financial crisis led to large losses and failure and closure of many banks, and forced the intervention of both central banks and governments around the world. Short-term responses have been manifold and included: government purchase of distressed assets; changes in rules surrounding assets accepted as collateral; nationalization or part nationalization of financial institutions which were thought 'too big to fail'; and increased government guarantees of consumer deposits and bank liabilities. Poor monetary policies, misaligned incentives for investors, banks and credit rating agencies, poor disclosure, accounting rules, lax lending standards and loopholes in regulation and supervision, and fraud have all been cited as contributory factors to the ongoing financial crisis.[15]

Governments around the world have responded with a variety of policies aimed at improving disclosure and transparency and reducing the potential for moral hazard via the safety nets instituted by government agencies.[16] Specific action has been taken, such as: extension of coverage of bank regulation based on economic substance rather than legal form; increased capital requirements; countercyclical capital requirements; enhanced regulation and supervision of liquidity; enhanced supervision of credit rating agencies; codes covering executive pay and benefits; improved arrangements for regulation of the activities of cross-border banks; reform of accounting disclosure rules; and the establishment of consumer protection agencies.[17]

There has been an erosion of trust between banks themselves (evidenced by the freeze of the interbank markets in 2008); between banks and investors (marked by episodes of market participants short-selling shares of financial institutions); and between banks and their customers (evidenced by the dramatic depositor run on Northern Rock and then later on a number of other financial institutions).[18]

In recent years, economists have begun to explore whether any link can be established between trust and (individual or aggregate) economic performance.[19] To measure trust, a number of sources have been used including the World Values Survey and the European Social Survey.[20] Respondents are asked general questions of the form: 'Generally speaking, would you say that most people can be trusted, or that you can't be too careful in dealing with people?' Trust is measured using some form of scale with responses ranging from no trust to full trust.

A number of studies have examined whether there is a link between trust and economic performance. For example, Knack and Keefer (1997), using a dataset comprising

29 countries covering the period 1980–1992, find a positive link between the level of trust and gross domestic product (GDP) growth. Guiso et al. (2008) use a sample of 1943 Dutch households as part of the annual Dutch National Bank Household survey, to assess whether there is a link between trust and stock market participation. The authors find that stock market participation is lower where the corresponding level of trust is low. In order to test for whether there is trust in institutions, they augment their analysis with a second dataset comprising 1834 bank customers of a large bank in Italy. In this survey customers were asked: 'How much do you trust your bank official or broker as financial advisor for your investment decisions?' The authors find that a lack of trust in the bank affects individual decisions to invest in risky assets. Guiso et al. (2009) use survey data compiled by Eurobarometer covering the period 1970 to 2005 and find a positive relationship between the level of bilateral trust and the extent of trade between countries. Butler et al. (2009) utilize European Social Survey data (from 2004 and 2005), and find an inverted U-shaped relationship between trust and individual income. The authors also find, unsurprisingly, that there is a positive relationship between an individual's level of trust and the probability of being cheated when buying goods and services. This appears to be particularly acute in banking (compared to other goods and services such as food, second-hand goods, plumbing and repairs). Finally using a subsample of immigrants, the authors find some evidence that individuals moving from low-trust to high-trust countries are much less likely to be cheated than their counterparts moving from high-trust to low-trust countries.

Economists have also begun to look explicitly at trust in financial services. A good example of this is the Financial Trust Index Survey (FTIS). The FTIS was designed by Luigi Guiso, Paola Sapienza and Luigi Zingales, and conducted by the University of Chicago and North Western University. The survey comprises a telephone survey on a representative sample of about 1000 US households. The households are asked questions relating to: trust in financial institutions and markets; investment intentions and expectations; and views on the underlying causes and effectiveness of government policies during and since the global financial crisis. The first survey took place in December 2008. Surveys have since been conducted at a quarterly frequency. The results of the first seven stages (or waves) are now available along with a detailed commentary written by Sapienza and Zingales.[21] These results provide us with invaluable information as to the extent and evolution of trust in banking. Guiso (2010) utilizes the results of the first seven waves of the FTIS to assess the evolution of trust in financial institutions during this financial crisis. He finds a collapse of trust, which is linked to the emergence of frauds and scandals (such as the recent Madoff scandal) in the financial services industry. This collapse in trust has led to investors switching towards safer portfolios. He argues that switching behaviour could have serious implications for the availability and cost of credit to both businesses and households. He suggests that reforms (including a ratings system to measure the trustworthiness of financial institutions, and the creation of a financial services consumer protection agency) are required to restore trust in financial institutions and markets.

Knell and Stix (2009) utilize household survey data to assess whether trust in banks declined during the financial crisis, and if so, what factors determine the level of trust (mistrust) in banks. The authors employ a dataset drawn from a series of quarterly surveys conducted by the Austrian National Bank between 2004 and 2009. These data provide information about evolution of trust in banks over time and compared with other institutions. The authors observe high levels of consumer trust in banks that is comparable to other institutions such as the police force and the central banks. In fact, around 65 per cent of consumers still maintained high levels of trust in banks even at the height of the financial crisis.

Overall, the evidence presented in this section suggests that trust is of the utmost importance in banking, and in individual and aggregate economic performance more generally. By extension, trust is likely to influence the behaviour of both depositors and investors, and ultimately have implications for financial stability. Consequently, further research is required to understand the linkages between trust, contagion, financial stability and the design, implementation and enforcement of prudential regulation.

24.6 SUMMARY

To the best of our knowledge, this chapter provides the first overview on social, environmental, ethical and trust (SEET) issues in banking. The interest in social and environmental issues (particularly climate change) in banking has experienced rapid growth in 2000–2009. Ethical and trust issues have also gained attention during the recent global financial crisis. The importance of SEET issues in banking is illustrated by a number of international initiatives such as the United Nations Environment Programme Finance Initiative, the Equator Principles and the United Nations Principles for Responsible Investment that have promoted a sustainable economic and social development agenda. The rate of adoption of these initiatives (especially the PRI) by banks and other financial institutions has increased in recent years, and is likely to continue to do so.

A structured literature review highlights the importance of social, environmental and ethical issues for the risk management, reputation and performance of banks and other financial institutions. Finally, we discuss the relevance of consumer trust especially for banking, and the degree to which the recent global financial crisis led to an erosion of consumer trust in banks in some parts of the world. Consequently, given the increased relevance of especially trust and environmental changes (brought about by climate change), we conclude that our overview is timely and relevant for academics, policymakers and practitioners alike.

NOTES

*   We are very grateful to Jim Barth, Barbara Casu, Andreas Lehnert, Bert Scholtens and Raj Thamotheram for comments. We also thank Natalie Beinisch at the Principles for Responsible Investment (PRI) for information provision. Any remaining errors or omissions are the sole responsibility of the authors. The views expressed in this chapter are not necessarily shared by the Principles for Responsible Investment.
1.   In the words of the United Nations Millennium Ecosystem Assessment (2005: 5) the decline of two-thirds of the natural capital assets provided by nature to humanity is '[i]n many cases .. literally a matter of living on borrowed time'.
2.   A detailed treatment of the recent financial crisis is beyond the scope of this chapter. Brunnermeier (2009) and Barth (2009) provide an excellent overview of the crisis, while Goddard et al. (2009a, 2009b) and Petrovic and Tutsch (2009) provide a detailed treatment of policy interventions taken by governments in Europe to stabilize the banking system.

3. A number of papers and reports have proposed new forms of micro- and macro-prudential regulation to restore and maintain the stability of the financial system. The most comprehensive to date are the Stern School volumes edited by Acharya and Richardson (2009) and Acharya et al. (2010), and the Centre for Economic Policy Studies (CEPS) Report produced by Carmassi et al. (2010). Stephanou (2010) discusses a number of ways in which the market can be used by supervisors to assess bank risk and discipline the activities of bank managers. Explicit discussions of ethics in banking are rather scarce. Kane (1977, 2010) provides a welcome exception to provide an extensive discussion of ethical dimensions related to bank regulation and supervision.

4. We separate the discussion of SEE issues and trust into two sections, since the latter is inherently linked to the recent financial crisis, while the former issues have generally gained in importance over the last decade.

5. We use 'climate change' as search term for environmental issues, since terms like 'environment', 'sustainability' or 'green' are ambiguous and climate change is the dominant environmental issue of 2000–2009.

6. We approximate the attention to trust in banking by searching for the keywords 'bank' and 'fear'. We search for 'fear' as an antithesis to trust, since the term 'trust' is ambiguous (e.g., unit trust) and its synonyms (e.g., confidence) are too much part of a general not necessarily trust-related business language.

7. For smaller initiatives, see Peters (2003).

8. We concentrate in this and the next section on research directly focused on SEET issues in banking. For discussion of research on related areas such as microfinance, credit unions, responsible investment and Islamic banking and finance, see Cull et al. (2009), McKillop et al. (2010), Hoepner and McMillan (2009), Beck et al. (2010), Čihák and Hesse (2010) and Hoepner et al. (forthcoming), respectively.

9. This is somewhat reduced from a previous estimate of $2.8 trillion (IMF, 2009).

10. The precautionary principle essentially represents a risk management approach. It reads as follows: 'When an activity raises threats of harm to human health or the environment, precautionary measures should be taken even if some cause and effect relationships are not fully established scientifically' (Wingspread Conference on the Precautionary Principle, 1998: 1).

11. Boot and Thakor (2010) provide an excellent discussion of the increasing integration of banks in capital markets.

12. For more information on the BankTrack network, see http://www.banktrack.org/.

13. By estimating stock return data based on industry-specific Carhart models with country controls, Hoepner et al. (2010) investigate the effect which CSR has on shareholder value directly, instead of the effect which it has on an indicator of corporate financial performance that might to some degree transform into shareholder value (e.g., ROA, ROE, Tobin's Q). The industry specifications, Carhart model control variables and country controls ensure hereby that all known stocks return drivers are ruled out as alternative explanations of any observed effect.

14. Recent evidence suggests, however, that mortgage defaults and property foreclosures were much lower in US states which had passed anti-predatory lending laws (Ding et al., 2011). Other studies assessing the importance of anti-predatory lending laws on the type, availability and costs of mortgage credit are reviewed in Bostic et al. (2008) and Durkin and Elliehausen (2010).

15. Mian and Sufi (2009) note that mortgage credit expansion and income growth are negatively correlated in the run-up to the subprime crisis, and that this coincided with an increase in securitization of subprime mortgages. Keys et al. (2010) use a large dataset of securitized loan contracts to examine whether the securitization process reduces the incentives of financial intermediaries to screen borrowers carefully. They find that securitized portfolios of mortgages default more than a similar risk portfolio with a lower probability of securitization. Subsequently, they conclude that securitization does adversely affect the screening incentives of lenders. In a companion study the authors find that more heavily regulated institutions and those that retain a portion of securitized assets have greater incentives to screen borrowers (Keys et al., 2009). Igan et al. (2009) find that lobbying by financial institutions may have contributed to the financial crisis. Specifically, they find that lenders lobbying more on specific issues related to mortgage lending originated mortgages with higher loan-to-income ratios and securitized loans at a rapid rate. This suggests that lobbying may be linked to lenders expecting favourable regulatory treatment. For a general overview of the evolution of the subprime mortgage market in the US and the subsequent increase in mortgage defaults, see Chomsisengphet and Pennington-Cross (2006) and Mayer et al. (2009). For a method for testing for fraud in the mortgage market, see Carrillo (2009). For an excellent analysis of the political economy of the subprime mortgage expansion and subsequent defaults, see Mian et al. (2010). Finally, Barth and Landsman (2010) and Laux and Leuz (2010) provide a detailed discussion of the extent to which fair value accounting rules contributed to the crisis.

16. Kane (1977, 2010) contends that the regulation and supervision of the banking industry is a repeated game of move and counter-move, with government agencies inevitably playing catch-up with the banks they are charged with regulating.

17. The Consumer Financial Protection Agency Act of 2009 established the Consumer Financial Protection

Agency as an independent executive agency to regulate the provision of consumer financial products and services in the US.
18. The trustworthiness of banks plays an important role in the demand for financial services, given that financial products can be classified as credence services. A credence good or service is one whose quality cannot easily be assessed before or after consumption, because a judgement about quality requires the consumer to have specialized knowledge of the product or service (Darby and Karni, 1973). Bucks and Pence (2006) find that borrowers with less income or education seem especially likely not to understand the terms of their mortgage contracts and the implications for repayments should interest rates increase.
19. Glaeser et al. (2000), Sapienza et al. (2007) and Fehr (2009) each provide excellent discussions and over-views of a wide range of issues related to how to measure and understand trust. The inspiration of much of this work lies with Arrow (1972).
20. Details of the World Values Survey can be found at http://www.worldvaluessurvey.org/, while details of the European Social Survey can be found at http://www.europeansocialsurvey.org/.
21. The results of seven surveys and associated discussions are available at http://www.financialtrustindex.org/results.htm.

REFERENCES

Acharya, V., T.F. Cooley, M. Richardson and I. Walter (2010), *Real Time Solutions for US Financial Reform*, New York: Stern School of Business.
Acharya, V. and M. Richardson (eds) (2009), *Restoring Financial Stability: How to Repair a Failed System?* New York: John Wiley & Sons.
Argandoña, A. (2009), 'Can corporate social responsibility help us understand the credit crisis?', Working Paper, IESE Business School, University of Navarra, available at http://www.iese.edu/research/pdfs/DI-0790-E.pdf.
Arrow, K. (1972), 'Gifts and exchanges', *Philosophy and Public Affairs*, **1**, 343–362.
Bailey, M., D. Elmendorf and R. Litan (2008), *The Great Credit Squeeze: How It Happened, How to Prevent Another*, Washington, DC: Brooking Institution.
Barkemeyer, R., F. Figge and A.G.F. Hoepner (2010), 'Sustainability-related media coverage in 41 countries: regional-level patterns or a North/South divide?', Working Paper, Queen's University Management School.
Barnett, M.L. (2007), 'Stakeholder influence capacity and the variability of financial returns to corporate social responsibility', *Academy of Management Review*, **32**(3), 794–816.
Barth, J. (2009), *The Rise and Fall of the US Mortgage and Credit Markets*, Washington, DC: Milken Institute.
Barth, M.E. and W. Landsman (2010), 'How did financial reporting contribute to the financial crisis?', *European Accounting Review*, **19**, 399–423.
Becchetti, L., R. Ciciretti and I. Hasan (2009), 'Corporate social responsibility and shareholder's value: an event study analysis', Federal Reserve Bank of Atlanta Working Paper 2007-6, available at http://papers.ssrn.com/sol3/papers.cfm?abstract_id=928557#PaperDownload.
Beck, T., A. Demirgüç-Kunt and O. Merrouche (2010), 'Islamic vs. conventional banking: business model, efficiency and stability', World Bank Policy Research Working Paper 5446.
Boot, A.W.A. and A. Thakor (2010), 'The accelerating integration of banks and markets and its implications for regulation', in A.N. Berger, P. Molyneux and J.O.S. Wilson (eds), *Oxford Handbook of Banking*, Oxford: Oxford University Press.
Bostic, R.W., K.C. Engel, P.A. McCoy, A. Pennington-Cross and S.M. Wachter (2008), 'The impact of state anti-predatory lending laws: policy implications and insights', *Journal of Economics and Business*, **60**, 47–66.
Brown, M. and P. Whysall (2010), 'Performance, reputation, and social responsibility in the UK's financial services: a post- "credit crunch" interpretation', *Service Industries Journal*, **30**(12), 1991–2006.
Brunnermeier, M.K. (2009), 'Deciphering the liquidity and credit crunch 2007–08', *Journal of Economic Perspectives*, **23**, 77–100.
Bucks, B. and K. Pence (2006), 'Do homeowners know their house value and mortgage terms?', Federal Reserve Board of Governors, Washington, DC.
Butler, J., P. Giuliano and L. Gulso (2009), 'The right amount of trust', Centre for Economic Policy Research Paper Number 7461.
Callado-Muñoz, F.J. and N. Utrero-Gonzalez (2011), 'Does it pay to be socially responsible? Evidence from Spain's retail banking sector', *European Financial Management*, **17**(4), 755–787.
Carhart, M.M. (1997), 'On persistence in mutual fund performance', *Journal of Finance*, **52**(1), 57–82.
Carmassi, J., E. Luchetti and S. Micossi (2010), *Overcoming Too-Big-to-Fail: A Regulatory Framework to Limit Moral Hazard and Free Riding in the Financial Sector*, Brussels: Centre for European Policy Studies.

Carrillo, P. (2009), 'Fools or crooks: testing for fraud in the residential mortgage market', George Washington University Working Paper.

Carroll, A.B. (1999), 'Corporate social responsibility: evolution of a definitional construct', *Business and Society*, **38**(3), 268–295.

Carroll, A.B. and K.M. Shabana (2010), 'The business case for corporate social responsibility: a review of concepts, research and practice', *International Journal of Management Reviews*, **12**(1), 85–105.

Chomsisengphet, S. and A. Pennington-Cross (2006), 'The evolution of the subprime mortgage market', *Federal Reserve Bank of St Louis Review*, **88**, 31–56.

Čihák, M. and H. Hesse (2010), 'Islamic banks and financial stability: an empirical analysis', *Journal of Financial Services Research*, **38**, 95–113.

Coulson, A.B. (2009), 'How should banks govern the environment? Challenging the construction of action versus veto', *Business Strategy and the Environment*, **18**(3), 149–161.

Cowton, C.J. (2002), 'Integrity, responsibility and affinity: three aspects of ethics in banking', *Business Ethics: A European Review*, **11**(4), 393–400.

Cowton, C.J. (2010), 'Banking ethics', Working Paper, Financial Ethics and Governance Research Group, University of Huddersfield, available at http://eprints.hud.ac.uk/6933/1/FEGREG_WP_10-01%5B1%5D.pdf.

Cowton, C.J. and P. Thompson (2000), 'Do codes make a difference? The case of bank lending and the environment', *Journal of Business Ethics*, **24**(2), 165–178.

Crouhy, M.G., R.A. Jarrow and M. Turnbull (2008), 'Insights and analysis of current events: the subprime credit crisis of 2007', *Journal of Derivatives*, **16**, 81–110.

Cull, R., A. Demirgüç-Kunt and J. Murdoch (2009), 'Microfinance meets the market', *Journal of Economic Perspectives*, **23**(1), 167–192.

Darby, M. and E. Karni (1973), 'Free competition and optimal amount of fraud', *Journal of Law and Economics*, **16**, 67–88.

de la Cuesta-González, M., M.J. Munoz-Torres and M.A. Fernández-Izquierdo (2006), 'Analysis of social performance in the Spanish financial industry through public data: a proposal', *Journal of Business Ethics*, **69**(3), 289–304.

Decker, S. and C. Sale (2009), 'An analysis of corporate social responsibility, trust and reputation in the banking profession', in S.O. Idowu and W. Leal Filho (eds), *Professionals' Perspectives of Corporate Social Responsibility*, Heidelberg: Springer.

Ding, L., R.G. Quercia, C.K. Reid and A.M. White (2011), 'State antipredatory lending laws and neighborhood foreclosure rates', *Journal of Urban Affairs*, **33**, 451–467.

Durkin, T. and G.E. Elliehausen (2010), *Truth in Lending: Theory, History and a Way Forward*, New York: Oxford University Press.

The Economist (2006), 'Stern warning', *The Economist* print edition, 2 November, available at http://www.economist.com/opinion/displaystory.cfm?story_id=E1_RTDRNNT.

Equator Principles (2010), 'About the Equator Principles', available at http://www.equator-principles.com/documents/About_the_Equator_Principles.pdf.

Factiva (2010), 'Fast facts about Dow Jones Factiva content', Dow Jones & Company, available at http://factiva.com/sources.asp.

Fehr, E. (2009), 'On the economics and biology of trust', *Journal of the European Economic Association*, **7**, 235–266.

Foote, C.L., K. Gerardi, L. Goeete and P.S. Willen (2008), 'Subprime facts: what (we think) we know about the subprime crisis and what we don't', Federal Reserve Bank of Boston Public Policy Discussion Papers, No. 08-2.

Freshfields Bruckhaus Deringer (2005), 'A legal framework for the integration of environmental, social and governance issues into institutional investment', United Nations Environment Programme Finance Initiative (UNEP FI), available at http://www.unepfi.org/fileadmin/documents/freshfields_legal_resp_20051123.pdf.

Gerardi, K., A. Lehnert, S.M. Sherland and P.S. Willen (2009), 'Making sense of the subprime crisis', *Brookings Papers on Economic Activity*, **2**, 1–61.

Glaeser, E., D. Laibson, J.A. Scheinkman and C.L. Soutter (2000), 'Measuring trust', *Quarterly Journal of Economics*, **115**, 811–846.

Goddard, J., P. Molyneux and J.O.S. Wilson (2009a), 'The financial crisis in Europe: evolution, policy responses and lessons for the future', *Journal of Financial Regulation and Compliance*, **17**, 362–380.

Goddard, J., P. Molyneux and J.O.S. Wilson (2009b), 'The crisis in UK banking: lessons for public policy', *Public Money and Management*, **29**, 276–284.

Griffin, J.J. and J.F. Mahon (1997), 'The corporate social performance and corporate financial performance debate: twenty-five years of incomparable research', *Business and Society*, **36**(1), 5–31.

Guiso, L. (2010), 'A trust-driven financial crisis: implications for the future of financial markets', European University Institute Working Paper ECO2010-07.

Guiso, L., P. Sapienza and L. Zingales (2008), 'Trusting the stock market', *Journal of Finance*, **63**(6), 2557–2600.

Guiso, L., P. Sapienza and L. Zingales (2009), 'Cultural biases in economic exchange?', *Quarterly Journal of Economics*, **124**, 1095–1131.

Hawley, J. and A.T. Williams (2000), *The Rise of Fiduciary Capitalism: How Institutional Investors can Make Corporate America more Democratic*, Philadelphia, PA: University of Pennsylvania Press.

Hoepner, A.G.F. and D.G. McMillan (2009), 'Research on "responsible investment": an influential literature analysis comprising a rating, characterisation, categorisation and investigation', Working Paper, School of Management, University of St Andrews, available at http://papers.ssrn.com/sol3/papers.cfm?abstract_id=1454793.

Hoepner, A.G.F., P.-S. Yu and J. Ferguson (2010), 'Corporate social responsibility across industries: when can who do well by doing good?', Working Paper, School of Management, University of St Andrews, available at http://papers.ssrn.com/sol3/papers.cfm?abstract_id=1284703.

Hoepner, A.G.F., H.G. Rammal and M. Rezec (forthcoming), 'Islamic mutual funds' financial performance and international investment style: evidence from 20 countries', *European Journal of Finance*.

Hortacsu, A. and E.N.O. Gunay (2008), 'Vignettes to identify the ethical domain of an emerging country's banking sector: the experience of Turkey', *Business Ethics: A European Review*, **17**(2), 121–137.

Igan, D., P. Mishra and T. Tressel (2009), 'A fistful of dollars: lobbying and the financial crisis', IMF Working Paper 09/287.

International Monetary Fund (IMF) (2009), *World Economic Outlook, October 2009*, Washington, DC: International Monetary Fund.

International Monetary Fund (IMF) (2010), *World Economic Outlook, April 2010*, Washington, DC: International Monetary Fund.

Kane, E.J. (1977), 'Good intentions and unintended evil: the case against selective credit allocation', *Journal of Money Credit and Banking*, **9**, 55–69.

Kane, E.J. (2010), 'Regulation and supervision: an ethical perspective', in A.N. Berger, P. Molyneux and J.O.S. Wilson (eds), *Oxford Handbook of Banking*, Oxford: Oxford University Press.

Kelly, M. and A. Huhtala (2001), 'The role of the United Nations Environment Programme and the financial services sector', in J.J. Bouma, M. Jeucken and L. Klinkers (eds), *Sustainable Banking: The Greening of Finance*, Sheffield: Greenleaf.

Keys, B., T. Mukherjee, A. Seru and V. Vig (2009), 'Financial regulation and securitization: evidence from subprime loans', *Journal of Monetary Economics*, **56**, 700–720.

Keys, B., T. Mukherjee, A. Seru and V. Vig (2010), 'Did securitisation lead to lax screening? Evidence from subprime loans', *Quarterly Journal of Economics*, **125**, 327–362.

Knack, S. and P. Keefer (1997), 'Does social capital have an economic payoff? A cross-country investigation', *Quarterly Journal of Economics*, **112**, 1251–1288.

Knell, N. and H. Stix (2009), 'Trust in banks? Evidence from normal times and from times of crises', Oesterreichische Nationalbank Working Paper.

Laux, C. and C. Leuz (2010), 'Did fair-value accounting contribute to the financial crisis?', *Journal of Economic Perspectives*, **24**, 93–118.

Llewellyn, D.T. (2005), 'Competition and profitability in European banking: why are British banks so profitable?', *Economic Notes*, **34**(3), 279–311.

MacDonald, D., M. Jeucken, P. Clemens-Hunt and G. Power (2007), 'Principles for responsible investment hit $8 trillion mark on first year anniversary', UN Principles for Responsible Investment, an investor initiative in partnership with UNEP Finance Initiative and the UN Global Compact, available at http://www.unpri.org/media/PRI_media_release_29-04-07.php.

Margolis, J.D. and J.P. Walsh (2003), 'Misery loves companies: rethinking social initiatives by business', *Administrative Science Quarterly*, **48**(2), 268–305.

Maslakovic, M. (2008), 'Fund management 2008', IFSL – International Financial Services London, available at http://www.ifsl.org.uk/upload/CBS_Fund_Management_2008.pdf.

Mattison, R., M. Trevitt, L. van Ast, J. Gifford, N. Mnatsakanian, O. Watson, C. Zimmerman, V. Piani and A.G.F. Hoepner (2010), *Univeral Ownership and Environmental Externalities*, New York: United Nations Environment Programme.

Mayer, C., K. Pence and S. Sherlund (2009), 'The rise in mortgage defaults', *Journal of Economic Perspectives*, **23**, 27–50.

McKillop, D.G., J.O.S. Wilson, C. Brown and K.T. Davis (2010), 'Credit unions: a theoretical and empirical overview', University of St Andrews Working Paper.

Mian, A.R. and A. Sufi (2009), 'The consequences of mortgage credit expansion: evidence from the US mortgage default crisis', *Quarterly Journal of Economics*, **124**, 1449–1496.

Mian, A., A. Sufi and F. Trebbi (2010), 'The political economy of the US mortgage default crisis', *American Economic Review*, **100**, 1967–1998.

Mintzberg, H. (1983), 'The case for corporate social responsibility', *Journal of Business Strategy*, **4**(2), 3–15.

Orlitzky, M., F.L. Schmidt and S.L. Rynes (2003), 'Corporate social and financial performance: a meta-analysis', *Organization Studies*, **24**(3), 403–441.

O'Sullivan, N. and B. O'Dwyer (2009), 'Stakeholder perspectives on a financial sector legitimation process: the case of NGOs and the Equator Principles', *Accounting, Auditing and Accountability Journal*, **22**(4), 553–587.

Peneda Saraiva, P. and Z.M. Silva Serrasqueiro (2007), 'Corporate sustainability in the Portuguese financial institutions', *Social Responsibility Journal*, **3**(2), 82–94.

Peters, H. (2003), 'Sustainable development and the role of the financial world', in L. Hens and B. Nath (eds), *The World Summit on Sustainable Development*, Heidelberg: Springer.

Petrovic, A. and R. Tutsch (2009), 'National rescue measures in response to the current financial crisis', ECB Legal Working Paper no.8.

PRI (2008), 'Signatories to the Principles for Responsible Investment', UN Principles for Responsible Investment, an investor initiative in partnership with UNEP Finance Initiative and the UN Global Compact, available at http://www.unpri.org/signatories/.

PRI (2010a), 'About us', Principles for Responsible Investment, United Nations, available at http://www.unpri.org/about/.

PRI (2010b), 'Become a signatory', UN Principles for Responsible Investment, an investor initiative in partnership with UNEP Finance Initiative and the UN Global Compact, available at http://www.unpri.org/sign/.

PRI (2010c), 'Signatories to the Principles for Responsible Investment', UN Principles for Responsible Investment, an investor initiative in partnership with UNEP Finance Initiative and the UN Global Compact, available at http://www.unpri.org/signatories/.

Sapienza, P., A. Toldra and L. Zingales (2007), 'Understanding trust', National Bureau of Economic Research Working Paper Number 13387.

Scholtens, B. (2006), 'Finance as a driver of corporate social responsibility', *Journal of Business Ethics*, **68**(1), 19–33.

Scholtens, B. (2009), 'Corporate social responsibility in the international banking industry', *Journal of Business Ethics*, **86**(2), 159–175.

Scholtens, B. and L. Dam (2007), 'Banking on the equator: are banks adopting the Equator Principles different from non-adoptors?', *World Development*, **35**(8), 1307–1328.

Schrader, U. (2006), 'Ignorant advice – customer advisory service for ethical investment funds', *Business Strategy and the Environment*, **15**(3), 200–214.

Siegel, D.S. and D.F. Vitaliano (2007), 'An empirical analysis of strategic use of corporate social responsibility', *Journal of Economics and Management Strategy*, **16**(3), 773–792.

Simpson, W.G. and T. Kohers (2002), 'The link between corporate social and financial performance: evidence from the banking industry', *Journal of Business Ethics*, **35**(2), 97–109.

Statman, M. (2004), 'Fairness outside the cocoon', *Financial Analysts Journal*, **60**(6), 34–39.

Stephanou, C. (2010), 'Rethinking market discipline in banking: lessons from the financial crisis', World Bank Policy Research Working Paper, 5227.

Stern, N. (2006), *The Economics of Climate Change. The Stern Review*, Cambridge: Cambridge University Press.

Thompson, P. and C.J. Cowton (2004), 'Bringing the environment into bank lending: implications for environmental reporting', *British Accounting Review*, **36**(2), 197–218.

UNEP FI (1997), 'UNEP statement by financial institutions on the environment and sustainable development', UNEP FI, available at http://www.unepfi.org/fileadmin/statements/fi/fi_statement_en.pdf.

UNEP FI (2009), 'Fiduciary responsibility: legal and practical aspects of integrating environmental, social and governance issue into institutional investment', United Nations Environment Programme Finance Initiative Asset Management Working Group, available at http://www.unepfi.org/fileadmin/documents/fiduciaryII.pdf.

UNEP FI (2010a), 'About UNEP FI', UNEP FI, available at http://www.unepfi.org/about/index.html.

UNEP FI (2010b), 'Background', UNEP FI, available at http://www.unepfi.org/about/background/index.html.

UNEP FI (2010c), 'Our members', UNEP FI, available at http://www.unepfi.org/signatories/index.html?&no_cache=1.

United Nations Millennium Ecosystem Assessment (2005), 'Living beyond our means: natural assets and human well-being', United Nations, available at http://www.millenniumassessment.org/documents/document.429.aspx.pdf.

Wackernagel, M., N.B. Schulz, D. Deumling, A. Callejas Linares, M. Jenkins, V. Kapos, C. Monfreda, J. Loh, N. Myers, R. Norgaard and J. Randers (2002), 'Tracking the ecological overshoot of the human economy', *Proceedings of the National Academy of Sciences of the United States of America*, **99**(14), 9266–9271.

Watchman, P.Q., A. Delfino and J. Addison (2006), 'EP2: the Revised Equator Principles: why hard-nosed bankers are embracing soft law principles', Working Paper, LeBoeuf, Lamb, Greene & MacRae, available at http://www.equator-principles.com/documents/ClientBriefingforEquatorPrinciples_2007-02-07.pdf.

Weber, O., M. Fenchel and R.W. Scholz (2008), 'Empirical analysis of the integration of environmental risks into the credit risk management process of European banks', *Business Strategey and the Environment*, **17**(3), 149–159.

Weitzner, D. and J. Darroch (2009), 'Why moral failures precede financial crises', *Critical Perspectives on International Business*, **5**(1–2), 6–13.

Wingspread Conference on the Precautionary Principle (1998), 'Precautionary Principle', Science and Environmental and Health Network, available at http://www.sehn.org/wing.html.

Wright, C. and A. Rwabizambuga (2006), 'Institutional pressures, corporate reputation, and voluntary codes of conduct: an examination of Equator Principles', *Business and Society Review*, **111**(1), 89–117.

25 Corporate social responsibility, financial performance and selection bias: evidence from Taiwan's TWSE-listed banks

Chung-Hua Shen and Yuan Chang

25.1 INTRODUCTION

The worldwide surge in corporate social responsibility (CSR) shows that companies are becoming increasingly worried about the impact of their business activities on society.[1] More and more firms highlight their CSR activities, which aim to balance their business operations with the concerns of external stakeholders such as customers, unions, local communities, non-governmental organizations (NGOs) and governments. Thus, although generating profits is important, the social and environmental consequences of operations are also weighed against economic gains.

Corporate governance and CSR are both extraordinarily important to a corporation. This is because corporate governance involves a set of processes, customs, policies, laws and institutions which affect the way in which a company is directed, administered or controlled. It also includes the relationships among the many stakeholders involved and the goals for which the corporation is governed. The principal stakeholders are the shareholders, the management and the board of directors, and other stakeholders include employees, customers, creditors, suppliers, regulators and the community at large. Thus, companies with well-formed corporate governance systems take care of most CSR issues.

CSR is not separate from corporate governance. For example, good corporate governance is basically concerned with making better decisions for the long-term health of the company, such as enhancing the brand value of a company. Taking care of CSR is like taking care of risk management, where the risk is related to the value of a company brand. The 2008 Chinese milk scandal is a notable example.[2] Taking care of CSR is likely to enable the firm to benefit from fewer disruptions to its business from strikes, boycotts and regulations. It is thus able to safeguard the suppliers of finance to corporations, who can then be assured that they are getting a return on their investment, which is in accordance with Shleifer and Vishny (1997).

The UN Global Compact shows that, in a more globalized, interconnected and competitive world, the way in which environmental, social and corporate governance issues are managed is part of the overall management quality that companies need to compete successfully. Companies that perform better with regard to these issues can increase shareholder value by, for example, properly managing risks, anticipating regulatory actions or by accessing news markets while at the same time contributing to the sustainable development of the societies in which they operate. Moreover, these issues can have a strong impact on reputation and brands, an increasingly important part of company value.

Based on our view, CSR is an extended version of corporate governance. However, in spite of the growing interest in CSR and the anecdotal evidence, doubts still remain concerning whether such social initiatives could finally lead to improvements in a firm's financial performance. One may be concerned that there are clear costs associated with these CSR activities, but their correlation with better financial performance appears to be hard to prove.

From an academic point of view, those who advocate the adoption of CSR claim that a positive relationship exists between CSR and performance because such practices may improve employee productivity, and enhance social reputation, trust, brand image and product competitiveness (Bowman and Haire, 1975; Alexander and Buchholtz, 1978; Porter and van der Linde, 1995; Fombrun et al., 2000; Porter and Kramer, 2006). Those who suspect the function of CSR suggest that such activities lead to inefficiency in the use of resources, and to limitations in terms of product development. Other negative outcomes include cost pressures and non-profitability with a lack of public awareness and feedback in regard to performance (Friedman, 1970; Bragdon and Marlin, 1972; Vance, 1975; Aupperle et al., 1985; Walley and Whitehead, 1994; Henderson, 2002).[3]

The concern over CSR is also relevant to the banking industry. By taking the role of financial intermediation for channeling funds into consideration, banks engaging in CSR practices could bring social legitimacy to bear through the ethical screening of their loan and investment decisions or else they could establish social initiatives by themselves. If a specific bank runs into financial difficulties, its impact will extend to corporate borrowers as well as to other customers and depositors. Moreover, since transactions between banks involve enormous amounts of funds, the failure of a single bank may trigger a chain reaction. Thus, bank managements are required to maintain a healthy financial base to a much greater extent than the managements of other companies.

As regards the international development of bank CSR such as in the case of socially responsible investment (SRI), an investment strategy may seek to maximize both financial return and the community's benefit, namely, the environment, society and governance (ESG) in relation to target assets. The United Nations and some well-known financial institutions have established financing criteria which place emphasis on ESG, such as the Principles for Responsible Investment (PRI), the Equator Principles Financial Institutions (EPFIs) and the Carbon Disclosure Project (CDP). The Community Reinvestment Act (CRA) of 1977 is a US federal law that requires banks and thrifts to offer credit throughout their entire market area and prohibits them from targeting only wealthier neighborhoods with their services. The purpose of the CRA is to provide credit, including home ownership opportunities to underserved populations as well as commercial loans to small businesses.

There is a famous example of philanthropic behavior in the form of the Grameen Bank, a microfinance organization and community development bank started in Bangladesh that extends small loans (known as microcredit) to the impoverished without requiring collateral.[4] Some have doubted whether the business model of the bank is a sustainable one without the explicit and implicit donor support that it receives. At the same time, it is often cited as a success story in microfinance and serves as a model for financial institutions with a similar CSR philosophy worldwide.

The CSR philosophy is also important for Taiwan's financial institutions. Following the global trend of CSR, financial conditions are not the only criteria that need to be examined in determining the extension of credit; it is also necessary to consider social and public welfare. Some financial institutions have included environmental protection and the relationship between labor and capital in their evaluations. Banks would not want to lend money to companies that might have to shut down at any time because they are polluting the environment or having their employees go on strike. For example, Fubon FHC is engaging in the promotion of the concept of corporate citizenship such as having a better corporate governance system, providing excellent financial services to customers, and leading employees towards growth and better and more efficient use of corporate resources. It has also established the Fubon Foundation for facilitating credit card bonuses for charity, lotteries for charity, and voluntary work aimed at contributing to society.

To the best of our knowledge, while the number of studies on CSR and financial performance in the context of the banking industry is small, Llewellyn (2005) has found that the average performance of banks in Germany falls short of that of banks in the UK, with the former banks taking CSR into consideration (by adopting the stakeholder model), while the latter do not (by adopting the shareholder model). Another focus of this study is Islamic banking, which strives for a just, fair and balanced society as envisioned by Islamic economics, for instance by prohibiting lending to those with an interest in gambling, and those who take excessive risks, and protecting the interests and benefits of all parties involved in market transactions. This implies that these practices of Islamic banks are parallel to the globally accepted framework of CSR (Lewis and Algaoud, 2001; Iqbal and Molyneux, 2005).[5]

While the above developments of CSR in banking are prevalent in modern economies, from an academic standpoint there are few empirical investigations of the association between CSR and bank performance based on single-country or cross-country data. For example, Scholtens (2009) and Prior and Argandoña (2009) provide an assessment of the social responsibility of banks operating internationally without an evaluation of the relationship between social responsibility and bank performance. This provides us with the motivation to fill this gap. In order to understand the status of CSR awareness and its fulfillment among Taiwanese corporations, and to help bring Taiwan into line with global trends in this area, one of Taiwan's leading commercial magazines, *Global Views Monthly* (GVM), conducted its first Survey of Corporate Social Responsibility, which was based on three criteria, namely, social participation, environmental protection and financial transparency, to evaluate the companies listed on the Taiwan Stock Exchange (TWSE). It also established the 2005 CSR Award to commend domestic companies for CSR excellence and encourage specific action and attention in this area. The five top-scoring banks from the survey were selected to receive the CSR Award and in this study are referred to as CSR-banks. The other TWSE-listed banks are defined as NonCSR-banks. Analyzing the performance measures between the two groups of banks helps us to evaluate the CSR's effects on the risk-return profiles of banks.

Before comparing performance measures between CSR-banks and NonCSR-banks, the condition of 'other things being equal' has to be taken into consideration. To be specific, if the characteristic variables of the two groups of observations are systematically different due to the non-random assignment (thus incurring sample selection bias) of the samples, the attributes of performance differences in terms of the effects of adopting CSR will be contaminated by differences in the characteristic variables. For example, if the assets of CSR-banks are larger on average, then whether the superior performance of CSR-banks is due to the CSR-effect or a scale factor cannot easily be identified. According to Rubin (1997), a complication associated with using large databases to draw causal inferences regarding the effects of actions, treatments or interventions is that they are almost always observational rather than experimental; that is, they are not based on the results of carefully conducted randomized clinical trials, but rather represent data collected through the observation of systems as they operate in normal practice without any interventions implemented by randomized assignment rules. It is thus necessary to control for naturally occurring systematic differences in background characteristics between the treatment group and the control group, such as the age or sex distributions, that would not occur within the context of a randomized experiment.

Matching theory, which was developed by Rubin (1973) in the medical and biological field, has recently been widely applied in economics and finance to eliminate the sample selection bias problem.[6] The basic concept of matching theory is that, when examining the treatment effect (the effect of adopting CSR on bank performance), the treatment sample (e.g., the CSR-banks) should have similar characteristics to those of the controlled sample (e.g., the NonCSR-banks). If the two samples have similar characteristics, then the resulting difference between the two matched observations is theoretically the treatment effect. In other words, the other characteristics of banks in the two groups should be roughly the same to ensure that the sample is randomly determined and is not exogenously given. When the dimension of matching is large, the matching, once successful, often reduces the available sample substantially. Rosenbaum and Rubin (1983, 1985a, 1985b) proposed propensity score matching (PSM) to resolve this problem as it reduces multidimensional matching to one-dimensional matching. PSM involves two steps, of which the first step is to estimate the probability of including in the experiment all samples using characteristic variables as the explanatory variables. Then, for each bank in the treatment sample, banks in the control samples are selected as matched samples according to the closeness of the above-estimated probability. See Shen and Chang (2009) for the details.

This study investigates the relationship between CSR and the financial performance of banks within the context of an emerging economy – namely, Taiwan – and uses four matching methods to control for the sample selection bias problem. In this way, it seeks to add a new dimension to the existing literature.

The remainder of this chapter is organized as follows. Section 25.2 introduces the principle of matching theory, and several matching methods. Section 25.3 describes the CSR measures, and how GMV compiled the CSR data bank and the bank's performance measures (CAMEL). Section 25.4 discusses the statistical methods, while section 25.5 reports the main empirical results. Section 25.6 provides the conclusion.

25.2   MATCHING THEORY AND PROPENSITY SCORE MATCHING METHODOLOGY

25.2.1   Principle of Matching Theory

Matching theory has been developed to address the problem of bias due to the non-random selection of samples. Following Dehejia and Wahba (2002) and Shen and

Chang (2009), let Y_{i1} denote the performance variable of bank i when bank i is subject to treatment, that is, it is a CSR-bank. Y_{i0} is the value of the same performance variable when bank i is exposed to control, that is, it is a NonCSR-bank. The performance difference between i being a CSR-bank and being a NonCSR-bank, which is regarded as a treatment (or experimental) effect of engaging in CSR, is defined as $\tau_i = Y_{i1} - Y_{i0}$. The expected treatment effect over the treated population is (the subscript i is omitted below for simplicity):

$$\tau|_{T=1} \equiv E(\tau|T = 1) = E(Y_1|T = 1) - E(Y_0|T = 1),$$

which is defined as the average treatment effect on the treated (ATET), where $T = 1(0)$ if the observation is a CSR-bank (NonCSR-bank). The basic problem in identifying ATET is that the variable of interest is observed under either the treatment or control regimes, but not both, which is why we can estimate $E(Y_1|T = 1)$, but not $E(Y_0|T = 1)$.

We could use $\tau^d \equiv E(Y_1|T = 1) - E(Y_0|T = 0)$ as a proxy estimator for $\tau|_{T=1}$, because $E(Y_0|T = 0)$ can be estimated. If the treatment and control groups do not systematically differ from each other, they are regarded as drawn from the same population, that is, $Y_1, Y_0 \perp T$, where $\perp$ is the symbol for independence. In this situation, $E(Y_1|T = 1) = E(Y_0|T = 1)$. In the terminology of Rubin (1973), the ignorability of treatment condition (ITC) is satisfied, and thus $\tau^d = \tau|_{T=1}$. However, if the treatment and control groups systematically differ in their characteristics, we have to consider them to be a non-random sampling of the same population or as being drawn from different populations, and thus τ^d is a biased proxy estimator for $\tau|_{T=1}$, with the difference from τ^d to $\tau|_{T=1}$ being the selection bias.

Based on the ITC, Rubin (1973) proposed that, conditional upon the observable co-variates X, the assignment of observations to treatment has become random, such that $Y_1, Y_0 \perp T|X$, that is, there is conditional independence (CI), and:

$$
\begin{aligned}
\tau|_{T=1} &\equiv E(Y_1|T = 1) - E(Y_0|T = 1) \\
&= E_x[\{E(Y_1|X,T = 1) - E(Y_0|X,T = 1)\}|T = 1] \\
&= E_x[\{E(Y_1|X,T = 1) - E(Y_0|X,T = 0)\}|T = 1] \\
&= E_x[\tau^d|_{T=1,x}|T = 1].
\end{aligned}
$$

As long as the two groups of observations have similar characteristic variables, comparing the samples of treated and untreated observations is approximately equivalent to comparing those two samples in a random-sampling experiment, so that $\tau^d = \tau|_{T=1}$.

25.2.2   Dimensionality Reduction through Propensity Scores

When the number of variables increases, the chances of finding exact control matches for each treatment sample decrease, because it is more difficult to find control samples which have exactly the same observed characteristics as a given treatment sample when the number of characteristics becomes larger. Rosenbaum and Rubin (1983, 1985a, 1985b) suggest using the propensity score – the conditional probability of the treatment being given a set of characteristic covariates – to reduce the dimensionality of matching. Let $P(X)$ be the probability of a bank being subject to treatment (a CSR-bank), that is:

$$P(X) = P(T = 1|X) = E(T = 1|X).$$

Furthermore, according to Rubin (1973), conditional upon the propensity scores $P(X)$, as projections of observable covariates are made, the assignment of samples to treatment is random:

$$Y_i, Y_i \perp T|X \Rightarrow Y_1, Y_0 \perp T|P(X),$$

and:

$$\tau|_{T=1} = E_{P(X)}[\tau^d|_{T=1,P(X)}|T = 1].$$

The ITC and CI may be extended to using propensity scores. Selection bias is mitigated as well as the dimensionality of matching.[7] We can use the probit or logit model to estimate the propensity scores.

25.2.3 Matching Algorithm

Given the observed characteristic covariates X and the propensity scores $P(X)$ obtained for all CSR-banks and NonCSR-banks, a specific CSR-bank is paired with one or more NonCSR-banks according to one of the following four matching criteria.[8]

First, define bank i as being subject to treatment, that is, as a CSR-bank, and bank j as being exposed to control, that is, as a NonCSR-bank. The propensity scores of sample bank i and j are P_i and P_j, respectively. The first criterion, Nearest-Neighbor Matching (Nearest), matches each treatment sample to the control sample that has the nearest propensity score. In terms of mathematics:

$$C(P_i) = \min_j |P_i - P_j|,$$

where $C(P_i)$ is a set which contains a control sample that has the nearest propensity score for bank i.

The second criterion is Caliper Matching (Caliper), which matches each treated sample to the control samples with propensity scores falling within a pre-specified caliper. That is, when $|P_i - P_j| < \eta$, bank j is contained in the $C(P_i)$ set, namely, the matched sample for bank i. Note that, under this criterion, the number of control samples contained in $C(P_i)$ is arbitrary, ranging from zero to the full number of control samples. According to Shen and Lee (2006) and Shen and Chang (2009), η is specified as one-quarter of the standard error for all estimated propensity scores.

The third criterion is Mahalanobis Metric Matching (Mahala). This criterion does not make use of propensity scores in matching, but instead just uses observed characteristic variables. Define the Mahalanobis distance as:

$$d(i, j) = (u - v)^T C^{-1}(u - v)$$

where u and v are vectors of observed characteristic variables of treated bank i and control bank j, respectively. C is a variance–covariance matrix of observed characteristics. For purposes of illustration, suppose that there are five characteristic variables, thus $k = 5$, and that there are five characteristic variables, X_{ik}, X_{jk}, $k = 1, 2, \ldots, 5$ belonging to each of banks i and j. Then the Mahalanobis distance between them is:

$$d(i,j)_{1 \times 1} =$$

$$\begin{bmatrix} X_{i1} - X_{j1} \\ X_{i2} - X_{j2} \\ X_{i3} - X_{j3} \\ X_{i4} - X_{j4} \\ X_{i5} - X_{j5} \end{bmatrix}_{5 \times 1}^{T} \begin{bmatrix} Var(X_1) & Cov(X_1, X_2) & Cov(X_1, X_3) & Cov(X_1, X_4) & Cov(X_1, X_5) \\ | & Var(X_2) & Cov(X_2, X_3) & Cov(X_2, X_4) & Cov(X_2, X_5) \\ | & & Var(X_3) & Cov(X_3, X_4) & Cov(X_3, X_5) \\ | & & & Var(X_4) & Cov(X_4, X_5) \\ | & \rule{1cm}{0.4pt} & \rule{1cm}{0.4pt} & \rule{1cm}{0.4pt} & Var(X_5) \end{bmatrix}_{5 \times 5} \begin{bmatrix} X_{i1} - X_{j1} \\ X_{i2} - X_{j2} \\ X_{i3} - X_{j3} \\ X_{i4} - X_{j4} \\ X_{i5} - X_{j5} \end{bmatrix}_{5 \times 1}$$

The steps involved in the Mahala approach are as follows. First, calculate the Mahalanobis distance for bank i and bank j. Second, match each treatment sample to the control sample that has the least distance with the other.

The fourth criterion is Mahalanobis Metric Matching with Caliper (Mahala Caliper), which matches each treated sample to the control samples with a Mahalanobis distance smaller than a pre-specified caliper. That is, when $d(i,j) < \eta$, bank i and bank j are matched samples. Similarly to the Caliper, the number of matched control samples of bank j for bank i is arbitrary, and also according to Shen and Lee (2006) and Shen and Chang (2009), η is specified as one-quarter of the standard error of all estimated propensity scores.

25.2.4   Verification and Comparison of Matching Results

Once we select the matching NonCSR-banks, we then verify the matching by examining the null hypothesis of $H_0: (\overline{X}_i - \overline{X}_j) = 0$, where $\overline{X}_i$ and $\overline{X}_j$ are the averages of the characteristic variables of treated bank i and control bank j, respectively. The two groups have the same characteristics if the null is not rejected.[9]

25.3   DATA AND VARIABLES

25.3.1   CSR Measure

While it is a matter of dispute whether firms should adopt CSR or not, academics seem to favor the concept that banks should pay attention to CSR (Scholtens, 2009; Prior and Argandoña, 2009). Firstly, they have to maintain sound, transparent and trustworthy management practices, as well as healthy credit and financial conditions to protect depositors and stockholders. Secondly, they should enhance their business management abilities to ensure the effectiveness of their CSR activities and extend these abilities to their customers – namely, through the ethical screening of lending or investment decisions – or else establish social initiatives by themselves. They should also make responsible loans and investments in relation to their customers' projects by providing sustainable development to the society that cannot be achieved through their core activities. Thirdly, they should formulate a quick and accurate decision-making process and build a corporate governance framework that is centered on implementing CSR throughout the entire group of stakeholders.

Recently, a number of research and financial institutions, such as the FTSE, have developed widely acknowledged social responsibility criteria that have gradually become an international standard. Firms included in FTSE4Good indices must meet specific criteria in three areas: the environment; society and stakeholders; and human rights. In addition, those companies whose business interests encompass tobacco, nuclear weapons and power stations, as well as uranium, are excluded from the index. These indices have been widely employed.[10]

In Taiwan, *Global Views Monthly* conducted its first Survey of CSR for around 700 publicly listed companies in 2005. The magazine also established the annual Corporate Social Responsibility Award to commend domestic companies for CSR excellence and encourage specific action and attention in this area.

As we have already mentioned, the framework for evaluating the performance of social responsibility is based on the three dimensions of social participation, environmental protection and financial transparency. To be more specific, the GVM magazine referred to OEKOM, an independent research and rating agency for CSR in Germany, to design a questionnaire regarding the engagement and effectuation of the above three aspects for firms listed on the Taiwan Stock Exchange. They then calculated scores for each of the three dimensions of the CSR activities based on the respondents' replies. Finally, they ranked the companies according to their total scores after excluding firms characterized by the following from rating: negative events challenged by government agencies such as the Environmental Protection Administration or the Council of Labor Affairs; major controversies between labor and capital; troubles with consumers; litigation pertaining to and restrictions on the departure of the chief executive officer (CEO); and losses over a period of years.

Once the rankings were generated, the top five banks which were elected to have the CSR Award conferred upon them were defined as CSR-banks. Other TWSE-listed banks were defined as the control sample, there being a total of 29 NonCSR-banks. The announcement regarding these rankings was made in May 2005, and because this CSR rating considered the firm's social performance for three years prior to the announcement date, this determined our sample period from 2002Q1 to 2006Q2.

One may wonder whether our classification of CSR-banks versus NonCSR-banks is ad hoc. That is to say, since the scores provided by the GVM CSR rating are in descending order, a decisive classification between the fifth and sixth banks is less meaningful because one is a CSR-bank and the other is a NonCSR-bank. Although there are numerous data on the corporate social performance of firms around the world, such as the KLD, FTSE4Good indices, the Dow Jones Sustainability Group Index, and so on, their evaluation does not consider listed companies in Taiwan. In the future, as these international CSR rating agencies declare their CSR rating in Taiwan, we could compare them with those for our sample of CSR-banks as a robustness check.

25.3.2 Measures of Bank Financial Performance: CAMEL

We use CAMEL criteria, which include 15 items, to evaluate bank performance (Shen, 2002). CAMEL denotes a bank-rating system which is proposed by the Federal Financial

Institution Examination Council in the US, to examine capital adequacy, asset quality, management ability, earnings ability and the liquidity risk of banks.

As for capital adequacy, two sub-assessment indicators are employed. The first is the capital adequacy ratio proposed by the Bank for International Settlements (*BISCAR*), and its calculation is based on a bank's Tier 1 plus Tier 2 capital divided by its risky assets. The second is the equity ratio (*EQUITY*), which is total equity divided by total assets. Larger values of *BISCAR* and *EQUITY* represent higher degrees of capital adequacy.

For asset quality, three sub-assessment indicators are used. The first is the ratio of non-performing loans (*NPL*), which is the current-period level of non-performing loans divided by total loans. A lower *NPL* represents better asset quality. The second is the ratio of loan loss reserves (*LLR*), which is calculated by loan loss reserves divided by average total assets. A bank with a large *LLR* implies lower asset quality.[11] The third is the coverage ratio (*COVERAGE*), which is defined as total equity plus loan loss reserves minus current-period nonperforming loans and then divided by total assets. A larger coverage ratio represents better asset quality for a bank.

For management ability, four sub-assessment indicators are introduced. The first is the efficiency ratio (*INEFFICIENCY*), which is calculated as non-interest expense divided by net interest income and non-interest income. The second is the burden ratio (*BURDEN*), defined as non-interest expense minus non-interest income and then divided by total assets. The third, the expense ratio (*EXPENSE*), is calculated as total expense divided by total assets. The above three ratios are negatively correlated with management ability. The fourth is the deposits-to-loans ratio (*DEPLOAN*), which is defined as the average balance of lending divided by the average balance of deposits, and is positively correlated with management ability.

For earning ability, there are also four sub-assessments. The first and second are the return on assets (*ROA*) and return on equity (*ROE*), of which the former is net income divided by total assets, and the latter is net income divided by total equity. The higher *ROA* and *ROE* give rise to better earning ability. The third is the ratio of the net interest margin (*NIM*), which is the net interest income (interest income minus interest expense) divided by total assets. The fourth is the ratio of non-interest income (*NONINT*), which is non-interest income divided by total assets. The latter two indicators can be seen as the distribution of the bank's earnings between traditional and fee-oriented business.

For liquidity risk, two sub-assessments are employed. The first is the liquidity ratio (*LIQUID*), which is current assets divided by total assets. The second is the ratio of liquidity reserves (*LIQUIDREV*), which is defined as the provision of eligible current assets divided by total deposits which required a provision of current reserves by the central bank. Banks with higher values of the above two ratios will have lower liquidity risks.

25.4   ECONOMETRIC METHODS

25.4.1   Propensity Scoring Function (PSM)

The use of PSM requires estimating the propensity scores function based on the Probit model, which is:

$$Pr(D_{CSR} = 1) = F(\beta'X) \tag{25.1}$$

where D_{CSR} is a dummy variable which is equal to 1 if it is a CSR-bank, and 0 otherwise, $F(\cdot)$ is the cumulative probability density function of a normal distribution, β is a vector of marginal impact coefficients and X is a vector of characteristic variables.

According to Dierkes and Coppock (1978), Trotman and Bradley (1981) and Fombrun and Shanley (1990), the larger the scale of a company, the more attention that company attracts from the public; namely, the response from its philanthropic activities is noticeable. Thus, scale is considered to be a crucial characteristic variable and its expected effect on the probability of adopting CSR is positive. Here, three scale variables, *ASSET* (the total assets), *BRANCH* (the number of branches) and *EMP* (the number of employees) are considered.

McGuire et al. (1988) and Moore (2001) proposed the available funds theory to argue that firms with abundant resources have more ability to engage in CSR activities. On the contrary, Posner and Schmidt (1992) and Alkhafaji (1989) suggested that firms that earn sufficient profits could exhibit egocentric behavior without fear of being challenged for not noticing the interests of the public. Here, two variables that measure bank financial worthiness, *NETINC* (the net income) and *DEBT* (the debt ratio), are considered.

Note that Dehejia and Wahba (2002) have stressed that the role of the score is only to reduce the dimensions of the conditioning; as such, it has no behavioral assumptions attached to it. Thus, while these variables are close to the determinant of being selected as CSR-banks, the main focus is that they serve as the basic characteristics of the two groups of banks.

Our characteristic variables (X) include *ASSET, BRANCH, EMP, NETINC* and *DEBT*, which are used in the four matching methods mentioned above. Our main objective is to find the NonCSR-banks whose characteristics are 'sufficiently' close to those of the CSR-banks.

25.4.2 Two Approaches to Estimate the Treatment Effects

Following Hofler et al. (2004) and Shen and Chang (2009), two approaches are implemented to determine whether adopting CSR activities affects the bank's performance. The first is the basic statistical method, which computes the mean differences in financial performance between two pairs of groups, based on before- and after-matching samples. Bootstrapping methods (1000 repetitions) are used to establish confidence intervals to determine the significance of the differences.

Second, we perform regression analysis with a D_{CSR} dummy variable which is equal to 1 if it is a CSR-bank, and 0 otherwise, to examine the differences in financial performance between the two groups of banks. The model is:

$$PERFORMANCE = \alpha + \beta\,ASSET + \gamma D_{FHC} + \lambda D_{CSR} + +\varepsilon \tag{25.2}$$

where *PERFORMANCE* comprises the performance variables, namely, *BISCAR, EQUITY, NPL, LLR, COVERAGE, INEFFICIENCY, BURDEN, EXPENSE, DEPLOAN, ROA, ROE, NIM, NONINT, LIQUID* and *LIQUIDREV. ASSET* is the control variable, and D_{FHC} is a dummy variable which is equal to 1 if it is a financial holding company (FHC)-bank,[12] and 0 otherwise, in order to capture the effects of banks being subordinated to the FHC in terms of performance. The estimated λ captures the effect on bank performance of adopting CSR.

Note that the 15 ratios above reflect different aspects of bank performance. For example, while the larger *ROA* represents sounder financial strength, a lower *NPL* indicates the same situation. Thus, for simplicity, we categorize those ratios with positive and negative effects on the banks' financial health as 'positive financial ratios' and 'negative financial ratios', respectively. The positive ratios include *BISCAR*, *EQUITY*, *COVERAGE*, *ROA*, *ROE*, *NONINT*, *LIQUID* and *LIQUIDREV*, whereas the negative ratios include *NPL*, *LLR*, *INEFFICIENCY*, *BURDEN* and *EXPENSE*. The direction of effect is uncertain for *NIM* and *DEPLOAN*. A positive λ suggests that the CSR-banks perform better than the NonCSR-banks if *PERFORMANCE* is proxied by positive financial ratios; by contrast, a negative λ suggests that the CSR-banks perform better when *PERFORMANCE* is proxied by the negative financial ratios.

The characteristic and financial performance variables are derived from the *Taiwan Economic Journal* (TEJ) database and are summarized in Table 25.1.

25.5   EMPIRICAL RESULTS

25.5.1   Basic Statistics before Matching

Our sample period covers 2002Q1 to 2006Q2 with 90 and 489 bank-quarter observations for CSR-banks and NonCSR-banks, respectively. Table 25.2 reports the descriptive statistics of the characteristics and 15 CAMEL performance variables for our sampled observations – namely, banks, CSR-banks and NonCSR-banks – before matching. We find that, on average, CSR-banks have larger assets, more branches and employees, and greater net income, but also have higher debt ratios. For example, the average assets of CSR-banks and NonCSR-banks are 875.87 and 477.07 billion NTD (New Taiwan Dollars), respectively. The average numbers of branches of CSR-banks and NonCSR-banks are 106 and 66, respectively. These basic statistics provide preliminary evidence that these two groups of banks have systematic differences in their characteristic variables, at least on average.

With respect to the performance variables, for capital adequacy, CSR-banks perform better than NonCSR-banks in regard to *BISCAR* but not to *EQUITY*. For asset quality, the CSR-banks perform better than the NonCSR-banks in regard to *NPL*, *LLR* but not *COVERAGE*. As for management ability, CSR-banks perform better in regard to *INEFFICIENCY*, *BURDEN* and *EXPENSE*, but not *DEPLOAN*. As for earning ability, CSR-banks have higher *ROA*, *ROE* and *NONINT*. As for liquidity risk, CSR-banks perform better than NonCSR-banks in regard to *LIQUID* and *LIQUIDREV*. As an illustration, the average NPL ratios for CSR-banks and NonCSR-banks are 2.6286 percent and 5.132 percent, respectively, and the average *ROA* values for CSR-banks and NonCSR-banks are 0.4644 percent and 0.1092 percent, respectively.

Two caveats should be noted. First, although most of the evidence shows that CSR-banks have better performance, this evidence lacks information regarding the statistical

Table 25.1 Mnemonics and definitions of characteristic and performance variables

Variable	Definition	Expected sign of taking CSR
Characteristic variable		
D_{CSR}	A dummy variable which equals one if the bank is a winner of the CSR Award (CSR-banks), conferred by *Global View Monthly* in 2005. Otherwise, it is equal to zero (NonCSR-banks).	
Scale factors:		
ASSET	Current assets + Long-term investment + Total fixed assets + Total other assets	+
BRANCH	Number of branches	+
EMPLOY	Number of employees	+
Financial factors:		
NETINC	After-tax net income	Uncertain
DEBT	(Total debt/Total assets) × 100	Uncertain
Performance variable (CAMEL)		
BISCAR	BIS capital adequacy ratio	+
EQUITY	Total equity to total assets	+
NPL	Non-performing loans to total assets	−
LLR	Loan loss reserve to total assets	−
COVERAGE	Total equity plus loan loss reserve minus current-period non-performing loans and then divided by total assets	+
INEFFICIENCY	Non-interest expense divided by net interest income and non-interest income	−
BURDEN	Non-interest expense minus non-interest income and then divided by total assets	−
EXPENSE	Total expense to total assets	−
DEPLOAN	Average balance of loans to average balance of deposits	+
ROA	Net income to total assets	+
ROE	Net income to total equity	+
NIM	Net interest income to total assets	Uncertain
NONINT	Non-interest income to total assets	Uncertain
LIQUID	Current assets to total assets	+
LIQUIDREV	Provision of eligible current assets divided by total deposits which required provision of current reserves by central bank	+

significance. Second, although one cannot judge whether or not CSR-banks have performed better than NonCSR-banks so far, there exists an obvious systematic divergence in terms of the characteristic variables between the two groups of observations. We therefore cannot attribute the difference in performance purely to the banks' engagement in CSR activities, and we have to use matching methods to fix the differences in

Table 25.2 Basic statistics of all samples, CSR-banks and NonCSR-banks

	All samples				CSR-banks				NonCSR-banks			
	Mean	Std. dev.	Min.	Max.	Mean	Std. dev.	Min.	Max.	Mean	Std. dev.	Min.	Max.
Characteristic variable												
ASSET	539.06	462.26	40.837	2380.5	875.87	402.66	302.69	1521.9	477.07	445.82	40.837	2380.5
BRANCH	72.447	45.943	3.0000	289.00	106.43	38.802	55.000	184.00	66.192	44.421	3.0000	289.00
EMPLOY	2959.2	1963.2	467.00	8453.0	5242.4	1948.5	2043.0	8375.0	2539.0	1653.5	467.00	8453.0
NETINC	0.1496	3.0403	−31.681	6.0701	0.8002	4.0058	−22.060	4.5018	0.0300	2.8159	−31.681	6.0701
DEBT	91.868	10.347	30.440	99.840	93.569	1.5789	90.230	96.960	91.555	11.213	30.440	99.840
Performance variable (CAMEL)												
BISCAR	10.668	4.6425	−0.1900	41.680	10.900	1.5089	8.1100	13.990	10.646	4.9917	−0.1900	41.680
EQUITY	8.1316	10.347	0.1553	69.557	6.4310	1.5783	3.0394	9.7654	8.4446	11.213	0.1553	69.557
NPL	4.7422	4.4526	0.3800	29.750	2.6286	1.6486	0.7400	8.9900	5.1320	4.6920	0.3800	29.750
LLR	1.1142	0.9062	0.2492	6.8875	0.8648	0.4393	0.3972	2.8510	1.1604	0.9615	0.2492	6.8875
COVERAGE	5.9457	11.490	−13.792	69.182	5.6092	2.1835	−0.0891	9.6941	6.0082	12.477	−13.792	69.182
INEFFICIENCY	95.879	61.473	10.784	646.12	80.564	31.887	58.743	254.46	98.698	65.109	10.784	646.12
BURDEN	0.9700	1.4188	−4.9688	9.7410	0.8898	0.9012	−0.1065	4.9993	0.9848	1.4951	−4.9688	9.7410
EXPENSE	2.6297	1.8079	0.3396	13.286	2.5654	1.5342	0.5719	8.0763	2.6415	1.8550	0.3396	13.286
DEPLOAN	85.125	28.491	50.820	458.04	76.937	5.7343	58.650	90.680	86.632	30.672	50.820	458.04
ROA	0.1646	1.1404	−8.0800	5.3400	0.4644	0.6880	−2.0300	1.8500	0.1092	1.1979	−8.0800	5.3400
ROE	0.1962	1.2123	−8.0800	5.4300	0.5252	0.8622	−2.6500	2.2700	0.1354	1.2578	−8.0800	5.4300
NIM	2.9991	1.6548	0.4377	8.5087	2.9966	1.6156	0.7027	8.0251	2.9996	1.6635	0.4377	8.5087
NONINT	0.6640	0.6588	0.0227	6.5082	0.8372	0.5317	0.0816	2.2267	0.6321	0.6752	0.0227	6.5082
LIQUID	26.801	7.9454	11.764	55.117	30.770	7.3457	12.140	48.997	26.071	7.8416	11.764	55.117
LIQUIDREV	21.822	17.206	1.1900	167.22	23.312	9.7919	12.190	51.260	21.548	18.240	1.1900	167.22

Notes:
1. See Table 25.1 for the definitions of variables. Source of data: *Taiwan Economic Journal* (TEJ).
2. The unit for ASSET and NETINC is billions of New Taiwan Dollars (NTD). Quarterly data are used, and range from 2002Q1 to 2006Q2.
3. There are 579 bank-quarters for all samples, where there are 90 and 489 CSR-banks and NonCSR-banks, respectively.

Table 25.3   Estimation results of propensity score function: Probit model

Variable	Estimated coefficients	
	Model I	Model II
Constant	−2.479	−2.390
	(−1.30)	(−1.27)
ASSET	−0.003***	−0.003***
	(−4.98)	(−4.74)
BRANCH	0.001	0.001
	(0.30)	(0.27)
EMPLOY	0.001***	0.001***
	(8.80)	(8.52)
NETINC	0.045*	
	(1.81)	
NETINC$_{t-1}$		0.044*
		(1.77)
DEBT	−0.004	−0.005
	(−0.20)	(−0.25)
No. of obs.	579	545
Pseudo R^2	0.3696	0.3721

Note: The *t*-statistics are given in parentheses, and ***, ** and * denote the significance at the 1%, 5% and 10% levels, respectively.

the characteristics to obtain a purer and more identifiable effect on the performance of CSR-banks.

25.5.2   Basic Statistics after Matching

Table 25.3 presents the pooled estimated results of the propensity score function using the Probit model.[13] We have specifications depending on the number of explanatory variables being included. For Model I, all the variables are contemporaneous (Model I contains all of the contemporaneous variables). We find that the coefficients for *ASSET, EMP* and *NETINC* are positive and significant, with values of 0.003, 0.001 and 0.045, respectively, suggesting that banks with large scale, more employees and high net income tend to engage in CSR. The coefficients for *BRANCH* and *DEBT* are not significant.

Because McGuire et al. (1988) and Moore (2001) proposed the available funds theory to argue that firms with abundant resources have a better ability to engage in CSR activities, we consider the last year's profit level (proxied by *NETINC$_{t-1}$*) as an explanatory variable to replace *NETINC*. Thus we have Model II and leave this part of the analysis to a robustness check.

Based on the estimation results of Model I for the propensity score function, we obtain the propensity scores for each of the banks. We can then select the samples based on the four matching methods, namely, the Nearest, Caliper, Mahala and Mahala Caliper.

Table 25.4   Mean differences of characteristic variables: before- and after-matching samples

Characteristic variable	Before matching			After matching		
				Nearest-neighbor matching (Nearest)		
	CSR-banks	NonCSR-banks	difference (t-value)	CSR-banks	NonCSR-banks	difference (t-value)
ASSET	875.87	477.07	398.80*** (7.91)	875.87	1178.2	−302.30*** (−4.22)
BRANCH	106.43	66.192	40.238*** (8.05)	106.43	142.88	−36.444*** (−4.99)
EMPLOY	5242.4	2539.0	2703.4*** (13.9)	5242.4	5838.6	−596.20* (−1.93)
NETINC	0.8002	0.0300	0.7702** (2.22)	0.8002	1.3138	−0.5136 (−0.91)
DEBT	93.569	91.555	2.0140* (1.70)	93.569	94.853	−1.2840*** (−5.51)

Notes:
1. The numbers are averages for CSR-banks and NonCSR-banks, respectively, and their differences.
2. The numbers under 'Before matching' denote the average of the raw sample of the two groups before adopting any matching methods. There are a total of 579 bank-quarter samples, of which 90 are CSR-banks, and 489 are NonCSR-banks.
3. The numbers under 'After matching' denote the averages of the sample that have been matched by adopting the Nearest, Caliper, Mahala and Mahala Caliper methods, respectively. The numbers of observations for the independent banks are 90, 70, 80 and 5 based on using the above four matching methods.
4. The *t*-statistics are presented in parentheses.
5. ***, ** and * denote significance at the 1%, 5% and 10% levels, respectively.

Table 25.4 compares the means of the characteristic variables between the two groups using the samples before and after matching. We find that, firstly, before matching, the five characteristic variables between the two groups of banks are statistically different based on t-tests of their means. Second, under the Nearest matching method, significant differences exist in regard to *ASSET, BRANCH, EMPLOY* and *DEBT*, but not in relation to *NETINC*. Third, when Caliper matching is employed, *BRANCH* and *DEBT* are still significantly different between the two groups of banks, and under the Mahala matching method, significant differences still exist in *ASSET* and *EMPLOY*. Fourth, under the Mahala Caliper method, four of the five characteristic variables between the two groups of samples are still significantly different, at least on average. It should be recalled that better matching methods could reduce characteristic differences between the two groups of samples, and thus from this point of view, the Mahala matching method is a better matching method.

It is worth noting that the matching process reduces the control sample. For example, the degrees of freedom are substantially reduced from 489 to 5 when the Mahala Caliper method is adopted. On the contrary, under the Mahala, Nearest and Caliper methods, the number of degrees of freedom still remain at 80, 90 and 70, respectively. Therefore, there exists a trade-off between the closeness in matching and the losses in terms of

	After matching								
Caliper matching (Caliper)			Mahalanobis metric matching (Mahala)			Mahalanobis metric matching with Calipers (Mahala Caliper)			
CSR-banks	NonCSR-banks	difference (t-value)	CSR-banks	NonCSR-banks	difference (t-value)	CSR-banks	NonCSR-banks	difference (t-value)	
875.87	989.09	−113.22 (−1.46)	875.87	666.70	209.17*** (2.99)	875.87	1467.9	592.07*** (−3.27)	
106.43	127.86	−21.424*** (−2.86)	106.43	96.425	10.008 (1.43)	106.43	180.80	−74.367*** (−4.26)	
5242.4	5118.9	123.51 (0.37)	5242.4	4029.9	1212.5*** (4.11)	5242.4	7045.4	1802.9** (−2.06)	
0.8002	1.2110	−0.4108 (−0.81)	0.8002	0.1727	0.6275 (1.07)	0.8002	2.4131	1.6128 (−0.90)	
93.569	94.413	−0.8447*** (−3.08)	93.569	93.626	−0.0573 (−0.23)	93.569	95.594	−2.0253*** (−2.85)	

degrees of freedom. Because no method is overwhelmingly superior to the others, we report the regression results using all four methods.

25.5.3 Performance Comparisons

As in subsection 25.4.2, there are two ways of examining the effects of being CSR-banks on financial performance. The first involves a comparison of the financial performance ratios between the two groups.

Table 25.5 presents the basic statistical results of the financial performance differences between the CSR-banks and NonCSR-banks. Recall that we have distinguished them into positive and negative financial ratios if they have beneficial and adverse impacts, respectively, given a one-unit increase in the ratios. Before the matching, as shown in the second column, there is significant evidence of the CSR-banks having lower *EQUITY, NPL, LLR, INEFFICIENCY* and *DEPLOAN,* and higher *ROA, ROE, NIM* and *LIQUID.* A total of seven of these nine performance variables show that the CSR-banks outperform the NonCSR-banks, at least on average.

When we observe columns 3 to 6, the performance comparison results become diversified when different matching methods are applied. First, under Nearest, the extent of the striking outperformance of the CSR-banks is mitigated but still exists in relation to *EQUITY, NPL* and *COVERAGE.* Secondly, under Caliper, CSR-banks outperform NonCSR-banks in regard to *EQUITY* and *COVERAGE* with statistical significance. Third, under Mahala matching, ten performance measures demonstrate the superiority of the CSR-banks, which are *BISCAR, NPL, COVERAGE, INEFFICIENCY, BURDEN, ROA, ROE, NONINT, LIQUID* and *LIQUIDREV.* Finally, when we use the Mahala Caliper method, there are only two ratios of differences that are significant, which reveals that the CSR-banks outperform the NonCSR-banks in regard to *BISCAR* and *EQUITY.*

From the above performance comparison results, we observe that, before matching,

Table 25.5 *The differences in performance variables: CSR-banks and NonCSR-banks: before- and after-matching samples*

Variable	Before matching	After matching			
		Nearest-neighbor matching (Nearest)	Caliper matching (Caliper)	Mahalanobis metric matching (Mahala)	Mahalanobis metric matching with Calipers (Mahala Caliper)
BISCAR	0.254	−0.168	−0.010	0.611***	−0.755*
	(0.48)	(−0.51)	(−0.03)	(2.67)	(−1.80)
EQUITY	−2.014*	1.285***	1.066**	0.286	0.548***
	(−1.70)	(3.35)	(2.08)	(1.27)	(3.13)
NPL	−2.503***	−0.764*	−0.747	−1.332***	1.305
	(−5.00)	(−1.67)	(−1.47)	(−3.13)	(0.72)
LLR	−0.296***	0.067	0.021	0.043	0.071
	(−2.86)	(0.86)	(0.24)	(0.53)	(0.80)
COVERAGE	−0.399	1.772***	1.485**	1.177***	−0.450
	(−0.30)	(4.17)	(2.26)	(2.94)	(−0.37)
INEFFICIENCY	−18.13***	0.349	−0.912	−16.54***	−2.651
	(−2.58)	(0.05)	(−0.10)	(−3.36)	(−0.45)
BURDEN	−0.095	0.327	0.221	−0.393*	0.101
	(−0.58)	(1.60)	(0.90)	(−1.68)	(0.66)
EXPENSE	−0.076	0.330	0.302	−0.046	0.154
	(−0.37)	(0.90)	(0.91)	(−0.12)	(0.27)
DEPLOAN	−9.695***	0.676	−0.338	0.781	−0.550
	(−2.99)	(0.45)	(−0.17)	(0.68)	(−0.32)
ROA	0.355***	0.180	0.184	0.358***	0.039
	(2.73)	(1.33)	(1.22)	(4.02)	(0.28)
ROE	0.390***	0.151	0.154	0.392***	0.021
	(2.82)	(0.97)	(0.90)	(3.57)	(0.12)
NIM	−0.003	0.258	0.324	0.125	0.472
	(−0.02)	(0.63)	(0.88)	(0.33)	(0.61)
NONINT	0.205***	0.131	0.140	0.268***	−0.134
	(2.73)	(0.93)	(1.33)	(2.98)	(−0.55)
LIQUID	4.700***	0.246	0.629	2.038*	−2.908
	(5.28)	(0.09)	(0.32)	(1.91)	(−0.90)
LIQUIDREV	1.765	0.025	1.202	4.181***	−0.582
	(0.84)	(0.01)	(0.55)	(3.36)	(−0.25)

Notes:
1. The numbers are the differences in the means for the two groups: CSR-banks and NonCSR-banks.
2. The bootstrap *t*-statistics are presented in parentheses by repeating the sampling 1000 times.
3. ***, ** and * denote the significance at the 1%, 5% and 10% levels, respectively.

CSR-banks perform better in relation to more than half of the performance measures. When Nearest, Caliper and Mahala Caliper are used, the significant evidence of the CSR-banks outperforming the NonCSR-banks decreases and most of the evidence shows that the CSR-banks and NonCSR-banks are not statistically different, at least on average. The exception is the result under the Mahala matching method, where there is significant evidence of the CSR-banks' outperformance.

It is arguable that the above basic statistical comparisons may be subject to the criticism that they are missing a third variable. Thus we use regression analysis to examine the robustness of our results.

Table 25.6 presents the estimated results using regression analysis. Before the matching takes place, the coefficients of D_{CSR} are significantly positive when the performance measures are *BURDEN, ROA, ROE, NIM* and *NONINT*, while the coefficients of D_{CSR} are significantly negative when the performance measures are *EQUITY, COVERAGE, DEPLOAN* and *LIQUIDREV*. This means that CSR-banks perform better for all profitability measures, but perform worse in regard to equity to total assets, the coverage ratio, burden ratio, loans-to-deposits ratio and liquidity reserve ratio. Because the coefficients of D_{CSR} are insignificant for *BISCAR, NPL, LLR, INEFFICIENCY, EXPENSE* and *LIQUID*, this means that CSR-banks and NonCSR-banks are not statistically different in relation to these performance measures.

The estimated results are slightly changed as we use after-matching samples under Nearest, Caliper, Mahala and Mahala Caliper, which are reported in Panel B to Panel E of Table 25.6. Firstly, under Nearest, when the performance measures are *BISCAR, EQUITY, LLR* and *LIQUIDREV*, the estimated coefficients of D_{CSR} are significant with values of 0.558, −0.767, 1.151 and 0.123, respectively. This means that CSR-banks have a higher capital adequacy ratio, loan loss reserve ratio and liquidity reserve ratio, but a lower ratio of equity to assets. Only two of these four variables provide evidence of the CSR-banks outperforming the NonCSR-banks. Second, under Caliper, CSR-banks have significantly higher *LLR, LIQUID* and *LIQUIDREV* and lower *EQUITY*, which means that CSR-banks perform better in terms of their liquidity ratios and liquidity reserve ratios, but perform worse in relation to the equity to assets and loan loss reserves ratios. Third, under Mahala, although more performance variables exhibit significant differences between the two groups of banks, half of these ten variables show that CSR-banks significantly outperform NonCSR-banks, these variables being *INEFFICIENCY, DEPLOAN, ROA, LIQUID* and *LIQUIDITY*. Finally, when we use Mahala Caliper as the matching method, the regression results suggest that CSR-banks outperform NonCSR-banks in relation to *COVERAGE* but underperform in regard to *INEFFICIENCY* and *ROA*, with statistical significance.

To sum up, before matching, although CSR-banks outperform NonCSR-banks in regard to *ROA* and *ROE*, and have higher coefficients of *NIM* and *NONINT*, they perform less well in relation to *COVERAGE, BURDEN, DEPLOAN* and *LIQUIDREV* compared to NonCSR-banks. After matching, the empirical evidence shows that the significant outperformance of CSR-banks is reduced, and is still combined with evidence of underperformance. Because we cannot judge which performance measures are more important than others, each measure is equally weighted for the sake of simplicity. Under such circumstances, CSR-banks do not have all-round performance superiority.

The specifications of Table 25.7 are the same as those of Table 25.6 except for the estimation of PSF based on the results of Model II. Based on the estimation results of Model

Table 25.6   Do CSR-banks perform better? OLS estimation results
$$PERFORMANCE = \alpha + \beta\ ASSET + \gamma\ D_{FHC} + \lambda\ D_{CSR} + + \varepsilon$$

Panel A. Before Matching

	BISCAR	EQUITY	NPL	LLR	COVER-AGE	INEFFI-CIENCY	BURDEN
Constant	9.495	7.946	7.389	1.538	4.070	108.9	1.4E−00
	(31.6)	(11.7)	(27.2)	(25.8)	(5.49)	(25.9)	(14.9)
ASSET	−0.001	−0.005	−0.001	0.000	−0.004	0.001	−5.1E−04
	(−2.13)	(−5.43)	(−3.97)	(−5.41)	(−4.21)	(0.14)	(−3.86)
D_{FHC}	3.736	6.920	−3.685	−0.389	9.513	−25.19	−5.0E−01
	(9.90)	(8.12)	(−10.8)	(−5.15)	(10.2)	(−4.76)	−(4.15)
D_{CSR}	−0.813	−2.614**	−0.507	0.035	−2.231*	−8.928	3.0E−01*
	(−1.53)	(−2.19)	(−1.06)	(0.33)	(−1.70)	(−1.20)	(1.76)

Panel B. Nearest-Neighbor Matching (Nearest)

	BISCAR	EQUITY	NPL	LLR	COVER-AGE	INEFFI-CIENCY	BURDEN
Constant	8.007	4.106	0.942	6.197	82.70	1.259	3.229
	(27.1)	(8.94)	(10.6)	(13.3)	(9.80)	(5.76)	(9.57)
ASSET	−0.035	0.020	−0.001	−0.052	0.201	0.002	−0.006
	(−8.17)	(2.98)	(−0.67)	(−7.72)	(1.64)	(0.56)	(−1.19)
D_{FHC}	0.002	−0.003	−0.001	0.004	−0.026	−0.001	0.000
	(4.15)	(−4.75)	(−0.49)	(6.31)	(−2.13)	(−2.37)	(−0.28)
D_{CSR}	0.558***	−0.767**	0.071	1.151***	−0.332	0.111	0.077
	(2.90)	(−2.56)	(1.22)	(3.80)	(−0.06)	(0.78)	(0.35)

Panel C. Caliper Matching (Caliper)

	BISCAR	EQUITY	NPL	LLR	COVER-AGE	INEFFI-CIENCY	BURDEN
Constant	8.985	4.405	1.030	7.046	78.18	1.138	3.083
	(28.8)	(8.44)	(10.9)	(13.4)	(10.3)	(5.19)	(8.78)
ASSET	−0.040	0.017	−0.002	−0.058	0.212	0.003	−0.005
	(−8.68)	(2.24)	(−1.21)	(−7.41)	(1.90)	(0.88)	(−1.00)
D_{FHC}	0.002	−0.003	0.001	0.004	−0.026	−0.001	0.000
	(3.79)	(−3.52)	(−0.12)	(5.47)	(−2.38)	(−2.62)	(−0.35)
D_{CSR}	0.185	−1.295***	0.030	1.024***	2.524	0.168	0.186
	(0.91)	(−3.79)	(0.48)	(2.95)	(0.50)	(1.17)	(0.81)

Panel D. Mahalanobis Metric Matching (Mahala)

	BISCAR	EQUITY	NPL	LLR	COVER-AGE	INEFFI-CIENCY	BURDEN
Constant	8.903	4.960	0.988	6.792	82.30	1.622	3.144
	(38.3)	(10.8)	(9.60)	(16.5)	(10.1)	(6.66)	(8.70)
ASSET	−0.041	0.011	−0.001	−0.054	0.340	0.005	0.003
	(−10.6)	(1.49)	(−0.53)	(−7.82)	(2.51)	(1.26)	(0.52)
D_{FHC}	0.002	−0.002	−0.001	0.004	−0.031	−0.001	−0.001
	(5.49)	(−3.16)	(−0.35)	(6.03)	(−2.26)	(−2.67)	(−1.54)
D_{CSR}	0.022	−1.424***	0.026	0.905***	−11.09*	−0.328*	−0.102
	(0.12)	(−3.99)	(0.33)	(2.83)	(−1.76)	(−1.74)	(−0.36)

EXPENSE	DEPLOAN	ROA	ROE	NIM	NONINT	LIQUID	LIQUID-REV
3.1E-00	8.4E-01	−1.5E-02	0.010	3.496	0.583	21.25	14.55
(25.0)	(43.7)	(−0.19)	(0.12)	(31.0)	(13.5)	(44.0)	(12.2)
−8.0E-04	−7.3E-03	−9.6E-05	0.001	−0.001	0.001	0.006	0.004
(−4.70)	(−2.74)	(−0.88)	(−1.14)	(−5.22)	(−4.85)	(8.49)	(2.33)
−1.8E-01	1.4E-01	4.0E-01	0.446	−0.260	0.442	5.140	12.16
(−1.18)	(5.78)	(4.04)	(4.24)	(−1.83)	(8.16)	(8.59)	(8.15)
3.1E-01	−1.2E-01***	2.4E-04*	0.276*	0.419**	0.152**	0.535	−4.346**
(1.43)	(−3.56)	(1.76)	(1.88)	(2.10)	(2.00)	(0.64)	(−2.07)

EXPENSE	DEPLOAN	ROA	ROE	NIM	NONINT	LIQUID	LIQUID-REV
80.72	0.594	0.750	3.812	0.946	29.30	14.75	0.420
(63.1)	(4.05)	(4.16)	(10.9)	(8.48)	(17.1)	(7.48)	(4.96)
0.019	−0.007	−0.009	−0.006	−0.007	−0.079	0.000	−0.005
(1.02)	(−3.49)	(−3.63)	(−1.21)	(−4.12)	(−3.18)	(0.02)	(−3.85)
−0.006	0.001	0.001	0.000	0.001	0.011	0.008	0.001
(−3.22)	(3.11)	(3.27)	(−0.32)	(3.66)	(4.19)	(2.72)	(6.94)
−0.472	0.070	0.023	−0.016	0.071	0.578	1.459	0.123**
(−0.57)	(0.73)	(0.19)	(−0.07)	(0.98)	(0.52)	(1.13)	(2.24)

EXPENSE	DEPLOAN	ROA	ROE	NIM	NONINT	LIQUID	LIQUID-REV
80.9	0.706	0.876	3.780	0.914	26.7	11.68	0.148
(59.9)	(4.85)	(4.78)	(10.5)	(8.33)	(17.9)	(5.81)	(1.71)
−0.001	−0.009	−0.012	−0.006	−0.007	−0.046	0.033	−0.002
(−0.04)	(−4.29)	(−4.30)	(−1.08)	(−4.41)	(−2.10)	(1.10)	(−1.60)
−0.005	0.001	0.001	0.000	0.001	0.010	0.007	0.001
(−2.39)	(3.73)	(3.80)	(−0.57)	(4.19)	(4.90)	(2.31)	(6.05)
0.095	0.048	0.001	0.080	0.102	−0.224	2.203*	0.213***
(0.11)	(0.50)	(0.01)	(0.34)	(1.41)	(−0.23)	(1.65)	(3.75)

EXPENSE	DEPLOAN	ROA	ROE	NIM	NONINT	LIQUID	LIQUID-REV
75.63	0.505	0.623	3.486	0.806	29.22	13.95	0.176
(63.0)	(3.79)	(3.70)	(9.79)	(8.20)	(23.5)	(8.22)	(2.62)
0.008	−0.008	−0.010	0.003	−0.005	−0.082	−0.024	0.005
(0.40)	(−3.71)	(−3.64)	(0.53)	(−3.04)	(−3.94)	(−0.82)	(−4.40)
−0.002	0.001	0.001	−0.001	0.000	0.013	0.011	0.001
(−1.01)	(2.90)	(2.84)	(−1.79)	(2.87)	(6.27)	(3.83)	(9.52)
2.227**	0.272***	0.289**	0.105	0.149*	−1.132	2.276*	0.214***
(2.39)	(2.63)	(2.21)	(0.38)	(1.95)	(−1.17)	(1.71)	(4.10)

Table 25.6   (continued)

Panel E. Mahalanobis Metric Matching with Calipers (Mahala Caliper)

	BISCAR	*EQUITY*	*NPL*	*LLR*	*COVER-AGE*	*INEFFI-CIENCY*	*BURDEN*
Constant	8.422	3.431	0.855	7.061	21.49	−0.075	2.036
	(11.5)	(3.60)	(2.97)	(7.02)	(1.08)	(−0.13)	(2.01)
ASSET	−0.044	0.020	−0.001	−0.061	0.401	0.004	−0.003
	(−9.49)	(3.40)	(−0.69)	(−9.69)	(3.21)	(1.16)	(−0.52)
D_{FHC}	0.003	−0.003	−0.001	0.005	−0.021	0.000	0.000
	(5.96)	(−5.21)	(−0.06)	(8.31)	(−1.73)	(−1.04)	(−0.21)
D_{CSR}	0.343	−0.334	0.152	0.638	34.69**	0.834*	0.996
	(0.62)	(−0.47)	(0.70)	(0.84)	(2.32)	(1.88)	(1.30)

Notes:
1. This table reports the pooled OLS estimation results of the regression analysis for the relationship between CSR-banks and financial performance.
2. The data range from 2002Q1 to 2002Q2. Before sample matching, there are 90 CSR-banks and 489 NonCSR-banks. After matching, the number of NonCSR-banks for the Nearest, Caliper, Mahala and Mahala Caliper categories are 90, 70, 80 and 5, respectively.
3. The *t*-statistics are presented in parentheses.
4. ***, ** and * denote significance at the 1%, 5% and 10% levels, respectively.

II, we employ four matching methods and then use the after-matching samples to run the regression analysis, for which the results are reported in Panels A, B and C. Because the Mahala method does not use the propensity score, its estimated results should be the same as those in Panel C of Table 25.6, and are thus omitted from Table 25.7.

The three findings are as follows. First of all, under Nearest, the coefficients of D_{CSR} are positive when the performance variables are *BISCAR*, *LLR* and *LIQUIDREV*, and are 0.498, 0.952 and 0.225, respectively. The coefficient of D_{CSR} is negative when the performance variable is *LLR*, which is 0.952. This means that CSR-banks perform better in terms of their capital adequacy ratios and liquidity ratios, but worse in terms of their ratios of equity to assets and loan loss reserve ratios. Second, under Caliper matching, five significant estimates of D_{CSR} reveal the relative weakness of CSR-banks. Third, under Mahala Caliper, all of the estimated coefficients of the CSR dummy variables are insignificant, and this means that CSR-banks and NonCSR-banks are approximately equal for all performance variables, at least on average.

To sum up the above results of the regression analysis, when we use the before-matching sample, CSR-banks do not outperform NonCSR-banks for all performance measures. After matching, the above evidence is reinforced so that fewer performance variables reveal the superiority of CSR-banks.

25.6   DISCUSSION AND CONCLUSION

Because banks possess abundant funds and have an important and public role to play in financial intermediation in order to channel resources, their ethical screening of lending and investment decisions merits increased attentiveness to CSR practices and

EXPENSE	DEPLOAN	ROA	ROE	NIM	NONINT	LIQUID	LIQUID-REV
78.66	1.752	2.198	3.050	1.390	36.23	22.23	0.365
(22.1)	(4.44)	(4.45)	(2.90)	(4.31)	(8.01)	(3.45)	(1.92)
0.024	−0.013	−0.016	−0.005	−0.009	−0.081	−0.004	−0.004
(1.07)	(−5.05)	(−5.13)	(−0.69)	(−4.55)	(−2.86)	(−0.10)	(−3.53)
−0.006	0.001	0.001	0.000	0.001	0.010	0.006	0.001
(−2.98)	(2.48)	(2.58)	(−0.67)	(2.97)	(3.66)	(1.56)	(8.26)
1.362	−0.472	−0.654*	0.811	−0.078	−5.575	−3.907	0.050
(0.51)	(−1.59)	(−1.76)	(1.02)	(−0.32)	(−1.64)	(−0.82)	(0.35)

related academic research. While most empirical studies which provide examples of CSR and financial performance rarely focus on banks, this chapter examines the effect of corporate social responsibility on financial performance (resulting from the CAMEL concept) by using TWSE-listed CSR-banks and NonCSR-banks defined by *Global Views Monthly*. We also employ four matching methods to match samples with similar characteristic variables so as to remove the selection bias due to the non-random assignment of samples. The four matching methods are the Nearest, Caliper, Mahala and Mahala Caliper matching methods.

Before matching, the CSR-banks performed well on some of the performance measures but worse on others. After matching, although the results were slightly mixed, the empirical results still showed that the CSR-banks did not have an overall advantage for all the performance measures. On the contrary, some measures for the CSR-banks were significantly weaker than those for the NonCSR-banks. This result could be partially explained by Llewellyn (2005), who shows that the average performance of English banks (after adopting the stockholder business model) is better than the performance of German banks (which adopt the stakeholder business model).

In this chapter we consider four matching methods, with the first two methods being based on the propensity scoring method and the second two on the characteristic variables method. In regard to matching efficiency, the best method is the Mahala Caliper method, because the five characteristic variables in the two groups are nearly the same at the conventional statistical level. The first three methods are only the second-best methods. However, when we use regression analysis and the Mahala Caliper is employed, the performance ratios of the two groups are almost the same. The gaps for all performance measures between the two groups become insignificant, implying that CSR-banks can hardly outperform the NonCSR-banks. Although the four matching methods yield different and mixed results, we hope that the comparisons can be based on similar characteristic variables, which are successfully achieved by using the Mahala Caliper method. Thus, we prefer its results, which suggest that there is little effect on performance in terms of being a CSR-bank, given that the characteristic variables of the two groups are statistically insignificant.

There are two points worth noting in future research. First, better matching results in a loss in sample size (and a loss in terms of the efficiency of estimation), and thus matching

Table 25.7   Do CSR-banks perform better? OLS estimation results (using Model II to estimate PSF)

Panel A. Nearest-neighbor matching (Nearest)

	BISCAR	EQUITY	NPL	LLR	COVER-AGE	INEFFI-CIENCY	BURDEN
Constant	8.271	3.259	0.968	7.074	87.60	1.341	3.287
	(31.0)	(7.76)	(10.7)	(18.0)	(8.79)	(6.25)	(9.78)
ASSET	−0.039	0.023	−0.001	−0.058	0.402	0.004	−0.005
	(−10.2)	(3.83)	(−0.67)	(−10.4)	(2.82)	(1.37)	(−1.07)
D_{FHC}	0.002	−0.003	0.000	0.004	−0.047	−0.001	0.000
	(5.38)	(−4.80)	(−0.64)	(7.76)	(−3.36)	(−3.43)	(−0.37)
D_{CSR}	0.498***	−0.576**	0.060	0.952***	−8.266	0.017	−0.018
	(2.91)	(−2.14)	(1.04)	(3.78)	(−1.29)	(0.12)	(−0.08)

Panel B. Caliper matching (Caliper)

	BISCAR	EQUITY	NPL	LLR	COVER-AGE	INEFFI-CIENCY	BURDEN
Constant	8.360	5.220	1.133	5.942	84.61	1.403	3.608
	(28.0)	(9.27)	(10.8)	(11.3)	(8.24)	(6.05)	(10.2)
ASSET	−0.041	0.028	0.000	−0.063	0.505	0.004	−0.004
	(−9.21)	(3.40)	(−0.21)	(−8.14)	(3.34)	(1.20)	(−0.76)
D_{FHC}	0.002	−0.004	0.000	0.006	−0.054	−0.001	−0.001
	(5.16)	(−5.23)	(−1.44)	(7.03)	(−3.44)	(−2.85)	(−1.12)
D_{CSR}	0.336	−1.677***	−0.033	1.468***	−10.79	−0.071	−0.089
	(1.64)	(−4.33)	(−0.46)	(4.07)	(−1.53)	(−0.45)	(−0.37)

Panel C. Mahalanobis metric matching with Calipers (Mahala Caliper)

	BISCAR	EQUITY	NPL	LLR	COVER-AGE	INEFFI-CIENCY	BURDEN
Constant	8.108	2.418	0.765	7.312	43.55	0.646	2.659
	(14.0)	(3.16)	(3.36)	(9.18)	(2.71)	(1.35)	(3.30)
ASSET	−0.043	0.021	−0.001	−0.061	0.382	0.004	−0.004
	(−9.59)	(3.52)	(−0.68)	(−9.89)	(3.04)	(1.00)	(−0.63)
D_{FHC}	0.003	−0.003	0.000	0.005	−0.026	−0.001	0.000
	(6.28)	(−5.00)	(0.01)	(8.51)	(−2.16)	(−1.48)	(−0.43)
D_{CSR}	0.582	0.458	0.228	0.445	18.83	0.306	0.555
	(1.37)	(0.82)	(1.37)	(0.77)	(1.60)	(0.87)	(0.94)

Notes:
1. Based on model specification II for estimating PSF, this table reports the pooled OLS estimation results of the regression analysis based on the relationship between CSR-banks and financial performance.
2. The data range from 2002Q1 to 2002Q2. Before sample matching, there are 90 CSR-banks and 489 NonCSR-banks. After matching, the number of NonCSR-banks for the Nearest, Caliper, Mahala and Mahala Caliper categories are 90, 70, 80 and 5, respectively.
3. The t-statistics are presented in parentheses.
4. ***, ** and * denote significance at the 1%, 5% and 10% levels, respectively.

EXPENSE	DEPLOAN	ROA	ROE	NIM	NONINT	LIQUID	LIQUID-REV
81.03	0.594	0.719	3.854	0.921	26.54	14.92	0.223
(59.3)	(3.94)	(3.82)	(10.8)	(8.00)	(15.9)	(6.82)	(2.53)
0.016	−0.010	−0.013	−0.007	−0.008	−0.064	−0.007	−0.004
(0.81)	(−4.64)	(−4.68)	(−1.35)	(−4.63)	(−2.70)	(−0.24)	(−3.12)
−0.006	0.001	0.001	0.000	0.001	0.011	0.009	0.001
(−3.21)	(4.38)	(4.50)	(−0.14)	(4.53)	(4.72)	(2.95)	(7.05)
−0.325	0.113	0.094	−0.061	0.080	1.287	1.627	0.225***
(−0.37)	(1.17)	(0.78)	(−0.27)	(1.09)	(1.20)	(1.18)	(3.97)

EXPENSE	DEPLOAN	ROA	ROE	NIM	NONINT	LIQUID	LIQUID-REV
78.49	0.599	0.763	4.202	0.996	27.61	12.23	0.269
(57.3)	(3.84)	(3.97)	(11.6)	(9.12)	(18.9)	(6.09)	(3.22)
0.019	−0.011	−0.014	−0.001	0.001	0.011	0.008	0.001
(0.96)	(−4.93)	(−5.03)	(−1.07)	(4.39)	(5.13)	(2.52)	(8.47)
−0.005	0.001	0.001	−0.047	0.085	−0.152	2.657	0.192
(−2.51)	(4.34)	(4.42)	(−0.19)	(1.13)	(−0.15)	(1.90)	(3.33)
0.951	0.172	0.149	−0.006	−0.008***	−0.062***	0.015	−0.006***
(1.01)	(1.61)	(1.13)	(−1.12)	(−5.14)	(−2.90)	(0.48)	(−4.59)

EXPENSE	DEPLOAN	ROA	ROE	NIM	NONINT	LIQUID	LIQUID-REV
77.21	1.238	1.620	3.621	1.170	32.96	19.34	0.245
(27.4)	(3.85)	(4.05)	(4.34)	(4.66)	(9.13)	(3.80)	(1.62)
0.025	−0.012	−0.016	−0.005	−0.009	−0.079	−0.002	−0.004
(1.12)	(−4.85)	(−4.97)	(−0.78)	(−4.67)	(−2.82)	(−0.05)	(−3.50)
−0.006	0.001	0.001	−0.001	0.001	0.011	0.007	0.001
(−2.94)	(2.96)	(3.04)	(−0.86)	(3.31)	(3.96)	(1.75)	(8.71)
2.467	−0.093	−0.231	0.382	0.102	−2.986	−1.692	0.140
(1.20)	(−0.40)	(−0.79)	(0.63)	(0.56)	(−1.13)	(−0.46)	(1.27)

methods require a large sample. Second, in order to investigate the effects of taking CSR into consideration on performance, it is often suggested that the performances of banks be compared both before and after taking CSR into consideration. In this chapter, we do not perform such a comparison, one reason being that the macro environment may not be the same for the two periods, and the other being that we could hardly identify the exact starting date of taking CSR into consideration for each bank. To control the time trend effects and differences in the characteristics between samples, the difference in differences (DID) method could be employed (Nguyen et al., 2005).

NOTES

1. Regarding the definitions of CSR, see Frooman (1997), Carroll (1999) and McWilliams and Siegel (2001).
2. The 2008 Chinese milk scandal was a food safety incident in the People's Republic of China (PRC) involving milk and infant formula, and other food materials and components that had been adulterated with melamine. It is reported that there were an estimated 300 000 victims, with six infants dying from kidney stones and other kidney damage, and a further 860 babies being hospitalized.
3. Empirical studies of CSR and performance are classified based on measures of performance. The measures of the first kind of study are accounting-based, such as return on assets (ROA) and return on equity (ROE) (Griffin and Mahon, 1997; Guenster et al., 2005; Aigner, 2006; Nelling and Webb, 2006; Shen and Chang, 2009). Those of the second kind are market-based, using measures such as stock returns (Hamilton et al., 1993; Guerard, 1997a, 1997b; Brammer et al., 2005a, 2005b; Anderson and Smith, 2006). The third method is based on event studies regarding the impact on short-run stock returns from engagement in or contravention of CSR activities (Posnikoff, 1997; Wright and Ferris, 1997; Teoh et al., 1999; Brammer et al., 2005b; Becchetti et al., 2007).
4. The origin of Grameen Bank can be traced back to 1976 when Professor Muhammad Yunus (awarded the Nobel Peace Prize in 2006), a Fulbright scholar and Professor at the University of Chittagong, launched a research project to examine the possibility of designing a credit delivery system to provide banking services targeting the rural poor. In October 1983, the Grameen Bank Project was transformed into an independent bank by government legislation.
5. According to Ahmad (2000) and Warde (2000), Islamic banking is characterized by a moral filter based on the definitions of *halal* (permissible) and *haram* (prohibited and undesirable) which targets the conscience of an entrepreneur or firm, thereby promoting a positive social climate for society, and providing an expedient legal framework. Islamic banks are not allowed to finance projects which violate the moral value system of Islam, such as a brewery, a casino, a nightclub or any other activity which is prohibited by Islam or known to be detrimental to society.
6. See Shen and Chang (2009).
7. Rubin and Thomas (1992) demonstrated that using the estimated probability of being treated based on observable characteristics X, $\hat{P}(X)$, instead of $P(X)$, still reduces selection bias.
8. We need not match samples by industry because all firms in our sample are banks.
9. We can also compute the percentage change from before-matching to after-matching for a given characteristic variable for each matching criterion. Please refer to Shen and Chang (2009) for details.
10. Chih et al. (2008) applied the FTSE4Good index to study the relationship between earnings management and CSR and found evidence of a positive association.
11. According to Shen (2002), because the order for the provision of loan loss reserves is revenue, then retained earnings, to which paid-in capital and equity are then added, more provision means more erosion of the profitability of banks. More provision also implies increased apprehension regarding the asset quality on the part of bank managers.
12. To alleviate the overbanking and overcompetition problem and in an attempt to bring the financial industry in line competitively with the global financial markets, the Taiwan government decided to conduct banking financial reforms. Also, almost at the same time, in the United States, the announcement of the Citigroup merger sped up the process of financial consolidation, and afterwards Congress passed the Gramm–Leach–Bliley Act (GLBA). Under the FHC structure, a financial institution can engage in banking, insurance and securities at the same time. The GLBA encouraged the financial regulators in Taiwan to speed up the reforms. Taiwan passed the amended Banking Law and the Financial Institutions Consolidation Law in 2000. In 2001, the Financial Holding Company Act was promulgated to encourage the consolidation within and across banking sectors. The FHC holds at least 25 percent

shares of banks, insurance and securities, hoping to create economies of scale and scope. Since the passage of the FHC Act, 14 FHCs were established successively. In the early stages, 13 banks joined the FHCs. Subsequently, an additional four banks joined in. Thus, there are in total 17 FHC-banks and 17 independent banks in our sample between 2002 and 2006. See Shen and Chang (forthcoming) for details.

13. We obtain similar results when propensity score function (PSF) is estimated using the Logit model.

REFERENCES

Ahmad, K. (2000), 'Islamic finance and banking: the challenge and prospects', *Review of Islamic Economics*, **9**, 57–82.

Aigner, D.J. (2006), 'Corporate social responsibility and the bottom line', Working Paper, Paul Merage School of Business, University of California, Irvine.

Alexander, G.J. and R.A. Buchholz (1978), 'Corporate social performance and stock market performance', *Academy of Management Journal*, **21**, 479–486.

Alkhafaji, A.F. (1989), *A Stakeholder Approach to Corporate Governance: Managing in a Dynamic Environment*, New York: Quorum Books.

Anderson, J. and G. Smith (2006), 'A great company can be a great investment', *Financial Analysts Journal*, July/August, 86–93.

Aupperle, K., A. Carroll and J. Hatfield (1985), 'An empirical examination of the relationship between corporate social responsibility and profitability', *Academy of Management Journal*, **28**, 446–463.

Becchetti, L., R. Ciciretti and I. Hasan (2007), 'Corporate social responsibility and shareholder's value: an event study analysis', Working Paper, Federal Reserve Bank of Atlanta.

Bowman, E.H. and M. Haire (1975), 'A strategic posture toward corporate social responsibility', *California Management Review*, **18**, 49–58.

Bragdon, J. and J. Marlin (1972), 'Is pollution profitable?', *Risk Management*, **19**, 9–18.

Brammer, S., C. Brooks and S. Pavelin (2005a), 'Corporate social performance and stock returns: UK evidence from disaggregate measures', *Financial Management*, **35**, 97–116.

Brammer, S., C. Brooks and S. Pavelin (2005b), 'The stock performance of America's 100 best corporate citizens', Working Paper, Cass Business School, City University, London.

Carroll, A.B. (1999), 'Corporate social responsibility: evolution of a definitional construct', *Business and Society*, **38**, 268–295.

Chih, H.L., C.H. Shen and F.C. Kang (2008), 'Corporate social responsibility, investor protection, and earnings management: some international evidence', *Journal of Business Ethics*, **79**, 179–198.

Dehejia, R.H. and S. Wahba (2002), 'Propensity score matching methods for nonexperimental causal studies', *Review of Economics and Statistics*, **84**, 151–161.

Dierkes, M. and R. Coppock (1978), 'Europe tries the corporate social report', *Business and Society Review*, Spring, 21–24.

Fombrun, C.J., N.A. Gardberg and M.L. Barnett (2000), 'Opportunity platforms and safety nets: corporate citizenship and reputational risk', *Business and Society Review*, **105**, 85–106.

Fombrun, C. and M. Shanley (1990), 'What's in a name? Reputation building and corporate strategy', *Academy of Management Journal*, **33**, 233–258.

Friedman, M. (1970), 'The social responsibility of business is to increase its profits', *New York Times Magazine*, **13**, September.

Frooman, J. (1997), 'Socially irresponsible and illegal behavior and shareholder wealth: a meta-analysis of event studies', *Business and Society*, **36**, 221–249.

Griffin, J.J. and J.F. Mahon (1997), 'The corporate social performance and corporate financial performance debate: twenty-five years of incomparable research', *Business and Society*, **36**, 5–31.

Guenster, N., J. Derwall, R. Bauer and K. Koedijk (2005), 'The economic value of corporate eco-efficiency', Academy of Management Conference Paper.

Guerard, J.B., Jr. (1997a), 'Is there a cost to being socially responsible?', *Journal of Investing*, **6**, 11–18.

Guerard, J.B., Jr. (1997b), 'Additional evidence on the cost of being socially responsible in investing', *Journal of Investing*, **6**, 31 35.

Hamilton, S., H. Jo and M. Statman (1993), 'Doing well while doing good? The investment performance of socially responsible mutual funds', *Financial Analysts Journal*, November, 62–66.

Henderson, D. (2002), *Misguided Virtue: False Notions of Corporate Social Responsibility*, London: Institute of Economic Affairs.

Hofler, R., J. Elston and J. Lee (2004), 'Dividend policy and institutional ownership: empirical evidence using a propensity score matching estimator', Discussion Papers on Entrepreneurship, Growth and Public Policy, No. 2004-27, Group for Entrepreneurship, Growth and Public Policy, Max Planck Institute of Economics.

Iqbal, M. and P. Molyneux (2005), *Thirty Years of Islamic Banking: History, Performance and Prospects*, New York: Palgrave Macmillan.

Lewis, M.K. and L.M. Algaoud (2001), *Islamic Banking*, Cheltenham, UK and Northampton, MA, USA: Edward Elgar.

Llewellyn, D.T. (2005), 'Competition and profitability in European banking: why are British banks so profitable?', *Economic Notes*, **34**, 279–311.

McGuire, J., A. Sundgren and T. Schneeweis (1988), 'Corporate social responsibility and firm financial performance', *Academy of Management Journal*, **31**, 854–872.

McWilliams, A. and D. Siegel (2001), 'Corporate social responsibility: a theory of the firm perspective', *Academy of Management Review*, **26**, 117–127.

Moore, G. (2001), 'Corporate social and financial performance: an investigation in the UK supermarket industry', *Journal of Business Ethics*, **34**, 299–315.

Nelling, E. and E. Webb (2006), 'Corporate social responsibility and financial performance: the virtuous circle revisited', Working Paper.

Nguyen, A.N., J. Taylor and S. Bradley (2005), 'The estimated effect of Catholic schooling on educational outcomes using propensity score matching', Working Paper, Department of Economics, Lancaster University.

Porter, M. and M. Kramer (2006), 'Strategy and society: the link between competitive advantage and corporate social responsibility', *Harvard Business Review*, **84**(12), 78–92.

Porter, M.E. and C. van der Linde (1995), 'Green and competitive: ending the stalemate', *Harvard Business Review*, September–October, 120–135.

Posner, B.Z. and W.H. Schmidt (1992), 'Values and the American manager: an update updated', *California Management Review*, **34**, 80–94.

Posnikoff, J.F. (1997), 'Disinvestment from South Africa: they did well by doing good', *Contemporary Economic Policy*, **15**, 76–86.

Prior, F. and A. Argandoña (2009), 'Best practices in credit accessibility and corporate social responsibility in financial institutions', *Journal of Business Ethics*, **87**, supplement 1, 251–265.

Rosenbaum, P. and D. Rubin (1983), 'The central role of the propensity score in observational studies for causal effects', *Biometrika*, **70**, 41–55.

Rosenbaum, P. and D. Rubin (1985a), 'Constructing a control group using multivariate matched sampling methods that incorporate the propensity', *American Statistician*, **39**, 33–38.

Rosenbaum, P. and D. Rubin (1985b), 'The bias due to incomplete matching', *Biometrics*, **41**, 103–116.

Rubin, D. (1973), 'Matching to remove bias in observational studies', *Biometrics*, **29**, 159–183.

Rubin, D. (1997), 'Estimating causal effects from large data sets using propensity scores', the Sixth Regenstrief Conference: Statistical Methods, Annals of Internal Medicine, Harvard University.

Rubin, D.B. and N. Thomas (1992), 'Characterizing the effect of matching using linear propensity score methods with normal distributions', *Biometrika*, **79**, 797–809.

Scholtens, B. (2009), 'Corporate social responsibility in the international banking industry', *Journal of Business Ethics*, **86**, 159–175.

Shen, C.H. (2002), 'CAMEL in financial holding company banks and individual banks: 1997–1998', *Taiwan Banking and Finance Quarterly*, **3**, 73–94.

Shen, C.H. and Y. Chang (2009), 'Ambition versus conscience, does corporate social responsibility pay off? The application of matching methods', *Journal of Business Ethics*, **88**, 133–153.

Shen, C.H. and Y. Chang (forthcoming), 'To join or not to join? Do banks that are in a financial-holding-company perform better than banks that are not?', *Contemporary Economic Policy*.

Shen, C.H. and C.C. Lee (2006), 'Estimating the effects of hedging by derivatives on the firm's value: application of propensity score matching methods', manuscript.

Shleifer, A. and R. Vishny (1997), 'A survey of corporate governance', *Journal of Finance*, **52**, 737–783.

Teoh, S.H., I. Welch and C.P. Wazzan (1999), 'The effect of socially activist investment policies on the financial markets: evidence from the South African boycott', *Journal of Business*, **72**, 35–89.

Trotman, K.T. and G.W. Bradley (1981), 'Associations between social responsibility disclosure and characteristics of companies', *Accounting, Organizations and Society*, **6**, 355–362.

Vance, S. (1975), 'Are socially responsible firms good investment risks?', *Management Review*, **64**, 18–24.

Walley, N. and B. Whitehead (1994), 'It's not easy being green', *Harvard Business Review*, **72**, 2–7.

Warde, I. (2000), *Islamic Finance in the Global Economy*, Edinburgh: Edinburgh University Press.

Wright, P. and S. Ferris (1997), 'Agency conflict and corporate strategy: the effect of divestment on corporate value', *Strategic Management Journal*, **18**, 77–83.

PART VI

GOVERNANCE IN NON-BANK FINANCIAL INSTITUTIONS

26 Management turnover, regulatory oversight and performance: evidence from community banks

Ajay A. Palvia*

26.1 INTRODUCTION

Bank shareholders, like shareholders of unregulated firms, delegate the monitoring of top management to company boards of directors. Unlike other firms, however, banks are also subject to regulatory monitoring, which has the potential to improve oversight by providing bank boards with additional information or by prodding bank boards to consider existing information more dutifully. To the extent regulatory oversight helps, or forces, bank boards to discipline ineffective management, it has the potential to improve bank governance.[1]

Regulatory monitoring of banks largely consists of rating banks, communicating the rationale behind the ratings to banks, and initiating either formal or informal actions when important deficiencies in banks are found.[2] If regulatory monitoring uncovers information signifying ineffective or inept management, it may lead to the replacement of senior management. This chapter considers the role of regulatory monitoring in promoting better bank governance. In particular, it examines whether regulatory evaluations influence top management turnover and whether such regulatory-induced turnover is associated with better subsequent performance.

Numerous past instances of top management replacement suggest that regulatory monitoring can play a disciplinary role in banks. For example, an Office of the Comptroller of the Currency (OCC) bank examination found poor internal controls at a community bank in 2001; soon thereafter, the bank's chief executive officer (CEO) was fired by its board (OCC, 2002). In more recent cases, Coast Bank of Florida and Westsound Bank, both facing pressure from investigations by bank regulators for loan fraud, announced the resignations of their CEOs (Frater and Pollick, 2007; Gardner, 2008). These actions support the view that regulatory oversight, at least in some cases, is associated with turnover of ineffective or inept bank management. This chapter explores whether the association between regulatory oversight and top management dismissals is systematic. Further, it examines whether regulatory-linked turnover of top management improves bank performance.

Overall, this chapter finds that, consistent with past studies of large, publicly traded firms, poorly performing community banks are more likely to have top management turnover. It also finds that greater regulatory pressure, as indicated by recent regulatory examinations, weak regulatory ratings and recent rating downgrades, is associated with more executive turnover after controlling for bank performance. Finally, turnover linked to regulatory monitoring is significantly, positively related to future profitability. Taken as a whole, the evidence suggests that regulatory oversight improves bank discipline and can help to improve bank performance and, implicitly, bank governance.

A key distinguishing feature of this study is a unique dataset of about 3000 community banks and over 74 000 observations spanning a decade.[3] The large sample and the large number of years allow for significant variation in both management turnover and bank financial performance. The study focuses on community banks – which tend to be small, geographically concentrated and privately held – for two reasons.[4] First, neither the effect of performance on turnover nor the impact of regulatory monitoring on turnover is well understood for smaller or private banks. Additionally, because market and board oversight may not be as strong for community banks, and if managerial replacements induced by regulatory monitoring lead to improvements in bank governance, the improvements should be easier to identify in community banks relative to larger, publicly traded banks.

A large number of studies have examined the relationship between past stock performance and CEO turnover and usually found a negative relationship.[5] The benefits of such turnover on subsequent performance, and implicitly on bank governance, are not as clear, however. The existing literature does document a positive relationship between turnover of poorly performing management and subsequent performance (Denis and Denis, 1995; Hotchkiss, 1995; Khorana, 2001). These studies suggest that managerial discipline linked to traditional monitoring by boards can improve performance. In contrast, the impact of management turnover on performance arising from non-traditional monitoring mechanisms, such as regulatory oversight, is less clear. This is the first study, to my knowledge, to explore the performance impact of management turnover arising from such non-traditional monitoring mechanisms. In providing evidence that management turnover linked to regulatory monitoring is associated with improved bank performance, this chapter suggests that regulatory monitoring of bank management leads to better bank governance and is not entirely driven by compliance with regulation.

In the next section, I describe the key aspects of the regulatory examination process of banks and consider its role in bank governance. The data are described in section 26.3. In sections 26.4 and 26.5 I present the empirical results, and in section 26.6 I draw some conclusions.

26.2   REGULATORY OVERSIGHT, BANK EXAMINATIONS AND BANK GOVERNANCE

The US bank regulatory system is complex and composed of both state and federal regulators. Banks with state banking charters are overseen jointly by their state regulatory agency and by either the Federal Reserve or the Federal Deposit Insurance Corporation (FDIC). The OCC oversees nationally chartered banks.[6] Regardless of regulatory agency, federal regulators examine vast amounts of information during the examination process and a major product of the examination process is a regulatory rating of a bank's overall condition, commonly referred to as a CAMELS rating. It is used by all the three federal banking regulators.

The CAMELS rating is an overall assessment of a bank based on six individual ratings; the word CAMELS is an acronym for these individual elements of regulatory assessment (capital adequacy, asset quality, management, earnings, liquidity and sensitivity to market risk).[7] The overall CAMELS rating and each individual component rating are private and confidential. Regulatory agencies do not release ratings; even historical CAMELS ratings or ratings of banks no longer in existence are not released.

All individual component ratings as well as the overall ratings are coded on a scale of 1 to 5 with 1 being best (no regulatory concern) and 5 being worst (very serious regulatory concerns). Banks with weak CAMEL ratings (generally 3, 4, and 5) tend to be monitored more aggressively by regulators and are often faced with informal and sometimes formal regulatory actions. Thus, weaker ratings should be associated with greater regulatory pressure.

Although many of the individual components of CAMEL are likely to be correlated, they are not identical. This chapter's focus is on the management ratings. According to the OCC definition, regulatory management ratings are based on:

> a) technical competence, leadership, and administration ability, b) compliance with banking regulations and statutes, c) ability to plan and respond to changing circumstances, d) adequacy of and compliance with internal policies, e) depth and succession, f) tendencies toward self-dealing, g) demonstrated willingness to serve the legitimate banking needs of the community.

Although much of the information in the CAMEL or management component ratings can be deduced from publicly available financial information, an increasing number of studies indicate that the regulatory information in these ratings cannot be fully explained by publicly available information (DeYoung et al., 2001; Peek et al., 1998). Given that most of the guidelines upon which the management regulatory rating is based are consistent with good corporate governance, regulatory actions based on private information contained in these ratings could potentially help improve the governance of banks.

Previous evidence implies that the bank examination process may lead to improved bank governance in terms of forcing banks to report loan losses more fully (Dahl et al., 1998; Gunther and Moore, 2003). Although several studies have also implied that regulatory oversight drives management turnover in banks (Houston and James, 1993; Palvia, 2011; Prowse, 1995; Webb, 2008), results from these studies may not necessarily indicate that such oversight is beneficial. For example, if the turnover attributable to regulatory pressure is primarily a result of compliance issues and not because of ineffective or inept management, then regulatory-linked replacement of top management may not improve governance. Furthermore, if regulatory-linked managerial discipline simply replaces the disciplinary role of boards (Cook et al., 2004), regulatory oversight of bank management may not improve bank governance.

To address the question of whether regulatory oversight is beneficial in improving bank governance, this chapter focuses on community banks, where the potential benefits of regulatory oversight should be the greatest. Detailed governance data on these banks, however, are not available to address this question directly. Fortunately, because improved governance is generally associated with better performance, improved governance owing to regulatory oversight can be inferred if the management turnover linked to this oversight is also related to better subsequent performance. By examining whether bank regulatory oversight is associated with turnover, and then exploring whether turnover linked to regulatory oversight is related to improved performance, this chapter explores whether regulatory monitoring of bank management can lead to improved bank governance.

26.3   DATA

All financial data are based on call report data, which is publicly available for all US banks. Private regulatory variables are obtained from the OCC. Because regulatory data are only available for national banks, the sample is restricted to these banks. Regulatory ratings of bank management are used, rather than information regarding the issuance of formal actions. Regulatory ratings implicitly factor in both formal and informal actions and also incorporate the effects of communication between regulators and bank boards that do not culminate in a specific formal or informal action. Accordingly, the use of regulatory ratings allows for a more comprehensive measure of regulatory oversight than indicators of whether a bank is facing an explicit enforcement action.

The key data on executive turnover are only available for community banks, defined as banks having assets of up to $100 million, between 1984 and 1994.[8] Additionally, the sample is restricted to banks that are not part of a multibank holding company (MBHC) for two reasons. Firstly, this reduces the likelihood that banks in the sample are indirectly influenced by market pressures of large organizations through an affiliation with an MBHC. Secondly, bank management may have multiple roles within a holding company or may be influenced by the holding company board. Because the data do not allow the identification of roles of senior bank management or the make-up of boards within the subsidiaries of a holding company and its parent organization, the role of regulatory ratings of bank management is more difficult to interpret in these types of organizations. The elimination of banks affiliated with MBHCs reduces the sample further by about 25 percent. Because of the data restrictions, the results of the chapter will apply to community banks that are not part of MBHCs and may not necessarily apply to larger banks or banks that are part of larger banking organizations. Despite these data restrictions, the sample contains an overwhelming majority of national banks and the results apply to a broader number of banks and bank classes than previous studies focusing on large, publicly traded banks.[9]

For the most part, banks in the sample are included for all time periods in which data are available.[10] Thus the dataset consists of an unbalanced panel, in which banks remain in the sample for a varying number of years during the observation period (as new banks form and existing banks are acquired or exit for other reasons). The data are not restricted to banks remaining in the sample over the entire period, because this would have greatly reduced the sample size and would lead to considerable survivorship bias. All financial variables are winsorized, at the bottom 1 percent and top 1 percent levels, to minimize the effect of outliers. After creating lagged values of key variables, the final dataset consists of about 3000 banks and over 74 000 bank-quarter observations during the ten-year period between 1985 and 1994.[11]

26.3.1   Variables

The key variable in the analysis indicates whether a change in senior executive officer occurred during the quarter (*EXTURN*). A senior executive officer is defined as any one of the top three officers in the bank; these officers, regardless of their official titles, perform the functions of a chief executive officer, president or senior lending officer. A change can occur for any reason, including resignation, retirement, death, or demotion (to a non-senior officer). For banks with fewer than three senior officers, an additional officer being hired to a senior role is also counted as a change.[12]

Three variables are used to measure regulatory monitoring of banks. The first of these is the regulatory rating for management (*MANRAT*); like CAMEL ratings, *MANRAT* ranges from 1 (best) to 5 (worst). Secondly, I include the change in the management rating during the quarter. Positive values of the change in rating variable (*CHANGERAT*) indicate regulatory downgrades. I use the change in the rating, rather than a dummy indicating a downgrade, to allow for the fact that downgrades of more than one notch may have a different impact relative to downgrades of only one notch.[13] The variables *MANRAT* and *CHANGERAT* capture different dimensions of regulatory oversight. While *MANRAT* captures the current regulatory opinion of bank management (and implicitly the effect of past downgrades), *CHANGERAT* captures a recent change in the regulatory opinion of bank management. All else being equal, we should expect poorly rated bank management and management whose ratings have been recently downgraded to be associated with greater regulatory pressure on management and thus higher turnover. The third regulatory oversight variable included is a dummy indicating whether an examination was conducted in the last 18 months (*EXAMINED*). Typically, bank exams are conducted every 12–18 months; sometimes, banks are not examined for years. Faced with limited resources, regulators typically prioritize examinations to focus on banks with suspected problems. The inclusion of *EXAMINED* acknowledges that banks may not always be examined with equal regularity and a decision by regulators to conduct an exam may itself indicate a lack of regulatory confidence in a bank or its management.

Bank performance is measured by the return on assets (*ROA*), which is defined as net income to assets. To control for other aspects of bank financial condition, I include measures for financial leverage, liquidity, and credit risk. I proxy for credit risk using the dollar amount of loans more than 90 days past due or under nonaccrual status divided by assets (*PDUE90*). Liquidity (*LIQUID*) is proxied by the amount of nonvolatile liabilities scaled by assets.[14] Financial leverage is controlled for using the capital ratio based on Tier 1 capital (*CAPRAT*).[15] To control for size, I also include the log of total assets (*LGASSET*).

Lastly, I include controls relating to bank organizational structure and market factors. Given the large dataset of mostly private firms, detailed data regarding organizational, board and ownership structure are not available. Instead, several other observable characteristics that may cause executive turnover are accounted for. First, I include a dummy indicating whether the bank has acquired another bank during the quarter (*ACQUIRE*); banks that have acquired other banks are more likely to have redundant management and are more likely to have higher executive turnover.[16] Additionally, because newer banks are likely to have less experienced management, management turnover could be different for these banks. To control for this, I include a dummy indicating that the bank is a de novo bank (*DENOVO*); I define 'de novo' as being chartered within the last five years.

Although ownership structure of the bank is not available, it is possible to identify when a bank moves from non-affiliated status to becoming a bank holding company member, when a bank moves from being affiliated to a holding company to being affiliated with a different holding company, and also when a bank goes from being a member of a holding company to being unaffiliated. A measure of change in ownership,

OWNCHANGE, indicating any of the above changes, is included in the analysis because these changes may lead to redundant management or reorganizations resulting in executive turnover.[17]

Because executives may leave a bank voluntarily, it would be beneficial to control for other potential causes of executive turnover, such as retirement or accepting employment elsewhere. Unfortunately, no information is available about average executive age or other factors that may affect a decision to retire. A bank executive's decision to accept employment elsewhere, however, is likely to be affected by the number of bank executive positions in the market where the bank operates. To control for voluntary turnover, I include two additional variables. First, I include the percentage of other banks in the market (metropolitan statistical area or rural county) experiencing turnover during the quarter (*EXTURNMKT*). Secondly, the variable *BANKSMKT*, which indicates the number of banks currently operating in the market, is included.[18] *BANKSMKT* may also proxy for higher market-level competition; banks located in markets with greater competition may be more willing to replace poorly performing management.[19]

Finally, executive turnover is likely to depend on executive tenure for multiple reasons. First, relatively new senior executives are less likely to be entrenched and are, therefore, more vulnerable to being disciplined. An additional factor could be that senior management turnover happens in waves. Because our measure of turnover, *EXTURN*, includes turnover in any of the top three executive positions of a bank, it is possible that turnover in one quarter could be associated with turnover in the following quarter, as subsequent quarters could be associated with different executives. Thus short tenure of top management (*TENSHORT*) is measured as turnover in the prior quarter and is included in the analysis.

26.3.2 Descriptive Statistics

Summary statistics for all variables are provided in Table 26.1. The mean for the turnover variable, *EXTURN*, shows that about 8.5 percent of banks had senior executive changes in any given quarter during the observation period. The regulatory variable *MANRAT* has a mean of 2.33 and a median of 2. This suggests that the majority of banks are rated highly, (i.e., 1 or 2). The regulatory variable *CHANGERAT* is reported in Table 26.1 only for observations when a change in a rating has occurred.[20] *CHANGERAT*, for banks with ratings changes, has a mean of 0.06 and 5th percentile and 95th percentile values of −1 and 2, respectively. This suggests that while the overwhelming majority of ratings changes are only one notch up or down, sometimes larger changes do occur. The mean of the last regulatory variable, *EXAMINED*, is about 88 percent, which indicates that most banks have been examined in the previous 18 months.

The average log assets (*LGASSET*), measured in thousands of dollars, is 10.48, which implies the average bank size is $35 million during the entire time period. Similarly, the 5th percentile, median and 95th percentile sizes are roughly $11 million, $38 million and $92 million, respectively. Thus, there is a wide range of bank sizes within the sample of community banks. The mean of change in log assets (*CHLGASSET*) is 0.07 while the 5th percentile and 95th percentile are −0.09 and 0.30, respectively; this indicates that, on average, banks grow from quarter to quarter, but some banks shrink.

Table 26.1   Variable names, definitions and summary statistics

Variable name and definition	Number of obs	Mean	Percentiles				
			5th	25th	50th	75th	95th
EXTURN Indicates senior officer change	73 269	8.51%	0.00%	0.00%	0.00%	0.00%	100.00%
MANRAT Supervisory rating (i.e. 1, 2, 3, 4, or 5)	73 269	2.33	1.00	2.00	2.00	3.00	4.00
CHANGERAT Indicates change in *MANRAT*	5 420	0.06	−1.00	−1.00	1.00	1.00	2.00
EXAMINED Indicates exam occurred in last 18 months	73 269	88.46%	0.00%	100.00%	100.00%	100.00%	100.00%
LGASSET Log of assets	73 269	10.48	9.30	10.03	10.54	10.98	11.43
CHLGASSET Change in log assets (since last quarter)	73 269	0.07	−0.09	0.00	0.05	0.11	0.30
CAPRAT (Tier 1) Capital ratio	73 269	9.24%	4.98%	7.23%	8.66%	10.62%	15.36%
ROA Return on assets	73 269	0.77%	−1.48%	0.55%	0.99%	1.36%	2.02%
PDUE90 Loans 90 days past due to assets	73 269	1.27%	0.01%	0.28%	0.79%	1.69%	4.36%
LIQUID Non-volatile liabilities to assets	73 269	88.67%	70.92%	84.60%	90.86%	95.04%	98.55%
DENOVO Indicates new bank (5 or fewer years)	73 269	11.58%	0.00%	0.00%	0.00%	0.00%	100.00%
ACQUIRE Indicates acquired another bank	73 269	0.53%	0.00%	0.00%	0.00%	0.00%	0.00%
OWNCHANGE Indicates change in bank ownership	73 269	1.01%	0.00%	0.00%	0.00%	0.00%	0.00%
BANKSMKT Number of banks in market	73 269	35.34	2.00	4.00	7.00	26.00	170.00
EXTURNMKT % of other banks in market with turnover	73 269	8.10%	0.00%	0.00%	0.00%	13.30%	31.45%

Notes: Summary statistics detailed in this table are primarily based on quarterly call report data from 1985 to 1994. Regulatory variables are derived from data obtained from the Office of Comptroller of the Currency. The variable *CHANGERAT* is summarized only for bank observations when there was a change in the rating (about 7.4 percent of observations); this is done to present a meaningful distribution of ratings changes. Finally, all financial variables are winsorized to the bottom and top 1 percent values. *LGASSET* and *CHLGASSET* reflect assets measured in thousands of dollars.

The variation in performance (*ROA*) and financial condition is considerable in the sample. The 5th and 95th percentile *ROA* values are −1.48 percent and 2.02 percent, respectively. Similarly, large ranges between the 5th and 95th percentile values of past-due loans (*PDUE*), capital ratio (*CAPRAT*) and liquidity (*LIQUID*) indicate that other elements of financial condition also vary dramatically across the sample. The 5th percentile to 95th range for *PDUE90, CAPRAT* and *LIQUID* are 0.01 percent, 4.36 percent; 4.98 percent, 15.36 percent; and 70.92 percent, 98.55 percent; respectively.

The mean value for *DENOVO* indicates that newer (de novo) banks make up about 11.58 percent of the banks in the sample. A very small portion of banks, that is, about 0.53 percent, acquire (*ACQUIRE*) other banks in any given quarter and about 1.01 percent of banks have had a change in ownership (*OWNCHANGE*) in any given quarter. The average and median numbers of banks in the market (*BANKSMKT*) in the sample are about 35 and 7, respectively; these numbers suggest that most markets have relatively small numbers of banks but a few very competitive markets lead to a higher overall average market size. Finally, the mean and median percentages of other banks in the market with turnover (*EXTURNMKT*) are 8.1 percent and 0.0 percent, respectively; thus most markets witness no turnover in other banks, while some witness a relatively large amount.

26.4   EMPIRICAL RESULTS

To examine how top manager turnover relates to regulatory pressure and performance, I first conduct univariate tests relating managerial turnover to regulatory pressure and performance. Next, the same question is examined through multivariate techniques. Further tests explore the question of whether regulatory-linked managerial turnover is related to future performance.

26.4.1   Univariate Tests: Performance and Regulatory Pressure – The Effect on Turnover

Table 26.2 divides the sample by time period and by whether executive turnover occurred in the quarter. The first three years of the sample (1986–1988) represent a period immediately following bank deregulation, with high levels of competition in the industry and an increasing number of bank failures; the next three years (1989–1991) are characterized by even more bank failures and the enacting of new, risk-based capital standards to limit risk-taking incentives by bank management. The last few years (1992–1994) are characterized by a more stable banking environment and improved bank profitability.

The results indicate that there are some differences in the performance and regulatory variables over time. Performance (*ROA*) tends to improve in later time periods relative to the first time period. Ratings downgrades, as indicated by higher values of *CHANGERAT*, are also somewhat more widespread in the earlier two periods of the sample relative to the later period. Finally, the percentage of banks examined in the last 18 months (*EXAMINED*) seems to be somewhat smaller in the earliest period relative to the later periods. Nevertheless, performance (*ROA*) is worse, regulatory ratings are worse

Table 26.2   Regulatory oversight and performance: univariate tests

Time period	Variable	No executive changes	At least 1 executive change	No change vs change
		(N = 30 497)	(N = 3245)	
1985–1988	*ROA*	0.72%	−0.02%	***
	MANRAT	2.26	2.64	***
	CHANGERATE	0.01	0.08	***
	EXAMINED	80.15%	89.46%	***
		(N = 19 463)	(N = 1763)	
1989–1991	*ROA*	0.79%	0.16%	***
	MANRAT	2.33	2.72	***
	CHANGERATE	0.01	0.06	
	EXAMINED	93.62%	94.84%	***
		(N = 17 071)	(N = 1230)	
1992–1994	*ROA*	1.06%	0.64%	***
	MANRAT	2.31	2.72	***
	CHANGERATE	−0.03	0.01	***
	EXAMINED	95.89%	97.89%	***

Notes: In the table, results of univariate tests examining the effect of performance and regulatory oversight on top management turnover are presented. Tests of differences are done using standard unpaired t-tests. Test significance is denoted by *** (p-value < 0.01), ** (p-value between 0.05 and 0.01), and * (p-value between 0.1 and 0.05). The variables *MANRAT* and *CHANGERAT* indicate regulatory ratings of bank management and changes in management ratings, respectively. *EXAMINED* indicates an exam occurred in the previous 18 months. *ROA* refers to return on assets.

(higher *MANRAT*), rating downgrades are more prevalent (higher *CHANGERAT*), and recent examinations are more likely to have occurred (*EXAMINED*) for banks when there was executive turnover regardless of time period. The differences between banks with and without executive turnover are statistically significant in every time period of the sample.

The tests described in Table 26.2 indicate that both performance and bank regulatory pressure play a part in bank executive turnover but do not account for these factors simultaneously. To address this issue, additional tests are conducted to examine the simultaneous impact of regulatory monitoring and performance. The results of these tests are shown in Table 26.3. Here, the level of performance (*ROA*) is divided into quartiles and the regulatory variables are summarized for each of these quartiles separately, for banks that did and did not experience turnover. It can be observed that regulatory pressure is stronger for banks with worse performance (i.e., worse ratings, greater prevalence of downgrades and increased likelihood of recent exams). Despite the correlation between performance and greater regulatory pressure, the results clearly indicate that the management ratings tend to be worse, downgrades are more widespread, and recent regulatory examinations are more likely to have occurred for banks with turnover for each quartile of performance. Overall, the results of Table 26.3 are consistent with both performance and regulatory pressure being drivers of executive turnover.

Table 26.3   Simultaneous effects of regulatory oversight and performance: univariate tests

ROA quartile	Variable	No executive changes	At least 1 executive change	No change vs change
		(N = 15 252)	(N = 2803)	
ROA – Quartile 1	*MANRAT*	2.75	3.04	***
(Lowest)	*CHANGERAT*	0.04	0.12	***
	EXAMINED	0.94	0.95	***
		(N = 16 812)	(N = 1444)	
ROA – Quartile 2	*MANRAT*	2.29	2.48	***
	CHANGERAT	0.00	0.01	*
	EXAMINED	0.90	0.93	***
		(N = 17 461)	(N = 1039)	
ROA – Quartile 3	*MANRAT*	2.12	2.28	***
	CHANGERAT	−0.01	0.00	*
	EXAMINED	0.86	0.89	***
		(N = 17 506)	(N = 952)	
ROA – Quartile 4	*MANRAT*	2.07	2.32	***
(Highest)	*CHANGERAT*	−0.02	0.01	***
	EXAMINED	0.82	0.89	***

Notes: This table describes univariate tests that simultaneously examine the effects of regulatory oversight and performance on management turnover. Quartiles of *ROA* (return on assets) are taken for each time period.. Tests of differences are done using standard unpaired t-tests. Test significance is denoted by *** (p-value < 0.01), ** (p-value between 0.05 and 0.01), and * (p-value between 0.1 and 0.05). The variable *MANRAT* represents regulatory ratings of bank management and *CHANGERAT* indicates changes in *MANRAT*. *EXAMINED* indicates an exam occurred in the previous 18 months.

26.4.2   Multivariate Tests: Performance and Regulatory Pressure – The Effect on Turnover

While the univariate statistics are clearly consistent with managerial turnover being driven by both performance and regulatory evaluations of bank management, they may not adequately adjust for other aspects of bank financial condition or non-financial factors that may influence turnover. If these other factors are really driving executive turnover, then not adequately accounting for them may lead to inaccurate conclusions. To control for these factors, multivariate regressions are conducted, controlling for key financial variables and other controls. A logistic model is employed for these tests as shown in the following equation:

$$Log\left(\frac{\text{Prob}(EXTURN_{i,t-1})}{1 - \text{Prob}(EXTURN_{i,t-1})}\right) = B_0 * MANRAT_{i,t-1} + B_1 * CHANGERAT_{i,t-1}$$

$$+ B_2 * EXAMINED_{i,t-1} + B_3 * ROA_{i,t-1} + \sum_{j=4}^{8} B_j * FC_{j;i,t-1+t-1}$$

$$+ \sum_{j=9}^{14} B_j * NFC_{j;i,t} + TIME_t + BANK_i + \varepsilon_{i,t} \tag{26.1}$$

In equation (26.1), FC is a vector of financial controls (*PDUE90*, *CAPRAT*, *LIQUID*, *LGASSET* and *CHLGASSET*). The second vector, *NFC*, includes the non-financial controls (*DENOVO*, *ACQUIRE*, *OWNCHANGE*, *TENSHORT*, *BANKSMT* and *EXTURNMKT*). To mitigate the effect of other omitted bank variables, I include bank fixed effects. Time dummies are also included to minimize the effect of unobserved macro-economic or industry factors. In each of these regressions, *MANRAT*, *CHANGERATE*, *EXAMINED*, *ROA* and the other financial variables are lagged to minimize potential endogeneity problems. The implicit assumption in these regressions is that the regulatory monitoring variables are in part driven by a bank's performance, financial condition, macroeconomic factors, market factors and bank-specific factors. Controlling for these other factors should help in isolating the impact of regulatory pressure on management turnover.

The primary specification results, based on the logistic regression described in equation (26.1), are reported in columns (1) and (2) of Table 26.4.[21] The number of observations drops from over 74 000 in the univariate tests to about 59 000 in these multivariate regressions. This is because bank fixed effects are included and the logistic regression drops observations without any change in the turnover variable across time.[22] If the dropped observations constitute banks that are systematically different from those remaining, the coefficients may be biased. To explore whether this materially affects the results, variations of equations (26.1) and (26.2) are explored in columns (3)–(6). Columns (3) and (4) report the same results as in columns (1) and (2), respectively, based on a logistic regression without bank fixed effects; the last two columns present these results using a linear probability model with bank fixed effects.

Column (1) of Table 26.4 reports the results of regressing turnover (*EXTURN*) on performance (*ROA*), financial controls (*FC*) and non-financial controls (*NFC*). The results suggest that poor performance (*ROA*) is strongly associated with executive turnover. Column (2) reports the same regression as in column (1) but includes the regulatory monitoring variables *MANRAT*, *CHANGERAT* and *EXAMINED*. Each of the regulatory variables has a positive and significant coefficient suggesting that greater regulatory pressure is a driver of bank executive turnover. Also, the adjusted R-square increases in column (2) relative to column (1). The effect of regulatory monitoring appears economically significant as well. Results in column (2) indicate that having a poor managerial rating (*MANRAT*) increases the odds of executive turnover by e(0.25) = 1.28 and a ratings worsening (*CHANGERAT*) leads to an increase in turnover odds by e(0.14) = 1.14.[23] Finally, banks that have been examined recently also have higher turnover odds by e(0.13) = 1.14.

The results in column (2) also indicate that the poor performance (*ROA*) and higher *PDUE90* are significantly associated with executive turnover and that *CAPRAT* and *LIQUID* are not. The coefficients of *ROA* and *PDUE90*, while diminishing somewhat from column (1), are still significant in the expected directions; this suggests that board discipline based on these variables is not replaced by regulatory oversight. The magnitude of the coefficient of *CAPRAT*, however, does drop down significantly from column (1). This drop suggests that regulatory oversight, besides focusing on private, non-financial information obtained in bank examinations, also considers poor risk management, as captured by low capital ratios. Taken together, the significance and direction of the coefficients of the performance and financial condition variables indicate that, after

Table 26.4   Determinants of executive turnover: multivariate test

	(1)	(2)	(3)	(4)	(5)	(6)
MANRAT		0.2527***		0.2846***		0.0219***
		(9.77)		(13.93)		(9.26)
CHANGERAT		0.1365***		0.1188***		0.0168***
		(3.58)		(3.01)		(4.11)
EXAMINED		0.1280**		0.1924***		0.0057*
		(2.15)		(3.62)		(1.79)
ROA	−11.9272***	−8.9338***	−15.0209***	−11.3523***	−1.5705***	−1.2729***
	−(9.10)	−(6.67)	−(13.08)	−(9.74)	−(9.56)	−(7.69)
PDUE9O	7.3103***	4.6546***	8.2877***	3.5639***	0.7715***	0.5173***
	(6.03)	(3.74)	(8.99)	(3.65)	(5.82)	(3.84)
CAPRAT	−1.6632**	0.0228	−2.6545***	−1.0192**	−0.1624*	−0.0195
	−(2.05)	(0.03)	−(5.62)	−(2.19)	−(1.91)	−(0.23)
LIQUID	0.0875	−0.0291	−0.6068***	−0.5136***	−0.0010	−0.0084
	(0.26)	−(0.09)	−(3.61)	−(3.06)	−(0.03)	−(0.26)
LGASSET	−0.1931**	−0.1033	−0.1136***	−0.0605***	−0.0200**	−0.0134
	−(2.26)	−(1.19)	−(5.09)	−(2.67)	−(2.44)	−(1.63)
CHLGASSET	−(0.81)***	−(0.63)***	−(0.72)***	−(0.53)**	−(0.09)***	−(0.08)***
	−(4.08)	−(3.17)	−(2.93)	−(2.19)	−(3.72)	−(3.20)
DENOVO	0.1185*	0.1287*	0.2644***	0.2877***	0.0164**	0.0165**
	(1.80)	(1.95)	(5.77)	(6.28)	(2.39)	(2.41)
ACQUIRE	0.7088***	0.6823***	0.7766***	0.7703***	0.0627***	0.0604***
	(4.08)	(3.91)	(4.80)	(4.72)	(3.70)	(3.56)
CHANGEOWN	0.4865***	0.5044***	0.6255***	0.6564***	0.0445***	0.0456***
	(4.06)	(4.21)	(5.53)	(5.79)	(3.63)	(3.72)
BANKSMKT	0.0001	0.0004	0.0012***	0.0011***	0.0001	0.0001
	(0.09)	(0.50)	(6.48)	(6.42)	(0.66)	(0.98)
EXURNMKT	1.9632***	1.9542***	1.8435***	1.8286***	0.1760***	0.1751***
	(21.63)	(21.45)	(25.09)	(24.71)	(17.71)	(17.67)
TENSHORT	0.3752***	0.3450***	1.0380***	0.9846***	0.0540***	0.0513***
	(10.27)	(9.39)	(28.23)	(26.43)	(10.09)	(9.57)
Constant term			−0.7087**	−2.2553***	0.3041***	0.1770*
			−(2.27)	−(6.83)	(3.15)	(1.81)
Bank fixed effects	+	+			+	+
Time fixed effects	+	+	+	+	+	+
Number of observations	58 155	58 155	73 272	73 272	73 272	73 272
Adjusted/pseudo R-square (%)	3.55	4.07	7.67	8.35	1.98	2.25
F-statistic/chi-square p-value	0.00	0.00	0.00	0.00	0.00	0.00

Notes: The dependent variable, in each of the regressions summarized in this table, is *EXTURN* (executive turnover in the current quarter). Regulatory oversight, performance, and financial condition regressors are lagged. Columns (1)–(4) represent logistic regression results; columns (5) and (6) present linear probability model results. The reported R-squares represent adjusted R-squares for the linear probability models and pseudo R-squares for the logistic regressions. Similarly, overall regression p-values are for F-tests and chi-square tests for the linear probability models and logistic models, respectively. T-stats are presented in parentheses below each regression coefficient. The asterisks indicate significance of the regression coefficients. Significance at the 1 percent level is indicated by ***. Similarly ** and * indicate significance at the 5 percent and 10 percent levels, respectively. The variables *MANRAT* and *CHANGERAT* indicate regulatory

Table 26.4 (continued)

ratings of bank management and changes in these ratings, respectively. *EXAMINED* indicates an exam occurred in the previous 18 months. *ROA*, *PDUE90*, *CAPRAT* and *LIQUID* represent return on assets, loans 90 days past due to assets, and ratio of nonvolatile to volatile assets, respectively. *LGASSET* and *CHLGASSET* represent log of assets and change in log of assets. *DENOVO* indicates a bank chartered within the last five years. *ACQUIRE* indicates that a bank has acquired another bank and *CHANGEOWN* indicates a change in bank affiliation. *BNKSMKT* indicates the number of banks in the metropolitan statistical area or rural county. *EXTURNMKT* indicates the percentage of banks with turnover in the quarter and *TENSHORT* indicates short tenure, i.e., executive turnover in the last quarter.

factoring in regulatory pressure, non-financial controls, bank fixed effects and time fixed effects, bank boards of directors and shareholders consider performance (*ROA*) and to some extent credit risk (*PDUE90*) to be the primary metrics for judging bank executives' performance.[24]

Many of the other controls have significant relationships with turnover. The size variable, *LGASSET*, seems to be negatively related to turnover in most specifications and significant in many of these. One explanation could be that smaller banks are less stable and more likely to be acquired; alternatively, because larger banks tend to be more profitable and better governed, they have less need for forced turnover. The change in size (*CHLGASSET*) variable is strongly and negatively related to turnover in all specifications; this may indicate bank owners punish bank management for poor growth.

The variable *ACQUIRE* is significantly and positively associated with executive turnover across all specifications; this is consistent with the explanation that firms undergoing merger activity have redundant executive positions and experience more turnover. The coefficient for *DENOVO* is positive and mostly significant across specifications, which indicates that newer banks tend to have more management turnover.

Unsurprisingly, banks with changes in ownership (*OWNCHANGE*) are found to be more likely to have turnover; this is likely because of redundant management or other organizational changes initiated by changes in ownership. The number of banks in the market (*BANKSMKT*), on the other hand, is not related to turnover in any specification; the percentage of other banks with turnover (*EXTURNMKT*) is strongly associated with more turnover. Lastly, short tenure (*TENSHORT*) is associated more executive turnover in all specifications.

Results from the logistic regression without fixed effects, reported in columns (3) and (4), and the linear probability model, reported in columns (4) and (5), generally confirm the results in columns (1) and (2). The degree of significance and relative impact of each variable varies, however. For example, the coefficient of *EXAMINED* is almost twice that of *CHANGERATE* in column (4), whereas the coefficient of *EXAMINED* is less than the coefficient of *CHANGERATE* in columns (2) and (6). This suggests that a model without fixed effects, while confirming the overall relationship of the primary specification, may result in biased coefficients because of the treatment of observations from the same bank as independent. The results based on the linear probability model, reported in columns (5) and (6), also must be interpreted with caution because of the well-known problems of estimating linear models with dummy dependent variables;

still, estimates from this model can be seen as convenient approximations, because linear probability models generally give acceptable estimates for common values of the explanatory variables.[25]

Because of potential problems with estimating the effect of regulatory oversight and performance on turnover without bank fixed effects or with a linear probability model, the remaining analysis in this chapter focuses on the results in columns (1) and (2). Still, the additional tests in columns (3)–(6) by and large confirm the results in columns (1) and (2) and are important in showing that the results from columns (1) and (2) do not depend on the exclusion of banks without turnover.[26] Overall, the results in Table 26.4 are consistent with the explanation that both performance and regulatory oversight are factors in driving top management turnover in banks and that regulatory oversight serves to complement the role of board oversight.[27]

26.4.3   Multivariate Tests: Future Profitability and Managerial Turnover

The results of univariate and multivariate tests relating managerial turnover to regulatory oversight suggest that regulatory oversight serves a complementary role to board discipline in the sense that both weak performance and greater regulatory pressure are related to increased likelihood of turnover. If regulatory-linked management turnover in banks is solely driven by compliance issues, however, this turnover may not prove directly beneficial to banks. On the other hand, if regulatory-linked turnover leads to improved governance, it should also lead to improved bank performance. To explore this issue, I next examine whether management turnover attributable to regulatory oversight is related to future bank performance.

These additional tests may also help evaluate whether the results from tests relating regulatory oversight to turnover were due to misspecification. The implicit assumption in these previous tests was that bank regulators pressure bank boards to fire their management primarily if inefficient or self-dealing tendencies in management are found; thus it is also implicit that regulatory-linked turnover is likely to improve bank performance. However, if the regressions relating executive turnover to regulatory oversight are misspecified, the positive association between *EXTURN* and the regulatory variables could be spurious. In particular, if *EXTURN* is not really driven by *MANRAT*, *CHANGERAT* or *EXAMINED* and instead is driven by variables correlated with the regulatory variables, then the interpretation of these results would not be correct and management turnover induced by the regulatory variables should not be positively related to subsequent performance. Alternatively, if turnover linked to regulatory pressure is found to be positively related to future performance, then equation (26.1) is likely to be correctly specified.

To explore whether regulatory-linked turnover is beneficial to bank owners, I relate performance (*ROA*) to the predicted likelihood of executive turnover attributed to the regulatory variables. The predicted likelihood of executive turnover is estimated by means of the procedure used by Core et al. (1999), Bertrand and Mullainathan (2001), and others. This involves obtaining the predicted value of *EXTURN* from the regression of *EXTURN* on regulatory oversight, performance, and other controls, (i.e., the results based on equation (26.1) reported in column (2) of Table 26.4). However, instead of estimating predicted values in the usual sense, I estimate the predicted value using only the regulatory variables. Thus *EL_EXTURN* ('excess' likelihood of executive turnover) is defined as:

$$Log\left(\frac{EL\_EXTURN_{i,t}}{1 - EL\_EXTURN_{i,t}}\right) = b_0 * MANRAT_{i,t-1} + b_1 * CHANGERAT_{i,t-1}$$

$$+ b_2 * RECENTEXAM_{i,t-1}. \tag{26.2}$$

In equation (26.2), b_0, b_1 and b_2 are the estimated coefficients for *MANRAT*, *CHANGERAT* and *EXAMINED* reported in Table 26.4, column (2). After obtaining estimates for *EL_EXTURN*, I next execute regressions of performance on lagged *EL_EXTURN* and other controls.[28] $EL\_EXTURN_{i,t-k}$ in equation (26.3) represents regulatory-linked turnover for bank i exactly k quarters in the past ($k = 4, 8, 12,$ and 16 in columns (1), (2), (3) and (4), respectively); the results of these regressions are reported in Table 26.5. As before, FC indicates the financial control variables *PDUE90, CAPRAT, LIQUID, LGASSET* and *CHLGASSET*. I include lagged *ROA* on the right-hand side of equation (26.3) because past performance is a key indicator of future performance:

$$ROA_{i,t} = \emptyset_0 * EL\_EXTURN_{i,t-k} + \emptyset_1 * ROA_{i,t-1} + \sum_{j=2}^{7}\emptyset_j * FC_{j:i,t-1} + TIME_t$$

$$+ BANK_i + \varepsilon_{i,t} \tag{26.3}$$

Because the regressions in columns (1), (2), (3) and (4) of Table 26.5 require banks to survive for 4, 8, 12 or 16 quarters after the quarter of regulatory-linked turnover, there is the potential for substantial selection bias. For example, only banks that survive 16 quarters (i.e., four years) past the quarter of regulatory-linked turnover are included in the regression indicated by column (4) of Table 26.5. If banks that face regulatory-linked management turnover fail during this four-year period because of poor performance, then the effect of regulatory-linked turnover on performance will be overstated; alternatively, if these banks exit primarily because of superior performance (i.e., if better-performing banks are acquired), the effect of turnover attributable to regulatory pressure on performance will be understated.

In either case, the bias will be strongest in regressions with the four-year lag and less strong for the regressions with shorter lags. To minimize the impact of selection bias, the regressions reported in Table 26.5 are re-estimated using a Heckman two-step procedure (Heckman, 1979) to control for the likelihood of surviving long enough to remain in the sample. The first step of the Heckman estimation, not reported, uses a probit model and estimates whether a bank survives over a given time period as a function of performance (*ROA*), the financial condition variables (*FC*) used in equations (26.1) and (26.3), market competition (*BANKSMKT*), and economic environment (*TIME DUMMIES*). A transformed version of the predicted probability of survival arising from the estimation, the inverse-mills ratio (*INVERSEMILLS*), is then added to the regression specified by equation (26.3). This is the second step of the procedure and is reported in Table 26.5 columns (5)–(8) for regulatory-linked turnover one, two, three and four years in the past, respectively.

The results in Table 26.5 columns (1)–(4) and (5)–(8) indicate that turnover

Table 26.5 Future profitability and regulatory-linked turnover: multivariate tests

	(1)	(2)	(3)	(4)	(5)	(6)	(7)	(8)
EL_EXTURN (4 qtrs ago)	0.0026*** (3.25)				0.0020** (2.40)			
EL_EXTURN (8 qtrs ago)		0.0057*** (7.67)				0.0037*** (4.84)		
EL_EXTURN (12 qtrs ago)			0.0038*** (5.51)				0.0026*** (3.71)	
EL_EXTURN (16 qtrs ago)				0.0033*** (5.21)				0.0024*** (3.64)
LGASSET	-0.0007*** -(3.74)	-0.0003** -(2.05)	-0.0005*** -(3.34)	-0.0004*** -(3.08)	-0.0006*** -(3.12)	-0.0001 -(0.54)	-0.0003** -(2.29)	-0.0003** -(2.19)
CHLGASSET	0.0027*** (6.77)	0.0018*** (5.39)	0.0020*** (5.78)	0.0009*** (3.01)	0.0026*** (6.64)	0.0017*** (4.97)	0.0019*** (5.54)	0.0008*** (2.77)
CAPRAT	-0.0269*** -(13.13)	-0.0191*** -(9.57)	-0.0131*** -(6.82)	-0.0081*** -(4.52)	-0.0228*** -(10.33)	-0.0143*** -(6.97)	-0.0109*** -(5.60)	-0.0070*** -(3.84)
PDUE90	-0.1311*** -(43.09)	-0.1115*** -(37.10)	-0.0963*** -(32.13)	-0.0799*** -(26.97)	-0.1315*** -(43.22)	-0.1134*** -(37.68)	-0.0964*** -(32.18)	-0.0793*** -(26.73)
ROA	0.5982*** (173.000)	0.6092*** (173.54)	0.6195*** (172.29)	0.6257*** (172.33)	0.5968*** (172.14)	0.6063*** (172.21)	0.6174*** (171.10)	0.6247*** (171.89)
LIQUID	0.0088*** (11.70)	0.0077*** (10.50)	0.0063*** (8.94)	0.0054*** (7.99)	0.0085*** (11.27)	0.0076*** (10.38)	0.0064*** (8.99)	0.0054*** (8.01)

	(1)	(2)	(3)	(4)	(5)	(6)	(7)	(8)
INVERSE MILLS					0.0133***	0.0069***	0.0031***	0.0022***
					(5.04)	(9.41)	(6.21)	(5.59)
Constant term	0.0041*	−0.0015	0.0021	0.0022	0.0032	−0.0035*	0.0007	0.0011
	(1.86)	(−0.76)	(1.19)	(1.39)	(1.46)	(−1.79)	(0.38)	(0.67)
Bank fixed effects	+	+	+	+	+	+	+	+
Time fixed effects	+	+	+	+	+	+	+	+
Number of observations	58 124	55 470	52 776	50 145	58 124	55 470	52 776	50 145
Adjusted R-square %	44.26	44.86	44.32	44.53	44.28	44.95	44.36	44.57
F-statistic p-value	0.00	0.00	0.00	0.00	0.00	0.00	0.00	0.00

Notes: This table presents multivariate tests of the effect of regulatory-linked turnover (*EL_EXTURN*) on future profitability. *EL_EXTURN* is calculated based on equation (26.2) and the estimated coefficients in Table 26.4 column (2). The dependent variable is *ROA* in each column. Columns (1)–(4) utilize values for *EL_EXTURN* (the portion of the likelihood of executive turnover explained only by the regulatory variables) 4, 8, 12, and 16 quarters ago, respectively. All other regressors represent values in the prior quarter. Columns (5)–(8) report the same results as columns (1)–(4) while utilizing a Heckman-type selection procedure to minimize the impact of firms without enough history to compute the effect of lagged *EL_EXTURN* on profitability; the reported inverse-mills ratio (*INVERSE MILLS*) in these columns is a measure of the likelihood of firm survival. T-statistic significance at the 1 percent level is indicated by ***. Similarly ** and * indicate significance at the 5 percent and 10 percent levels, respectively. The variables *LGASSET* and *CHLGASSET* represent the log of assets and change in log of assets. *ROA, PDUE90, CAPRAT* and *LIQUID* represent return on assets, loans 90 days past due to assets, and ration of non-volatile to volatile assets, respectively.

attributable to regulatory pressure (*EL_EXTURN*) is positively related to future *ROA* for each of the four years following this turnover. The results are significant, but weakest, one year after regulatory-linked turnover. This is not unexpected because new management may need time to implement positive change.[29] The results appear weaker, but still significant, after factoring in the likelihood of firm survival (i.e., inclusion of *INVERSEMILLS*); the significance of the *INVERSEMILLS* ratio suggests that controlling for survival bias is important.

The estimated coefficients in columns (5)–(8) indicate that as the portion of executive turnover likelihood implied by regulatory actions (*EL_EXTURN*) increases from 0 to 1, *ROA* increases by 20, 37, 26 and 24 basis points in one, two, three and four years, respectively. Alternatively, turnover attributable to a downgrade of one level (*CHANGERAT* = 1) that results in *MANRAT* going from a 1 to a 2 with an exam having been conducted in the last 18 months (*EXAMINED* = 1) is associated with an *ROA* higher by about 9 basis points in one year, 16 basis points in two years, 11 basis points in three years, and 10 basis points in four years. If *MANRAT* instead goes from 3 to 4 and *CHANGERAT* and *EXAMINED* are as above, then regulatory-linked turnover leads to a higher *ROA* in one, two, three and four years of 11, 21, 15 and 13 basis points, respectively.[30]

In all columns of Table 26.5, higher lagged *ROA* is associated with better future *ROA*, as might be expected, because past performance is an excellent predictor of future performance. In contrast, higher capital (*CAPRAT*) is associated with lower future *ROA* in all specifications. This may be because higher financial leverage (or lower capital ratios) may be indicative of poor financial condition only at very high levels. In general, a lower capital ratio may be indicative of higher risk, which implies a higher *ROA*.[31] Also, better liquidity (*LIQUID*) and lower past-due loans (*PDUE90*) are associated with better performance, as might be expected.

The regressions also indicate bank size (*LGASSET*) and change in size (*CHLGASSET*) affect future profitability. The *LGASSET* term is significantly and negatively related to future *ROA* in all specifications. A possible cause of any negative relationship between bank size and future profitability is that larger firms, although possibly enjoying economies of scale, may be less efficient than smaller firms. The results also indicate that *ROA* tends to be higher in growing firms (higher *CHLGASSET*); the results for this variable are significant in all columns.

26.5   SENSITIVITY/ROBUSTNESS TESTS

26.5.1   Timing of Regulatory Interventions

Equation (26.1) assumes that *MANRAT* implicitly factors in the effect of past downgrades and thus the *CHANGERAT* variable is included only for the most recent lagged quarter. To the extent downgrades at other time lags are important in explaining turnover, the results in Table 26.4 could be biased. To explore this possibility, I experiment with including lagged rating changes six quarters in the past. Though the coefficients of some of the earlier lags (i.e., second, third and fourth quarters) are somewhat significant, the inclusion of these variables dramatically reduces the coefficients of the supervisory rating variable, *MANRAT*, and does not lead to an improvement in the overall R-square of the regression. These additional tests suggest that the supervisory rating, *MANRAT*, already largely incorporates the effect of past downgrades beyond one quarter and the inclusion of the variable indicating downgrade in the most recent quarter along with the managerial rating leads to an appropriate specification.[32]

Another issue is whether bank regulators really provide new information to the board or simply confirm a board's findings by downgrading a bank's management ratings when poor governance or other evidence of ineffective management is found. If a bank's board observes the same things bank regulators do and acts on these independently of regulatory actions, then the regulatory variables may be correlated with unobserved board variables and the board variables may really be driving executive turnover. The inclusion of bank fixed effects in equation (26.1) and the use of lagged indicators of regulatory pressure greatly reduce the likelihood of this possibility. To explore the issue further, I examine bank executive turnover in relation to the timing of regulatory downgrades of management ratings. If management turnover is driven by supervisory oversight and not by board variables correlated with this oversight, then turnover should occur more frequently in the quarter after a ratings downgrade than in the quarter before. Additional tests, not reported, suggest that rating downgrades are much more likely to be associated with executive turnover when the downgrade occurs in the quarter prior to turnover, relative to the quarter after turnover. This suggests that regulatory oversight, as opposed to unobserved board variables, is driving executive turnover in banks.

26.5.2   Direct Impact of Regulatory Intervention and Performance

Bank examinations may lead to improved bank performance independent of executive turnover. But, because management is more likely to leave poorly performing and poorly rated banks, the results in Table 26.5 might represent a spurious correlation between regulatory-linked turnover and performance. To examine this possibility, the results in Table 26.5 were re-estimated while replacing *EL_EXTURN* (regulatory-linked turnover) with the ratings and downgrade variables directly. The results suggest that past downgrades, in general, are associated with worse performance and recent exams have no discernable effect on performance. The effect of past management ratings on performance is positive but small in magnitude. Overall, the additional test results suggest that it is more the regulatory-linked turnover, and not as much the direct impact of regulatory oversight, that leads to better subsequent performance.

26.5.3   Impact of 'Forced' Dismissals

In some cases, bank regulators order banks to remove executives. To the extent that these orders are given in conjunction with a ratings downgrade, the relation between the departure of an executive and the downgrade would be spurious. Because regulator-ordered removals of executives are rare events, this is unlikely to affect the results. In cases when executives are ordered to be dismissed, the orders are typically associated with formal regulatory actions. To examine whether the effect of formal actions alters the results, an additional variable was added to equation (26.1) indicating that a formal action occurred in the quarter. The inclusion of this variable did not materially affect the results.[33]

26.5.4   Omitted Observations

The regression described by equation (26.1) measures performance using *ROA* and to some extent *PDUE90*, *LIQUID* and *CAPRAT*. To the extent other measures of perform-ance are excluded, the results could be biased. One important measure of performance is bank survival, especially because bank failure can be the ultimate failure of bank gov-ernance. Because failed banks fall out of the sample, regression (26.1) implicitly excludes the effect of bank failure. This problem is minimized in part because banks that fail will have low levels of financial performance as captured as *ROA*, *PDUE90*, *LIQUID* and *CAPRAT* and the inclusion of these variables helps to capture the impact of potential failure. As an additional test, equation (26.1) was re-estimated while excluding banks that failed during the sample. The results, not reported, were qualitatively similar to those reported in Table 26.4.

26.5.5   Reversals

A central theme of this chapter is that regulatory-linked management changes are associated with better bank governance. As an additional test of this central theme, I explore the issue of whether turnover attributable to regulatory oversight is associated with future regulatory upgrades. Such a reversal effect, to the extent it is observed, adds weight to the argument that regulatory-linked turnover leads to better bank governance. A simple correlation analysis, not reported, indicates that regulatory-linked turnover (*EL_EXTURN*) in the past is strongly related to upgrades in the future; this suggests that subsequent ratings upgrades are not independent of regulatory-induced turnover and that there is a reversal effect.

26.6   CONCLUSIONS

This chapter has provided evidence that both weak performance and regulatory monitor-ing are related to greater executive turnover in banks; the results suggest that regulatory evaluations of management serve to complement the role of board oversight. Further, the evidence is consistent with the explanation that regulatory-driven executive turnover is beneficial for banks in that it leads to improved subsequent performance. Finally, because this chapter utilizes a unique sample of predominantly small and private banks, the results imply that neither board oversight nor regulatory oversight depends on the market pressures of publicly traded firms.

   The results also add to the growing body of evidence that regulatory oversight, more generally, can be effective as a monitoring mechanism. The results may be especially relevant in the context of the current debate on reforming financial regulation. Although the results do not imply that all forms of financial regulation are beneficial in all con-texts, they do imply that regulatory oversight focused on improving governance can be valuable.

NOTES

* The views expressed in this chapter are those of the author alone and do not necessarily reflect the views of the Office of the Comptroller of the Currency or the US Department of the Treasury. The author would like to thank Irina Barakova, Michael Carhill, Fred Finke, Yaniv Grinstein, Mark Levonian, Min Qi, Gary Whalen, Peihwang Wei, Office of the Comptroller of Currency seminar participants, International Conference on Business and Finance participants, and Southwestern Finance Association conference participants for helpful suggestions. The author takes responsibility for any errors.

1. Because bank assets tend to be opaque (Iannotta, 2004; Morgan, 2002), regulatory monitoring of banking firms may be especially beneficial.

2. Typical informal actions include commitment letters, memorandums of understanding, and safety and soundness plans, and are not publicly disclosed. Formal actions are generally more severe and publicly disclosed. The US bank regulatory system is described further in the next section.

3. The dataset is based on executive turnover data from 1985 to 1994 for nationally chartered US banks. Although the full dataset contains over 74 000 bank-quarter observations, some of the multivariate tests utilize a somewhat reduced observation set because of econometric issues; these issues are discussed later in the chapter.

4. While there is no formal definition of 'community banks', such banks generally have very small branch networks and low levels of assets; consistent with available data, this chapter defines community banks as banks with assets of $100 million or less.

5. Brickley (2003) provides a good review of this literature.

6. For more details on the organization of the banking system, see Fabozzi et al. (2002), Chapter 3. For information on banking laws and regulations, see www.fdic.gov/regulations/laws.

7. The last component in the acronym CAMELS, sensitivity to market risk, is a relatively new feature and was introduced in 1997. Because the period of study in this chapter precedes 1997, the rest of this chapter will refer only to CAMEL.

8. The executive turnover variable was only required to be reported for banks filling out a Federal Financial Institutions Examination Council (FFIEC) 034 reporting form. This excludes banks with assets of $100 million or more and was only available between 1984 and 1994.

9. Although virtually all banks in the sample are private, the data do not allow for the identification of those few that are not. Given the very small number of publicly traded banks in general, and even smaller number of small publicly traded banks, the number of publicly traded banks in this sample is likely to be inconsequential.

10. An exception to this is banks that failed during the sample period. Observations from banks that failed for the one-year period immediately preceding failure are excluded, because financial data so close to failure may not be reliable. This reduces the sample size by about 1 percent. Additional tests, not reported, indicate the results are not affected by this exclusion.

11. There is a total of about 3000 banks in the sample over the entire period. Because of bank acquisitions, bank failures, and newly chartered banks, the actual number of observations at any given point ranges from about 1400 to about 2300.

12. The turnover variable is derived from a call report variable indicating whether a change in senior officers has occurred in a given quarter. A limitation of these data is that turnover cannot be attributed to a particular senior officer.

13. In practice, only a small percentage of downgrades (about 10 percent) are associated with changes in the management rating by more than one notch; for robustness, I replace *CHANGERAT* with a dummy indicating that a downgrade occurred. The results are unchanged.

14. Volatile liabilities are defined as including large certificates of deposit, federal funds purchases, demand notes issued to the US Treasury, foreign office deposits, and adjusted trading liabilities.

15. The Tier 1 capital ratio is defined as: (Tier 1 Capital) / (Average Total Assets − Disallowed Intangibles). Tier 1 capital is considered the most reliable and is a key measure of capital used by bank regulators. It generally consists of common stock, irredeemable and non-cumulative preferred stock, and retained earnings.

16. The variable defines an acquisition as an unassisted acquisition (not assisted by the FDIC or other federal agencies in any way).

17. Although banks belonging to multi-bank holding companies are excluded from the sample, some banks still choose to operate as single-bank holding companies. Ownership structure can change when a bank becomes affiliated as a holding company or when a bank's affiliation to a holding company is ended.

18. Although the univariate and multivariate tests include only national community banks, all US banks were included in defining *BANKSMKT*. All banks were included because national banks are likely to face competitive pressures not only from other national banks but also non-national banks.

19. Market-level data, from which measures such as the Herfindahl index could be computed, are not available during this time period. Because banks in the sample are mostly local community banks, the number of banks in the market may serve as a good proxy for competition in the local metropolitan statistical area or county in which a bank is located.
20. Because most banks (over 90 percent) are not downgraded or upgraded in any given quarter, presentation of *CHANGERAT* in this form is helpful in describing the distribution of ratings changes. In all univariate and multivariate tests, *CHANGERAT* is set to 0 when no rating change occurred in the quarter.
21. Because the logit specification has bank fixed effects, no constant term can be estimated.
22. Without variation in the dependent variable, observations of a given bank will have either all positive or all negative outcomes and computation of a fixed effect becomes impossible for this procedure.
23. As an alternative to *MANRAT*, I also experiment with a dummy indicating a 'good' versus 'bad' rating (i.e., a rating of 1 or 2 versus a rating of 3, 4 or 5. I also estimate equation (26.1) while replacing *MANRAT* with dummies for each individual rating. The latter of these methods best addresses any potential nonlinear relationship between ratings and turnover. Tests using these alternative measures, not reported, lead to similar results.
24. An alternative measure of performance to *ROA* is *ROE* (return on equity). Additional tests, not reported, indicate these results are robust to the use of *ROE* to measure performance.
25. The linear probability model is associated with heteroskedastic error terms, non-normally distributed errors, and predicted values that can be outside the range of (0, 1). A more complete explanation of the benefits and drawbacks of linear probability models is provided in Wooldridge (2002, Ch. 15).
26. The multivariate tests, reported in Table 26.4, were also estimated for each of the periods 1985–1988, 1989–1991, and 1992–1994. The results were similar in terms of directions of coefficients but weaker in terms of significance, especially in the latter two time periods, perhaps owing to not enough observations. Further multivariate tests using the subperiod 1989–1994 were similar in both direction and significance.
27. The results, while finding strong associations between performance and turnover and regulatory oversight and turnover, do not definitively establish that performance and regulatory oversight cause turnover. For example, to the extent executive turnover is indicative of poor governance, turnover could also lead to poor performance and, given this possibility, the results should be taken with some caution. Still, given the use of lagged measures of performance and regulatory oversight, which greatly reduce the possibility of endogeneity and reverse causality in the findings, the results are consistent with performance and regulatory oversight driving turnover.
28. To be consistent with the estimation equation (26.1), I only include banks that had at least one change in senior management during the entire observation period. Additional tests, not reported, indicate that the results for equation (26.3) do not depend on this data reduction.
29. Robustness tests, using ROE to measure performance, were conducted. The results, not reported, were very similar.
30. These estimates are calculated using equation (26.2) to first estimate the *EL_EXTURN* implied by *MANRAT*, *CHANGERAT* and *EXAMINED*. The estimated value for *EL_EXTURN* is then applied to the estimated coefficient for *EL_EXTURN* in equation (26.3) to estimate the effect as described. For example, if a downgrade (*CHANGERAT* = 1) leading to a managerial rating of 3 (*MANRAT* = 3) leads to an increase in *EL_EXTURN* of X, the implied increase in *ROA* in one year is 0.0020 * X.
31. Traditional corporate financial theory suggests a risk–return trade-off. That is, investors must be compensated for higher risk by receiving a higher expected return.
32. I also experiment with a 'time-to-ruin model', where the time to a turnover event is related to past downgrade events. The results suggest that downgrades are related to a reduced time to turnover for the first three quarter lags, but that the effect is much more significant in the quarter immediately prior to the turnover. As before, the inclusion of lagged *CHANGERAT* more than one quarter in the past significantly diminishes the coefficient of *MANRAT*.
33. In these tests, a formal action is defined as a 'cease and desist order', a 'civil money penalty', a 'prompt corrective action', a 'formal agreement', or a 'removal or prohibition order'.

REFERENCES

Bertrand, M. and S. Mullainathan (2001), 'Are CEOs rewarded for luck? The ones without principals are', *Quarterly Journal of Economics*, **116**, 901–932.
Brickley, J.A. (2003), 'Empirical research on CEO turnover and firm-performance: a discussion', *Journal of Accounting and Economics*, **36**, 227–233.

Cook, D., A. Hogan and R. Kieschnick (2004), 'A study of the corporate governance of thrifts', *Journal of Banking and Finance*, **28**, 1247–1271.

Core, J., R. Holthausen and P. Kumar (1999), 'Corporate governance, chief executive compensation, and firm performance', *Journal of Financial Economics*, **51**, 371–406.

Dahl, D., J. O'Keefe and G. Hanweck (1998), 'The influence of examiners and auditors on loan-loss recognition', *FDIC Banking Review*, **11**, 10–25.

Denis, D. and D.K. Denis (1995), 'Performance changes following top management dismissals', *Journal of Finance*, **50**, 1029–1058.

DeYoung, R., M. Flannery, W. Lang and S. Sorescu (2001), 'The information content of bank examination ratings and subordinated debt prices', *Journal of Money, Credit and Banking*, **33**, 900–925.

Fabozzi, F., F. Modigliani, F.J. Jones and M.G. Ferri (2002), 'The role of government in financial markets', in *Foundations of Financial Markets and Institutions*, 3rd edn, Saddle River, NJ: Pearson Education, Chapter 3.

Frater, S. and M. Pollick (2007), 'Bradenton's Coast Bank ordered to fire its CEO', *Herald Tribune*, Online Edition.

Gardner, S. (2008), 'Westsound CEO to resign', *Kitsap Sun*, Online Edition.

Gunther, J. and R. Moore (2003), 'Loss underreporting and the auditing role of bank exams', *Journal of Financial Intermediation*, **12**, 153–177.

Heckman, J. (1979), 'Sample selection bias as a specification error', *Econometrica*, **47**, 153–161.

Hotchkiss, E.S. (1995), 'Postbankruptcy performance and management turnover', *Journal of Finance*, **50**, 3–21.

Houston, J. and C. James (1993), 'Management and organizational changes in banking: a comparison of regulatory intervention with private creditor actions in non-bank firms', *Carnegie-Rochester Conference Series on Public Policy*, **38**, 143–178.

Iannotta, G. (2004), 'Testing for opaqueness in the European banking industry: evidence from bond credit ratings', SDS Boccon Working Paper.

Khorana, A. (2001), 'Performance changes following top management turnover: evidence from open-ended mutual funds', *Journal of Financial and Quantitative Analysis*, **36**, 371–393.

Morgan, D. (2002), 'Rating banks: risk and uncertainty in an opaque industry', *American Economic Review*, **92**, 874–888.

Office of the Comptroller of the Currency (OCC) (2002), 'Outsourcing your audit function', transcript of presentation by J.D. Hawke, Jr., Z. Blackburn, M. Blair, C.S. Schainost, R.T. Riordan and W.E. Baker.

Palvia, A. (2011), 'Banks and managerial discipline: does regulatory monitoring play a role?', *Quarterly Review of Economics and Finance*, **51**(1), 56–68.

Peek, J., E. Rosengren and G. Tootell (1998), 'Does the Federal Reserve have an informational advantage? You can bet on it', Federal Reserve Bank of Boston Working Paper.

Prowse, S. (1995), 'Alternative methods of corporate control in commercial banks', *Economic Review*, Federal Reserve Bank of Dallas Working Paper.

Webb, E. (2008), 'Regulator scrutiny and bank CEO incentives', *Journal of Financial Services Research*, **33**, 5–20.

Wooldridge, J. (2002), 'Discrete response models', in J. Wooldridge, *Econometric Analysis of Cross Section and Panel Data*, Cambridge, MA: Massachusetts Institute of Technology, Chapter 15.

27 Redeemability as governance: a study of closed-end and open-end funds under common management

Peter MacKay*

27.1 INTRODUCTION

The ability to reclaim resources from managers is perhaps the most direct way to moderate principal–agent relations. This point is made by Fama and Jensen (1983a, 1983b, 1985) who argue that the option shareholders have to liquidate an organization's assets as an ultimate recourse acts as a powerful corporate governance mechanism. Despite its appeal, this argument has received little attention in the literature.[1] Instead, most research studies the role of board structure, large shareholders and managerial ownership in aligning claimant interests, particularly within non-financial firms.

This chapter examines the importance of reclaimable assets as a governance mechanism by comparing the performance and operation of redeemable and non-redeemable assets under common management, namely, open- and closed-end funds run by the same investment fund company (fund family). I hypothesize that the difference in share redeemability across funds within a family induces managers to favor their open-end funds over their closed-end funds (favoritism). This might entail channeling superior trades and resources toward their open-end funds, a hypothesis I also test.

My research design draws on four features of investment funds in China. Firstly, redeemable open-end funds have only been allowed in China since 2001; only closed-end funds were available prior to this. In many cases, open- and closed-end funds belong to the same fund family. Importantly, opening closed-end funds was not allowed until 2006. This stark difference between open- and closed-end funds in China avoids the identification and endogeneity problems that plague the US setting. Thus, the years 2001 to 2006 offer a natural experiment where completely redeemable and completely non-redeemable shares often fell under common management.

Secondly, unlike in the US, where investment funds need only disclose their security holdings, investment funds in China must also report securities bought or sold. Thus, in addition to comparing the performance of affiliated open- and closed-end funds, these disclosure rules allow for testing whether any detectable family favoritism can be linked to cross-fund subsidization strategies such as trade coordination.

Thirdly, unlike in the US, where fees and redemption conditions vary widely, even within families, fund fees and redemption conditions in China are regulated – and therefore uniform – which greatly simplifies the comparison of fund performance.

Finally, Chinese fund families are centralized, with a single board of directors and common research and trading departments servicing all affiliated funds. Therefore, although each fund is headed by its own management team, the organization of Chinese fund families is such that coordination among funds is greatly facilitated.

Thus, while one might at first hesitate to use Chinese data to study investment funds and corporate governance, it turns out that the regulatory environment, the availability of detailed data, the uniformity of fees and redemption conditions, and the centralized organization of investment fund families in China present a unique laboratory with which to analyze the role of reclaimable assets in corporate governance. The ideal test would isolate the effect of favoritism while controlling for all other systematic differences between affiliated open-end funds and closed-end funds. I propose a variety of approaches to this test, which I present in ascending order of reliability and, as it turns out, in increasing order of statistical and economic significance.

Firstly, I run simple difference tests between open- and closed-end funds, where I compare the funds in terms of financial performance (raw investor returns, market-adjusted and three-factor adjusted returns, holding returns and return gap) and in terms of accounting performance (net profit per share). Secondly, I run multivariate regressions where, besides controlling for fund and family characteristics, I test whether the difference in returns of paired open- and closed-end funds depends not only on family affiliation but also on the resources a family has to support favoritism, namely, the combined assets of its non-redeemable, closed-end funds.

Thirdly, following Gaspar et al. (2006), I refine the paired-fund differences approach by replacing each fund by an unaffiliated style- and size-matched fund. Because cross-fund subsidization is more likely to be concealed in interim trades than reflected in portfolio holdings, I repeat the matched paired-fund approach using the return gap (investor returns minus holding returns) instead of investor returns. Finally, I avoid comparing open- and closed-end funds altogether by investigating whether the closed-end fund discount relates to family affiliation and family resources.

The empirical results support my hypotheses, regardless of estimation method. Firstly, I find that open-end funds outperform closed-end funds in general, which suggests that open-end funds have stronger incentives to perform, either because they are better rewarded for performance (inflows chase performance) or because their governance structure is better, perhaps thanks to the redeemable nature of their shares.

Secondly, the difference in performance is significantly greater when open- and closed-end funds are affiliated, and even more so when closed-end (open-end) funds represent a large (small) fraction of family assets. This suggests that investment-fund families deliberately enhance the performance of their open-end funds to the detriment of their closed-end funds. This finding supports my conjecture that redeemability is a prime determinant of the differential performance of investment funds in particular and that reclaimable assets are a key dimension of corporate governance in general.

How is cross-fund subsidization – or favoritism – actually achieved? First, fund families might engage in tandem trades where a given security is bought or sold, first by the open-end fund, then by the closed-end fund. In this way, the closed-end fund supports prices (provides liquidity) to the benefit of the open-end fund, at the expense of its own performance. Although the data do not identify transaction dates precisely, I find that returns on comparable trades (interim trades involving the same security) yield significantly higher returns for open-end funds than for their closed-end siblings. This is evidence of cross-fund subsidization through trade coordination.

Second, fund families might direct better resources to their open-end funds. Consistent with this hypothesis, I find that managerial turnover is lower for closed-end funds than for open-end funds within the same fund family. More specifically, I find that the probability that a closed-end fund manager is replaced is not sensitive to past fund performance but that the probability that an open-end fund manager is replaced is inversely related to past performance. This suggests that fund families rationally direct their best talent to the funds where accountability and the incentive to perform well are greatest, namely, their redeemable-share, open-end funds.

This study adds to the nascent empirical literature on favoritism that documents preferential allocation of initial public offerings (IPOs) (Löffler, 2003), human resources (Guedj and Papastaikoudi, 2004) and trades (Gaspar et al., 2006) among affiliated funds. But, given the obligation funds have to maximize shareholder value, why do fund families appear to favor the performance of one fund over another? Why does favoritism occur?

The literature implies that because fund compensation depends more on assets under management than on performance, behavioral biases such as return chasing (Nanda et al., 2004) and convex flow-performance sensitivity (Chevalier and Ellison, 1997; Sirri and Tufano, 1998) can rationalize favoritism. Alternatively, affiliated funds might have different performance incentives (Nohel et al., 2006). While I agree that differences in incentives are important, I believe that the definition of incentives must extend to all facets of governance, not just compensation. Differences in governance – and accountability – across affiliated funds, say between redeemable and non-redeemable shares, thus offer a broader explanation of favoritism.

The study most closely related to mine is Nohel et al. (2006), who establish that hedge funds and mutual funds run by the same manager respectively underperform and outperform their peers. This is contrary to their prediction that the higher-powered compensation structure of hedge funds would induce managers to prioritize the performance of hedge funds over that of mutual funds. I suggest that this prima facie surprising result supports the thesis and findings of our study. Specifically, I argue that the lengthy lock-in period imposed by hedge funds represents a substantial reduction in the redeemability of investors' assets which compromises governance and lowers hedge fund performance, despite the incentive of high-powered compensation.[2]

This chapter makes three contributions. Firstly, I link share redeemability to fund performance and governance. Secondly, I provide evidence of favoritism in a controlled, non-US setting thanks to detailed data on investment funds in China. Thirdly, I propose favoritism as a new agency explanation for the closed-end fund discount.

The chapter is organized as follows. Section 27.2 develops my hypotheses. Section 27.3 describes the data. Sections 27.4 and 27.5 relate family affiliation to fund performance differences and the closed-end fund discount. Section 27.6 links favoritism to trade coordination and resource allocation. Section 27.7 generalizes. Section 27.8 concludes.

27.2 HYPOTHESIS DEVELOPMENT

Favoritism will occur when fund families have both the incentive and the scope to pursue cross-fund subsidization strategies. Firstly, the incentive arises when the fund family owners (its residual claimants, not its fund participants) surmise that they are better off if they boost the performance of some of their funds over others. Thus, since a fund family's main source of profit is the fees it earns on assets under management, any strategy that maximizes family inflows (or minimizes outflows) might make sense.[3] Secondly, the scope for cross-fund subsidization arises when fund families are not fully accountable to their fund shareholders. Lack of accountability could result from limited disclosure, such as when trading activity is not reported (e.g., the US), or from differences in governance across funds, such as when a family manages both redeemable open-end funds and non-redeemable closed-end funds (e.g., China) or when a mutual fund manager also runs a hedge fund (Nohel et al., 2006).

The literature already offers examples of favoritism in the context of limited disclosure, namely, in the US setting. For instance, Nanda et al. (2004) argue that because investors seem first to pick a fund family and then the individual fund within that family, running a 'star' performing fund can have positive spillover effects on the inflows of the other funds in the same family. In other words, fund families might be better off running one above-average fund and several under-average funds than average funds only.

This argument is bolstered by Chevalier and Ellison (1997) and Sirri and Tufano (1998), who show that fund inflows are more sensitive to good performance than outflows are to bad performance. Clearly, whether convex or not, the flow-performance sensitivity of open-end funds is greater than that of closed-end funds, where inflows and outflows are ruled out by definition. Put differently, favoritism is hard-wired in fund families that manage both open-end funds and closed-end funds.

In this study, I stress the lack of accountability that results from differences in governance rather than from limited disclosure. This is not to say that investment funds in China are subject to full disclosure of their trading activity. However, the data are revealing enough to allow testing of whether the cross-fund subsidization strategies I can detect favor funds subject to strong governance (redeemable open-end funds) over funds subject to weak governance (non-redeemable closed-end funds). What is more, open- and closed-end funds in China are subject to the same disclosure rules. This means that the lack of accountability linked to incomplete disclosure is the same for both types of funds; that is, the rest is attributable to differences in governance.

27.2.1   Hypotheses on the Detection of Favoritism

In light of the preceding discussion, I formulate the following hypotheses:

Hypothesis 1   All else being equal, open-end funds should outperform closed-end funds in general, that is, regardless of family affiliation.

This hypothesis follows directly from Fama and Jensen (1983a, 1983b, 1985), who argue that by exerting constant discipline on managers, redeemable shares represent a powerful form of governance, especially compared to non-redeemable shares. Thus, redeemable open-end funds should outperform non-redeemable closed-end funds.

Hypothesis 2   All else being equal, open-end funds should outperform affiliated closed-end funds, above and beyond any difference explained by Hypothesis 1.

This hypothesis follows from the idea that fund families may be better off if they treat their funds differently rather than evenly. Thus, families having both the incentive and the scope to engage in favoritism probably will. The incentive arises from differences in flow-performance sensitivity and accountability (redeemability) across funds in a family. The scope arises when a family manages both open-end funds and closed-end funds, which opens up cross-fund subsidization strategies not available to unaffiliated funds. Consequently, open-end funds should not simply outperform affiliated closed-end funds; they should outperform them beyond any general difference between the performance of open- and closed-end funds (that is, that explained by Hypothesis 1).

Hypothesis 3   All else being equal, the difference in performance between affiliated open- and closed-end funds should rise (fall) as the fraction of family assets represented by closed-end (open-end) funds rises.

This hypothesis reflects the idea that cross-fund subsidization strategies, such as trade coordination, tax a family's resources. Viewing closed-end fund assets as the supply of resources and open-end fund assets as the demand of resources, it follows that the relative supply and demand of resources determines the scope a family has to favor the performance of its open-end funds. Thus, open-end funds in families where open-end funds represent a small (large) fraction of total family assets should outperform their closed-end siblings to a greater (lesser) extent.

Finally, I also consider two corollaries of the previous hypotheses:

Hypothesis 2a   All else being equal, open-end funds in families that also manage closed-end funds should outperform open-end funds in families that do not.

Hypothesis 2b   All else being equal, closed-end funds in families that also manage open-end funds should underperform closed-end funds in families that do not.

These hypotheses follow from Hypotheses 2 and 3, which imply that open-end funds without affiliated closed-end funds cannot be subsidized by resources from the latter. I consider these corollary hypotheses to address partly the concern that even though I control for likely differences between open- and closed-end funds, it is hard to rule out the possibility that other factors besides favoritism might explain why open-end funds outperform affiliated closed-end funds. Thus, comparing open-end (closed-end) funds among themselves serves to mitigate this possibility.

27.2.2   Hypotheses on How Favoritism Might Work

Suppose I do find evidence of favoritism in the data. What more can I say? Can I test whether plausible cross-fund subsidization strategies are also supported? The answer is yes. First, thanks to the availability of data on funds' trading activity I am able to test for trade coordination that favors the open-end funds within a family. Second, by collecting data on managerial turnover, I can also test whether families tend to allocate their best talent to their open-end funds. Answering these questions also serves as a check on my first set of hypotheses, as it is doubtful that I would conclude that families are channeling superior trades and talent to their open-end funds if they were not trying to favor these funds in the first place. I reserve the details of these tests for section 27.6, but the corresponding hypotheses are straightforward:

Hypothesis 4   All else being equal, families that manage both open-end funds and closed-end funds will engage in trade coordination strategies that benefit the open-end fund at the expense of the closed-end fund.

Hypothesis 5   All else being equal, families that manage both open-end funds and closed-end funds will assign better managers to their open-end funds.

27.3   DATA

27.3.1   Data Sources and Sample Selection

I obtained investment funds' periodic reports (quarterly, interim and annual) from the Shanghai and Shenzhen stock exchange websites and from fund companies' own websites. Monthly data on fund and stock performance are from Tinysoft.NET, a Chinese financial data provider. Fund type and style classifications are from Morningstar China. Stock-market index data are from the CITIC Security Company.

Chinese investment funds produce quarterly, interim and annual reports. The quarterly reports contain data on quarterly returns, total net assets (TNA), expense ratios, load fees, fund launch dates, and so on. I use TNA to measure fund size, which is net asset value (NAV) per share times the number of shares at the end of the quarter. The interim (semi-annual) and annual reports contain data on trading activity during the reporting period, which is a key feature of the Chinese data, not available for US funds. Combining the interim and annual reports allows the construction of a semi-annual time series of funds' trading activity, which I later use to test for trade coordination.

The first Chinese closed-end fund went to market on 27 March 1998, and the first open-end fund was launched on 11 September 2001. My sample period runs from January 2002 through June 2005. I start the sample in January 2002 to ensure that both open- and closed-end funds were available for at least a few months. I end the sample in June 2005 to make sure every fund had at least six months of data as of early 2006. There were then 181 Chinese investment funds in existence.

Of these 181 funds, three funds have dual-class shares, which I exclude. To delineate clearly between redeemable and non-redeemable funds I also drop five listed open-end funds and another one offered as an exchange-traded fund (ETF).

Since part of my analysis relies on Morningstar China's classification of domestic equity fund styles, and because data on securities other than stocks are hard to obtain, I drop bond, money-market and capital-protection funds, retaining only stock and hybrid funds that primarily invest in equity securities. This leaves an unbalanced panel of 142 funds, of which 54 are closed-end and 88 are open-end. Note that the sample is free of survivor bias since no fund has yet delisted in China.

I compile the sample funds' investment styles from Morningstar China, which includes the following possible styles: BlendLarge, BlendMid, BlendSmall, GrowthLarge, GrowthMid, GrowthSmall, ValueLarge, ValueMid and ValueSmall.

Table 27.1 presents descriptive statistics for the sample funds (Panel A) and the fund families that manage them (Panel B). The first thing to note is that the number of funds and families grew dramatically over a short period, going from 54 funds offered by 15 families in June 2002 to 95 funds offered by 25 families in December 2003. However, almost all of this growth is explained by open-end funds, which went from three in June 2002 to 41 by December 2003. Notice that by December 2003, not a single fund family only managed closed-end funds; most of them offered both open-and closed-end funds, and eight of the ten new families only operated open-end funds.

In support of my claim that the fee structure is very uniform among Chinese investment funds, the last two columns of Panel A show that fund management and load fees vary very little over time (note the lack of time trends) or across funds (note the standard deviations at each point in time). This uniformity in fees is why they can be safely ignored. For closed- and open-end funds alike, dividends are assumed to be reinvested in the shares held in the fund at the end of the month they are distributed.

27.3.2   Performance Measures

Partly for economic reasons and partly for robustness, I ground my analysis on both market-based and accounting-based measures of fund performance. Within market-based measures I distinguish between investor returns, what the investor earns by owning a share of the fund, and holding returns, the returns hypothetically earned on the fund's holdings. For open-end funds, investor returns are given by the percentage change in the fund's NAV per share. Investor returns can also be computed this way for closed-end funds but they are more accurately computed from the market price per share. This is because a closed-end fund's NAV is notional since its shares cannot be redeemed but must instead be traded at the going market price. NAV-based returns and price-based returns only differ if the closed-end fund discount changes over the return period. To guard against this possibility, and to ensure that I capture true investor returns, I use NAV-based returns for open-end funds and price-based returns for closed-end funds.

The crux of my analysis lies in comparing the performance of open-end funds and closed-end funds, whose returns might differ for many reasons besides favoritism. As a first attempt at controlling for confounding effects, I also use market-factor-adjusted returns and Fama and French (1993) three-factor-adjusted returns.[4]

I implement the market- and three-factor models using style indexes from CITIC to construct factor-mimicking portfolios. I estimate the following regressions to obtain the factor loadings (betas) and excess returns (alphas) for each fund:[5]

$$R_{it} - RF_t = \alpha_i + \beta_{iRMRF}RMRF_t + \beta_{iSMB}SMB + \beta_{iHML}HML + e_{it}$$

where R_{it} is the return of fund i in month t, RF_t is the one-month interbank rate, R_{mt} is the return on the market factor, $RMRF_t \equiv R_{mt} - RF_t$ is the excess market return, SMB_t (small minus big) is the return on the size factor mimicking portfolio, HML_t (high B/M minus low B/M) is the return on the book-to-market factor mimicking portfolio, α is the three-factor model excess return, the βs are the factor loadings, and e_{it} is the residual for fund i in month t. Following Nanda et al. (2004) and others, I use the sample data, the

Table 27.1 *Descriptive statistics: funds and fund families*

A) Funds

Date	Number of funds	Number of open-end funds	Number of closed-end funds	Total net assets (TNA)	Value of stocks held	Fund age	Management fees	Front- and back-end load fees
30 June 2002	54	3	51	1661.55 (1192.83)	1068.62 (738.50)	2.22 (1.04)	1.5 (0)	2.8 (1.04)
31 December 2002	66	12	54	1629.82 (1131.56)	835.85 (584.10)	2.30 (1.31)	1.49 (0.09)	2.55 (0.86)
30 June 2003	70	16	54	1603.19 (1015.75)	987.41 (670.60)	2.67 (1.36)	1.48 (0.11)	2.42 (0.81)
31 December 2003	95	41	54	1574.12 (1076.30)	1079.31 (759.72)	2.46 (1.68)	1.45 (0.17)	2.07 (0.61)

B) Fund families

Date	Number of families	Families with both open- and closed-end funds	Families with open-end funds only	Families with closed-end funds only	Number of funds per family	No of closed-end funds per family	No of open-end funds per family	Average TNA per family	Average closed-end funds' TNA per family*	Average open-end funds' TNA per family*
30 June 2002	15	3	0	12	3.6 (1.59)	3.4 (1.40)	1 (0)	5981.57 (3080.88)	6487.94 (334.20)	3992.80 (667.62)
31 December 2002	17	11	0	6	3.88 (1.87)	3.18 (1.47)	1.09 (0.30)	6327.53 (3381.03)	4834.30 (1435.40)	3260.01 (1568.33)
30 June 2003	17	14	0	3	4.12 (1.83)	3.18 (1.47)	1.47 (0.36)	6601.36 (3238.44)	5186.645 (1719.27)	2367.30 (1444.69)
31 December 2003	25	17	8	0	3.8 (2.08)	3.18 (1.47)	1.64 (0.76)	5981.67 (4516.03)	5070.53 (2182.73)	2894.84 (2517.61)

Notes: Shown are descriptive statistics for funds (Panel A) and fund families (Panel B) in China. Although the entire sample runs from January 2002 through June 2005, the data presented are a subset of that period (2002–2003). For comparability, the sample only includes equity funds (money-market, bond, and capital-protection funds are excluded). Total net assets (TNA) is the weekly closing market value of fund assets under management, in millions of yuan, computed as NAV per share times the number of shares outstanding. Standard deviations are reported in parentheses.
* This figure only includes families with both open- and closed-end funds.

estimated coefficients ($\hat{\alpha}_i$, $\hat{\beta}_i$), and the residuals ($\hat{e}_{it}$) to compute the three-factor-adjusted return ($\hat{\alpha}_{it}$) for fund i in month t as:

$$\hat{\alpha}_{it} \equiv \hat{\alpha}_i + \hat{e}_{it}.$$

The market-factor return is based on the CITIC Composite Index, which is a free-float value-weighted average of all A shares (only available to Chinese nationals). The risk-free rate is the repurchase (repo) rate on government bonds. The size-factor return (small-minus-big, SMB) is the difference in returns on the CITIC Small-cap Index and the CITIC Large-cap Index. The book-to-market factor return (high-minus-low, HML) is the difference in returns on the CITIC Value Index and the CITIC Growth Index.

Investor returns are useful in that they reflect all factors driving performance. This is something of a liability in trying to detect favoritism since cross-fund subsidization is likely to operate through covert trade coordination strategies rather than through differences in reported holdings, which I control for anyway by adjusting for factor loadings and other observables. Chen et al. (2000) suggest another reason why it might be preferable to strip away holding returns. They argue that managers' active stock trades reflect more strongly held views than those reflected in passive stock positions, especially as the latter might be driven by factors other than performance, such as style constraints, transactions costs and taxes. Thus, stock selection ability should be more discernible in trades than in holdings.

One way to neutralize the effect of portfolio holdings on fund performance is to use the return gap, namely, investor returns minus holding returns.[6] The return gap suits my purpose because, as Kacperczyk et al. (2008) argue, it measures how much of a fund's performance derives from unobservable actions by managers, such as interim trades, as opposed to observable portfolio holdings.

Another way to remove passive holding decisions from fund performance is to use the accounting-based measure 'net profit per share', which reflects capital gains and losses on securities sold, interest and dividend income earned, and expenses such as management fees. Net profit per share is a good indicator of managers' trading ability because it not only reflects gains and losses on long-term holdings (securities on record since at least the last reporting date) but also, more importantly, gains and losses on interim trades (securities bought and sold since the last reporting date). What net profit per share usefully excludes is the change in market value of fund holdings.

27.4   FAMILY EFFECTS AND FUND PERFORMANCE

27.4.1   Basic Performance Comparisons

As a first set of tests of my hypotheses on favoritism, Table 27.2 presents sample averages for all the proposed performance measures across various fund groupings. Panel A compares the performance of open- and closed-end funds in general. This tests my first hypothesis, which holds that because redeemability is a powerful form of governance, redeemable open-end funds should outperform non-redeemable closed-end funds in

Table 27.2 *Closed-end versus open-end funds*

A) Closed-end versus open-end funds in general

	Closed-end funds	Open-end funds	Difference p-value
Share-price return	−1.0507	n/a	n/a
NAV return	0.1030	0.2868	0.4083
Market-adjusted return	0.0079	0.0086	0.0000
Three-factor-adjusted return	0.0052	0.0065	0.0000
Net realized profit per share	−0.0155	0.0212	0.0000
Unrealized profit per share	0.0712	0.0680	0.8534
Total net assets (TNA)	1499	2527	0.0000
Observations (months/qrt/s-a)	2285/748/375	1659/585/321	

B) Closed-end and open-end funds under common management

	Closed-end funds	Open-end funds	Difference p-value
Share-price return	−1.0169	n/a	n/a
NAV return	0.1224	0.2715	0.4173
Market-adjusted return	0.0080	0.0087	0.0000
Three-factor-adjusted return	0.0053	0.0062	0.0000
Net realized profit per share	−0.0158	0.0243	0.0000
Unrealized profit per share	0.0710	0.0721	0.7592
Total net assets (TNA)	1492	2527	0.0000
Observations (months/qrt/s-a)	1901/646/338	1066/373/202	

C) Open-end funds in different fund-family types

	Open funds in families managing open funds only	Open funds in families managing open and closed funds	Difference p-value
NAV return	0.2396	0.2715	0.4834
Market-adjusted return	0.0086	0.0087	0.3119
Three-factor-adjusted return	0.0076	0.0062	0.9990
Net realized profit per share	0.0139	0.0243	0.0402
Unrealized profit per share	0.0546	0.0721	0.1204
Total net assets (TNA)	1828	2527	0.0002
Observations (months/qrt/s-a)	593/212/119	1066/373/202	

Notes: Reported are average performance measures and fund size (*Total net assets, TNA*) for a sample of 142 Chinese investment funds from January 2002 to June 2005. Panel A compares closed- and open-end funds in general. Panel B compares affiliated funds, that is, closed- and open-end funds under common management. Panel C compares open-end funds in families that manage open-end funds only and open-end funds in families that manage both closed- and open-end funds. *Share-price return* (only available for closed-end funds) is the percentage change in the fund's market price per share. *NAV return* is the percentage change in the fund's net asset value (NAV) per share. *Market-adjusted return* accounts for the return on the stock-market index (using the CITIC A-share index as the market proxy). *Three-factor-adjusted return* accounts for market return, size (SMB), and book-to-market (HML). *Net realized profit* is capital gains and losses on securities traded plus interest and dividend income earned, minus all expenses such as management fees. *Unrealized profit* is the change in the market value of securities held since the fund's last reporting date. *Total net assets (TNA)* is closing market value, in millions of yuan, computed as NAV per share times the number of shares outstanding. Returns are monthly (months), TNA is quarterly (qtr), and profits are semi-annual (s-a).

general, that is, regardless of family affiliation. Except for NAV returns and unrealized profit per share, the results show that open-end funds significantly outperform closed-end funds, both statistically and economically. For instance, monthly market-adjusted (three-factor-adjusted) returns average 0.0086 percent (0.0065 percent) for open funds and 0.0079 percent (0.0052 percent) for closed funds, a difference of 9 percent (25 percent). Closed-end funds do poorly, even in absolute terms, with monthly share-price returns averaging −1.05 percent and an average semi-annual net realized profit per share of −1.55 percent (versus 2.12 percent for open-end funds).

Panel B also compares open- and closed-end funds performance but restricts the sample to fund families that manage both open- and closed-end funds. I find very similar results to those in Panel A, which reflects the fact that this sample contains most of the observations found in the broader sample. The samples largely overlap because all fund families launched open-end funds shortly after they were allowed to do so, that is, when open-end funds were instituted by Chinese securities regulation in 2002. Thus, a direct comparison of panels A and B is not a powerful test of our central prediction (Hypothesis 2) that open-end funds should outperform affiliated closed-end funds, above and beyond any general difference in performance. The sections which follow propose more powerful tests, which overcome this limitation of the sample.

Panel C of Table 27.2 tests one of my corollary predictions (Hypothesis 2a), namely, that all else being equal, open-end funds in families that also manage closed-end funds (type II) should outperform open-end funds in families that manage open-end funds only (type I). I run this test to address partly the concern that even though I control for likely differences between open- and closed-end funds, such as different factor loadings, it is possible that other factors besides favoritism explain why open-end funds outperform affiliated closed-end funds.

At one level, the results in Panel C show that this concern is justified since I find no statistical difference in the return-based measures of performance across the two categories of open-end funds. However, I find that the hypothesis is supported based on accounting performance: average net realized profit per share is 1.39 percent for type I funds, which is significantly lower than the 2.43 percent observed for type II funds. I view the difference in results across financial and accounting measures of performance as a clue that strategies aimed at favoring open-end funds are primarily conducted through trading activity and are therefore concentrated in net realized profit.

One might also want to contrast the performance of closed-end funds in families that also manage open-end funds and closed-end funds in families that do not (this would be a test of my corollary Hypothesis 2a). However, because there are so few cases when families manage only closed-end funds, I omit the test for lack of power.

Given the limitations of these essentially univariate tests of fund performance, I propose a series of multivariate tests that examine the role of family affiliation in explaining the difference in performance between pairs of open- and closed-end funds.

27.4.2   Paired-Fund Performance Differences

Although I account for some of the possible differences between open- and closed-end funds (e.g., market-adjusted and three-factor-adjusted returns), open-end funds might outperform affiliated closed-end funds for reasons other than favoritism. In this subsection, I check whether my results survive the addition of control variables such as fund and family size and age and year fixed effects. Because I am interested in explaining the differences in fund performance rather than fund performance itself, I adopt a paired-fund approach from this point onwards. As explained below, the way I pair open- and close-end funds depends on whether I simply test for family effects with the addition of control variables or if I also match on fund style and size.

Multivariate analysis of paired-fund return differences

I construct a sample of paired funds as follows. For every month in the sample period (January 2002 through June 2005), each open-end fund is paired with every closed-end fund in the sample – they need not belong to the same family. For instance, if there are 50 open-end funds and ten closed-end funds in a given month, then the pairing procedure generates 500 fund pairs for that month. This yields a total of 85 261 fund-pair months for the entire sample period.

I difference the paired funds' returns and run the following regression:

$$Open\_end\_return_{i,t} - Closed\_end\_return_{j,t} = \alpha + \beta \ Open\&Closed + controls + \varepsilon,$$

where $Open\_end\_return_{i,t}$ is the return for open-end fund i in month t, and $Closed\_end\_return_{j,t}$ is the contemporaneous return for closed-end fund j. The indicator variable $Open\&Closed$ is set to one if the open-end fund belongs to a family that manages both open-end and closed-end funds, and zero otherwise. A positive β would support my hypothesis that fund families favor open-end funds over their closed-end siblings. I use the same control variables as Gaspar et al. (2006), namely, the size and age of each fund in the differenced pair (four variables), the size and age of the families managing the paired funds (four variables), and three year dummies. The fund- and family-age controls allow for the possibility that funds are managed differently at various stages of their development, particularly near inception.

Hypothesis 3 states that open-end funds should outperform affiliated closed-end funds most dramatically when the scope for cross-subsidization is greatest. This would happen when closed-end fund assets represent a large fraction of total family assets under management. I test this hypothesis using the following regression:

$$Open\_end\_return_{i,t} - Closed\_end\_return_{j,t} = \alpha + \beta \ Family\_CF\_size + controls + \varepsilon,$$

where $Family\_CF\_size$ is the sum of closed-end fund total net assets (TNA) managed by the open-end fund's family. The set of control variables is the same as above. According to Hypothesis 3, β should be positive.

The sample of paired funds is constructed differently than before. This time, each open-end fund is paired with every closed-end fund in the same fund family (before I matched to every closed-end fund in the sample). For instance, if a family has two open-end funds and three closed-end funds, then the procedure generates six fund pairs for this family. This sample can be viewed as a subset of the previous sample in the sense that non-family pairings are excluded and only multi-fund families' fund pairs are retained. This yields a sample of 57 289 fund-pair months.

Table 27.3 reports results for raw fund returns and three-factor-adjusted returns.

Table 27.3   Family effects and paired-fund performance differences

A) Family affiliation

	Raw returns	Three-factor-adjusted returns
Open&Closed	0.3750[a]	0.0020[a]
	(6.61)	(3.40)
Adjusted R-square	0.0719	0.1431
Observations (fund-pair months)	85 261	85 261

B) Family resources

	Raw returns	Three-factor-adjusted returns
Family_CF_Size	0.3681[a]	0.0013[c]
	(4.91)	(1.74)
Adjusted R-square	0.0285	0.0735
Observations (fund-pair months)	57 289	57 289

Notes: Reported are multivariate regression results on the role of family affiliation (Panel A) and family resources (Panel B) in explaining the difference in returns between paired open- and closed-end funds. The sample used in Panel A is constructed as follows: for every month in the sample period (January 2002 through June 2005), each open-end fund is paired with every closed-end fund in the sample – they need not belong to the same family. In Panel B, each open-end fund is paired with every closed-end fund in the same fund family rather than every closed-end fund in the sample. The dependent variable for both panels is the difference between the paired funds' returns, alternatively measured in terms of raw returns (left column) and three-factor adjusted returns (right column). The variable *Open&Closed* is set to one if the open-end fund belongs to a family that manages both open- and closed-end funds, and zero otherwise. This variable tests whether open-end funds outperform affiliated closed-end funds. The variable *Family_CF_size* is the sum of closed-end fund total net assets (TNA) managed by the open-end fund's family. This variable tests whether open-end funds outperform affiliated closed-end funds more if the family has more resources (closed-end assets) to support cross-fund subsidization strategies. The regressions include unreported control variables, namely, the size and age of each fund in the paired funds (four variables), the size and age of the families managing the paired funds (four variables), and three year dummies. t-statistics appear in parentheses. a, b and c indicate statistical significance at the 1 percent, 5 percent and 10 percent confidence levels or better.

Consistent with my hypotheses, the βs are positive and statistically significant. The results are stronger for raw fund returns but remain statistically significant for three-factor-adjusted returns. Thus, results in Panel A support the hypothesis that families with closed-end funds subsidize their open-end funds. Results in Panel B support the hypothesis that families with a larger fraction of closed-end fund assets to total family assets can draw on greater resources to support their cross-subsidization strategies, which leads to greater performance differences.

Multivariate analysis of matched fund-pair return differences
The control variables included in the previous section might not exhaust the ways in which affiliated open- and closed-end funds can differ. I therefore propose a matching algorithm inspired from Gaspar et al. (2006) to improve the paired-fund differences approach by matching funds on management style and size.

   I then apply a matching routine to this sample of family-paired funds where each fund

Table 27.4 Family effects and matched paired-funds performance differences

A) Matched paired-funds return differences		
	Raw returns	Three-factor-adjusted returns
Affiliated	0.3023[a]	0.0021[b]
	(2.95)	(1.92)
Adjusted R-square	0.0575	0.1012
Observations (fund-pair months)	32 891	32 891
B) Matched paired-funds return gap differences		
	Raw returns	Three-factor-adjusted returns
Affiliated	0.5517[a]	0.4163[a]
	(4.24)	(3.86)
Adjusted R-square	0.1243	0.1957
Observations (fund-pair months)	32 891	32 891

Notes: Reported are multivariate regression results on the role of family affiliation in explaining the difference in returns between style- and size-matched pairs of open- and closed-end funds. Panel A uses investor returns (what investors earn by owning the fund) and Panel B uses the return gap (the difference between investor returns and the hypothetical returns earned on the fund's holdings; see Grinblatt and Titman, 1989). The sample period runs from January 2002 through June 2005 and each open-end fund is paired with every closed-end fund in its fund family. Following Gaspar et al. (2006), we then replace each paired fund by an unaffiliated, style- and size-matched fund. Funds without a suitable style match are dropped from the sample. The dependent variable is the difference between the matched paired-funds' returns, alternatively measured in terms of raw returns (left column) and three-factor-adjusted returns (right column). The variable *Affiliated* is set to one if both funds in the matched pair belong to the same family. This variable tests whether open-end funds outperform affiliated closed-end funds. The regressions include unreported control variables, namely, the size and age of each fund in the paired funds (four variables), the size and age of the families managing the paired funds (four variables), and three year dummies. t-statistics appear in parentheses.
a, b and c indicate statistical significance at the 1 percent, 5 percent and 10 percent confidence levels or better.

is replaced by an unaffiliated, style- and size-matched fund.[7] For instance, suppose a particular fund pair contains a large-cap growth open-end fund and a mid-cap value closed-end fund. The open-end fund is replaced by the large-cap growth open-end fund that is closest in size (TNA) but does not belong to the same family. Similarly, the closed-end fund is replaced by the mid-cap value closed-end fund that is closest in size (TNA) but does not belong to the same family. I then difference the matched paired-funds' returns and run the following regression:

$$Open\_end\_return_{i,t} - Closed\_end\_return_{j,t} = \alpha + \beta \; Affiliated + controls + \varepsilon,$$

where the indicator variable *Affiliated* is set to one if the paired funds belong to the same family. Under Hypothesis 1, I expect β to be positive.

Table 27.4 (Panel A) presents the results. As in Table 27.3, statistical significance is higher for raw fund returns than for three-factor-adjusted returns, but the results are significant at conventional levels in either case. These findings for matched fund-pair return differences corroborate my earlier results in suggesting that open-end funds outperform affiliated closed-end funds thanks to favoritism within families.

Multivariate analysis of matched fund-pair return gap differences

The pursuit of strategies that favor the performance of open-end funds over closed-end funds should be reflected in funds' trading activity and give rise to abnormal returns that cannot be explained by their portfolio holdings. In other words, the effects of such strategies should be concentrated in the return gap, that is, the difference between investor returns and holding returns.

I therefore adapt the previous section's analysis by using differences in the return gaps of matched fund pairs instead of differences in investor returns. In other words, I strip away holding returns from investor returns. I implement this test by estimating the following regression:

$$Open\_end\_ReturnGap_{i,t} - Closed\_end\_ReturnGap_{j,t} = \alpha + \beta \ Affiliated + controls + \varepsilon,$$

The only difference between this specification and the previous one is in the dependent variable, which is now computed from return gaps rather than investor returns. As before, Hypothesis 1 implies that β should be positive and significant.

Table 27.4 (Panel B) presents the results. This time, the statistical significance for raw fund returns is only slightly higher than for three-factor-adjusted returns, and in both cases the results are significant at the 1 percent confidence level. These findings form the strongest and most convincing evidence so far that open-end funds outperform affiliated closed-end funds, and that some type of cross-fund subsidization is at work.

27.5   FAMILY EFFECTS AND THE CLOSED-END FUND DISCOUNT

Despite my attempts to control for confounding effects, one still might worry that the difference in performance I document between affiliated open- and closed-end funds is caused not by favoritism but by an omitted correlated factor. I address this concern by proposing a test that relies solely on the cross-section of closed-end fund discounts rather than the comparison of open- and closed-end fund performance.

It is now well established that closed-end funds typically trade at a discount to the market value of their holdings, that is, below their NAV.[8] As many have argued, the closed-end fund discount – the difference between NAV per share and market price per share – should reflect the severity of the agency problems that depress a closed-end fund's market value. In line with this reasoning, I conjecture that the incentive and scope fund families have to engage in cross-fund subsidization will be reflected in the closed-end fund discount.

I formulate two empirical predictions corresponding to Hypotheses 2 and 3. First, I predict that closed-end funds managed by families that also manage open-end funds trade at a deeper discount than those without open-end fund siblings. Second, I predict that the closed-end fund discount increases and decreases with the supply and demand of resources involved in cross-fund subsidization strategies. I measure the supply of resources as the sum of closed-end fund assets (own fund excluded) in the closed-end fund's family (*CFSIZE*) and the demand of resources as the sum of open-end fund assets in the closed-end fund's family (*OFSIZE*). Both *CFSIZE* and *OFSIZE* equal the number of shares in the fund times NAV per share.

This specification serves several functions. First, subsumed in the *OFSIZE* variable is a test of the base prediction that the discount deepens when closed-end funds are affiliated with open-end funds. This is because *OFSIZE* takes on a value of zero if the closed-end fund has no open-end fund sibling, but a positive value otherwise. Second, although *CFSIZE* and *OFSIZE* are expressed in absolute terms rather than normalized by family TNA, including both of them together achieves the same purpose. Finally, by including *CFSIZE* and *OFSIZE* together, I account for all the assets within a family and therefore control for overall family size. I compute the fund discount as:

$$DISC_{i,t} = \frac{NAV_{i,t} - PRICE_{i,t}}{NAV_{i,t}}$$

where $DISC_{i,t}$ is the discount for closed-end fund i at the end of quarter t, $PRICE_{i,t}$ is the fund's share price and $NAV_{i,t}$ is its net asset value (NAV). A positive (negative) value of $DISC_{i,t}$ indicates that the fund is trading at a discount (premium) to NAV.

My proposed specification is therefore:

$$DISC_{i,t} = \alpha + \beta_O OFSIZE + \beta_C CFSIZE + controls + \varepsilon$$

where the control variables are suggested by prior literature, such as those used by Chan et al. (2005) in their study of Chinese closed-end funds, namely, fund size (using the fund's TNA), liquidity (number of shares traded in the quarter divided by the number of shares outstanding, *TURNOVER*), industry concentration (weight of the top five industries held by the fund, *TOP5_IND*), and portfolio concentration (weight of the top ten stocks held by the fund, *TOP10_STOCK*). Since closed-end funds have a contractual maturity, which determines when a fund's assets can finally be redeemed, I also control for the number of years until maturity (*TIME_TO_MATURITY*).

For this test, I extend the sample period back to the first quarter of 2001, when only closed-end funds were available in China (as before, the sample ends with the second quarter of 2005). This introduces additional variation in the sample in the sense that the *OFSIZE* variable is set to zero for quarters prior to 2002. In other words, this allows the sample to reflect not only cross-sectional variation in the size of open-end funds but also the time-series effect of their introduction in September 2001.

The sample uses different data than those used in the earlier tests. First, I collect quarterly data on fund prices, fund trading volume, and net asset values. Second, I compute the top five industry and top ten stock portfolio weightings for each fund using hand-collected data from quarterly reports. Third, I obtain fund name, size, years to maturity, and family affiliation from Tinysoft.NET.

The results are reported in Table 27.5. I find a positive relation between the closed-end discount and the size of the fund family's open-end funds (*OFSIZE*). The relation is

Table 27.5   Family effects and the closed-end fund discount

	Model 1	Model 2	Model 3
CF_SIZE	−0.7958[a]		−0.8430[a]
	(−4.49)		(−4.71)
OF_SIZE	0.7226[b]		0.7835[a]
	(2.34)		(2.49)
CF_NO		−0.5047[a]	
		(−2.75)	
OF_NO		0.7498[b]	
		(2.43)	
FUND_SIZE	0.0019[a]	0.0017[a]	0.0020[a]
	(4.50)	(4.10)	(4.65)
TURNOVER	−0.0770[a]	−0.0774[a]	−0.0761[a]
	(−11.37)	(−11.25)	(−11.13)
TOP5_IND			0.0594[c]
			(1.71)
TOP10_STOCK			−0.0576[c]
			(−1.65)
TIME_TO_MATURITY	0.4147[a]	0.4742[a]	0.4097[a]
	(3.48)	(3.98)	(3.43)
Adjusted R-square	0.8204	0.8179	0.8209
Observations (fund-months)	748	748	746

Notes: Reported are multivariate regression results relating the closed-end fund discount to fund family effects. The dependent variable is the closed-end fund discount, namely, the difference between a fund's NAV per share and its market price per share, divided by its NAV per share. *CF_SIZE* is the sum of closed-end fund assets (TNA) within the closed-end fund's family (own fund excluded). *OF_SIZE* is the sum of open-end fund assets (TNA) within the closed-end fund's family. TNA (total net assets) equals the number of shares in a fund times its NAV per share. These variables measure the supply (*CF_SIZE*) and demand (*OF_SIZE*) of resources potentially associated with cross-fund subsidization strategies by the closed-end fund's family. *CF_NO* (*OF_NO*) is the number of closed-end (open-end) funds managed by a family. *FUND_SIZE* is the closed-end fund's TNA. *TURNOVER* is the number of shares traded in the quarter divided by the number of shares outstanding. *TOP5_IND* measures industry concentration (weight of the top five industries held by the fund). *TOP10_STOCK* measures portfolio concentration (weight of the top ten stocks held by the fund). *TIME_TO_MATURITY* is the number of years until the closed-end fund matures.
a, b and c indicate statistical significance at the 1 percent, 5 percent and 10 percent confidence levels or better.

significant whether I control for fund size and liquidity alone (Model 1) or additionally control for the fund's industry and portfolio concentration (Model 3). This finding supports my prediction that the discount deepens when closed-end funds are affiliated with open-end funds and confirms my earlier evidence of favoritism.

I find a negative relation between the closed-end discount and *CFSIZE*, which is statistically significant, regardless of what controls are included (Model 1 or Model 3). Consistent with the idea that cross-subsidization strategies tax the resources of affiliated closed-end funds, this finding suggests that the burden favoritism imposes on any one closed-end fund lowers – the discount falls – as the portion of closed-end funds in a family increases.

As an alternative proxy for the relative importance of open- and closed-end funds in a family, I use the number of funds of each type (*CF_NO* and *OF_NO*) instead of their assets. As Model 2 shows, this yields qualitatively similar results.

Finally, consistent with the idea that a fund's maturity reflects its redeemability, I find that the closed-end discount is significantly deeper when time to maturity is longer: governance is weaker when fund assets will not be released for a long time.

27.6 HOW MIGHT FAVORITISM WORK? SOME CROSS-FUND SUBSIDIZATION STRATEGIES

Although the evidence strongly suggests that open-end funds significantly outperform affiliated closed-end funds, my claim that this outcome is the result of cross-fund subsidization remains conjectural. In this section, I seek to test more directly that the difference in performance actually does derive from cross-fund subsidization. I consider two fund family strategies that could favor open-end funds over affiliated closed-end funds, namely, trade coordination and resource allocation.

27.6.1 Trade Coordination

Suppose a fund family wished to draw on the resources of its non-redeemable closed-end funds to boost the performance of its redeemable open-end funds.[9] How might it proceed? First, it probably would wish to do so covertly, which suggests that cross-fund subsidization strategies are likely to center on hidden trading activity rather than publicly disclosed portfolio holdings. The previous sections support this hypothesis in that differences in affiliated open- and closed-end fund performance are stronger for measures of unobserved actions (e.g., net realized profit per share, return gap) than measures of observed actions (e.g., unrealized profit per share, holding returns). By the same logic, strategies that can be completed within a reporting period, that is, interim trades, should be preferred over strategies that overlap reporting periods. This is because the latter would appear as reported portfolio holdings, and therefore be detectable, whereas interim trades need never be revealed, at least not in detail.[10]

Fund families might coordinate trades to favor their open-end funds through a pump-and-dump strategy, which I call a tandem trade. A tandem trade involves a sequence of four transactions. First, the open-end fund buys a security, which the closed-end fund then also buys. Second, the trade is reversed: the open-end fund sells the security and the closed-end follows suit. In this way, the closed-end fund is used – to its own detriment – to nudge prices up to benefit the open-end fund. To the extent that these trades are quick to execute and profitable for the open-end fund, they can be done on several illiquid securities at once or repeated many times within a reporting period without being disclosed (interim trades). This is true in the US context, but in China these trades may leave a paper trail, which I use to test for trade coordination.

The trading data used in this chapter represent a substantial improvement over the quarterly portfolio-holding data typically found in literature. For example, Gaspar et al. (2006) investigate intra-family trade coordination by testing for opposite trades, which occur when one fund sells the same security that a sibling fund buys during a given reporting period. They resort to this rough measure of trade coordination because interim trade data are not available for the US, so comparing quarter-to-quarter portfolio-holding reports is the only option.[11] For China, select data on interim trades *are* available, which leads us to propose tandem trades as a finer measure of intra-family trade coordination.

So, how do I test for trade coordination in this study? I simply apply the measure developed by Gaspar et al. (2006) to the interim trade data instead of the period-to-period changes in fund portfolio holdings used in their study. There are two facets to the measure, which reflect the frequency and relative importance of similar interim trades executed by the funds in a given pair of open- and closed-end funds.[12] Keep in mind that although I know the number of shares involved in each reported interim trade, I do not know the dates or prices of the purchase or sale.

For instance, suppose open-end fund O reports that it bought and sold 50 shares of stock X and 200 shares of stock Y, and paired closed-end fund C reports that it bought and sold 100 shares of stock X and 100 shares of stock Z during the same reporting period. In this case, only the round-trip trades involving stock X represent a potential tandem trade. I note this as one matched interim trade. If C had traded in stock Y instead of stock Z I would note two matched interim trades.

I express the relative importance of matched interim trades by dividing the value of the securities traded by each fund (number of shares times the end-of-period price) by its TNA. Since this yields two fractions (one for each fund), I record only the lesser of the two. This follows the approach of Gaspar et al. (2006) and represents a conservative estimate of the potential trade coordination reflected in a given matched interim trade.

Continuing my example, suppose that funds O and C each have a TNA of $1000 and that stocks X and Y are trading for $1 and $0.80 at the end of the reporting period. Then the trade involving X represents 5 percent of fund O's TNA ($1 × 50 ÷ $1000) and 10 percent of fund C's TNA ($1 × 100 ÷ $1000). I therefore associate a value of 5 percent with this matched interim trade. If C had traded in stock Y instead of stock Z I would note a second matched interim trade, with an associated value of 8 percent: the minimum of 16 percent = $0.80 × 200 ÷ $1000 (stock Y's relative importance to fund O) and 8 percent = $0.80 × 100 ÷ $1000 (stock Y's relative importance to fund C). Because fund pairs can share many matched interim trades, I sum the relative importance of all matched interim trades noted for a given fund pair (e.g. 13 percent = 5 percent + 8 percent) to gauge total potential trade coordination between these funds (the *Coordination* variable).

This leads to the following regression specification:

$$OF\_performance_{i,t} - CF\_performance_{j,t} = \alpha + \beta \; Affiliated$$

$$+ \gamma \; Coordination + \theta \; Affiliated \,|\, Coordination + controls + \varepsilon$$

where the indicator variable *Affiliated* is set to one if the paired funds belong to the same family, *Coordination* measures trade coordination, and *Affiliated* × *Coordination* is their interaction, which is actually the variable of interest. Indeed, I want to know whether trade coordination by affiliated funds can explain why open-end funds outperform closed-end funds. If so, θ should be positive and significant.

Since my previous analyses show that favoritism appears to be concentrated in trading returns rather than holding returns, I only show results for net profit, which I alternatively divide by beginning-of-period NAV or number of shares outstanding.

Table 27.6 Family effects and trade coordination

A) Performance measure: net profit divided by net asset value

	Coefficient	t-statistic
Intercept	0.0537[a]	11.39
Affiliated	−0.0025	−0.37
Coordination	0.3460[c]	1.64
Affiliated × Coordination	3.4465[b]	2.16
Adjusted R-square	0.1360	
Observations (fund-pair half-years)	3857	

B) Performance measure: net profit per share

	Coefficient	t-statistic
Intercept	0.0439[a]	11.39
Affiliated	−0.0032	−0.50
Coordination	0.4174[b]	2.07
Affiliated × Coordination	3.3601[b]	2.20
Adjusted R-square	0.1384	
Observations (fund-pair half-years)	3857	

Notes: Reported are multivariate regression results on the role of family affiliation and trade coordination in explaining the difference in performance between paired open- and closed-end funds. For every six-month reporting period between 2002 and 2003 (disclosure rules changed in 2004, which is why we use a restricted sample for this test), each open-end fund is paired with every closed-end fund in the sample – they need not belong to the same family. The dependent variable is the difference in paired fund performance, measured as net profit divided by NAV (Panel A) and net profit per share (Panel B). *Coordination* is our proxy for trade coordination, which we construct as follows. We note whether the paired-funds report interim trades involving the same security (we call these matched interim trades). If so, we express the relative importance of the trade to each fund in the pair by dividing the value of the trade (number of shares times the end-of-period stock price) by the fund's TNA. Since this yields two fractions (one for each fund), we record only the lesser of the two as a conservative estimate of trade coordination. Finally, we sum the minimum relative importance of all the matched interim trades noted for a given pair of funds (the *Coordination* variable). The variable *Affiliated* is set to one if both funds in the pair belong to the same family. The interaction variable *Affiliated × Coordination* tests whether trade coordination among affiliated funds can explain why open-end funds outperform closed-end funds.
a, b, and c indicate statistical significance at the 1 percent, 5 percent, and 10 percent confidence levels or better.

I again need to adjust my sample compared to earlier sections of the chapter. First, trading data are only reported semi-annually, so the frequency of the data is now semi-annual. Second, since the disclosure rules changed at the beginning of 2004, I restrict the sample to 2002–2003 to avoid mixing periods that span a structural break in disclosure rules. Since the disclosure rules that took effect in 2004 require funds to report more detail than before, I plan to refine my tests later to use the richer data.

Results are presented in Table 27.6, where one finds that the interaction variable, *Affiliated × Coordination*, is indeed positive and statistically significant. This supports my prediction that coordinated trades between affiliated funds serve to boost the performance of the open-end fund at the expense of the closed-end fund.

Table 27.7   Family effects and resource allocation

	ret_t	ret_{t-1}	TNA_t	TNA_{t-1}
Closed-end funds	1.50	0.04	0.36	−0.22
	(0.71)	(0.02)	(0.38)	(−0.23)
Open-end funds	1.35	−6.06^c	−0.22	0.10
	(0.35)	(−1.62)	(−0.41)	(0.20)

Notes: Reported are multivariate logistic regression results relating managerial turnover to performance in open-end and closed-end funds. The dependent variable is set to one if fund management has changed and zero otherwise. The independent variable *ret* is the monthly three-factor-adjusted return and *TNA* controls for fund size. The model is estimated using monthly data from January 2002 through June 2005. Z-statistics are reported in parentheses.

27.6.2   Resource Allocation

One of the key resources a fund family can allocate across funds is managerial talent. This is corroborated by the fact that managerial turnover during the sample period is high relative to the number of funds in circulation: one observes 170 changes in fund management for closed-end funds and 102 for open-end funds.[13]

I propose to examine whether managerial talent is preferentially allocated to open-end funds by testing whether the probability that a manager is replaced (retained) following bad (good) performance is higher for open-end funds than closed-end funds. I reason that because redeemability increases accountability, fund families watch the performance of their open-end funds closely, quickly dismissing bad managers and retaining their stars. Conversely, because non-redeemability decreases accountability, families have little incentive to monitor or act upon the performance of their closed-end fund managers. I therefore specify the following logit model to test whether the probability of replacing a fund manager depends on past fund performance:

$$\Pr(Manager\_changed) = \Lambda[\beta_1 + \beta_2 ret_t + \beta_3 ret_{t-1} + \beta_4 TNA_t + \beta_5 TNA_{t-1}]$$

where *ret* is the monthly three-factor-adjusted return and *TNA* controls for fund size. I consider both current and lagged returns since it is not clear how quickly fund performance will affect the manager's fate. Λ denotes the log-likelihood function (logit assumes the residuals follow a standard logistic distribution). I estimate the model using monthly data from January 2002 through June 2005. The dummy variable *Manager_changed* is set to one if fund management has changed and zero otherwise. I run separate regressions for closed-end funds and open-end funds and test whether the coefficients for returns (β_2 and β_3) differ significantly across the two subsamples.

Results are presented in Table 27.7. For closed-end funds, the probability that management changes is not sensitive to performance; both β_2 and β_3 are insignificantly different from zero. However, for open-end funds, the probability that management changes is inversely related to past fund returns: bad (good) past performance makes changes in management more (less) likely. These results support my hypothesis that fund families care more about their open-end funds and their closed-end funds, and that because of this, they tend to skew their management policy in favor of the former.

27.7 GENERALIZATIONS

The findings of this study have implications for the organization and regulation of financial institutions. The main conclusion of my study suggests that differentially redeemable claims can lead to preferential treatment across investors. In this section, I discuss how this conclusion might generalize to other situations.

First, I can generalize the idea of redeemable claims. In this study, the laws regulating closed-end and open-end investment funds in China create a stark contrast between redeemable and non-redeemable claims. In most other cases, redeemability is a matter of degree, which makes it a more nuanced but therefore pervasive concept. For instance, mutual-fund backload fees deter investors from redeeming their funds, at least relative to front-load and no-load fee schemes, where investors can redeem their funds with impunity. My results show that such differences in redeemability put fund managers in a conflict of interest, which can result in wealth transfers across investors.

This conflict of interest can be mitigated internally through self-regulation, and externally through regulatory intervention. Institutions can seek internal solutions by adjusting managerial incentives (e.g., the compensation structure) or by revisiting the contractual terms that give rise to the differences in redeemability in the first place. Failing such self-regulation, market regulators might have to forbid institutions from servicing clienteles marked by material differences in redeemability, or at least require that these clienteles' assets be segregated and managed independently.

This conflict of interest is surely exacerbated by lack of transparency. For instance, hedge funds, which are notoriously opaque and require long redemption notices, could be particularly prone to these types of incentive problems. Therefore, hedge funds might be asked to disclose – voluntarily or compulsorily – the existence of investor classes as well as the contractual terms governing each class, terms which effectively determine the relative redeemability of their claims and potential conflicts.

Globalization and consolidation of the financial services industry means that, now more than ever, financial institutions span many services and diverse clienteles. For instance, many countries have witnessed the ascent of universal banking, often facilitated – even promoted – by regulators under the banner of one-stop banking. This has been a longstanding trend in Europe and more recently in North America, with the repeal of the Glass–Steagall Act that traditionally separated investment banking and commercial banking functions in the United States. While this consolidation no doubt fosters economies of scale and scope, the synergies thus gained could be partly offset by the introduction of unrecognized differences in redeemability across clients within these financial conglomerates. For instance, might liquidity kept to cover on-demand liabilities in the banking division come at the expense of skewed portfolio positions that compromise returns to long-term insurance policy holders? Does divisional accountability properly map to material differences in redeemability? Sufficient transparency and adequate separation of accounts seem advised.

Redeemability – as liquidity – also has implications for the macro-regulation of financial institutions. For instance, the fear of mass redemptions (runs) induces banks to maintain sufficient liquidity, profitability and capital to keep bank runs from materializing and thus serves as a powerful disciplinary device. Yet, certain macro policies that are meant to further reduce the risk of runs can sap this natural discipline: schemes such as deposit insurance, implicit insurance and liquidity support (lender of last resort) all shift the risk from the private hands of bankers to the unwitting public. As a result, banks rationally lower their natural defenses against bank runs, including redeemable claims, making them less accountable and raising the risk of moral hazard.

27.8   CONCLUSIONS

This study examines the role of reclaimable assets in corporate governance. Specifically, I investigate the idea advanced by Fama and Jensen (1983a, 1983b, 1985) that the ability that holders of redeemable shares have to remove assets unilaterally from managerial control exerts a strong discipline over management and is therefore a powerful form of governance. Absent the discipline of redeemable shares, managers become less accountable and governance weakens. I test the implications of Fama and Jensen's argument by comparing the performance and operations of redeemable open-end funds and non-redeemable closed-end funds under common management.

My analysis draws on a natural experiment surrounding investment funds in China where, unlike in the US, the institutional setting allows us to make a relatively clean comparison between open- and closed-end funds. Through a variety of empirical strategies, I make the case that open-end funds outperform closed-end funds in general, and affiliated closed-end funds in particular. The difference in performance is even higher when families have large pools of closed-end fund assets available to boost the performance of their open-end funds. Perhaps most convincingly, I find that the closed-end fund discount deepens for funds with affiliated open-end funds.

Corroborating my evidence of favoritism, I find that fund families appear to coordinate trades that help their open-end funds but hurt their closed-end funds. Fund families also appear to direct their best managerial talent to their open-end funds. I argue that these cross-fund subsidization strategies arise rationally when governance is skewed, which causes accountability and incentives to vary across funds in a family.

NOTES

*   This chapter was previously circulated under the title: 'Closed-end and open-end: share redeemability and cross-fund subsidization'. I thank Sugato Bhattacharya, Kalok Chan, Sudipto Dasgupta, Jie Gan, Doseong Kim, Tim Kruze, Cen Ling, Michael Skully, Laurence Swinkels, Mungo Wilson, Youchang Wu and Lu Zheng for helpful discussions and participants at the Hong Kong University of Science and Technology (HKUST) PhD workshop, the 2007 Conference on Professional Asset Management (Rotterdam), Singapore Management University, National University of Singapore, Tsinghua University (Beijing), the International Conference on Economics, Finance, and Accounting (Taipei – Best Paper), the China International Conference in Finance (Chengdu), the 2nd Asia-Pacific Corporate Governance Conference (Hong Kong), the 2nd International Conference on Asia-Pacific Financial Markets (Seoul – Outstanding Paper Award), and the AsianFA-NFA 2008 International Conference. The usual caveats apply.
1. Admati and Pfleiderer (2005) examine the discipline that large informed shareholders can exert by selling shares. However, in their analysis assets are transferred to new shareholders, not removed from managerial control.
2. It is not uncommon for hedge funds to close, which makes them even more akin to traditional closed-end funds.
3. I say 'might' make sense to acknowledge that legal and ethical considerations also weigh in the equation.

4. Much of this study aims to control for confounding effects through a variety of approaches presented later.
5. For the market-model, we simply set β_{iSML} and β_{iHML} to zero.
6. The idea of comparing investor returns to holding returns dates back to Grinblatt and Titman (1989) who use the approach to study mutual-fund transaction costs. The return gap has since been used to investigate stock-picking talent and investment style (Wermers, 2000), window-dressing (Meier and Schaumburg, 2004), the effect of tick size on trading costs (Bollen and Buse, 2006), and hidden actions (Kacperczyk et al., 2008).
7. Note that the set of candidate matching funds is not restricted to multi-family funds. However, because not every fund can be matched on style and size, some fund pairs drop out of the sample, leaving 32 891 fund-pair months.
8. See Berk and Stanton (2007) for a review of the stylized facts on closed-end fund pricing and a theory relating the dynamics of the discount to managerial ability and incentives.
9. I confine my analysis to strategies that I believe are legal (in the strictest sense) but ethically questionable in that they favor open-end fund shareholders over affiliated closed-end fund shareholders. In other words, I rule out outright fraud and accounting manipulation as possible strategies. Implicit in my analysis is that cross-fund subsidization strategies make economic sense – and are therefore discernable – to the extent that they serve to maximize the value of the residual claims of the fund family, although not each fund individually. It is this basic assumption – that cross-fund subsidization makes sense and is discernable – that my results so far support.
10. This is true for the US but in China interim trades must be reported, although not exhaustively and key data are omitted when they are divulged. The Chinese disclosure rules can be summarized as follows. Until 2003, funds had to disclose the number of shares (not the prices) of each security bought or sold in a reporting period. Since 2004, they must report the market value paid and received for securities sold if they belong to the fund's top 20 holdings or if they represent more than 1 percent of beginning-of-period TNA. One way funds can avoid reporting interim trades (securities bought and sold between reporting dates) is to hold a token amount of the security. For instance, if a fund buys 10 000 shares and sells 9900 shares of stock A between reporting dates, it need only report a position of 100 shares at the next reporting date, without divulging the large shadow interim trade involving the other 9900 shares. (Some funds in the sample report some unusually small, odd-lot holdings that seem to betray this practice.) The gain or loss on the trade would be reflected in the period's net profit; however, it would be impossible for outsiders to detect the shadow interim trade or isolate the associated gain or loss. In short, only interim trades that are fully closed out are reported. This quirk in the disclosure rules means that the reported interim trades represent a lower bound on the true level of trading activity.
11. Given the punctual nature of holdings data and my conjecture that fear of detection vies with trade coordination strategies that can be traced through holdings, it is all the more remarkable that any type of trade coordination can be inferred from portfolio-holding reports.
12. Note that, as in section 27.6.2, I again consider all possible pairings of open- and closed-end funds and capture family affiliation through a family indicator variable.
13. Ideally, I would like to distinguish between promotions and demotions, voluntary departures and terminations. However, the data only allow me to identify changes in management, regardless of the cause of replacement.

REFERENCES

Admati, Anat R. and Paul C. Pfleiderer (2005), 'The "Wall Street Walk" as a form of shareholder activism', Stanford Law and Economics Olin Working Paper No. 315.

Berk, Jonathan and Richard Stanton (2007), 'Managerial ability, compensation, and the closed-end fund discount', *Journal of Finance*, 62(2), 529–556.

Bollen, N.P. and J.A. Busse (2006), 'Tick size and institutional trading costs: evidence from mutual funds', *Journal of Financial and Quantitative Analysis*, **41**, 915–937.

Chan, Kalok, Hung Wan Kot and Desmond Li (2005), 'Portfolio concentration and closed-end fund discounts: evidence from the China market', Working paper, Hong Kong University of Science and Technology.

Chen, Hsiu-Lang, Narasimhan Jegadeesh and Russ Wermers (2000), 'The value of active mutual fund management: an examination of the stockholdings and trades of fund managers', *Journal of Financial and Quantitative Analysis*, **35**, 343–368.

Chevalier, Judith and G. Ellison (1997), 'Risk taking by mutual funds as a response to incentives', *Journal of Political Economy*, **105**, 1167–1200.

Fama, Eugene F. and Kenneth R. French (1993), 'Common risk factors in the returns on stocks and bonds', *Journal of Financial Economics*, **33**, 3–56.

Fama, Eugene F. and Michael C. Jensen (1983a), 'Separation of ownership and control', *Journal of Law and Economics*, **26**, 301–325.

Fama, Eugene F. and Michael C. Jensen (1983b), 'Agency problems and residual claims', *Journal of Law and Economics*, **26**, 327–349.

Fama, Eugene F. and Michael C. Jensen (1985), 'Organizational forms and investment decisions', *Journal of Financial Economics*, **14**, 101–119.

Gaspar, Jose-Miguel, Massimo Massa and Pedro Matos (2006), 'Favoritism in mutual fund families? Evidence on strategic cross-fund subsidization', *Journal of Finance*, **61**, 73–104.

Grinblatt, Mark and Sheridan Titman (1989), 'Mutual fund performance: an analysis of quarterly portfolio holdings', *Journal of Business*, **62**, 393–416.

Guedj, Ilan and Jannette Papastaikoudi (2004), 'Can mutual fund families affect the performance of their funds?', Working Paper, MIT.

Kacperczyk, Marcin, Clemens Sialm and Lu Zheng (2008), 'Unobserved actions of mutual funds', *Review of Financial Studies*, **21**(6), 2379–2416.

Löffler, Gunter (2003), 'Anatomy of a performance race', Working Paper, University of Ulm.

Meier, I. and E. Schaumburg (2004), 'Do mutual funds window dress? Evidence for US domestic equity mutual funds', Working Paper, Yale University.

Nanda, Vikram, Z.J. Wang and L. Zheng (2004), 'Family values and the star phenomenon', *Review of Financial Studies*, **17**, 667–698.

Nohel, Tom, Z. Jay Wang and Lu Zheng (2006), 'Side-by-side management of hedge funds and mutual funds', Working Paper.

Sirri, Erik and P. Tufano (1998), 'Costly search and mutual fund flows', *Journal of Finance*, **53**, 1589–1622.

Wermers, Russ (2000), 'Mutual fund performance: an empirical decomposition into stock-picking talent, style, transaction costs, and expenses', *Journal of Finance*, **55**, 1655–1703.

28 The role of venture capitalists in the acquisition of private companies
Paul A. Gompers and Yuhai Xuan*

28.1 INTRODUCTION

The motivation for and the performance implications of acquisitions have been important areas for corporate finance researchers. We explore the characteristics of one particular type of acquisition, the acquisition of venture capital-backed private companies. Unlike other companies, young, private venture capital-backed companies have values that are primarily based upon real options, that is, future investment opportunities. For most companies, their values may be determined more by assets in place. Venture capital-backed companies, on the other hand, are generally small with relatively minor sales, but substantial technology and intellectual property. Large public companies may be motivated to purchase these companies because they represent potential future investment opportunities for them or because the young start-up may be a future competitor of the firm. As such, we expect that the characteristics of acquirers of venture capital-backed private companies as well as the market's reaction to their announcement and long-run performance may differ from other types of public or private acquisitions.

Prior research on acquisitions (Jensen and Ruback, 1983) has shown that announcement period event returns for acquiring firm shareholders tend to be insignificant or slightly negative. Cash mergers have consistently higher announcement period abnormal returns than those financed with stock. Moeller et al. (2004) find that shareholders of small acquirers gain from acquisition announcements and those of large acquirers suffer losses. In addition, acquirer announcement period returns for private targets are typically higher than those for public targets. Within the sample of acquisitions for private firms, stock offers typically experience higher abnormal returns than cash offers while both enjoy non-negative abnormal returns at merger announcements. In addition to announcement period event studies, Loughran and Vijh (1997) find that acquirers in cash mergers earn positive five-year post-merger abnormal returns, and acquirers in stock deals earn negative long-run abnormal returns, although the results are somewhat sensitive to the estimation methodology. Finally, other research that focuses on the pre-merger and post-merger accounting performance of the event firms (Healy et al., 1992) finds that while the acquirers show no evidence of superior industry-adjusted pretax operating cash flow returns prior to the mergers, their post-merger operating performance improves relative to the industry benchmarks.

Our focus on acquisition of venture capital-backed private companies highlights many differences from these prior results. First, when the characteristics of acquirers of venture capital-backed companies are compared to the characteristics of the acquirers of non-venture capital-backed companies, they are typically larger and have higher Tobin's Q.

535

The acquirers of venture capital-backed companies are more likely to buy firms in related industries and use stock transactions.

Our event study analysis of announcement period returns shows that the market reacts more negatively to the announcement of an acquisition of a venture capital-backed company as compared to other private company acquisitions. Within the sample of venture capital-backed acquisitions, stock deals and related deals tend to have more negative announcement period returns. Our results indicate that at the time of the announcement, the market potentially views venture capitalists as being particularly good at negotiating high prices for their companies in acquisitions or it believes that the adverse selection problem of buying real options due to greater asymmetric information and uncertainty is quite high.

When we examine long-run stock market and operating performance, however, the results differ substantially from both the short-run stock price reaction and the existing literature on acquisitions. First, acquirers of non-venture capital-backed companies have universally negative stock market performance while acquirers of venture capital-backed companies have positive risk-adjusted stock returns over the three-year period following acquisition. In addition, acquisitions with stock and of firms in related industries perform significantly better on average. Finally, acquirers of private companies have positive industry-adjusted pre-merger and post-merger operating performance. Acquirers of venture capital-backed companies, in particular, continue to have high industry-adjusted capital expenditure and Tobin's Q indicating that these firms continue to have significant investment opportunities that they are exploiting. Overall, the results suggest that acquirers of venture capital-backed private companies are superior-performing, high-investing firms that continue to invest and perform well even after the acquisition. In addition, the use of stock to motivate the management of the acquiring company is potentially an important part of the acquisition process, and the use of equity in the acquisition appears not to be a signal of overvaluation.

By focusing on acquisitions of private, venture capital-backed companies, this study contributes to our understanding of the sources of value creation in mergers and acquisitions as well as our understanding of the value-added role that venture capital investors play in the young private firms above and beyond capital provisions. In addition, the use of stock in the acquisitions potentially to align the incentives of the management and shareholders echoes the widespread use of stock grants and stock options by venture capitalists as a governance mechanism to motivate entrepreneurs in private companies (Baker and Gompers, 2003a, 2003b). Thus, applied in a broader context, our results highlight the important link between governance (in particular incentive compensation) and value creation (Gompers et al., 2003), especially when human capital is critical to the long-run performance. The rest of the chapter is organized as follows. Section 28.2 highlights the venture capital industry and the usefulness of focusing on private venture capital-backed companies as real options that large public companies seek to acquire. Section 28.3 reviews the literature on acquisitions and outlines our research design. Section 28.4 describes our data, while Section 28.5 presents our analyses. Section 28.6 concludes.

28.2 VENTURE CAPITAL INVESTORS AND PRIVATE COMPANIES

28.2.1 The Role of Venture Capital Investors

Venture capital firms specialize in collecting and evaluating information on start-up and growth companies. These types of companies are prone to information gaps – due to the highly specialized nature of their products and their early stage of development – and capital constraints are likely to be a significant problem. These firms are primarily composed of future investment and growth opportunities, have few assets in place, and have little history of revenues and cash flows. Because the intensive involvement of the venture capitalist alleviates some of the information gaps, these firms are likely to be better organized and perform better while still private than similar firms financed with other sources of capital.

One of the most common features of venture capital is the meting out of financing in discrete stages over time. Sahlman (1990) notes that staged capital infusion is the most potent control mechanism a venture capitalist can employ. Prospects for the firm are periodically re-evaluated. Staged capital infusion keeps the owner-manager on a tight leash and reduces potential losses from bad decisions.[1] Gompers (1995) examines the staging of venture capital and finds that it is utilized to alleviate moral hazard and the asymmetric information problem. Consistent evidence regarding the strength of contractual terms in these agreements is found in Kaplan and Stromberg's (2003) analysis of 130 venture investment agreements.

In addition to the staged capital infusions, venture capitalists will usually make investments with other investors. One venture firm will originate the deal and look to bring in other venture capital firms. This syndication serves multiple purposes. For example, it allows the venture capital firm to gain additional insights and advice about the firm. The syndication of investment also allows the venture capitalist to diversify his portfolio across a greater number of investments.

A third mechanism utilized by venture capitalists to avoid conflicts is the widespread use of stock grants and stock options. Managers and critical employees within a firm receive a substantial fraction of their compensation in the form of equity or options. This tends to align the incentives of managers and investors. Baker and Gompers (2003a, 2003b) examine the role that venture capitalists play in setting compensation and incentives of entrepreneurs. They find that venture capitalists increase the sensitivity of management's compensation to the firm's performance relative to similar non-venture capital-financed companies. Fixed salaries are lower and the size of the equity stake held is higher for venture capital-backed chief executive officers (CEOs).

In addition to the control mechanisms employed, venture capitalists are value-added investors. The advice and recruiting networks that venture capitalists maintain add considerably to a company's value. The venture capitalists put better boards of directors into place and align the incentives of management (Baker and Gompers, 2003a). Similarly, a recent paper by Sorensen (2007) examines whether specific venture capitalists are value-added to the firm. He shows that there are identifiable value-added effects of having seasoned venture capitalists involved with a company.

28.2.2   Venture Capital Backing: Importance to the Acquirer

Two critical distinguishing features motivate our use of venture capital-backed acquisitions by public companies. First, as mentioned above, the value of a venture capital-backed start-up is typically composed of primarily future growth opportunities, not current revenues or cash flow. Cash flows at the time of acquisition are likely to be rather low. The future value is highly dependent upon the successful execution of these growth options. As such, the characteristics of the acquisition as well as the long-run performance implications of the purchase may be substantially different from the purchase of other private companies whose value is largely dependent upon existing assets in place.

A second, related feature of the value of venture capital-backed acquisitions is the importance of human capital to the future value of the opportunity. Because, many times, the market or product will not be proven and because of the importance of the entrepreneur who developed the idea, the skills and experiences of the people associated with the venture capital-backed company will be critical to its future success at the acquirer. Their management of the future investment opportunities may be required to ensure success. Similarly, the acquirer would not want the entrepreneur to start a competing firm. This might influence the structure of the purchase transaction as we discuss in the next section.

28.3   MERGERS AND ACQUISITIONS, REAL OPTIONS AND SOME EMPIRICAL PREDICTIONS

The traditional literature on mergers suggests that acquisitions often take place for efficiency-related reasons. Mitchell and Mulherin (1996) document that mergers occur in waves and strongly cluster by industry. Mergers are seen as a response to industry shocks. Andrade et al. (2001) show that merger activity in the 1990s was largely driven by deregulation. Another category of theories of mergers focuses on the behavior of managers. Mergers offer an opportunity for managers pursuing self-interest to build up their own empires with private benefits of control (Jensen and Meckling, 1976; Jensen, 1986). Managers affected by hubris are likely to overestimate their ability to run the targets and thus make expensive and unnecessary acquisitions (Roll, 1986; Heaton, 2002). In addition, bad managers can entrench themselves through manager-specific acquisitions to improve their job security (Shleifer and Vishny, 1989). A recent theory based on inefficient markets and rational managers (Shleifer and Vishny, 2003) sees mergers as a form of arbitrage by which managers take advantage of the stock market's misvaluation of the acquiring firm's stock and its perception of resulting synergies.

A particular type of acquisition that we focus on in this chapter is the acquisition of real options (or growth options). Rather than acquiring assets in place or existing sales as in more traditional takeovers, acquisition of real options are strategic investments that afford acquirers the opportunity to develop capabilities and the flexibility to make larger subsequent investments, to increase the scale or widen the scope of operations in the future when and if new market conditions warrant the desirability and timing of such expenditures. Values of these real options are typically accounted for not by current operations and cash flows, but by future growth and investment opportunities. This type of acquisition is very likely more prevalent for venture capital-backed private targets. Such targets are typically young start-ups in high-tech industries with limited sales or earnings track records yet high future growth opportunities.

The characteristics of real options and venture capitalists' typical involvement in such companies suggest that venture capital backing may have an effect on the structure of the acquisition of private targets by public acquirers. As with financial options, real options have great uncertainties about their future pay-offs. Assets in place generate current cash flow that can be better estimated, whereas future cash flows and contingent investment for real options entail a great deal of uncertainty. When facing high uncertainties for the target's value, an acquirer would prefer to make stock offers because any cost of overpayment due to the difficulties in target valuation would be partially borne by the target shareholders themselves, referred to as the 'contingency pricing effect' of stock offers by Hansen (1987). Moreover, because human capital may be important to these growth options, an acquirer is more likely to want to tie managers of the private firm to the public company. Typically, such 'tying in' is done by buying the firm with stock rather than cash in order to align the incentives of the target managers with those of the acquirer, and to tie the target managers' future personal returns to their abilities to generate future pay-offs.

Additionally, because of the greater uncertainties and the importance of human capital associated with real options, an acquirer might find it less daunting to estimate the target's value and manage the acquired personnel in the future if the target is in a line of business related to the acquirer. Therefore, if we believe young venture capital-backed start-ups are more likely to be growth options, we would expect such acquisitions to be more likely in the form of stock and to come from acquisitions in a related industry.

Merger research has also focused on determining shareholder value gains or losses resulting from mergers and their distribution between stockholders of the acquirers and those of the targets. Researchers (Jensen and Ruback, 1983; Andrade et al., 2001) conducting announcement period short-term event studies show that target firm shareholders normally enjoy significantly positive announcement period abnormal returns from merger transactions while acquiring firm shareholders tend not to gain from mergers. Form of payment in the financing of the merger transactions is found to make a significant difference in stock market reaction, with mergers financed without any stock earning consistently higher announcement period abnormal returns than those financed with stock. Moeller et al. (2004) find firm size to be a key factor in determining acquirer returns, with shareholders of small acquirers gaining from acquisition announcements and those of large acquirers suffering losses. This size effect remains after controlling for the organizational form of the acquired assets (public, private or subsidiary) and the method of payment and seems to play a more important role in affecting abnormal returns than the other determinants of acquirer returns.

When acquisitions of private firms alone are examined, however, the above results for value implications associated with mergers do not generally hold (Hansen and Lott, 1996; Chang, 1998; Fuller et al., 2002). In particular, acquirer announcement period returns for private targets are typically higher than those for public targets. Additionally, within the sample of acquisitions for private firms, stock offers typically experience higher abnormal returns than cash offers, while both enjoy non-negative abnormal returns at merger announcements. The positive wealth effect associated with acquisitions of private firms is often attributed to a price discount captured by the acquirers for purchasing such firms resulting from the limited competition in the acquisition market for private targets and their relative illiquidity compared to publicly traded firms. In addition, monitoring activities by large blockholders created from the target shareholders, reduced information asymmetries and favorable tax effects together contribute to the higher abnormal returns for stock-financed acquisitions compared with cash transactions when privately held firms are targets.

Acquisitions of real options, however, might be a distinct group among acquisitions of private targets in terms of the price reaction to the acquisition announcement. The greater uncertainties associated with real options, coupled with the fact that many such targets are less mature companies without much prior record, make an accurate valuation of the target by the acquirer and by the market at the time of the merger announcement more difficult than in acquisitions of assets in place. Moreover, when the level of uncertainty is high, leading to a high level of perceived heterogeneity in the target's value, the winner's curse problem is aggravated. Thus, a buyer in an auction of a venture capital-backed private company may be more susceptible to adverse selection problems. If they win the bid for the private company, it is more likely that they overpaid for the firm than it would be if they were buying another private firm with a long history of revenues and cash flows. Furthermore, if most of the acquisitions for real options are venture capital-backed targets, the market might expect the venture capitalists to negotiate better-priced deals for the targets with the acquirers.[2] All these factors imply that acquirers of venture capital-backed start-ups would likely experience larger price declines at announcement than acquirers of other, non-venture capital-backed start-ups. In particular, if such an acquisition is financed by stock, the market might take it as a signal that the value of the target is of greater uncertainty, as suggested before. If such an acquisition is related, the target might be more certain of its value to the acquirer and demand a higher offer price, thus minimizing the price discount. Moreover, the market might perceive such a related acquisition as a sign that the acquirer is running out of its own internal growth opportunities and/or that it is overpaying to pre-empt future competition. If these are the cases, we would expect venture capital-backed acquisitions that are stock-financed and/or related to have even lower announcement period returns.

In the long run, if the real options prove to be strategically valuable to the long-term development and thriving of business (and the market incorrectly incorporates these benefits into the stock price), we would expect to see strong relative stock performance of the acquiring companies. In particular, if related acquisitions turn out to provide helpful research and development (R&D) capabilities, complementary technologies and competitive strengths, and if stock-financed deals show their advantages in human capital management, as discussed earlier, one would expect to see a positive drift in the long-run stock price of companies undertaking venture capital-backed transactions.

Instead of relying on abnormal returns to measure the value effect of mergers, some researchers have directly examined the pre-merger and post-merger accounting performance of the event firms to see whether mergers lead to improvements in asset productivity relative to their industry peers. Healy et al. (1992) find that while the acquirers show no evidence of superior industry-adjusted pretax operating cash flow returns prior to the mergers, their post-merger operating performance improves relative to the industry benchmarks. Similarly, Andrade et al. (2001) show that cash flow-to-sales for the sales-weighted average of the target and the acquirer outperforms the industry peers before the merger and cash flow-to-sales for the acquirer improves slightly relative to the industry benchmark after the merger.

We expect similar results for the acquirers of real options. Before acquisitions, such acquirers are most likely leaders in their respective industries, with better than average operating performance. Because of the great amount of uncertainty involved in acquisitions of real options, one would expect that only relatively strong performers that have the necessary experience and capability would be willing and able to take part in such transactions. Thus, a typical acquirer of venture capital-backed private companies is likely to be an industry leader that not only regularly undertakes a great number of investments but also has considerable growth capabilities so that it can fully take advantage of the real options acquired once the opportunities arise in the future.

28.4 DATA

We identify a sample of mergers and acquisitions for which the targets are venture capital-backed US private companies obtained from Venture Economics and Securities Data Corporation. We consider only transactions in which the acquiring firm is a US public company listed in the Center for Research in Security Prices (CRSP) and Compustat databases during the event window. This dataset, which is our primary sample for analysis, includes 1234 transactions, with announcement dates between 1976 and 2001, the majority of which, approximately 97 percent, occur between 1990 and 2001. For comparison purposes, we also gather a second sample of mergers and acquisitions from the Securities Data Company's US Mergers and Acquisitions Database. We select the sample of transactions with announcement dates between 1990 and 2001 in which the target is a private company, and the acquirer is a US public company listed on CRSP and Compustat during the event window. We then exclude from this sample all the observations by the same company within the one-year window (six months before and six months after) of the announcement date of any transactions in the primary sample. This gives us our sample of acquisitions of non-venture capital-backed private targets, consisting of 10 178 transactions.

Table 28.1 shows the number of acquisitions by year for both samples. The total number of acquisitions and the number of acquisitions of non-venture capital-backed private targets exhibit the same time pattern, mainly because the majority of transactions in a given year are non-venture capital-backed targets. The numbers increase through time (except for a dip in 1995) and peak in 1997 before declining. A similar pattern exists for the sample of acquisitions of venture capital-backed private targets, although the number of such transactions increases monotonically until its peak in 1999, which seems to suggest a lag in the decline for the acquisitions of venture capital-backed private targets.[3] The percentage of all acquisitions that have venture capital-backed targets is reasonably steady around 10 percent, except for the beginning of the 1990s when fewer transactions involve venture capital-backed targets and in 1999 and 2000 when such transactions make up about 17 percent and 13 percent of all mergers respectively.

Table 28.2 reports sample summary statistics for all the acquisitions of private targets, divided according to whether the targets were venture capital-backed or not. Panel A

Table 28.1   Number of acquisitions of private companies by year

Year	VC-backed targets	Non-VC-backed targets	Total	VC-backed/Total (%)
1990	11	237	248	4.44
1991	18	323	341	5.28
1992	59	495	554	10.65
1993	75	700	775	9.68
1994	78	914	992	7.86
1995	99	805	904	10.95
1996	133	1 062	1 195	11.13
1997	141	1 583	1 724	8.18
1998	172	1 512	1 684	10.21
1999	214	1 071	1 285	16.65
2000	148	970	1 118	13.24
2001	48	506	554	8.66
Total	1196	10 178	11 374	10.52

Notes: The table indicates by year the number of observations in the two samples of acquisitions of private companies for the period 1990–2001. The acquirers are US public companies. The targets are US private companies, differentiated by whether or not they are venture-backed.

contains the characteristics of the transactions. From Panel A, we see that the transaction values are much larger both in dollar value and as a percentage of assets (or market capitalization) for deals involving venture capital-backed private targets than for those with non-venture capital-backed private targets. The two samples also differ significantly in the method of payment. Stock is used more frequently in payment for acquisitions of venture capital-backed private companies, and cash, on the contrary, much less often. In fact, the percentage of pure equity deals is more than twice as large for acquiring venture capital-backed private companies as for acquiring non-venture capital-backed ones, and the percentage of pure cash deals is more than 50 percent smaller for acquiring venture capital-backed targets than for acquiring non-venture capital-backed ones.

Finally, we focus on the relatedness of the acquisitions. A merger is classified as related if the target is acquired by a company that has the same two-digit Standard Industrial Classification (SIC) code as it does, and unrelated otherwise.[4] Our results show that an acquisition is less likely to be unrelated if the target is venture capital-backed. These results are consistent with our prediction that acquisitions of real options are more likely to be stock-financed and related.

Panel B concentrates on characteristics of the acquiring firms. Acquirers of venture capital-backed private targets are much larger in both assets and market capitalization than acquirers of non-venture capital-backed private targets. Firms acquiring venture capital-backed private targets are also more liquid than firms acquiring non-venture capital-backed private targets, having a much higher percentage of assets in cash and short-term investments. Note that although these companies have more cash on hand, cash is less frequently used in their acquisitions of private targets, while stock is their preferred method of payment, consistent with the 'contingency pricing effect' and the incen-

Table 28.2   Sample summary statistics for acquisitions of private companies

	VC-backed targets		Non-VC-backed targets	
Panel A: Deal characteristics	Mean	Median	Mean	Median
Transaction value (TV) ($ millions)	397.173	75.000	44.423	11.500
TV/Assets	0.339	0.128	0.327	0.052
TV/Market capitalization	0.286	0.081	0.276	0.060
Cash in payment (%)	34.05		68.29	
Stock in payment (%)	70.84		45.74	
Pure cash deals (%)	20.84		42.94	
Pure equity deals (%)	57.63		26.47	
Related deals (%)	64.83		57.20	
Panel B: Acquirer characteristics	Mean	Median	Mean	Median
Assets ($ millions)	6018.270	674.416	2779.710	267.293
Market capitalization ($ millions)	13890.026	930.686	1485.263	202.971
Cash/Assets	0.226	0.154	0.132	0.058
Book to market equity	0.426	0.271	1.246	0.440
Q	2.920	1.832	1.704	1.164
Small acquirer (%)	25.65		55.08	

Notes: The sample is acquisitions of private companies (mainly for the period 1990–2001), where the acquirers are US public companies and the targets are US private companies, differentiated by whether or not they are venture-backed. The first panel presents the characteristics of the transactions. A deal is classified as related if the target and the acquirer have the same two-digit SIC code. The second panel reports the characteristics of the acquirers. Cash includes cash and short-term investments. Q is calculated as the sum of the market value of equity and the book value of debt, divided by assets. A small acquirer is defined to be an acquiring firm whose market capitalization in the event year is equal to or less than the smallest quartile of NYSE-listed firms.

tive advantage of stock financing in acquisitions of growth options, as argued before. Next, acquirers of venture capital-backed targets have on average a much lower book-to-market ratio and a much higher Tobin's Q (calculated as the sum of the market value of equity and the book value of debt, divided by assets). This suggests that the acquirers of private, venture capital-backed start-ups are higher-growth companies than acquirers of non-venture capital-backed private firms. Lastly, the group of acquirers of venture capital-backed private targets has a much lower percentage of small acquirers than their counterparts in the non-venture capital-backed target group, where a small acquirer is defined to be an acquiring firm whose market capitalization in the event year is equal to or less than the smallest quartile of New York Stock Exchange (NYSE)-listed firms.[5]

Moeller et al. (2004) provide summary statistics for their sample of mergers and acquisitions between 1980 and 2001, organized by the organizational form of the assets acquired. The characteristics of the deals and acquirers in our non-venture capital-backed private target group are pretty much in line with those of acquirers of private targets in their sample, except that the company size is on average larger for the acquirers in our non-venture capital-backed target group. The statistics for our main sample of acquirers of venture capital-backed targets, however, are very different from those of average acquirers of private targets in their study. In fact, except for Tobin's Q, acquisitions of venture capital-backed private targets look very similar to acquisitions of public targets in Moeller et al. (2004) in both deal and acquirer characteristics: they are on average bigger transactions, more often financed by equity and less likely to be unrelated. In addition, the acquirers are generally larger in size and have fewer small companies in composition. Moeller et al. (2004) show that acquirers of public targets generally have much lower Q values than acquirers of private targets. We can see from Panel B of Table 28.2 that the Q of acquirers of venture capital-backed private targets is higher than average within the group of acquisitions of private targets and thus is much higher than the Q of acquirers of public targets. Overall, the summary statistics suggest that within acquisitions of private targets, those involving venture capital-backed targets are very different from those of non-venture capital-backed ones.

28.5   RESULTS

28.5.1   Event-Period Abnormal Returns

In this section, we explore the market's reaction to the announcement of the acquisition of private companies, examining the relationship between the characteristics of the acquisition and the return from one day before the announcement of the acquisition until one day after the announcement of the acquisition. Announcement period abnormal returns are calculated following the standard estimation methodology for event study with daily returns as in Brown and Warner (1985). For each observation in the sample, we use days -200 through -20 relative to the event date as the estimation period. We regress the daily returns for our sample of acquirers on the value-weighted returns on the market portfolio for this period. We require a stock to have no more than 90 missing daily returns in days -200 through $+60$ in order to be included in the estimation. From the regression results, we take the estimated factor loadings to estimate a market model predicted return for each day from -20 through day $+60$. The difference between the actual daily return and the market model prediction during the event period is the measure of abnormal performance. For the purpose of our event time analysis, we focus on the cumulative abnormal return (CAR) over the three-day event window ($CAR[-1,+1]$).

Table 28.3 tabulates the CAR from day -1 to day $+1$ for both venture-backed and non-venture-backed targets. In addition to tabulating total sample average CARs, we tabulate average CARs based on whether the deal was pure cash or pure equity as well as if the deal was related to the acquirer's business or not. A deal is classified as related if the target and the acquirer have the same two-digit SIC code.

The results in Table 28.3 show that the market has very different reactions to the announcement of an acquisition of a venture-backed company. The CAR from day -1 to day $+1$ is 0.64 percent for venture-backed acquisitions, significantly smaller than the 1.58 percent CAR for non-venture-backed acquisitions. There are also differential effects of deal structure on these two subsamples. The abnormal return for pure cash deals is large and positive for venture capital-backed targets while it is negative for pure equity deals of venture-backed targets. Both types of deals have average positive CARs for non-venture capital-backed deals, but pure equity deals actually have a higher (more positive) abnormal return than pure cash deals. This is different from the literature on

Table 28.3   Announcement period abnormal returns for acquirers

	VC-backed targets			Non-VC-backed targets		
	CAR [−1,+1] (%)	t-statistic	N	CAR [−1,+1] (%)	t-statistic	N
Full sample	0.64	2.62	1120	1.58	13.13	8960
Pure cash deals	1.73	4.32	202	1.15	8.09	3845
Pure equity deals	−0.58	−1.60	531	1.96	9.60	2436
Related deals	0.40	1.24	723	1.23	8.92	5110
Unrelated deals	1.06	2.96	397	2.09	12.42	3850

Notes: The sample is acquisitions of private companies (mainly for the period 1990–2001), where the acquirers are US public companies and the targets are US private companies, differentiated by whether or not they are venture-backed. Announcement period abnormal returns are calculated following the standard estimation methodology for event study with daily returns as in Brown and Warner (1985). For each observation in the sample, we use days −200 through −20 relative to the event date as the estimation period where we regress the daily returns on the value-weighted returns on the market portfolio. We require a stock to have no more than 90 missing daily returns in days −200 through +60 in order to be included in the estimation. The difference between the daily return and the market model prediction during the event period is the measure of abnormal performance, and we focus on the cumulative abnormal return over the three-day event window (CAR[−1, + 1]). A deal is classified as related if the target and the acquirer have the same two-digit SIC code. N is the number of observations.

acquisition of public targets in which pure stock deals have a more negative abnormal return at announcement. The literature typically views equity acquisitions as being similar to seasoned equity offerings and signaling overvaluation of the firm's equity. Surprisingly, the market views all equity transactions as being bad for acquirers of venture capital-backed firms, but positive for acquirers of non-venture capital-backed firms.

Relatedness appears to have a similar effect on the abnormal return of both venture-backed and non-venture-backed companies. Unrelated deals have higher (more positive) CARs than do related deals. In particular, the acquisition of unrelated private non-venture capital-backed companies has a positive 2 percent impact on the acquirer when the acquisition is announced. This suggests that, at least at the time of the acquisition, the market does not have a negative view of these acquisitions of private companies.

These results are explored in Table 28.4 in which we regress the event window (day −1 to day +1) on controls for the size of the acquirer, the relative size of the acquisition, the acquirer's book-to-market ratio, how related the acquirer and target are, whether the deal was pure cash or pure stock, and whether the target was venture capital-backed. The results show that the price reaction for the larger acquirer is more negative. The effect is not driven by relative transaction size because we control for how large the acquisition was relative to the firm's market value. There are a couple of potential explanations. First, larger acquirers may be more likely to acquire firms in a competitive bidding process that would increase the adverse selection problem. Second, because the average price reaction on announcement is positive, maybe the market believes that the acquisition will have a larger positive effect on the value of the smaller acquirers.

It is also interesting that related acquisitions have a more negative announcement reaction. This is unusual because one might expect unrelated, diversifying acquisitions

Table 28.4 *Regressions for acquirer announcement period abnormal return controlling for firm and deal characteristics*

Panel A: Venture-backed and non-venture-backed targets

Independent variables	Dependent variable: CAR in event window [−1,+1]							
	Coefficient	t-statistic	Coefficient	t-statistic	Coefficient	t-statistic	Coefficient	t-statistic
Logarithm of acquirer's size (market equity)	−0.0061	−9.59	−0.0061	−9.69				
Small?					0.0156	6.63	0.0157	6.69
Relative size (transaction value/size of acquirer)	0.0003	0.71	0.0003	0.72	0.0006	1.40	0.0006	1.42
Acquirer's book-to-market ratio	−0.0001	−1.35	−0.0001	−1.37	−0.0001	−1.06	−0.0001	−1.08
Related on the 2 digit level?	−0.0067	−2.88	−0.0048	−2.01	−0.0075	−3.24		
Related on the 4 digit level?			−0.0010	−0.37			−0.0054	−2.25
Pure cash deal?	−0.0013	−0.45	0.0023	0.76	−0.0030	−1.07	−0.0027	−0.98
Pure stock deal?	0.0028	0.92	−0.0034	−0.85	0.0013	0.42	0.0007	0.23
Venture-backed?	−0.0034	−0.84			−0.0086	−2.17	−0.0087	−2.20
Constant	0.0857	8.19	0.0842	8.06	0.0096	1.19	0.0071	0.89
Adjusted R²	0.016		0.016		0.011		0.010	
Number of observations	8693		8693		8693		8693	

Panel B: Venture-backed targets only

Independent variables	Dependent variable: CAR in event window [−1,+1]							
	Coefficient	t-statistic	Coefficient	t-statistic	Coefficient	t-statistic	Coefficient	t-statistic
Logarithm of acquirer's size (market equity)	−0.0031	−1.62	−0.0030	−1.54				
Small?					0.0356	3.93	0.0357	3.93
Relative size (transaction value/size of acquirer)	0.0011	0.20	0.0014	0.26	−0.0015	−0.27	−0.0012	−0.23
Acquirer's book-to-market ratio	0.0003	0.11	0.0001	0.02	0.0002	0.07	−0.0001	−0.04
Related on the 2 digit level?	−0.0106	−1.32			−0.0104	−1.30		
Related on the 4 digit level?			0.0068	0.91			0.0075	1.02
Pure cash deal?	−0.0016	−0.14	−0.0008	−0.07	0.0001	0.01	0.0010	0.09
Pure stock deal?	−0.0226	−2.38	−0.0229	−2.41	−0.0197	−2.11	−0.0199	−2.12
Constant	0.0324	0.29	0.0307	0.28	−0.0168	−0.16	−0.0164	−0.16
Adjusted R²	0.016		0.015		0.031		0.030	
Number of observations	868		868		868		868	

Notes: The sample is acquisitions of private companies (mainly for the period 1990–2001), where the acquirers are US public companies and the targets are US private companies. Panel A includes both venture-backed and non-venture-backed targets, and Panel B includes only venture-backed targets. The dependent variable is the cumulative abnormal return (CAR) over the three-day event window, calculated following the standard estimation methodology for event study with daily returns as in Brown and Warner (1985). The independent variables include a dummy variable (*Small*) that equals one if the acquirer's market capitalization in the event year is equal to or less than the smallest quartile of NYSE-listed firms, dummy variables that equal one if the acquirer has the same two-digit or four-digit SIC code as the target, a dummy variable that equals one if the transaction is a pure cash deal, a dummy variable that equals one if the transaction is a pure equity deal, and a dummy variable that equals one if the target is venture-backed. The other independent variables are the logarithm of the acquirer's market equity, the acquirer's book-to-market ratio, and the ratio of the transaction value to the acquirer's size (relative size). Year fixed effects are also included.

547

would be more likely to be associated with poor future performance and hence a negative reaction at announcement. The market, however, may believe that bidders overpay for related acquisitions, even if they are better from a strategic operating perspective. This might result if the public company is viewed as overpaying to pre-empt its future competition.

We find no relation between the method of payment and the price reaction at the announcement of the acquisition. On the other hand, the presence of venture capital investors in the target firm leads to lower abnormal returns for the acquirer on announcement of the acquisition. Because venture capitalists have considerable experience with selling companies (between a quarter and a third of all venture capital-backed firms are sold via an acquisition), they may be able to negotiate better terms for the seller and, hence, the market may believe that less of the value will accrue to the acquirer.

In Panel B, we examine the reaction of the market for the venture capital-backed sample of acquisitions. Much like the entire sample, larger size for the acquirer appears to be associated with lower abnormal returns. The other results appear to be less significant than they were in the full sample. The one difference is the effect of method of payment on the price reaction at the announcement of the acquisition. Pure stock deals have significantly lower announcement returns as the sorts in Table 28.3 demonstrated. Because the acquirers of venture capital-backed firms are typically low book-to-market growth companies, the market may view equity acquisitions as signals of market timing and overvaluation.

28.5.2   Long-Run Buy-and-Hold Abnormal Returns

In this subsection, we explore whether or not there are long-run abnormal returns following the acquisition of private venture and non-venture capital-backed companies. For each acquirer, we calculate the firm's buy-and-hold abnormal return (BHAR). BHARs are calculated as the difference between the three-year buy-and-hold return for the event firm and the benchmark portfolios.[6] The benchmark return is computed by calculating the buy-and-hold return on the matched portfolio from 25 value-weighted, non-rebalanced portfolios formed on size and book-to-market equity using NYSE breakpoints, as recommended by Mitchell and Stafford (2000). In forming the benchmark portfolios, we exclude all event firms but include all other stocks available on CRSP and Compustat that can be assigned to a size-book-to-market group. We first sort benchmark stocks independently into five size quintiles and five book-to-market quintiles at the end of each June based on NYSE breakpoints, and then construct the benchmark portfolios by intersecting these size and book-to-market quintiles. An event firm is then matched to its benchmark based on its book-to-market equity for the last fiscal year and market capitalization as of the event date. Missing event firm returns over the three-year period are replaced by the corresponding benchmark portfolio returns in the calculation of BHARs. For all event firms, we report the mean BHAR as well as the wealth relative, calculated as the ratio of the average three-year gross returns of the event firms to the average three-year gross returns of the benchmark portfolios.

In Table 28.5, we tabulate the three-year buy-and-hold return for the full sample as well as the venture and non-venture capital-backed cohorts. When the full sample is examined, the acquirers of private firms underperform substantially, whether the results

Table 28.5 *Three-year buy-and-hold abnormal returns (BHARs) for acquirer*

Panel A	Wealth				
	Sample	Benchmark	Relative	BHAR	N
Equal-weight					
Full sample	0.5135	2.1602	0.4789	−1.6467	4788
Venture-backed	0.5254	1.8013	0.5445	−1.2759	659
Non-venture-backed	0.5116	2.2175	0.4698	−1.7059	4129
Value-weight (unstandardized)					
Full sample	0.4901	0.8994	0.7845	−0.4094	4788
Venture-backed	0.5907	0.7707	0.8984	−0.1800	659
Non-venture-backed	0.4113	1.0001	0.7056	−0.5888	4129
Value-weight (standardized)					
Full sample	0.6315	0.9166	0.8513	−0.2850	4788
Venture-backed	0.8230	0.8451	0.9880	−0.0221	659
Non-venture-backed	0.4950	0.9675	0.7598	−0.4726	4129

Panel B: Venture-backed targets	Wealth				
	Sample	Benchmark	Relative	BHAR	N
Equal-weight					
Full sample	0.5254	1.8013	0.5445	−1.2759	659
Pure cash deals	0.5323	1.5403	0.6032	−1.0080	125
Pure stock deals	0.4586	1.7788	0.5249	−1.3203	286
Related deals	0.5755	1.8789	0.5472	−1.3035	405
Unrelated deals	0.4456	1.6775	0.5399	−1.2319	254
Value-weight (unstandardized)					
Full sample	0.5907	0.7707	0.8984	−0.1800	659
Pure cash deals	0.6397	0.8049	0.9084	−0.1653	125
Pure stock deals	0.7081	0.8163	0.9404	−0.1083	286
Related deals	0.6330	0.7546	0.9307	−0.1216	405
Unrelated deals	0.5030	0.8041	0.8331	−0.3011	254
Value-weight (standardized)					
Full sample	0.8230	0.8451	0.9880	−0.0221	659
Pure cash deals	0.8544	0.8716	0.9908	−0.0172	125
Pure stock deals	0.9804	0.9045	1.0399	0.0760	286
Related deals	0.9471	0.8334	1.0620	0.1136	405
Unrelated deals	0.6579	0.8606	0.8910	−0.2027	254

Panel C: Non-venture-backed targets	Wealth				
	Sample	Benchmark	Relative	BHAR	N
Equal-weight					
Full sample	0.5116	2.2175	0.4698	−1.7059	4129
Pure cash deals	0.6593	2.1495	0.5269	−1.4902	1642
Pure stock deals	0.4924	2.1653	0.4715	−1.6729	1145
Related deals	0.5818	2.2469	0.4872	−1.6652	2381
Unrelated deals	0.4161	2.1775	0.4457	−1.7613	1748

Table 28.5   (continued)

Panel C: Non-venture-backed targets	Wealth				
	Sample	Benchmark	Relative	BHAR	N
Value-weight (unstandardized)					
Full sample	0.4113	1.0001	0.7056	−0.5888	4129
Pure cash deals	0.4635	0.9814	0.7386	−0.5179	1642
Pure stock deals	0.4224	0.9927	0.7138	−0.5702	1145
Related deals	0.3963	1.0450	0.6828	−0.6486	2381
Unrelated deals	0.4289	0.9473	0.7338	−0.5184	1748
Value-weight (standardized)					
Full sample	0.4950	0.9675	0.7598	−0.4726	4129
Pure cash deals	0.5265	0.9333	0.7896	−0.4068	1642
Pure stock deals	0.5283	0.9410	0.7874	−0.4127	1145
Related deals	0.5233	1.0600	0.7395	−0.5367	2381
Unrelated deals	0.4659	0.8727	0.7828	−0.4068	1748

Notes: The sample is acquisitions of private companies (mainly for the period 1990–2001), where the acquirers are US public companies and the targets are US private companies (venture-backed and non-venture-backed). Multiple observations on the same firm that occur within three years of the initial observation are excluded. BHARs are calculated as the difference between the average three-year returns for the event firms and the benchmark portfolios. Wealth relatives are calculated as the ratio of the average three-year gross returns of the event firms to the average three-year gross returns of the benchmark portfolios. The expected return benchmarks are 25 value-weighted, non-rebalanced portfolios formed on size and book-to-market equity using NYSE breakpoints. Event firms are excluded from benchmark portfolios. Missing sample firm returns over the three-year period are replaced by corresponding benchmark portfolio returns. Equal-weighted and value-weighted (unstandardized and standardized) averages are reported. Standardized value weights are based on market capitalizations at the event month, divided by the level of CRSP value-weighted market index. Panel A reports BHAR results for the entire sample. Panel B and Panel C focus on the subcategories in the samples of venture-backed targets and non-venture-backed targets, respectively. A deal is classified as related if the target and the acquirer have the same two-digit SIC code. N is the number of observations.

are calculated using equal or value weighting. We use two methods of value weighting returns as in Mitchell and Stafford (2000). In the first method, we just weight by the acquiring firm's market capitalization. Standardized value weighting utilizes changes in the market index to avoid putting more weights on more recent observations. These weights are based on market capitalizations divided by the level of CRSP value-weighted market index at the event month. This result is consistent with the existing long-run post-acquisition performance literature which documents poor performance in samples of public acquisitions.

This pattern is similar when we examine the returns in the non-venture capital-backed cohort. In fact, the magnitude of underperformance is larger for the non-venture capital-backed acquirers than it was for the entire sample. Once again, value weighting appears to reduce the magnitude of underperformance.

The sample of venture capital-backed acquirers shows a very different pattern. While the equal-weighted sample shows underperformance relative to matched size and book-to-market benchmarks, value-weighted acquirers of venture capital-backed companies do not underperform comparable size and book-to-market companies.

In Panel B, we examine the pattern of long-run abnormal returns in the sample of acquirers of venture capital-backed companies. When returns are equal-weighted, all types of deals underperform with no clear pattern emerging within the type of payment or relatedness. When returns are value-weighted, only unrelated acquisitions show any underperformance.

Panel C tabulates the long-run performance for acquisition of non-venture capital-backed private companies. Once again, every category of acquirer for non-venture capital-backed companies shows strong underperformance. When returns are equal-weighted, there is no pattern across various types of acquisitions. For value-weighted returns, related acquisitions appear to perform more poorly than other types of acquisitions.

These patterns are examined in greater detail in Table 28.6 in which we examine the calendar time returns of the acquirers in our sample. For each month starting from January 1990 to December 2001, we form equal-weighted and value-weighted event portfolios by including all event firms that made an acquisition within the previous three years.[7] We then regress monthly excess event portfolio returns (PR) on the three Fama–French factors (Fama and French, 1993). The excess event portfolio returns are event portfolio returns in excess of the one-month Treasury bill rate or the returns on a zero-investment event portfolio (e.g., long venture-backed portfolio and short non-venture-backed portfolio). The three Fama–French factors are: the excess market return (RM-RF), which is the value-weighted market return on all NYSE/AMEX/NASDAQ firms (RM) minus the one-month Treasury bill rate (RF); the mimicking return for the size factor (SMB), which is the difference between the returns on small firms and big firms; the mimicking return for the book-to-market equity factor (HML), which is the difference between the returns on a portfolio of high book-to-market stocks and a portfolio of low book-to-market stocks.

In Table 28.6 the equal-weighted regressions reveal that while the intercepts are negative, they are not significant. In addition, there are several differences between the coefficients on the portfolio of the acquirers of venture capital-backed companies and acquirers of non-venture capital-backed companies. Acquirers of venture capital-backed companies have higher factor loadings on both the market and HML, that is, acquirers of venture capital-backed companies have returns that move more closely with low book-to-market growth firms.

Value weighting the returns gives intercepts that are now positive and significant, that is, the acquirers of venture and non-venture capital-backed companies have positive excess returns when performance is measured relative to the Fama–French three-factor model. Similarly, value-weighted results increase the venture capital-backed acquirers' factor loading on HML.

In Panel B, we examine the pattern of returns for the acquirers of venture capital-backed companies. When returns are equally weighted, there is no pattern in the performance of various types of acquisitions when acquirers are sorted by method of payment or whether the acquisition is related or unrelated. Value-weighted returns, however, demonstrate a clear pattern in returns performance. Acquisitions that are financed by pure equity perform significantly better than pure cash acquisitions. Similarly, related acquisitions perform better than unrelated acquisitions. These patterns are the opposite of the announcement return pattern that we see in Tables 28.3 and 28.4.

Table 28.6   Calendar-time Fama–French three-factor model portfolio regressions of acquirers

Panel A: Venture-backed vs. non-venture-backed

	a	$t(a)$	b	$t(b)$	s	$t(s)$	h	$t(h)$	Adj. R^2
Equal-weighted									
VC-backed	−0.0018	−0.63	1.3243	17.47	0.8736	11.02	−0.2567	−2.60	0.8583
Non-VC-backed	−0.0020	−0.85	1.0425	15.93	0.8008	11.90	0.0824	0.98	0.8155
Long VC-backed – short non-VC-backed	−0.0007	−0.31	0.3197	5.56	0.0834	1.39	−0.3115	−4.15	0.4861
Value-weighted									
VC-backed	0.0134	5.66	1.0760	16.72	−0.0301	−0.45	−0.5699	−6.79	0.8303
Non-VC-backed	0.0098	6.55	1.1030	26.93	0.1608	3.82	−0.0632	−1.20	0.8960
Long VC-backed – short non-VC-backed	0.0029	1.02	0.0044	0.06	−0.1820	−2.30	−0.4839	−4.90	0.1830

Panel B: Venture-backed targets

	a	$t(a)$	b	$t(b)$	s	$t(s)$	h	$t(h)$	Adj. R^2
Equal-weighted									
Pure cash deals	−0.0050	−1.29	1.1234	10.56	0.5861	5.27	0.2377	1.71	0.5667
Pure equity deals	−0.0008	−0.23	1.3684	13.79	0.8998	8.67	−0.7090	−5.48	0.8354
Long cash – short stock	−0.0042	−0.88	−0.2450	−1.90	−0.3137	−2.32	0.9467	5.63	0.4462
Related deals	−0.0013	−0.41	1.3919	15.64	0.9228	10.65	−0.3458	−3.15	0.8676
Unrelated deals	−0.0027	−0.74	1.3310	13.56	0.7562	7.37	−0.0413	−0.32	0.7415
Long related – short unrelated	0.0038	0.90	−0.2963	−2.61	0.0110	0.09	−0.5281	−3.57	0.0924

Value-weighted								
Pure cash deals	0.0074	1.71	1.1326	9.57	−0.0724	−0.59	−0.2189	−1.42	0.5233
Pure equity deals	0.0212	6.25	1.0838	11.73	−0.0453	−0.47	−0.7835	−6.51	0.7440
Long cash – short stock	−0.0138	−2.43	0.0488	0.32	−0.0271	−0.17	0.5646	2.80	0.0736
Related deals	0.0203	5.21	1.0648	9.72	−0.0703	−0.66	−0.7429	−5.50	0.7156
Unrelated deals	0.0129	4.21	1.1106	13.35	−0.0485	−0.56	−0.4794	−4.42	0.7361
Long related – short unrelated	0.0049	1.02	−0.2470	−1.91	−0.0528	−0.39	−0.3131	−1.86	0.0124

Notes: The sample is acquisitions of private companies from 1990 through 2001, where the acquirers are US public companies and the targets are US private companies (venture-backed and non-venture-backed). Multiple observations on the same firm that occur within three years of the initial observation are excluded. Equal-weighted and value-weighted event portfolios are formed by including all sample firms that made an acquisition within the previous three years, and are rebalanced monthly. The dependent variable is excess event portfolio return (*PR*), the event portfolio return in excess of the one-month Treasury bill rate or the return on a zero-investment event portfolio. The independent variables include the excess market return (*RM-RF*), which is the value-weighted market return on all NYSE/AMEX/NASDAQ firms (*RM*) minus the one-month Treasury bill rate (*RF*); the mimicking return for the size factor (*SMB*), which is the difference between the returns on small firms and big firms; the mimicking return for the book-to-market equity factor (*HML*), which is the difference between the returns on a portfolio of high book-to-market stocks and a portfolio of low book-to-market stocks. All regressions are for January 1990 through December 2001 for a total of 144 observations. Panel A reports regression results for the sample of venture-backed targets versus the sample of non-venture-backed targets. Panel B focuses on the subcategories within the sample of venture-backed targets. A deal is defined as related if the target and the acquirer have the same two-digit SIC code.

$$PR(t) = a + b[RM(t) - RF(t)] + sSMB(t) + hHML(t) + e(t)$$

The results appear to indicate that the acquisition of real options is different from the acquisition of assets in place. The use of equity (potentially to align incentives) and the importance of understanding the opportunity (when the acquisition is related) are central to the long-run performance of the acquisition.

28.5.3   Pre- and Post-Acquisition Operating Performance

In this subsection, we explore how operating performance changes around the acquisition date. For each acquirer, we examine its operating performance relative to the industry one year prior to and one year after the acquisition.[8] Our measures of operating performance include operating income (scaled by assets and by sales), capital expenditure (scaled by assets and by sales), sales growth, operating income growth, and Q. To arrive at industry-adjusted operating performance, we take the difference between the sample firm value and the median value in the same industry, defined by the same two-digit SIC code.

Table 28.7 tabulates the median industry-adjusted operating performance one year before and one year after the acquisition for the full sample as well as the venture capital-backed and non-venture capital-backed cohorts. On the whole, acquirers of private targets perform better than their industry medians both before and after the acquisitions. While sales growth and operating income growth improve subsequent to the acquisitions, operating income seems to deteriorate after the transactions, although still remaining above the industry median. When we separate the full sample into venture-backed and non-venture-backed cohorts, this pattern holds for both groups. However, we discover that venture capital-backed acquirers have significantly stronger operating performance than non-venture-capital backed acquirers relative to their industry peers both before and after the acquisitions. In particular, acquirers of venture capital-backed companies have higher capital expenditures relative to the industry peers prior to and after the acquisitions, while acquirers of non-venture-capital-backed companies do not spend more on capital investments than industry medians at any time.

In Panel B, we examine the industry-adjusted operating performance in the venture capital-backed sample of acquisitions. Much like the entire sample, industry-adjusted operating performance appears to decline after the acquisition, albeit still beating the industry peers. One thing to note is that acquirers of venture capital-backed companies carrying out pure equity deals and related deals have significantly higher Q not only compared to the industry medians, but also compared to the acquirers of venture-backed companies undertaking pure cash transactions and unrelated transactions. In fact, for acquirers with pure equity deals, there is even an increase in Q after the acquisitions.

We further examine the pre- and post-acquisition industry-adjusted operating performance for the acquirers of private targets in a regression setting in Table 28.8. We run median regressions on all firms with valid operating performance data in Compustat each year from 1989 to 2000 for pre-acquisition operating performance analysis and from 1991 to 2002 for post-acquisition operating performance analysis, and report the averaged coefficients across the 12 years, following the Fama and MacBeth (1973) methodology, to account for cross-sectional correlation in performance measures due to the clustering of merger activities (Andrade et al., 2001). The dependent variables are industry-adjusted operating performance including operating income (scaled by assets

Table 28.7   Pre- and post-acquisition median industry-adjusted operating performance

Panel A: Venture-backed vs. non-venture-backed targets

	Median industry-adjusted operating performance measures						
	Operating income (over assets)	Capital expenditure (over assets)	Operating income (over sales)	Capital expenditure (over sales)	Sales growth	Operating income growth	Q
Full sample							
t − 1	0.0115[a]	0.0000	0.0237[a]	0.0000	0.0596[a]	0.1024[a]	0.1314[a]
t + 1	0.0042[a]	0.0000	0.0118[a]	0.0007[a]	0.1470[a]	0.1248[a]	0.1192[a]
VC-backed							
t − 1	0.0421[a, d]	0.0090[a, d]	0.0501[a, d]	0.0137[a, d]	0.0832[a]	0.1498[a]	0.4641[a, d]
t + 1	0.0120[a, d]	0.0050[a, d]	0.0252[a, d]	0.0110[a, d]	0.1296[a]	0.1026[a]	0.3872[a, d]
Non-VC-backed							
t − 1	0.0090[a]	0.0000	0.0201[a]	0.0000	0.0557[a]	0.0971[a]	0.1016[a]
t + 1	0.0035[a]	0.0000	0.0102[a]	0.0000	0.1490[a]	0.1276[a]	0.1003[a]

Panel B: Venture-backed targets

	Median industry-adjusted operating performance measures						
	Operating income (over assets)	Capital expenditure (over assets)	Operating income (over sales)	Capital expenditure (over sales)	Sales growth	Operating income growth	Q
Pure cash deals							
t − 1	0.0691[a, f]	0.0104[a]	0.0767[a, e]	0.0078[c, d]	0.0685[a, d]	0.1807[a]	0.2391[a, d]
t + 1	0.0330[a, d]	0.0011[e]	0.0628[a, d]	0.0016[d]	0.0808[a, e]	0.0777[b]	0.1160[b, d]
Pure equity deals							
t − 1	0.0413[a]	0.0166[a]	0.0464[a]	0.0245[a]	0.1729[a]	0.2359[a]	0.7593[a]
t + 1	0.0052	0.0099[a]	0.0048	0.0230[a]	0.1942[a]	0.0947[b]	0.8182[a]

Table 28.7 (continued)

Panel B: Venture-backed targets

	Median industry-adjusted operating performance measures						
	Operating income (over assets)	Capital expenditure (over assets)	Operating income (over sales)	Capital expenditure (over sales)	Sales growth	Operating income growth	Q
Related deals							
t − 1	0.0473[a]	0.0092[a]	0.0554[a]	0.0179[a, d]	0.0921[a]	0.1775[a, f]	0.5299[a, e]
t + 1	0.0114[a]	0.0059[a]	0.0183[b]	0.0146[a, e]	0.1379[a]	0.1005[a]	0.4797[a, d]
Unrelated deals							
t − 1	0.0368[a]	0.0083[b]	0.0452[c]	0.0050[a]	0.0596[a]	0.1073[a]	0.2967[a]
t + 1	0.0139[a]	0.0034	0.0301[a]	0.0037	0.1145[a]	0.1108[a]	0.2297[a]

Notes: The sample is acquisitions of private companies from 1990 through 2001, where the acquirers are US public companies and the targets are US private companies (venture-backed and non-venture-backed). Multiple observations on the same firm that occur within three years of the initial observation are excluded. Industry-adjusted measures of operating performance, pre- (t − 1) and post- (t + 1) acquisition, include operating income, capital expenditure, sales growth, operating income growth, and Q (calculated as the sum of the market value of equity and the book value of debt, divided by assets). Industry-adjusted operating performance is calculated as the difference between the sample firm values and the median values in the same industry, defined by the same two-digit SIC code. Panel A focuses on the sample of venture-backed targets versus the sample of non-venture-backed targets. Panel B focuses on the subcategories within the sample of venture-backed targets. A deal is defined as related if the target and the acquirer have the same two-digit SIC code.

a. Significantly different from zero at the 1% level, using a two-tailed test.
b. Significantly different from zero at the 5% level, using a two-tailed test.
c. Significantly different from zero at the 10% level, using a two-tailed test.
d. Significantly different from the corresponding subcategory for the same time period (i.e., VC-backed vs. non-VC-backed, pure cash deals vs. pure stock deals, and related deals vs. unrelated deals), at the 1% level.
e. Significantly different from the corresponding subcategory for the same time period (i.e., VC-backed vs. non-VC-backed, pure cash deals vs. pure stock deals, and related deals vs. unrelated deals), at the 5% level.
f. Significantly different from the corresponding subcategory for the same time period (i.e., VC-backed vs. non-VC-backed, pure cash deals vs. pure stock deals, and related deals vs. unrelated deals), at the 10% level

and by sales), capital expenditure (scaled by assets and by sales), sales growth, operating income growth and Q. We use dummy variables as independent variables to investigate the effect of acquisition of private targets and venture capital-backing on operating performance before and after the acquisition. For pre-acquisition operating performance regressions in Panel A, we include a dummy variable that equals one if the firm makes an acquisition of a private target in the next year, and an interaction between this dummy and another dummy variable that equals one if the target in the acquisition is venture capital-backed. Similarly, for post-acquisition operating performance regressions in Panel B, we include a dummy variable that equals one if the firm makes an acquisition of private targets in the prior year, and an interaction between this dummy and another dummy variable that equals one if the target is venture capital-backed. The acquirer's log market equity and book-to-market ratio are included as control variables.

The regression results in Table 28.8 basically confirm our findings in Table 28.7. In the year before the acquisition as seen from Panel A, acquirers of private targets generally perform significantly better than non-acquirers in their industry. In particular, acquirers of venture capital-backed companies have above-the-median operating performance in all our performance measures, especially in capital expenditure and Q, surpassing not only non-acquirers in the industry but also acquirers of non-venture capital-backed companies. These results hold after controlling for the fact that acquirers of venture-backed targets generally have bigger size and lower book-to-market ratio. From Panel B, we see that the evidence of continued superior performance of the acquirers into the year after the acquisition is mixed. While sales growth, operating income growth and Q increase, operating income declines, a pattern similar for both acquirers of venture-backed targets and non-venture-backed targets.

Table 28.9 tabulates the post-acquisition abnormal operating performance for the acquirers. Following Healy et al. (1992), post-acquisition abnormal industry-adjusted operating performance for acquirers is estimated by the intercept term from the cross-sectional regression for event firms, where the dependent variable is the industry-adjusted operating performance measure for an event firm in the year after the acquisition, and the independent variable is the same measure for the same company in the year before the acquisition. This procedure controls for persistence of the performance measures in time, and a significant and positive intercept indicates an improvement in the post-acquisition operating performance.

Panel A compares the abnormal operating performance of the venture capital-backed and non-venture capital-backed cohorts. Both cohorts display an increase in capital expenditure and Q, with the venture capital-backed group posting a higher increase. While there is no significant decline in operating income for acquirers of venture capital-backed targets, acquirers of non-venture capital-backed targets experience a significant weakening in operating income following the acquisition.

From Panel B, we see that within the venture capital-backed group, there is a post-acquisition increase in capital expenditure and Q only for acquirers undertaking pure equity deals and related deals. Acquirers with pure cash deals and unrelated deals in general experience no significant improvement or decline in any performance measures.

These results are somewhat different from the existing literature on post-acquisition operating performance for acquirers of public companies, which documents statistically significant improvements in operating performance following the merger (Healy et al.,

Table 28.8   Regressions for pre- and post-acquisition industry-adjusted operating performance

Panel A: Pre-acquisition operating performance

Independent variables

	Dependent variable							
	Operating income (over assets)		Capital expenditure (over assets)		Operating income (over sales)		Capital expenditure (over sales)	
	Coeff.	t-stat.	Coeff.	t-stat.	Coeff.	t-stat.	Coeff.	t-stat.
Logarithm of firm size	0.0121	25.19	0.0025	11.67	0.0194	48.77	0.0029	19.81
Acquirer's book-to-market ratio	1.2E-05	1.63	3.8E-06	1.69	4.4E-05	3.89	3.2E-05	4.25
Acquisition next year?	0.0064	3.80	-0.0017	-2.99	0.0123	5.85	-0.0011	-1.28
(Venture-backed?)*(Acquisition next year?)	0.0160	2.09	0.0063	2.80	0.0070	1.24	0.0096	2.95
Constant	-0.1387	-25.11	-0.0281	-14.77	-0.2206	-38.35	-0.0327	-26.15

Independent variables

	Dependent variable					
	Sales growth		Operating income growth		Q	
	Coeff.	t-stat.	Coeff.	t-stat.	Coeff.	t-stat.
Logarithm of firm size	0.0079	5.39	0.0137	7.41	0.0590	8.89
Acquirer's book-to-market ratio	-2.0E-05	-0.71	-1.2E-05	-0.29	-0.0005	-3.68
Acquisition next year?	0.0427	6.66	0.0738	7.32	0.0692	3.30
(Venture-backed?)*(Acquisition next year?)	0.0453	1.86	0.0726	1.75	0.2992	5.70
Constant	-0.0800	-4.62	-0.1483	-6.28	-0.6576	-8.19

Panel B: Post-acquisition operation performance

Independent variables	Dependent variable							
	Operating income (over assets)		Capital expenditure (over assets)		Operating income (over sales)		Capital expenditure (over sales)	
	Coeff.	t-stat.	Coeff.	t-stat.	Coeff.	t-stat.	Coeff.	t-stat.
Logarithm of firm size	0.0115	23.99	0.0021	11.00	0.0197	45.65	0.0027	18.75
Acquirer's book-to-market ratio	4.7E-06	1.09	3.3E-06	1.13	3.4E-05	3.31	2.2E-05	3.59
Acquisition last year?	−0.0060	−3.35	0.0002	0.36	−0.0013	−0.46	0.0011	1.64
(Venture-backed?)*(Acquisition last year?)	−0.0005	−0.07	0.0005	0.16	−0.0115	−0.98	0.0054	1.90
Constant	−0.1320	−23.88	−0.0248	−13.58	−0.2266	−37.00	−0.0313	−24.35

Independent variables	Dependent variable					
	Sales growth		Operating income growth		Q	
	Coeff.	t-stat.	Coeff.	t-stat.	Coeff.	t-stat.
Logarithm of firm size	0.0083	6.65	0.0139	7.24	0.0686	10.54
Acquirer's book-to-market ratio	−1.1E-05	−0.47	−2.0E-05	−0.59	−0.0004	−2.74
Acquisition last year?	0.1356	10.34	0.1057	7.04	0.0545	3.90
(Venture-backed?)*(Acquisition last year?)	−0.0421	−1.85	−0.0614	−2.50	0.1505	2.14
Constant	−0.0894	−5.66	−0.1554	−6.33	−0.7761	−9.74

Notes: The dependent variables are industry-adjusted measures of operating performance including operating income, capital expenditure, sales growth, operating income growth, and Q (calculated as the sum of the market value of equity and the book value of debt, divided by assets). Industry-adjusted operating performance is calculated as the difference between the sample firm values and the median values in the same industry, defined by the same two-digit SIC code. The independent variables in Panel A include a dummy variable that equals one if the firm is to make an acquisition of private targets in the year after and an interaction between this dummy and another dummy variable that equals one if the target in the acquisition is venture-backed. The independent variables in Panel B include a dummy and another dummy variable that equals one if the firm made an acquisition of private targets in the year before and an interaction between this dummy and another dummy variable that equals one if the target in the acquisition is venture-backed. The other independent variables are the logarithm of the acquirer's size (market equity), and the acquirer's book-to-market ratio. The Fama–Macbeth methodology (Fama and Macbeth, 1973) is employed where cross-section median regressions are run on all firms with valid data in Compustat each year from 1989 to 2000 for Panel A and from 1991 to 2002 for Panel B and coefficients are averaged across the 12 years. Panel A reports results for pre-acquisition operating performance and Panel B reports results for post-acquisition operating performance.

Table 28.9   Abnormal post-acquisition industry-adjusted operating performance for acquirers

Panel A: Venture-backed vs. non-venture-backed

	Dependent variable						
	Operating income (over assets)	Capital expenditure (over assets)	Operating income (over sales)	Capital expenditure (over sales)	Sales growth	Operating income growth	Q
Venture-backed targets							
a	0.0018	0.0051	-0.3166	0.0538	0.2377	0.0676	0.7316
	0.24	**2.63**	**-1.23**	**2.69**	**3.08**	**0.94**	**3.97**
b	0.4373	0.5416	0.0721	0.0370	0.0646	-0.0652	0.5095
	15.97	**15.15**	**3.83**	**1.05**	**1.76**	**-3.19**	**7.08**
Non-venture-backed targets							
a	-0.0184	0.0046	-0.3320	0.0431	3.7746	0.1444	0.2450
	-2.26	**4.28**	**-2.57**	**2.79**	**1.18**	**1.26**	**5.82**
b	0.6992	0.4759	0.0082	0.3848	-0.0533	0.0088	0.4942
	17.13	**34.73**	**3.81**	**16.08**	**-0.08**	**0.29**	**21.91**

Panel B: Venture-backed targets

	Dependent variable						
	Operating income (over assets)	Capital expenditure (over assets)	Operating income (over sales)	Capital expenditure (over sales)	Sales growth	Operating income growth	Q
Pure cash deals							
a	-0.0105	0.0015	-0.0155	0.0047	0.1060	-0.0654	0.0502
	-0.90	**0.38**	**-1.24**	**0.84**	**3.07**	**-0.75**	**0.16**
b	0.8186	0.5999	1.0731	0.3481	0.2549	0.4940	1.2215
	9.75	**7.22**	**15.01**	**4.42**	**2.39**	**3.57**	**6.91**

Pure equity deals

	(1)	(2)	(3)	(4)	(5)	(6)	(7)
a	-0.0069	0.0070	-0.5926	0.0918	0.2320	-0.0025	1.2134
	-0.51	**2.31**	**-1.01**	**2.08**	**5.23**	**-0.01**	**3.10**
b	0.4577	0.5765	0.2585	0.0579	0.0627	-0.1178	0.5241
	10.32	**11.39**	**2.03**	**0.75**	**4.38**	**-0.71**	**3.95**

Related deals

	(1)	(2)	(3)	(4)	(5)	(6)	(7)
a	-0.0013	0.0075	-0.5192	0.0770	0.2363	0.0152	1.0604
	-0.11	**2.93**	**-1.26**	**2.50**	**1.88**	**0.14**	**3.72**
b	0.3934	0.4940	0.0707	0.0307	0.2547	-0.0682	0.4334
	11.79	**11.57**	**2.96**	**0.70**	**2.29**	**-2.87**	**4.20**

Unrelated dea s

	(1)	(2)	(3)	(4)	(5)	(6)	(7)
a	-0.0096	0.0008	0.0131	0.0038	0.1558	0.1128	0.2299
	-1.32	**0.27**	**1.01**	**0.84**	**5.32**	**1.32**	**1.55**
b	0.8278	0.6909	0.5690	0.3564	0.0267	0.0767	0.6538
	16.80	**10.31**	**19.51**	**7.41**	**2.81**	**0.87**	**9.63**

$$AOP_{post,i} = a + b * AOP_{pre,i} + e_i$$

Note: The sample is acquisitions of private companies from 1990 through 2001, where the acquirers are US public companies and the targets are US private companies (venture-backed and non-venture-backed). Following Healy et al. (1992), abnormal post-acquisition industry-adjusted operating performance for acquirers is estimated by the intercept term from the cross-sectional regression on event firms, where the dependent variable is the industry-adjusted operating performance measure for an event firm in the year after the acquisition and the independent variable is the same measure for the same company in the year before the acquisition. Measures of operating performance for the event firms include operating income, capital expenditure, sales growth, operating income growth, and Q (calculated as the sum of the market value of equity and the book value of debt, divided by assets). Industry-adjusted operating performance is calculated as the difference between the sample firm values and the median values in the same industry, defined by the same two-digit SIC code. Panel A reports results for the sample of venture-backed targets versus the sample of non-venture-backed targets. Panel B focuses on the subcategories within the sample of venture-backed -argets. A deal is defined as related if the target and the acquirer have the same two-digit SIC code. t-statistics are reported below the coefficients in bold.

1992; Andrade et al., 2001). The operating performance of acquirers of private companies, especially non-venture capital-backed ones, generally declines relative to the industry peers one year after the acquisition. This seems to be inconsistent with the on-average positive announcement period stock market reaction. One possible explanation is that private companies are operated quite differently than public companies before being acquired. Thus, it might take some time for the acquirers to adjust and integrate the operations of the acquired private targets into those of their own and make an improvement upon overall performance, especially when the targets are less mature companies consisting mainly of future growth options. Moreover, if mergers cluster in industries and occur as a response to industry shocks as Mitchell and Mulherin (1996) point out, the industry peers might themselves be responding to industry shocks by taking on mergers and internal restructuring at the same time that these acquisitions of private targets take place (Andrade et al., 2001). Within the sample of acquirers of private companies, the venture capital-backed cohort has stronger performance than the non-venture capital-backed cohort both before and after the acquisition. A typical acquirer of venture capital-backed private companies, especially in pure equity and related deals, appears to be an outperformer in its industry with high growth opportunities which consistently takes on a significantly higher-than-average amount of investment.

28.6   CONCLUSIONS

The value of venture capital-backed start-ups is typically dependent primarily upon real options, that is, future investment opportunities. Examination of the characteristics of acquirers of private venture capital-backed companies provides an opportunity to explore how the acquisition of real options by public companies differs from acquisition of assets in place. We find that acquirers of private venture capital-backed companies tend to be larger and have higher Tobin's Q than do acquirers of other private companies. In addition, acquirers of venture capital-backed companies are more likely to use pure equity transactions and to purchase companies in related industries.

Upon announcement of the purchases of private companies, the acquiring firms experience a positive announcement period return on average, but the market reacts more negatively to the purchase of venture capital-backed companies. Similarly, the use of equity and purchase of related firms by acquirers of venture capital-backed companies lowers the announcement period returns. The results seem to indicate that the market either believes that venture capitalists are better at negotiating higher prices for their companies in the public market, or that the adverse selection problem from purchasing real options is higher than for purchasing assets in place. Similarly, the use of equity in the purchase of venture capital-backed companies is not seen as a positive attribute.

The long-run performance of these acquisitions, however, is quite different from the announcement period returns. Long-run buy-and-hold abnormal returns are very negative for acquisition of private non-venture capital-backed companies. These acquirers appear to be unable to meet market expectations for further improvements in performance for these existing assets in place, although operating performance remains above industry peer performance both prior to and after the acquisition. On the other hand, acquirers of venture capital-backed companies appear to have substantially better performance. The use of stock in the purchase and the acquisition of related companies predicts superior long-run performance.

Finally, industry-adjusted operating performance both pre-merger and post-merger is positive. In particular, the acquirers of venture capital-backed firms have high Tobin's Q and high investment both prior to and after the acquisition. Industry-adjusted Tobin's Q actually increases for the acquirers of venture capital-backed companies.

Overall, our results suggest that the acquirers of venture capital-backed companies are high-performing, high growth opportunity and high-investment companies both prior to the acquisition and after. At the time of the acquisition announcement, the market views these acquisitions less favorably, particularly if they are purchased with stock indicating that there is the perception that an adverse selection problem exists and/or the acquirer's stock is overvalued. The superior long-run performance for stock acquisitions indicates that the human capital may be critical to the performance of real options, and providing incentives to existing management may be important. Similarly, firms that 'stay close to home' by buying companies in related industries may be able to utilize their expertise to enhance the value of the investment opportunities.

NOTES

* We thank participants at the 2008 American Finance Association meetings for helpful discussions and comments. Support for this research was provided by the Division of Research at the Harvard Business School.
1. Two related types of agency costs exist in entrepreneurial firms. Both agency costs result from the large information asymmetries that affect young growth companies in need of financing. First, entrepreneurs might invest in strategies, research or projects that have high personal returns but low expected monetary pay-offs to shareholders. For example, a biotechnology company founder may choose to invest in a certain type of research that brings them great recognition in the scientific community but provides little return for the venture capitalist. Similarly, entrepreneurs may receive initial results from market trials indicating little demand for a new product, but may want to keep the company going because they receive significant private benefits from managing their own firm. Second, because entrepreneurs' equity stakes are essentially call options, they have the incentive to pursue highly volatile strategies, such as rushing a product to market when further testing may be warranted.
2. Venture capitalists specialize in exiting private investments. Many venture capitalists will have sold numerous private companies and hence may have better negotiating skills and an ability to extract higher prices.
3. This later peak in venture capital-backed acquisitions also reflects the surge in venture capital investing which increased dramatically from 1993 through 2000.
4. The results are qualitatively similar if relatedness is defined as the acquisition being in the same four-digit SIC code.
5. This definition of small acquirer follows Moeller et al. (2004).
6. Each acquirer firm is used as the unit of observation only once within any three-year event window. Multiple acquisitions by the same firm that occur within three years of the initial observation are excluded.
7. Each acquirer firm is used as the unit of observation only once within any three-year event window. Multiple acquisitions by the same firm that occur within three years of the initial observation are excluded.
8. Each acquirer firm is used as the unit of observation only once within any three-year event window. Multiple acquisitions by the same firm that occur within three years of the initial observation are excluded.

REFERENCES

Andrade, Gregor, Mark Mitchell and Erik Stafford (2001), 'New evidence and perspectives on mergers', *Journal of Economic Perspectives*, **15**, 103–120.

Baker, Malcolm P. and Paul A. Gompers (2003a), 'The determinants of board structure at the initial public offering', *Journal of Law and Economics*, **46**, 569–598.

Baker, Malcolm P. and Paul A. Gompers (2003b), 'Executive ownership and control in newly public firms: the role of venture capitalists', Working Paper, Harvard Business School.

Brown, Stephen J. and Jerold B. Warner (1985), 'Using daily stock returns: the case of event studies', *Journal of Financial Economics*, **14**, 3–31.

Chang, Saeyoung (1998), 'Takeovers of privately held targets, methods of payments, and bidder returns', *Journal of Finance*, **53**, 773–784.

Fama, Eugene F. and Kenneth R. French (1993), 'Common risk factors in the returns of stocks and bonds', *Journal of Financial Economics*, **33**, 3–55.

Fama, Eugene F. and James D. MacBeth (1973), 'Risk, return, and equilibrium: empirical tests', *Journal of Political Economy*, **81**, 607–636.

Fuller, Kathleen, Jeffry Netter and Mike Stegemoller (2002), 'What do returns to acquiring firms tell us? Evidence from firms that make many acquisitions', *Journal of Finance*, **57**, 1763–1793.

Gompers, Paul A. (1995), 'Optimal investment, monitoring, and the staging of venture capital', *Journal of Finance*, **50**, 1461–1490.

Gompers, Paul A., Joy L. Ishii and Andrew Metrick (2003), 'Corporate governance and equity prices', *Quarterly Journal of Economics*, **118**, 107–155.

Hansen, Robert G. (1987), 'A theory for the choice of exchange medium in mergers and acquisitions', *Journal of Business*, **60**, 75–95.

Hansen, Robert G. and John Lott (1996), 'Externalities and corporate objectives in a world with diversified shareholders/consumers', *Journal of Financial and Quantitative Analysis*, **31**, 43–68.

Healy, Paul, Krishna G. Palepu and Richard S. Ruback (1992), 'Does corporate performance improve after mergers?', *Journal of Financial Economics*, **31**, 135–175.

Heaton, J.B. (2002), 'Managerial optimism and corporate finance', *Financial Management*, **31**, 33–46.

Jensen, Michael C. (1986), 'The agency cost of free cash flow, corporate finance and takeovers', *American Economic Review*, **76**, 323–329.

Jensen, Michael C. and William H. Meckling (1976), 'Theory of the firm: managerial behavior, agency costs and the ownership structure', *Journal of Financial Economics*, **3**, 305–360.

Jensen, Michael C. and Richard Ruback (1983), 'The market for corporate control: the scientific evidence', *Journal of Financial Economics*, **11**, 5–50.

Kaplan, Steven N. and Per Stromberg (2003), 'Financial contracting theory meets the real world: an empirical analysis of venture capital contracts', *Review of Economic Studies*, **70**, 281–315.

Loughran, Tim and Anand M. Vijh (1997), 'Do long-term shareholders benefit from corporate acquisitions?', *Journal of Finance*, **52**, 1765–1790.

Mitchell, Mark L. and J. Harold Mulherin (1996), 'The impact of industry shocks on take-over and restructuring activity', *Journal of Financial Economics*, **41**, 193–229.

Mitchell, Mark L. and Erik Stafford (2000), 'Managerial decisions and long-term stock price performance', *Journal of Business*, **73**, 287–329.

Moeller, Sara B., Frederik P. Schlingemann and Rene M. Stulz (2004), 'Firm size and the gains from acquisitions', *Journal of Financial Economics*, **73**, 201–228.

Roll, Richard (1986), 'The hubris hypothesis of corporate takeovers', *Journal of Business*, **59**, 197–216.

Sahlman, William A. (1990), 'The structure and governance of venture capital organizations', *Journal of Financial Economics*, **27**, 473–521.

Shleifer, Andrei and Robert W. Vishny (1989), 'Management entrenchment: the case of manager-specific investments', *Journal of Financial Economics*, **25**, 123–139.

Shleifer, Andrei and Robert W. Vishny (2003), 'Stock market driven acquisitions', *Journal of Financial Economics*, **70**, 295–311.

Sorensen, Morten (2007), 'How smart is smart money? A two-sided matching model of venture capital', *Journal of Finance*, **62**, 2725–2762.

29 Governance and microfinance institutions
Rients Galema, Robert Lensink and Roy Mersland

29.1 INTRODUCTION

Since the mid-1990s, much has been written on microfinance (e.g., see for recent overviews Hermes and Lensink, 2007, 2011; Armendáriz and Morduch, 2010). The literature on microfinance is diverse. It includes theoretical studies on the design of optimal contracts and, more recently, the testing of these theories through randomized control experiments. It also includes impact studies that try to find out whether microfinance measurably improves the lives of the poor. Finally, there are macro studies that study how microfinance institutions (MFIs) are affected by the macroeconomic environment in which they operate and how they trade off outreach and financial sustainability. Yet, comparatively little has been written on the corporate governance of MFIs; most of the existing studies on MFI governance consist of consultancy reports that assume that MFIs are comparable to regular commercial firms (Labie and Mersland, 2011).

The lack of scientific studies on microfinance governance is unfortunate, because a number of recent MFI failures have been attributed to bad governance systems. Until recently, researchers and policymakers considered microcredit as an important instrument to lift poor people, especially women, out of poverty. An enormous amount of anecdotes and simple empirical analyses support the positive view on microcredit. Policymakers became almost euphoric about the possible role of microfinance as a development instrument after Mohammad Yunus received the Nobel Peace Prize in 2006. Yet, recently the rosy view of microfinance has started to come to an end, especially after stories about loan-shark-style MFIs who have driven borrowers to suicide in the Indian state of Andhra Pradesh. Bateman (2010) even suggests that microfinance is the main obstacle to sustainable development. To explain why some MFIs are successful where others fail, we need a better understanding of governance issues. These include ownership and board-level decisions on important areas like staff incentives and attracting funding. Good governance is important since it can support the viability of MFI operations in terms of both performance and risk management.

According to agency theory, microfinance governance should deal with ways in which suppliers of finance – donors and investors – ensure that they get a return on investment and the MFI reaches its social mission. In many organizations, including most MFIs, there is a separation of ownership and control. Even though non-profit MFIs have no owners, in almost all MFIs the suppliers of funds are different from those who manage the MFI. Because managers and suppliers of funds have different interests and there is information asymmetry, there are agency problems and thus a need to control managers. The main function of governance is to control self-interested managers to solve agency problems. When sufficient oversight is lacking, managers are likely to enrich themselves or pursue other self-interest at the MFI's expense. This is illustrated by the collapse of the Colombian Corposol, where a powerful chief executive officer (CEO) who did not receive proper board oversight played a large role in Corposol's eventual bankruptcy (Steege, 1998).

Some MFIs have the legal status of banks, which makes their agency problems very comparable to those of banks. Oddly, very little theoretical governance literature has been written specifically for banks. Instead, corporate governance perspectives are usually directly applied to banks, which is unfortunate, for banks face very specific governance problems (Macey and O'Hara, 2003). A problem with bank governance is that deposit insurance and capital controls give much stronger incentives to shareholders to push banks to take more risk (Laeven and Levine, 2009). Deposit insurance removes the incentive for depositors to push the bank to take less risk, and banks tend to hold little debt such that there are no other fixed claimants that incentivize the bank to take less risk. Most MFIs do not have the legal status of banks and are typically unregulated, so they are not allowed to take deposits. Instead, they rely much more on other sources of funds like commercial borrowing, non-commercial borrowing and donations (Cull et al., 2009). A greater dependence on debt holders and a lack of deposits make unregulated MFIs more similar to corporations in which debt holders prevent an organization from taking too much risk. So, depending on their funding sources, MFIs face different governance problems.

According to a more broad definition of governance, microfinance governance is the determination of how an MFI uses its resources and resolves conflicts of interest of the organization's myriad participants (Daily et al., 2003). Good directors can bring valuable resources to the firm, and advise and counsel CEOs. For instance, they can provide experience from other MFIs, banking knowledge and a network of possible donors. The initial survival of non-profits depends very much on whether they can attract sufficient donations. In this process the connections of board members to donors could be an important asset. So, instead of a sole focus on the board's task of controlling executives, other roles of the board deserve investigation as well. Such a broad definition could be more appropriate to MFIs because they have both financial and social objectives. Setting a proper social mission and achieving it is not as clear-cut as maximizing profits, but involves other stakeholders' active involvement in the decision-making process.

In non-profit MFIs that have the largest focus on social objectives, other stakeholders have much more influence. Glaeser (2003) shows that due to the fact that non-profit governance is weak, workers and donors have much more influence. Non-profits have boards, but these boards are ultimately not accountable and they are very difficult to incentivize because of their opaquely defined mission and lack of stock ownership by managers. The result is that the CEO and the board have an almost unparalleled degree of autonomy. One the one hand this calls for more board oversight and incentive structures that align the board's interests with those of donors and debt holders. On the other hand, given that many non-profits operate with very weak governance structures without managers appropriating all the resources, this suggests that there are other factors that explain their success. It would be worthwhile to investigate what determines MFI success, instead of a sole focus on incentive issues. It is likely that managers and board members of non-profits are very much intrinsically and socially motivated. To the extent that this is key to an MFI's success, giving too many incentives could undermine people's natural motivation. Therefore, a more broad view on governance that includes the resources the board provides to the MFI could provide additional insights regarding to what extent microfinance governance would benefit from incentive structures.

The aim of this chapter is to review the microfinance performance and governance literature and provide an agenda for future research. In reviewing the microfinance governance literature two issues stand out. First, most papers concentrate on the relation between corporate governance and financial and social performance. Section 29.2 provides an overview of this literature. It also introduces the different organizational types, which all have a very different ownership structure and performance. Although MFI performance literature is interesting and important, at the same time it covers only a limited number of questions related to microfinance governance. With the exception of Galema et al. (forthcoming) and Galema (2010), issues related to governance and risk management are virtually uncovered. Therefore, section 29.3 deals with governance and MFI risk-taking. It presents an example of an empirical study that links governance with MFI risk and gives suggestions for future research in this area. In the empirical study we try to find out whether larger boards make less extreme decisions by testing whether the larger boards are associated with less return variability (Cheng, 2008).

Second, empirical microfinance governance studies are guided by agency theories developed for corporations and Western non-governmental organizations (NGOs). Corporations maximize profits, whereas MFIs have dual objectives, which theories on optimal incentive structures have to take into account. Within the microfinance industry, there are many different types of MFIs ranging from the most commercial bank to the least commercial NGO. They all decide on a different trade-off between their financial and social objectives. Moreover, one-size-fits-all governance arrangements do not exist. MFIs' funding structures are very different, which creates a very heterogeneous set of governance problems. Section 29.4 pleads for new theory on how optimal incentives throughout the institution can stimulate the MFI to reach its dual objectives, and shows how different funding structures create different governance problems.

29.2 GOVERNANCE, OWNERSHIP AND MICROFINANCE PERFORMANCE: A SURVEY

An important topic in the microfinance governance literature deals with the question whether the type of ownership of MFIs explains the performance. The microfinance sector is characterized by various organization types, such as banks, non-bank financial institutions (NBFIs), credit unions and NGOs. The category of banks includes rural banks and banks which can be both publicly owned or privately owned (Mersland, 2009). Also among banks in developed countries we observe various organizational types. For example, the Dutch cooperative bank Rabobank ranks among the world's 25 largest banks, and in Germany the ownerless Sparkassen holds more than 40 percent of the banking market. Nevertheless, the many organizational types in microfinance can be a particular challenge since they operate in markets with normally limited competition and under different regulatory regimes (Mersland, 2009). Table 29.1 presents a characterization of different MFI ownership types.

Banks are formal, for-profit financial institutions, usually regulated by central banks, that offer savings accounts. Although NBFIs are comparable to banks, they are limited

Table 29.1   Definition of microfinance institutions (MFIs) according to ownership type

Non-governmental organization (NGO)	An organization registered as a non-profit for tax purposes or some other legal charter. Its financial services are usually more restricted, usually not including deposit taking. This institution is typically not regulated by a banking supervisory agency.
Non-bank financial institution (NBFI)	An institution that provides similar services to those of a bank, but is licensed under a separate category. The separate license may be due to lower capital requirements, to limitations on financial service offerings, or to supervision under a different state agency. In some countries this corresponds to a special category created for microfinance institutions.
Cooperative/ credit union	A non-profit, member-based financial intermediary. It may offer a range of financial services, including lending and deposit taking, for the benefit of its members. While not regulated by a state banking supervisory agency, it may come under the supervision of a regional or national cooperative council.
Bank	A licensed financial intermediary regulated by a state banking supervisory agency. It may provide any of a number of financial services, including: deposit taking, lending, payment services, and money transfers.

Note: Definitions based on MIX-Market Taxonomy, http://www.mixmarket.org/mix-market-development-roadmap/inline-glossary)/http://www.mixmarket.org/en/glossary.

by law in the range of services they can offer; some cannot provide savings accounts. Among the non-profit institutions, credit unions are owned and controlled by their members, who obtain and supply its funding. Finally, NGOs were the pioneers in the microfinance industry and are usually the first to start offering services to the poor in a particular region or to a particular segment of the population. They are often supported by donors and should thus be better able to serve the poorest segments of the population.

In contrast to NGOs, cooperatives and credit unions, NBFIs and banks are shareholder firms which in theory have clear financial objectives and distribute excess profits to their shareholders (Glaeser, 2003). However, their objectives are often not clear cut, because many banks and NBFIs are still fully or partly owned by NGOs. Cooperatives and credit unions are allowed to distribute profits to their members, but in practice they tend to do this by decreasing lending rates or increasing deposit rates. NGOs are subject to a so-called non-distribution constraint: they cannot distribute profits to their stakeholders.

The non-distribution constraint may create organizational slack and managerial discretion, because any excess profits are returned to the organization (e.g., Glaeser and Shleifer, 2001; Hansmann, 1980). Moreover, NGOs' non-executive board members do not have a financial stake in the organization, so they have less incentive to monitor (GTZ, 2000). These board members are generally independent persons who may wish to support the organization but in practice lack the technical knowledge and the time needed to assure proper board oversight and control. Sometimes NGO boards also include donors and clients, who do have a stake in the organization but seldom have financial knowledge and experience with risk management. In addition, NGOs are less affected by external governance mechanisms like public banking regulation and hence are normally not allowed to offer savings products. Because they do not offer savings products and cannot issue equity, they are more limited than other MFIs in obtaining funding. However, NGOs are better able to obtain donor money; due to their non-distribution constraint donations cannot be expropriated (Mersland, 2009). Donations shield NGOs somewhat from competition, which is another external governance mechanism.

Many authors argue that non-profit MFIs should transfer into shareholder owned firms (SHFs) (see Mersland and Strøm, 2009 for references). SHFs can be regulated by banking authorities, accept deposits, provide a larger range of better quality services, are independent from donors, attract private equity capital and benefit from superior corporate governance because they are privately owned. However, a recent study by Mersland and Strøm (2008) contradicts this hypothesis. They compare NGOs and shareholder MFIs (SHFs) on five aspects of the MFI performance dimensions: cost, depth, breadth, length and scope. 'Cost' is defined as the sum of monetary costs and transaction costs to clients; 'depth' is defined as clients' poverty level or other social factors, such as for instance the percentage of women reached; 'breadth' is defined as the number of clients served; 'length' is defined as the time frame of the supply of services; and 'scope' is defined as number of types of financial contracts supplied. They use a dataset containing 200 non-governmental or shareholder MFIs in 54 countries. Surprisingly, their results suggest that the difference in social and financial performance between SHFs and NGOs is minimal.

Some recent studies use stochastic frontier analysis (SFA) to examine the effect of corporate governance on MFI efficiency. Servin et al. (2011) examine whether MFIs with different ownership types differ in technical efficiency and technology. Using a sample of 315 MFIs from 18 Latin American countries, and applying the methodology of Lansink et al. (2001), they estimate separate production functions for MFIs characterized as NGOs, cooperatives/credit unions, NBFIs and banks. The study suggests that the technology of NBFIs and banks is better than that of NGOs and cooperatives/ credit unions. This is probably due to the fact that NBFIs and banks offer larger loans to richer clients, which allows them to use more efficient technologies. Moreover, they find that NBFIs and banks are more technically efficient than NGOs and cooperatives, which implies that given their own technology, NGOs and cooperatives perform worse than NBFIs and banks. Servin et al. (2011) argue that this may be due to a suboptimal monitoring system in non-shareholder MFIs. In contrast, Gutiérrez-Nieto et al. (2007), in a study of 30 MFIs in Latin America, find that NGOs are more efficient than MFIs. The reason for the difference in outcomes is not clear. What is clear, however, is that both studies clearly show that ownership type, and thus governance, matters for the MFI efficiency.

The dual mission of financial sustainability and outreach to the poor could create a trade-off, because serving the poor is costly. Hermes et al. (2011) demonstrate that there is a trade-off between these objectives. They use data for 435 MFIs for the period 1997–2007 to provide new evidence on the existence of the trade-off between sustainability and outreach. In particular, the study focuses on the relationship between cost efficiency of MFIs (as a measure of sustainability) and the depth of outreach measured by the average loan balance, average savings balance and percentage of women borrowers. Clearly, clients have very different interests than employees or investors, so the trade-off between financial and social performance makes microfinance governance extra challenging.

Also researchers that study the influence of governance on MFI performance need to take into account the double objectives. Mersland and Strøm (2009) regress governance mechanisms on financial and social performance separately and generally find little effect of governance on MFI performance. Hartarska and Mersland (2011) take the research one step further as they apply stochastic cost frontier analyses to capture simultaneously the cost minimization goal and the goal of serving many poor clients. Their study suggests that MFIs are less efficient if the positions of the CEO and the board chair are combined, and when MFIs have a larger proportion of insiders (employees) on the board.

29.3   MFI GOVERNANCE AND RISK-TAKING

This section deals with the impact of MFI governance on risk. Governance risk is an underestimated topic in the banking literature. The current financial crises shows that bank governance did not protect banks from taking excessive risks, so good governance is especially important for investors. The success of microfinance has induced more commercial debt and equity holders to invest in microfinance. Commercial investors are typically more concerned about investment risks than traditional, non-profit-driven microfinance investors. In addition, there are strong indications that the current financial crisis has severely affected MFI performance, which in turn has induced managers in MFIs to take excessive risks.

Within the field of corporate finance some recent papers have emerged on the relationship between corporate performance variability and board member characteristics. When board members have different opinions, decisions depend on the decision-making power of different members. For example, some firms have very large boards in which the decisions are outcomes of consensus, while other firms have boards in which the CEO makes all the major decisions. Regarding the first, Cheng (2008) looks at the relationship between board size and variability of performance and finds a negative relation. The explanation is that firms with larger boards make less extreme decisions and therefore have lower performance variability. Regarding the latter, Adams et al. (2005) investigate the relationship between CEO power and the variability of performance. They find that when CEOs have more power, their companies have higher performance variability. The explanation offered for this is that CEOs that have more power can make more extreme decisions, which leads to higher performance variability.

Although governance appears to be very relevant for MFI risk-taking, with the exception of Galema et al. (forthcoming) and Galema (2010) there are almost no studies that look at this. Galema et al. (forthcoming) develop a framework that substantiates that MFI managers have sufficient managerial discretion such that CEO power leads to more extreme decisions. Their main finding is in line with the results of Adams et al. (2005): CEO power is associated with more MFI risk-taking. Galema et al. (forthcoming) also find that the increase in risk is especially pronounced for NGOs. They explain this by arguing that: (1) an NGO's non-distribution constraint creates more organizational slack; (2) the double bottom line objectives make it hard for the board to practice active oversight; and (3) NGOs typically are not regulated by a central bank. Therefore, compared to other MFI types, an NGO offers executives the most managerial discretion

In this section we contribute to the literature on governance and MFI risk-taking by examining whether, in line with Cheng (2008), a larger board reduces MFI risk-taking. We argue that the same relationships between board size and performance variability may also exist for MFIs, even though they typically have different objectives and different boards than regular firms. In general, their main objectives are reducing poverty while simultaneously being financially sustainable. Due to this double bottom line, boards of MFIs are typically composed of many different types of board members, such as employees, donors, clients and, in particular, independent board members. These board members all have different interests, which have to be balanced. For instance, employees might be more interested in financial returns, while donors would be more interested in achieving higher poverty reduction. Due to the higher diversity of board members, it is even harder for MFI boards to reach consensus. This suggests that MFIs with larger boards have less performance variability.

For the analysis we use the dataset that has been developed and explained in Mersland and Strøm (2009). This dataset contains information from risk assessment reports on MFIs from five microfinance rating agencies: MicroRate, Microfinanza, Planet Rating, Crisil and M-Cril. The dataset contains a maximum of four years of MFI data, including information on their financial position, and MFI governance characteristics such as board size and board composition. The sample contains 278 MFIs from 60 countries over the 2000–2007 period, with the vast majority from the last four years. The dataset primarily provides information on commercial and professionally oriented institutions that have decided to be rated to improve access to funding. For more information on the dataset, the reader is referred to Mersland and Strøm (2009).

Similar to Adams et al. (2005) and Cheng (2008), we define within-firm, over-time variability as the standard deviation of MFI performance over the sample period. We regress the standard deviation of performance on a set of independent variables, which are averaged over the sample period:

$$std(roa_i) = \alpha + \beta_1 \overline{ceochair}_i + \beta_2 \overline{INTboards}_i + \beta_3 \overline{femceo}_i + \beta_4 \overline{indiv}_i + \beta_5 \overline{regulated}_i$$

$$+ \beta_6 \overline{urban}_i + \beta_7 \overline{boardsize}_i + \beta_8 \overline{age}_i + \beta_9 \overline{PaR}_i + \beta_{10} \overline{size}_i + \beta_{11} \overline{compet}_i$$

$$+ \beta_{12} \overline{writeoff}_i + \beta_{13} \overline{roa}_i + \beta_{14} \overline{leverage}_i + \varepsilon_i. \tag{29.1}$$

The explanatory variables are similar to those used in Mersland and Strøm (2009). *Ceochair* indicates that the CEO and the chairman of the board of directors are the same person. *INTboards* indicates the number of international board members. *Femceo* is a dummy indicating that the CEO is female. *Indiv* indicates that an MFI uses mainly individual lending. *Regulated* is a dummy stating whether the MFI is being regulated by banking authorities in the country. *Urban* is a dummy indicating that the geographical area the MFI is emphasizing is mainly urban. *Boardsize* indicates the number of board members. *Age* indicates the MFI age. *PaR* (portfolio at risk) is the percentage of the gross loan portfolio that is more than 30 days in arrears. *Size* is the natural logarithm of assets. *Compet* is microfinance market competition, as indicated by the rating agencies.

Table 29.2   Return on assets variability and MFI characteristics

Ceochair	0.021	[0.106]
INTboards	0.013**	[0.034]
Boardsize	−0.003*	[0.052]
Femceo	−0.002	[0.869]
Indiv	−0.008	[0.347]
Regulated	−0.009	[0.223]
Urban	0.012	[0.217]
Age	−0.001***	[0.005]
PaR	−0.022	[0.460]
Size	−0.003	[0.364]
Compet	−0.009***	[0.005]
Writeoff	0.201	[0.138]
ROA	−0.141*	[0.074]
Leverage	−0.002	[0.687]
Constant	0.157***	[0.001]
Observations	76	
R-squared	0.511	

Notes: * Significant at 10%; ** significant at 5%; *** significant at 1%. P-values between brackets.

Writeoff is the ratio of loans that have been written off and accounted as a loss in the MFI. *ROA* is the return on assets and is incorporated to control for the mean effect of the left-hand side variable. *Leverage* is the debt-to-equity ratio.

All explanatory variables are averaged over time, as indicated by the bar on top of each variable, so every sample MFI has only one observation. The independent variables chosen are similar to those used in performance regressions by Mersland and Strøm (2009). In addition, we include the write-off ratio and leverage since we believe they capture MFI risk.

In performing regression (29.1) with return on assets, we find that the results are very much influenced by outliers. To get an indication of these outliers, we use the graphical tool proposed by Rousseeuw and Van Zomeren (1990). We construct a graph (not presented for reasons of space, but which can be obtained on request) by plotting on the vertical axis the residuals, standardized by their standard deviation. We plot on the horizontal axis a measure of the (multivariate) outlyingness of the explanatory variables, known as the Mahalanobis distance. This is a measure similar to the Euclidean distance, but it also takes into account the correlation structure between the explanatory variables. In order to control for the outliers, we drop the four observations with the largest Mahalanobis distance.

The results of the performance variability regressions are reported in Table 29.2. Consistent with Cheng (2008), we can confirm our hypothesis that larger boards are associated with less performance variability. Also consistent with Adams et al. (2005) and Cheng (2008) we find that older MFIs have less variable return on asset performance. A novel finding we report is that MFIs that face less competition have less performance variability. A straightforward explanation is that markets with higher competition are more mature and therefore show less growth and have more stable lending rates over time. The finding that international board members increase performance variability could at first sight be considered surprising. However, this finding supports a recent finding in Mersland et al. (2011) showing that international directors in MFIs have a negative influence on financial performance while they have a positive influence on the MFI's social performance. Probably international directors in MFIs are there to control poverty outreach and do not have the knowledge needed to enhance financial performance and reduce MFI risk. Finally, in line with Galema et al. (forthcoming) we find some evidence for the hypothesis that more CEO power is associated with more performance variability, with significance just below 10 percent.

29.4 DISTINCTIVE FEATURES OF MICROFINANCE: DUAL OBJECTIVES AND FUNDING STRUCTURES

There are many features that make banks and corporations different from MFIs. This section discusses two of these features and their implications for governance. First, MFIs have dual objectives which greatly complicates setting optimal incentives to loan managers and the board. Second, MFIs' funding structures are very different. Commercialized banks rely mostly on deposits, whereas NGOs rely very much on donations. This has important implications for the board's fiduciary duties.

29.4.1 Incentive Schemes: A Plea for New Theory on MFI Governance

To ensure that the MFI achieves both objectives, it needs properly designed incentive schemes. The main question is how incentives should be designed such that financial sustainability is stimulated while social goals are not undermined. The current theoretical literature almost exclusively focuses on incentive issues between borrowers and lenders, mostly in the context of group lending, such as explaining how joint liability lending solves asymmetric information problems (see, e.g., Banerjee et al., 1994; Ghatak, 2000; Gangopadhyay et al., 2005; Ghatak and Guinnane, 1999; Laffont, 2003; Stiglitz, 1990). Group lending is a lending contract in which group lenders are required to guarantee each other's loan repayments; they have joint liability. When lenders are jointly liable, peer monitoring and peer selection help to overcome adverse selection and moral hazard problems, which reduces a lender's agency costs. There are also some papers that focus on other characteristics of group lending schemes. Chowdury (2005, 2007) and Guttman (2008), for instance, deal with the dynamic incentive aspects of group schemes. So the existing 'incentive' literature on microfinance focuses almost entirely on reducing asymmetric information problems in the context of group lending, while it hardly pays attention to the incentive schemes the board gives to loan managers.

Another distinguishing feature is that most MFI clients lack a wage earner's stable income. They often operate in the informal sector, which offers variable and uncertain income flows. Moreover, most MFI clients lack collateral, which implies that MFIs need to develop other instruments to ensure repayment. Usually, the microcredit methodology is based on a field evaluation of the client's character and ability to pay. Related to the type of clients, the products that most MFIs traditionally offer are very different from normal bank loans. In particular, lenders typically take repeated loans which are unsecured, small and short term.

When there are many MFIs operating in a region, staff incentives can have perverse consequences like overindebted clients and excessive peer pressure. The theoretical literature lacks analyses on the adverse effects of peer pressure in group lending. While group lending theories help to explain why poor customers repay their loans to MFIs, the theories make little attempt to explain how excessive peer pressure could push non-performing group members into increased misery. For MFIs that want to improve the lives of the poor, excessive intra-group peer pressure constitutes a governance problem which existing theories fail to explain. How can the MFI design incentive structures for its staff and its credit groups that assure loan repayment without introducing excessive enforcement methods? This is especially important for lenders that take uncollateralized loans in markets where customer protection is nonexistent. Under such conditions an unpaid loan can easily lead to excessive peer pressure.

Probably the most important distinction of MFIs with obvious implications for the governance system is that most microfinance lenders pursue both financial and social objectives. On the one hand, they try to contribute to development and poverty reduction, which involves reaching more clients and poorer clients. On the other hand, MFIs want to be financially sustainable and become independent from donors. Controlling an organization with dual objectives is more difficult than controlling one solely dedicated to profits, especially when we take into account that Hermes et al. (2011) find that there is a trade-off between these objectives.

A difficulty MFIs face in designing optimal incentive schemes is that their two aims often conflict. The trade-off between the social and financial performance implies that MFI managers can justify their bad performance on one criterion by referring to the other; poor financial performance could be attributed to the MFI's social mission, especially because social performance is so difficult to measure. This problem is well known in multitask agency theory but difficult to solve. Holmström and Milgrom (1991), for instance, show that it is suboptimal to offer variable incentive schemes to the CEO when the firm has dual objectives, one of which is difficult to measure. It is not clear, however, to what extent the insights of Holmström and Milgrom (1991) directly apply to MFIs. Relatedly, Hartarska (2005) reveals that performance-based compensation schemes are not associated with better performance. In addition, variable incentive schemes are often forbidden by NGOs, so that even if social performance could be measured easily an optimal incentive scheme cannot be developed (Hartarska, 2005).

A possible solution to the multitask-incentive problem is to make different staff responsible for different tasks and reward them accordingly, that is, to seek for 'functional specialization' (Dewatripont et al., 1999). In addition, functional specialization matches staff to the tasks in which they have a comparative advantage. For example, loan officers of ASA, one of the major MFIs in Bangladesh, only provide basic financial services, while better-educated staff provide training sessions (see Armendáriz and Morduch, 2010: 368).

Despite the importance of MFI incentive structures there is almost no scientific literature available that deals with the topic. The only literature on staff incentives is case studies from which it is hard to draw any general lessons. Many for-profit MFIs have now introduced bonuses for their agents based on repayment rates. These bonuses are often based on individual incentives, such as bonuses related to the percentage of the portfolio not at risk, the number of clients and the value of the outstanding loan portfolio. A drawback of individual monetary incentives may be that they can conflict with attempts to build social cohesion within an MFI. Therefore, sometimes incentives based on branch performance or performance of the entire institution are introduced. Obviously, incentives at the higher level may lead to free-riding problems, and hence work less efficiently. For this reason, Bank Rakyat Indonesia (BRI) has introduced incentives at the individual, branch and institution-wide levels. In particular, staff of BRI receive bonuses that depend on the profit of their unit, the entire bank and the value of collected but already written-off loans (see Armendáriz and Morduch, 2010: 364).

29.4.2   How Funding Determines Governance

The standard view in economics regarding fiduciary duties is that directors owe fiduciary duties only to shareholders, as shareholders are the residual claimants with the appropriate incentives to make decisions in the corporation's best interest. Still, in every corporation there is a conflict of interest between shareholders and debt holders. Shareholders are interested in increasing risk, while debt holders want to decrease risk as the extra risk gives them no additional returns. In microfinance there is potentially an additional conflict between those that provide funds with a social motive (e.g., non-commercial investment and donations) and those that provide commercial funds. Compared to corporations, microfinance boards face a more difficult task, because in their fiduciary duties they have to strike the right balance between multiple interests. Boards have some discretion in deciding which interests are more important, but logically they give priority to those that provide the most funds.

The funding structure of MFIs is very different than that of corporations and also within the population of MFIs there are large differences. Cull et al. (2009) show that equity represents only 13 percent of MFIs' funding, whereas 26 percent consists of donations and 34 percent consists of borrowing, so shareholders are much less important than in corporations. Considering the different organizational types, banks and credit unions obtain most of their funding from deposits (71 percent and 64 percent, respectively). NBFIs are often not allowed to take deposits, so they obtain most of their funds from commercial borrowing (28 percent) and donations (23 percent). Finally, NGOs obtain most of their funds from donations (39 percent) and commercial borrowing (26 percent). Depending on its funding structure, each MFI type faces different governance issues.

First, we consider banks. Empirical contributions on bank governance are to a large extent based on agency theory (e.g., Laeven and Levine, 2009). Shleifer and Vishny (1997) conclude that legal protection of investors and some form of concentrated ownership are essential elements of a good corporate governance system. Although this works for corporations, Macey and O'Hara (2003) argue that special governance problems of banks weaken the case for giving shareholders so much power. In a corporation, debt holders have an incentive to limit risk-taking, for instance, by demanding a higher return when the firm is more levered. Banks are different in that their capital supply consists mainly of deposits. Deposit insurance removes the incentive of the depositors to reduce risk and thereby increases the room for shareholders to push for higher risk levels. This is confirmed by Laeven and Levine (2009) who find that deposit insurance increases risk when the bank has a large equity holder that has the power to act on the increased risk-taking incentives created by deposit insurance. In response, capital requirements try to reduce shareholders' risk-taking incentives by forcing owners to put more of their wealth at risk in the bank. Yet, Laeven and Levine (2009) find that capital regulations only increase bank risk, which they explain as being motivated by shareholders' desire to compensate for the utility loss from capital requirements. Because of the excessive power of bank shareholders and the public's desire for a safe banking system, Macey and O'Hara (2003) argue that boards should weigh the interests of debt holders and depositors more heavily in their fiduciary duties.

To some extent, lessons can be learned from credit unions which are owned by their members – savers and borrowers – and which often also have other stakeholders like employees and donors on their board. Like banks, NBFIs are often for-profit institutions. Yet, their funding structure is very different: most of them are not allowed to take deposits, so they rely much more on debt and donations. To some extent this alleviates problems associated with deposit insurance and capital requirements, but it also creates possible conflicts between commercial debt holders and donors. Donors want MFIs to reach out to the poorest clients, which involves extra costs and risks, whereas debt holders want a safe return on their investment. This problem is more severe for debt holders of NGOs, which focus on even poorer clients than the NBFI.

29.5   CONCLUSIONS

This chapter shows that the existing literature on governance and microfinance is small, and conflicting. Some studies find that governance issues are rather unimportant for MFI performance, others come to the opposite conclusion. These results call for much more study on governance and microfinance in order to come to a definitive view on how governance affects MFIs. We have made a first step by providing some new empirical support for the view that larger boards reduce risk-taking of MFIs.

The unequivocal results of existing empirical studies could indicate that we currently lack good theoretical models that allow us to test the right hypotheses. Currently, most empirical studies are explorative and not based on theories tailored to microfinance. We make a plea for theoretical governance research that considers the specific features of MFIs. This includes how to set optimal incentive structures given microfinance's dual mission and how to determine governance arrangements given MFIs' different funding structures.

We end this chapter by referring to some recent developments in microfinance that have important implications for the governance system and should be taken into account in new theoretical and empirical governance research. First, MFIs that traditionally have been funded mainly by subsidies from private and public donors and aid organizations have started to commercialize and attract funds from private capital markets. Some microfinance institutions, such as Compartamos in Mexico and SKS microfinance in India, have even gone public. The transformation of a traditional NGO into a listed company obviously has important governance implications. Second, MFIs have started to become involved in other activities than lending. Whereas originally they were mainly focused on providing credit, nowadays they are involved in micro savings, micro insurance and financial literacy training; and the list is growing. In addition, new banking technology, such as charge cards, automated teller machines (ATMs), points of payment, the use of cellphones and the Internet, has begun to enter the microfinance business. Finally, many governments in developing countries have started installing regulations to help improve the stability of the microfinance business, which has far-reaching consequences for the governance policies of MFIs.

In many ways microfinance represents the future of banking. Already more than 150 million people are loan clients in MFIs (www.microcreditsummit.org) and many are starting to open savings accounts as well (Christen et al., 2004). In the years to come the number of microfinance customers will probably by far outnumber the number of customers in traditional banks. This implies important responsibilities for microfinance actors which need to be handled through proper governance systems.

REFERENCES

Adams, R.B., H. Almeida and D. Ferreira (2005), 'Powerful CEOs and their impact on corporate performance', *Review of Financial Studies*, **18**(4), 1403–1432.

Armendáriz, B. and J. Morduch (2010), *The Economics of Microfinance*, second edition, Cambridge, MA: MIT Press.

Banerjee, Abhijit, Timothy Besley and Timothy Guinnane (1994), 'The neighbor's keeper: the design of a credit cooperative with theory and a test', *Quarterly Journal of Economics*, **109**, 491–515.

Bateman, M. (2010), *Why Doesn't Microfinance Work? The Destructive Rise of Neoliberalism*, London: Zed Books.

Cheng, S. (2008), 'Board size and the variability of corporate performance', *Journal of Financial Economics*, **87**(1), 157–176.

Chowdhury, Prabal Roy (2005), 'Group-lending: sequential financing, lender monitoring and joint liability', *Journal of Development Economics*, **77**, 415–439.

Chowdury, Prabal Roy (2007), 'Group-lending with sequential financing, contingent renewal and social capital', *Journal of Development Economics*, **84**, 487–507.

Christen, R.P., R. Rosenberg and V. Jayadeva (2004), 'Financial institutions with a double bottom line: implications for the future of microfinance', GGAP Occasional Paper no. 8.

Cull, R., A. Demirgüç-Kunt and J. Morduch (2009), 'Microfinance meets the markets', *Journal of Economic Perspectives*, **23**, 167–192.

Daily, C.M., D. Dalton and A. Cannella (2003), 'Corporate governance: decades of dialogue and data', *Academy of Management Review*, **28**, 371–382.

Dewatripont, Mathias, Ian Jewitt and Jean Tirole (1999), 'The economics of career concerns, part II: Application to missions and accountability of governance agencies', *Review of Economic Studies*, **66**(1), Special Issue (Contracts), 199–217.

Galema, R. (2010), 'Debt enforcement and microfinance risk', University of Groningen, working paper.

Galema, R., R. Lensink and R. Mersland (forthcoming), 'Do powerful CEOs determine microfinance performance?', *Journal of Management Studies*.

Gangopadhyay, Shubhashis, Maitreesh Ghatak and Robert Lensink (2005), 'On joint liability and the peer selection effect', *Economic Journal*, **115**, 1012–1020.

Ghatak, Maitreesh (2000), 'Screening by the company you keep: joint liability lending and the peer selection effect', *Economic Journal*, **110**, 601–631.

Ghatak, Maitreesh and Timothy W. Guinnane (1999), 'The economics of lending with joint liability: theory and practice', *Journal of Development Economics*, **60**, 195–228.

Glaeser, E.L. (2003), 'Introduction to the governance of not-for-profit organizations', in E.L. Glaeser (ed.), *The Governance of Not-for-Profit Organizations*, Chicago, IL: University of Chicago Press.

Glaeser, E.L and A. Shleifer (2001), 'Not-for-profit entrepreneurs', *Journal of Public Economics*, **81**, 99–115.

GTZ (2000), *A Risk Management Framework for Microfinance Institutions*, Eschborn: GTZ.

Gutiérrez-Nieto, B., C. Serrano-Cinca and C. Mar Molinero (2007), 'Microfinance institutions and efficiency', *Omega*, **35**(2), 131–142.

Guttman, Joel M. (2008), 'Assortative matching, adverse selection, and group lending', *Journal of Development Economics*, **87**, 51–56.

Hansmann, H.B. (1980), 'The role of nonprofit enterprise', *Yale Law Journal*, **80**(5), 835–901.

Hartarska, V. (2005), 'Governance and performance of microfinance institutions in Central and Eastern Europe and the newly independent states', *World Development*, **33**(10), 1627–1643.

Hartarska, V. and R. Mersland (2011), 'Which governance mechanisms promote efficiency in reaching poor clients? Evidence from rated microfinance institutions', *European Financial Management*, doi: 10.1111/j.1468-036X.2009.00524.x.

Hermes, N. and R. Lensink (2007), 'The empirics of microfinance: what do we know?', *Economic Journal*, **117**(517), F1–F10.

Hermes, N. and R. Lensink (2011), 'Microfinance: its impact, outreach and sustainability', *World Development*, **39**, 875–881.

Hermes, N., R. Lensink and A. Meesters (2011), 'Outreach and efficiency of microfinance institutions', *World Development*, **39**, 939–948.

Holmström, B. and P. Milgrom (1991), 'Multitask principal–agent analyses: incentive contracts, asset ownership, and job design', *Journal of Law, Economics, and Organization*, **7**, 24–52.

Labie, M. and R. Mersland (2011), 'Corporate governance challenges in microfinance', in Beatrice Armendáriz and Marc Labie (eds), *The Handbook of Microfinance*, Singapore and London: World Scientific Publishing, pp. 283–300.

Laeven, L. and R. Levine (2009), 'Bank governance, regulation and risk taking', *Journal of Financial Economics*, **93**, 259–275.

Laffont, Jean-Jaques (2003), 'Collusion and group lending with adverse selection', *Journal of Development Economics*, **70**(2), 329–348.

Lansink, A.O., E. Silva and S. Stefanou (2001), 'Inter-firm and intra-firm efficiency measures', *Journal of Productivity Analysis*, **15**, 185–199.

Macey, J.R. and M. O'Hara (2003), 'The corporate governance of banks', *Economic Policy Review*, **9**(1), 91–107.

Mersland, R. (2009), 'The cost of ownership in microfinance organizations', *World Development*, **37**(2), 469–478.

Mersland, R., T. Randoy and R.Ø. Strøm (2011), 'The impact of international influence on microbanks' performance: a global survey', *International Business Review*, **20**, 163–176.

Mersland, R. and R.Ø. Strøm (2008), 'Performance and trade-offs in microfinance organizations – does ownership matter?', *Journal of International Development*, **20**, 598–612.

Mersland, R. and R.Ø. Strøm (2009), 'Performance and governance in microfinance institutions', *Journal of Banking and Finance*, **33**(4), 662–669.

Rousseeuw, P.J. and B. Van Zomeren (1990), 'Unmasking multivariate outliers and leverage points', *Journal of the American Statistical Association*, **85**, 633–639.

Servin, R., R. Lensink and M. van den Berg (2011), 'Does the ownership type of MFIs affect MFIs technology and efficiency: evidence from Latin America', Wageningen University, mimeo.

Shleifer, A. and R.W. Vishny (1997), 'A survey of corporate governance', *Journal of Finance*, **52**(2), 737–783.

Steege, J. (1998), 'The rise and fall of Corposol: lessons learned from the challenges of managing growth', USAID Microfinance Best Practice, Washington, DC.

Stiglitz, Joseph E. (1990), 'Peer monitoring in credit markets', *World Bank Economic Review*, **4**, 351–366.

PART VII

REGIONAL AND COUNTRY STUDIES

30 Bank governance: the case of New Zealand
Don Brash

30.1 THE 1980S: LIBERALIZATION AND CRISIS

Until the mid-1980s, New Zealand had just four banks: one fully owned by the government, one owned by Lloyds Bank in the UK, and two owned by large Australian banks. In the mid-1980s, as the New Zealand economy experienced a far-reaching liberalization across virtually every area of policy, non-bank financial institutions were allowed to convert to full banking status, and foreign banks were allowed to establish branches or subsidiaries. By the time I became Governor of the Reserve Bank of New Zealand in September 1988, there were a total of 15 registered banks, including the four 'original' banks.

The Reserve Bank had responsibility for issuing licences to the new banks – the original four were deemed banks by legislation, and so did not need to get a licence – and for supervising all of them. In keeping with the policy environment in New Zealand at that time, supervision was light-handed, and regulation even more so. We did not dream of on-site inspection and were relaxed about whether foreign-owned banks operated as subsidiaries incorporated in New Zealand or as branches of the foreign parent. When I first arrived at the Bank, there was no limit on risk concentration.

I was particularly surprised at the absence of any limit on risk concentration, having just come from a commercial banking environment, and soon after my arrival we instituted a limit of 35 per cent of bank equity for any single counterparty.

But then in the late 1980s New Zealand was hit by recession. In part, this was a result of an aggressive attack on inflation by the central bank and in part a result of a dramatic fall in share and property prices following the October 1987 crash on Wall Street. (The fall in share prices was much more abrupt in New Zealand than in the US.) The government-owned bank, the Bank of New Zealand, suffered severe loan losses and would almost certainly have failed had the government not stepped in and injected additional capital. One of the new banks, owned by a foreign-owned insurance company, would also have failed had it not been for massive support from its British parent. And a near-bank, DFC, did fail: the largest failure of any financial institution in New Zealand history. The failure of DFC was particularly traumatic for financial markets because until a year or two earlier it had been wholly owned by government, and its 'privatization' was seen by many of its creditors (which were mainly US and Japanese banks and other institutions) as still leaving the government primarily responsible for the institution (80 per cent of the shares were purchased by the National Provident Fund, a government agency responsible for providing pensions to many thousands of public servants).

30.2   SUPERVISORS VERSUS ECONOMISTS: TOWARDS A NEW REGIME

The more or less automatic reaction of those of us in the Reserve Bank was that we needed to intensify our supervisory activities, and get a great deal more information from the banks than we had been receiving previously. Where we had been getting information from banks quarterly, we moved to get it monthly, and in some cases even more frequently. We adopted the Basel I rules for minimum capital, both Tier 1 and Tier 2.

But some of the senior economists at the Bank began asking questions about the rationale for what we were doing. In particular, they asked whether the additional information we were seeking from banks was intended to be an alternative to more intensive regulation or an addition.

And thus began an internal debate which raged for several years. The economists tended to argue that supervision and regulation were largely futile and could even be counterproductive. They pointed out that in the almost five decades since World War II the only major banks which had failed in the developed world had failed for one of two reasons. First, they may have failed because of fraud – think BCCI (or a little later, Barings) – and bank supervisors almost never detect fraud, especially if there is collusion between bank management and bank customers. Second, they more often failed because of a dramatic fall in asset prices, usually property prices – and bank supervisors seem no better able to anticipate those than the management of banks. Therefore, claiming to be able substantially to reduce the probability of bank failure risks damaging central bank credibility when the inevitable bank failures eventually come. The economists argued that compelling banks to make more disclosure to the public could be a substitute for tighter regulation.

Moreover, the economists were worried that gathering substantial amounts of confidential information from banks significantly increased the problem of moral hazard. As supervisors, we – but not bank customers or the wider public – would know about the strength of the banks and would feel some responsibility if a problem began to emerge. We would be 'fixed with knowledge' and face all the wrong incentives.

On the other side of the debate, our bank supervisors were absolutely sure that regulation and supervision of banks was essential and cited the usual arguments of asymmetric information and systemic risk. They were convinced that our regulation and supervision were essential to keep the banks sound, and that without our oversight the banks would quickly get into trouble – as, indeed, they had done in the late 1980s.

An economist by background myself, I was sympathetic to the argument of the economists, and I was strengthened in that view when one of my predecessors as Governor told me he thought that the Bank was on a hiding to nothing by carrying responsibility for bank supervision. When things are going well, the Bank will get no credit; but when things turn sour, the Bank will be blamed.

In September 1992, a chance conversation strengthened my conviction that the economists were right. I was a guest at one of the innumerable dinners which mark the annual meetings of the International Monetary Fund (IMF) and World Bank in Washington, and found myself sitting beside a man who had had a very distinguished career in the UK Treasury. He had just been appointed a director of one of the largest British banks. I asked him how he found being a bank director after a lifetime of working in the Treasury. 'Funny you should ask that', he replied. 'Banking is all about measuring and pricing risk, and in the Treasury I haven't had experience of that.' So I was greatly relieved to discover that all I had to worry about as a director of the bank was whether we were complying with the Bank of England's rule (this was before the creation of the Financial Services Authority, FSA, of course).

In the end, we announced a new regime to take effect from the beginning of 1996. We retained the minimum capital rules from Basel I because we were not quite brave enough to reject totally the international orthodoxy, and we retained rules on related-party exposures. But we scrapped any limit on credit concentration; we had no minimum requirements for liquidity; we had no rules on foreign exchange exposure; we had no rules about risk control systems; we did not reserve the right to approve bank directors; we still had no on-site inspections.

Instead, we had three things. Firstly, we required a high level of financial disclosure, not just to the central bank but also – and primarily – to the market, on a quarterly basis. So, for example, banks had to disclose the extent of their risk concentration: how many exposures they had to individual counterparties which exceeded 10 per cent of equity, how many which exceeded 20 per cent of equity, and so on. Similarly, banks had to disclose the extent of any open foreign exchange position, and the maturity structure of their assets and liabilities. We reasoned that the obligation to disclose this information would in itself impose a strong discipline on the banks without the Reserve Bank having to specify some arbitrary rules.

Secondly, we required all bank directors – executive directors and non-executive directors – to sign off these quarterly disclosure statements, attesting to their belief both that the information therein was accurate and that the bank's risk control systems were appropriate to the nature of the bank's business.

These director attestations prompted a reaction. Shortly before they were implemented, the managing director of the Australian parent of one of New Zealand's largest banks flew to Wellington to protest that it was quite wrong of us to require these attestations. Most bank directors, he claimed, know absolutely nothing about banking, so it is totally unfair to expect them to sign these attestations.

I had to accept his statement that many bank directors did not know a lot about banking – and that was partly because the bank supervisor had been willing to make key decisions about capital adequacy, risk control systems and all the rest for them. Too often banks had appointed people as directors because of their strong connections in the corporate world, or their reputation for probity and integrity; and while those things are clearly advantageous, it was also, in our view, important that bank directors took primary responsibility for bank governance.

Thirdly, we required all banks to have an independent chairman and at least two independent directors – independent from any parent bank, that is. We wanted to ensure that if the bank group of which the New Zealand operation was a part got into difficulty, there were at least some strong independent voices at the board table to look out for the interests of the New Zealand operation.

30.3   DISCLOSURE AND GOVERNANCE

Has this approach to bank regulation worked? It is impossible to be dogmatic because of course nobody knows what the counterfactual would have been.

But we do know that banks themselves keep a close eye on the disclosure statements of other banks, and this has to be constructive. Shortly after the new regime was introduced, the New Zealand subsidiary of an American bank was forced to disclose in its quarterly disclosure statement that it had lent more money to its parent than it had equity in New Zealand. Another bank protested vigorously to that subsidiary because it had had very substantial funds on deposit with the subsidiary at a time when the latter effectively had a negative net equity position in New Zealand. To the best of my knowledge, the American bank never repeated that behaviour.

There is no doubt in my mind that the requirement for bank directors to make quarterly disclosure statements has improved the quality of bank governance in New Zealand. Early on, it was established that signing the attestations does not require bank directors to become internal auditors, but it does require them to put in place policies and procedures designed to give them a high degree of confidence that what they are being asked to sign is in fact accurate and reliable. And I have no doubt that that has strengthened bank governance. Some years after I resigned as Governor of the Reserve Bank in 2002, I became a director of the largest commercial bank in New Zealand – and I can personally confirm that bank directors take signing these attestations very seriously indeed.

As an aside, the disclosure statements come in two forms: a so-called Key Information Summary of no more than three or four pages, which must be available on demand in every branch of the bank; and a much longer and more comprehensive statement, which must be provided within five days of any request being made. This reduces the number of forests that must be felled in producing the more comprehensive statement in a situation where the number of people who will actually read it carefully can almost certainly be counted on the fingers of two hands (though a few toes may be needed also). On reflection, I think the Bank (and I take full responsibility for the decision) required an excessive level of detail in the comprehensive statements: the sheer volume of that detail probably obscures more than it reveals to all but the most diligent and determined of observers.

But can it be claimed that the New Zealand approach to banking regulation and supervision has actually worked? If an improvement in bank governance is the criterion for making that assessment, I would argue that it has done so, as noted above. And there have not been any bank failures since the regime was introduced in the mid-1990s.

However, New Zealand is not a good laboratory to test the regime. Until the last few years, almost every bank in the country has been a subsidiary or a branch of a major international bank, and the four largest banks, which overwhelmingly dominate the New Zealand banking sector, are all wholly owned by financially strong Australian banks. Those Australian 'parents' are supervised by the Australian Prudential Regulation Authority, which operates an entirely orthodox supervisory regime. The fact that there is a widespread assumption that the Australian parent banks would support their New Zealand subsidiaries means that very few people, even very few financial analysts, pay any attention at all to the quarterly disclosure statements.

Moreover, since I left the Reserve Bank in 2002 the New Zealand regime has drifted gradually towards a more orthodox regime also. The Bank still does not conduct on-site inspections but it does, for example, now stipulate that a minimum percentage of every bank's funding should come from retail or long-term wholesale funding to reduce reliance on short-term (and therefore potentially fickle) wholesale funding. And all directors and senior management of banks must be approved by the central bank. I have a good deal of sympathy for putting in place rules around the maturity structure of bank funding, given the vulnerability that banks which are heavily dependent on short-term wholesale funding have. I am much less convinced of the merit of requiring a central bank tick for all bank directors and senior management: if something should go wrong with the bank, depositors could with some justification come to the central bank demanding compensation.

30.4   DEALING WITH FOREIGN CONTROL

The Bank's thinking has evolved in other areas also, during my own time as Governor and subsequently. When I first became Governor, we were entirely relaxed about whether a foreign bank operating in New Zealand chose to incorporate locally or simply operate as a branch, without local incorporation. We could see considerable merit in having foreign-owned banks operating as a branch because this enabled the local operation to derive the full benefits of the parent's balance sheet.

This indifference began to change after the failure of BCCI in 1991. We saw central banks and other official organs put their hands around whatever assets of BCCI happened to lie within their jurisdiction, regardless of legal form; but that appeared to be somewhat easier to do without legal challenge when the operations were incorporated locally.

Then we became focused on the implications of the Australian Banking Act: the legislation provided that in the event of an Australian bank being wound up, a priority would be given to Australian depositors of the bank at least insofar as the Australian assets were concerned. But what constituted the 'Australian assets' of the bank? Could a court find that the 'Australian assets' included assets owned through a branch structure in New Zealand? To make matters worse, US legislation was changed during the 1990s, providing the same kind of priority to American depositors in the event of a US bank being wound up. What would happen to New Zealand depositors with the local branch of a US bank which got into trouble?

While the Reserve Bank had (and still has) no legal obligation to protect bank depositors (our responsibility was to protect the stability of the banking system), we decided that the political implications of a situation where an Australian or American bank in liquidation was able to pay out its own national depositors in full but able to pay nothing or very little to New Zealand depositors would be intolerable. In the end, we decided that all foreign banks which engage in substantial retail banking business in New Zealand and which are based in countries which give their own national depositors a priority in the event of the bank's being liquidated must be incorporated locally. We decided that banks which are only engaged in commercial or corporate banking can choose to incorporate or not as they please, on the assumption that commercial and corporate customers are mature enough to make an informed judgement about the risks themselves. (Of course, banks which come from countries where all depositors, whether local or foreign, are treated *pari passu* have no obligation to incorporate in New Zealand, whatever the nature of their banking business.)

As a consequence of this policy, one large Australian bank which had operated in New Zealand for more than a century as a branch was obliged to incorporate locally, while an American bank which had a small retail banking operation in New Zealand and which was not incorporated locally withdrew from retail banking operations but continued with commercial and corporate banking business.

30.5   'TOO BIG TO FAIL' AND OPERATIONAL SEPARABILITY

One of the major issues confronting any banking supervisor is how to deal with a bank which gets into serious trouble. Like all central bankers with responsibility for supervising banks, I steadfastly maintained the public stance that no bank was 'too big to fail'. But when we actually did some analysis of what would happen if one of our four big banks did fail, it was rapidly apparent that closing the bank would be out of the question – not just because of the effect on those with deposits in the bank, or even those dependent on loans from the bank, but because of the disastrous consequences for the payments system if one of the four largest players were to close. So we started trying to work out how a systemically important bank might be allowed to fail without actually being closed – or at least without being closed for more than, say, 24 hours.

I understand that the Reserve Bank has continued to work on this issue since I left in 2002. It is entirely consistent with moves in some other countries to require banks to provide 'living wills' to their supervisors, so that in the event that a bank gets into trouble the supervisor is able to step in and either wind up the bank in a sensible manner or alternatively keep it going, perhaps by imposing some form of haircut on one or more categories of bank creditors. (We referred to this as BCR, for bank creditor recapitalization.)

But of course for it to be feasible to continue the operations of a failed bank it would be essential that whoever steps in to run the bank has the practical ability to do so; in other words, has the ability to access the bank's loan processing facilities, its computer systems, and so on. If these are inside the international headquarters of the parent bank, that could be very difficult in practice, particularly if, as is likely, the foreign parent is itself in difficulty and could even be under the direct control of a foreign supervisor. For this reason, the Reserve Bank has required foreign-owned banks in New Zealand to maintain control over their own back-office processing facilities. They do not need to be in New Zealand, but there must be robust contractual arrangements which provide a high degree of confidence that, in the event of a crisis, they would be under the effective control of whoever has stepped in to take control of the bank in New Zealand.

Having said that, I acknowledge that all those responsible for the regulation and supervision of banks, whether in New Zealand or elsewhere, are only too aware that what to do with a systemically important bank in serious difficulty remains a major conundrum. Nobody wants to acknowledge that a major bank is too big to fail, but everybody recognizes the serious dilemmas involved in letting a major bank close its doors. While bank creditor recapitalization might conceivably work for a bank specific crisis, where everybody could see that the problems facing one bank were unlikely to be facing other banks in the system, it seems unlikely to be a sufficient solution to a crisis which extended to the banking system as a whole – the sort of crisis which has affected the banking systems of the US and Europe over the last few years.

30.6   THE LIMITS OF SUPERVISION

I think there is a role for bank supervision,[1] but I am more than ever convinced in the light of the bank failures internationally over the last few years that bank regulation and bank supervision are only part of the answer. Neither supervision nor regulation can prevent all bank collapses: after all, despite the public myth that banks were entirely free of regulation and supervision over the last couple of decades, large US banks at least were subject to intensive supervision, with supervisors on site permanently. Not only did that not prevent some major banks getting into serious trouble, but also that level of supervision may even have made matters worse, by encouraging both bank management and bank directors to assume that, as long as the supervisors did not blow the whistle, things must be just fine. Nothing could be further from the truth.

NOTE

1.   See also D.T. Brash (2010), 'Banking regulation after the global financial crisis', speech to the Alamos Alliance conference, 19 February, http://donbrash.com/banking-regulation-after-the-global-financial-crisis/.

31 Corporate governance in European banking

Francesca Arnaboldi and Barbara Casu*

31.1 INTRODUCTION

Since the signing of the Treaties of Rome in 1957, the European Union (EU) has grown to a union of 27 member states and a population of nearly half a billion citizens. Nowadays, the EU is the largest integrated economic area in the world, accounting for more than 20 per cent of the world's GDP.[1] The financial sector has played a key role in the process of EU economic growth. Since the introduction of the First Banking Directive in 1977 (77/780/EEC), the deregulation of financial services, the establishment of the Economic and Monetary Union and the introduction of the euro have helped to create the Single Market for financial services. European authorities consider financial integration one of the key issues for making Europe more efficient and competitive and, ultimately, for contributing to sustainable economic growth (ECB, 2005). Indeed, EU financial integration has brought with it a range of benefits, from increased income generation to improvements in technology and risk management, increased access to funds, risk diversification and deepening of financial markets.[2]

Despite the positive achievements, critics argue that the Single Market can never operate properly across an area with such different cultures and levels of wealth. Whether it is a question of North to South or East to West, there seem to be identifiable cultural fault lines across the European continent. There are, of course, common values and some European common culture, but definitions are complex.[3] It is therefore apparent that, even with the recent emphasis on integration, Europe is not a monolithic bloc of countries. Quite to the contrary, EU authorities struggle to find a common European identity that can generate widespread support in all member states. Europeans mostly identify themselves with their own nation, and the dominance of national interest over the common EU interest became all the more obvious during the recent financial crisis. The injection of public funds into troubled financial institutions highlighted the gap between the rhetoric of an integrated Europe and the reality of national interests. Still, far from being powerless, the EU has been at the forefront of the coordination of the rescue plans designed by the member states and of the reform of the financial system (EC, 2008, 2009a).[4]

It is argued that the Single Market for financial services was in a way too successful, as it allowed the creation of cross-border financial institutions that are too large relative to individual member states, thus highlighting the need for an integrated framework for cross-border crisis management and resolution (EC, 2009b; Fonteyne et al., 2010). Regulators have also begun to question the suitability of financial institutions' supervisory systems and investigate whether existing corporate governance mechanisms in financial institution are incomplete or poorly implemented (EC, 2010).

The impact and outcomes of the crisis have however been different within the EU member states, with some countries' banking systems worse affected than others. For example, because of their conservative business models, Italian banks have done better than their larger UK and continental peers. While this conservatism and lack of global ambition were previously seen as major weaknesses, analysts now applaud Italian banks for their focus on traditional banking models.[5]

Post-crisis, European bank managers are facing a difficult business environment and the strategic implications of this could be substantial. It is likely that the future of EU banking will be shaped by regulatory initiatives that will favour stability over profitability (ECB, 2010). Against this backdrop, this chapter surveys the corporate governance features of banking institutions in the 15 countries that were members of the European Union prior to the latest enlargement (Fourth Enlargement, Phase 1 in 2004 and Phase 2 in 2007).[6] While we aim to account for European diversity, there is still a large disparity between the countries comprising the EU-15 area and the newer member states. This is true in terms of the overall standards of living,[7] but also in terms of management and corporate culture. For this reason, we focus on the area also known as 'old Europe', comprising: Austria, Belgium, Denmark, Finland, France, Germany, Greece, Ireland, Italy, Luxembourg, the Netherlands, Portugal, Spain, Sweden and the United Kingdom. The remainder of this chapter is structured as follows: section 31.2 reviews the different systems, structures and models in EU banking. Section 31.3 offers an insight on bank corporate governance features in the EU-15, taking into account national and cultural differences. Finally, section 31.4 concludes.

31.2   EU BANKING: SYSTEMS, STRUCTURES AND MODELS

The banking systems of the EU-15 countries present varied characteristics, including features from the Anglo-Saxon market-based system, prevalent in the US, the UK and the Netherlands, and a more bank-based system, prevalent in Germany and in most of continental Europe.[8] In recent years, the demarcation lines of this common classification of financial systems have become increasingly blurred and it is nowadays generally accepted that bank intermediation and capital market funding activities are complementary. Nevertheless, to understand better the different characteristics of the EU-15 banking systems, it is useful to address briefly the main typology that distinguishes the two common types of financial systems. These differences are also reflected in two main models of corporate governance: the more liberal Anglo-Saxon model and the more concentrated Continental model.

In a bank-based system, banks are the most important source of external financing for firms, although to a various extent. Bank–client relationships are close and the universal banking model is widespread. Informational barriers are more significant, as incumbent banks have informational advantages over new entrants (Petersen and Rajan, 1994; Dell'Ariccia, 2001; Hauswald and Marquez, 2006). In countries where the universal banking model prevails, the share of foreign ownership is lower, consistent with the idea that entry is more difficult (Steinherr and Huveneers, 1994; Affinito and Piazza, 2008). The corporate governance regime is pluralistic and mainly stakeholder-oriented, and allows different stakeholder groups to play an active governance role. Ownership is often concentrated and corporations tend to be controlled by large shareholders (including banks).

In a market-based system, on the other hand, capital markets usually are the main sources of firm financing. Bank–client relationships are typically at arm's length and thus have less contractual flexibility than relationship-based finance. Even though universal banking activities are allowed in all EU countries following the implementation of the Second Banking Directive (89/646/EEC) (European Council, 1989), market-based systems tend to favour bank specialization, either by law or by tradition. In addition, in market-based countries, non-bank financial intermediaries also play an important role. Corporate governance is shareholder-oriented rather than stakeholder-oriented, ownership tends to be dispersed and the mechanism of management control relies mostly on market forces.

Llewellyn (2006) considers two further dimensions when describing the different structures of EU banking systems: shareholder value models (SHV) and stakeholder value models (STV). The former is based on the notion that banks are primarily firms whose main objective is to maximize shareholder value. In contrast, in the STV model, a bank has many stakeholders and profit maximization, while important, is not necessarily the exclusive, or even primary, objective of bank management. This distinction is also a reflection of cultural difference: the SHV model is typical of Anglo-Saxon systems while the more general STV model is found in continental Europe, where there is a legacy of state ownership, pluralist ownership structure is more prevalent and the market in corporate control is less active.

In terms of EU banking systems integration, until 2007 the trend was towards a degree of convergence in the direction of a more market-based approach with emphasis on return on equity (ROE) maximization. Post-crisis, because of the vast losses and the substantial government intervention in the banking sectors across the EU, there is little public support for banks returning ROE ratios of well above 20 per cent, as these have mostly proved to be unsustainable (ECB, 2010). The emphasis is now to ensure that bank profitability is 'sustainable' and returns to investors are 'fair'.

In this context, the pluralistic structure of EU banking systems, the varied nature of corporate governance arrangements and different business models represent a strength of the EU. In the remainder of this chapter we will present a brief analysis of EU banking structures and corporate governance arrangements to identify factors that might contribute to the emergence of a truly European banking model as well as factors that may increase the existing segmentation of EU banking markets.

31.2.1   EU Banking Structure

National banking systems within the EU vary considerably in terms of bank size, types of banks and ownership structure. Table 31.1 illustrates the main structural characteristics of the EU-15 banking sectors in the year 2009. Market differences are apparent, in terms of both number of banks and overall size of the banking sector. Larger countries, such as Germany, Italy and the United Kingdom, have more fragmented markets; whereas smaller countries, such as the Netherlands, Finland and Greece, are characterized by more concentrated banking sectors.

Table 31.2 illustrates the breakdown of each country's banking sector total assets into size groups and into domestic (large, medium-sized and small banks) and foreign-controlled branches and subsidiaries.[9] Large banks dominate the banking sector in the UK, Sweden, the Netherlands and France, whereas no bank passes the 'large' threshold

Table 31.1   EU banking structure

	No. of banks	No. of branches	No. of employees	Total assets (EUR millions)	HHI	CR5
AT	790	4167	77246	1036597	414	37.2
BE	104	4316*	65985*	1155506	1622	77.1
DK	164	1996	50101	1104536	1042	64.0
FI	349	1538	24879	387630	3120	82.6
FR	712	38479	492367*	7155460	605	47.2
DE	1948	39411	685550*	7423967	206	25.0
GR	66	4078	65673	490134	1184	69.2
IE	498	1228	38178	1323584	881	58.8
IT	801	34035	322575	3691965	353	34.0
LU	147	229*	26416	797460	288	27.8
NL	295	3137	110000	2217008	2032	85.0
PT	166	6430	62221	520188	1150	70.1
ES	352	44431	267383	3433283	507	43.3
SE	180	2147	49071	934534	899	60.7
UK	389	12360	471095	9420998	467	40.8

Notes:
AT = Austria; BE = Belgium; DK = Denmark; FI = Finland; FR = France; DE = Germany; GR = Greece; IE = Ireland; IT = Italy; LU = Luxembourg; NL = Netherlands; PT = Portugal; ES = Spain; SE = Sweden; UK = United Kingdom. HHI = Herfindahl Index. CR5 = five-firm concentration ratio.
All values refer to the year 2009. * denotes 2008 values when 2009 figures are not available.

Source: European Central Bank (2010).

definition of the European Central Bank (ECB) in Austria, Finland, Greece, Ireland, Luxembourg and Portugal.[10] Indeed, British banks account for nearly 18 per cent of the total consolidated assets of EU banks, followed by German and French banks, with 13 per cent and 15 per cent respectively.

A large share of the domestic banking sector in some EU countries is foreign-owned, particularly in Ireland, Belgium, Finland and Luxembourg. Traditionally, foreign banks specialized in the commercial and wholesale markets, but in recent years they have made significant acquisitions in the retail banking business.

In terms of banking models, the EU banking landscape is dominated by large universal banking groups that have also considerable activities abroad; over the last two decades EU large banks have grown in size and have broadened geographically and in terms of products offered. Although both diversified and specialized banks were affected by losses, write-downs and recapitalizations during the crisis, diversified institutions have proven to be more resilient, possibly owing to clearer synergies between private, retail, corporate and investment banking. Also, diversified or universal banks are based on strong bank–customer relationships and more stable sources of funding (deposits), making them on average better able to withstand liquidity shocks (ECB, 2010).

Recent developments therefore support the view that the universal banking model will gain further importance within the EU, although the development will be shaped by the new regulatory framework implementing stricter capital and liquidity requirements.

Table 31.2   EU bank size groups (domestic and foreign banks)

	Total assets of credit institutions (EUR millions)			
	Large	Medium	Small	Foreign-controlled
AT	0	747	121	272
BE	514	75	2	600
DK	592	108	41	164
FI	0	103	15	264
FR	5849	249	4	215
DE	5057	1976	607	77
GR	0	385	1	104
IE	0	517	0	822
IT	1747	656	12	236
LU	0	86	5	783
NL	2149	379	2	118
PT	0	396	6	109
ES	2073	1291	44	333
SE	1105	109	8	3
UK	6941	326	32	2352

Notes: Data are based on the consolidated banking data (CBD) provided by members of the Banking Supervision Committee. The CBD data cover nearly 100% of the EU banking sector. Large domestic banks are defined as banks with assets totalling more than 0.5% of the total consolidated assets of EU banks, whereas medium-sized banks have total assets of between 0.005% and 0.5% of total consolidated assets. Banks with total assets of less than 0.005% of total consolidated assets are considered small. The total consolidated assets for the year 2010 are €39 589 billion. Foreign banks are defined as subsidiaries and branches that are controlled by either an EU or a non-EU parent that is 'foreign' from the reporting country's point of view (ECB, 2010).

The next step is to investigate whether a particular corporate governance structure also appears to support a banking model that has proven more favourable to financial stability.

31.3   BANK CORPORATE GOVERNANCE IN THE EU-15

To analyse the corporate governance features of EU banks, we collected an original dataset which includes data on all listed commercial banks and bank holding companies (BHCs) incorporated in a EU-15 country as at June 2009.[11] We restrict the analysis to banks with comparable corporate governance structures, and therefore we exclude co-operative, savings, private and Islamic banks. These exclusions do not prevent full sample representativeness for our specific purposes: the aggregate market capitalization of the banks in the sample accounts for more than 96 per cent of the total EU-15 bank market capitalization (see Table 31A.1 in the Appendix).

Table 31.3 illustrates the main features of our sample. While our main focus is on EU banks, for comparative purposes we also collected information on a sample of over 800 US-listed, US incorporated banks. Our final EU-15 sample is composed of 165 observations, of which 114 are commercial banks and 51 are bank holding companies.[12] Adams

Table 31.3 Sample features: by country, legal system and language family

	Number of banks (percentage)	Number of BHCs (percentage)	Total number of observations
Country			
AT	2	3	5
	40%	*60%*	
BE	–	6	6
	0%	*100%*	
DE	18	1	19
	95%	*5%*	
DK	33	2	35
	94%	*6%*	
ES	8	1	9
	89%	*11%*	
FI	2	3	5
	40%	*60%*	
FR	20	3	23
	87%	*13%*	
GR	9	3	12
	75%	*25%*	
IE	–	1	1
	0%	*100%*	
IT	17	4	21
	81%	*19%*	
LU	–	2	2
	0%	*100%*	
NL	2	5	7
	29%	*71%*	
PT	1	4	5
	20%	*80%*	
SE	2	2	4
	50%	*50%*	
UK	–	11	11
	0%	*100%*	
Overall EU	114	51	165
	69%	*31%*	
US	133	740	873
	15%	*85%*	
Legal system			
Civil law	114	39	153
	75%	*25%*	
Common law	–	12	12
	0%	*100%*	
Language family			
Romance	46	14	60
	77%	*23%*	
English	–	12	12
	0%	*100%*	

Table 31.3   (continued)

	Number of banks (percentage)	Number of BHCs (percentage)	Total number of observations
Language family			
German	22	15	37
	59%	*41%*	
Nordic	37	7	44
	84%	*16%*	
Greek	9	3	12
	75%	*25%*	
Proximity			
Southern Europe	35	12	47
	74%	*26%*	
Anglo-Saxon countries	–	12	12
	0%	*100%*	
Continental Europe	42	20	62
	68%	*32%*	
Nordic countries	37	7	44
	84%	*16%*	

and Mehran (2008) argue that the organizational structure of a bank may have a significant impact on corporate governance features. This is because holding companies often have complicated hierarchical structures through their ownership or control of banks and other subsidiaries, each separately chartered with its own board. Thus, it is plausible that the coordination of activities across subsidiaries occurs through these boards. This seems particularly relevant in countries such as the US and the UK where publicly traded banks are all organized as BHCs.

In an attempt to relate the corporate governance features of EU banks not only to the country of origin but also to cultural features that some EU countries may share, we further analyse the sample by origin of the legal system and language family. The notion that corporate governance is influenced by cultural values is largely accepted by economic theorists, policymakers and market practitioners (Stulz and Williamson, 2003; Beck et al., 2003; Pagano and Volpin, 2005; Guiso et al., 2006, 2009; Tabellini, 2010).

Referring to the vast literature on the links among legal systems, institutional environment and corporate governance structures, La Porta et al. (1999) indicated that the efficiency of corporate governance rules differs between legal traditions and showed that common law countries have stronger legal protection of investor rights than civil-law countries. Empirical research indicates, for example, that the Anglo-Saxon system of common law proves more efficient in protecting shareholders' rights (La Porta et al., 2002; Gugler et al., 2003). Laws in different countries are typically not written from scratch, but rather taken from a few legal families or traditions (La Porta et al., 1998). Two broad traditions may be identified: common law, which is prevalent in Anglo-Saxon countries; and civil law, which developed from Roman law. Nowadays, the resulting legal systems reflect both the influence of these two traditions and the changes introduced by individual countries over time. La Porta et al.'s (1998) classification of countries' legal systems has become a standard reference; we therefore divide the EU-15 countries according to the origin of their legal system into common-law countries (the UK and Ireland) and civil-law countries (the remaining 13 countries).[13]

To classify countries by language family, we adopt the official language classification by Haveman[14] and identify five main linguistic areas: Romance, English, German, Nordic and Greek. We then cluster EU countries according to their linguistic origin: Romance (i.e., languages that derive from Vulgar Latin) in the case of Spain, France, Italy, Portugal and Luxembourg; English in the case of Ireland and the UK; and German (i.e., languages that derive from Western German) for Germany, Austria, the Netherlands and Belgium. We then form a fourth group (Nordic) to include those countries not belonging to one of the above-mentioned linguistic areas (Denmark, Finland and Sweden). These countries should be separated according to their different origin (Nordic and Finno-Ugric); nevertheless it would add an excessive fragmentation to the analysis. We finally separate Greece, as the Greek language does not share its origin with any of the above-mentioned groups.

We further group countries according to their geographical proximity. The geographical distance between two countries and their proximity can have significant effects on bilateral trust, affecting both economic and financial exchanges (Guiso et al., 2009). We thus identify four main groups according to their proximity: (1) Southern Europe, which includes Portugal, Spain, Italy and Greece; (2) Anglo-Saxon countries (Ireland and the UK); (3) continental Europe – Austria, Belgium, France, Germany, Luxembourg and the Netherlands; and (4) the Nordic countries group – Denmark, Finland and Sweden.

In the remainder of this chapter we apply these cultural classifications to the analysis of corporate governance features, with reference to both the characteristics of the board and the characteristics of the chief executive officer (CEO). In particular, as far as the features of the board are concerned we look at board size, type of board (one-tier versus two-tier) and average board tenure. In addition, to account for cultural characteristics and board diversity, we consider the presence of women, employees, external and other firms' representatives as well as the presence of international board members. For the CEO, we consider age, gender, average tenure in the bank and average tenure in the sector. We also gathered information on whether the CEO holds an MBA, and was previously employed in the same bank or in the financial sector.

31.3.1   Main Features of Boards of Directors in EU Banks

The size and composition of the board of directors constitute the two dimensions of board structure that have been studied most extensively. Improving board structure is one of the core objectives of corporate governance initiatives undertaken by international regulators (OECD, 2004; Basel Committee, 2006, 2010).

Board size
Several studies have hypothesized a negative correlation between board size and firm performance (Jensen, 1993; Hermalin and Weisbach, 2003). As board size increases, boards become less effective at monitoring management because of free-riding problems amongst directors and increased decision-making time. In the financial services industry, though,

Table 31.4   Board size and specifications: by country, legal system and language family

	Size (avg)	1-tier board (%)	2-tier board (%)	Average board length of tenure (years)
Country				
AT	19.6	20	80	6.2
BE	15.8	67	33	6.0
DE	13.6	12	88	3.6
DK	11.2	58	42	5.2
ES	13.8	89	11	7.0
FI	10.5	50	50	4.7
FR	18.1	43	57	6.1
GR	14.3	33	67	2.1
IE	21.0	100		3.0
IT	17.8	38	62	3.3
LU	14.0	100		5.4
NL	12.0	100		3.5
PT	18.8	60	40	6.7
SE	23.8	25	75	3.8
UK	15.3	64	36	3.6
Overall EU	15.2	44	56	4.5
US	12.9	89	11	8.2
Legal system				
Civil law	15.2	42	58	4.6
Common law	15.8	58	42	3.6
Language family				
Romance	17.2	53	47	5.1
English	15.8	58	42	3.6
German	14.5	20	80	4.4
Nordic	12.6	53	47	5.0
Greek	14.3	33	67	2.1
Proximity				
Southern Europe	16.2	49	51	4.0
Anglo-Saxon countries	15.8	58	42	3.6
Continental Europe	15.8	29	71	4.8
Nordic countries	12.6	53	47	5.0

the negative relationship between board size and bank performance seems not to hold and overall results are mixed. Possible explanations rely on regulatory issues, on informational asymmetries and on organizational structure (Eisenberg et al., 1998; Spong and Sullivan, 2007; Adams and Mehran, 2003, 2008; Andrés and Vallelado, 2008).

The mean size of a board in the banking sector ranges from 16 to 18 directors (Adams and Mehran, 2008; Andrés and Vallelado, 2008). In our sample of EU-15 listed banks, board size is 15 members on average. As illustrated in Table 31.4, differences at the country level are relevant. Swedish banks have the largest boards, with approximately 24 members, followed by Irish banks (21) and Austrian banks (19). Finnish banks, on the other hand, have the smallest boards (10.5 members on average), followed by Danish and Dutch banks (11.2 and 12 members on average).

One-tier versus two-tier board

Looking at board specification, differences among European countries are relevant. A first distinction is between one- and two-tier boards.[15] Broadly speaking, in a one-tier structure the board performs all tasks, while in a two-tier structure advisory and monitoring functions are carried out separately. While a one-tier structure is thought to favour information sharing, a two-tier structure can minimize interference from large shareholders (Adams and Ferreira, 2007). Therefore a two-tier board may have developed as a valuable option in continental Europe where firm ownership is more concentrated. The two-tier structure is predominant in Germany and was recently adopted by some Italian banks. On the other hand, a sole board is prevalent in Anglo-Saxon countries, where the emphasis is on board independence through the presence of external directors (Hermalin and Weisbach, 2003).

Table 31.4 illustrates the breakdown of board specification by country, legal system, language family and proximity. Fifty-six per cent of the banks in the sample have a two-tier board system. The preference for a dual board system is confirmed in civil-law countries, whereas a sole board system prevails in common-law countries. In the US, 88.5 per cent of banks adopt a one-tier board. In the EU sample, country-specific differences are relevant. In Austria, Germany and Sweden more than 75 per cent of banks have a two-tier board. In contrast, a one-tier board has been chosen by 100 per cent of banks in Ireland, Luxembourg and the Netherlands. Interestingly, 89 per cent of Spanish banks favour a one-tier board. In recent years, Spanish banks have been particularly active in the UK banking market, characterized by one-tier board prevalence. Looking at language families, German-speaking countries predominantly choose two-tier boards (80 per cent) for their banks.

Average length of tenure

The second board specification of interest is the average length of tenure.[16] Longer tenure may have a positive effect on bank corporate governance, leading to major stability and deeper knowledge of the bank's business model. This could help the board to carry out better both the advisory and the monitoring tasks. In addition, as longer tenure is linked to higher entrenchment, an established board should be able to counterbalance a CEO's power more effectively. However, longer tenure can also signal lower board dynamism (Shleifer and Vishny, 1997). Despite the potential relevance, factors determining the board length of tenure and turnover have received less attention in the literature compared to other board features. Reasons include that the composition of the board changes only moderately over time. Turnover is also influenced by the rules for election to the board (e.g., proposal from previous board; nomination by the CEO or by a nomination committee). Yermack (2004) documents a positive correlation between board turnover and CEO turnover, thus casting doubts on inference drawn on the correlation between board turnover and firm performance. Interestingly, he also documents significantly lower turnover rates for female directors, while Faleye (2007) finds that electing boards on staggered terms has no significant effect on board turnover. Del Guercio et al. (2008) find that firms attacked by activist investors (for example mutual funds and private investment groups) experience a higher level of director turnover.

Average tenure of bank boards in the EU-15 is four and a half years. In the US, on average directors remain in charge nearly twice as long (8.2 years). In civil-law countries tenure is longer compared to common-law countries (4.6 versus 3.6 years). Countries belonging to the Romance language group have the longest tenure in the EU (5.1 years) whereas English-speaking countries have the shortest length of tenure (3.6 years). Looking at proximity, Nordic countries have the longest tenure, whereas Anglo-Saxon countries still remain at the bottom of the ranking. Once again differences among countries are striking: length of tenure ranges from seven years in Spain to two years in Greece.

Board composition and board diversity

Board composition is another relevant board feature, crucial to aligning the interests of management and shareholders (Hermalin and Weisbach, 2003). The composition of boards varies according to the representation of insiders, outsiders, shareholders or stakeholders, which have different monitoring capacities and interests. The literature has focused mainly on the relative proportion of non-executive directors and outside directors, including other firm representatives, employees' representatives and external members. More recently, board diversity has become the focus of public debate as well as academic research, with the emphasis towards fostering gender diversity, together with ethnic diversity and age dispersion of board members. The main argument to support diversity is that a more diverse management team tends to be more creative, more innovative and, when making decisions, may consider a wider range of alternatives. In addition, more diverse boards should protect minorities, guarantee that differing opinions are taken into account, and be harder to manipulate. However, diversity may also bring costs: heterogeneous boards may be less efficient; the decision-making process may be slower and the likelihood of reaching consensus may be smaller (Carter et al., 2003, 2010).

As women directors add to the diversity of the board, their inclusion can also have mixed outcomes. Although the literature on the impact of women's presence on the boards of directors of banks is still in its infancy, Mateos de Cabo et al. (2009) indicate that women are less likely to appear on smaller boards and where a preference for homogeneity is stronger. In other words, homogeneous boards that are male-dominated will continue holding back the access of women to top positions in banks. As a consequence, they suggest that cultural differences explain part of the heterogeneity in the presence of women on the boards, and that differences among European countries are significant. In general, empirical studies focusing on firm demand for female directors underline the role of the country's socio-political beliefs and attitudes towards women, work and families, the gender-historical role in the government, and public and private initiatives in increasing the possibility of individual women's career progression (Terjesen et al., 2009).

Differences in board composition in EU banks are illustrated in Table 31.5. In European bank boards, other firms' representatives and external members usually account for around 15 per cent of the board members, while women and employee representatives are respectively 9 and 7 per cent. EU banks include a wider array of representatives in their boards compared to US banks. External and other firm representatives are present in Spain and Luxembourg (51 and more than 20 per cent of board members).

Table 31.5   Board features: by country, legal system and language family

	External members (%)	Women (%)	Employees' representatives (%)	Other firms' representatives (%)	International boards (%)
Country					
AT	0	11	26	19	40
BE	21	11	0	12	67
DE	0	8	25	26	29
DK	3	12	18	2	4
ES	51	10	0	51	22
FI	26	14	2	14	
FR	8	12	2	12	26
GR	20	9	2	10	17
IE	5	14	0	10	
IT	24	4	0	13	29
LU	25	0	0	21	50
NL	0	6	0	8	14
PT	12	3	0	28	60
SE	18	19	7	7	25
UK	32	11	0	7	70
Overall EU	15	9	7	15	27
US	3	12	7	0	8
Legal system					
Civil law	14	9	7	15	24
Common law	29	11	0	7	64
Language family					
Romance	20	8	1	19	30
English	29	11	0	7	64
German	4	9	16	19	34
Nordic	9	14	14	4	6
Greek	20	9	2	10	17
Proximity					
Southern Europe	26	6	0	20	28
Anglo-Saxon countries	29	11	0	7	64
Continental Europe	6	10	10	16	32
Nordic countries	9	14	14	4	6

The presence of other firms' representatives is usually associated to bank cross-holdings; hence a higher percentage is noticeable in those EU countries such as Austria, Germany and Portugal where cross-holdings are common practice.

Heterogeneity in board composition may be also partially explained by differences in legal systems: in common-law countries board diversity seems greater in terms of external and women members (29 and 11 per cent versus 14 and 9 per cent). In contrast, employee and other firm representatives are present predominantly in countries with civil-law systems (7 and 15 per cent versus 0 and 7 per cent). These differences may be caused by existing laws; in some EU countries regulations guarantee a minimum presence of employee and other firm representatives on boards of directors.[17] As a consequence, in Austria and Germany the average number of employee representatives is more than twice the average of all other European countries.

Cultural differences among countries in terms of board diversity can also be identified by looking at language families and proximity. As can be seen from Tables 31.4 and 31.5, in German-speaking countries the average size of a board of directors is 14.5 members, which includes employee representatives (16 per cent) and other firms' representatives (21 per cent) but few external representatives. In English-speaking countries, on the other hand, board size is slightly larger (15.8 members on average), and includes external representatives (29 per cent) and women (11 per cent) but no employees' representatives. As expected, in Southern European countries (which are often under the spotlight for perceived gender inequalities in the workplace due to more traditional cultural values), women's presence is below the EU average (although this is not the case in Spain). In Nordic countries, on the other hand, we find the largest presence of women on boards, greater than in English-speaking countries, including the US.

Table 31.5 also illustrates a proxy for the cultural diversity of the board. In this context, we measure cultural diversity by the number of nationalities represented by board members. This spans from one (i.e., all directors are nationals of one country and no foreign directors are present) in Finland and Ireland, to seven different nationalities (in Italy). Among the EU-15 countries, only Belgium, Portugal and the UK have a prevalence of multicultural boards (67, 60 and 70 per cent of banks have foreign board members). In contrast, Denmark, Greece and the Netherlands have a prevalence of domestic board members (only 4, 17 and 14 per cent of banks have international members, respectively). Multicultural board members can increase board diversity and therefore add new perspectives to board discussions. However, cultural misunderstanding and mistrust may occur and cause inefficiency in board meetings. These cultural biases are so rooted that they affect even the equity portfolio allocation of professional investors in equity funds (Guiso et al., 2006).

English-speaking countries host the higher number of multicultural boards (63.6 per cent). Nordic countries have the least international boards (6 per cent). Interestingly, Southern and continental Europe show similar patterns (28 versus 32 per cent of banks with international boards). Even if European Union laws guarantee the free movement of workers within the EU (Article 30 EU Treaty), cultural barriers such as differences in languages still prevent full board internationalization. English-speaking countries seem to represent the preferred destination for the foreign workforce (including high-flying international bankers). To compare the EU and the US, almost all US banks have fully domestic boards (only 8 per cent of banks have foreign board members). A possible explanation relies on different immigration policies. In the US, immigrants have to apply for work visas, and green card applications can be part of the hiring package. In the EU, working visas are required only for non-EU citizens.

31.3.2   CEO Features in European Banking

This section of the analysis concentrates on the impact of CEO features for corporate governance. Bank CEOs are key decision-makers and their personal attributes and behavioural biases (for example risk-aversion or overconfidence) affect both the quality of the information available to the board of directors and corporate investment decisions (Adams and Ferreira, 2007; Malmendier and Tate, 2005, 2008; Goel and Thakor, 2008).

The managerial power hypothesis argues that CEOs may be able to control board decisions due to higher managerial influence.[18] This situation is more likely to arise where shareholding is dispersed and passive; where boards are large and heterogeneous; and where CEOs are older, and with longer tenure in the bank. This may exacerbate the agency problem, since the board becomes less effective in monitoring CEO behaviour. Adams et al. (2005) argue that in firms run by powerful CEOs – that is, those who can consistently influence board decisions – the risk of judgement errors is higher, thus increasing the variability of firm performance. There is a vast literature on managerial compensation in the financial sector and its impact on managerial decision-making and risk-taking (John and Qian, 2003; Chen et al., 2006). More recently, the emphasis has been on the role of managerial compensation in the recent financial crisis, but results are mixed (Fahlenbrach and Stulz, 2009; Beltratti and Stulz, 2009; DeYoung et al., 2009; Erkens et al., 2009; Chesney et al., 2010).

To investigate CEO features in EU banking we refer to the following variables: age, gender, average tenure in the bank, average tenure in the financial sector, education (MBA) and career trajectory, as illustrated in Table 31.6.

European banks' CEOs are on average 56 years old, similarly to US banks' CEOs. CEO career trajectories are mostly internally focused (employee to executive): 52 per cent of CEOs have been previously employed in the same bank. The average tenure in the bank (as employee as well as CEO) is ten years and the average length of employment in the banking sector is almost 29 years. EU banks' CEOs therefore have long-standing expertise in the industry, which is likely to provide them with reputation and power. In Belgium, Finland, Luxembourg, Portugal and Ireland more than 80 per cent of bank CEOs are promoted internally. This guarantees continuity in bank management policy and culture, resulting in longer tenure and lower turnover. Internal managerial promotion and CEO succession planning are important strategic decisions for companies, as they affect managerial incentives, firm valuation and CEO entrenchment. However, insider CEOs may have increased control over the board of directors and this may hinder change.

Another variable that can both increase CEO control over the board of directors and hinder change is CEO age. On average, older CEOs with longer tenure are, *ceteris paribus*, more powerful. In Austria and Portugal, bank CEOs are on average 62 years of age, with long tenure both in the bank and in the financial sector (more than 20 and more than 32 years, respectively). On the other hand, relatively younger bank CEOs are found in Finland, Ireland and Sweden (50 years old or younger, on average). Italian banks have relatively young CEOs (53 years old, on average), despite the fact that CEO tenure is below the EU average. A possible explanation may be that a relatively higher percentage of CEOs (38 per cent) are outsiders rather than internal promotions. Interestingly, banks in English-speaking countries not only have on average older CEOs, but also have CEOs with the longest tenure in the sector (34 years). Furthermore, 75 per cent of CEOs are internally hired. As internal career advancement is notoriously slower, banks in English-speaking countries have far more entrenched and conservative CEOs on average than other EU countries.

Table 31.6   CEO features: by country, legal system and language family

	Average CEO's age	Average tenure in the bank at 2010 (years)	Average tenure in the sector at 2010 (years)	CEO previously employed in the same bank (%)	CEO previously employed in the banking sector (%)	MBA (%)	Female CEO (%)
Country							
AT	62	28.5	38.0	60	60	0	0
BE	63	10.2	33.3	83	100	17	0
DE	57	8.6	30.3	42	42	5	0
DK	53	10.7	30.0	31	40	0	0
ES	58	15.7	33.8	78	67	33	0
FI	47	10.3	14.0	80	60	20	0
FR	57	5.8	26.6	35	22	4	4
GR	62	8.0	20.8	42	50	25	0
IE	50	2.0		100	100	100	0
IT	53	9.7	28.6	62	62	19	0
LU	55	9.0	28.5	100	50	0	0
NL	53	6.4	23.3	43	86	14	0
PT	62	20.4	32.0	80	60	0	0
SE	47	11.8	20.5	75	75	0	25
UK	59	7.9	34.7	73	73	27	9
Overall EU	56.1	10.4	28.7	52	52	12	2
US	56.6	15.7	30.4	64	61	14	2
Legal system							
Civil law	54.3	5.0	34.7	86	86	64	5
Common law	56.0	11.9	27.7	62	59	11	2
Language family							
Romance	56.0	10.9	29.5	57	47	13	2
English	57.8	7.4	34.7	75	75	33	8
German	58.3	11.3	30.2	51	62	8	0
Nordic	50.8	10.8	23.6	41	45	2	2
Greek	62.1	8.0	20.8	42	50	25	0
Proximity							
Southern Europe	57.2	12.0	28.2	62	60	21	0
Anglo-Saxon countries	57.8	7.4	34.7	75	75	33	8
Continental Europe	57.7	9.6	29.2	47	47	6	2
Nordic countries	50.8	10.8	23.6	41	45	2	2

The proportion of women reaching top positions is still very low in most EU countries: only 2 per cent of European bank CEOs are women, the same representation as in the US. Sweden (with 25 per cent women CEOs), the UK (9 per cent) and France (4 per cent) are the only European countries above the average. In absolute terms, 'Latin-speaking' countries have the same number of women CEOs as Nordic and English-speaking countries.

However, confirming commonly held beliefs about the role of women in the workplace in Southern Europe, there are no female bank CEOs. This evidence reflects the mixed results in the literature. Given the fact that not all banks have women in senior positions, it is difficult to identify the relationship between female participation and firm performance. Levi et al. (2008) examine whether the gender of CEOs or corporate directors plays a role in the pricing of and returns on mergers and acquisitions. Their results suggest differential abilities of men versus women in discovery of target company values, with women appearing to be able to reach more realistic values. Huang and Kisgen (2009) analyse whether men and women differ in corporate financial decisions. They find that acquisitions made by female CEO firms have significantly higher announcement returns, and argue that women appear to undertake greater scrutiny and exhibit less hubris in acquisition decisions. While the academic literature may recognize the benefits of female participation in firms' top management, this recognition is still poorly reflected in the actual appointments.

Without entering the debate as to whether an MBA makes a better CEO, we collected data on specialized postgraduate qualifications. On average, 12 per cent of EU bank CEOs hold an MBA. In the US this percentage is slightly higher (14 per cent). MBAs are popular among bank top executives in Ireland, Spain and the UK: over 27 per cent of CEOs hold an MBA. This may be the case because both Spain and the UK host the highest-ranked business schools in Europe.[19] Usually firms can better gauge the value of an MBA qualification if the business school awarding the degree has a strong reputation in the same country where the firm's prevalent business and headquarters are located. It may also be the case that MBA students pursue careers in the same country where they obtain their qualifications. This may be particularly the case for the UK, currently the most developed financial market in the EU. MBAs are popular in English-speaking countries, where 33 per cent of CEOs hold the qualification compared to 8 per cent of CEOs in German-speaking countries and 2 per cent of CEOs in Nordic countries. This result points to the higher relevance attached to MBA education in Anglo-Saxon countries and in Southern Europe.

31.4   CONCLUSIONS

Despite the EU efforts towards financial integration and the creation of a EU banking model, our survey of the corporate governance features of banking institutions in the EU-15 countries indicates that country-specific characteristics still play an important role. Working on the notion that corporate governance is influenced by cultural values, we have presented an analysis clustering EU countries on the basis of their legal system, language family and proximity as indicators of cultural differences.

The standard classification of a more market-based Anglo-Saxon system versus a more bank-based continental European system seems to be still prevalent in shaping corporate governance arrangements. Looking at board characteristics, a two-tier board is the predominant structure in continental Europe (particularly in German-speaking countries). On the other hand, a sole board is prevalent in Anglo-Saxon countries and, interestingly, in Spain.

In continental European civil-law countries board tenure is longer, and boards are more heterogeneous but less multicultural. CEOs tend to be younger and to have followed an external career path to the top job. In English-speaking, common-law countries, boards are slightly larger, board tenure is shorter, and boards are less diverse in terms of employees' and other firms' representatives, but include a larger proportion of external representatives, women and foreign members. CEOs are on average older. Furthermore, the majority of CEOs are internally hired and a significant proportion hold an MBA.

Cultural and legal differences are still strongly embedded in national cultural identities and these seem to drive the majority of differences in corporate governance arrangements. Prior to the crisis, it was possible to notice a certain degree of convergence towards a more market-based, shareholder value-oriented model. The financial crisis has reversed this trend and brought about a revival of more traditional banking models. On the other hand there are signs that this reversal may only be temporary, as increased labour mobility, standardized postgraduate specialized MBA courses and the emergence of more diverse and multicultural boards may act as a catalyst to reduce structural and cultural differences within the EU.

The sole common feature of both Anglo-Saxon and continental European countries seems to be the under-representation of women on boards. The proportion of women CEOs of EU banks is only 2 per cent, the same as in the US. However, some interesting insights can be drawn from cultural classifications. Firstly, differences among language families do not fully reflect commonly held beliefs. 'Latin-speaking' countries have more women and more international representatives on bank boards than German-speaking countries, and equivalent numbers to Nordic countries. Southern Europe also has banks with younger CEOs compared to both continental and Anglo-Saxon peers.

We would have expected stronger similarities between 'Latin'- and German-speaking countries, since both have adopted a universal banking model. However, individual countries' banking systems have shaped it according to their different requirements and backgrounds. Similarities can be found in terms of CEOs' features, but there are noticeable differences in terms of board size and board structure, where 'Latin-speaking' countries display features closer to the Anglo-Saxon model rather than to the traditional continental European universal banking model. This is also reflected in differences in the percentages of external and employees' representatives. It seems that a third possible model, combining features of the two baselines models, has emerged in a number of EU countries.

NOTES

*   This work forms part on an ongoing research project on Governance, Risk and Performance in European Banking. The authors gratefully acknowledge financial support from Cass Business School, City University London Pump Priming Scheme. While the chapter is the result of intense collaboration between the two authors, sections 31.1 and 31.2 are attributable to B. Casu and section 31.3 to F. Arnaboldi. Section 31.4 is a joint effort.
1. World Economic Outlook Database (IMF, 2010).
2. There is a vast literature on EU financial integration. Freixas et al. (2004) review the objectives of the Financial Services Action Plan (FSAP) to integrate European financial markets. Most studies find some evidence of integration in money, bond and equity markets and in wholesale banking (Emiris, 2002; Cabral et al., 2002; Hartmann et al., 2003; Baele et al., 2004; Manna, 2004; Guiso et al., 2004; Cappiello

et al., 2006). However, most empirical evidence suggests that significant barriers to the integration of retail banking markets still exist, driven mainly by cultural and political differences (Berger, 2003; Berger et al., 2003; Heuchemer et al., 2009). Gropp and Kashyap (2009) propose a new test of integration based on convergence in banks' profitability (return on assets, ROA) while Casu and Girardone (2010) propose the use of efficiency measures.

3. Guiso et al. (2006) define culture as customary beliefs and values that ethnic, religious and social groups transmit fairly unchanged from generation to generation. In other words, it refers to those inherited, long-standing traditions, or 'slow-moving' components of culture that remain fairly unaltered during an individual's lifetime. These include commonality of religion, commonality of language, somatic and genetic distance, and geographic proximity. In addition, there are factors that may capture more recent aspects of cultural tradition but unlikely to be substantially altered during an individual's lifetime (hence contributing to their cultural norms); these include the origin of the legal system, a country's history of wars and history of political institutions (Guiso et al., 2006, 2009; La Porta et al., 1997; Tabellini, 2010). A full analysis of the different components of culture is outside the scope of this chapter. Nevertheless, cultural factors may affect corporate governance features. Consequently, we attempt to include a cultural perspective in our analysis, as detailed in section 31.3.

4. See also De Larosière Group (2009) report.

5. The impact of the financial crisis on the Italian banking system has been relatively moderate compared to other countries. Italian banks have largely remained focused on traditional retail operations and corporate lending, relying on customer deposits to fund day-to-day operations. Because of the limited presence in their balance sheets of the assets hit hardest by the crisis and their lower dependence on wholesale funding, Italian banks mostly avoided the huge losses and publicly funded bailouts (Bank of Italy, 2010).

6. On 1 May 2004, Cyprus, the Czech Republic, Estonia, Hungary, Latvia, Lithuania, Malta, Poland, Slovenia and the Slovak Republic joined the European Union. Bulgaria and Romania joined in 2007.

7. Although standards of living have improved considerably over the past decade (in the new member states, income per capita rose from 40 per cent of the old member states' average in 1999 to 52 per cent in 2008) significant differences among member states remain (European Commission, 2009c).

8. For a review of the literature on comparative financial systems see Allen and Gale (1995, 2000a, 2000b) and Thakor (1996). For a review of banking structures in the EU, see Goddard at al. (2010).

9. The ECB defines foreign banks as subsidiaries and branches that are controlled by either an EU or a non-EU parent that is 'foreign' from the reporting country's point of view. The data for these institutions are excluded from the definition of the domestic banking sector (ECB, 2010).

10. 'Large' banks are defined as credit institutions with assets totalling more than 0.5 per cent of the total consolidated assets of EU banks. The total consolidated assets equalled €39 589 billion in 2009 and relates to the total consolidated assets of the EU-27 banks, as estimated by the European Central Bank (2010).

11. We considered all banks listed on a major stock exchange (NYSE Euronext, London Stock Exchange, Deutsche Börse, Mercado Continuo Espanol, Luxembourg Stock Exchange, Irish Stock Exchange, Athens Stock Exchange, NASDAQ OMX, Nordic Exchange and Wiener Börse). We also considered banks listed on additional stock exchanges in Europe (e.g., Berlin, Hamburg, Munich and Stuttgart Stock Exchanges; and Xetra). Data are gathered from Thomson OneBanker, a Fitch dataset which includes comparable market and accounting information on banks.

12. Following Bankscope's classification – a Fitch/Bureau Van Dijk dataset on banks' financial statements, and ratings – we define as commercial those banks mainly active in a combination of retail banking (individuals, small and medium-sized enterprises), wholesale banking (large corporates) and private banking and not belonging to groups of savings banks or co-operative banks; and as BHC the holding companies of banking groups.

13. It is common to distinguish civil law countries further in terms of French, German and Scandinavian legal origin. However, we do not adopt this further classification for the purpose of this analysis.

14. Following, among others, Guiso et al. (2006), we gather data from Jon Haveman's website, http://www. macalester.edu/research/economics/PAGE/HAVEMAN/Trade.Resources/TradeData.html.

15. In some countries this choice might be dictated by the existing regulatory framework.

16. Turnover is usually computed as one over the length of tenure and gives the probability of changing the board in the following year (Weisbach, 1988; Perry and Peyer, 2005).

17. *Mitbestimmung* (co-determination, i.e., the presence of workers on firms' boards) was introduced in Germany by law. Co-determination is regulated by three statutes for different sectors of the economy and sizes of company. The system which provides the most extensive form refers to the coal, iron and steel industry, governed by the 1951 Montan-Mitbestimmungsgesetz. Companies in other industries with between 501 and 1999 employees are covered by the corresponding provisions of the 1952 Betriebsverfassungsgesetz, under which employee representatives occupy only one-third of seats on the supervisory board. Lastly, the 1976 Mitbestimmungsgesetz covers all standard forms of company

normally employing more than 2000 employees. This provides for equal numbers of representatives from the employee side and the company side on the supervisory board, which consists of 12, 16 or 20 members according to the size of the company.
18.   On the role of CEO compensation in overcoming the agency problem see, among others, Oxelheim and Wihlborg (2008).
19.   According to the *Financial Times* Global MBA Rankings 2011, in the highest 20 positions, ten schools are based in the US, three in Spain, two in France, and one in the UK: http://rankings.ft.com/businessschool rankings/global-mba-rankings-2011.

REFERENCES

Adams, R.B., H. Almeida and D. Ferreira (2005), 'Powerful CEOs and their impact on corporate perform-ance', *Review of Financial Studies*, **18**(4), 1403–1432.
Adams, R.B. and D. Ferreira (2007), 'A theory of friendly boards', *Journal of Finance*, **64**(1), 217–250.
Adams, R.B. and H. Mehran (2003), 'Is corporate governance different for bank holding companies?' *Economic Policy Review*, Federal Reserve Bank of New York, April, 123–142.
Adams, R.B. and H. Mehran (2008), 'Corporate performance, board structure, and their determinants in the banking industry', FRB of New York Staff Report No. 330, June.
Affinito, M. and M. Piazza (2008), 'What are borders made of? An analysis of barriers to European banking integration', Banca d'Italia, Temi di Discussione, 666, April.
Allen, F. and D. Gale (1995), 'A welfare comparison of intermediaries and financial markets in Germany and the US', *European Economic Review*, **39**, 179–209.
Allen, F. and D. Gale (2000a), *Comparing Financial Systems*, Cambridge, MA: MIT Press.
Allen, F. and D. Gale (2000b), 'Corporate governance and competition', in X. Vives (ed.), *Corporate Governance: Theoretical and Empirical Perspectives*, Cambridge: Cambridge University Press.
Andrés, P. and E. Vallelado (2008), 'Corporate governance in banking: the role of the board of directors', *Journal of Banking and Finance*, **32**(12), 2570–2580.
Baele, L.M., A. Ferrando, P. Hordahl, E. Krylova and C. Monnet (2004), 'Measuring financial integration in the euro area', *Oxford Review of Economic Policy*, **20**, 509–530.
Bank of Italy (2010), 'Annual Report', May.
Basel Committee on Banking Supervision (2006), 'Enhancing corporate governance for banking organisa-tions', available at www.bis.org/publ/bcbs122.htm.
Basel Committee on Banking Supervision (2010), 'Consultative document – Principles for enhancing corporate governance', June, available at http://www.bis.org/publ/bcbs168.pdf.
Beck, T., R. Levine and N. Loayza (2003), 'Finance and the sources of growth', *Journal of Financial Economics*, **58**, 261–300.
Beltratti, A. and R.M. Stulz (2009), 'Why did some banks perform better during the credit crisis? A cross-country study of the impact of governance and regulation', NBER Working Papers 15180, National Bureau of Economic Research, July.
Berger, A.N. (2003), 'The efficiency effects of a single market for financial services in Europe', *European Journal of Operational Research*, **150**(3), 466–481.
Berger, A.N., Q. Dai, S. Ongena and D.C. Smith (2003), 'To what extent will the banking industry be glo-balized? A study of bank nationality and reach in 20 European nations', *Journal of Banking and Finance*, **27**(3), 383–415.
Cabral, I., F. Dierick and J. Vesala (2002), 'Banking integration in the euro area', ECB Occasional Paper Series 6.
Cappiello, L., P. Hordahl, A. Kadareja and S. Manganelli (2006), 'The impact of the euro on financial markets', ECB Working Paper 598.
Carter, D.A., F.P. D'Souza, B.J. Simkins and W.G. Simpson (2010), 'The gender and ethnic diversity of US boards and board committees and firm financial performance', *Corporate Governance*, **18**(5), 396–414.
Carter, D.A., B.J. Simkins and W.G. Simpson (2003), 'Corporate governance, board diversity and firm value', *Financial Review*, **38**(1), 33–53.
Casu, B. and C. Girardone (2010), 'Integration and efficiency convergence in EU banking markets', *OMEGA, The International Journal of Management Science*, **38**(5), 260–267.
Chen, C.R., T.L. Steiner and A.M. Whyte (2006), 'Does stock option-based executive compensation induce risk-taking? An analysis of the banking industry', *Journal of Banking and Finance*, **30**(3), 915–945.
Chesney, M., J. Stromberg and A.F. Wagner (2010), 'Risk-taking incentives, governance, and losses in the financial crisis', available at SSRN, http://ssrn.com/abstract=1595343.

De Larosière Group (2009), 'Report by the High-Level Group on Financial Supervision in the EU', chaired by J. De Larosière, Brussels.

Del Guercio, D., L. Seery and T. Woidtke (2008), 'Do boards pay attention when institutional investor activists "just vote no"?', *Journal of Financial Economics*, **90**, 84–103.

Dell'Ariccia, G. (2001), 'Asymmetric information and the structure of the banking industry', *European Economic Review*, **45**(10), 1957–1980.

DeYoung, R., E.Y. Peng and Y. Meng (2009), 'Executive compensation and business policy choices at US commercial banks', available at SSRN, http://ssrn.com/abstract=1465996.

Eisenberg, T., S. Sundgren and M. Wells (1998), 'Larger board size and decreasing firm value in small firms', *Journal of Financial Economics*, **48**, 35–54.

Emiris, M. (2002), 'Measuring capital market integration', *BIS Papers*, **12**, 200–221.

Erkens, D., M. Hung and P.P Matos (2009), 'Corporate governance in the 2007–2008 financial crisis: evidence from financial institutions worldwide', available at SSRN, http://ssrn.com/abstract=1397685.

European Central Bank (ECB) (2005), 'Indicators of financial integration in the euro area', September, http://www.ecb.de/pub/pdf/other/indicatorsfinancialintegration200509en.pdf.

European Central Bank (ECB) (2010), 'EU banking structures', September, http://www.ecb.int/pub/pdf/other/eubankingstructures201009en.pdf.

European Commission (EC) (2008), 'A European economic recovery plan', Communication from the Commission to the European Council COM(2008).

European Commission (EC) (2009a), 'Economic crisis in Europe: causes, consequences and responses', DG Economic and Financial Affairs, European Economy 7/2009.

European Commission (EC) (2009b), 'An EU framework for cross-border crisis management in the banking sector', COM(2009) 561/4.

European Commission (EC) (2009c), 'Five years of an enlarged EU: economic achievements and challenges', DG Economic and Financial Affairs, European Economy 1/2009.

European Commission (EC) (2010), Green paper on 'Corporate governance in financial institutions and remuneration policies', http://ec.europa.eu/internal_market/company/docs/modern/com2010_284_en.pdf.

European Council (1989), 'Second Council Directive of 15 December 1989 on the coordination of laws, regulations and administrative provisions relating to the taking up and pursuit of the business of credit institutions and amending Directive 77/780/EEC (89/646/EEC)'.

Fahlenbrach, R. and R.M. Stulz (2009), 'Bank CEO incentives and the credit crisis', NBER Working Papers 15212, National Bureau of Economic Research, August.

Faleye, O. (2007), 'Classified boards, firm value, and managerial entrenchment', *Journal of Financial Economics*, **83**(2), 501–529.

Fonteyne, W., W. Bossu, L. Cortavarria-Checkley, A. Giustiniani, A. Gullo, D. Hardy and S. Kerr (2010), 'Crisis management and resolution for a European banking system', IMF Working Paper WP/10/70.

Freixas, X., P. Hartmann and C. Mayer (2004), 'The assessment: European financial integration', *Oxford Review of Economic Policy*, **20**, 475–489.

Goddard, J., P. Molyneux and J.O.S. Wilson (2010), 'Banking in the European Union', in A.N. Berger, P. Molyneux and J.O.S. Wilson (eds), *The Oxford Handbook of Banking*, Oxford: Oxford University Press.

Goel, A.M. and A.V. Thakor (2008), 'Overconfidence, CEO selection, and corporate governance', *Journal of Finance*, **63**, 2737–2784.

Gropp, R. and A. Kashyap (2009), 'A new metric for banking integration in Europe', NBER Working Paper 14735.

Gugler, K., D.C. Mueller and B.B. Yurtuglo (2003), 'The impact of corporate governance on investment returns in developed and developing countries', *Economic Journal*, **113**, 511–539.

Guiso, L., T. Jappelli, M. Padula and M. Pagano (2004), 'Financial market integration and economic growth in the EU', *Economic Policy*, **40**, 523–577.

Guiso, L., P. Sapienza and L. Zingales (2006), 'Does culture affect economic outcomes?' *Journal of Economic Perspectives*, **20**(2), 23–48.

Guiso, L., P. Sapienza and L. Zingales (2009), 'Cultural biases in economic exchange?' *Quarterly Journal of Economics*, August, 1095–1131.

Hartmann, P., A. Maddaloni and S. Manganelli (2003), 'The euro area financial system: structure, integration and policy', *Oxford Review of Economic Policy*, **19** 180–213.

Hauswald, R. and R. Marquez (2006), 'Competition and strategic information acquisition in credit markets', *Review of Financial Studies*, **19**(3), 967–1000.

Hermalin, B.E. and M. Weisbach (2003), 'Boards of directors as an endogenously determined institution: a survey of the economic literature', *Economic Policy Review*, **9**, 7–26.

Heuchemer, S., S. Kleimeier and H. Sander (2009), 'The determinants of cross-border lending in the euro zone', *Comparative Economic Studies*, **51**(4), 467–499.

Huang, J. and D. Kisgen (2009), 'Gender and corporate finance', Working Paper.

International Monetary Fund (IMF) (2010), 'World Economic Outlook Database', October.
Jensen, M. (1993), 'The modern industrial revolution, exit, and the failure of internal control systems', *Journal of Finance*, **48**, 831–880.
John, K. and Y. Qian (2003), 'Incentive features in CEO compensation in the banking industry', *Economic Policy Review*, April, 109–121.
La Porta, R., F. Lopez-De-Silanes and A. Shleifer (1999), 'Corporate ownership around the world', *Journal of Finance*, **54**, 471–517
La Porta, R., F. Lopez-De-Silanes, A. Shleifer and R. Vishny (1997), 'Legal determinants of external finance', *Journal of Finance*, **52**, 1131–1150.
La Porta, R., F. Lopez-De-Silanes, A. Shleifer and R. Vishny (1998), 'Law and finance', *Journal of Political Economy*, **106**(6), 1113–1155.
La Porta, R., F. Lopez-De-Silanes, A. Shleifer and R. Vishny (2002), 'Investor protection and corporate valuation', *Journal of Finance*, **62**, 1147–1170.
Levi, M.D., K. Li and F. Zhang (2008), 'Mergers and acquisitions: the role of gender', Working Paper.
Llewellyn, D.T. (2006), 'European financial integration: convergence or diversity in banking?' SUERF Paper, May.
Malmendier, U. and G. Tate (2005), 'CEO overconfidence and corporate investment', *Journal of Finance*, **60**, 2661–2700.
Malmendier, U. and G. Tate (2008), 'Who makes acquisitions? A test of the overconfidence hypothesis', *Journal of Financial Economics*, **89**, 20–43.
Manna M. (2004), 'Developing statistical indicators of the integration of the euro area banking system', ECB Working Paper 300.
Mateos de Cabo, Ruth, Ricardo Gimeno and Maria J.J Nieto (2009), 'Gender diversity on European banks' board of directors: traces of discrimination', 18 March, available at SSRN, http://ssrn.com/abstract=1362593.
Organisation for Economic Co-operation and Development (OECD) (2004), 'OECD principles of corporate governance', October.
Oxelheim, L. and C. Wihlborg (eds) (2008), *Markets and Compensation for Executives in Europe*, Bingley: Emerald.
Pagano, M. and P.F. Volpin (2005), 'The political economy of corporate governance', *American Economic Review*, **95**(4), 1005–1030.
Perry, T. and U. Peyer (2005), 'Board seat accumulation by executives: a shareholder's perspective', *Journal of Finance*, **40**(4), 2083–2123.
Petersen, M. and R.G. Rajan (1994), 'The benefits of lending relationships: evidence from small business data', *Journal of Finance*, **49**(1), 3–37.
Shleifer, A. and R.W. Vishny (1997), 'A survey of corporate governance', *Journal of Finance*, **52**(2), 737–783.
Spong, K. and R.J. Sullivan (2007), 'Corporate governance and bank performance', September, available at SSRN, http://ssrn.com/abstract=1011068.
Steinherr, A. and C. Huveneers (1994), 'On the performance of differently regulated financial institutions: some empirical evidence', *Journal of Banking and Finance*, **18**(2), 271–306.
Stulz, R.M. and R. Williamson (2003), 'Culture, openness, and finance', *Journal of Financial Economics*, **70**(3), 313–349.
Tabellini, G. (2010), 'Culture and institutions: economic development in the regions of Europe', *Journal of the European Economic Association*, **8**(4), 677–716.
Terjesen, S., R. Sealy and V. Singh (2009), 'Women directors on corporate boards: a review and research agenda', *Corporate Governance*, **17**(3), 320–337.
Thakor, A. (1996), 'The design of financial systems: an overview', *Journal of Banking and Finance*, **20**, 917–948.
Weisbach, Michael S. (1988), 'Outside directorships and CEO turnover', *Journal of Financial Economics*, **20**, 431–460.
Yermack, D. (2004), 'Remuneration, retention, and reputation incentives for outside directors', *Journal of Finance*, **59**, 2281–2308.

APPENDIX

Table 31A.1   Sample composition

Country	Sample features
AT	All banks and bank holding companies listed on the Wiener Stock Exchange. Oesterreich Volksbanken AG and Volksbank Vorarlberg have been excluded because they are savings banks. Wiener Privatbank is not considered as it is not a commercial bank
BE	All listed banks and banking groups on NYSE Euronext Brussels and incorporated in Belgium
DE	All commercial banks and bank holding companies listed on the Berlin, Frankfurt, Hamburg, Munich and Stuttgart Stock Exchanges and Xetra and incorporated in Germany. We exclude investment banks, non-credit institutions, real estate, cooperative and savings banks
DK	All listed banks and banking groups listed on NASDAQ OMX Nordic Exchange and incorporated in Denmark
ES	All banks listed on the Mercado Continuo Espanol and incorporated in Spain. Our sample does not include Caja de Ahorros del Mediterraneo CAM, since it is classified as a savings bank
FI	All listed banks and banking groups listed on NASDAQ OMX Nordic Exchange and incorporated in Finland
FR	All listed banks on NYSE Euronext Paris and incorporated in France
GR	All banks listed on the Athens Stock Exchange and incorporated in Greece, except the Bank of Greece and T Bank S.A.
IE	We consider the only listed bank on the Irish Stock Exchange incorporated in Ireland. We exclude the national central bank, the Bank of Ireland.
IT	All commercial banks and bank holdings listed on LSE Borsa Italiana. Banca Popolare di Milano, Banco Popolare di Sondrio, Banco Popolare, Credito Valtellinese and UBI have been excluded since they are classified as cooperative banks. Mediobanca is classified as an investment bank
LU	All banks on the Luxembourg stock exchange and incorporated in Luxembourg
NL	All banks and bank holding companies listed on NYSE Euronext Amsterdam and incorporated in the Netherlands
PT	All banks listed on NYSE Euronext Lisbon and incorporated in Portugal
SE	All banks listed on NASDAQ OMX Nordic Exchange and incorporated in Sweden, with the exception of Swedbank as it is classified as a savings bank.
UK	All banks and banking groups listed on the London Stock Exchange and incorporated in the UK at 1 January 2009. We exclude Islamic Bank of Britain and European Islamic Bank.

32 Debt forgiveness during Japan's lost decade
*Satoshi Koibuchi**

32.1 INTRODUCTION

The Japanese economy experienced a prolonged slump after the collapse of the asset price bubble in the late 1980s. Although there were considerable factors that led to the 'lost decade', it is widely recognized that the problem of non-performing loans constituted one of the major factors responsible for the prolonged slump. However, this decade-long problem was suddenly resolved after a turning point around 2003.

Figure 32.1 depicts the outstanding risk management loans for the major and regional banks. The non-performing loan problem for the major banks peaked in March 2002, though the amount of risk management loans and its share to the total lending continued to decline steeply until March 2005.

Impetus for resolving the bad loan problem was provided by the announcement of the Anti-Deflation Package and the Financial Revitalization Program in October 2002. Under these programs, the Japanese government declared that the bad loan outstanding share to the total lending for the major banks would be forced to decline from 8.4 percent at that time to around 4 percent in the next two and half years. In reality, in May 2003, Risona Bank, one of the most ailing major banks, was nationalized; and in November, Ashikaga Bank, a large regional bank, was liquidated under the Financial Reconstruction Law.[1]

The Industrial Revitalization Corporation of Japan (IRCJ) was established in response to the Financial Revitalization Program to resolve the debt overhang problem in the corporate sector in Japan. From its commencement in May 2003, it supported the restructuring of 41 debt-ridden companies including the symbolic bad large companies, such as Daiei and Misawa Homes, and it was resolved in March 2007, a year before its planned termination.

Figure 32.2 presents the cumulative abnormal returns of the Japanese banking sector, measured by the stock price of TOPIX Banks ETF, during the period from July 2002 to March 2005. Apparently, the stock price of the Japanese banking sector significantly recovered during the period from 2003 to 2004, which was almost the same period during which several policies, including the establishment of the IRCJ, were implemented under the Financial Revitalization Program.

In this chapter, I focus on the cases of debt forgiveness of large Japanese companies during the period from 1998 to 2004, which includes the lost decade of Japan. As Hoshi et al. (1990), Sheard (1994), and Hoshi and Kashyap (2001) indicate, in the traditional Japanese bank–firm relationship, a main bank maintaining a long-term relationship with client firms had a strong incentive to rescue the financially distressed clients to protect its reputation as a 'sound main bank'. In this sense, until the 1980s, the main bank-led corporate restructuring had been expected to function as a scheme to resolve the debt overhang problem of the corporate sector swiftly and efficiently. However, the

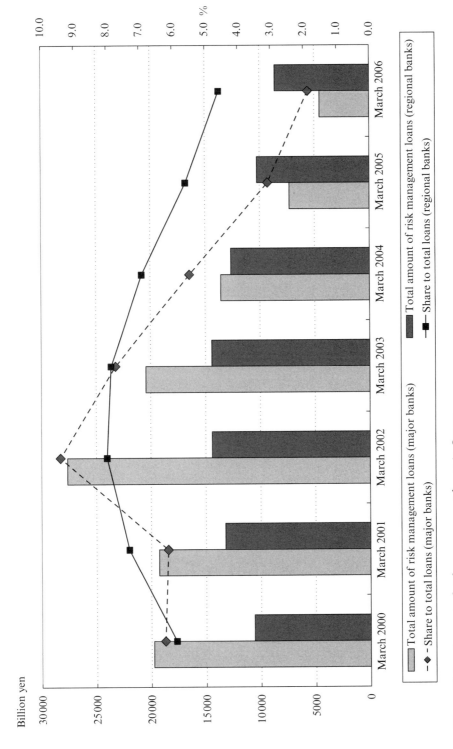

Billion yen

Total amount of risk management loans (major banks)
- Share to total loans (major banks)
Total amount of risk management loans (regional banks)
- Share to total loans (regional banks)

Figure 32.1 Amount of risk management loans in Japan

CAR (benchmark: TOPIX)

─── CAR of Topix Banks ETF (TSE, code:1615)

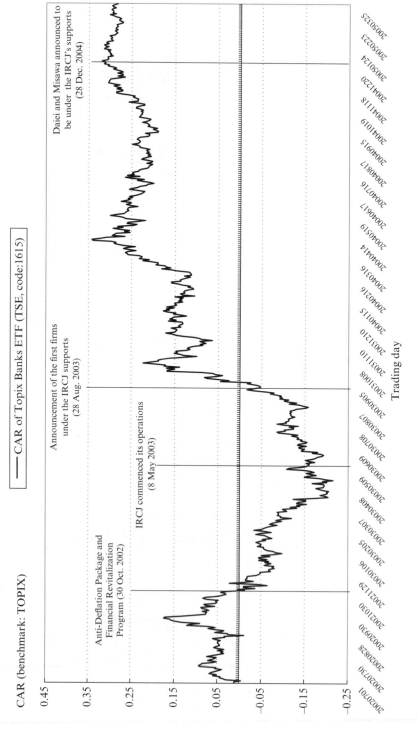

Figure 32.2   Cumulative abnormal returns of the Japanese banking sector (1 July 2002 to 31 March 2005)

prolonged non-performing problem during the 1990s heavily impaired Japanese bank capital; further, the effectiveness of the main bank-led corporate restructuring was rapidly reducing because the ailing main banks were unable to support the huge amount of the burden of debt forgiveness. Under these circumstances, the IRCJ assumed the role of the main banks to lead the negotiations among many lenders and successfully introduced the new rule of the burden of debt forgiveness proportionate to their loan shares.

Given the excess burdens on the traditional main bank-led resolution of the debt overhang problem, market participants may perceive a request for debt forgiveness by a debt-ridden client as negative news on the valuation of its main bank. In contrast, if the request for debt forgiveness accompanies the IRCJ's support, then market participants may expect that the excess burdens of the main banks would be substantially mitigated and perceive the request as positive news on the valuation of the main bank. In this chapter, I will examine this difference in impact between the ordinary cases and the cases supported by the IRCJ, by employing the standard event study methodology with the financial data and equity price of the main banks.

This chapter proceeds as follows. Section 32.2 explains theoretically the evolution of the corporate restructuring schemes in Japan by employing the simple cooperative game model. Section 32.3 examines the impacts of the IRCJ's support on the excess burdens of debt forgiveness. Section 32.4 proposes the hypothesis and discusses the methodology of an event study. Section 32.5 presents basic empirical results, and section 32.6 concludes the chapter.

32.2 EVOLUTION OF THE CORPORATE RESTRUCTURING SCHEMES IN JAPAN

32.2.1 The Simple Cooperative Game Model

In order to consider the evolution of the corporate restructuring schemes in Japan, I first explain why debt forgiveness is necessary for resolving the debt overhang problem. I suppose a firm with a project whose net present value of cash flow is X, liquidation value is L, and existing outstanding debt is D. If I focus on the case of $D > X > L$, then this inequality indicates that positive profits are expected from a continuation of the project; however, X is not sufficiently large to repay all the existing debts D. In this situation, the project is socially beneficial, though for its continuation, someone has to incur the cost of $D-X$. In a joint-stock company, the first stakeholders that bear this cost are the existing shareholders. However, if under the limited liability of the shareholders the amount of equity is below $D-X$, then the firm would be filed for bankruptcy and liquidated unless the existing lenders accept debt forgiveness. However, it is known that the acceptance of debt forgiveness generally does not become the Nash equilibrium of a non-cooperative game (Gertner and Scharfstein, 1991). This situation is known as a debt overhang problem.

The most important problem is determining the manner in which the burdens of debt forgiveness are shared among multiple lenders. The simplest solution would include a proportional allocation of burdens (pro rata) on lenders on the basis of their loan shares in a firm's total borrowing. However, the actual burdens of debt forgiveness largely deviate from the proportional allocation if there exists a disproportionate cost among lenders when the firm files for bankruptcy.

In this section, I present a simple model that determines the burdens of lenders as a solution of the Shapley value, which constitutes one of major solutions for the cooperative game, with disproportionate bankruptcy costs among lenders.[2] I consider a firm borrowing from three lenders, A, B and C, whose loan shares are a, b and g, respectively, where $a + b + g = 1$ and $a \geq b \geq g$. Therefore, lender A is the largest lender and known as a 'main bank'. Further, I define a characteristic function, $v(S)$, as pecuniary returns for lenders who participate in any coalition S. The Shapley value is employed in order to determine uniquely the return for each lender on the basis of the weighted average of the marginal contribution of each lender to the possible coalitions in which the lender participates. Therefore, the return for lender A, x_A, is determined as:

$$x_A = (1/3)[v(ABC) - v(BC)] + (1/6)[v(AB) - v(B)] + (1/6)[v(AC) - v(C)] + (1/3)v(A).$$

I impose the following three assumptions for specifying the values of $v(S)$:

- A1: $aD \geq bD \geq gD > X$.
- A2: Liquidated assets, L, are allocated among lenders in proportion to their loan shares when the firm is liquidated.
- A3: Only the largest lender A suffers from private cost, $Z > 0$, when the firm is liquidated.

First, assumption (A1) indicates that all the three lenders must agree on debt forgiveness because the firm cannot even repay the principal of the debt borrowing from the smallest lender C. In this case, each single lender possesses a veto to block any coalition of $v(S)$ in which the other two lenders participate. Second, assumption (A2) indicates that for pecuniary returns, the rule of proportional (pro rata) allocation is applied to all lenders when the firm files for bankruptcy and its project is liquidated. Third, assumption (A3) presents that there exist disproportionate non-pecuniary private costs on lenders, so that only the largest lender (the main bank) inevitably suffers from a large cost when the firm is liquidated.

Based on these assumptions, I specify the values of $v(S)$: $v(ABC) = X$, $v(AB) = (a + b)L - Z$, $v(AC) = (a + g)L - Z$, $v(BC) = (b + g)L$, $v(A) = aL - Z$, $v(B) = bL$ and $v(C) = gL$ and derive the Shapley value of x_A for lender A as follows:

$$x_A = (1/3)(X - L) + \alpha L - (2/3)Z. \tag{32.1}$$

On the other hand, the Shapley values for lenders B and C are $x_B = (1/3)(X - L) + \beta L + (1/3)Z$ and $x_C = (1/3)(X - L) + \gamma L + (1/3)Z$, respectively. By simple calculation, it is confirmed that the Shapley values for all lenders are larger than the returns in the case of liquidation as long as $X + Z - L > 0$.

Lender A's share of burdens is measured by $(aD - x_A)/(D - X)$. If $x_A = aX$, it is the case of the proportional allocation of burdens on lenders on the basis of their loan shares, which indicates that lender A's share of burdens coincides precisely with lender

A's loan share, $(aD - x_A)/(D - X) = a$. If $x_A < aX$, it is the case that lender A incurs disproportionately large excess burdens of debt forgiveness in comparison to its loan share, $(aD - x_A)/(D - X) > a$.

Equation (32.1) shows that even in the case of no bankruptcy cost for the largest lender A, $Z = 0$, the Shapley value deviates from the proportional allocation as every single lender obtains one-third of the cash flow exceeding the liquidation value, $X - L$. However, this distortion is marginal as long as a is not significantly different from 1/3.

On the other hand, if I suppose that only the main bank has the disproportionate cost of Z, then the deviation of the main bank's Shapley value from the proportional allocation is considerably larger than its loan share as Z increases, and small lenders bear the relatively smaller burdens than their loan shares. If it is inevitable for the main bank to incur the private cost of Z when its client is liquidated and all small lenders precisely understand this situation, then the bargaining power of the main bank in the negotiation among lenders is very weak. Therefore, the main bank with large Z is forced to bear huge burdens while negotiating debt forgiveness among lenders.

32.2.2 Traditional Main Bank-Led Corporate Restructuring

The above-mentioned simple model enables us to answer three important questions about the scheme of the traditional main bank-led corporate restructuring in Japan: why it worked well for a long time, particularly during the high-growth era in the 1960s and the 1970s; why it malfunctioned in the late 1990s; and why the new scheme did not emerge voluntarily during the period from the 1990s to the early 2000s.

In the Japanese bank–firm relationship, a main bank maintaining a long-term relationship with client firms had a strong incentive to lead the negotiation among lenders when the clients underwent financial distress to protect its reputation as a 'sound main bank' (Hoshi et al., 1990; Sheard, 1994; Hoshi and Kashyap, 2001, Chapter 5). Under the traditional main bank-led corporate restructuring, the main bank having a large inherent cost Z was expected to incur large excess burdens to rescue its distressed clients. The main banks could afford to bear large excess burdens as the financial condition of most of the Japanese banks had been rather sound until the late 1980s, and more importantly, cases where its clients were financially distressed were uncommon.[3] Therefore, the main bank-led corporate restructuring was working well as a scheme to swiftly and efficiently resolve the debt overhang problem of the corporate sector in Japan at least during the high-growth era.

However, the situation was transformed in the 1990s in two ways. First, many debt-ridden large companies were prevailing in the Japanese economy, and Japanese bank capitals had been heavily impaired as a result of the huge amount of disposal of non-performing loans (Sekine et al., 2003; Caballero et al., 2008). Second, the regulatory capital requirement was introduced in the early 1990s and a prompt corrective action was also implemented from 1998. In this situation, the additional cost as a result of the bankruptcy of large client firms could have a crucial influence on the continuation of its main bank (Peek and Rosengren, 2005). Moreover, even in the case in which the main bank prevented the bankruptcy of its debt-ridden clients by debt forgiveness, the main bank having close relationships with its clients (and having large Z) could inevitably suffer from disproportionately large burdens of debt forgiveness, which would create a large negative shock for the already impaired bank capital. Therefore, the main bank tended to choose the forbearance lending to debt-ridden clients, and consequently the effectiveness of the main bank-led debt forgiveness as the scheme to swiftly resolve the debt overhang problem for its clients was substantially eroded. On the other hand, while the alternate schemes of corporate restructuring were very slow to develop, the stakeholders of debt-ridden companies including their small lenders continued to expect the main banks to bear disproportionately large burdens of debt forgiveness. The main bank could not introduce the new rule on debt forgiveness that mitigated excess burdens because, for a long time, the main bank itself had a large inherent cost Z accumulated through the bank–firm relationship.

32.2.3   Emergence of the IRCJ

Description of the IRCJ
In this chapter, I will consider the impact of the IRCJ on the Japanese financial system. The movement for establishing the IRCJ was initiated with the promulgation of the Anti-Deflation Package and the Financial Revitalization Program in October 2002. The IRCJ was expected to resolve the excess obligation problem in the corporate sector after the non-performing problem in the banking sector in response to the Financial Revitalization Program (known as the Takenaka plan) that was considered a hard-landing policy. Thereafter, the government introduced the Industrial Revitalization Corporation Act, which was enforced in April 2003. The IRCJ was established as a joint-stock company with only two shareholders including the Deposit Insurance Corporation of Japan (DIC, 98.5 percent) and Norinchukin bank (1.5 percent). The city and regional banks also funded the IRCJ by indirect equity participation through the DIC. The IRCJ first operated in May and announced the first three companies it supported on 28 August.

The brief description of the process surrounding the IRCJ's support to a company is as follows. First of all, the company or its main bank informally asks for the IRCJ's support and due diligence (DD) prior to obtaining the formal decision on the support. The IRCJ briefly examines the possibility of the support and then adopts the full-scale DD to prepare the corporate rehabilitation plan. After negotiating with various stakeholders, the company formally asks the IRCJ's assistance on the completion of the corporate revitalization plan. Immediately after the Industrial Revitalization Committee decides to provide formal support to the company, the decision will be formally announced and the corporate revitalization plan will be released. The corporate revitalization plan usually includes the total amounts of financial assistance (debt forgiveness, debt–equity swaps and equity participation) and its share of burdens among lenders. Together with the formal announcement of its support, the IRCJ announces cessation of the collection of money by lenders and by itself begins to coordinate the negotiations among lenders. After all lenders accept the share of the burdens of debt forgiveness, the IRCJ purchases the debts held by the non-main lenders. The IRCJ is supposed to sell all of the claims and shares, referred to as 'exit', within three years from the purchase of debts from the non-main lenders.

After the IRCJ announced its support for three companies – Kyushu Industrial Transportation, Dia Kensetsu and Usui Department Store – initially, it provided assistance to a total of 41 firms until February 2005. In March 2006, the IRCJ sold all stakes in Skynet Asia Airways and completed support for all 41 companies.

The total debt outstanding for the 41 supported companies amounts to 3.3 trillion yen (almost 10 percent of the outstanding non-performing loans in the Japanese banking sector in March 2002). The total amount of financial assistance (including equity participation and new loans) attained 1.7 trillion yen, while the amount of debt purchased by the IRCJ amounted to a total of 1.0 trillion yen.

In the following analysis, I focus on nine major cases, namely Kyushu Industrial Transportation, Dia Kensetsu, Mitsui Mining, Kimmon Manufacturing, Kanebo, Taiho Industries, Daikyo, The Daiei and Misawa Homes Holdings. Total debt outstanding for these nine companies amounts to 87 percent in all 41 cases, 88 percent for all debt purchases, and 84 percent for all financial assistance. All the main banks of the nine major companies are mega banks, including Mizuho and Mizuho Corporate Bank, SMBC, UFJ Bank, and Risona Bank.[4]

Delegation to the IRCJ
The most important role of the IRCJ includes assuming the role of a negotiator to coordinate the allocation of the burdens of debt forgiveness from the main bank. This is a significant difference in the cases under the Guidelines for Private Liquidation, which were introduced by the major players in the Japanese financial sector in September 2001. Under the guidelines, the main bank has to pursue the role of leading the coordination among lenders. According to my discussion using the cooperative game, the main bank having a large inherent cost of Z has to bear extremely large burdens as its bargaining power against small lenders in the negotiation is extremely low.

However, if the IRCJ, which is free from the main bank's cost of Z as a third party, leads the coordination among lenders, it has the power of enforcing the new rule of proportional burdens of debt forgiveness on the basis of the loan shares of lenders. Therefore, I argue that the IRCJ's support significantly mitigates the excess burdens of the main bank in debt forgiveness to resolve the debt overhang problem. By delegating the role of coordination among lenders to the third party, the debt overhang problem of the corporate sector could be resolved under the new scheme where the main bank and small lenders bear in proportion the burdens of debt forgiveness.[5]

In the following sections, I will compare the cases supported by the IRCJ with the ordinary cases without the IRCJ's support, by employing case and event studies using the stock price of the main banks.

32.3 IMPACTS ON BURDENS OF MAIN BANKS

32.3.1 Excess Burdens on Main Banks

During the late 1990s and the early 2000s, in the Japanese economy, many large companies underwent debt forgiveness to resolve their debt overhang problem. In this section, I will first consider the major cases of debt forgiveness, known as 'the ordinary cases', that were announced by the large companies during the period from 1998 to 2005. These included 39 cases related to 35 firms where I could identify the actual share of their main banks' burdens of debt forgiveness by financial statements, disclosure information, and news reports.

A bank provides three types of financial assistance to its client firm: waiver of an obligation, debt–equity swaps and acceptance of preferred shares. First, in the waiver of an obligation (debt forgiveness for lenders), lenders forgive some parts of claims, and the borrower's obligations are completely waived. Profits from the waiver are generally included in the income statement of the firm in the fiscal year-end immediately after the debtor and its lenders agree on debt forgiveness. Second, debt–equity swaps (DES) are financial instruments aiming to issue shares to the bank by exchanging some parts of the claims held by the bank. Therefore, the debt–equity swaps are accompanied by a direct reduction of the outstanding debt of the firm, although there exists no waiver profit in the income statement. Third, in the acceptance of the preferred shares by the bank, capital will increase, though there occurs no direct reduction in the outstanding debts of the firm. I include only debt forgiveness and debt–equity swaps to calculate the total amount of debt forgiveness for each case because these two instruments are accompanied by a direct reduction of the outstanding debt of the firm.

While I identify a main bank as the largest lender for the company, the 'main bank's share of burdens' is defined as the main bank's burdens of debt forgiveness divided by the total amount of debt forgiveness and the 'main bank's loan share' is calculated as the firm's borrowing from the main bank divided by the total borrowing of the firm at the fiscal year end immediately before the announcement of debt forgiveness. In the case of the proportional allocation of debt forgiveness, the 'main bank's share of burdens' is equal to the 'main bank's loan share'. If the 'main bank's share of burdens' exceeds the 'main bank's loan share', then the main bank bears the positive excess burdens of debt forgiveness.

Figure 32.3 depicts the relationship between the 'main bank's share of burdens' and the 'main bank's loan share' in the ordinary cases. Surprisingly, the 'main bank's share of burdens' exceeds the 'main bank's loan share' in all cases. This indicates that during the lost decade in Japan, the main bank had disproportionately borne most of the burdens of debt forgiveness, while small lenders had borne small burdens.

Figure 32.4 depicts the same relationship for the nine cases supported by the IRCJ. As it is easily recognized, all cases are scattered around a 45-degree line, which indicates that the proportional allocation of the burdens of debt forgiveness is applied to those lenders under the IRCJ's support. Therefore, the main bank only bears the burdens proportional to its loan share in the cases supported by the IRCJ.

I now consider regressing the 'main bank's share of burdens' on the 'main bank's loan share' with a constant term. Table 32.1 reports the result using alternative samples. In the estimation using all the samples for the ordinary cases, reported in the first row, the estimated coefficient of the 'main bank's loan share' is 0.51 and the estimated constant term is about 0.52; further, both are statistically significant at the 1 percent level. Therefore, we can interpret that the average excess burden on the main bank, which is not explained by the 'main bank's loan share', amounts to about 50 percent in the ordinary cases.

The second row of Table 32.1 reports the regression result using the sample of six cases (Iwataya Department Store, Toyo Shutter, Nippon Yakin Kogyo, Seibu Department

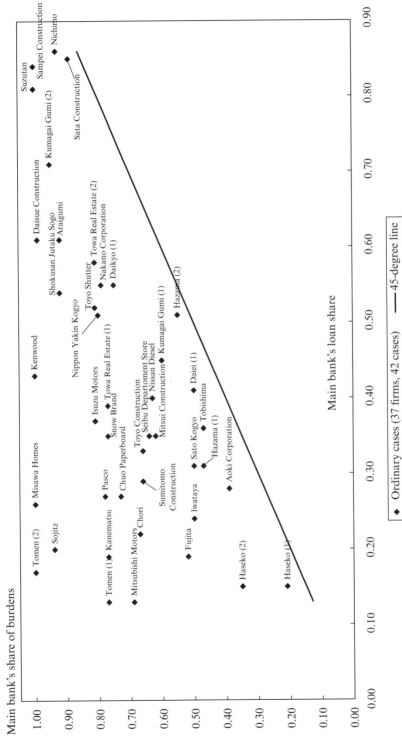

Figure 32.3 *Main bank's burdens in the ordinary cases*

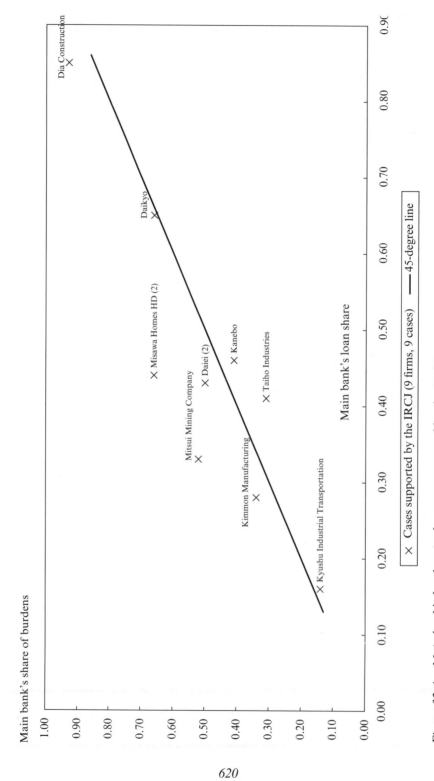

Figure 32.4 Main bank's burdens in the cases supported by the IRCJ

Table 32.1   Determinants of the main bank's burdens of debt forgiveness

	Ordinary cases		Cases supported by the IRCJ
	All cases	Cases under the Guidelines on Private Liquidation	All cases
Constant	0.519	0.397	0.039
	(0.000)	(0.032)	(0.691)
Main bank's loan share	0.511	0.606	1.026
	(0.000)	(0.059)	(0.001)
Adjusted R-squared	0.252	0.537	0.767
Observations	42	6	9

Notes:
Sample: ordinary cases (37 firms, 42 cases) and cases supported by the IRCJ (9 firms, 9 cases).
Dependent variable: main bank's burdens of debt forgiveness.
The p-values based on t-test are reported in parentheses.

Store, Hazama Corporation (2) and Sata Construction) whose debt forgiveness was conducted following the Guidelines for Private Liquidation. In this case, the estimated constant term is 0.39 and is statistically significant at the 1 percent level. This result shows that the guidelines failed to mitigate the large excess burdens of debt forgiveness on the main bank.

In contrast, the result of the estimation using the sample of the cases supported by the IRCJ shows that the estimated constant term takes a very minimal value, 0.03, that is not different from 0 at any significant level. This indicates that in cases where there was the IRCJ's support, the excess burden of the main bank suddenly disappeared.

In the traditional main bank relationship in Japan, the main bank was supposed to lead the corporate restructuring by bearing disproportional burdens compared to its loan share. The results from Figure 32.1, Figure 32.2 and Table 32.1 suggest that although this special role of the main bank at the time of corporate distress had been observed until the mid-2000s, this role was dramatically transformed as a result of the intervention of the IRCJ.

32.3.2   Burdens on the IRCJ

Excess burden on the main bank disappears in the cases supported by the IRCJ, while large excess burdens are observed in the ordinary cases. Who bears the burdens of debt forgiveness in these cases? One possibility is that the IRCJ subsidizes the company by fixing the price of debts for the non-main lenders at an extremely high level.

In order to assess this possibility, Table 32.2 reports the burdens of the IRCJ and the non-main lenders calculated from the data published by the IRCJ. According to these data, the purchasing prices of the debts from the non-main lenders, denoted by (B), range from 30 percent to 70 percent against their book value. Substantial burdens of the non-main lenders exceed the total amount of financial assistance (sum of debt forgiveness and debt–equity swap) in six cases, excluding Kanebo, Taiho Industries and The Daiei. This indicates that small lenders bear all of the burdens of debt forgiveness and that the IRCJ

Table 32.2 Burdens on non-main bank and the IRCJ in the nine major cases supported by the IRCJ (unit: million yen)

Company supported by the IRCJ	Main bank(s) that offered the IRCJ's support to the company	Total borrowing of company	(A) Amount of debt purchased by the IRCJ	(B) Purchasing price ((B)/(A))	(D) Burdens of the non-main banks (A)-(B)	(E) Amount of financial assistance from the IRCJ	(F) Debt forgiveness	(G) Debt-equity swap
Kyushu Industrial Transportation	Misuho Bank	52 598	36 182	18 733 (52%)	17 449**	16 187	15 590	597
Dia Kensetsu	Risona Bank	193 998	18 397	9 476 (52%)	8 921**	8 507	8 507	0
Mitsui Mining Company	SMBC	242 400	179 543	58 843 (33%)	120 700**	87 148³	67 148	20 000
Kimmon Manufacturing	Risona Bank	30 010	15 878	11 990 (76%)	3 888**	3 517	3 517	0
Kanebo	SMBC	555 654	103 971	47 235 (45%)	56 736*	66 543	56 543	10 000
Taiho Industries	UFJ Bank	8 903	4 271	4 057 (95%)	214*	850	0	850
Daikyo	UFJ Bank	484 300	84 771	56 588 (67%)	28 183**	27 075	27 075	0
The Daiei	U F Bank, Mizuho Corporate Bank, SMBC	1 020 562	366 646	247 022 (67%)	119 624*	152 583	(112 583)	40 000
Misawa Homes Holdings	UFJ Bank	294 152	43 411	14 274 (33%)	29 137**	28 452	28 452	0

Notes:
1. Sample firms include 8 large companies listed in the stock exchanges and Kyushu Industrial Transportation whose financial statements are available in 2002–2004.
2. '(D) Burdens of non-main bank' are defined as '(A) amount of debt purchased by the IRCJ' minus '(B) purchasing price'. ** attached to the number in (D) depicts that (D) exceeds (E), while* depicts that (D) exceeds at least (F).
3. In the case of Mitsui Mining Company, the IRCJ offered a new loan of 19 578 million yen to the company besides providing the direct financial assistance. The loan was completely repaid by the company by 17 March 2007.

Source: Author's calculation using the data from IRCJ's news releases available at the Cabinet Office's website, http://www8.cao.go.jp/sangyo/ircj/ja/index.html.

Table 32.3 Profit on the sales in the cases of equity participation by the IRCJ (unit: million yen)

Company name	Equity participation by IRCJ Total amount (DES)	Name of sponsor to whom the IRCJ sold the shares Proceeds from the sale of the shares	IRCJ's profit on the sale (rate of returns)
Kyushu Industrial Transportation	Kyushu Industrial Transportation 700 (DES 350)	HIS 3194	2494 (356%)
	Kyushu Sanko 1250 (DES 250)	Footwork Express N.A.[1]	N.A.[1]
Mitsui Mining Company	20 000 (DES 20 000)	Daiwa SMBCPI, Nippon Steel Corporation, Sumitomo Corporation 18 200 Nomura Securities 9237	7437 (37%)
Kimmon Manufacturing	3000 (DES 0)	Yamatake Corporation 4650[2]	1 650[2] (55%)
Kanebo	Kanebo Cosmetics 236 000 (DES 150 000)	Kao Corporation 263 401	27 401 (11%)
	Kanebo 20 000 (DES 10 000)	Trinity Investment N.A.[3]	N.A.[3]
Taiho Industries	850 (Des 850)	Ichinen Co,.Ltd. 1631[4]	781[4] (92%)
The Daiei	50 000 (DES 40 000)	Marubeni Corporation 69 800	19 800 (40%)

Notes:
1. It is obvious that, overall, the IRCJ did not suffer any losses because the profit on the sale of Kyushu Industrial Transportation (2494 million yen) exceeds the total amount of equity participation to Kyushu Sanko by the IRCJ (1250 million yen).
2. This value is the author's estimation using the evidence that the proceeds from the sale of the preferred shares held by the IRCJ, Risona Bank and Mizuho Corporate Bank were in total 9300 million yen.
3. It is obvious that, overall, the IRCJ did not suffer any losses because the profit on the sale of Kanebo Cosmetics (27 401 million yen) exceeds the total amount of equity participation to Kanebo by the IRCJ (20 000 million yen). According to the Nikkei Newspaper (*Nikkei Kinyu*, 21 December 2005), the IRCJ is expected to earn a total profit of 20 000 million yen in by selling the shares of Kanebo and Kanebo Cosmetics.
4. This value is the author's estimation using the calculation based on a TOB price (225 yen per share) by Ichinen Co. Ltd.

Source: News releases of the related companies and press reports.

bears nothing at all. In addition, in the other three cases, where the substantial burdens of the non-main lenders exceed at least the total amount of debt forgiveness, the IRCJ's burden depends on the *ex post* profit from the sales of the shares that the IRCJ acquired through debt–equity swaps.

Table 32.3 reports the IRCJ's profit from the sales of shares in the case of equity participation by the IRCJ. Surprisingly, the IRCJ earned a substantial amount of profits in all cases, while its rate of returns varies from 11 percent for the sales of Kanebo

Table 32.4   *Reduction of equity, stock consolidation and capital increase in the corporate revitalization plan (unit: million yen)*

Company name	'Shareholder responsibility' in the corporate revitalization plan		
	Reduction of equity	Stock consolidation	Capital increase
Kyushu Industrial Transportation	Kyushu Industrial Transportation: 'massive reduction' Kyushu Sanko: 100.0%	–	DES and the third-party allocation of the newly issued shares to the IRCJ
Dia Kensetsu	99.0%	–	–
Mitsui Mining Company	91.1%	2 shares to 1	Capital increase
Kimmon Manufacturing	90.0%	–	The third-party allocation of the newly issued share
Kanebo	99.7%	10 shares to 1	The third-party allocation of the newly issued share
Taiho Industries	95.0%	–	The third-party allocation of the newly issued share and issue of the preferred stock
Daikyo	99.2% for common stock 50% for prefered stock	–	The third-party allocation of the newly issued share
The Daiei	99.6%	10 shares to 1	Massive capital increase
Misawa Homes Holdings	99.0%	10 shares to 1	Capital increase by the sponsor

Note: Sample firms include 9 major companies with support from the IRCJ (8 listed companies and Kyushu Industrial Transportation).

Source: This table is based on IRCJ's news releases available at the Cabinet Office's website, http://www8. cao.go.jp/sangyo/ircj/ja/index.html.

Cosmetics to 356 percent for those of Kyushu Industry Transportation. According to these data, in all cases, the IRCJ did not suffer from any losses through purchasing and selling debts held by the non-main lenders.

Existing shareholders of the debt-ridden company also shared the burdens to resolve the debt overhang problem. The corporate revitalization plan published by the company includes a section on the 'shareholder's responsibility'. Table 32.4 shows that the plans were accompanied by a substantial degree of equity reduction exceeding 90 percent in all cases. Together with a substantial amount of capital increase, reduction of equity is believed to dilute the value attributable to incumbent shareholders.

Overall, the results in this section strongly suggest that the non-main lenders bear the proportional burdens of debt forgiveness through the appropriate purchasing price by the IRCJ. The IRCJ successfully sold the supported firms at an adequately high value and did not suffer from any *ex post* losses by supporting the debt-ridden companies.

32.4   HYPOTHESIS AND METHODOLOGY

32.4.1   Hypothesis

In the traditional Japanese financial system, the main banks have always led the nego-tiation among lenders to resolve the debt overhang problem for their client firms by disproportionately bearing the larger share of the burdens of debt forgiveness compared to small lenders. As discussed in the previous section, extremely large excess burdens on the main bank were commonly observed even in the ordinary cases of the major Japanese listed companies until the mid-2000s. Moreover, the bank capitals for most of the major Japanese banks were heavily impaired by huge amounts of disposal of non-performing loans until the late 1990s. Therefore, given the excess burdens on the main bank in the resolution of the debt overhang problem, market participants may perceive a request for debt forgiveness by a debt-ridden client as negative news on the valuation of its main bank. In this case, we would observe significant negative impacts on the equity price of the main bank when the client announced the request for debt forgiveness for its lenders. However, it is quite natural that market participants perceive the deterioration of the financial condition of the debt-ridden company and expect the approaching request for debt forgiveness prior to the formal announcement by the company. To the extent that investors expected the possibility of debt forgiveness *ex ante*, negative impacts on the valuation of the main bank might be less significant when the request was formally announced.

In contrast, if the IRCJ announced that the company would include debt forgive-ness under its support, then the IRCJ would apply the proportional allocation of the burdens of debt forgiveness to all lenders. This indicates that excess burdens of the main banks would be substantially mitigated. If market participants precisely predict the consequences under the IRCJ's scheme, they might perceive the announcement of debt forgiveness with the IRCJ's support as positive news on the valuation of the main bank. In this case, we would observe significant positive impacts on the equity price of the main banks when the IRCJ announced its support to its client firms.

Moreover, although announcement of the IRCJ's support could also positively impact on the equity price of non-main lenders through resolving their client's debt overhang problem, the impact on the main bank would be largest among lenders, reflecting market participants' perception that the IRCJ scheme disproportionately mitigates the main bank's burdens of debt forgiveness that were extremely large under the traditional scheme. Therefore, we would observe larger positive impacts on the equity prices of the main banks compared to those of non-main lenders including the secondary banks.

In the following section, I will test these hypotheses by examining how the abnor-mal returns of the main banks responded to the events in which their troubled clients requested debt forgiveness.

32.4.2   Identifying the Event Day

In order to examine the hypotheses, I construct the abnormal returns over two kinds of event windows for the main and secondary banks: the largest and the second-largest lenders, respectively, whose client firms requested debt forgiveness during 1998–2004.

A first event window is around an event day when a news report on the possibility of a request for debt forgiveness (or financial assistance including debt–equity swap) was released to market participants for the first time. In the cases supported by the IRCJ, the company (and/or its main bank) has to ask informally whether the company is eligible to accept the IRCJ's support and has to obtain a two-step DD prior to the formal decision of the Industrial Revitalization Committee. Though the IRCJ enforced a strict rule to maintain the confidentiality of the informal offer by the company, in most cases newspapers actually reported the evidence on '*ex ante* informal offer' of the companies before the decisions on the IRCJ's support were formally announced.

I define this event day as a 'first news report' on the request for debt forgiveness with or without the IRCJ's support. This event day is a first point in time when the investors perceive the possibility of the debt forgiveness of the company and determine whether its scheme would receive the IRCJ's support; therefore, impacts on the equity price of its main bank are expected to be large. I specified the date of the 'first news report' for each case by searching all articles including the company name in major newspapers (four *Nikkei* papers, *Asahi*, *Yomiuri*, *Mainichi* and *Sankei*) compiled in Nikkei Telecom 21 during the period from 1998 to 2004.

A second event window is around an event day when the company formally announces its corporate revitalization plan including the request for debt forgiveness for its lenders. Particularly, for the cases supported by the IRCJ, this event day is precisely specified as the day when the IRCJ formally announces the name of the company that it will support, and releases its corporate revitalization plan including a request for debt forgiveness for its lenders. I define this event day as a 'formal announcement of the (corporate revitalization) plan', which is expected to include more concrete information on the debt forgiveness of the company than the 'first news report' event. The corporate revitalization plan usually includes information on the total amount of debt forgiveness and the main bank's consent to debt forgiveness. More importantly, at this point in time, market participants are aware whether the company formally receives the IRCJ's support, which substantially impacts the main bank's burdens of debt forgiveness, as discussed in section 32.2. I specified the date of this event window for each case by searching for articles using Nikkei Telecom 21 for the ordinary cases and by news releases on the IRCJ's website for the cases supported by the IRCJ.

Table 32.5 presents the list of the event days of the 'first news report' and the 'formal announcement of the plan' under the IRCJ's support for each of the cases supported by the IRCJ together with the list of main banks and secondary banks of companies. The '*ex ante* informal offers' by the companies were reported by the major newspapers for the seven cases supported by the IRCJ excluding the Kimmon Manufacturing and Taiho Industries, which were relatively smaller and less influential in the industry than the others. In reality, based on the news, investors actively traded the stocks of related companies and their major lenders including main and secondary banks.

Table 32.6 shows the list of the event days of the 'first news report' and the 'formal announcement of the plan' for each of the ordinary cases together with the list of main and secondary banks of the companies. Only 14 cases among all of the 42 cases include the news reports on the request for debt forgiveness prior to the formal announcement of the plan by the company.

If the case includes both the event days of the 'first news report' and the 'formal

Table 32.5   *List of debt forgiveness cases with the IRCJ's support during the period from 2003 to 2004 (cases supported by the IRCJ, 9 firms, 9 cases)*

Code	Company	Industry	Main bank	Secondary bank	Event date	
					First news report on request for debt forgiveness under the IRCJ's support	Formal announcement of the corporate revitalization plan under the IRCJ's support
unlisted	Kyushu Industrial Transportation	Transportation	Mizuho Bank	Bank of Tokyo-Mitsubishi	20030724	20030828
8858	Dia Kensetsu	Real estate	Resona Bank	(Mizuho Corporate Bank)	20030724	20030828
1501	Mitsui Mining Company	Mining	SMBC	Chuo Mitsui Trust	20030725	20030828
7724	Kimmon Manufacturing	Manufacturer	Resona Bank	Bank of Tokyo-Mitsubishi	–	20040128
3102	Kanebo	Manufacturer	SMBC	Mizuho Corporate Bank	20040216	20040310
4953	Taiho Industries	Manufacturer	UFJ Bank	Chuo Mitsui Trust	–	20040520
8840	Daikyo (2)	Real estate	UFJ Bank	Mizuho Corporate Bank	20040921	20040928
8263	The Daiei (2)	Retailer	UFJ Bank	Mizuho Corporate Bank	20041014	20041228
1722	Misawa Homes Holdings (2)	Construction	UFJ Bank	Chuo Mitsui Trust	20041129	20041228

Note: The bank in parentheses is excluded from the sample of event studies because the main bank (Mizuho Bank) of Kyushu Industrial Transportation at the same event day and the secondary bank (Mizuho Corporate Bank) of Dia Kensetsu, whose event days coincide with Kyushu Industrial Transportation, belong to the same financial holding company (Mizuho Financial Group).

Table 32.6 List of debt forgiveness cases (ordinary cases) during the period from 1998 to 2004 (Ordinary cases, 37 firms, 42 cases)

Code	Company	Industry	Main bank	Secondary bank	Event date	
					First news report on request for debt forgiveness	Formal anouncement of the corporate revitalization plan
1886	Aoki Corporation	Construction	Asahi Bank	IBJ	—	19981119
1808	Haseko Corporation (1)	Construction	Daiwa Bank	Chuo Mitsui Trust	19981118	19981218
1806	Fujita Corporation	Construction	Sakura Bank	Tokai Bank	19981114	19981224
1920	Shokusan Jutaku Sogo	Construction	Sanwa Bank	Sakura Bank	—	19990122
8834	Towa Real Estate Development (1)	Real estate	Tokai Bank	Sumitomo Trust	19981114	19990205
1804	Sato Kogyo	Construction	Daiichi-Kangyo Bank	Hokuriku Bank	—	19990223
9232	Pasco Corporation	Transportation	Bank of Tokyo-Mitsubishi	Sanwa Bank	—	19990301
3887	Chuo Paperboard	Manufacturer	Juroku Bank	(Nippon Credit Bank)	19981124	19990430
8020	Kanematsu Corporation	Wholesaler	Bank of Tokyo-Mitsubishi	(Norinchukin Bank)	—	19990518
8003	Tomen Corporation (1)	Wholesaler	Tokai Bank	Sakura Bank	—	20000209
1837	Hazama Corporation (1)	Construction	Daiichi-Kangyo Bank	Mitsubishi Trust	—	20000525
1861	Kumagai Gumi (1)	Construction	Sumitomo Bank	(Shinsei Bank)	20000810	20000901
1814	Daisue Construction	Construction	Sanwa Bank	Sumitomo Trust	—	20000926
1821	Mitsui Construction	Construction	Sakura Bank	Chuo Mitsui Trust	20001124	20001228
8263	The Daiei (1)	Retailer	UFJ Bank	Mizuho Corporate Bank	20020109	20020118
1808	Haseko Corporation (2)	Construction	Chuo Mitsui Trust Bank	Sumitomo Trust	—	20020221
8246	Iwataya Department Store	Retailer	Mizuho Bank	Fukuoka Bank	—	20020226
1923	Misawa Homes (1)	Construction	UFJ Bank	Chuo Mitsui Trust	—	20020301

5936	Toyo Shutter	Manufacturer	Mizuho Bank	UFJ Bank	20011122	20020308
1823	Sumitomo Construction	Construction	SMBC	Sumitomo Trust	—	20020426
2262	Snow Brand Milk Products Company	Manufacturer	(Norinchukin Bank)	UFJ Bank	—	(20020503)
8840	Daikyo (1)	Real Estate	UFJ Bank	Mizuho Corporate Bank	—	20020514
7202	Isuzu Motors	Manufacturer	Mizuho Corporate Bank	UFJ Bank	—	20020814
1854	Arai-Gumi	Construction	SMBC	Sumitomo Trust	—	20020823
5480	Nippon Yakin Kogyo	Manufacturer	Mizuho Corporate Bank	UFJ Bank	—	20020918
6765	Kenwood Corporation	Manufacturer	Asahi Bank	Chuo Mitsui Trust	—	20020927
8834	Towa Real Estate Development (2)	Real Estate	UFJ Bank	(Shinsei Bank)	—	20021105
8003	Tomen Corporation (2)	Wholesaler	UFJ Bank	SMBC	—	20021226
unlisted	Seibu Department Store	Retailer	Mizuho Corporate Bank	(Shinsei Bank)	20021218	20030114
1837	Hazama Corporation (2)	Construction	Daiichi-Kangyo Bank	Mitsubishi Trust	—	20030117
8014	Chori	Wholesaler	Mizuho Corporate Bank	UFJ Bank	20030222	20030328
1861	Kumagai Gumi (2)	Construction	SMBC	Sumitomo Trust	—	20030403
1805	Tobishima Corporation	Construction	Mizuho Corporate Bank	SMBC	20030403	20030416
1890	Toyo Construction	Construction	UFJ Bank	Mizuho Corporate Bank	—	20030610
7210	Nissan Diesel Motor	Manufacturer	Mizuho Corporate Bank	Risona Bank	20030917	20030930
8193	Suzutan	Retailer	UFJ Bank	Bank of Tokyo-Mitsubishi	—	20031027
1827	Nakano Corporation	Construction	Bank of Tokyo-Mitsubishi	Bank of Tokyo-Mitsubishi (Mitsubishi Trust)	—	20031121
8838	Nichimo	Real Estate	Risona Bank	Yokohama Bank	—	20031125
1908	Sampei Construction	Construction	Resona Bank	(Shoko Chukin Bank)	—	20031126
1826	Sata Construction	Construction	Gunma Bank	(Ashikaga Bank)	—	20040127
7211	Mitsubishi Motors Corporation	Manufacturer	Bank of Tokyo-Mitsubishi	(Mitsubishi Trust)	20040517	20040521
2768	Sojitz Holdings Corporation	Wholesaler	UFJ Bank	Mizuho Corporate Bank	20040720	20040726

Note: The banks whose names are in parentheses are excluded from the sample of event studies because their equity prices are unavailable. For Nakano Corporation and Mitsubishi Motors Corporation, only equity prices of their main bank (Bank of Tokyo-Mitsubishi) are available because their secondary bank (Mitsubishi Trust) is a subsidiary under the same financial holding company (Mitsubishi Tokyo Financial Group, MTFG).

announcement of the plan', then I define the two different event days as the first event (e = 1) and second event (e = 2), respectively. If the case does not include the event day of the 'first news report', I define the 'formal announcement' as the first event (e = 1) and nothing as the second event. Summing these first and second events for all cases, in total, 70 event windows associated with 15 event days for the cases supported by the IRCJ and 55 event days for the ordinary cases are present.

32.4.3   Event Study Methodology

In order to obtain the estimates of abnormal returns for the main banks and secondary banks, I conduct standard market model regressions of the realized daily stock return for main bank i (main bank or secondary bank) of client firm j, R_{ijt}, on a measure of the realized daily return of market index, R_{mt}, and three daily dummies for each event e, $D_{ijk,e}$, $k \in [-1,1]$, which take the value of 1 for days inside the event window and 0 outside:

$$R_{ijt} = \alpha_{ij} + \beta_{ij}R_{mt} + \sum_{e}\sum_{k=-1}^{1}\gamma_{ijk,e}D_{ijk,e} + \varepsilon_{ijt}. \tag{32.2}$$

The coefficients $\gamma_{ijk,e}$ for bank i measure the daily abnormal returns inside the event window. ε_{ijt} is a random error. Estimation period includes 150 trading days before the first event day (e = 1) and 40 trading days after the second event day (or the first event day if nothing in e = 2). The duration of these sample periods conforms closely to those used in the previous studies (e.g., Ongena et al., 2003; Brewer et al., 2003). Sums of the daily abnormal return estimates $\hat{\gamma}_{ijk,e}$ during the event windows yield cumulative abnormal return (CAR) estimates. In the following section, I consider three event windows: single day abnormal returns, AR[0], cumulative abnormal returns, CAR[−1,0], including one day before the event day, and CAR[0,1], including one day after the event day.

Figure 32.5 reports estimated single-day abnormal returns of the main bank, AR[0], over the events of the 'first news report' and the 'formal announcement of the plan' for each of the ordinary cases (40 cases excluding Snow Brand Milk Products whose main bank, Norinchukin Bank, is an unlisted company; in chronological order from the left) and the cases supported by the IRCJ (last nine cases). The figure shows that, in the ordinary cases, the announcement of client firm's request for debt forgiveness generally negatively impacts the stock price of its main bank in many events excluding several events like the 'formal announcement of the plan' of Toyo Shutter and Nissan Diesel. Even in these cases, their abnormal returns at the event of the 'first news report', which constitutes the first event day when market participants perceive the possibility of debt forgiveness for the first time, are marginal and much smaller than those of the formal announcement of the plan.

In contrast, most of the abnormal returns of the main bank for the cases supported by the IRCJ exhibit positive signs regardless of the choice of the event days, which indicates that the announcement of a client firm's request for debt forgiveness positively impacted the stock price of the main bank under the scheme with the IRCJ's support. Interestingly, on the first event day for the Kyushu Industrial Transportation, one of the first three cases supported by the IRCJ, the abnormal return of its main bank, Mizuho Bank (Mizuho HD), accounted for 9.5 percent, the highest among all cases.

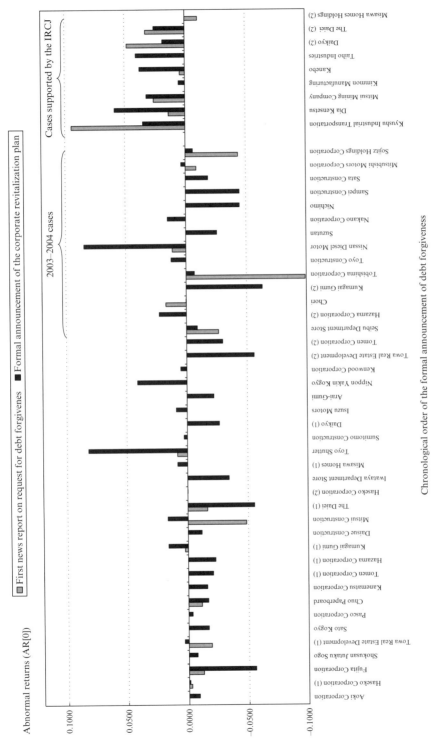

Figure 32.5   Main bank's abnormal returns on the event day of the announcement of debt forgiveness

32.5   EVENT STUDY RESULTS

32.5.1   Simple Mean Test

For analyzing the statistical importance of the difference between the ordinary cases and the cases supported by the IRCJ, first I take a simple average of ARs (and CARs) of main banks within each sample under the assumption that the estimates are independent across events, and then I use the t-test to judge its significance. Table 32.7(A) reports the sample average and p-value for AR[0], CAR[−1,0] and CAR[0,1] of main banks by using all events including the 'first news report' and the 'formal announcement of the plan' during all of the sample period from 1998 to 2004.

From a main bank's perspective, the events exert a differential impact on the stock price depending on whether the case receives the IRCJ's support. In the cases supported by the IRCJ, the sample average of (cumulative) abnormal returns of main banks are about 0.03 (3 percent) and have a statistically significant positive value at the 1 percent level for the AR[0] and CAR[−1,0] and at the 5 percent level for the CAR[0,1]. In contrast, in the ordinary cases without the IRCJ's support, the sample average of AR[0] of a main bank is −0.01 and is statistically significant at the 5 percent level. In this case, the average cumulative abnormal returns of the other event windows, CAR[−1,0] and CAR[0,1], are about 0 and not statistically important at any significance level. Next, I conduct an equality test of mean between the ordinary cases and the cases supported by the IRCJ. The results reported below the main banks for the ordinary cases show that the differences between sample means are statistically significant at all event windows, AR[0] at the 1 percent, CAR[−1,0] at the 5 percent, and CAR[0,1] at the 10 percent level, respectively. Even if I extract the 14 cases during the period 2003–2004 from the ordinary cases – that is, those in a same period when the cases supported by the IRCJ were announced to be granted debt forgiveness – the sample average never exhibits a statistically significant positive value in all the event windows, and especially, its AR[0] is different from the sample mean of the cases supported by the IRCJ at the 1 percent level.

The impact of the announcement of debt forgiveness on a main bank is different between the cases supported by the IRCJ and the ordinary cases; this is consistent with my hypothesis that the investors precisely predict the importance of the IRCJ's involvement while negotiating among lenders. If a debt-ridden company only requests debt forgiveness for its lenders, then the main bank's burdens of debt forgiveness are expected to be disproportionately large due to the rule of the traditional main bank system. However, when the company requests debt forgiveness under the IRCJ's support, the allocation of burdens will be proportional to lenders' loan shares and the burdens of the main bank could be significantly lightened as a result of the IRCJ-led negotiation among lenders. Therefore, the results in Table 32.7 show that the announcement of debt forgiveness exerted statistically significant positive impacts on the stock prices of the main banks in the cases supported by the IRCJ, while it tended to exert negative impacts on those in the ordinary cases. Further, this difference was observed even when I restricted the sample to the most recent years during the period from 2003 to 2004.

Table 32.7(B) reports the sample mean and its p-values using the sample of secondary banks for cases supported by the IRCJ and for the ordinary cases. In the cases supported by the IRCJ, the sample average of (cumulative) abnormal returns of secondary banks

Table 32.7 Average (cumulative) abnormal returns of main and secondary banks across events

(A) Average (C)ARs of main banks across events (both first news report and formal announcement of the plan) within each sample

Sample	Number of events		AR[0]	CAR[−1,0]	CAR[0,1]
Main banks for cases supported by the IRCJ (9 cases)	15	Sample mean	0.030	0.036	0.033
		p-value	(0.000)	(0.000)	(0.019)
Main banks for ordinary cases (42 cases)	55	Sample mean	−0.010	−0.000	0.003
		p-value	(0.019)	(0.920)	(0.655)
	Test for equality of mean	t-value	4.685	2.291	1.952
		p-value	(0.000)	(0.025)	(0.055)
Main banks for 2003–2004 ordinary cases (14 cases)	23	Sample mean	−0.001	0.007	0.013
		p-value	(0.830)	(0.625)	(0.217)
	Test for equality of mean	t-value	2.729	1.396	1.158
		p-value	(0.009)	(0.171)	(0.254)

(B) Average (C) ARs of main banks across events (both first news report and formal announcement of the plan) within each sample

Sample	Number of events		AR[0]	CAR[−1,0]	CAR[0,1]
Secondary banks for cases supported by the IRCJ (9 cases)	14	Sample mean	0.011	0.023	0.008
		p-value	(0.092)	(0.030)	(0.324)
	Test for equality of mean	t-value	2.054	0.995	1.695
		p-value	(0.049)	(0.328)	(0.108)
Secondary banks for the ordinary cases (33 cases)	43	Sample mean	−0.001	0.008	0.004
		p-value	(0.776)	(0.345)	(0.435)

Notes:
1. The sample in the table includes main and secondary banks' ARs (or CARs) at the event days of both first news report and formal announcement of the plan) corporate revitalization.
2. '2003–2004 ordinary cases' includes 12 cases that formally announced the request for debt forgiveness in 2003–2004.
3. I take a simple mean of ARs (or CARs) within each sample under the assumption that the estimates are independent across events, and use a t-test to judge significance. The sample mean and p-value are reported in the first row and the second row, in parentheses, respectively.
4. To check the differences comparing to mean of (C)ARs for main banks for cases supported by the IRCJ, t-value and p-value of 'test for equality of mean' are reported below each sample.

ranges from around 0.008 to 0.02, and statistically significant positive value at the AR[0] and CAR[−1,0]. Result of the test for equality of mean shows that secondary banks' sample average AR[0] is different from that of the main banks for the cases supported by the IRCJ at the 1 percent level.

These results show that announcement of the IRCJ's support could benefit not only the main banks of the debt-ridden companies but also their secondary banks, mainly due to the resolution of the debt overhang problem. However, we tend to observe larger positive impacts on the valuations of main banks compared to those of secondary banks, especially in the abnormal returns of the single day event window, AR[0].

32.5.2   Cross-Sectional Regressions

In order to gain a better understanding of the patterns underlying the abnormal returns documented in Table 32.7, I consider regressing the (cumulative) abnormal returns of the main and secondary banks on a set of variables related to the size of debt forgiveness, firm's stock price, and the bank–firm relationship characteristics. A description of the variables and summary statistics is provided in Table 32.8.

The first variable is the 'proportional burdens of debt forgiveness divided by the bank's capitalization', which measures the impact of the minimum burdens of debt forgiveness on the lender's valuation under the assumption that the lender's burden is proportional to its loan share. A bank's capitalization is calculated by using the bank's stock price of one day prior to the event day (window). A sample summary in Table 32.8(A) reveals that the impact is very significant for the bank's valuation. The sample means of this variable for main banks include 0.047 for the cases supported by the IRCJ and 0.040 for the ordinary ones. On the other hand, though the impacts are smaller for the secondary banks than for the main banks in both of the cases, the sample means take still significant values: 0.012 for the cases supported by the IRCJ and 0.025 for the ordinary cases. I expect a negative coefficient of this variable, which indicates that the case with the larger amount of debt forgiveness potentially has a larger negative impact on the main and secondary banks' equity price, on the event of the announcement of debt forgiveness.

The second variable includes the 'firm's (cumulative) abnormal returns times the market value of equity holding divided by the bank's capitalization' to control the direct impact of the transformation of a firm's stock price on the event day (window) on the bank's valuation. The firm's stock price underwent significant transformation on the event of the announcement of debt forgiveness. In the Japanese main bank system, the major lenders, especially main and secondary banks, usually hold a substantial amount of a client's stock; therefore, a change in the client firm's stock price can substantially impact the bank's valuation in an ordinary situation. Therefore, the expected sign of the coefficient of this variable is positive. However, as the sample summary in Table 32.8(B) shows, these direct impacts on the banks' valuation through equity holdings are nearly 0 in all cases and all event windows. This reflects the evidence that the stock price of the debt-ridden company had been very low and that the change in the value of the stock holding relative to the major bank's capitalization had been negligibly small until one day prior to the announcement of debt forgiveness.

The third variable consists of the dummies for the closeness of a bank–firm relation-

Table 32.8 *Sample summary of explanatory variables*

	Cases supported by the IRCJ				Ordinary cases			
	Main banks		Secondary banks		Main banks		Secondary banks	
	9		9		42		33	
Total number of cases	Mean (Medium)	Max (Min)	Mean (Median)	Max (Min)	Mean (Median)	Max (Min)	Mean (Median)	Max (Min)
(A) Debt forgiveness (First events)								
Proportional burdens of debt forgiveness/Bank capitalization	0.0468 (0.0223)	0.2216 (0.0001)	0.0120 (0.0043)	0.0582 (0.0003)	0.0401 (0.0155)	0.1758 (0.0012)	0.0251 (0.0072)	0.2076 (0.0000)
(B) Firm's abnormal returns (First events)								
Firm AR[0] * Market value of firm equity holdings/Bank capitalization	−0.0000 (0.0000)	0.0000 (−0.0001)	0.0000 (0.0000)	0.0002 (−0.0001)	0.0000 (0.0000)	0.0010 (−0.0017)	−0.0000 (0.0000)	0.0004 (−0.0010)
Firm CAR[−1,0] * Market value of firm equity holdings/Bank capitalization	−0.0000 (0.0000)	0.0000 (−0.0001)	0.0000 (0.0000)	0.0002 (−0.0001)	0.0000 (0.0000)	0.0014 (−0.0017)	0.0000 (0.0000)	0.0008 (−0.0008)
Firm CAR[0,1] * Market value of firm equity holdings/Bank capitalization	−0.0000 (0.0000)	0.0000 (−0.0002)	0.0000 (0.0000)	0.0015 (−0.0010)	0.0000 (0.0000)	0.0007 (−0.0013)	−0.0000 (0.0000)	0.0007 (−0.0015)
(C) Bank–firm relationships	Number of relevant cases	% to total cases	Number of relevant cases	% to total cases	Number of relevant cases	% to total cases	Number of relevant cases	% to total cases
Bank top equity holder immediately before debt forgiveness	5	56	0	0	21	50	3	9
Bank representation on the president immediately before debt forgiveness	4	44	0	0	27	64	1	3
Stable lending relationship since 1990	7	78	2	22	37	88	21	64
Bank top equity holder since 1990	4	44	0	0	13	31	1	3
Bank representation on the president since 1990	2	22	0	0	8	19	1	3

ship in terms of lending, equity ownership and bank representation on management, which are considered as proxy variables for the excess burden of debt forgiveness borne by the main and secondary banks.

I employ two kinds of dummies with different time horizons indicating, respectively, a relationship immediately before debt forgiveness and a more stable longer-term relationship during a decade from the beginning of the 1990s. The first includes 'the bank top equity holder among outsiders', which is a dummy variable that takes 1 if the main (secondary) bank is the largest shareholder excluding the insiders (owner and owner's family, employee stock holders) in the fiscal year-end prior to the announcement of debt forgiveness and 0 otherwise.[6] In terms of the bank representation on the board, almost all companies in the sample included at least one official from their main bank on their board prior to the announcement of debt forgiveness. Therefore, I choose a more strict definition, 'the bank representation on president', as a dummy indicating the close relationship with the bank, which takes 1 if the bank representation is a president (including a chairman and a vice-president with *daihyoken*) of the company and 0 otherwise.[7] Moreover, if these two kinds of relationships are observed for consecutive years since 1990, I identify the case as having a stable long-term relationship with its main (secondary) bank prior to debt forgiveness. Last, I consider another measure of relationships, 'the stable lending relationship since 1990', which takes 1 if the case is that the main (secondary) bank is the largest (the second-largest) lender for consecutive years since 1990 and 0 otherwise.

A sample summary in Table 32.8(C) shows that sample firms had close relationships with their main banks prior to debt forgiveness. For example, more than half of the main banks in cases supported by the IRCJ and the ordinary cases were top equity holders and sent the banks' personnel as presidents immediately before debt forgiveness. In terms of the lending relationship, the main bank relationship continued over a decade prior to debt forgiveness. In contrast, there are no such strong relationships between sample firms and their secondary banks except the 'stable lending relationships since 1990' in the ordinary cases. In total, we observe no significant difference between the cases supported by the IRCJ and the ordinary cases in terms of bank–firm relationships. The expected sign of the coefficients of these dummies is negative because market participants anticipate larger excess burdens of debt forgiveness on the bank if the bank relationship is stronger.

Finally, the most important variable constitutes a dummy for the cases supported by the IRCJ. If market participants predict that the excess burdens of the main bank will be significantly mitigated and that the new rule of the proportional burden of debt forgiveness will be introduced, then the announcement of debt forgiveness with the IRCJ's support will positively impact the stock price of the main bank. If the sign of coefficient of the IRCJ dummy is statistically significant and positive even after controlling the other variables related to various characteristics of the case, I can conclude that the IRCJ's support will positively impact the bank's valuation in the process of resolution of the debt overhang problem.

32.5.3   Regression Results

First of all, I regress AR[0], CAR[−1,0], and CAR[0,1] on the explanatory variables using a sample with only main banks. Table 32.9 reports the results on various combinations of the explanatory variables. Most of the coefficient estimates exhibit the same signs as

Table 32.9 Cross-sectional examination of main banks' (C)ARs: all events

Sample	Main banks, all events										
Dependent variable	AR[0]					CAR[−1,0]			CAR[0,1]		
Constant term	−0.003 (0.552)	−0.000 (0.963)	0.010 (0.326)	0.012 (0.243)	0.013 (0.205)	0.019 (0.091)	0.019 (0.096)	0.031 (0.108)	0.021 (0.051)	0.013 (0.221)	0.034 (0.065)
Proportional share of debt forgiveness/Bank capitalization	−0.095 (0.180)	−0.126 (0.073)	−0.144 (0.045)	−0.151 (0.036)	−0.156 (0.031)	−0.273 (0.036)	−0.173 (0.181)	−0.289 (0.034)	−0.260 (0.033)	−0.211 (0.082)	−0.289 (0.023)
Firm AR * Bank equity holdings/Bank capitalization	2.812 (0.815)	0.870 (0.941)	3.740 (0.745)	2.750 (0.811)	−0.415 (0.972)	12.1501 (0.509)	10.542 (0.572)	11.232 (0.557)	8.887 (0.710)	15.784 (0.508)	4.563 (0.853)
Bank top equity holder immediately before debt forgiveness	−0.010 (0.155)					−0.023 (0.086)			−0.018 (0.161)		
Bank representation on the president immediately before debt forgiveness		−0.004 (0.588)					−0.023 (0.096)			−0.003 (0.771)	
Stable lending relationship since 1990			−0.017 (0.076)	−0.017 (0.073)	−0.016 (0.094)			−0.019 (0.294)			−0.017 (0.315)
Bank top equity holder since 1990					−0.008 (0.368)			−0.009 (0.563)			−0.022 (0.166)
Bank representation on the president since 1990				−0.010 (0.274)	−0.006 (0.553)			−0.018 (0.330)			0.005 (0.752)
IRCJ's support dummy	0.041 (0.000)	0.043 (0.000)	0.041 (0.000)	0.041 (0.000)	0.042 (0.000)	0.044 (0.007)	0.036 (0.026)	0.042 (0.012)	0.035 (0.021)	0.032 (0.038)	0.035 (0.025)
Adjusted R-squared	0.228	0.248	0.261	0.263	0.261	0.103	0.100	0.081	0.076	0.049	0.068
Observations	70	70	70	70	70	70	70	70	70	70	70

Note: Coefficients and p-values based on t-test are reported in the first row and in parentheses, respectively.

expected above. The 'proportional burdens of debt forgiveness divided by the main bank's capitalization' exhibits a negative and statistically significant coefficient estimate that remains robust across all specifications. The estimates suggest that a 10 percent increase in the minimum burden of debt forgiveness on the main bank leads to a decrease by about -1.5 percent in AR[0] and between -2.1 and -2.7 in CAR[$-1,0$] and CAR[$0,1$]. Second, the 'firm's (cumulative) abnormal returns times the market value of equity holding divided by the main bank's capitalization' exhibits a positive but statistically insignificant estimate in all specifications. This result provides the evidence that this variable is very small in all samples. Third, dummies for the bank–firm relationship prior to the announcement of debt forgiveness exhibit negative coefficient estimates, particularly statistically significant for the 'stable lending relationship since 1990' for AR[0] and the two measures of bank–firm relationships immediately before debt forgiveness for CAR[$-1,0$]. If the main bank has a close relationship with a client firm measured by these dummy variables, then the (cumulative) abnormal returns decrease by -1.5 percent to -2.3 percent.

In terms of a dummy for the cases supported by the IRCJ, the coefficient estimates are positive and statistically significant at the 5 percent level across all specifications and event windows. The estimates suggest that the stock price of the main bank would increase by about 3.2 percent to 4.3 percent when debt forgiveness would be announced with the IRCJ's support.

These results are consistent with my hypothesis that the IRCJ's support significantly mitigates the excess burdens of debt forgiveness and positively impacts the main bank's valuation. Market participants precisely predicted the consequences under the IRCJ's scheme and the announcement of debt forgiveness to resolve the debt overhang problem as the client firms positively impact their main bank's valuation.

Similar results are reported in Table 32.10, which represents the results for the sample including the main and secondary banks. Even controlling after explanatory variables on size of burdens of debt forgiveness and bank–firm relationships, we observe the statistically significant positive coefficient on the dummy for cases supported by the IRCJ in all specifications and event windows. More importantly, in the specifications incorporating a cross-dummy variable for the main bank of the IRCJ's support case, their estimated coefficients take the positive values from 0.02 to 0.04 in all event windows, and statistically significant on AR[0] and CAR[$0,1$] at the 5 percent level. Similar results are also confirmed in Table 32.11, which represents the results for the selected samples including the main and secondary banks, only first events (the first news report or the formal announcement of the plan) on the left-hand side and cases from 2003 to 2004 on the right-hand side of the table, respectively.

These results show that though it positively impacted on the valuation of the company's main and secondary banks, announcement of debt forgiveness under the IRCJ's support favored its main bank more, compared to the secondary bank. These results are consistent with my hypothesis that the IRCJ scheme disproportionately mitigates the main bank's burden of debt forgiveness that was extremely large under the traditional scheme.

32.5.4   Impacts on Non-Main Lenders and Existing Shareholders

The results presented above strongly support my hypothesis that main banks' burdens of debt forgiveness were mitigated substantially under the new scheme introduced by the

Table 32.10 Cross-sectional examination of main and secondary banks' (C)ARs: all events

Sample	Main banks and secondary banks, all events										
Dependent variable	AR[0]					CAR[−1,0]			CAR[0,1]		
Constant term	−0.000 (0.911)	0.002 (0.612)	−0.001 (0.702)	−0.002 (0.422)	0.004 (0.435)	0.014 (0.105)	0.018 (0.058)	0.019 (0.042)	0.010 (0.067)	0.014 (0.012)	0.017 (0.034)
Proportional share of debt forgiveness / Bank capitalization	−0.043 (0.410)	−0.068 (0.197)	−0.076 (0.152)	−0.070 (0.188)	−0.064 (0.231)	−0.185 (0.072)	−0.210 (0.044)	−0.216 (0.039)	−0.184 (0.029)	−0.231 (0.006)	−0.231 (0.007)
Firm AR * Bank equity holdings / Bank capitalization	2.025 (0.831)	3.103 (0.739)	0.134 (0.988)	3.158 (0.737)	3.404 (0.715)	12.969 (0.402)	13.631 (0.377)	11.159 (0.478)	25.612 (0.089)	23.775 (0.111)	24.2601 (0.108)
Stable lending relationship since 1990	−0.006 (0.252)	−0.009 (0.082)				−0.009 (0.356)	−0.012 (0.222)	−0.010 (0.331)	−0.004 (0.614)		
Bank top equity holder since 1990			−0.012 (0.074)				−0.007 (0.636)			−0.016 (0.144)	−0.017 (0.190)
Bank representation on the president since 1990				−0.009 (0.257)				−0.015 (0.388)	−0.000 (0.984)		
Main bank dummy					−0.005 (0.381)						
IRCJ's support dummy	0.026 (0.000)	0.012 (0.149)	0.014 (0.084)	0.015 (0.058)	0.010 (0.248)	0.026 (0.024)	0.011 (0.465)	0.009 (0.550)	0.017 (0.083)	−0.003 (0.786)	−0.005 (0.704)
IRCJ's support dummy * Main bank dummy	0.026 (0.017)	0.027 (0.016)	0.023 (0.031)	0.030 (0.011)		0.027 (0.199)	0.032 (0.138)		0.041 (0.022)	0.042 (0.021)	
Adjusted R-squared	0.131	0.164	0.165	0.152	0.162	0.046	0.051	0.048	0.042	0.081	0.068
Observations	127	127	127	127	127	127	127	127	127	127	127

Note: Coefficients and p-values based on t-test are reported in the first row and in parentheses, respectively.

Table 32.11   Cross-sectional examination of main and secondary banks' ARs: selected events

Sample Dependent variable	Main and secondary banks, first events				Main and secondary banks, 2003–2004 cases			
	AR[0]				AR[0]			
Constant term	−0.005	0.003	0.000	0.000	−0.004	−0.000	−0.000	0.000
	(0.131)	(0.418)	(0.925)	(0.869)	(0.426)	(0.980)	(0.995)	(0.919)
Proportional share of debt forgiveness / Bank capitalization	−0.092	−0.121	−0.120	−0.107	−0.052	−0.134	−0.126	−0.112
	(0.127)	(0.042)	(0.045)	(0.073)	(0.542)	(0.134)	(0.152)	(0.209)
Firm AR * Bank equity holdings / Bank capitalization	9.908	7.918	7.361	9.045	11.568	2.262	11.438	9.711
	(0.329)	(0.428)	(0.467)	(0.365)	(0.813)	(0.963)	(0.808)	(0.838)
Stable lending relationship since 1990			−0.005				−0.003	
			(0.388)				(0.651)	
Bank top equity holder since 1990		−0.012	−0.010	−0.008		−0.017		
		(0.100)	(0.198)	(0.282)		(0.095)		
Bank representation on the president since 1990	−0.003		−0.000		−0.021		−0.031	−0.030
	(0.688)		0.974		(0.136)		(0.031)	(0.041)
Main bank dummy			−0.009					−0.005
			(0.160)					(0.594)
IRCJ's support dummy	0.025	0.007	0.005	0.003	0.030	0.013	0.014	0.012
	(0.000)	(0.434)	(0.600)	(0.725)	(0.000)	(0.161)	(0.152)	(0.271)
IRCJ's support dummy * Main bank dummy		0.034	0.037	0.041		0.031	0.032	0.035
		(0.008)	(0.006)	(0.003)		(0.014)	(0.013)	(0.024)
Adjusted R-squared	0.114	0.181	0.169	0.190	0.170	0.219	0.234	0.235
Observations	91	91	91	91	62	62	62	62

Note: Coefficients and p-values based on t-test are reported in the first row and in parentheses, respectively.

IRCJ. However, the resolution of the debt overhang problem by debt forgiveness could impact on other stakeholders surrounding the companies supported by the IRCJ, especially on non-main major lenders and existing shareholders.

To see these possibilities, Table 32.12 reports the estimates of single-day abnormal returns, AR[0], on 12 event days related to 'first news report' and 'formal announcement

Table 32.12   Impacts of the IRCJ's support on equity values of the supported firms and their major lenders

Firm supported by the IRCJ	Main bank	Secondary bank	Other major banks with more than 3% loan share (rank among lenders)*			
24 July 2003: First report on the IRCJ's support for Kyushu Industrial Transportation and Dia Kensetsu						
Kyushu Industrial Transportation NA	*Mizuho* 0.094	BTM 0.026	Chuo-Mitsui Trust (3) 0.016	Sumitomo Trust (4) 0.028	Fukuoka (6) −0.025	Kumamoto Family (7) −0.004
Dia Kensetsu 0.356	Risona 0.013	*Mizuho* 0.094				
25 July 2003: First news report on the IRCJ's support for Mitsui Mining Company						
Mitsui Mining Company 0.193	SMBC 0.025	Chuo-Mitsui Trust −0.043				
28 August 2003: Formal announcement of the IRCJ's support for Kyushu Industrial Transportation, Dia Kensetsu, and Mitsui Mining Company						
Kyushu Industrial Transportation NA	Mizuho 0.034	BTM 0.046	*Chuo-Mitsui Trust* (3) 0.041	Sumitomo Trust (4) 0.039	Fukuoka (6) 0.011	Kumamoto Family (7) NA
Dia Kensetsu −0.295	Risona 0.058					
Mitsui Mining Company −0.101	SMBC 0.031	*Chuo-Mitsui Trust* 0.041				
28 January 2004: Formal announcement of the IRCJ's support for Kimmon Manufacturing						
Kimmon Manufacturing 0.230	Risona 0.005	Tokyo-Mitsubishi 0.000	Mizuho Corporate (3) 0.015	Musashino (4) −0.000		
16 February 2004: First news report on the IRCJ's support for Kanebo						
Kanebo −0.162	SMBC 0.004	Mizuho Global −0.006	UFJ (3) −0.021			
10 March 2004: Formal announcement of the IRCJ's support for Kanebo						
Kanebo 0.029	SMBC 0.037	Mizuho Global 0.019	UFJ (3) 0.028			

Table 32.12 (continued)

Firm supported by the IRCJ	Main bank	Secondary bank	Other major banks with more than 3% loan share (rank among lenders)*		
20 May 2004: Formal announcement of the IRCJ's support for Taiho Industries					
Taiho Industries −0.100	UFJ 0.040	Chuo-Mitsui Trust 0.041	Mizuho Project (3) −0.009	SMBC (5) −0.007	
21 September 2004: First news report on the IRCJ's support for Daikyo					
Daikyo −0.137	UFJ 0.048	Mizuho Corporate −0.007	Risona (4) −0.015		
28 September 2004: Formal announcement of the IRCJ's support for Daikyo					
Daikyo −0.064	UFJ 0.018	Mizuho Corporate 0.013	Risona (4) 0.018		
14 October 2004: First news report on the IRCJ's support for The Daiei					
The Daiei −0.029	UFJ 0.032	Mizuho Corporate 0.016	SMBC (3) 0.023		
29 November 2004: First news report on the IRCJ's support for Misawa Homes HD					
Misawa Homes HD 0.072	UFJ −0.010	Chuo-Mitsui Trust −0.003	SMBC (3) 0.002	BTM (4) 0.012	Mizuho Corporate (6) −0.003
28 December 2004: Formal announcement of the IRCJ's support for The Daiei and Misawa Homes HD					
The Daiei 0.031	UFJ (0.025)	*Mizuho Corporate* 0.021	SMBC (3) 0.010		
Misawa Homes HD −0.005		Chuo-Mitsui Trust −0.000	SMBC (3) 0.010	BTM (4) 0.004	*Mizuho Corporate* (6) −0.003

Notes:

* 'Other major banks' are defined as the listed lenders, excluding the (unlisted) insurers and the government financial institutions, with more than 3% loan share prior to the IRCJ's support. *Italic bank names* depict that those banks were major lenders for plural companies supported by the IRCJ on the same event day.

1. The single day abnormal returns (AR[0]) on each event day are reported below the firm and bank names.

Table 32.13 Firm's equity return during the period under the IRCJ's support

Firm supported by the IRCJ	Formal announcement of the IRCJ's support	Date of exit	Buy-and-hold return of firm's equity (comparing to TOPIX)
Dia Kensetsu	20030828	20050810	17.5% (−5.1%)
Daikyo	20040928	20050408	50.0% (40.3%)
The Daiei	20041228	20061110	−4.9% (−44.4%)
Misawa Homes HD	20041228	20060331	117.2% (65.0%)

Notes:
1. The 'Date of exit' is defined as the day when the IRCJ sold all the equity and credit of the supported firm.
2. I use the split adjusted equity price in order to calculate the buy-and-hold return of the firm's equity.

of the IRCJ's support' for firms supported by the IRCJ, their main and secondary banks, and other major lenders with more than 3 percent loan share.[8]

First, for comparing the largest lender with the second-largest, abnormal returns of the main banks exceed those of the secondary banks in ten of all 14 samples. Furthermore, if focusing on abnormal returns for major lenders with rank under the second, I observe that the bank with lower rank among lenders tends to have lower abnormal returns. Especially, on the 'first event' day for six of all nine cases including Kyushu Industrial Transportation, Mitsui Mining Company, Kimmon Manufacturing, Kanebo, Taiho Industries and Daikyo, abnormal return of the bank with lowest rank takes a negative value, while that of the main bank takes a positive value. This shows that though the IRCJ's support could have a positive impact on equity prices of major lenders, their magnitudes are statistically less significant than those of the main banks.

Next, for the stock prices of firms, abnormal returns of the first cases supported by the IRCJ including Dia Kensetsu and Mitsui Mining Company on the event day of 'first news report' take large positive values, 0.36 and 0.19, respectively. However, equity prices of these two companies underwent significant negative decline, −0.29 and −0.10, on the event day of the 'formal announcement of the IRCJ's support' mainly because market participants perceived that, under the IRCJ's scheme, a degree of equity reduction in tandem with debt forgiveness would exceed 90 percent when the corporate revitalization plans were released to the public for the first time. Interestingly, in the following events, we observe that equity price of supported firms declined on the event days of 'first news report' except Kimmon Manufacturing and Misawa Homes HD. This evidence suggests that the market participants strongly perceived that the incumbent shareholders of firms supported by the IRCJ also bore a substantial amount of the burden of debt forgiveness through dilution of value by massive reduction of equity.

Table 32.13 reports equity returns from the announcement of the support through the date of exit for four firms that continued to be listed in the stock exchange after the IRCJ's support. Excluding the Daiei's small decline of equity returns, the other three firms underwent substantial increase of equity values during the support, especially for Daikyo (50 percent) and Misawa Homes HD (117 percent). Moreover, as I discussed in section 32.3.2, the IRCJ substantially benefited from equity participation to all supported companies including the remaining five companies delisted from the stock exchange after the IRCJ's support. Therefore, I conclude that the IRCJ's support was a scheme to improve the valuation of supported firms in the medium- and long-term perspective, though it caused a loss to the incumbent shareholder by a substantial degree of equity reduction.

32.6   CONCLUSION

Until the late 1990s, it had been widely recognized that the traditional main bank-led corporate restructuring malfunctioned under the circumstances that the main bank's financial conditions were heavily impaired by the large amount of disposal of non-performing loans. However, alternate schemes such as proportional allocation of debt forgiveness did not emerge voluntarily, and the application of the traditional rule of the disproportionately large excess burdens on the main banks continued.

The IRCJ, which was founded by the initiative of the government, significantly mitigated the excess burdens of debt forgiveness on the main bank by introducing the new rule on the burdens of debt forgiveness proportional to the loan shares of lenders. This is in contrast with the ordinary cases in which the main banks disproportionately bore large burdens of debt forgiveness. Moreover, market participants precisely incorporated the new rule of the burdens of debt forgiveness in the main bank's valuation, and the performance of the Japanese banking sector was improved under the IRCJ's support. By using the standard methodology of event study, I have confirmed that the announcement of debt forgiveness with the IRCJ's support positively impacted the equity price of the main bank, while such announcement in the ordinary cases that followed the traditional rule of the main bank-led resolution of the debt overhang problem tended to impact negatively the equity price of the main bank.

Although a number of factors prevailed that had led to the lost decade, it is widely recognized that the prolonged problem of non-performing loans constituted one of the major factors leading to the slump in the Japanese economy. This chapter's results strongly suggest that the large excess burden on the main bank under the traditional Japanese main bank system constituted one of the major impediments to resolving the non-performing loan problem in Japan.

NOTES

*   The original version of this chapter was published in October 2008 in the Japanese journal, *Kinyu Keizai Kenkyu* (Review of Monetary and Financial Studies) **27**, 1–24. This chapter also includes a theoretical model and new empirical results based on the updated dataset. This work was supported by the Grant-in-Aid for Young Scientists (B) (#21730259) of the Japan Society for the Promotion of Science (JSPS).

1.   Sakuragawa and Watanabe (2009) provide an event study on the impacts of the resolution of Risona and Ashikaga banks on the entire banking sector.
2.   Fukuda and Koibuchi (2006) attempt to determine the burdens of debt forgiveness on lenders as a solution of the cooperative game model including the Core and the Shapley values.
3.   By assessing the 42 cases that Sheard (1994) documented as the major cases of the main bank rescue, Fukuda and Koibuchi (2006) found that there existed only three cases of debt forgiveness, including Ataka

Sangyo (in 1977, its main bank was Sumitomo Bank), Japan Line (in 1987, IBJ), and Fuji Kosan (in 1992, Tokyo Bank), among the Japanese listed companies during the period from the 1960s to the early 1990s. In all three cases, the main banks bore most of the burdens of debt forgiveness.

4. A list of the main banks that offered the IRCJ's support, together with the supported companies, is reported in Table 32.2.

5. This type of discussion is not new for macroeconomics and corporate finance. It resembles Rogoff's (1985) discussion on delegation of monetary policy to a conservative central banker and Aghion and Bolton's (1992) incomplete contracting approach to corporate finance.

6. The average percentage of equity held by the main bank immediately before debt forgiveness amounts to 3.31 percent for the cases supported by the IRCJ and 4.38 percent for the ordinary cases.

7. The *daihyoken*, usually translated as 'representative powers', is the legal authority to commit the firm in external matters. See Hoshi and Kashyap (2001: 155) for details.

8. In order to obtain the estimates of abnormal returns for firms and other major lenders, I employ the same standard market model as equation (32.2) with the same estimation period.

REFERENCES

Aghion, P. and P. Bolton, (1992), 'An incomplete contract approach to financial contracting', *Review of Economic Studies*, **59**, 473–493.

Brewer, E., H. Genay, W.C. Hunter and G.G. Kaufman (2003), 'The value of banking relationships during a financial crisis: evidence from failures of Japanese banks', *Journal of the Japanese and International Economies*, **17**, 233–262.

Caballero, R., T. Hoshi and A. Kashyap (2008), 'Zombie lending and depressed restructuring in Japan', *American Economic Review*, **98**(5), 1943–1977.

Fukuda, S. and S. Koibuchi (2006), 'Furyo Saiken to Saiken Hoki: Mein Banku no Choka Futan' (Non-performing loans and debt forgiveness: excess burdens of the main bank), *Keizai Kenkyu* (Hitotsubashi University), **57**(2), 110–120.

Gertner, R. and D.S. Scharfstein (1991), 'A theory of workouts and the effects of reorganization law', *Journal of Finance*, **46**(4), 1189–1222.

Hoshi, T. and A. Kashyap (2001), *Corporate Financing and Governance in Japan*, Cambridge, MA: MIT Press.

Hoshi, T., A. Kashyap and D. Scharfstein (1990), 'The role of banks in reducing the costs of financial distress in Japan', *Journal of Financial Economics*, **27**(1), 67–88.

Ongena, S., D. Smith and D. Michalsen (2003), 'Firms and their distress banks: lessons from the Norwegian banking crisis', *Journal of Financial Economics*, **67**, 81–112.

Peek, J. and E.S. Rosengren (2005), 'Unnatural selection: perverse incentives and the misallocation of credit in Japan', *American Economic Review*, **95**, 1144–1166.

Rogoff, K. (1985), 'The optimal degree of commitment to an intermediate monetary target', *Quarterly Journal of Economics*, **100**, 1169–1189.

Sakuragawa, M. and Y. Watanabe (2009), 'Nippon no Kinyu Kaikaku no Hyoka: Shijo wa Do Miteitanoka?' (in Japanese) (Assessments on financial reform in Japan: how did market participants evaluate?), *Keizai Kenkyu* (Hitotsubashi University), **67**(1), 60–74.

Sekine, T., K. Kobayashi and Y. Saita (2003), 'Forbearance lending: the case of Japanese firms', *Monetary and Economic Studies*, **21**, 69–91.

Sheard, P. (1994), 'Main banks and the governance of financial distress', in M. Aoki and H. Patrick (eds), *The Japanese Main Bank System: Its Relevance for Developing and Transforming Economies*, Oxford: Oxford University Press, pp. 188–230.

33 Corporate governance of banks in Korea
Heungsik Choe and Byungyoon Lee

33.1 OVERVIEW

Since the 1997 Asian financial crisis, Korea has established an outside director system and has been working towards improving corporate governance (Choe and Lee, 2003). The outside director system was implemented in response to the financial crisis of 1997, which was partially the result of inadequate monitoring of majority shareholders and management by the board of directors. After the system was introduced, the Commercial Code and the Securities Exchange Act were amended to ensure that half of the board of large listed companies would be composed of outside directors, and a one-fourth from other listed and KOSDAQ-listed companies. Korean banks followed the same path, as the number of outside directors increased to account for half of the board and more than half of the outside director recommendation committee.

After the financial crisis, the outside director system was established in Korean companies and banks, but it has been criticized by some on the grounds that it is not effective from the point of view of shareholder wealth maximization. There have been complaints that lack of independence and relevant expertise have prevented outside directors from carrying out their duties in controlling major shareholders and management effectively. For example, banks competed to increase their assets from 2005 to early 2008, exposing them to larger risks. The boards did not keep their managements in check, which made the boards the target of criticism. Recent criticism of the system has been aimed at outside directors themselves; specifically, that they tend to pursue their own personal interest by taking advantage of regulations that were intended to enhance the independence of the directors at banks and bank holding companies.

Faced with growing complaints with respect to the banking board system, the Financial Services Commission (FSC) and commercial banks have been aiming to improve banking corporate governance in Korea. Best Practices for Outside Directors of Banks and Related Institutions were announced in January 2010 (Korea Federation of Banks, 2010). To enhance independence and expertise, the Best Practices contained several important clauses: separation of the posts of chief executive officer (CEO) and board chairman; limitations on the term of outside directors; introduction of staggered terms for the CEO and outside directors; enhancement of impartiality in the selection process of outside directors; prevention of conflicts of interest for outside directors; and strengthening of the *ex ante* and *ex post* expertise of outside directors.

In addition, the FSC is trying to introduce the Act on Corporate Governance of Financial Institutions to improve the governance system including the board system, audit committee, executive directors, major shareholders and compliance officers of all the financial institutions.

In this chapter, we will review the history of the board system adopted by Korean banks and bank holding companies, highlight problems in its application, and present solutions. This discussion will provide a background for the Best Practices announced in January 2010. We provide an overview of these suggested practices and discuss what needs to be done to improve corporate governance at Korean banks. Finally, we discuss how the Act on Corporate Governance of Financial Institutions can be improved.

33.2   HISTORY OF BANK AND BANK HOLDING COMPANY BOARD SYSTEMS

In January 1997, the Banking Act was amended for the purpose of reorganizing the board system by adopting a non-standing director-based system (renamed the 'outside director system' in January 2000), which would limit the number of standing directors to less than 50 percent of the total number of directors. The non-standing directors would constitute the CEO candidate recommendation committee.

In February 1998, the Rules on Securities Listing were amended so that the outside director system could be introduced in listed companies, and included the requirement that more than a quarter of the board should be composed of outside directors.

In February 1999, the basic framework for current corporate governance was implemented at banks' regular shareholder meetings: the board was to be largely composed of non-standing directors in order to enhance its governing function; the board's roles in decision-making and execution were to be separated by assigning the executive function to management and by strengthening the board's checks-and-balances role relative to management. Furthermore, a variety of subcommittees were to be formed under the board. The Commercial Code was amended in December 1999 to permit the formation of different committees under the board and of an audit committee (optional).

In January 2000, the Securities Exchange Act was amended to lay the legal groundwork for the outside director system and the audit committee system. The amendment urged listed companies to fill over one-fourth of their board with outside directors, and large listed companies (over 2 trillion won in total assets) to select more than three outside directors and make up over half of the board with outside directors. Large listed companies were required to set up an outside director candidate nomination committee and to fill more than one-half of the committee with outside directors. Qualifications for outside directors (such as being a major shareholder) were specified, and large listed companies were required to create an audit committee and make up more than two-thirds of the committee with outside directors.

The Banking Act was also amended in January 2000 to require at least three outside directors making up more than half of the board, and that an audit committee be established with at least two-thirds of the committee composed of outside directors.

In March 2000, some operational problems were addressed by clarifying the roles of the board and the CEO; promoting the active operation of the board and committees; requiring a performance evaluation of the directors; shortening an outside director's term to one year (to coincide with the evaluation period); and developing an evaluation system that linked performance to pay.

In March 2001, the Securities Exchange Act was amended to apply the outside director and audit committee systems to KOSDAQ-listed companies. Under the revised Act, the outside director system that was introduced for listed companies was applied to KOSDAQ-listed companies (except for venture businesses with less than 1 trillion won in total assets). Large-scale KOSDAQ-listed companies were required to put an audit committee in place, and large-scale KRX- and KOSDAQ-listed companies were required to include board member candidates recommended by minority shareholders (1 percent or higher) in their recommendation list to the general shareholder meeting. Also, the voting rights of majority shareholders were to be restricted for those exceeding the 3 percent threshold when appointing outside directors to serve on the audit committee. The audit committee chairman was required to be appointed from among outside directors.

In July 2002, the Banking Act was amended such that the bank CEO nomination committee system was abolished, and a special clause on the appointment of outside directors was replaced by the outside director candidate nomination committee system.

In December 2003, the Securities Exchange Act was amended to require that outside directors in large listed companies comprise more than 50 percent of the board, and that at least one of the audit committee members was an accounting or finance expert.

In December 2008, an amendment to the Banking Act was submitted to the National Assembly. It added a clause mandating that a 'major shareholder and his or her special related parties' would be disqualified from becoming outside directors, and a majority of outside directors on the board became a requirement.[1]

In January 2009, the Commercial Code was amended. New clauses on the board system and outside directors were introduced to make the Code consistent with the Securities Exchange Act. In January 2010, the Korea Federation of Banks announced Best Practices for Outside Directors of Banks and Related Institutions. In June 2010 the FSC organized public hearings before promulgating the Act for the Corporate Governance of Financial Institutions.

33.3   CURRENT STATE OF THE BANK AND FINANCIAL HOLDING COMPANY BOARD SYSTEM

33.3.1   The Current State of Outside Directors on Bank and Holding Company Boards

Currently, outside directors hold the majority of positions on the boards of banks and bank holding companies (Table 33.1). The proportion of outside directors on the boards of banks and bank holding companies has continuously increased. As a result, the average number of outside directors in banks and financial holding companies (FHCs) exceeds half of the board directors as required by the Banking Act and the Financial Holding Company Act. Thus, it is fair to say that in the case of banks and bank holding companies, major resolutions and activities of committees under the board are completely controlled by outside directors.

33.3.2   The Current State of the Bank Outside Director System

Qualifications for outside directors of a bank
On 17 May 2010, the Banking Act was partially amended.[2] The previous qualifications for outside directors were stipulated in Articles 18 and 19 of the Regulations concerning

Table 33.1 Composition of the boards of banks and financial holding companies as of 16 August 2010 (unit: person, %)

	FHC					Bank										
	KB	Shinhan	Hana	Woori	Kookmin	Shinhan	Hana	Woori	SC first	KEB	Daegu	Busan	Kwangju	Cheju	Jeonbuk	Kyungnam
Total no. of directors (A)	11	12	13	12	7	10	9	11	10	11	7	7	6	6	8	6
No. of outside directors (B)	9	8	9	7	4	8	6	8	7	8	5	5	4	4	6	4
B/A	81.8	66.6	69.2	58.3	57.1	80.0	66.6	72.7	70.0	72.7	71.4	71.4	66.7	66.7	75.0	66.7

Sources: Mid-year reports of each company.

the Supervision of Banks. The newly amended Banking Act combined these two clauses into one in Clause 7 of Article 22.

The qualifications for outside directors in the amended Banking Act can be classified into two types of criteria: negative criteria, which stipulate the disqualification rules; and positive criteria, which prescribe what constitutes a qualified person.

According to the disqualification rules, a person falling under one of the following criteria is ineligible to become an outside director: a minor, an incompetent or quasi-incompetent person, a person who has been declared bankrupt, a person who has been sentenced to imprisonment,[3] or a person who has been officially disciplined due to regulatory violations.[4] Other subparagraphs disqualify persons based on factors that could potentially compromise the independence of an outside director: a major shareholder or person specially related to him/her; a person who is or was a standing employer of the bank, its subsidiary, its branch or the bank holding company within the last two years; a person who is or was a standing employer of the legal entity that is involved in an important transaction with the bank as designated by presidential decree; or a person who is or was in a competitive or cooperative position in business terms within the last two years.

The positive criteria are more broadly and abstractly defined in Clause 2 of Article 18 of the Banking Act. The Article refers to a qualified person as 'a person who has experience and knowledge in finance and cannot possibly harm the public interest of a financial institution, its sound management and the credit system'.

Composition of bank boards

The composition of bank boards in Korea is prescribed in Article 22 of the amended Banking Act. As noted above, the number of outside directors for a bank should exceed three and form a majority of the board (Clause 2 of Article 22). Also, a bank should set up a nomination committee to recommend outside director candidates (based on Clause 2 of Article 393 of the Commercial Code). The outside directors are to be selected at the shareholders meeting from among the appropriately recommended candidates (Clause 4 of Article 22).

Authority of bank boards

The authority of bank boards in Korea is prescribed in Articles 23 and 35.2 of the Banking Act. Specifically, Clause 1 of Article 23 stipulates the following items as subjects for deliberation and resolution by the board: management goals and assessment; revisions to Articles of Incorporation; budgets and settlement of accounts including compensation for executive officers and employees; material changes in the organization such as dissolution, transfer or merger; and internal control guidelines.

Clause 2 of Article 23 specifies the board's authority as prescribed by Clause 1 of Article 393 of the Commercial Code referring to the possibility of delegating certain decisions in accordance with the Articles of Incorporation of the financial institution. The decisions that can be delegated this way are the rights to nominate or dismiss a manager and to open, transfer or close a branch. Additionally, Clause 2 of Article 35 dictates that a board resolution is required for the bank to provide credit exceeding an amount designated by a presidential decree (the lesser of one-thousandth of total equity capital and 5 billion won).

33.4   PROBLEMS IN THE BANK BOARD SYSTEM AND SUGGESTIONS FOR IMPROVEMENT

33.4.1   Problems in the Bank Board System

Lack of independence of outside board directors

The outside director system in Korea was first adopted by banks as a non-standing director system through an amendment to the Banking Act in 1998. Since then, a variety of improvement measures have been taken to reinforce the independence of outside directors. Among these have been to include major shareholders and related parties among those disqualified to be outside directors as a way to limit the influence of majority shareholders. The same objective is served by the requirement that properly nominated outside directors comprise at least 50 percent of the board. Furthermore, the influence of senior management and major shareholders on nominations for outside directors was reduced by the revised nomination procedures mentioned above. In spite of these substantial reforms one cannot conclude that the attempts to increase the independence of outside directors have delivered results that clearly serve the best interest of banks as a whole. There are several reasons for this skepticism with respect to the role of the outside directors.

First, many observers have claimed that outside directors lack management expertise since they often do not meet expertise criteria, and because information from management to the outside directors is not always provided in a timely manner. In such cases, it can be difficult for outside directors to make independent decisions at a board meeting without being influenced by major shareholders or management.

Second, major shareholders and management may join the outside director nomination committee. This raises the likelihood that major shareholders or management could influence outside director recommendations, thereby weakening the independence of outside directors.

Third, lack of independence may persist for a long period as a result of 'path-dependence' in the nomination process, which can result if the process of appointing outside directors is dominated by outside directors. In other words, once a less-independent outside director is elected, the consequences persist. To prevent such path-dependence in the UK, Code Provisions state that non-executive directors should be evaluated with stricter yardsticks in cases where they serve more than six years (two three-year terms).

Fourth, there are concerns that a self-contained organization created by outside directors could lead outside directors to form a 'clubby board' that pursues personal gain at the expense of the best interests of the company. To avoid such conflicts of interest, institutions should be put in place to ensure that outside directors can make independent decisions free from the influence of management, major shareholders, the government or other interests. This would enable outside directors to perform their role of overseeing management more effectively.

Lack of relevant expertise of outside board directors

Lack of expertise and independence due to collusion between management and directors result in a situation where outside directors cannot keep management in check. In other words, a lack of expertise results in an inability to understand corporate management. In such cases, outside directors become unable to determine their own agenda for the board. They may passively follow the executive's opinion. Therefore, it is necessary to verify the expertise of outside directors to encourage independent decision-making, as well as appropriate management decisions.

The expertise of outside directors can be divided into two categories: *ex ante* and *ex post*. *Ex ante* expertise means that an outside director has work-related knowledge of relevance for the business prior to the appointment as director. In other words, the director has experience or education in a field related to the business. *Ex post* expertise refers to knowledge that can be acquired through training and the information provided by company management after the appointment as director.

Under the current Banking Act, the criteria[5] regarding *ex ante* expertise of outside directors are very broadly prescribed. As a result of this vagueness, many people without related expertise in the banking sector are elected as outside directors of banks and then criticized for not adding value to the bank. Toughening the *ex ante* qualification criteria for outside directors would serve as a screening tool in appointing those with greater *ex ante* expertise. This would enhance the level of expertise of outside directors as a whole.

Even if outside directors with *ex ante* expertise are appointed, it is essential that they be provided with *ex post* training and relevant management information to improve the level of their *ex post* expertise, especially since the banking industry requires very specialized knowledge. Considering that most board agendas revolve around making financial decisions, outside directors should be continuously educated with regard to decision-making and training in order to perform their role properly and effectively monitor management. Outside directors must ensure that they have access to relevant management information to ensure that they can help guide the company in the right direction.

33.4.2   Best Practices for the Bank and BHC Board System

The Best Practices for Outside Directors of Banks and Related Institutions, proposed in January 2010, were aimed at providing outside directors with more independence, as well as protecting the interests of the entire company. The system was designed in such a way that the guidelines were prepared as 'best practices' that can be flexibly adjusted by each bank or bank holding company depending on its specific needs. Although the best practices generally are in compliance with international practices of 'comply or explain',[6] each bank and bank holding company is permitted to tailor the system to its specific circumstances.

Separation of CEO and board chairman posts

There are two competing theories regarding the benefits and costs to be obtained by separating or combining the roles of the CEO and chairman of the board. Practices vary from country to country. The rationale for separation is that the board's independence as the representative of shareholders increases, since the board can monitor the CEO and the management without internal conflicts of interest. In contrast, proponents of combining the roles argue that the integration of CEO and chairman of the board enhances the efficiency of corporate management, particularly the speed and accuracy of decision-making. Thus, if emphasis is placed on board independence, separation would be the best option, whereas combining the roles would be preferred if efficiency of corporate decision-making is the dominant consideration. Looking at different countries, the UK has adopted separation, whereas Germany has separated the management board and supervisory board, thereby detaching the CEO and the chairman. A French company can choose between separation and combination, while the United States has no specific regulations in place. US companies often combine the roles of CEO and chairman of the board.

If the separation of the roles of CEO and chairman of the board causes efficiency losses, the senior outside director system can serve as a substitute mechanism for achieving efficiency. In this system, senior directors preside over their own meetings with outside directors and play the role of mediator between management and the chairman of directors. Senior outside directors promote communication as well, and they can play a central role in overseeing management. Korea has already introduced the senior outside director system in the public sphere. All public and quasi-government agencies are required to appoint one non-standing senior outside director in accordance with Article 21 of the Act on Management of Public Institutions.

The Best Practices suggest that the CEO and chairman should be appointed separately so that board members can monitor management effectively. The chairman of the board is recruited from among the outside directors. However, to prevent inefficient management decision-making, the board is allowed to operate a senior outside director system as an alternative in cases where the risk of inefficiency is deemed significant.

Limits on the terms of outside board directors
If the terms of outside directors are short, outside directors may not be able to gain a sufficient understanding of the company, but if they are long, there is the risk that collusion with management impairs board independence. In Korea, the term for most outside directors of banks is one year, which can be considered too short from the point of view of developing expertise. The short term also raises concerns about independence, since directors with little expertise are easily led to collude with management, who can influence their reappointment. Hence, the term of directors should be lengthened without being too long.

Other countries are moving toward shortening of board terms that may be excessively long. In the UK, an outside director working for the same company for more than six years (two three-year terms) is subject to a more rigorous evaluation for re-election. It is generally thought that independence could diminish substantially after nine years (three terms). In France, it is stipulated by statute that the tenure of directors must not exceed four years.

The Best Practices require that the term and the total duration of tenure of outside directors be limited to two and five years, respectively (Article 11 of the Best Practices).

Staggered terms between CEO and outside board directors
In cases where outside directors and the CEO share the same terms of tenure for many years, there is a risk that collusion might arise between them. However, there is no regulation suggesting that concurrent terms of management and directors be restricted in Korean banks and bank holding companies.

The Best Practices suggest that one-fifth of the board should be replaced by new directors every year to minimize the number of outside directors whose terms overlap with those of the CEO and the chairman of the board.

Enhancing the transparency of the selection process of outside board directors

There is a concern that the independence of directors might deteriorate if management and controlling shareholders exert influence, directly or indirectly, on the process of selecting candidates for outside director seats within the outside director recommendation committee. The objectivity and transparency of the recommendations of the nomination committee can be enhanced if the outside director recommendation process is disclosed publicly and subject to market evaluation. Therefore, the Best Practices require the nomination committee members to publicly disclose their relationship with recommenders, officers and shareholders when recommending candidates as outside directors.[7] Also, there is cause for concern that advisors recommend themselves considering that the nomination committee consists mainly of outside directors. In order to address these potential issues, the Best Practices recommend that directors nominated by the board shall be excluded from voting.

Prevention of conflicts of interest for outside board directors

Since financial institutions have been allowed to expand their footprint into new sectors of finance, banks and bank holding companies can now compete in other sectors, thus giving rise to potential conflicts of interest. For example, when a bank's outside director holds a post in another financial company as an outside director, a conflict of interest can occur. The new guidelines prohibit, as a rule, outside directors, non-standing directors or non-standing auditors of financial institutions that are not an affiliate of a bank from becoming an outside director of the bank.

There was a provision in the original Regulations on Supervision of Banking Business that stipulated that any person who holds an important trading relationship with a bank cannot become an outside director of that bank. However, the scope of regulation was too narrow to address any real world problems. The Regulations on Supervision of Banking Business were thus amended to define broadly[8] the terms of a trading relationship with a bank, so that anyone who has a stake in the bank could not become an outside director.

Improvement of relevant expertise of outside board directors

In order to monitor management properly, outside directors must be 'qualified' in terms of industry expertise. The independence of outside directors and their expertise can be said to have an organic relationship. Some observers have pointed out that the positive qualification criteria for gauging the expertise of outside directors at the time of nomination are insufficient to prevent the appointment of outside directors with low levels of expertise. To deal with this problem, the Best Practices contain a provision that qualified outside directors should be those with sufficient financial, economic, business, legal, accounting, media or other professional knowledge and practical experience in related fields.

In addition, outside directors must have access to the same information as the CEO of the company in order to monitor management. Thus, it is necessary for the company to provide management information and training for the directors. To this end, the Best Practices require designation of a department that officially supports directors and provides them with management information and training. Thereby, outside directors can strengthen their *ex post* expertise.

Evaluation and compensation of outside board directors and proper disclosure
Evaluating the activities of outside directors is essential in ensuring that they perform their roles effectively. Therefore, the Best Practices require that any activities[9] performed by outside directors on the board and in subcommittees during the previous month must be disclosed by the 15th of the following month. They also require that outside directors conduct self-assessment, and that the board and employees assess outside directors on the basis of their activities. Furthermore, they state that the evaluation methods must be disclosed along with information on whether to evaluate the performance of the previous year.

Outside directors were once compensated with stock options linked to performance in addition to base salary, but there was criticism that it was inappropriate to pay compensation linked to performance to outside directors who are responsible for the evaluation and compensation of the management officers. Therefore, such practices were prohibited. However, it can be difficult to motivate outside directors with basic compensation without performance-based incentives. Therefore, the Best Practices allow outside directors to be compensated in accordance with their responsibilities and activities. Information about the total compensation of outside directors should be disclosed along with details about base salary and other benefits of committee members (in audit, evaluation, compensation and risk management committees).

33.5 FUTURE AGENDA TO IMPROVE CORPORATE GOVERNANCE

As mentioned above, the Best Practices for outside directors of banks in Korea were announced in early 2010. They were followed by a similar announcement for investment companies, leading to some improvement in the board system across the industry. However, after the global financial crisis in 2008 the global demand for better governance practices for financial firms grew. In response, the Korean government took advantage of this opportunity to improve the corporate governance of financial companies. The government is currently seeking to integrate corporate governance-related legislation by combining separate laws for each type of financial institution into one law that will apply to all financial institutions. The intention is to solve the existing governance issues with one comprehensive piece of legislation. In this section, we will exemplify the need for comprehensive regulation as well as key elements of the proposed legislation.

33.5.1 Need for Comprehensive Legislation

The main purpose of the Act on the Corporate Governance of Financial Institutions is to enhance the stability of the entire financial system, to achieve effective supervision through the integrated regulation of corporate governance, and to ensure compliance with international standards throughout the financial industry.

First, the Act on the Corporate Governance of Financial Institutions is aimed at enhancing the accountability of the entire financial system by ensuring consistent governance across the industry, which should help to minimize differences between sectors and secure more solid governance structures for financial institutions. These structures reinforce responsibilities, controls and monitoring of management. The consistent governance structure is also essential in securing a stable financial system, as well as in promoting the interests of depositors, insurance policy holders and investors.

Second, it is necessary to bring about more effective supervision through the integrated regulations on governance by, for example, improving internal control and risk management systems. By linking the high-level structure of the board with substructures such as internal controls, compliance and risk management, the corporate governance of financial institutions in general can be expected to be upgraded. Additionally, effective regulation of the governance system can be achieved through consistent improvements in qualification and assessment reviews, and through improved discipline for officers, executives and key business personnel.

Third, the Act on the Corporate Governance of Financial Institutions can be viewed as one part of a policy to improve the consistency of governance and compensation practices. Such consistency has been emerging as a key challenge in the international community since the global financial reform.

33.5.2   The Direction for Legislation

The Act on the Corporate Governance of Financial Institutions is expected to reshape institutions with respect to the independence, expertise and accountability of outside directors, to enhance the credibility and monitoring role of the board. The Best Practices reshaped the banking sector in these aspects. The Act will lead to greater accountability for management, as well as stronger monitoring of operations of boards led by outside directors. In addition, tougher regulations on executive officers will help to improve the monitoring process for registered directors as well as for officers with significant influence on the management of a financial institution.

A plan is being prepared to operate audit committees as an outside director-centered system to ensure that their roles of monitoring and controlling management take root through greater independence. Additional measures will be taken to reinforce the support system for the audit committee, with stronger internal audits and internal control systems to ensure effective *ex post* audit. Also, the Act is expected to reinforce the stature of the entire board of directors, and strengthen confidence in internal–external audit functions. This will be achieved through increased independence and expertise of the audit committee, and through the stabilization of the committee-led monitoring functions.

Efforts will be made to toughen eligibility requirements for executives and shareholders, including major shareholders. First, the accountability of major shareholders of a financial institution will be enhanced by requiring *ex post* qualification reviews in order to maintain eligibility. In other words, the legal system will be revamped to maintain dynamically the eligibility of major shareholders of financial institutions across the industry by pressuring them into acting responsibly with respect to financial consumer protection, sound management and system stability. In addition, the credibility of the internal governance structure will be enhanced over time by means of an eligibility suspension system, which will make qualification criteria stricter for employees.

The practical role of compliance officers and risk managers will be continually upgraded. Levels of protection, appointment procedures and compensation schemes will be improved throughout the legal system. Internal controllers or compliance officers are in effect in charge of *ex ante* monitoring for financial companies. Additionally, by introducing the risk manager system and by establishing risk management committees, Korea will be in line with the international trend toward strengthened risk management. Thus, the risk management system, which has been operating autonomously, will be subject to corporate governance law, as is common internationally. The system will provide a legal basis for regulating the risk management system of financial institutions. Authority and responsibility for risk management will be clearly defined.

A compensation-related regulation system will also be overhauled and institutionalized. Compensation issues that can be regulated by law based on international and local best practices (for example compensation committee) will also be reflected in the law in order to build a systematic incentive system. This system is expected eventually to facilitate the functions of the board by strengthening the authority of the board over management.

Governance regulation of financial institutions will be applied in a more consistent and fair manner by applying the same legislation in similar cases, whenever possible. In other words, comprehensive rules will be drawn up for matters that need to be regulated by one standard across the industry in order to ensure fair regulation and prevent regulatory arbitrage across the industry. Examples of such matters are the organization of the board, minority shareholder rights, and a cooling-off period.

33.6   CONCLUSION

Since a system of outside directors on boards in the Korean banking industry was adopted in 1997, efforts have been made to improve the independence and expertise of outside directors. However, there are still some who doubt that outside directors are able to carry out their roles independently of influence from CEOs. If this is the case, risk management in banks may not be effective. Hence, in January 2010, banks announced the Best Practices for Outside Directors of Banks and Related Institutions, with the objective of enhancing the level of independence and expertise of outside board members. Currently, the FSC is preparing the Act on Corporate Governance of Financial Institutions to improve policies regarding the corporate governance of financial institutions, including banks. It is generally believed that such efforts will be successful in helping Korean banks to build the effective control systems for corporate governance.

Historically, corporate governance problems in the banking industry could not be solved solely by means of system improvement. Further processes were periodically required to achieve systemic improvement. All parties in a bank have to bear in mind that the value of banks will increase through the build-up of efficient corporate governance and the establishment of effective 'checks and balances' between the CEOs and the board of directors.

Moreover, market participants have incentives to consider whether a bank has appropriate corporate governance when evaluating the bank. In Korea, where corporate governance systems are already well developed, further governance problems in banking can be avoided if all interested parties and market participants recognize the need for reform and pursue appropriate measures.

NOTES

1. However, the clause was not applied to non-listed banks which did not have a strong need for minority shareholder protection (although they were still required to have more than three outside directors).
2. The new law came into effect on 18 November 2010.
3. A person who has been sentenced to imprisonment and for whom five years have not passed since the execution of the penalty was terminated; a person who has been sentenced to a penalty by violating any banking or other finance-related laws and for whom five years have not passed since the execution of the penalty was terminated; and a person who has been sentenced to probation and for whom the probation period has not yet expired.
4. A person who has been officially disciplined (dismissal or reprimand) in accordance with the Banking Act, the Bank of Korea Act, the Act concerning the Establishment of the Financial Supervisory Organizations, or financial laws of other countries, and for whom five years have not passed since the discipline was determined; a person who served as employee of a financial institution which was subjected to an administrative measure such as taking timely corrective actions or accepting to transfer a contract concerned, and for whom two years have not passed since the measure was announced; and a person who worked as employee of a corporation whose license was revoked in accordance with the Banking Act or finance-related laws, and for whom five years have not passed since the date of revocation.
5. The qualifications for outside director are stipulated, in Clause 2 of Article 18 of the Banking Act, as a person who has experience and knowledge of finance and would not harm the order of the credit market, sound management and the public interest of banks and financial holding companies.
6. OECD (2009) and Walker (2009).
7. Specifically, the following information should be disclosed: (i) overview of outside director candidate nomination process; (ii) committee member list and profile; (iii) adviser list and profile, in the case of setting up an advisory committee; (iv) information on proponent and relationship with candidate; (v) relationship of outside director candidate with the bank (including affiliates), officers, and major shareholders; (vi) whether to satisfy the qualification conditions described in applicable laws and Article 6, and supporting grounds; and (vii) reasons for nominating as candidate.
8. Legal counsel, management consulting and agreements, and information technology (IT) services, financial surveys, research, real estate and asset management services contracts, legal entities whose past transactions amount to more than 10 percent of sales revenue, whose single-trading contracts amount to over 10 percent of sales income, and whose paid-in-capital amounts to over 5 percent of equity, and legal entities that are under a technology transfer contract.
9. Outside director's attendance and vote results such as approval, opposition, abstention, and so on.

REFERENCES

Choe, Heungsik and Bong-Soo Lee (2003), 'Korea bank governance reform after the Asian financial crisis', *Pacific-Basin Finance Journal*, **11**, 483–508.
Financial Services Commission (FSC) (2010), *The Act on Corporate Governance of Financial Institutions*, preliminary version, June.

Korea Federation of Banks (2010), *Best Practices for Outside Directors of Banks and Related Institutions*, January.

OECD (2009), *Recommendation on Reforming Board of Directors of Financial Institutions*, June.

Walker, David (2009), 'A review of corporate governance in UK banks and other financial industry entities', 16 July, available at http://webarchive.nationalarchives.gov.uk/+/http://www.hm-treasury.gov.uk/d/walker_review_consultation_160709.pdf.

34 Banking regulatory governance in China: a legal perspective
Yufeng Gong and Zhongfei Zhou

34.1 INTRODUCTION

The past decades have witnessed that bank failure is more or less regulatory failure. In financial crises in East Asia, Ecuador, Mexico, Russia, Turkey and Venezuela, weak regulatory governance – for example political interference in the regulatory process, regulatory forbearance, weak regulation, and lack of public sector accountability and transparency – is considered a contributing factor to the depth and size of the systemic crises.[1] Since these crises, the importance of good banking and financial regulatory governance to financial stability had begun to attract attention from international standard-setting bodies such as the Basel Committee on Banking Supervision (hereinafter Basel Committee), the International Association of Insurance Supervisors, and the International Organization of Securities Commissions as well as the International Monetary Fund (IMF) and the World Bank.

Notwithstanding its prominence, the definition of and guidance on regulatory governance of a banking regulatory agency are not so clear in contrast to corporate governance. Udaibir Das and Marc Quintyn define regulatory governance as the capacity to meet the delegated objectives, protection from industry capture and political interference, and the respect of the agency for the broad goals and policies of the legislature.[2] They identify independence, accountability, transparency and integrity as the four key institutional underpinnings for good regulatory governance.[3] As the basic contents of integrity are included in the other three components, this chapter will employ independence, accountability and transparency to analyze regulatory governance of China's banking regulatory agency, the China Banking Regulatory Commission (hereinafter CBRC) from a legal perspective. Centering upon the conceptual framework, the authors will discuss advantages and disadvantages in Chinese banking legislation with respect to regulatory governance and attempt to outline a legal framework for guaranteeing sound regulatory governance of the CBRC.

34.2 INDEPENDENCE OF THE CBRC

Regulatory independence refers to independence from political and industry interference from the government and interest groups. Regulatory independence can be assessed with respect to performance independence, personnel independence, financial independence and legal immunity of supervisory liability. To ensure regulatory independence, the contents of the four components should be stipulated in the form of law.

34.2.1   Performance Independence

Performance independence refers to the autonomy of a banking regulatory agency to perform statutory functions. The extent of performance independence depends on whether legislation has clear provisions with respect to the regulatory objectives, legal status and regulatory powers of a banking regulatory agency.

Regulatory objectives

Legislating of regulatory objectives empowers a banking regulatory agency to refuse any intervention and request from the government or interest groups which are in violation of any regulatory objective. Although legislation in different countries has different statutory objectives of the banking regulatory agency,[4] the protection of the banking (or financial) system stability and the protection of the interests of banking customers are commonly two of the statutory objectives. For example, under the Banking Supervision Law of China, banking regulatory objectives include contributing to safe and sound operations of the banking industry and maintaining the public's confidence in the banking industry.[5]

The regulatory objectives of the banking regulatory agency partially overlap with the overall objectives of the government. This overlap, combined with the strong initiative of the government to achieve the short-term goal of economic growth and financial stability, may lead to interpretation of safe and sound operations of the banking industry as preventing individual banks from failing during the government's term of office. In this case, the intervention of the government in the banking regulatory agency is unavoidable. Where a bank failure is taken as reflecting the regulatory agency's impotence or regulatory failure by the public or by itself, out of concern for its future destiny the agency is likely to accept the government's order of not closing a failed bank. In the authors' opinion, the objective of contributing to safe and sound operations of the banking industry requires the regulatory agency to focus on the stability of the whole financial system rather than prevent an individual bank from failing. As a practical and theoretical matter, bank failure is itself conducive to protecting the stability of the financial system as a mechanism of market discipline. This is why the authors suggest that the Chinese banking law should explicitly provide that the banking stability objective does not mean zero bank failure. Clarification of the objective would enhance the autonomy of the CBRC in making a decision of bailing out or closing a bank.

Legal status

Without legitimate establishment and delegation, no agency can truly independently fulfill its regulatory obligations. In many countries such as Canada, Finland and Australia, specific legislation regarding banking or the financial regulatory agency is enacted. In the UK, even if there is no specific law for the Financial Services Authority (FSA), the Financial Services and Markets Act specifically spells out the details of the FSA in Part One, 'Regulator'. The CBRC was established before the Banking Supervision Law was enacted. On 26 April 2003, the second session of the Standing Committee of the National People's Congress (NPC) of China made a decision according to which the CBRC was established to take over banking regulatory responsibilities from the People's Bank of China (PBOC). On 27 December 2003, the Standing Committee of the NPC passed the Banking Supervision Law, under which the CBRC is legally authorized to be responsible for regulating and supervising banking financial institutions and their activities.[6]

However, where banking regulatory responsibilities are distributed among different banking regulatory agencies, it is more probable that each regulatory agency would be captured by interest groups, even if all of them are set up according to law. Regulatory competition[7] arising from a multiple banking regulatory agency regime enables regulated banks to switch among regulators. On the one hand, any regulatory agency is reluctant to lose its regulatory turf and therefore reduce its regulatory budget because regulated banks switch charters. As a result, the banking regulatory agency may have to succumb to the influence of regulated banks. On the other hand, regulated banks themselves work to support such a fragmented regulatory structure and protect their business turf from other potential competitors. It is an open secret that the insurance industry would rather be regulated by '50 monkeys than one big gorilla'.[8]

Regulatory powers

From the perspective of protecting regulatory independence, the statutory objectives and legitimate status of a banking regulatory agency only bear a more or less theoretical meaning. In the authors' opinion, a clear-cut legal definition regarding regulatory powers would be a more operational approach to protecting regulatory independence. In this sense, the power of a banking regulatory agency both to enact and to implement regulatory rules independently needs to be confirmed clearly by law.

Basically, there are two different legislative practices with respect to making rules. In some countries, primary legislation and secondary legislation are so detailed that the regulator has no room for making rules. In other countries, primary and secondary legislation only produces broad-brush principles, leaving ample room for regulatory initiatives.[9] Some authors argue that in the first case, regulatory independence is limited as regulatory agencies are allowed to issue non-binding guidelines while regulatory independence under the second system is great because the agency can fine-tune technical regulations.[10] Although the authors doubt the causality between limited rule-making power and limited regulatory independence, it is argued that granting rule-making power to a regulatory agency should essentially enhance regulatory independence. The reasons for granting regulatory rule-making power to regulatory agencies are the technicality of banking regulatory rules and the fast-changing financial environment. Banking regulatory rules – prudential rules in particular such as capital adequacy, large exposure and loan loss provisioning – deal with the technicalities of banking regulation. Neither the legislator nor the government has expertise to understand these rules precisely, as banking regulatory agencies do. On the other hand, financial markets and financial products are fast-changing in nature. In this environment, banks would make endless efforts to escape regulation. In this cat and mouse game, only when the banking regulatory agency has the autonomy to issue or amend regulatory rules in time can it more or less avoid regulatory arbitrage by banks through financial innovation. In China, under the Banking Supervision Law, the CBRC has the power to make regulatory rules and bank prudential operational rules according to laws and regulations.[11]

As far as regulatory independence is concerned, however, legal protection for how to make rules independently is more important than legislative arrangements for rule-making power. In several countries it is common that the government intervenes in the regulatory agency's rule-making process, where the government forces the agency to lower loan classification standards and provisioning rules for loans to problematic economic sectors in order to facilitate lending to these sectors.[12] In China, the Legislation Law and the Banking Supervision Law divide responsibilities between the NPC, the State Council and the CBRC in setting regulatory rules. The general law on the banking sector is made by the NPC or its Standing Committee. The State Council has the power to enact administrative regulations both for the purpose of implementing laws and within the confines of the administrative and managerial functions defined by the Constitution,[13] while the CBRC may set and issue rules regarding banks and their activities according to laws and administrative regulations.[14] However, these general prescriptions result in ambiguities in dividing legislative responsibilities, which may frustrate the independence of the CBRC in setting regulatory rules. Generally speaking, regulatory rules can be classified in three main categories: economic rules, relating to bank entry, exit and resolution; prudential rules, dealing with capital adequacy, large exposure and liquidity adequacy; and finally, information rules, involving information disclosure to the public and supervisors.[15] Both economic rules and information rules are mostly fundamental and rigid. They should not be subject to too many changes over time and are therefore stipulated in the form of the NPC's laws and the State Council's regulations.[16] By contrast, prudential rules with regard to capital, risk asset, risk weight, and liquid liabilities and assets are technical. The definitions and the rules on these issues should adapt to the increasingly changing financial activities and products as well as regulatory purposes. For this reason, the authors argue that the setting of prudential rules – except those relating to basic standards or principles such as a capital adequacy ratio of 8 percent and a large exposure ratio of 15 percent that are defined by law or regulation – should be left to the CBRC's autonomy.

In addition to the independence to make regulatory rules, performance independence of banking regulatory agencies depends to a great extent upon their independence to implement regulatory rules. In other words, regulatory independence reflects the extent to which a banking regulatory agency is free from political interference and regulatory capture in licensing and revoking a license, conducting on- and off-site examinations and imposing penalties on violations. However, most of the regulatory activities are invisible so that the regulatory agency is vulnerable to interference from politicians and the supervised banks.[17] Therefore, it is suggested that legislators should fill in legislative gaps to the extent possible to prevent the regulatory agency from being interfered with in performing functions. Taking the Chinese legislation for example, the Banking Supervision Law provides that the CBRC shall not be subject to interference from governments and individuals.[18] This general provision, however, does not make any sense in safeguarding the CBRC's performance independence. Lack of legal guarantee can be illustrated through the CBRC's prompt corrective action. In China, prompt corrective action is a regulatory measure defined by the CBRC's rules. Under the CBRC's Measures on the Administration of Capital Adequacy of Commercial Banks (hereinafter, Measures on Capital Adequacy), the CBRC may take over a significantly undercapitalized bank.[19] Both the Commercial Banking Law and the Banking Supervision Law, however, provide that only a bank which has been or is likely to be in a credit crisis with the result that the interests of depositors and other customers are significantly affected may be taken over.[20] So far, neither Chinese primary legislation nor secondary (at the State Council's level) legislation has clearly linked significant undercapitalization to a credit crisis which significantly affects the interests of depositors. As a result, on the one hand, once the CBRC takes over the significantly undercapitalized bank, the bank may lodge a lawsuit with the court on the grounds that the CBRC's prompt corrective action lacks legal foundation. On the other hand, the government may revise this provision in the form of secondary legislation or directly stop the CBRC from taking prompt corrective action against the problem bank.

Under circumstances where the regulatory process is opaque, the more discretion banking regulatory agencies have, the more possibly they are prone to government interference and interest-group capture. To some degree, legislative technique affects the correlation between the former and the latter. Chinese banking laws set forth many qualitative standards under which the CBRC may take action against a violating bank. The qualitative standard – for example 'serious damage' – is subject to the CBRC's interpretation. It is highly probable that the CBRC may make different interpretations due to government and interest group pressure.

34.2.2   Personnel Independence

Personnel independence refers to legal arrangements for banking regulatory agency independence regarding the terms and procedures of appointment and dismissal of its senior officials, conflicts of interest and internal structure. The more rational the legal arrangements for personnel independence are, the less a banking regulatory agency suffers from political or interest-group interference.

Appointment and dismissal
Staff, especially senior officials in the banking regulatory agency, must have expertise, regulatory skill and integrity appropriate for performing their functions, which constitutes a basis for professional independence. Professional independence provides a guarantee for regulatory independence as regulatory staff with professional skills and good moral standing would have more ability to resist undue influence. Contrary to central banking law, under which the qualification requirements for a central banker are explicitly set forth, few banking laws or banking regulatory agency laws in the regime of central bank and banking regulatory agency separation stipulate the qualification requirements for banking regulatory officials. The Banking Supervision Law generally requires a banking regulatory official to have expertise and relevant experience appropriate for his position.[21] The silence of legislation on qualification requirements for banking regulatory staff reflects the fact that the legislators have not recognized the importance of these requirements to regulatory independence. In the modern banking industry in which bank risk management is a top focus, regulatory agencies will be subservient to banks if they have no capability to understand risk management models and techniques employed by banks. In the authors' opinion, qualification requirements, especially those relating to supervisory expertise, should be legally compulsory for a regulatory official.

The independence of a banking regulatory agency head(s) determines largely the independence of the whole regulatory agency. Therefore, legislation should establish an effective mechanism for protecting appointment of the head(s) from being influenced illegally by the government or interest groups. To ensure appointment of a qualified head(s) and depoliticized appointment, a doubt-veto approach is adopted in many banking laws, under which one body nominates and another body appoints, or one body appoints and another body approves. In the US, Hungary and Japan, the head of the regulatory agency is nominated by the government, prime minister or president, and approved by the president or Congress. In contrast, Australia, Belgium, France and Korea adopt a one-vote approach with the head being directly appointed by the government. The Chinese banking laws are silent on appointment of the chairman of the CBRC. According to China's political practices the chairman of the CBRC, which is an institution directly affiliated to the State Council, is directly appointed by the State Council. However, the CPC Central Committee's Regulations on Promotion and Appointment of Communist Party and Government Cadres (hereinafter, Regulations on Cadres) should be taken into account in discussing appointment and dismissal of Chinese government officials. According to the Regulations on Cadres, the appointment of government officials (including the head of the CBRC) must go through a series of processes including democratic assessment, review, deliberation and decision-making after the party committee's collective discussions.[22] The complex procedures may more or less reduce politicized appointment.

In a sense, the legal protection against arbitrary and non-procedural dismissal of a regulatory official is more important than the legal provisions on appointment for safeguarding regulatory independence. Relevant legislation must be in place to prevent regulatory officials from being removed during their term of office without any legal grounds. As one of the essential criteria in assessing compliance with the Core Principles for Effective Supervision, the Basle Committee's Core Principles Methodology states that the head(s) of the supervisory authority can be removed only for reasons specified in law.[23] Legally specified reasons for dismissal should relate to the regulatory official's professionalism and integrity rather than his failure to follow the instructions of political authorities. In the cases where central bank and banking regulatory agency are separated, only a minority of countries specify the reasons for dismissal of banking regulatory officials in the form of law. Under the Australian Prudential Regulation Authority (APRA) Act, the appointment of a supervisory member is terminated due to their becoming a director, officer or employee of a regulated entity; misbehavior or physical or mental incapacity; becoming bankrupt; absence from duty for a certain period; and others.[24] The Banking Supervision Law does not directly specify the grounds for firing a CBRC official. Article 43 of the law lists the cases where CBRC officials may assume administrative and criminal liability. Apparently, an official sentenced for a crime must be dismissed from their position at the CBRC. In addition, the Regulations on Cadres spell out the grounds for dismissing a Communist Party or government cadre, including unsatisfactory performance assessment, incapacity, gross misconduct and negligence, and so on.[25] As a common practice in China, the Regulations on Cadres apply equally to the removal of CBRC officials.

Conflict of interest

Where a regulatory official simultaneously holds jobs in other sectors during his term of office in the regulatory agency, a conflict of interest would not be avoided and personal independence would be compromised. For this reason, many banking laws provide for a number of measures to compel a regulatory official to be fully devoted to his responsibilities. The measures involve performance of duty on a full-time basis and prohibition from becoming an officer or director, or holding stock in financial institutions and even in any private and public entity. Under the Banking Supervision Law, the CBRC officials are prohibited from obtaining undue benefits by taking advantage of their position, and from doing part-time jobs in banks and other enterprises.[26]

In some central banking laws, the conflict-of-interest restriction is even extended to the activities conducted by a central banker after his term expires. Its basic intention is to restrain a central banker, after he leaves office, from being employed by a public or private entity which could exert influence on the central banker concerned while in office, so that he can avoid being captured, typically in the later term of office. In the US for example, the members of the Federal Reserve Board (Fed) shall be ineligible for two years after the term has expired to hold any office, position or employment in any member bank, if they fail to complete their entire 14-year term.[27] In contrast, however, very few banking laws impose restrictions on a regulatory official's employment during a certain period after he leaves office. In China, similar restrictions are prescribed by the Law on Civil Servants. A civil servant is not permitted to hold office in enterprises or other profit-making entities directly related to his original job, or engage in profit-making activities directly related to his original job, for three or two years, depending on whether the position is senior, after he resigns or retires.[28]

Internal structure

From a perspective of sound regulatory governance, regulatory agency independence should not be an excuse employed by an individual within the regulatory agency for his arbitrariness and autocracy. To ensure that regulatory policies are consistent and less likely to be decided by only a few individuals of the regulatory agency, legislation usually arranges the agency's internal structure to establish checks and balances. In the UK, the FSA consists of a chairman and a governing body. In exercising its legislative functions, the FSA must act through its governing body.[29] Through its non-executive committees, the governing body keeps under review the question of whether the FSA uses its resources in the most efficient and economic way, and whether the FSA's internal financial controls secure its proper conduct.[30] This structure is similar to that in a typical corporation: the governing body is analogous to the board of directors while the chairman is to the chairman of the board. In China, the Banking Supervision Law is silent on the internal structure of the CBRC. In practice, the CBRC has a chairman's meeting in operation. All of the members of the meeting are the CBRC's officials, and the meeting is chaired by the CBRC's chairman. It is doubtful whether the chairman's meeting, within which the members are ranked in seniority, can establish effective checks and balances against the chairman's abuse of power. For this reason, the authors suggest that banking legislation should design sound governance structure within the CBRC to ensure effective checks and balances.

On the other hand, where the law permits the government's representative to sit on or chair the board of a regulatory agency, without doubt it gives leeway for the government to intervene in the daily operation of the agency. According to Marc Quintyn et al.'s survey, 20 countries have a government representative to chair or sit on the board of the regulatory agency, while in 12 countries the law gives the minister of finance the right to intervene in the operations of the agency.[31] In Poland, the Financial Supervisory Authority must have voting members from the ministers responsible for financial institutions and social security or their representatives.[32] In Australia, the minister may give APRA a written direction about APRA's policies based on the Act-defined procedures and APRA must comply with the direction.[33]

34.2.3 Financial Independence

It is generally argued that even if a banking regulatory agency obtains performance and personnel independence, its overall independence would not be safeguarded if it does not have the autonomy to determine the financial resources to fulfill its mandate. Thus, any assessment of an agency's independence must analyze the degree to which it is subject to the power of the purse.[34] Financial independence refers to the ability of a regulatory agency to determine the size of its own budget and the allocation of resources and priorities that are set within the budget.[35] A banking regulatory agency is funded through either appropriations from the government budget or levies on regulated banks. In theory, the two funding sources can be used to interfere with regulatory independence. On the one hand, the government imposes its own will on a regulatory agency through controlling the source, size and use of the agency's budget; on the other hand, regulated banks may influence the regulatory agency through whether they pay fees or how much they would like to pay. So, legislation should arrange a mechanism under which a regulatory agency has discretion to propose its own budget in the case of funding from the government, and to determine together with the government the levy level in the case of funding via a levy.[36]

The CBRC is funded by the central government budget and levying on banks. Under the Budget Law and Implementation Regulations on the Budget Law, the classification of income and payment in the CBRC's budget is determined by the State Council, and the CBRC proposes its budget for the review of the Ministry of Finance through which the proposal is approved by the NPC or its Standing Committee. It is apparent that the CBRC does not have autonomy to determine its own budget, while the approval of the NPC or its Standing Committee is more procedural. In other words, the CBRC's budget is actually determined by the Ministry of Finance or the State Council. The government's say on the CBRC's budget creates the possibility for the government to interfere with the supervision of banks by the CBRC, particularly government-owned banks. In the authors' opinion, to ensure the budgetary independence of the CBRC, the law should grant the CBRC autonomy to determine its own budget proposal, which is directly submitted to the NPC for approval.[37]

The CBRC is partly funded by levies on regulated banks. According to the relevant rules of the State Council, levies are directly handed over to the central treasury, and the Ministry of Finance appropriates the levies to the CBRC according to the ministerial budget procedure. This approach cuts the direct relation between the CBRC and its regulated banks, and the door for industry capture through this channel is closed.

34.2.4   Legal Immunity of Supervisory Liability

The Core Principles for Effective Banking Supervision state that a suitable legal framework for legal protection of supervisors is necessary.[38] One of the essential criteria for assessing compliance with the Core Principles for Effective Banking Supervision is that the law provides protection to the supervisory authority and its staff against lawsuits for actions taken and/or omissions made while discharging their duties in good faith.[39] Legal immunity of supervisory liability refers to exemption or severe limit of tort liability of banking agencies and banking supervisors in discharge of their supervisory functions in good faith. According to Marc Quintyn et al.'s survey, about 78 percent of the countries surveyed have included legal immunity for all supervisory staff in their legislation.[40] In some countries, banking supervisors benefit from generic statutory protections or immunities for all government employees, while some other jurisdictions have specific statutory protections for regulatory agencies and supervisors. For example, paragraph 19 of Schedule One of the Financial Services and Markets Act of the UK clearly provides that the FSA is 'not to be liable in damages . . . for anything done or omitted in the discharge, or purported discharge', of its functions. That is to say, banking regulatory agencies cannot be sued by depositors for losses as a result of actions or omissions by agencies in the bona fide exercise of any functions conferred under law.

In China, laws and regulations do not provide specific statutory immunity for the CBRC and its staff. In the context of ensuring regulatory independence, it is essential to provide specific rules on granting full or partial immunity from tort liability to the CBRC (including its supervisors). In our opinion, the CBRC may be exempt from tort liability if it meets the following criteria. Firstly, the CBRC must perform its legally defined functions. Under the Banking Supervision Law, the CBRC's functions include setting and issuing regulatory rules, granting and revoking bank licenses, conducting on- and off-site examinations, and taking prompt corrective action. According to Chinese administrative law theory, these functions can be classified into two categories: abstract administrative action (e.g., setting regulatory rules) and specific administrative action. Although there is debate regarding whether an abstract administrative action falls within the scope of administrative liability, the authors suggest that tort liability arising out of any abstract administrative action can be exempted unless it is unconstitutional or taken in bad faith.

Secondly, the CBRC must perform its functions in good faith. Absence of good faith can be interpreted as bad faith, negligence, gross negligence or unlawfulness. In Chinese administrative law circles, there are different views about the liability criterion for administrative tort, including fault liability, non-fault liability, illegality liability, and fault and illegality liability. For the purpose of this chapter, the authors do not discuss these criteria in detail. Given the importance of banking regulation to financial stability, it is argued that supervisory liability should be limited and the law should confine liability to situations of fault and illegality. By this is meant that the CBRC is liable for damages only caused willfully or negligently and unlawfully.

Thirdly, the CBRC owes a duty of care to depositors. It should be noted that 'depositors' here is defined as depositors as a whole rather than individual depositors. The risk of imposing liability on the supervisory authority arising from two judgments of the German supreme court in 1979 forced Parliament to revise the German Banking Act in 1984 by prescribing that banking supervision exclusively served the public rather than private depositors' interests.[41] In Hong Kong, the judge in 1988 held that the banking regulator's duties were owed to the public at large, not to individual depositors, and the granting of a license could not form the basis of a claim by the depositors.[42] Apparently, the argument that the CBRC's duty of care is owed to depositors as a whole rather than individual depositors should be adopted by the Chinese banking law.

Fourthly, there is a causal relation between the CBRC's alleged breach of its duty of care and the loss incurred by the claimant. Generally speaking, the CBRC's approval of a license does not amount to a warranty that all banks are sound and safe. Even if it breaches a duty of care in approving a bank license, the CBRC is not liable for the losses of depositors of the bank concerned. Only when a particular breach of duty directly leads to loss by depositors can the CBRC not be granted immunity from liability.

34.3 ACCOUNTABILITY OF THE CBRC

Regulatory independence is relative rather than absolute. Absolute independence would lead to dictatorship, autocracy and corruption. Therefore, banking regulatory independence is mutually complementary to regulatory accountability. As the essential criterion for assessing whether a supervisory authority is accountable for the discharge of its duties, the Basel Committee's Core Principles Methodology requires that the law prescribe the operational accountability.[43] 'Accountable', according to the *Oxford English Dictionary*, is defined to mean not only to be held responsible for one's action, but also to be required to justify and explain actions and decisions.[44] Based on this definition, regulatory accountability implies that bank regulatory agencies should explain, justify and assume responsibility for their performance to the body or bodies delegating authority to them. Therefore, the basic concept of accountability involves accountable for what, to whom and how. The focus of accountability is on not only *ex post* punishment but also ongoing monitoring. Accordingly, regulatory accountability consists of performance accountability and institutional accountability. Legislation should properly design arrangements for the two types of accountability.

It should be noted that 'accountable to whom' should not be interpreted as 'control by whom' or even 'intervention by whom'. Unfortunately, legislation in many countries holds a banking regulator accountable through control; for instance, the government or its representatives sit on the board of the regulatory agency.[45] In our opinion, accountability is a mechanism of checks and balances exerted by the accountor on the accountee, which depends to a great extent on legal arrangements, ensuring that no one controls the independent agency, yet the agency is under control.[46]

34.3.1 Performance Accountability

Performance accountability refers to the extent to which regulatory objectives are achieved and delegated functions are performed. Typically, the objectives and functions are explicitly defined in the form of law. Legally defined objectives are both a precondition and a yardstick for evaluating banking regulatory agency accountability, because a banking regulatory agency can be held accountable by assessing whether it achieves the objectives.

In contrast to the central bank's measurable objectives (e.g., inflation does not exceed 2 percent), regulatory objectives are usually multiple, general and unquantifiable, leading to difficulty in assessing the performance accountability of a regulatory agency. For instance, how could safe and sound banking operations be measured? Can we use the number of financial crimes and failed banks to measure the objective? The decline of the number of financial crimes and failed banks may be the result of a success or failure of the regulator's policy.[47] With respect to the objective of the public's confidence in the banking system, this concerns more the state of mind and thinking. How exactly are we to measure these?[48] It is for this reason that regulatory objectives are embodied or complemented in operating principles, standards or methodologies. The Financial Services and Markets Act of the UK requires the FSA to have regard to the way of using resources, cost–benefit analysis, innovation, and so on.[49] The CBRC announces on its website that its regulatory purposes are to protect the interests of depositors and consumers; enhance confidence in the market through prudential regulation; promote public understanding of modern finance through education and information disclosure; and reduce financial crime. The standards which the CBRC tries to meet in performing its functions are to facilitate both financial stability and financial innovation; promote the competitiveness of China in international financial services; set reasonable regulatory limits; encourage orderly competition; make regulators and regulated banks more accountable; and use regulatory resources in an efficient and economic way. All these purposes and standards are declared informally by the CBRC on its website and not defined or clarified by any law. It is left unknown whether the CBRC's accountability can be assessed according to these purposes and objectives.

In the authors' opinion, the embodiment of regulatory objectives in the form of standards or principles is not sufficient for enabling regulatory objectives to be measurable. Even so, however, it does not mean that legislation could abolish regulatory objectives. It is argued that legal certainty with respect to regulatory objectives is the utmost guarantee for regulatory accountability. Whether they are unquantifiable, multiple or too general, the law-based objectives in themselves provide a sound basis for holding banking regulatory agencies accountable in pursuing their objectives.

In addition to assessing the extent of achieving regulatory objectives, the importance of substantive and procedural arrangements for the process of achieving regulatory objectives to regulatory accountability should not be biased. In other words, the substantive and procedural legislation on the CBRC's setting and implementation of regulatory rules is another aspect of protecting and assessing regulatory accountability. This is because regulatory power has a tendency to expand and escape control, and therefore substantive law must prescribe its boundaries and procedural law must standardize its operations.

The main methods by which substantive law constrains regulatory power involve legal reservation and explicit authorization. Both of the methods may apply to the division of responsibility in setting banking laws, regulations and rules between the NPC, the State Council and the CBRC. As discussed above,[50] the authors' proposal that economic rules and information rules are prescribed in the form of law or regulation, and prudential rules are set by the CBRC, is still helpful to constrain the CBRC's expansion of its rule-setting power. However, no matter how clear and detailed the rule-setting power is in law, it is still impossible to have a clear-cut division of the rule-setting responsibility between these different rule-setting bodies. The role of substantive law in constraining the expansion of the rule-setting power is, thus, limited. To offset the weakness, procedural law is required to monitor the whole process of setting banking regulatory rules.

In China, procedural monitoring of the CBRC's rule-making process includes administrative review by the State Council, judicial review by the court and public participation. Under the Constitutional Law and the Legislation Law, the State Council has the power to amend or abolish inappropriate orders, instructions and rules issued by its ministries.[51] By contrast, any judicial review of a banking rule is prohibited by the Administrative Procedural Law as rule or law is considered an abstract administrative action.[52] With respect to the public participation in the banking rule-setting process, Chinese legislation (the State Council's Regulations on the Procedures for Rule-Setting for instance) does not grant stakeholders a right to move for a banking rule and is ambiguous about whether to seek public consultation for a rule proposed by the CBRC. To ensure regulatory accountability in the CBRC's rule-making process, it is argued that an operational legal guarantee for the public's (especially stakeholders') participation is essential.

As with the rule-making process, the implementation of regulatory rules should be subject to substantive as well as procedural constraints. Sanctioning powers of the CBRC, for instance, is an important aspect of its regulatory accountability. The banking laws enable the CBRC to sanction violations of laws, regulations and rules in the form of warnings, fines, confiscation, suspension of business, revocation of license, dismissal of senior management, and other legally defined penalties. To ensure objectivity, properness, preciseness and fairness of an administrative penalty, the CBRC's Stipulations on Administrative Penalties separate the investigation and decision-making processes. The investigation department of the CBRC is responsible for investigating a case and proposing a penalty while the legal department is responsible for examining the legitimacy of the penalty and organizing a hearing. The final decision on whether a penalty is imposed is made by the chairman's meeting of the CBRC or the president's meeting of the CBRC branch. The CBRC's Stipulations on Administrative Penalties detail the warning notice system stipulated in the Law on Administrative Penalties, granting the person concerned a right to make representations, defend themself and apply for a hearing. These stipulations are similar to Parts XIV and XXVI in the Financial Services and Markets Act of the UK.

In contrast to monitoring of the CBRC's sanctioning powers, the legislation seems unclear about how to monitor the CBRC's exercise of other powers. The Banking Supervision Law and Commercial Banking Law give the CBRC extensive regulatory powers including approving and revoking a license, determining the business scope of a bank, conducting a fit and proper test for senior management, taking prompt action, taking over a bank, and so on. Under Chinese administrative laws and administrative procedural laws, actions taken by the CBRC such as approving and revoking a bank license and dismissing a senior manager fall within the scope of administrative reconsideration and the jurisdiction of an administrative court as a specific administrative action. However, for other actions such as taking over a bank and restricting the rights of shareholders or senior management, the law is silent on whether the person concerned has a right to administrative reconsideration or to appeal to a court, because it is not clarified whether they are specific administrative actions. For instance, the Regulations of the Administration of Foreign Banks of 2006 (hereinafter, Foreign Bank Regulations) enacted by the State Council grant the CBRC the power to take special regulatory actions against violating foreign banks including suspending part of their business activities and removing senior management.[53] The Implementation Rules on Foreign Bank Regulations issued by the CBRC expand the number of special regulatory actions, under which the CBRC gives itself the power to have a warning talk with senior management, send special regulators to guide daily operations of a bank, and restrict funds and profits from flowing out to overseas.[54] On the one hand, it remains uncertain as to whether these expanded special regulatory actions fall within the category of specific administrative actions and then are subject to legal remedy. On the other hand, it is just because no legal remedy is applied that the CBRC itself has the incentive to expand regulatory powers by issuing rules. Without doubt legal uncertainty and ambiguousness in this regard would greatly undermine regulatory accountability.

34.3.2   Institutional Accountability

When a banking regulatory agency is delegated authority, it must be subject to checks and balances by any of the parties involved. In a democracy, these parties involved are three branches of government: legislature (parliament), executive and judiciary. In addition, a banking regulatory agency is accountable to the industry as it is financed partly or fully by regulated banks.

Parliamentary accountability
Given that banking regulation is a public good, the banking regulatory agency is in the broadest sense accountable to the public at large. However, the public would not directly check the performance of a banking regulatory agency, and they elect parliament to represent their interests. This is why banking regulatory accountability relates first and foremost to parliament. Parliament holds banking regulatory agencies accountable through its law-making powers, described as *ex ante* accountability and *ex post* accountability.[55] By *ex ante* accountability is meant that parliament has power to grant the legitimacy of the banking regulator's existence, determine its objectives and mandate, and set the rules with which a banking regulator must comply. *Ex post* accountability refers to a mechanism whereby parliament has power to change the legal basis of the banking regulatory agency, and reformulate its objectives, mandate and rules.[56] To enhance *ex ante* and *ex post* accountability, parliament requires the banking regulatory agency to establish institutionalized contacts with itself, normally in the form of law, so that parliament has the opportunity to review and assess the performance of the agency on a regular basis.

Institutionalized contacts take various forms such as submission of regular reports, appearance before parliament, ad hoc inquiries, and so on.[57] However, the Banking Supervision Law does not require the CBRC to report to the NPC or its Standing Committee directly or through the State Council. In practice, the main mechanism through which the NPC holds the CBRC accountable is that the relevant heads of the CBRC may be summoned by the NPC or its Standing Committee to appear or to report. Because of the complexity and technicality of banking regulation, few politicians of the NPC possess expertise in finance and economics sufficient for understanding the reports. In our opinion, it would be optimal that parliamentary monitoring of the CBRC can be included in the daily work of the special committees under the NPC, as the members of the special committees – for example the finance committee of the NPC – are able to devote more expertise and energy to monitor the CBRC's discharge of its functions.

Governmental accountability

In virtually all countries, the government bears the ultimate responsibility for maintaining financial stability and financial development. Therefore, a banking regulatory agency needs to have a direct line of accountability.[58] The arrangements for the government to hold a regulatory agency accountable include four types: reporting; direct involvement in operations; appointment and dismissal; and issuing regulations and instructions.

Based on its responsibility for the whole financial system, the government has the power to require the banking regulatory agency to submit reports to it on a regular basis. In countries where the banking supervisor is independent from the government, the law usually prescribes the details of the reporting requirements; for example, reporting frequency. For instance, the Financial Services and Markets Act requires the FSA to make a report at least once a year to the Treasury on the discharge of its functions and so on.[59] The CBRC, as an institution directly affiliated to the State Council, has a duty to provide supervisory information to the latter upon request, although banking laws are silent on information communication between them.

In some countries, the government sends its representative to sit on or vote at the board of the regulator. As discussed above, Marc Quintyn et al.'s survey found that 20 countries have a government representative chair or sit on the board of the regulatory agency, while in 12 countries the law gives the minister of finance the right to intervene in the operations of the agency.[60] In this case, political influence on the banking regulatory agency is not avoided. Fortunately, Chinese banking laws do not have any such provision permitting the government to participate in the CBRC's operations, at least on paper.

As an instrument of regulatory accountability, the government determines or recommends the appointment or dismissal of senior officials of a banking regulatory agency. To prevent political intervention through appointment and dismissal, the procedures for appointment and dismissal in particular must be legalized, as a guarantee for regulatory accountability as well as regulatory independence. In Australia, the appointment of an APRA member is terminated if the member becomes a director, employee of a regulated institution, bankrupt, physically or mentally incapable, absent from duty for a certain period of time, and so on.[61] Unlike in Australia, Chinese banking laws do not legalize the reasons and procedures for dismissing banking regulatory officials. It should be noted, however, that the Communist Party of China (CPC) Central Committee's Regulations on Cadres illustrate this issue for appointing and removing Communist Party and government officials, which applies equally to the CBRC's officials.

To achieve its objectives, the government may issue regulations against the banking industry and the banking regulatory agency for the latter's compliance. In China, the State Council has the constitutional right to issue banking regulations for the CBRC's compliance or as guidelines by which the CBRC makes its regulatory rules. In the Banking Supervision Law, there are many provisions which prescribe that the CBRC conduct regulatory activities according to the State Council's stipulations, even though many of the stipulations have not been issued. However, it is well known that the government has its own interests which may be inconsistent with social well-being. Therefore, the danger exists that the government intervenes in a banking regulatory agency through its regulation-making power but in the name of holding the agency accountable. Again, the authors argue that the division of rule-making responsibilities between the State Council and the CBRC, discussed above,[62] still apply.

Judiciary accountability

The separation of powers makes it impossible for Congress to scrutinize and monitor the daily operations of the banking regulatory agency on a case-by-case basis. Governmental accountability is only an internal approach to monitoring the banking regulatory agency. In many cases, banking regulatory failure means government failure, which results in an insufficiency of governmental accountability. For these reasons, the law provides legal redress in court for the purpose of compensating for the insufficiency. Judicial authority and transparency, and the judge's independence and professionalism, can guarantee the legality and due process of the performance of regulatory functions on the one hand, and provide the right of legal remedy to regulated banks and persons who are affected by the regulatory agency's decisions and activities on the other hand. In China, as discussed above,[63] it seems that the person or bank concerned is not granted legal remedy against some regulatory measures taken by the CBRC, as it is unknown whether these measures are reviewable.

Legal redress against banking regulatory activities should not be unlimited. In several countries, excessive appeals to the court are allowed, which apparently results in disadvantages.[64] For instance, in the case where a decision for closing a failed bank is made by the regulatory agency, banking law in many countries permits the closed bank to file a suit with the court against the decision. The arrangement has the following disadvantages. Firstly, it allows the failed bank to prolong its existence under unsound conditions that may affect financial stability. Secondly, it allows the judge, who may lack expertise in banking, to intervene in the regulatory activities, which undermines the integrity and reputation of the regulatory agency. Thirdly, it distracts the attention and energy of the agency from the discharge of its responsibilities because the agency may be involved in a time-consuming lawsuit. Fourthly, it increases the possibility of regulatory capture through the court.[65] These disadvantages require the law to strike a trade-off between legal remedy and supervisory integrity. Establishment of a special tribunal consisting of judges having banking expertise – for example the Financial Services and Markets Tribunal in the UK – may be a practicable solution to these disadvantages.

Industrial accountability

A banking regulatory agency is accountable to its supervised industry, which pays a levy to the former. Proper legal arrangements for industrial accountability may prevent supervised banks from capturing the banking regulatory agency, and establish effective mechanisms for granting banks the freedom to air their opinions on regulatory policies and activities. These mechanisms include consultation, participation and representation of supervised banks. In the UK, for instance, the law requires the banking regulatory agency to make arrangements for consulting regulated institutions on its general policies and practices.[66] A practitioner panel in which regulated institutions participate is established to represent the interests of practitioners.[67] In Germany, France and the Netherlands, the financial industry is represented in the regulatory agencies.[68] In China, although the CBRC is partially funded by the banking industry, the CBRC, banks and legislator are not aware that the CBRC should be accountable to the banking industry. As a result, there has been no legislation in relation to the accountability of the CBRC to the industry.

34.4 TRANSPARENCY OF THE CBRC

Transparency refers to a mechanism under which banking regulatory agencies disclose information about regulatory activities to the public or stakeholders. Transparency is not only an instrument for regulatory accountability but also a factor affecting the degree of regulatory accountability, as accountability of a banking regulatory agency to the public or stakeholders depends to a great extent on the information that the agency discloses and its quality. Publicity of the regulatory process may press the banking regulatory agency to make well-reasoned and consistent decisions. In addition, transparency is a guarantee for regulatory independence. The regulatory process is usually conducted in an invisible manner, which makes the banking regulatory agency vulnerable to interference from both the government and interest groups. By contrast, more transparency could give rise to more scrutiny, leading the government and interest groups to have more scruples in dealing with the agency.

As transparency should not be left to the discretion of a banking regulatory agency, legislation should prescribe information disclosure with respect to the agency's discharge of its functions. In China, the Banking Supervision Law only requires the CBRC to make its regulatory process known to the public,[69] but detailed implementing rules have never been issued. Apparently, the general provision does not enable the CBRC to become a transparent regulator. Generally speaking, regulatory information is disclosed through bulletins, annual reports, press conferences and websites. In the UK, to ensure sufficient communication between the FSA and the public, the FSA must hold a public meeting not later than three months after making an annual report to the Treasury, so as to discuss the contents of the annual report, and publish a report of the proceedings of the public meeting.[70]

There is debate about whether transparency would be improved if the minutes and voting records of banking regulatory agency meetings were made public. Legislation in many countries is silent on this issue. In our opinion, publication of minutes and voting records enables the public to follow the course of debate among the banking regulatory agency members, and understand the decision-making process, so that it is easier to hold the members accountable for their behavior. In this case, to protect their own reputation and professional integrity, the members have to comply with a fiduciary duty and air high-quality and independent opinions commensurate with their expertise.

Nonetheless, publicity of regulatory activities, in particular corrective actions taken by the regulatory agency against a problem bank, would adversely affect the stability of the bank and even the stability of the whole banking system. Immediate publication of a real-time regulatory decision is likely not only to impede the investigation of the problem bank but also to impair the confidence of depositors in the bank, which may lead to a bank run. In the authors' opinion, it is more proper that the regulatory agency publishes the minutes and voting records as to actions decided at the meeting a certain period of time after the event. As far as ensuring regulatory independence and accountability is concerned, the issue is not that the regulatory decision is disclosed *ex ante*, real-time or *ex post*, but that there is legal provision imposing on the banking regulatory agency the obligation to disclose such information. Publicity, even if *ex post*, may effectively encourage banking regulatory agency members to make responsible decisions.

34.5   CONCLUDING REMARKS

Fears that a banking regulatory agency would be captured by the government and interest groups on the one hand, and would not be subject to the usual political checks and balances if it becomes highly independent on the other hand, lead to the need to ensure banking regulatory agency independence and accountability. A widespread perception is that independence and accountability are of a trade-off nature and ultimately incompatible: more independence means less accountability, and vice versa. This view misunderstands the relationship between banking regulatory independence and accountability. Eva Hüpkes et al. argue that independence and accountability are complementary, and therefore properly structured accountability arrangements are fully consistent with agency autonomy.[71] An independent banking regulator may still have a high degree of accountability, while a less independent banking regulator may be unaccountable. In our opinion, heavier government interventions in banking regulation would make it hard to hold a banking regulatory agency accountable for its performance, as the line between the banking regulatory agency's performance and the government behavior is blurred. In this case, it can be concluded that a less independent banking regulator may not always have more accountability; rather it may have less accountability. The authors also argue that banking regulatory agency independence and accountability are complementary and mutually reinforcing. Both of them are law-based. Properly designed legal arrangements should include mechanisms for granting a banking regulatory agency sufficient independence, while holding it accountable for its delegated powers.

In a market characterized by asymmetric information, legal arrangements for regulatory independence and accountability without the support of transparency do not guarantee the availability of sound regulatory governance. Publicity of regulatory decisions and processes exposes banking regulatory agencies to public and stakeholder monitoring, which presses the regulatory agencies, the government and interest groups to behave properly. Again, legal certainty with respect to regulatory transparency matters must be in place.

However, a properly designed legal framework is only the first step towards sound regulatory governance. *De jure* regulatory governance does not represent de facto sound regulatory governance. Only when legal arrangements for regulatory governance fit into the political culture of a country, and are implemented effectively, can they yield policy effectiveness. However, few people acknowledge that financial stability can be achieved in a way that the regulatory governance of the banking regulatory agency is improved. Once a financial crisis occurred, regulatory governance would not be a top priority of the government. What the government assuming ultimate responsibility for maintaining financial stability really needs to do is to defuse the crisis as soon as possible. More importantly, actions taken by the government which may undermine regulatory governance during a financial crisis are more or less recognized and supported by law and the public. In this sense, each financial crisis leads to a retrogression of regulatory governance, although improvement is repeatedly conducted post-crises.

NOTES

1. Das, Udaibir S. and Marc Quintyn (2002), 'Crisis prevention and crisis management: the role of regulatory governance', IMF Working Paper WP/02/163, September, p. 5.
2. See ibid., pp. 7–8.
3. See ibid., pp. 9–12.
4. Statutory objective has different expressions in different countries. It can be expressed as purpose or objective of the banking regulatory agency in Australia and Finland; regulatory objective in the UK and China; or legislative purpose in Canada.
5. Banking Supervision Law, Art. 3. The Banking Supervision Law of China was enacted in 2003 and amended in 2006.
6. Banking Supervision Law, Art. 2.
7. On discussions of regulatory competition, see generally Scott, Kenneth E. (1977), 'The dual banking system: a model of competition in regulation', *Stanford Law Journal*, **30**; Kane, Edward J. (1984), 'Regulatory structure in futures markets: jurisdictional competition among the SEC, the CFTC and other agencies', National Bureau of Economic Research Working Paper, No. 1331, April; Butler, Henry N. and Jonathan R. Macey (1988), 'The myth of competition in the dual banking system', *Cornell Law Review*, **73**(May); Weinberg, John A. (2002), 'Competition among bank regulators', *Federal Reserve Bank of Richmond Economic Quarterly*, **88**(4).
8. Ramirez, Steven A. (2000), 'Depoliticizing financial regulation', *William and Mary Law Review*, **41**, 563.
9. Quintyn, Marc and Michael W. Taylor (2002), 'Regulatory and supervisory independence and financial stability', IMF Working Paper WP/02/46, March, p. 16, Box 2.
10. See ibid.
11. Banking Supervision Law, Art. 15.
12. Quintyn, Marc and Michael W. Taylor (2002), 'Regulatory and supervisory independence and financial stability', IMF Working Paper WP/02/46, March, p. 15, n. 19.
13. Legislation Law, Art. 56.
14. Banking Supervision Law, Arts. 15 and 21.
15. See Quintyn, Marc and Michael W. Taylor (2002), 'Regulatory and supervisory independence and financial stability', IMF Working Paper WP/02/46, March, p. 15.
16. See ibid.
17. See ibid., p. 17.
18. Banking Supervision Law, Art. 5.
19. Measures on Capital Adequacy, Art. 41. A significantly undercapitalized bank is defined as one whose total and core capital adequacy fall below 4 percent and 2 percent, respectively. See ibid., Art. 38.
20. Commercial Banking Law, Art. 64; Banking Supervision Law, Art. 38.
21. Banking Supervision Law, Art. 9.
22. Regulations on Cadres, Chapters 3, 4, 5 and 6.
23. Basel Committee, *Core Principles Methodology*, October 2006, p. 6.
24. APRA Act, Sec. 25.

25. Regulations on Cadres, Chapter 11.
26. Banking Supervision Law, Art. 10.
27. See Federal Reserve Bank Act, Sec. 242.
28. Civil Servant Law, Art. 102. The China Securities Regulatory Commission (hereinafter CSRC) also prohibits its staff from holding office at the regulated firms within 12 months after they leave the CSRC, unless otherwise approved. CSRC, Conduct Code of CSRC Staff, Art. 13.
29. Financial Services and Markets Act, Schedule 1, para. 5 (2).
30. See ibid., para. 4.
31. Quintyn, Marc, Silvia Ramirez and Michael W. Taylor (2007), 'The fear of freedom: politicians and the independence and accountability of financial sector supervisors', IMF Working Paper WP/07/25, February, p. 23.
32. Act on Financial Markets Supervision of Poland, Arts 5 and 11.
33. APRA Act 1998, amended up to Act No. 82 of 2010. Before 1 July 2003, if the Treasurer and APRA fail to agree with APRA's policy, the Treasury may then give the Governor-General a recommendation as to the solution and the latter determines the policy to be adopted by APRA. See APRA Act 1998, amended up to Act No. 36 of 2003, sec. 12.
34. Ramirez, Steven A. (2000), 'Depoliticizing financial regulation', *William and Mary Law Review*, **41**, 517.
35. Quintyn, Marc, Silvia Ramirez and Michael W. Taylor (2007), 'The fear of freedom: politicians and the independence and accountability of financial sector supervisors', IMF Working Paper WP/07/25, February, p. 10.
36. See ibid.
37. Take the PBOC, for example; under Article 38 of the PBOC Law, the PBOC has its own independent budget separate from the government budget. However, the PBOC's budget must be subject to the review and approval of the Ministry of Finance. See Ministry of Finance, Financial Administration System for the PBOC, Arts 3 and 41.
38. Basel Committee, *Core Principles for Effective Banking Supervision*, October 2006, p. 2.
39. Basel Committee, *Core Principles Methodology*, October 2006, p. 9.
40. Quintyn, Marc, Silvia Ramirez and Michael W. Taylor (2007), 'The fear of freedom: politicians and the independence and accountability of financial sector supervisors', IMF Working Paper WP/07/25, February, p. 23.
41. See Tison, Michel (2004), 'Who's afraid of Peter Paul? The European Court of Justice to rule on banking supervisory liability', *Financial Regulator*, **9**(1), 63.
42. See Proctor, Charles (2002), 'Regulatory immunity and legal risk', *Financial Regulator*, **7**(3), 30.
43. Basel Committee, *Core Principles Methodology*, October 2006, p. 6.
44. See *Oxford Dictionary of English*, 2nd edn, 2005, p. 11.
45. See *supra* nn. 31–33 and accompanying text.
46. See Hüpkes, Eva, Marc Quintyn and Michael W. Taylor (2005), 'The accountability of financial sector supervisors: principles and practice', IMF Working Paper WP/05/51, March, p. 5.
47. See generally Goodhart, Charles A.E. (2001), 'Regulating the regulator: an economist's perspective on accountability and control', in Eilis Ferran and Charles A.E. Goodhart (eds), *Regulating Financial Services and Markets in the Twenty First Century*, Oxford: Hart Publishing, p. 152.
48. See ibid., p. 153.
49. Financial Services and Markets Act, Sec. 2(3).
50. See *supra* n. 15 and accompanying text.
51. Constitutional Law, Art. 89 (13); Legislation Law, Art. 88 (3).
52. See Administrative Procedural Law, Art. 12.
53. Foreign Bank Regulations, Art. 50.
54. Implementation Rules on Foreign Bank Regulations, Art. 94.
55. See generally Hüpkes, Eva, Marc Quintyn and Michael W. Taylor (2005), 'The accountability of financial sector supervisors: principles and practice', IMF Working Paper WP/05/51, March, pp. 19–20.
56. In the central bank field, it has been argued that the mere threat of a change of the law will ensure that even independent central banks will in general be in accordance with the wishes of elected politicians. See Jakob de Haan, F. Amtenbrink and S.C.W Eijffinger (1998), 'Accountability of central banks: aspects and quantification', manuscript, May, p. 13.
57. See Hüpkes, Eva, Marc Quintyn and Michael W. Taylor (2005), 'The accountability of financial sector supervisors: principles and practice', IMF Working Paper WP/05/51, March, pp. 22–23.
58. See ibid., p. 24.
59. Financial Services and Market Act, Schedule 1, para. 10.
60. Quintyn, Marc, Silvia Ramirez and Michael W. Taylor (2007), 'The fear of freedom: politicians and

the independence and accountability of financial sector supervisors', IMF Working Paper WP/07/25, February, p. 23.

61. APRA Act, Sec. 25.
62. See *supra* n. 15 and accompanying text.
63. See *supra* nn. 53–54 and accompanying text.
64. Quintyn, Marc and Michael W. Taylor (2002), 'Regulatory and supervisory independence and financial stability', IMF Working Paper WP/02/46, March, p. 18.
65. See ibid., pp. 18–19.
66. Financial Services and Markets Act, Sec. 8.
67. Ibid., Sec. 9.
68. Hüpkes, Eva, Marc Quintyn and Michael W. Taylor (2005), 'The accountability of financial sector supervisors: principles and practice', IMF Working Paper WP/05/51, March, p. 30.
69. Banking Supervision Law, Art. 12.
70. Financial Services and Markets Act, Schedule 1, paras 11 and 12.
71. Hüpkes, Eva, Marc Quintyn and Michael W. Taylor (2005), 'The accountability of financial sector supervisors: principles and practice', IMF Working Paper WP/05/51, March, p. 4.

35 Corporate governance and bank performance in Thailand

*Tientip Subhanij and Wanvimol Sawangngoenyuang**

35.1 INTRODUCTION

As the Asian financial and subprime crises have shown, one of the main causes of the crises was poor corporate governance and risk management from borrowers as well as from banks. Poor governance from borrowers often leads to overborrowing and poor investment decisions, while poor governance at banks usually leads to improper credit assessment and inefficient credit allocation. Furthermore, banks with poor corporate governance could not monitor and discipline borrowers.

In the wake of financial crisis and a more globalized financial sector which results in more competition, more complex financial products and risk, good governance is a key factor to strengthen the soundness and stability of the banking sector. In this respect, corporate governance in the banking industry in Thailand has changed significantly. Many new regulations and measures have been initiated and implemented by the Bank of Thailand (henceforth, BOT) to improve corporate governance (henceforth, CG) practices as well as supervision.

The rest of the chapter is organized as follows: section 35.2 discusses the background of the Thai banking sector after the 1997 crisis; section 35.3 provides an overview of policies implemented by the BOT to enhance CG of banks; section 35.4 presents the impact of CG on bank performance and section 35.5 concludes.

35.2 CHANGING FINANCIAL LANDSCAPE OF THE THAI BANKING SECTOR

The Thai banking sector has undergone significant transformation through the financial crisis episode in 1997 and the Financial Sector Master Plan (FSMP). The first phase of the FSMP was implemented in 2004, followed by phase II in 2010. The first phase aimed to increase the financial access of especially the grass-roots sector, enhance consumer protection and increase efficiency. The second phase of the FSMP, which was announced in late 2009, aims to improve further the financial efficiency and financial access by reducing system-wide operating costs, increasing competition and strengthening institutional infrastructure, especially in risk management.

Prior to the FSMP, multiple types of licenses were issued to a large number of financial institutions that provide many of the same services to customers. These systems allowed for regulatory arbitrage. Therefore, the FSMP I simplified the licensing system by offering two types of Thai financial institutions: commercial banks and retail banks; and two types of foreign financial institutions: foreign bank branches and subsidiaries. Financial

Table 35.1 Number of financial institutions, pre-crisis and June 2010

Types of financial institutions	Pre-crisis (Jan 1997)	Current (June 2010)
Commercial banks	31	32
Domestically registered	15	16
Commercial bank	15	14
Retail bank*	–	2
Foreign bank branch♣	16	15
Foreign bank subsidiary♦	–	1
Finance and securities companies	91	3
Credit foncier companies	12	3
International banking facilities (IBF)	42	–
Total	176	38

Notes:
*   Retail banks provide virtually all types of financial transactions with the same exceptions as commercial banks, but are not allowed to conduct businesses related to foreign exchange and derivative products. They may offer basic financial services to every type of customer, with the limitation that they may only provide credit, or other similar transactions, to retail customers and SMEs.
♣   Foreign bank branches enjoy the same scope of business as Thai commercial banks but with only one branch.
♦   Subsidiaries enjoy the same scope of business as Thai commercial banks and are allowed to open five branches in addition to one head office – two branches in the Bangkok metropolitan area, and the remaining three outside the Bangkok metropolitan area.

Source: Bank of Thailand.

institutions whose license types were eliminated were given the option to apply for a new license through a merger with another institution.

With those changes, the structure of the Thai banking sector remains largely unchanged since the pre-crisis period. The number of commercial banks is almost the same as before the 1997 crisis (see Table 35.1). However, over the period 1998–2010, a number of banks have been closed down, merged or acquired by other financial institutions (see Table 35.2) and many new banks have been established.[1] The FSMP I also encouraged financial institutions such as securities and finance companies, credit foncier companies and international banking facilities (IBFs) to upgrade, or merge and upgrade to become banks. Hence, the number of these types of financial institutions declined dramatically to around six companies while IBFs were completely phased out in 2006. Finance companies and credit foncier companies that have not applied for bank licenses may continue to function as finance or credit foncier companies; but will face tougher competition.

In terms of bank size, there is no change in the ranking (Figure 35.1). The six largest banks remain the largest ones. The combined asset shares of the six largest banks declined from 71 percent of the banking industry assets in December 2000 to 68 percent in June 2010. The deposit share and loan share account for 77 percent and 74 percent of the market, respectively.

Although the market remains concentrated to the six largest banks, the industry has become more competitive. As can be seen from Figure 35.1, the shares of deposits and

Table 35.2   Mergers and acquisitions of locally incorporated commercial banks from 1998 to June 2010

Date	Acquirer	Target	Type of stake	Note
Jan 98	Development Bank of Singapore	Thai Danu Bank	Majority stake	Sold to TMB in 2004
Jun 98	ABN Amro Bank	Bank of Asia	Majority stake	Sold to UOB in 2004
Sep 99	Standard Chartered Bank	Nakornthon Bank	Majority stake	
Nov 99	United Overseas Bank (UOB)	Radanasin Bank	Majority stake	
Jan 09	CIMBT	Bank Thai	Majority stake	
Apr 10	ICBC	ACL	Majority stake	
Jun 10	Thanachart Bank	Siam City Bank	Majority stake	
Sep 08	ING	TMB	Controlling stake	
Jan 07	GE Capital	Bank of Ayudhya	Controlling stake	
Jul 07	Bank of Nova Scotia	Thanachart Bank	Controlling stake	

Source: Herberholz et al. (2010) and Bank of Thailand.

loans from Bangkok Bank (BBL) are declining from 21 and 19 trillion baht in 2000 to 18 and 17 in April 2010, respectively. Some foreign banks have started to compete with domestic banks. HSBC and Citibank, although facing a one-branch limitation, are starting to compete in the retail markets such as credit cards (Nakornthab, 2007).

Furthermore, there is a shift in ownership structure (Tables 35.2 and 35.3). The ownership is changing from family to government and to foreign investors. After the 1997 financial crisis, family-owned banks almost disappeared from the market as their shares were sold to foreign investors or they were bailed out by the government in order to raise capital. Those banks were later sold to selected qualified foreign investors who have been allowed to hold more than 49 percent of the share for a period up to ten years – these banks are called hybrid banks. Nevertheless, the share of assets of the foreign banks and hybrid banks remains around 20 percent of the total banking assets, the same level as in 2001.

35.3   CORPORATE GOVERNANCE

To enhance corporate governance in Thailand, the National Corporate Governance Committee (NCGC) was established in 2002 to set out policies, measures and schemes to upgrade corporate governance. The NCGC has appointed four subcommittees. One of them is the subcommittee on the Enhancement of Corporate Governance in Commercial Banks, Finance Companies and Insurance Companies which is chaired by the governor of the Bank of Thailand. The main responsibility is to raise the standard of business operations in the financial sector by having good corporate governance such as a sound management structure and controlling system.

The BOT also implemented several initiatives aimed to promote GC and self-regulation to promote corporate accountability and prevent conflict of interest. Such

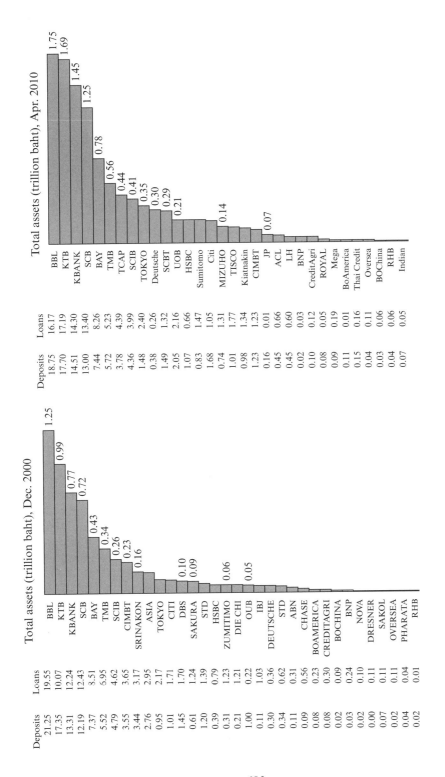

Source: Bank of Thailand.

Figure 35.1 Assets, deposit shares and loan shares of banks in Thailand

Table 35.3   Shareholder structure for selected banks

Bank	Holder (5)	1975	2000	2004	2010Q3
BBL	Family	22.3	<10	<5	<5
	Thai investors		41.08	52.98	57.51
	Foreign investors		48.77	47.01	42.49
KBANK	Family	10.5	<7	<5	<5
	Thai investors		52.41	51.97	51.37
	Foreign investors		48.98	48.02	48.63
BAY	Family	22.8	6.1	<5	<5
	Thai investors		49.58	73.70	52.87
	Foreign investors		30.38	26.30	47.12
BMB*	Family	24.9	0		
	Thai investors		0		
	Foreign investors		0		
	Government		100		
SCIB	Thai investors				100
	Foreign investors			9.96	
	Government		100	79.35	

Note: * BMB or Bangkok Metropolitan Bank later merged with SCIB in 2002.

Source: Wailerdsak (2006) and SETSMART.

policy initiatives include guidelines for the structure of a financial institution's board of directors, lending, information disclosure, equity investment and the Financial Sector Master Plan and supervision.

35.3.1   Board of Directors and Other Committees

Directors of financial institutions are important not only to organizations, but also to the economy and the financial system as a whole. It is important for financial institutions to have directors with competence, integrity and honesty, as the performance of the financial institutions can magnify the business cycle and may end up in crisis if not properly managed. Several measures, therefore, have been initiated to enhance the effectiveness of the board of directors.

The Financial Institutions Business Act B.E. 2551 provides the BOT with the authority to define the appropriate structure of the board of directors and subcommittees of financial institutions to establish checks and balances. The appointment of the directors must receive approval from the BOT. To obtain approval, the directors must satisfy 'fit and proper' criteria by not having prohibited characteristics[2] and additional prohibited characteristics categorized under three aspects: (1) honesty, integrity and reputation; (2) competence, capability and experience; (3) financial soundness (Notification of the Bank of Thailand No. ThorPorTor SorNorNor 13/2552; Notification of the Bank of Thailand No. ThorPorTor SorNorNor 14/2552). Furthermore, directors should have at least five years of experience with well-run financial institutions, and they should not serve as a director with full signatory authority in more than three business groups so that they can devote sufficient time and effort to the bank (Bank of Thailand, 2000, 2003). To enhance board monitoring, a director is also required to attend at least 50 percent of the annual board meetings (Polsiri and Wiwattanakantang, 2005).

Apart from general duties and responsibilities to enhance the stability of the financial system in the long run, the board of directors must have main duties in four major areas: (1) risk management; (2) monitoring the capital adequacy; (3) rules and regulations compliance; and (4) duties in accordance with good corporate governance (Notification of the Bank of Thailand No. ThorPorTor SorNorNor 15/2552). In particular, the board of directors must perform those four major duties with honesty, loyalty and care under the framework and methods of the Business Judgment Rule.[3] The decisions must be made in good faith, must be reasonable, and must be made in the belief that they are in the best interests of the company.

The BOT also requires that a board must have at least nine members, and not more than one-third of the board must be executive directors. Furthermore, at least three members or one-quarter of the board (whichever is higher) must be independent directors. The independent directors, who play an important role in maintaining a proper balance among board members in exercising the board's roles and responsibilities, should not be involved in any commercial banking-related business or work that may affect their decisions. Furthermore, they must not: (1) be an employee of the bank; (2) have a closed relationship with top executives or major shareholders of the bank; (3) hold shares in excess of 1 percent of the issued shares of the bank; or (4) have any direct or indirect interest or benefit in related entities of the bank (Bank of Thailand, 2002; Notification of the Capital Market Supervisory Board No. TorChor. 28/2551).

In addition, banks are required to set up audit and risk management committees. The audit committee's main responsibilities are to review the bank's financial report to ensure accuracy and adequacy; review the bank's internal control and audit procedures system; and ensure the bank's compliance with applicable laws and regulations. The audit committee is to consist of at least three members who are independent directors and should not be committee members of related firms. The risk management committee is to ensure that the bank has a sufficient capital base, while risk portfolios are constantly monitored and managed within limits. The committee should have at least five members who are board directors and/or management who have knowledge and understand the overall risks.

In addition, banks are recommended to set up two other committees: a nominating committee and a remuneration committee. The former is to formulate policy, criteria and methods for proposing candidates to the board for consideration and appointment of directors and board members as well as top management. The latter committee is to recommend the remuneration and benefits of directors, committee members and top management. The BOT also advises that the chairperson of these committees be an outsider (Hoontrakul and Karnchanasai, 2010; Limpaphayom and Connelly, 2004).

35.3.2   Lending

Banks are, by law, prohibited from lending to directors, their immediate family, and the enterprises where they, individually or in aggregate, hold more than 30 percent of the shares. This prohibition also covers exposure arising from guaranteeing any debts, or accepting, providing aval to, or intervening in any bills of which the director is a drawer, a maker or an endorser. Lending to or investing in enterprises related to the bank, or its directors or senior management (where the stake is more than 10 percent), and lending to the bank's shareholders with a substantial or controlling interest or its senior management are permitted but must not exceed the limits and must conform to normal lending practices, with no special terms and conditions. The limits are 5 percent of the bank's Tier 1 capital; 25 percent of the total liability of such an enterprise; or 50 percent of such an enterprise's equity, whichever is the smallest (Bank of Thailand, 2002).

35.3.3   Information Disclosure

In order to increase transparency and promote market discipline, banks are required to disclose details of the following information in addition to those required by the BOT: (1) transactions relating to senior management of the banks in which directors or senior management have interest equal to or more than 10 percent of the enterprise's paid-up capital; (2) compensation or other benefits, both cash and non-cash, paid to directors, or senior management apart from their usual compensation; (3) non-performing loans; (4) loans to related parties; and (5) violations against the BOT's rules and regulations, and the amount paid on such violations (Pathan et al., 2008a; Bank of Thailand, 2002). Some other information must be disclosed on a monthly basis.

35.3.4   Equity Investment

To avoid moral hazard and the principal–agency problem, the BOT sets rules to limit bank investment and the share structure. In terms of investment, banks are not allowed to: (1) hold more than 10 percent of a company's shares; (2) invest in a company's shares more than 5 percent of bank total capital funds; and (3) invest in shares of all companies exceeding 20 percent of the bank capital. With regard to the share structure, any single shareholder holding more than 5 percent of the bank's total distributed shares must be reported to the BOT. Furthermore, shareholding exceeding 10 percent of total distributed shares by a single shareholder is prohibited, unless otherwise approved by the BOT.

35.3.5   Financial Sector Master Plan and Supervision

Besides regulation on corporate governance, the BOT also enhances its supervisory role by implementing the Financial Sector Master Plan (FSMP) as well as restructuring the supervisory process of the BOT. These changes are intended to create a more competitive environment and reduce structural weakness in the banking system. The key measures include reducing the number of small players and eliminating regulatory arbitrage by a licensing rationalization scheme and the 'one-presence' policy. Licensing rationalization reduces the licenses for deposit-taking institutions to four types: two for domestically registered banks (commercial banks and retail banks), and two for foreign banks (foreign bank branches and subsidiaries of foreign banks). In addition, a one-presence policy restricts financial conglomerates with many deposit-taking institutions within their groups to merging their holdings and maintaining only one type of deposit-taking institution. With these measures, the authorities have removed the overlapping scopes of business that posed regulatory arbitrage problems.

To ensure that banks follow the guidelines on CG, banks are subject to both off-site and on-site examination from the BOT. The off-site examiner conducts quarterly reports, serving as an early warning system to help change and improve the condition of each bank. The report from the off-site examiner will be used to develop the scope for the on-site examination. After the on-site examination, banks are rated internally according to their aggregate level of risk.

35.4 BANK GOVERNANCE AND BANK PERFORMANCE

35.4.1 Literature Review

This section explores the effect of better bank governance on bank performance. Many past studies have examined the relationship between the two. There is, however, no conclusive evidence on this. Some suggest that a small board of directors may be more profitable since they have a better monitoring role. Some argue that large boards could create a free-rider problem (Pathan et al., 2008a). The paper by Bhagat and Black (1999) found that there is an uncertain relationship between board composition and firm performance. Using the survey data from firms listed in Standard & Poor's (S&P), they found that there was no convincing evidence that larger numbers of independent directors relative to the normal practice among large American firms improves firms' performance. Apart from the US, it was found that European banks' performance is negatively related to the size of the board of directors (Staikouras et al., 2007). Using data from 1984–1991 for 425 large public corporations, Yermack (1996) found an inverse relationship between CG and bank performance. Given the large average size of US boards, it is possible that the correlation may have a convex shape.

On the other hand, a number of empirical studies found the opposite result. Larger board size allows more diverse experience and opportunities. Klapper and Love (2004), using the survey data from Credit Lyonnais Securities Asia (CLSA), found that better corporate governance is highly correlated with better operating performance such as return an assets (ROA) and Tobin's Q. Recent studies by Sofia and Vafeas (2010), focusing on smaller firms with poor operating performance history, found that board size is positively correlated with firm value. Kiel and Nicholson (2003) found that board size was positively correlated with firm value for Australia's largest publicly listed companies.

Brown and Caylor (2009) relate CG to operating performance. Based on the 51 governance provisions (51 CG) provided by Institutional Investor Services (ISS), they found that some governance provisions are significantly and positively related to ROA or return on equity (ROE), depending on specification. Such provisions, for instance, include the following: (1) the governance committee meets at least once during the year; (2) at least one member of the board has participated in an ISS-accredited director education program; (3) the nominating committee is composed solely of independent outside directors.

35.4.2   Data and Model

In this chapter, we use the annual data of the financial statement and the management team spanning from 2000 to 2009. Eight Thai commercial banks are included in the study. Our data are primarily based on the SETSMART database. A list of banks, variables used and basic statistics are provided in the Appendix.

To measure the impact of CG on bank performance, we estimate a panel data regression model with time fixed effect.[4] Following the specification used by Pathan et al. (2008b), the bank performance is regressed against corporate governance and the bank-specific variables as follows:

$$Performance_{i,t} = \alpha + \beta_1 BoardSize + \beta_2 BoardSize^2 + \beta_3 \frac{Independent}{BoardSize}$$

$$+ \beta_4 size + \beta_5 capitalstructure + \beta_6 NPL$$

where i indexes banks i and t indexes time t. Five measures of performance, namely return on asset (*ROA*), net interest margin (*NIM*), economic profit (*Econ_profit*), economic value-added (*EVA*[5]) and cost to income (*Cost/Income*) are used. Detailed calculation of each measurement is discussed in the Appendix.

The traditional bank performance measures such as *ROA*, *NIM* and *Cost/Income* are easy to calculate and readily available; however, they have shortcomings since they are bound to accounting standards, and do not include cost of equity. Here, we include *Econ_profit* and *EVA* to overcome such shortcomings.

Econ_profit, adjusted for cost of capital, should be a more appropriate measure of performance. Usually, when we determine the true performance of a firm, we take earnings before interest and tax (*EBIT*) and subtract taxes and cost of capital which includes cost of borrowing and cost of equity. However, in the case of banking business, banks create value from the liability side such as deposits. Therefore, cost of borrowing should not be considered part of the source of capital. For this reason, economic profit is expressed as:

$$Econ\_profit_t = Net\ income_t - (Equity_{t-1} * Cost\ of\ equity_t).$$

Nevertheless, it should be noted that net income and equity are still taken from the financial statement which is prepared according to accounting standards. To overcome the shortcoming, we also use the *EVA* which is expressed as:

$$EVA = Adjusted\ net\ income_t - (Adjusted\ equity_{t-1} * Cost\ of\ equity_t).$$

Uyemura et al. (1996) narrowed down the adjustment of balance sheet and income statement into five items: (1) loan loss reserves and loan loss provisioning; (2) taxes; (3) extraordinary items; (4) securities; and (5) goodwill. Due to a lack of data availability, no adjustments can be made for taxes, gains and losses from the sale of securities and goodwill in this chapter. *EVA* is a performance measure that explicitly charges for the use of equity and thus implicitly reflects bank-specific risk preferences and is not bound

Table 35.4   Comparison of performance measures

	Main advantages	Main disadvantages
Return on asset (*ROA*)	• Availability of information	• Is bound by accounting standards
Economic profit (*Econ_profit*)	• Charges for the use of equity	• Is bound by accounting standards
Economic value-added (*EVA*)	• Charges for the use of equity • Uses adjusted net income and equity	• Suffers from subjectivity inherent in adjustments • Does not remove depreciation effect

Table 35.5   Correlation between different performance measures

	ROA	*NIM*	*Econ_Profit*	*EVA*	*Cost/Income*
ROA	1				
NIM	0.4922	1			
Econ_profit	0.0338	0.057	1		
EVA	0.1120	0.2194	0.9600	1	
Cost/Income	−0.9800	−0.5230	−0.0393	−0.1351	1

by generally accepted accounting standards (Herberholz et al., 2010). A comparison of performance measures is given in Table 35.4.

The capital asset pricing model (CAPM) is used to determine the cost of equity where the beta is estimated for each month using the Stock Exchange of Thailand (SET) index as proxy for the future on the overall stock market. Since there is no risk-free rate that is comparable to rates on US Treasury bills, the minimum lending rate which is the interest rate charged on the most creditworthy borrowers is used instead. Due to the lack of historical price information, especially due to government interventions, and subsequent suspensions of trading as well as delisting that occurred during the study period, many commercial banks were dropped out of the observation. A ten-year monthly rolling window is used to determine the beta of each bank.

Due to the adjustment discussed above on the items in the financial statement, the performance measures based on accounting standards have low correlation with the performance measures based on adjusted items, but quite high correlation within the group (Table 35.5). The correlations between *ROA* and *Econ_profit* and between *ROA* and *EVA* are 0.03 and 0.11, respectively; while the correlation between *ROA* and *NIM* is 0.49.

The board size (*BoardSize*) and the ratio of independent directors to board size are used as a proxy for CG. Since there is no conclusive evidence regarding the pattern of association between CG and bank performance, it may suggest that there may be a convex relationship. Therefore, to test this hypothesis, the board size is entered as an absolute value and a square term to examine whether there is any inverted-U shape relationship between CG and bank performance. Bank size, capital structure and ratio of non-performing loans (NPL) to gross loans are bank-specific variables. The natural

Table 35.6   Composition of boards

	Board size		Chairman		Vice-chairman		Director		Independent director	
	2000	2010*	2000	2010*	2000	2010*	2000	2010*	2000	2010*
ACL	9	11	1	1	0	1	5	5	3	4
BAY	8	11	1	1	0	0	4	6	3	4
BBL	13	16	1	1	1	1	9	8	2	6
CIMBT	7	8	1	1	0	1	4	2	2	4
KBANK	12	13	1	1	1	1	6	4	4	7
KTB	10	10	1	1	1	1	5	4	3	4
SCB	11	15	1	1	0	0	8	5	2	9
SCIB	6	12	1	1	0	1	3	5	2	5
TMB	16	12	1	1	1	0	12	7	2	4
UOBT	9	10	1	1	0	1	6	5	2	3
Average	10.1	11.8	1.0	1.0	0.4	0.7	6.2	5.1	2.5	5.0

Note: * Data as of September 2010.

Source: SETSMART and bank websites.

Table 35.7   Correlation between corporate governance and bank performance

	ROA	NIM	Econ–Profit	EVA	Cost/Income
Board size	0.1753	0.4058*	−0.1743	−0.0951	−0.1864
Independent/Board Size	0.3439*	0.4875*	0.2702*	0.3157*	−0.3195*

Note: * Denotes significant at 95% confidence interval or higher.

Source: SETSMART.

log of the bank's assets is used to control for bank size. The capital structure, which is the ratio of total liabilities to total assets, measures the level of risk. *NPL* or banks' non-performing loans is the ratio of non-performing loans to gross loans, which represents loan quality.

Table 35.6 shows that on average the number of board directors meets the minimum requirement set by the BOT (the board should comprise at least nine members). Over a decade, the average board size increased from 10 to 11 members. Larger banks tend to have larger board sizes than smaller ones. The number of independent directors more than doubled for many banks.

Table 35.7 shows the correlation between the measures of CG and five different measures of bank performance. The board size is positively correlated with bank performance, namely *ROA* and *NIM*. The ratio of independent directors is positively related to *ROA, NIM, Econ_profit* and *EVA*, suggesting that better CG enhances bank performance. Furthermore, CG is negatively related to cost-to-income ratio, suggesting that good CG can help lower the cost of banks.

Table 35.8   Regression results (fixed effect: year)

Variables	ROA	NIM	Econ–Profit	EVA	Cost/Income
Independent/Board Size	0.0301**	0.0033	3.8076*	4.5182*	−0.4839***
	(3.189)	(0.853)	(2.047)	(1.879)	(−3.680)
Board Size	0.0011	0.0048**	−0.4689	−0.2599	−0.0226
	(0.320)	(2.850)	(−1.282)	(−0.521)	(−0.335)
Board Size²	−0.0001	−0.0002**	0.0179	0.0089	0.0014
	(−0.491)	(−2.759)	(1.259)	(0.456)	(0.462)
Debt/Asset	−0.1230*	−0.0577**	−5.1234	−7.1178	1.8888*
	(−2.209)	(−2.580)	(−0.575)	(−0.653)	(2.119)
ln(Asset)	0.0107**	0.0039**	−0.4494	−0.4127	−0.2065**
	(2.479)	(2.327)	(−1.231)	(−0.912)	(−2.511)
NPL	−0.0393	0.0037	−1.0414	−0.5214	0.6390
	(−1.417)	(0.809)	(−0.752)	(−0.317)	(1.532)
Constant	−0.1083	−0.0317	15.4129	14.8149	3.5416
	(−1.001)	(−0.686)	(0.939)	(0.724)	(1.689)
Observations	80	80	80	80	80
R-squared	0.350	0.474	0.153	0.119	0.346
F	5.876	9.762	4.585	4.741	8.541

Note: t-statistics in parentheses. ***, **, * significant at the 1%, 5% and 10% levels respectively.

35.4.3   Regression Results

The regression results are shown in Table 35.8. The positive coefficient of CG suggests that banks with better CG have better bank performance. The coefficient of the ratio of independent directors to board size (*Independent/Board Size*) is positive and significant to almost every measure of bank performance except cost-to-income ratio, suggesting that the higher share of independent directors would increase bank performance. The negative coefficient for the cost-to-income column implies that banks with a higher ratio tend to have lower costs.

   With regard to board size, there is some weak evidence that the size of the board will influence the performance of banks. The impact of the board size has a non-linear relationship, particularily an inverted U-shape relationship with *NIM*. The coefficient of the board size (*BoardSize*) is positive and becomes negative for *Board Size²*, suggesting that when the size of the board is small, the increase in board size would benefit bank performance. However, if the board size becomes too large, the benefit from larger board size decreases. The positive coefficient of the size variable *ln(Asset)* indicates that banks benefit from economies of scale.

35.5   CONCLUSION

The banking sector has always been one of the most important sectors in Thailand. The size of the Thai banking sector has also been much larger than that of the capital market.

Past experience indicates that weak corporate governance and lack of prudential controls were among the most important factors that caused banking crises throughout history. Weak corporate governance allowed banks to engage in risky lending that was based on overvalued collateral and connection with the bankers (related-party lending). This chapter discusses the government's and the Bank of Thailand's efforts to reform corporate governance of the banking sector and evaluates the effect of corporate governance on the performance of Thai banks, using both accounting and economic profit measures.

Our analysis reveals that since 2000, the increased proportion of independent directors relative to board size has improved Thai banks' performance and reduced the cost-to-income ratio. However, only weak evidence of the relationship between board size and banks' performance was found. Having a higher number of independent directors is crucial to banks' profitability because independent directors are able to discuss corporate matters without being interfered with by the bank's management. Despite the significance of corporate governance on banks' performance, other factors can also play important roles. These include, for example, overall macroeconomic conditions, banks' financing structure, level of NPL, and so on.

Our findings suggest that it is important to design a mechanism that promotes good corporate governance in the Thai banking industry. Opening up the banking sector, as envisioned by the FSMP, is a step in the right direction as it could strengthen the monitoring process via increasing competition from rival banks. Overall, improving corporate governance of banks and ensuring a good governance environment have been a positive development for the Thai banking sector as a whole. This in turn should reduce the likelihood of moral hazard and future banking crises in Thailand.

NOTES

*   The views expressed in this chapter are the views of the authors and do not necessarily reflect the views or policies of the Bank of Thailand.
1.   New banks are Kiatnakin Bank, Thanachart Bank, Tisco Bank, Land and Houses Retail Bank, Thai Credit Retail Bank, AIG Retail Bank and GE Money and Retail Bank (the latter two were already closed down in Sep 2009 and Jan 2007, respectively).
2.   Financial Institutions Business Act B.E. 2551 Section 24 (1)–(9) defines 9 prohibited characteristics as follows: (1) has been declared bankrupt within the last 5 years, (2) has been convicted of a criminal offence, (3) has been dismissed or asked to resign from government agencies due to fraudulent or dishonest conduct, (4) was a director or in the management team of a financial institution that has gone into insolvency, liquidation, (5) has been removed from a management position under Section 89(3) or Section 90(4) of the securities law, (6) was a director, manager or employee or a member of management team of other financial institutions simultaneously, (7) was a manager or member of management team of a firm that received a loan from the financial institution, (8) was a political official, a member of the House of Representatives or senator, and (9) was a BOT employee. Some of these restrictions, however, can be relaxed with the BOT's approval.
3.   It states that a director will not be liable for any business decision if he or she can establish the following elements (Low, 2004):
     i.   The judgment was made in good faith and for a proper purpose;
     ii.   There was no material personal interest in the subject matter of the judgment;
     iii. He or she informed himself or herself about the subject matter of the judgment to the extent he or she reasonably believed to be appropriate; and
     iv.   The judgment was rationally believed to be in the best interest of the corporation.
4.   For the specificiation test, we also run a regression with a bank dummy. The signs of coefficients remain the same. The results are shown in Appendix Table 35A.4.
5.   EVA® is a registered trademark of Stern Stewart & Company

REFERENCES

Bank of Thailand (2000), 'Supervision Report 2000'.

Bank of Thailand (2002), 'Supervision Report 2001–2002'.

Bank of Thailand (2003), 'Supervision Report 2003'.

Bhagat, Sanjai and Bernard Black (1999), 'The uncertain relationship between board composition and firm performance', *Business Lawyer*, **54**, 921–63.

Brown, Lawrence and Marcus Caylor (2009), 'Corporate governance and firm operating performance', *Review of Quantitative Finance and Accounting*, **32**(2), 129–144.

Herberholz, Chantal, Wanvimol Sawangngoenyuang and Tientip Subhanij (2010), 'The impact of the changing financial landscape on Thai banks', *Sixth National Conference of Economists Conference Proceedings*, Bangkok, 29 October.

Hoontrakul, Pongsak and Chatsurang Karnchanasai (2010), 'The evolution of corporate governance in banking industry of Thailand from the 1997 Asian crisis to the 2008 global credit crisis', available at SSRN, http://ssrn.com/abstract=1555423.

Kiel, Geoffrey and Gavin Nicholson (2003), 'Board composition and corporate performance: how the Australian experience informs contrasting theories of corporate governance', *Corporate Governance: An International Review*, **11**(3), 189–205.

Klapper, Leora and Inessa Love (2004), 'Corporate governance, investor protection and performance in emerging markets', *Journal of Corporate Finance*, **10**(5), 703–728.

Limpaphayom, Piman and J. Thomas Connelly (2004), 'Corporate governance in Thailand', Review of Corporate Governance in Asia, available at http://www.adbi.org/conf-seminar-papers/2004/08/18/531.corporate.governance.thailand/, 30 September.

Low, Chee Keong (2004), 'A Road Map for Corporate Governance in East Asia', *Northwestern Journal of International Law and Business*, **25**, 164–203, available at: http://www.oecd.org/dataoecd/4/57/37499034.pdf

Nakornthab, Don (2007), 'Thai commercial banks one decade after the crisis: assessment of risk to financial stability', Discussion Paper DP/03/2007, Bank of Thailand.

Notification of the Bank of Thailand No. ThorPorTor SorNorNor. 13/2552 Re: Corporate Governance for Banks. Dated 9 July BE 2552.

Notification of the Bank of Thailand No. ThorPorTor SorNorNor. 14/2552 Re: Approval Criteria for Board of Director, Manager, Management Team and Financial Consultant. Dated 9 July BE 2552.

Notification of the Bank of Thailand No. ThorPorTor SorNorNor. 15/2552 Re: Board of Director's Roles and Responsibility. Dated 9 July BE 2552.

Notification of the Capital Market Supervisory Board No. TorChor. 28/2551 Notification of the Capital Market Supervisory Board. Dated 15 December BE 2551.

Pathan, Sham, Michael Skully and J. Wickramanayake (2008a), 'Reforms in Thai bank governance: the aftermath of the Asian financial crisis', *International Review of Financial Analysis*, **17**(2), 345–362.

Pathan, Sham, Michael Skully and J. Wickramanayake (2008b), 'Board size, independence and performance: an analysis of Thai banks', *Asia-Pacific Financial Markets*, **14**(3), 211–227.

Polsiri, Piruna and Yupana Wiwattanakantang (2005), 'Corporate governance of banks in Thailand', CEI Working Paper Series No. 2005-20, Hitotsubashi University.

Sofia, Larmou and Nikos Vafeas (2010), 'The relation between board size and firm performance in firms with a history of poor operating performance', *Journal of Management and Governance*, **14**(1), 61–85.

Staikouras, Christos K., Panagiotis K. Staikouras and Maria-Eleni K. Agoraki (2007), 'The effect of board size and composition on European bank performance', *European Journal of Law and Economics*, **23**, 1–27.

Uyemura, Dennis G., Charles C. Kantor and Justin M. Pettit (1996), 'EVA® for banks: value creation, risk management, and profitability measurement', *Journal of Applied Corporate Finance*, **9**(2), 94–109.

Wailerdsak, Natenapha (2006), *Business Groups and Family Business in Thailand Before and After the 1997 Crisis*, Bangkok: BrandAgebooks. (in Thai)

Yermack, David (1996), 'Higher market valuation of companies with a small board of directors', *Journal of Financial Economics*, **40**(2), 185–212.

APPENDIX

Table 35A.1   Banks included in this study

1. Bank of Ayudhya Public Company Ltd. (BAY)
2. Bangkok Bank Public Company Ltd. (BBL)
3. CIMB Thai Bank Public Company Ltd. (CIMBT)
4. KasikornBank Public Company Ltd. (KBANK)
5. Krung Thai Bank Public Company Ltd. (KTB)
6. Siam City Bank Public Company Ltd. (SCIB)
7. Siam Commercial Bank Public Company Ltd. (SCB)
8. TMB Bank Public Company Ltd. (TMB)

Table 35A.2   Descriptive summary

Variable	Obs	Mean	Std. dev.	Min.	Max.
Performance measurement					
ROA	80	0.002	0.018	−0.074	0.025
NIM	80	0.023	0.010	−0.008	0.038
Economic Profit	80	−0.103	1.560	−3.928	9.060
EVA	80	−0.393	1.964	−5.352	10.729
Cost to income	80	0.947	0.339	0.552	2.324
Corporate governance					
Independent/Board Size	80	0.349	0.146	0.000	0.636
Board Size	80	11.488	3.222	4.000	17.000
Board Size²	80	142.213	74.231	16.000	289.000
Bank specific					
Debt/Asset	80	0.930	0.029	0.877	1.004
ln(Asset)	80	20.307	0.605	18.749	21.277
NPL	80	0.109	0.082	0.001	0.592

Table 35A.3   Calculations

Variable	Calculation
Performance measurement	
ROA	Earning Before Tax/Total Assets
NIM	(Interest Income – Interest Expense)/Total Assets
Economic Profit	$Net\ Income_{i,t} - (Equity_{i,t-1} * Cost\ of\ Equity_{i,t})$
EVA or *Economic Value Added*	$Adjusted\ Net\ Income_{i,t} - (Adjusted\ Equity_{i,t-1} * Cost\ of\ Equity_{i,t})$ where *adjusted income* = net income + loan loss provisions – reversals of loan loss provisioning – chargeoffs, *adjusted equity* = equity + loan loss reserves + unrealized loss on changes in value of investment – revaluation gain on change in value of investment; $chargeoffs$ = loan loss provision$_t$ + loan loss reserve$_{t-1}$ –loan loss reserve$_t$; cost of equity is calculated from the CAPM model
Cost to income	(Interest Expense + Loan Loss Provision + Overhead / (Interest Income + non-Interest Income)
Corporate governance	
Independent/Board Size	Independent Director/Board Size
Board Size	Director + Independent Director + Chairperson + Vice Chairperson
Bank specific	
Debt/Asset	Total liabilities/Total Assets
ln(Asset)	*ln(Asset)*
NPL	Non-performing Loan/Gross Loan

Table 35A.4   Regression results (time fixed effect with bank dummy)

Variables	ROA	NIM	Econ-Profit	EVA	Cost/Income
Independent/Board Size	0.0141	−0.0033	5.2871**	5.7200**	−0.1586
	(1.231)	(−1.115)	(2.829)	(2.323)	(−0.870)
Board Size	0.0051*	0.0052***	−0.0923	0.4475	−0.1107**
	(1.881)	(4.301)	(−0.157)	(0.659)	(−2.957)
Board Size²	−0.0003**	−0.0002***	0.0002	−0.0207	0.0056**
	(−2.740)	(−3.883)	(0.00814)	(−0.829)	(2.564)
Debt/Asset	−0.0407	0.0383	5.5540	16.2765*	−0.2517
	(−1.066)	(1.689)	(0.805)	(1.903)	(−0.303)
ln(Asset)	0.0110	−0.0140***	−1.5026	−2.1689*	−0.1812
	(0.992)	(−4.826)	(−1.599)	(−2.143)	(−0.927)
NPL	−0.0302	−0.0225**	−4.7407*	−7.2137**	0.6213
	(−0.876)	(−2.603)	(−1.867)	(−2.605)	(1.231)
Constant	−0.2098	0.2443***	24.0616	24.4618	5.3580
	(−0.881)	(4.203)	(0.949)	(0.911)	(1.259)
Observations	80	80	80	80	80
R-squared	0.544	0.866	0.340	0.377	0.570
F	4.875	86.56	74.56	16.74	3.712

Notes: *t*-statistics in parentheses. ***, **, * significant at the 1%, 5% and 10% levels, respectively.

36 Governance issues in Indian microfinance
Shubhashis Gangopadhyay and S.K. Shanthi

36.1 INTRODUCTION

In the 1970s and the 1980s, the developing countries were using public sector institutions as the main providers of financial services to the poor. These institutions lent to small and marginalized farmers at subsidized interest rates (Martin et al., 2002). However, lending to this group of rural poor is generally associated with higher risks and this, together with poor institutional structures, resulted in formal institutions failing to deliver financial services effectively to the rural poor (Basu and Srivastava, 2005).

The 1980s and 1990s saw the emergence of formal and semi-formal financial institutions which attempted to reach out to the rural poor through various microfinance models. The success of the Grameen Bank in Bangladesh, in terms of productivity improvement, poverty alleviation and women's empowerment, encouraged other countries, including India, to use the microfinance route to reach populations that were otherwise completely bypassed by the formal banking sector. The joint liability group (JLG) model employed by Grameen was a concept that caught on in other countries which came up with slight contextual modifications of the original idea to reach out to the poor. The most widespread model used was that of forming rural women into groups, called self-help groups (SHGs), and lending to these groups instead of to individuals. These loans were savings-linked. The groups save and borrow as collective units, thus reducing the risk of default to the lender. Many non-governmental organizations (NGOs) act as facilitators in this model and link the SHGs to banks that offer savings accounts and also lend to them. There are also other models in operation which do not use the concept of group lending, though they specialize in reaching out to the poor. There are two main characteristics that separate such microfinance institutions from the formal institutions: lower loan amounts and greater frequency of loan repayments. A microfinance institution, or MFI, can be an NGO, a bank, a co-operative society, a non-bank finance company (NBFC) or a public limited company with diverse ownership and governance structures.

In section 36.2 we describe the current debate among MFI-watchers. Sections 36.3 and 36.4 discuss, respectively, the international literature on governance and the role of women in governance. Section 36.5 gives a description of the MFI sector in India. Section 36.6 discusses the new set of proposed recommendations for regulating the Indian MFI sector. Section 36.7 concludes.

36.2 MICROFINANCE DEBATE

The current debate going on in the academic community, and among policymakers, is centered on a few fundamental questions regarding the operation of MFIs. Can we find enough justification for subsidizing the microfinance industry with public funds? Do increased interest rates exacerbate agency problems, as detected by lower loan repayment rates and less profitability? Is there evidence of a trade-off between the depth of outreach to the poor and the pursuit of profitability or self-sustainability? Is there evidence of 'mission drift' in the functioning of MFIs; that is, are they moving away from serving the poorer and/or female clients in pursuit of commercial viability? What role does governance play in resolving these questions? (Cull et al., 2007)

Microfinance has increasingly become a poverty reduction tool in many developing countries, along with that of the financial inclusion of the poor. In particular, it was expected to reduce poverty by taking profit-making banking practices to low-income communities. Given that existing financial institutions were unable to customize their loan portfolios for the poor, more flexible and context-driven MFIs were expected to act as specialized institutions to achieve financial inclusion. Indeed, in many countries, they were often conceived as 'extension services' to formal institutions, with banks playing an active role in supplying funds to MFIs.

Empirical evidence on the effectiveness of this strategy is mixed. One view is that microfinance has little or no impact on poverty. This finding is based on randomized evaluations of microfinance (for example, Banerjee et al., 2010; Karlan and Zinman, 2009; Feigenberg et al., 2010). On the other hand, Kai and Hamori (2009) examined the relationship between microfinance and inequality across 61 countries, and found that microfinance does have an equalizing impact on the incomes of the poor and reduces inequality. Their conclusion was that poorer countries need to focus more on microfinance to reduce inequality. Similar inferences were drawn by Ahlin et al. (2010) and Ahlin and Lin (2006).

In a recent study, Imai et al. (2010) also test the hypothesis that microfinance reduces poverty at the macro level using cross-country and panel data, and find that taking account of the endogeneity associated with loans from MFIs, a country with a higher MFI gross loan portfolio tends to have lower levels of poverty measured by the FGT (Foster–Greer–Thorbecke) indices. Microfinance loans are negatively associated not only with the poverty head count ratio, but also with the poverty gap and squared poverty gap, implying that even the poorest of the poor benefit from them. These findings are also reflected in others that have used household-level datasets (Khandker, 2005; Gaiha and Nandhi, 2009; Imai et al., 2010).

Cull et al. (2007) study patterns of profitability, loan repayment and cost reduction with data on 124 MFIs in 49 countries, and find evidence to show that while there is a possibility of making profits while serving the poor, a trade-off emerges between profitability and serving the poorest. They further find that raising interest rates and fees does not necessarily lead to greater profit, and the benefits of cost-cutting diminish when serving relatively better-off customers.

36.3   GOOD GOVERNANCE

In microfinance literature, the term 'governance' was first used by the CGAP (Consultative Group to Assist the Poor) in 1997 when it was defined as: 'a system of checks and balances whereby a board is established to manage the managers. Governance is sometimes conceived as a virtuous cycle that links the shareholder to the board, to the management, to the staff, to the customer, and to the community at large' (CGAP, 1997). MFIs, whether they are for-profit or non-profit, are institutions that include a social mission, which is that of providing financial services to the low-income population. The financial objectives of this provision are to enable the poor to attain self-sufficiency and independence along with generating surpluses for the owners of these funds. MFIs are, therefore, constantly balancing the dual purpose of maximizing social impact with profitability or sustainability (Mersland and Strøm, 2010). The extent to which they maintain the dual focus is shaped by their governance structure.

Good governance is the process by which a board of directors, working through management, guides the institution's corporate mission and protects its assets. In any corporation, the board and the management deal with the same issues but at different levels. While the board is the policymaking entity, the management deals with the actual day-to-day operations of the corporation. Effective governance strikes the appropriate balance in the relationship between the board of directors and management in their combined efforts to move forward the institution and its mission. Each brings unique skills to the joint effort and views the institution through a different lens. Together they add value precisely because they are complementary (PRISMS, 2005).

Ownership of MFIs is another factor that contributes to the effectiveness of not only the governance but also the delivery of their social mission. Four types of ownership structures are found among the MFIs throughout the world:

1. Government or public ownership.
2. Non-profit (NGOs).
3. For profit (banks/financial institutions).
4. Co-operatives (credit unions).

Each of the above has its own strengths and weaknesses. Most of the publicly owned MFIs have performed poorly due to misguided government policies that distort markets, through targeted subsidies, political interference or corruption. The one notable exception is BRA, Indonesia. NGO-run MFIs have no owners, and failed governance in their case is often because of power concentration in the hands of an executive without oversight. But the NGO model has also succeeded in many cases when the board members have identified strongly with the mission and have provided strategic guidance to the institution. For MFIs that do not want any regulation and are driven by a strong commitment to the social mission and have adequate resources, the NGO model perhaps is the most viable. But most of them face challenges when they grow 'too big'. There are two types of for-profit MFIs. The first type includes the commercial banks, financial institutions and other non-bank finance companies (NBFCs) that move downmarket to offer financial services like deposit accounts and loan products to serve the micro enterprise sector. The second type includes non-profit NGOs establishing for-profit MFIs. While the primary motive of the first type of MFI is profit, in the case of the second type the motivations differ depending on their funding agencies. They access NGO funds, public entity funds from governmental agencies, specialized equity funds and private investment funds. Each investor group has its own interests and the future course of the MFIs will depend on how well the board negotiates through those interests (PRISMS, 2005).

As the microfinance industry is transitioning from an infant stage to a growth and maturity stage of development, governance becomes important. Many organizations in this sector are struggling with issues of long-term sustainability and with the challenges of becoming for-profit organizations without losing their social missions. Most of them have been started by a visionary with little regard for sustainability, giving pre-eminence to the social mission. The boards of their NGOs, therefore, had members who owed a strong allegiance to the visionary as well as to the vision. The funding mostly came from donations for which the board felt little fiduciary obligation. When the NGOs become financial intermediaries, then legal and other fiduciary responsibilities catch up and the board has to balance the various demands placed upon it. Commercial interests catch up when the NGO finally transforms itself into a for-profit financial institution that attracts investors who come in with different expectations of return on their investments. All these factors combine to make governance of MFIs different and more challenging than that of other entities (Rock et al., 1998).

The governance of MFIs stands on four main pillars: (1) ownership; (2) board size and composition; (3) chief executive officer (CEO), management, remuneration structures, transparency in accounting procedures and auditing; and (4) information and establishing mechanisms to manage risks. The last is very important since the risks faced by MFIs are many. They face operational risks (risk of default); information-related risks due to unreliable management information systems (adverse selection and moral hazard); and organizational risks relating to internal control and other market related risks such as competition, regulation and political risks (Keasey et al., 1997).

Hatarska (2004) studies the impact of governance mechanisms on the outreach and sustainability of MFIs in Central and Eastern Europe and finds that among the external governance mechanisms auditing has a positive effect on outreach, while regulatory supervision and rating by outside agencies are not effective mechanisms of control. Among the internal governance mechanisms, the board plays an important role. Local boards achieve better sustainability than international boards. The study also finds that larger boards and boards with greater representation from insiders exhibit poorer financial performance. The inclusion of women on the board is found to improve the depth and breadth of outreach as well as the financial performance. Presence of donors on the board is found to improve the depth of outreach but not necessarily the breadth, and the presence of financiers on the board is found to improve the financial performance.

Kyreboah-Coleman and Osei (2008) study a sample of 52 MFIs in sub-Saharan Africa and find that governance plays a critical role in their performance, and that the independence of the board and a clear separation of the positions of the CEO and the board chairperson have a positive correlation with both the outreach and the profitability of MFIs. The study highlights the need to clearly balance the multidimensional and sometimes conflicting objectives facing MFIs.

Tchakoute-Tchigoua (2010) explores the relationship between the legal status of the MFIs and their performance in a sample of 202 MFIs in Latin America. NGOs, private finance companies and co-operatives are compared, and the results show that private corporations perform better than NGOs only when the quality of the portfolios is used as an indicator. Surprisingly, they also find that for-profit MFIs are more socially efficient than not-for-profit MFIs, thus leading to the conclusion that a commercial approach of microfinance does not seem inconsistent with its social mission.

Mersland and Strom (2009) find that the performance of MFIs improves with local rather than international directors, an internal board auditor and a female CEO. The number of credit recipients increases when the chairman and the CEO are different, and outreach is lower in the case of individual lending as opposed to group lending. Interestingly, they find no difference in financial performance and outreach in a for-profit as opposed to a not-for-profit MFI. They further argue that their findings highlight the need for an industry-specific approach to MFI governance.[1]

Kyreboah-Coleman (2007) examines the impact of capital structure on the performance of MFIs from sub-Saharan Africa. Analyzing panel data for a ten-year period (1995–2004), he finds that most of the MFIs are highly leveraged and finance their operations with long-term debt. They perform better on outreach, enjoy economies of scale and are therefore better able to deal with moral hazard and adverse selection, thus improving their ability to deal with risk.

36.4   WOMEN AND MICROFINANCE

Women and microfinance are inextricably linked. The objective of the Microcredit Summit Campaign, which plays a key role in developing and promoting microfinance, is 'to ensure that 175 million of the world's poorest families, especially women, receive credit for self-employment and other financial and business services'. The Norwegian Nobel Committee, while awarding the prize in 2006 to Muhammad Yunus and the Grameen Bank, emphasized the role of microfinance in women's liberation. Globally there are about 1000 MFIs that provide financial services to 150 active clients, three-fourths of whom are women. In the early years, most of the microfinance clients were women organized into self-help groups, following the Grameen Bank model, and many studies have documented this fact. Morduch (1999) concludes that this is one of the main reasons for the success of the MFIs. Armendáriz de Aghion and Morduch (2005) also document the focus of MFIs on female customers. They argue that targeting a female clientele is perfectly compatible with financial sustainability, since female repayment rates are much better. D'Espallier et al. (2009a, 2009b) investigate the anecdotal evidence of the supposed positive performance effect from female targeting, using a global dataset. Their results confirm that the targeting of women leads to higher repayment rates to micro banks, but their second study finds that the overall profitability of micro banks is not enhanced since the benefits arising out of better repayment are offset by the increasing costs of servicing the much smaller loans that female customers usually want. Some studies also point to the dangers involved in commercialization and that profit-making among MFIs may lead to 'mission drift', where they may turn to more profitable customers. This shifts them away from the rural poor to the urban poor who, in general, are more bankable; and away from female borrowers to male borrowers (Cull et al., 2008).

The gender issue therefore has a greater relevance in the microfinance industry, given that its customers are mostly women. Intuition suggests that having women managers in leadership roles must imply that MFIs are better able to customize their products to suit the needs of the clients and thereby lead to better financial performance. But, on this issue, the findings are somewhat mixed.

Bassem (2009) conducts an empirical examination of the relation between governance mechanisms and the performance of MFIs in the Euro-Mediterranean region. He finds that performance-based compensation to the managers is not associated with better performance of the MFI. He identifies trade-offs between MFIs' outreach and sustainability on larger board size and on a higher proportion of independent directors. The study shows that greater representation of women on the board is associated with better performance and external supports help them to perform better financially. However, it finds that MFIs acting as NGOs seem to be more consistent with their social mission than with their financial performance.

Strom et al. (2010) investigate the relationships between female leadership, firm performance and corporate governance in a panel of 379 MFIs across 73 countries, and find that female leadership is significantly associated with larger boards, younger firms, non-commercial legal status and more female beneficiaries or clients. They further find that female leadership is positively related to the MFI performance, but this result is not driven by improved corporate governance. The improved performance again is restricted to female chairpersons and CEOs, and not to female members of the board. Indeed, Kanter (1977), Smith et al. (2006) and Adams and Ferreira (2009) make the argument that female directorship is more a token of gender equality in the composition of the board.

36.5 MICROFINANCE INDUSTRY IN INDIA

India is one of the largest markets for microfinance in the world, with about 260 million people living below the poverty line. Microfinance in India has been growing impressively in the first decade of this century. While the global microfinance industry posted a compounded annual growth rate (CAGR) of 12 percent in the borrower base and a CAGR of 34 percent in the portfolio outstanding, in India the CAGR of the borrower base was 86 percent and that of outstanding portfolio was 96 percent. Latin America continues to lead in terms of portfolio outstanding with US$16 billion (36 percent of the world total).

As of 31 March 2009, the total client base of the sector was estimated to be about 22.6 million, four-fifths of them being women, with an outstanding portfolio of US$2 billion. A total of 6.1 million SHGs are estimated to be participating, with total savings of about US$1.2 billion. Microfinance loan size in India mostly falls in the range of US$100 to US$500, carrying interest in the range of 25 percent to 35 percent. In the coming years, with industry maturity, the growth rate of the outstanding portfolio is expected to level off to about 30 percent. The future of the sector currently lies in product innovations, through product diversity, insurance linking, client targeting, and creative financial and non-financial offerings. More sophisticated growth strategies will be needed to keep this sector on a continued growth path.

The sector is also attracting equity funding as microfinance is gaining ground as a viable investment opportunity. The return on equity in the range of 20 percent to 30 percent is driven by strong operating efficiency and high portfolio quality. The total primary investments in Indian MFIs from 2006 to 10 January 2010 amounted to US$295 million. While most of the investors are socially focused, pure commercial investors are also beginning to play a significant role by participating in a few large transactions. In the years to come, more reliance will be placed on equity capital, especially in light of the Reserve Bank of India's (RBI) capital adequacy requirement for the sector which is currently at 12 percent and is set to increase to 15 percent.

The RBI has instituted measures towards ensuring financial inclusion and priority sector lending (lending targeted to agriculture), and the commercial banks follow the norms to fulfill their financial inclusion quotas. With the active support of the RBI, Indian banks and financial institutions are aggressively participating in the micro-finance sector. Their total exposure to microfinance in 2009 stood at US$2.45 billion, a jump of almost 150 percent over the previous year. Out of the total 267 banks that have reported the data, 181 banks (67.8 percent) had more than 90 percent of SHG loans as of 31 March 2009. The bank lending to MFIs has also grown substantially, from US$0.4 billion to US$0.9 billion, approximately. The National Bank for Agriculture and Rural Development (NABARD), a major player in India in this sector, estimates that by 2014 the borrower base will exceed 110 million with US$30 billion in borrowings.

Nevertheless, around September 2010, all hell broke loose when elected representatives of the state of Andhra Pradesh picked up on reports that MFI members were committing suicide as a result of harassment by MFI staff for recovery of loans. The State Assembly (legislature) passed an ordinance (on 15 October 2010) that put severe restrictions on the operations of MFIs in the state. First, all new MFIs had to register with state authorities before they could begin operations and, for the existing ones, all operations had to stop till they registered. The Ordinance also mandated that no one could be a member of more than one self-help group (SHG); those who had already become members in more than one SHG had to withdraw from all but one SHG. This had to be done within three months of the Ordinance. Of course, they had to settle all their dues and responsibilities to the SHGs from which they were dropping out. There were many other stringent conditions, but the two important ones were that MFIs could not lend to those who were already indebted to banks or other MFIs (the MFIs were responsible for ensuring this) and coercive recovery practices were made criminal offences.

For two reasons, this had an immediate impact on MFI activities throughout India. First, Andhra Pradesh accounts for more than 30 percent of the nation's MFI operations. Second, many of the big (and even some small) MFIs in Andhra Pradesh operate in other states also. Though this ordinance was for MFI operations in Andhra Pradesh only, MFIs correctly inferred that this would create repercussions throughout the country.

It is important to understand the Indian MFI sector in some detail. There are three major forms of organization: the SHG–bank linkage model, non-bank finance companies (NBFCs) and others (trusts, cooperative societies, and so on). The first two account for around 92 percent (58 plus 34, respectively) of all MFI activities. The SHG–bank linkage model was pioneered by NABARD. Women-only SHGs were formed; they were encouraged to save and lend to their members with these accumulated savings that were generously supplemented by bank funding. The loans were for income generation and livelihood concerns only. It was pointed out that once these SHGs were formed, other MFIs started making short-term loans to them with repayment schedules that were shorter than those of the banks. As a result, even though the banks were the 'senior' creditors, other MFIs had their loans serviced before the banks could get their repayments. In fact, a poor household in Andhra Pradesh (AP) services, on average, four loans at a time.

The NBFCs usually follow the JLG (joint liability group) model. The early ones were mostly not-for-profit, but as the market expanded they found it increasingly difficult to attract funds fast enough. Consequently, many of them became for-profit organizations.[2]

Even though many of these MFIs themselves obtained funding from the banks, they lent at what the government claimed were 'usurious' interest rates. The effective rates of interest on MFI loans were mostly no more than 36 percent but there were enough reports of MFIs charging 40–60 percent rates of interest. This coexistence of the 'bad' with the good, and the high returns on the MFI equity holdings, prompted the local government to take drastic steps since it felt that MFIs were making money off the poor from funds subsidized by the nation.

It is not unusual that poor households borrow from more than one source, formal as well as informal. In fact AP leads in this statistic with an average four loans per family, 86 percent served by informal sources. In principle, having access to multiple sources of any service is indeed a good thing since healthy competition helps in keeping the exploitative tendencies of monopolies at bay, and clients would have a wide choice to work with. However, excessive supply, especially of credit, to ill-informed clients and by poorly trained staff driven by perverse incentives, often leads to disaster. Andhra Pradesh stands out with respect to the availability of a variety of lenders, thanks to proactive government programs and aggressive microfinance initiatives led by for-profit MFIs, in addition to super-active traditional informal sources.

While there is tremendous potential for further growth, the need for good governance has become more acute than ever. The high growth of nearly 90 percent over the first decade of this century has become unsustainable. Problems of staff quality, portfolio management and information management are now beginning to surface. The increased competition in the sector has also resulted in some MFIs engaging in multiple lending to attract clients, resulting in excessive indebtedness of some borrowers. Combined with the type of staff engaged for loan recoveries, with stringent schedules and zero tolerance for delinquency, this resulted in a crisis in the state of Andhra Pradesh in 2010, when a number of farmers reportedly committed suicide because they could not repay their loans to MFIs.

36.6 MFI REGULATION IN INDIA

The Malegam Committee set up by the RBI to look into the regulatory aspects of this sector, and fill the 'regulatory gap', submitted its report in January 2011 (Malegam, 2011). The important thing about the report is that it has asked for MFIs to be treated as special NBFCs, and has developed a set of regulations for a new organization called an NBFC-MFI. The special features of this new regulation are based on the fact that microfinance clients are very poor and, often, with little or no financial literacy. An additional reason for regulating them, according to this Report, is that they compete directly with the SHG-Bank Linked lending activities which, somehow, are not to be impaired by unbridled competition from for-profit NBFC-MFIs. However, quite correctly, they also point out that about 75 percent of the NBFC funds for microfinance activities come from the same banks that are pushing through the SHG-Bank Linked model. The definition of these NBFC-MFIs is: '(any company) which provides financial services predominantly to low-income borrowers, with loans of small amounts, for short-terms, on unsecured basis, mainly for income-generating activities, with repayment schedules which are more frequent than those normally stipulated by commercial banks'.

An NBFC-MFI must have 90 percent of its assets in specific types of loans. These loans cannot be more than INR 25 000, given to individuals whose annual incomes are not more than INR 50 000, and the total amount of indebtedness of the borrower cannot be more than INR 25 000. This last condition is similar to the Andhra Pradesh dictum on multiple loans but a bit relaxed. In Andhra Pradesh, multiple lending was not allowed; here, multiple borrowing is allowed provided the total indebtedness is not more than INR 25 000. Furthermore, at least 75 percent of the loans must be for income-generating purposes. This last bit smacks of the pre-1990s banking practices. According to the RBI guidelines then, banks were allowed to give out only 'production' loans and not 'consumption' loans. With money being fungible, there is little meaning to this term, especially when it comes to monitoring and implementation.

Of course, the Report could not ignore the issue of interest rates. It went further and also introduced a 'margin cap'. And, once again, it has gone back to the pre-reform days – not only in the very concept of a cap but also by providing a looser cap for small compared to large MFIs. The latter discrimination between large and small played havoc with industry efficiency as companies multiplied with no consolidation (or economies of scale) as owners wanted to partake of the sops and subsidies available to a 'small' firm. The Malegam Committee Report has divided up NBFC-MFIs into those with a loan portfolio of more than INR 100 crore (1 crore is equal to 10 million) and those with less than that. The margin cap for the large has been set at 10 percent while for the small it is 12 percent. In addition, maximum allowable interest rate (for both sizes) is 24 percent. Also, an MFI can levy only three charges, namely: a processing fee, interest and an insurance charge. In other words, all the financial repression experienced in the pre-reform days is being brought back 20 years after the reforms started. Of course, to make it seem new, new entities have been created; to make it acceptable (politically correct, if not economically wise), the poor have been invoked. And so, to complete the process, all lending to NBFC-MFIs by banks will be counted as priority sector lending: that is, banks will lend at subsidized rates.

The Committee has made a number of recommendations to mitigate the problems of multiple lending, overborrowing, ghost borrowers and coercive methods of recovery. A Credit Information Bureau has to be established and the Reserve Bank must prepare a draft Customer Protection Code to be adopted by all MFIs. Further, the primary responsibility for avoidance of coercive methods of recovery must lie with the MFI and its management. All MFIs must observe a specified Code of Corporate Governance and there must be grievance redressal procedures and establishment of ombudsmen. The Committee has also made suggestions on ensuring compliance and for regular monitoring of MFI activities.

Finally, the Committee has cautioned that while recognizing the need to protect borrowers, it is also necessary to recognize that if the recovery culture is adversely affected and the free flow of funds in the system interrupted, the ultimate sufferers will be the borrowers themselves as the flow of fresh funds to the microfinance sector will inevitably be reduced.

36.7   CONCLUSIONS

The microfinance sector in India has experienced rapid growth since its inception in 1992. This growth and the worldwide euphoria regarding such institutions encouraged Indian policymakers to push this sector even further. Indeed, MFI activities were often viewed as a panacea for the poor, especially in terms of financial inclusion. However, reports of exorbitant profit-making by MFIs, households burdened with multiple loans, coercive recovery by MFI agents and, to top it all, suicides by defaulters after being harassed by MFI loan recovery agents created a furore in government and policy circles. This led to a swing in the pendulum: a draconian state ordinance followed by a national-level set of recommendations that are trying to push a hitherto unregulated fast-growing sector into becoming a highly shackled industry of the pre-reform days.

Of course, these are still 'recommendations', but even a watered-down version could be detrimental to the industry since the basic idea of interest caps and margin caps, along with specification of the type of loans (income-earning), is based on a philosophy that has been tried before and failed whenever and wherever it has been used. In other words, we have to wait and see in which direction the Indian MFIs evolve. It would be unfortunate if knee-jerk regulatory thinking stifles the growing maturity of the sector.

NOTES

1. As we will see later, the recent recommendations for regulating Indian MFIs also make this point.
2. Indeed, the demand growth made operations highly profitable and attracted organizations that started off as for-profit companies and immediately attracted private equity. This encouraged not-for-profits also to transform themselves into commercial ventures. Many NGOs operating in other spheres also set up their own for-profit NBFCs. MFIs have become big business opportunities in India.

REFERENCES

Adams, R.B. and D. Ferreira (2009), 'Women in the boardroom and their impact on governance and perform-ance', *Journal of Financial Economics*, **94**(2), 291–309.
Ahlin, C. and J. Lin (2006), 'Luck or skill? MFI performance in macroeconomic context', Bureau for Research and Economic Analysis of Development, BREAD Working Paper No. 132, Centre for International Development, Harvard University.
Ahlin, C., J. Lin and M. Maio (2010), 'Where does microfinance flourish? Microfinance institution perform-ance in macroeconomic context', *Journal of Development Economics*, **95**(2), 105–120.
Armendáriz de Aghion, B. and J. Morduch (2005), *The Economics of Microfinance*, Cambridge, MA: MIT Press.
Banerjee, A., E. Duflo, R. Glennerster and C. Kinnan (2010), 'The miracle of microfinance? Evidence from randomised evaluation', Cambridge, MA: Department of Economics, MIT Mimeo.
Bassem, B.S. (2009), 'Governance and performance of microfinance institutions in the Mediterranean countries', *Journal of Business, Economics and Management*, **10**(1), 31–43.
Basu, Priya and Pradeep Srivastava (2005), 'Scaling-up microfinance for India's rural poor', World Bank Policy Research Working Paper 3646.

CGAP (1997), 'Effective governance for microfinance institutions', *FOCUS*, March, p. 2.

Cull, R., A. Demirgüç-Kunt and J. Morduch (2007), 'Financial performance and outreach: a global analysis of leading banks', *Economic Journal*, **117**(517), F107–133.

Cull, R., A. Demirgüç-Kunt and J. Morduch (2008), 'Microfinance meets the market', Policy Research Working Paper No. 4690, Washington, DC: World Bank.

D'Espallier, B., I. Guerin and R. Mersland (2009a), 'Women and repayment in microfinance', Working Paper RUME 2009-02, Provence University/Rume Project, Marseille, France.

D'Espallier, B., I. Guerin and R. Mersland (2009b), 'Gender bias in microfinance', Working Paper RUME 2009-08, Provence University/Rume Project, Marseille, France.

Feigenberg, B., E.M. Field and R. Pande (2010), 'Building social capital through microfinance', Cambridge, MA: RWP 10-019, Kennedy School, Harvard University.

Gaiha, R. and M.A. Nandhi (2009), 'Microfinance, self-help groups and empowerment in Maharashtra', in R. Jha (ed.), *The Indian Economy Sixty Years after Independence*, London: Palgrave Macmillan.

Hatarska, V. (2004), 'Governance and performance of microfinance institutions in Central and Eastern Europe and the newly independent states', William Davidson Institute Working Paper No. 677.

Imai, Katsushi S., Thankom Arun and Samuel Kobina Annim (2010), 'Microfinance and household poverty reduction: new evidence from India', *World Development*, **38**(12), 1760–1774.

Kai, H. and S. Hamori (2009), 'Microfinance and inequality', MPRA Paper No. 17572.

Kanter, R.M. (1977), *Men and Women of the Corporation*, New York: Basic Books.

Karlan, D. and J. Zinman (2009), 'Expanding credit access: using randomized supply decisions to estimate the impacts', New Haven, CT: Innovations for Poverty Action.

Keasey, K., S. Thompson and M. Wright (1997), *Corporate Governance: Economic and Financial Issues*, Oxford: Oxford University Press.

Khandker, S.R. (2005), 'Microfinance and poverty: evidence using panel data from Bangladesh', *World Bank Economic Review*, **19**(2), 263–286.

Kyreboah-Coleman, A. (2007), 'The impact of capital structure on the performance of microfinance institutions', *Journal of Risk Finance*, **8**(1), 56–71.

Kyreboah-Coleman, A. and Kofi A. Osei (2008), 'Outreach and profitability of microfinance institutions: the role of governance', *Journal of Economic Studies*, **35**(3–4), 236–248.

Malegam (2011), 'Report of the Sub-Committee of the Central Board of Directors of the Reserve Bank of India to Study Issues and Concerns in the MFI Sector', Reserve Bank of India, January.

Martin, I., D. Hulme and S. Rutherford (2002), 'Finance for the poor: from microcredit to microfinancial sevices, policy arena on finance and development', *Journal of International Development*, **14**(2), 273–294.

Mersland, R. and R.O. Strøm (2009), 'Performance and governance in microfinance institutions', *Journal of Banking and Finance*, **33**, 662–669.

Mersland, R. and R.O. Strøm (2010), 'Microfinance and mission drift?', *World Development*, **38**(1), 28–36.

'Microfinance Industry in India' (2010), *Lok Capital*, March issue.

Morduch, J. (1999), 'The microfinance promise', *Journal of Economic Literature*, **37**(4), 1569–1614.

PRISMS (USAID Nigeria Prisms Project) (2005), 'Governance issues in microfinance', paper presented at the International Year of Microcredit (IYMC) Workshop, 16 December.

Rock, R.M., M. Otero and S. Saltzman (1998), 'Principles and practices of microfinance governance', ACCION International, August.

Smith, N., V. Smith and M. Verner (2006), 'Do women in top management affect firm performance? A panel study of 2300 Danish firms', *International Journal of Productivity and Performance Management*, **15**(7), 569–593.

Strom, R. Oystein, Bert D'Espallier and Roy Mersland (2010), 'Gender, performance and governance in microfinance institutions', mimeo, http://www.rug.nl/feb/onderzoek/events/workshopmicrofinance2010/pdfMicro/StromEspallierMersland.pdf.

Strom, O., B. D'Espallier and R. Mersland (2010), 'Gender, performance and governance in microfinance institutions', in N. Smith, M. Verner and V. Smith (eds), *Proceedings of the Workshop on Women in Top Corporate Jobs: Compensation, Promotion and Firm Performance (Online)*, Aarhus: Aarhus University, http://www.asb.dk/article.aspx?pid=24169.

Tchakoute-Tchigoua, Hubert (2010), 'Is there a difference in performance by the legal status of microfinance institutions?', *Quarterly Review of Economics and Finance*, **50**(4), 436–442.

Index